Montague A Holbein in 1890 pictured astride his Whippet sprung safety cycle with cushion tyres, on which he rode 336 miles, and in 1895 he improved to 397 miles on a Swift cycle.

# THE 24 HOUR STORY    1882 – 2008

## A COMPLETE HISTORY OF THE 24 HOUR CYCLE RACE, INCLUDING MANY CLASSIC RRA LONG DISTANCE ROAD RECORD DESCRIPTIONS

## BY JOHN TAYLOR

This book is dedicated to the riders, whether male or female, on bicycle, tricycle, tandem or tandem tricycle, irrespective of whether they have ridden 200, 300, 400 or 500 miles in a day.   The fact that they have faced the timekeeper and have ridden as far as possible in 24hrs is a true measure of their bravery, courage, dedication and self-esteem.   Whether competing against other riders or as lone record breakers, it is a tribute to them all.

It is also a dedication to the skilled race organisers, timekeepers, checkers observers and also the cycling clubs and club folk who have turned out, sometimes two or three times a year, annually to promote these famous events or long distance records covering some 130 years.   One must include in these dedications the marshals who have braved the elements and traffic for hours at a time, to see the rider has a safe direction to ride.
I must also mention the skilled feeding teams including the riders own family and friends who have given up possibly some 36 hours to help.

All of the above have, in one way or another, combined to create the rich history of the 24hr Cycle Race and Long Distance Road Records that link the 19th, 20th and 21st Centuries.

To Jim Turner, a most generous man who, along with his wife Anne has put his heart and soul into promoting and organising the Mersey RC 24 hour and supporting long distance time trialling and record breaking for over two decades.  His enthusiasm and persuasive powers knew no bounds when it came to recognising a rider's potential to succeed.   Most of the End to Ends and 1,000 mile records that took place between years 2000 and 2002 had a massive input from Jim, helping Lynne, Andy and Gethin to realise their dreams with those records.

In 2003 Jim had a guiding influence over the successful Walsall RCC ladies team of Lynne Taylor, Marina Bloom, Tracey Maund and Ann Wooldridge.  They not only took many individual awards and Championship team wins, but also broke team Competition records at 100 miles, 12 hours and 24 hours.   Jim made them all realise just how good they are and helped them all to extend their racing careers to gain these top honours.

A special dedication to Paul Histon who, on many occasions, worked alongside Jim Turner, firstly as a roving marshal in the Mersey RC 24hr, checking on the leading riders etc. and then as a 'mentor' to Andy Wilkinson on many of his record exploits since the early '90's'.   Paul's observations on those occasions have formed some of Andy's ride descriptions and make interesting reading.  In more recent years, Paul has played a large part in Lynne Taylor's road record breaking successes since 2000, raising her expectations to ride at record speed and beyond her normal limits to break seemingly impossible records in adverse conditions.   In 2007 he pushed her to 459.21 miles in the Mersey RC 24hr, the second highest ladies mileage ever.   In 2008 he personally supervised Lynne's training programme, and took her to over 30 events, resulting in 2nd place in the Women's BBAR

I also dedicate this book to my wife Liz for transferring my handwritten scribble onto the word processor, so making sense of it all.   Liz has worked tirelessly over the years to help Lynne and myself with our favourite pastime.

On a much lighter note, my book is also dedicated to our first grandchild, Noah Bruin Taylor, born to Kate and Mike on 24th September 2006, so that he knows what fun his Grandad and later Auntie Lynne have had whilst riding 24hr events over the last 45 years. I had just started writing this book on the day he was born.   Secondly, twenty months later Noah's sister, Poppy Beatrice came into the world on 21st May 2008, just as I was finalising the last few photos to finish the book.

Published in the United Kingdom by
Btown Bikes Ltd.
Unit 7, Lakeside Plaza
Bridgtown, Cannock, WS11 OXE
Tel: 01922 411180
www.btownbikes.com

A catalogue record for this book is available from the British Library

ISBN 978-0-9562023-1-4

Produced by Set & Match Ltd.
Edited by Inky Moss & Andy Harper

'When I said bring out my night clothing I meant my long-sleeved
racing top and my leg warmers.'

# Acknowledgements

To Bob Beaman for the many hours spent at the computer and helping with the general layout of the book, the photos and the result sheets.

To the Committee and Members of the 24hr Fellowship for allowing me to plunder the pages of the Fellowship Journals and to reproduce material written therein.

To Johnny Helms for permission to draw on fifty years worth of cartoons to enlighten my pages.

To John Arnold, Syd Parker and John Williams Senior for imparting their own personal knowledge of this history of long distance racing.

To Tom Lodge for his help with Wessex RC 24hr history details.

To Mrs Mary Cook for her help with details of the North Road CC 24hr history

To the Mersey R.C. for the use of material from their club history and in particular the late Frank Mumford for his unique style of reporting the 24hr in 'The Record'.

To the Williams Family for their input to the Mersey RC 24hr history.

To the Anfield Bicycle Club for allowing me to use details of their early 24hr history, from the 'Black Anfielders' book.

To Roger Sewell for loaning me his early history book on the First 50 Years of the North Road CC.

To Peter Barlow, Ian Dow, Stuart Jackson, Ian Shaw, Roy Cromack and the late Bernard Thompson, for their enlightening articles found in the 24hr Fellowship Journal.

To Pat Kenny, Pete Swinden, Les Lowe and Jim Hopper for their help with details of long distance records and racing.

To the RRA for allowing me to use their logo and race and record data from their handbooks.

I am grateful to Gregory Houston Bowden, the great grandson of Sir Frank Bowden the founding owner of Raleigh, for information found in a book published by him in 1975 titled 'The Story Of the Raleigh Cycle'. It is a compact history of Raleigh Cycles, cataloguing the expansion of this vast cycle making business empire, from its beginning in 1888 up until 1975.

## And finally

To Dave Threlkeld, Brian Jones, Kimroy Photography, the late Harold Harvey, Les Brown, John Arnold, the late Bernard Thompson, Ron Good and Darren from Avid Photography, for allowing me to use photos from their collections.

I also acknowledge riders who've kindly loaned me photos to use for this book, although they are too numerous to mention everyone individually.

My sincere thanks to you all for making this unique history possible to put on paper.

# CONTENTS

# INTRODUCTION

**THE TIME**      3.05 pm   Sunday July 27th 1997

**THE PLACE**     Timekeeper 8, Handley Village, a few miles south of Chester

"Wilko" lay panting for breath on a grass verge where the timekeeper had stopped him. He was desperately tired but also relieved to have finished. His helpers had to lift him bodily off his bike, so exhausted was he. After the initial euphoria and adrenalin rush from victory and achievement had faded slightly, he felt sick, he tried to talk but was now shivering feverishly and uncontrollably as his helpers tried to cover him with blankets and rub some warmth back into his cold clammy limbs.

After being violently sick he lay huddled under blankets for a well deserved few minutes sleep. Andy Wilkinson 'Wilko' to his friends, riding for the Port Sunlight Wheelers and sponsored by Adidas Sci-Con, had ridden at almost 22mph flat out and virtually non stop for 525 miles, so breaking the RTTC National 24hr Time Trial Competition Record by a massive 18.07 miles. It was a record that had stood for 28 years to Roy Cromack, Clifton CC whose 507 miles had survived many attempts by all of the top long distance men from 1969 until this memorable day.

Handley Village is on the finishing circuit of some 15 miles of quiet back lanes used by the Mersey Roads CC for their 54th annual promotion incorporating this R.T.T.C. National Championship event. It's a sporting course that is not recognised as being particularly 'fast' or easy on any of its various circuits or directions. There are no flat, tree-lined, sheltered dual carriageways or fast flowing, traffic assisted sections for its riders, it's just an undulating, interesting and fairly safe rural course, so this made Andy's ride even more superb!

Wilko had ridden a very controlled race as suggested and planned by Roy Cromack. He hadn't chased down or stamped his superiority on three or four other very respected top 'distance' riders earlier in the event, he'd let them have their own battles and he'd stayed aware of their positions hour by hour throughout the race. Andy knew his own body and mind and its limitations, he'd also experienced a poor season up to this point. His training mileages hadn't been as good as in previous years resulting in him being slightly overweight, but he knew he could stand the pain and pressure to rise to any challenge. This knowledge and experience was probably gained from winning previous 24hr races on this course in 1995 with 496.16 miles and 1996 with 501.39 miles, and breaking the Lands End to John o Groats record twice. He'd gone through all of the 'mind over matter' situations that are likely to crop up en route, not to mention his record breaking B.B.A.R. of the previous year. All of these past performances gave him his ultimate confidence on this day.

One may perhaps deduce from this result and record of Andy Wilkinsons in 1997, that the ultimate performance and distance had been achieved, and that it would create an anti-climax which would affect entries for this challenging event from up and coming and also established long distance riders, but one would be very mistaken.

Since 1997 competitors have entered this event knowing they have only the slimmest chance of beating Wilko's mileage. They know that if everything goes well for them they may win, or possibly beat 500 miles, or both. They may amass a 'personal best' mileage in the event, count as a team member to win the team prize or gain Championship Honours.

Riders such as Edwin Hargraves who won a year later in 1998 with 462.20 miles at 48 years of age, a real triumph for him. It's a good job he won, as the following year he was struck down by the deadly Salmonella bug which led to a pulmonary embolism, consequently ending his competitive career and very nearly his life. Karl Austin won in 1999 with 448.16 miles. He is a regular jovial sturdy 24hr competitor who generally rides a track machine with a fixed single speed gear, usually of 90". Karl has been riding 24hr races since the early 90's and this was his first win.

Gethin Butler in the year 2000 followed his famous grandfather Stan's footsteps (or should that have been wheel tracks). Stan broke Competition Record in 1950 with 458.18 miles. Gethins tremendous mileage of 509.25 in year 2000 was the second fastest ride ever done at that time; interestingly it's just over 50 miles further, 50 years later. Gethin won again in 2001 with 485.88 miles and later that year went on to break Andy Wilkinsons Lands End to John o' Groats record by nearly 58 minutes. You will see from this performance of Gethins that Andy's awesome 24hr record hadn't deterred him from having a crack at his 'End to End'.

V

In 2002 David Shepherd won with 482.12 miles. He was another fine rider who, like Andy, rode well beyond his limit to achieve this result, he looked ashen and absolutely exhausted at the end.

Gethin Butler won again for the third time in 2003 with 471.21 miles. He was still enjoying his riding and racing even after a full career from schoolboy 10 mile time trialling to winning top premier league road races and the ultimate distances of the RRA 24hr, End to End and 1,000 miles.

For the next three years in succession, it was Nikolaus Gardiner with 479.131, 493.081 and finally in 2006 he realised his goal of 504 miles, exactly 21 mph. Nik like Gethin and Andy is a very popular rider with always a quick word of encouragement for other riders as he passes them. Like other true champions, he has pushed beyond his limits to record these distances.

In 2006 at the prize presentation after the event at Farndon, Nik when questioned about his performance said that the last hour or two of his ride was a real battle for him as he had been running 'on empty', but once he had reached the 500 mile point, he really enjoyed the last 4 miles.

In 2007, a superbly fit 48 year old postman, Eamonn Deane from Bournemouth, riding his first 24hr race, won with 501 miles. To be honest, he looked as though he was an old hand at the game, riding comfortably but controlled from the very start. With a smooth style and a low 'tuck' position which he maintained for the full 24hrs, he looked a winner at any stage of the race. The only concession he made to his speed was to remove his aero helmet before the halfway point in favour of a cloth cap. Here is a man who could possibly push Andy's record higher, he certainly looks as though he's got a few years of 24hr riding to come.

In 2008, Nik Gardiner with 513.65 took his 4th Championship Gold Medal. He now joins the ranks of multi-Championship winners, Stuart Jackson with four and Nim Carline with six. This was Nik's second ride over 500 miles, it becomes the second highest mileage in time trial history, and must surely qualify him to be our next 'End to End' aspirant and record breaker?

This praise and awe, as men have won and records have fallen, has been evident since it all started in the early 1880's, when the 'Ordinary' cycle nicknamed the 'Penny Farthing' or 'High Bicycle' became a machine on which young men of reasonable fitness could explore the countryside over a wide area. It was inevitable that sooner or later the question would arise – "How far can you ride in a day?"

*I will at this point include my own personal introduction to this great history and add a few paragraphs describing my early cycling days, which started in the 1950's.*

*I had always been interested in general history from quite an early age and I suppose my Grandad was the oldest person I knew. He lived a very frugal and meagre existence and very rarely spoke to us grandchildren. He was one of the 'old school' who believed that children should be seen and not heard. The closest I ever got to him was when he cut a chunk of tobacco for his pipe he would then let me roll it in the palms of my hands and shred it until it fitted his pipe. My mom told me that he was a 'Master Upholsterer' and had worked on Queen Victoria's carriage and I assumed that by living near to a railway depot it was a railway coach, although I found out later that he also worked on some of the earlier cars. So at the time I could brag to my friends at school that my Grandad worked for Queen Victoria.*

*I loved going to my local cinema in Tyseley to a Saturday matinee where my favourite films were Cowboys and Indians and War Stories, but I wasn't sure whether these epic gunfights and battles had really taken place or whether it was just 'make-believe' for kids.*

*As a young teenager and adolescent I was 'tubby' even though I felt that I was always on the go. As well as being sent to play football and anything else one played in those days on the local recreation ground while your Mom did the housework or went to work, I also borrowed my sister Margaret's bike. I say borrowed, although it was only for an hour or two, it was usually without her knowing. My Mom would ask me later where I had been all morning or afternoon and I would reply "Oh, just playing marbles or football, or riding around local streets with my friends". The truthful reality was that I'd been out along the main Stratford Road astride my sister's 'New Hudson' bike with semi-dropped handlebars and Sturmey Archer gears. My route would take me through Shirley, out into the countryside to Tanworth-in-Arden, Earlswood Lakes and home again, a round trip of about 20 miles I guess, as I wasn't sure of distances at that time. I knew that as long as I retraced back along the same roads, then I wouldn't get lost.*

The feelings of freedom, secret achievement and independence were immense. I was about 12 years of age at that time and both of my sisters, Barbara and Margaret were regular touring cyclists. Later they both youth hostelled with their future husbands John and Les, riding with groups of other young cyclists who lived locally or even in the same street as us. Nobody in my family had a car or even a motorbike at that time.

Moving on a year or two, I now had my sister Barbara's 'B.S.A' Tour of Britain sports-racer and used it to go everywhere on. I attended one of the first Comprehensive schools to be built, in Sheldon, Birmingham. It was a journey of some 5 miles to school through the back streets, past factories such as Dawes Cycles, Renolds Chains and numerous cycle component manufacturers. I rode along the Coventry Road dicing daily with the traffic, which included the almost silent trolley buses, to my destination.

My favourite subjects at school were history and geography. Victor Skipp, my history teacher, was such an enthusiastic man, he made me realise that I hadn't to go more than a mile to find real history as there was a 12th century church within sight of the school. I was hooked from that day onwards and the only school trips I went on were to Museums and Roman sites.

At the age of 13 my sister Margaret introduced me to the Birmingham St Christopher's Catholic Cycling Club via her work colleague Joan Knox, and that was it, I never looked back. I wasn't a fast rider but I could ride all day from 8am to 8pm or even later if the trip home from the tea stop wasn't on my side of the town. I was also reliant on the older club members getting me home at that time, as I was only a novice map reader. The club run Captain would generally choose a ride that included somewhere of historical importance, either to a castle or the scene of a battle; even Mrs Sherwood's café at Kenilworth was a 400 year old cottage on the green opposite the castle.

I soon started to ride local time trials, mainly 25 and 50 mile events and was 'roped in' to help John Withers on his early 24hr races, one of his first being the Mersey RC event in 1960. The names being bandied about at that time were Ken Usher, Cliff Smith, Dave Keeler, Fred Burrell, Jim Hanning, Arch Harding, Dick Poole, Reg Randall, Ron Coukham, Dave Duffield and John Arnold to name but a few.

With only an interest in History, Geography and Art I was not deemed academically gifted and so started work at 15 earning up to £4.00 per week as an apprentice letterpress printing plate 'half tone etcher'. I now felt totally independent with my £1.50 a week pocket money, most of which went on bikes, components and race entry fees. I rode everywhere at that time and could hardly wait for the weekends, especially the Bank Holidays when I would finish work on Saturday dinner time and ride to the Welsh coast and back overnight. Eventually I would stretch that mileage and take rides south to Exeter and back, sleeping only when I had to, usually in bus shelters, eating and drinking mainly by means of transport cafes and milk machines en route. Most of these expeditions were done on my own.

The fitness and stamina gained from these journeys enabled me to ride my first Oldbury and District 12hr race at 16 and my first Mersey RC 24hr at 18. Both rides were of mediocre mileages compared with the men who took the top ten places in these events and also in the case of the 12hr the women who had beaten me. I had a terrific respect for all of them.

Just to be on the same road and be passed by such names as Fred Burrell, Cliff Smith and Ron Coukham was more than enough for me. I could return to work the next morning knowing that I had done something magnificent with my weekend. I found that the euphoria gained from my effort would carry me through the negative or mundane situations that cropped up in life.

I've always had a very active imagination and throughout my life I've always been interested in epic voyagers and their expeditions; men such as Shackleton, Scott and Darwin. Mountaineering exploits always gripped me, with climbs from Hillary, Tensing, Bonnington, Dougal Haston and more recently the near death exploits of Joe Simpson. Lone yachtsmen or women such as Sir Francis Chichester, and later Dame Ellen MacArthur, oarsmen Chay Blyth, Robin Knox Johnston and Sid Genders. The most touching and poignant to me being Ellen MacArthur's two epic lone yacht voyages at the very start of the 21st century.

The preparation, the doubts and the intrepidation that these brave people must have experienced before their tremendous lone journeys must be the same set of emotions that a rider feels for their first ride in a 24hr race or long distance road record. The question "What am I doing here on this start line?" must be a very relevant one for all competitors and aspirants. I was lucky, I had no worries about riding all night at 18 years of age, I'd already experienced many long trips of 250 miles or more and felt invincible and full of 'bravado', after all, if John Withers, Pat Kenny and Pete Swinden could do it, then so could I.

VII

*I mentioned earlier about my lifelong interest in historical episodes, either wars, battles, expeditions, conquests etc. I was also always amazed at inventions and medical cures and how short a time some of these discoveries have been around. I also love to see old photos of the way things were, especially anything to do with cycling. Therefore, throughout this book I have tried to fit in a few historical moments in time to run like a thread interwoven with our own 24hr and record breaking achievements.*

*The first incident to run parallel with our history is* **'The Gunfight at the O.K. Coral'.** *For years I thought it was just another cowboy story and was amazed to find out it really took place in 1881, within a few months of the first recorded Lands End to John o Groats ride by the Hon. Ion Keith Falconer in 12 days 23 hrs and 15 mins. By mentioning (usually in italics or different type) these few historical moments, I hope to break up the generally repetitive nature of the annual events and to also give a chronological depth to that particular era. The same applies to the inclusion of strategic long distance 'R.R.A' Road Records. It all goes to show just how good these men's and women's rides were throughout this 125 year history.*

*In a Cycling Paper published in 1880 it stated "man is a social animal and directly he finds a new amusement he proceeds to form a club to be able to pursue it in company". So it was with our sport. There was only one club in 1870, but by 1879 there were 55 and one year later the numbers had risen dramatically to 213 Cycling Clubs.*

*Early long distance rides are not without interest; back in the 1870's there was a tremendous keenness on the part of cyclists to cover 100 miles in a day. A special supplement of 'The Cyclist' in March 1881 gave a list of all the 'century' rides, the first being in 1874 with just one ride recorded – Bath to Hounslow, on a machine weighing 65lbs. In 1880 there had been 136 'century' rides in total.*

**By 1878 a ride from London to Bath and Back, by Wat Britten, was the longest authenticated 24hr ride 'on record'.** *Soon there would be challenges amongst the young men in a club having already completed their 100 mile rides, it would be "I bet I can ride farther than you in 24 hrs!" In Victorian times, the majority of people would not have travelled much further than the extremities of their towns or villages. It was probably only wealthy people who could afford or had access to, a cycle, a horse, or a horse-drawn vehicle, that ventured out far into the countryside. Railway travel was in its infancy and restricted to certain routes between towns for people with money.*

**On December 28th 1879 The Tay Bridge in Scotland collapsed.** *A train carrying 300 passengers fell from the bridge and all were feared dead. Faulty girder design was deemed to be the cause of the collapse of the longest bridge in the world at that time.*

**On October 26th 1881**, *the cemetery at Boot Hill in Tombstone Arizona, received three more inmates when Wyatt Earp and his two brothers Morgan and Virgil along with Doc Holliday won a gun battle at the O.K. Corral. Within a minute, three outlaws consisting of the two McLowery brothers and Billy Clanton were shot dead.*

**June 1882 saw the Honourable Ion Keith-Falcone**r *of the Cambridge University CC, attempt and set the* **First Lands End to John o' Groats Record**, *on an 'Ordinary Bicycle' without using ferries in Scotland, in* **12 days 23 hours 15 minutes.** *A few weeks later,* **Alfred Nixon** *rode from top to bottom,* **John o' Groats to Lands End** *on a tricycle weighing 110 lbs, covering 1000 miles en route in* **13 days 23 hrs 55mins.**

# CHAPTER ONE      PIONEERS OF THE 'PACED' ERA   1882 – 1900

The first recorded 24hr race, where more than one competitor took part (and there may have been others previously but not known to me) was held on the **30th September 1882,** and confined to riders of **The 'Facile'** a lever driven bicycle where two levers connected to the front wheel were worked by foot in a treadling action.

The race was run from **London to Bath and back** and was won by **W. Snook** of Winchester.   He rode **214.5 miles in 24 hrs,** and his time for getting back from Hyde Park Corner to Fleet Street where the race had started, took another 30mins & 42secs.   A lot of these early races and challenges were instigated by newspapers wanting to get the full story of these rides.  Manufacturers of certain types of cycle such as the 'Facile' or 'Coventry Rotary' tricycle would organise races restricted to owners of these particular machines only.    The manufacturers would link up exclusively with a newspaper to get good coverage and advertising for their products.

## 1883

On the 26th May 1883 The Speedwell Bicycle Club ran a 24hr race for their own club members.   The weather was poor and caused distances to be low.  **F. Clarke won the event with 207.5 miles.**

The **first 'Open' 24hr** race was held by the **London Tricycle Club in July 1883,** for tricyclists only.   There were 67 starters.   A gold enamelled medal was given for rides over 200 miles, silver for 150 miles and bronze for 100 miles.   The winner was **T.R.Marriot** (soon to be a founder member of the North Road CC), he covered **218.75 miles.**   Another founder member of the North Road CC rode that day and gained a silver medal, **A.J.Wilson** ("FAED").  *A.J. Wilson's nickname 'Faed' was a reversal of deaf, which he had been profoundly, since a young age.   His deafness did not appear to be a handicap to him in any way, as he rose to high positions of esteem both in industry and in the cycling world.*   Wilson would have won a higher award but his tricycle broke down – "greatly to his joy" as he wrote to Bidlake some years later.

A week or two later **The Speedwell Bicycle Club also held a 24hr tricycle race, won by Alfred Bird,** later Sir Alfred of 'Bird's Custard fame with **221.5 miles.**  This race started at the Small Heath Railway station yard, literally a stone's throw from my Grandparents house.    I used to ride past Alfred Bird's custard factory in Bradford Street, Digbeth, Birmingham on my way to work in the late 1950's.  The smell was wonderful, it was an aroma similar to freshly ground or roasted coffee beans.  I digress, but it's a little bit of history I've seen, touched and smelt for myself.

## 1884

*In October 1884, Greenwich was adopted as the Universal Meridian so creating 'Greenwich Mean Time'. Also at that time Louis Pasteur developed a cure for Rabies.  It was usually a fatal disease spread by the bite of a rabid dog, as at that time there were no quarantine laws or controls between the various continents.*

**In September 1884 W.F. Sutton** increased the **24hr** mileage to **230.75 miles.**   The competitive spirit was developing in the Liverpool and Cheshire area and also encompassed South Lancashire, the main clubs being the 'Anfield Bicycle Club' and the 'Manchester Athletic Bicycle Club' (which became The Manchester Wheelers Club in 1890).   These clubs started awarding stars for specific mileages and performances; silver for 100 miles, gold for 175 miles on a tricycle or 200 miles on a bicycle or tandem tricycle.  The first 24 hour run by the Anfield BC was an experimental one, and started on the outskirts of Liverpool near Rainhill, where riders took the London Road and turned at Coventry.   It was won by Mercer with 161.5 miles.

All of the 24hr rides started at midnight on a Friday night at the actual start of the day, as it hadn't occurred to anybody that a different arrangement of the 24hrs might have been more convenient, such as starting in daylight. It must be remembered that at that time in history, the observance of the Sabbath was strictly enforced and no official races were allowed to take place on that day.

The Manchester club event started south of the city, sometimes it was from 'Brooks Bar' or 'Trafford Bar'. They were two of Manchester's surviving 'Road Tollhouses'. Another point for the start was the 9th milestone from Manchester, near Altrincham. The route went via Chester, Whitchurch, Wem and Shrewsbury, where there were extensions either south to Ludlow or east to Wolverhampton.

*The Tollgate at Trafford 'Trafford Bar' was at the end of an old turnpike road that dated from before the year 1800. The tollgate was manned by a toll keeper who would charge stage coaches a fee for using the road. The Great North Road was the first turnpike toll road from London in about 1700. I think it possibly terminated at 'Potters Bar' near London. By 1750 there were 143 turnpike 'trusts' responsible for the collection of tolls and the maintenance of some 3,386 miles of roads, mainly radiating from in and around London.*

*The journey from London to Bristol, running close to the river Kennet and now known as the A4 would have originally taken 40 hours by stage coach. By 1785 the journey had been reduced to 19 hours.*

One interesting anecdote worth mentioning here at this time, was from G.P. Mills on the subject of roaming wild dogs, which were an absolute menace to a cyclist. He carried a pistol on his winning ride in the 'Bordeaux Paris' in 1891 and he disposed of at least five.

THIS one is yours, son

## 1885

*January 26th 1885, General Gordon is killed by Mahdi Dervishes at Khartoum.*

**June 1st 1885** saw the 'End to End' record being reduced again when **M.R. Lennox** riding an 'ordinary' brought the time down to **6 days 16 hours and 7 minutes.**

**July 1st 1885 C.H.R. Gosset achieved 231.75 miles riding a tricycle.** This became the first **'RRA' (Road Records Association) tricycle 24hr record.** Less than one week later **Mrs Allen** of Birmingham became **the first woman to ride 200 miles in 24 hours on a tricycle.** This created much press comment about the desirability of ladies performing such athletic feats and many were the prophecies of dire consequences such efforts would make to the fragile female form.

The **22nd August 1885 saw the first Anfield Bicycle Club 24hr** race for club members only; from 'Knotty Ash' (an area of Liverpool made famous by comedian Ken Dodd) to Weedon Beck and back. **G.P. Mills won the event** with an officially credited **259 miles,** followed by **G.B. Mercer** with **211 miles** and **F.W. Mayor** with **207 miles.** Mill's ride is the one listed in the RRA Handbook as the best on an ordinary with solid tyres.

'The Cyclist' **Sept 23rd 1885** tells how two Manchester 'scorchers' **Henry Feay and W. Riley,** gained long distance medals by riding **175 miles** and **205 miles** respectively in the day. Feay crashed heavily, damaging his pedal crank and bruising himself badly, but managed to limp home with the help of Riley who had turned at Shifnal. Feay only got as far as Shrewsbury before turning for home. The state of the main roads at the time we cannot begin to imagine. If the road was surfaced with macadam (compacted shale and earth) it became porous over time and water bound. After a few weeks of horse drawn traffic leaving ruts, potholes and mounds of manure, one can only imagine the foul mud the riders had to endure if it rained heavily, riding bicycles or tricycles that weighed in excess of some 60lbs (27kgs) over 4 times heavier than the latest carbon fibre cycles of the 21st century.

**On 24th September 1885, a 24hr race for riders of the Coventry Rotary Tricycle** was promoted by its makers. The race was run on the Great North Road which ran from London to Scotland on the eastern side of the country (now the A1). It was the first all day race to be held on it and was won by **J.H. Adams,** his distance being **233.5 miles.** Billson of Leicester was 2nd with **224 miles** and **D.G. Duncan,** Beretta CC 3rd with **179 miles.**

Quite a lot of End to End records are attempted and broken in the years between Blackwell and Harman in 1880 and G.P. Mills in 1891 and this is a history on its own. Quite a lot of the record breakers over this journey were accomplished 24hr riders, and, at this time, most record breakers were assisted by 'pacers' and 'followers'. As road record breaking is inextricably linked to 24hr racing, I will endeavour throughout this book to keep abreast of the End to End and RRA 24hr records as they appear during this history.

In October 1885 A.J. Wilson issued a circular to other keen cyclists and clubmen that he knew, with a view to starting a club purely for racing men, for the purpose of promoting and encouraging fast and long distance riding chiefly, but not exclusively, in the Great North Road district. Membership would be restricted to riders who had ridden at least 100 miles in a day. Being a member of this club did not mean you couldn't belong to another one for social riding, and on the **21st of December 1885 The North Road Cycling Club was formed.**

It was decided to hold two long distance races in 1886, a 100 mile race and a 24hr race in September. **G.P. Mills won the 24hr race** on an 'ordinary' bicycle which you may know as a 'penny farthing' or 'high bicycle', with **227 miles.**

But first of all let us start this year of 1886 with the events listed chronologically. It will be evident that this period of time was ruled over by one outstanding rider: **G.P. Mills.**

# 1886

*In March 1886 Coca Cola went on sale in Georgia USA*

**In 1886 The Anfield B.C.** held their **24hrs** road race for club members only, over a course from Liverpool to Lichfield, Derby and return, which was **won by G.P. Mills (George Pilkington) with 227 miles. N. Cooke was second with 218 miles,** and only four other members finished.

⟫•◇•⟪

**June 1886 saw A.H. Fletcher** riding a Humber 'Cripper' Tricycle increase the 24hr record to **250.5 miles** which was later authenticated by the **NCU** (National Cyclists Union) and later adopted by the **RRA.**

**In July G.P. Mills** of the Anfield B.C. set out and **broke the Lands End to John o Groats** record with **5 days 1 hr 45 mins** on a Beeston Humber Ordinary. This remains the 'Best on Record' for an Ordinary with solid tyres. *To put some sort of modern day context to this record, Alex Baxter, Southport CC, riding a similar 'Penny Farthing' machine attempted to break this record in 1999 and failed to do so by 6.5 hours, despite the vastly improved modern road surfaces. Alex did however take considerably more sleep than Mills. Whereas Mills had taken 6 hours in total, Alex told me he took 6 hrs a night on his journey, although in all fairness Alex wasn't a young man, he was very strong, even though well into his middle age. G.P. Mills' rides over the End to End route were 'raced' all the way even though he had pacers and helpers wherever he could. His ride was a performance that a stagecoach with relay teams of fresh horses would be hard pushed to beat. In a lot of areas en route the road was reduced to tracks, especially where they were trying to lay a railway line on top of the existing road in parts of Scotland.*

The **M.A.B.C. (Manchester Athletic Bicycle Club) ran its 24hr race on August 20th 1886,** starting at Brooks Bar at midnight. **Dave Foulkes** took the lead from the start, dressed in a white flannel suit. Chester was reached via Northwich by 3.15am. Whitchurch by 5.10am to stop at Shrewsbury at 7am with 79 miles covered. He continued through Wellington, Shifnal and Stretton to turn at the Lichfield turnpike at 12 noon, 124 miles. He retraced with a helpful wind to reach Chester at 8.55pm. He was met outside the town by pacemakers W.E. West and James Reilly. They reached *Dunham Park and finished at Bowdon having covered **241 miles,** breaking the existing Manchester record held by C. McSmith by 18 miles.

**(Dunham Park is now the Dunham Massey Estate, owned by the National Trust)*

Less than 1 month later **Mills rode 268 miles in 24hrs** to create what is considered to be the best ever performance on an 'ordinary'. For some strange reason due to course measurement this distance never became a record. **Mills** wasn't too bothered and used it as a training ride. Just two weeks later he was back at Lands End to reduce the tricycle **End to End** by 30 hours with **5 days 10 hours.**

⇒•◇•⇐

**September 1886 The North Road CC ran their first ever 24hr race** and despite having only a few days rest after his trike 'End to End' **G.P. Mills won the race** on an 'ordinary' with another **227 miles.** The start took place in the station yard at Hatfield on the stroke of midnight. The course followed the Great North Road via Stevenage and Baldock, Peterborough, Wisbech, Sutton Bridge, Kings Lynn to turn one mile from Norwich and retrace to Biggleswade at which point the mileage was 267. As luck would have it, the weather was bad, a dark wet and windy night followed by as bad a day. The leaders ran out of time long before Biggleswade was reached, milestones would have been used to measure the riders distances, probably with a following rider to witness the time and place **T.W. Waterhouse was second with 225 miles and B.F. Huntsman was 3rd with 217 miles. T.R. Marriot** (another North Road Founder member) was the **fastest trike rider with 190 miles.** These distances show just how badly riders were affected by wet roads, where the hard packed surfaces just turned into mud.

⇒•◇•⇐

**One month later** in dry conditions **G.P. Mills** produced **295 miles** to become the record holder for **24 hours.** This mileage and other records were adopted by the **RRA** when it was formed in **1888.** Mills was racing for the first time on a 'safety bicycle' At the time these records were broken **G.P. Mills** was just **18 years of age !**

He went on to a distinguished military career and fought in many wars. He lived on to refute the medical professions claim that riding for 24 hours without sleep would take 10 years off one's life. These were Victorian times of course, where most medical matters were looked upon with pessimism. G.P. Mills carried out at least twenty such rides.

**When Lieutenant-Colonel George Pilkington Mills, D.S.O. died in 1945 he was 78 years old.**

## 1887

1887 was a quieter year with only the **North Road CC** holding a 24hr in September. This attracted 37 entries, **Tinsley Waterhouse winning with 270.5 miles** riding a 'safety' bicycle (the forerunner of today's cycle). **G.P. Mills riding a tricycle** improved Laurence Fletcher's record with **264 miles. D. Belding** was the best 'ordinary' with **237.5 miles.** September 20th 1887 saw C.W. Brown and W.C. Goulding set the tandem tricycle **record for 24hrs with 259 miles,** but days later **G.P. Mills partnered by R. Tingey** increased this to **298.5 miles.**

## 1888

*On March 16th 1888 the first recorded purchase of a Benz car was in Paris to Emile Roger.*

*In December 1888, Frank Bowden, a Solicitor, who had realised the healthy way of life that a cycle can bring, negotiated with a small two-man Company of Woodhead and Angois', and founded the* **Raleigh Cycle Co.** *The name Raleigh was taken from the street name where the small workshop was situated, producing just 3 or 4 cycles a week.*

⇒•◇•⇐

**The North Road CC** ran two events over **24 hrs** in this year. The first on the **25th August** going from Hatfield to Wisbech and back. The race attracted 55 starters: 31 'safeties', 11 ordinarys, 11 trikes and 1 tandem. It was a wild and stormy night and as bad next day. **The race was won by Monty Holbein of the Catford CC with 266.5 miles** riding a 'safety' bicycle. **F.T. Bidlake was the fastest trike with 155.5 miles,** he finished some 5 hours too early for this mileage. A Mrs Maughan entered on a tricycle and covered 25 miles before retiring. This was the first and last time an entry was accepted from a woman in this race until Anne Dunk in 1980.

**29th September** the club decided to run a second event due to inclement conditions in the August event. A slightly different course was used starting at Hitchin market place. **Monty Holbein led from the start to run out time with 292.5 miles, 2nd place went to W. Chater-Lea with 282.5.** Older readers will recognise this name Chater-Lea as being famous later for producing slim-line chrome plated cottered steel cranks and chain rings with a CL motif forming part of the chain ring structure. They also produced pedals and various other lightweight steel transmission components, all of which were very popular from the 1930's to 1970's, when they were superceded by aluminium cotterless chainsets mainly from continental Europe. Campagnolo, Stronglight, 'T.A.', Zeus etc. **W.C. Goulding won the tricycle prize with 252 miles.** Holbein, Chater-Lea and Browne all rode 'safety' bicycles, this race undoubtedly established the supremacy of this bike over the 'ordinary'.

---

*The 'Ordinary' bicycle was also known as a 'High Ordinary' or 'High Bicycle' but its most common nickname was a 'Penny Farthing', so called because of its very large diameter front wheel in relation to its very small trailing rear wheel, and would have a very upright position compared to a modern day cycle. The pedals and cranks were connected to the front hub and were a direct drive with no chains or cogs involved. To slow down, the rider would resist against the turning pedals and eventually stop.*

*To mount the cycle one would use a high step or low brick wall to stand on, although many riders would launch themselves by putting one foot on the fork crown holding the rear wheel and scooting along. Another form of braking was by a device rather like a metal shoehorn being pressed directly onto the front solid rubber tyre. Many riders would dismount while the bike was still moving slowly by dropping over the back of the saddle. Using lampposts was also a good way of dismounting. The very aloft position gave the rider a view from about 8ft high off the ground, but could also startle cattle and animals in the fields because of the silent approach. The large diameter front wheel rode well over small potholes. The 'safety' bicycle was the forerunner of a modern day cycle with two*

THIS is the latest model - it's got aerodynamic footrests

*wheels equal in diameter of approximately 26". The rider's position was now much closer to the ground and obviously much safer. The saddle was now further away from the handlebars giving the rider a more comfortable position and better control. The drive was now by pedals and cranks turning a toothed chain ring transmitting power to a fixed toothed cog on the hub of the rear wheel via a linked roller chain. Braking was again performed by resisting against the turning pedals and the crude friction device braking directly onto the tyre surface could now be operated by pushrods and a brake lever fitted to the handlebars.*

1888 was the inaugural year of the RRA but only produced one record in October. **Percy Nix raised the bicycle 24hr record to 297 miles.** In 1888 the Catford CC awarded six gold medals for riders of their own **club 24hr race.** The winner being **E.R. Scantlebury with 249 miles and Holbein second with 246 miles.**

## 1889

*On March 31st The Eiffel Tower was completed.*

F.T. Bidlake was apppointed to the office of Club Secretary to the **North Road CC;** a service he provided until his death in 1933. The club ran various races in this year but the **24hr** which took place on **September 7th** was a memorable event for many reasons.

A cool calm day preceeded a fine moonlit night. At the **12 hour** point in the race 4 men broke records. **Holbein** was out on his own and led the field from 40 miles. He was the first to break the **12hr record with 175.5 miles.** G.T. Langridge on an 'ordinary' rode to record with **154 miles.** **Goulding and Ward both on tricycles covered 151 miles** in a previously agreed 'dead heat'.

*At this point you may have noticed that 12hr mileages produced during the 24 hr race were being classed as records. These mileages subsequently were listed in the RRA results handbook from this day on. Once pacing had stopped however, this practice seems to have died out.*

*Holbeins total 24hr mileage of 324 miles was the only time that 300 miles had been surpassed in 24hrs on solid tyres. Frank Shorland was 2nd with 291.5 miles after breaking the Edinburgh to London record by 10 hours with 44hrs 49 mins only eight days previously. Third was W.C. Goulding on a trike with 280 miles also breaking the 24hr record by 16 miles.*

This was the first year 'out and back' detours were used from Wisbech, probably of some 20 miles in length. If a rider such as Holbein or Shorland was way ahead of the main field and going fast, a controller would send them on a detour at Wisbech for some ten miles only to be turned and retraced by a stationary marshal.

━━━▷◆◁━━━

**F.T. Bidlake** got his name on the **RRA** record books this year with a **100 mile tricycle ride in 6hrs 55 mins 58 secs, also taking the London to York in 18 hrs 28 mins.**

Thus the decade ended with several important changes having occurred. **Racing on the road was declining due to Police intervention.** The RRA had taken over the control of road records from the **NCU.** Performances on the **'Ordinary'** 'High Bicycle'or 'Penny Farthing' had been eclipsed by the lower **'Safety Bicycle'** and the **pneumatic tyre** had been re-invented by **John Boyd Dunlop**, although its effect on cycle racing had yet to be seen. **The Motor Car** had also come into being and slowly through the next decade it would influence further changes to cycle racing.

<h1 style="text-align:center">1890</h1>

This year saw the first appearance of the 'pneumatic' cycle tyre used in club races. John Boyd Dunlop invented his tyre in 1888 but it had been found to be hard to remove and replace when a puncture occurred. Improvements to the design were quickly made and by 1890 it became a practicable device. *Strangely enough incompatibility is a problem that still exists between certain tyre and rim combinations, some 110 years or more later!* These new tyres were much bulkier than the slim solid ones and were a source of ridicule to the average man in the street, but it didn't take long for them to realise the benefits of the invention. Men won races with these new tyres right from the outset. The benefits were so good that the North Road CC handicapped riders for using this type of tyre by 5 minutes, but even so, every club race was won by men riding pneumatics. *Whether by design or accident, the early 'place to place' rides challenged comparison with the times of the mail coaches, which in good weather averaged 10 mph over a journey of about 200 miles. The mailbags reached York or Liverpool from London in about 20 hours and it was 1890 before the bicycle beat that. Hence the start and finish was at the head G.P.O's in the centre of these towns wherever possible.*

This was the year that **Frank Shorland** achieved the ambition of **beating the stage coach time** for travelling from **London to Brighton and back of 7hrs 50 mins.** A team of four riders had beaten the coach time, but it fell to **Shorland to be the first man to accomplish it single handed. His time was 7hrs 19mins.** At that time Brighton and back was not a record recognised by the RRA but as a result of the ride it was placed on the list and Shorland's time passed as the first record over the route. Racing on the road was now being frowned upon by the N.C.U. (National Cyclists Union) and a lot of clubs looked to using enclosed 'paths' or tracks to run their shorter events. The Anfield and the North Road CC continued with their 24hr races on the road, but the instructions given to the riders with their official route and start card stated that *'Competitors are particularly requested to avoid all appearance of racing through towns'*.

Pacing was still an accepted part of all forms of racing, but from being a gentlemanly assistance of one's club mates and a returning of favours, it was becoming more organised with the better riders creating a team of skilled pacers who could assist their man under any conditions.

⎯⎯◇•⎯⎯

**May 2nd 1890 The Anfield BC** promoted a 24hr road ride for club members only, starting at midnight on a course that ran from Knotty Ash, going first into Cheshire and then down into Newport, Shropshire, then linking with the Watling Street (A5) to retrace at Weedon. The weather was so bad that the event was cancelled, but one of their members J.A. Bennett, 'Artie' to his friends, insisted on finishing, to obtain his club standard badge and managed **215 miles.**

⎯⎯◇•⎯⎯

**The 30th August 1890** saw the first **North Road CC 24hr** event where pneumatic tyres were used, although the **winner, Monty Holbein with 336.5 miles,** was using cushion tyres, a solid tyre with air-spaces, like a honeycomb, which were claimed at that time to be as good as 'pneumatic', but puncture free. **F.T. Bidlake** rode these same 'cushion tyres' on his **trike** to produce a record like Holbein. **Bidlake's mileage was 289 miles.** Holbein and T.A. 'Tommy' Edge led the race right from start till the end where Edge sprinted past Holbein, thinking he had won, but Holbein had covered more miles than him due to a 'detour'. **Edge was 2nd with 333 miles and H.H. Spencer took 3rd with 302 miles.** Holbein's bicycle was a sprung-framed 'Whippet' which he claimed was more comfortable for the road surfaces at that time.

**The Northern Road Records Association** was formed in this year in December. The NRRA took in the areas in the north of England to include the counties of Lancashire, Yorkshire, Cheshire, Derbyshire, Staffordshire, Northumberland, Durham, Cumberland and Westmorland. Eighteen clubs affiliated and later the counties of Flintshire and Denbighshire and parts of Nottinghamshire and Lincolnshire became subject to NRRA rules.

**The Catford CC** awarded gold medals for riders attaining records for 24hrs. **W.H.Grimwade rode 247 miles** on Western roads but was later outclassed by **Holbein with the North Road and RRA record of 336.5 miles.**

*On December 29th 1890, 100 Sioux Indians were massacred at Pine Ridge, Dakota, by U.S Cavalrymen under the command of Colonel James Forsyth. Half of the casualties were women and children.*

## 1891

*In this year Frank Bowden offered G.P. Mills £1,000 a year to design cycles for him with a view to producing a more simple method of multiple gearing. This led eventually to a lengthy series of test rides to perfect the new 3 speed hub gear. Mills with his expertise and fitness did a fair amount of the testing himself. The final designs were completed by Henry Sturmey and James Archer.*

**'The Cyclist'** A prominent paper of the day states "The North Road Club now boasts 132 members, amongst whom are the cream of the earths road fliers".

**May 1891** saw the first race take place from Bordeaux to Paris on very muddy roads, **British riders dominated. G.P. Mills won** despite a fall and having to borrow a bike from one of the pacers. **He took 26hrs 34mins 57secs for the 360 mile ride. Holbein was second in 27hrs 50mins 47secs.** S.F. Edge was third in 30hrs 13mins 49 secs. J.E. Bates fourth in 30hrs 13mins 57secs. **The first Frenchman to reach Paris was Jiel-Laval some 5.5 hours slower than Mills. How times have changed!**

⎯⎯◇•⎯⎯

**The North Road CC 24hr** took place on August 22nd. The police objected to the event starting in Hitchin, so it was moved to Henlow Crossing. Holbein wanted to avenge his defeat by Mills in the Bordeaux-Paris race by stamping his authority and race to a high mileage, but 4 miles from the start, Holbein fell heavily and was badly hurt, unable to continue.

**Frank Shorland** now came to prominence and at 12 hours had got well ahead of Mills with **192.5 miles,** a new record. Any performance records like this in an event are also being used for the RRA record books. At 3pm the weather turned with heavy rain spoiling any more records. **Shorland** on a 'safety' finished his ride early with 326 miles knowing he wouldn't break the record. **J.F. Walsh, Bath Road CC was 2nd** on an 'ordinary' with **312 miles. F.T. Bidlake on a trike broke his own record with 304.5 miles.** All riders were now riding on pneumatic tyres.

---

**September 19th saw the Anfield BC** hold their closed **24 hrs** ride, which was won by **A.J. Jack** riding a pneumatic tyred 'ordinary' with **286 miles**, a 'NRRA' record. **J.A. Bennett was 2nd** and **T.B. Conway third.**

**Also this year saw records by Holbein at 24hrs on a trike with 311.5 miles, an RRA record.** P.A. Ranson took the RRA London to Edinburgh bicycle record down to 43 hrs 25 mins.

**Midnight September 29th 1891:** After two unsuccessful starts due to bad weather G.P. Mills finally got away from Lands End on a starlit September night. The southwest wind suited his urgent style. He lost one of his 'pacers', fellow Anfielder, J.D. Siddeley after six miles when he hit a cart and he stopped to make a repair. Mills left and passed through Penzance just before the first hour was up and members of the 'First and Last CC' helped pace him to Redruth and Bodmin.

One of the party slipped on the gravel and fetched everybody but Mills down. He pressed on through Cornwall and into Devon and by the time he reached the border into Somerset the dawn was up. Just after Bridgwater he stopped to borrow one of his pacers mounts, feeling that it would be lighter than his 50lb machine. By the next evening Mills was fairly flying, Bristol, 196 miles was reached after 18.5 hours. At 11.40 pm he'd reached Worcester inside 24hrs for 256 miles. He took a stop for refreshment and then pressed on to Kidderminster, Wellington, Hodnet, & Whitchurch. 300 miles passed and he battled on through Nantwich, Middlewich and Northwich. The dawn rose at Warrington where he stopped for breakfast; rain started to fall atNewton Le Willows and the bad cobbled roads of Wigan were slippery in the wet. It rained for 48 hours, covering his Black Anfielder's tunic in mud. At Lancaster he stopped to change into dry clothing; Kendal, The Lake District and Penrith were passed by 10.30 pm. **He'd covered 456 miles from Lands End inside 2 days.** He stopped for a short sleep and extra clothing to see him through till his 3rd dawn and he struggled through Carlisle and the Borders. By 6am he'd completed 500 miles, but the last few hours had been spent slipping through the thick mud. A large crowd waited to see him through Edinburgh; one of his pacers caught a train to Pitlochry to get well ahead of him. The rain was relentless and the roads in Scotland were worse than England. Through the Grampians to Inverness he struggled on with his pacers. Dingwall, Tain and Golspie at 802 miles was reached by 8pm Thursday and Mills had only stopped for one and a half hours sleep since leaving Lands End. Dry clothes were borrowed at almost every stopping place and the wet ones discarded. The pace slackened and as the last night drew on, Mills began to feel very drowsy. At Helmsdale village on the Scottish coast with only 54 miles left to cover, he asked P.C. Wilson, one of his pacers, to see if the chemists shop had got anything to keep him awake. Wilson returned with a white powder and a cup of coffee. He put a large teaspoonful of the powder in the coffee, Mills drank it and continued with his journey.

The drink soon took effect and the speed began to increase rapidly; the pacemakers couldn't keep up with Mills and he seemed to be 'flying' dementedly. Suddenly he lost consciousness and remembered nothing until awakened the following morning. His pacers recalled that he was fast asleep but still pedalling hard. He obeyed their instructions and followed their lead, like an automatic machine. Thirty five miles were reeled off in this manner of riding until they came to a signpost and in the darkness they did not know which way to take. At this point at 4.50am after seemingly negotiating the route through Berriedale and Wick to this position where they were lost, Mills fell from his machine and couldn't be set in motion again. They carried him to a nearby crofter's cottage where he was put to bed and slept for over six hours. When his helpers finally roused him he was astonished to find he was only three miles from John o' Groats. Within minutes he was back on his machine and away again and in spite of everything that had happened he reached his destination at 11.17am.
He'd taken 14hrs 28 mins off his own previous record for the 874 mile journey ridden on an 'ordinary' to a new time of **4 days 11 hrs 17 mins.**

Mills hadn't quite understood what had happened over those last 50 miles and asked Wilson what it was he'd given him at Helmsdale: "cocaine" was the reply. Nine months later when his doctor questioned him as to how he kept going for days non stop and had he taken anything to keep awake, Mills replied he'd taken cocaine just once. "How much?" the doctor asked. When Mills told him it was a large teaspoonful in a cup of coffee, the doctor looked aghast and replied "You took enough to kill two men!" The doctor went on to say that Mills was fortuitous to have kept on pedalling for so long after taking the drug and keeping his circulation going at a brisk rate as otherwise such a large dose would have killed him.

Mills described the roads in Cornwall as being very loose and stony resembling a sea beach rather than a road. He had to walk over a mile before reaching Sennen and was pitched out of the saddle twice before reaching Penzance. On his first End to End riding an 'ordinary' with no brakes he averaged over 200 miles a day and had a total of five hours sleep, all this at 19 years of age. He mentions crossing Bodmin Moor which was in very bad condition as the road was very rarely used. His mileage at midnight after his first 24hrs was 215, reaching north of Bristol.

*The road over the Grampians even in 1924 was described by Roy Green in his book titled '100 years of Cycling Road Records' as being 'no more than two cartwheel tracks with grass and heather growing in the middle'.*

*Later in the ride leaving Blair Atholl with 642 miles covered, he encountered the full force of a gale and was frequently blown out of the saddle, and the last 23 miles to Dalwhinnie took over 4 hours. On the 'Ord of Caithness' the wind regularly reduced him to walking for miles.*

*Roy Green mentions riders being paced over many of their records and races at all distances 'but the extent to which it benefitted the rider varied considerably according to his, or his clubs, wealth and ability to put up pacing teams'.*

Finally the last record of the year went to **Monty Holbein** riding a Swift safety bicycle at the Herne Hill Track he covered **361.8 miles** in 24 hrs. **A new track 24 hr record.**

# 1892

The Anfield B.C. 24 hr was for club members only and was won by 'Artie' J.A. Bennett with 305.5 miles. Lawrence Fletcher increased the NRRA tricycle record to 268.5 miles. 2nd bike was S.H. Keeling with 268 miles; 2nd trike was H.C. Siddeley with 260 miles.

⇒·◇·⇐

**8pm Friday July 22nd** saw nine men start away at **Herne Hill Track** to ride for 24hrs to try and win a 100 guinea Challenge Cup from the proprietors of **CUCA Cocoa**. Spectators could pay to come in and watch the riders, they could even place a bet on the winner and have something to eat and drink. **Frank Shorland** broke away early, at 84 miles into the race, gradually increasing his lead until the end. Holbein stopped at 167 miles with saddle-soreness, all of the riders were paced throughout by single bicycles and the day was good with no wind or rain. Only four men finished **F.W. Shorland** was 1st with **413.9miles**, 2nd **J.M. James North Road CC**, 407.3 miles, J.F. Walsh Bath Road Club, 3rd with 384.5 miles, and A. Brundrett, Keighley CC was 4th with 379.45 miles.

It was a great success for the promoters, and was the first time **400 miles had been reached in an all day ride.** One press report said that "Shorlands winning distance was so phenomenal, it will become a fixture on the record book". A rash statement to make!

A few days before Shorland's ride at Herne Hill, a Frenchman, **Stephane,** the winner of the second Paris-Bordeaux race, rode **392.6 miles** on the Buffalo Velodrome in Paris in **24 hrs.**

On hearing of Shorlands ride, **Stephane** made a 2nd attempt on the same track and covered **421.25 miles.**

In June 1892, Tommy Edge succeeded in beating G.P. Mills record for the Lands End to John o Groats with **4 days 40 minutes,** a beating of over 10.5 hours. **Edge went on and completed the 1000 miles in 5 days 11 hrs 38 mins.** *Some years later the RRA added the 1,000 miles to the list of records.*

———⊃•◇•⊂———

The **North Road CC open 24hr** was run on **September 10th.** The day was a good one and Shorland rode away from his fellow riders after 100 miles, never to be caught. His winning distance was **a new RRA record of 366.5 miles.** 2nd was Artie Bennett with 352.5 miles and fastest trike was once again **F.T. Bidlake** with **207 miles,** having stopped early.

———⊃•◇•⊂———

August of that year saw **Lawrence Fletcher of the Anfield BC break the End to End** with **3 days 23 hrs 55 mins.** In that same month he broke the **NRRA Trike 24hr record** with **268.5 miles.** R.H. Carlisle broke the London to Edinburgh record with 33hrs 55 mins and Holbein improved the RRA bicycle 24hr record to 359 miles and later rode 337 miles on a trike.

## 1893

The mileages achieved on the Herne Hill Track, which was a wooden board surface, seem a little unreal for the date in time but one must remember that these races and indeed virtually all races at this time were 'paced'. The pacers themselves were very capable of good mileages and I would imagine that they were paid by the 'stars' they were helping. **July 21st** saw the second **24hr track race for the 'Cuca Cocoa Cup';** it was another success for **Shorland with a record 426.25 miles,** but the 2nd man was the sensation of the day **F.T. Bidlake riding a trike and achieving 410.625 miles,** beating all of the remaining bike riders.

A few weeks previously, **in June, G.P. Mills brought the End to End record down by another 7 hours on a trike.** This is the first time a trike had been faster than a bike over this journey. He recorded **3 days 16 hours 47 mins.** It was a paced tricycle record and was not beaten by another tricycle until 1949, by Bert Parkes.

**29th July 1893 The Anfield 24hr** road ride took place. A rare phenomenon was achieved when **a trike ridden by H. Hellier won the event with 281.75 miles creating a new NRRA record beating A.G. White with 280.75 miles,** K.B. Saunders with 272.87 miles and T.B. Conway with 271 miles.

———⊃•◇•⊂———

The **North Road open 24hr** took place on August 26th. **F.W. Shorland won with 370 miles, a new record, and also breaking the 12hr record with 195 miles.** F.T. Bidlake was 2nd on his trike with 331 miles. H. Hammond was 3rd with 325 miles. 62 year old **Joseph Atto** of the Pickwick BC rode **281 miles** to gain a gold medal award from his club.

The French also held a **24hr track** race at the **Velodrome D'Hiver** in Paris. **Williams of Nevers won the event with 428.5 miles** from Huret with 423 miles and Duanip 3rd with 409.

## 1894

*Queen Victoria opened the Manchester Ship Canal, linking Manchester to the sea via the River Mersey in this year.*

The **Anfield BC** was the first event in the 24hr calendar held in July. **W.J. Neason won the event with 335 miles – a new NRRA record.** Lawrence Fletcher was 2nd with 324 miles and W.R. Hood was 3rd with 280.5. Eight riders finished.

*The course had altered for this year to try and get better roads. The start was moved to the Chester area, then using various 'loops' of roads on the Wirral before going to Whitchurch, then Congleton, to High Legh, back to Whitchurch, followed by various triangles of road in Shropshire. Newport is probably as far south as the riders will now travel to, before retracing back towards Chester.*

⇒·◇·⇐

In the southern half of Great Britain things were a little different as police were cracking down on cyclists racing furiously on the road. The cause of this police purge was an accident during a 50 mile race on July 21st. There were 50 riders and probably as many 'pacers' if not more, and with the way the riders were handicapped on their past performances, it was inevitable that there would be large bunches of riders on the road.

The accident happened on the Great North Road at the 57th milestone, F.T. Bidlake was being paced by J.W. Stocks, and Arthur Ilsley was inches away from Bidlake's back axle. A horse and carriage driven by a lady was ambling along towards the riders, and on seeing them she lifted the reigns, pulling the wrong one. The horse slewed across the rider's path causing them all to fall into the ditch. No actual harm was done but the woman complained to the police who subsequently banned all cycle racing from the carriageway. *The Chief Constable of Huntingdonshire went to extraordinary lengths to stop the annual 24hr race taking place. 'Cycling' reported "Constables were all over the place; at Stilton 22 sprang out of hedgerows when three harmless cyclists came along. It was also reported that horse reins had been stretched across the road, and at Hitchin the police planned to snare the cyclists in nets. The police however had a long fruitless wait on a wet night, as Bidlake and Wilson had quickly revised a new course eliminating 'hostile' areas."*

Undeterred, the **North Road 24hr** race went ahead but it started outside of the county boundary at Peterborough at 11pm instead of midnight. **C.C. Fontaine** of the Polytechnic **CC won** the event with **376 miles.** A new **open 24hr RRA record.** Edwin Buckley, Anfield BC, was **2nd** with **358.5 miles.** F.T. Bidlake again won the **tricycle** event with **356.5 miles.** At the twelve hour point he'd reached **194.5 miles.** Both of those mileages became records on a trike. **The first tandem** to finish a **24hr** road race did so with **317 miles,** ridden by **J.Van Hooy Donk and Park Highatt.**

⇒·◇·⇐

The **'CUCA' Cup 24hr** goes down in history as the one in which **Frank Shorland** had his **third successive win** so making the cup his own. The promoters had gone to great measures to find a good challenger to Shorland, as earlier in the year, in June, **Constant Huret,** the French professional, had raised the record to **457 miles** on the Paris track. This left Shorland needing over 31 miles to get his record back.

The challenger was **Fontaine,** he made a 'Herculean' effort to combat Shorland. The race which had started at 8pm before a crowd of about 9,000 enthusiasts, saw Shorland take the lead immediately, and by 4 miles he had lapped the field. By midnight the crowd had increased to 15,000, most of whom stayed until morning to see their heroes get to the 12hr point. Fontaine had to confess himself beaten, and gave up the chase. He finally retired at 17 hours. Bidlake had started on a bicycle but gave up at 100 miles, whereupon he continued to coach and keep Shorland ahead of his schedule. Huret (later to become involved in producing cycle components and mechanisms for multiple derailleur gearing) had come over to England to see Shorland ride and sportingly steered one of the pacing tandems to the great delight of the spectators.

As the day wore on, more spectators crowded in to swell the crowd to 25,000. At the finish **Shorland** had amassed **460.68 miles.** The band played "Rule Britannia", "Marseillaise", and "Yankee Doodle". **Petersen** of Denmark was **2nd** with **431.57, Chapple** was **3rd** with **427.3 miles.** This was Shorland's last race, he was a much liked and very popular man and quick-tongued. During the race, Fontaine had jocularly shouted to Frank "I've got my eye on the cup"; to which Shorland replied "yes, but you'll never get your ruddy hands on it".

*Record breaking on the road was mainly over the End to End route. R.H. Carlisle broke the bicycle record with 3 days 14 hrs 15 mins. Then G.P. Mills lowered this to 3 days 5hrs 49 mins. Mills also reduced the London to Edinburgh record that year with 29hrs 28 mins. This record didn't last long though, C.C. Fontaine brought it down to 28 hours 27 mins in September. E. Oxborrow and H.H. Sampson set the tandem bicycle record over the same route in 27 hrs 33 mins and created a new 24hr mileage of 340 miles on the way.*

*The first x-ray experiments took place in this year*

The **Anfield B.C.** was the only one to promote a **24hr race** using the open road this year, it was a very close finish, and was restricted to club members only, and run in July.   **F. Watkins** won with **343.5 miles.**   2nd was **J.R. Thompson, 343 miles** and **H. Hellier** broke the **NRRA Tricycle record** with **326.75 miles.**

⋙—◇—⋘

Track 24hr races are now becoming popular and in early June **The Anerley B.C.** promoted an event on the Putney cement track, the prize was the Carwardine Cup.   Out of eight riders who started, only three finished.   **C.C. Fontaine** of the Polytechnic CC won with **474.8 miles, J.J. Patterson,** North London CC was **2nd** with **466.38 miles** and **J. Bowie 3rd, 338 miles.**

The **North Road CC held their invitation track 24hrs race** at Wood Green.   Out of twenty riders invited, eighteen started and only four finished.   **R.H. Carlisle** of the Anfield B.C. won with **417 miles, J.P. Clark,** North Road CC was **2nd 403 miles** and **H.W. Standish** of the London Century RC **3rd 395m,** and **F.R. Cook,** North Road CC **372 miles.**   High winds and hours of heavy rain almost ruined the event.

The **CUCA Cup 24hr race** took place at Herne Hill.   Fifteen riders started and only five finished.   **George Hunt** of the Notts Corinthians **won with 458 miles.**   **Artie Bennett,** Anfield B.C. **2nd  with 447 miles** and C. Chapple Chelsea CC **3rd with 409 miles.**   Hunt led the race almost from start to finish.

A French man, Cordang, won a motor paced 24hr race at The Crystal Palace Track with **615.5 miles.**   The **Bol D'or race** at the Paris track was **won by Huret with 515.08 miles.**

Although there have been lots of track races and the results for the winners have been very good, the events generally have been poorly supported, both by riders and spectators.   On the record-breaking scene **W.J. Neason** lowered the **London to Edinburgh bicycle record to 27hrs 38mins.**   In July **Mills and Edge** lowered the **Tandem End to End record to 3 days 4 hrs 46 mins** and this record remained unbroken until 1938.   They rode a Raleigh tandem and also **improved the 24hr record to 377 miles.**   In September **Holbein and Artie Bennett** bettered this **24hr record** with **397.5 miles.**   **Holbein** just prior to his tandem record had improved the **single bicycle record** to **397 miles** riding a **Swift bicycle** with **Dunlop tyres.**

Also in 1895, B. Winchurch won a 24hr race on Aston Track with 421 miles.

*Marconi conducts his first 'wire-less' transmission.*

*The first British Cinema opened in London.*

The **Anfield B.C.** was again the only club to promote a **24hr** on the road.   It was **won by E. Buckley with 373.5 miles, G.R. Deakin was 2nd with 363.5 and F. Watkins 3rd with 355 miles.**   Edwin Buckley and G.R. Deakin were in the lead almost to the 12hr point with Deakin 196 miles, Buckley 194, and Watkins 187 miles. They stayed two miles apart until Buckley closed the gap around the Sandbach area.    He then increased his lead by 10 miles and ran off the route card at Latchford and so turned to finish towards Lymm.

⋙—◇—⋘

This was the year when two different track races clashed on the same weekend. The 'Cuca Cup' and the 'North Road'. Also with various races going on in France, the top riders were thinly spread around, again resulting in poor fields and poor crowds. **Rivierre won the Bol D'or tandem paced track event with 533.5 miles** from Williams and Buffel, all Frenchmen. **The North Road CC** professional race was **won by Huret with 460 miles**. **The Cuca Cup race was won by F.R.Goodwin** of the North Roads CC with **476.95 miles. John Hunt was 2nd with 467.45 miles**, 3rd was **A.P. Pepper,** Luton Town CC **425.21 miles.**

In Paris the new Velodrome D'Hiver saw a two man match race between Rivierre and **Huret,** paced with teams of quad's (four men machines) and triplets. At 11hours Rivierre retired leaving Huret to continue and reach **a new world record of 545.728 miles in 24hrs.**

The annual Bordeaux to Paris race saw 41 professionals take part, including four British riders; Arthur Linton, W.J. Neason, R.H. Carlisle and George Hunt. Arthur Linton went into the lead towards the end but on approaching Paris he went off course and took a longer route to the finish. Rivierre finished 1st with Linton closely behind him. The judges decided to award a dead heat. Two months after the race Arthur Linton died. The press and medical opinion at that time considered the cause of death to be an excessive amount of riding in long distance races, but shortly afterwards, his brother Tom and team-mate Jimmy Michael both died. All three men were in their early twenties and had been trained by 'Choppy' Warburton. Doping was prominent amongst professional riders even in those days, and later Warburton was accused of having used excessive amounts on the three men, which helped cause their early demise.

So 1896 showed a distinct reduction of long distance events, with so few riders and a pathetic number of finishers in these track events, it is little wonder that they went into decline. They must have been boring to both ride and watch.

*There were now more and more motorists in and around the London area. The law requiring a motor vehicle to have a man walking a few yards in front, with a red flag, was dropped and by 1896 he was no longer required at all. The speed limit was also raised from 4mph to 14 mph, although I also have literature stating 12 mph in rural areas and 8 mph in towns.*

## 1897

**The Anfield 24hr** was again a club event for members only and was won by **W.A. Lowcock with 330 miles.** F. Watkins 2nd with 304 and 3rd E.A. Tooth 250 miles. Eight other riders plus three tandems failed to finish.

⟫◇⟪

**The North Road CC 24 hr** was back on the open road this year, eight riders started but only two finished. **Ernest Gould with 340 miles and W.M. Crosbie with 315 miles. This would be the last North Road event to allow the pacing of riders.**

⟫◇⟪

There were still two **24hr track races** held in this year. In June an International race at **Crystal Palace** saw **G.A. Patterson** win with **502.125 miles.** In September a motor paced event at the same track saw **Frenchman Mathieu Cordang** win with **616 miles.** In France the **Bol D'or** track 24 hr race was won by **Frenchman L. Stein** with **474.95 miles.**

There were three more paced records in **1897.** The first one was **Monty Holbein's 24hr** attempt being paced on the road by a Daimler car for some of the **403.5 mile** distance. The law governing speed for motor vehicles at that time meant that the car was either breaking the speed limit constantly, or of no use at all. Later in the year this record was improved by **G. Hunt with 411.5 miles. He went on to break the London to Edinburgh with 26hrs 46 mins.** The value of pace-making was discovered very early in cycling club life but was used very casually in the first few years of racing. It was more a case of you help me in this race, and I'll help you in the next one. There would probably have been monetary involvement as well.

With the development of the tandem and larger multi-rider cycling machines in the middle 1890's, pace-making became a great art. Holbein in particular used to make very thorough preparations to ensure he was adequately served by pacing machines, he even had printed instructions to issue to his pacers before a race, and here is an extract: "the order of pacing is to be: tandem leading, tandem tricycle next, record breaker to follow, spare 'safety' rider to follow, last. When the wind is on the side, the tandem tricycle should lead, and the tandem to ride at the side of the record breaker to shelter him."

*With a cavalcade like that it's a good job there was little or no other traffic on the road!*

**These extracts, like many others on the North Road Club 24hr race, were taken from the History of the North Road Cycling Club 1885 to 1935.**

Later that year Monty Holbein had an accident which finished his cycling career. He had broken more cycling road records than any other man and had been the first to cover 300 and 400 miles in 24 hours. He went on to become a great long distance swimmer, specialising in Channel swimming. He tried to emulate his idol, Captain Mathew Webb, who swam the 21 mile English Channel between Dover and Calais in 21 hrs 45 mins some 22 years earlier. But Holbein never got to break that record, or indeed complete the full crossing, after many attempts. He was nevertheless an authority on the subject.

# 1898

By 1898 there wasn't a single track 24 hr race held in this country. Promoters of these events had seen spectator figures dropping rapidly over the last two years and with riders failing to finish it had become a dull spectacle.

The only club to run a 24hr road race that year was the **Anfield BC** in July. Nine solo bicycles and one tandem started. **T.B. Conway won with 353 miles. B.H. Glover was 2nd 340, and M. Montgomery 3rd with 330.75 miles.**

⟹◆⟸

At home **F.R. Goodwin** attacked the **bicycle 24hr record.** It was a motor paced ride and although he broke the record with 428 miles, his pacers were fined for speeding in several counties. This led to the RRA banishing motor paced rides from 1900. A new category of **unpaced riding** was introduced by the **RRA** in this year **1898.** One of the first records to be broken was the **12hr** by **Arthur Ilsley** on a **bike** with **187 miles.** Then **Gould** attacked it twice and beat it twice in that same year with rides of **191 miles** and **201.5 miles, all unpaced.**

*September 2nd 1898, General Kitchener's army slaughters a huge Mahdist Dervish Army in the Sudan, and finally avenges Gordon's massacre of 1885.*

# 1899

The years 1899 to 1902 encompass the Boer War. Cycle racing was in decline and the cycle trade in general didn't pick up until 1920. This year of 1899 was the poorest year to date for long distance records. The **Anfield B.C. 24hr** was run in appalling weather conditions and although all the riders retired, **F.H. Wood** completed the greatest distance achieving **255 miles** before he stopped at 23 hours.

⟹◆⟸

**F.H. Goodwin** of the North Road CC attacked the **London to Edinburgh** riding a bicycle with a **Bricknell hand gear.** This was a device that drove the front wheel by pumping special handlebars up and down and combined with the rear wheel drive, it was thought that a much greater performance could be achieved. Although Goodwin broke the record with 25 hours 26 mins it was felt that the new device didn't provide any real advantage. Goodwin was also paced by a motor tricycle to Newcastle and from there on by two single bicycles. This was probably because the speed limit in Scotland was 10 mph.

A final record was performed at the 'La Hague' velodrome in the Netherlands when **Mathieu Cordang,** paced by eight tandems, pushed the **24hr track record to 649.1 miles.** However, the record was not recognised as at the time, Cordang was under suspension by the UVF (Union Velocipedique Francaise) the French ruling body of cycling at that time.

One or two attempts were started around this time to establish cycle mileage records for a years riding, many such attempts would take place over the next 40 years culminating with Tommy Godwin's record in 1939.

It was about this time at the turn of the Century that F.T. Bidlake took the first steps to find a solution of getting cycle races back onto the roads in this area. He proposed that instead of bunches of racing cyclists and their pacers attracting police hostility, a method of setting riders off individually at intervals according to their ability and handicap mark, would be more appropriate and so the BIRTH OF 'TIME TRIALLING' TOOK PLACE.

*Road Race 1886*

*In late November 2008 Lynne Taylor was the Guest of Honour at the 60th Anniversary of the A5 Rangers CC annual dinner and prize presentation. We were made most welcome by Sue and Mick Holliday, Trevor Parrish, and all of the members present, at the Saracen's Head Inn at Towcester. Before Lynne presented the prizes she gave a short speech describing her trials and experiences on her 'End to End' rides and also how she reprogrammed herself to become 2nd in the BBAR in 2008. Mention was also made of her many wins in 15 successive Mersey RC 24hr races. Up until the 1990's the A5 Rangers had a keen 24hr rider, Mick Holliday, and this made his fellow club members more aware of long distance riding. In 1979 the club took 2nd team in the Mersey RC 24hr and in 1987 Mick rode 408.90 miles for 4th place in that same event, helped by his wife Sue. With another past 24hr rider, Joe Summerlin, giving a toast to the club and an amusing speech, it was a most memorable and enjoyable evening.*

*Lynne and I had travelled there by car along the old Roman road, the Watling Street, otherwise known as the A5, the original route from the north west to London. We live not far from Brownhills on route to the Anfield 24hr turn at Weedon near Towcester, and our comfortable car journey through the fog and cold going via Tamworth, Hinckley and Weedon, was nearly two hours in duration. It made me realise just how far from home the competitors in that Anfield event of 1885 must have felt after riding from Knotty Ash in Liverpool, down through Cheshire and Shropshire to the A5, roughly 70 miles. They then had a similar distance to ride from there to the turn at Weedon, making an outward journey of nearly 140 miles, retracing to finish in the dark again at midnight, somewhere in the Cheshire area. I think there was also an alternative turn at the Lichfield turnpike for the slower riders at this time, but what a journey they must all have had on their heavy cumbersome bikes nearly 120 years ago. G.P. Mills won that year with 259 miles riding a high ordinary cycle with solid tyres.*

# CHAPTER TWO

## THE UNPACED TIME TRIAL ERA 1900 – 1939

### 1900

If we consider that 1900 was the last year of the Century, we can finish by commenting on the two 24 hour events that were held.

**The Anfield BC** continued as always, their event being won by **R.L. Knipe with 332.75 miles. W.R. Oppenheimer was 2nd with 330.75 miles and R. Barton 3rd with 265.875 miles.** The weather had been more kind to the riders this year. Knipe had led Barton by 14 miles at 12 hrs, Barton then touched his pacing tandems rear wheel. He fell heavily damaging his knee but struggled on until the pain forced him to stop at 265 miles.

———————⋙◇⋘———————

After a gap of three years with no event, the **North Road CC** ran their event for club members on a strictly unpaced basis, so avoiding the problems of the previous years when F.R. Goodwin was prosecuted for furious riding while being paced. Sixteen riders were despatched at 15 minute intervals and alternate riders were sent on different routes. This must have required tight organisation but success came to **T.G. King Jnr who won with 346.5 miles. A.R. Childs covered 322 miles and L. Diespecker was 3rd with 306 miles.** In his winning ride, King covered 170 miles in the first 12 hrs and 176.5 in the second. Sixteen riders started and 8 gold medals were presented.

———————⋙◇⋘———————

*By the year 1900 Raleigh Cycles were producing 10,000 bikes a year.*

There was now a noticeable decline in 24hr riding; track racing had attracted very poor fields and few spectators, and this led to most of the tracks closing. The motor cars, which had up to now been mechanically unreliable, were now becoming reliable and sought after by the young wealthy men who had previously been the backbone of cycle racing, they now took to racing motor cars. Even the famous Catford Hill Climb in 1900 included motor vehicles.

*I would like to thank the late Ron Sant, a good friend of mine for having the foresight to collate information on these early years of long distance cycle racing. Ron was a keen 24hr rider and 24hr fellowship member. He owned quite a large collection of antique cycles and memorabilia. Ron passed away in 2003 when leading a procession of antique cycles through Telford. While writing this early period of cycling history, I've dipped into Ron's authorative writings on the subject, many times.*

*One of my other main sources of information is a book entitled '50 Years of Road Riding'. The history of the North Road Cycling Club by S.H. Moxham. It covers a period of years from 1885 to 1935, and I am very grateful to the North Road CC for allowing me to use their yearly diary of events contained in this book. My thanks also to Mr Lancaster and Mr & Mrs Cook for their kind help.*

*Also my sincere thanks to Roger Sewell who ran the more recent 24hr events for the North Road CC until 1999, for loaning me this historic book.*

*My thanks to the Anfield Bicycle Club for allowing me to extract information from their Centenary edition of 'The Black Anfielders' the story of the Anfield Bicycle Club 1879 to 1978.*

# 1901

*Queen Victoria died on January 22nd at Osborne house on the Isle of Wight at the age of 81, so ending a 64 year reign.*

**The Anfield 24hr** was still a paced event and was expected to be a duel between Knipe and Oppenheimer. It was for the first 12 hours when Knipe led by 5 miles with 214.25 miles, a new NRRA record. By Whitchurch he'd gained 28 mins. Oppenheimer's problem was due to his pacing tandems not being fast enough, whereupon he rode on his own. At Newport he hadn't a chance of catching Knipe and so retired at 303 miles. **Knipe finished with 385.25 miles, another NRRA record. The tandem of Wood and Owen finished 2nd with 305.75 miles, again another NRRA record.**

⬅⬦➡

**The North Road CC 24hr** took place in late August with just six club members only. The weather was bad with persistent rain, only 2 men finished. **T.G. King Jnr won again with 357 miles and broke the RRA record for an unpaced solo bicycle. H.S. Price covered 337 miles** in his first 24hr race.

*On December 12th Marconi made his first wireless signal transmission across the Atlantic to Newfoundland from Poldhu in Cornwall.*

In the years covering the period from 1870 to 1920 so many new things were either discovered or invented, almost at the rate of one a month, that its hard to keep up with. Things that we now consider to be so basic in the 21st century, they seem almost commonplace in today's society. Items such as cars, aircraft, electricity, television, telephones, radio, rail travel, cures for diseases etc, etc. The list is endless, everything is now taken for granted. I've listed odd items of important historical interest as they've happened interspersed between the races because I'm still in awe of the men on cycles who covered over 400 miles in 24 hours, when Cowboys and Indians still fought battles on America's plains, and where in England an electric light was still a novelty, enjoyed by the very 'well off'.

# 1902

**The Anfield 24hr** saw the first 'paced' rider reach and **beat 400 miles** with **R.L. Knipe's 406.5 miles.** He also took the 12hr record on the way with 217 miles, both new NRRA records. He was the favourite and was out in the lead day and night. **R.E. Prichard was 2nd with 344.5 miles and E.H. Fox 3rd with 342 miles.** Knipe's record is the first 400 on the Northern RRA books, and the last as from now on, pacing isn't allowed.

⬅⬦➡

1902 saw eight **North Road** club riders contest the annual 24hr race. The first three places were taken by novices (first time riders at 24 hrs). **E.A. Cully won with 359.5 miles, P.S. Murray was 2nd with 342 miles and A. Mackenzie 3rd with 340 miles.**

# 1903

*The Sturmey-Archer 3 speed hub gear went on sale to the cycling public in 1903*

**Anfield 24hr.** Bad weather thwarted Bob Knipe's chances of breaking any more records this year. **J. Park won with a ride of 326 miles.** Pacing was still allowed in this event but only by using a solo bicycle.

⬅⬦➡

**The North Road** 1903 event was cancelled due to lack of entries.

*December 17th: The Wright Brothers made their first flight. Also in this year the first weather reports by wireless telegraph were received in London.*

# 1904

*There were now 20 million people living in Great Britain*

The Anfield 24hr was won this year by Kendrick and Holt on a tandem with 345 miles, an NRRA record. H. Roskell was 2nd with 326 miles and W.C. Tierney and R. Barton 3rd (both with 307.5 miles) paced.

———◆———

The North Road 24hr run on August 26th and 27th was a reasonably good day weather- wise. **W.E. Ward won the race with 363.5 miles.** It was an **event record** for an unpaced ride. Six other riders finished, all qualified for gold medals. **W.W. Robertson won the trike prize with 292 miles.**

A few more long distance records were either set or broken this year as **all RRA records are now unpaced,** and possibly slower for the place to place records compared to a paced one. The fixed time records such as the 12hr and 24hr may be of less mileage also.

Two North Road men **E. Bright and E.H. Grimsdell** set a new **tandem** record for riding from **London to Liverpool in 12hrs 25 mins.**

M.A. Crosbie: London to Portsmouth and back by tricycle, 9hrs 26mins 47 secs.

**E.H. Grimsdell** on a solo bicycle, **London to Edinburgh in 28hrs 3mins.** **W.E. Ward** who won the 24hr rode the **London to Portsmouth and back** on a **bike in 7hrs 50 mins 37 secs** breaking the record.

The Wingrave brothers **R.A. and F.H. broke the tandem record for London to Portsmouth and back,** and finally **Dr. F.W. Wesley,** a G.P. from Nottingham broke C.J. Mather's **Lands End to John o' Groat's** record by nearly 22 hours with **4 days 7 hrs 25 mins.** But of course this ride is still nearly a day slower than G.P. Mills paced record of 1894.

An amusing couple of incidents connected to road records is when W.H. Nutt who was in charge of feeding the two lots of riders on the London to Portsmouth and back had to fend off a pack of ravenous dogs who attacked his food supply on the side of the road, as well as feed the riders. Another is when **E.H. Grimsdell** broke the **London to Edinburgh bicycle record in 28hrs 03mins** riding a 91" single speed gear. He thought it was a 78" gear and didn't find out until a week later. He just assumed it was a hard route! When he got to Newcastle he had to cross the High Level penny toll Bridge. He only had a gold sovereign and couldn't get change so pleaded poverty until another sportsman came along and paid his toll to get across.

A short time later, **George Olley** broke Grimsdell's **London to Edinburgh** by nearly an hour with **27hrs 10 mins.**

*The first pedestrian was killed by a car in London this year. The speed limit is raised to 20 mph for all vehicles.*

# 1905

This years **Anfield 24hr race** was won by E.J. Cody with 362 miles. Edwin Buckley was 2nd with 359 miles after a closely fought day long battle between them. **F. Bird was 3rd with 290 miles,** all paced.

———◆———

*The Austin Motor Company was formed.*

**The North Road CC 24hr** August 18-19th saw rain, gale force winds throughout and a very dark night. Nine riders started but only four finished. **W.E. Ward won** for the second time with **333 miles, Dr. F.W. Wesley with**

306 miles was 2nd and **C. Hillhouse with 288** came 3rd. **E. Bright** on a **tricycle** was **4th with 224.5 miles.** Although there have been many bad days experienced in the running of this event, the consensus of opinion was that 1905 was the worst ever 24hr.

⇒•◇•⇐

Although many place to place 'RRA' and 'Regional RRA' records are being broken almost on a weekly basis, **I must now concentrate on the 'London to Edinburgh', 'The 24hr', and 'The End to End' and '1,000 mile' records to augment my history of the 24hr time trial.**

I feel that these important RRA records are very closely linked to the 24hr history and most of these record breakers would all have ridden a 24hr club time trial to have measured their fitness and stamina reserves by. **(Although saying that, I have no record of Goss Green, Tom Peck, George Olley or W. Welsh ever riding a 24hr time trial).**

**E.H. Grimsdell** retook his **London to Edinburgh Bicycle record** from George Olley with a ride of **26hrs 10 mins,** a one hour beating. **E. Bright and P.H. Miles** on a **tandem** were the **first unpaced** crew to take the **Edinburgh London record** with **27hrs 54 mins,** and **Dr F.W. Wesley** on a **trike** set a record time for that same journey of **32 hrs 42 mins.**

**George Olley** reduced Wesley's **bicycle End to End** record to **3 days 20 hours 15 mins** also in this year of 1905.

*The 'AA' (Automobile Association) was formed this year and would soon have AA patrolmen on bicycles riding the roads, not only to help at breakdowns but also to warn approaching motorists of police 'speed-traps' ahead. The patrolman would signal by saluting the driver – so nothing changes much does it! In the 'AA's latest Centenary road atlas all of the Gatso speed cameras are marked as to their location on each road (2005).*

*In December 1905 the first Ambulance service started in London.*

## 1906

This report of the **Anfield BC** event is rather ironic, it continues - **'The club ran its first unpaced 24hr** road ride this year, **no followers were allowed'** (these were riders who would follow the competitor some good distance behind and would administer food and help throughout the ride. Most of the 'followers' would obviously be very fit men but would probably ride no more than 50 miles at a time, then they might possibly pick up a train to get ahead of the rider, so passing the duties onto another follower, or wait for their rider to retrace and return, and then follow him to the finish to witness his correct distance and time). The report goes on to say 'although the start had taken place at the new earlier time between 9 and 10pm on the Friday in fair weather, it soon came on to rain heavily as the riders left the Manchester Toll Gate. Normally the followers would have carried the riders waterproofs, extra clothing, food and drink etc, but with the torrential rain, darkness and a gale force wind blowing through 'the Cheshire Gap' the two survivors at 3 am 'declined' to leave the comforts of Chester and retired'.

⇒•◇•⇐

*The first village signs appear in this year and between now and 1939 the 'AA' (Automobile Association) oversees the instalment of many road warning signs and place signposts, due to most local authorities not having enough funds.*

Later on August 31st, **The North Road CC ran their first open invitation 24hr event.** An excellent entry of thirty three riders from twelve different clubs took part. The North Road club had no fewer than thirteen of their own men riding. A longer than normal course was arranged, of some **385 miles.** Competitors were required to provide their own food, but the club had also arranged for various conveniently placed hotels to remain open all night (I would imagine 'Fullers' at Girtford Bridge would have been one of them). Prizes of five, three and two guineas were on offer for the first three riders. The weather conditions were almost the exact opposite of the ones experienced in the Anfield; intense, torrid heat this time but it had almost the same effect in reducing the field to just four finishers. **Charles Hillhouse** from the host club **won** the event with **350.75 miles.** **F.T. Bone,**

Polytechnic cc **2nd with 345.25 miles.** Frank Newell, Vegetarian C & AC **335.25m, 3rd,** and **F.T. Hawkes 330 miles 4th.**

*The first suffragette uprisings take place in England.*

## 1907

In March of this year **George Olley** became the first man ever to have a **1000 miles record** recognised by the RRA. He was timed by F.T. Bidlake on a course taking in many of the same roads used by the North Road 24hr. Based on the Great North Road (The A1) with stretches into the Fen district and then north up the A1 to Doncaster and retrace. He beat the standard set by the RRA by nearly nine hours to record **4 days 9 hrs 3 mins.**

In June 1907 **Tom Peck** took seven hours and 22 minutes off George Olley's 1905 **Lands End to John o' Groat's record with 3 days 12 hrs 53 minutes.**

—————◆—————

The **Anfield 24hr** this year was blessed with better weather which at least saw riders finish the event. **J.J. Rogers won with 325.75 miles. A.P. James was 2nd with 318.75 and G.E. Carpenter 314 miles, 3rd.** There were no special features recorded, but the distances must be considered satisfactory under the new and strange 'unpaced' 'no followers' rules. These were now Edwardian times and Cycling club racing was still a rich man's sport.

—————◆—————

The **North Road CC 24 hrs** race took place in perfect conditions on the 23rd August. From nineteen starters, eight riders finished with mileages over 350. The event was won by **T.A. Fisher,** Unity CC, taking the **bicycle** prize with **377.75 miles. A.G. Markham** won the **trike** prize with **301.5 miles. J.G. Naylor** was **2nd with 372.5** miles and 12 riders finished in total.

A week after the North Road event, **W. Welsh** made history by being the first man to break the **End to End** and then simply retrace back towards Inverness to complete the **1000 miles record.** He got to John o' Groat's in **3 days 8 hrs 4 mins and reached his 1000 miles in 4 days 7 hours 41 mins.**

## 1908

Record breaking started early in 1908 when, in May, **T.A. Fisher** who won the previous North Road 24hr, broke the **1000 mile** record using similar roads as used in the 24hr race and very similar to Olley's 1907 ride. Fisher went as far north as York before turning. He beat Welsh's record by 12 hrs 40mins giving a time of **3 days 19 hrs 1 min.**

A description of this man Fisher, was that he was a 'meat-eater' unlike many of his vegetarian predecessors. He was lean, very fit, and 'trained to the minute'. He rode a Rudge-Whitworth racer, geared to 74" with 'Constrictor' tyres on wooden rims.

**George Olley** was the first man this year to break the **End to End** with a record of **3 days 5hrs 20 mins.**

On July 20th **Tom Peck** took the **End to End** record to become the **first man to break the three day barrier** with **2 days 22 hrs 42 mins.**

Seven days later on the 27th July 1908, **Harry 'Goss' Green** left Lands End and after a terrible journey reached **John o' Groats 2 days 19 hrs 50 mins** later, to break the record.

—————◆—————

The **Anfield 24hr** was won this year by **A.P. James** with **328.625** miles after taking 2nd place the previous year. **G.E. Carpenter** was **2nd with 322.875** and **J.C. Band 3rd with 312.25 miles.**

*On August 12th 1908, the first 'Model T' Ford rolled off the production lines in Detroit, and over a nineteen year period, more than 15 million were sold.*

⟫⟩·◇·⟨⟪

**The North Road CC 24 hr** race this year was won by another Unity CC rider, **G.H. Briault** with **368.5 miles.** **E.J. Bass** won the **trike** prize with **288.5 miles.** The race took place on the 11th and 12th September and conditions during the night were cold and wet for the 21 riders. **Frank Wingrave** of the North Road CC was **2nd bike** with **360.5 miles.** **F.W. Wesley** with **357 miles was 3rd, F.T. Bone 4th 355.25 miles** and **C. Hillhouse 5th with 351.**

**Dr. F.W. Wesley** who came 3rd later set up a new **RRA Tricycle 24 hr record** with **326 miles.** He broke many records during his career. Later in life he took to helping and checking riders through the North Road 24hr during the night. He sadly passed away in 1935.

# 1909

*January 9th - Ernest Shackleton's expedition fails by 11 miles to reach the South Pole.*

**The Anfield** event this year was a 'scratch' race combined with a handicap. E. Buckley gave away 25 miles to R.A.Fulton. E. Buckley won the event with 363.5 miles. R.A. Fulton rode 342 miles plus 25 miles to record 367, so winning a cup presented by Mr. F. Gee. The possibility of winning a silver cup this year had boosted the field so that there were 8 finishers including two trikes, all with good mileages, better than in previous years. At this time the Anfield 24hr was a club member only event, and I wonder what would have happened to the size of the 'fields' of riders if the race had been open to all-comers.

Also at this time in history, riders of long distance races such as 24hr events didn't seem to travel much out of their own regions. The Anfield riders tend to be from the counties of Shropshire, Cheshire, Denbighshire, Flintshire, Lancashire etc, and the North Road riders tend to be from the counties near to London or Cambridge. In fact if you drew a line across the country running from east to west through Birmingham, this would just about divide the two catchment areas.

*Raleigh produce a ladies cycle, fully equipped weighing 27.5 lbs for £7.19s.6d.*

*July 25th 1909, Louis Bleriot flies across the English Channel.*

⟫⟩·◇·⟨⟪

**The North Road** event on 27th & 28th August produced **383.75,** the highest mileage ever since pacing was disallowed. **Frank Wingrave** with this mileage broke the event record. **E.J. Bass** on a **trike** produced **288.5 miles.** Wingrave had been having good successes in other races, winning the Anfield 100 in 1904, 1905 and 1907. A.G. Keen and C.W. Shadford, both of the Unity CC were 2nd and 3rd with 379.75 and 377.5 miles respectively from a field of thirteen finishers.

⟫⟩·◇·⟨⟪

In 1909 there was a revival of the **Track 24hr** by the **NCU** and **J.H. Bishop** of the Beaumont CC won with **513.7 miles.** He won again in 1910 but with a lesser mileage. To my knowledge these are the last two track 24hr races until the Polytechnic events in 1927.

On August 31st using much of the same roads as the North Road 24hr, **William Welsh of the MC & AC (Midlands Cycling & Athletic Club) broke the 1000 miles record in 3 days 15 hrs 57 mins.**

# 1910

*We are now in the reign of George V.*

1910 was a year for slightly lower results in the **Anfield 24hr.** The top rider was **W. Jones** with **345.5 miles,** 2nd was **C.H. Turnor** with **342 m** and **J.C. Band 3rd** with **334 miles.** At the 12 hr point Jones had been 10 miles behind Turnor, but in the last hour Jones caught and passed him to win by 3.5 miles.

*Vehicle taxation and road fund licensing starts around this time. Petrol duties were also introduced.*

---

**Frank Wingrave won the North Road 24hr** again for the second time with **365.75 miles.** The **trike** race was won by **L.W.B. Martin** of the Bath Road CC with **301.75.** The race was held on August 19th and 20th and will be ever memorable for the tremendous duel fought between Wingrave and R.V. Gillvray of the Sheffield RC. There was a ding dong struggle all day. At 12 hours the Yorkshire man led Wingrave by 1.75 miles, at 273 miles their times were equal, and by 322 miles Wingrave was a minute ahead. As the previous winner of the event, Wingrave had started last man with Gillvray ten minutes before him, but that little interval was not bridged until the last half hour, when Frank rode alongside Gillvray on the last Bedford detour with the greeting "I've been looking for you all day", and finally ran out a winner with **365.75** miles to his credit, with Gillvray covering **362.5 miles.**

It was destined to be a very long time before a North Road club member again won the 24hr, in fact some 17 years passed before W.A. Ellis 'Billy' had three consecutive wins in 1927, 1928 and 1929. Breaking competition record twice with 410.5 in 1927 and 413.5 in 1928.

By his two successive wins in the 24hr Frank Wingrave set the seal upon his reputation as a great long distance rider, but we think one of his greatest claims to fame is as a '100 miler'. His three fastest times in the 'Anfield 100' in 1904, 1905 and 1907, beating the course record on the last two occasions, and in the 'Bath Road 100' in 1905 and 1906. Both the Anfield and Bath Road events being 'classics' form a series of performances which no other North Road man has ever equalised.

# 1911

**The Anfield 24hr** was **won** by **E. Buckley** with **375 miles,** possibly the highest unpaced mileage for the Anfield event so far, beating **J.A. Grimshaw's 364 miles.** These two leading riders had been practically level on performance up to 300 miles. **G. Poole** was **3rd** with **339 miles.**

---

**H. Bennett** of the Unity CC on September 9th, won the **North Road 24hr** with the **highest unpaced mileage so far, 386 miles.** **G. Brown** ran in 2nd with **365.5 miles** and **R.W. Gillvray 3rd** with **365 miles.**

The first 'North Roader' home was Henry Norman 4th with 360.25 miles. Frank Wingrave had started this event but was compelled to retire with punctures and mechanical problems at 12hrs.

One amusing incident that had taken place in the Club 12hr race in July was about W.R. Lempriere who broke the club record with 205 miles. Lempriere will always be remembered for his great politeness, and we believe it was in this race, after overtaking C.J. Cole, he apologised for passing and dropping him with the remark: "I'm awfully sorry to leave you, old chap, but I feel so beastly fit that I really must get on with it!"

# 1912

*January 17th, Scott the Explorer reaches the South Pole only to find that Amundsen had beaten him by a month.*

*April 14th sinking of the Titanic with very few survivors, after colliding with an iceberg. The same thing happens in 2007, to a cruise ship, but luckily this time all are saved.*

*On Whit Monday, Charles Moss won his 3rd Anfield 100 in succession and proved to be a top class road man at this distance, although he did go on to take many longer MRRA road records. He also won the Bath Road Cup outright for his successive wins in the famous Bath Road 100. He rode in the Stockholm Olympics with Charlie Davey but suffered a damaged knee during the event which was a 200 mile time trial. Charles Moss's family recall him having to pay for his own boat journey and passage to Stockholm. Stephen 'Inky' and Christopher Moss, two of his grandsons, recalled his tales of being harassed by farmers and other road users when out riding and training with his MC & AC club mates around the Warwickshire lanes.*

**The Anfield event** was run off in awful rain with **J.A.Grimshaw** battling it out with **G.E. Carpenter** to take the title with **329.5 miles** to **303.75 miles** respectively, and three other riders finished. Don't forget, the roads under a deluge of rain would be turned into a quagmire, clogging the tyres and chain. The poor rider would be covered with stinking glutinous mud, from the horse-drawn vehicles and farms on these rural roads.

---

**The North Road CC 24hr** saw **Maurice Selbach** of the Unity CC produce a massive **394 miles** with **W.W. Robertson** North Road CC taking the **trike** prize with **287 miles.** From a good entry of 42 riders, 34 started and 24 finished. **H.G. Cook** was **2nd** with **379 miles** and **F.C. Higgins,** Polytechnic **3rd** with **374.75 miles.** Frank Wingrave was **4th** with **371.25 miles,** the highest placed **North Road rider.** Heavy flooding made the course around Ely very dangerous and at least one rider missed the bridge at Mepal and went into the river.

# 1913

Another wet **Anfield** event saw **J.A.Grimshaw win** again with **340 miles.** A 10 mile improvement on 1912's figures with **L. Cohen 2nd** with **318 miles.** Three others finished.

*Gradient signs on hills were introduced this year and the Panama Canal opened.*

---

**The North Road CC 24hr** was won by **F.G. 'Frank' Thomas** of the Century RC with **381.5 miles.** **F.J. Parker** of the Unity CC ran 2nd with **373.25 miles.** **C.A. Stevens** of the Polytechnic was **3rd** with **371.5 miles.** The first **'North Road'** man home was **Henry Norman,** 5th with 357.25 miles in a field of 18 finishers; no trike was recorded. The event took place mid-September.

*Frank Thomas, the winner of the event, was the father of Ivy Mitton. Ivy became a famous timekeeper and officiated on many high profile RRA records including Eric Tremaine's End to End in 1982. She helped, Observed and Timekept for Pat Kenny and myself plus many other Midland record breakers in the late 1970's, and 80's.*

# 1914

In this year **the Anfield** made their **24hr** an **'invitation event'.** Their top rider **Grimshaw,** won the event by a mile from **J.E. Brown,** Walton C & AC with **379.75 miles** to **378.75m.** **T.P. Nichols,** Leeds RC took **3rd** spot with **360.75.** At the 12 hr point Brown had a lead of four miles, and it was only late in the afternoon when Grimshaw got level. Towards the end of the event some 'busybody' misdirected Brown off course, but the committee very rightly waived the strict rules and credited Brown with the miles actually ridden. Six other riders finished.

No event was recorded for the North Road CC due to the imminence of war, with troops being mustered from all over the British Isles.

# 1914 – 1918 - THE GREAT WAR

On August 4th - 5th 1914 Britain gave Germany a 'War Ultimatum' after German troops had invaded many countries adjacent to its borders with Europe, including France, Belgium and Russia.

September 3rd 1916 – England was raided near London by thirteen Zeppelin Airships.

November 11th 1918 – The Germans surrendered.

November 15th 1918 – 'Victory Day' marking the end of the first world war 'The Great War'.

*It is estimated that the total number of lives lost in this war was 9 million with another 27 million injured, rendering it the most destructive war the world has ever seen.*

*During the war years, roadside petrol pumps were introduced and Lloyd George became Prime Minister.*

# 1919

In 1919 when peacetime allowed the **Anfield BC** to resume its 24hr race again, the distances the riders performed over roads wrecked by war-time traffic and troop movement were much better than could have been expected. **J.S. Blackburn** with **349.25** miles won the event by ten miles from **G.E. Carpenter.** **A. Warburton** was 3rd with **330 miles.** They were all Anfielders'. Three other riders finished.

*The Ministry of Transport was established in this year.*

*Two 50 mile events were won by C.E. Sewell, in the first event with 2 hrs 30 mins beating Bill Best , and the second 2 hrs 40 mins beating Frank Armond by over 3 minutes   These performances were from a man whose son and grandsons went on to ride many time trials including 24 hrs over the next 80 years.*

——⟹·◆·⟸——

**Maurice Selbach** re-opened competition in the **North Road CC** event with a fine outstanding mileage of **405 miles** to win for the second time and become the **first man in history to ride unpaced for 24hrs and break the 400 mile barrier.** Earlier in the year he'd won the **Anfield 100** mile event with **5 hrs 15 mins 39 secs.** **A.G. Markham** North Road CC won the trike race with **223 miles.** **F.M. Inwood** was 2nd with **382 miles** and **Frank Armond** covered **360 miles** for **4th.** It is interesting to note that of the 12 finishers, 6 were 'North Roaders'; the last of them **J. Foxley Norris** covering **287 miles** at 63 years of age.

A remarkable feature of Selbach's ride was that he covered 202 miles in the first 12hrs and 203 miles in the second.

*Frank Armond, in an interview with Cycling's Dennis Donovan, remembers going off course at Long Sutton around the half distance point and having to climb up signposts, front lamp in hand, to find his way.  If there wasn't a moon in the sky in those early years deep in the countryside it was pitch black, as 'light polution' was unheard of.  In later years when Frank took to promoting the event, he always made sure there was a marshal at Long Sutton.  He remarked that Selbach's 405 miles was 'out of this world'!*

The **Anfield** club members provided the riders for the first four places.   **Grimshaw** being **1st** with **352.25 miles.** **G. Molyneux** 2nd with **322.25** miles and **A.E. Walters** 3rd with **314 m.**  **G.F. Hawkes** with **313.75 miles** should have beaten Walters but with 16 minutes left to ride, he stopped to feed, so giving Walters the advantage.

---

**North Road CC.**  In these early days the relationship with the Police was again a hostile one towards cyclists. Several North Road clubmen were stopped in Eaton Socon and had their names and addresses taken, resulting in fines, which were paid for by the club.   **The 24hr** was won by **Jack Rossiter** of the Century road club with **378.75 miles.**  A new name but one we would see and hear a lot of over the next 15 years or more, with RRA road records broken at 100 and 1000 miles, 12 hrs, London-York, Bicycle End to End and Lands End to London and 24hr on a tricycle.

**T. H. Pryor** of the Anfield BC won the **tricycle** race with the highest mileage ever in a 24hr race, **354.5 miles.** When one considers the higher mileages attained in this the North Road event, held on or around what is now known as the A1, taking in roads into the Fen district, then I think compared to the Anfield course these are possibly better, faster roads.

Fifteen riders finished from an entry of twenty three.   **Frank Armond** led at the halfway mark with 197.75 miles but at 13 hrs he 'croppered' a chicken which ran through his front wheel, damaging himself badly.   Bravely he retained the lead until Rossiter found that 'little bit extra' in the last hour, to win by **one mile.  C.A. Sewell** was 'lanterne rouge' (last man) on the day with **291.125 miles,** but he was better known as a '50 miler' winning many races.

C.A. Sewell was the grandfather of Roger and David Sewell who raced in the 1970's, 80's and 90's, and the father of Jack Sewell. 'C.A.' rode with 'E.M' Sewell on a tandem trike in 1925 and broke the RRA 100 mile record with 4hrs 59 mins.

Here is a passage about Roger's grandfather, and Roger kindly gave me permission to use it.

*'The last man in the race was C.A. Sewell with 291.75 miles.   Sewell in his day was a good racing man, but not at 24hrs and we think the following extract from the account of the race published in the club gazette will not be without interest: "Sewell, of course, finished; he always does.  Probably the family motto is something to the effect that Sewells may die, but they never 'chuck'.  As a matter of fact, Sewell did 'die' at about 11 hours but for the remainder of the time the corpse gave a series of spasmodic kicks which propelled the bicycle along at about 8 mph.   We admire Sewells determination to finish, but as somebody said: 'He rides a very fine '30' but he can't seem to manage 12 of them on the same day'! We believe he rode something like 120 races in his career and finished in all but one of them'.*

Frank Armond knew that Rossiter could be beaten mentally in a race if he wasn't winning, so after requesting an early starting position in the event Frank was out on his own at the front of the field and held that position for 12 hours, with Rossiter struggling to gain on him.  But around the 12 hour point Rossiter started to gain slightly on Frank, then with 13 hours ridden misfortune struck, when Frank was brought down by a chicken.   He crashed heavily, damaging both knees and his hip.   Still Rossiter hadn't caught him and he rode pluckily on.   Frank held onto his lead at the front of the field until the last few minutes of the event when Rossiter finally caught him.  At the end, Rossiter lay exhausted on the ground, he'd beaten Frank by one mile. Even though Frank was bruised and battered his role as a first aid man came first and he knelt down over Rossiter to make sure he was okay and not in any danger.

After that 24hr in 1920, Frank's club The North Road CC told him to attempt the Lands End to London record. They gave him a long list of pubs to write to for food as motor vehicles were not used on record attempts at that time.   Frank was followed by cyclists every inch of the way, and so wrote to these pubs and sent them all a five 'bob' (25p) postal order telling them what food he wanted.   He was assured of a good spread and a huge crowd of locals to cheer him on his way.

Frank said "I remember riding down the steep hill out of Launceston, it was a frightful road and there'd been timber carting and tree felling both sides during the war, so I'm bumping down the hill and a copper shouted 'you'll break your bloody neck!' but I didn't.   Charlie Sewell followed me going into London and said 'mind those bloody tramlines, you're going too fast!"   Frank broke the record by nearly an hour with 19hrs 46 mins, ironically, that same year the RRA passed a rule allowing motor vehicle assistance.

# 1921

If **The Anfield** events of recent years have suffered from bad weather with rain reducing the finishers to just two or three, then this years weather was the opposite, but had exactly the same effect.   Many riders had to give up from heat exhaustion.  Of the ten who finished, **J.A. Grimshaw,** Anfield BC **won with 357.5 miles, J.G. Shaw,** Sharrow CC, **2nd 350.75m,** and **A.R. Bamford,** Manchester Wheelers, was **3rd with 324.5 miles.**

⋗◆⋖

**The North Road CC** event run on 16th & 17th September was won by **Charlie Davey** of the Vegetarian C & AC with **401.5 miles.**   He was another rider we were destined to see and hear about in the future.

In 1923 Charlie Davey went on to break three tough RRA records.   The London to Bath and back; Lands End to London, and 24 hr, all records were on a bicycle.   In later years he helped other Vegetarian riders and organised their racing and record rides.   One of his most prominent in the future would be Dave Keeler's End to End in 1958.

But I digress:  back to 1921 and **A.E. Burt won the trike race with 320.75 miles.**  A good entry of thirty one men started, of whom twenty three finished.   **Jack Rossiter was 2nd with 392 miles.**   **Frank Armond** was the first North Road man home with **383.25 miles.**  Later that year, Frank took the tandem 24hr record with Frank Thomas, covering 399 miles after a good deal of chain trouble.

*A code of uniform hand and arm traffic signals is established for police to instruct, direct and inform all road users.*

*Tax discs are introduced and the road fund licence was raised to £1.00 per horse power of engine.*

*Road surfaces are now generally improving all across the country with bitumen and tar providing a more resilient, smoother surface capable of withstanding heavy rain.   The rubber tyred cars and lorries cause less damage.  'Tar and Feathering' (gravel and small chippings spread over wet tar and then rolled) seems to be a popular method of surfacing and one that is still used present day.*

# 1922

Conditions generally were by now getting back to normal.   There had been no invasion from the enemy, just the terrible loss of life amongst the mainly male conscripts and volunteers in the war, and only the roads had suffered damage, mainly from troop movement.   The production of peacetime mechanical objects, such as cycles, had been put on hold for making ammunition and items for the war effort.  The economy had suffered, but life for the working and rural classes was much the same.   Those who had nothing before the war still had nothing.

Anybody who had a bike at this time, especially a lightweight racer would have had either a very good job i.e. a qualified engineer, chemist, doctor, teacher etc, or be fairly 'well off'.   Other people if they were lucky enough to have a bike would probably be riding a heavy 'roadster' that was quite often too big for them and had more than likely been passed down through two or three generations.

**The Anfield** as mentioned earlier was an invitation event and still started with only a handful of riders. **Albert Lusty** of the host club **won the event with 351 miles** by 'steady' riding.   There was hardly any change all day in the position of the leading riders.   **C. Hunt,** Liverpool Century was **2nd** with **346.5 miles** and **W.A. Tuplin 3rd** with **343.5m.**  Two others finished.

The event still used the same format as 1894, starting between 9 & 10 pm on Friday in the Chester area and using various loops of road on the Wirral before riding south to Whitchurch and Newport, Shropshire, to retrace and finish back in the Chester area.

*The Austin Seven was launched this year and the state of Palestine was set up.*

⸺⸻◆⸻⸺

**Maurice Selbach won the North Road CC** event in fine style again, with **402 miles.** Over a five year period Selbach had won the event three times. *A photo from 1922 shows Selbach at 345 miles in this North Road event, on his single speed bike with a small wicker basket that fitted neatly between his brake levers and large chime bell. He carried in it his sandwiches, drinks and tools.* He'd also broken four RRA road records: **The 24 hr with 397.25 miles** and the **Lands End to London in 17hrs 47 mins** taking Charlie Davey's record, which Davey promptly regained with 17 hrs 29 mins in 1923. Selbach also broke the **100 mile tandem record** with **A.R. Woods** in **4hrs 27 mins 58 secs.** He also took the London to Bath and back record with 11 hrs 55 mins 30 secs.

*Frank Fisher recalled that Selbach worked for a cycle maker in the early 1920's and both he and his boss entered for the Anerley 12 hr race run on a Saturday. Selbach was told he could not have the day off but he took it just the same and during the event he caught and passed his boss, who called out "You're sacked!" to which Selbach replied "You're wrong, I've already resigned!" He later had a successful career as a professional and then had his own flourishing cycle making business in South London. He was killed when he skidded in tramlines when cycling to work in 1935*
.

**V.J. Viel** of the same club as Selbach, the Unity CC was **2nd** with **395 miles. Jack Rossiter** was **3rd** with **378.5 miles.** Of four North Road starters, only two finished, the best being **F.J. Tunmer** with **360.25 miles.**

It was at this time in history that the North Road President. F.T. Bidlake, had the initiative to instigate a movement to collectively form a **'Road Racing Council'**, made up of ten like minded officials from clubs who, like the North Road CC, were promoting road racing (time trials). Officials included F. Maton, Anerly BC, W.P. Cook, Anfield BC, J. Burden-Barnes, Bath Road Club, G.H. Stancer, Century RC, S.E. George, Etna CC, H. Farmer, Kingsdale CC, Frank Urry, Midland C & AC, F.T. Bidlake, North Road CC, J.F. Ditchman, Polytechnic CC and A. Shillito, Unity CC.

The items discussed were:- The definition of unpaced riding; the limitation of the number of entries in road events; the prescribing of suitable costume; the avoidance of undue publicity; the provision of adequate intervals between starters; the avoidance of clashing of events and courses; the adoption of the non-advertising regulation; and, to act as referee in any appropriate matter voluntarily referred to them.

The **'Council'** formed from this meeting was unquestionably a great success. Rules for the conduct of 'Road time trialling' were drawn up and membership was open to any like-minded club which promoted an 'open event'.

*This 'Council' held good until 1937 when the sport had flourished to the extent that new guidelines, in view with modern traffic conditions, were needed. From 1937 it was known as 'Road Time Trials Council' – 'RTTC'.*

# 1923

*In February the first 'Flying Scotsman' train service between London and Edinburgh started. It reached constant speeds of 100 mph.*

**Charlie Davey** who won the North Road 24hr in 1921 went on in this year of 1923 to break three separate RRA records. The **London to Bath and back** with **11hrs 47 mins 52 secs, The Lands End to London** with **17hrs 29 mins** and the **24 hr** with **402.5 miles.** They were all records held by Maurice Selbach. It was the first motor accompanied (followed) attempt allowed by the RRA.

In the **Anfield event** their top riders were beaten by **W.A. (Bill) Tuplin** of the Gomersal CC with a mileage of **366.** The writer of the race report went on to say "this successful mileage gave us as much pleasure as a loser can be expected to feel!" Its good to see a humorous wit of the day, like a forerunner of Frank Mumford, the Mersey 'Scribe'. **J.G. Shaw** and **J.A. Grimshaw** with **360** and **356.25 miles,** both saved the credit of the club and gave Tuplin a mileage worth beating. Eleven other riders had close finishing mileages despite bad weather. I suppose fourteen finishers in total is very similar to some non-championship events run in more recent years.

---

*It was this year of 1923 that the* **RRA** *allowed riders to attempt records on a Sunday as up till now the Sabbath had been very strictly observed. It has proved very difficult to find whether any of the 24hr races were held using any part of Sunday. The earliest mention of a time trial being held very early on a Sunday morning was the 'Memorial 50' race on Sunday 10th July 1927 for the North Road CC. The history of the club mentions –* **'After very serious consideration by the Committee it was felt that the presence of a large number of motor vehicles on Saturday afternoons made cycle racing increasingly dangerous.'**

*For good or ill the decision was taken to hold the event in the early hours of Sunday! Whether this was the first Sunday race or not, I do not know, but this is certainly the first mention of one.*

In the **North Road CC** event **Jack Rossiter** took his **second win** putting 24 miles onto his 1920 figures with **402.5 miles,** and its also just .5 of a mile more than Selbach's the previous year. These two riders were so evenly matched physically and performance wise. The RRA records they tussled over between themselves are also very close in quality and performance.

**A.G. Keen** took the **trike** win with **310.25 miles;** another Unity CC rider. The event run in late August saw a field of 43 starters with 22 finishers. **H.D. Hall,** Oak CC was **2nd bike** with **383.5 miles** and **F.E. Sandford,** Highgate CC, **3rd** with **376.25 miles.** The only host club member to finish was again **F.J. Tunmer** with **338.50 miles.**

Things may have been different if Frank Armond hadn't been put 'out of the running' at about 100 miles when he collided 'head on' with W.S. Gibson of the Century RC. Both riders were very badly cut about the head and nose.

Up until this year of 1923, the club had resisted 25 mile 'novelty' events. 50, 100 miles, 12 hr and 24hr time trials were the 'norm', but under increasing pressure from members, a 25 mile race was introduced with a cup donated by Dr. Kilham Roberts. The 25 mile race was looked upon by the 'elders' as an event for the 'boys'.

*The first road islands or roundabouts appeared this year.*

# 1924

Conditions were more pleasant for the **Anfield 24 hr** this year. **J.G. Shaw,** an 'Anfielder', with **363.5 miles** brought the clubs pride back with a **4 mile win** over **Tuplin. A. Hancock,** Grosvenor Wheelers, took **3rd** place with **352.5 miles.** Twelve more riders all with good mileages made up the finishing list.

*Ramsay Macdonald becomes Prime Minister.*

---

**Jack Rossiter** had another win in this years **North Road event** with **377.75 miles. F.R. Fisher** took the **trike** prize with **342.5 miles,** riding for the Essex Road CC. The event held on the 12th & 13th September attracted a field of 61 starters. It can be deduced from Rossiter's mileage that it was a very hard ride. A gale force wind swept across the Fens and reduced the competitors at times to walking pace and only 25 riders finished. **E.C. Pilcher,** Polytechnic CC was **2nd** with **373 miles. J.B. Dilley,** Crescent Wheelers **3rd** with **365.75 miles.** Only two North Road men finished, **F.J. Tunmer 330.5** and **F.G. Thomas** on a **trike 323.5 miles.**

It is quite noticeable that riders still did not venture much from their 'home' racing courses, even with good rail travel. The Anfield seems to attract riders from Liverpool, Lancashire, Shropshire, The Potteries and from as far south as Wolverhampton. The North Road catchment area seemed to be the 'Home Counties' of Middlesex, Essex, Sussex, Bedfordshire, Hertfordshire, Cambridge and the East Coast clubs.

It is also interesting to note that only a few top riders were prepared to travel to a 'classic' 100 mile event, such as 'North Roader's' riding the 'Anfield 100' in May, or the 'Bath Road 100' in August. It isn't until well after the Second World War that increasing car ownership enabled riders and their helpers to travel to two or three 24hr events a year.

**The large field of 61 starters was a record for a 24hr race so far in history.**

The Porter brothers failed in their attempt to break the End to End record, when they got to the Meikle Ferry at 750 miles only to find it wasn't running, causing them to abandon.. This incident plus the fact that professionally backed riders were getting faster boats to ferry them across stretches of water, led to the RRA banning the use of ferries on the End to End route. This ban came into force in 1925.


# 1925

**The Anfield Club** had to settle for their top men being second and third in this years event. **A. Hancock** of the Grosvenor Whls **won** the event with **369 miles**. **C. Randall 2nd** with **362.75** and **J.A. Grimshaw 3rd** with **359.5 miles**. **A. Gunn,** Liverpool Century had been leading at 12 hrs but met with an unfortunate accident with a car and was badly hurt. Eleven other riders finished.


## The Catford Era   1925 – 1975

This famous Essex Club held its inaugural event this year. An event that was to see many champions come and go and competition records broken on many occasions. It ran for exactly 50 years and it drew many riders from the south who quite possibly wouldn't have ventured north of London to ride a 24hr race.

The actual course took in an area on the south side of London, stretching to the south coast. Everyone thought that the roads would be too hilly, and only 401.5 miles were mapped out for this reason. Roads that the Anerly BC 12 hr and 'Southern 100's' were run on were adopted as a foundation, down to Fareham, various detours to Guildford, Portsmouth road to the Kingston by-pass, Windsor, back to Guildford, Horsham, Cowfold, Offington, Littlehampton, Chichester, Clapham and Billinghurst. Pease Pottage seems to have been one of the popular start and finish areas for this famous event, held in early July.

1925 saw **Jack Holdsworth** with **408.5 miles win** this first event and put up a **new 24hr record.** Jack had previously ridden to 4th place in the 1924 North Road event with 365 miles. He also led the **Kentish Wheelers** to their **first win of 1,127.5 miles** with **F.R. Buckle** riding **367 miles** and **W.A. Whyler 352m** making up the team. **This is the first time to my knowledge of trawling through records that a team has been mentioned and given a collective mileage.**

Jack Holdsworth won the event riding a 78" fixed gear. He also had a puncture. I only have provisional mileages for **2nd** and **3rd** riders. **H.D. Hall,** Oak CC, **384.5 miles** and **H. Page,** Catford CC, **375m.** From 39 entries, 35 started and 26 finished.

Here is a short passage from Sid Hayward who questioned Jack Holdsworth on his win. "Jack replied that he knew Competition Record was held by Maurice Selbach with 405 miles and that Rossiter had the 2nd greatest of 402.5 miles. Both were riders he knew well. Jack felt that the 'Catford' would be too hilly to produce a big mileage and as was mentioned earlier, there was only 401.5 miles of measured road available. (At that time, a rider was only allowed to cover any part of the course once in each direction). So that when Jack found himself near to the 400 miles mark with time to go, the Catford officials went into a huddle and directed him over the only optional road left, the Cowfold to Horsham road, climbing over a steep hill. Jack recalled riding a single fixed gear with no 'low gear' for the hills. The roads were very bumpy, the lower road from Offigton corner towards Littlehampton in particular. He was so bruised after his ride that it was two weeks or more before he could sit down with any comfort, and even though he'd bound his handlebars with rubber sponges and crepe bandages prior to the event, his hands were still sore."

Glancing through the History of the Catford CC's first 50 years, I've come across one or two passages in the book, which for me are steeped in nostalgia. A meeting was called in early January 1925 and about a dozen 'old timers' gathered in a little old pub in Bush Lane, Cannon Street, London. They mounted a rickety old staircase and entered a dingy old room without any light, but with plenty of gas, which had been escaping. They opened the window and let the gas out and the fog in. A match was struck to light the gas mantle and the meeting began, and from this meeting it was thought that the seeds of running a 24 hour race were sewn, possibly by Jack Dueters, and it was thought that a great deal of helpers would be required. Twenty clubs showed interest, and another meeting was called to discuss arrangements of feeding and marshalling etc. The 4th and 5th of July was to be the date, the only weekend available for most people in a busy club and racing calendar. The meeting was chaired by F.T. Bidlake and finalised by H.W. Bartleet.

On that date mentioned earlier, the first Catford CC invitation 24 hour road ride took place. I would imagine the invitation to ride would have been made to riders belonging to those 20 local clubs. Jack Holdsworth, who won this very first event, wrote to the club thanking them for their hospitality, and he mentions "the ride seemed to me to be a series of runs between bands of willing helpers and friends, all anxious to assist. If it had not been for the bumpy roads, the ride would have been almost a picnic. The run from Chichester to Fareham and back was perhaps the most delightful, the night was so glorious that I wished I was on tour and could have ambled lazily along. I enjoyed the bread and milk, provided at Steadmans in the middle of the night, more than anything else on the ride".

Jack finished by saying "I'm afraid I became somewhat tired and irritable near the end and I hope the checkers will accept my apologies if I was not quite as polite to some of them as I should have been".

Norman Tullett, a rider with the Kentish Wheelers, remembers seeing Jack ride this first Catford. Norman was out helping during the event at 17 years of age. "Jack Holdsworth sat very low with his face down almost to the handlebars and I wondered how he could ride in that position for such a long time. At Guildford Jack stopped at the night feed, he quickly dashed in, sat down and shovelled minced beef down his gullet as quickly as possible, heeding no-one." Holdsworth went on in 1927 and 1929 to ride in 'paced' 24 hr events at Herne Hill track, winning both events.

Norman Tullett, not many seasons later in 1931, was himself a member of the competition record breaking team in this event.

⟫⋅◆⋅⟪

**The North Road 24 hr** was won by **J.W. Dougal** of the Marboro AC with **394 miles.** The event took place on September 4th and 5th. The club had experienced difficulties in previous years, handling very large fields of riders and so, decided to restrict the entries to fifty maximum of which 49 started and 26 finished. Conditions were again hard. A very cold night followed by a very windy day with heavy rain in the closing hours, that battered the riders. **W.E. Sandford** was **2nd** to Dougal with **383.5m** and **Rossiter** was **3rd** with **382.5miles.** Only one North Road man finished, **F.W. 'Robby' Robinson** with **357 miles.** He later went on to take up timekeeping with the 'End to End' records of Syd Parker and Jim Letts on tandem trike in 1947 and Jim Letts trike record in 1949, being just two of his successes.

## 1926

*May 4th, a 'General Strike' took place this week as a protest by workers over wage reductions.*

**The Anfield BC 24hr** this year was won by **E. Sutton** of the Cheadle Hulme club. He had to be persuaded to get back on his bike at Chester after a feed and went on to pile up a mileage of **388.75 miles.** A. Hancock couldn't be persuaded to resume riding so **L. Butterworth**, Oldham Century RC came **2nd** with **376.25 miles.** Anfields own **J.G. Shaw** took **3rd** place with **369 miles,** and five other riders finished.

⟫⋅◆⋅⟪

The Catford 24 hr was won by **Jack Rossiter** with **405.5 miles.** Jack Holdsworth who came **2nd** with **386m** seemed to vie for either first or second place with Rossiter over this long period of time. **R.G. Hughes,** Bell Vue CC came **3rd** with **378.75 miles.** **Catford CC won the team race** with **1048.5 miles.** 33 riders started. *This event made a loss of £7.00, a lot of money at that time.*

*Television was invented*

*August 6th 1926, an American woman Gertrude Ederle became the first woman to swim the English Channel in 14hrs 31 mins, beating Matthew Webb's record by 1hr 59 mins.*

**The North Road CC 24 hrs** a short time later in mid September saw **Jack Rossiter** of the Century Road Club win his second 24hr of the season, with a very fine **407.5 miles,** beating Maurice Selbach's 1919 course and event record by 2.5 miles. This was Rossiter's fourth and last win in this event, which attracted an entry of 45 riders of whom 28 finished. **Jack Holdsworth** was **2nd** with **383.25 miles.** **Fred Fisher,** Essex Roads CC was **3rd** with **381.5 miles,** again only one North Roader finished, **F.W Robinson 4th** with **379.25 miles.**

In an article to the 24hr Fellowship Journal in 1976, Wally Perkins recalls the terrible bike that Jack Rossiter rode in those days, cranks and pedals bent, bottom bracket loose, frame out of alignment, a bike not even good enough for winter riding. 'A real case of 90% man and 10% bike'.

## 1927

*May 21st Lindbergh flies the Atlantic from New York to Paris. It was the first solo flight over this route.*

**The Anfield 24** hrs was **won** by **L. Butterworth,** Oldham Century CC with 377.25 closely followed by **E.B. Barnes,** Walton C & AC with **376 miles.** **H.F. Pullan** with **353.75** and **W. Martin 353** made up **3rd** and **4th** places in the event and secured the **team** win for the Walton C & AC with **1092.75 miles.**

⇒•◇•⇐

In 1927 **The Polytechnic CC** decided to resurrect the **Track 24 hr races** at Herne Hill in London, none of which had been held since the N.C.U. races of 1909 and 1910. They were supported very well by the press with their venture and 'Cycling' alone gave thirteen pages of coverage and photos. They even printed bus, train and tram routes and times for the public's benefit, but despite all this, the crowds were quite poor for the first event in 1927.

The 1927 race began at 7pm Friday 8th July and there were fourteen entrants, all with their own teams of pacing tandems. They were H. Grant, E.C. Pilcher, Jack Holdsworth, W.S. Almond, H. Fowler, W.W. Perkins, D Marsh, A.G. Keen, E.J. Winn, H.M. Oxley, G. Sibthorpe, W.G. Hazel, J.J. Lee and C.G. Bowtle.

Frank Shorland, the winner of the Cuca Cup 24hr in 1892, 93 & 94, fired the starting pistol and Jack Holdsworth took the lead to record 27.8 miles in the first hour. Sibthorpe duelled with Holdsworth for the first three hours but then slowed. At the 100 mile point Holdsworth took his first 4 minutes rest after recording 3 hrs 53 mins. Almond tried hard to make up time but by 6 hrs he'd 'cracked' and retired. At this point Holdsworth led with 149.15 miles, Fowler was 2nd with 147 miles and Perkins 3rd with 142 miles. Hazel had a nasty crash at around 8 hrs when two pacers ran down the banking and hit Hazel's tandem broadside on, bringing down all three men. He bravely continued after being patched up. At 12hrs Holdsworth had covered 284 miles, 1470 yards, just 370 yards more than J.H. Bishop, the original record holder, had covered in 1909.

At the 400 mile point, **Holdsworth** still held the lead comfortably in 17hrs 47 mins, over 16 minutes better than the record. He started to suffer stomach problems from this point, but with careful coaching he continued at record pace. During the last hour he maintained 19 mph to beat Bishop's 1909 track record by 4 miles with an astounding **517.3 miles.** **W.W. Perkins** with **489.8 miles** was **2nd,** Sibthorpe **3rd** with **469 miles.**

31

A programme of boxing and running had also taken place in the track centre to maintain the spectators interest and swell the gate proceeds.

Frank Shorland who had fired the starting pistol was apparently not only a past winner of this event, he'd also earned himself a reputation as an all-round crowd entertainer and on one occasion rode around the track 'no handed' communicating with 'Faed' Wilson in deaf and dumb sign language.

—————◆—————

**The Catford 24hr** saw **Harry Pearson** of the Marlboro club almost **equal** Jack Holdsworth's **competition record** with **408.25 miles**. **Harry Jukes** came **2nd** with **391.5 miles** and **J. Emerson** was **3rd** with **390.5**. The Marlborough C & AC won the team race with 1134 miles. From 42 starters, 31 finished. On the back of the Catford Club Gala programme in 1927 was advertised "400 miles for £1, the cheapest tour in England, comfortable travelling (on your bike); Excellent cuisine (including rice and tea): Special Free Accommodation (under any hedge): Tour embraces the best scenery in Surrey and Sussex (If you can complete the course)!

*Traffic Lights were introduced in Leeds and Wolverhampton.*

—————◆—————

**The North Road** event a few weeks later on September 9th and 10th saw a North Road man **Bill Ellis** break **Competition record** with his first of three consecutive wins with **410.5 miles**. This year turned out to be a very good one for Bill Ellis as he had already won the club 12hr race with 215.25 miles. The 24hr race had 51 starters of whom 28 finished and at last it was a North Road man who won for the first time in seventeen years. Ellis had a very fierce duel with Jim Dougal the winner in 1925. **Dougal** recorded **409.75** just .75 of a mile less than **Ellis**. **Jack Rossiter** was **3rd** with **405.5 miles** and for the first time ever, a man topped 400 miles without getting a place, **Cyril Neale's 401.75** giving him 4th position. *Cyril Neale later in life went on to become the Organiser of the Wessex RC 24hr, a job he did for many years.* Evans did 397.5 miles and Robinson did his 'personal best' with 395.5 for 6th place.

Scraps on the road during the 24hr ensued when Rossiter caught Holdsworth and they in turn caught Dougal who had suffered two punctures. All three riders then rode for mile after mile 'neck and neck', one on each side of the road and one in the middle, out to Rippingale and back to Long Sutton. At the feed Rossiter's helpers took his food outside to save him time, unwisely, Holdsworth cut his feed out. Ellis came to life on this section of the course after being in the 'doldrums' and soon established himself in fourth place. At the 12hr point Rossiter had covered 218.75 miles, Evans and Holdsworth 216 each and Ellis 215.25. Rain, cold and a piercing wind set in at about 14 hours, but despite Bill Ellis suffering a rear wheel collapse, he still managed to lead the field by 7 minutes at the 297 mile point (Eaton Socon). Ellis was also delayed at the level crossing at Wansford, both ways, while Jim Dougal suffered two punctures. Ellis stopped for a feed which resulted in Dougal getting within 2 minutes of him, but Ellis held his lead by a slim margin to win the event.

*A proposal by Frank Wingrave favouring the use of motor vehicles where possible to assist with feeding and helping the riders was accepted by the North Road Club's committee. Will Townsend suggested 'The Bull' at Long Sutton could be kept open all night, provided the landlady was willing to cater for the riders and helpers. She and her staff looked after the club's needs excellently for seven years.*

*The club had now accepted that the feeding and welfare of the riders was one of its responsibilities and was grateful to other clubs in or around the area for their help. These annual gatherings over the years became a social occasion for many people.*

We should not have been so surprised at Ellis's win really because he'd been the only finisher in the clubs annual Doncaster and back race, due to bad weather, in June. He recorded 19hrs 8 mins for that tough ride.

*January 9th Alexander Fleming discovers Penicillin*

**Anfield B.C. 24hr  A. Hancock,** who'd previously ridden for the Grosvenor  Wheelers was now riding for the Anfield.   Following the disappointments of his last two years in this event, where he'd retired without getting a place, he more than made  up for this by **winning** with **384 miles.**  Hancock had a very fast first 12 hours which yielded 205.5 miles.   **J. Smith,** Lancs R.C. was **2nd** with **368.5 miles, J. Long,** Anfield BC was **3rd** with **362.75.** The first half of the race had been a battle between Hancock and Long; the second half was between Smith and Long.  A.E. Edge of the Speedwell BC finished 4th with 360.25 miles and ten other riders finished.

---

**The Catford 24hr** had now become accepted as a real top-notch event by the long distance men.   It was won again this year by **Jack Rossiter,** his second win, with **400.4 miles.**  The mileages produced in this event by the top riders were easily on a par with any other event, especially the North Road.    **E.J. Doubleday,** Catford CC was **2nd** with **392.25 miles, L. Cooper** was **3rd** with **386.5 miles** and led the **Kentish Wheelers to a team win of 1119.5 miles.** The weather for the event was strong winds and rain.

47 riders battled against the wind to Offington where the helpers experienced a hectic time.  The first man arrived considerably outside schedule, but in the meantime three 'charabancs' had pulled up in front of the 'Coach and Horses' so that when the riders did roll in, in batches of fives and sixes, helpers were dodging each other around the vehicles. The checker was holding three bikes and writing down six men's times at once; the helpers were pumping tyres with one hand and filling bottles with the other.  The lady helpers dished out food to eight men at once and filled their pockets with fruit.

Rossiter was leading the field here, 59.5 miles in 3hrs 2mins, followed by Young, Perkins, Bridges, Baker and 'Doub' E.J. Doubleday.  After the Chichester detours were complete the next major feed was at Fareham, late at night. One of the last riders to turn up was J. Curtis of the Carlyle CC, at about 12.30am.   The door of the café was closed but he was ushered in and directed to a 'feed' table.  He silently devoured rice pudding, fruit, bread and butter and bananas.  When he finished eating he exclaimed that he'd never eaten fruit and rice pudding before in his life, and that this was his first 24hr, having only ever ridden a 25 mile race before.   He went off into the night quite cheerfully after cadging a 'fag' and having his bottles filled with ale.  After a fine night where Rossiter covered just over 213 miles at Guildford in 12 hours, Doubleday had crept into 2nd place 48 mins behind him.  At the Beverley Brook turn one of the Catford helpers had arrived at 5.25am to do the checking.   There was a night-watchman asleep in his hut at the side of the road, and a short while later, more clubmen arrived and set to making a field kitchen on the side of the road.  They even constructed a table from some old planks and piping and all this was done without waking the night-watchman, who was thought to be a 'specialist' at his job!

Rossiter appeared at 6.05am looking very fresh and happy whilst Doubleday followed 32 mins later, closely marked by Baker.  By this time the night-watchman had awoken and was taking an interest in proceedings and went on to tell them how he used to ride a solid tyred 'Kangaroo' Ordinary cycle, back in the good old days.

By Guildford at around 20 hours, Cooper had run into 3rd place behind Rossiter and Doubleday, and that's how the final result came about.  The strong winds had played havoc with the riders during daylight hours for Rossiter to win with 400 miles.

---

**Polytechnic 24hr Track Race** at Herne Hill, Friday 7pm July 12th.   The main contenders this year were Jack Holdsworth of the Kentish Wheelers who was expected to win again, Harry Pearson, Marlboro AC a previous 24hr road winner in the 1927 Catford , G. Sibthorpe and E.J. Winn, third and fourth respectively in last years event.  Vic Jenner, F. Harris and Wally Perkins who took 2nd place last year.

Other entries were E.J. Evans, F. Wingrave, F. Bowler and C.G. Bowtle. The weather on Saturday turned out to be the hottest day for 5 years and yet even in this blazing heat only 4 riders retired although every exposed part of their bodies was painfully red causing terrible distress and sunburn. *Obviously the luxury of suntan creams and the dangers of exposure to U.V. rays were not known about at that time.*

Jack Holdsworth the favourite didn't have the runaway win he had in 1927, in fact, at 7hrs into the ride he was 4th behind Fowler, Pearson and Wingrave. It was around this time that Pearson took his first heavy fall in the semi-darkness between the lights from two of the acetylene flares dotted around the track. He touched the wheel of his pacing tandem and was badly grazed and shaken, but 15 minutes later he was back in the field lying in 3rd place.

At 12 hrs the leading distances were Fowler with 288.9 miles (a new track record) Pearson 282 miles, Holdsworth 281m, Wingrave 278 miles with Perkins and Sibthorpe level on 277m. By mid-morning the heat had taken its toll and many riders could hardly keep awake. From 3pm to 6pm Pearson increased his lead over Holdsworth to 10 miles, but then Pearson started to fade in the last hour and when Holdsworth retaliated Pearson finally cracked. He'd been reeling backwards and forwards across the track absolutely exhausted. With 23 mins to go he again hit his pacing tandem and fell heavily on the track, becoming unconscious. This left **Holdsworth** to win with **a new 24 hr track record of 531.75 miles,** to Pearson's 528.7 miles. Fred Wingrave was the discovery of the race, coming 3rd with 498.5 miles. E.J. Evans made a remarkable recovery after starting much too fast, to take 4th with 491.7 miles, Fowler 5th 487.8 miles, W.E. Jones, 466.4, W.J. Mason, 464, A.V. Jenner, 461, Scott , 458m. C.G. Howtle, 434, and J.H. Emmerson, 425 miles.

⊱•◈•⊰

Jack Rossiter, this years Catford winner, went on in 1929 to break the **End to End** record, being the first solo bicycle rider to use an all land route after the RRA banished the use of ferries in Scotland. His record time was **2 days 13 hours 22 mins.**

In 1974 Frank Clark of the Wessex RC sent in some of his memories of these early Catford events of 1926, 27 and 28, to the 24 hr Fellowship Journal. "A few of us gathered on the course at Fareham outside Mrs Briggs café on the Saturday night where riders were being fed and retraced. It was here that I first met Doc Miller, then aged about 63, who rode the event to get fit. After a leisurely wash he would shake hands with everyone in sight including other competitors before sitting down to eat. Here you could get anything from lamb chops to strawberries and cream. I know Jack Rossiter was partial to a lamb chop. Afterwards, I suppose half the riders left here with cigarettes alight, a habit seldom seen in these days (1974)".

*When reading old books on cycling clubs history I've come across various references to 'smoking contests' being part of the evening's entertainment. Now in 2007 smoking has been banned from everywhere except the privacy of ones own home. The last person I saw in a 24hr race, smoking a cigarette, was Arch Harding in about 1960 just after he'd downed a glass of beer going into the early evening.*

Frank continues "As there weren't optional detours in those days, the time lag between first and last man on the road could be four or five hours. We then rode over to help at Guildford, the old 'workhouse' being used as a feeding station. After having a late tea at Horsham on the Sunday evening it was still a long 60 miles ride home, getting in about midnight at Southampton, feeling very weary".

⊱•◈•⊰

**The Wessex RC 24 hr** was first run in this year of 1928, as a club event only. It was promoted to meet the long distance aspirations of certain members of the club. It was held on September 29th and 30th, entry fee £1 inclusive of feeding. At the beginning of September it was feared that the event would be cancelled due to lack of volunteers to help run the event, but it did take place and went down in the club history as 'the race of retirement' as only 4 riders from 13 starters finished the 24hrs, due to the very strong cold wind, plus many punctures suffered by the riders.

At 116 miles Harry Jukes led Charlie Lane by 10 mins and at the 12 hr point Jukes led Lane by 3 miles with 204 miles. They duelled for the lead until about 250 miles where a 6 mile spell off course by both riders, led to Lane's retirement.

Jukes continued strongly to run out an excellent winner with **386 miles**. **Bert Brown** riding his second 24hr of the year was a very good **2nd** with **378 miles**. **Jones** was his usual cheerful self for **3rd** place with **368 miles** and **Frank Clark 4th** with **348.5 m.**

━━━►•◄•►•◄━━━

The North Road 24hr in 1928 was run on August 31st and September 1st, and attracted a field of 57 riders with 32 finishers. **Bill Ellis** started a strong favourite after his previous years win in this event. He **won** the event with **413.5** beating **Rossiter** by 10.5 miles. **413.5 was a new competition record** by 3 miles. **3rd** was **T.F. Maddex**, North Road CC with **395.5 miles**. Other North Road members to finish were **Bill Frankum** with **354.75 miles** and **E.J. Foot** on a **trike** with **331m**; both were novices at 24hrs. Bill Ellis had topped off a very successful season with his win, as earlier in the year he'd proved himself by winning two 50 mile events and also the 'Doncaster and back' in 17hrs 5 mins. He had also taken the club 12 hr with 213.75 miles, also a good pointer as to his fitness.

**The Tricycle race was won by Frank Fisher with 365.25, (a new Competition Record by 10.75 miles)** although it is 1939 before trike Comp Record is listed. This '24' was the last one ridden by two men who were responsible for a series of performances each unique in its way. The first one was Jack Rossiter who rode in every race from 1920 to 1928 and was placed each time. He won four times (a distinction he shares with Holbein) was second twice, and third three times – a wonderful record on its own. The other rider was C.A.Stevens, Polytechnic CC. He rode his first 24 in this event in 1908 and by 1928 he'd started in 14 events, and finished in 13. He rode to 3rd place in 1913, certainly a record of consistency.

At the first full moon following the 24 hr event, **W.A. Ellis** attacked the **Edinburgh to London** figures and was successful, covering the distance in **21 hrs 53 mins.** A beating of the old record by nearly two hours.

# 1929

In the **Anfield 24hr** only six men finished from fifteen starters, due to excessive heat. **A.Power,** Cheshire Roads CC **371.5 miles** won, from. **J S. Heath,** Anfield BC, **371**, a very close result. **E.W. Robinson,** Palatine CC was 3rd with **364.75 miles.**

*Since records began in the late 1880's End to End riders had been allowed to use Ferries in Scotland to cross the Firth of Forth etc, or any stretch of water, but on 21st June 1929, Tom Hughes of the Palatine CC riding a trike and using an all-land route beat the new RRA standard for the End to End with 3 days 21 hrs 55 mins.*

*In those early years, one peculiar incident occurred when G.P. Mills and Tommy Edge reduced the tandem record for the End to End to 3 days, 4hrs 46 mins in 1895. They rode the whole journey without sleep, but lost two hours recovering from sea-sickness after a very rough ferry crossing in Scotland, probably the Firth of Forth at Granton, near Edinburgh.*

*Ed Zoller a Scottish rider and RRA Observer mentioned in Roy Green's book that in 1924 he travelled the main route over the Grampians north to Inverness and noted that the road was nothing more than cart tracks with grass and heather growing in the middle. He said "imagine that, on a dark wet night, even with a good acetylene lamp".*

━━━►•◄•►•◄━━━

The Polytechnic Track 24 hr gave **Jack Holdsworth** his third outright **win** and a **new record of 534.8 miles.** At the 100 mile point L. Cave started to assert his supremacy by lapping the field. By the time 200 miles had been covered Cave was 14 laps ahead of Holdsworth. Wingrave fell heavily for the second time and at 9 hours of riding the positions were Cave 221miles, Holdsworth 217 miles, Rose 200m, Scott 196, Wingrave 189 and Tom Hughes

188m.   Forty two minutes later the race pattern changed dramatically when Cave touched his pacing tandem, fell and then was run over by Scott's tandem.   Scott did a somersault over his handlebars, landed on his feet and grabbed a spare bike to continue.  Cave's injuries were all in the wrong place, knees, back and the palms of his hands and by the time he'd been patched up he'd lost over 30 minutes.   He eventually retired at 259 miles.

By the 12 hr point, Holdsworth had amassed 285.75 miles with Rose at 30miles, Scott at 34 miles and Wingrave at 35 miles.   By the end of the race Wingrave had pulled through the field to finish 2nd.  **Jack Holdsworth** won with **534.8 miles, Fred Wingrave was 2nd** with **481.8 miles** and **Scott** was **3rd** with **476.8 miles,** Jones 469m, Tom Hughes 448.3m, W.H. Rose 439.65 and F.H. Freeborn 418.5 miles.

Tom Hughes of the Palatine CC who produced 448.3 miles in this event is the same Tom Hughes who broke the 'End to End' on a trike just one month earlier.   That is an amazing feat of endurance and fitness.   The organisation of this race had been superb with better track lighting and informative result board to keep the crowd happy but despite all of this, **the event was very poorly attended and the Track 24 hr race was again to disappear from the calendar, but this time forever.**

Geoff Dring goes on to say that Fred Wingrave was one of the riders on the pacing tandem for E.C. Pilcher in 1927 and this is what fired his enthusiasm for riding in 1928.   Fred's ride must have been a great family affair as his five brothers got together 20 tandems and riders and his father looked after them all with food and drink on the hottest day of the year.   Fred's 498.5 mile ride didn't sap his stamina as he got up early the next morning to ride the Southern 12 hr.   Ethel Brambleby mentions that Wally Perkins who received a cup for 2nd place in the track 24hr of 1927, later donated the cup to the Kentish Wheelers, as a memorial trophy for those who had fallen in the war. The cup eventually was used for the Surrey/Sussex ladies 'BAR' trophy.

The track events of the late 1880's, 1909 and 1910 and these last three would have had 'betting' taking place, although I don't know whether it was legal or illegal at that time.   Or was there even a law governing gambling at that time?   Most of the race promoters also had boxing matches and running events taking place to enliven the proceedings.

*My many thanks to the late Geoff Dring and Bill Frankum for having the foresight to preserve these last three Polytechnic results for us all to see.   Geoff wrote many interesting reports for the 24hr Fellowship Journal including this one.*

⇒•◇•⇐

**The Catford 24 hr on the 20th July was won by Eric Doubleday, Catford CC with 397.125 miles.   Harry Jukes was 2nd with 394m, E.B. 'Bert' Brown was 3rd with 390m.   Frank Clark with 366 miles enabled the Wessex RC to win the team race.**

Frank Clark of the Wessex RC recalls being persuaded to ride the Catford '24' earlier in the springtime by Bert Brown and Harry Jukes.  Bert had told Frank "We want you just to ride and finish, we will look after the 'fireworks'!" The day came and Frank had lunch at Crawley and then pottered the few miles to the start at Pease Pottage. "Armed with a packet of 20 'Craven A' cigarettes, I heeded my colleagues instructions to take it steady from the start.  It was north of Guildford on the long haul to Beverley Brook that I caught Jack Spackman, then riding for the Windsor Wheelers.  It was the first of many such encounters during the next 20 years.  He assured me that he would do 360 miles, but he didn't manage it.  However, Bert Brown and Harry Jukes did their stuff.  Harry came 2nd in the event behind Doubleday (Doubleday being a very appropriate name for a 24hr winner!)  Bert was 3rd and my modest mileage enabled the Wessex RC to win the team race, by the way I had '5 fags' left at the finish."

All kinds of weather was experienced during the event; heavy rain, lightning, cold wind, and burning heat during the day.   The night was pitch black and troop movements in the Arundel area caused some very narrow escapes. Sporting instinct was shown by Maurice Draisey at Fareham, where one or two riders were having trouble with their equipment.  He replaced a broken pedal with one off his own trike, and also exchanged a faulty light for a rider during the night.  Maurice was last seen trying to repair a broken toe strap for another rider, - a true sportsman. There were 66 entries for this race.

Frank Fischer of the Kentish Wheelers remembered one of his fellow team members in this event, 'Sailor' Cooper, who finished with 327.6 miles having a stack of punctures. Rumour has it that he was seen stitching up punctured 'tubulars' in the middle of the night, cursing profusely and probably profanely.

**E.B. (Bert) Brown** went on to win the North Road 24hr in 1931 and broke many **solo bicycle RRA records** that same year, so following a pattern that a lot of long distance men have taken, and still do over the years, of riding from 'London to Edinburgh', or vice versa, and then continue for the 24hr and possibly include the 'York to Edinburgh' all in one ride. In that same year, **Bert** broke the **'Lands End to London'** with **16 hrs 35 mins**, beating Charlie Davey's eight year old record by 54 minutes.

**Earlier in 1930 Bert** had teamed up with **Cyril Neale** and had broken the **'London to Edinburgh' tandem record** with **21hrs 35 mins**.

*12th August 1929 saw* **Les Meyers** *take nearly two hours off Tom Hughes'* **End to End trike record** *with* **3 days 19 hrs 56 mins.**

⟫⟩◆⟨⟪

**The Wessex 24hr** was run again this year for club members only. **Bert Brown** was the **winner** with **371 miles**, **Charlie Jack** was **2nd** with **360.5** and **Frank Clark 3rd** with **352.5 miles**.

*In August 1929* **Jack Rossiter,** *the Raleigh professional, broke the* **End to End** *record using an all land route in* **2 days, 13 hrs and 22mins.** *He suffered very heavy rain for the first 24hrs and was apparently the first man to climb Berriedale without walking. He rode a Sturmey Archer 3 speed gear.*

*In September 1929, Logie Baird was invited by the BBC to carry out experimental T.V. transmissions.*

⟫⟩◆⟨⟪

**The 1929 North Road 24hr** was held in late September on the 20th and 21st. It turned out to be a very hard day with strong to gale force winds. **Ellis,** who seemed to ride better as conditions got worse, **won the event for the third time** with **406 miles.** Ellis had a hard struggle with **F. Stott,** Century RC who finished **2nd** with **401.5 miles, 3rd** was **W. Low,** Kent RC with **394.75m.**

Twenty three riders finished this very hard race. The **trike** event was won by **Les Meyers,** nicknamed 'Uncle', with **332.5 miles,** riding for the Southgate CC. His ride came just some five weeks after breaking the **End to End** on a **trike** with **3 days 19 hrs 56 mins.**

This was Ellis's third win in succession and had come after another very tough season for him, having taken 2nd place in the Gayler 12hr with 226.25 miles and 2nd place in the Leicester 12 hr. In June he'd recorded the fastest time ever in the clubs history for the Doncaster and back with 17hrs 18 mins.

Bill Ellis retired from racing at the end of 1929, to his clubs joy at him winning for the third time and likening his rides to Frank Shorland's some forty years earlier. All of his rides were won on a hard day, especially the last one. What could this man have done in favourable conditions?

*October 29th Wall Street Stockmarket crashes in America.*

## 1930

This years **Anfield BC 24hr** saw even less finishers than the previous years, when rain and extreme cold reduced the field from eleven to four. **W.T. 'Tom' Melia,** Mersey Roads CC was an **easy winner** with **380.5 miles** with fellow clubman **A.L. Alan Littlemore 356.5 miles 2nd** and **N.S. Heath** of The Anfield BC **354miles 3rd.**

*We are now in a short period of years where there were up to five 24hr races a year. The Anfield, The Catford, The Wessex, The Irish RC and The North Road, but the only two events that seemed to be getting good entries and lots of good riders were*

37

G P Mills

"Artie" Bennett in characteristic pose.

J A Bennett

Monty Holbein

F T Bidlake

George Olley

C Moss

G H Stancer

F Shorland & F T Bidlake

G P Mills & T A Edge

Maurice Selbach

Jack Rossiter

Frank Armond

Bill Ellis

Charlie Davey

Tom Hughes

Cyril Heppleston

Hubert Opperman

Sid Ferris

Alec Smith

Frank Southall

Eric Wilkinson

*The Catford and The North Road.   Popularity for these two events is shown by the fact that competition record 'bounces' between the two promotions.   The other three events are destined in their present format to eventually disappear from the calendar.*

---

**The Catford 24hr** this year produced a **competition record** with **another win** by E.J. Doubleday with **416.25 miles**.   **Jim Dougal,** Marlborough, was **2nd** with **413.25.   Catford** won the **team** race with **1,134.25miles** and there were 34 finishers.   **Jack Perkins** was a fine **3rd** with **408.125 miles.** Dougal had been in the first six riders all day, he then suffered two punctures and a collapsed rear wheel.   He had to borrow a clubman's bike with a Sturmey Archer three speed, having a top gear of 92", and he rode 28 miles on this heavy bike.   Bert Brown covered 405 miles for 4th place.

At that time it was prophesied that it would be a long time before anyone rides further in 24hrs and the fact that J.W. Dougal, after having trouble with his bike, managed to ride a distance of 413 miles and only came second with such a high mileage, was even more astounding.   The winner, Doubleday, sympathised with Dougal after the event and said that had he not suffered with mechanical problems it is quite possible that Dougal would have won, as his own lead in the race, at that time, was only about two minutes at the most.

*Amy Johnson flies solo from London to Australia in 19 days.*

---

**The Wessex RC 24hr** winner for the second year running was **Bert Brown** with **374 miles.**

*The Road Traffic Act makes third party insurance compulsory.*

**Jack Rossiter** *riding as a professional for Raleigh on August 3rd 1930 broke the* **solo bicycle 1000 miles record** *using a course based on the Great North Road, using much of the 24hr course.   He took the record with* **3 days 11 hours 58 mins.**

---

**The Irish Road Club** was one of the oldest in the British Isles having been formed in 1890.   Bill Finn instigated the first running of their open **24hr event.** It took place in the 'Bog of Allen' area, running north from the Wicklow Mountains to Navan, and then westwards from Dublin towards Athlone.

**Frank Shubert,** a member of Cheltenham and County CC and Vegetarian C & AC provided us with most of our knowledge and details on this popular event that took place on the Irish August Bank Holiday each year.   The event ran annually until 1937.

**T. Masterson** won this 1930 event with **362 miles and 88 'perches'** (perch, rod or pole = 5.5 yards i.e. 1 x 320th of a mile) – a new Irish record.   **N.J. Troy** was **2nd** with **352 miles.   W.J. 'Bill' Finn** was **3rd** on a **trike** with **345.830** also a new Irish trike record.   J. Murphy, Loraine CC was 4th with 344miles.

*The Clubs long distance 12hr and 24hr events prior to 1930 were for club members only and the results are hard to find.*

---

**The North Road 24hr** this year took place on September 5th and 6th, 47 riders started.   The race was a very open one as Bill Ellis had now retired from racing. The **winner W.A. Low,** Kent RC fought hard all day and beat Ellis's previous event record by .25 of a mile with **413.75.   2nd** place went to **R.J.J. Coe,** University CC with **405.75 miles.**   The third placed rider came very close with **405.5 miles.**   He was **L.W. Brown,** Luton Wheelers.

**The North Road CC** won the **team** race with **G.H.M. Pitt,** 391.5 miles, **F.W. Robinson** 390.25 m and **T.F. Maddex** with **383.75,** totalling l,165.5 miles.   The **trike** prize was won by **E.H. Cooper,** Highgate CC with **324 miles.**

*There are now more than one million cars on the road.*

# 1931

**F. Hancock** of the Grosvenor Wheelers won this years **Anfield B.C. 24 hrs** after having a magnificent battle with **G. Gilbert,** East Liverpool Whls.    Hancock's mileage was **389.5,** to Gilberts **387.**    **H. Rothwell** was **3rd** with **379.5 miles.**    Seven more riders finished.

*The first Highway Code is published.*

⤙⧫⤚

**The Catford** again produced more superb competition records firstly of **430.75** beating the previous years record by a massive 14 miles.  **Jim Dougal** was the new record holder.

Its also interesting to note that the **Kentish Wheelers team** amassed **1,206.75 miles** -another **competition record. J.T. Perkins 418.25 m, Norman Tullett 400.75** and **L. Cooper 387.75.**    Perkins was actually **2nd** in this event. His mileage would have been a new competition record if Dougal hadn't beaten him.  This was the first time the team distance gave an average of over 400 miles per man.  Norman Tullett with 400.75 came 4th in the event in his first ever 24hr.  **Sid Ferris** was **3rd** with **409.25 miles.**

Norman recalls his memories of the event:

"Every year until 1939 I'd been a helper, and was probably one of the slowest in the club, everyone passed me in races especially SCCU 50's, so riding a 24hr was just a case of sheer bloody obstinacy for me.  I had a 73" single speed gear and a bottle on my handlebars, which Jack Holdsworth 'J.E.' took off in no uncertain manner saying "why carry the extra weight when the whole club is looking after you?"  The help of the Catford Club was superb, Sandy's and Mrs 'H' especially.

On the way to Fareham I was riding in company with two other competitors, both older and better than me.  I was doing the talking and it was a long slope up, when I suddenly realised I was talking to myself, I was astonished. Some many miles later on the way back from where I'd turned at Fareham, I saw them and they looked dreadful. They must have thought I was a horrible little b.....d!

At the little feeding station near Roundstone, I saw Ferris with half his face covered in blood.  Sid Ferris had only one eye, the other was covered with an eye patch due to blindness.  He looked awful and he warned us of a bad hole in the road close to the feed.  It was being repaired and was badly lit.  Sid had hit it hard and had to return to the feeding station for repairs and treatment for his injuries.  Doubleday going for his third win had also hit the pothole and had to retire due to his injuries.  He had not long ago recovered from Scarlet Fever, and at the time of this accident was leading the race by 5 minutes from Ferris.

It was wet in that area very often and although the Catford tried to choose a moonlit night for their event, it often was not.  This in time became a bit of a joke.  I also remember 'Gentleman' Jim Dougals unforgettably smooth riding style."

Frank Clark, who also rode this event, remembers Dougals effortless pedalling especially going up Washington Hill on the A24, as he caught and passed 5 or 6 riders on the hill.  Frank added "that year, I missed the Guildford to Windsor detour of 40 miles so I saw Jim towards the end, coming out of detours as I was entering them; it was said he was averaging 22mph for the last few hours."

During the night, two or more detours had taken the riders from Guildford to the outskirts of London, where 7 million people were asleep, blissfully unaware of the riders urging their machines forward with ever tiring limbs. The writer of this passage continues "If this had been the Tour De France, those riders would have been welcomed by the cheers from thousands of throats and the townsfolk would have gone without sleep.  But I digress."

By dawn a slight drizzle had set in and then later in the morning heavy rain fell, leaving a depleted field of 27 finishers from 45 that started. The club and its members were now in the grip of a severe depression, similar to the rest of the country, and the entry was the lowest since the event started in 1925. Such was the price of gold, the club this year could only present medals with a small gold centre, and many members couldn't afford to race.

Sid Ferris went on to win the North Road CC 24hr three times consecutively from 1932. In 1937 he broke the End to End and 1,000 miles in one ride and later the 'London to Edinburgh'. In 1938 he broke the RRA 24hr record with 465.75, a record previously held by Cyril Heppleston. Sid's record breaking had started on a tandem with brother Harry in 1927 breaking the London to Portsmouth and back.

---

**The Wessex RC 24hr** was won by **Frank Clark** with **360 miles.**

---

**The Irish RC 24 hr** was won this year by **D. Lundstrom** with **367miles 243 perches.** J.J. Masterson who led for the first 20 hours was overcome by tiredness and fell into a ditch. This enabled Lundstrom to go first on the road. **Masterson** recovered to finish with **362 miles. J.J. Killean** was **3rd** with **354** and **F. Dawson** Veg C & AC who was about to start a fortnights holiday in Ireland finished **4th** with **339 miles.**

**Bert Brown** broke the **Edinburgh to London** record with **21hrs 49mins** knocking just 4 mins off Ellis's record.

---

**The North Road 24hr** event suffered from a low entry of thirty three riders of whom only fifteen finished. The winner was **Bert Brown**, Wessex RC who covered **407.75 miles. L.W. Brown** of the Luton wheelers was **2nd** with **403 miles** and **R.J.J. Coe** 3rd with **399.75.** W,A, Low was well up with the leaders and riding very strongly hoping to repeat his previous years win, but at about 12hrs he crashed into the rear of a stationary vehicle when riding with his head down, and was too badly knocked about to continue. It was felt that this incident had a definite effect on the outcome of the leadership in the event. This is a bad habit that has been prevalent amongst riders over the years and can still be seen in time trialling in 2007.

# 1932

**In the Anfield 24hr** 21 riders started and 15 finished. **G.H.M. Pitt** had travelled up from the North Road club to **win** the event with **394.75 miles,** certainly one of the highest mileages ever attained in this event, if not **the** highest! It's interesting to note that quite a lot of riders in this era have three or four very good seasons winning most of their own clubs events and then retire. Pitt was no exception, having won various 12hr races in the club calendar and getting high places in his own clubs 24hr. He also won the Doncaster and back race in 17 hrs 38 mins. **G. Gilbert** was **2nd** overall, another high mileage of **392 miles** and **J.S. Jonas,** Anfield BC was **3rd** with **374.5 miles.** He won a special prize for trikes only. Others to finish were C. Randall (bike) 351.75, N.S. Heath (trike) 351.7 and Alan Littlemore, Mersey RC (trike) 323.25 miles.

---

**The Catford CC 24hr. Bill Low,** Kent RC who had won the North Road event in 1930 with 413.75, improved on his mileage to **win** this Catford event with **423.625 miles. Norman Tullett** was **2nd** with **408 miles,** Frank **Clark** was **3rd** with **400.8m.**

Frank recalled "this was my vintage year, starting No 15 I was first on the road just after Fareham. Near Chichester, Bill Low caught me and we rode together to Clapham where he got away due to missing a feed. By Windsor he was five miles ahead. It was on the 'Roman Gate' detour to Billingshurst that Norman Tullett caught me. I soon recovered but could not bridge the gap, I finished 3rd and Bert Brown retired with a bad back."

Norman Tullett in 2nd place remembers "there were some new detours south of Chichester and I went 'off course'. Then I had to go like mad to make up the distance and thus finished taking a 'hell of a packet', in contrast to my first effort the previous year. During the event I could see Frank, who I was catching, keep looking back at the top of every rise to see if I was any nearer, of course this was bad for him psychologically and when I did get to catch him he just faded. It was a wet, cold night and I pedalled like mad just to keep warm."

━━━━◆━━━━

The Wessex RC 24hr on the 22nd May was won by **Frank Clark** with **353.5 miles, Arthur Moss 2nd** with **341.6** and **3rd R.E. Gage** with **311.75.**

━━━━◆━━━━

The Irish RC 24hr was won by **J.J. Kilean** with **359.87 miles.**

━━━━◆━━━━

The North Road 24hr was run off in the best weather seen for many years on September 16th and 17th. **Sid Ferris** of theVegetarian C & AC **won** with **429.75 miles, a new course and event record** for the North Road club. He was just one mile short of Competition Record. **L. Hall** of the Century Road Club was **2nd** with **413.25m, L.W. Brown,** Luton Whls was **3rd** with **406.75 miles.** Five men beat 400 miles.

Ferris's win was the first of three consecutive wins for him in this event. No trikes finished.

## 1933

**In the Anfield BC 24hr** this year, Pitt of the North Road was expected to win and repeat the success of his previous years ride, but it wasn't to be. He hadn't reckoned on one, Tom Melia of the Mersey RC. Tom had won in 1930, it was his local event on roads he knew well.

**Tom Melia** won the event with **401 miles, a record** as no-one had ever beaten 400 miles unpaced in this event until now. His 12hr mileages were 201 first half and 200 to finish with. Steady riding was the fashion of the day. Just reading the only mention of this 1933 event in the 'Black Anfielders' book, one wouldn't sense the underlying facts of this brave ride by Melia. The actual passage from the book reads: *"After a wet cold night, Gilbert, Hancock and Jonas had retired about midday but other riders seem to have stood up to the weather very well. W.T. Melia's 401 miles was not much ahead of Pitt, North Road CC whose 398 miles was worthy of his club. R. Hepworth, Huddersfield RC was a good 3rd with 389.75 miles. Eight other riders finished from 17 starters.*

*Frank Fischer, one of the riders, supplied the 24hr fellowship with these other eight results. Tommy Hegginbotham 385 m, Harry Gawthrop, Mersey Roads CC 367 m, F.E. Fischer, Altrincham Ravens, 363.5 miles, F. Ashton, Huddersfield RC, 357.25, S. Leach, Lancs RC, 352.25, W. Hudson, West Pennine RC, 350.7, A.C.Pluck, Warrington RC, 332.75m, H.A. (Howard) Saunders, Walsall RCC, 331.5 miles.*

Whoever wrote these descriptions and details about the Anfield 24hr in 1933 seems to have been more in praise of Pitt of The North Road CC, another famous old cycling club with a 50 year history, compared with a relatively new club, The Mersey Road CC, which was only founded in 1924. Maybe they didn't like the 'underdog' winning, don't forget, class structure, times and attitudes have altered immensely in 70 years.

When reading the North Roads early history (pre 1900) there is mention of the class structure at that time and *"whether it was wise for Jack to be seen riding with his master?"* It was at the end of the Victorian era when this question was posed. It would be after the First World War, roughly the 1920's, before relatively cheaper cycles produced by such companies as Raleigh and Hercules could be afforded by a person who was in regular work, but even then it would have been an expensive item for most people.

When researching those earlier years, 1885 to 1939 one realises that the hierarchy who ran the clubs and the benefactors who designed the administration of the sport in their area were fairly 'well off'. They would probably be local tradesmen, shop, store or company owners and directors. Professionals such as Doctors, Lawyers, Academics and retired military personnel etc, they would most likely have 'dabbled' with the sport on a personal basis or would have had a bicycle in their earlier years and were re-living their youth.

I think 'class culture' or the awareness of it, disappeared from **most** cycling club life after the Second World War. Although I was aware of 'posh' people in other walks of life in the 1960's it was certainly not evident in any of the clubs or club folk I knew at that time, although there was still plenty of 'male chauvenism', which hasn't been eradicated from the sport, even in 2008.

Early in 2007, I had a chance meeting with John Williams of the Mersey RC. He comes from a family steeped in the history of cycling, time trialling and record breaking in the north west. I mentioned that I was now writing my next book on the history of the 24hr and had he got any bits of information on pre-war events. Straight away he said **"Don't forget our own Tommy Melia, the first man to beat 400 miles in the North"** and that's how I found out about some very interesting and touching facts behind the figures.

With the 1930's came the 'Depression' or 'Slump'. Employment was hard to find in many areas and by 1933 Tom had been out of work for quite some time, like thousands of others. There was no 'dole money' or 'unemployment benefits' in those days, in fact it would be well after the Second World War some 20 years into the future, before plans instigated by the Beveridge Committee were implemented by the Government, so creating 'The Welfare State'.

Men and, sometimes whole families, were roaming the countryside and towns looking for work. Tom was luckier than some in as much as he was a single man and living in meagre lodgings. He was fit and although he was always hungry he still managed to ride quite hard most days in between looking for work. One of the benefactors of the Mersey RC learnt of Tom's plight and the fact that he was very fit, and offered to help. He came up with a few expenses for Tommy that enabled him to carry on training. In those early years, if a rider won a prestigious or 'classic' open time trial such as the Anfield 100 or 24hr or the Bath Road 100 it was a real 'feather in the cap' for the riders club.

The Benefactor paid Tommy's entry fee as well as his own sons as he was also out of work. With the food Tom would get in the event he was in for a real treat, it was reckoned that Tom rode well above himself to make sure he did the full course just to get to the extra feeding stations on route.

Another Historian now in his mid 80's, and an expert on anything connected to 24hr riding and record breaking in the north, is Peter Barlow. He would have been a young teenager in the 1930's and he used to help his dad, Tommy Barlow, to check the riders through various places on the road. He recalls *"Most of the competitors were, I suppose, hard riding tourists and clubman brought up on all night rides and CTC '250 miles in 24 hr' events, and were content to ride for 'club standards'. The 1st prize in the Anfield 24hr was 5 guineas (£5.25p) a not indifferent sum of money in those days, indeed probably two or three weeks wages. What therefore should a 1st prize be today? I'll leave you to judge. Dwelling on the subject of hard riding tourists, it seems ironic that 50 years on, it's the hard riding 'Audax' members who are bringing new entries into the 24hr scene. There's nothing new is there?"* Peter wrote that passage over 20 years ago in 1987.

I was really intrigued by Tom Melia's story, so much so that I delved deep into the Mersey RC past history and found that Tom had edited the Mersey RC newsletter 'The Record' between 1929 and 1933, and I now include an abridged account of those years by him.

*Tom said that the 'deep depression' which had been slowly moving across the country in the previous two years had now firmly settled. Four million people were unemployed with Liverpool and St Helens being black spots in the North West. He lived in 'digs'(lodgings) at that time and said that a few of the lads like himself were unemployed so couldn't afford the club 'subs' and race entry fees.*

*He rode the Anfield 24hr with Alan Littlemore on August 22nd 1930. Ten men started from the 'Bull and Stirrup', Chester, at 2 minute intervals from 8pm on a calm warm Friday night. Tommy rode a fixed gear of 76" on a wooden sprint rim which was split but repaired with tape to bind it together. He had been loaned two new tyres by Bill Clarke, but only had an oil lamp on the front of his bike, which threw very little beam.*

The first feeding station came after darkness had fallen back at Chester. After stocking up with goodies donated by club members for the long night ahead, he continued on his way, but found it very difficult to see the road. It was such a dark night that he had to reduce his speed. At 140 miles the course ran back through Chester to the same feeding station for the last time and then came the long 50 mile drag into the wind to Chetwynd Church near Newport. It was now daylight as he picked up speed, but the daylight also brought heavy rain at Broxton.

Whitchurch, Chetwynd and then back to Shawbury was the next part of the course, with another sit down feed at the 'Three Greyhounds' at Shawbury. Tommy was cold and very wet, he took his shoes off and sat with his feet in a bowl of hot water while he ate. He was leading the field at this point and as he left the 'feed' he filled his jacket pockets with food. He arrived at Toft Corner, Knutsford to find only four riders left in the race. Alan Littlemore, who came 2nd with 365.5 miles, Heath of the Anfield rode 354 miles and Durran 333m. This left Tommy with a winning mileage of 380.5 after being 'followed out' by Frank Da Costa, and Jack Farrar on a tandem. They all stayed the night at Knutsford, then met the club for lunch the next day at Pickmere Lake, riding home later.

In 1933 in order to recognise other club members they were allowed to wear the Mersey RC coloured armband of blue and white on their black Alpaca jacket sleeve.

In 1933 Tommy mentioned that he'd been out of work for 3 years and was very hard up, very thin and lean, mostly living on bread and jam. Although very fit he had doubts about his stamina. His friend in the club, Harry Gawthrop, had a father with a good job in insurance and as such he was happy to pay for Harry and Tommy's entrance fees for the Anfield 24hr. Tommy openly admitted to giving it deep thought and selfishly thinking not about what mileage he could produce, but more to the point, how much food he could consume, having gone almost without for the last three years!

The start as usual was from the 'Bull and Stirrup' on a cold wet Friday night and Tommy soon settled down despite the conditions and proceeded to eat his way around the course; as well as feasting at the stops he also kept his pockets full and ate almost constantly. At the Shawbury feed he found he was equal 3rd with Pitt, both having covered 201 miles in 12 hours. Ted Gilbert was leading with 203.5 miles and Fred Hancock was 2nd with 202 miles. It was now getting a little warmer and he felt good, he caught both Gilbert and Hancock and as he headed back north he found he was leading by 7 minutes. He stopped for a feed at Byley (320 miles) run by Guy Pullan, and took a load of food including 3 raw eggs beaten up into a cup of tea, and then told Guy he would now only take drinks. So is salmonella poisoning just a modern day issue? On the return from 'Broken Cross', Middlewich, Tommy said his 'stomach went over his back' and his legs turned to jelly. He lost all interest in the event, he wanted to pack but his club mates wouldn't let him. As he left 'Toft' he saw Pitt coming up having taken 7 mins out of him. This made Tommy more determined and he rode painfully through his bad patch to be finally 'run out' followed by Tommy Barlow in a car with his son Peter, who was in school uniform. His final mileage finishing outside the 'Old Toll Cottage' on the Knutsford road was 401 miles. He'd beaten Pitt by 4 miles and his friend Harry had ridden 367 miles for 5th place. Tommy said he was very pleased to have given his benefactor his moneys worth and become the first rider in the North of England to beat 400 miles.

In modern times when food gets left on plates and is thrown away and over a fifth of the nation are classed as 'obese', it's hard to imagine anyone riding a 24hr cycle race just for the food, and the prize money of 5 guineas to live on. Just reading the only mention of this event of 1933 in the 'Black Anfielders' history book one wouldn't sense the underlying facts of this brave ride by Tommy Melia. I'm so glad I had that chance meeting with John Williams and found out the story behind the ride. But I wonder how many more interesting stories like this have disappeared forever, untold?

On a slightly lighter note, after that last race description and the dire hardships caused by 'the depression', and the way the hero of the day overcame all odds to win, I'm reminded of a comic book hero I read about when I was young, "Alf Tupper – The Tough of the Track". He would win every time he ran on the track. He ran in bare feet as he couldn't afford shoes but he still beat all of the 'posh' kids. He lived on bread and jam and six 'penn'orth' of chips was his treat. He ran everywhere because he couldn't afford the bus fare, and whatever hardships and obstacles were put in his way to stop him winning, he would always overcome them. 'Alf Tupper' was a model of triumph over adversity and when researching Tom Melia's story and background I kept thinking of 'Alf Tupper'.

Later in this book there are many heroes and characters who would fit the Alf Tupper mould for triumph over adversity.

Tommy was still competing in the Mersey RC races in the 1970's and I remember passing him in 1972, probably without so much as a word or a courteous 'dig em in'. I was an ignorant youth knowing nothing of his achievements and not realising that one day I would be writing at length about him and many other 'stars'. Tom rode 353 miles that year of 1972, virtually at the end of a 40 year career.

<hr>

The Catford 24hr 1933; **Norman Tullet** at his 3rd attempt **wins with 412.5 miles.** The **2nd** man, **Ted Vahey,** rode **399.4m.** **Frank Clark** of the **Wessex RC** was **3rd** with **393.8m** and together with **Jack Warhurst** and **Bill Kiddle** won the team prize. **Jack Spackman** was **4th** with **395.6 miles.** Norman Tullet recalls: "I think I was experimenting with different crank lengths of 6.75" (170 mm) from my usual ones, as I hadn't struggled as badly as the previous year, the only thing I do remember was the vile weather. The night was as black as your hat, bobby dodger lamps were all that was available and mine were worse than most. I came out of the black night between Roundstone and Horsham and as dawn broke I patted my crossbar and said 'still there old friend'; and to my legs 'still going up and down like piston rods, that's the style!'
George, my brother was riding and he amused us all by often saying 'Oh dear, Oh dear', when doing a 387 mile ride without too much effort."

Frank Clark remembers that it was the year of the thunderstorms during the night. "we had about eight storms between 6pm and 6am, then Sunday dawned bitterly cold, no sun and with a northerly wind. There were 39 entries.

<hr>

The **Irish RC 24hr** was won by **Phil Brady** with **384 miles, Frank Shubert,** who gave us the information on these Irish events, crashed heavily when charged by a bull escaping from market, which badly damaged his cycle. He was loaned a bike by a marshal and continued, even though the bike was the wrong size and he'd sustained a few injuries. **Frank** eventually came **3rd** with **370 miles.** **Killean** rode a strong race to come **2nd** with **377 m.**

<hr>

The **Wessex RC 24 hr** event was cancelled this year due to lack of entries. *Tom Lodge sent me lots of information on the history of the Wessex Road Club, for which I am most grateful.* It covers the 24hr races between 1928 and 1955, and this next passage reiterates my observations when writing about other 24hr races in that same period of time, especially the Anfield event. Here is a passage from that history:

*"It is sad to relate that the Wessex RC 24 was abandoned due to insufficient entries. Judging by the small entries experienced in other 24hr races this season, it seems as though long distance riding is passing through a depression. There are several reasons for this. Finance is one, as this class of event is expensive for competitors; The All Rounder competition is another, but I think the real secret is to be found in the decline in long distance club riding. I admit that club runs must cater for the weakest, the slowest and the laziest of riders, but they should also consider those at the other end of the scene. I know it will be argued that the hard rider will make his own runs, but what about the new blood which is constantly entering the club. One or two long distance runs per year are not good enough.*

*There is no need to revert to that "blessed state" of night rides every weekend but here is a point that members will do well to ruminate upon before they attend their A.G.M. I hope the result will be a classic 'scrap' for the possession of Mr and Mrs Carter's 'Waverley Cup'*

I noticed in an earlier report that the entry fee for this club 24hr was £1 including all food. Although this sounds a piffling amount to us in 2008, I would imagine in 1933 that £1 would make the difference between a family eating well for a week, or living on scraps. I know that my wages in 1970 were £20 a week and I had a house, a mortgage and a young family. £1 in 1970 would purchase 5 gallons of petrol, so even at that time it was certainly an important amount of money.

I also noticed a sad and poignant passage that made me realise that even in 1933 the motor car was a 'killer' of cyclists. *"The Club is poorer for the loss of Myrtle Tolley. She was riding home to Weymouth with Donald Middleton when a car ran into their tandem. The only comfort we have is that she must have died instantly. Although not yet 19 years old she had cycled regularly for three years with the Wester section and her unfailing good nature made her one of the most popular members. She lies in Wyke Regis Cemetery. Donald was seriously injured and it was thought he may lose a leg, but the doctors have now promised a full recovery."*

One other interesting snippet gives a 'nostalgic air' to these times, when a rider describing a club run homeward journey after a weekend away in Salisbury said how a passing steam wagon "gave us a farewell with a shower of cinders from Devon".

---

**The North Road** event was held on September 1st and 2nd and out of 25 entries only 14 finished. **Sid Ferris won** the event with **431.25** setting a **new competition record.** The greatest distance ever covered in 24hrs of un-paced riding on the road. It would appear that the Catford and the North Road either have the fastest courses or the best riders, or both. **Les Hall,** Century Road Club was **2nd** again with **414.25 m. 3rd** was **F.M.E. Parry,** Unity CC with **403.5m.** The weather for the race was very favourable. **Jack Spackman** was **4th** with **401.5 miles,** a high mileage for Jack, but he was much younger then. **Stan Mortimer** of the Calléva RC came **7th** with **388.75m.** In an article he submitted to the Fellowship Journal in year 2000, he mentions going off course for some miles, but his main trouble apart from that was having broken spokes in his rear wheel which caused his tyre to rub away on the frame. He used up all of his 'spares' due to this. Stan mentions that a genius came along "He must have thought I was a tramp sitting in a ditch mending umbrellas. He was a mass of nipple keys. He lent me a back wheel to go to the next turn and back, and while I was away, he and his pals took spokes out of their wheels and made my wheel like new". Stan also mentions being fed by Charlie Davey as it was too far north for his Calleva club mates to ride and help him. All the food that Stan had was what was in his pockets at the start, but Davey looked after him and fed him very well throughout.

The Timekeeper was Mr. S.H. Moxham and the Event Secretary was Arthur Smith.

1933 had been a very sad year for the North Road club. In July, Stanley Artaud collapsed unconscious and died at a young age. He was a winner at all distances up to 12 hours, and was always an encouragement to younger riders, passing on his knowledge. He possessed a very smooth, effortless style.

A month later, the President of the Club, F.T. Bidlake 'Biddy' as he was affectionately known, was knocked from his bicycle by a motorist, while descending Barnet Hill. At the time he was not thought to be seriously hurt, but three weeks later, to the intense sorrow of the Club and indeed the whole cycling world, he passed to his eternal rest. Bidlake had won the trike prize six times in the earlier days of the 24hr from 1888, succeeding G.P. Mills. He was a timekeeper of esteem and formulated many of the guidelines to which our sport in modern day still uses.

*Frank Armond, who was 87 years old in 1976 and still riding regularly at that time, remembers Bidlake well. To some his nickname was 'Biddy' but to the older members of the North Road he was known as 'The Bishop' due to his attire, which was more akin to a Victorian clergyman. Frank said "We called him the Bishop, but he could ride like the bloody devil!"*

A National Memorial fund was set up to provide a fitting tribute to a great man, from which 'The Bidlake Memorial Garden' at Girtford Bridge evolved; along with the **'Bidlake Memorial Plaque'.**
The North Road Club members themselves raised £ 112 to provide a special prize known as the 'Bidlake Memorial Prize' to be presented to the member accomplishing the best ride in the North Road CC 24hr.

**G.H.M. Pitt was its first recipient**

# 1934

*Hubert Opperman* on **16th July 1934,** *set out to break the* **End to End** *and* **1,000 miles** *RRA record.* *On the way* *he also broke* *Bert Brown's* **24hr record** *by getting almost to Shap Summit with* **431.5 miles.** *He reached* **John o'** **Groats** *in* **2 days 9hrs 1m** *and completed the* **1,000 miles** *in* **3days 1hr 52 mins,** *after suffering horrendous stomach problems for 30 hours.*

*The reason why Opperman isn't mentioned in time trial or club history up until now is due to him being an Australian Professional riding for the BSA Cycles Company. Later he became a Government Minister and Ambassador in Australia and became Sir Hubert.*

*A short time later,* **Frank Southall,** *who was by now, I think, a Professional for Hercules Cycles was successful in beating Opperman's RRA* **24hr record** *with* **454 miles.**

*In 1935, Opperman before returning to Australia, pushed the RRA 24hr record up to 461.75 miles.*

———◆———

**The Anfield 24hr** event this year had a very small field with only seven men finishing. **R. Hepworth** who had taken 3rd place the previous year, **won** the event with **397 miles.** **T.W. Hegginbotham,** Manchester Wednesday CC was **2nd** with **384 miles,** Frank Fischer **354.5,** J.R. Band, Anfield BC, **321m,** R. Wood, Warrington RC **318m.**

When reading through result sheets, one discovers many strange club names such as: Manchester Wednesday CC; Hull Thursday RC; Kettering Friendly etc. I suppose out of simplicity when choosing a club name a group of cyclists would just be known by the day they met, socially or for club rides, as well as a Sunday run and the location i.e. Hull Thursday RC. Recently in 2007, quite a few young clubs and club folk can be found by a website name only such as; timetrial.co.ukrt or Agiscoviner.com.

———◆———

**The Catford** event was **won** by **Norman Tullett** for the second year running with **427.625 miles** even after suffering 3 punctures. **Team Competition record** was broken again this year with an improvement of nearly five miles by the **Calleva RC** with a total of **1211.625 miles.** The team comprised of **Edgar Seeley 425.5 miles, G.A. Hallifax 403.625m** and **L.E. 'Ted' Vahey 382.75m.** **Seeley** took **2nd** overall and **W. Birkin,** Anerley B.C. **3rd** with **407m.**

*Frank Clarke said "This was the heat wave year, I started with a splitting headache which eased in the cool night. By 10am the next day, the tar was melting on the road. I retired after leaving Guildford, Bert Brown also climbed off. At one time there were about ten of us crawling back to base, we passed other riders who were hiding on the banks of the road for shade".*

Norman Tullets comments were "Yes, this was my year, and the coming of Edgar Seeley, the new 'demon rider' in those days. At 12hrs he led me with 225 miles to my 219m. At 280 miles I was 28 minutes down on him as I retraced home. The Guildford to Horsham stretch passed by safely and with two hours to go, Seeley's lead was down to 8 minutes. He was in the grip of lethargy and tumbled off his bike in the heat, fast asleep. At this point there was no-one ahead of me, I just had to win. Seeley did recover and gained some time back in the last hour but it was too late. At the end, Seeley who had finished before me, was off his bike and handing me a drink, what sportsmanship. During the ride I'd had three punctures and suffered a bee sting on the way back from Horsham".

The results of the race were late in being published due to a course alteration at Guildford towards the end. The 'Cycling' magazine picked up on this and tried to create a controversy that didn't actually exist.

The Editor of 'Cycling' was told that, in future, his photographers and reporters wouldn't be welcome at the race due to the fact that they interfered with the smooth running of the latter part of the race, by trying to gain information from checkers etc. "We run our '24' for the benefit of long distance men, irrespective of financial loss or gain, and not for the purpose of 'Cycling' to try to increase its circulation!"

---

*Belisha Beacon crossings are introduced.*

**The Wessex event** was back on the calendar this year as support had improved. It was 'open' to members of other local clubs. Eleven riders started but only three finished due to bad weather. **Frank Clark won** with **371.5 miles, J.H. Draper,** Bournemouth Arrow CC was **2nd** and **Beadle** was **3rd** after suffering with a damaged knee.

*'Cats Eyes' invented by Percy Shaw were introduced in this year of 1934 and appeared on many roads in 1935.*

---

**The Yorkshire branch of the Vegetarian C & AC** had decided to promote the **first open 24hr** cycling event for the North East region of England. The Clubs enthusiastic leader, Norrie Ward of Leeds was responsible for the expert promotion. **Frank Shubert** took his **first win** in a 24hr in this event with **411 miles** against very stiff opposition from English and Scottish riders, such as L. Kershaw of Leeds Westfield, W.F. Sykes of Sheffield Phoenix and J. Dickson of Edinburgh. **Archie Telfor,** a local rider from the Clifton CC came **2nd** with **409 miles.** One week later, Frank travelled to Ireland to ride their 24hr race.

---

**Irish RC 24hr 1934,** held on the Irish August bank holiday. **Frank Shubert** won with **380 miles,** beating the best of Irish 24hr riders, also contestants from Lancashire, Yorkshire, The Midlands and Herefordshire. Two 24hr wins on consecutive weekends must surely be a record on its own at this time in history.

*I have conflicting reports upon which year the heavy continuous rain occurred. Frank Shubert himself reports it to have been 1935 but other reports have the rain being constant in 1934. Some of the mileages are also a little conflicting between the different reports but usually only by a mile or so. The winning positions of the riders all seem to be correct which is the important thing.*

*Winning two 24hr races, two weekends in succession, one would think that Shubert was a glutton for punishment, but not so, Tommy Barlow said he never looked distressed, always finishing fresh. Tommy recalls Frank setting off to ride home over the Pennines some 70 miles or more after a 24hr race.*

Frank said that the road conditions and surfaces were not in quite such good fettle as in England at that time, but the organisation of the race was second to none. Lots of Inns and Taverns were kept open all night to serve the riders and helpers. What did concern him was the high percentage of cyclists, mainly local riders, who didn't use lights at night at all, endangering everyone, and themselves.

---

**The North Road CC 24hr** had 36 starters. **Sid Ferris** who already had two wins to his credit, wanted to make it a 'hat-trick' and join the cherished band of riders who had won **three consecutive 24hrs on the North Road.** Riders such as Holbein with four, Shorland, three and Ellis, three.

The night was almost perfect for speed and at 12hrs Ferris had covered 220.75 miles and was riding strongly enough to attain another competition record. In the 'small hours' conditions changed and a strong southerly wind sprang up, bringing with it a band of heavy rain which dashed all of the riders hopes of high mileages. To give some idea of the merit of **Ferris's win** which realised **421 miles,** the **2nd** man **Les Hall,** Century RC, just managed **400 miles** and **Norman Tullett, 396.75.** Hall has now run 2nd to Ferris on all three occasions. There were twenty finishers in all. **G.H.M. Pitt** was the best North Road man coming in **6th** place with **383.25m** and thus becoming the first recipient of the **'Bidlake Prize'.**

On 24th October, **Frank Southall** took 1hr 27 mins off Bert Browns **Lands End to London record** with **15hrs 08mins,** and then went on to put 22.5 miles onto Hubert Oppermans **24hr record** with **454 miles.** Although Southall was a professional, he rarely waited to take advantage of the wind and weather, and in fact he often broke the records by large margins of time in very poor conditions.

In this year of 1934 you will have noticed six 24 hr events listed, and only one that I'm aware of was for club members only, that being the Wessex RC event.

*Adolf Hitler became German Chancellor.*

# 1935

*Driving Tests were first introduced in this year; also 'L' plates, Provisional Licences and 30mph urban speed limits.*

**The Anfield** took its usual place on the calendar this year. **Harry Jackson,** Wolverhampton Wheelers, took **first** prize with **398 miles.** **Bill Coupe** of the Potteries CC was **2nd** with **377.75 miles** and **A.E. Whitbread,** Withington Wheelers **3rd,** with **373m.** **Arthur Powell,** Wolverhampton Whls **370m,** Frank Fischer **361.5m** **W.A.G. 'Wag' Onslow,** Wolverhampton, **357.25,** Bert Parkes trike Mersey RC **333m.** An extract from 'The Black Anfielders' book in 1935 – "This event of recent years was now in decline. Support from riders and helpers was waning and although the old club members reminded the current day membership at the time (1935) that the Anfield B.C. was built on long distance work, it was felt that the club could only sustain one more years event".

Bill Coupe (Senior) who came second has just passed away aged 99. (2008) He wrote many articles for the 24hr fellowship journal and here are a few interesting 'snippets' from his description of the 1935 Anfield.

*"I rode round on a 72" freewheel with five spare tubs strapped to the saddle and an Alpaca jacket full of ham sandwiches and an aluminium bottle on the bars full of egg and milk. As the race started at 9pm on a Friday night round Chester I went to work as usual that day and put my bike in my motorbike and sidecar and got up to the start in time to get into tights and Alpaca jacket with my spare batteries strapped in a silk stocking and the bike weighing about 40 lbs".*

*Next day was the hottest for 40 years and the road ran rivers of tar. Bill remembers having a line of tar chippings up his back and front and by the middle of next day he was parched and hadn't had a drink for hours. Luckily he found his brother Ray and scrounged a drink to see him through to Cranage where the feed was situated on a grass verge, with buckets of cold water. There was no finishing circuit in those days, just a lop-sided figure of eight section of lanes around Holmes Chapel and Knutsford Bill called the 'Midden'. This part could be ridden twice and then the riders had to head North towards Chester. With 30 minutes to go your timekeeper followed on your wheel and counted off the minutes to go. With 5 mins to go, Bill remembers dropping him, but could just hear him in the distance hollering 'times up'.*

*An hour later he got deposited at his 'digs' in Middlewich and his landlady, who had taken his 'five bob' the day before, refused to have him in the place. Her words were "take him away, I'm not having him in here, he'll not last the night". Bill had ridden 377.75 miles and was in a right state. He ended up in a hotel and fell asleep on the billiard table. Next morning he pedalled off very saddle sore to find his motor bike which was hidden in a hedge somewhere near Chester.*

*His racing career was built on sheer hard work and effort and Bill was still racing well after my debut at 24hrs in 1962. He is of course, Mick Coupe's father. Mick himself was a prolific 24 hr winner over a period of some 20 years but more importantly, he broke the bicycle End to End in 1982 with 1day 22hrs 39mins 49secs. Mick's hard riding days spent with his dad and brother Bill prove that you have to put the effort in to get the results.*

## Cycling July 17th 1935

"H. Jackson won the Anfield 24 with 398 miles. Twelve men started at 9pm and Hepworth (last years winner) forged ahead to a clear lead to be 30mins up at 12hrs with 215 miles covered. Four men had already dropped out and just before noon Saturday, Hepworth retired from digestion problems, leaving Jackson with a good lead that he kept to the end. Powell came 4th after going off course for miles, and Frank Fisher who had lost valuable time from sleepiness in the afternoon, finished 5th".

Bert Parkes who rode a trike in this event went on some 14 years later to break the End to End trike record with 3days 13hrs 3mins. W.A.G. 'Wag' Onslow I saw on a regular basis riding in South Staffs CA time trials from the late 1950's onwards. Like 'Ed' Green 'Wag' would be found usually on a trike. He was another 'larger than life' character. Both men rode their trikes right to the end of their lives.

———❖———

**The Catford 24hr 1935** saw **Edgar Seeley,** described as the new demon rider by his predecessor, break **competition record** with another massive mileage of **444.75m** to win this popular event. It was a beating of Sid Ferris's record by over 13 miles. **Ted Vahey** again joined Seeley in the team along with **Harry Ferris,** Sid's brother. **Ted Vahey** rode **400.25 miles,** and **Harry 390.75. They took the 24hr team competition record up to 1,235.75 miles.** An improvement of over 24 miles. Seeley's ride was a very well judged one. Tullett who had possibly started off too fast had been caught by Seeley, then he tried very hard to chase Seeley down over a period of hours, while in second place. Norman Tullett retired from the race as did Sid Ferris, much to their regrets, leaving second place wide open. Seeley was a prolific mile eater, totalling more than 20,000 miles a year and often 400 in a weekend, despite working Saturday morning. He enjoyed a smoke and a drink, like a lot of riders in those days and he favoured a single fixed gear for all of his riding.

Seeley breaking the Competition Record was the major hi-lite of the year for the Catford CC. Despite having to change bikes due to a broken chain and having a puncture in the last five miles, it was noted that his mileage was only nine miles short of the wind assisted straight out RRA 24hr record held by professional Frank Southall. It was said that Seeley rode so fast from the start, that he took many marshals and checkers by surprise.

*Seeley's record ride became the **first officially recognised** one by the RTTC in their handbook.* **C. Harris,** *Charlotteville CC was overall* **2nd** *with* **420 miles** *and* **Frank Robertson,** *Veg C & AC* **3rd** *with* **404.8 miles.**

———❖———

**The Wessex RC 24 hr** in 1935 became an invitation event where members of other clubs were invited to ride. **J.H. Draper** of the Bournemouth Arrow CC won with **377 miles.**

———❖———

**The Yorkshire RC and Vegetarian C & AC 24 hr** was run again, following the success of the previous year. **Frank Shubert** repeated his previous years performance by **winning** with **412 miles** and then 'doing the double' by winning again in Ireland a week later.

*Malcolm Campbell takes the World Land Speed Record to over 300 mph.*

———❖———

**The Irish RC 24hr** held mid August on the Irish Bank holiday that year, proved to be one of the most extraordinary ever experienced with over 30 hours of continuous heavy rain, covering the start through to the finish of the event. Many competitors, including Ireland's best all rounder, Phil Brady, punctured all of their tubular tyres including all of the spare ones they carried usually looped over their shoulders or strapped in a bundle under their saddles. **Frank Shubert,** as mentioned, **did the 'double' and won the event again with 397 miles.** Frank rode on high pressure standard wired-on tyres and a single speed fixed gear of 71". He led the field at every checkpoint and beat **P. Deegan** of the promoting Irish RC by 41 miles. **C. Shaffrey** I.R.C. was **3rd** with **345 m, P.G. Jones,** Cheltenham & County CC **4th, 344m, F. Dawson** Yorks RC, **288m.**

*An anecdote from Bill Finn who organised the Irish R.C. 24hr races, mentions Brady being in front of Shubert on the road as they came to a marshal. Brady mistook the marshal's signal and went off course. Shubert realised the situation and before the marshal could leave his post, Shubert chased after Brady and got him back on the right road to Dublin.*

⟫◇⟪

**The North Road** event marked the **Club's 50 year history** which has seen the change in bicycle styles from the 'ordinary' (High Bicycle or Penny Farthing) to the 'safety'. The safety bicycle was lower and closer to the ground and the forerunner of today's style of cycle. Another transformation in those 50 years has been from solid tyres to pneumatic ones, and finally paced racing to un-paced time trials. The North Road has played a leading role in all of these changes.

Conditions in the '24' commenced well, but later the weather changed to high winds and heavy rain in which **Dick Goodman** of the Luton Wheelers did well to cover **406 miles.** The severity of the weather led to the retirement of 15 out of the 47 starters. **Frank Robertson was 2nd with 394.5 miles** and **L. Davis,** Viking RC was **3rd** with **382.5 miles. G.H. Pitt** came **4th** with **375.875 miles** and **A.B. Marsh 375m** was **5th.**

*Hubert Opperman took Southall's Lands End to London by nearly an hour and carried on into East Anglia for the 24hrs to re-take his record from Southall with 461.75 miles.*

I have noticed when researching from about 1910 onwards, that I've known, or have seen, quite a lot of the riders mentioned in either the 'North Road' or 'Anfield' history books. Riders such as Frank Armond, Jack Middleton, Bill Coupe, Charles Holland, Frank Greenwood, C.E. 'Ed' Green, President of the 'T.A.' (Tricycle Association), Maurice Draisey, trike record breaker in 1928, and getting closer in time to the fifties, Crimes and Arnold.

I was so pleased I went to the RRA Triennial dinner at the Connaught Rooms in London in 1981, where over 200 members were present and I remember seeing such a lot of old record breakers. This large room was filled with mainly elderly gentlemen, officials of the RRA and past record breakers, some from the turn of the century – Victorian times. It made me aware of the rich history I'd stepped into and was lucky enough to be a small part of. I think that at 37 years of age I was probably the youngest record breaker there at that time.

These elderly gentlemen with moustaches and some with hearing aids and walking sticks were our past heroes. It was hard to imagine that they had been the dashing young men who had sped from capital to capital in 24hrs in the early 1900's, or had ridden from Lands End to John o' Groats on all sorts of different machines, some inside 3 days, since the turn of the century.

I was so proud to be there to pick up a record certificate with Pat Kenny and now felt in some way that I'd worked hard enough on the tandem trike to be amongst their company. My only regret is that I wasn't writing books at that time and that bits of information gleaned from these wonderful characters weren't committed to paper for future reference.

I only have one or two living sources of information left alive who I can converse with, the main one being Syd Parker who can take me back to the late 1920's. He raced from the early 1930's to the 1950's gaining RRA records on a trike and winning trike 24's. He was well placed in many high profile 24 hr races at that difficult time before and after the Second World War. In 1947 he set new figures for the End to End and 1000 miles with Jim Letts on a tandem trike. Syd still keeps in touch with Lynne and myself, sending me information he's stored for years, and at 92 years of age I'm hoping he gets to read this book.

John Arnold coming forward slightly in years has been another very good source of knowledge from the late 1940's onwards, not forgetting Pat Kenny, my present day mentor, both of whom I will mention later.

*The Raleigh Cycle Company in 1935 produced close on half a million cycles and one million Sturmey Archer hub gears. The average cost of a cycle at that time was from £5.00. This cheaply priced cycle was not actually a Raleigh, it was called a 'Gazelle' and it was just marketed through Raleigh.*

# 1936

*On May 15th 1936, Amy Johnson flew solo from Great Britain to the Cape of Good Hope and back. She became famous for her many solo record-breaking flights, her first one being in 1930 from England to Australia. She died on 5th January 1941 flying over the Thames while working as an air ferry pilot.*

**The Anfield 24 hr. This was to be the last event ever by this famous club due to falling entries.** Ironically, the winning mileage by **Tommy Heginbotham** of the Manchester Wednesday CC was the highest recorded in this event by an unpaced rider of **402.25 miles. J.R. Sutton,** Warrington RC was **2nd** with **386.5m** and **A.J. Carr,** Anfield BC **3rd** with **372 miles.**

Jim Carr, an uncle of Mick Coupe's had gained a slight lead on the rest of the field but then found he couldn't keep the pressure on and rode himself out, having to stop with 1hr 49 mins still to go. Six other riders finished.

To digress slightly, an amusing incident happened during Jim Carr's career in 1939 when **Tommy Godwin** of the Potteries was attempting his year's mileage record. **Tom's average mileage was just over 200 miles a day.** Throughout the year he had many ups and downs, suffering crashes, cramps, punctures and light failures. He used to get so stiff on his bike that he quite often crawled off and walked the last two miles home just to straighten up.

One night Tommy turned up at Jim Carr's house for a bath and a rub down. He had been feeling beaten and down from the effort. Jim came in from work, fed him, rubbed him down and then dragged poor old Tommy out to Shrewsbury and back before letting him fall into bed. It was a long time before he crawled into Jim's house, looking for sympathy, again.

"At mid summer **Tommy had three days when he covered 290, 360 and 290 miles consecutively.** By the end of July he'd covered 42,461 miles. **Tommy ended the year with a total of 75,065 miles,** beating Ossie Nicholson's Australian record of 62,657 m ridden in 1937."

*This report was taken from a writing by Bill Coupe and appeared in the '24hr Fellowship Journal' of April 1985. My sincere thanks to Bill and the Fellowship for having permission to print.*

Peter Barlow was at this last event promoted by the Anfield in 1936 and recalls " I can remember checking riders through at Toft Corner towards the end of the race. The entries were so low with long waits between the riders, it appeared that nothing was happening. Old man Tuplin, who had won the event in 1923, came through and lapped on what was then a sort of finishing circuit. The finishing system at that time was such that each rider had to find his own 'follower'. The 'follower' would have checked his watch against 'timekeeper's time' and then rode behind his rider until time expired. A note was then taken of the finishing point and it was subsequently measured. There were stories of followers catching their rider, riders dropping their followers and watches whose times were not always coincidental with timekeeper's time. It did not matter a great deal I suppose, for finishing mileages were usually given to the nearest eighth or quarter of a mile".

Peter continued " I have the 1936 route card in front of me and it makes interesting reading. The start of what we now call a finishing circuit was at Allostock crossroads at 338 miles 7 furlongs and 132 yards. The timekeeper was stationed here and provided accurate time of day for the followers, not to worry too much that the timekeeper had a 'Kew-A' watch and many of the followers had a 5 bob (Shillings) (25p) 'Ingersol' pocket watch.

The circuit, as we know it, was 33 miles round and followed a lop-sided 'figure of eight' as follows: "Allostock crossroads to Broken Cross canal bridge, Twemlow Smithy, Siddington, Laundry Lane, Knutsford, Allostock, Middlewich Station, Allostock, Twemlow Pump, Monks Heath, Toft Corner and round again."

*My thanks to Peter Barlow and the 24hr Fellowship for this information.*

Immediately after the 1936 event had finished, plans were made, between the Anfield BC and the Mersey RC for the event to carry on in 1937, and be run by the Mersey RC. The Anfield BC had a 12hr and a 100 mile race to run each year; in fact the Anfield '100' mile is still a very popular early season 'classic' event and to win it is still a much coveted achievement amongst time triallists even now. The '100' has been run virtually every year, except for the two wars, since 1889, so a period of some 118 years.

The transition from the Anfield BC 24hr to the Mersey RC was a very amicable one and various elders of the Anfield gave it their seal of approval. Men such as Frank Marriott, Rex Austin, Albert Lusty and Guy Pullan all helped to make sure that riders in the Midlands and the more Northerly areas had a 24hr race kept in the area.

⇒•◇•⇐

**The Catford 24hr** held on the 18th and 19th July 1936 will be remembered for its really rough weather. Almost a gale force wind buffeted the riders at the start. Heavy rain in the night coupled with the darkness and wind made it a dangerous time with branches off trees littering the road.

**Sid Ferris** who **won** with **418.125m** had by no means a trouble free ride, he had to change his rear wheel no fewer than six times and he ended the event using his brother Harry's wheel after he had packed. Ferris had fought a day and night long battle for supremacy with **T. Crawley**, Comet CC who finished **his first 24hr in 2nd place** with **412.5 miles.** Ferris didn't actually catch Crawley who had started just 18 mins in front of him, until 5 mins to go and that was only due to Crawley having a collapsing rear wheel. **E.R. Staplehurst** was **3rd** with **406.875 miles.**

**George Lawrie,** on a bike this time, rode **387.5 miles** to be pipped by **Syd Parker,** Ealing CC, also riding a bike instead of his usual trike, by just over a mile with **388.625 miles.**

**A.G. Oxbrow with 402m and D.E. Powell 385m along with Ferris, gave the Vegetarians the team win with 1205 miles.** Other notable finishers were C.A.Prior with 401.75 miles, S.E. Armstrong, 397.375 and Arthur Zenthon with 394.5 miles. 34 riders finished from an entry of 53.

*Frank Robertson who rode in the same event as Sid Ferris recalled in a Fellowship Journal in 1992.*

"Sid was the man for hard conditions, nothing ever worried him, the harder the day, the harder he tried. Both Ferris and Edgar Seeley performed top three rides at other distances. I knew both of these riders very well at one time as the unofficial racing HQ of both the Calleva and the Vegetarians was the home of the Ferris brothers in Hounslow".

⇒•◇•⇐

**The Wessex RC 24hr** was again an invitation event and was won by **J.H. Draper.** It was held on August 8th and 9th and was Drapers 2nd win in this event. He beat his fellow clubman H. Cox by just over 5 miles with **388.5m** to Cox's **383.25m.** **R. Silk** was first man for the Wessex RC with **380m, Frank Clark** rode **366.25** and **L. Edwards** Vectis RC was **5th** with **355.75.** Draper's mileage of 388.5 miles was a new course record for the Wessex RC.

⇒•◇•⇐

**The Irish Road Club** event this year was won by **Paul Brady** with **395 miles.** This was his second win in this event. Frank Shubert, who had earlier in the year set up a new MRRA 24 hr record, suffered with severe stomach trouble in this Irish event and retired at 187 miles. The event started in a gale that blew throughout. Brady who had won in 1933 beat his fellow clubman **J. Keenan** by 34 miles. **R.S. Walkden,** Lancashire RC, **359 miles.** **F. Moran,** Irish RC, **348 miles. C. McQueen,** IRC **330m, R.G.Wheeler** IRC **300m.**

⇒•◇•⇐

54

The North Road CC 24 hr on September 5th 1936 was the 50th Anniversary of the event that had run since 1886.   Heavy rain storms during the second 12 hours and a strong breeze during daylight hours didn't prevent **Les Hall,** Century RC from accumulating **420.75 miles** to win this event at his 5th attempt.   He'd finished 4th in his first ride and has been placed second on three occasions.   **Norman Tullett** was **2nd** with **416.5m.**   It had been a three cornered fight for the 'solo' bicycle places between Les Hall, Norman Tullett and an 'unknown' W.R.A. Howlett.   Howlett led the field for the greater part of the day, using a standard 3 speed hub gear to amass 414.75 miles to finish 3rd.   Tullett, who stayed in the faster half of the field, came to life in the second 12 hours. When 301 miles had been reached, Hall went into the lead with 17 hours elapsed.   He put 9 minutes into Howlett and Tullett with R. Mence at 57 minutes.   Just before the 400 miles point, Hall punctured both tyres but despite that he still covered 16.5 miles into the tough wind in those last 57 minutes.

The tricycle trophy went to **A.G. Oxbrow** of the Vegetarian C & AC with **382.5 miles,** a new **trike competition record.**   Ted Vahey was **2nd trike** with 380 miles, Vahey also had a puncture in that last hour which possibly cost him the record.   These two experienced trike men had been locked in a fierce battle almost from the 'off'.   A bit like the Crimes and Arnold battles to come.   **George Lawrie** of the Viking RC was 3rd trike with 369.75m after starting 20mins late.   **The Unity CC** pulled off the **team** win with **1,167.125 miles.**   R. Mence, K. Davies and **J.A. Davis** were the victors over the 'Essex Roads' by six miles.

It was a Saturday night start this year, from an entry of ten trikes and forty two bikes, a total of 32 riders finished. High winds, punctures and mechanical problems sorted out the 'men from the boys'.   **George Lawrie went on in 1938 to create a new 1,000 miles tricycle record in 4 days 6 hrs 32 mins** in almost continuous rain, using a lot of the roads he had just covered in this 24 hr.

The Catford History Book mentions that Monty Holbein, aged 75, swam from Richmond Lock to London Bridge this year.   He covered the 16.5 miles in 5hrs 14 mins.   The last 2 hours were spent in the dark and he finished his swim just before midnight.

*Jarrow Marches – October 5th 1936.   Two hundred people started out on this day to march to London in protest at the 'Depression' suffered by the Tyneside area since 1934.   It was called the 'Jarrow Crusade' and was commonly known as a 'Hunger March'.*

*November 30th 1936.   Crystal Palace is destroyed by fire.*

*December 11th 1936.   King Edward V111 abdicated the throne.   This was also the night of the annual North Road dinner and prize presentation.   The records show that a 'Wireless' was brought into the room, and the dinner was interrupted so that those present could listen to the speech broadcast from Windsor Castle.   Edwards brother George reluctantly took over the realm of Monarch and became King George V1 in December.*

*The production of VW cars started this year.*

*The Spanish Civil War starts.*

## 1937

**The Catford 24hr** on June 26th and 27th was the first 24hr on the calendar this year, due to the demise of the Anfield event.   It was won by **Cyril Prior,** Ilford RC with **427.5 miles.**   The modern C.T.T. handbook shows the **Vegetarian C and AC team** mileage as being **1,254.62 miles,** but the actual Catford result sheet loaned to me by Syd Parker shows **1,254.675 miles,** for a **new team competition record.**   The team comprised of **Frank Robertson** with **421.125,** Geoff Guy, 419.675 and **A.G. Oxbrow, 413.675m.**   In this event three teams finished with over 1,200 miles.   **2nd** team were **Kentish Wheelers, 1222.875m** and **Ilford RC** with **1,200, 3rd.**

Prior who won the race was one of the Ilford Road Clubs small but select band of long distance road men. He took the lead in the second half of the event, to win by 6 miles with 427.5 of which 222m were produced in the first 12 hours.   Although Frank Robertson who came 2nd with 421.125, actually rode more miles in the second 12 hours.

**Norman Tullett,** Kentish Wheelers with **418.75** took **4th** place.   **Oxbrow** was **5th** with **413.675.  Frank Fischer,** Kentish Wheelers **6th, 407 miles.  Gordon Basham 7th** with **402.375** and **Syd Parker,** Ealing CC took **8th** place with **402.6 miles,** in this his second event at the distance.   **George Lawrie,** Viking RC with **371.3 m took top trike place.**  Gordon Basham up to now has been better known as a Wessex RC short distance man, but I'm sure we will see a lot of this rider in the next few years.

The night had been excellent, but the daylight hours were very warm, too warm for black tights and Alpaca jackets, but the riders had no option but to wear them.   Out of 64 entries, 45 riders finished, a tribute to their endurance.

———◇◆◇———

*Early in June, Sid Ferris took Opperman's Edinburgh to London record with 20 hrs 19 mins for the 397 mile journey.*

*July 17th – 19th 1937.   , Sid Ferris now riding as a professional for Raleigh Cycles broke the End to End and 1,000 miles record in 2 days 6 hrs 33 mins, and 2 days 22hrs 40 mins respectively.   They were both Hubert Opperman records, but Ferris didn't have an easy ride and was well down on Opperman's records until Bonar Bridge at 777 miles.*

There was no Yorkshire event this year but **Frank Shubert** went over to ride the **last Irish RC 24 hr to be held. Frank won the 'Challenge Cup' outright by producing the first ride ever over 400 miles with 404m.**   The weather was very good and Frank had undying memories of the lovely 'Bog of Allen' countryside, including the tempting displays of huge luscious blackberries by the side of the road, the many fields with free growing white mushrooms, the hee-hawing of the many donkeys and the fascinating spasmodic cry of the corncrake, moving about in the marshlands at eventide.   The sheer joy of riding alongside the long stretches of the Irish Grand Union Canal made the miles seem easier.   **P.G. Jones,** Hereford Whs, was **2nd** with **352 m** beating his clubmate **P.J. Meredith** by .5 of a mile into **3rd** place.

———◇◆◇———

**The Mersey RC Subscription 24hr** run in late **July,** was the inaugural event for the Mersey Roads Cycling Club who had taken over the slot that was left by the demise of the Anfield event in this North West region.   **It was won by Alec Smith,** a relative of the Williams Family, riding for the Vegetarian C & AC with **420.50 miles.   The Liverpool Century RC were the fastest team with 1,117.5 miles,** the team consisted of J.A. Gerrard 388m, A.G. Morris 375.5 m and Ossie Dover 354m.   Mersey RC with 1,082m were 2nd team, Tom Heginbotham,362m Bert Parkes 361m, and Bill Booth Jnr 358.

As the title suggests the event was mainly funded by donations from clubs and club folk, sometimes relatives or friends of the riders donated either before or after the event.   Food and drink was also donated to help the club in these early years.   If you were a donor then your name would be printed in a list on the start or result sheet of the event as a way of saying thank you.   The event is still run even to this day on a subscription basis.   That and the wonderful enthusiasm of the Mersey RC and Friends have shone through to make this event the only one left on the calendar at this present time of 2008.

Whereas the Anfield was run starting on a Friday night at 9pm, the Mersey RC event started on the Saturday teatime at 5 o'clock.   This first event attracted 19 entries and that in itself was heartening, for it more than doubled the 1936 Anfield entry.   The course used was a similar one to the Anfields, based on Chester as an axis, running down to Battlefield, Shrewsbury, much of Shropshire, Cheshire and The Wirral were used.   One of the main differences was the finish being on a smaller circuit of some 12.5 miles from Cholmondley School to Ridley Green and Acton Windmill.   The complete course at the end of two complete finishing circuits was 384.75 miles after which the riders peeled off and continued on the course for as long as time allowed.

With a fair percentage of the field being slower than to need more than about 350 miles, Tommy Barlow set about making sections of the course to be omitted for these riders whilst mindful of the fact that Tommy Melia and Tommy Heginbotham had both beaten 400 miles in the last few Anfields, and riders of their 'ilk' would probably need another twenty added on.   In fact by 1938 the full course had been increased to 419.875 miles running out at Duddon Heath.   Alec Smith had to turn right into the lanes to avoid going over the finishing circuit again, and so have this mileage disallowed.   He had to negotiate the tricky twisting lanes via Huxley Chapel and Tiverton, and then climb from Beeston Brook to Ridley Green and return.

One humorous diversion in these early years was when a helper had been designated to replace the carbide in rider's acetylene lamps. In due time when all of the riders had gone, he was left with a pile of carbide. He shovelled this down a drain grid and departed. Later, an itinerant pipe smoker threw away a still lighted match and had the shock of his life from the flash explosion as it erupted from below the ground and through the drain.

*I've used passages and lines from the Mersey RC 'Record' to describe this first 24hr time trial - the first of many. This first paragraph is a very poignant one: -*

'The day of the event was a very clammy one, hot and uncomfortable with a troublesome humid wind which affected riders and helpers alike. There is always something awe-inspiring about the start of a 24hr event, a feeling as though somehow the rider is giving up this earthly normal life. The ordinary tones of conversation are subdued, there comes an almost irresistible impulse to crack a joke with some particular rider to try and keep his mind off it, but he needs no diversion. The rider is the calmest man there. Quietly and unobtrusively he slips away, a voice here and there calling out an occasional "good luck". Nineteen times the timekeeper gives the word "go", and as the last man slips away there comes into our minds the thought that the greatest adventure in the history of the club has started.

Clethero was already in the lead on the Saturday night, amongst the busy traffic. At the Cranage feed he was the main topic of conversation. The general feeling was that he wouldn't last the night out; they thought they knew his capabilities and told him to ease off, but he continued at a cracking pace. With the coming of darkness, an even greater test came. For the next 100 miles these riders, many of them strangers to these roads, had to be guided on their way through the hours of darkness. At Mickle Trafford feeding station, an amusing incident occurred which showed what thoroughness and silence was used to carry out the feeding of a rider. First of all he would be spotted in the distance and his imminent arrival was signalled by a flashlight from up the road. A dark form was just visible and six eager pairs of hands went out to help him. This rider didn't seem to want to stop, but the helpers took his bike, helped him off and assisted him to a table full of food. It was only when he passed across the beam of light from the cars headlights that it was realised he was one of the locals dressed in a dark suit, and it was all done without a sound!

It was now after midnight, some helpers were tired, some snatched an hours sleep knowing they had a full day ahead, some were wide awake and some wanted to see Sid Ferris go through on his End to End. He'd left Lands End at 10am and was due at Warrington before daybreak on Sunday. His route took him within a few miles of the 24hr course just north of Whitchurch.

A battle was now raging between Alec Smith and Clethero. It lasted all night and well into the morning, finally Smith came out on top. Apparently there had been no more that 100 yards between them for all of those hours. Smith then led the field all day without faltering, the pace and style of this tall athletic vegetarian was a beauty to behold. The printed course was made to cover just over 400 miles and it was realised he would outrun the course by 20 miles or more.

Plans were put into place under the guidance of Tommy Barlow assisted by the head timekeeper Rex Austin, they had to guide him north through Chester to Farndon and then turn him to retrace through the busy Chester streets again. The same plan had to be implemented for Clethero who was just 30 mins behind. The two riders crossed each other between Farndon and Chester; Clethero was dark around the eyes from lack of sleep but as soon as he saw Smith he found a second wind and trod even harder on the pedals.

After a nail biting time guiding the winner through Chester, the event came to an end when **Alec Smith** reached **420.5 miles. Clethero** came **2nd** with **410.25,** and **Frank Pulman 3rd** with **402.624m.** While Smith sat resting and eating strawberries the club officials were signing forms to witness his breaking of the Northern Twenty Four Hours Record. Clethero's 2nd place mileage was such a surprise for an un-seeded rider. Everyone thought that this man must surely have an enviable record at the shorter distances. When asked, he said "Oh, I've ridden a 25, two 50's and a 100" – that's all!

Tommy Heginbotham for the Mersey RC did a sparkling 362 miles on a trike to take the club record. He also led the 2nd team of Bert Parkes and Bill Booth Jnr. *The winning team from Liverpool Century RC had as their 3rd man, Ossie Dover with 354 miles. I notice also that he rode in 1938 on a trike and did 339 miles. I only knew Ossie when his health was failing towards the latter part of his life. His wife Hilda used to push him around in a wheelchair, and by then he had gone blind. A charitable trust was set up in his/their names to help the sport and all of those years I knew of him and didn't realise he was a 24hr man.*

'Club Officials and helpers at that time were Rex Austin, Timekeeper, Tommy Barlow, Detour Controller, Harry Wilson who provided much needed transport, George Rooney, Ralph Fer, Allan Littlemore and young Johnny Williams who when faced with a rider, P.L. May of the Broad Oak CC who'd taken an almighty 'packet' supplied him with a bottle of white 'dope' (milk I hope?)

Alec Smith was presented with the Percy Brazendale Cup to hold for one year, by Percy Brazendale himself, the President of the Mersey Roads Club.

A gold medal was also presented to Alec Smith by Albert Lusty for his record ride. A.N. Clethero received a silver medal for 2nd place.'

<hr>

*Dipped headlights on cars are introduced for safety purposes to other road users.*

1937 was the year when the British Nation was still getting over the shock of Edward V111's abdication and the storm clouds were gathering over Europe as Hitler prepared to wage war on his neighbouring countries. And what did the British do? – they carried on riding their favourite 24hr races, still dressed the same as before the previous war, from head to toe in black tights and Alpaca jackets, 'undertakers outfits' as the colourful Australian rider Opperman described us. Even the helpers were dressed in jackets and trousers or 'plus fours' and there was not a coloured racing vest in sight at this time.

*By this time many engineering firms, including cycle manufacturers, had allotted production space in their factories for the supply of 'munitions' for the war effort.*

<hr>

**The Wessex RC 24hr** held on 7th and 8th August was won by **L.E. 'Ted' Vahey,** Wessex RC with a **record course and event mileage of 407.** The weather was extremely good and produced a spate of very high mileages. **Ivor Jones,** Viking RC was 2nd with **402.875 miles** and **Arthur Zenthon, 3rd,** with **402.75m.** From 32 starters, 14 finished (another record). **Wessex RC won the team race with 1,112.2 miles. L.R. Voss and F.L. Cooper made up the team with Vahey.**

*Tom Lodge informed me that Ted Vahey had quite an important job, possibly an Engineer. His employers were very understanding and they allowed Ted to have the summer months off for training and racing. This is probably what gave him his winning 'edge'.*

<hr>

**The North Road CC event** this year was **won again** by **Les Hall** of the Century RC with **418 miles. G.S. Smith** of the Southgate CC, a clubmate of the **trike** 'End to Ender' Les Meyers, won the trike prize with **351.375 miles.** Timekeeper Frank Armond despatched 71 riders on the Friday evening from 6 pm, into a gusty wind. At 85 miles Brumell was leading in 4hrs 23mins, closely followed by Parry at 4mins, Mence 5mins & Powell 6mins. Hall was outside 4hrs 30m at this stage but time was on his side, he knew how to pace himself. At 154 miles Hall had pulled level with Brumell in 8hrs 20mins, Jim Purves was 3rd, 5 mins down. At the 12 hr halfway mark, Hall led the field by 10mins. He then punctured and Brumell closed the gap to 7 mins. With 360 miles covered there were three hours to go. Hall was increasing his lead again and the Century R.C. 'stayer' rode on to win by 4.5 miles.
Forty three riders finished this tough event. **Hall with 418 miles won, 2nd was A.W. Brumell,** Veg C & AC with **413.4m, Parry,** Unity CC 3rd with **408.5m, and Ted Vahey 4th with 404.2m.**

**The Unity CC won the team race, the Parry brothers and R. Mence totalling 1,191.125 miles.**

The start of the event had been a very wet one with roads awash from hours of continuous rain, but luckily most of the riders got away just as the rain stopped, as if by order. It was a long dark night for this mid-September event, with glimpses of a harvest moon. Most of the riders missed the detour that came after 12 hours. Only seven 'fast men' went on this out and home stretch of road known as 'the wilderness'. It is dead straight for 7 miles, so 14 miles in total proved to be a graveyard for Purves hopes, for when he returned at 238 miles, he was so saddle sore he had to retire. After a 57 mile trek south, Hall emerged still in the lead by 13 minutes from Brumell. It was a lead that Hall sustained to the end, even after two hilly detours in the closing stages dashed the hopes of many riders wanting to beat 400 miles, he maintained his superiority.

Many riders paid the price of inexperience, not pacing themselves for 24 hours and falling by the wayside exhausted, but one ride of note goes to A.V. Lancaster (Arthur), who only having ridden one 50 mile race in his life, and also had only ridden his bike three times in the previous month, rode out the 24 hrs with 344 miles to his credit.

Seventy five riders had entered representing 40 clubs and there were seven teams of three riders started. **This was surely a record.** Fensom of the Spalding CC crashed at Ely and broke a crank. He dashed into the town, had it welded and was back in the race in 50 minutes! There were a good many crashes during the night due to the wind, mud on the road, and poor lighting. Couzens of the North Road cut a detour without consent and was disqualified. 'Fullers' at Girtford Bridge and 'The Marshmoor' at Hatfield were two favourite feed stops for these hungry riders on route. One must remember that in those times there would only be a few cars involved in the event, most of the riders would rely on other cyclists to help them. Various clubs would get different jobs to carry out during the event. There would be numerous drink and a sponge locations where helpers would stretch out along the road and pass a bottle, (aluminium in those days) up to the rider, he would then throw it down at the next helper who would pass up a sponge soaked in water for the rider to wipe the sweat and grime off his face.

One can imagine just how grubby these bottles and sponges got in earlier days with only blocks of rough soap to clean them with, unlike the eco friendly grease busting citrus liquids we have in this day and age. Many reports are heard, through the history of cycle racing, of cyclists suffering sickness and diaorrhea and failing to finish. One wonders whether it was picked up from a bottle or a sponge, or raw eggs? The 'sit-down' feeds would have been situated at about every 100 miles in a 24hr race, and as mentioned various hostelries were used, some even stopping open all night for the riders to use. In my first 12hr race in 1959, there was a good 'sit down' feed at about 120 miles. The Oldbury and District CC ran a very good event for about 30 years. Being a novice at 16 years of age, I think I also stopped for more food on the way back past this feeding station. In modern times of 2007, it's great to think that the Mersey RC have carried on this tradition with a mobile comfort stop just beyond Hodnet manned by

"Dad sent me to bed early last night, so I've put a dead mouse in his feeding bottle".

Mike Johnson and Yvonne Crane, and there is the ever popular Raven Café at Prees, Nr Whitchurch, which stays open all night, just for this event.

## 1938

*By 1938 nearly every major RRA bicycle record was held by a professional rider. Competition was intense, particularly between two men and two records. Sid Ferris and Cyril Heppleston on the Edinburgh to London and 24hr routes.*
**The Catford 24hr** was won by **Geoff Guy** of the Vegetarian C & AC with **433.25 miles. C.A. Prior,** Ilford RC was **2nd** with **430 miles. A.D. Slane,** Calleva RC was **3rd** with **426.625m.** A very creditable mileage for this 'novice' rider. Geoff Guy's mileage was the second highest ever, after Seeley's 444.75m competition record ridden in this same event in 1935. It was a record entry of 77 riders this year.

The troublesome south westerly wind, luckily a dry one, made conditions hard for all the riders, especially in the closing hours of the race.  The fourth placed rider, A.G. Horwood, Bath Road CC was a serious challenger to Guy for the first 12 hours, and at 215 miles was only a minute behind.  Norman Tullett with 407m suffered a lot of punctures, four in all, which delayed his reaching 'detours' in time.  Being a 'seeded' rider who would normally cover the full course, this set him back, but he pushed on regardless.

George Lawrie took the **trike** prize again with **376 miles.**  Horwood came **4th** with **424.875 miles,** Jim Purves, **5th, 418m.**  The team prize was won by the Vegetarian C & AC, comprising Geoff Guy, Jim Purves and S.C. Oxford with **390.75 miles,** giving a total of **1,242.25 miles,** with the Calleva RC team just 3 miles less.  Reading down the finishing list. E.S. Walker, Twickenham CC 413.5m, Syd Parker, Ealing CC, broke his own club record with 412.25m.  Arthur Zenthon crashed heavily when his gear broke, but continued to finish with 394m.  Harry Ferris, Sid's brother, retired around the 120 mile point due to being seriously troubled by the heavy night time coastal traffic.

⎯⎯⎯►◄⎯⎯⎯

**Syd Parker** later in the year went on the break the London to York and 12hr trike records with **10 hours 24 mins and 230 miles.**  This 12hour record of 230m remained on the RRA books for 17 years until David Duffield added just .75 of a mile on.

1938 was also a very busy record breaking year for other riders, most of whom were regular 24hr men such as: **B.F. Gough and G.E. Lawrie,** who broke the London to Edinburgh and 24hours on a tandem trike with **23hrs 37m.**  George Lawrie went on to set the **trike 1,000 mile reord in 4 days 6hrs 32 mins** in almost continuous rain.  **Innes & Thompson,** broke the End to End tandem record with **2days 14hrs 48m.**

*On the 22nd of July 1938, Lilian Dredge set the ladies End to End record with 3 days 20hrs 54mins.  She went on to set the 1,000 mile record at 4days 19hrs and 14mins.*

⎯⎯⎯►◄⎯⎯⎯

The Wessex RC 24hr was won by **Ted Vahey** with another course and event record of **419 miles. Don Chalmers** was **2nd** with **403m, Charlie Geall** did **399.**  From 15 starters only 5 finished.  The daytime heat caused many to retire.

⎯⎯⎯►◄⎯⎯⎯

The Mersey RC event was again **won** by **Alec Smith** now riding for the Colne Valley CC.  This tall vegetarian improved 17 miles to record **437.5 miles. A.E. Byrnes,** Mersey RC was **2nd** with **411.75m** and **Owen Musgrave** was **3rd** with **406m.**

Solihull CC were the only team to finish.  **B. Knight** with **390.375m, F. Baker 383.5m** and **H. Sandford** with **363.125m** made the team mileage of **1,137 miles.**

*The Nazi's invade Czechoslovakia.*

*After his disqualification from last year's North Road 24hr event, Les Couzens went on to break the London to Brighton and back with 5hrs 20mins 57secs and the London to Portsmouth and back with 7hrs 40m 38secs.  Both rides done on a trike, so pleasing his father and the North Road Club immensely.*

⎯⎯⎯►◄⎯⎯⎯

The North Road CC 24hr saw **Les Hall** gain his **hat trick** in this event with **422.125 miles.**  He now joins the 'greats' who have had three consecutive wins; Holbein, Shorland, Ellis & Ferris.   **H.V. Rourke,** Liverpool Century **won** the **trike prize** with **350.5 miles.** P.F. Rohr, Veg C & AC put up a splendid ride to finish 2nd overall with **418.125m.**  A great ride considering he had not long recovered from a badly smashed leg which had sidelined him for three years.  **Frank Robertson** was **3rd** with **415.25miles.**

The ride had started at 6.31pm on Friday and right from the start Alec Smith, Colne Valley Wheelers, who had won the first two Mersey RC events took a flying lead and had 5 minutes in hand by the 100 miles point, but he'd also got a buckled wheel, which he changed.    Minutes later, he punctured again losing valuable time at which point, he retired.

Geoff Guy who was also challenging Hall for the lead was suffering from very sore feet after losing his big toe nails in the previous Catford 24hr, and at 191 miles when lying in 4th place he also 'packed'.    By this time, Hall was really feeling the effects of sickness that he'd had from the first hour, but he still bravely battled on, knowing that he still held the lead.    F.N. Robertson and F. Parry 'scrapped' for **3rd** place, that **Robertson** won, sealing the team win for the 'Vegetarians' who had battled day and night against the Unity CC.  A poacher hunting pheasants put paid to trike rider McLarens chances, just south of Stretham early in the morning, at 243 miles.    He received pellet wounds to his face and was taken to hospital covered in blood.    To add insult to injury, his trike went missing while he was receiving treatment.

**A.F. Smith** of the Warren CC was **5th** with **408.25,** Les Hall got his 'hat trick' of wins, a true test of unflappable riding, judging the pace perfectly on his 78" single geared bike.    The riders this year had been dogged by a cool northerly wind, which dropped slightly during the night to give patches of moonlight to help them.    Alfred Marsh was the best 'North Roader' with 396.5 miles.    There were 57 entries from 32 clubs.

---

On October 27th 1938 the battles between Professionals Ferris and Heppleston were fought out over the Edinburgh to London and 24hr route.    Heppleston left Edinburgh at 6.02am and went via Coldstream and Newcastle towards London.    Charlie Holland left Edinburgh at 7.02 am bound for York and Sid Ferris Left at 7.17am bound for London, but via Carter Bar for Newcastle.  Holland suffered badly with cold feet and retired (don't forget overshoes are a luxury from about 1980 onwards).    Heppleston finished first and broke Opperman's Edinburgh to London, with 19hrs 18 mins and was given a provisional 24hr mileage of 463m.    Ferris finished at 7.17am next day with 465.25m.    There was then a controversy over the course distances covered, as both men had used slightly different routes at the start.    Early in 1939 it was announced that Heppleston had covered 464.75m and Ferris 465.75m and these are the mileages given in the current RRA handbook.

# 1939

*Tommy Godwin in this calendar year of* **1939** *produced a* **new record mileage** *of* **75,365 miles.**   *His best mileage for one week in June was just under 2,000 miles.   He was supplied with equipment by Raleigh and Sturmey Archer.   He set a new world record with this mileage, a record that has never been beaten.*

In May of this year, a revenge match between Ferris and Heppleston took place over the Edinburgh to London and 24hr records.    The two men again set out from Edinburgh within an hour of each other.    Ferris 'cracked' leaving Heppleston to improve both records.    He'd finally stamped his authority on the Edinburgh to London with 18hrs 57mins and then rode on to 467.5 miles in 24hrs.    To my knowledge he had never ridden in an open 24hr time trial.

---

**The Catford 24hr** event started at 4pm and Geoff Guy, the previous years winner, led from the start.    At 50 miles he'd pulled away from his team mates, S. Oxford and P. Rohr, on time.    Powell of the Catford was lying 3rd followed by Zenthon, Carr and Purves.    Darkness fell and by 162 miles Guy led in 8hrs 25 mins, just about 18 mins outside 'evens' pace.    Purves at this point was close behind at 5 mins, but the rest of the field were 28mins or more adrift.

The night was very cool and the wind by dawn was very troublesome.    At 200 miles the positions were much the same, and despite the strong winds throughout the day, Guy seemed to be at his best.    Between 350 miles and the finish Guy had sustained a puncture but he still finished nearly 2 miles ahead of his team mate Jim Purves.  With A. Zenthon of the Westerly RC 3rd.

So the **first three** were **Geoff Guy 427.5m, Jim Purves 425.875m, A. Zenthon 419.625m.** S. Oxford continued valiantly for the Vegetarian C & AC team with **396.625m,** giving them the **second highest total ever** with **1,251 miles.** Bailey was 4th with 415.375m, Rawlinson 5th with 415m, T. Powell, Catford, 6th with 410.125, 7th R. Mackrory, Ross Wheelers with 399.675, E. Derham, Westerley RC, 8th 397.625, S. Oxford 9th 396.45625, F. Darnell, Viking RC 10th 391.25m. This was the Vegetarian C & AC's 4th team victory.

*I'm certain that in this Catford event, **George Lawrie broke the trike 24hr Competition Record with 387.37 miles,** as listed in the CTT handbook.*

———⟫◆⟪———

**The Wessex RC 24hr** in 1939 was to be the last one for 12 years due to the war, although the 'WTTA' ,Western Time Trials Association, ran the event on a slightly more westerly course from 1947 until 1950. The 1939 Wessex was won by **Ted Vahey** with **409.2 miles.**

———⟫◆⟪———

**The Yorkshire 24hr.** In this event Alfred Marsh, North Road CC, had a personal best result with 407 miles, and the event was won by **Benny Hudson** with **415 miles.**

*Up until recently, my reports on the Irish RC 24hr and the Yorkshire 24hr have been researched exclusively from writings by Frank Shubert, but I happened to come across an article by Norris Ward who was heavily involved in the Yorkshire events, and I've discovered a few discrepancies and additions, albeit only minor ones. Norris has **1936** as having no event, and that the event of 1937 was won by J. Dickson, Edinburgh RC with 433 miles. F.W. Atkinson was 2nd with 410 miles and Harold Binns was 3rd with 404 miles. Out of 16 starters, 10 riders finished. In 1938 it was another Scot who won the Yorkshire 24hr. D. Findlay, Edinburgh RC with 408m, Lewis Kershaw was 2nd 407 miles and D.A. Eld was 3rd with 406miles. Apparently Findlay rode another 19 miles 'off course' that day which couldn't be counted in his total!*

*This brings us back up to 1939 and Norrie Ward mentions one or two very heroic rides. The first being Jack Riley a one legged rider who managed 279 miles; previous to that in 1935, Walter Greaves rode 328 miles with only one arm. Greaves, the following year put up a world record mileage of 45,380 miles in the full 12 months.*

———⟫◆⟪———

**The Mersey RC 24hr was won for the third year running by Alec Smith.** This Vegetarian member of the Colne Valley CC, Huddersfield, produced his best winning mileage so far, a mileage that is the second highest ever recorded by an unpaced rider of **438.375m.** **Owen Musgrave** of the Cheshire RC was **2nd** with **416.125m** with **3rd** placed **C.R. McCracken,** Midland Veg C & AC the only other rider over 400 with **401 miles.** **Allan Littlemore** of the Lancs Veg C & Ac was the best trike mileage of **318.375m.**

Alec Smith collected his gold medal awarded by Albert Lusty for breaking the course record again. This medal was his third for such an annual achievement so far. Smith from his position as last man off, worked his way quickly through the field so that by Tarporley at 84 miles, the only uncaught rival was Musgrave. He eventually overhauled him and after a cleanly fought tussle, drew away to perform his usual solitary ride at the head of the field. At Whitchurch Alec Smith was sent on an optional detour to Nantwich and back, a distance of approx 20 miles. While he was on this detour, Musgrave went though to be the first man on the road. When he reached the finishing circuit he stopped as his time ran out and then saw Smith approaching with 8 minutes to go. For one brief moment maybe Musgrave thought he had won.

Both riders had ridden virtually solo performances with no one to catch since the 84 mile point. Heavy rain fell almost till the time of the first riders departure and then cleared to give an ideal night and a bright Sunday. From seventeen starters, twelve finished. Tommy Barlow worked wonders organising the course and the timekeeping and Frank Marriott of the Anfield loaned motorised assistance to the club and Frank Slemen was the principal timekeeper.

*These details were from the Mersey RC 'Record' of 1939, the Editor at that time was Guy Pullan. My thanks to the 24hr Fellowship Journal for this information.*

Whilst on the subject of the Mersey RC and time trialling in general at that time, Peter Barlow's comments on the subject of course measurement and accuracy are interesting. He said *"In the period before the second war, course measurement was not of guaranteed accuracy and there were no strict time-keeping standards applicable to time trials".* In the late 1950's he helped on various RRA record attempts and the timekeepers involved at that time were very proficient at their job. They were quite often much older men and were generally very serious about their tasks.

The concentration required when starting or finishing riders in either a time trial or a record attempt meant that virtually nobody except the assistant timekeeper or recorder was allowed anywhere near the principal timekeeper. When stopwatches were being synchronised before an event or being checked for accuracy afterwards it was a hushed and tensely concentrated atmosphere.

Many of the top timekeepers in cycling events were just as respected and revered in athletic circles using tenths and hundredths of a second for track events. In the Midlands, two men that spring to mind were Alan Tomkins and Fred Allcoat. They would have been 'AAA', RTTC and RRA approved.

To become a fully fledged timekeeper one has to train as an assistant, working under and with an approved timekeeper for a least a year. The assistant would then have to undergo a strict test or exam to gain full timekeeping powers. In recent years digital timepieces have taken over from mechanical ones, but they still have to be checked and tested for accuracy by a qualified tester.

Course measuring whether it be for the time trials or Road Records Association purposes has to be very accurate. Course measurers also have to be very careful and serious about their work. Their measurements have to be checked over and over again using a revolution counter on a wheel. Each District Council would have a 'measured mile' that is as accurately measured and documented as it's possible to be. The course measurer would take his wheel revolutions gained from riding the 'measured mile' and then apply them to the road he was measuring, stopping every mile to mark the road and note revolutions etc. A very time consuming job, a job requiring much accuracy.

Tommy Barlow, Peters father, was a wizard with a stopwatch and course measurements. He was actively involved in the sport virtually all of his life, as was Peter. Tommy was the man who, in his spare time, ran the British Best All Round Competition, from its inception in 1944 until 1977, when Frank Minto took over and ran it for over 20 years.

**Here is a list of pre Second World War record-breaking 24hr riders with mileages over 400m.**

| Year | Name | Event | Miles |
|------|------|-------|-------|
| 1919 | M.G. Selbach | North Road | 405 |
| 1925 | J.E. Holdsworth | Catford | 408.5 |
| 1927 | W.A. Ellis | North Road | 410.5 |
| 1928 | W.A. Ellis | North Road | 413.5 |
| 1930 | E.J. Doubleday | Catford | 416.25 |
| 1931 | J.W. Dougal | Catford | 430.75 |
| 1933 | S.H. Ferris | North Road | 431.25 |
| 1935 | E.B. Seeley | Catford | 444.75 |

On a lighter note, Roy Lomas remembers racing in the 1930's where, on occasions, there was no timekeeper at all. One man would set them all off at minute intervals and then would set himself off, leaving the watch at the roadside. The first man back would check the watch and see what he'd done, and then time the others in This became riotous in wet weather when the watch had been hidden under one of the dozens of capes lying in the grass. The question was 'which one?'

**Famous quotes from the last 39 years**

*"All that I have to say about 24hr races is that I'm not in favour of them; I have had bad experiences"*
(F.H. Wingrave – North Road winner 1909)

*"24hr riders are mostly crazy folk who can do little else anyway"*     (W.A. Ellis – North Road Winner 1927, 28, 29)

The North Road Club History in 1939 has a few paragraphs that are a poignant reminder as to the severity of the upheaval in everyday life the war would bring.

"As the time of war approached, the preparations for it, took men from all spheres of life and livelihood to the armed services and civil defence services.   Many jobs associated with war or defence were moved from areas believed to be likely to suffer air attack, to places in Wales and the North and West Counties.   London and Home Counties club member's wives and children were evacuated to rural areas.   Clubs lost their organisers.   Government, whilst encouraging the continuation of sports and pastimes as essential to the Countries health and morale, was at times forced by circumstances to ask the population to make minimum use of roads and rail.   Food and petrol rationing made difficulties for non-essential activities.   Club cycling and racing was affected, as was all civilian life, by the war.   George Bullen, who had put the usual huge amount of work into the promotion of the North Road 24 hr by starting his preparations months in advance, now had the sad task of sending out 116 telegrams to cancel the event, quite close to the date fixed.   Fifty one riders had entered.

**War was declared on Germany – September 3rd 1939.**

*Petrol rationing is introduced – there are now two million cars in Britain.*

Club life carried on although with very much depleted gatherings due to our brave men and women either serving in the armed forces or civil defence, including the Home Guard and Women's Land Army.   Troop movement by convoys made the roads a dangerous place for cyclists, although one or two time trials were organised by various clubs.

*By 1939 all local authorities were responsible for more than 30,000 village signs, all road signs, and they had taken over the role started by the 'A.A'.*

*Travel by cycle was also made very difficult due to signposts and milestones being removed in case of invasion.   Night-time movement was very restricted and dangerous due to lack of lighting, car headlamps had to have the lenses reduced to allow just a small slit of light to be emitted.*

*A 20mph speed limit is imposed for all night driving.*

*Winston Churchill becomes Prime Minister.*

One or two road records were broken during this time.   Probably the most notable one was by **Marguerite Wilson** who started out from **Lands End** on **September 1st 1939** after waiting days for decent weather.   She reached **John 'o' Groats** in record time with **2 days 22hrs and 52 mins.**   She bravely went on to accomplish this once in a lifetime opportunity of completing the **1,000 miles** in **3days 11hrs 44 mins** arriving back at John 'o' Groats as wartime blackout restrictions were being implemented.   As she looked out towards the Orkneys, British Battleships and Destroyers could be seen gathering at Scapa Flow.

Many brave men and women gave their lives for our freedom including members of cycling clubs and organisations from all across the British Isles.

We also lost two of our most famous racing cyclists who had been there at the start of this 24hr record breaking history we've inherited.   Mercifully they both died of natural causes at a ripe old age.

**Monty Holbein died in 1944.** He had proved to be a tough bullish competitor over many distances, favouring the long rides. He pioneered the use of proper training and diet for racing. He gained his stamina by walking long distances at a brisk pace, swimming and weight training were also methods used by this great man. A bad accident caused him to retire from cycle racing and he then took up long distance swimming. His many exploits took him well into old age.

**George Pilkington Mills** was our most exciting young pioneer over long distances and the 'End to End' route became his battle ground. Starting at 18 years of age he crammed more successful road records and time trials, into a ten year period, than anybody else in history at that point in time. He then went on to a very distinguished military career, fighting in many battles. **He died in 1945** at the age of 78. (*So dispelling the Victorian myth that for every 24hr cycle race one rode, ten years would be knocked off one's life. Mills carried out twenty such rides*)

**A.J. Wilson (Faed)** who rode his first tandem trike12hr in 1891 and was a North Road founder club member **also died this year of 1945.**

**Ted Vahey** of the Wessex Road Club who had won his club's last three 24hr races and gained many high placings in the Catford CC and North Road 24hrs over a seven year period didn't return from the War. He died in a concentration camp in Italy. **W.T. Shepherd,** North Roads CC, and **Alfred Marsh,** a young 24 hr rider, also a North Road club member, both died in action flying with the Royal Air Force over Germany. Other Wessex men also died at war – **George Ansell, Gerry Tilley and Ewart Warne.**

**May 7th 1945**     Nazi Germany surrendered to the Allies early this morning and the war in Europe has ended.

**May 8th 1945**     Parties are held all over Britain as 'VE' day is celebrated marking the end of the World War 11 in Europe.

**September 2nd 1945**     The war in Japan is finally over.

While researching the details of races since the 1930's up until the outbreak of war, I've noticed one or two features common to all three of the main club histories. The Wessex RC, the North Road CC and the Catford CC all mention the emergence of the team race and that, generally speaking, if a club could field a team of three or more riders for an event, at any distance or duration, it helped lesser riders to strive harder for the team, or when part of a team, rather than as a sole entrant, and we are now seeing evidence of this, especially in 24 hour races. This team effort and awareness culminates post Second World War with the battle for team honours, especially for Championship events by the larger clubs that have historically always had a long distance and road record breaking background. Prominent clubs are the Luton Wheelers, Addiscombe CC, Middlesex RC, Vegetarian C & AC, North Road CC, Catford CC, Wessex RC, and Kentish Wheelers.

The second noticeable feature common to these clubs histories between 1920 and 1950, are the accounts of deaths and injuries to cyclists due to lunatic motorists with  riders suffering loss of limbs due to their vulnerability to larger vehicles. Street lighting that is non existent in many areas and many cars having poor lighting, poor brakes and steering, and in most cases, drivers with poor ability due to lack of tuition, as testing wasn't introduced until 1935, and car MoT testing in 1960. Horrific injuries were also caused by motor cycles and trams, with cyclists getting stuck in tram lines in the large cities.

Whilst modern day fatalities and injuries to cyclists due to speeding and dangerous drivers is still totally unacceptable, it is probably only marginally worse than in those earlier years. In 1939 there were two million cars on Britain's roads, and now in 2008, there are more than 25 million cars.

# CHAPTER THREE

## AFTER THE SECOND WORLD WAR - "THE GOOD OLD DAYS" 1945-1967

### 1945

The first 24 hour to take place after the war was run on 15th & 16th September 1945. It was run by the **North Road CC** at 2.00 pm. **Eric Wilkinson (Wilkie) of the Luton Wheelers won the event with 390.75 miles.**

'Bob' R.J. Haythorne also Luton Wheelers was **2nd** with 387.75m and **3rd** was **Basil Hudson** of the Scala Wheelers with **385.125m.** The team race was won by the North Road CC with 1,030.625 miles. The team comprised of **Arthur Lancaster** with **367miles** who was glad to be home on leave after several years in the Holy Land with the Armed Forces. **C.E. 'Ed' Green** was the **2nd** member of the team on a **trike** with **335.875m** and **E.J. Foot** with **328 miles.** Syd Parker on a bike this time was **5th** overall with **372.25 miles.** **Jack Spackman** riding for the Century RC won the **trike** prize with **349.875m.** Jack went on to become one of the most prolific 24hr riders, completing over 55 rides in his racing career.

The weather for this event was a very tough south-westerly wind that blew for the whole 24 hours. There were 26 finishers.

F.W. 'Robby' Robinson was the timekeeper this year and whereas Bidlake in the past had just uttered 'Get Ready–Go' when starting the riders, Robby counted the seconds '5,4,3,2,1, Go'. A method still used to this day both for RRA and RTTC purposes.

Eric Wilkinson who won this event was a good long distance rider before the war with 100 mile and 12 hr events being his favourites. He went on in later years to become a much revered timekeeper for this North Road event and indeed many RRA records, including the Swinden and Withers tandem End to End in 1966. Eric, with his wife Jan, were a most energetic pair when help was needed.

**Frank Fischer** of the **Kentish Wheelers** rode 362.375 in this event and he along with Frank Shubert became regular contributors to the 24hr Fellowship Journal with memories of long distance events from the past. We are indebted to them both.

There were no other 24 hr events in 1945 as most clubs were still suffering from not only lack of man and woman power, but also funds. It would be quite a few years before food rationing was finally over and 1953 before food stuffs required for a long distance race were easily available. Syd Parker told me that if club folk knew there was to be a long distance record or time trial, they would all dip into their rations and provide the riders with enough food for their journeys. On Syd's tandem trike End to End and 1,000 mile record with Jim Letts in 1947, they were well looked after by club folk for the whole length of the country. Another factor that affected long distance events and indeed any cycle ride, was the state of the roads after the war.

'Conscription' was to become another factor affecting the sporting lives of many young men. They had to serve 2 years in the Armed Forces either in the UK or abroad in Occupied Countries. It quite often meant that budding time triallists, by the time they had served their years for King and Country, would have lost interest in the sport and quite often stopped riding bikes altogether.

### 1946

*In this year, nationalisation of some of our main industries started to take place; coal, steel etc. Eventually shipbuilding, railways, transport, civil aviation, broadcasting, electricity, banking, health, gas and water were also nationalised.*

The south of the country, London and the Home Counties, in cycling terms, seems to have recovered quicker than the North, whether it was club funds, manpower, state of the roads I do not know, but there were to my knowledge, only two events in this year, both of them in the southern half of the country.

---

The Catford CC 24hr in July, saw **S.E. Ellis** of the Woolwich CC taking **1st place** with **422.75 miles**, **Geoff Guy** who was **2nd** with **417.625** led his **Vegetarian C & AC colleagues to win the team event with 1,179.875m**. **L.E. Bailey with 389.125m was the 2nd** counter for the team and **F.R. Clayden 3rd 'Veg'** home with **373.125m**. **G.F. Ely** of the Hull Thursday RC was **actual 3rd** in the event with **415.5 miles**. Another rider I knew of from the 24hr Fellowship was **Andy Burnett**, riding at that time for the Middlesex RC. Andy came **5th** with **402.675m**, and **Alf Layzell** on a **trike** rode **335.70 miles**.

Ely at the 12hr point led Ellis by 7 minutes, Guy by 15 mins, Hoare 21mins and Burnett 30m. At 367 miles Ellis led Ely by 7 mins but Geoff Guy, who missed a detour, battled on unaware that he was actually going fast enough to make 2nd place and that is how they finished. Ellis, 422.625 and Ely, 415.5m. The event was run with virtually no vehicle assistance due to petrol rationing.

**Jack Spackman** on a bike finished with **369.625**. He was one of the most resilient and helpful characters I knew. My first memory of Jack was on one of the many long distance RRA records I helped on in the 1960's and 70's. Jack would just appear at the side of the road complete with overnight rucksack and offer his help, sometimes being out for three or four days and nights. He would have got out onto the course by hitching a lift by car or lorry. Jack was a very knowledgeable man, especially on matters of 24hr rides or riders and RRA records, and I often wish he were still here to confer with over the result of a pre or post war event or record.

Jack died in 1992 having ridden some fifty five 24 hour races, with at least fifteen before the Second World War. He was almost a life long member of the Century RC although he started with the Windsor Wheelers, riding the Catford CC 24hr in 1929. Jack's last event was to my knowledge the Wessex 24hr in 1960 when he covered 299.17 miles.

**The 24hr Fellowship was the brainchild of Jack Spackman and Sid Genders and when it formed in 1960, Jack became the Founder President.**

---

**The North Road CC 24hr** took place from 12.00 noon on 7th and 8th September with much better weather than the previous year. This reflects on the improved mileages of the riders, the first 12 men in this event beat the winner's mileage of the 1945 race. **R.J. 'Bob' Haythorne** of the Luton Wheelers **won** the event with **435 miles**. A forty seven mile improvement on his 2nd placed ride the year before. **G.F. Ely** of the Woolwich CC was **2nd** with **431.450 miles** having previously come 3rd in the Catford 24hr some weeks earlier. **R.E. Finnimore** was **3rd** riding for the North London CC with **415.65 m**. **Andy Burnett** was **5th**.

**Luton Wheelers won the team race with 1,237.1 miles. E.S. Ellingham was 2nd team member and actual 4th with 405.5m. M.C. Pain** completed the team with **396.6 miles**. Two other teams finished; the North Road CC and Kings Lynn CC. **Alf Layzell won the best trike with 335.75m.** Thirty four riders finished from 55 entries. **Frank Pulman** of the Manchester Roads CC covered **391.4** in just one of his many events. Frank has been another regular source of knowledge for the 24hr Fellowship Journal over the years.

# 1947

1947 saw the running of four 24hr races. The first one being **the Catford** that was **won** by **Jim Purves** of the Vegetarian C & AC with **428 miles**. **2nd** man was **Andy Burnett**, Middlesex RC with **410.625 miles**. **J.G. Whitcombe**, Twickenham CC took **3rd** with **409.875m**. **J. Vallack** who was **4th** with **409 miles** led his **team the Norwood Paragon CC to victory with 1,183.125 miles. The 2nd team counter was H.G. Greatwood with 403.5 and third was F. Sams with 370.625m. Arthur L. Wilkins was the fastest trike with 356.625m.** Thirty nine riders finished

---

**The 'WTTA' (Western Time Trials Association)** promoted their first 24 hr in late July 26/27th in this year. The 'WTTA' consisted of clubs belonging to the South Western Region i.e. Chippenham and District Wheelers, Bristol RC, Bath CC, Bristol South CC, Avon RC. Four other non-association clubs were represented: the North Road Club, Century RC, Warwickshire RC and North London CC.

⪥•◇•⪤

**Jack Nunn,** Chippenham and District Whls **won** with **433 miles, R. Finnimore,** North London CC was **2nd** with **420.375m** and **L. Holt** was **actual 3rd** for the **Chippenham Whls** with **402.375. P. Ellery** was the other **winning team** member with **366.825m,** totalling **1,202.35 miles.** Two other teams finished and a total of 16 riders completed the 24hrs.

⪥•◇•⪤

That same weekend of July 26/27th 1947, saw the resumption of the **Mersey RC 24hr.** Held on roads in or around Cheshire, the Wirral, Shropshire and Wales. **Harry Skinner** of the Walton C & AC **won** the event with **411.625m** from **Les Russell** of the East Liverpool Wheelers by over 11 miles. **3rd** placed rider was **Frank Pulman,** back on his local roads for the Manchester RC scoring **386.75 miles. 'Lol' Innes** of the Seacroft and Crossgate CC was **4th** with **373 miles. Alan Littlemore** of the Mersey RC was **6th** with **360.25** and together with **H. 'Bert' Parkes** on a **trike** with **350.25** and **Vic Bone** with **334m** they **won the team** race for the **Mersey RC** with a total of **1,044.5m.** Fifteen riders finished.

**'Lol' Innes** together with **Bill Thompson** put up the **first un-paced Tandem End to End record in 1938** with **2 days 14hrs 48mins,** using an all land route. Apart from 'Lol' Innes we also had *Bert Parkes.* He went on to break the **End to End** on a **trike** in 1949 and then retook it in 1950, after Jim Letts had taken it from him. Two other larger than life characters contested the trike prize. C.E. 'Ed' Green who later took on the roll of President of the 'T.A' (the Tricycle Association) and W.A.G. 'Wag' Onslow, North Worcester's CC . One can deduce from these comments on the End to End riders that they used 24hr time trialling as a yardstick to measure and maintain their endurance and fitness training for future record attempts.

The winter and spring of 1947 had been very hard with over four months of ice, snow, rain and freezing conditions all over Britain, but affecting the north and east of the country for longer than other areas. March had been the worst month when 2 metres of snow fell in the east, particularly on the flat lands of the Fen District and the East Coast, Wisbech, Norwich, Cambridge, Spalding and Kings Lynn. The ground in those areas that contained a fair amount of peat was already frozen to a depth of nearly a metre, locking millions of gallons of water in. Then 2 metres of snow fell and that froze. Finally when it rained heavily this started the 'thaw'. The land drainage systems consisting of deep dykes or ditches that were already full of flood water, couldn't cope. Rivers rose, roads were underwater, houses were flooded and thousands of people had to be evacuated to higher ground. Eventually the flood waters receded but it had proved that the flood defence infrastructure was not adequate and miles of extra dykes had to be cut. This changed the landscape in certain areas forever.

*August 2nd, Jim Letts and Syd Parker rode from* **Lands End to John o' Groats** *to establish a new* **Tandem Trike** *record in* **2 days 22hrs 41 mins.** *They then continued for the* **1,000 miles,** *that took a total of* **3 days 12 hrs 25 mins.**

⪥•◇•⪤

By the time the **North Road 24hr** took place in September, the main roads had returned to normal. The event, judging by the entries, was the most popular one of the year. **Gordon Basham** of the Wessex RC took **1st** place with **443.5 miles,** just missing competition record. **Dick Goodman** of the Luton wheelers was **2nd** with **432.625** and **Stan Harvey** of the Addiscombe CC, a very close **3rd** with **431.3 miles.**

**Syd Parker** of the Ealing Paragon **won** the **trike** prize with **368.875 miles,** riding a 78" fixed gear. Quite a high gear for a trike in those early years but Syd was strong enough to turn it with ease and to good advantage. After all he hadn't long broken the tandem trike End to End with Jim Letts, going on for the 1,000 miles record, so just a mere 24hr ride was easy, wasn't it?

**Luton Wheelers won the team race** and **broke competition record with 1,283.5 miles.** The team consisted of **Dick Goodman, E.S. Ellingham** who came **4th** in the event with **427.25m** and **H. Walker 6th** with **423.615m.** Four teams finished, the Luton Whls, Wessex RC, Century RC and the North Road CC.

F.W. 'Robby' Robinson despatched 67 riders off on that long northward trek into the wind that caused 7 retirements by 100 miles. At Cambridge, 120 miles, Gordon Basham with 6hrs 4 mins, led Stan Harvey by 3 mins, with Jack Nunn at 7 mins and Syd Parker was leading the trike race with 7hrs 13 mins. At Market Deeping, 249 miles, Basham and Harvey were still in the lead and Goodman had moved into 3rd place. At Cambridge, 354 miles, with nearly 5 hours to go, it became apparent that the competition record could well be broken. News flew around the course and at Girtford Bridge with just under 2 hours to go, a large crowd had gathered to see Basham through. An extra detour of eight miles had to be found for him to run out time but the wind took its toll, and sadly Basham missed the record by 1 mile.

**Jack Sewell** beat Bill Medgett to win the 'North Roaders' prize, 'The Bidlake Trophy' with **383.6 miles.**

*Richard Hulse finished with a very fine 371.1 miles and J.G. MacDonald rode to 340m. Both were members of the Speedwell BC and I will mention Richard Hulse in more detail later in the history.*

*John George MacDonald was known as 'Mac' and his untimely demise in 1954 is written about in Nostalgic Moments – Chapter 8.*

Cecil Paget, Bill Frankum and Frank Armond were all to be congratulated on their faultless promotion, along with all the North Roaders and neighbouring clubs. Jack Sewell is the son of Charlie Sewell the pre-war rider for the North Road. Jack is the father of Roger and David Sewell, both 24hr riders. Roger went on in the 1990's to be secretary and organizer of this famous event.

F.W. 'Robby' Robinson, the main timekeeper had just a few weeks previously, timed Syd Parker and Jim Letts of their successful End to End and 1,000 miles tandem trike record.

71 entries were received, 67 started in intense heat and a very strong north easterly wind, followed by a very cold night with a very heavy, wet, mist falling that chilled the riders causing 26 retirements.

It is now quite noticeable from the many photos in 'Cycling' that the ruling on tights and Alpaca jackets has been eased, as many riders are wearing shorts and a jumper or singlet. Some are seen in shorts and a jacket so they're half way there. It is thought that wartime clothes rationing finally put paid to Alpaca jackets and tights.


# 1948

*January 30th Mahatma Ghandi is assassinated.*

*On May 14th 1948 the State of Israel was formed.*

**The Catford CC 24hr** on July 17th/18th 1948 was a very good one for **Syd Parker.** He broke trike competition **record by nearly 4 miles with 391.04miles.** Geoff Guy won the event with **430.5 miles.** S.F. Wynne, De Laune CC was **2nd** with **407.125m,** F. Sailing was 3rd with **405.5m.** Syd Parker was 4th. **I think this is the highest position a trike rider has ever aspired to in a 24hr time trial to date,** since unpaced road time trials started almost at the start of the century. **Bill Shillibeer** was 5th with **389.5 miles** riding for the **Vegetarian C & AC** and this gave them the **team win** with **1,225.5 miles.** 28 riders finished from a field of 67.

**The WTTA 24hr July 24th/25th.** I hadn't realised until checking the RTTC 'CTT' handbook that just one week after the Catford event, **Len Holt,** a member of the same club as Syd Parker, the Ealing Paragon, also broke trike competition record beating Syd's ride by just 1.6 miles with **392.65m.** He also came **4th** overall in this event. It's a good job Syd chose the Catford to do his ride in. **Jack Nunn** of the Vegetarian C & AC **won** the event in fine style with **431.5 miles** beating **L. Killbe,** Avon RC by 30 miles. **A. Herrington** was 3rd with **392.9 miles.** J. Burgess, Ernie Haldane and Bill Medgett came 10th, 11th & 12th to take the **team prize** for the **North Roads CC** with **1,075.3 miles.**

⬤▸◆◂⬤

**The Mersey RC 24hr** run on the same weekend in July as the WTTA event still attracted a decent field with 26 riders finishing. **Harry Okell** of the Mersey RC **won** the event with **412.625 miles,** leading the **Mersey Road Club** to a fine **team win** with **1,196.75 miles.** **Frank Mumford,** a young man at the time came **4th** with **396 miles,** and **A.E. Byrne** was 5th with **388.625** making the team. Frank Mumford, years later became the 'scribe' who penned 'The Record' a Mersey RC journal and also wrote the very interesting articles on the Mersey event for the 24hr Fellowship Journals until 2003. **2nd** to Harry Okell was **Les Russell,** East Liverpool Wheelers with **407.5miles.** **3rd** was **B.G. Knight** of the Solihull CC with **406m.**

*Dave Threlkeld informed me that Les Russell's 2nd place mileage of 407.5 was his club's record, and for that he was presented with an engraved 18 carat gold medal. Dave also mentioned that the club had been formed at the turn of the century by three Liverpool pawnbrokers.*

**The fastest trike** was none other than **Albert Crimes,** Crewe Wheelers, making his debut I think, with **377 miles** in **11th place. 2nd trike** was another prolific RRA record breaker, **Ed Tweddell** of the Barras CC with **361.75m.** He broke no less than 15 records on either trike or tandem trike with various partners, in fact the End to End and 1,000 are about the only two not on his list.

Another 'future' End to Ender apart from Albert Crimes that day was **Bert Parkes** on a **trike** with **353.25 miles,** probably using this 24hr as training for the following years attempt. Harry Okell, the winner, was Bert's following helper on the End to End in 1949, trailing him at a distance, just about visible and carrying tools, food, clothing and spares for when Bert stopped. Don't forget in 1949 one couldn't guarantee the help of motorised transport due to petrol rationing.

I have reliable information from Peter Barlow that Harry followed Bert from Bristol to Perth, but Harry was so cold by Perth he had to climb off and let Bert continue alone without help. They were hard in those days!

⬤▸◆◂⬤

**The North Road 24hr** a month later on 21st and 22nd was the **lst Official National Championship 24hr for the RTTC.**

**Gordon Basham won the event with a new Competition Record of 454.37m.** It was a 10 mile improvement on the 13 year old record of Edgar Seeleys. This Wessex RC long distance star rider led from the start and didn't relinquish his lead for the whole 24hrs. This was definitely the best ride of his life. **Stan Harvey,** Addiscombe CC was **2nd** with **442.375m** and 3rd was **Geoff Guy,** Veg C & AC with **425.625 miles.** **Luton Wheelers won the team race to become the first Official Championship 24hr team with 1,252.62 miles.** The **team** comprised of **G. Valentine 4th** overall with **424.5m,** Bob Haythorne 7th, **416.25m** and **Dick Goodman 8th** with **412.125m.** 'Ed' Green, North Road CC won the **fastest trike** with **346.625m** beating **Alf Layzell** by just .375 of a mile. **This was the 50th North Road 24hr promotion** and probably one of its best so far with a collection of the countries elite distance riders gathered to do battle. Messrs Paget, Armond and Frankum who organised the event, had fought to make sure that although it was a Championship event, there should still be provision made for the slower riders and trikes, who form the bulk of the field, to be able to do 'detours' and so make sure of getting back to the finishing circuit. The RTTC hierarchy had wanted to make it an elitist event where detours for slower riders weren't recognised. This stand by the North Road committee set the precedence for all future long distance events.

*The Blazer Brigade of the RTTC would regularly, throughout the next 50 years, intervene with the running of our long distance events, and as late as 1996 they imposed a June date for the North Road CC Championship 24hr.*

It was also an historic time for the club in as much as a "24" Society was formed from interested members of all clubs to help with the running of the event, whether financially or by playing an active part or both, 250 members were involved.

Conditions at the start were fair, but at around four hours into the event the rain and wind started. This lasted for some seven hours at gale force severity. At the 202 miles checkpoint where the weather was at its worst, Harvey was trailing Basham by 20 mins. Basham seemed to improve in the bad conditions.

By morning the rain had stopped and sun shone over the course. Harvey at the 375 miles point was still only 25mins behind Basham so had held him well. Geoff Guy was still 3rd at 1.5 hours. On the 11.6 miles finishing circuit Basham lapped at 38 mins, **Ron Diplock** of the Ealing Paragon rode the fastest circuit with 35.5 mins. He finished **5th** overall with **420.625m.** **Fensom** of the Spalding CC was **6th** with **418.25m.**

It was the first time that a properly organised finishing circuit with 7 stationary timekeepers had been used by the North Road CC. Basham completed 3 circuits and then had to be detoured to 'run out time' as the RTTC ruling only allowed the circuit to be used 3 times.

'Cycling' reported a few days later that two large elephants had been seen walking along the road during the early hours of Sunday morning and that in the North Road 24hr in 1897, one Ernest Gould had collided with an elephant during that race. I can only suggest, having read many reports of North Road events, that one or two riders had mentioned that in either the Cambridge or Ely area, they had passed a fairground late on the Saturday night, and had seen the flashing contacts of the dodgem cars lighting the sky. I suppose the elephants could have belonged to the fairground, or even a circus. It also said in that same report, that Gordon Basham drank 10 pints of beer during his ride and his first act on finishing was to drink 2 more. He is photographed with an empty glass at the finish, looking very happy. Did he see the elephants? Maybe that's the secret. (writing this in 2007 I think we should forego the aero helmets and disc wheels, tri bars and carbo drinks, and instead have a pint of beer every two hours) This was also Basham's first time on multiple gears of 65,76,81,86", maybe that was his secret weapon.

The hard luck story is of Jim Purves, Veg C & AC after having 3 punctures early in the race, found he had no more spare tubular tyres and so retired just before the 200 miles point. He's now started in four North Road events and failed to finish in any. One of the most gallant of performances was by **Roy Lomas** who rode **330m** with the use of **only one leg.** Out of a record 78 entries, 50 riders finished with 13 over 400 miles. All of these statistics are records so far.

"WHEN you said you would give me a drink at the Millstone, I thought you would be outside with a bottle of glucose."

*In 1949 Reg Harris signs to become a professional track sprinter for Raleigh. This is probably the beginning of their most popular advertising promotion* **'Reg rides a Raleigh'**

## 1949

Wally Summers set a new record from Pembroke to London, riding on John Bull 'Safety Speed Tyres', in 11 hours 46 minutes, on February 27th.

The **Catford 24hr** produced many good rides this year with 51 solos including 2 trikes, plus 1 tandem finishing. **Jim Purves** after the disappointment of packing in the North Road 24hr in 1948, at last rode to success with **440.39 miles,** a 12 mile improvement and a personal best for his **2nd Catford win. Bill Shillibeer** who also produced a personal best with **433.075m** took **2nd** place. **R.P.F. Hare,** Norwood Paragon took **3rd** place with **420.75m.** **Geoff Guy** came **4th** overall with **410.75** to clinch the **Competition Team Record** win for the **Vegetarians** with **1,284.19 miles. Cliff Prior** riding a trike also broke competition record with **402.11m, the first time 400 miles had been topped on a trike.** Prior's ride came 12years after he won the Catford 24hr on a bike. The tandem of E.G. Widdows and J.M. Robinson produced a fine 421 miles. This is the first tandem to appear on an official result sheet in more modern times, (I say 'modern' because it is post world war two) although I dare say there have been others. **Widdows and Robinson** broke many **RRA tandem tricycle records** in the early 1950's including the **24hr** with **404 miles,** taking the **London to Edinburgh** on the way, with **22 hrs 57 mins.**

Jim Purves said that "this event would be his swan song", he'd tried so hard to win four North Road events and failed to finish in any of them, he really deserved this win. Jim nearly always started steady and rode his own race. He lay 10th at 92 miles, but by 12 hours he'd taken the lead with 230 miles, a well-judged second 12 hours gave 210 miles for him to win by seven miles. Conditions were very good, if a little hot.

⟾⬦⟽

*18th June 1949 saw **Bert Parkes** of the Mersey RC start from **Lands End** to arrive at **John o' Groats** in **3days 13 hours 3 minutes,** beating the trike record set by Les Meyers, some 20 years previously, by nearly 7 hours.*

*One month later Bert had lost his **trike record** to **Jim Letts** by over 3 hours with Letts recording **3 days 9 hrs 27 mins.***

⟾⬦⟽

The **WTTA** ran its 3rd promotion at 24hrs and as an open event will rank high in the history of all day speed. Not only did it produce the second highest mileage of the year, it also produced new talent amongst the nine men who topped 400 miles. **Vernon Wills,** just two days after his 19th birthday **won** this, **his first 24hr** with a magnificent total of **445.5 miles. Jack Nunn** was **2nd** with **430.25.** He had been the favourite to win, needing just one more success to make the 'Fred Baker Cup' his own. He'd won this event in 1947 and 1948 with 433m and 431.25 respectively and this **2nd** place **430.25m** ride makes him a 'stayer' of some distinction. **Jack Thomas** of the Bristol RC was **3rd** with **413.75 miles,** but the other revelation of the day apart from Wills, was the ride by **Len Holt** who **won the trike** event with a staggering **409 miles.** *This mileage isn't recorded as a Competition Record in the RTTC book, so I can only assume that his performance was just beaten chronologically by Albert Crimes some 200 miles further north in the Mersey RC event.* **But what a ride !**

There were 7 trikes riding that day, **Arthur Wilkins,** North Rd CC took **2nd prize** with **364.75** and **Syd Parker,** Ealing Paragon, **3rd trike** with **361m. Vernon Wills** led the Bristol RC team to a win with **1,267.5 miles. Jack Thomas** with **413.75** and **Dennis Smith 409.25** completed this team of 'youngsters' as both were in their early 20's. Wills was the youngest rider ever to win a 24hr race. He rode a single speed gear of 77" and was quite happy throughout the ride, finishing remarkably fresh. He actually covered about 450 miles due to over-running a turn despite the call of the marshal. Strangely enough his team mate Den Smith did the same in the early stages losing about 40 mins. He only blames himself for not studying the route card. This lapse may have cost them the team competition record.

A special ovation for the man placed 20th, **J.C. Bertrand,** South Western RC who's beautiful pedalling style won the admiration of fellow riders and officials all around the course. Starting nearly 20 mins late, his total of **345.75 miles** was a magnificent effort for a **one legged competitor.**

**Jack Wrightson,** whose wife Wynn went on to break the Women's Road Records Association (WRRA) Amateur 1,000 mile record in 1953, rode to 8th place with 408 miles. Jack was later involved with many RRA record rides as an official of the RRA, for riders such as Reg Randall, Pete Swinden and John Withers tandem 'End to End' in 1966.

72

The Mersey RC 24hr on July 22/23rd was a very hot weekend. The club also hosted the **2nd National 24 hr Championship for the RTTC.** **Stan Harvey of the Addiscombe CC won the event with 439.97 m Benny Hudson** who had quite a few placings in rides around this time came **2nd** riding for Rutland CC with **432.10 miles. T.W. Read,** East Midlands Clarion was **3rd with 429.33m.** But the revelation of the day was **Albert Crime's trike Competition Record of 411.79 miles.** This ride of Alberts was to be the first of many fine records by him over the next fifteen years of which I will try and keep you informed in this history. The **4th** placed rider overall was **Stan Bray,** Solihull CC who rode to **422.35m** and led a **Solihull team to victory.** The other team members being **G.A. Juggins** with **409.49** and **B.G. Knight, 401.41m.**

Stan Harvey deserved this win after coming 2nd in last years Championship. This veteran rider didn't have an easy ride, due to the excessive heat that caused him to have 3 punctures.

*This was an event where I look at the result sheet and think 'I knew quite a lot of these riders'. Although I was only five at the time of this event, it would only be another eight years before I joined Birmingham St Christopher's CCC and went out to watch time trials with some of these men riding. Stan Bray was one I saw regularly, he was a science teacher and probably into his forties when I first saw him ride. Stan was a tough rider and very hard with himself. On quite a lot of occasions he pushed himself so hard that he was sick at the finish of an event or in a state of collapse, looking like 'death warmed up' (a Birmingham saying I think). His claim later in life was that he'd ridden for over 50 years without 'packing' in an event. I didn't know at that time whether I could ever be ruthless enough to push myself that hard, but within a few years I was riding 100's, 12hrs, 24hrs and nodding my head to him regularly.*

*I joined the Midland Road Records Association (MRRA) in the late 1970's and Stan was there playing an important part on the Committee. He'd retired from racing by then after gaining MRRA records including the 24hr with 425m in 1952. Another rider on the result sheet was Richard Hulse, of the Speedwell B.C. I knew Richard from record breaking days and he would also attend the MRRA meetings. He was one of the most outstanding characters I've ever known. I can only describe him as an 'apparition' of a cyclist from the early 1900's. Dressed in a proper tweed cycling suit comprised of a finely tailored jacket and 'plus fours', long socks and collar and tie, with his hair slickly combed and parted in the middle. He wore a watch on a chain tucked into his waistcoat pocket. His attire was finished off by leather cycling shoes that had a large flap covering the laces. If the weather was bad he wore an oilskin cape and 'deerstalker' hat. He rode a 3 speed Raleigh Record Ace and on his handlebars he had a large chrome 'chime' or 'chalice' bell.*

*Tony Shardlow described his appearance as "stepping straight out of a Patterson sketch" Richard had been rewarded with his Raleigh cycle by his father for passing his 'metriculation' exam while still at school. Richard used those skills gained early in life to become an Engineer at Fort Dunlop in Birmingham, back in the days when we made products not only for ourselves but also for the whole world.*

*When an RRA record was taking place, Richard could be found miles from home, checking and observing the record breakers, nothing was too much trouble for him, sheltering from the winds and puffing on his pipe. One could never envisage him breaking into a sweat but he must have done, because in this Mersey event of 1949 he produced 362.06 miles, and you can't do that without trying hard.*

Another team to finish that day was **The Walsall Roads CC headed by Sid Genders with 417.24m, Bill Perrett 388.74m and Bill Bradley, 365.78 miles.** Sid later became a founder member of the 24hr Fellowship and also broke MRRA records, but his most famous claim to fame was **rowing single handed across the Atlantic.** Bill Perrett owned a local bike shop in Bloxwich and along with Bill Bradley and Al Harper they were instrumental in keeping the 'South Staffs Cycling Association' alive for about 40 years or more.

Syd Parker

Stan Butler

Eddie Mundy

G A T Laws

Stan E Harvey

Nick Carter

A Jones, C Bate, P Carter, L Heald
J Spackman, S Genders,  D Cane

Gus Andrews

Albert Crimes

Ed Green

Ken  Price

Gordon Basham

Bert Parkes

Letts & Parker

Tweddell & Stott

Cowsill & Denton

Innes & Thompson

A Crimes & J F Arnold

## NORTH ROAD 1948 RESULT

| Pos. | Name | Club | M. | F. |
|------|------|------|----|----|
| 1. | G.H.Basham | Wessex R.C. | 454.4. | * |
| 2. | S.E.Harvey | Addiscombe C.C. | 442.1 | |
| 3. | E.G.Guy | Vegetarian C.& A.C. | 425.5 | |
| 4. | G.Valentine | Luton Whs. | 424.4 | |
| 5. | R.D.Diplock | Ealing Paragon C.C. | 420.6 | |
| 6. | T.W.Fensom | Spalding C.C. | 418.2 | |
| 7. | R.J.Haythorne | Luton Whs. | 416.2 | |
| 8. | R.Goodman | Luton Whs. | 412.1 | |
| 9. | R.K.Masterman | Rutland C.C. | 409.6 | |
| 10. | H.Walker | Luton Whs. | 405.6 | |
| 11. | R.Walker | University C.C. | 405.0 | |
| 12. | R.C.Robinson | Century R.C. | 403.6 | |
| 13. | W.W.Clague | Essex Roads C.C. | 403.0 | |
| 14. | J.Griffiths | Willesden C.C. | 399. | 3. |
| 15. | B.Hudson | Rutland C.C. | 397. | 7. |
| 16. | B.A.Kelly | Peterborough C.C. | 397. | 1. |
| 17. | G.S.Smith | Southgate C.C. | 394.55. | |
| 18. | E.J.Foot | North Road C.C. | 387. | 7. |
| 19. | S.W.Parker | Ealing Paragon C.C. | 387. | 6. |
| 20. | L.Gane | Parkhill C.C. | 386. | 6. |
| 21. | M.W.Ling | Nomads (Hitchin) C.C. | 386. | 4. |
| 22. | E.Lane | Flixton C.C. | 383. | 5. |
| 23. | C.Harvey | Forest C.C. | 379. | 1. |
| 24. | W.Stott | Tyneside Vagabonds C.C. | 379. | 0. |
| 25. | S.H.Kern | Crusader C.C. | 378. | 5. |
| 26. | L.H.Armstrong | Century R.C. | 378. | 2. |
| 27. | H.P.Short | Sharrow C.C. | 377. | 7. |
| 28. | E.G.Kings | Bruce Castle C.C. | 376. | 5. |
| 29. | C.J.Sewell | North Road C.C. | 376. | 4. |
| 30. | D.E.Dowie | East Mid.Clarion C.& A.C. | 374. | 0. |
| 31. | J.J.Cox | Deal R.C. | 373. | 2. |
| 32. | A.L.Wilkins | North Road C.C. | 372. | 0. |
| 33. | J.S.Spackman | Century R.C. | 369. | 0. |
| 34. | M.C.Pain | Luton Whs. | 368.2. | |
| 35. | W.J.Medgett | North Road C.C. | 367. | 2. |
| 36. | D.Robinson | Century R.C. | 363. | 4. |
| 37. | W.G.Smith | Speedwell B.C. | 360. | 7. |
| 38. | R.Hulse | Speedwell B.C. | 351. | 7. |
| 39. | T.Hubbard | Marlboro A.C. | 350. | 1. |
| 40. | H.J.W.Worth | Essex Roads C.C. | 346. | 6. |
| 41. | C.E.Green | North Road C.C. (T) | 346. | 5. |
| 42. | A.Layzell | Westerley R.C. (T) | 346. | 2. |
| 43. | H.E.G.Ferris | Hounslow & Dist. (T) | 339. | 7. |
| 44. | G.E.Martindale | Southgate C.C. | 335. | 2. |
| 45. | G.W.A.Cutts | Coventry C.C. | 333. | 7. |
| 46. | J.G.MacDonald | Speedwell B.C. | 333. | 5. |
| 47. | G.E.R.Lomas | Kentish Wheelers | 329. | 5. |
| 48. | H.Rickett | Bruce Castle C.C. | 321. | 4. |
| 49. | J.H.Doggett | Hayes Swifts C.C. | 316. | 2. |
| 50. | J.C.Caukwell | Sheff.Central C.C. (T) | 307. | 7. |

| Team: | | | |
|-------|---|------|--------|
| | 1. | Luton Wheelers | 1252. 7. |
| | 2. | Century R.C. | 1151. 0. |
| | 3. | North Road C.C. | 1136. 3. |
| | 4. | Speedwell B.C. | 1046. 3. |

* comp record

# MERSEY/NATIONAL 1949

| | | | |
|---|---|---|---|
| 1. | S. E. Harvey | Addiscombe CC | 439.97 |
| 2. | B. Hudson | Rutland CC | 432.10 |
| 3. | T. W. Read | East Mids Clarion | 429.33 |
| 4. | S. P. V. Bray | Solihull CC | 422.35 |
| 5. | L. V. Russell | East Liverpool Wh | 417.86 |
| 6. | S. J. Genders | Walsall Roads CC | 417.24 |
| 7. | L. Newstead | Huddersfield RC | 411.92 |
| 8. | A. Crimes | Crewe Wh  (T) | 411.79 |
| 9. | H. Okell | Mersey RC | 411.77 |
| 10. | G. A. Juggins | Solihull CC | 409.49 |
| 11. | J. Morrall | Dukinfield CC | 405.28 |
| 12. | B. G. Knight | Solihull CC | 401.41 |
| 13. | E. F. Twiss | Manchester Wh | 398.23 |
| 14. | F. Mumford | Mersey RC | 397.56 |
| 15. | W. J. Godkin | Preston Wh | 395.28 |
| 16. | D. Jones | Mersey RC | 395.00 |
| 17. | E. V. Shackleton | Yorkshire Century RC | 391.90 |
| 18. | W. M. Perrett | Walsall Roads CC | 388.74 |
| 19. | E. Wagstaffe | Broad Oak RC | 388.64 |
| 20. | A. R. Craig | Coventry CC | 386.35 |
| 21. | J. E. Boot | Sharrow CC | 386.33 |
| 22. | H. Wright | Coventry CC | 383.98 |
| 23. | M. L. Gapper | N. Worcestershire RC | 383.03 |
| 24. | E. Roberts | Manchester Wh | 382.68 |
| 25. | J. Else | Leeds Atlas RC | 379.12 |
| 26. | E. R. Salkeld | Mersey RC | 378.62 |
| 27. | G. W. A. Cutts | Coventry CC | 377.08 |
| 28. | L. Huskins | Coventry CC | 375.15 |
| 29. | H. Buckley | Manchester Wh | 371.91 |
| 30. | G. B. Whiteman | Nottingham Wh | 367.00 |
| 31. | W. L. Bradley | Walsall Roads CC | 365.78 |
| 32. | G. A. Wilkinson | Manchester Wh | 364.79 |
| 33. | R. Hulse | Speedwell BC | 362.06 |
| 34. | G. C. Richmond | Mersey RC | 361.61 |
| 35. | D. E. G. Rixom | Coventry CC | 357.37 |
| 36. | A. L. Goldie | Crewe Wh | 356.37 |
| 37. | J. J. Cox | Deal RC | 352.34 |
| 38. | A. R. Cooper | Solihull CC | 341.19 |
| 39. | C. E. Green | North Road CC  (T) | 341.16 |
| 40. | J. Shelton | Broad Oak RC | 336.37 |
| 41. | R. B. Crosthwaite | Barras RC | 329.00 |

Team: Solihull CC, 1233.25m

## W.T.T.A. 1950 (NATIONAL)

| | | | M | Y | |
|---|---|---|---|---|---|
| . | S.M.Butler | Norwood Paragon | 458. | 321 | * |
| . | E.Mundy | Addiscombe C.C. | 455. | 1600 | * |
| . | S.E.Harvey | Addiscombe C.C. | 445. | 129? | |
| . | S.E.Armstrong | Addiscombe C.C. | 440. | 545 | |
| . | G.A.Juggins | Solihull C.C. | 438. | 1237 | |
| . | B.Hudson | Rutland C.C. | 434. | 925 | |
| . | J.C.Leversidge | Rutland C.C. | 431. | 724 | |
| . | J.M.Wrightson | R.A.F.Gloucester C.C. | 431. | 443 | |
| . | L.W.Killbe | Avon R.C. | 429. | 1634 | |
| 0. | D.W.Osmonde | Solihull C.C. | 429. | 700 | |
| 1. | R.K.Masterman | Rutland C.C. | 428. | 1545 | |
| 2. | J.F.Watts | Addiscombe C.C. | 421. | 1272 | |
| 3. | S.P.V.Bray | Solihull C.C. | 418. | 964 | |
| 4. | G.J.Waller | Middlesex R.C. | 415. | 289 | |
| 5. | R.Walker | University C.C. | 414. | 11 | |
| 6. | C.R.Whatley | Bristol R.C. | 412. | 1322 | |
| 7. | S.J.King | Colchester Rovers (T) | 411. | 806 | |
| 8. | W.R.Moulsdale | University C.C. | 410. | 1182 | |
| 9. | R.E.Cook | Salisbury R.C. | 410. | 925 | |
| 0. | G.W.A.Cutts | Coventry C.C. | 406. | 27 | |
| 1. | R.C.V.Kirby | Oxford City R.C. | 405. | 1024 | |
| 2. | W.Jones | Swindon & Dist.R.C. | 400. | 904 | |
| 3. | J.Winter | Solihull C.C. | 393. | 58 | |
| 4. | C.H.Williams | Frome & Dist.Whs. | 391. | 1735 | |
| 5. | P.S.Launchbury | Oxford City R.C. | 390. | 1607 | |
| 6. | H.V.Brown | Solihull C.C. | 389. | 1557 | |
| 7. | J.Bragg | Warwickshire R.C. | 388. | 1092 | |
| 8. | S.C.Holyday | Bournemouth Jubilee Wh. | 387. | 541 | |
| 9. | M.C.Rees | Middlesex R.C. | 386. | 517 | |
| 0. | A.R.C.Miller | Colchester Rovers | 386. | 515 | |
| 1. | F.Knowles | Charlotteville C.C. | 380. | 843 | |
| 2. | J.E.Weller | Oxford City R.C. | 380. | 35 | |
| 3. | R.I.Timms | Coventry C.C. | 377. | 173 | |
| 4. | J.R.Parker | Belle Vue C.C. | 374. | 1334 | |
| 5. | J.S.Spackman | Century R.C. | 368. | 706 | |
| 6. | G.Tyler | Crescent Whs. | 364. | 130 | |
| 7. | L.M.Grant | University C.C. | 362. | 77 | |
| 8. | C.R.Coupland | Warwickshire R.C. | 361. | 37 | |
| 9. | J.T.Bassnett | Rutland C.C. | 356. | 872 | |
| 0. | J.C.Burgess | North Road C.C. | 348. | 1543 | |
| 1. | S.C.Price | Rover R.C.C. | 347. | 416 | |

| | | M | Y | |
|---|---|---|---|---|
| m: 1. | Addiscombe C.C. | 1341. | 1674 | * |
| 2. | Rutland C.C. | 1294. | 1434 | |
| 3. | Solihull C.C. | 1286. | 1141 | |
| 4. | University C.C. | 1186. | 1269 | |
| 5. | Oxford City R.C. | 1176. | 906 | |

\* comp record

Catford National 1951

| | | | | | |
|---|---|---|---|---|---|
| 1. | G.Andrews | Addiscombe C.C. | 461 | 546 | * |
| 2. | G.A.T.Laws | Catford C.C. | 459 | 1243 | |
| 3. | S.E.Harvey | Addiscombe C.C. | 450 | 162 | |
| 4. | S.E.Hayward | Kentish Whs.C.C. | 446 | 722 | |
| 5. | J.F.Watts | Addiscombe C.C. | 440 | 918 | |
| 6. | F.P.Wright | Rednon C.C. | 435 | 552 | |
| 7. | H.T.Corby | Norwood Para.C.C. | 434 | 442 | |
| 8. | F.Sailing | Vegetarian C.& A.C. | 433 | 1540 | |
| 9. | S.E.Armstrong | Addiscombe C.C. | 428 | 1600 | |
| 10. | J.H.Trenowden | Addiscombe C.C. | 427 | 1400 | |
| 11. | L.Newstead | Huddersfield R.C. | 427 | 462 | |
| 12. | A.D.Thorne | Bournemouth Arrow C.C. | 425 | 1178 | |
| 13. | S.P.V.Bray | Solihull C.C. | 425 | 842 | |
| 14. | L.H.Sanwell | Westerley R.C. | 425 | 282 | |
| 15. | R.Wilmot | Delta R.C. | 424 | 842 | |
| 16. | J.Davey | Cambridgeshire R.C. | 423 | 579 | |
| 17. | E.G.Guy | Vegetarian C.& A.C. | 423 | 8 | |
| 18. | W.T.Fraser | De Laune C.C. | 421 | 442 | |
| 19. | W.R.Moulsdale | University C.C. | 420 | 942 | |
| 20. | G.L.Redman | Oxonian C.C. | 419 | 368 | |
| 21. | F.C.Smith | Balham C.C. | 417 | 1166 | |
| 22. | B.R.Thompson | Middlesex R.C. | 417 | 402 | |
| 23. | J.F.Wise | Rednon C.C. | 415 | 694 | |
| 24. | J.Parsonson | Norwood Para.C.C. | 412 | 681 | |
| 25. | C.H.Press | Balham C.C. | 410 | 402 | |
| 26. | H.P.Short | Sharrow C.C. | 410 | 40 | |
| 27. | E.G.Kings | Bruce Castle C.C. | 408 | 1075 | |
| 28. | A.R.How | De Laune C.C. | 408 | 1075 | |
| 29. | F.W.Jones | Balham C.C. | 406 | 1418 | |
| 30. | G.Sanderson | Gomersal O.R.C. | 400 | 1662 | |
| 31. | H.A.Wenman | Bec C.C. | 397 | 804 | |
| 32. | F.W.Miles | West Kent R.C. | 396 | 839 | |
| 33. | J.E.Weller | Oxford City R.C. | 395 | 1174 | |
| 34. | D.C.Goodfellow | Cen.Sussex C.C. | 394 | 1056 | |
| 35. | W.P.Plowman | Gosport C.C. | 394 | 122 | |
| 36. | E.C.Baldwin | Fountain C.C. | 393 | 792 | |
| 37. | L.S.Webber | Dragon R.C. | 388 | 1428 | |
| 38. | M.J.Hall | Coventry R.C. | 388 | 1320 | |
| 39. | C.W.J.Harrison | Gosport R.C. | 387 | 1726 | |
| 40. | D.C.Kean | University C.C. | 386 | 170 | |
| 41. | D.Chambers | Victoria C.C. | 382 | 1460 | |
| 42. | C.J.H.Harvey | Forest C.C. | 381 | 1517 | |
| 43. | P.S.Launchbury | Oxford City R.C. | 381 | 560 | |
| 44. | D.P.Brooks | Priory Whs.C.C. | 381 | 260 | |
| 45. | A.Dixon | Southern Rds.C.C. | 379 | 780 | |
| 46. | C.H.Thomas | Catford C.C. | 379 | 776 | |
| 47. | R.Davis | Southern Rds.C.C. | 379 | 389 | |
| 48. | B.R.Constable | Braintree Whs.C.C. | 379 | 280 | |
| 49. | H.Streeton | Crescent Whs.C.C. | 378 | 1363 | |
| 50. | W.H.Chappell | Bristol South C.C. | 376 | 1348 | |
| 51. | F.Wells | Dragon R.C. | 376 | 700 | |
| 52. | R.Wiltshire | De Laune C.C. | 373 | 1039 | |
| 53. | G.E.Moore | Sorian C.C. | 372 | 492 | |
| 54. | J.S.Spackman | Century R.C. | 370 | 1243 | |
| 55. | A.J.Baker | Victoria C.C. | 370 | 826 | |
| 56. | E.F.Butt | Hampshire R.C. | 369 | 1653 | |
| 57. | J.Pellett | Rodney C.C. | 359 | 1189 | |
| 58. | L.J.Jarvis | Hampshire R.C. | 355 | 1568 | |
| 59. | K.E.Walker | Oxonian C.C. | 353 | 708 | |
| 60. | D.F.Lamb | Mercury C.C. | 347 | 1094 | |
| 61. | A.L.Capel | Rodney C.C. | 326 | 1407 | |

Team:

1. Addiscombe C.C.   1351m. 1626 y.   *
2. Balham C.C.       1234m. 1226 y.
3. De Laune C.C.     1204m.   36 y.

* Comp. record.   93 entries, 91 started, 61 finished.

## NORTH ROAD/NATIONAL 1952

|     |                   |                    | m   | yds  |
|-----|-------------------|--------------------|-----|------|
| 1.  | **E. Mundy**      | **Addiscombe CC**  | **467** | **595** |
|     | **(Competition Record)** |             |     |      |
| 2.  | V. Callanan       | Norwood Paragon    | 459 | 94   |
| 3.  | G. Andrews        | Addiscombe CC      | 448 | 878  |
| 4.  | J.H. Ward         | Notts Castle       | 447 | 957  |
| 5.  | S.E. Harvey       | Addiscombe CC      | 445 | 1588 |
| 6.  | S. Thompson       | Rutland CC         | 444 | 1555 |
| 7.  | R.W. O'Dell       | Luton Whs          | 440 | 582  |
| 8.  | G.L. Redman       | Oxonian CC         | 439 | 1135 |
| 9.  | E.W.G. Osborne    | Watford RCC        | 436 | 1046 |
| 10. | F.R. Thwaites     | Eagle RC           | 436 | 83   |
| 11. | A.E. Moggeridge   | Shaftesbury CC     | 435 | 176  |
| 12. | E. Wade           | Bedlington RC      | 429 | 485  |
| 13. | B.A. Kelly        | Peterborough CC    | 429 | 452  |
| 14. | E. Watts          | Hemel Hempstead    | 427 | 1347 |
| 15. | J. McCluskey      | Port Talbot Whs    | 424 | 483  |
| 16. | L.H. Samwell      | Westerley RC       | 423 | 495  |
| 17. | G.A. White        | Eagle RC           | 422 | 1685 |
| 18. | J.C. Nelmes       | Aylesbury CC       | 422 | 720  |
| 19. | E.C. Guy          | Veg C & AC         | 421 | 796  |
| 20. | J. Griffiths      | Willesden CC       | 414 | 1238 |
| 21. | D.W. Buswell      | Leicester Forest   | 413 | 1230 |
| 22. | E.S. Ellingham    | Luton Whs          | 413 | 364  |
| 23. | E.G. Kings        | North Road CC      | 411 | 1215 |
| 24. | R.C. Robinson     | Century RC         | 411 | 535  |
| 25. | J. Turner         | Fountain CC        | 408 | 310  |
| 26. | E.C. Baldwin      | Fountain CC        | 407 | 112  |
| 27. | G. Nixon          | Century RC         | 406 | 1050 |
| 28. | H. Crumbley       | Addiscombe CC      | 406 | 1035 |
| 29. | P. Allpress       | Suffolk RC         | 404 | 1715 |
|     | J.W. Stott        | North Road CC      | 404 | 1715 |
| 31. | W.F. Finnimore    | St Neots & Dist CC | 401 | 1169 |
| 32. | A. Stacey         | Herts Whs          | 398 | 1529 |
| 33. | W. Lowe           | Comet CC           | 396 | 427  |
| 34. | E. Haldane        | North Road CC      | 395 | 1107 |
| 35. | B. Holt           | Sheffield Sports   | 395 | 725  |
| 36. | M.L. Gopper       | Oldbury & Dist     | 388 | 880  |
| 37. | M.J. Hall         | Coventry RC        | 388 | 77   |
| 38. | R. Ward (T)       | Veg C & AC         | 384 | 24   |
| 39. | H. Streeton       | Crescent Whs       | 383 | 748  |
| 40. | J. Leonard        | Archer RC          | 383 | 554  |
| 41. | D.H. Grant        | Cambrian RC        | 380 | 1575 |
| 42. | R. Coupe          | Tunstall Whs       | 379 | 435  |
| 43. | N.G. Potter       | Chelmer CC         | 379 | 227  |
| 44. | D.G. Wicks        | Verulam CC         | 375 | 1355 |
| 45. | G.W.A. Cutts      | Coventry CC        | 374 | 1285 |
| 46. | W.B. Noble (T)    | North Road CC      | 370 | 892  |
| 47. | J.R. Rankin       | W. Scotland Clar.  | 368 | 1195 |
| 48. | A. Layzell (T)    | North Road CC      | 364 | 1340 |
| 49. | J.C. Pavely       | Mercury RC         | 359 | 680  |
| 50. | T.A. Percival     | Wisbech Whs        | 359 | 145  |
| 51. | R.G. Sibley       | Luton Arrow        | 350 | 1009 |
| 52. | R.B. Crosthwaite  | North Road CC      | 349 | 995  |
| 53. | C.E. Green (T)    | North Road CC      | 348 | 1687 |
| 54. | J.S. Spackman (T) | Century RC         | 337 | 443  |
| 55. | T. Hubbard        | Marlborough        | 324 | 440  |
| 56. | K. Boyd           | Broad Oak RC       | 324 | 210  |

Team: Addiscombe CC, 1361 m 1301 yd (Comp. Record)

## 1953 Mersey National

| | | | | | |
|---|---|---|---|---|---|
| 1. | P.E.A. Carter | S. Lancs. R.C. | | 459.48 | 1st. |
| 2. | J.F. Arnold | Middleton C.C. | (Trike) | 457.33 | * |
| 3. | E. Mundy | Addiscombe C.C. | | 448.02 | 2nd. |
| 4. | A. Turner | Warrington R.C. | | 445.50 | 3rd. |
| 5. | S.E. Harvey | Addiscombe C.C. | | 435.37 | |
| 6. | S. Thompson | Rutland C.C. | | 433.91 | |
| 7. | R. Ballance | Maryland Wh. | | 433.32 | |
| 8. | C. Bate | S. Lancs. R.C. | | 430.36 | |
| 9. | A.E. Denton | Lancs. R.C. | | 429.81 | |
| 10. | S.P.V. Bray | Solihull C.C. | | 426.22 | |
| 11. | E.V. Shackleton | Yorks. Century R.C. | | 425.60 | |
| 12. | A. Crimes | Crewe Whs. | (Trike) | 424.33 | |
| 13. | S. Lea | Warrington R.C. | | 423.77 | |
| 14. | P.J. Bates | S. Lancs. R.C. | | 415.67 | |
| 15. | H. Benson | W. Pennine R.C. | | 415.37 | |
| 16. | J.F.W. Broad | Birkenhead C.C. | | 414.10 | |
| 17. | A. Vale | Warrington R.C. | | 412.83 | |
| 18. | D.F. Perks | N. Worcs. R.C. | | 406.81 | |
| 19. | G.E. Jones | Birkenhead N.E.C.C. | | 403.90 | |
| 20. | N. Eckersley | Abbotsford Park R.C. | | 396.62 | |
| 21. | R.H.W. de Looze | Seamons C.C. | | 395.87 | |
| 22. | E. Wild | N. Worcs. R.C. | | 385.70 | |
| 23. | C.B. Blow | S. Lancs. R.C. | | 385.16 | |
| 24. | T.V. Simcock | N. Shropshire Wh. | | 382.20 | |
| 25. | A.E. Barker | Eckington Wh. | | 380.81 | |
| 26. | R.A. Jones | S. Lancs. R.C. | | 369.38 | |
| 27. | C.H. Motley | Rutland CC. | | 360.07 | |
| 28. | J.T. Bassnett | Rutland C.C. | | 348.67 | |
| 29. | L.J. Rees | Walton C. & A.C. | (Trike) | 343.19 | |
| 30. | H. Nelson | Royal Oak R.C. | | 331.50 | |
| 31. | P.L. White | Speedwell B.C. | (Trike) | 330.83 | |
| 32. | A.G. Russell | Merseyside Wh. | (Trike) | 314.58 | |

*Comp. Record but Not eligible for Championship on a tricycle.

| Teams:- | 1. | S. Lancs R.C. | 1305.51 |
|---|---|---|---|
| | 2. | Warrington R.C. | 1282.10 |
| | 3. | Rutland C.C. | 1142.65 |

## Wessex National 1954

| | | | | |
|---|---|---|---|---|
| 1. | S. Thompson | Rutland C.C. | 469.666 | Comp Record. |
| 2. | A. Turner | Warrington R.C. | 457.807 | |
| 3. | S.J. King | Colchester Rovers C.C. | 457.750 | |
| 4. | G. Andrews | Addiscombe C.C. | 455.882 | |
| 5. | E. Mundy | Addiscombe C.C. | 453.802 | |
| 6. | A.G. Ramsey | Hounslow & District Wh. | 453.152 | |
| 7. | S.E. Harvey | Addiscombe C.C. | 447.814 | |
| 8. | R.F. Randall | Harlequins C.C. | 447.466 | |
| 9. | B.R. Taylor | Wessex R.C. | 447.030 | |
| 10. | P.C. Hill | Haslemere & Dist. C.C. | 446.623 | |
| 11. | J. Nelmes | Watford Rds. C.C. | 440.956 | |
| 12. | E.R. Stainer | Yeovil C.C. | 438.085 | |
| 13. | G.G. Hood | Middlesex Clarion C.C. | 431.455 | |
| 14. | L.F. Morgan | Salisbury R.C. | 425.455 | |
| 15. | G.W. Siddle | Spartan Whs. C.C. | 416.756 | |
| 16. | R. Pearson | Colchester Rovers C.C. | 414.170 | |
| 17. | D.A. Rout | Colchester Rovers C.C. | 408.855 | |
| 18. | E.G. Guy | Vegetarian C. & A.C. | 407.566 | |
| 19. | R.E. Cook | Salisbury R.C. | 393.428 | |
| 20. | W.W. Brown | Cwmcarn Paragon R.C. | 388.182 | |
| 21. | C.W.J. Harrison | Gosport C.C. | 386.468 | |
| 22. | E. Potter | Doncaster Wh. C.C. | 384.315 | |
| 23. | H.A. Tribe | Gosport C.C. | 377.849 | |
| 24. | B.J.V. Daltry | Actonia C.C. | 375.270 | |
| 25. | E.F. Butt | Hampshire R.C. | 349.100 | |
| 26. | T.G.E.M. Ryder | Portsmouth N.E.C.C. | 340.956 | |
| 27. | A. Gould | Actonia C.C. | 332.252 | |
| 28. | R. Smith | Actonia C.C. | 327.600 | |

| Team:- | | | |
|---|---|---|---|
| Addiscombe C.C. | 1357.498 | 49 Entered. | |
| Colchester Rovers C.C. | 1280.773 | 48 Started. | |
| Actonia C.C. | 1035.128 | 8 Teams Entered. | |

81

In the year 2000 Lynne Taylor (my daughter), David Edwards and myself rode the Mersey RC 24hr and broke the Walsall RC team record that these 'lads' had held for 51 years, by 14 miles.

*I think it was possibly a 'first' for a Father and Daughter finishing in the same 24hr event.*

Sid Genders, who rode this 1949 Mersey RC event, remarked that in the dressing room after the event, (probably the 'Bulls Head' at Clotton) some chap asked "which one are you riding next?" and received the usual 'first timers' reply – "don't be daft, do you think I would do that again? – once is enough".  From a dark corner came a weary chuckle (it was J.G. MacDonald of the Speedwell BC) "Don't kid yourself boy, now you've been through the mill you're one of us.  You'll be there again next year and the year after!"  Sid said that remark just about summed it up; it is the finest game we know and we think the chaps taking part are the salt of the earth.

---

**North Road CC 24hr** September 3rd & 4th was not only a success for Bob Mynott and Ed Green but also at last a success for the North Road club.  **Bob Mynott's 447.1 miles** was a club record and **Ed Green's trike** performance of **366.1** was also a club record.  It had been twenty years since Bill Ellis had won for the North Road and forty years since Wingrave and Bass had pulled off the 'double' of bike and trike victories for the club.

The weather was very hot, sixty four riders started and forty six finished.  The **2nd** placed rider, **Stan Argill**, did **436.5m,** and **Mike Pain** was **3rd** with **431m.  The Century RC won the team prize with R. Robinson, W. Budge and F.J. Taylor** totalling **1,232.7 miles.**  Four teams finished.

This was Bob Mynott's first 24hr race as was Argills.  At 12hrs Mynott lay in 3rd place, Fensom who was leading at the time, later crashed and had to retire at 300 miles, his bike was wrecked.  Bill Shillibeer also crashed heavily in the later stages, so thwarting his teams chances of a win, and his own.

## 1950

*In June of this year, Harry 'Goss' Green died after suffering Rheumatism for many years.  He broke many road records including the End to End in 1908 with 2 days 19hrs 50 mins.*

---

**The Catford CC 24hr** started the year off in the long distance calendar, held in mid July.  **Stan Butler,** after a career lasting some twenty years so far, was tackling his first 24hr.  Riding for the Norwood Paragon CC, he **won** the event by a clear 25 miles from **Mike Aycliffe, Clarencourt CC.**  Butler's winning mileage of **450.85m** was the **2nd greatest ever,** just under 4 miles less than Basham's two year old competition record.  Aycliffe's mileage was **425.85** and **R.P. Hare,** Norwood Paragon CC was **3rd** with **421.25m.  Geoff Guy** led the Vegetarian C & AC **to a team win of 1,236.02m.**  His mileage was **421.01,** Oxford and Bailey were the other team members.  There were 70 riders in this event.

Stan Butler is of course, Gethin Butler's grandfather and would have been so proud of Gethin and his father Keith's achievements in later years.

---

**The WTTA 24** hr two weeks later at the end of July was a **National RTTC Championship event** and a record breaking event in many ways, receiving 82 entries being just one of them.  **Stan Butler** was on marvellous form this year, having won the Catford event just a fortnight previously.  He went even faster to **win** this event and produced a **new competition record of 458.18 miles.**  But we must not forget **Eddie Mundy,** Addiscombe CC riding his first 24hr.  He had started in front of Butler by 21 mins so finishing before him.  **Eddie also broke competition record** that day with **455.91 miles,** in fact, **he broke two comp records that day** when he led the **Addiscombe team,** managed by Charlie Davey, to a **massive 1341.95 miles,** a 57 mile improvement over the Veg C & AC record of the previous year.  **Stan Harvey** with **445.7m,** a personal best for him, and **Syd Armstrong** with **440.3m**  both did outstanding rides to complete the team, but then Harvey had won the Championship the previous year.

Another outstanding ride of the day was **Jack Kings,** Colchester Rovers, on a **trike with 411.5m,** just missing Albert Crimes record by .25 of a mile. He actually stopped just before his time was up, so this was probably the amount he missed the record by.

Butler and Mundy were so evenly matched, there was never more than 10 minutes between them throughout the race. Conditions were far from ideal with winds and heavy rain in the 2nd 12 hours. Butler suffered with backache during the race and had to stop for a massage. The backache was probably due to riding his spare 'hack' bike after breaking the handlebars on his race bike and riding one handed for a long time. All of these problems possibly cost Butler 20 mins or more, so one can only imagine what mileage was lost. Mundy meanwhile was steaming along despite the weather, and when the two riders reached the finishing circuit there was nothing between them on time.

Mundy turned onto the sixteen mile finishing circuit for the last time with 446 miles covered and 30 mins left to run, he was so close to Butler. Then he 'cracked', for two miles his speed dropped to less than 10 mph. He rolled on his bike like a drunken man and I assume he'd got the 'knock', a condition caused by very low blood sugar level, medically termed, 'hypoglycaemia'. Luckily he pulled out of it ten minutes later and picked up speed once more.

Mundy passed the original competition record distance and then ran out of time. Then all eyes were trained on the road looking for Butler to see if he would beat him. Despite the heavy rain, Butler flew on that last circuit, sometimes over 25 mph with the following car unable to keep up. It was such an exciting finish to a record breaking event held on roads that reached into Somerset, Wiltshire, Warwickshire, and coming as far north as Worcester. At the 103 mile check 'Lofty' Joe Leversidge, Rutland CC had a 6 mins lead on Butler and a 15 mins lead on Mundy but by 12 hours just 10 mins covered the first four riders. Butler was now in the lead with 235 miles, and the rest, as they say, is history.

*I noticed when looking through the provisional results for this event that the Solihull CC consisting of G. Juggins with 438.6m, Doug Osmonde 429.5 and Stan Bray 418.375, giving a total of 1,286.45m, and also the Rutland CC with Leversidge 431.45, Ron Masterman 430.45 and Benny Hudson 420.5 giving a total of 1282.40. Both teams came so close to equalling the 'Vegetarians' record of the previous year, in fact the Solihull mileage was greater by over 2 miles. But I only have the provisional results to go on.*

—▸◆◂—

**The Mersey RC 24hr** this year, was one of the wettest on record. Probably the same band of rain that had been experienced in the WTTA event held on the same weekend. **Cliff Bate,** Mercury RC won the event with **437.71 miles** from **Stan Lea,** Warrington RC who clocked **422.08 m. Frank Cowsill,** Lancashire RC was **3rd with 413.04m.** He was probably using this event as a build up for an End to End and to test his endurance and night riding abilities.

Cliff Bate's win came in spite of 17 hours of rain, often torrential. The riders actually started in heavy rain, the conditions were so bad that only 16 of the 38 starters survived the 24hrs. At the 12 hour point, **Bate** had covered **226 miles,** but the gaps were now appearing in the field. By 251 miles, at the Shawbirch check, he went through at 1.15am. Les Russell was at 46 mins, Twiss was 3rd at 56 mins and Lea was at 1hr 4mins, Cowsill 1hr 8mins and Harry Okell 1hr 9mins. Okell who had won the Mersey event in 1948, retired at Shawbury, 279miles and at Wem, 299m, Bate was 1.5 hours ahead of the field.

By the time the finishing circuit was reached, Lea had battled to 2nd place but still couldn't bridge the gap, and although he had pulled some time back on Bate, he finished 15 miles behind. Cowsill, who had a good battle with Twiss in the closing stages, came out best by just over 2 miles. This was Bate's first season and his entry form only showed a best 25miles of 1hr 7mins and a 50 mile of 2hrs 9m and nothing else. He'd done a 235 mile 12 hour the previous week but there was little clue he was going to dominate the event as he did.

The Mersey RC won the team race with 1,191.97miles. R.Head, Frank Mumford and D. Jones who were 5th, 6th and 7th in the event made up the team and, despite there being only 16 finishers in total, this figure included two more teams.

⟫•◇•⟪

One month later, August 26th & 27th, saw the **North Road event with a record field of 100 riders,** of whom 63 finished, including two riders who had made the journey from Scotland. G. Handley, Lomond Roads CC and J. Ranking, West Scotland Clarion. Twenty six riders beat 400 miles. I think these statistics above are all record amounts so far.

**Bob Mynott,** North Road CC, who had won last years race wasn't to be outdone by Butler's record breaking spree. He pulled out another **Competition Record ride** of **459.50m,** the third competition record this year for a bicycle 24hr, and the 4th if you count the team win of the Addiscombe CC.

**Bob Haythorne,** Luton Wheelers, was **2nd** with **447.5m** and **E. Ellingham** also Luton Whls, **3rd** with **434.2miles.** One would think that having a third team member **R. O'Dell** with **414 miles,** the Luton had got the team race sewn up, but one would be wrong. **The North Roads CC** beat them by 4 miles. **The team consisted of Mynott, Alan Blackman 430.4m and Arthur Wilkins with 408.4, producing 1,299.5miles.** This was the second year running that the North Road had cause to be jubilant, fielding the winning rider and winning team

Five teams finished, another record I think. **Syd Parker,** Ealing Paragon, on a **bike, rode to one of his best mileages with 410.3miles** to take 15th place. **Cliff Prior,** Ilford RC, had another outstanding ride to **win the Trike event with 408.5m.**

Butler and Mynott were the two favourites and were neck and neck for 160 miles. Butler, who had already ridden two 24hr races in quick succession, winning both, was now feeling the effects and at 12hrs his knees started to give him a problem. Mynott was now in the lead by 3 miles with 242m. Butler struggled on but finally at 255miles, he climbed off and retired.

Bob Haythorne and John Arnold both gave Mynott a very hard battle earlier in the race, but by the time night fell, conditions started to change. The night was cold, wet and miserably dark. The heavy showers soaked the riders and the Fenland winds cut through their clothing. John Arnold of the Middleton CC got to the 259 miles point, where his feet were troubling him, and retired.
*This complaint was to 'dog' John's career for the next 20 years causing him many problems.*

Prior's trike mileage of 408.5 miles was the greatest distance ever covered on a trike in a North Road event, and at one time it was thought that Crimes's record would fall to him, but the relentless wind got to him in the end. He'd also had to replace his front wheel due to a broken spindle, quite a common thing, especially on trikes, before quick release (Q/R) systems came along.

Bob Mynott finished, absolutely exhausted, and unable to stand unaided, but within minutes he was revived by a pint of Black and Tan. (no 'Rego' recovery drinks in those days!) Both Mynott and Butler had pushed themselves to breaking point this year and one wonders where the limits of exhaustion lie in terms of mileage.

This was the start of a 27 year period of organising this event by Sid Mottram.

*One other ride worthy of mention was Joe Pond of the Hertfordshire St Christopher's CCC with 335 miles. At first look one might think 335 miles 'so what' but considering he stopped early on the Sunday morning and had another club member take him to church in a car, where he attended mass, and then travelled back to where he'd left his bike on the course, that puts his mileage into context. Joe Pond was a tourist at heart and he was probably the first St Christopher's rider to enter a 24hr race. In the 1950's the Catholic Church was strict on attending mass on a Sunday, and at that time, there were no Saturday evening masses, not that it would have made much difference in Joe's case. When I first started racing in time trials or riding with the club, one always had to attend mass either before or after the ride, otherwise one would be scorned or 'ticked off' by Club 'elders' for not fulfilling ones religious duties.*

*The outcome of it all was a 'Joe Pond' trophy presented by his club, and to win it, one had to be a St Christopher's member and beat 335 miles in a 24hour, including attending mass during the race.   There was usually a club in most large conurbations i.e. London, Coventry, Liverpool, Leeds, Glasgow, North Staffordshire and Hertfordshire.   Birmingham had two sections, North and Central.*

*On a more amusing note, being a member of Birmingham St Christopher's CCC, along with Pete Swinden, John Withers and Pat Kenny, we rode the Mersey RC 24hr on many occasions and always managed to get to the church, St. Werburga's, in Chester for 7.30 evening mass, after finishing the event at about 6.00 pm.  You can imagine the state we were in, usually exhausted and probably whiffed a bit.   As soon as we got into a crowded warm church, lack of oxygen and dim lighting took over, our eyelids got heavier and although we usually sat or stood at the back of the church, we normally ended up slipping out one by one, having taken a 'turn for the worse'.   One year there were three of us sitting on the steps outside with our heads between our knees feeling very faint!   John Withers was our only member to win the Joe Pond Trophy with 403 miles.*

<hr>

We are now into the 1950's and so many things are changing in all walks of life.   Optimism is in the air for a brighter future, a future perhaps without the threat of war, with our forces joined with other peaceful nations occupying parts of Europe.   Germany and Japan were both beaten nations and would cause no more problems.

Prosperity is the keyword, a lot of our industries and services were already nationalised, helping the country pull together at this time.   The bicycle isn't now just for people with money, or just to use for sport.   Many bicycle companies were producing large quantities of relatively inexpensive machines of all types, from a 'tourer' to a 'racer' a utility bike or sports model.   All could be purchased from about £15.00 and some shop owners were now offering 'hire purchase' terms.

Raleigh, Hercules and B.S.A. were I think the main volume suppliers at that time, with Professionals, both male and female, being signed up to promote their products.   I know that before the war Jack Rossiter had ridden for Raleigh on his End to End and 1,000 mile record, and they displayed the bike he used in Curry's Peckham showroom window in 1930.   Sid Ferris rode for Raleigh with Sturmey Archer gears on his End to End in 1937.   The record he beat was Hubert Opperman's who rode for 'B.S.A.', the Birmingham Small Arms Company that produced rifles, motor bikes and other machinery as well as cycles.   Marguerite Wilson rode for 'Hercules', another Birmingham manufacturer, on her record rides in 1939.

This was all before the war and whether it had the desired effect on the public's purchasing power, I don't know, coupled with the fact that these Companies would have suffered a severe loss of manpower during the war and the factories and existing workers would have been producing munitions or machinery for the war effort, I think the professional's efforts would have had minimal effect.

If a rider wanted to turn professional between 1930 and 1960, he or she had to make sure that they had done all that they had wanted to do as an amateur sports man or woman whether in time trialling circles or in 'massed start' road racing.   Once they had taken part in any race or promotion as a professional sportsperson, they could not then ride as an Amateur cyclist.

Things became more relaxed later, but certainly at this time and until the 1970's this was the ruling.   So these professionals really had to make sure that they had ridden all the club racing they had wanted to do at Amateur level.   Only one governing body, the 'RRA' (Road Records Association) allowed either 'status' to compete for their various records and that's always been the case for the men.  The women's association, 'WRRA' had separate records for each status until 1989.

*How different conditions are now in 2008, anything goes, and a fair percentage, probably a third of riders, maybe more in Championship events, are sponsored, with living expenses to train and travel to events, have cycle equipment and entry fees paid for, and be rewarded for good results; in fact virtually professionals.  This to me makes a mockery of the description Amateur Racing Cyclists, but I'm proud to still be associated with many proper Amateur riders who are just happy to give their all for a trophy, a medal, a certificate, or just a free cup of tea.*

Back in the 1950's, as far as record breaking is concerned for this books interests, only a few professional riders, who rode at Amateur time trial level originally, get mentioned.   Rossiter, Ferris, Ken Joy, and the ladies, Lilian Dredge, Marguerite Wilson, and Eileen Sheridan.

Employment was on the increase although there were large areas where the bombings and blitz had left utter devastation.   Bus and train travel routes by this time were almost back to normal, providing mass transport to and from work, and for people to get around the country generally or to go to the coast for a holiday.

Cycle use was well on the increase.   At 7 or 8 years of age, I remember walking to a local recreation ground, passing large factories such as 'Joseph Lucas' and 'M.E.M' on the way.   If you happened to be just going past either of their large exit gates at dinner time or 'knocking off' time, you ran the gauntlet of about 200 cyclists, and as many on foot as they spilled out of the factory gates and filled the roads around the area.   I lived in Tyseley, Birmingham and within a 5 mile radius of home there were numerous cycle manufacturers including B.S.A., Dawes, James, Hercules, Armstrong, Co-op, Phillips and Parkes.   Within a 10 mile radius, component manufacturers almost too numerous to remember; Cyclo Benelux, Bayliss-Wiley, T.D. Cross,   Reynolds Tubing, Renolds Chains, Brampton, Miller Dynamos, Dunlop Tyres, the list was endless.   Nottingham and Coventry were really the only other areas for mass production of cycles and components.   Nottingham of course was Raleigh and Sturmey Archer, who had been producing since 1887.

Of course there was a plethora of smaller individual cycle makers such as Claud Butler, Hobbs, Rotrax, Holdsworth, Grubb, Bates, Hetchins plus many frame builders dotted around the country, although most of the lightweight companies were in the London and Home Counties area.   I know that Claud Butler had numerous outlets for his bikes dotted all round London.

*At this present time in 2008, apart from a few individual frame makers, such as Mercian and Bob Jackson etc. and one or two small engineering companies making hubs, disc brakes, chainrings and small c.n.c. parts, we have no cycle industry left at all.   Everything comes in a box marked either 'Made in China, Taiwan, Phillipines, Vietnam, Spain, Japan, France, Italy, India' - in fact everywhere but Great Britain.   All that we have is an overcrowded road system with thousands of lorries daily transporting boxes with foreign goods in, from one massive warehouse to another.*

By 1950, if you turned up to a race in Alpaca jacket and black tights you would have received some very strange looks;  shorts, albeit they had to be black, were by now the order of the day, and the women's shorts seem to be shorter than the mens.

I have in front of me as I am writing a 1949 'Cycling' magazine with photo's of Mary Capell, Stella Farrell, Eileen Sheridan and Janet Gregory, all in shorts, and now wearing coloured racing tops.   I say tops, because many have long sleeves.   The men were equally dressed much the same, but wearing racing vests that had pockets at the front, across the chest, and at the rear.

The road racing 'massed start' fraternity are seen at this same time with lighter coloured, and even multicoloured, tops on.   All are riding on multiple derailleur gears, an influence from Europe, the 'Tour de France' and 'Giro'. At this time I would think that men's time trials were still dominated by the fixed wheel single speed bike.

Certain top long distance riders like Gordon Basham, Stan Butler, Eddie Mundy, Bob Mynott and Stan Harvey were at the 'cutting edge' all using derailleur gears.   Whether multiple gears were the reason for the increase in mileages by these top riders, attaining competition records, year on year, I don't know.   I personally think that the larger fields attracted to these classic races, The Catford, The Mersey and The North Road 24 hours, making them more hotly contested, is the real reason.

The main interest at the moment is still the events in the Southern half of the country with the Mersey event still waiting to gain Competition Record status.

*In November of this year British Troops were actively engaged in the Korean War.*

# 1951

*On May 3rd 1951 "The Festival of Britain' was opened by the King and Queen on the South Bank of the Thames.*

*The first Zebra Crossings were introduced in this year.*

⎯⎯►◄⎯⎯

There were only three events this year, the first to be run was the **Catford CC 24 hr.** There was a huge entry of 93 riders for this popular Championship event run in June, at almost mid-summer. 91 started, 61 finished and **30 riders beat 400 miles** and that's definitely a record so far.

**Gus Andrews** of the Addiscombe CC **won** the event with another new **Competition Record of 461.31 miles,** beating **George Laws** who was better known as a track rider, from the Catford CC, by over a mile. **Law's 459.7m** ride would probably have just beaten Mynotts 1950 mileage by a whisker, but Georges' day will come. **Stan Harvey, Addiscombe CC was 3rd with 450.1 and along with 5th placed Jack Watts, 440.5m, they clinched the team win and put another 10 miles onto Competition Team Record so keeping the honours for the Addiscombe CC with 1,351.92m.**

At the 156 mile point, the furthest west on the course at Fareham, Stan Butler, the favourite had re-caught George Laws after many tussles on the road. The battle between these two had left the field behind. Another new name at 24hr riding, 'Gus' Andrews was 18 mins down on Butler at this point. At Bucks Farm, 206m Butler who was going all out, was 14 mins up on 'evens'( a 480m ride) and 10 mins up on Laws, the hills and the Downs slowed the riders and at 12 hours Butler had slowed slightly to 241 miles. At 309 miles, Butler wasn't looking happy, he'd stopped gaining ground on his rivals and by 338 miles, Stan Butler had retired with sickness and breathing difficulties. He'd pushed himself so hard in an effort to win.

The race was now 'wide open'. Laws was leading Andrews by 2 minutes at 360 miles. By the time the finishing circuit was reached, Andrews had taken the lead; Laws had, by now got backache from the massive effort. They ran out of road to ride as the finishing circuit in those days could only be used 4 times and they ended up on a detour heading towards Brighton, to finish their terrific rides so bringing a very exciting race to a close.

With the death of popular timekeeper, F.W. Robinson in 1950, Alan Gordon now takes his role.

**Jock Wadley who covered this Championship event for the 'Cycling' magazine describes 'following out' Gus Andrews' last 23 mins in the company of the timekeeper, in George Newman's car.**

*'As he left the last permitted circuit to strike off on new ground it was still touch and go for the record, with no margin in hand for even a short spell of the 'slows'. The roads were busy; a motorised tandem thought Andrews was trying to 'dust them up' and had to be called out of the way; a Policeman's hand shot up to stop the rider, but mercifully shot down again when he sensed the urgency of the job in hand.*

*With 12 minutes to go, Charlie Davey sprinted down the road with Andrews's last drink of the race. Refreshed, the Addiscombe rider continued strongly and steadily, his arms bent rather curiously outwards. To finish a 24hr at any speed is an achievement; to be called upon to ride as hard as if riding a 25mile race with a National Record at stake was an ordeal. A traffic island mix up through the wanderings of a Sunday driver brought him almost to a halt, and several times he hesitated, thinking the blasting of the klaxons was a signal that his time was up. But the record point was passed with several minutes in hand, and as if the boy hadn't already worked hard enough, the final three quarters of a mile was up a hill that you wouldn't blame a cycling club for walking.*

*After he'd straightened his back, Andrews was in really good shape shortly after finishing and it seemed impossible that this slightly built cyclist could have ridden over 461 miles in a day'.*

**Sid Hayward,** Kentish Wheelers, came **4th with 446.4 miles;** he also enjoyed the event. I've used one or two of his comments from a 24hr Fellowship Journal to describe some of the conditions in the race.

'At Pease Pottage for the mid-day start on the Saturday, I was started No 90 out of 93 riders. The weather was just about right, although it turned out very dark during the night with lots of insects and moths in the air. Pockets of mist covered the road at dawn. At Chichester roundabout, a rider who had packed, offered me his food, which was a parcel of whole chicken, boned and sliced. I accepted with enthusiasm. I caught a lot of riders during the night and have memories of pounding along the Horsham to Guildford road in the pitch black with a poor front light focussed on the white line down the middle so as to detect the bends, catching many dim rear lights in the process, a memory one can only collect in a 24hr race!

At the start of the finishing circuit I called in at my pre-race 'lodgings', Mrs Bridgelands, for a glass of ginger beer and milk. I passed Norman Tullett's club record of 427.25 miles on my third finishing circuit with an hour to go, in that I put another 19.25 miles.

Gus Andrews rode gears of 76,81 and 86". He had a 1min 43secs late start after puncturing on the start line, he had no sit down feeds and only 5 mins off the bike throughout the event. Runner up George Laws said afterwards "first and last!" and like most people he'd changed his mind by the following year. He rode the same size gears as Andrews and had a very low flat back '25 milers' position on his bike, probably another reason for his backache towards the end of the race. Laws stopped at all of the 'sit down' feeds provided, not only because he was very hungry, but also because he felt that having breaks was very wise in this, his first 24hr race.'

Jack Spackman did 370 miles, in this his 21st Catford CC 24hr race, having ridden everyone so far, since it started in 1925.

Jack (John) Watts, the 3rd Addiscombe CC team member was a regular 24hr man. I think this mileage of 440.5 and 5th place overall was probably one of his best performances, if not the best for him. He and his wife, Christine, have been involved with time trialling and record breaking for a period of some 60 years. Christine holds tandem records at 50 miles, 100 miles and the London to Brighton and back with D.R. Grist. In 1954, Christine broke the Ladies Competition Record for 12 hours, beating Eileen Sheridan's record by .375 of a mile with 237 miles. Both Eileen and Christine are Vice-Presidents of the RRA.

**My thanks also to Keith Hyatt who supplied me with a photocopy of the original result sheet and souvenir Catford newsletter. Keith rode 397 miles in the last Catford event in 1975.**

⟹◈⟸

**The Mersey RC 24hr.** Apart from the weather this years event was looking very similar to the previous years race, with Cliff Bate dominating the proceedings for the first 200 miles. He was now starting to suffer the after effects of a chill and had an attack of sickness. By Battlefield at 207 miles he started to slow and soon retired. Arthur Vale who had been trailing Bate in 2nd position now took over the lead but hadn't seen him pack and assumed that he was still in front of him on the road and 'stormed' on powerfully hoping to catch Bate.

After riding the Hodnet to Shawbirch detour, Vale began to pay for his efforts; he now knew he was in the lead but not by much. At the Wem Road fork he'd covered 299 miles in 16 hours. Les Russell was the closest to Vale at 8 minutes. Vic Bone was third on the road at 33 mins, Stan Lea was 4th followed by Denton, Cowsill, Okell and Sandham. On the 'Bangor on Dee' detour, Lea started to pull back time as he had done the previous year.

By the time they had reached the finishing circuit, the positions for finishing were now set with **Vale** running out a very well judged **winning** mileage of **437.83 miles. Russell 433.32m** and **Lea 432.52m.** Alec Denton rode well to pull back to **4th** place with **427.49m.**

"You're still leaning the wrong way going round corners."

88

Behind the leaders on the road another battle raged with **John Arnold versus Jack King on trikes.** King had previously missed Albert Crimes record of 411.79 by only a third of a mile in the WTTA event of 1950. This time it was a physical battle man to man, mile for mile on the road. At 70 miles Arnold led by 7 minutes but then punctured, so losing time. King then led all night and by 278 miles had still got a lead of 6 mins. 20 miles later, Arnold had caught King and by the finishing circuit had 12 mins in hand. With just 26 mins left to run, Arnold 'over-cooked' a bend and crashed. He quickly remounted, grinning all over his face and thrashed on with a buckled wheel to record 419.26m beating King by 4 miles. King deserved full praise for his fight that improved his personal best to 415.05 miles, which ironically would have been another Competition Record if he had started 20 or more minutes in front of Arnold.

So for **John Arnold of the Middleton CC this was a new Competition record for a trike at 24hours of 419.26 miles.** The first of many heroic rides by him.

Newcomer Cliff Sandham finished 10th with 411.49m. Four years later he would gain honours by winning the Wessex 24hr. Vic Bone of the Mersey RC omitted the Aston detour at Whitchurch without authority, for that the **Mersey** Committee decided to exclude him from the **winning team** comprised of **Harry Okell 422.76m, J.P. Thomas 421.13m and Frank Mumford 407.72m.**

**Frank Cowsill** produced 404.78 for 13th place and in 1952 he teamed up with **Alec Denton** to break the **tandem End to End in 2 days 8hrs and 47 mins,** carrying on for the **1,000 miles record in 3 days 7hrs 41m.** So their 24hr time trialling had paid off as good training! Incidentally they are the only modern day (post 1929) riders to simply retrace at John o' Groats and ride back towards Inverness for the completion of their 1,000 miles.

⟹·◇·⟸

*On August 24th 1951 the Mau Mau rebellion began led by Kenyan nationalists. It was a terrorist war that Britain helped to quell by arresting Jo Mo Kenyatta on October 21st 1952.*

**The North Road 24hr** was again a very popular one even though it was a non championship event. Of the 65 finishers there were 32 riders who beat 400 miles; again both statistics were records. **A.E. Warden** of the Rapier CC **won with 442.375 miles** beating **T.W. Fensom,** Spalding CC on his local roads, riding to **440.25m. E.S. Ellingham,** Luton Wheelers was **3rd with 435.5m. The Luton Wheelers, consisting of Ellingham, Pain and Palmer won the team race with 1,253.875 miles. W.B. Noble, North Road CC won the trike race with 396.625m** - other than his success it had been an event of dashed hopes for the promoting club. Bob Mynott who was expecting to gain a hat-trick of wins, failed to start. Only days before he'd put up a gallant attempt on the RRA 24 hour record but didn't succeed. Alan Blackman for the club was expected to produce a good ride and up to the 400 miles mark was comfortably in the lead with Fensom and Warden shadowing him. Blackman suddenly lost the use of his arms and had to 'pack'. **Arthur Wilkins** was the best club finisher on a bicycle with **411.125m,** for the North Road CC.

During daylight hours the weather was bright and warm, but during the night it was very dark and a very strong wind rose to trouble the riders.

*The Catford History Book mentions that trams had now been removed from busy London streets, but it would be many years before the tramlines disappeared. Alf Muncey, a very popular member, was killed just days before Christmas from this hazard.*

## 1952

*February 6th 1952. King George V1 died peacefully at Sandringham. He had taken the throne when his brother Edward V111 abdicated in 1936. King George V1 and Queen Elizabeth, the Queen Mother, were popular with the general public for their care and concern shown in wartime, as was Winston Churchill.*

*We have been in a remarkable period of time, this last 17 years. A time that has seen the emergence of the **team race** and the mileage that a **man** can cover **in 24hrs riding unpaced** has risen well. From **Edgar Seeley** with **444.75m** in **1935** we've seen a steady increase after the war by riders such as **Gordon Basham, Eddie Mundy, Stan Butler, Bob Mynott, Gus Andrews, George Laws,** and again this year **1952, Eddie Mundy with 467.52m.**

*Before the war the **Unity CC** and the **Vegetarian C & AC** were vying for supremacy in the team race. Directly after the war it was the turn of the **North Road CC**. By 1949 the Team Competition Record was 1,284.19m held by the **Vegetarian C & AC**. By 1952 another team had emerged, the **Addiscombe CC**. They took **Competition Record** up three times to 1,361.94m.*

*In the later events, fields of **100 riders** are becoming quite common with as many as 35 riders beating 400 miles in each event. Up to 6 teams are also completing these rides. More coverage is now being given to these 24hr races throughout the year by the cycling press, with magazines such as 'Cycling' and 'The Bicycle' running stories and photos of these heroic riders, pushing the mileage boundaries, month after month, and now creating as much interest as the fastest 25, 50 or 100 mile events, probably more in fact.*

*Now that the trike battles have begun, they too have drawn readers eyes to their exploits, coupled with the 'Place to Place' records by Hercules Professionals, Eileen Sheridan and Ken Joy, this next few years looks a very interesting time for long distance racing.*

*We were blessed with four events this year, **The Wessex RC 24hr** was back on the calendar after a gap of 12 years, including the war years.*

*May 2nd 1952. Jet age travel was born today as the first De Havilland Comet Jet Airliner with 36 passengers on board, flew from London to Johannesburgh on the first scheduled jet flight.*

⇒◇⇐

**The Catford** was again the first event of the year, using roads south of London, starting at Pease Pottage and taking in Guildford, Horsham and Chichester. The event was won in fine style by a fairly new name in long distance racing, **George Laws** with **463.29m** not only a new name but also a **new Competition Record. 2nd place** was taken by **Reg Randall** of the Harlequins CC with **438.3 miles.** This was also the first time Reg's name or that of his club had taken any long distance honours. Reg was a short, stocky, powerful rider who would punch the pedals round very effectively, in contrast to other more fluid pedallers. His aggressive riding style obviously paid off and he usually went faster the further he rode. **Mike Aycliffe** of the Clarencourt CC was **3rd** with **436.3 miles. Gosport CC won the team race with 1230.85m, the team comprised of Harrison, 417.5m, Tribe, 407.8m and Ploughman 405.7m.**

Jock Wadley wrote a special report for the Catford Gazette and he mentioned that George Laws only made sure of beating Competition Record in the last hour. He'd lost 12mins earlier in the race due to punctures, but rallied strongly in his last two circuits. Jock went on to say that 10 days after the event he heard that J. Holland, Rodney CC, lost a great deal of time helping at the scene of a fatal motor cycle accident, but still finished with 384 miles.

Shortly after the 1952 season, George Laws disappeared from cycling club life completely after a recurring slipped disc problem and increased family commitments.

⇒◇⇐

*The floods at Lynton and Lynmouth caused death and destruction in this year.*

**The Wessex RC 24hr** that hadn't been run since 1939 was **won** by **Stan Harvey** of the Addiscombe CC with **441.4 miles.** The event was now a fully open one and traversed roads slightly more south and central than the WTTA had used. Ringwood and roads over the New Forest and Salisbury formed part of the course. Looking down the list of riders who finished this event shows they were nearly all from local areas. **D.R. Chalmers**, Bournemouth Arrow CC was **2nd** with **429.06m** and **S.T. Hollinrake**, Wessex RC was **3rd** with **423.2m leading a Wessex RC team win of 1,241.75 miles. L.J. Jones and C.W. Gannaway were the other team members with 411.875 and 406.650 miles respectively.** Bert Bishop of the Hampshire RC whose team came 2nd mentions their 3rd counting member F.G. Randall having a collapsed rear wheel at 50 miles into the event, and losing nearly an hour rebuilding it then carrying on to finish with 355.9 miles. Fifteen riders finished from nineteen.

On **July 28th Cowsill and Denton** started on their successful **End to End and 1,000 miles record** on a **tandem**.

**The Mersey RC 24hr** event was won by **P.E.A. 'Nick' Carter** of the South Lancs Road Club with **451.96 miles**, even after going off course for 4 miles.   **Arthur Turner** of the Warrington RC took **2nd** place with **436.59**, **Peter Duncan**, Vegetarian C & AC was **3rd** with **434 miles**.   This was Nick Carter's first foray into 24hr riding and what a start to his career, breaking course and event record by over 13 miles.   **Stan Lea** was **4th** overall with **431.4 miles**. **Harry Okell** was **5th** with **425.44m**.   He'd already won in 1948.

**Albert Crimes put over 3 miles onto John Arnold's trike Competition Record with 422.40 miles** and gained 6th place.   This was the 2nd time he'd broken competition record in this event, on roads that were local to him. Crimes and Arnold would eventually have their battle for trike 24hr supremacy in 1953 on these same roads. **Frank Mumford** rode to a fine **407.59 miles** followed by **Jack Duckers** with **404.81**.   Jack was one of the many riders who in later years could be found either marshalling or organising feeds in long distance events and record attempts in this area; attempts such as Crimes and Arnolds End to End in 1954.

**Warrington RC won the team race with 1,285.57m.   Turner, Lea and Bentham were the riders.   Alan Gordon** of the Solihull CC tied with **J.W. Stott** of the North Road CC in **402.92 miles**.

Cliff Bate had started this event as one of the favourites.   As usual he started fast and by 69 miles had pulled a 5 minutes lead on the main contenders, Carter, Russell and Lea.   It was very windy going up the coast road to Prestatyn this year and by the time the riders had got back to Queensferry, 164 miles, Carter was only 3 mins behind Bate.   Both riders were on an 'evens' ride (20 mph) and the battle had drawn them well ahead of the field, Lea was at 17 mins, Duncan 33m.

On the way back to Whitchurch the wind was favourable and Carter caught Bate.   At Shawbury, 240 miles, and still on 'evens', Carter looked strong, Bate was now 25mins adrift and unhappy.   At 327 miles Peter Duncan took over 2nd position, leaving Turner and Lea 15 mins behind him; by Redbrook, Bate had retired.

Carter was now nearly an hour ahead of the field, Turner really battled with Duncan and had pushed him into 3rd place by 380 miles.   Nick Carter reached the finishing circuit at Waverton Corner and promptly got sent off course by an unauthorised person, so losing approximately 4 miles, but he wasn't put off by this and continued to pound his way round the circuits and won the event by 25 miles.   A very worthy winner.

Carter went on to win this event three more times and also gained many placings over the years.   Peter Duncan went on to ride some pretty high mileages on bike and trike in 24hr events and eventually promoted the only Scottish 24hr time trial ever run, in 1967.   J.W. Stott broke many tandem trike records with Ed Tweddell around this time, in fact seven RRA records fell to them; 12hrs, London to York, London to Edinburgh, 24hr, Lands End to London, London to Bath and back, Pembroke to London plus many regional road records.   'Wilson' Stott was using the Mersey event to harden himself up for these journeys to come.

*John Arnold, Middleton CC, broke the RRA 'straight out' 24hour trike record this year, adding 43 miles on to Jack Rossiter's 19 year old record.   Arnold produced 428.5 miles, a record that was to last 13 years until Pat Kenny updated it by 3 miles in 1965, which included breaking the Edinburgh to London in 20 hrs 48 mins 52 secs on the way.   This record earned Pat a lot of praise and acknowledgement from John and many other trike men.*

**Tweddell and Stott broke the tandem trike RRA 24hr record around this time on a course based in Scotland, with a mileage of 412.5 miles.**

**This North Road CC event** in 1952 was known as **"The Cold 24".** It was a **National Championship this year,** and as such drew a huge full field of 100 riders. The weather was awful, it was cold, wet and a strong north easterly wind decimated the field to a mere 56 finishers. Using different variations over the years, this is a course that had been in use for nearly 70 years so far. It's based mainly on or around the Great North Road, the A1. It is very open and as its name implies the road runs south to north from London to Edinburgh.

Starting at Crosshall on the Northampton Road (A45) the course took in villages and towns such as Kimbolton, Brampton Hut, Thrapston, Wansford, Oundle, Eltisley, Ely, March, Wisbech, Long Sutton, Spalding, Market Deeping, Guyhirn, Peterborough, Cambridge, Eaton Socon, Tempsford and finally finishing on a circuit in the Girtford Bridge area. The roads that deviate off the A1 and into the Fen District in the east are running in a very unfavourable direction if there is any east or north east in the wind. If any bike rider reading these course details has traversed these roads, especially to Ely, Chatteris and Wisbech, then they will know what I am describing. The 'Fens' are dead flat and are sectioned into large square portions of land by drainage ditches, almost the size of rivers or canals, called dykes.

The roads tend to run straight for five miles or more, and then turn sharp left or right at 90 degrees and then carry on again, dead straight for miles and usually running alongside the dyke on a high exposed bank, making the wind unbearable on a bike if it's in the wrong direction. Riders have been known to get off and walk some of the more exposed sections for fear of being blown off the road. A lot of the land is below sea level and has been reclaimed by various schemes since the middle ages.

I digress, but felt that it was important to describe what the riders had to endure in conditions that are unique to this event.

"CANCELLED! Why has it been cancelled?"

Eddie Mundy rode steadily throughout the first 12 hours, so covering 237.5 miles. He was still lying in 2nd position behind Vin Callanan of the Norwood Paragon who was having a 'storming' ride. At the 18 hour point, Mundy had reduced his deficit to just 3 minutes and he soon caught Callanan and from that point on was clearly in a class of his own producing 230 for his second 12 hours.

What a ride, adding over 4 miles onto George Law's competition record set only a few weeks previously. So, a brand **new Competition Record for Mundy, Addiscombe CC,** yet again of **467.5 miles. Vin Callanan** also had a marvellous ride for his first try at a 24hr race, he finished with **459.04 miles. 'Gus' Andrews,** also of the **Addiscombe rode to 3rd place with 448.5m along with Stan Harvey at 445.19m, created another new Competition Record of 1,361.943 miles,** in hard conditions!

**J.H. Ward** of the Notts Castle CC was **4th** with **447.5 miles. Stuart Thompson,** Rutland CC who was **6th** with **444.870** is a name to watch for in the future, also the Rutland CC, a club from the Sheffield area. **The fastest trike was A. Ward,** Vegetarian C & AC with **384 miles.**

*I have no recollection of seeing Vin Callanan riding another 24hr, before or after this event, but I did notice he was in the Norwood Paragon Comp. Record breaking 12 hour team behind B.J. Brown and P.H. Kitchiner with 740.09 miles in 1948, so he did have some 'previous'! Another point of absolute coincidence is J.W. 'Wilson' Stott in this event, again tying with another rider P. Allpress of the Suffolk RC with 404.9 miles after doing exactly the same thing with Roy Gordon in the Mersey RC event just weeks previously.*

Stuart Thompson recalled at a later date, in a Fellowship Journal, as to just how hard the conditions were, and I've taken some observations from his writings.

After 100 miles the rest of the Rutland squad consisting of Benny Hudson, Joe Leversidge and Johnny Basnett had 'packed'. Stuart had a good first 12 hours, covering some 242 miles and putting him at the head of the field. The team were without any mobile help and because of the 'out and home' nature of the course it was not easy to get help. He remembers having a bag with a large currant loaf, cut and buttered, which was tied under his saddle, unfortunately spray from the rear wheel had reduced it to a somewhat doughy mess! As dawn broke over the fens with 300 miles covered, he turned onto the 'wilderness leg', a dead straight out and home, desolate stretch of road. Eddie Mundy was catching him and on the return trip the wind rose even more and Stuart became very cold. Mundy caught and dropped him very quickly. Thompson's legs went numb and stiff, he was so weary, but he plodded on hoping to get club record.

He said "Consciousness almost deserted me on several occasions when I found myself swerving on the wrong side of the road, but I managed to make it to the finishing circuit before sleep finally overcame me, and I fell from the bike into a deep ditch."

Stuart doesn't know how long he slept for, but vaguely remembers climbing back out of the ditch up to road level, and climbing wearily back on his bike with only an hour to go. He stumbled on; he had dropped from 2nd to 5th place in that time and finished with 444.870m, so breaking his club record by 10 miles. In spite of the very hard conditions 31 of the 56 finishers broke the 400mile barrier with 7 riders over 440m.

*The actual results are courtesy of Gordon Dennis and the North Road 'Gazette' with narrative from Stuart Thompson and myself.*

# 1953

On January 31st 1953 heavy flooding occurred in East Anglia and the South East Coast. Whereas in 1947 the flooding had been caused by melting snows, this latest tragedy was the result of heavy seas that were 10ft higher than normal. A total of 307 people lost their lives, with Canvey Island losing 58 souls. The heavy seas invaded the lower coastlines in the South Eastern areas, such as the Fen District, for miles inland. People died not only from drowning, but also from exposure and freezing conditions. Those same seas also invaded Holland where 1,800 lives were lost. The state of emergency lasted for more than two weeks.

*On April 25th 1953 the science of 'DNA' was established by British scientist, Francis Crick and American biologist, James Watson.*

**Edmund Hillary and Sherpa Tenzing conquer Everest just 4 days before Queen Elizabeth 11 is crowned on June 2nd.**

⋙◈⋘

**The Catford 24hr** is the first event this year, **Reg Randall,** Harlequins CC, riding only his second 24hr race was the **winner** out of a field of 57 finishers. Reg won by just over 3 miles with **457.86 miles** from **John Mortimer** of the Westerly RC with **454.55m. S.J. King,** Colchester Rovers was **3rd** with **447.380m** just beating **A.E. Wright** by nearly a mile into **4th** place. 82 riders started in this popular event.

**The Westerly RC won the team race with 1,293.6 miles, Mortimer was joined by R. Park 427.25m and G.H. Samuel with 411.76m.**

Out of 57 finishers, 37 riders beat 400 miles. *This is the largest amount of riders over 400 miles so far, that I can recall. This result is outstanding, and amazing to think that over 50 years later, for our one and only event left on the calendar, we can't always muster fields anywhere near the size of this non-championship Catford event of 1953. In fact the special millennium event in Year 2000 had 54 finishers and ok, Gethin Butlers 509 miles was a very high mileage, but there were only 5 riders in this special event who beat Reg Randall's mileage, and only 21 riders in total who beat 400 miles, compared with 37 in 1953. These certainly were 'the good old days'!*

*In June, Wyn Wrightson* set a new **Ladies Amateur 1,000 miles record** with **3 days 15 hrs 53 mins,** ridden on a star shaped course near her home in Gloucestershire. The roads she used were generally ones that the Western Time Trials Association 'WTTA' used for their 24hr and other time trials.

---

**The Wessex RC 24hr** was held on the 25th & 26th July, the same weekend as the Mersey RC Championship event, and subsequently suffered with a poor entry. **Don Chalmers,** Bournemouth Arrow, **won** the event with **428.08 miles,** just under a mile less than his 2nd place ride the previous year behind Harvey. **Roy Cook,** Salisbury RC was **2nd** with **420.5 miles** and **J. Trenowden,** Addiscombe CC was **3rd** with **419.25 miles.** Cook led the **Salisbury RC to a team win of 1,213.2 miles. L. Morgan, 402.6m and P. Leaney 390.09 making up the team.** 26 riders finished out of 37. Five trike riders contested the **Tricycle Trophy.** It was won by **R. Turner,** Doncaster Wheelers, with **389.2 miles.**

---

**The Mersey RC 24 hr on 25th & 26th July was an RTTC Championship event. This race ended with one of the most controversial results ever seen in a time trial, let alone a 24hr National Championship.**

The Saturday teatime start was very wet, but within the hour a spirited south westerly wind blew the clouds away to reveal a clear blue sky, but this was the only favour the wind did for the riders.

Albert Crimes, Crewe Wheelers, on a trike was off number 15. At 49 miles, Simcock of the North Shropshire Wheelers was just in front as Albert came through. John Arnold, Middleton CC also on a trike, off number 37, thundered past here very strongly and was already 8 mins up on Albert. These two top trike men were leading a 'star-studded' field that included Nick Carter, Eddie Mundy, Cliff Bate, Stan Harvey, Arthur Turner, Stuart Thompson and Stan Bray. John was out to catch Albert as early as possible, to establish an early lead. The first feeding station at 88 miles was manned by John (Jack) Williams and Alec Smith, who had won the first three Merseys' in succession. Charlie Davey of the Vegetarian C & AC called in for some milk to make up some vegetarian drinks for the 'lads' he was helping who I'm pretty sure were Mundy and Harvey of the Addiscombe CC . Carter was already 'up' on Mundy and Stan Harvey was already having problems with his bike.

The night was a fine one with a full moon just rising. The south-west wind was freshening as it passed over the Flintshire 'mountains'. Many of the club folk were manning the feeds and checkpoints wearing nothing more than shirts and shorts. Some of them had pitched small tents so that they could grab a couple of hours sleep before they rode down into Shropshire to take up duties the next day. Our next check point was at Shotton where the glare of the great steel works lit up the sky and area around. At 102 miles Crimes and Arnold were the first two on the road with 14mins between them, then Thompson at 5 mins, Carter and Mundy. Arthur Turner was in close contention with three bottles on his handlebars and a map of the course. Various bags and mussettes were lashed to the rest of his bike. (A mussette is a thin fabric bag with a long thin tape sewed onto it acting as a shoulder strap. The mussette is usually slung across the shoulders and worn on ones back to carry food. It is of French origin and used in the Tour de France).

Dave Threlkeld, a young Mersey RC member at that time, says he remembers riding out with the club to help. John Williams (the Elder) had a night-watchman's metal brazier strapped to the back of his bike, and one of the other riders had a sack of coke. They set up camp on the island at Prees and provided food and drink for the riders and marshals day and night.

Stuart Thompson was now first on the road at 6hrs 6mins, Carter at 2 mins, Arnold 6 mins, Turner 10mns, Crimes 15mns, Mundy 17minutes. The long ride up the Welsh coast road to Nant Hall, Prestatyn, was a real battle for Crimes and Arnold, and by the time they had turned and retraced towards Chester, John Arnold was just 5 mins in front of Crimes having taken 1hr 55mins for the 37 miles.

At the 200 mile point Carter had slipped past Thompson and was leading the race with 9hrs 52mins. Thompson was at 13mins; he was feeling the effects of the cool night although many of the helpers and marshals were still only dressed in shorts and a top. Cliff Bate had crept up into 3rd place followed by Mundy and Andrews. Arnold had punctured and had lost 10mins. By the next feeding station at 241 miles, Carter was on 'evens' but stopped for his breakfast. He was just on his cereals when Arnold came flying past to take the lead on the road. Crimes was the next to pull in and stop for breakfast. When told that Arnold had fled past without stopping for food, Albert muttered 'bugger him!' Thompson was last to stop having lost 15 miles 'off course' "no use rushing now" he said, tucking into his cereal.

The wind which had been a stiff breeze all night, was now bending the trees, although it didn't seem to bother Arnold at all, cornering beautifully, slipping into 83" gear for the easy bits and 73" for the slopes and out of the saddle for the real hills. Peter Barlow called out "How's it going John?" to which John replied thoughtfully and inquisitively " I don't really know". I don't think John realized at that time that he was gaining on Carter.

At the start of the finishing circuit, Carter's lead had come down to 13 mins with Arnold still chasing very hard. Everyone at the crossroads to the entrance of the circuit was looking at their stop watches to see the other riders positions on the road. The roar from the crowd "man up" was exciting, just to see who it was. (nowadays with mobile phones and an abundance of cars, there isn't that mystique as to who is coming through). The shout "Albert" heralded Crime's entry onto the circuit, weaving through the lines of club folk waiting to see their hero. Albert leant over his machine to take a bend, just to keep the wheel from lifting up, rather like a motorcyclist with a sidecar has to. His backside was nearly touching the tyre and his head skimmed the bushes.

Carter had felt happy that his few minutes lead over Arnold was enough, as surely with all the tight bends on the circuit, and there were many of them, **Arnold couldn't possibly stay with him at that speed.** But the country's **top trike man** was fighting that hard, he gained back 6 minutes in 3 hours riding to **finish with 457.33m to Carter's winning 459.48m. Mundy was 3rd with 448m.** And Crimes? he rode so powerfully but he knew he couldn't match that extra speed needed to redress the situation. **Crimes** finished with **425 miles, a 2.5 mile improvement** on his own 1952 Competition record. **Although actually timed as 2nd placed rider, Arnold was unplaced in the incorporated RTTC National Championships, which was open said the rules, only to riders of bicycles!**

The club world's indignation on learning this, was only soothed by the decision of the RTTC to make a special presentation to John Arnold at the 'BBAR' Champions concert in the Royal Albert Hall, London   At the next National Council meeting, delegates voted that tricyclists would be eligible for future National Championships and the BBAR competition, should the situation ever arise again.

So **Eddie Mundy** took the **silver medal** with **448.02 miles** and **bronze** went to **Arthur Turner** with **445.50m. Stan Harvey 5th** with **435.37m, Stuart Thompson, 433.91, R. Balance, 433.32, Cliff Bate, 430.36, Alec Denton 429.81** and **Stan Bray** was **10th** with **426.22m.
South Lancs RC won the team race with 1,301.51m. P.J. Bates** with **415.67** making the **3rd team member.**

A word of explanation is needed here I think, for the reader who has never ridden a trike and who may not have realised that it is possibly as much as 10% slower than a bike, with three points of contact on the road and generally 3 kilos heavier than a bike. Being harder to steer makes it difficult to ride with one hand, even on a flat road. Cambers on a road tend to throw the rider towards the verge, but then T.A. (Tricycle Association) members wouldn't have it any other way!

A lot of this race information came from Jock Wadley's report in 'Cycling' and in Alf Arnold's description of John's rides throughout his career. Alf who was John's brother was present at virtually all of his major races and records. His help as a driver, mechanic, feeder, marshal and advisor was paramount to John and Albert and indeed to many long distance record breakers at that time; Dave Duffield and Arthur Render to name but two more.

The pinnacle of Crimes and Arnold's efforts was the combined 12 hour, 24hr, End to End and 1,000 miles (4 in 1) record on the tandem trike in 1954.  **Albert and John were the two most talented trike riders in history, performing feats of speed and endurance that were 40 years ahead of time.**

Stuart Thompson of the Rutland CC who went off course in this 24hr event for about 15 miles and losing nearly an hour, said he wanted to carry on to the end, just to see how the battle between Carter and Arnold finished up. It was a thrill to see one of the greatest rides of all times!

**John Arnold added nearly 35 miles onto Competition Record that day.  It took another 19 years to add on just another half a mile in 1972, with another epic ride by Eric Tremaine.**

***On July 27th 1953 Edith Atkins set out from Lands End to become the first amateur lady rider to break the End to End.***  *It was a record held by Marguerite Wilson, a professional.  Edie took 4 hrs 48 mins off Miss Wilson's 1939 record with* **2 days 18 hrs 4 mins.**  *Her toes were still sore from raising the 24hr record to 422 miles a few weeks earlier!*

&gt;—&loz;—&lt;

In the **North Road 24hr** event one month later, **Stuart 'Joe' Thompson** who had missed bronze or possibly silver medal in the Mersey Championship by going off course, was vindicated by **winning** his first North Road CC 24hr with **449.80m.**   Thompson was a lone rider from the Rutland CC.  **2nd** placed was **Tom Fensom,** Spalding CC with **445.65m.**   **3rd** was **R. O'Dell** with **439.01m,** another lone rider from the Luton Wheelers, in fact the first four riders hadn't got team support.  **Alan Fowler** was the **fastest trike** rider with **392.125m,** leading **Harold Bridge** with **380.875m on a bike** and **Wilson Stott on a trike** with **378.25m** to a **North Road Team win of 1,151.3 miles.**

Alan's winning trike mileage was the third best ever in this event, and later he teamed up with Roy Cook and broke the London to York tandem trike record with 9 hrs 9 mins.   Stuart Thompson, the winner, said that the race was a 'see-saw' battle between him and Tom Fensom right from the start, passing each other 5 or 6 times before managing to wear Tom down just before the finishing circuit and win his first 24 hour.

"Youth triumphs over experience" proclaimed the caption in the North Road Gazette, but only after a prolonged struggle where Fensom led at the 12 hrs point with 238 miles to Thompson's 234m, but on the long run south from Rippingale in the early hours of Sunday morning, the position was reversed.   An absorbing duel ensued until the Rutland CC man steadily forged ahead to win.

# 1954

*On May 6th 1954 the first sub 4 minute mile was run by Roger Bannister.*

*On July 3rd all rationing finally officially finished.*

*Flashing indicators became a legal requirement this year.*

**The Catford CC 24 hrs** was again the first 24hr event of the year.  It was **won in fine style by Reg Randall,** of the Harlequins CC for the 2nd year running, with a mileage of **453.35m.**   In **2nd** place was **E.W. Crawley,** Kentish Whls with **439.30m** and 3rd was **P.J. Tester,** Redhill CC **433.95m.**   The fastest team was the **Balham CC with 1,239.6m** consisting of **F.C. Syred, 427.31m, D.A. McCowan, 409.95,** and **C.H. Press, 402.3 miles.**

Reg Randall was proving to be a regular 'stayer', this being his 2nd win in this event and only his 3rd 24hr.   At 29 years of age he was building himself up for greater feats of endurance to come.   He was primarily a long distance tourist at heart.   He always thanked the marshals at the same time as he called his number out.   Reg valued highly, anybody who helped him in his racing or long distance records.

As I look down at this Catford result sheet of 51 riders, I see about 95% of the field are from London and the Home Counties.  Sadly a lot of the clubs listed are no longer in existence, clubs such as Oval CC, Watford CC, Balham CC, London Clarion.   **The South Eastern RC created the first recognised trike 24hr competition record team with 1,054.30m.**   **D.G. Ivey, A.J. Waller and L.G. Smalden were the team members.**

The Wessex 24hr in July 1954 was a **National Championship** with 44 riders entered.   **Stuart Thompson,** Rutland CC, **had a terrific win with a new Competition Record of 469.66miles.**  After his disappointment of going off course in 1953's Mersey Championship event when in contention for the title, this win more than made up for it. He also beat a very strong field for this victory and it also proved that the Wessex RC course and event on the right day is as good and as fast as any in the country.   **Arthur Turner** took silver and **2nd** place with **457.807m.   Stan King** was **3rd** by only .057 of a mile with **457.750m.   Gus Andrews** with **455.882** led the Addiscombe CC to a **very high mileage team win of 1,357.498,** just missing comp record by 5 miles.  **Eddie Mundy** was the **2nd** team member with **453.802** and **5th** overall.   **Stan Harvey** completed the team with **447.814m.   A.G. Ramsey,** Hounslow and District CC was **6th** with **453.152.     Reg Randall,** Harlequins CC was riding his 2nd 24 hour of the year and his 4th in total to finish with **447.466.**

Competition Record mileage keeps getting nudged up higher and higher almost year upon year, with everyone wondering "can it get any higher, is 480 miles (20 mph) a possibility?"

This tall lean 25 year old Rutland CC rider from Sheffield, a draughtsman by trade, rode multiple gears and used his top gear of 92" to good advantage.  'Joe' to his fellow club mates who said he never looked happy even when he was winning.  This was his 4th 24hr and his 3rd win.  Thompson rode the first 18 hours at 'evens' pace as did Nick Carter, but the relentless cold rain from then on ruined Carter's ride, and at 390 miles he collapsed unable to go on.   After this departure, Thompson got stronger and stormed away to win.   Stan King and Arthur Turner had a terrific battle on the road for medal places.   King, who had been in 2nd place for the last few hours, was pipped at the end by Turner.

Thompson recalled that he'd chatted to Nick Carter earlier in the season and they both agreed to see who would be the 'best man' in the Wessex!   After some of the early 'fliers' had shot their bolt, Carter and Thompson were well out in front of the field and Carter had taken the lead.   Thompson had taken a spill on the wet roads and the gap increased to 15 minutes; try as he might, he couldn't catch him back.   At about 350 miles when Thompson was making a quick time check on Nick, he realised he was only a minute down and that Nick had lost 13 mins on him.  "Its all yours Joe" he shouted.   A minute or two later, Nick Carter climbed off his bike; he was locked up badly with cramp and retired, leaving Thompson to get his Competition Record win.

Before I continue with the History of the 24 Hour, I will include here a brief account of the two most extraordinary feats of endurance to enhance the list of long distance riding and record breaking so far in the 20th Century.   They both happened literally just over a week or so before the Mersey RC 24hr in 1954.

**Friday 9th July saw Eileen Sheridan,** a petite Coventry housewife, start out on the longest, most demanding cycle race of her life, the **Lands End to John o' Groats record, and carrying on for the 1,000 miles.**  Eileen, now a Professional riding for **Hercules Cycles** rode very strongly up through the West Country, reaching Worcester in 14 hours.  Here she was 36 minutes faster than Sid Ferris had been.   Whitchurch and 323 miles was reached at 3.37am and Preston at 7.08am.  On through Lancaster, Kendal and just before Shap was climbed, she broke a gear cable and changed bikes.   Eileen rode Shap on a 72" gear, reaching the summit having completed **432 miles in 24 hrs.**

**This was the furthest anyone had travelled on the End to End route in 24 hours,** covering a mile more than the Australian Professional, Hubert Opperman's distance in 1934.   At Carlisle with 470 miles ridden in 27 hours, Eileen took her first break, suffering from the cold and fatigue.  After a change to warmer clothing she climbed to Beattock Summit with icy rain battering her from all directions.   At Perth she took on lights and extra clothing for the 2nd night through the cold 'Grampians'; dawn broke to a freezing cold morning.
At Dalwhinnie with 673 miles covered she took her second break.   After a short sleep and some hot food, Eileen continued with her assault on the Cairngorms to reach Inverness at 9.00am in brilliant sunshine.   She had beaten a coach load of tourists who had seen her a day earlier back in England.   They were amazed at her progress.

Aultnamain mountain was climbed and then a hair-raising descent to the flatter coast road, but with the climbs onto the 'Ord of Caithness' still to come it wasn't over yet.   Helmsdale and Berriedale Hills were climbed, so reaching **John o' Groats** just before nightfall, having taken **2 days 11 hours 7 mins,** breaking Edith Atkins' amateur record by 6hrs 57mins.

After nearly 2 hours sleep, Eileen climbed wearily back onto her bike and rode back out into the cold dark third night.   She suffered hallucinations from sleep deprivation, hypothermia and exhaustion and **completed her 1,000 mile journey** next morning at 11am, in **3 days 1 hour.**  What an achievement!

**This 1,000 mile record would stand for nearly 49 years.**

Just two hours later back at John o' Groats, **the tandem trike record breakers, Crimes and Arnold,** sped over the finish line outside the hotel.   **They had broken no less than 3 records up to this point.  The 12 hour, 257.745m,** getting them just south of Worcester, then hammering through the first night for the **24 hour record of 466.25 miles.**   Despite mechanical problems, even more serious were Albert's stomach problems, bouts of severe pain for which they lost 1.5 hours, worth at least 30 miles.   So could 490m or even 500m have been attained in 24 hours?

Albert suffered two lots of severe pain, but nevertheless they reached **John o' Groats in 2 days, 4 hrs, 26 mins, the fastest of any men on any machines over this route so far in history.**   It would be four years before Dave Keeler reduced their time by 1hr 15mins in 1958, on a bike.

After a short break and a chat to Eileen and her team, they carried on for the 1,000 miles, roughly another 130 miles.     The first 100 miles from the hotel was covered in 4hrs 15mins such was their speed on those roads around Caithness, Castletown, Wick and Thurso.   They finished at one minute to 11pm, just going into the 3rd night with the **fastest End to End and 1,000 miles time ever.   The 1,000 miles time was 2 days 13 hours 59 minutes.**

Jock Wadley, who was a travelling reporter for 'Cycling' at the time, covering both Eileen's and Crimes and Arnold's records over this period of 4 days, caught an express train back from the Scottish borders after seeing Eileen. He described the steam locomotive thundering along and "roaring at near 100 mph down the 'Shap' slopes," enabling Jock to pick up the tandem trike entourage as they came up through Lancashire on the A6.   Jock said at the end of his article that "Albert and John had cornered so fast at the end of their 1,000 miles record, he felt that they must fall, but Albert and John didn't fall, and neither, I think, will the four records they achieved!"

*I felt that these magnificent rides had to be recorded here although they can also be found in more detail along with 45 more End to End and 1,000 mile record rides, in my book "The End to End Story" published in 2005, covering a period from 1929 to present day.*

Over the years, John Arnold had always suffered severely with his feet and in 24hr races they swelled up very badly. Years later he told me that he had arthritic problems in and around the years of his record breaking career, he even resorted to riding in clogs which were bolted to his pedals to alleviate his discomfort.  He recalled that even on the day of his End to End he remembers finding it impossible to walk more than 10 yards without sitting down to ease the pain in his feet.   At the guesthouse where he and Albert stayed, John recalled trying to stand and have a wash and then having to rest on the side of the bath, with Albert laughing and saying how could they be attempting the End to End when John couldn't even stand up!

<hr>

Despite this physical condition, **John, two weeks after breaking the records, went on to win the Mersey RC 24hr with 466.73 on a bike this time.** He was probably   **riding** high on the 'euphoria' most riders seem to get after completing something as tough as the End to End where your brain tells you that after riding for nearly three days non-stop, what is a mere 24hr going to do to you?  He beat **Stan Bray,** Solihull CC who recorded a personal best up to this point with **442.84m** and **3rd** was **Alec Denton,** Lancs RC with **441.76 miles,** a personal best ever for him. **Peter Duncan in 4th place with 440.90 miles won the trike championship from nine other trikes.**

Duncan's ride ranks alongside those of Crimes, Arnold, Tremaine and Jackson, and at that time it was actually the 2nd greatest ever after Arnolds'. **Harold Nelson** rode that day; I've noticed his name in various events. He finished with **357.01m** riding for the Royal Oak CC. Harold Nelson went on in later years to be the main feeding organiser for the Mersey RC event covering a period of some 40 years. He was also a physio, a masseur and trainer. He taught many people the art of massage in sport and was also instrumental in Eric Matthews successes, especially his 24hr rides and wins. Harold Nelson was later awarded a B.E.M. for his work and contributions to sport.

**The team race** was won by the **Merseyside Wheelers,** the team consisted of **three trike riders. L. Thomason, A.G. Russell and S.D. Wallace** with a total distance of **965.19 miles. J.J. 'Jim' Hutton** of the Speedwell BC with **381.94,** who beat Harold Nelson by one place on the result sheet, was probably better known in 'MRRA' circles as a long distance Midlands Road Record breaker. I broke his Birmingham to York and back record by 33 minutes in 1982, but his ride had been undertaken just after the Second World War in 1946, without the aid of dual carriageways and a following car. I also attacked his Birmingham to Holyhead and back record of 16hrs 56mins but failed. Needless to say, I have the greatest respect for Jim and indeed all of the record breakers whether at regional or national level.

⇒•◇•⇐

*At the very end of* **July 1954, Ken Joy,** *set out from Lands End hoping to break the 'End to End' record that had been held by Sid Ferris since 1937. Ken was a professional for Hercules Cycles and had enjoyed a very successful amateur time trial career winning the BBAR four years running from 1949. The End to End was always the natural progression for any aspiring Professional and he was also attacking Cyril Hepplestons 24hr record en route.*

*He started very fast and completed his first 50 miles in 2 hrs amidst showers and sunshine. He crashed on a slippery hairpin bend at Launceston but remounted. There were no town or city bypasses of any use to a cyclist on that route at that time. The first 100 went by in 4hrs 18mins. He reached Bristol in 8hrs 36mins, his second 100 took 4hrs 32mins and he ran out his 12 hours in the Bridgnorth area with 271 miles.*

*The temperature dropped drastically overnight as he passed through the Lake District, still nearly an hour up on schedule. At Lancaster the 400 miles had taken him 19hrs 32 mins. He suffered sickness and couldn't keep warm, it was now not only cold but very wet. He got beyond Carlisle in* **24hrs** *and retired exhausted at* **475 miles,** *adding 8 miles onto Heppleston's record.*

⇒•◇•⇐

**The North Road CC 24hr** on the 11th and 12th September saw **Stuart Thompson, Rutland CC win his 2nd 24hr in 2 months with 456.630 miles. Alan Blackman,** North Road CC came **2nd** with **451.70m** and **Tony Fouldes,** another Rutland man, came **3rd** with **447.5 miles.**

**Blackman led Geoff Edwards, 429.875m and Ken Davis with 422.9 miles to a North Road Team win with 1,304.5 miles. A.E. Moggridge was the best trike rider with 398.875 m.**

A bumper field of eighty entries was reduced to 45 by the end. At the 100 mile point, Blackman had led Thompson by 6 mins in 4hrs 40 mins. A violent storm during the afternoon proved a trial for a lot of riders, but Blackman's 12 hour of 240m looked to be setting a seal on the race, but he hadn't reckoned on Thompson's aggressive riding and slipped away to 2nd place.

Stuart Thompson recalled that he had painful memories of that event. "Looking back, I was fortunate enough to win this event, so many times was I near to packing, everything seemed to go wrong.

I started the event with a large abscess in the most inconvenient place, the relic of a very bad season and it was in trying to ease the pressure that caused agonising backache in the later stages, coupled with this, I suffered punctures at 50 and 100 miles causing a loss of over 20 minutes. These things put me in a dejected state of mind, only tempered when I gradually forged ahead to win a duel with Alan Blackman for the lead. Tony Fouldes, who finished third, is perhaps the toughest and most determined rider I know.

## 1955

The Catford 24hr on July 2nd 1955 was a **National Championship event** and as such drew a magnificent field of 100 riders, made up from some of the top long distance men in the country. **Ken Price** of the Cardiff 100 mile RC, a new name in 24hr racing **won** the event with **478.55 miles, a new Competition Record. Stuart Thompson** of the Rutland CC rode into **2nd** place with **474.120m, breaking Competition Record** himself by way of starting in front of Ken Price, who was No 91 from a field of 100 men. This was **Thompson's second Comp Record,** having previously broken it in the Wessex event of 1954.

**The Rutland had at last mustered a fine team of riders, Ron Coukham took bronze with 462.05m and Tony Fouldes came overall 4th with 460.950 to give a new Competition Record Team mileage of 1,397.**13m adding 35 miles onto the Addiscombe record of 1952. Both Ron Coukham and Ken Price were 'novice' riders. Kens' only 'previous' was having won two 12hr time trials in South Wales, both were Championship events.

The start in the lane at Pease Pottage was a hustling, bustling hive of activity. There were lots of different accents with riders from the Provincial regions. There was a strong Welsh contingency to see and help Ken Price; Lancashire was represented by Nick Carter and his team; Len Jenkins from the Rhondda Valley, the Rutland team and helpers; so different from last years field of mainly London and Home Counties riders.

Nick Carter who had experimented all winter with riding multiple gears, decided two weeks before the event to go back to riding a fixed wheel gear. Ken Price hadn't done any specific long distance training for the event and was suffering with a head cold, not ideal for a 24hr ride. The last man off was Reg Randall, a position always given to the winner of the previous years event.

The Steyning turn at 90 miles saw Price in the lead and pulling away from Thompson, Blackman and Carter were 'looking good' at this stage, although Carter was suffering from stomach trouble which was to last until the end of the event. Arthur Turner looked happy as usual even though he had suffered a puncture earlier on. The 'Rutlanders' team were all moving very well, and at 90 miles were leading the team race by 23 minutes from the 'North Roaders'.

At 6.5 hours Price led Thompson by just one minute with Pat Wright of the Redmon CC 12 minutes behind Thompson. The leaders and most of the main field were now down in the Selsey and West Wittering area, their helpers were usually found on the Chichester by-pass as it gets to nightfall. Extra clothing and lights are called for and quite a crowd gathers as the riders 'come in' to where their respective helpers are stationed. One of the old riders, Tom Hubbard, who rode the first 'Catford' in 1925, turned up and predicted, as he did every year, that he felt that a winning ride of 444 miles would be the outcome due to the north west wind that had been troubling the riders from the start, but his predictions were a long way out, the weather was now changing, the wind had dropped and there was a full moon rising.

At 160 miles Price had still got the lead from Thompson and was nearly 30 minutes inside 'evens'. Later, on crossing the traffic lights to turn towards Fareham, Price stopped for a pullover and when asked why he had now dropped behind Thompson, he replied that he had to stop for food, as he couldn't eat while riding because of his head cold. Jack Spackman wasn't in so much of a hurry as these youngsters. He stopped and turned the water tap on his enormous carbide lamp, ready to light up further along the road. Geoff Guy missed the Fareham detour and retraced to Arundel. The teams of helpers were now waiting in anticipation for their riders to return from Fareham. Some had got campfires burning on the grass verges with flashing beacons for their riders to pick them out.

Jenkins was first man back, but lost his lead on the road almost immediately by stopping to fix his rear lamp. Ron Coukham flashed by, he was now the 'pathfinder' for those who were riding the full course. Price and Thompson were still almost neck and neck. Reg Randall was riding steadily into 4th place behind Tony Fouldes.

The speed of the riders this year meant that most of them were arriving at various strategic timing points much earlier than other years. Fred Churchill who was to drive Alan Gordon the timekeeper to Billingshurst, further up the course, muttered "I know they're all up on schedule this year" to which Gordon agreed, pulling out last years check sheets to confirm this. "I don't need to see that", said Fred, "I go by the pub closing time!" The Roman Gate check on the way back from Guildford was at the 246 miles point and was a good check to see what riders were doing for their 12hr mileages. In the case of Thompson he came through with exactly 10 seconds to spare. Price at this point had a comfortable lead of over 6 minutes, so his estimated 12 hour mileage was nearly 249 miles. The next stretch of 16.75miles that took in Codmore Hill, had everyone struggling. Thompson took 56 minutes while most people were outside the hour.

Back at Guildford, the streaks of daylight were showing at 5am. George Hunton, another distinguished timekeeper who timed John Woodburn's End to End at a later date, and indeed many RRA records in his lifetime, was stationed here. We found out that Arthur Turner had collided with an inebriated jay-walker in Arundel and had sustained a badly cut eye and head, but he was still happy despite having to pack. Peter Bate stopped to help him and lost so much time, he too abandoned his ride. The South Lancs RC team of helpers had been looking after Turner, of the Warrington RC, like he was one of their own riders, such is the camaraderie of long distance cyclists and their helpers.

Bill Brown was one of the bystanders, he'd broken a pedal at 200 miles and had to retire saying "I'll be back next year". He will be 60 next year. Another Welshman was with Bill, a lad from the 'Acme Wheelers' in the Rhondda Valley. Bill told us he'd ridden over from Wales in 2 days with this young Len Jenkins who was now riding so well at the head of the field. Jenkins was a coal miner and working in the famous Nant-Garw Pit and it was his first 24hr, but he had twice finished 2nd to Ken Price in South Wales Championship 12 hour races.

The Kentish Wheelers had lots of helping cars but only two riders left to feed as Joe Crawley had pulled out at 90 miles with an attack of malaria. At Windsor Island, Coukham was holding off Thompson and Jenkins. With Price showing no signs of cracking there was much talk of a 480 miles ride being a possibility. The riders were now on their way back to Guildford towards the Crawley area and to the finishing circuit. Thompson was the first man to enter just ahead of team mate Coukham.

The timekeepers were briefed as to the riders performances from their checking cards, they then took up their positions around the circuit. Price's first lap took 58 mins for the 17.6 miles, his next lap was 5 mins faster. Thompson had to stop and blow his tyre up which added to his worries, young Coukham on the other hand was revelling in the situations, he re-caught and dropped Thompson, who I am told never looks very happy on a bike.

Hurried arrangements were being made by the Organisers to 'follow out' the leading riders who were likely to break Competition Record, or win. So not only the two leaders but also Coukham and Randall would have to leave the circuit at 458.75 miles as RTTC rules forbade the circuit to be covered more than 4 times. They would have to be followed independently by car to Crawley and beyond, towards Brighton. Coukham was first off the circuit with 20 mins to go, then Thompson, with 57 mins, Price with 69 mins. Fouldes and Randall also had to be followed out and stopped at their 24hr point.

To beat 480m Price had to ride the next 25 miles in 1hr 12 mins, which sounds easy enough if you are fresh, but he had the problem of negotiating Crawley and getting onto the Brighton Road, then retrace at Woodlatch back into a stiff wind. First of all he passed Coukham, being congratulated at 462 miles, then Thompson's finishing spot, where he got a rousing cheer from the Rutland Team. **Price** finished his ride, stylish pedalling to the end, just missing evens with **478.55m,** a wonderful **Competition Record win.** Arch Harding who helped in a Middlesex-Welsh squad bought Ken a very welcome pint to round off his remarkable ride. What a wonderful weekend, **3 Competition Records, Ken Price, Stuart Thompson and the Rutland Team** win. This was the first of their five Championship Team wins from 1955 to 1959 and ended the 4 out of 5 team wins the Addiscombe had powered to in five years.

*A lot of this information was taken from an article by Jock Wadley which appeared in the 24hr Fellowship Journal. Jock, who covered the Tour de France every year for the Cycling Press, took up training for a 24hr at a very late age, and fulfilled his ambition with 397 miles in 1972.*

**The Wessex RC 24hr** 1955, was **won** by **Cliff Sandham,** Maryport CC with **443.57 miles.** A.R. **Chamberlain,** Hounslow and District Wheelers, was **2nd** with **442m** and **Roy Cook,** Salisbury RC was **3rd** with **440.68.** **Cook led Len Morgan, 408.75** and **P.G. Leaney, 392.5m** to a Salisbury RC team win with **1,241.93m. Ed Tweddell was the fastest trike rider with 390.34m.** An interesting article appeared in the Fellowship Journal in the year 2000, entitled "The Wessex Ghost", written by Ronald Smith of the Actonia CC, one of the old 24hr riders.

*I had just left the Cadnam roundabout going towards Lyndhurst, Lymington, Ringwood, Wimborne and Upton when suddenly I saw a light in the road, then a front wheel and heard the whirr of tyres. I was not surprised to be caught by a better rider, as this happened quite often and they regularly gave us slower riders words of encouragement. The passing rider asked "how far to the all night feeding station?" I quickly calculated the mileage via the towns on route and replied "about 38 miles I should say". The rider said "thanks" and then suddenly disappeared. The light from his lamp went. There was no sign of his wheel and no sound from his tyres – all gone. I slowed right down and looked all around. There was no side road, footpath or track, or even a gate to a meadow – just nowhere to go. I was really unnerved for a time, and it was a few miles before I recovered from this experience.*

*Later in the event I retired and ended up helping to marshal the riders towards the finishing circuit. Much later on when the event was over, I was having a meal at the café where other riders had stayed overnight. From a group of riders at the table opposite, I heard a Middlesex Clarion rider telling the other three the same story as the episode I'd experienced the previous night. The location was exactly the same and the Middlesex mans answer of "about 38 miles, I should say" was uncanny. Needless to say, his passing rider said "thanks" and disappeared completely. I then told them that the same thing had happened to me at exactly the same location.*

*Since those days, my wife Margaret and I have cycled past that same spot on holidays, and just a few years ago everything looked exactly the same as that moonlit night in July 1955"*

Ron went on to say that he never did get round to contacting the Wessex RC or anyone else about his experience and also wished that he had contacted the Fellowship earlier. At 84years of age in year 2000, he asked if anyone riding the Wessex RC 24hr since then has had a similar experience? Had a rider been killed at that spot, then to have his spirit return and ask "How far to the all-night feeding station?"

---

**The Mersey RC 24hr** on 23rd and 24th July 1955 saw David Stapleton the Organiser and Secretary have a very busy build up to the event, with a three week old son to contend with and course alterations at the last minute, all added to his worries. There was also the fact that the event may be a slightly lack-lustre one.

Nick Carter had won in 1952 producing a new course and event record, then in 1953 he won again. The event had been a Championship one and Carter had been chased by Arnold on the trike, creating controversy on the status of a trike with John Arnold coming second and having no Championship medal. Then in 1954, Arnold showed what he could do on a bike, winning the event and raising the **course record to 466.73 miles.** So what could 1955 possibly bring? A lot of the big hitters had ridden the Catford championship a couple of weeks earlier and were absent. Crimes and Arnold had by now done it all especially after their epic records. They were out helping around the course as you would expect, but Dave Stapleton needn't have worried. The event was a success for him, the club and the riders.

First of all the weather was near perfect, no rain or strong wind, a dark night but not cold, a dull Sunday morning and a dry sunny finish, but not too hot. Every rider in this event got a medal, either a bronze or a silver, according to their performances. 360 miles or more on a trike or 400 plus on a bike, won you a silver medal; 320 to 360 on a trike or 360 to 399 miles on a bike, won a bronze.

*It would be another nine years before Eric Matthews was presented with a Gold Mersey RC medal for beating 480 miles. He did so handsomely, with a new Competition Record ride of 490.03 miles.*

The riders started in beautiful sunshine, Cliff Bate failed to start making it easier for either Carter, Render or Bray to get top three possibly.    By the eighty mile point at Parkgate Island (Chester) Nick Carter was fastest by 8 minutes from Holt of the Eckington Wheelers, then Stan Bray at 9 mins and Arthur Render at 10 mins.    There was a new feed this year at the Two Mills Café, courtesy of Mr Donelly.    Up until this point in time, Miss Lloyd at Great Sutton had provided a feeding station which was manned by John Williams (the elder) and his wife, but sadly Miss Lloyd had passed away.

An optional detour controlled by Tommy Barlow at Saltney sent the faster riders to Marford and back.    At 119 miles the positions here were, Carter 5hrs 41 mins, Bray at 19 mins, Holt, Gaskell and Duncan (trike) all at 21 mins, together with Heald, Astall, Render, Shuttleworth and Cowling.    These were all of the leaders on time here.    The course went through Flint, Mostyn and along the coast road to 'Nant Hall', Prestatyn, to turn and retrace, a round trip of 37.75 miles.    The traffic along here was heavy, even in this day and age, getting worse with holiday camps and caravan sites along the coast.    Motorists on a night out to Chester were dazzling the riders with their headlights.

Back at Queensferry Island, 169 miles, and Carter was still in command with 8hrs 12mins, Bray at 26 mins, and Duncan had crept into 3rd place at 30 mins.    On the long ride to Whitchurch, Carter hit something in the road and took a tumble, but got back on unhurt.    Peter Duncan on his trike was holding his own with the bikes on this stretch and it looked likely that he would do a very good ride.    Arthur Render moved up in the positions along here and so did Heald.    At Whitchurch, Carter was now 31 mins ahead of the field with Stan Bray 2nd.

After an optional detour to Nantwich and back, the riders continued south to 'Battlefield' near Shrewsbury, an apt name, but this battlefield was named after a famous old battle.

*Sir Henry Percy, known a 'Harry Hotspur', was killed in battle near Shrewsbury while trying to overthrow King Henry 1V, this took place here in 1403.*

This is the 12hr point for the faster riders and they arrive usually in daylight.    Carter was just inside 'evens' here with 11hrs 55mins, Bray was at 36 mins, Duncan 42mins and Render 44mins.    The riders go to Hodnet and then either detour to Shawbirch, Telford (Wellington in those days) and return, or they work their way via Tern Hill, Prees and Wem back to the finishing circuit.    If there is any fear that a rider may not be going fast enough, he will be got away from the Shropshire border by 11.00am.    The riders doing the full course will be sent via Wem and 'Redbrook Pump', Bangor on Dee, and then retraced to the finishing circuit.    At Redbrook Pump, 353 miles, Carter had a massive lead of 48 mins over Bray with Render at 62 mins.    Duncan was now out of the picture, having fallen asleep on the roadside at about 310 miles.    It's a pity as he was well on his way to a personal best.

The Bangor on Dee small section, although lumpy, is an interesting stretch and isn't really as hard as everyone thinks, the trike riders in previous years have always had good 'scraps' on this section.    Bray was still holding second place and on to a 'p.b.' ride, Render was 3rd but very tired.    The riders now gritted their teeth and headed for the finishing circuit at Waverton, in perfect conditions.    Carter arrived at 2.38pm with time to set up a new course record, if he kept the pressure up.    Bray came on at 3.19 pm and 3rd place would have been between Les Heald and Arthur Render after battling it out on the way to the circuit.    Render won the battle and arrived first.    Carter stopped for refreshment on his second lap and lost a lot of time, 6 minutes in fact, which actually cost him the course record that Arnold held.    He failed by two miles.    In the absence of Duncan, Dave Duffield was easily the fastest trike, finishing with 414 miles and Ed Green on a trike as usual, produced his best ever mileage to win a silver medal. I can imagine Dave Duffield just about to pass Ed Green and saying "permission to pass, Mr President?" as Ed was the top man in the T.A. (Tricycle Association).

**Nick Carter** won in fine style, his third win in this event with a superb **464.65 miles, Stan Bray** was **2nd** with **449.24** and **Arthur Render** was **3rd** with **439.87 miles** in his first ever 24hr; what a ride.    **The South Lancs RC won the team race with 1,328.30; Heald** with **438.17m** and **Tyson 425.48m** completed the team along with Carter, making a record mileage for this event.

It's very interesting to note that four prominent riders in this event went on to gain National RRA Records. Heald and Tyson took the Liverpool to Edinburgh tandem record with 9hrs 21 mins in this same year, 1955. Dave Duffield broke the trike 1,000m with 3days 12hours 15mins in 1956, and then went a year later from John o' Groats to Lands End in 2 days 20 hrs 9 mins, the first and only person to ride from North to South in record time.

**Arthur Render** went on two weeks later to produce **427 miles** in the **North Road 24hr.** He was using the two events this year as a build up for his attempt on the **1,000 miles Bicycle record** which he broke in 1956 with **2 days 16hrs 50 mins.**

*As I put the finishing touches to this race report in 2007, a report may I add that was originally penned by Dave Stapleton, I learn the sad news of his death at 93. I spoke to him only recently at the end of the Mersey RC 24hr in 2006. He was a very hard working organiser for the sport we love and we owe him a debt of gratitude.*

⸻ ◈ ⸻

**The North Road CC 24hr** on September 3rd and 4th **was won by Len Fensom** of the Holbeach Wheelers, with **463.047 miles. Nim Carline,** Monckton CC was 2nd with **453.693** and **3rd T. Fensom** of the Spalding CC with **451.546m.** This was the Spalding rider's best result and placing so far. **Cliff Smith,** East Midlands Clarion was 4th with **446.219m** and **Reg Randall,** 5th with **445.691m.**

The **fastest trike** was **E.J. Smith,** Bedfordshire RC with **384.280m.** The Luton Wheelers took the team prize with a total of **1,294.184m** comprised of **Ken Palmer** overall 6th, **433.604m,** Bob Haythorne 8th, **432.316m** and Adrian Forde, 18th with **408.264m.** Syd Parker rode one of the best performances of his 20 year career with **407.4 miles.**

The event drew 70 entries despite an unfortunate clash with the National Championship 12 hour. Conditions were the best for many years. A remarkable feature of Fensom's winning ride was the fact that he rode the last 343 miles as the first man on the road, having caught the field and put them behind him. He displayed a model judgement of pace and a refusal to be rattled by the battles raging behind him. Alan Blackman of the North Road CC had actually been the fastest until around the 375 miles point, when his efforts to close the Fenman down took their toll and left him shattered. He retired soon after.

*It is interesting to note that the Fensoms' are brothers even though they rode for different teams. Information courtesy of Frank Fischer.*

It's also interesting to note the promising debut of **Nim Carline** of the Monckton CC, a young man whose strength and grit in these events was to earn him respect over the next two decades. Another rider, rising to a high position and mileage in one of his earliest outings in a 24hr race was **Cliff Smith,** East Midlands Clarion.

*Nim and Cliff between them will almost dominate the 24hr scene especially Championship Events and will share the podium places between themselves over the next 15 years.*

## 1956

*Over the May Whitsun holiday, **Dave Duffield,** Beacon Roads CC, broke George Lawrie's **1,000 mile trike record** by 18hrs, 17mins with a time of **3 days, 12 hours and 15 mins,** on a course that took in St Albans, Thetford, Birmingham, Shrewsbury and Worcester.*

1956 was a bumper year for 24hr races. There were to be **five events** this year, the extra one being **'the Ealing Paragon CC event'.**

**The Catford CC 24 hr** this year was again won by **Ken Price** of the Cardiff 100 mile RC. It wasn't a record ride but it was a convincing **win of 461.90m,** in fact he won by nearly 20 miles from **Ken Davey,** Kingston RCC with **442.3m. J.W. Smith,** West Kent RC was 3rd with **440.55m,** he just narrowly pipped E.W.J. 'Ted' Crawley, Kentish Wheelers by .5 of a mile. **Bromley RC won the team race with 1,313.995 miles** amassed by three very evenly matched riders: **R.C. Poore 438.875m, D.C. Palmer 437.590m and R.E. Lessett 437.530m.**

**Peter Duncan was the fastest trike rider** with another very high mileage of **435.125m** for **8th** place. B. Wray was 9th with 432.88 and Reg Pinkham 10th 432.75m. Ian Shaw riding for the Saracen RC, a club based in Shirley, South Birmingham, produced a fine 408.9m for one of his first 24hr rides. In 1971 Ian came back from New Zealand after a spell of work there and took over as Editor of the 24hr Fellowship Journal, and was one of the Fellowship stalwarts at that time.

———⟫•◇•⟪———

*20th June 1956 – Arthur Render, Oldbury and District CC, after riding to 439 miles in the previous years Mersey event, had been persuaded by his club mates to attack the **1,000 mile bicycle record**, held by Sid Ferris. This he did on the above date, beating it by 4hrs 50 mins to record **2 days 16 hours 50 mins**. He used a course based in the Midlands, but going as far North West as Prestatyn and as far South as Bristol, and as far east as Lincoln. After a meal of specially prepared chicken, he suffered with terrible stomach pains early on in his ride, and was worried when he had protrusions the size of tennis balls appear on his stomach. As he approached 'Nant Hall' Prestatyn later in the ride he had a heavy nose bleed, but other than a spot of double vision in the Droitwich area, the remainder of his attempt was trouble free! Arthur said that being a tourist at heart he was able to let his imagination carry him away as he rode through some beautiful countryside with his legs pumping up and down as if on auto pilot.*

———⟫•◇•⟪———

**The Wessex RC 24hr 1956. The 480 mile 'evens' record was at last broken most convincingly by Dennis White,** Swindon Wheelers, with a mileage of **484.64 miles.** It was a 6 mile improvement over Ken Price's record. His riding style was steady and methodical, almost text book. His first 12 hours yielded 246 miles, his 2nd 238m. He didn't fight for position at the start like a lot of riders do, he just rode his own race at his own speed and waited for other riders to drop away over the first 12 hours. Another unusual feature of his ride was that he had two or three short breaks built into his schedule where he stopped for food.

White was on what were for him 'local roads' and as far as I can gather he never ventured out of this area to ride any other 24hr. I remember as a youngster, getting hold of the Cycling magazine, before my sisters Barbara and Margaret, got home from work, looking for the results, and seeing the headlines about Dennis White being the first man to beat evens for 24hrs. At that time I could almost beat 'evens' for a 10 mile event, and I thought "how can his heart and lungs keep working at that pressure for 24hrs, and what about the pains in his legs, how did he manage?" I was 13 years old at the time and suffered what I called 'growing pains' mainly in my legs and usually when sitting or lying down. It was always worse after a heavy weeks mileage or a long hard club run. After my first few 25mile races in 1958, I remember lying on the grass for ages panting heavily for breath. They would call it hyperventilating nowadays and my legs felt like they would burst from the effort. It was years before I learned what lactic acid was and also about the perils of smoking. Having helped my club team at the Mersey 24hr by handing up drinks and sponges and trying to stay awake all night, I often wondered what Dennis White would have done on this course. I have digressed from the plot slightly but these were my thoughts at that time in the late 1950's.

The **2nd** placed rider was **Jim Hanning,** another strong rider scoring **465.37miles,** his team mate **Peter Duncan** was **3rd** overall with **464.42m** for the Veg. C & AC. Peter was at the peak of his career having had some excellent trike rides in previous years. A.R. Chamberlain was 4th with 458.57m, D.W. Jordan 5th with 452.47m. The rider in 6th place, Dave Keeler, made the Vegetarian team complete with his 439.5 miles. He had been better known as a short distance champion, especially at the track 'pursuit'. He was 25 and 50m Champion, breaking Competition Record twice in 1951 for the 25 mile with 57m.15s and 57m.11s..

**Keeler's mileage in this 24hr gave the Vegetarian C & AC another superb team win with 1,369.29 miles.**

This Wessex RC event was his first foray into long distance riding. Looking down the list of 20 finishers, the Salisbury RC team of Hathaway, Cook and Morgan rode a very even race with 431.7, 431.3 and 426.3 to take 2nd team, but just one place lower was A.D. White, Swindon Whls with 415.25m. I wonder if he was in any way related to the winner?

⟹ ⬩◇⬩ ⟸

**The Mersey RC 24hr 1956** was **won for the 4th time by Nick Carter** of the **South Lancs RC with his second highest mileage of 461.08m, taking the South Lancs RC to another high mileage team win, in fact a record in this event so far, with 1,374.14 miles. K.W. Benson was 2nd with 453.4miles.** He is a rider I haven't noticed before but he rode very strongly for the South Lancs team with **Les Heald** being the **third counter** with one of his best mileages ever, **431.94,** giving him **7th** place overall. **B. Holt,** Eckington Whls was actual **3rd** overall with **439.4m. G. Arstall,** Seamons CC with **436.56** was **4th, Albert Crimes** was **5th** on a trike with another high mileage of **436.5 miles.** He was no doubt keeping himself up to the metal for his forthcoming trike attempt on the End to End in 1957. **Arthur Turner,** Warrington RC was **6th** with **433.6 miles.**

It looks as though the South Lancs RC were the only club to finish a team, in fact they had another two riders both on trikes who also finished. **Cliff Bate** with **396.19m** and **P. Duce** with **350.71 miles.** Another rider who was a tough man to beat is **Terry Kelly,** Yorkshire Century RC on a trike with **403.69 miles,** making his first appearance. I rode a bike against him in the 1960's and 70's and he beat me nearly every time. He seemed to have an insatiable appetite for pain and always had a smile on his face, like Cliff Smith. I can't say I ever saw Terry with a helping team, so that made his efforts even more outstanding. Granville Olive produced 404.83m, Harold Nelson rode to probably his best mileage with 373.5, just beating Bill Coupe, Wigan Wheelers by 2 miles. Bill had been a regular 24hr rider in the late 1930's in the Anfield event and he was still riding in the 1970's. Bill is of course the father of End to Ender Mick Coupe. Benny Hudson, riding for the Sheffield Phoenix was having a 'lull' in his career, but still rode a good mileage at 398.25m. Stan Bray, 8th overall and Doug Osmonde, both Solihull CC riders, were just .06 of a mile different at the end with Bray 423.86m to Osmonde's 423.80m.

⟹ ⬩◇⬩ ⟸

*On August 6th, 1956,* **Ray Booty** *produced the* **first sub four hour hundred miles ride with 3 hrs 58mins 28 secs,** *in the Bath Road CC time trial. To all British cyclists, it was as important as Roger Bannister's mile record was to the world of athletics.*

⟹ ⬩◇⬩ ⟸

**The Ealing Paragon 24 hrs** August 11-12th **1956. L.R. Jenkins,** Acme Wheelers (Rhondda) won the event with **446.09 miles. Reg Pinkham,** Westerley RC was **2nd** with **435.375m, E.W.J. Crawley,** Kentish Wheelers was **3rd** with **431.75m.**

This was just a one-off. It had been hoped to make it an annual event but it never materialised. Using a different course to most events, it started at Chalfont St Peter, continuing through Aylesbury, Buckingham, Brackley, Banbury, Bicester, Oxford, Witney, Abingdon, Wallingford, Pangbourne, Wantage, Thame, and Princes Risborough, finishing on a circuit in the Thame area. Twenty two riders out of thirty three finished; **Syd Parker** who sent me the course and event details completed **375.2 miles,** riding for the promoting club.

106

**'Young' Jenkins** as Jock Wadley had referred to him came **7th** in the Catford Championship event of 1955 with **449.1 miles.** I daresay that he had ridden to the start at Chalfont St Peter in the previous days, as he had done for the Catford. **Derek Evans,** Ealing Paragon CC who came **5th** in this, his own club's event, with **410.90m** gives us an insight as to the conditions during the event. He admitted to being a bit of a 'scrubber' compared to Messrs Harding, Poole, Carline, Price etc, and was just out to beat his own previous best of 404m and possibly get near the Club record of 421miles. He also wanted to get around the course on 10 cigarettes and not 20. He had taken a tip from Arch Harding of having no handlebar end 'bungs' or plugs so that he could store the 'dog-ends' inside the handlebars! As it happened he ran out of cigs and his club mates gave him bananas to eat instead.

"JUST hang on for a moment until I've finished this cigarette".

Derek rode to the start in heavy rain; the first 50 miles were straight out against the wind via Amersham, Aylesbury and Buckingham, to turn just short of Banbury. By Aylesbury, the rain had stopped and the weekend was dry from then on. He reached the 50 mile check point in 2hrs 45mins having caught at least a dozen riders. Derek in turn was only caught by the eventual winner Len Jenkins, and Don Picking. The return journey to Aylesbury should have been easy, but alas the wind had dropped and it seemed just as hard. After Aylesbury the course turned North West to Bicester to turn again just short of Banbury. His 100 miles had taken 5hrs 35mins.

He and other slightly slower riders were missed off the next 20 mile detour to Buckingham and back and sent straight through to the feed at Kidlington, he wasn't too happy about this but found out later that as he was from the promoting club and one of the only riders who knew the course well, it was felt he could detect if any important marshals were missing and so avert problems for other riders. Bob Stevens a fellow competitor and club mate battled it out for the lead during the night and the decision proved right for them to be pathfinders, as they managed to get a man sent to Frilford Crossroad to marshal a very dodgy junction.

At the Kidlington feed, Derek was sent to have a wash which made him most indignant. His retaliation was "I'm riding a 24hr and have no time for 'titivating!" After a quick wash he was away into a moonlit night. By Witney he'd caught Jock Dawson after a hard battle and was now first man on the road, a position he kept until Len Jenkins caught him at 6 am. Derek's 12hr mileage was 203 and he was disappointed with this and felt like packing until he found out that Jenkins wouldn't beat 220 and that his 203 miles would put him in the first 12 riders.

The course had taken the riders via Kingston-Bagpuize, Abingdon, Wallingford, Pangbourne and out onto the Bath road. The stretch from Newbury to the turn at Savernake was a very lonely one, but from there on, the last ten hours were 'flyers' and many riders produced better mileages in the last half of the race to the first half.

Derek Evans was the only rider that Jenkins hadn't caught. At Pangbourne Derek stopped for a 'cuppa' from the Carlyle CC and Jenkins went past. Reg Pinkham was the only other rider who completed the full course. At Witney, a ride down the Oxford by-pass was a real 'float' for the riders on a glorious sunny morning, the breakfast feed back at Kidlington was dispensed with as Derek preferred to ride the last four hours on cold milk only.

The riders went back to Bicester then the A41 to Blackthorn, then a right hand turn to Thame and onto the finishing circuit with 352 miles done and with 3 hrs 13 mins riding time left, Derek managed 58.5 miles. There were many 'scraps' around the 19 mile circuit based on Thame-Longwick and Stone, it was said that the tussle between Jenkins and Pinkham nearly finished the Welshman off. Reg Randall was out handing up drinks on the circuit as was Dick Poole who hadn't yet ridden a 24 hr. **Evans** finished more than happy, having covered nearly **411 miles** creeping from 12th place at 12 hours to **6th** at the finish. **The Camberley Wheelers won the team race. K. Wisker with 402.70, T.E. Jones, 389.7 and J. Fairgreive, 381.880, giving a total of 1,174.28m.**

**The North Road CC National Championship 24hr was won by Fred Burrell** of the Middlesex RC with **477.70 miles.** He beat a classy field that day by 'controlled riding'. He was very similar in his approach to 24hr racing as Dennis White, letting everybody have their battles, but keeping an eye on the position of other riders. Fred generally rode a single speed gear of 79" and probably was an exponent of counting the 'revs' per minute to check his speed (pedal revolutions). He beat two very good riders who were on form that day, **Stuart 'Joe' Thompson,** Rutland CC with **467.68m** and **Jim Hanning,** Veg C & AC, **463.80m.**

**The Rutland CC took the team prize with Thompson 467.68, Ron Coukham 462.60m and Tony Fouldes 434.78m, a total of 1,365.06 miles.**

'Joe' Thompson recalled 'fighting the wind which swoops across the unsheltered Fenland roads as dawn breaks, presenting a real challenge. The first half of the race ran pretty true to form, Hanning and myself disputing the lead with Tony Fouldes and Ron Coukham (his Rutland team mates). Not far away also in the picture was a rider unknown to most of us at that time, Fred Burrell of the Middlesex RC. Ken Price, not riding to his usual form had retired earlier. Coming back from the Peterborough turn with 300 miles covered, I was able to discern two or three riders in pursuit. "You're just up on Hanning" shouted one of our helpers. "Never mind that" I said "a chap I passed 15 hours ago is catching me fast!" Sure enough, Fred Burrell soon came by, I tried to hold him for a while but paid for it dearly later, however I was not alone and only Burrell did not falter on the hard trek to the finishing circuit.

Tony Foulds overcame many bouts of sickness that day to give us our second Championship Team win. I also formed the opinion at the time that Fred Burrell was the finest 24hr rider in hard conditions I had ever encountered, and subsequent events have given me no reason to change that view'.

**A.C. Stacey,** Hertord Wheelers, **won the trike** prize with **366.342m** and out of 57 starters, 38 of them were on variable gears. Each new racing season saw a slight decrease in the proportion of fixed or single speed gear riders at all distances. Conditions were cool and breezy with some heavy rain before a cold damp night. Fred Burrell with 246 miles was 3rd at the 12 hour point behind Jim Hanning, 250m, and Thompson 249m, but his steady unruffled progress in the critical 'small hours' brought him a lead that he wasn't to lose, and victory by 10 miles. The 'elders' pointed knowingly to Fred's 79" fixed gear and wired on tyres as factors in an effort which would surely have resulted in a better than 'evens' ride but for the hard conditions.

*In July 1956, President Nasser of Egypt nationalised The Suez Canal. The British Prime Minister intervened with British and French troops to protect oil supplies. This action by Sir Anthony Eden made him very unpopular with the British public and he resigned in January 1957.*

*Petrol rationing was re-introduced around this time.*

## 1957

*Two trophies were donated to the RTTC by the Charlotteville CC. Both were oblong wooden plinths upon which were mounted engraved shields and plaques. The trophies were both to be awarded for the Championship 24hr. One for the solo champion and one for the winning team.*

*On May 15th 1957 Britain tested its first 'H' (Hydrogen) Bomb by dropping it on the Christmas Island in the Pacific.*

The Catford 24hr on July 13th and 14th was won by **L.G. Bowerman** of the Charlotteville CC with **453.692m.** Len Jenkins, Acme Wheelers was **2nd** with **451.555** and **Reg Randall**, **3rd** riding for the Harlequins CC with **448.996miles.** 2nd placed rider **Jenkins led a Welsh team of N.J. Yeo and D. Thomas to a win of** 1,272.303 miles. This was Jenkins best mileage so far I think, and was the first time L.G. Bowerman had come to my notice. Reg Randall went on to many great achievements and **Terry Kelly** was the **fastest trike** rider with **402 miles.** Riders mileages are now calculated by timekeepers stationed around the finishing circuit in this event for the first time.

*Friday June 7th 1957 was the day* **David Duffield** *started at 8pm from John o' Groats on a* **trike to break the End to End** *some* **2 days 20 hours and 9 mins** *later.* **This is the only record that has ever succeeded from a northerly direction.** *He suffered terribly with the cold in Scotland. Duffield took 4hrs and 29 mins off Bert Parke's record. As we all know David went on to become a famous T.V. reporter for the 'Tour de France'.*

⇒◇⇐

**The Wessex 24hr** this year had a slightly depleted field compared with other years, especially the previous one, when Dennis White had won with Competition Record mileage from a star studded field. Nevertheless the rider who had taken 4th place in the 1956 event behind Peter Duncan was **this years winner. A.R. Chamberlain** of the Hounslow and District CC with **450.8 miles.** He was the first of 12 finishers, beating **Len Morgan** from the Salisbury RC by 27 miles. His **423.8m** was another good mileage on this his local course. **J.E. Jones** was **3rd** with **401.38m** riding for the 'R.E.M.E.'(The Royal Electrical and Mechanical Engineers) CC. **Bill Suttie** was **4th**, **Roy Cook 5th** and **Reg Pearce**, Stafford Road Club, **6th. No team finished.**

⇒◇⇐

**The Mersey Rc 24hr** on July 27th & 28th was a National Championship event. Joe 'Lofty' Leversidge won in fine style with **467.82m**, leading a Rutland CC team to their **3rd Championship win in succession**, with **Ron Coukham** taking a hard won **2nd** place of **462.2 miles.** **Jimmy Hall** surprised everyone to beat George Steers to a place in this **winning team** with **448.73** to give a **1,378.75 miles total.** This was a record team mileage for this event so far.

The Rutland CC beat the Vegetarian C & AC, the 'favourites' to win. **Peter Duncan** was the fastest Vegetarian with **460.22m** coming **3rd** in the Championship. **Dave Keeler** took **4th** place with **453.12 miles.**

Looking down the finishing list I can now see lots of riders names that I'm familiar with. Stan Bray, Solihull CC, 9th with 443m; John Arnold, 12th, with 432.5m on a bike; Jack Forrest, North Lancs RC 2nd trike with 389.96, he went on in 1960 to break the tandem End to End record with Jim Bailey. **R.W. Prowse won the fastest trike prize with 392.57m.**

*Frank Cooper, Stone Wheelers, with 372m was a regular rider in the Mersey event, over a period of some 20 years. I would see him as I travelled up to the race by car, usually around the Woore to Nantwich area, riding to the start at Tarvin after working Saturday morning in Stone, and arriving just in time to start at 5pm. When he finished on the Sunday teatime, he would ride back home to the 'Potteries'.*

Ed Green, President of the 'TA' on a trike, recorded 356.39m a very good mileage, in fact I don't think he ever raced on a bike to my knowledge. Alf Layzell, another 'trikie' with 336.61m was just 6 miles short of his 1937 mileage in the Catford. He's been around a long time, sometimes completing 4 x 24hr races a year, similar to Jack Spackman also on a trike with 318.77m. No less than 10 trikes finished the event, but then it was their Championship as well.

⇒◇⇐

**16th August 1957, Albert Crimes** *started on his successful* **trike End to End** *but going south to north (the usual way). He broke David Duffield's two month old record by 7.5 hours with* **2 days 12 hours 37 mins.**

*Albert started at the unorthodox time of 4pm; whether it was to tie in with missing heavy traffic in the large towns on route, or to be passing through Shropshire, Cheshire and Lancashire when club folk would be available to see and help him during the daytime of Saturday, I don't know.*

*He quickly gained time on his schedule, so much so that by the Midlands he was two hours ahead, and caused many of his local club folk to miss him. After a two and a half hours sleep at Brock in Lancashire, he carried on through Kendal to climb Shap. He had a sit down feed before Carlisle, of liver, bacon, eggs, tomatoes and chips, which set him up for his next tough section, climbing to Beattock Summit into the wind. He had a very bad patch and lost all interest, he was so tired, but Peter Barlow was very firm with him and told him that 10 mph was better than stopping! He continued with a steady struggle through Scotland, over the Grampians and picked up a favourable south-westerly wind with 140 miles to go.*

*Albert came to grief on the '1 in 4' hairpin climb of Berriedale when his drive wheel slipped and he ended up hitting the road. This incident unnerved him and it was Wick before he settled down again. He arrived at John o' Groats just after 4.30am, with another great record under his belt.*

"I caught him loitering near the bank, and he told me a cock-and-bull story about waiting for somebody riding a tricycle from Land's End to John o' Groats!"

In the **North Road 24hr, Dave Keeler** had his **first classic win** and beat 'evens' with **480.783m.** He was out for his first win after only coming 4th in the Mersey event some weeks previously with 453 miles. **Jim Hanning,** Vegetarian C & AC with **460.242 miles** was **2nd** and **Len Fensom,** Spalding CC **3rd** with **454.263m. Cliff Smith,** East Midlands CC was **4th** with **448.235m,** a 2 mile improvement over his 4th place ride two years previously in the same event.

Keeler was riding his notorious, almost unique, 'Paris Roubaix' gear, which looked like a fixed wheel gear and hub, but was actually a multiple speed gear operated by levers and rod, situated on the right hand seat stay. It was just a crude method of unshipping the chain from one cog to another by loosening the rear wheel. This multiple speed gear shift required a lot of concentration and agility to use by the rider, and it was said that using this gear and constantly reaching down to the seat stay was the reason for Keeler's bad back pain suffered during his End to End, the following year.

**The Luton Wheelers won the team prize** much to the pleasure of Eric Wilkinson, the timekeeper. He'd been the first man to win this event riding for the Luton Wheelers in 1945, just after the war. **The Luton team comprised of Rob O'Dell who'd been 5th overall with 445.047, Ken Palmer 428.299 and Alan Forde, 419.276, for a total of 1,295.579m.** The North Road team of Ken Davis with 426.978, Ted Kings, 421.620 and B. Hay, 406.425m were beaten into 2nd place by just over 40 miles. **W.A. Cliff,** Southgate cc was the **fastest trike** rider with **399.170miles.**

The North Road Gazette's description of the ride said that 76 entries were received by Sid Mottram and the hot favourite won in immaculate style. Conditions were very windy for the first seven hours or so and Alan Blackman's early efforts on a fixed wheel to keep on terms with Keeler proved too much, and he was forced to 'pack' at 360 miles.

*Reading this last item made me realise that this is almost a repeat of Blackman's ride in 1955, after a long battle with Fensom. If only he could have ridden his own race, I'm sure he could have won.*

**Joe Summerlin** of the Wellingborough CC with a very good debut ride of **431** miles for **6th** place was referred to as a 'young novice'. He was heard to mutter "never again" shortly after finishing. Joe in later years became Principal Timekeeper for this event.

It is noticeable that a new breed of winners seem to be shunning the old, tried and tested method of 'steady riding' and seem to be going almost flat-out from the start, trying to catch another opponent as soon as possible, in an effort to stamp their authority on the race. It takes a lot of patience and judgement to play a waiting game and as a rider it can only be done if you know in your own mind that you can react, if necessary, at a later stage.

One more item of interest, more of a correction really was in 1973, when Ted Kings wrote to the 24hr Fellowship Journal and disclosed that all of the riders mileages printed in this 1957 North Road result sheet, barring Keeler's, were two miles short. Ted Kings had actually designed the course as well as riding the event. He remembered being turned on the Saturday afternoon on the Royston leg, one mile further along the road than they should have been. I haven't adjusted any mileages in this text, as there has never been to my knowledge, an amended result sheet. Both the North Road History Book and their 24 hr result cards had the lower mileages on for all but Keeler.

The North Road club had been well represented in this event with 3 more riders finishing: Ernie Haldane, Harold Bridge and J. Riley. Harold Bridge later emigrated to Canada, but still kept in touch with the Fellowship, writing many interesting articles.

# 1958

On 30th May 1958, **Dave Keeler** *started on his epic* **'End to End'** *journey to try and become the first amateur solo bike rider in 20 years to break the record. This he did in* **2 days 3 hrs 9 mins.** *This tall 6ft 2" 13 stone rider was deemed to be too tall for an 'End to Ender' but proved them all wrong with this record which makes the 2 days barrier so much closer.*

Charlie Davey, who had come to prominence in the North Road 24hr of 1921, winning with 401.5 miles was Keeler's Organiser and helper on this epic journey. He was aided by Eddie Mundy and his wife Pat for most of the ride. This was another triumph for a vegetarian rider and writing and researching has made me realise what a strong force the 'Vegetarians' were, right from the start of cycle racing, before the turn of the 20th Century. Vegetarianism seems to be a family thing as well as a way of life. Dave Keeler's father was a long distance walker who fared well in competitions to a ripe old age and was also a 'veg'. When I started riding and racing in the late 50's there seemed to be a lot of famous riders all in the Vegetarian C & AC, riding all the time trials throughout the country. Their club network was nationwide, like my own Club, St Christopher's CCC, but looking at result sheets of the time trials in recent years, there is very little mention of Vegetarians, and I assume that although the strong club structure isn't there, the Vegetarian riders are, but they probably belong to other clubs.

*Vegetarian riders were always distinctive and easily recognisable by white flashes on their upper arms.*

———————◆◇◆———————

**The Catford 24hr in 1958 was won by Jim Hanning with 462.98m.** A well deserved win after being overshadowed for many years by other Vegetarian C & AC top riders. **A. Brook,** Bec CC was **2nd** with **443.3 miles** and **Ted Crawley** was **3rd** with **438.2m. Bec CC won the team race** from the Bromley RC with **1,290.3 miles. Alf Layzell** was the only trike rider with **340.925 miles.** From 35 starters only 18 finished but of those 18 finishers, 13 beat 400 miles.

———————◆◇◆———————

**The Wessex RC 24hr was a National Championship event and won** for the second time by **Dennis White,** Swindon Wheelers with **484.75m.** George Herbert Stancer (G.H.S.) writing in the Cycling Magazine on August 6th, said that the most remarkable thing about Dennis White's second 24hr Competition Record was that it was almost a carbon copy of his first one, with just a few hundred yards (.110 of a mile) added on. His first 12 hour distance on both record rides yielded 246 miles, almost text book riding.

**"How often have we seen riders fade away in the closing stages of a 24hr through the effect of their premature indiscretions in struggling for an early lead. Perhaps the most surprising feature of the champion's performance was that he made three 'refresher' stops of several minutes each. This is contrary to current non-stop practice, but it showed supreme confidence on White's part in his ability to pick up lost time again."**

*Dennis White's rides were both done in the Wessex RC 24hr and both were ridden in good conditions. He rode a 79" single speed gear and his performances were very similar to Fred Burrells', who also had identical winning mileages ridden at, or very close to White's winning years. Burrell's 1956 mileage was 477.70 and 1960, 477.70 and both were Championship North Road events, the only difference to White's being that Burrell had tough conditions for both of his rides.*

Ron Coukham with **477.75m** took **2nd** place behind White and **led the Rutland CC to their 4th National Championship Team win and their 2nd Competition team record with a mileage of 1,402.69m.** Stuart Thompson was **3rd** with **469.83** and together with **George Steers** made up the victorious Rutland team. Steers mileage of 455.43 put him 8th in the event. Dave Keeler came 4th overall with 466.29m. Stuart 'Joe' Thompson gave us his perspective on the event, made easier for him because this year there had been no pressure on him to win.

*"Should it seem that these team wins were a piece of cake, I might say that rarely did we start the race as favourites and on this occasion it was thought that the Vegetarian C & AC who were strongly represented, would have the beating of our lads, but even riders of the calibre of Keeler, Hanning and Duncan couldn't match Ron Coukham and George Steers onslaught. Despite lack of training I entered the event with no pressure to win. I rode an 86" fixed wheel, forsaking my usual gears. I had the easiest ride of my 24 hr riding career without the tension of fighting for the lead; these roles were taken by White, Keeler and Coukham.*

*It was my first view of White, the 'wonder', who had beaten 'evens', many were dubious as to whether he could stand up to the strain of Championship competition. What I saw impressed me greatly, but he needed all of his style and stamina to stave off first the mighty Keeler and later a tenacious Ron Coukham.*

*The fight for team honours was developing into a battle of the highest merit with the 'Veg' boys matching us man for man. Gradually we gained the ascendancy and suddenly they cracked, leaving Keeler to fight on alone for individual honours, but even this was to be denied him. White went majestically on his way to equal his own record of 484 miles and I repeated the mileage that had earned me the title four years earlier to push Dave Keeler out of 3rd place. George Steers pulled out a personal best to earn his first team medal, helping us to a new record of 1,402.69m. Four team wins in a row, could we keep it up for any longer?"*

**H. Kellie** was **5th, 462.60m,** D. Thomas 6th, 462.48, **A.R. Chamberlain** produced a personal best for **7th** place with **461.72.** Thirty two riders beat 400 miles that day, out of 42 finishers. **Tony Fouldes** was the 4th team member for the Rutland CC with **451.25 miles** and **9th** place, a mileage that could easily have won any lesser event, and one that would still ensure a Rutland team win should any of the others have failed. On reflection, Dave Keeler, had probably overstretched himself on his successful 'End to End' at the end of May, so it wasn't surprising as to his 4th place.

⋙◆⋘

*Britain's first motorway 'The Preston By-Pass' opens.*

**Mersey RC 24hr 1958** late July. After a gap of 8 years, **Cliff Bate** came back to **win** this event once again, with a personal best mileage of **458.64m** an improvement of 21 miles over his 1950 win. **He led a South Lancs RC 'A' team to a win of 1,351.29m.** They had two teams finish. **Stan Bray,** Solihull CC came **2nd** with his best ever performance of **455.70m.** I can just imagine the state he must have been in to produce this mileage. He used to push himself so hard and was merciless with himself every time he raced. **Nick Carter,** South Lancs RC was **3rd** with **453.52m, Ken Usher,** Crouch Hill CC was **4th** with **448.94m.** This was a new name appearing on the 24hr scene and one we were destined to see more of. **Alec Denton,** Lancashire RC was **5th** with **443.76m.** He had previously broken the tandem End to End record in 1953 with Frank Cowsill in 2 days 8hrs 7 mins. They had then carried on for the 1,000 mile record in 3 days 7 hrs 41 mins. **6th** place went to **B. Holt,** Eckington Wheelers with **441.27m** while **Les Heald** in **7th** place was the remaining South Lancs RC 'A' team rider with **439.13m. Derek Middleton,** West Pennine RC was **8th** with **435.58. Don Spraggett** in **9th** place with **434.04** was making his debut appearance in this event I think and this is the start of a very long relationship with the Mersey 24 for Don, covering more than 40 years either as a rider (placed on many occasions, 2nd being his best) or as a helper. Fred Cowling, Tyne RC was 10th with 420.83m. Ray Burnett, Jim Shuttleworth, Norman Maggs on a bike! with 387.77m. I didn't know he could ride a bike, I think I've only ever seen him on a trike. Cliff Farrar, trike, 372.97, Arthur Comer, trike, 348.78, Jack Spackman, 346.85 and Alf Layzell, trike, 340.07m. Both Jack and Alf must surely be getting close to the end of their careers in 24hr racing.

I only found out recently, from Stan Bray's son Eddie, that Cliff Bate had been allowed to start on a bike, even though he had entered on a trike. Stan wasn't aware of this until it was too late in the ride to close the gap on Bate's winning margin of nearly 3 miles. Stan's efforts in the closing stages on the finishing circuit had him nearly 'taking off' every time he rode over 'Pooly Bridge' on his 92" gear.

<hr>

**On 29th July 1958, Reg Randall** who had won the Catford 24 hr in 1953 and 1954 with mileages of 457m and 453m and in 1955 had ridden 458 miles in that same event, decided to attack the **'End to End'** that Dave Keeler hadn't long broken. Reg was a stocky, short rider with a totally different build and riding style to Keeler. **He broke the record** by 1 hr 11 min, taking **2 days 1 hr 58 mins.**

*August 14th – 17th* **Albert Crimes,** *Crewe Wheelers,* **broke the tricycle 1,000 miles record** *held by David Duffield by 14 hours 38 mins, giving a* **new record** *of* **2 days 21 hours 37 mins.** *It was performed on a course reaching as far as Morecambe Bay and Preston, starting and finishing near Middlewich, and took in much of the Mersey RC 24hr course used at that time.*

<hr>

A few weeks later, **Dave Keeler,** who had been out of the Country working in France, came back to England to finish off his racing season. *He'd been back quite a while before he found out that he'd lost his 'End to End' record to Reg Randall and it came as quite a shock to him.* However, he did finish in fine style by winning the **North Road 24hr** race by 19 miles from **L. Fensom,** Spalding CC **471.37.** Keeler's winning mileage of **490.311** although 6 miles more than White's **could not be a new Competition Record as 7 miles of it had been covered off the prescribed course after being misdirected in the night.**

Even though an accurate measurement of the exact amount was made, the mileage could only be used for the overall position in the race. **Jim Hanning,** Vegetarian C & AC was **3rd** with **456.217** and along with **W. Penyman's** mileage of **416.176,** the **Vegetarians won the team race with 1,362.704 miles.** **J.R. Westcott** was **4th** with **456.109** and **Cliff Smith** proved that his previous performances were not beginners luck by taking **5th** place with **448.813m.**

"I think they should bring back hanging for missing marshals."

Conditions were good, and out of 56 starters, 34 finished. Keeler's winning ride had shaken some of the pundits with his 2 hrs 8 mins first 50 mile, and his crouched 'aero' style, but there were those who recognised the arrival of a new generation of 24hr men who were to make speed the basis of some superlative long distance rides.

Another name I recognised on that result sheet was Jim Bailey, Nelson Wheelers. He came 7th with 437.945m and was testing himself out for an RRA tandem 24hr to take place the following year with Jack Forrest who also rode this event on a trike with 408.849m. Just above Jack on the result sheet, was **Terry Kelly, the trike event winner with 414.035m,** riding his first North Road event. Les Lowe was one place above Terry on the result sheet in 15th place with 414.578m riding his first North Road event and possibly his first 24 hr. Les went on to enjoy a very long 24 hr and long distance record-breaking career covering nearly 40 years. This event was also a first try for **John Withers, Birmingham St Christopher's CCC.** **He finished with 403.648 and really this was the start of the Birmingham Sections record breaking and long distance time trialling 'spree' that would last for nearly 30 years.** I say 'section' because there were numerous St. Christopher CCC's situated in most of the major Cities in Great Britain, and whereas one or two single riders from these clubs rode the 24hr event, the two main clubs to produce teams were Birmingham and, later of course, the North Staffs section.

On the record breaking scene in the 1960's, John Withers and Pete Swinden broke the tandem End to End and 1,000 mile records, and Pat Kenny broke the tricycle, Edinburgh to London and 24hr records. Later Pat broke many tandem trike RRA records, some with myself, culminating in his solo trike End to End. These earlier activities eventually led to my daughter, Lynne Taylor, riding 24hr events, following in her father's footsteps and eventually taking three End to End records. One on a tandem with Andy Wilkinson and two solo bike End to End's with a continued 1,000 miles added to her last record.

Even though all of Lynne's riding has been done in the colours of the Walsall Roads CC, her early days were spent helping a St Christopher's team either in the Oldbury 12 hour or at the Mersey 24 hr, handing up bananas and malt loaf and mingling with us 'old uns' listening to our tales and stories, it must have rubbed off on her! After all, the stories that John Withers brought back to the clubroom about his first 24hr had rubbed off on all of us, tales about the exploits of Keeler, Fensom, Hanning, Smith, these were his latest heroes. We already knew about Eileen Sheridan's End to End and by now she had already retired. Being a professional record breaker meant that she wasn't eligible to ride an amateur time trial, so her exploits were mainly seen on film. However, we'd seen Crimes & Arnold, Reg Randall, Ron Coukham and Fred Burrell in the flesh and it was they that we tried to emulate.

1958 had been a wonderful year for long distance record breaking either at 24hrs or on the End to End and 1,000 mile route:

| | |
|---|---|
| May 20th: | Dave Keeler's End to End      2 days 3 hrs 9 mins |
| Late July: | White wins Wessex National Championship 24hr with another Comp Record of 484.75m. |
| 29th-31st July | Reg Randall takes Dave Keeler's 2 month old End to End record in 2 days 1 hr 58 mins. |
| 14-17th August | Albert Crimes breaks the trike 1,000 mile record, 2 days 21 hrs 37s |
| September | Dave Keeler pushes the 24hr mileage barrier to 490.311m. *(even though it couldn't be used as a Competition Record)* |

*Over a 5 month period we have seen five amazing records take our sport forward. It will be another 24 years before more multiple long distance records are broken by our 24 hr 'stars' all in one season.*

# 1959

*Fidel Castro conquers Cuba.*

*Double white lines introduced in this year*

**The Catford 24hr was a National Championship event. It was won by Ron Coukham with 469.17m.** This was his first win in a 24hr event let alone a Championship, although to be fair he'd had a pretty high profile career so far, taking bronze in 1955 with 462.05m, 4th in 1956 North Road Championship with 462.60, and silver in 1957 in the Mersey championship with another 462.2 m. How about that for consistency, three almost identical mileages, even better than Burrell's and White's matching performances. In 1958, Ron again took silver in the Wessex Championship with 477.75 miles.

Coukham dominated this Championship almost from the start. **Arch Harding** was **2nd** with **463.12 miles.** He was a very fast 'vet' (over 40 years of age) and he set the foundation of some future high mileage team wins for the Middlesex RC when Burrell returned in 1960 to the North Road event. **Joe 'Lofty' Leversidge** returned for **3rd** overall position with **460 miles** and **George Steers** was again on top form with **456m** for **5th** place for this the **Rutland CC's 4th team win 1,386 miles,** 133 miles ahead of the Bec CC. Leversidge who was 3rd was still recovering from a serious car accident the previous year, so his mileage was particularly good. Joe Thompson who was absent from this event described the Rutland team as dominating this star-studded field right from the start, with Dennis White, Arch Harding and the 'Veg' boys in close attendance.

There was little to choose between the leaders at the 100 mile point. Dennis White led in 4 hrs 34 mins, Coukham and Stone were at 1 minute, Steers at 3 mins, Joe Leversidge and young Les Lowe were at 4 mins, Poole and Hanning at 6 mins, Duncan at 8, Harding, Smith & Usher jointly at 9 mins. At 225 miles, White narrowly held his lead with Coukham still at 1 min, Steers was at 5 mins, Leversidge at 6 mins, Poole at 8, Harding moved swiftly into 6th place, Cliff Smith was steady at 17 mins, Hanning, Usher and Keeler had now dropped out of contention. At 293 miles Coukham had taken the lead with the gusty conditions suiting him, he was just outside 'evens', White had dropped away and Harding was now 2nd, Poole lay 3rd. The finishing circuit was reached at 400.75 miles and Coukham had increased his lead over Harding to 12 mins, Leversidge was 3rd at 19 mins, Steers at 25 mins. Poole and Smith were at 30 mins, Randall & White were both at 45 mins, but Randall was actually pulling away from White. Keeler had by now 'packed' and Cummings pulled away from Jubb and Stone to ride into 10th place.

Coukham meanwhile rode stronger than ever to increase his lead on Harding and Leversidge to finish with 469 miles. Steers lost heavily on the three leaders and was eventually beaten by both Poole and Smith, who battled it out right to the finish, where Poole gained 4th place by only 46 yards!

*Ron had an extra special incentive to win this year's Championship Gold Medal. It was his wife Brenda's 25th birthday and he'd promised her the medal!*

Besides the Rutland CC another 3 teams finished, the Bec CC, Doncaster Wheelers and Hants RC. Dennis White finished down in 9th place with 449m and I think this was his last appearance in a 24hr race. Les Lowe riding his first Catford finished 25th overall with 424.2m, out of a field of 48 riders of whom 38 beat 400 miles. **Terry Kelly rode a very strong race on his trike with 408.15 miles.**

---

**The Wessex RC 24hr** was won by H. Kellie, Exe Valley RC with **452.77 miles**. A.R. Chamberlain, Hounslow & District was **2nd** with **446.79m,** and making a long trip south was **3rd** placed rider J. Taylor from the Calder Clarion CC with **435.13m**. Many of the riders were from the area where the course was based. **Bill Suttie** was the **fastest** of three **trikes** with **377.73m**. **No team finished from a total of 17 riders.**

---

*Britain now has Five Million cars on its roads.*

**The Mersey RC 24hr** was won by a new name in 24hr racing. **G.J. Kay** of the Lancashire RC with **458.10 miles**. **Barrow Central Whls won the team race with 1,179.79 miles.** **Ken Usher,** Crouch Hill CC came **2nd** with **454.44m** and J. **Goodwin,** Eckington Whls, was a very close **3rd** with **453.08m**. **Stan Bray,** Solihull CC rode to a fine **4th** place with **439.88 miles.**

Jeff Sanders, North Worcestershire CC who I knew more as a fast Midlands BBAR man came 11th with 420.72m after having problems in a previous 24hr with not being able to see properly in the mist, rain and dark. Anyone with perfect eyesight and not having to wear glasses wouldn't realise the restrictions that poor vision imposes on a rider. Benny Hudson, Sheffield Phoenix CC with 415.28m has been a regular 24hr participant for a good few years, as had Fred Cowling, Tyne RC with 417.20m. **Jim Shuttleworth on a trike with 409.79m** had a fine ride. Gerry Jones, Liverpool St Christopher's CCC 402.74, Ray Burnett, Middlesborough Co-op CC 393.90, Frank Cooper, Jack Duckers, Norman Maggs and Norman Brocklehurst, another St Christopher's rider from the Manchester section.

Some of the riders are linked to record attempts, such as Jack Ducker, North Shropshire Whls who played a part in End to Ends and many other records as they passed through Shropshire and Cheshire. He provided hospitality at his home for the riders and helpers and along with Norman Maggs was a regular marshal and helper in the Mersey events.

**Dave Keeler**

**Stuart Thompson**

**Ken Joy**

**Dennis White**

**Reg Randall**

**Graham Fouldes**

**Sid Hygate**

**Dick Poole**

**Ken Lovett**

**Ron Coukham**

**Arch Harding**

**Den Mills**

**Joe Leversidge**

**Fred Burrell**

Johnny Pardoe

David Duffield

Stan Bray

Ken Usher

John Arnold

Ken Hughes

Jack Watts

Taff Brissenden

Peter Duncan

Forrest & Bailey

117

## Catford National 1955

| | | | Miles | Yards | |
|---|---|---|---|---|---|
| 1. | K.Price | Cardiff 100 M.R.C. | 478 | 980 | * |
| 2. | S.Thompson | Rutland C.C. | 474 | 215 | * |
| 3. | R.Coukham | Rutland C.C. | 462 | 89 | |
| 4. | G.Fouldes | Rutland C.C. | 460 | 1679 | |
| 5. | R.F.Randall | Harlequins C.C. | 458 | 327 | |
| 6. | S.J.King | Colchester Rovers | 452 | 269 | |
| 7. | L.R.Jenkins | Acme Whs.(Rhondda) | 449 | 213 | |
| 8. | F.P.Wright | Redmon C.C. | 448 | 596 | |
| 9. | P.E.Carter | South Lancs.R.C. | 444 | 968 | |
| 10. | S.Avely | Tooting B.C. | 437 | 1412 | |
| 11. | R.J.Way | North Road C.C. | 437 | 1051 | |
| 12. | R.E.Yates | University C.C. | 436 | 660 | |
| 13. | R.A.Mackinlay | Addiscombe C.C. | 433 | 1578 | |
| 14. | R.Waddington | Doncaster Whs. | 431 | 244 | |
| 15. | W.Marchant | Tooting B.C. | 430 | 1638 | |
| 16. | R.Rance | Balham R.C. | 430 | 1578 | |
| 17. | W.E.Thorncroft | Brentwood R.C. | 430 | 850 | |
| 18. | R.F.Shiret | Redmon C.C. | 429 | 701 | |
| 19. | G.L.Redman | Oxford City R.C. | 428 | 1638 | |
| 20. | A.G.Williams | Viking R.C. | 424 | 1675 | |
| 21. | J.W.Smith | West Kent R.C. | 424 | 1638 | |
| 22. | I.Eley | Tooting B.C. | 424 | 1638 | |
| 23. | R.Jessett | Bromley R.C. | 422 | 1206 | |
| 24. | E.Osborn | Watford R.C. | 422 | 452 | |
| 25. | P.D.Barton | Castlenau C.C. | 421 | 378 | |
| 26. | G.W.Siddle | Spartan Whs. | 420 | 302 | |
| 27. | D.A.Wright | Cambrian Whs. | 419 | 628 | |
| 28. | C.King | Kentish Whs. | 416 | 97 | |
| 29. | W.W.Leonard | Fountain C.C. | 415 | 590 | |
| 30. | P.Pearson | Colchester Rovers | 414 | 1276 | |
| 31. | J. Beard | Redmon C.C. | 412 | 1171 | |
| 32. | D.E.Challis | Sorian R.C. | 411 | 1603 | |
| 33. | G.D.Seward | Middlesex R.C. | 411 | 1236 | |
| 34. | G.Crough | Kingston Phoenix R.C. | 411 | 316 | |
| 35. | J.Lawrence | Bromley R.C. | 411 | 110 | |
| 36. | D.C.Hall | Rodley Whs. | 409 | 1683 | |
| 37. | P.Pinkham | Westerley R.C. | 409 | 578 | |
| 38. | R. Walker | University C.C. | 408 | 758 | |
| 39. | L. Wilson | Bromley R.C. | 404 | 1098 | |
| 40. | E. Potter | Doncaster Whs. | 401 | 1551 | |
| 41. | E.G.Guy | Vegetarian C.& A.C. | 400 | 1428 | |
| 42. | D.Hutchinson | Crouch Hill C.C. | 399 | 553 | |
| 43. | G.Haslam | Manchester Clarion | 398 | 556 | |
| 44. | M.Hayler | Brighton Mitre C.C. | 394 | 639 | |
| 45. | A.R.How | De Laune C.C. | 394 | 556 | |
| 46. | B.Hudson | Rutland C.C. | 392 | 236 | |
| 47. | R.V.Iles | Greenford C.C. | 391 | 451 | |
| 48. | D.A.Rout | Colchester Rovers | 389 | 1336 | |
| 49. | P.S.Birbeck | Harp R.C. | 383 | 1483 | |
| 50. | H.A.Wenman | Bec C.C. | 377 | 188 | |
| 51. | M.C.Tillett | Kentish Whs. | 377 | 160 | |
| 52. | R.L.Cass | Viking R.C. | 375 | 1464 | |
| 53. | N.Meadows | Harp R.C. | 375 | 888 | |
| 54. | S.E.Knight | Castelman C.C. | 374 | 867 | |
| 55. | R.I.Gill | North Road C.C. | 373 | 443 | |
| 56. | A.D.McGowan | Balham C.C. | 372 | 677 | |
| 57. | J.H.Doggett | Clarence Whs. | 369 | 904 | |
| 58. | A.J.Baker | Victoria C.C. | 366 | 820 | |
| 59. | N.J.Carter | Epsom C.C. | 366 | 141 | |
| 60. | J.S.Spackman | Century R.C. | 365 | 1056 | |
| 61. | F.Wells | Carlyle C.C. | 360 | 856 | |
| 62. | E.F.Butt | Hants R.C. | 354 | 429 | |

```
Teams:  1. Rutland C.C.      1397 m.   233 y. *
        2. Tooting B.C.      1291 m.  1133 y.
        3. Redmon C.C.        290 m.   708 y.
        4. Colchester Rovrs. 1256 m.  1121 y.
        5. Bromley R.C.      1238 m.   654 y.
```

100 riders accepted, 96 started, 62 finished.

* comp record

118

# NORTH ROAD/NATIONAL 1956

| | | | |
|---|---|---|---|
| 1. | **F.A. BURRELL** | **MIDDLESEX RC** | **477.70** |
| 2. | **S. Thompson** | **Rutland CC** | **467.68** |
| 3. | **J.A. Hanning** | **Veg C & AC** | **463.80** |
| 4. | R. Coukham | Rutland CC | 462.60 |
| 5. | L. Fensom | Holbeach Whs | 461.37 |
| 6. | K. Davis | North Road CC | 445.24 |
| 7. | J.A. Westcott | Icknield RC | 443.36 |
| 8. | S.E. Harvey | Addiscombe CC | 442.90 |
| 9. | P.J. Marsh | Shaftesbury CC | 442.65 |
| 10. | R.W. O'Dell | Luton Whs CC | 442.10 |
| 11. | E. Mundy | Addiscombe CC | 437.25 |
| 12. | G. Fouldes | Rutland CC | 434.78 |
| 13. | W.E. Thorncroft | Brentwood RC | 424.23 |
| 14. | R.S. Ward | Spalding CC | 411.69 |
| 15. | J.A. Bailey | Nelson Whs | 409.58 |
| 16. | P.J. Cox | Beeston RC | 408.61 |
| 17. | E.W. Haldane | North Road CC | 406.41 |
| 18. | D. Rains | Allondon RC | 403.59 |
| 19. | J.S. Marriott | Myriad RC | 397.48 |
| 20. | L.J. Holmes | Elite CC | 391.33 |
| 21. | J.J. Nice | Colchester Rovers | 388.92 |
| 22. | G.W. Arnot | Priory Whs | 388.16 |
| 23. | J. Bowman | Hertfordshire Whs | 384.92 |
| 24. | J. Walton | Leamington C & AC | 384.20 |
| 25. | D. Thomas | Long Eaton CC | 379.22 |
| 26. | D.C. Kean | University CC | 372.57 |
| 27. | H.J. Francis | Elite CC | 371.23 |
| 28. | J.E. Boot | Sharrow CC | 369.25 |
| 29. | J.S. Pugh | Godric CC | 367.94 |
| 30. | R.I. Gill | North Road CC | 367.33 |
| 31. | A.C. Stacey (T) | Hertfordshire Whs | 366.35 |
| 32. | R. Williams | Finchley CC | 361.13 |
| 33. | D. Shaw | Long Eaton CC | 353.70 |
| 34. | H. Nelson | Royal Oak CC | 353.56 |
| 35. | J.S. Spackman | Century RC | 342.99 |
| 36. | L.E. Davey | Boston Whs | 315.19 |
| 37. | S. Gold | Hounslow & Dist Whs | 306.20 |

Team: Rutland CC, 1365.06

## Mersey National 1957

| 1. | J.Leversidge | Rutland C.C. | 467.82. |
|---|---|---|---|
| 2. | R.Coukham | Rutland C.C. | 462.20. |
| 3. | P.Duncan | Vegetarian C&AC. | 460.22. |
| 4. | D.J.Keeler | Vegetarian C&AC. | 453.12. |
| 5. | A.Turner | Warrington R.C. | 451.11. |
| 6. | J.W.Hall | Rutland C.C. | 448.73. |
| 7. | W.McGuigan | Hamilton C.C. | 443.54. |
| 8. | J.A.Hanning | Vegetarian C&AC | 443.40. |
| 9. | S.P.V.Bray | Solihull C.C. | 443.02. |
| 10. | G.Steers | Rutland C.C. | 442.80. |
| 11. | R.Pratt | Vegetarian C&AC. | 433.59. |
| 12. | J.F.Arnold | Middleton C.C. | 432.54. |
| 13. | L.Heald | S.Lancs.R.C. | 429.21. |
| 14. | L.Newstead | Huddersfield R.C. | 427.83. |
| 15. | G.Arstall | Seamons C.C. | 423.02. |
| 16. | B.Holt | Eckington Whs. | 418.35. |
| 17. | H.Benson | W.Pennine R.C. | 417.85. |
| 18. | W.Rowe | Abbotsford Park R.C. | 416.50. |
| 19. | J.M.Hargreaves | Pendle Forest C.C. | 411.98. |
| 20. | J.Walton | Leamington C&AC. | 409.82. |
| 21. | J.F.W.Broad | B'head C.C. | 409.44. |
| 22. | A.J. Halls | Cheltenham & County C.C. | 408.52. |
| 23. | A.Ingham | Nelson Whs. | 406.46. |
| 24. | L.Hornby | Phoenix (Aintree) C.C. | 403.60. |
| 25. | B.Hudson | Sheffield Phoenix C.C. | 403.49. |
| 26. | K.M.Gardiner | Leicestershire R.C. | 403.26. |
| 27. | W.R.Bentham | Warrington R.C. | 402.02. |
| 28. | F.Rodway | Lancaster C.C. | 398.60. |
| 29. | F.V.Randall | Fleetwood R.C. | 395.77. |
| 31. | J.E.Brownhill | Sheffield Phoenix C.C. | 392.22. |
| 30. | R.W.Prowse (T) | West Pennine R.C. | 392.57. |
| 32. | D.Beckett | M/c.Clarion C&AC. | 391.00. |
| 33. | J.Forrest (T) | N.Lancs.R.C. | 389.96. |
| 34. | L.J.deMouilpied | Beacon R.C.C. | 386.12. |
| 35. | J.Gallimore (T) | Warrington R.C. | 383.00. |
| 36. | M.G.Burns (T) | Barrow Cent.Whs. | 379.33. |
| 37. | J.T.Shuttleworth (T) | Stretford Whs. | 377.03. |
| 38. | A.Moore (T) | Beighton Whs. | 374.25. |
| 39. | H.Knipe (T) | Barrow Cent.Whs. | 373.41. |
| 40. | R.H.W.de Looze | Seamons C.C. | 373.26. |
| 41. | F.J.Cooper | Stone Whs. | 372.00. |
| 42. | R.T.Hamlett (T) | Janus R.C. | 358.00. |
| 43. | C.E.Green (T) | North Road Club. | 356.39. |
| 44. | A.Layzell (T) | Ealing Paragon C.C. | 336.61. |
| 45. | E.Lane | Flixton C.C. | 335.07. |
| 46. | J.S.Spackman (T) | Century R.C. | 318.77. |

Team:-1. Rutland C.C. (J.Leversidge, R.Coukham, J.W.Hall)   1378.75 miles.
      2. Veg. C&AC   1356.76 miles.
      3. Warrington R.C.   1236.13 miles.

## WESSEX 1958
### (NATIONAL CHAMPIONSHIP)

| | | | | | |
|---|---|---|---|---|---|
| 1. | D.H.White | Swindon Whs.C.C. | 484.75 | * | |
| 2. | R.Coukham | Rutland C.C. | 477.43 | | |
| 3. | S.Thompson | Rutland C.C. | 469.83 | | |
| 4. | D.J.Keeler | Vegetarian C.& A.C. | 466.29 | | |
| 5. | H.Kellie | Exe Valley R.C. | 462.60 | | |
| 6. | D.Thomas | Long Eaton C.C. | 462.48 | | |
| 7. | A.R.Chamberlain | Hounslow & Dist.Wh.C.C. | 461.72 | | |
| 8. | G.Steers | Rutland C.C. | 455.43 | | |
| 9. | G.Fouldes | Rutland C.C. | 451.25 | | |
| 10. | E.R.Stainer | Wessex R.C. | 450.49 | | |
| 11. | D.Free | Oxonian C.C. | 447.63 | | |
| 12. | S.M.Searle | Hampshire R.C. | 441.02 | | |
| 13. | W.E.Thorncroft | Brentwood R.C. | 440.63 | | |
| 14. | D.E.Issitt | Beacon Rds.C.C. | 431.85 | | |
| 15. | R.A.Jubb | Army C.U. (H.Q.) | 429.37 | | |
| 16. | P.J.Johnson | New Forest C.C. | 422.79 | | |
| 17. | D.Shaw | Long Eaton C.C. | 422.63 | | |
| 18. | J.A.Westcott | Icknield R.C. | 422.09 | | |
| 19. | R.H.Ross | Crescent Whs.C.C. | 422.04 | | |
| 20. | R.G.Barlow | Kingsgate & Venta C.C. | 420.19 | | |
| 21. | W.Suttie | Bournemouth Jubilee Whs. | 418.65 | | |
| 22. | R.Dane | Faversham C.& A.C. | 417.96 | | |
| 23. | S.Aldridge | Brentwood R.C. | 417.63 | | |
| 24. | H.J.Bartlett | Frome & Dist.Wh.C.C. | 416.23 | | |
| 25. | L.F.Morgan | Salisbury R.C. | 415.84 | | |
| 26. | J.H.Clarke | Royal Navy C.A. | 413.72 | | |
| 27. | I.J.Jones | Wessex R.C. | 412.11 | | |
| 28. | N.C.Anderson | Sittingbourne C.C. | 411.63 | | |
| 29. | K.H.Bazer | Wessex R.C. | 408.23 | | |
| 30. | R.E.Cook | Salisbury R.C. | 407.93 | | |
| 31. | W.A.Walton | 29th Wh.C.C. | 404.04 | | |
| 32. | C.A.Taylor | Southampton Wh.C.C. | 402.90 | | |
| 33. | R.J.Pearce | Stafford R.C. | 399.16 | | |
| 34. | P.F.Holt | Long Eaton Par.C.C. | 391.40 | | |
| 35. | A.R.Martin | Becontree Wh.C.C. | 388.21 | | |
| 36. | C.C.P.Davies | Hampshire R.C. | 378.07 | | |
| 37. | M.G.Bell | Cheltenham & Cty.C.C. | 360.31 | (T) | |
| 38. | I.D.Thompson | Hampshire R.C. | 352.03 | | |
| 39. | J.S.Healey | Medway Wh.C.C. | 351.21 | (T) | (A) |
| 40. | J.W.Turner | Medway Wh.C.C. | 349.39 | (T) | (B) |
| 41. | J.Johnson | Stafford R.C. | 346.02 | | |
| 42. | J.S.Spackman | Century R.C. | 317.52 | (T) | |

| | | | | |
|---|---|---|---|---|
| Team 1. | Rutland C.C. | 1402.69 | * | |
| 2. | Wessex R.C. | 1270.83 | | |
| 3. | Hampshire R.C. | 1171.12 | | |

\* Comp.Record.

## Catford National 1959

THE RESULT

| Pos. | No. | Name | Club | Distance | | |
|---|---|---|---|---|---|---|
| 1 | 60 | R.Coukham | Rutland C.C. | 469 | miles | 297 yds |
| 2 | 48 | A.C.Harding | Middlesex R.C. | 463 | " | 248 " |
| 3 | 40 | J.C.Leversidge | Rutland C.C. | 460 | " | 1,196 " |
| 4 | 58 | R.W.Poole | Middlesex R.C. | 458 | " | 790 " |
| 5 | 70 | C.Smith | East Mids.C.C. | 458 | " | 744 " |
| 6 | 35 | G.Steers | Rutland C.C. | 456 | " | 406 " |
| 7 | 55 | R.F.Randall | Harlequins C.C. | 455 | " | 690 " |
| 8 | 54 | E.D.Cummings | Delta R.C. | 450 | " | 976 " |
| 9 | 65 | D.H.White | Swindon Wheelers | 449 | " | 304 " |
| 10 | 53 | R.Jubb | Doncaster Wheelers | 448 | " | 1,312 " |
| 11 | 47 | P.W.Stone | West Kent | 448 | " | 57 " |
| 12 | 63 | B.Wray | Bec C.C. | 440 | " | 400 " |
| 13 | 75 | J.Hanning | Vegetarian C&AC | 440 | " | 6 " |
| 14 | 56 | W.A.Dunk | Forest C.C. | 438 | " | 192 " |
| 15 | 61 | R.Pinkham | Westerley R.C. | 437 | " | 720 " |
| 16 | 67 | S.M.Searle | Hants.R.C. | 432 | " | 1,700 " |
| 17 | 69 | A.Warrington | Wombwell Wheelers | 432 | " | 795 " |
| 18 | 52 | B.Cornwell | Westbourne Rovers | 432 | " | 691 " |
| 19 | 72 | A.Brook | Bec C.C. | 431 | " | 1,420 " |
| 20 | 43 | P.D.Issett | Eclipse C.C. | 431 | " | 1,042 " |
| 21 | 39 | L.C.Clare | Kingston Phoenix | 430 | " | 517 " |
| 22 | 20 | J.W.Hall | Rutland C.C. | 429 | " | 454 " |
| 23 | 14 | K.Gadd | Redmon C.C. | 426 | " | 1,570 " |
| 24 | 32 | W.Heseltine | Old Portlians C.C. | 426 | " | 1,290 " |
| 25 | 29 | L.E.Lowe | Long Eaton | 424 | " | 390 " |
| 26 | 68 | D.C.Palmer | Bromley R.C. | 423 | " | 875 " |
| 27 | 27 | J.Hefferman | Castlenau C.C. | 422 | " | 430 " |
| 28 | 59 | E.H.Barrett | Tooting B.C. | 419 | " | 682 " |
| 29 | 36 | D.Shaw | Long Eaton | 419 | " | 34 " |
| 30 | 18 | D.Bell | Spartan Wheelers | 410 | " | 1,629 " |
| 31 | 66 | E.Osborn | Redmon C.C. | 410 | " | 1,620 " |
| 32 | 37 | W.H.Welsh | Doncaster Wheelers | 410 | " | 1,359 " |
| 33 | 44 | E.Boorman | Southboro C.C. | 408 | " | 935 " |
| 34 | 64 | D.G.Ivey | South Eastern R.C. | 408 | " | 462 " |
| 35 | 12 | T.Kelly (TRI) | Yorks Century | 408 | " | 309 " |
| 36 | 41 | J.Hardman | Brighton Excelsior | 405 | " | 1,730 " |
| 37 | 30 | P.Duncan | Vegetarian C&AC | 404 | " | 1,398 " |
| 38 | 3 | K.Graham | Brighton Excelsior | 402 | " | 1,108 " |
| 39 | 33 | R.Baynham | Thanet R.C. | 399 | " | 823 " |
| 40 | 24 | E.J.Hodges | Medway Wheelers | 393 | " | 1,734 " |
| 41 | 42 | C.Tapley | Southern Wheelers | 383 | " | 1,093 " |
| 42 | 6 | J.A.Wenman | Bec C.C. | 381 | " | 1,608 " |
| 43 | 17 | I.D.Thompson | Hants.R.C. | 372 | " | 856 " |
| 44 | 38 | C.R.Davies | Hants.R.C. | 371 | " | 682 " |
| 45 | 15 | E.Potter | Doncaster Wheelers | 365 | " | 1,471 " |
| 46 | 26 | A.J.Creed | Brighton Excelsior | 365 | " | 1,407 " |
| 47 | 23 | D.A.Porter | Glendene C.C. | 361 | " | 942 " |
| 48 | 2 | J.W.Turner (TRI) | Medway Wheelers | 341 | " | 410 " |

Team:

| | | |  |  | | |
|---|---|---|---|---|---|---|
| 1 | | | Rutland C.C. | 1,386 | miles | 139 yds |
| 2 | | | Bec C.C. | 1,253 | miles | 1,668 yds |
| 3 | | | Doncaster Whs | 1,225 | miles | 622 yds |
| 4 | | | Hants R.C. | 1,176 | miles | 1,478 yds |

## North Road National 1960

| | | | |
|---|---|---|---|
| 1. | F.A.Burrell | Middlesex R.C. | 477.702 |
| 2. | A.C.Harding | Middlesex R.C. | 474.728 |
| 3. | L.Fensom | Spalding C.C. | 460.906 |
| 4. | J.F.Arnold | Middleton C.C. | 460.175 |
| 5. | R.W.E.Poole | Middlesex R.C. | 454.806 |
| 6. | W.H.Shearing | Salisbury R.C. | 450.016 |
| 7. | L.E.Lowe | Long Eaton C.C. | 446.707 |
| 8. | W.A.E.Dunk | Veg.C.&.A.C. | 446.566 |
| 9. | D.E.Mills | Sth Ruislip C.C. | 443.385 |
| 10. | D.Atter | Harworth & Dist.C.C. | 438.707 |
| 11. | J.W.Hall | Rutland C.C. | 434.564 |
| 12. | B.Goldstein | Leicestershire R.C. | 433.460 |
| 13. | G.W.Siddle | Spartan Whs. C.C. | 433.283 |
| 14. | K.E.Davis | North Road C.C. | 430.106 |
| 15. | A.Warrington | Rutland C.C. | 429.608 |
| 16. | A.Comer | Veg.C.&.A.C. | 428.698 |
| 17. | P.J.Marsh | Shaftesbury C.C. | 427.830 |
| 18. | L.T.Launspach | Ealing Paragon C.C. | 427.477 |
| 19. | J.A.Hanning | Veg.C&.A.C. | 426.483 |
| 20. | G.Whitehouse | Verulam C.C. | 425.678 |
| 21. | S.J.Genders | Walsall Roads C.C. | 425.052 |
| 22. | J.Withers | B'ham.St.Chris.C.C.C. | 423.008 |
| 23. | F.J.Summerlin | Nene Valley Whs. C.C. | 418.435 |
| 24. | G.Russell | Hull Thursday C.C. | 413.578 |
| 25. | T.K.Kelly | Yorks Century C.C. | 410.410 |
| 26. | C.E.Metcalfe | North Bucks R.C. | 408.580 |
| 27. | C.B.Burgon | Kentish Whs. C.C. | 407.825 |
| 28. | H.N.Cooke | Rutland C.C. | 405.879 |
| 29. | N.Brocklehurst | Man.St.Chris.C.C.C. | 405.131 |
| 30. | D.A.Porter | Glendene C.C. | 401.522 |
| 31. | E.J.Hodges | Medway Whs.C.C. | 398.982 |
| 32. | J.A.Lovell (T) | Kettering A.C.C. | 396.365 |
| 33. | C.A.Taylor | Southampton Whs. | 393.649 |
| 34. | J.M.Walker | Willesden C.C. | 390.934 |
| 35. | D.L.Sykes | Nomads C.C. | 390.743 |
| 36. | S.F.Wynne | De Laune C.C. | 390.563 |
| 37. | A.J.King | North Road C.C. | 384.776 |
| 38. | N.T.Channon | Medway R.C. | 365.997 |
| 39. | J.D.Taylor | Parkhill C.C. | 353.506 |
| 40. | J.Gray | Parkhill C.C. | 343.121 |

Team:

| | | |
|---|---|---|
| 1. | Middlesex R.C. | 1407.236 * |
| 2. | Veg.C.&.A.C. | 1301.747 |
| 3. | Rutland C.C. | 1270.051 |

* Comp record

As mentioned at the beginning **Barrow Central Whls** led by **Bert Dodds** with **425.57 won the team race**. He was backed up by two trike riders **M.G. Burns** with **379.12** and **H. Knipe** with **375.10 miles**. Barrow in Furness is of course, the location for one of the largest ship building yards in Great Britain. It has always been famous for producing submarines, even to this present year of 2008.

<hr>

**Jim Bailey and Jack Forrest** who had both ridden the North Road 24hr in 1958, Bailey on a bike and Forrest on a trike, **teamed up on a tandem and broke the RRA 24hr record with 492 miles,** and it's a record that still stands today (2008).

<hr>

**The North Road CC 24hr** was won by **Cliff Smith,** East Midlands CC with **464.304** miles. This was his **first win** in a 24hr event and like Coukham he had been well placed in a fair amount of '24 hrs' including Championships. This was to be the first of many for Cliff **Vic Stringer,** Bedfordshire RC was 2nd with **451.757m** and **J.R. Westcott,** Icknield RC. was 3rd with **448.490m.**

The event was held on the 3rd weekend in August and it's interesting to note that this was a rare instance where the old practice of following the harvest moon and the modern day Bank Holiday weekend coincided, but a poor entry of 45 riders was thought to be the result of following the Championship 12 hour too closely. This year of 1959 saw the emergence of a man who was to win the event on no less than ten occasions in 16 years, and whose familiar smooth pedalling and remorseless style was to become a regular sight to all followers of the distance game.

In this year he won the event typically with a well judged ride, surviving the challenge from Alan Blackman for 12 hours. Both men had 243 miles apiece and a 'Veg' rider, Bill Dunk with 235m. Drama in the night at March where British Rail had closed the level crossing all night, for track repairs, and tired riders were glad of help in negotiating the barriers. **Alan Blackman** went for a 'nocturnal perambulation' in an orchard and then fell asleep like a dormouse, eventually waking to finish with **445.916 m** taking **4th** place.

**Ken Usher was the fastest trike with 423.226m. This Crouch Hill CC rider led a team of trikes to a new competition record of 1,216.53m.** D. Hutchinson with **399.962 miles** and **H.K. James 393.342** added 152 miles onto a 5 year old **South Eastern RC** record. This distance of 152 miles at this point in time is the highest mileage ever to improve a **Team Competition Record** with. Ken Usher came to prominence in the Mersey of 1958 taking 4th place with his first ride at that distance.

**The actual team winners were the North Road CC trio of Alan Blackman with 445.916, Ernie Haldane, 430.715m and Tony King with 390.124m giving a total of 1,250.475 miles.**

# 1960

**The 24 Hour Fellowship was formed this year.**

The first organised Fellowship meeting was at Bickenhill near Meridan on December 18th 1960. Its founder members were: Jack Spackman, Sid Genders, Nick Carter, Arvon Jones, Dave Cane, Les Heald, and Cliff Bate, soon to be joined by Stan Bray, Ian Shaw and Les Lowe.

*Annual MOT tests are made compulsory for all 10 year old cars.*

<hr>

**The Catford 24 hr** on July 9th and 10th was **won by E.J. Stagg,** Old Portlians CC with **461.17m. Jim Hanning,** Veg C & AC **2nd** with **457.769** and 3rd **B. Wray** with **451.323.** Reg Randall, Harlequins CC was 4th with **450.257m,** having a last race in competition with other long distance 'stars' before his lone attempt at the 1,000 mile RRA bicycle record due to take place in just over a months time. **Peter Duncan,** Veg C & AC was 5th with **447.333 and Bill Dunk completed the team in 7th** place with **434.770 miles,** giving a **total of 1,339.872** out of 53 starters 35 finished.

*On July 11th 1960, **David Duffield** broke Albert Crimes **trike End to End record** with **2 days 10 hrs 58 mins,** riding the popular way this time from south to north.*

⟩•◇•⟨

**The Wessex RC** 24hr was **won** by **Bill Shearing** with **438.75 miles.** He led a Salisbury RC team to victory with **a total of 1,268.67 miles.** 2nd placed rider **Roy Cook** with **422.57m** and **M.M. Lambourne** with **404.35m** were the other members of the team. Considering only 12 riders in total finished due to 'arduous conditions' it's amazing to think that **another full team** from the **Hampshire RC** also finished. **S.M. Searle,** Hampshire RC was **3rd** overall with **416.82m, C.C.P 'Chris' Davies,** Hampshire RC with **388.21m** and **I.D. Thompson, 364.24** completed this **2nd team** with **1,169.37.**

This ride by Chris Davies was, I think, one of his first at 24hrs. He was on his way to his first 300,000 miles, so becoming one of the founder members of the '300,000 Miles Club' and at this present day (2007) he has so far covered more than 875,000 miles and is surely on his way to a million. Pete Luxton, Exeter Wheelers CC with 366.97 was another rider and regular supporter, who with his wife Jean, was always out on route in the West Country to marshal and help or observe, when a record breaker was passing through the area. **Bill Suttie,** Bournemouth Jubilee Whls beat Jack Spackman, **350.77m** to 299.17 so taking the **fastest trike** position.

⟩•◇•⟨

*Ron Coukham, who had won the Catford National Championship 24hr race in 1959, attempted to break the Lands End to John o' Groats record as a few of his 'peers' had done before him, but unkind weather conditions thwarted his efforts. The attempt finally drew to a close along Glen Annan, after completing nearly 500 miles. Coukham had battled against sickness, cold, wind and rain with grim determination. From Warrington onwards the teeming rain had lashed the rider and when the wind finally turned to howl down on him from due north, he bowed to his powerful foe - the weather. Rutland CC's champion had taken over 27 hours for the 500 miles to this bleak part of Dumfriesshire.*

⟩•◇•⟨

**The Mersey RC 24 hr** on July 23rd 1960 started in its usual place in a lane leading to Austins Hill near Tarvin As usual it drew a huge crowd of not just helpers, riders and officials, but also many interested club folk who regularly made the annual pilgrimage into Cheshire to see the riders off and then come back next day to see them finish. The weather was fair with one or two isolated showers. Although not a huge 'star-studded' field, it consisted of a fair selection of seasoned hard men and tough all day riders. Looking at the names on the start sheet and knowing the rides that these men had already produced and were capable of, there were a possible seven or more winners from a field of 45 starters. Ken Usher, Cliff Bate, Ken Hughes, 'Taff' Brissenden, Jeff Sanders, Don Spraggett and Vic Stringer, who had ridden to 2nd place in the North Road event of 1959 with 451 miles.

At 80 miles into the race, Bate led Spraggett by 1 minute with 3hrs 46 mins. Owen, Solihull, was at 3 mins, Sanders, Clowes and Jeavons were at 7 mins. Hughes, Brissenden and Hussey were at 8 mins, Reg Pearce at 9 mins and Malcolm Jones and Ken Usher at 10 mins. By the 120 mile point Spraggett led with 5 hrs 55 mins elapsed, Bate was 2nd at 1 min and Usher had crept through the field into 3rd place at 5 mins. At 170 miles, Bate had regained the lead with 8hrs 33mins, Usher was 2nd at 1 min. At the 12 hour point Ken Usher had taken the lead from Bate and Ken Hughes had just 'packed'. Between Whitchurch and Battlefield, Usher actually caught Cliff Bate on the road and the battle for supremacy was over. Usher wasn't really challenged again. Another battle was going on behind Usher; that of Brissenden and Sanders, with Sanders eventually coming out on top.

A south west wind helped the riders back to the finishing circuit at Waverton where Usher had a 17 mins lead on Jeff Sanders and 27 mins on Brissenden and that's how the race result eventually evolved. **Ken Usher,** Crouch Hill CC **won** with **454.59 miles, 2nd** was **Jeff Sanders,** North Worcs RC with **452.04,** a fine mileage for him and his best ever, finally overcoming the problems of misted glasses. **'Taff' Brissenden,** Mid Shropshire Whls was **3rd** with **448.75m, Alan Owen,** Solihull CC was **4th** with **445.62m** and **Vic Stringer,** Bedfordshire RC **5th** with **434.75 miles.**

Stan Bray was the 2nd fastest trike after Jim Shuttleworth, Stretford Whls 409.38m. Stan's 396.83m gaining him a new 'vets' record and the 2nd counter in the Solihull CC winning team, Dave Cane was the 3rd team member with 391.57m giving them a total of 1,234.17 miles.

A Birmingham St Christopher's CCC team of Pete Swinden, John Withers and Pat Kenny took the 2nd team medals with 1,187.33m. Swinden, with 410, Withers, 399m and Kenny, 377m.

One or two amusing incidents took place during this year's event. The first was at Marford where five club members who were checking and waiting at the turn, were surprised when a bus drew up for them to enter. They were dismayed at the scowl from the bus conductor when they failed to get on. They saw the funny side of things when they realised that as well as the checkpoint being at telegraph pole 15 (TP15) there was also a bus stop! The second incident was when the South Lancs RC's helping team tried to blow everyone up with what was a faulty pressure cooker!

*If John Arnold had been there he would have chuckled and said "you can' t beat a good old fashioned frying pan!"*

---

*On July 26th 1960 Jim Bailey and Jack Forrest broke the tandem End to End record in 2 days 4 hrs 48 mins. Although they reached Exeter 20 mins ahead of schedule they had experienced very heavy holiday traffic in the West Country. They reached Tewkesbury before the 12hr point at 243 miles and took on night clothes. At Nantwich they had a sit down feed at Jack Duckers house at 2am. Shap was climbed in a thick cold mist at dawn and their 24hrs yielded 448 miles, but by Carlisle they were an hour down on schedule due to heavy traffic. As they climbed through the Grampians on their second night they had two frights, the first one being a 'D.U.K.W.' amphibious landing craft hurtling towards them in the middle of the road with its headlights blazing, and the second was a high speed train that seemed to appear from nowhere on a track that ran alongside the road. From Inverness they had a very tough ride over Aultnamain and a very wet and windy grovel over the Ord of Caithness, into the teeth of a northerly gale, where at times they were reduced to walking. Despite the conditions they took nearly four hours off the previous record.*

*On Friday August 19th 1960, Reg Randall started on his mammoth 1,000 mile journey at 6 am, using roads that had formed part of the WTTA 24hr course just after the Second World War. 2 days 10 hrs and 40 mins later he'd broken Arthur Render's four year old record by over 6 hours. This 35 year old Harlequin CC rider standing at just 5ft 2" and weighing 10.5 stone had now proved that he was not only a winner at 24hr races, he was also the best man over the End to End route and 1,000 miles record route, and that height and stature weren't important to a record breaker.*

*His first 100 miles were done into the teeth of a strong south-westerly wind in 4hrs 44 mins. His course took in many towns such as Guildford, Reading, Marlborough, Langport, Taunton, Frome, Bristol, Gloucester, Worcester, Evesham, through the Cotswolds to Chippenham and Newbury. He covered 448 miles in the first 24 hours. Instead of getting slower at the 600 mile point he started to increase his speed and as dawn came up on his 2nd day, he'd completed 800 miles. By 900 miles he was 3.5 hours up on schedule with 51 hrs 42 mins and at the end he'd improved Arthur Render's figures by over 6 hours. This record will stand for 41 years.*

*Reg always put the help that he received from his friends and club mates as being a paramount feature in his successes, always stressing how important their help was to him. Reg is now a sprightly 85 year old and Lynne and I see him at various dinners and functions. He is still very interested in the current long distance, 24hr and End to End record breaking scene, but prefers to go walking with his old friends. He says it's a bit safer than riding a bike. Over the years he has been on a fair amount of record attempts as an Observer for the RRA, or as a helper.*

*Whenever one gets into conversation with him he always mentions the helpers that were on his many races against the clock, stating that without them he couldn't have broken records or gained decent positions in 24hr races. He once showed me a large photo that he treasures, of his crew of helpers, probably about 30 in all, stood with him at the end of this 1,000 mile record, but Reg sadly admitted that over half of them had now passed away. I last chatted to Reg at the 2006 Frome and District Wheelers Dinner.*

**The North Road CC 24hr** on August Bank Holiday 1960 was a **National Championship.** If we thought that the field for the Catford National of 1959 was a good one for 'star' riders, then this North Road production was to be the icing on the cake, harkening back to the 'heady' days of the early 1950's when battle raged between 'stars' such as Mundy, Harvey, Butler, Laws, Basham, Andrews, Crimes, Arnold, Carter and Thompson. The field for this 1960 Championship promised to be an even better one. The winners of the previous seven North Road events were present and champions such as Coukham, Burrell and Thompson were riding. Harding, Fensom, Keeler and Smith were all after 'honours'. After five successive championship team wins the Rutland had a record 7 entries, The Vegetarian C & AC had 5, The Middlesex, 4, the Leicester Forest, Hull Thursday and North Road also had teams.

The weather according to the 24hr Fellowship Journal was cool, showery and windy, but the North Road Gazette describes it as good conditions throughout, with a still and brilliantly moonlit night? Sixty eight riders faced the timekeeper Eric Wilkinson. A check at 54 miles showed Keeler setting a fast pace and leading Coukham by 4 mins. Cliff Smith had already punctured but wasn't far behind with George Steers in front of him. At Hitchin, Tony Fouldes came off his bike and suffered concussion. At 91 miles, Keeler had caught Coukham for 5 mins and was having a real scrap on the road for supremacy. Smith and Steers were 7 mins down on the leaders, Burrell at 8.5 mins, Harding at 10m, Duncan 10.5m and Poole at 15m. At Wansford with 170 miles behind them Coukham had retired having overdone things, 'blown' is the modern expression. Cliff Smith had taken the lead, Arch Harding was at 1m 45secs, Keeler at 3.45m, Den Mills at 5.45m, Burrel 6.30m, Steers, John Arnold, making a rare appearance, and Dick Poole, were all within 18 mins of the leader. The Middlesex RC were leading the team race by 20 mins at this point.

At 224 miles Harding had taken the lead with Burrell 1 min behind, Smith was now at 4 mins. After the Godmanchester to Ely and back 'leg' the position was much the same but Keeler was suffering badly from his earlier efforts. Across the 'Fens' the Middlesex battle continued and at 294 miles, Burrell had taken the lead with Harding at 1 min. Smith was at 17 min, Mills 24m, Duncan 30, Fensom 32, Arnold 48, Thompson 55m and Dick Poole who was suffering badly but being urged on to greater efforts for the sake of the team. By 315 miles, Keeler and Steers had retired.

Jock Wadley writing in the Sporting Cyclist, described 'young' Fred Burrell who was 38 years old, in comparison to Arch Harding being 47, gladdening the hearts of the North Road 'Old Timers' riding a 79" fixed wheel on the same bike he'd ridden to victory in 1956. His steady pedalling riding 'wired-on' tyres, was a joy to see. Mal Rees writing about that same event described Arch Harding's disappointment at never winning a Championship event but regularly taking 2nd place and how Burrell was the unknown force in the team until the day of the race, never giving any indication of his fitness or showing any optimism.

Mal Rees heaped great acclaim on Dick Poole's performance, despite poor preparation due to being newly wed and painting his new home. Realising that the team competition record was within their grasp, Dick was urged to hold his speed and that around 445 miles would secure the win. For hour after hour his support team urged him on; they realised how much he was suffering by the way he reacted to their demands. Usually he was cheerful, but he was now stone faced and at the end, his efforts left him in agony. Tears welled in his tired eyes as he was helped off his bike, he'd earned his third place in the team and secured a new Competition Record.

By the time the finishing circuit was reached with 406 miles covered, Fred Burrell had increased his lead over Harding to 18 minutes. Fensom was 3rd at 54 mins, Duncan and Smith had 'packed', Smith due to severe cramp. John Arnold was at 65 mins, Mills at 71mins and Dick Poole was now at 81mins.

Burrell went round the finishing circuit steadily at 18 mph while Harding went round nearer to 20 mph to try and bridge the gap, but when the gap was down to 8 minutes at 457 miles, **Burrell matched Hardings speed to win the Championship with exactly the same mileage as his first one, 477.702m.** **Arch Harding** produced his best mileage ever to take **2nd** place with **474.728m** and **Fensom** who had battled it out in the closing stages with Arnold, got **3rd** place with **460.906m** to **Arnolds best ever mileage of 460.175m.** **Dick Poole took 5th place with 454.806m to secure the Team win for the Middlesex RC with a new Competition record of 1,407.236 miles.**

**Shearing** of the Salisbury RC took **6th** place with a **450.016m** ride and **Les Lowe** rose to his highest ever mileage of **446.707m** for **7th** place. **Bill Dunk,** Veg C & AC, was very close to Les with **446.566m. Den Mills** who is now a Committee member and Official of the RRA came **9th** with **443.385. The fastest trike was J.A. Lovell with 396.365 miles.**

*Stuart 'Joe' Thompson recalled 'the end of an era' when his club, the Rutland CC failed to get a rider into the first ten positions. Although he had hardly touched his bike for the previous two years, he was lured back to give the team race one last try. They faced the timekeeper with numerically the largest force they had ever mustered, but even so, there was no 'air of confidence' about the team.*

*The strain of the years of high level competition was more than ever apparent amongst the more seasoned riders, men who had once lived only for their cycling now had other pressing commitments. After a six week crash training programme and three time trials at 25, 50 and 100 miles, Thompson felt he was up to it, but a touch of flu the week preceding the race left him feeling very despondent. This feeling was heightened during the race when he punctured at 20 miles and felt that this wasn't to be his day, but that he must press on for the team. It is this next part of his description that I can relate to very easily. Thompson said he witnessed the most amazing occurrence ever seen in a 24hr Championship, due to a freak chance in the order of start. About half a dozen of the top riders had congregated together before the 100 miles mark was reached and were scrapping it out mile after mile, for all the world as though they wanted to settle the issue there and then. Ron Coukham was amongst this group battling with Keeler, Harding, Burrell and Hanning. Thompson thought at this stage that a 'trial of strength' would prove disastrous.*

*His fears were confirmed when Coukham retired, the first casualty of this fierce private battle. The shades of night were falling fast as the riders rejoined the A1 for the long run north, a bobbing tail light ahead turned out to be that of Dave Keeler, he was now the second casualty of the earlier battles. The Middlesex RC were in full flight with the team race sewn up as well as 1st and 2nd positions on the road. The heavy flow of traffic in the darkness on the A1 made Thompson feel unnerved and he said that whereas five years previously it wouldn't have bothered him, he now couldn't help thinking of his responsibilities to his wife and three little girls at home. His friend George Steers who's cheery grin had brightened many a 24hr race 'called it a day' and as Stuart Thompson rode on through the old familiar places, small market towns and sleepy villages he had a sudden tiredness overcome him.*

*He was pleased to see his old friend John Arnold going very well on his come back ride, but as the first rays of the morning sun broke through on that dreaded stretch from Guyhirn Bridge to Cambridge he felt he couldn't go on any further. He'd covered 350 miles, the cold was intense, his legs were lifeless and no amount of care and cold sponges could keep him awake. His brain was numb and muddled and he felt that this was where he came in 8 years previously. Whereas he had something to continue for then, he felt that any reward now couldn't repay the agony. After watching the battle on the finishing circuit and seeing the Middlesex RC eclipse the Rutland Competition Record, Stuart Thompson felt that this was the end of the Rutland era and a notable chapter in his club's history was complete.*

I too was there that day, helping my club mate John Withers, Birmingham St Christopher's CCC who came 22nd with 423 miles, and I also remember seeing that same battle erupt between those top men. The atmosphere was electric with no one willing to give way or drop back, and I felt that they couldn't possibly ride at that speed all night. One very fond memory I have, is of seeing Arch Harding downing a pint of beer outside the pub and riding away puffing on a cigarette that same evening. (Both criminal offences in public places in 2007).

*My many thanks to Stuart Thompson for his many 'insights' of the 24hr race scene at that time, especially the battle for team supremacy.*

*For many years I thought it was amazing that a County as small as Rutland could field so many excellent 24hr riders and it was only on researching this book that I realised Rutland doesn't exist on modern day maps and that the 'Rutland CC' was a club formed in a small area of Sheffield known as Rutland Hall, and nothing to do with the small area that used to be adjacent to Leicestershire, on its eastern border. My large scale map shows Rutland Water and Rutland County Museum, close to Oakham and Stamford but doesn't even list Rutland in the index.*

# 1961

*The Soviet Union puts the first man into space.*

The **Catford CC 24hr** was the first event of the year, and was **won by Bill Best** of the Orpington CRC with **446.85 miles.** Reg Randall of the **Harlequins CC** was **2nd** with **439.30** and **M.J. Wilkins,** Surrey Roads CC was **3rd** with **432.53m.** D.P. Knight with 432.20 and G. Holton, 388.74 completed the Harlequins CC team for a win of 1,260.44 miles. Twenty riders finished and the **fastest trike rider** was P.W. Hennessy, Southborough Wheelers with **363.90 miles.**

———⟫•◇•⟪———

The **Wessex RC 24hr** on July 15th-16th was **won by Bill Shearing,** Salisbury RC with **448.39m,** Vic Stringer, Bedfordshire Roads CC was **2nd, 446.27m** and **A.R. Chamberlain,** Hounslow & District Wheelers was **3rd** with **443.33m.** S.M. Searle who was 4th with 416.83m led Chris Davies, 401.72 and J.H. Taylor, 367.71 to a Hampshire RC team win with 1,186.26m. Fourteen finished from twenty starters and **Bill Suttie was the fastest trike** with **365.87 miles.**

———⟫•◇•⟪———

The **Mersey RC 24hr** on July 22nd and 23rd was a **National Championship event won by Arch Harding with a course and event record of 470.36 miles.** He also led the Middlesex RC team consisting of Fred Burrell and **Dick Poole to a Championship Team win for the 2nd year running with 1,398.93m.** Another team record for this Mersey course and event.

This National Championship had drawn some very good riders to the field. Fred Burrell as well as Arch Harding had a race long battle with Cliff Smith, and Dick Poole produced possibly his best mileage so far, and less than 10 miles covered the first four riders, **Arch Harding, 470.36, Fred Burrell, 2nd with 467.42, Cliff Smith, 3rd with 464.78 and Dick Poole 4th with 461.15m.**

Harding's win was an amazing achievement for a 48 year old. The Middlesex beat the **Mid Shropshire Whls team** by 81 miles. Their top man **'Taff' Brissenden** improved on last years Mersey mileage to finish 5th with **455.66m,** his clubmate **Ken Hughes** was **6th** with **454.50m** and along with **Ray Page, 408.19m** they completed the **2nd team** with **1,318.35 miles.**

First onto the finishing circuit at 2.48pm was Poole looking immaculate and riding on the tops, as he had been for most of the event. Harding arrived one minute later and Burrell was third, attired in the old inconspicuous all-black of the pre-club colours era. Only fifteen riders had covered the complete course prior to reaching the circuit. The gallery of spectators at Waverton Corner gave Harding an extra loud cheer each time he flashed through, until he finally ran out of time to achieve a great ambition of at last becoming the 24 hour Champion. He suffered severe backache from the 10 hour point until the finishing circuit. In fact it was so bad he didn't think he would finish. Arch said "everything ached except my legs", he hadn't got anything complimentary to say about the Cheshire and Shropshire road surfaces, and felt that the event should have started at mid-day in line with other 24hr time trials.

Fred Burrell rode a 79" fixed wheel again and commented that his gear was too high for this course, which he described as 'hard touring country'! Jock Wadley went on to mention how the championship result was decided in Wales on the arid, pub-less (*pubs in Wales didn't open on Sundays in the 1960's*) drags out through Flintshire to the Denbigh border at Bangor-on-Dee. At that period in the race Harding was slowing badly and described his own speed as just "balancing".

The fastest trike rider in this 1961 event was Terry Kelly with 410.78 miles.

**Jeff Sanders,** North Worcestershire RC although down to **7th** place this year, his mileage of **454.12** was a personal best in his 3rd event. **Don Spraggett** had a good ride for **8th** place with **438.08,** despite being hit by a car. **John Thompson,** Manchester Whls CC with **433.21m** was **9th,** John Withers, Birmingham St Christopher's CCC with one of his best mileages of **430.11m** was **10th,** with **Pat Kenny, 427.47m** and Pete Swinden, **402.44m.** They completed the **3rd team** with **1,260.02.** **John Pugh,** Godric CC with **410.12m** was another young rider like myself, whose interests lay mainly in long distance riding and 24hr events, a trait that would last him most of his life.

⟫═◇═⟪

**The North Road 24hr** was **won by Cliff Smith** with **460.625 miles.** **Den Mills,** South Ruislip CC was **2nd** with **438.807** and **Reg Randall** was **3rd** with **436.210m.** The North Road history book described it as a 'Cliff Smith benefit race' due to him winning it twice in 3 years, despite the presence of some good men such as Reg Randall, Ken Usher and Bill Dunk. The report goes on to say that it became apparent from the first check at 50 miles, that nothing short of an earthquake would stop Smith winning his 2nd North Road 24 hr race.

The North Road club at this particular time were experiencing problems of only attracting small fields, and from 42 starters, only 25 riders finished. **Joe Summerlin** came **4th** with **433.212m.** **Reg Randall** led **J. Randall** and **S. Holton** to a Harlequins CC team win of **1,234.086m.** Their 2nd team win in as many years. **Stan Spelling beat Cliff Tremaine** by 5 miles to take the fastest trike award with **395.833m.** **Stan Bray** took **8th** place for the Solihull CC with **417.983m** and **Howard Bayley** rode his debut 24hr race for the Solihull on a **trike** with **362.26m.**

*On December 22nd 1961 the first U.S. Soldier was killed in Vietnam. His death came months before America's direct military involvement. The war was to last some eleven years, until President Nixon declared on January 23rd 1973, that war was over.*

1962

**The Catford CC** event started the 24 hour season off in the south. It was **won by Cliff Smith,** East Midlands CC with **462.16 miles.** This was the first of Cliff's eight wins in this event spread over the next ten years. **Reg Randall** came **2nd** with **453.2 miles** and led a Harlequin CC team to a win of **1,302.88 miles.** The other riders in the team were **Les Randall,** with **424.88,** and **G. Horton, 424.80m,** (both very close performances). **Mick Dunn,** Catford CC was overall **3rd** with **449.625m, Vic Stringer,** Bedfordshire RC was **4th** with **443.2 m, Ray Burnett** in **5th** place had one of his best mileages in this event with **433.88m.**

A prominent non-finisher was Ken Usher who two weeks later went on to win the Mersey event Mick Dunn had progressed from a junior with the Catford CC over a period of years, to taking 3rd place in this event. It was a natural progression as he'd been the club champion and record holder at nearly every discipline from track racing to 12hours prior to this event. Dunn also excelled at road record breaking both on bike and trike.

⟫═◇═⟪

**The Wessex RC** in 1962 hosted the **RTTC National Championships.** It was **won** by **Nim Carline** now riding for the Morley CC with **472.05 miles.** The race was held in very windy weather and was the first time appearance of 12 hr 'star' Carline in this Wessex event. His only other ride at the distance had been in 1955 coming 2nd in the North Road event with 453.693m. Harding, Poole and Burrell were present as probably the team favourites, as were the Mid Shropshire Whls. **The Middlesex RC** were leading the **team** race when suddenly Burrell 'packed' in the last few hours, leaving **George Seward** to rise to the Championship occasion with **417m** to secure the **team win** with **1,334 miles,** just ahead of the Mid Shropshire Whls 1,326m. **Cliff Smith,** East Midlands CC fresh from his Catford win came **2nd** with **463.67** and **Arch Harding** a very close **3rd** with **462 miles.**

130

*I will now use sections, paragraphs and details from an article by Ian Shaw who covered the event for the 24hr Fellowship.*

'The time was 3.02 Saturday afternoon; the last man had just been despatched by the timekeeper, officials and helpers looked at their watches and checked when the riders would be due back again while they chatted with last years friends, and this years acquaintances. Stocks of food and drink had to be secured for the day and night ahead. It was cloudy and a gale was buffeting large trees back and forth as if they were just flimsy hedgerows; hopes were expressed that it would calm down a bit in the evening, meantime it was fairly cool. The course went straight out for 36 miles and it was heard that the later riders had gone through a heavy storm at the end of the 'leg' that completely soaked them.

Conversation swung round to riders prospects and likely winners. The name Wilkings buzzed around a lot, it had been quite a while since a current 12hour champion had entered a 24hr Championship, especially one who had beaten 271 miles, it was said he had a schedule for 504 miles taped to his top tube! Arch Harding was known to be very fit and as a proved 24hr man, a very hard one to beat. Fred Burrell as a Champion in 1956 and 1960 was wagered on and many knew how keen and fit Dick Poole was, to complete a Middlesex RC trio. Cliff Smith was mentioned as a 'near outsider'. The name Nim Carline was remembered by a few but got rather lost among the other names.

Someone shouted "man up" and number 10, Tucker, came through followed a minute later by a hard riding No 30, a quick check on the start card, Oh yes, it's Carline, in 3hrs 6 mins for approximately 71 miles, or about the rate for a 4hr 27 minute 100 miles. Hmmm he's flying. Several others flew past including the big names, Burrell 14 minutes slower than Carline, Poole at 11 mins, Wilkings at 4 mins, Brissenden at 20 mins, Goulding at 16 mins, Smith at 11 mins, Hughes after mechanical trouble at 24 mins and Harding at 16 mins.

They were all flying before the wind now as they rode on in the direction of Southampton, along the straight rolling roads of the New Forest. A check at 148 miles at Lyndhurst showed the positions as before but even more so, so to speak. Carline was at 6hrs 44mins, 38 mins inside 'evens'. Wilkings was holding him at just over 8 mins, Smith at 15 mins, Poole at 24m. Burrell and Harding at 26m. The light began to fail and so did some of the predictions. The wind, for instance, did not moderate and the same can be said for Nim Carline riding largish gears, uninhibited by caution, Carline continued to forge ahead.

*Large gears were Nim's trademark plus a very stripped down bike, no spares and quite often no bottle or bottle cage. At night he would concede to wearing a flat cap and if the weather was really cold maybe a thick sweater. I only ever saw Nim wearing thin long trousers over his shorts just once in a 24 hour. Apart from shorts and a racing vest most people resorted at that time to fairly normal warm top clothing. Don't forget this was 1962 and whereas Professional cyclists and Olympic team riders would probably be supplied with a tracksuit etc, these clothes were not that easily available or affordable to just club cyclists.*

The helpers and spectators predicted that either the more experienced 24hr men would bide their time and then whistle past Carline, one by one, when he eased off in the second half as surely he must do, or that a large explosion would be heard in the early hours as he 'blew'! Meanwhile Cyril Neale, the Event Organiser, began to worry a little about his marshalling schedule being threatened by this fast riding. Through Ringwood at 184 miles, Carline had a substantial lead, having taken just 8hrs 40 mins, and the time being 11.10pm. After a 22 mile detour leg from Lyndhurst to Bull Hill and back only Wilkings was anywhere near Carline at 9 mins. Smith was at 17 mins, Burrell 27m, Harding 29m, Poole 29.5m Davies, Exeter Whls at 33mins. Goulding now slowing at 47 mins, Tucker at 43m, Owen 44m and Ken Hughes at 46m.

Soon after this stretch Wilkings retired to everyone's disappointment. It was said that he had stomach trouble and double vision but he was also downhearted at being over an hour down on his schedule, in fact he was seen examining it rather sadly under a street light despite being reassured that schedules go wild on a day or a night with such weather as this. He was firmly in 2nd place when he retired.

At the 12 hour point Carline went through with 246 miles covered, Cliff Smith was now second just below 240 miles, riding powerfully, smoothly and very steadily. Dawn came to the roundabout at Bailey Gate, many watches timed Carline through 292 miles in 14 hours 33 mins, just 3 mins inside evens and 25 mins ahead of Fred Burrell on the road who was now pulling back time on the leader as he had done many times before. Cliff Smith at this point was still 2nd, Burrell 3rd, Harding 4th and Poole 5th. Back at Bailey Gate the second time it was thought that either Carline was slowing a little or had stopped for a few minutes as he had lost time to all the medal contenders who were chasing him. Fears were expressed that Carline's great 17 hr ride in the lead with continuously grim conditions was beginning to sap his strength. A lot of people were quite unaware that he had already proved himself to be a proficient 24hr and 12hr rider and many of his rides were done in far from ideal conditions.

At 370 miles all of the speculations had proved fruitless as Carline was still there in the lead with Smith at 12 mins, Harding at 22 and Poole at 29 mins. Surprisingly Burrell had retired when in 3rd place at about 360 miles, he was quite cheerful but he had just had enough.

It had been very cool at dawn with that relentless wind, but as Carline entered the finishing circuit just before 11 am, the sun came out and it was a little warmer for the first time in 21 hours. The circuit was just over 15 miles round, and by the time Cliff Smith rode onto it Carline was just about to complete his first lap. As he had started 30 mins before Smith this meant that effectively Smith was only 5 or 6 miles behind him at the most. Carline's response was to raise his speed and pull out an even greater effort and in the next lap he had put another 5 minutes or nearly 2 miles onto his lead. Try as he might, Cliff Smith couldn't match Carlines strength. The lead grew until at the finish Carline beat Smith by over 8 miles, and Harding by 10m.

So **Gold for Carline** with **472.05m, Silver** for **Smith, 463.67m** and **Bronze** for **Harding, 462.00m.  Dick Poole** took **4th** place with **454.21m** to give the **Middlesex RC team** a good lead over the Mid Shropshire Whls, even without Burrell finishing, the Middlesex still had another good **3rd team counter** in **George Seward** with **417.83 miles.**

While the medal positions were being sorted out during the event, there had been some pretty tough riding from the lads in the 2nd team, the Mid Shropshire Whls, consisting of 'Taff' Brissenden, Ken Hughes and Norman Kellett. **The Middlesex totalled 1,334.04m and the Mid Shropshire Whls, 1,326.39 miles.**

Ian Shaw finished his report by saying "Again we saw some close riding from Brissenden, 454.21 and Hughes, 441.29m. This club appears to be a new force in the long distance world. Few believed Nim Carline would keep it up, perhaps not even he himself, but he started brilliantly, held on steadily, then ground down the remaining opposition on the circuit with a flashing fast finish, all over 472 unbelievably tough miles. A new star has emerged in the 24hr world."

⇒·◇·⇐

After pulling out of the Catford event earlier in the month, **Ken Usher,** Crouch Hill CC **won the Mersey RC 24hr.** It was his second win in this event with a **new Course and Event Record of 474.02m.** The Solihull CC won the team race with 1,287.09 miles. Eric Matthews made his debut in this event and what a debut, **coming 2nd with 467.12m. Don Spraggett** who was on his 5th Mersey produced his best mileage so far to take **3rd** place with **452.88m. Stan Bray** who came 4th with **445.81** led the winning Solihull Team of Dave Cane with **423.91 and Howard Bayley on a trike** was vastly improved from previous years with **417.37m.** His colossal training mileages mixed with his daily work routine had made all the difference. **Terry Kelly** also on a **trike** with **415.89m** was a very hard man to beat. Eric Matthews led the Altrincham RC trio of R. Metcalfe with 400.81 and M. McAllister 381.95m to secure 2nd team with 1,249.88m. **B. Holt** took **5th** place with **437.88, Charlie Alexander** was **6th** with **432.47m, Brian Haddock,** Oldbury and District CC **429.07.** I also made my debut at 24hr riding that day aged 18. The Elders in the club said "You're much too young son, you'll do yourself harm; but here I am at 64 years of age and still feeling like a spring chicken! My 380.46 helped Pete Swinden with 419.70 and John Withers 403.58 to get Birmingham St Christopher's the 3rd team spot with 1,203.74m. My participation in long distance racing made me feel different about myself and it gave me confidence in life, in fact throughout life, and the euphoria just from finishing a 24hr lasted right through until the winter. Whenever I got a knock backwards at work or at home, I would think to myself, at least I can ride for 24 hrs with the 'men'.

⇒·◇·⇐

**The North Road 24hr** event was rather late this year, being in the middle of September, consequently there was a reduced field, however, out of all the 24hr races in 1962, this one had the closest result. There were 37 riders on the card; prominent names amongst these were Reg Randall, John Arnold and Cliff Smith. Reg Randall had hoped to go for the London to Edinburgh record and as the wind appeared to be from the right quarter, he duly attempted it. His name isn't in the RRA record book for this place-to-place record, so I can only assume it was abandoned. With Reg out of the reckoning everybody knew it would be a colossal day long battle between Arnold and Smith. Already this year Smith had won the Catford with 462m and was 2nd in the National Championship with 463m. For John Arnold, it was his first 24hr race since the North Road of 1960 when he had ridden to 4th place with 459.9m. This 24hr race was also said to be the first time he had raced this year at any distance, but knowing John he wouldn't have skimped on his training. The weather was breezy and dry with sunny periods but not over warm at the start at 12.01pm. Later however the breeze turned into a cold, strong, south-westerly wind, and a chilling rain led to the retirement of over half of the 37 riders.

At 100 miles Smith led with 4hr 41m 12 secs. Arnold was at just over 6 mins, Joe Summerlin, Oundle was 3rd at 12 mins, Ken Davis 4th at 13m, Vic Gibbs at 14m and Nigel Stark at 15m. At the 147.5 mile point, Arnold had closed up to Smith with 3.5 mins and was really putting on the pressure. Harold Nelson, busily brewing yet more porridge for Arnold, looked thoughtful and said this was really like the old trike days of the early 1950's when John fought many battles on the road against Crimes, Carter and Thompson. By 160 miles Smith had lost his lead on the road and Arnold took over the role, pressing on up the North Road A1 into the cold night, riding an 84" single freewheel gear. Cliff Smith rode his usual Sturmey Archer hub gear giving a variable of 75", 81 and 86", *although for some reason he didn't like it publicised, and Cliff was the sort of chap who would have shunned anything to do with professionalism or sponsorship.* We were now witnessing a duel worthy of a Championship event. At 203 miles Arnold led in 9 hrs 50 mins and Smith was at 4 mins. Vic Gibbs was 3rd at 39 mins. At 12 hours Arnold had done 246 miles and Smith 245, so it was getting very close again. There was very little wind in the night and it was mainly clear, but very cold, especially by dawn. Smith lost a little time when he lost his helpers due to their car breaking down. By 301 miles Arnold was 8 mins up on Smith in 14hrs 56 mins and Gibbs was still 3rd at 61 mins. Heading back from the Fens the riders had a tough ride into a very cold, strong, westerly wind. At 393 miles Arnold came through Eltisley, a prize winning best-kept village, but he had little time to admire the well kept green. Nearly thirty mins later Smith came through, now 15 mins down on Arnold, but he was fighting back hard. John Arnold was slowing slightly but his considerable efforts over the last 13 hours had given him a sufficient lead, enough to win. He entered the finishing circuit nearly 12 mins up and lapped in 57 mins, 55m and 54m. Smith actually got within 3.5 mins of Arnold but when time was called, Arnold had won by 1.5 miles.

**John Arnold, 462.982 miles, Cliff Smith 461.429m, Vic Gibbs 438.041m. A. Dalton, 4th 431.252m. John Baines 5th 431m** was riding his first 24hr. **Chris Davies with 386.282m led a Hampshire RC team comprising of S.M. Searle 377.517 and D.C. Culverwell, 373.240 to a winning total of 1,137.039m. Bill Sargeant,** one of the trike riders rode 363.9 miles, he was a regular helper on many record attempts in that area. **A.C. Jones was the fastest trike with 372.409 miles.**

*In the October of this year, George Herbert Stancer 'G.H.S' died and again the North Road CC had lost another stalwart member who'd been with them since 1904, although he was also Acting President of the Century R.C. He had been the Editor of 'Cycling' from 1910 to 1930 and then he became Secretary and Editor of the CTC. He later became President of the 'C.T.C' and the 'T.A' (Tricycle Association). He was a cycling statesman who in his earlier years had guided many long distance racing men through their careers, men such as Harry Green who took many records in the early 1900's including the End to End. He was also very encouraging to women long distance riders such as Kate Green, Lilian Dredge and Marguerite Wilson.*

# 1963

**The Catford** was the first event this year and it was a **National Championship won by Nim Carline with 475.18 miles.** He dominated the event and this year he'd come with a full team, hoping to get the 'double', but although Arch Harding had retired at 12 hrs, the **Middlesex RC still won the team race with Dick Poole, Fred Burrell and newcomer John Dean,** filling Harding's place. Cliff Smith also came with a full team this year.

When the event started in the old familiar lane, nothing could have been more daunting to the riders than the prospect of riding through torrents of rain that were falling. Elsewhere, Wimbledon was washed out, Cricketers were sitting huddled in pavilions, but here on the Brighton Road, men were setting out in a deluge with the prospect of it lasting through until the next day. One old timer remarked "I can only remember it raining as hard as this in the Anfield of 1928" and this could be believed. It was like a tropical downpour but without the mild temperature to make it bearable. Despite that, noticeably fast rides were done over the first stages of this event.

At the 'Lower Beeding' turn which was very tricky in the wet, Carline led with Poole at 1 min, Brissenden, 90 secs, Smith at 2 mins, Duncan at 3m, Harding at 4.5m and Jenkins at 5 minutes. Arch Harding wasn't very complimentary about the weather as he came by and he was already threatening to retire. Arch wore glasses and I would imagine the prospect of trying to see and judge the road ahead for him was quite frightening and this was only daylight. It seemed strange to look down the start sheet and read only one vegetarian riders name, and to think back, not so long ago, of the roll call of great vegetarian 'stayers' such as Purves, Guy, Ferris, Marshall, Cave, Lawrie, Keeler, Hanning, Duncan and Davey, plus many others over the years.

Carline was already setting the race alight, setting a cracking pace at just under 24 mph and in those conditions. It was difficult to believe that he could keep up such pressure, but he was the Champion and we had to assume that he knew what he was doing. At the 50 mile check, Alan Gordon recorded the following times: Carline, 2hrs 9 mins, Poole at 4 mins, Brissenden, 5 mins, Smith 7 mins, Jenkins and Usher 8m, Dunn, 8m 35 secs.

"DIG IN - ONLY 22 HOURS TO GO."

Usher of the Edgeware RC was a new arrival amongst the leaders and who could tell how he might do? At Dale Hill the rain reached new heights of fury, lashing the riders as they rode under the edge of the mist laden 'Devil's Dyke. As the riders turned onto the Brighton Road they could watch the tattered stragglers in the Brighton and back walk struggling home towards London, four or five hours behind the winner, and after over 30 hours on their feet. (*Sounds worse than 24 hr riding to me!*) Later the riders headed towards Steyning and they could see the rain, lightening and easing slowly. At that point (90.9 miles), Carline was at 3 hrs 58 mins, Poole at 10m, Smith 11m 34s, Jenkins 13m, Brissenden (who fell heavily at the turn) 14m, Cooke 15m, Usher 15m 47s and Dunn at 16m 48 secs.

The field was now falling into some sort of order, but at the 'Frankland Arms' sit down feed very few riders stopped. One or two riders had mislaid their bags with their spares and food rations due to an organisational mishap; one or two riders had suffered multiple punctures and were desperate for spares, as was Ray Burnett. Baker was leading the trike contingency at this point, very strongly, as they plugged into a stiff breeze. Bill Best who won the Catford two years previously didn't look so good at this point and could be seen struggling out of the saddle. I would think a sore backside caused by a wet saddle and shorts was probably the reason.

At the 150.43 miles checkpoint on the Chichester by-pass, Carline still led the field, doing 22.5 mph, in 6 hrs 51m, Smith was 2nd at 14 mins, Poole at 15m, Usher 18m, Dunn 24m, Jenkins 26m, Brissenden 27m and Burrell at 31 m. It was here that a car ran into the rear of a scooter rider on the wet road at the traffic lights. No blood was spilt luckily and only superficial damage was done to the scooter, but it was a bad omen as only a few miles away, Bill Best who earlier had been struggling, was struck down by a motor-cyclist and taken to hospital with a suspected broken leg, collar bone and facial injuries. Later when we heard the full story it seemed that it wasn't as serious as first thought and his wife, although greatly upset, insisted on going back to the event to keep the other Orpington rider, Fred Manus going. She earned a great deal of respect that day for her efforts at a very trying time.

By Selsey, Stockbridge and Wittering darkness had fallen and riders were cautiously helped around a traffic island by a conveniently positioned cars headlight. Bill Sargeant was overcome by sickness and retired. At the 212 miles point, Carline had an almost unassailable lead with 9hrs 56 mins. Poole and Usher were at 29 mins, Jenkins 35m, Brissenden 38m, Cooke 41m and Mick Dunn at 43 mins.

Earlier in the event, on Plummers Plain in the afternoon's heavy downpour, we had seen a cyclist who was obviously an 'old timer', reminiscent of the helpers of many years ago. On the back of his saddlebag was a kettle, and at every convenient point on his machine there were drinking bottles, hooked on with string; sponges for the canvas bucket also hung there, towels, frying pan, you name it, he'd got it, in fact everything a good helper should have. We met him at Chichester and discussed the rest of the route. John had ridden a long way to help the Mid-Shropshire Whls team and was not concerned at riding virtually the whole of the course with them, not that a little thing like a 24hr would worry him, for this was the legendary John Arnold! On to Guildford and the day started to dawn as the riders went to Esher and back to Guildford. The leaders then went out to Windsor and the long trek back to the finishing circuit. At 277 miles, Carline had a huge lead of 34 mins over Poole, Burrell 40m, Jenkins 43m, Cooke 47, Cliff Smith 52m, Dunn 61m, Dean, Middlesex RC and Brissenden 1hr 12mins. Nobody could understand how Fred Burrell had crept into 3rd place on the leader chart, but they shouldn't really have been surprised as this is what he nearly always does. (*The first time I noticed him was in the 1956 North Road Championship event at about 300 miles, when Stuart Thompson shouted to his helpers "Who is the chap I passed 15 hours ago and is catching me very fast?" That was Fred Burrell!*) Burrell was the only one who was gaining significantly on the leader, could he keep it up? Carline had also lost a few minutes to Dick Poole in these last few miles up to Guildford, so were these hills getting to him? And where were Usher and Brissenden?

Back at the Shalfords feed, Mike Rees, Middlesex RC came in. There is a point of exhaustion beyond which courage, discipline and loyalty cannot go and Rees was already past that point. His head was rolling from side to side, his mouth hung open, his hands dangled from strengthless wrists and arms and as he walked his knees were buckling under him, but the Middlesex RC had its sights set on the team prize and no one who could 'keep going' (*another way of saying 'was still alive'*) would be allowed to stop in case they were needed. Harding was already out and if Rees went too, there would only be four riders still going for the Club. So after refreshment, he was cruelly persuaded back onto the bike, and sent wearily on his way. Automatically his feet slid back into his toe clips and he disappeared from view. Jenkins, who had been prominent throughout the race up until about the 340 mile point, suddenly cracked. He'd had a fair amount of tough luck, having been off course two or three times when leading on the road.

Most of the riders were back on the finishing circuit with just a few hours left. Mick Dunn from the promoting club decided to make his mark for a higher mileage than last year and was in a storming mood. Through Bucks Green and Broadridge Heath the riders vied for their places on the road. Carline was still in the lead and his speed was still high which tempted people to think that Competition Record could possibly be broken, but it had been a very hard event and as he passed Roffey Church, he was visibly slowing and I think Carline was just riding to win, which he did handsomely by over 6 miles with **475.18 miles, Poole 2nd** with **468.815m**. A personal best for both men. **Fred Burrell** maintained his **3rd** place with **464.746m** and **John Dean** getting **7th** place with **439.895miles,** this gave the **Middlesex RC their 4th Championship team win with 1,373.456m.** **D. Cooke**, Apollo CC was **4th** with **458.934m, Cliff Smith,** who had a miserable ride and never really got warm, came **5th, 451.695m,** and **Mick Dunn,** Catford CC, **6th, 440.900m.**

The team that backed **Carline** consisting of **D.Robertson, 436.868m** and **R.W. Metcalfe, 400.784** took the **2nd team** prize for the **Morley CC** with **1,312.830m.** **Cliff Smith** also had a **team** backing him for the first time with **Eric and Cliff Tremaine,** both making their debuts, **Eric** with **413.181** and **Cliff 410.785** for a **3rd team** total of **1,275.660m** for the **East Midlands CC.** We shall see much more of the Tremaine brothers. **Taff Brissenden** with **430.883** led **Ken Hughes, 426,237m** and **Norman Kellett, 416.772** to a **4th team** mileage of **1,273.892m** for the **Mid Shropshire Wheelers.** **Ian Shaw** riding for the Bromsgrove Olympique CC produced **425.512** and **Ray Burnett** finished with **414m** despite punctures, and from 67 starters, 45 finished.

An interesting note that was printed in the Fellowship Journal, post Catford 24hr event, from Nim Carline, explains his methods and the 'specialist' feeding regime for this Champion.

"I found I could tolerate the first 18hrs, but found the last six hours agony. If I hadn't had such a substantial lead at 400 miles I would probably have packed. The reason why I set off fast this time was because it worked last time and I'm willing to try 'owt' twice. As for eating, I can take and enjoy anything succulent, especially surprise pancakes. I got two fried sausages straight from the frying pan and an iced lolly off John Arnold I usually like hot tea and plenty of big wet sponges even when its raining. At home I eat whatever comes along, fish and chips and ale for supper."

*I am grateful for this fine 24hr report from the Catford CC Gazette by W.A. Walsh with a few comments from myself.*

---

**The Wessex RC 24hr** on the 20th and 21st July **was won by Tony Harris,** Viking RC with an impressive **473.325m.** The weather conditions were good this year with a dry and sunny daytime, a warm but dark night with light breezes next day. Cyril Neale reported that there were no big 'star' riders entered this year, just very experienced ones and with some very good class 12hr riders making their debut at 24 hours. It was also the 'VTTA' Championship event this year (Veterans Time Trial Association).

At the turn at Landsford (106 miles) Clark was in the lead with 4hrs 52mins 25 secs with Wright at 38 sec, Betteridge at 5.17 secs and Harris at 6 mins. By the checkpoint at Lyndhurst, Wright had gained the lead in 6hrs 54 mins, with Betteridge at 2 mins, Clark at 4 mins and Harris at 11 mins. Darkness fell as the riders returned through the New Forest, Wright was well in the lead and when he passed the night H.Q. at Upton (199 miles) he gave the appearance of being set for an outstanding ride. However, within the next 5 miles, he had retired complaining of trouble with his knees. At Corfe Castle where Bert Brown was checking, Clark was back in the lead with 209 miles covered in 10hrs 8 mins with Betteridge at 2 mins 15 secs and Harris at 4 mins 15 secs.

The leading riders now passed to the western detours towards Weymouth and Gallows Hill. Dawn came during the detour to Puddletown via Blandford and back at Bailey Gate at 303 miles, Harris had displaced Clark and was leading in 15 hrs 8m 29s with Clark at 3m 13s and Betteridge 7m 6secs. Harris's time equates to 31 seconds inside 'evens'. The speed of the leading riders was proving a worry for the organisers who had their work cut out to get marshals into place in time. At 345 miles Harris was only 8 mins outside 'evens' and 16 mins and 21 mins ahead of Clark and Betteridge respectively.

The return to Ringwood and the finishing circuit was accomplished by Harris in 20hrs 16mins, Betteridge had re-caught Clark and was at 19 mins, Clark was at 22 mins. The circuit of fifteen miles was covered by **Harris** four times in almost exactly 47 mins per lap. He **won the event** with a well judged and splendid ride of **473.325m.** Pete Betteridge beat **Bob Clark** by the narrowest of margins, **461.876m to 461.441m.** Clark led a Wessex RC team of Ivor Jones, 403.194 and G.N. Herbert, 378.693m to a win with 1,243.328 miles. The 'VTTA' Championship was won by **Charlie Alexander.**

---

**The Mersey RC 24hr** on July 27th-28th was won by Eric Matthews with 473.30 miles. He made his debut at 24 hour riding in this event the previous year. I have used paragraphs and details extracted from a 24hr Fellowship report of the event by rider, **Ken Hughes,** who came **2nd** in the event with **444.45 miles and led a winning Mid Shropshire Whls team of Taff Brissenden, 439.47 and Norman Kellett 424.14m for a total of 1,308.06m.** Ken's 2nd placed ride came only three weeks after taking a hammering with the weather and stomach trouble for a 12th placed ride of 426.24 in the Catford event. Ken's best ride was in the 1961 Mersey Championship with 454.5 miles.

"It was with some misgivings that I had entered the 1963 Mersey RC 24hr having arrived home after taking a terrible hammering in the Catford and finding two completed entry forms plus postal orders, along with a scribbled note from my clubmates, Norman and Taff, who were still on holiday in the south of England, asking me to enter the Mersey event to make up the team. I did enter however and when the day came, the prospect of riding another 24 hr so close to the last one, didn't seem very inviting, the fact that I had only managed a 2hr 14min in the Oldbury and District 50m event the week before, didn't make matters any better.

The day came, it was sunny and warm; the lane near Tarvin was crowded with club folk and vehicles. We sat on the grass and had a sandwich, a cup of Rona's tea to compensate for the fact that the Mersey event starts at the time when most people are having their evening meals. After the bikes were prepared I had a quick chat to Dave Stapleton, the Organiser, Jack Spackman and Les Russell who had set the standard for long distance racing in our club just after the war.

Norman was the first in the team to start and he went off like a sprinter obviously out to 'do a ride'. I was next, seven minutes later, and starting a lot more sedately, not feeling at all energetic in the sultry conditions. As I plodded along the road towards Tarporley, the heat seemed even more oppressive and there was no life at all in my legs. The thought of keeping going for 24 hours was very sobering indeed. I wasn't a bit surprised to be caught after eight miles by Brian Haddock, Oldbury and District CC , he'd caught me for 1 minute. We were two of the 'primitives' left, still using a fixed wheel gear and after a quick natter he soon became a speck in the distance. Before the first turn at Alpraham Green I was caught for 4 minutes by an old friend and rival, Don Spraggett who seemed to be really flying and my opinion was soon confirmed by Alan Littlemore at the turn who said that Don was the fastest so far, a minute up on Eric Matthews.

On retracing my tracks I was able to note the early pattern of the race and how my two club mates were doing. Norman had crept away from me with that rapid start. 'Taff' was difficult to estimate but seemed to be a shade up, but he had been caught by last years winner and course record holder, Ken Usher, who always seems to do his best rides in the Mersey event, although it's a long way from his native London.

Just after the turn, Ray Burnett drew alongside, at this rate it seemed that all seven of the riders who had started behind me were going to catch me. I decided that although it was a little early in the race, I would go a bit faster and give Burnett a run for his money, but he seemed much too strong, so I gave that up and just plodded on at about 'evens' as I had been doing up to then. Ken Usher had disappeared and I heard later that he had packed with mechanical troubles. I had now caught one or two of the slower riders so I was in no danger of being the 'last man' on the road, or 'lantern-rouge'.

It still seemed hot and stuffy and I was quite looking forward to the cool night ahead. On my way back towards Backford, 'Taff' caught me and told me he had broken his gear lever and had jammed the mechanism in a gear somewhere near 80". Little did he know that this was the first in a series of mishaps to befall him during the race. I seemed to be moving a little better now and passed through the calculated 100 miles point just inside 5 hours. 'Taff' obviously was faster and so was Norman, for whom it was quite exceptional to beat 5 hours for 100 miles. Soon after this I recaught Brian Haddock and returning from Gayton I passed Burnett and was soon having a 'do' with 'Taff' who seemed troubled by the cars headlights, as they returned home to the towns on the Wirral. On the way to the Sealand turn we passed Albert Crimes who was out feeding a club mate and he had a collection of cooking utensils hanging from his trike. Along this section 'Taff' punctured and I was able to tell our helpers just up the road, as to where he was, but by the time they had found him he had changed the tyre. On the controlled detour from Saltney to Marford the figure of Don Spraggett re-appeared ahead, probably paying the penalty for his very fast start. I also spotted Norman changing a tubular at the side of the road. Arriving at Queensferry I stopped to put on my sweater, it was getting on towards 1 am. As I set off toward Prestatyn with Don Spraggett just behind me, 'Taff', came flying past on Cliff's (one of our helpers) track iron that was on loan to him while the lads replaced his broken gear lever. The long straight North Wales coast road took its usual toll of riders and I dropped Don who later retired. On the way back from the turn at Nant Hall, 'Taff' reappeared on his own bike and stayed fairly close to me on the road all the way back to the Chester area where he had to stop twice, firstly to tighten the hurriedly fitted gear lever that had worked loose and secondly to change a softening tubular tyre.

It was now getting quite light as we headed south for Whitchurch and the Nantwich detour of some 20 miles. Eric Matthews who was my 'minute man' had already completed this detour before I had even started it! Eric already had the race 'sewn up' now with a 20 miles plus lead, Alan our mathematician told me there were about six of us in the running for 2nd place. Somewhere in this vicinity I had caught Lionel Lea of the Wigan Wheelers who was moving very well and surely going to do a ride that was a great improvement on anything that he had done before; I told him this, but he didn't seem too sure himself at the time.

I reached the early morning breakfast feed at Edgebolton feeling quite fresh, but the temptation of the porridge that I had sampled there the previous year was too strong, so I pulled up for a quick snack.

As I set off I was told that Norman and 'Taff' had gone through close together some five minutes earlier. I was now determined to catch them, which I did on the way back from the 'Raven' turn at Prees. Norman seemed about shot but 'Taff' started a battle that lasted on and off till Wem at 357 miles; here I managed to shake him off for the last time.

I thought now that all I had to do was to take 5 minutes out of him in the last 4 hours to be sure of 2nd place, but when I started to retrace from Redbrook, Lionel Lea was moving up and seemed all set to catch me again, so I tried my hardest as I headed north towards the finishing circuit, but it was not hard enough, for he caught me at Broxton. This was not too bad however because there were 400 miles now covered and I thought that I should be able to hold onto some of the ten minutes that I had on Lionel.

It was a great struggle though as we scrapped on and around the circuit, Lionel finally taking about two or three minutes out of me but leaving me to take 2nd place, two miles ahead of his very creditable 442 miles, an improvement I think of about some 20 miles for him. This gave Lionel 3rd place, an actual 442.36 miles and 'Taff' Brissenden 4th with 439.46 miles.

I was fairly satisfied with my ride, for although it was a long way off my best, it was the only success I had in a poor season. The fact that we had won the team race with 'Taff' and Norman in 4th and 7th places was very inspiring, for that had been our main ambition.

So it was the end of another memorable Mersey RC 24hr with Eric Matthews running out time with 473.30 miles, very close to course record, and with no real competition to speak of. Eric had undoubtedly great potential and might easily get near competition record if there was anyone to push him."

*My thanks to the late Ken Hughes for his in-depth enlightenment on this event.*

<hr/>

Pete Swinden was 5th with 438.64 miles which I'm sure for him was one of his best, if not the best, mileage ever. H.G. Clowes, Crewe Whls, was 8th with 424.01m. This is the fellow clubman that Albert Crimes was out to help, what a distinguished helper, I bet Clowes felt he had to do a real ride with Albert there, and didn't he do well! 9th was Pat Kenny 421.47, on one of his 'much better' rides, he won't mind me being honest, but like me, he had some quite low mileage rides and when one considers the amazing RRA road records he broke, through sheer tenacity in quite often very hard conditions, it makes you wonder whether he rode these 24hr events just to get used to 'suffering' and 'not giving up'. Pat also seemed to ride much better when he was under pressure time-wise, such as on a record attempt where there wasn't much room for manoeuvre. I owe a lot to my club mates, Pete Swinden, John Withers and Pat in particular, for encouraging my record breaking rides at a later date, and making me realise I was capable of such a discipline.

Brian Haddock was 10th with 421.02m, he was another good fixed-wheel man, a good all round clubman and time triallist at all distances. This event also saw a friendly bond struck between the Mid Shropshire Whls lads, who later included Malcolm 'Mal' Jones, Ray Page, 'Ken' and 'Taff', and the Birmingham St Christopher's lads. Over the next few years we had quite a few 'ding dongs' on the road with them. They usually won but not by too many miles, they were and still are, a friendly bunch.
Pete Swinden was a solid rider, one of the 'old school' of hard riding 'fast tourists' who aspired to some great long distance road records on a tandem with John Withers, both at 'Regional' and 'National' RRA levels, with their End to End and 1,000 mile records being 'epics' and records that still stand to this day.

Pete only spent a small percentage of his time racing in time trials and usually would only have ridden maybe two preliminary 100's before the 24hr in July, and then afterwards he could sometimes be cajoled into riding the Oldbury and District 12 hr in September with his club mates. The main proportion of his time spent on a bike was riding to work and generally using the bike for transport, as we all did. Plus he would go on all the club runs, weekends away touring, looking at viable record breaking courses for future use, most of these later trips were done on a tandem with John.

Touring on the Continent and extensively in England on bikes was also another favourite way of training for Pete, John, Pat, Ant Burke, Barry 'Bas' Blagg and Pete Hambley (all St Christopher's team members). With full saddlebags riding from coast to coast, then from ferry to home with daily mileages generally exceeding 120 miles. Journeys through five European Countries were commonplace, all in a fortnights annual works summer holiday.

They would carry all their own kit in one big canvas saddlebag, not like on many of today's modern 'tours' where riders travel light on probably the best of bikes, with 'back up' trucks carrying their kit and helping them on their way on a bad day. No wonder the 'lads' of 1960 were tough riders, and I'm sure that went for many hardy clubmen tourists in clubs dotted around the British Isles.

At that time, I know that Reg Randall's favourite training was a foreign 'tour' on the bike, done in the same way.

I suppose the closest equivalent we have to this in modern times are the tough regular Audax riders who tackle any distances in set times, rides like London-Edinburgh-London, & Paris-Brest-Paris. Even longer mileages are performed by certain riders such as Steve Abrahams, his epic ride being 2,100 miles in 9 days, a triangular ride of Great Britain riding from his home to Dover then to Lands End, up to John o' Groats and back down to home at Milton Keynes. Over 233 miles every day, needless to say, Steve is another very good 24hr man who rides without 'back up' of any kind and produces rides of 440 miles plus on a fixed wheel (as at 2007).

But all of this obviously took up a lot of time in ones life, endurance sports and sportsmen were still in vogue in the 1960's. Time consuming, brain numbing, body degenerating television was luckily still in its infancy, cars hadn't completely taken over the roads and peoples lives, they were very costly and it was still cheaper to catch the bus or train to commute or better still, cycle or walk. Phones were still an item of luxury, and people generally kept their messages short and to the point. In the 1960's eating and drinking hadn't become a huge industry of gut-busting magnitude. People only ate when they needed to, 'snacking' hadn't become part of everyday life, although the extra calories burnt off when cycling long distances at decent speeds meant the cyclists were nearly always ready to eat. Going out for the day for most people at that time meant taking a bag of sandwiches from home and a thermos flask or bottle of diluted cordial.

On a Sunday club run the teatime stop was usually the 'treat' of the day for many Midland cycling clubs, where a tea place would be pre-booked by the club secretary. Egg and beans on toast was a favourite and so was a salad tea in the summer, followed by fruit and custard and gallons of hot tea, as coffee wasn't quite so popular or easily available. This put the riders back into good condition to tackle the last 30 miles back home before nightfall, if it was summertime, or done in the cold and dark, through the winter. *"Did I hear you say people were still out on bikes at that time of day, on a Sunday, with lights on, and they'd been out since early morning, some of them after attending church? Good lord, now you are really having me on! Girls and youngsters, wives as well, and they looked happy and did I also hear you say that some of them sang popular songs of the day, or whistled as they rode along, now that is a likely story. Were they a cult of some kind?"*

*I will stop now from ranting on about the 1960's and the good old days before the decline in our domestic sporting standards\* generally and not just in Cycling but in any pastime that required a raised pulse rate for any longer than ten minutes, as I have another 44 years of our rich history to write about. For more enlightenment on the decline of our sport see Chapter 6, entitled "The gradual decline and possible remedies'.*
*\*By sporting standards generally, I mean ordinary people at club amateur level and not at County or International standard, whether it be cycling, running, athletics etc.*

⟹•◇•⟸

**The North Road CC 24hr in 1963 was won for the third time by Cliff Smith, East Midlands CC with 454.693 miles.** It was very windy and rather cool at the start near St Neots, though the sun was doing its best to shine. The only time the wind eased up was around dawn; the night was clear but cold after a pale sunset over the fens.

Thirty one riders started, ten of whom were novices, seven entries were on trikes, 23 rode derailleur gears, 2 on hub gears and 6 on fixed. Smith led from the start and apart from Pete Swinden and Eric Tremaine being just 15 and

16 mins behind him at the 101.5 miles point in Shefford, Smith was never seriously challenged from about 10 hours onwards. At the end of the 2nd circuit near Peterborough at 197 miles, Smith led in 9 hours 53 mins, Pete Swinden was 2nd at 31 mins with Eric Tremaine 3rd along with Griffiths, Luton Wheelers at 33 mins. Cambridge at 258 miles saw Smith take 13 hrs 12min, Swinden at 42m and Vic Gibbs was now at 46 mins. By the time the riders had returned from Spalding many had missed controlled detours in an effort to keep the field together. At Long Sutton, Smith led from Vic Gibbs and Pete Swinden, with Tremaine 4th. It seemed nothing could stop Smith now, but a considerable battle continued for the next few places, from the 350 mile point to the finish. The main feature of this struggle was a very powerful effort from Smith's East Mids CC team-mate Eric Tremaine. Pete Swinden slowed off considerably and **F. Brown,** Cambridge Town and County on a **trike** rode powerfully to finish **4th** and record the 3rd best trike ride so far in this events history, with **414.017m.**

At March, Vic Gibbs made a tough effort to pull away from Swinden and Tremaine but the effort cost him 2nd place which went to **Tremaine with 430.455m.** Gibbs 3rd with **423.510, Ray Burnett 5th** with **410.886** and **Swinden,** B'Ham St Christopher's CCC came **6th** in this tough event with **410.14m.** With **Cliff Tremaine** (Eric's brother) finishing **7th** with **409.947** this gave the **East Midlands** the **team** prize with **1,295.095 miles.** 'Ant' Burke and **John Withers** for the **B'ham St Christopher's CCC** team produced **401.977** and **370.418** respectively to take the **2nd team** spot with **1,182.538m.**

It was felt that the small entry for this event was due to its very late position on the Calendar, but it was also felt that the riders were just being selective and riding mainly the Championship events. One comical note from the North Road history book for this event was of a Mr Beech of the Comrades CC who kept disappearing from the action at intervals, to have supplementary sit down feeds in cafes and enjoy 'post prandial recitals' on the juke box. He finished some 166 miles behind the winner and strained the detour controller's arrangements to the limit. He was noted as the event judges 'bogey man'!

In 1963, Johnny Pardoe broke the York to Edinburgh trike record taking just under two minutes off J. Parr's record with 10hrs 21mins 15secs. Later, Parr retaliated by taking another 16 mins off with 10 hours, 4mins, 24secs. A short time later that year, John Arnold took another 1hr 16mins off, with a time of 8hrs 48mins 28secs. Such exciting times!

>─•◇•─<

On November 22nd 1963, President John F Kennedy was assassinated.

# 1964

*The Forth Road Bridge in Scotland opened this year, which was good news for End to Enders*

**The Catford 24hr in 1964 was another win for Cliff Smith with 471.22 miles.**

*I've used a report by Ian Shaw for the coverage of this event.*

"It was very pleasant to return to 'Catford Country' to witness the event, although the numbers were lower due to it being a non championship event, the field of 31 riders included Cliff Smith, twice a winner here and busting fit after a personal best 4hr 24mins 100 mile event a few weeks previously. Ken Usher, always a good distance rider who usually wins away from home, was riding. Super long distance man Reg Randall, who had also won the Catford twice, was having a serious comeback in this event.

The weather was very hot, in fact so hot that it was melting the butter in the helpers cars and Peter Duncan whom I was helping accused me of heating up his milk and ginger beer drinks. In fact it was rather too warm for the riders and there was a strong south westerly wind, but what a change to take the rain cape off and shirt too! There were many 24hr Fellowship riders in this race and it was pleasing to see and meet up with Fellowship members who were out helping in this event, such as Ken Porter, Ken Smith, Gordon Hinder, Peter Reeves and John Coulson. Later I met Ann and Bill Dunk, Jack Spackman and Bill Sargeant, sporting a beard and riding a trike.

On top of the 'Downs' at about 112 miles, Smith led with Thompson riding well at 7 mins, Hadfield 3rd at 10m, Randall 4th at 14m and Burnett at 16 mins.   In between my feeding Peter Duncan I managed to get a rough time check at 173 miles where Smith was 9 mins inside 'evens', Thompson was 2nd still at 13 mins and Randall had moved into 3rd place at 17 mins.   Peter Duncan, had now 'packed' so I was able to rejoin the main field and get a view of what everyone was doing.

Despite a fracas with a police car, wondering what was happening and why our car was full of happy cyclists at 1.45am, we continued to Guildford and pressed on to pass Reg Randall who was still in his shorts with it being mild and less windy now.  He was moving very well and using his gears to gain more speed.  In the small hours we pitched the tent and got the stoves roaring with ham, eggs and coffee to see us through the day.

At 300 miles Smith came through in 15 hours 7 mins just outside 'evens', Randall was now 2nd at 39 mins, Thompson at 44m and only these three riders did the Windsor detour.  At Crawley we met Ivy and Bert Brown, Mick Dunn and George Seward and we were in time to see the riders do the return leg to Cowfield Heath and back.  Smith was averaging 19.3 mph now and demonstrated what a powerful rider he was, especially in the second half of the race.  He came through the 373 miles in 18hours 54 mins, or just 15mins outside 'evens'.  Randall was 54mins slower here and on the finishing circuit, Smith was still riding hard at 19.6 mph, even over newly tar sprayed roads.  His approximate 242 and 228 miles in the two halves of the race showed how he took advantage of a fast warm latter half of the night and early morning.   This powerful riding came at a time when most riders were in a 'tired groove'."

**Cliff Smith won handsomely with 471.22, Reg Randall was 2nd, 451.79m and J.B. Thompson 3rd with 442.54m.   Tony Brook 4th with 439.75, led a BEC.CC Team of Ken Davey, 428.08m and P.G. Wells, 417.24m to a total of 1,285.07m  Brian Kent, Mephisto CC was the fastest trike with 363 miles.**

*My thanks once again to Ian Shaw for this report on the Catford race.  He found that both Ken Usher and Reg Randall were riding the new small wheel Moulton cycles, but we can only measure Reg's success as Usher didn't finish. I can only say that this new and revolutionary machine doesn't seem to have made much difference as Reg usually does around the 450 mile plus on his 'normal' bike. These are only my own comments of course.  Ian's report is one that I've amended and shortened slightly.*

Whereas 35 riders was considered a low entry for the 1963 event, this years was even lower.   Dissent was being shown by the youngsters in the club and feelings were becoming hostile towards the 24 hour.   One or two broke the club rule by riding events the same weekend as the 24hr without gaining permission to be exempt from helping. This same dissent would be expressed by young members of the North Road CC in the 1980's, eventually leading to the events demise.

⤐●⤙

**The Wessex 24hr in 1964** had the smallest entry for a long time, one of only 24 riders.  **The winner was Brian Duignan** of the promoting club, by over 27 miles.   He had gained a commanding position early in the event to finish with **446.236 miles** and was also the only rider to complete the full course, and the first Wessex RC rider to win this event since 1939.  **Sid Hygate** of the Royal Naval CA was the only one to challenge Duignan, but at 267 miles he began to suffer badly with his knees and dropped away to finish **7th** with **407.563m**.  His team-mate **Owen Bryce** took **2nd** place overall with **418.790m. The team race** was a close run affair with the **Westerley RC winning** with **1,209.258** from the **Royal Naval CA 1,200.120m.  Bill Suttie was the fastest trike with 381.872** and **2nd fastest** was **Arthur Comer,** Veg C & AC with **358.865m**.   The **3rd** placed rider **overall** was **Harry Buck,** Frome and District Whls with **412.031m.**

The field had been further depleted before the start by a tragic accident that led to the death of Ken Lewis, Frome Whls whilst he had been taking part in a time trial on the Sunday prior to the Wessex event.

The weather was windy on both days, with a chilly night and cold showers at dawn.

*Les Lowe who was training for the Mersey 24hr used a trip to the Wessex event to help with marshalling and to write a report for the Fellowship Journal.  I've used some parts of Les's report to give a feeling for this event.*

"After riding from Derby to the start, I stocked up on food supplies and rode to the feeding station at 75 miles, where Brian Duignan had caught all but one of the field, and was about 10 mins inside 'evens' on an afternoon that was windy, and heavy traffic caused delays. The field was well split up already with the trikes bringing up the rear and Bill Suttie well in the lead.

As night fell, the riders were on the Bealieu leg, although several missed it and were sent straight on over the New Forest to Christchurch. At this point I was marshalling and while on this corner I met Gordon Basham, the first rider to beat 450 miles back in 1948. He was no longer cycling but was still interested in the 24hr game. The evening was now very chilly, at 116 miles Duignan was 17 mins inside 'evens' and 14 mins ahead of Pearce. At this same checkpoint, less than two minutes covered Tomkin, Pearson, Hygate, Andrews and Hughes. All of them were just over 20 mins behind the leader.

My next move was to follow the riders over the New Forest towards Christchurch. I was glad I wasn't going at racing speed as the night time traffic was very heavy and the dazzle from car headlights made the downhill sections very 'dodgy'. After a welcome cup of coffee from a marshal on the Christchurch by-pass and a quick natter, I pressed on to take a short cut through Bournemouth and Poole which seemed interminable, but finally brought me out at Fleets Bridge with just a short trip to the feed at Upton Cross. Here the riders were reluctant to leave the warmth of the tent and all that lovely food, to go back out into a chilly windy night.

Next, a marshalling duty at Lytchett Minster and then to Wareham Railway crossing, where there is a rather nasty bend. After seeing everybody through safely, my next point was Bailey Gate, known locally as Round House. This is an ideal place for seeing the riders in the early morning as they come from Upton Cross, turn left, (270m) to Dorchester and return, 299m, left again to Blandford and return, 311m, left again to Bear Cross and return, 344m, then left again to Upton Cross and on their weary way to the finishing circuit. Buck, Andrews, Bryce, Suttie (who was chasing his club trike record) and Duignan, were all moving well here.

Roadworks and missing marshals due to the postal strike caused a 'blip' on the way to the finishing circuit, but Cyril Neale, the Organiser soon got the situation under control. Finally the riders reached the circuit to run out time; they'd had a very hard event with a very troublesome wind.

*Les Lowe's 600 mile round trip obviously did the trick, as later in the Mersey RC event he rode to 4th place with 441.34 miles.*

⟐

**On Friday 17th July 1964, Pete Swinden and John Withers** *set out on the longest non- stop journey of their lives. They were hoping to break Cowsill and Denton's* **1000 mile tandem record** *of 3 days 7 hours 41 mins. Timekeeper Alan Tomkins sent them on their way from Alrewas to Coventry and back for the first leg of the journey. They went up to Nottingham and Newark to start the first of their many circuits based on the A1 and the roads that have formed the North Road 24hr course for many years. The calm conditions that were forecasted didn't materialise and so the attempt on the 492 mile tandem 24hr record held by Bailey and Forrest was abandoned. In the second 24hrs a lot of heavy rain was experienced. John's position directly over the rear wheel of the tandem became even more uncomfortable when the leather saddle he was riding lost its shape due to getting very wet. This problem came at a very bad time in the ride and got even worse, leaving John with massive open sores in his 'saddle area'. Despite all of this they finally broke the record by 13hours 32 mins to record* **2 days 18hrs 9mins.**

*Pat Kenny organised this attempt and was on the road either driving or helping for the duration. The Officials and Observers on that ride were Cyril Underhill, Jack Spackman, Mick De Mouilpied, Jack Clements and Richard Hulse. Pete Swinden's work colleagues from English Electric in Stafford, provided help for most of the attempt, along with club members from Birmingham St Christopher's CCC. I was also on that record attempt for the duration and I realised then the enormity of such a task. I felt that I was going round and round in never ending circles for 3 days and I formed the opinion that the End to End route was probably a more meaningful and direct way of doing it.*

The Mersey RC 24hr on 25th & 26th July saw Eric Matthews break Competition Record with the first RTTC recognised ride over 490 miles, in fact it was 490.03, so bringing the prospect of the 500 miles barrier that much closer. Considering that this event was not of Championship status it makes Eric's performance even better. Ken Usher failed to start, leaving 40 riders to battle it out for 2nd and 3rd place including 7 trikes. The weather at the start was dull but warm with a breeze to blow the riders to Nantwich.

At Acton Church (50.6m) Matthews led the field with 2hrs 8 mins with Don Spraggett at 5 mins, Gaskell 7m, Pat Kenny and Ray Burnett at 10m. At the 100 mile check on the Wirral, Matthews was in a clear lead and was first on the road with 4hrs 21m. By the time the riders had completed the Saltney to Marford detour at 130 miles, Matthews with 5hrs 49m led Gaskell by 16 mins, Burnett 25, Spraggett 26m. Ken Hughes, Pat Kenny and Les Lowe were all at 30 mins. It was at this point that Harold Nelson, who was Eric Matthews' coach, masseur and mentor, mentioned that Eric's schedule was made out to beat Competition Record by 2 miles.

After completing the Welsh Coast road to Nant Hall, Prestatyn and then retracing, Matthews reached Little Sutton at 2.50am with 195.5 miles covered in 9hrs 8mins. Here he turned south on the 27 mile run down to Whitchurch, the temperature had now dropped and the riders had to contend with several miles of cold mist patches.

Quite a large gathering at Whitchurch waited for Mathew's arrival, hot soup and tea was being brewed by the helpers here while waiting for their riders to appear. Tommy Barlow was waiting with stop-watch in his hand, ready to operate the optional detour of 20.6 miles to Nantwich and back. The atmosphere here, even at this 'small hour' was tense and exciting. Suddenly a cry went up "Here he is", and a very determined looking Matthews thrashed by at 33 mins inside 'evens'. With 222.4 miles covered at 4.16am, he'd taken just 10hrs 34 mins to do it. Gaskell was next through but after a severe bout of sickness he retired, leaving Ken Hughes in 2nd place, Les Lowe 3rd, Burnett 4th, Broad 5th and Pat Kenny 6th, just 58mins down on Matthews.

The course goes south again to Battlefield, nr Shrewsbury where the halfway point is reached, if you're going fast that is. Matthews' 12 hours produced 251 miles, Hughes 235, Lowe 232, Burnett 231 and Kenny 229. The Edgebolton feed is a hive of activity at 6am with riders either stopping for a quick breakfast or flashing through and taking a mussette of food and a bottle of tea. Bert Parkes, the Mersey RC trike record breaking End to Ender, was in charge here and with a team of willing hands was doing a magnificent job. Matthews was first to flash past at 6.23am, Brian Kirkham on a trike was next, over half an hour later but he'd missed two optional detours. The second fastest on the road, Ken Hughes, stopped for a quick 4 minute breakfast and was off again.

By 9.49am the sun had risen to be pleasantly warm as a crowd watched Matthews arrive at Shawbury with 330.5 miles covered. Ken Hughes arrived some 58 mins later. From here to Wem some terrific battles ensued between Jim Shuttleworth, Pete Broad, Haddock, Kenny and Lea. First and second places had already been allotted to Matthews and Hughes, but the battle for third was a severe one between half a dozen riders. While the riders were negotiating the Wem to Welshampton stretch, the skies went grey and the temperature dropped. A persistent cold rain fell all the way to the finishing circuit at Waverton near Chester.

Matthews arrived on the circuit at 1.51pm with 3hrs 51mins to go and 410miles already under his wheels, if the cold and wet didn't get to him it was just possible he could get that record. Ken Hughes, still as cheerful as ever, got to the circuit at 3.17pm. Matthews came through five minutes later to start his 3rd lap, to shouts of encouragement and enthusiastic clapping from the crowd, who always gather at the entrance to the circuit.

Eric meanwhile was 'flying' and hell bent on the record. On lap 5 with cheers all the way, he managed a smile as spectators checked their stop-watches when he flashed past. The cold dismal weather was completely ignored as Matthews hammered down this normally quiet country lane that was now lined with cheering, shouting, clapping people. That's it, Competition Record had gone and he still had four minutes to go. Principal timekeeper Ron Macqueen was in the following car with Tommy Barlow to 'run time out' for Matthews. A large cortege of cyclists chased after the car to witness Matthews as he finished at 30 mph coming to rest just before Hargrave Canal Bridge. This 27 year old Batchelor of Science had proved that he was without a doubt the best 24hr rider we had seen so far.

Like a lot of the top riders he was smooth in his style and had a good control of his power, whenever he passed me in a race he made it look so easy and he would be out of sight very quickly. Wilko and Ian Cammish were also riders who possessed these powers. Whenever Nim Carline came past you could feel the speed and urgency and the effort showed, as if he was being chased by a wild animal. Les Lowe who finished 4th remembered a few details from the race and I've put a few here to remind us that riders do struggle to complete this tough discipline for 24 hours.

With the cold misty dawn Les had to don lots of extra clothing to keep going. He remembers Terry Kelly on a trike struggling (that makes a change) and Les's helpers gave him hot soup. Several hours later Kelly had fully recovered and gave Les a right battle that lasted for miles. At the 12hr point Les was himself struggling and so were his helpers who were new to the game but doing a fine job. Unfortunately at that same time they had forgotten to feed themselves and were in a poor state, but Les said that luckily they were soon back at peak efficiency. Les later discovered, at about 300 miles, that rice pudding and tinned fruit went down very well. This had been a St. Christopher's speciality for many years.

Les kept seeing Eric Matthews as he crossed him on the various roads in Shropshire and says that Eric's solo effort was more like an 'RRA' attempt than a time trial, getting no benefit from catching 'lesser' riders. Later, Les set his sights on closing the gap between him, Pete Broad and Ken Hughes, but the wet and cold thwarted his efforts. He said "I felt that this slowing was as much psychological as physical as my pace back to the circuit dropped to 16 mph and my first circuit took almost an hour. Realising that I wasn't going to beat 440 miles at that speed, I upped the pace and did the second circuit in 52mins, thus proving to myself at least, that the trouble wasn't all physical".

"It's always like this at the end of a '24.'

Eric Matthews won by over 37 miles with 490.03, Ken Hughes had an excellent 2nd place ride with 452.46, Pete Broad, Rhos on sea CC was 3rd with 445.54 even with a late start, and Les Lowe 4th, with 441.34. Lionel Lea, Wigan Whls was on form with 434.06 as was Pat Kenny 6th with 432.21. Jim Shuttleworth had his best ride so far on a trike with 424.81. Ian Shaw led the Speedwell team of Stan Clabon and G. Spencer to a total of 1,232.08 miles.

---

**The North Road Championship 24hr 1964**

*For the report on this event I've used passages from Ian Shaws article that appeared in the 24hr Fellowship Journal with additional material from myself.*

"The sun shone brilliantly at the start near St Neots, a fairly strong breeze blew and it was rather warm. There were 72 riders in the field headed by National Championship winner for the last two years, Nim Carline, Morley CC. Last years winner and previously 3rd and 2nd in the Championship, Cliff Smith, looked confident especially after his fine early season win in the Catford event. Last years Championship runner up, Dick Poole, Middlesex RC was leading a good team in their bid to equal Rutland CC's five wins in a row. The team included Fred Burrell, who had won the last two Championships on this course, Arch Harding, perhaps fitter than ever this season, sadly had to pull out due to an infected finger, J.P. Dean their 3rd man last year was there and Mike Rees gave them a fourth rider.

Geoff Mayne, Godric CC and George Bettis, Elite CC were good 12 hour men and team warfare was also expected from the Mid Shropshire Wheelers, Bec CC and Morley CC, but the main interest centred on Nim Carline, who appeared very relaxed at the start. As usual he was riding very 'light' with no bottles or even a cage and when his start time came he was off like a track pursuiter.

At 73 miles he led Cliff Smith by 8.5 minutes, Poole was at 11 mins, Eric Tremaine 14 mins, Bettis was 14.5m, Dean 15min, Cliff Tremaine at 17m, 'Taff' Brissenden 17 m, Usher and Eyre were at 17.5 mins. At 101 miles with 4hr 28m 30secs Carline led Smith by 11 mins. Carline who was off No 60 became first man on the road by 135 miles, although his times for this distance were slower than his last two Championships, where the Wessex had near typhoon conditions and the Catford a monsoon.

At 174 miles it looked as though Carline was trying to make amends as he hammered away into the gathering dark (as if riding a late evening 10 mile event). He was now 15 mins up on Smith, 25m on Usher, 27 on Bettis, 32 on Dean, 36 on Tremaine and Poole, 37 on Brown and 45m on Burrell. Carline was now 48 mins inside evens (20 mph) !

At 213 miles it was interesting to see how the race was developing. An unhappy Poole had disappeared, Brissenden had stomach trouble, Usher had moved up to be at 19 mins, Smith had crept up to be just 9 mins behind Carline, who was thought to have stopped or slowed for some reason. Bettis was at 18 mins, Tremaine at 30 mins, Brown had moved up and rode strongly all night and Freddie Burrell was at 38 mins and 'waiting in the wings' to unleash his power.

Burrell then slowly and steadily regained the 18mins he had been dropped on the road by Carline, eventually to pass and drop him. Carline took a tremendous hammering and indeed when seen at 353 miles just after dawn, looked like death. Later near Cambridge he retired; he was suffering from back trouble, but later said he was just shattered after his bid to hold the 'night-flyer' Burrell. During this time, Smith had been maliciously sent off course by hooligans.

*Apparently it was around midnight when Cliff had ridden more than 240 miles and was beginning to stamp the ride with his class, a party of late night revellers leaving a wedding acted as marshals to put him and four other riders off course. When they had gone more than 3 miles some threw in their hand, disgusted, but Cliff, whose smile is legendary, just swallowed his anger and turned back the way he had come, to pedal on. No one was going to take away his title chance that easily. In the Fens at Guyhirn Crossroads (281 miles) Cliff Smith levelled his position with the flying Carline; obviously the adrenalin from the anger of being sent off course had helped Cliff to regain his high position with the leaders.!*

Usher and Dean had retired besides Carline, as had Mike Rees and Cliff Tremaine, both with severe stomach trouble. For a short time Carline's retirement threw Bettis into the lead and inspired him into too much effort. At Eltisley, 386 miles, Burrell took the lead (having gained 5.5mins on Smith in 33 miles). At the completion of the first lap of the finishing circuit (418 miles) Cliff Smith had crept back to be almost holding Burrell at 2.5mins. Bettis was adrift by 15 mins, Tremaine at 41m, Brown 78m and Brook at 79mins. For the next three laps Burrell and Smith fought on relentlessly and there was a grim determination from both men. Smith was after a first time Championship win and Burrell was out to get his 3rd and all taken on the North Road. At 420 miles it was all or nothing from both men, the wind was very strong and parts of the exposed circuit were very tough, and the heat made them struggle.

At the end of the 2nd lap, Smith had closed the gap to 1.5mins with Bettis at 23mins and Tremaine at 41m. On the 3rd lap, Burrell was visibly tiring. **Smith** on his 4th and last lap scented victory and took a lead of 2.5 mins to **win the event.** Knowing he had lost and with nothing left, Burrell was only doing 15mph on the straight road into the wind where he was run out. He then waited at the end of his ride for the inevitable sight of Cliff Smith, still thrashing along, to come past and stop just .9 of a mile further on. **Smith's 473.688m was a personal best for him. Fred Burrell** ran him a close race to finish a courageous **2nd** with **472.774m. George Bettis,** Elite CC, riding as a novice (first event) used his 12 hour riding experience to get a good **3rd** place with **463.573m. Eric Tremaine** improved 30 miles for a **p.b. 4th** place with **460.768** and **Tony Brown** who had previously taken a high mileage trike prize in this event came **5th** with **446.649.** **Ken Hughes** with **439.303** was below his Mersey performance, he said afterwards he had got little left after a full racing season. **Ray Burnett** with **432.6** had an excellent ride considering he'd already produced 432.4 in the Catford and 425m in the Mersey, earlier in the season.

**Stan France with 433.681 and Ray Page with 423.119 backed Ken Hughes to a Mid Shropshire Wheelers team win of 1,296.103 miles** beating the 2nd team by 48 miles. *By winning the team race the Mid Shropshire Wheelers had taken hold of this North Road CC event and out-ridden all of the established teams who had dominated all day racing for so long.*

Les Lowe said that the cold night got to him and he never recovered his speed, but nevertheless his 429.645 got him 10th place. Joe Summerlin now riding for the North Road CC and a regular 24hr man, rode 423 miles. Geoff Mayne, Godric CC, a good 12hr man did 423 miles. After being 7th at one stage earlier in the race, he had a bad patch but kept going in this, his first, 24hr race. **Stan Spelling, Wren Whls, with 389.335 miles, won the fastest trike award.** *My thanks to Ian Shaw for this report.*

*Pete Swinden, Birmingham St Christopher's CCC with 419.295 was using his fitness gained from the successful tandem 1,000 mile record with John Withers some six weeks earlier. John was on the start sheet to ride but was still very uncomfortable in the saddle area so decided not to start. Pat Kenny produced 400.415m, somewhat slower than his 6th placed Mersey ride of 432m, earlier in July. I was also on the start sheet for this North Road event but can't for the life of me remember what happened. I certainly didn't finish but it was a long time ago.*

*Looking back at the event one has to admire Nim Carline's way of riding. Charlie Burton had written a three part schedule for him to ride to, but that wasn't Nim's style, its all or nothing for this man. Nim's method often worked and this sometimes destroyed his adversaries, but occasionally he failed and this event was one of those times. I personally think Carline's way of riding was unique and exciting to watch, and I would go as far as to say that although a few riders have tried to emulate him in recent years, they have only won on the odd occasion. Generally the prolific winners have all ridden fairly controlled rides from the start.*

*Even Fred Burrell, when laid in blankets on the finishing circuit, waiting for Smith to go past, commented "but Carline is the rider".*

*On the other hand, one has to admire those riders who play a waiting game; they know their own minds and bodies and what they are capable of. Their way of winning is to go at a speed that they know they can maintain; riders such as Burrell, Smith, Harding and Poole. Eric Matthews is another high mileage 'run-a-way-win' type of rider but he doesn't seem to risk jeopardising his ride just to stamp his authority from the start.*

*Two other riders rose to prominence in the Championship event, namely, George Bettis and Eric Tremaine. Bettis of the Elite CC who came 3rd with 463.573m was a tough steady rider, and used his long high speed training rides to good advantage. Whereas most other riders would consider 50 or 60 miles fairly fast to be a good training spin a couple of times a week, George would tackle 90 or more miles roughly at 'evens' pace, four or five times a week using the A1 and roads in the Fens. Most of his racing took place in this area and I don't recall him travelling north or west to race very often. Like Carline, he was an excellent 12 hour rider.*

**Eric Tremaine** who came **4th** with **460.768 miles** *was just under three miles slower than Bettis. He was another very good rider, breaking into the scene at all distances. This was a personal best for him and although he probably didn't realise it, he had a long and illustrious career ahead of him, on both bike and trike.*

---

**Charlie Davey passed away in 1964.** He had been a tough 24hr man and RRA record breaker, mainly between the two wars, and later took on the role as a Manager and Coach for many top riders in the Vegetarian C & AC. Probably, his most high profile rider being Dave Keeler in the 1950's.

On Monday June 14th 1965 Dick Poole set out from Lands End on a quest to break the 'End to End' record, held by Reg Randall with 2 days 1 hr 58 mins since 1958. **1 day, 23 hours 46 mins 35 secs later, he arrived at John o' Groats.** He was the **first man to beat 2 days** and set a new benchmark for future record breakers. Dick carried on for the 1,000 miles record again held by Reg Randall with 2 days 10 hrs 40 mins. Poole rode through heavy cold rain and at the end of his 1,000 miles he was absolutely all in. He had covered what was thought to be well in excess of the 1,000 miles, **but when the course was measured soon afterwards, it was found to be 1.5 miles too short!** *For years, Reg Randall turned his 1,000 mile trophy to the wall and said that Dick's ride was far better than his.*

---

**The Catford CC 24 hr** on June 19th was **won by Cliff Smith for the 3rd time, with a mileage of 466.839m.** **Dan Hadfield,** Norwood Paragon CC was **2nd** with **454.18m** and **Pete Swetman,** East Surrey RC, **3rd** with **444.819m.** Arthur Brook led Ken Usher and P.G. Wells to a Bec CC team win with a total of 1,295.379m. **Bill Sargeant, Century RC was the fastest trike with 396.755m.**

The weather was hot, sunny and very breezy, but with a cold night. Dan Hadfield was the only real challenge to Cliff Smith during the first half of the event, but from there on, Smith surged ahead for another determined win. Twenty riders finished including four trikes.

---

**The Wessex RC 24hr** 17th & 18th July 1965. Brian Duignan who had won the event in 1964 had to retire after 120 miles due to stomach pains so leaving the race wide open for another Wessex RC rider to take **1st place.** **Bob Clark, with 451.74m,** Sid Hygate from Portsmouth Command RNCC took 2nd place with a 40 mile p.b. of **447.39, and led a team of submariners,** Dave Black and Pete Collard to a total of 1,240.72m. Not bad considering that this Royal Navy Team spent most of their lives under the waves. They resurfaced every now and then to win a cycle race, returning to the depths with their medals. **Dave Free,** Oxonian CC took **3rd** place with **436.40** and **Ian Shaw,** our roving Fellowship reporter and rider **4th** with **419.72m.**

The course had undergone several alterations to avoid the traffic on the busy Ringwood to Salisbury road during the Saturday afternoon, but little success was achieved as the riders arrived at busy junctions in the forest area earlier, to find even more traffic to delay them. At the Netherhampton turn (143m) Clark led in 6hrs 46mins with Lowe at 18m, Free at 22m and Hygate 26m. Jack Nunn had the misfortune to be run down by a car as darkness fell and was badly shaken enough to receive hospital treatment.

Clark retained his lead through the night, which turned cold and misty. At 202 miles he'd taken just 9hrs 59m so was inside 'evens', with Les Lowe at 19m, Free at 26m and Hygate 27m. By 251 miles the only team left on the road were the 'Royal Navy' lads. Back through Blandford and Wimborne to Cranbourne at 327 miles. Clark turned in 17hours 19mins with Hygate now in 2nd place at 5 mins, Free was 3rd at 32 mins. Les Lowe had been badly affected by the cold on this section and with his back being troublesome as well, retired when in 4th place.

At Salisbury, 385 miles, Clark still led with 20hours 25mins, Hygate at 20 mins and Free at 44mins. These positions remained the same to the very end, although Sid Hygate did close the gap slightly even with his knees troubling him. Fifteen riders finished including the **fastest trike rider, Bill Suttie with 371.95m.**

---

*The RTTC changed the ruling this year, allowing the same roads to be covered on the Saturday and the Sunday, which from now on made the Organisers job a little easier.*

**One week later** at 5.00pm on Saturday 24th July the field was assembled for the **Mersey RC 24hr Championship Race.**   Four previous Champions and the winners of the five previous Mersey's were on the card to start.   Cliff Smith, looking very fit was defending his title against tough competition, particularly the much fancied Eric Matthews and Nim Carline. Dick Poole, a good team man and record breaker, was also a dark horse to be watched. Fred Burrell and Arch Harding were both out to do a ride in support of Poole for the Middlesex RC who were just one of eight teams entered.   They were the favourites along with the East Midlands trio of Cliff Smith and the Tremaine brothers, Eric and Clifford.   Other teams were:  Solihull CC, Altrincham RC, Mid Shropshire Whls, Birmingham St Christopher's CCC, Mersey RC, Morley CC and Swadlincote Whls.

For this, their 22nd promotion, the Mersey RC had their 'gold standard' medals ready for rides over 480 miles that would surely be done from a huge entry of 86. 83 riders started and with virtually all of the current 24hr 'stars' down to ride, it would prove to be a nail biting, exciting race with personal bests the order of the day.   This was thought by many to be the finest 24hr field ever seen, but then they probably weren't present at some of the earlier Championship events of the 1950's and 60's; events such as the North Road 1950 (100 riders) WTTA 1950 (82 riders) Catford 1951 (93) North Road 1952 (100) Catford 1955 (100) and North Road 1960, to name but a few.

Looking at the start sheet, it was a difficult job to predict a winning team; it is so difficult to keep 3 riders going for 24 hours.   It was also difficult to pick an individual winner, although the obvious choice was Eric Matthews, the youngest of the 'stars'.   Cliff Smith the defending champion, a really fit, tough nut to crack, and one must not forget the 'magnificent failure' for that's what it was, of his attempt on the Edinburgh-London record during May of this year, in the vilest conditions imaginable.   Snow and bitterly cold rain for most of the way – a man not easily deterred.

This leads to another, not deterred at all, Dick Poole who in June had broken the End to End and put this record inside 2 days.   George Bettis an East Londoner from the Elite CC had shown promise the previous year, or Nim Carline that thrusting tough rider who had revolutionised the way a 24hr should be ridden.   Pete Broad, Rhos on Sea, was another tough rider, not afraid of 'mixing it' with the 'stars', he also could be a dark horse.

The weather was pleasant as the first rider was despatched by Ron MacQueen, the timekeeper.   Arch Harding was the only rider to start, puffing on a cigarette (no doubt a last minute 'fix'), although Norman Maggs who rode to 378 miles on his trike in this event usually started with his pipe in his mouth, but turned upside down to stop the wind blowing the smoke in his eyes.

As a fresh north-westerly wind pushed the 83 starters on their way, one notable non starter was Ken Usher.  This was a disappointment for him and his new Bec CC team mates as he was right on form and the 'Mersey' was his favourite event, but his wife had been taken seriously ill just before the event.

Nim Carline had no schedule this year (not that he ever looked at it) preferring to blast away from the start which he did and at 62 miles took the lead, 27 mins inside 'evens' trailed by Matthews, Broad, Gaskell, Bayley, Poole and Smith.   Carline passed the 100 mile point in 4hrs 20 mins and by 120 miles the pressure was really on causing George Bettis to crack and retire.   Matthews was losing time to Carline, although he was extremely fit and already had a 261 mile 12hr to his credit, he had caught a chill and was lacking the 'edge'.

The night was fairly calm, not too cool, no mist, overcast and good conditions.   At 222.4 miles Carline led the field 43 mins inside 'evens', Smith was at 11 mins, Gaskell at 20m, Poole 26m, Matthews 27m, Harding 39, Thomas 41, Broad 47, Bayley 52, Eric Tremaine 52.5 and Don Spraggett 54.5mins.

Carline was the only rider to gain time on the 'graveyard' stretch from Whitchurch to Nantwich and back, an optional detour of 20.6 miles that the riders reached between 2am and 4am Sunday, when at their lowest ebb.   At 242 miles Carline was still well inside 'evens' by 44 mins and Pete Broad who had struggled up till this point now really 'took off'.   From here to the finishing circuit at 410 miles he only lost another 7 mins on Carline.   Howard Bayley, Solihull CC on two wheels this year was moving well in 11th place even though he suffered with poor night vision.   Don Spraggett was 12th and Burrell 13th.

At the 12 hr point, Carline had slowed slightly and looked a bit rough. (On many occasions I saw Nim at his best and his face often looked flushed with puffy eyes. I'm sure that wrap-around clear glasses that are now used extensively by riders would have helped his eyes, and as for looking flushed, well he was riding almost flat out after all). I also heard that he suffered with sciatica during some of his events.

Carline's rough patch gave Smith, Poole and Matthews a chance to close up on him, but the positions remained very similar until Wem at 359 miles. By this time, Carline had lost ground to Poole and Poole in turn had caught Smith. From Wem to the 480m point the battle for 2nd place between Poole and Smith was nail-biting, with only seconds between them for hour after hour.

Carline entered the finishing circuit at 410 miles to great cheers, in 20hrs 6mins 40 secs, and was still 23 mins inside 'evens'. Poole entered in 2nd place at 15mins 46secs, Smith was 3rd at 16m 34s with Matthews at 34m 41s, and Broad at 57.02. The team race was a very close one; only 20 mins separated the Middlesex RC from the East Mids CC, but while Eric Tremaine 'flew' round the circuit as fast as Carline, Harding and Burrell lost ground and the East Mids trio took the team prize by less than a mile.

On the circuit, Smith closed back up on Carline and regained 2nd place from Poole by just 0.3 of a mile. Many retirements led to the collapse of several teams including the Morley CC, Swadlincote Whls and the Mid Shropshire Whls. Ken Hughes always a good top five contender in any event had suffered stomach trouble from the 80 miles point but struggled on until at 340 miles he found that his fellow team member, Stan France, had packed. This was the end for Ken who had been hoping to make this his last event. Ray Page rode a p.b. that day with 426 miles, but with the 'backbone' gone, one wonders will the Mid Shropshire Whls come again?

Johnny Pardoe on a trike in his first attempt at a 24hr had suffered in the Shawbirch-Hodnet area, but he managed to reach the finishing circuit for an excellent mileage of 419.94m. Other trike riders to win silver medals were Stan Spelling, 386m, Terry Kelly 415m, Brian Kirkham with a p.b.of 410; he'd been helped on the way by Les Lowe. Norman Maggs rode another p.b. of 378.54m. **The winning trike** with one of the highest mileages since John Arnolds record in 1953, was **Peter Duncan with 433.56** miles. Although Pete Swinden managed to 'pip' team mate Pat Kenny with 437.18 miles against Pat's 436.46 it was a p.b. (personal best) for Pat. This blue riband event raised the standard of many riders and when one looks at the performances of Stan Lea 443.85m, Gerald Stiff 443.84, and Cliff Tremaine 443.81m, they are all p.b.'s with only yards between them, so to speak.

But, at the end, **Carline** had **led** the field from the front to finish with **485.09 miles.** A fierce battle for **2nd and 3rd** place had been won by **Cliff Smith** with **480.93m** and **Dick Poole, 480.63m. Eric Matthews** was **4th, 477.37m, Pete Broad 5th** with **466.72,** after a tremendous second half fight back. Eric Tremaine again proved himself that day with 459.81m. Howard Bayley 458.29m led the Solihull CC team of Roy Gordon 428.65 and Derek Shuttleworth 427.58, to a third place total of 1,314.52 miles. W. Aitken, a new name, was 8th with 453.89 while Arch Harding and Fred Burrell turned in solid rides of 453.13 and 450.13 for the Middlesex RC teams second place total of 1,383.89m. The **Tremaine brothers, Eric and Clifford** backed **Cliff Smith** to a **team** win by almost one mile with **1,384.62m.**

This gigantic promotion was the main responsibility of Dave Stapleton, the hard working organiser who proved to be 'unflappable' on the day. He would obviously say that it takes team work, which it does, but there is usually only one man who makes the final decisions and ties up the loose ends and that was he. 39 of the 52 riders who finished beat 400 miles.

*For my details on this event, I have once again to thank Ron Henshall and Ian Shaw, for their excellent reports.*

⟫•◆•⟪

In 2008 I spoke to Johnny Pardoe about his 419mile trike ride in this 1965 event and he said he'd suffered badly with his knees during and after the event and this had deterred him from riding another 24hr. John was about 25 years of age at the time and we spoke about the fact that many of the successful long distance trike riders were only in their late 20's or 30's in these events. Even Peter Duncan who took the fastest trike prize that day with 433m was only 37 years of age at the time, and only 26 when he produced a 440 mile ride in 1954. When one looked down the start sheets of most 24hr events of that period, there were as many as ten trikes entered, compared with the events of the late 1990's, and 2,000 onwards where there has been just one or two, usually Jim Hopper and the average competitive long distance trike riders age is now 60 plus.

Over the years from about the 1950's onwards, I feel that there has been a gradual anti-trike campaign instigated by a few individuals who probably couldn't stand the thought that a trike rider could produce as fast a ride as a bike rider, even though a trike is rated at least 10% slower than a bike. Starting with the RTTC's non-recognition of John Arnold's second place ride in the Mersey 24hr Championship of 1953. I think that decision was an embarrassment that could have been avoided if they had listened to the groundswell of opinion from the grass root members, who were in favour of him winning the medal.

I too rode a trike in the 1960's, mainly for club riding and winter journeys when the roads were icy, and three wheels proved safer than two. The thought of me trying to compete on a trike, and be able to beat an average racing man on a bike over any distance of time trial, would have been pure fantasy!

In the late 1970's I rode thousands of miles at race speed on a tandem trike with Pat Kenny and it always felt as though we were dragging a trailer full of bricks, even though we broke National Road Records. The next day it was always such a relief to get back on two wheels and feel the surge of speed and the response of a bike, so I truly admire the long distance racing men of the 'T.A.'

In very recent times (2007) I've noticed that the V.T.T.A. hierarchy seems to have started a vendetta against its trike riding members who try harder, ride faster, and take awards that bike riders of the same age should theoretically win. Sour grapes perhaps?

⇒•◇•⇐

**The North Road CC 24hr** on 14th & 15th August 1965. **Cliff Smith,** just three weeks after his Mersey 2nd placed ride, **won this North Road event for the 5th time with 469.343m.** John Westcott, Icknield RC was **2nd** with **437.642** and **Derek Porter** was **3rd** with **424.759 miles.**

From 22 entries only 15 riders finished this tough event. A new configuration of roads was being used on both days, consisting of circuits based on Baldock, Royston, Wimpole and Biggleswade. It didn't prove to be universally popular with the riders, but it did reduce the marshalling and manpower required by the club, by cutting out the detours into the 'Fen District'. No teams finished and the **fastest trike** rider was **T.A. Lovell,** Kettering Amateur CC, **368.294.** John Withers, Birmingham St Christopher's CCC had a good start, riding a track bike with 3 speed Sturmey Archer fixed gears, and Joe Summerlin, North Road CC was riding a 77" fixed gear, but Ken Usher failed to start. It was a mild day at 72 degrees F, still and muggy with tiny black 'bugs' coming off the fields, plaguing the riders and most of the people at the start causing them to 'scratch away'.

At the 100mile point, Cliff Smith led by 11mins from Porter with Summerlin at 14 mins. At 158 miles only five riders had ridden the full course and by the early hours of Sunday only two riders, Smith and Westcott, had covered all of the roads. The night was moonlit with little wind and fairly mild. At 307 miles, Smith was 1 hour up on Westcott with Porter lying 3rd. After the completion of the new circuit during the night, the dawn turned grey and drizzly. Cliff Smith arrived at the end of his second circuit and someone shouted "Good ride Cliff" and Cliff's reply was "Good ride spoilt by a rotten course!"

I think it would be fitting at this point to analyse Cliff's ride. In spite of a poor field, a course that he did not like, and nothing to chase but 'Father Time', Cliff gave of his best. We are all familiar now with the Smith style of meticulously scything his way through the field, but when you are out there on your own, with nothing but your own personal suffering and the miles to devour as quickly as you can, it must be very tempting to ease up or stop and take a rest. Cliff did neither of these things, he went on fighting right up to the very end, even when he knew he had lost his chance of doing a personal best or his event best. Who then can be surprised when he became a little bitter, making the remark "I've won, so what!" Anyone who saw Cliff at the end, sick, tired and deathly white, lying beside the road as I have never seen him do before, must know that here is a truly great amateur sportsman.

Joe Summerlin completed 230 miles in his first 12 hours but slipped back before the finishing circuit to record 411 miles. He also disliked the new course and it was felt that the surface on the Baldock to Royston section was too rough to do 4 times in 2 days. **John Withers** finished **4th** with **418.60 miles** and said he preferred the 'circuits' to riding in the 'Fens'.

*This North Road description was courtesy of a race report by Tony King taken from the North Road Gazette and reprinted in the Fellowship Journal.*

—⟫•⟪—

On September 10th 1965, **Pat Kenny** set off at 5am from the Head Post Office in Edinburgh to attack **John Arnold's 24hr trike record of 428.5 miles.** On the way he hoped to break Ed Tweddell's Edinburgh to London record of 24hrs 11mins. Providing that the wind would blow from the North as forecasted, he was reasonably confident of getting Ed Tweddell's 16 year old record, but he knew that John Arnolds 428.5m 24 hr record would be a tough one. If he was to stand any chance of getting it he needed to be at the Head Post Office in London inside 21 hours, so leaving 3 hours for the run down towards the south coast through Purley, Crawley and Horsham, getting to Cowfold would just get him the record.

Pat had a storming ride from Edinburgh, even without a wind he was soon into the Lammermuir Hills and through Lauderdale. When you consider that Pat's best 24hr on a bike was 437 miles, then to beat a John Arnold trike record of 428.5 was demanding a lot of himself, but he pulled out all of the stops. By the time he'd reached the English Border the wind had picked up well in his favour. He passed through Coldstream, 48 miles, in 2 hrs 33 mins, and reached Newcastle, 108m, in 5hrs 46mins. At Borobridge he got caught up in a Saturday afternoon time trial and had to be careful not to infringe the strict RRA pacing rules. His 12hrs ran out between Blyth and Fulford with 234 miles. By nightfall he was well down the A1, heading towards the Capital. Dave Duffield was on hand to marshal him through some very busy junctions in the City and he reached **The Head Post Office at 1.48am with 386.5 miles covered and the first record broken by 3 hrs 23 mins.**

After a few minutes break he rode South, out of London, amidst very heavy all night London traffic, towards a very cold dawn, **to finish at Cowfold with 431.5 miles covered. St Christopher's could now brag that Pat Kenny was the first man other than Albert Crimes to beat a John Arnold record!**

I was on that record attempt as a helper and I had never seen six lanes of traffic going in and out of London (or anywhere) at 2 o'clock in the morning! What a culture shock for us 'Brummies' from the second city.

*After the racing season was well and truly over for most of us in November, Cliff Smith chased the Edinburgh to London record that cruelly eluded him in May. He waited for a north westerly to help him to London, but in the end when the wind didn't materialise, it was his own speed, strength and tenacity that got him through the cold and frost once again, to break the record with 7 minutes to spare. He broke a Professional record that day which had stood to Cyril Heppleston since 1939.* **Cliff's record of 18 hours 49 mins 42 secs then stood for another 24 years.**

## 1966

**On 6th June 1966 at 10am,** the Timekeeper, Eric Wilkinson, started **Pete Swinden and John Withers,** Birmingham St Christopher's CCC, on their **epic tandem 'End to End'** journey. They were attacking Bailey and Forrest's record of 2 days 4hrs 48 mins.

Heavy holiday traffic slowed them down in the West Country but they still managed 470 miles for their first 24hrs, the farthest anyone on any type of machine had travelled in the first 24hrs on a successful End to End at that time.

After more problems, and delays in Scotland with Pete's bad knee requiring hospital treatment at Perth and Inverness, they finally got to John o' Groats and **broke the record with 2 days, 2 hours 14 mins,** so beating the old record by 2 hrs 34 mins. **It is a record that still stands to this day, over 40 years later.**

Pete and John's performance was an example of a perfectly matched pair of hard riding 24hr men, who spent five years riding on the tandem in an effort to be ready for this journey. One can see from their performances in 24 hr events at this time, that they were not event winners as the solo record breakers have to be (Pete's p.b. 438 and John's 430m) they were just extremely fit, trained and prepared mentally and physically for the job. It was felt that without any of the delays they experienced, the two day barrier could also have been broken by them, as Dick Poole had done just one year earlier. There has been a few attempts at their record in recent years, the best one got as far as Lancashire.

---

A week or two later, **The Catford 24hr was won by Cliff Smith with 454.58 miles.** This was Cliff's fourth win in the event, but with one of his lowest mileages. **Gordon Hinder** was **2nd** riding for the Oxford City RC with **443.54m** and **Tony Brook,** Bec CC was **3rd** with **434.1m.** The event was run in 'vile' conditions with ten hours of rain from the 4th to the 14th hour. Gordon Hinder was making a comeback in this race and I've used parts of his report and memories of the event for the details.

*"The event started in bright sunshine giving no hint of the 'monsoon' conditions soon to hit us. I enjoyed the first 100 miles more than any event I have ever ridden. On the trip down to the South Coast the rain started, but I was convinced that it was only going to be a light shower, so I didn't bother to put on my racing cape. After about an hour, at the start of the Goring detour, I was forcibly made to cape up by my helpers who also provided the two vehicles. Peter Launchbury, Ray Chandler, Davy MacQuiston, Frank Needle, Don Dow, (Ian's dad)and John Gills (Gilly). They obviously knew more about the weather to come than I did.*

*The rain got heavier and heavier but it didn't seem to worry me, which was odd, because in all previous wet events I had decided to 'pack' if it ever rained in a 24 hr. Cliff Smith caught me returning on the Shrimpney leg and I soon speeded up after he had gone. He was soon out of sight but I didn't appear to lose much time on him over the next 250 miles. He may have eased up knowing that no-one was challenging him and it encouraged me no end.*

*Perkins was still out in front of the field but disappeared somewhere near the Havant by-pass, possibly when Cliff caught him. The rain was about at its heaviest now, bouncing off the road so hard it wouldn't drain away, and it was very dark. My helpers lost me due to not being able to keep up in the dangerous conditions. I suffered problems with lamps going on and off and struggled to see the road, but eventually reached the sit down feed where I nearly scalded my insides with boiling soup, rice pud and hot tea.*

*Restarting from here, I felt much better and with yet another new lamp I continued in the tracks of Cliff Smith who was now the only rider in front of me. Frank Needle informed me I had covered 236 miles in the 12 hours, eight more than I had scheduled. Soon after this I felt a pain in my knee so I borrowed tracksuit bottoms off John Gills. Luckily the roads were of quite a good surface as I had no way of seeing bumps or potholes, but finally dawn came and I at last saw Cliff in daylight as he returned from the Byfleet roundabout, and we wished each other 'Good Morning'; the same smiling Cliff, I wonder if he smiles in the dark?*

*On the way back to the finishing circuit later, I passed a few stragglers who, like me, were glad of my helper's directions and encouragement, as I had completely forgotten which direction the course took. Even when I reached the circuit I couldn't get inspiration and rode round for four laps, just glad to finish."*

From 25 starters only 13 finished on that hard day. **C. Sim,** South Bucks RC rode **430.69m** and **Ken Davey** with **412.14m** had his Bec CC team win hopes thwarted when Ken Usher retired in the night. **Stan Spelling, Wren Whls had a very good ride with 394.25m on a trike in 7th place.**

*My thanks to Gordon Hinder for this report.*

---

**The Wessex RC National Championship 24hr** on July 16th 1966 was won **by Nim Carline with a massive 496.37 miles, a new Competition Record by over 6 miles.**

Despite the remarkably small entry of 45 for a Championship event, the inclusion of the names of Carline, Smith, Poole, Eric Tremaine, Tony Harris and Rob Clark (2 of the previous winners), gave promise of a notable day and night, a promise which was fulfilled by Nim Carline with many other notable performances and personal bests.

The traffic problems in previous Wessex events made it necessary to re-arrange the course so as to avoid the use of the busy A338 during the peak afternoon period of traffic, and also to omit all the former detours laying north of Lyndhurst. This was made possible by taking advantage of the amended 'RTTC' regulation 33, allowing a second use on Sunday of roads already traversed on Saturday.

Weather conditions were promising when 41 riders were despatched from Crow Corner from 2pm. At 32 miles, Carline had passed Cliff Smith, Tony Harris and Dick Poole. At Bransgore (84 miles) Carline had become first man on the road and continued to draw away from the complete field. At the Heytesbury turn (123m) he clocked 5 hrs 25m, Clark was at 21 mins, Harris 22m, Hygate and Tremaine 31m, Dick Poole who was unhappy with his progress decided to call it a day and retired. Darkness had now fallen but Carline was so far ahead of the field that normal detours used at this time to Warmwell Cross and Gallows Hill had to be closed to most riders as Carline had already completed them. Carline had gone through in 8hrs 45m, Clark at 40m, Harris and Smith 44m, Tremaine 50 min, with the rest of the field well over one hour behind. At Woodbury Hill (228miles) Carline passed in 10hrs 21m at 1.05am. Westcott had arrived 2 mins earlier but he had missed out 29.6 miles of road.

Interest now centred on the **12 hour distances.** Cyril Neale the Organiser, drove Tom Barlow to follow **Carline** and pinpoint his 12hr mileage; **an amazing 260.97 miles or almost 22 mph.** Other riders approximate distances were, Harris 247m, Smith 245m, Tremaine 244m, Hygate 231 and Lowe 230. It will be seen that a keen battle was raging for silver and bronze medals at this stage.

At 300 miles, Carline came back to Ringwood in 13 hours 50 mins, Harris at 50 mins, Clark 56 m, Smith 61 and Tremaine 62m. Shortly after this check Clark called it a day. The field was now down to 30 riders and only the 5 leaders had followed the full course. On the Bailey Gate-Wimborne to Cranbourne section which was a tough one as a windy dawn was breaking, Carline appeared to be feeling the effects of his constant speed and effort, but on the return to Wimborne (375m) he was still firmly in the lead with 17hrs 46m followed by Harris at 49m, Smith 67m and Tremaine at 72m. At Crow Corner (405m) the riders started the finishing circuit. Carline finished his 1st lap (420m) in 20 hours 5 mins, 2nd lap (436) in 20 hr 52m, 3rd (451) 21h 40m, 4th (466) 22.25, 5th (481) 23.12, and 6th (496) 23.55m.

A terrific battle ensued on the circuit for 3rd place between Smith and Tremaine but Carline on the circuit was lapping in less than 45 mins and realised that the 500 would probably elude him. **Tony Harris produced a personal best for 2nd place with 478.63 miles. Eric Tremaine took bronze and 3rd place with another p.b. 475.4 and so led Cliff Smith with 472.73m 4th, and Eric's brother, Clifford, 438.89, to an East Midlands CC team win of 1,387.03 miles. Sid Hygate** took **5th** with a p.b. of **454.73m** for the RNCC.

Another ex-mariner, Stan Spelling had a very good ride with 444.79m for 6th place just beating **Les Lowe** by .5 of a mile. **Les led a Speedwell B.C.** team of Ian Shaw and Ken Smith to a 2nd place total of **1,278.39 miles.**

Cyril Neale, the Organiser of this event in 1966, wrote a poignant, historical note at that time.

*"Almost 50 years ago in cold and windy weather, Maurice Selbach riding in the Fens became the first man to attain the coveted target of 400 miles. The record has since increased by spasms. Jim Dougal's 430 during the 1920's Edgar Seeley's amazing 444 in the 30's then progression by smaller steps during the 40's and early 50's to 450, 460, 470 followed by Ken Price 478 and Dennis White's epic first inside evens ride and Dave Keeler's great but abortive accomplishment. In this decade we have seen Eric Matthews put the figure to 490miles, now Nim has raised it to 496m, and the position is very similar, relatively to the one which existed at the time of Selbach's ride."*

Tony Harris who came 2nd with 478.63 said that his only comment on Nim's ride is that, under these conditions, which were not perfect, only one person could have done it and that was Nim. It was a great ride and a pity that nobody was there to make him try that wee bit harder for the 500 miles. Sid Hygate who also pulled out a p.b. with 454.73 said that the start sheet amused him to think that he was at the back of the field with all the 'stars', Smith, Carline, Poole and Co. Tony Harris caught him for 4 minutes in 19 miles, they chatted for a minute or two and Harris was of the opinion that Carline wouldn't last. (How wrong can you be?) I saw Carline coming back from the first turn, crouched low, working like a '25 miler'. I'd asked Nim before the start how he planned to ride this one and his reply was "same as last year – ride like fury then hang on, so that everyone has to ride my way"! It's a brave and fit man who can do it that way, with success, but we all know the end result.

Sid mentions having a scrap on the road with a young lad riding a fixed wheel machine. He'd caught him, but the lad wouldn't be denied his moment of glory and kept coming past up the hills. This went on for some time and Sid didn't want to get drawn in so early in the race. After about 8 miles, Sid was just about to use some very nautical language when the problem was suddenly resolved; a car pulled out and the lad rammed it and fell off and as there were people to help him Sid carried on. Sid recalled having a bad stomach after 100 miles but later in the race his helping team realised the pre-mixed 'Complan' had turned sour. He went on to soup, took Disprin and the problem was solved. Sid had another bad patch with his knees hurting and had resigned himself to probably not finishing when Brian Lovegrove said "you're in 5th place". This jolted Sid into action and he gave his all to the finish.

A couple of amusing incidents occurred to the Speedwell team, and Ian Shaw described the first one when Ken Smith was found by his helpers in the night just about to start off in the wrong direction. He had fallen asleep at the side of the road and when he awoke he couldn't remember which direction he had come from. After a shock treatment of cold sponges and strong coffee he was sent off in the right direction but still protesting.

Les Lowe paid praise to Sid Hygate and Stan Spelling who both had excellent rides. Les mentioned using a bit of subterfuge in the night. Les's fellow competitors had got used to hearing the ticking of the milometer on his front wheel (no computers in the 1960's) and to baffle his rivals, such as Hygate, Free and Tremaine, Les disconnected the milometer. The trick didn't work completely as Sid Hygate remarked "crafty so and so" when he caught him.

---

**The Mersey RC 24hr on July 29th was won by Howard Bayley with 462.12miles. Newcomer Stan Richardson, South Lancs RC was 2nd with 444.74 and Ken Hughes, Mid Shropshire Whls, 3rd, 425.77m. Pete Swinden was 4th with 420.78 and led a Birmingham St Christopher's CCC team of John Withers 414.40 and Pat Kenny 408.37m to a winning total of 1,243.56 miles.**

A field of 52 riders, a fair size considering it was of non Championship status, had Pete Broad as its fastest rider on paper with a 466 to his credit, next was Howard Bayley with a 458, and Ken Hughes with two rides over 450m. Don Spraggett and Stan Lea were also in the frame for a place. The St Christopher's lads were the strongest team on paper and the event promised to be a good battle.

The weather at the start was mild but dull and cloudy with a moderate breeze. At 90 miles, Bayley was setting a very fast pace, 29mins inside 'evens' and was already stretching the field. Spraggett was very determined and had shot up from 7th to 2nd place, just 14mins behind. Tom Robson, Oldbury and District, had already put his warmer night clothing on although the weather was warm, he was at 15mins the same as Pat Kenny. Pete Broad wasn't happy at 17m and Richardson was steady at 19mins. After riding a p.b. first 100 of 4hrs 28mins Bayley now forged ahead.

At 152.8 miles, Broad had packed and Robson had also disappeared. He said he was bored and didn't fancy another 17 hours. Bayley, however, looked good, and was 33mins inside 'evens'. Spraggett was at 24mins, Hughes at 34m, Kenny 37m, Richardson 38m and Swinden at 46m. The wind that died down as dusk fell had now picked up to be very strong and gusty on the coast road to Prestatyn. On the way back to Queensferry at 184 miles, Bayley was at 34mins inside 'evens' and was causing further havoc with the rest of the field. Spraggett had lost more time but was still 2nd at 36mins and Hughes was at 41mins. *This was the event where Howard Bayley hopped over a churchyard wall to 'spend a penny'.  He emerged just as a drunk was staggering past.  Startled by Howard's gaunt black garbed figure, full black beard and piercing hypnotic eyes, the drunk ran off into the night shouting "repent, Christ has risen"!  or so the story goes.*

Bayley had a few minutes break at Whitchurch (220.5 miles) and then 'flew' up the Nantwich leg and checks showed he was moving 2 mph faster than his rivals.   Spraggett was still 2nd but had dropped to 42mins behind; next came Hughes 44m, Richardson, Shuttleworth, Swinden and Kenny.   Bayley passed through the 12 hour point with 248 miles, another p.b. for him.   The wind was nagging at the riders and on the return from the Raven to Ternhill at 284m Bayley's speed had dropped and he was just 13mins inside 'evens'.   Spraggett was holding 50mins, Hughes and Richardson were at 61m and 65m.

Most riders stopped at the sit down breakfast feed at Edgebolton, including Bayley.   The Mersey RC team as well as the Barrow Central Whls had fragmented, leaving the Birmingham St Christopher's lads the only team still riding.   From about 300 miles the weather deteriorated and very cold rain blew in through the 'Cheshire Gap'. Although Spraggett had lost no more time on the leader, the weather had got to him and by the time the pale dawn sun arrived, he had 'packed'.    It was also thought that the battle with Richardson had finished him.   Many retirements affected the field, but Richardson was now moving very well in 2nd place.   At Welshampton (364 miles) he had pulled back 17mins and was at 52mins behind Bayley.

The wind played a cruel trick here as the riders went from Wem to the finishing circuit; it turned from a south westerly to a north westerly, against the riders; it even reduced Bayley's speed to 17.7 mph from here to the finish, Richardson averaged 16.1 mph, Hughes 15.5 and Swinden 16.1 mph.

Further down the field of riders, as they had passed through the rain at 328 miles, was Charlie Alexander, who'd set a cracking pace but he was now suffering.   John Withers was moving well and was singing as he pedalled.  (Pete Swinden said that he usually did that when he was falling asleep on the back of the tandem).   Alf Cropper was moving well, Lea was steady and John Gills was slowing slightly.

"YOU'RE NOT PUSHING VERY HARD."

At the finish Bayley still looked strong and hung on to beat newcomer Stan Richardson by over 17 miles.   Ken Hughes proved that he wasn't finished yet with a 425 mile ride and said he would possibly return with a team next time. Strongman Pete Swinden held off Cropper and Shuttleworth for 4th place and **Brian Kirkham beat Terry Kelly for the trike award with 402.43 miles.**

Howard Bayley in an article written about the event said that his main thought was to get Pat Kenny behind him as soon as possible.  He mentioned stopping at Edgebolton breakfast feed for two eggs and beans, then pears and milk soda.  On his way to the start of the event at Prees, he'd had a hearty breakfast of two eggs, chips and peas plus fruit and ice cream, cake, followed by one egg, chips and peas!  (so perhaps that's his secret weapon).  Howard encountered his first herd of cows at Ternhill and got stung by nettles trying to squeeze by, and Johnny Arnold handed him up his usual peppermint potion at Prees.  At Edgebolton came his second brush with cows and after trying to get up the inside, the farmer told him to come round the other side as the cows were trained to keep to the left.   In all, Howard had six confrontations with cows in 24hrs.

On the cold wet Redbrook-Wem section, Stan and Eddy Bray got him into a cape to keep out the cold and so probably saved him time there.  Howard was in the main street at Wem when the wind direction changed; this demoralised him and the only comfort he had was the thought that if he could just last out to the finishing circuit he would win. Once on the circuit he met his 6th herd of cows going for milking.

Stan Richardson who came 2nd was amazed when he reached the final miles and said "what a circuit, its almost worth riding just for the applause and encouragement you get there, however, one thing bothered me, I kept feeling I ought to stop and bow, shake hands, or give some other form of acknowledgement".

*Just to prove that long distance training and racing doesn't necessarily affect your speed, Howard did eight 'personal bests' from and including the Mersey RC 24hr – 4hrs 18m for 4th place in the Speedwell '100'; 257 miles 1st place and 1st handicap 'MCCA' 12 hour; 1 hour for the Speedwell 25m; 2 hrs 4mins for the MC & AC 50 mile for 5th place; 4 hrs 37mins for Scottish trike 100 mile record; 1hr 3mins on a trike in the 'T.A.' 25, and finally 249 miles on a trike in the Oldbury 12hr for the Competition Record. In that same year, Howard Bayley took Pat Kenny's MRRA trike record off him with a ride of 430 miles. Strangely enough, whenever I have a mental picture of Howard, he's always riding a trike and I think this is what gave him his edge to win a 24hr on a bike.*

<hr />

*Just 3 weeks after his 496 miles Wessex ride, Nim Carline set out on August 7th on his quest to beat Dick Poole's End to End record. This tough 38 year old market gardener wanted to tackle this 'Blue Riband' record sooner rather than later as he believed Eric Matthews would soon 'put it on the shelf'.*

*After a warm start at a decent speed he missed his helpers in the West Country due to very heavy traffic. He probably suffered from dehydration as a result of this and he just failed to get the 12hr record. During the night he became very sleepy but he was still hoping to break Ken Joy's 475 miles 24hr record on the way, but after Wigan he slowed to below 'evens' (20 mph). He crossed the border into Scotland but failed to break the 24hr. Eventually he succumbed to sleep and climbed off at Ecclefechan.*

<hr />

**The North Road CC 24hr was won by George Bettis, Elite CC with 468.919m, Derek Porter, Glendene CC was 2nd with 434.072, and 3rd placed Cliff Hill, Leics Forest CC with 429.950m led Buswell and Ellway to a team win of 1,209.378 miles.**

Bettis who had set his heart on winning this event did a really excellent ride, setting the pace every inch of the way, on a far from easy day. His ride was a personal best by five miles. Derek Porter improved 2 miles to take 2nd place; his was a steady confident ride that held off a very vigorous fight for 3rd place between Cliff Hill and Bob O'Dell. It was Hill's first ride in a 24hr race and he led a Leics Forest team to a win, backed by D.W. Buswell with 395m and E.J. Ellway on a trike with 383 miles. Their total was 1,209.3. Stan Spelling took the trike award with a personal best of 407 miles and Ray Burnett finished his thirteenth 24hr in 5 years with 394.923m. Eric Wilkinson, the Principal Timekeeper, once his starting duties were over, took a trip around the course to see how riders and Officials were doing. Here are a few of his comments from that day.

*"Cliff Smith, five times winner of our event was the last man to start from 25 riders, in reasonable weather. Although having won the Catford '24' earlier in the season in heavy rain, he was not considered to be quite on top form this year and a few experts had predicted his defeat. The two most likely to topple Cliff from his throne were George Bettis and Ken Usher. Bettis was said to have been training specially for this event.*

*After lunch at St. Neots, I transferred to the luxury of Pat Phillip's Bentley and we travelled to Wimpole Lodge where Ted Kings informed us that Bettis was already in the lead at 61.5 miles with 2hrs 29mins. Smith was 2nd at 27mins and Usher 3rd at 29 mins. At 70 miles the position was the same, but Westcott had moved up into 4th place trying to improve on his 2nd placed Wessex ride of 438m.*

*We made our way to Eaton Socon to take the 100 mile times and to have a picnic tea provided by Mrs Haylock and her husband, Woodbine. He had been the Editor of the North Road Gazette for quite a few years. Bettis was still in the lead with 4hrs 36mins. Smith was still 2nd at 11mins, Usher 3rd at 14 mins and Westcott at 21mins. When we arrived at Norman Cross, concern was being expressed at the non-arrival of Cliff Smith. The possibility of his 'packing' was hardly considered, but alas it was so, his complete lack of form had shown and the fight had deserted him. At 10pm the wind was still fresh as it had been all day. At 182 miles after the second Peterborough circuit, only 7 riders had completed the full course. Bettis passed in 8hrs 35m, Usher 2nd at 21m and Porter 3rd, by just 1 minute from Westcott at 45mins.*

*The 12 hour mileages at Godmanchester were: Bettis 248m, Usher 242m, Porter 230, Westcott 227, Hill 226, King 224.5 and O'Dell 224. Ken Ushers helpers were having difficulty in keeping him going but Bettis was turning his 81" fixed gear and seemed very cheerful.*

*Usher retired on the way south from Guyhirne in the 'early hours'. Bettis went on to win with an undisputed lead".*

⪧◆⪦

**On October 21st 1966, a tragedy occurred at Aberfan, a coal mining community in Wales, when a 500 ft coal tip slipped, crushing Pantglas Junior School, a row of cottages and a farmhouse. The death toll of 144 included 116 children between the age of 7 and 11 years.**

*Also in 1966, the 'RRA' finally abolished its ruling on 'no prior publicity'. The rule had been introduced in the 1890's due to the hostility shown, to record breakers and racing cyclists, by the general public, car owners, other road users, Police and Magistrates. The only time the ruling was eased was if an End to End was taking place so that clubs along the route could prepare to supply food, drink and marshals, over the 870 mile route.*

*At this same time, since early days before the Second World War, the RTTC had similarly imposed a ruling that their event details and start sheets should have the words 'Private & Confidential' printed prominently on them. Time trial course details were also depicted by a code number that didn't give any road numbers or area details, unless you owned an RTTC handbook and could decipher the codes. The main aim of this was to prevent large crowds turning up to spectate, so blocking the roads and bringing the sport into disrepute. The Police have always been informed of time trials taking place and it's one of the first duties an event Secretary has to do, well in advance of any other procedures.*

"I THOUGHT YOU WOULD HAVE HAD SOMEBODY
IN THE CAR WHO CAN CHANGE A WHEEL."

# CHAPTER FOUR

## LIGHTWEIGHTS, LADIES, & THE MAGIC 507 / 525

### 1967 - 2008

**1967 heralded a very important landmark in the History of the 24hr Cycle Race. In this year, women were allowed to ride the Mersey RC 24hr for the first time ever.**

Prior to this, the only accurately timed 24hr solo ride would have been within the auspices of the Women's Road Record Association (WRRA), who at that time in 1967 still recognised two different categories, amateur and professional, with different performance figures and records for each. *To save duplication of information I have written more extensively on this Ladies history in my separate but complete account of women riding 24hr races in Chapter 5.*

At 5.06pm, Saturday, 22nd July 1967, history was made when Ron MacQueen despatched Christine Minto (nee Moody), Birdwell Wheelers to start her Competition record setting journey, followed one minute later by Mrs Ruth Williams, Liverpool Eagle RC, and then Mrs Wyn Maddock, Notts and Derby Clarion. I started two minutes later at 5.10pm and I didn't realise at the time that history was being made. I was 23 years old and at that time I probably just hoped that they didn't beat me by too many miles! This was also the first 24hr race promoted by the Merseyside Ladies Cycling Association and was incorporated in the main event.

Back in the 1960's women riding in time trials were placed at 1 minute intervals in succession to each other, as opposed to being dispersed evenly according to merit and speed throughout the complete field with the men, as is current procedure in 2007 and has been since the 1980's. In 1988 the 12 hour and 24 hour Championship became open to men and women integrated in one event and if a woman has a greater distance than a man then she is the winner and this also applies to the team race in the Championship, even a mixed team.

Prior to 1967 the only way a woman rider could prove her stamina and endurance powers to ride a long distance time trial was in a 12 hour event, and it will be noted from the CTT (RTTC) handbook that the men's 12hr competition record in 1945 was 251.8 by Arthur Overton. Two years later in 1947, Eileen Sheridan (still an amateur at that time) pushed the ladies competition record up to 237.82, so just 14 miles difference. In 1958, Owen Blower took the men's competition record to 271.8 but a year later in 1959, Beryl Burton raised the ladies record to 250.37 miles.

Then in 1967 an amazing thing happened. First of all, Mike McNamara raised the men's 12 hr record to 276.52m to win the men's BBAR at record speed, but in that event on the same day, Beryl Burton beat him by .73 of a mile with 277.25 miles. She became the fastest rider ever, male or female, over 12 hours. This also made 1967 an historical one for women. Apparently she gave Mike a sweet as she went past, just to soften the blow.

I know she was phenomenal and perhaps it seems a little unfair to just point to Beryl's unbelievable rides as being totally representative of women's performances compared to the men's, and although she stood out at the time, by her prolific winning rides in women's events, there were an increasing amount of other women who were finding that the longer the duration of a time trial, the better they fared against the men, from 100 miles to 12 hours.

*The RRA 24 hour record is a good example to use here, which in 1954 was taken by Ken Joy with 475.75 miles and like Ken, Eileen Sheridan broke her WRRA 24hr record that same year with 446.25 miles, the difference being that she was just over 6% slower.*

**From here on I will mention the women's rides and performances, but only in the context of the complete description of the event and its results.**

One more historical first for 1967 was the Scottish Cycling Union 24hr held in early August.

The first event on the calendar this year on June 24th was the 'Catford'. It was a National Championship event and won by Nim Carline, Morley RC with 480.27 miles. It was also the first time that 20 mph had been beaten in this event.

It was dull and overcast as the riders set off from Pease Pottage, near Crawley. From 63 entries, Carline was the strongest on paper, defending his Championship title with Cliff Smith and Dick Poole being his main opponents. Poole was still recovering from a bout of flu but he was a rider who was also capable of 480 miles and had numerous rides over 450 to his credit. Eric Matthews was having a year off from racing and the team title was also 'wide open' due to the Middlesex RC and East Midlands CC not having a team.

Dick Poole with newcomer Dave Meisner and veteran Bill Thorncroft made a good team for the Brentwood RC. The Speedwell BC were present with Les Lowe, Ian Shaw and Ken Smith as were the Buccaneers and the South Bucks RC. Gordon Hinder, Oxford City RC, who rode to 2nd place in the Catford event last year, was riding and thought to be very fit. Sid Hygate was reputed to be even less fit than last year due to Royal Navy commitments, but was determined to finish.

From the very start Carline unleashed his fury, and by the 75 mile point had caught three quarters of the field. During this time, the dull, humid, overcast conditions had given way to two hours of heavy cold rain and wind, but after the storm had passed over, the humidity rose to 85% and the temperature to 70 degrees F. For his first 100 miles Carline did 4hrs 18mins, Cliff Smith was 2nd, Tony Harris and Dick Poole were 3rd and 4th. The wind turned from the south-east to a southerly and made the exposed roads down to the south coast very hard. The heavy traffic in Arundel prevented Carline from seeing the marshal and he went off course here and lost 8 mins, but he seemed unperturbed and even more determined in his riding. A check at Chichester (150.2m) showed him to be 44mins inside 'evens' with Harris at 11mins, Smith at 12, Poole 17, Hinder 30m, Brook 31 and Lowe 33m. At Chichester on the return trip (196.7) as darkness fell, Carline was 51mins inside evens and led Smith by 16mins. Smith was now firmly in 2nd place with Harris back in 3rd with 23m, Poole 25m, Hinder and Brook were at 40mins. At 12 hours, Carline had ridden a remarkable 256 miles, Smith 251, Poole 246, and Harris 245. Retirements by this time had reduced the team race to the Brentwood RC leading the Speedwell BC by 38 mins.

Smith was hanging tenaciously onto Carline now and slowly pegging his lead, but this power struggle had drawn these two riders away from the field. The night was dry and warm, moonlit and with a light breeze, dawn gradually rose as Carline turned at Byfleet (290.7m) at 2.39am.

At 5 am the leading riders were returning towards Guildford, the only ones still riding the full course were Carline, Harris, Poole, Hinder, Hygate and Lowe. Carline returned from the Windsor detour looking very subdued and down to 18 mph, although he was still inside 'evens' by 26mins. Smith was still back in 2nd place just 24mins behind and Poole was 3rd at 51mins. Harris was also slowing at 57mins and everyone else was over one hour behind Carline, Hinder, Hygate and Lowe. Les said he suffered with the cold in the night.

It wasn't an easy wind assisted ride back to the finishing circuit this year, but it didn't deter Carline from averaging 19 mph on this stretch, he was still on to a 480mile plus ride at this point. As he entered the finishing circuit at 400 miles, Smith was 2nd, 40mins behind, but violent rain hit the riders on the circuit in those last two hours and caused many punctures. The lashing rain was very cold and thunder crashed all around.

Carline maintained his pace to finish with a well judged 480.27 miles. Cliff Smith as dogged as ever was 2nd with 469.55m. Dick Poole was pleased to get 3rd place with 465.65 miles, considering he wasn't fully fit, and Gordon Hinder even with a puncture had improved 12 miles for 4th place with 455.28m. Sid Hygate had ridden himself into fitness by sheer brute force and tenacity for 5th place with 445.22. Brook had a good ride with 437.72 and Ian Shaw came back very strongly in the last half of the race with 430.75, just beating Tony Harris by .2 of a mile, although Harris had to climb off with one circuit to go due to severe foot trouble; he'd already been riding in carpet slippers for an hour or two. There were 42 finishers from 59 starters and the fastest trike was Pete Cudmore with 393.1 miles.

**Dick Poole led Dave Meisner, riding his first 24hr race with 429.95m and Bill Thorncroft with 397.93m to a fine Brentwood RC Championship team win of 1,293.53 miles.** Ian Shaw, Les Lowe and Ken Smith totalled 1,240.03 for the Speedwell BC in 2nd place.

Poole recalled battling with Tony Harris for about 20 hours for 3rd place and said he timed his finish to perfection on the circuit, as he wasn't going to ride a yard further than necessary in that rain, and when he reached the timekeeper his luck was in, there was an empty telephone box to shelter in. He had consumed very little solid food during the race, preferring rice pudding and fruit cocktail, soup, 'Bengers' mixed with honey, tea and black coffee. Dick said "my congratulations to Nim on a fine effort – the 'Catford' is a real man's course in my opinion", *and that is from a man who at that time held the End to End record.*

Gordon Hinder praised the helpers around the course for being so encouraging and didn't think any other event was as friendly as a 24hr race and the atmosphere was terrific. By improving 12 miles he'd raised his own club record by that amount and for that his helpers didn't make him ride his bike home. His worst point was on the finishing circuit, when torrential rain washed sweat into his eyes, reducing his vision even more.

*Sid Hygate had little or no preparation at all before the race except for a 92 mile ride a week before the start. He'd spent the winter in a submarine and said "you try living in a confined space with six other men, boozing your way home from Australia via the U.S. at 10 knots an hour and see how fit you are." His only regret during the event was on the final lap of the finishing circuit, refusing a peppermint drink, not realising it was a 'John Arnold' special!*

Les Lowe remarked that the 'Catford' historically was never a good event for him, having grovelled all the way, when inexperienced in 1959. In 1963, punctures, wet and cold caused him to retire at 150 miles with severe foot and saddle chafing problems. This year he was more determined to do well, his first 100 mile and 12 hours were good and on schedule, but from then on, cold damp mist along the Thames put paid to his efforts. Although he did finish with 421.28, he hoped that his 184 miles in the last 12 hours would be his worst ever, but Les said he hoped to beat his Catford voodoo next year.

⇒•◇•⇐

In later years Les wrote many articles for the 24hr Fellowship Journal and here I've included a couple of quips and observations that Les wrote.

## Idolism

In my first 12 hour the Great L.J. Ross caught me at the entrance to the sit down feed at the 100 mile point, where teams of club girls were slaving over the primus stoves preparing choice dishes. Anxious to learn, I sat with Larry Ross and decided to eat what he did, starting with a bowl of honey porridge, followed by a huge plate of ham and eggs, and two large helpings of peaches and real cream. Larry then asked for two large hunks of chocolate cake. By now, 20mins had passed by and I was feeling like Falstaff; I suggested to the 'Great Man' that we should get going. He looked at me astonished and said "I've packed!"

## Dawn Caper

Two poachers slinking home around dawn with their 'catch' aroused Mersey RC stewards, Sam Moffat and his party who were lying 'Comatose' under a hedge wrapped in their capes while snatching a break from 24 hr duties. Simultaneously, Sam & Co leapt to their feet; the spectacle of four golden apparitions seemingly arising from the earth so startled the poachers, they dropped their catch and fled screaming with terror.

⇒•◇•⇐

**The Wessex 24hr** was the next event on the 15th July 1967. **Bob Clark** from the promoting club **won the event with 444.21m.** John Gills, Oxford RC had a personal best 2nd place ride that day with 426.68m and Charlie Alexander, Cardiff 100 mile RC was 3rd with 416.10m. Bob Clark led Ivor Jones, 400.64 and A.H. Vince, 369.77 to a Wessex RC team win of 1,215.35m. Bill Suttie was the fastest trike with 374.87 miles.

The Police had showed concern, prior to the event, of traffic congestion on the Saturday afternoon, so the Wessex RC tried experimenting by starting the riders at two minute intervals. The weather throughout the event was very good although there was a troublesome crosswind on the finishing circuit. Clark who was the favourite to win, took the lead early on although Dave Free challenged him at Heytesbury (124m) where Clark led in 5hr 49m. Free was at 19mins and Gills 34m. Between Wareham and Corfe Castle, Dave Free, who was still in 2nd place, was hit by a fast moving motorcycle coming towards him on the wrong side of the road. He was badly injured with broken limbs, several abrasions and contusions, and as a result he was hospitalised, but we have heard since the race that he made a good recovery.

At Warmwell Cross (197m) Clark went through in 9hrs 45mins with Gills at 52 mins and Alexander 67 mins. The positions of the leading riders remained pretty much the same through the night and well into the next day, and at the start of the finishing circuit at Crow Corner (405m) Clark had clocked 21hrs 40m 52secs, being the only rider to complete the full course up to that point. He maintained his lead over 2nd placed John Gills, to win by nearly 18 miles.

John Gills, a softly spoken, bearded, Oxonian and a good friend of the lads in the Birmingham St Christopher's CCC, gave the Fellowship Journal a few comments on his ride that day, from which I've chosen some poignant details. John mentions Bob Clark storming past him on the Salisbury Road at Ringwood which demoralised him, and this gave him the 'slows'.

Dave Free was the next to pass him and then some time later, John came to the scene of an accident and saw Dave lying there, several cars had already stopped to attend him and John was informed that there was nothing he could do to help. This obviously unnerved John and later at the traffic lights in Wareham he was confronted by Dave Free's helpers and had to break the news to them.

After riding the Gallows Hill section he refused to go on, such was the state of his mind, until his helpers informed him as to the extent of Dave's injuries. Once he knew, it put his mind at rest and from then on he started to pick up and close the gap between Bob Clark and himself. Eventually he caught and passed him while he was having a sit down feed; in fact John was easily matching Clark for speed., but of course he'd missed 11.6 miles of road earlier. John's ride was a personal best by 22 miles but he thought that without the upset of the accident, that 22 miles could have been a lot more.

⋙ ◆ ⋘

**The Mersey RC 24hr** on July 22nd and 23rd 1967 was **won in fine style by Rod Goodfellow,** Beacon Roads CC with **475.38m.** This was his first 24hr race but he'd already proved himself at the shorter distances and his best 12 hour on paper was 254 miles. Goodfellow, a Doctor by profession, beat last years winner Howard Bayley, by 17 miles. Weather conditions were just about perfect "just what the Doctor ordered" someone remarked.

There were 50 starters on the card including three ladies, Christine Minto (nee Moody), Ruth Williams, whose husband Bob knew he had his work cut out to beat her, and Wyn Maddock, a spritely 60 year old, who had sustained a slight fracture of the shoulder bone whilst training a week prior to the event.

The favourite to win the event was Howard Bayley, Solihull CC, but knew he would be hard pushed to beat Ken Usher, Edgeware RC. Bayley had won this event the previous year and Usher had won in 1960 and 1962. Pete Broad, Rhos-on-Sea CC had showed promise in previous years with high mileages, but it really was an open race, of course Rod Goodfellow had no previous 24hr results, so one could only take note of his good 12hr mileages.

Ron MacQueen dispatched 48 riders in fine sunny weather from 5pm with large crowds clapping the riders as each one rode away. Bayley started very fast and caught Usher within 20 miles, with Ken Hughes, Mid Shropshire Whls close behind. Christine Minto was the first rider on the road at Clives Green (40 miles). Back at Nantwich Cemetery she is still first through as Albert Crimes marshals the riders to the next turn. He marshalled this corner every year, and although I'd only heard about his and John Arnolds exploits from my club mates and reading about them, I didn't really know Albert, but I felt humbled to be directed on my way by him. I always took pride in saying "thanks Albert".

At Acton Church (50.5m) Bayley was actually the fastest through in 2hrs 9mins, Goodfellow was at 2mins, Broad 5mins, Clowes 6mins, Usher and Stan Lea 7m, Geoff Toon 8m, & Pete Swinden 10min. The three ladies were Christine at 13mins, Ruth 17m and Wyn at 35m. At Harold Nelson's 'mobile feed' operation at Tarvin, most of the riders took a sponge and a drink. At this point, Goodfellow started to put the pressure on as the field headed towards Chester. At Vicars Cross the riders detoured to Broxton (91.3m) where Bayley was now 5mins behind Goodfellow in 2nd place.

At the 100.4 miles check back at Vicars Cross, Goodfellow went through in 4hrs 27mins, Bayley at 5mins, Clowes 13m, Broad 14m, Usher 15m, Lea 18m. Christine is still the first rider on the road, due to her early starting position 40mins before Goodfellow, but the 'flying Doctor' was chasing her down just two minutes behind.

The course went through very dark back lanes and then the riders were sent on a detour from Saltney to Marford and back. This detour was controlled by Tommy Barlow and by the time the 13 riders had returned at 132 miles, Usher had moved in to 3rd place. The times here were: Goodfellow, 6hrs 1m, Bayley at 7mins, Usher at 15m, Clowes 18m, Broad 23m, Lea, 24m, Toon 27, Hughes 30. Christine is now at 58mins but Ruth is challenging her just 7mins slower and Wyn is riding steadily at the back of the field. Earlier as dusk fell at Chester, Harry Okell 'Okey', a past winner of this event who always marshals here, had mistaken her for a male competitor. I don't know why, but apparently he was very embarrassed about it. It's understandable really, after all, 24hr racing has been a male dominated sport for 82 years.

At Nant Hall, Prestatyn (171.6m) Goodfellow turned at 1.47am. This is 8hrs 1min riding time for him and he is only 5mins outside Eric Matthews' record-breaking ride of 1964 at this point. Bayley is at 9mins and Usher at 21mins. Back at Vicars Cross (201m) Goodfellow is still in the lead, the girls are riding at a steady 18mph at this point having covered 185miles in just over 10 hours.

It's a good clear night, no mist and not too cold as the riders return south to Whitchurch where the usual dawn assembly wait at the 'Hughes Hotel' to see the action. At 220.5 miles, Goodfellow took 10hrs 29mins, Bayley was at 19mins, Usher 26mins, with the next riders Clowes and Lea at 51 mins. The ladies had covered 205 miles here, Christine with 11hrs 23mins led Ruth by 25mins and Wyn by 29mins. Ruth is now leading husband Bob by 30 minutes.

After riding at over 'evens', Goodfellow completed this detour from Whitchurch to Nantwich and back, so finishing his first 12 hours, riding towards 'Battlefield' with 252 miles covered. He was still a fraction up on Matthew's record ride at this point. At the Edgebolton breakfast feed (263m) Bayley was suffering from the 'collywobbles' which he'd had all the previous week and Usher had moved into 2nd place, 34 mins behind Goodfellow. Bayley was at 39 mins, Pete Broad had recovered and moved up four places in the last 50 miles for 4th place.

It was a fine sunny morning as Tommy Barlow controlled the riders at Tern Hill and as Christine turned to his words of encouragement, she called back "don't worry, I'll finish". By Shawbury (293m) signs were that Bayley had come through his 'bad patch' and had drawn level with Usher to be 39mins behind Goodfellow who'd been having trouble with loose gear levers, leaving him with only large gears to use. At Shawbury the second time (329m) Goodfellow was 21mins inside 'evens' but as he took a sharp left he rolled his tyre off the rim, luckily, one of his helpers, Dave Duffield, a fellow Beacon RC member was on hand to give him a quick wheel change and get him back on the road in 20 secs.

Broad's 'comeback' was short lived as Stan Lea had caught him on the road, and between here and Wem, Pete retired. At Welshampton (344m) the leading riders were, Goodfellow 18hrs 43m, Bayley was at 24mins and Usher 45 mins.

After missing the Redbrook detour, Christine was now the first rider on the road as the field headed northwards towards the finishing circuit. Through Whitchurch and over the Broxton Hills, she was still two minutes ahead of Goodfellow on the road; could she keep up the speed and be the first rider to enter the finishing circuit? Alas, shortly after Handley he caught her with just two miles to go to the circuit. He entered the lane at Waverton Corner with 408.2 miles covered in 20 hrs 30mins, but he'd now dropped to 6mins outside 'evens'.

The effects of riding for many hours under a blazing sun had taken its toll on the riders and even **Goodfellow** by his 5th lap had gone from 6mins down on 'evens' to 14mins.  His **final mileage** was **475.38.**  **Howard Bayley** had pushed massive gears to maintain his lead over Usher and finished with **458.69m, Usher** was **3rd** with **455.17m, Stan Lea** had ridden consistently for **4th** place with **450.37.**  **Christine had won the ladies event with 409.16 miles to set up a Competition Record for the women's 24hr.**  **Ruth Williams** was 2nd lady with **403.70** and **Wyn Maddock 366.67.**  **The Otley CC were the only team to finish with 1,204.60 miles; Shuttleworth turned the tables on Kelly to win the fastest trike award with 416.91 miles.**  Bob Williams, Mersey RC did finally beat his wife Ruth by 11 miles and created a 'first' in history by becoming the first husband and wife to finish a 24hr in the same event.  I finished one place ahead of Terry Kelly by .16 of a mile with 404.13m.  Pat Kenny finished with 369.62 on a trike, but with our 'strongman' Pete Swinden retiring in the night, our team hopes were dashed. **Bill Griffiths,** Stone Wheelers, took **6th** place with **431.5** miles.  Bill was Phil Griffiths father and was a good all round time triallist.   In later years I met up again with Bill when he helped on Pat Kenny's End to End trike record in 1980, he proved to be a good solid support for us and said that he'd always wanted to help on an 'End to End'.

Phil Griffiths, Bill's son revealed some years later that after his 'B.A.R.' winning sprees in the 1970's he always intended to attack the End to End record, and ride a 24hr, to finish off his long and varied career.  Recurring back problems in the early 1980's put paid to all of this, but Phil went on to become one of the major figureheads in the cycle trade in the UK, a position he still holds at this present day in 2008.

Rod Goodfellow said that he was amazed to see so many trikes and beards in the group at the start, this was due to it being his first 24hr. His helper, Dave Duffield, had told him how easy it would be to demoralise Usher in the first 12hrs, saying that he would probably 'pack' if not winning by then! So much for Dave's prophecy.  From the start, Goodfellow had decided to give Bayley a run for his money, and at the end it was the heat that had got to him and pulled his speed down below 'evens'.

Howard Bayley had changed his training methods in preparation for this 24hr and had been piling in some colossal mileages on gears, higher than he would normally train on, his stomach problems really hit him hard as he rode towards Whitchurch at dawn.  He continued mainly for the team race and had got almost to 300 miles before his helpers told him that Graham Kelly and Derek Shuttleworth had both packed earlier in the event.  Bayley said that seeing Ken Usher coming towards him from the turn at Prees shocked him into action as he thought he was ahead of Usher.  He changed into a top gear of 117" and hammered after him, eventually to pass him on the climb to High Ercall.

On his first lap of the finishing circuit, Goodfellow caught him and said "I'm really enjoying doing this to you". Bayley then wished him luck.  On the last lap, Wyn Maddock went past Howard followed closely by Pat Kenny who exclaimed "and she's only 60!"  Goodfellow went on to have a varied 24hr career taking many wins and high places over a 25 year span.

---

**The North Road CC 24hr** on August bank holiday 1967, was **won for the 6th time by Cliff Smith with a personal best of 481.920 miles.  Stan Argill,** Beeston RC was **2nd** also with a p.b. of **458.896m.**  John 'Bomber' Baines, Icknield RC was **3rd** with another p.b. of **454.95 miles.**

Last year's winner, Bettis, wasn't entered due to a slipped disc problem and Ken Usher failed to start.  Conditions were excellent throughout for this small field of 29 riders who were sent off by Eric Wilkinson at 2 minute intervals. As expected, Cliff Smith led throughout and interest was focussed on whether or not he would join the select band of men who had beaten 'evens' (480 miles, a 20 mph average) for an all day ride.  With a 249 mile first half of the event and with a 232.9 second half, he reached his goal. Stan Argill and John Baines fought a battle for the placings with the Nottingham stayer running out time four miles ahead of his large geared adversary. **Tony King, North Roads, led Joe Summerlin and Ken Davis to a team victory with his 5th placed 434.4m ride.  Vic Stringer was 4th with 442.057 and Stan Spelling was the only trike with 399.480m.**

At the 100 mile point Smith led with 4hrs 39mins, Baines was 2nd at 12mins, just a few seconds ahead of Argill. Smith had reached the Cambridge control (249m) in exactly 12 hours  Argill rode 236 miles, Baines 231m, and Burnett 228.  The night was almost traffic free with a quarter moon helping the riders.  Tony King had a very tough time after 12 hours and was down to 8 mph, he was sick and feeling faint and didn't know if he could continue, but he did, and eventually moved so well he matched Cliff Smith's speed for hour after hour.  Argill finished with a 20 miles improvement over his 1949 ride in this event.  John Baines suffered severely at times to improve 23 miles from his previous ride in 1962.

But obviously the ride of the day was Cliff Smiths'.

---

**The Scottish Cycling Union 24hr** (In early August 1967) was the brainchild of Peter Duncan.  He organised the event and ran it from start to finish with a band of friends from the Glasgow area and one or two 24hr Fellowship members who were helping with marshalling etc.  Peter had always thought that there should be a permanent 24hr event on the calendar held in Scotland annually.   In the past he'd had to cross the border and travel hundreds of miles to ride his favourite discipline in a Sassenach event.   Duncan had ridden to some excellent mileages on a bike and trike in the 1950's and 1960's as a member of the Vegetarian C & AC.  His best trike ride of 440 miles was second only to John Arnolds record at that time and his best on a bike was 460 miles.

From the very early stages of trying to promote this event, Duncan had run up against hostility from Scottish C.U. officialdom and also received poor support from some of the clubs in the Glasgow area.  He had hoped to get 30 riders and was disappointed to get only 19.  The start of the event was held at the Highland Games and was quite an innovation that went down well with the assembled public.

Ken Price, probably the best 24hr rider in Scotland started, but was unwell and retired quite early on in the event, but there was another prolific 24hr rider in the making, George Berwick.

The course took in 'The Lochside' Loch Lomond, with a feed at Drymen organised by Hilary Cusker with Andy and Barbara McLeod.   On to Stirling where one or two places were un-marshalled; Jack Spackman and a few juniors came in very useful here.  Alloa had road works, however the riders found their way through; Kincardine Village was unmanned but Don McKinlay, after 'packing', helped out here.  In the Bells Dyke area the Glasgow Couriers provided a tented sit down feed, and the riders said that the efficiency and food here had the English sit down feeds 'licked'.

George Berwick was the only rider sent on the St Ninians detour and this consolidated his lead over the rest of the field.  Dave Gardiner was riding to a good second place and several others were within striking distance of him throughout the race including Sam Gilbert, St Neots CC.

Archie Barry, Lomond Roads, a Glasgow rider, renowned for 'packing' in events overcame a bad spell and finished happy.   Peter Duncan said that maybe it was the remarks he'd made over the P.A. system at the Highland Games had done the trick. (He told him that if he packed he would have to ride home to Glasgow)

Back over the Kincardine Bridge in daylight and despite missing marshals the riders managed to stay on course with direction arrows.  Sam Gilbert was struggling with drowsiness and despite a vigorous protest from him, he was dragged from his bike, plied with black coffee and doused with a cold sponge three times in 11 miles.

The stretches of road in the Fife area were very well marshalled and the riders returned safely to the finishing circuit in sunshine, to the cheers from one of the biggest crowd of supporters seen in Scotland for a long time.

George Berwick's **448.377 mile** winning ride became a **New Scottish Record, Dave Gardiner,** Kennoway CC was **2nd** with **437.790m** and **Sam Gilbert** was **3rd** with **431.815m. Stan Spelling's 395.619** mile ride became a new **Scottish Trike Record.** Over half of the 12 finishers were from Scottish clubs and the event was run under the rules of the Scottish Cycling Union.

Peter Duncan had hoped to make this an annual event, but whether it was apathy from the officials or clubs in Scotland I don't know, but this was the only 24hr event to take place in his native Scotland.

George Berwick must have caught the bug for riding 24hr races, as he can still be found riding his favourite Mersey RC event every year in late July, and has now, in 2008, ridden nearly 50 twenty-four hour events.

*'Drink Drive' laws came into force this year and Dr Christian Barnard performed the world's first heart transplant, at Capetown in December.*

# 1968

If 1967 was deemed remarkable for its historical content of '1st time happenings in 24's' to remember it by, then 1968 was to be equally as important a year for its close fought battles during the various events, by the 'stars', the 'newcomers', and the 'regulars', producing high mileages and courageous rides to make it an exciting 24hr season. With the return of Eric Matthews after a year out, making sure that the regular favourites had to fight for every one of their hard earned miles, it was to be a good year.

---

**The Catford CC 24hr on June 15th and 16th 1968 was won by Cliff Smith, East Midlands CC with 460.82 miles. It was his 5th Catford win and his 15th ride of 460 miles or over.** He rode a very tactical race after a slow start. Cliff was pushed hard in the first 12 hours by Ken Usher who was enjoying a spell of fitness and was now riding for the North Road CC. His brother Dick a relative newcomer to long distances was riding his first 24hr race. Bill Dunk completed the team for the 'North Roaders'. Other teams entered were the Balham CC and the Crawley Whls.

The timekeeper despatched 38 riders from noon onwards at two-minute intervals. For the first 4 hours the temperature was in the 80's and conditions must have been very trying for the riders. Cliff Smith started fairly fast and recorded 1hr 6mins for the first 25 miles, but then he seemed to struggle for the next few hours. By the 50 mile point many riders had closed up on him and by 80 miles at the completion of the second afternoon circuit, Ken Usher had taken the lead from Smith by 1 minute, Lee was 3rd at 5mins, Dick Usher and Stan Argill were at 8mins.

By the 116.69 mile check there had been retirements due to the intense heat, Ken Usher was really flying with Smith trailing 7mins down. Booth was now 3rd at 10mins, Lee at 13m, Dick Usher at 21m, and Les Lowe at 26mins. By Chichester with the cool of the evening, Smith was perking up a little and was now only 4mins adrift. The riders went on detours to Selsey and Havant after nightfall, and then returned again through Chichester at 196.73 miles. By this point Smith was riding with his usual zest and led Ken Usher by 1 minute. Dick Usher had moved into 3rd place, 32mins down on the leader.

After Chichester the route went east and then north over the 'Downs'. From the feed at Washington, the riders were sent on a short leg to Billingshurst and back, the mileage on the return was 228.35 miles and on this lovely calm warm night, Smith led Ken Usher by 5mins with his brother Dick at 38mins. Booth was at 43m, Chris Davies was having a battle with Les Lowe and led him by 5mins on the road and both of them were around an hour behind Smith.

At the 12hour point, Smith did 242.5m, Ken Usher 241m, and Dick Usher 231 miles. There were more retirements after the 12 hour point, probably due to the riders not being happy with their halfway distances; this left only the Balham CC with a complete team.

After the Roman Gate to Codmore Hill section at 264 miles in perfect temperatures and weather, Smith had actually caught Usher on the road and they were having a quick chat, then at the next check at Guildford (281 miles) he'd opened up a 3 minute lead over Usher on this hard section of road. He caught Dick Usher soon after and then became the first man on the road. Only 3 riders went on the Windsor detour of 39 miles, at 319 miles. Smith led Ken Usher by 19mins and Dick by 54m. At Alford 364.78m, Smith was riding at 18mph but Usher had closed up slightly. The morning was dull and gloomy with a very stiff rising wind, making the return to the finishing circuit a hard slog for the weary riders. Smith's lead was now 21 mins.

Despite a puncture and a heavy thunderstorm in the closing minutes, **Smith battled on to his 5th Catford win and his 11th 24hr win.** His **460.82** mile ride was a fine tactical victory, **Ken Usher** was **2nd** with **452.93m** and brother **Dick** on his first 24hr was **3rd** with **442.57. Alf Booth with 435.73m led the Balham CC to a team win.** Chris Davies rode a p.b.with 428.14m, Stan Spelling had a good ride with 418.19, so beating Les Lowe by less than a mile.

———◆———

**The Wessex RC 24hr** on the 13th and 14th July 1968 was a very open race with no previous Wessex winners amongst the field of 27 riders including 4 trikes. Only two teams were entered, the Hampshire RC and the Buccaneers CC. Previous riders of the Wessex event present were John Gills, Chris Davies , John Mortimer, Ivor Jones, Bill Suttie and Dave Free attempting a comeback after last years horrendous accident in which he sustained many injuries. One or two newcomers to 24hr riding were present, the most notable being Graham Mann.

The event started in good weather conditions, although the sky looked threatening. The course opened with the usual stretch across the New Forest to Fawley and Bull Hill, before returning to Ringwood. This was followed by a long 'leg' north-westerly through Salisbury to Warminster. At Lyndhurst, Arthur Comer who was no stranger to this event strayed off course and by the time he had retraced, he found himself so far adrift he became the first retirement.

The leading times at Heytesbury (124m) were Chris Davies, 6hrs 11mins, Mann at 1min, Gills at 2mins, Mortimer 3mins and Free 23mins. By 150 miles the weather had deteriorated and several sharp showers and a rising wind troubled the riders on the run from Heytesbury to Wimborne and back. Darkness had fallen by 175 miles and the rain had become a cold, steady, downpour and the outlook for the riders during the night was daunting. At the Corfe Castle turn, Ivor Jones for some reason ignored the marshals and rode straight on. It was later revealed that he had found himself on the sea front at Swanage and so became the 2nd retiree. At Warmwell Cross (198m) the leading times were; Davies 10hrs 6mins, Mann at 11min, Mortimer 22min, Gills 44m and Free, 66m.

The downpour was still relentless and at Leigh Common (248m) Davies led with 13hrs 5mins, Mann was at 12m. Many riders were struggling and were turned at Ringwood so missing the 32 mile detour to Salisbury and back. Dave Free was feeling the effects of his previous years injuries and retired at the Somerford turn (310m), Davies still led the field with 16hrs 51m, Mann was at 18m with Gills and Mortimer in 3rd and 4th place.

By the 20 hour point, conditions had improved, the rain had stopped but the strength of the wind became troublesome to the weary survivors. Davies arrived at the finishing circuit (404m) in 22hrs, 3mins, with Mann at 38m, they were the only two riders to have covered the full course. Mortimer was now ahead of Gills and Thomas. Eighteen riders reached the circuit to finish out their day in a very tricky crosswind.

**Chris Davies won the race with a well judged p.b. ride of 438.03 miles and led a Hampshire RC team including two trike riders, Malcolm Waters and Bill Vetcher, to a total of 1,188.28 miles. Graham Mann,** Hainault RC was **2nd** with **426.12** in his first 24hr race and **John Mortimer** was **3rd** with **415.80m. John Gills** struggled with the cold and wet affecting his knees very badly to finish **4th** with **407.15 miles. Dave Thomas** was **5th** with **395.39m** and led a Buccaneer CC team of John Coulson and Peter Reeve to 1,124 miles. **Ray Burnett** riding his 2nd 24hr in a month rode to **384.56.**

Bill Vetcher recalled that Malcolm Waters who beat him by 0.95 of a mile to be the fastest trike, had only ever ridden mainly short distance rides, 10's, 25's and 30 mile events, and on the day of the 24hr, Malcolm had consumed 5 pints of Guinness with his lunch and then ridden 18 miles to the start. His mileage was 375.60 and Bill's 374.65m.

"THEY'VE changed from glue sniffing to embrocation sniffing."

John Gills had suffered not only with bad knees but also with broken spokes, about the time that the rain started. He wondered if his helpers would let him pack and get into the car, but they would have none of it and sent him on his way with a new wheel. With his knees being his next worry, he tried all sorts of rubs and oils and confessed to having the most obnoxious smelling pair of knees in the whole of Wessex. He had wondered whether it was a form of 'housemaids knee', but somebody mentioned it was more likely to be 'barmaids knee'!

**The Mersey RC 24hr** on 27th and 28th July saw the return of **Eric Matthews,** Altrincham RC after a years break. He **won** the event with the 2nd highest mileage ridden on this course, **486.01miles.** He was just 4 miles short of his own Competition Record ridden in 1964. **Don Spraggett,** Birkenhead North End CC excelled himself to produce **471.88** for **2nd** place, and was for many hours the only rider to match Matthew's speed.

The start at Austins Hill saw one of the largest crowds ever gathered in the history of this event. Three ladies were at the front of the field again this year, but with an 8 minute gap between them and the first man, Norman Maggs of the promoting club. Joyce Blow, South Lancs RC on a trike was the first rider away to a huge applause, followed by Wyn Maddock, a 61 year old gran, and third off was reigning Competition Record holder, Christine Minto (nee Moody), hoping to improve on her mileage of the previous year.

Amongst the mens field were many regular 24hr riders, Frank Cooper, Fred Cowling, with Jim Shuttleworth and Terry Kelly both on trikes. Ray Burnett riding his 3rd 24hr of the year, Malcolm Jones, 'hardman' Pete Swinden, Richard Thomas, Geoff Toon, Malcolm Judge riding his first 24hr event, Don Spraggett, a 'regular' on his local roads, and Eric Matthews, after taking a year out to rest and try to eliminate a recurring stomach and digestion problem. Eric had shown real form only two weeks prior to the Mersey event by winning the Manchester and District 12hour with 266 miles, on an awful, wet and windy day.

The forty four riders got off to a good start on a fine but 'heavy' day. Christine was the first rider on the road at the Clive Green turn (40.1m) in exactly two hours. She was smiling broadly and obviously enjoying her ride. At Acton Church (50.5m) Matthews led Spraggett by 2mins in 2hrs 9min, Thomas was at 6mins, Swinden at 7mins, Judge was next but he had already punctured. 'The Nags Head' Haughton Moss at 61.3 miles was one of the tightest turns on any of the courses I've ever ridden. It's on a narrow country lane with high hedges, outside a quaint old pub set back slightly off the road. Many cyclists stopped here for a pint in the early evening and to find out how the race was unfolding. If a rider made a poor job of turning around the marshal by going wide, he or she could stray onto the forecourt of the pub where hundreds of ale supping supporters acted as a human barrier to keep the rider upright. The road was probably narrower than most peoples living room.

Christine was the first on the road to turn in 3hrs 5mins, Matthews was the fastest in 2hrs 40mins 48secs. Spraggett was at 3mins, Thomas 8mins, Swinden 11m and Judge 12m. Dusk fell as the riders headed north from Whitchurch to Broxton (91.3m), Christine was still the first to turn at 9.50pm with 4hrs 47mins elapsed. At Vicars Cross Island (100m) Eric Matthews went through in 4hrs 31mins with Spraggett at 6mins, Thomas 12m, Judge 17m, Swinden 20m; they were the only riders inside 'evens' pace.

As Christine went through the unlit dark lanes to Elton Green, a pig was wandering loose on the road and race officials had to knock up the farmer to lock it away before any riders were put at risk. At Saltney Corner (130m) only the leading 8 riders were sent to Marford and back. Matthews led with 6hrs 1m, Spraggett was at 5mins, Thomas 13m, Judge 16m, Malcolm Jones and Pete Swinden at 35m. Matthews is 9mins slower at this point, than on his epic ride of 1964, the girls times were Christine, 7hrs, Wyn 7hrs 32m and Joyce Blow, 7hrs 57mins.

On the Welsh coast road to Prestatyn, Andy Overall, was struck from behind by a hit and run driver, wrecking his trike and ruining his ride, landing him in hospital at Chester for a check up. For most of the riders, it was uneventful, with fast rides being done. Matthews maintained his lead of 8 mins over Spraggett and returned to Queensferry to ride south towards Whitchurch. Wyn Maddock was a victim to stomach pains on the coast road and retired. The night was kind to the riders as they headed south towards Shropshire, very little breeze, cool but not cold with no mist this year. At the start of the Nantwich detour (218.6m) Matthews had increased his lead to 15mins over Spraggett and arrived in 10hrs 32mins, by Battlefield (Shrewsbury) he'd completed 249 miles for his first 12hours. At this point he could have still broken competition record by maintaining this speed and producing 248 miles in the 2nd half, but it seemed unlikely.

Don Spraggett was unhappy with his progress, clocking 242 miles and swapped to his fixed wheel bike for a change. At the 290 mile point, Matthews was still 22mins inside 'evens', and feeling good and eating well.

Back at the Edgebolton feed on the return journey the aroma of frying bacon wafting slowly down the road was too much for most riders who are then tempted in. A fierce battle is going on for 3rd and 4th place between Richard Thomas and Malcolm Judge, with only 1min separating them on performance, but Judge is in trouble with his gears and can only ride in 'top'. At Shawbirch (299m) Matthews went through with 14hrs 36mins gone and Spraggett was at 21mins. Christine was actual 4th on the road and riding well. Harold Nelson, apart from organising earlier mobile feeding stations was also Mathew's main helper and was pleased with his progress but felt that the prospect of Competition record was remote and 500 miles even more so. A light southerly wind helped Eric on the hilly stretch back to Prees at 347 miles where he stormed through in 17hrs 23mins. Spraggett arrived exactly 30mins later, having changed back to his original bike with gears.

By the time the roads in the Wem to Welshampton section had been covered, the positions remained the same between the first four riders, with Spraggett matching Matthews for speed, mile after mile. Waverton Corner and the start of the finishing circuit was reached at exactly 2pm and Matthews had just under 4 hours to go. It was predicted at this time that 486 miles was a possibility for him. Spraggett arrived just 34 mins later to great applause from his many local supporters, he'd had an amazing ride. Judge was now leading Thomas by 4mins but the two were still locked in a fierce battle for 3rd place. **Stan and Cliff Richardson,** South Lancs RC were both still riding strongly and with **Richard Thomas they made sure of the team win for the South Lancs RC with 1,262.94 miles.** The Otley were the 2nd team with 1,232 miles.

So, **Matthews** ran out time with a predicted **486.01**miles and a Gold medal from the Mersey RC. He'd led from the start to the finish with that seemingly effortless style, smiling all the way this year. Forty one year old **Don Spraggett** rode way beyond expectations to **471.88miles. Malcolm Judge** on his first ever 24hr race took **3rd** place with **453.51m** and **Thomas** was 4th with **451.52m.** **Geoff Toon** was **5th** with **433.47m** and **Pete Swinden, 430.57m.**

Whilst we have been busy extolling the virtues of the men's winning mileages and performances, the two women riding that day both produced Competition records. **Christine** rode steadily to improve by 11 miles on her previous years ride for a new **Ladies Bike 24hr Competition record of 420.05m** and **Joyce Blow** proved that trike riding wasn't just a male preserve, by establishing a **Ladies Trike Competition record of 371.48 miles.** Christine's mileage would have placed her 7th in the men's race.

Ray Burnett finished his 3rd 24hr of the year with 410.22m and Terry Kelly was the fastest trike rider with 406.75. Barry Blagg, Birmingham St Christopher's CCC finished his first 24hr race with 388.91miles. He was a happy go lucky young chap, the same age as myself. He had a cheeky smile and never took anything very seriously. Barry was a Merchant Seaman who seemed able to spend months at sea and then just get on his bike and ride himself straight into fitness, with no proper training at all.

*Details for this report were taken from the Mersey 'Record' written by John Reid and reproduced in the Fellowship Journal with additional material from myself.*

———⪼•◆•⪻———

On Saturday, August 10th, **The North Road CC** held their 70th annual 24hr race incorporating the **RTTC National Championship.** The 64 entries, the most for many a year, contained the established 24hr Champions of the day plus some fast newcomers to the art of all day riding, and it was expected to be an exciting race. Nim Carline, 5 times champion in 1962, 63, 65, 66 & 67, was challenged by Eric Matthews in his 'comeback' year. With Carline capable of 496 miles and Matthews 490 miles, high mileages were expected on the day. Although it was wondered whether Matthews' 486 mile Mersey win just two weeks previously would affect him, Eric himself was quite confident that he had retained his fitness.

Eric Tremaine and Mick Ward, who was a novice to the 24hr scene, both wanted a win and high mileages; they led a Leicestershire RC team that day. John Baines and Rod Goodfellow were also trying for a winning place.

*Jock Wadley who was out at that event reporting for a magazine called 'International Cycle Sport', mentioned that he'd known Mick since he was a lad, and how Mick had ridden over from Haverhill on a Sunday morning for a Colchester Rovers CC '25', showing signs of the class that was to bring him a '25' and three '50' mile Championship wins, and how after a spell of semi-retirement for study and professional reasons, Mick was now riding seriously again. Jock guessed that his ambition in this, his first 24hr, was not merely to take just a team medal back to his new home in Leicestershire. Mick was still an East Anglian at heart and as he passed Jock there in Bedfordshire, obviously enjoying himself, he called out in music-hall Essex-Suffolk dialect "Aint yew acummin furer royd boy?"*

Cliff Smith who would normally be spoken of in the same breath as Carline and Matthews for Championship prospects, was recovering from being hit by a car a week before the race, and he rode the event with lacerations and broken cheek bones, to an excellent fourth place. Other riders in with a chance of a place were Ken Usher, Jeff Gould and Dick Poole, although Poole, who had just moved house, was unfit but riding for a Brentwood RC team win hopefully.

The weather was fine and sunny at the start with a north-easterly breeze. Of the 60 starters, 25 were 'novices' (first time 24hr riders). At 50 miles, Carline led Tremaine, Matthews and Gould by 1 minute. At 134 miles the breeze had dropped and the sun was blazing down. Carline led the field at this point by 7mins, he'd maintained 23mph on a new circuit using roads around Perten Hall and Cross Hall. Ward and Matthews were level in 2nd position, Matthews was suffering with the heat and could hardly wait for the cool night to come.

The stretch on the Great North Road to Norman Cross and back to Brampton Hut was ridden as darkness fell. Carline went through the 191.2mile point, 63 minutes inside 'evens' having so far averaged 22mph. This was the 'high point' of his ride however, as he later dropped to 'evens'. By the Woolpack he was only 5.5mins up on Matthews, with Ward at 12.5mins. Cliff Smith now clawed his way through the field and lay in 4th place at 34mins, with Tremaine and Goodfellow at 35mins.

Matthews levelled with Carline just before the 12hr point for 260.5 miles. *Jock Wadley caught up with the Barlow's, Tommy and Peter, around this point and asked them if they knew of other riders' mileages at 12hrs and the answer came back 'Carline 260 and Ward 254'. The Barlow's were always around when important rides were being done by the top riders and I would imagine they were 'rooting' for Eric Matthews that day.* Sam Gilbert and Ken Usher both retired on the return leg to Cambridge. At Streatham only 7 riders rode the detour to Needingworth, Poole and Baines went straight on. Heavy tidal flooding caused the detour to be cut some 4 miles short with the riders returning earlier than normal. The water was rising and in the dark it was deemed too dangerous to let the riders through to the normal turn.

Thick mist was also affecting the riders on this section of the course with the moon giving a tantalising appearance in the gaps. Matthews had stopped for a quick feed and Carline took his chance to fly past. At 338 miles, Matthews was back within a minute of Carline and both men were storming through the thick mist. Ward was at 31mins, Smith 52, Goodfellow 66m, but Tremaine had dropped to 73mins down on the leader.

Daylight came and at Soham, Matthews had a 13mins lead on Carline who appeared to be suffering. Matthews was riding so strongly but the very stiff early morning breeze had put paid to any records being broken. Only 4 riders had completed the full course by the time the field reached the finishing circuit; Matthews, Carline, Ward and Smith. The circuit was a new one and was thought by many riders to be too exposed on a windy day, and the riders speeds show this, with neither Carline or Matthews averaging more than 18mph for the remainder of their rides.

**Matthews' final mileage was 489.47m** on what could only be described as a fairly tough day. **Carline** rode through his bad patches to take a **Silver** medal with **481.52** miles, **Mick Ward** had a wonderful ride for 3rd place with **479m,** and **Cliff Smith** despite his many discomforts took **4th** place with **470.172m.** John Baines rode a well judged race with **465m** and **Rod Goodfellow** had delays and anxieties when his helpers were in a car crash but finished with **462 miles.** **Eric Tremaine struggled through many bad patches for 7th place and 458.311 miles with Eddie Cotterill's 443.347 and Mick Wards mileage, The Leicestershire RC took the team award with 1,380.753m.** Dick Poole rode steadily just to finish for his team with 442.437 miles. **Mick Henighan, Comet CC was the fastest trike with 410.416 miles.** 47 riders finished and 16 were 'dope tested' by the RTTC. (in line with new anti-drug legislation from the sporting council)

*The details for this report were provided by the North Road Gazette, with many observations from Ian Shaw, reporting for the 24hr Fellowship Journal.*

# 1969

*March 2nd 1969, Concorde made its maiden flight*

If one looks at 1967 with its historical ground breaking 'firsts' in 24hr racing, and then goes to 1968 with its exciting battles on the road for supremacy, resulting in some very high mileages, then one would wonder what 1969 could possibly hold in store? The answer was **Competition Record by over 10 miles, breaking the 500 mile barrier handsomely with 507 miles.** It wasn't performed by any of our regular champions of the day, who had pushed the mileage tantalisingly close to 500. No, the new **Champion and Record Holder was Roy Cromack,** Clifton CC riding his first and only 24 hour.

This year was also to be a very good one for another regular 'star', Cliff Smith, one of the old school of steady riding stayers. He opened his season by winning his sixth Catford 24hr with 455.17 miles. A month later he took 4th place in the Mersey RC Championship with 473.82m, followed by winning the North Road 24hr for the 7th time with 468.5 miles. All of this was achieved in the space of two months and Cliff was by now well into veteran status.

But I will leave the story there and continue with the history chronologically as the 24hr season evolves.

⇒·◇·⇐

**The Catford CC 24hr** on the 28th and 29th of June was **won for the sixth time by Cliff Smith, East Midlands CC with 455.17m. Mick Shaw,** Clarence Whls, was **2nd** with **417.63m** and **Steve Hawkes,** Oxonian CC was **3rd, 414.63m.** The weather was very hot with a muggy night and heavy conditions throughout.

Alf Booth and Henry Wootton were the only riders besides Cliff Smith to be inside 'evens' in the first stages of the race, but Booth went off course in the Bognor area and eventually 'packed'. Wootton now lay 2nd to Smith with Hawkes and Shaw moving rapidly through the field. The night was moon lit and provided excellent riding conditions but only if you weren't riding said Les Lowe, who was a spectator and roving helper that year.

By the 300 mile point Cliff Smith was the only rider to have covered the full course; Shaw was in 2nd place, Wootton was 3rd and Hawkes 4th. The morning dawned sunny and hot as the riders headed north to the finishing circuit. **Cliff Smith** rode way out in front to finish unchallenged for his **1st win of the year. Malcolm Waters with 411.09 led the Hampshire RC team, consisting of Chris Davies, 408.36 and Graham Jenkins, a young 18year old trike rider with 398.51 miles, to a winning total of 1,217.96 miles.** 18 riders finished from 26 entries.

---

**The Wessex RC 24hr** on July 12 and 13th, 1969, was run in even hotter conditions than the Catford 24. **Rod Goodfellow** won the event with **450.84 miles, Dick Usher was 2nd with 429.99** and **J. Lewis, 3rd with 412.87m.**

Torrid sunshine, temperatures in the 80's and a stiff breeze decimated the field causing many retirements, including Dick Poole, Chris Davies, Sid Hygate and Joe Summerlin. Dave Free made a successful comeback after sustaining injuries in 1967, to finish with 403.56m. **The Hampshire Rc trio of Culverwell, Vetcher and Waters on a trike, won the team prize with 1,162 miles.**

Rod Goodfellow had built a good lead to be the fastest rider by the time Salisbury was reached (107m). He led Dick Usher by 11mins, Culverwell by 19m and Lewis 30m. This order was maintained all the way to the finishing circuit where Lewis pipped Culverwell by .3 of a mile, after a fierce battle for 3rd place.

Rod Goodfellow who suffers particularly badly in the heat, being fair skinned, was in a good position to monitor his own progress after all he was a Doctor and knew the dangers of letting ones temperature rise too high. He paid attention to resting in the shade for a minute or two and soaking himself with cold water so as to keep his body temperature below 105 degrees F.

After Salisbury he was still in the lead but was demoralized with the fact that he was already below a 20 mph average (evens). The night was kinder to the riders with a temperature drop to 65 degrees F, but Rod Goodfellow did just enough to keep ahead of the field, by about an hour, to win. He recalled having nine sit down breaks for cooling off and feeds and lost probably an hour or more, but if that method secured his win, then that's all that mattered.

Rod found the course pleasant to ride, with the wooded sections giving shelter from the sun, although melting tar caused problems at times. Only 13 riders from the original 27 starters survived to the finish, the heat had taken many victims. *My thanks to Rod Goodfellow for details about his ride.*

---

*Meanwhile on July 21st 1969 American Astronaut, Neil Armstrong, walked on the moon after a successful Apollo mission. His words "that's one small step for a man, one giant step for mankind" became a popular catchphrase. So the American nation had gone from cowboys fighting and driving the Indians from their homeland, to putting a man on the moon, in less than 100 years.*

---

**Just five days later on 26th and 27th July 1969, The Mersey RC National Championship 24hr took place, incorporating the 3rd Merseyside Ladies CA event.** There were 74 men entered and 4 ladies. Eric Matthews, Nim Carline and Cliff Smith were the regular Champions entered and present; high mileages were expected. But this year was different, firstly **Beryl Burton** was entered and it was thought by many that she could set the race alight. It was rumoured that her husband, Charly, had worked out a 520 mile schedule for her; secondly, Roy Cromack, Clifton CC, another Yorkshireman was riding. He was a superb rider up to and including 12hr time trials as well as being the National 10 mile track Champion, Olympic Team Time Trial rider in Mexico and the National 12hr Champion. In weeks leading up to the Mersey, he had ridden 50 miles in 1hr 51m on two occasions and a 3hr 58m for 100 miles. His ambition since 1964 had been to ride a 24hr with a view to beating 500 miles.

The field was set out differently this year to accommodate Beryl who could not be placed amongst the men, according to RTTC regulations. The men's field was laid out as normal with the slower riders sent off first ahead of the seeded ones. From about the middle of the field a faster rider would be placed on a 5 or 10 minute position until the last quarter of the field, where most of the seeded riders were placed, including the previous years winner and National Champion who would start last. Then there was a few minutes gap before the ladies, Christine Minto, Wyn Maddock, Joyce Blow on a trike and Beryl Burton started. The Organisers would then detour the first 3 ladies inside the first 50 miles so as to put them back in front of the main field as they returned north to Chester, but Beryl was sent on to cover the full course with a time gap on the road to bridge, before making contact with the faster men.

Other notable riders in the field were Sid Hygate, Brian King, Malcolm Judge, Richard Thomas, Stan Lea, Stan Richardson and Stan Turner, a good 12 hr man, but a novice at 24 hrs. The Tyne RC looked to be the strongest team on paper with six riders including some very good 12 hr men. Dennis and Wes Clayton and John Yates. Other teams included were the South Lancs RC, Brentwood RC, Long Eaton CC, Barrow Central Whls and the Morley RC.

The first few riders started in a drizzle, which made the roads greasy for an hour or two especially in the narrow lanes. By the 20 mile point, Cromack had already lost time with a puncture and Carline led Matthews by a few seconds. Beryl was already ploughing her way through the field and was a few minutes up on the leaders on paper. Although she was not officially competing with the men, many spectators had added her name to the short list for the best ride of the day.

I think everybody knew what her intention was, especially after her phenomenal 12hr ride in 1967. She worked with Nim Carline on his rhubarb farm and she also trained long hard and fast miles with him after work, so it wasn't surprising that she was tough, with similar views to Nim on a 'do or die' style of riding.

The 'Nags Head' turn at 61 miles was always a good focal point to check the rider's progress. Tyne RC's Alan Robertson and Dennis Clayton were moving well. The three ladies, Christine, Wyn and Joyce were well up on the road, having been detoured already. Stan Turner held the fastest time for a while until Carline came through; his aggressive thrusting style had put him 8 minutes up on Turner. Cromack and Matthews turned 2 mins slower than Carline, but then hot on Matthews' trail came Beryl, she was now 4 mins faster than Carline and took the overall lead. The large crowd assembled at the 'Nags Head' was buzzing with excitement.

By the time the field reached the 100.4 mile check on the Chester by-pass, Nim Carline was the fastest and led the men's championship with 4hrs, 20.5mins, he was trying desperately hard to avoid being caught by Beryl for 18mins. At this point on paper she was 9 minutes up on him and recorded 4hrs 10mins for the 100 miles. Matthews was 2nd on the road, 2mins behind Carline with Cromack 3rd at 3mins 45secs. But of course Beryl was faster than all of them, she was trying so hard and rarely seemed to change down from her top gear of 107", even at the turns and islands. It was known that she had trained specifically for this event, but many found it very hard to believe she could last at such a pace.

At 130 miles Nim still led the men's race, but Beryl was nearly 15mins up on him and only just behind him on the road. Cromack now led Matthews by 2.5mins for 2nd and 3rd place in the men's race. King was 4th at 16mins, Turner was closing on him a few seconds behind and Cliff Smith was just over 20mins behind Carline. It was a good, fairly calm night as the riders returned from the Welsh Coast road with just a few small pockets of mist below the 'Broxton Hills'.

A large crowd had gathered to see Beryl Burton go left at Whitchurch (219.5miles). She was now the first rider on the road at 4.02am having caught everybody. A few minutes later Cromack came through followed by Carline at 1min, Matthews was 3rd man with Turner and Smith, 4th and 5th. Despite Beryl still pushing that huge gear over the trying 20mile detour to Nantwich and back, she was the first rider back with an incredible 58mins for the detour and 80mins inside 'evens' at 240 miles, so she was riding very close to a possible 270miles for her first 12hours at that speed. Carline caught Cromack back on the Nantwich section and they then rode together towards Battlefield with Carline's all hammer and bash, 'eyeballs out' style compared to Cromack's smooth resolute pedalling. Matthews had the fastest men's time on the Nantwich detour, just a few seconds inside the hour.

After the tough hilly road south to Battlefield, the course went sharp left to Tern Hill and left to Prees at 275 miles, so completing a triangle of roads. Beryl arrived at 6.45am still the leader on the road having completed 268miles for the first 12hrs. Cromack had the next largest distance of 259.5miles with Matthews on 257miles. Carline by this point had almost destroyed himself to produce 256.5m and was now slowing badly. Despite Beryl's demoralizing speed, both Matthews and Cromack continued to control their speed and ride their own races. Carline eventually packed at 291 miles.

The riders returned through Shawbury at 327miles to retrace to Battlefield and the weather was hotting up. Cromack led the men's championship here, with Matthews at just over 14mins. Turner at 48.5m, Smith 55m and Wes Clayton 66mins. Beryl led the field overall by 26mins, but her riding now looked strained and she was no longer gaining any time. At Quina Brook, a large crowd had gathered to see her through, but minutes passed and no Beryl. Then came the disappointing news that she had packed at 350 miles with severe knee pain, which apparently she had experienced while training prior to the event. The male pride could now be left intact!

By midday the heat was relentless with a stiff breeze affecting the riders on the Wem-Welshampton-Redbrook section, a tough hilly piece of road that can break riders spirits in the last stages of the race. Cromack who hadn't panicked when lying second to Beryl was now increasing his speed, even on this hilly section. He was over an hour inside 'evens', so definitely onto a 500 mile ride if he could maintain this speed. He called for an ice cream and luckily one was produced like a rabbit out of a hat, or more likely from a little shop in Wem. Matthews was still strong, smooth and positive and lay in 2nd place. Stan Turner was 3rd, Cliff Smith 4th, and still smiling. The Clayton brothers were still keeping their positions but most other riders were visibly wilting in the heat and slowing considerably.

Luckily the stiff breeze was from the south-west, which while not perfect in direction, helped the weary riders as they headed north to the finishing circuit. Cromack entered the circuit at 406 miles being 70 minutes inside 'evens' with nearly 5 hours left to run. He averaged nearly 21mph on this hot windy circuit, the huge crowds gathered on the roadsides were so pleased to see such a fine rider in action, with history being made. **Roy Cromack** timed his ride to perfection and coasted the last minute almost in a state of paralysis, **for 507 miles, a new Competition Record.** **Eric Matthews** despite having attacks of cramp from the heat and the massive effort, managed 19.8mph around the circuit to take **2nd** place with **492.88miles.** **Stan Turner,** who like Cromack was riding his first 24hr race, realised that once he got close to the finishing circuit, if he could average just under 20 mph he would beat 480 miles. He stormed around the circuit those last few hours at 19.6mph to take **3rd** place with **480.75miles. Cliff Smith** held off Wes Clayton for **4th** place by just .10 of a mile for **473.82m.**

**Wes Clayton's 473.72 miles for the Tyne RC gave them the team win with 1,396.48miles. Dennis Clayton with 467.68m and Alan Robertson, 455.08, filled the next two places to complete the team.** They beat the South Lancs RC trio of Stan and Cliff Richardson and Richard Thomas by 85 miles.

**Christine Minto broke her own Competition Record for the 2nd year running with 427.86 miles.** Wyn Maddock had better luck this year and finished with 386.59m, and **Joyce Blow broke her own trike Competition Record by 3 miles to record 374.15m.** The ladies performances seemed to have been overlooked from the progressive race report sheets but as already mentioned there is a separate and complete history of the ladies rides and performances in Chapter 5.

Although there were three or four outstanding rides at the head of the field, plus the Tyne RC team win with two novice riders, the rest of the men's field rode to their normal mileages.

Roy Cromack's 507 miles Competition Record that day amazed everyone. He was so focussed on his ride and what he had to do, not getting embroiled in the obvious scraps that were going on in the first 12 hours at the head of the field. His own excellent 259 mile first 12 hours, was followed by an amazing 248 mile second half in hot windy weather.

Roy's ride won him the Percy Brazendale Cup for winning the Mersey event, plus a Mersey RC Gold Medal, the National Championship Bowl and Gold Medal, the 24 Hour Fellowship '500' mile Trophy, and last but not least, a special Gold Medal presented by the North Road CC for the first man to beat 500 miles.

*"This following text describes Roy Cromack's feelings during the event. I've taken details from a Fellowship report written by him, and my thanks go to him for allowing me to use this material"*

*Roy's preparation for the 24 hour had been a normal season of time trialling at 25, 50, 100 miles and 12 hours. A final all night run of 170 miles in under 9 hours a week before the event and then a week of easy pedalling and relaxation. His schedule for the event was made out for 4hrs 27mins for the first 100, 258 miles for the first 12 hour and 500 miles with 2 minutes to go to the full 24 hours. He kept his gears fairly low throughout the event, 86" was his maximum for the first 12 hours. He had one or two punctures and lighting problems, which lost him a few minutes.*

*At Whitchurch as dawn broke Roy experienced a real bad patch as he rode the dreaded Nantwich detour; he couldn't keep awake and was convinced he would have to pack. He stopped just before he got back to Whitchurch and had a real good rub down, then several spoonfuls of honey, which seemed to perk him up. After his first 12 hours was up, with a mile or so on top of his schedule, he re-caught Carline who had clearly ridden himself into the ground. Roy then re-caught Beryl Burton on the road, but by the time he had taken command of the overall lead, she had packed.*

*In the last 12hours he felt quite good at times, and once on the finishing circuit he realised that all barring accidents etc, he would break Competition Record. Paralysis started to set in on his 6th circuit, but he passed the 496 mile record point with 32mins left to run, and at 500 miles he had got 20mins left. A quick thrash past the crowds lining the road before the final timekeeper brought on a dramatic seizure and numbness in his limbs, and Roy said that only instinct kept him upright for the last few minutes.*

*His feeding regime consisted of Kendal Mint Cake, fresh and tinned fruit, jelly, raisins, malt loaf, Complan, Ribena and peppermint, Coca-cola, yoghurt, ice cream and honey!*

**Eric Matthews wrote to the Fellowship Journal and congratulated Roy for what he had done for the sport of 24 hour riding and record breaking, proving that riding a 24 hour needn't affect your speed for BBAR purposes.**

I wouldn't normally extol the virtues of any rider who had 'packed' in a 24hr unless they had an unforeseen accident when having a storming ride, but I feel that in the case of Beryl Burton, it was a ride and a subsequent retirement on a totally different scale. **She had caught and passed the whole field of 82 riders including four of the fastest 12hr and 24hr riders in the country. Her riding demoralized Nim Carline to a point where he 'blew' and not many men have done that to Nim, let alone a woman.**

Beryl's first 100 miles was ridden in 4hrs 10mins, and her 2nd in 4hrs 31mins. At that point she was 21mins up on Cromack, 24m up on Carline and 29mins up on Matthews. **I'm pretty sure her first 100 miles was the fastest ever in this event, as was her 12 hour of 268 miles.**

It is lucky that **Eric Matthews** and in particular **Roy Cromack** weren't too phased by Beryl's riding, although there must have been moments around the 14hr point when even they must have thought "how long can she go on at this speed, and when is she going to crack?" They both knew of her tough 'do or die, win at all costs' type of riding from her glorious 12 hour ride of 1967, when she bettered the men's Competition record. Maybe one of Beryl's more forceful trusted helpers should have advised her to drop to a lower gear to save her ride and at least finish, but alas we shall never know.

I know that other critics will point to the fact that she didn't finish, with phrases such as 'a miss is as good as a mile' (excuse the pun) but her first 12 hours of 268 miles was the highest mileage ever ridden in a 24hr at that time as far as I can recall and even if she had dropped her speed drastically and completed the 2nd 12 hours with just 200 miles, she would have beaten today's current ladies Competition Record held by Christine Roberts. Again, this is all hypothetical and all I can conclude with is that her performance that day made the race a very exciting one, with Roy Cromack getting his very fitting reward at the end.

The last event on the Calendar, **The North Road CC 24 hour was won by Cliff Smith, East Midlands CC with 468.50 miles. This was Cliff's 7th North Road win,** and he met more than his usual amount of opposition in this event. On paper, John Baines and Malcolm Judge looked to be the main rivals. After a very fast first 50 miles in 2hrs 4mins Baines slowed, and after a valiant struggle against illness, later identified as the onset of influenza, he retired soon after 12 hours having ridden 241 miles. Malcolm Judge meanwhile had taken the lead, doing 251 at 12 hours, 3 miles more than Cliff Smith. At the 18th hour, Judge's speed dropped considerably and Smith did what he was best at, he maintained his steady pace to take the lead and win by over 12 miles. His winning mileage of 468.50m was considered to be one of his best, no doubt due to the pressure that **Malcolm Judge** had exerted to produce **455.87m** and **Eric Lobley** was **3rd** with **428.67 miles.**

The weather had been warm but dull, all 29 entrants started and 20 finished. **The Hampshire RC won the team race with 1,188.19 miles.** The North Road CC acknowledged the help received from friends, The Fenland Clarion, The Welland Valley Whls, The East Midlands CC, Solihull CC, and they concluded that without the continuing steadfast support of these many groups, this race could not go on for year after year.

There had been some interesting scraps in the closing stages of the race for the 'places' with Lobley eventually pushing **Bob O'Dell** down into **4th** by just .45 of a mile, with **Les Lowe 5th, 426.99m.**

**The North Road CC had a Gold medal specially struck for the first man to beat 500 miles, which of course went to Roy Cromack, but the clubs only regret was that it wasn't performed on their famous North Road course.**

---

That concluded the 1969 season, a very eventful one, but one can't help noticing when looking through the history of these famous races, that entries are not increasing and there are certain events that only ten or more years ago commanded fields of 90 or more riders, but now 19 is commonplace and one begins to wonder whether these events are still a viable proposition? Whether an event has 19 or 90 riders it still has to have roughly the same amount of marshals and timekeepers. Feeding teams may vary on field sizes but the cost of running a 24hr event relies upon there being at least 45 riders.

In 1969 the only event that seemed to be in a viable position was the Mersey RC with 83 entries and 55 finishers. The Mersey event was supported by voluntary donations or subscriptions from well wishers, and maybe that was the only way a 24 hour race will survive with the obvious voluntary help given freely year after year by a band of about 200 helpers. Events that incorporate the Championship for the year normally commanded a larger field, but this 'perk' only comes around every 4 years and it remained to be seen how long this situation could continue.

*Pelican Crossings were introduced this year and Britain now had 15 million cars on its roads.*

# 1970

The 1970 season got underway to its usual start on the 20th June with **The Catford CC 24hr.** It was won, for **the 7th time, by Cliff Smith with 451 miles.** Tony Roberts was **2nd** with **433.29m** and **Charlie Bruce** was **3rd** with **422.37 miles. Roberts led Bruce and Bavage to a Kentish Whls team win of 1,222.07 miles.**

From an entry of 29 riders, Cliff Smith was always the favourite although Ken and Dick Usher were entered for a North Road CC team including Tony King. Ken Usher insisted at the start that he was unfit and only there for the team win. The Kentish Whls team members were all 'novices' at 24hrs and Sid Hygate was using this event as training for the Wessex Championship.

George Bettis

Malcolm Jones

Rod Goodfellow

Dick Poole

Roy Cromack

Swinden & Withers

Pat Kenny & John Arnold

Eric Matthews

Cliff Smith

Nim Carline

Les Lowe

Charlie Bruce

Spelling & Purser

Stennett & Purser

Howard Bayley

Beryl Burton

Bill Griffiths

Christine Minto

# PHOTO PAGES SO FAR:

**Page : 38**

**G.P. Mills** at 18 years of age. **J.A. 'Artie' Bennett,** another 'Black Anfielder' in typical dress on his 'Ordinary' bicycle. **Monty Holbein,** Catford CC with his 'Safety' bicycle around 1886. Timekeeper **F.T. Bidlake** in typical pose in the early part of the 20th century. **George Olley** displaying his collection of trophies and aerodynamic bike, around 1910. **Charles Moss,** about to start another time trial on Warwickshire roads, around 1905. Frank Urry was the timekeeper. **'GHS' George Herbert Stancer** much later in life. **Frank Shorland** and **Frank Bidlake** on the Great North Road. **George Pilkington Mills** with **Tommy Edge** around the time of their 3 day 4 hrs 46 mins End to End tandem record in 1895.

**Page : 39**

**Maurice Selbach** pictured at around 345 miles in the North Road event of 1922. He went on to win this his third 24hrs with 402 miles, and to become the first unpaced man in history to beat 400 miles (note the food basket). **Jack Rossiter and Frank Armond** also pictured around this same time. **Bill Ellis** won the North Road 24hr in 1927/28/29. **Tom Hughes** on his trike End to End in 1929. He was the son of 'Owd Tom' also seen in the photo without a cap. Tom is being pushed on his way again by his brother, outside their cycle shop in Wigan. **Charlie Davey,** North Road winner in 1921 and multi RRA record breaker in 1923, he also managed and coached many top vegetarians in the 1940's and 50's. **Cyril Heppleston,** RRA record breaker at 24hrs in 1938, a superb time triallist and stylish rider. **Hubert Opperman,** an Australian professional riding for the 'BSA' Cycles team, he broke the End to End and 1,000 miles RRA record in 1934. **Sid Ferris,** North Road 24hr triple winner and multi RRA record breaker including the End to End and 1,000 miles in relaxed mode. **Alec Smith,** triple Mersey RC 24hr winner in 1937/38/39. **Frank Southall,** renowned timetriallist and Hercules professional road record breaker. **Eric Wilkinson,** winner of the first North Road 24 hr after the war in 1945, and celebrated time keeper.

**Page : 74**

**Syd Parker,** riding the Catford in 1948 and breaking trike 24hr comp record. **Stan Butler** on his way to competition record in 1950. **Eddie Mundy** in that same event also breaking comp record. **George Laws,** 2nd in the 1951 Catford 24hr. **Stan Harvey,** 3rd in that same event for the Addiscombe CC comp record team win. **Nick Carter,** South Lancs RC hill climbing. The original **seven founder members** at the inaugural meeting of the 24hr Fellowship at Bickenhill in 1960. **Aarvon Jones, Cliff Bate, Nick Carter, Les Heald, Jack Spackman, Sid Genders** and **Dave Cane.** **Gus Andrews** winning the 1951 Catford event with competition record mileage being given a drink by team mate, Eddie Mundy. **Albert Crimes,** Crewe Whls in record breaking position 1952. **Ed Green,** President of the Tricycle Association. **Ken Price,** 1955 comp record breaker with 478.55 miles.

**Page : 75**

**Gordon Basham** breaking competition record in 1948 with 454 miles. **Bert Parkes** almost at the top of Shap on his 2nd End to End in 1950 cheered on by Tom Barlow and Ed Green. **Jim Letts & Syd Parker** leaving Lands End in 1947 to set new End to End and 1,000 miles records. **Ed Tweddell & Wilson Stott** starting another RRA record in 1950. **Frank Cowsill & Alec Denton** somewhere in the Highlands in 1952, on the way to John o' Groats. **Lol Innes & Bill Thompson, 1938** tandem End to End record breakers. They are taking a drink from Alec Smith. **Crimes & Arnold** at Lands End waiting for the timekeeper, Tom Anderton and helper Tom Barlow, to see them on their way to John o' Groats, and a photo of them in training prior to the attempt.

**Dave Keeler** riding a 12 hour in 1957.    **Stuart Thompson** finishing a 100 mile time trial in 1953.    **Ken Joy** attacking another RRA record in 1954.    **Reg Randall,** End to End record breaker in 1958.    **Graham Fouldes,** Rutland CC looking at his watch on the finishing circuit.    **Dennis White,** the first man to beat 480 miles (20mph) in 1956.    **Sid Hygate,** 1965 2nd place, Wessex RC 24hr.    **Dick Poole,** the first man to reach John o' Groats from Lands End inside two days.    **Ken Lovett,** North Road 1974.    **Ron Coukham,** Catford winner 1959.    **Arch Harding,** 24hr Champion 1961.    **Den Mills,** personal best 443 miles in 1960.    **Joe Leversidge** Catford 24hr 1959, 3rd with 460 miles.    **Fred Burrell,** 24hr Champion 1960 with 477.7 miles.

**Johnny Pardoe,** Mersey, 1965, 419.9 miles.    **Dave Duffield,** End to End 1957 and 1960.    **Stan Bray,** Solihull CC, 2nd in the Mersey 24hr 1958 (on a bike) with a p.b. of 455.7m.    **Ken Hughes,** Mid Shropshire Whls, Mersey national 1961.    **Ken Usher,** starting away in the Mersey 24hr 1962, and winning with 474 miles.    **John Arnold,** trike competition record in the Mersey 24hr 1953 with 457.33 miles.    **Jack Watts,** Catford championship 1951, 5th place, 440.5 miles.    **Peter Duncan,** Mersey RC 24hr 1954 4th place on a trike with 440.9 miles.    **'Taff' Brissenden,** 5th in the Mersey RC championship 1961, 455.6 miles.    **Jack Forrest & Jim Bailey** with their End to End team in 1960.

**George Bettis,** 24hr champion in 1972 & 1976.    **Malcolm Jones,** Mersey 24hr 1970 2nd with 432.6.    A young **Rod Goodfellow,** Beacon RC.    **Dick Poole** on his way to John o' Groats in 1965.    **Roy Cromack** on his way to 507 miles in 1969.    **Pete Swinden & John Withers** climbing Hatton Bank during their MRRA 24hr attempt in the 1960's.    **Pat Kenny** on his RRA 24hr record in 1965, taking a drink from John Arnold, the previous record holder, somewhere on the A1.    What camaraderie    **Eric Matthews,** 24 hour champion in 1968 with 489 miles, taking a drink off Ron Coukham.    The ever-smiling **Cliff Smith,** winner of eighteen 24 hr races.

**Nim Carline** the winner of six championship 24hr races.    Mile-eater **Les Lowe** in the early 1980's.    **Charlie Bruce,** 3rd in the Catford  1970 with 422m.    **Stan Spelling & Martin Purser,** RRA record breakers in 1968.    **Hedley Stennett & Martin Purser** on the London to York record in 1976.    **Howard Bayley,** Solihull CC on his way to a 417 mile trike ride in the Mersey event of 1962.    The incomparable **Beryl Burton.**    **Bill Griffiths,** 431 miles in the Mersey event of 1967, coming 6th.    **Christine Minto,** the first ladies competition record breaker at 24 hrs.

## Mersey National 1961

| | | | | |
|---|---|---|---|---|
| 1. | A.C. HARDING * | | Middlesex Road Club | 470.36 miles |
| | | * Course and Event Record - 470.36 miles. | | |
| 2. | F.A. BURRELL | | Middlesex Road Club | 467.42 |
| 3. | C. SMITH | | East Midlands C.C. | 464.78 |
| 4. | R.W.E. Poole | | Middlesex Road Club | 461.15 |
| 5. | H.T. Brissenden | | Mid-Shropshire Wheelers | 455.66 |
| 6. | K.D. Hughes | | Mid-Shropshire Wheelers | 454.50 |
| 7. | J.T. Sanders | | North Worcestershire R.C. | 454.12 |
| 8. | D.G. Spraggett | | Birkenhead North End C.C. | 438.08 |
| 9. | J.M. Thompson | | Manchester Wheelers Club | 433.21 |
| 10. | J. Withers | | B'Ham St. Christophers C.C.C. | 430.11 |
| 11. | P. Kenny | | B'Ham St. Christophers C.C.C. | 427.47 |
| 12. | B. Holt | | Eckington Wheelers | 426.16 |
| 13. | A. Turner | | Warrington Road Club | 424.86 |
| 14. | T.H. Fuller | | Stretford Wheelers | 424.73 |
| 15. | G. Jones | | L'Pool St. Christophers C.C.C. | 423.70 |
| 16. | L.E. Lea | | Wigan Wheelers | 423.55 |
| 17. | D. Thomas | | Long Eaton C.C. | 422.70 |
| 18. | N.R. Kellett | | Crosby Cycling Club | 420.36 |
| 19. | A. Cole | | Barrow Central Wheelers | 418.05 |
| 20. | A. Jeavons | | Rotherham Wheelers | 417.78 |
| 21. | S. Lea | | Warrington Road Club | 417.34 |
| 22. | R.I. Burnett | | Middlesborough Co-op C.C. | 412.58 |
| 23. | R.B. Adshead | | Stretford Wheelers | 412.43 |
| 24. | T.K. Kelly | (T) | Yorkshire Century R.C. | 410.78 |
| 25. | J.S. Pugh | | Godric Cycling Club | 410.12 |
| 26. | R.H. Page | | Mid-Shropshire Wheelers | 408.19 |
| 27. | H. Okell | | Mersey Roads Club | 405.87 |
| 28. | J.T. Shuttleworth | (T) | Stretford Wheelers | 405.71 |
| 29. | L.J. de Mouilpied | | Beacon Roads C.C. | 404.57 |
| 30. | K.M. Gardiner | | Manchester Wheelers Club | 403.01 |
| 31. | P.M. Swinden | | B'Ham St. Christophers C.C.C. | 402.44 |
| 32. | R.L. Male | | Speedwell Bicycle Club | 401.95 |
| 33. | S.P.V. Bray | (T) | Solihull Cycling Club | 401.72 |
| 34. | G.D. Seward | | Middlesex Road Club | 401.46 |
| 35. | F.J. Cooper | | Stone Wheelers | 390.11 |
| 36. | D.R. Sedgley | | Oldbury & District C.C. | 388.99 |
| 37. | L.K. Barker | | Clifton Cycling Club | 372.97 |
| 38. | K.A. Hall | | Melling Wheelers | 372.21 |
| 39. | D.O. Davies | (T) | Speedwell Bicycle Club | 372.19 |
| 40. | M.G. Burns | (T) | Barrow Central Wheelers | 358.58 |
| 41. | D. O'Neill | | L'Pool St. Christophers C.C.C. | 355.67 |
| 42. | S. Crosby | | Spartan Wheelers | 329.00 |
| 43. | A. Layzell | (T) | Tricycle Association (N.E.). | 323.75 |

| Teams: | | | |
|---|---|---|---|
| | 1. | Middlesex Road Club | 1398.93 miles |
| | 2. | Mid-Shropshire Wheelers | 1318.35 miles |
| | 3. | Birmingham St. Christophers C.C.C. | 1260.02 miles |

## Wessex National 1962

| | | | | |
|---|---|---|---|---|
| 1. | N. CARLINE | MORLEY C.C. | 472.05 | miles |
| 2. | C. SMITH | EAST MIDLANDS C.C. | 463.67 | " |
| 3. | A C HARDING | MIDDLESEX R.C. | 462.00 | " |
| 4. | R.W.E. Poole | " " | 454.21 | " |
| 5. | H. Brissenden | Mid-Shropshire Whlrs. | 454.17 | " |
| 6. | A.E. Goulding | Gloucester City C.C. | 442.30 | " |
| 7. | K.D. Hughes | Mid-Shropshire Whlrs. | 441.29 | " |
| 8. | B.W. Tucker | Wessex R.C. | 438.16 | " |
| 9. | I.C. Davies | Exeter Whlrs. C.C. | 435.24 | " |
| 10. | R.H. Owen | Redmon C.C. | 433.08 | " |
| 11. | J.B. Matthews | Grimsby R.C. | 432.02 | " |
| 12. | A.B. Hellicar | Clarence Whlrs C.C. | 431.27 | " |
| 13. | N.R. Kellett | Mid-Shropshire Whlrs. | 430.93 | " |
| 14. | J. Cleeve | Norwood Paragon C.C. | 428.61 | " |
| 15. | C.W. Knight | Viking R.C. | 421.08 | " |
| 16. | G.D. Seward | Middlesex R.C. | 417.83 | " |
| 17. | W.T. Gladwin | Sth. Ruislip C.C. | 416.47 | " |
| 18. | R.E.J. Gale | Epsom C.C. | 409.33 | " |
| 19. | M.W. Rees | Middlesex R.C. | 408.27 | " |
| 20. | M.J. Wilkins | Surrey Road C.C. | 407.59 | " |
| 21. | F.J. Summerlin | Oundle Velo Club | 406.11 | " |
| 22. | D. Thomas | Long Eaton C.C. | 405.51 | " |
| 23. | S.W. Siddle | Spartan Whlrs. C.C. | 404.48 | " |
| 24. | H.N. Cooke | Rutland C.C. | 401.96 | " |
| 25. | A.G. Whittington | Frome & D. Whlrs. | 395.26 | " |
| 26. | N. Brocklehurst | St. Christophers C.C. | 390.91 | " |
| 27. | B. Hedges | Oxonian C.C. | 390.66 | " |
| 28. | P.W. Hennessey | Southboro & D. Whlrs. | 389.10 | " |
| 29. | D.M. Calverwell | Hampshire R.C. | 388.97 | " |
| 30. | W.E. Thorncroft | Brentwood R.C. | 387.15 | " |
| 31. | D.W. Buswell | Leicester Forest C.C. | 384.93 | " |
| 32. | J. Flanagan | Solent & D.R.C. | 384.81 | " |
| 33. | N.F. Channon | Medway R.C. | 378.26 | " |
| 34. | W. Suttie | Bath Jubilee Whlrs. | 374.33 | " |
| 35. | P. Corbin | Sthrn Paragon C.C. | 371.82 | " |
| 36. | T. Lovell (T) | Kettering Amateur C.C. | 367.89 | " |
| 37. | A.E. Comer (T) | Vegetarian C. & A.C. | 353.34 | " |
| 38. | K.V. Lewis | Frome & D. Whlrs | 352.77 | " |
| 39. | C. Tremaine (T) | Invicta C.C. | 346.39 | " |
| 40. | R.E. Cook | Salisbury R.C. | 343.07 | " |
| 41. | S. Crosby | Spartan Whlrs C.C. | 341.06 | " |
| 42. | E. Woodford (T) | Kingsgate & Venta R.C. | 337.53 | " |

Teams:  1.  Middlesex 1334.04 miles   2.  Mid-Shropshires 1326.39 miles.
Entries 62, Starters 58, Finishers 42.

## Catford National 1963

| | | | | | |
|---|---|---|---|---|---|
| 1. | N. | Carline | | Morley Cycling Club | 475.178 miles |
| 2. | R.W. | Poole | | Middlesex Road Club | 468.815 " |
| 3. | F.A. | Burrell | | Middlesex Road Club | 464.746 " |
| 4. | D. | Cooke | | Apollo Cycling Club | 458.934 " |
| 5. | C. | Smith | | East Midlands C.C. | 451.695 " |
| 6. | M.J. | Dunn | | Catford Cycling Club | 440.900 " |
| 7. | J.P. | Dean | | Middlesex Road Club | 439.895 " |
| 8. | D. | Robertson | | Morley Cycling Club | 436.868 " |
| 9. | P.N. | Swetman | | East Surrey Road Club | 431.068 " |
| 10. | H.T. | Brissenden | | Mid-Shropshire Wheelers | 430.883 " |
| 11. | G.W. | Siddle | | Spartan Wheelers C.C. | 427.924 " |
| 12. | K.D. | Hughes | | Mid-Shropshire Wheelers | 426.237 " |
| 13. | I.C. | Shaw | | Bromsgrove Olympique C.C. | 425.512 " |
| 14. | W.J. | Bull | | Wren Wheelers | 422.972 " |
| 15. | R.L. | Massett | | Charlotteville C.C. | 422.008 " |
| 16. | N.R. | Kellett | | Mid-Shropshire Wheelers | 416.772 " |
| 17. | E.J. | Hodges | | Medway Wheelers | 415.378 " |
| 18. | R.I. | Burnett | | Cleveland Wheelers | 414.233 " |
| 19. | E. | Tremaine | | East Midlands C.C. | 413.181 " |
| 20. | S. | Gilbert | | St. Neots & Dist. C.C. | 412.096 " |
| 21. | C. | Tremaine | | East Midlands C.C. | 410.785 " |
| 22. | J.A. | Goulson | | Elite Cycling Club | 403.897 " |
| 23. | J.S. | Pugh | | Godric Cycling Club | 401.990 " |
| 24. | R.W. | Metcalf | | Morley Cycling Club | 400.784 " |
| 25. | R.R. | Baker | (T) | Medway Wheelers C.C. | 396.259 " |
| 26. | R.H. | Douglass | | Worthing Excelsior C.C. | 393.195 " |
| 27. | P.W. | Hennessey | | Southborough & District Whs. | 388.809 " |
| 28. | H.N. | Hemsley | | Brighton Mitre C.C. | 387.383 " |
| 29. | M. | Haylor | | Brighton Mitre C.C. | 382.179 " |
| 30. | P. | Hammond | | Festival Road Club | 378.680 " |
| 31. | M.J. | Poland | | Worthing Excelsior C.C. | 376.528 " |
| 32. | P. | Reeve | | Elite Cycling Club | 369.761 " |
| 33. | F.P. | Hussey | (T) | Prescot R.C. | 361.641 " |
| 34. | R.J. | Burroughs | (T) | West Suffolk Wheelers C.C. | 360.576 " |
| 35. | L.A. | Howard | | Southern Roads C.C. | 360.368 " |
| 36. | J.D. | Hughes | | Dulwich Hamlet C.C. | 360.304 " |
| 37. | J.C. | Payne | | Brighton Mitre C.C. | 357.448 " |
| 38. | W.E. | Squirrell | (T) | South Western Road Club | 357.238 " |
| 39. | F. | Marns | | Orpington C.R.C. | 354.734 " |
| 40. | R. | Griffith | | Mephisto Cycling Club | 348.538 " |
| 41. | K.A. | Hall | | Melling Wheelers | 345.645 " |
| 42. | P.J. | Crowsley | | Southborough & District Whs. | 344.853 " |
| 43. | S. | Crosby | | Spartan Wheelers | 333.105 " |
| 44. | R.S. | Oxbrow | | South Eastern Road Club | 324.567 " |
| 45. | D.L. | Earle | | Charlotteville C.C. | 316.936 " |

| | | | |
|---|---|---|---|
| Teams: | 1. | Middlesex Road Club | 1,373.456 miles |
| | 2. | Morley Cycling Club | 1,312.830 " |
| | 3. | East Midlands C.C. | 1,275.660 " |
| | 4. | Mid-Shropshire Wheelers | 1,273.892 " |

70 Entries

3 D.N.S.

22 D.N.F.

## North Road National 1964

| | | | |
|---|---|---|---|
| 1. | C.SMITH | East Midlands C.C. | 473.688 |
| 2. | F.A.Burrell | Middlesex Road Club | 472.774 |
| 3. | G.M.Bettis | Elite Cycling Club | 463.573 |
| 4. | E. Tremaine | East Midlands C.C. | 460.768 |
| 5. | F.G.Brown | Cambridge Town & County | 446.649 |
| 6. | A. Brook | Bec Cycling Club | 444.806 |
| 7. | K.B.Hughes | Mid-Shropshire Wheelers | 439.303 |
| 8. | S.G.France | Mid-Shropshire Wheelers | 433.681 |
| 9. | R.I.Burnett | Mersey Road Cycling Club | 432.566 |
| 10. | L.E.Lowe | Long Eaton C.C. | 429.645 |
| 11. | R.H.Page | Mid-Shropshire Wheelers | 423.119 |
| 12. | F.J.Summerlin | North Road Cycling Club | 423.090 |
| 13. | G.G.Mayne | Godric Cycling Club | 423.081 |
| 14. | A.J.King | North Road Cycling Club | 420.423 |
| 15. | P.M.Swinden | B'han St.Christophers C.C.C. | 419.295 |
| 16. | W.J.Bull | Wren Wheelers | 412.397 |
| 17. | B. Eyre | Rugby R.C.C. | 409.395 |
| 18. | K.R.Rising | Comrades Cycling Club | 408.443 |
| 19. | B.J.Haddock | Oldbury & District C.C. | 406.338 |
| 20. | R.W.Metcalf | Morley Road Club | 404.590 |
| 21. | D.M.Macleod-Cullinane | Northern Cycling Club | 404.366 |
| 22. | K. Davey | Bec Cycling Club | 402.248 |
| 23. | P.G.Wells | Bec Cycling Club | 400.875 |
| 24. | R.J.Day | Morley Cycling Club | 400.692 |
| 25. | P. Kenny | B'han.St.Christophers C.C.C. | 400.415 |
| 26. | D.W.Buswell | Leicester Forest C.C. | 395.162 |
| 27. | H.S.Spelling (T) | Wren Wheelers | 389.335 |
| 28. | A.J.Perkin (T) | Godric Cycling Club | 386.915 |
| 29. | W.A.Cliff | Southgate Cycling Club | 385.362 |
| 30. | C.C.Davies | Hampshire Road Club | 383.166 |
| 31. | D.R.Shutt | Withington Wheelers | 382.415 |
| 32. | G.W.Arnot (T) | Priory Wheelers | 380.237 |
| 33. | G.W.Tolliday | Wren Wheelers | 374.769 |
| 34. | H. Bridge | North Road Cycling Club | 370.908 |
| 35. | R.W.Glover | Fenland Clarion | 363.949 |
| 36. | J. Lovell (T) | Kettering Amateur C.C. | 363.199 |
| 37. | R. Thomas | Star Cycling Club | 343.734 |
| 38. | J. Beech | Comrades Cycling Club | 312.129 |

Team: 1. Mid-Shropshire Wheelers    1,296.103 miles
2. Bec Cycling Club    1,247.949 miles.

## Mersey National 1965

| | | | | |
|---|---|---|---|---|
| 1. | N. | Carline | Morley Cycling Club | 485.09 miles |
| 2. | C. | Smith | East Midlands C.C. | 480.93 |
| 3. | R.W. | Poole | Middlesex Road Club | 480.63 |
| 4. | E.W. | Matthews | Altrincham Road Club | 477.37 |
| 5. | P.L. | Broad | Rhos-on-Sea C.C. | 466.72 |
| 6. | E. | Tremaine | East Midlands C.C. | 459.88 |
| 7. | H. | Bayley | Solihull Cycling Club | 458.29 |
| 8. | W.K. | Aitken | Swadlincote Wheelers | 453.89 |
| 9. | A.C. | Harding | Middlesex Road Club | 453.13 |
| 10. | F.A. | Burrell | Middlesex Road Club | 450.13 |
| 11. | S. | Lea | Warrington Road Club | 443.85 |
| 12. | G.W. | Stiff | Swadlincote Wheelers | 443.84 |
| 13. | C. | Tremaine | East Midlands C.C. | 443.81 |
| 14. | D.G. | Spraggett | Birkenhead North End C.C. | 441.54 |
| 15. | L.E. | Lea | Wigan Wheelers | 438.40 |
| 16. | P.M. | Swinden | Birmingham St. Christophers C.C.C. | 437.18 |
| 17. | P. | Kenny | Birmingham St. Christophers C.C.C. | 436.46 |
| 18. | P. | Duncan (Trike) | Vegetarian Outdoor Club | 433.56 |
| 19. | D.A. | Porter | Glendene Cycling Club | 431.72 |
| 20. | K. | Davey | Bec Cycling Club | 430.47 |
| 21. | R.J. | Gordon | Solihull Cycling Club | 428.65 miles |
| 22. | D.E. | Shuttleworth | Solihull Cycling Club | 427.58 |
| 23. | D.J. | Bishop | Hull Thursday Road Club | 427.17 |
| 24. | R.H. | Page | Mid-Shropshire Wheelers | 426.34 |
| 25. | A. | Brook | Bec Cycling Club | 425.48 |
| 26. | R. | Langman | Withington Wheelers | 424.67 |
| 27. | J.A. | Brayshaw | Middlesex Road Club | 422.87 |
| 28. | J.S. | Twigg | Manchester Wheelers' Club | 421.49 |
| 29. | J.S. | Pugh | Godric Cycling Club | 420.27 |
| 30. | J.K. | Pardoe (Trike) | Seamons Cycling Club | 419.94 |
| 31. | J.C. | Churchman | Otley Cycling Club | 418.65 |
| 32. | F.P. | Hussey | Prescot Road Club | 417.36 |
| 33. | M.S. | Shearer | Altrincham Road Club | 416.60 |
| 34. | T.K. | Kelly (Trike) | Yorkshire Century Racing Club | 415.27 |
| 35. | F.J. | Summerlin | North Road Cycling Club | 411.74 |
| 36. | R.I. | Burnett | Mersey Roads Club | 410.86 |
| 37. | W.D. | Nock | Birkenhead North End C.C. | 410.76 |
| 38. | W.E. | Thorncroft | Brentwood Road Club | 410.11 |
| 39. | B. | Kirkham (Trike) | North Lancashire Road Club | 410.08 |
| 40. | M.S. | Hickson | Macclesfield Wheelers | 409.38 |
| 41. | J.P. | Lea | Wigan Wheelers | 406.47 |
| 42. | C. | Williams | Mersey Roads Club | 401.19 |
| 43. | P. | Andrews | Andover Wheelers | 397.73 |
| 44. | P.J. | Robinson | Stone Wheelers | 397.51 |
| 45. | S.J. | Hall | Hull Thursday Road Club | 395.14 |
| 46. | J.W. | Taylor | Birmingham St. Christophers C.C.C. | 393.12 |
| 47. | M. | MacAllister | Altrincham Road Club | 390.79 |
| 48. | A. | Fell | Barrow Central Wheelers | 389.70 |
| 49. | H. | Spelling (Trike) | Wren Wheelers | 386.86 |
| 50. | F. | Mumford | Mersey Roads Club | 382.22 |
| 51. | N. | Maggs (Trike) | Mersey Roads Club | 378.54 |
| 52. | B. | Sanderson | Huddersfield Star Wheelers | 373.38 |
| 53. | L. | Robinson | Otley Cycling Club | 363.48 |
| 54. | H.G. | Hussey | Prescot Road Club | 348.03 |
| 55. | M. | Kirkham | Hyde Road Club | 346.57 |

Teams:-

| | | | |
|---|---|---|---|
| 1. | East Midlands C.C. | C. Smith, E. Tremaine, C. Tremaine. | 1,384.62 miles. |
| 2. | Middlesex R.C. | R.W.E. Poole, A.C. Harding, F.A. Burrell. | 1,383.89 miles. |
| 3. | Solihull C.C. | H. Bayley, R.J. Gordon, D.E. Shuttleworth. | 1,314.52 miles. |
| 4. | Altrincham Road Club | E.W. Matthews, M.S. Shearer, M. MacAllister. | 1,284.76 miles. |
| 5. | B'Ham St. Christophers | P.M. Swinden, P. Kenny, J.W. Taylor. | 1,266.76 miles. |
| 6. | Mersey Roads Club | R.I. Burnett, C. Williams, F. Mumford. | 1,194.27 miles. |

## Wessex National 1966

| | | | |
|---|---|---|---|
| 1. | N.CARLINE. | Morley Cycling Club | 496.37 miles. * |
| 2. | A.T.HARRIS | Viking Road Club | 478.63 |
| 3. | E.TREMAINE | East Mids.Cycling Club | 475.41 |
| 4. | C.SMITH | " " " " | 472.73 |
| 5. | B.R.HYGATE | Portsmouth Conn.R.N.C.C. | 454.73 |
| 6. | H.S.Spelling | Wren Whs.C.C. | 444.79 |
| 7. | L.E.Lowe | Speedwell B.C. | 444.29 |
| 8. | C.Tremaine | East Mids.C.C. | 438.89 |
| 9. | J.A.Westcott | Icknield Road Club | 438.56 |
| 10. | D.Free | Oxonian C.C. | 433.64 |
| 11. | I.C.Shaw | Speedwell B.C. | 429.15 |
| 12. | D.A.Porter | Glendene C.C. | 414.27 |
| 13. | M.B.Hutchinson | Westerley R.C. | 411.45 |
| 14. | R.E.Cook | Salisbury R.C. | 408.29 |
| 15. | P.F.Skelly | Maidenhead & Dis.C.C. | 406.22 |
| 16. | W.K.Smith | Speedwell B.C. | 404.95 |
| 17. | W.H.Wootton | Hounslow & Dis.Whs.C.C. | 402.80 |
| 18. | S.Winter | Maidenhead & Dis.C.C. | 396.80 |
| 19. | W.J.Suttie | Bournemouth Jubilee Whs. | 395.32 |
| 20. | W.E.Thorncroft | Brentwood R.C. | 395.24 |
| 21. | R.G.P.Edwards | Medway Whs.C.C. | 391.20 |
| 22. | D.J.E.Stokes | Viking Road Club | 389.09 |
| 23. | G.Martin | Clevedon & Dist.C.C. | 382.30 |
| 24. | A.R.Neale | Southbro' & Dist.Whs. | 381.58 |
| 25. | K.E.Bailey | South Bucks Road Club | 377.04 |
| 26. | A.G.Comer (T) | Vegetarian C.& A.C. | 366.32 |
| 27. | W.S.Dobbin | London Clarion C.& A.C. | 358.02 |

TEAM RACE

1. EAST MIDLANDS CYCLING CLUB — E.Tremaine,      1,387.03 miles
                  C.Smith, C.Tremaine.

2. Speedwell Bicycle Club — L.E.Lowe,I.C.Shaw,      1,278.39
                  W.K.Smith.


* comp record

## Catford National 1967

| | | | |
|---|---|---|---|
| 1. | N.Carline | Morley C.C. | 480.27 |
| 2. | C.Smith | East Mids.C.C. | 469.55 |
| 3. | R.W.E.Poole | Brentwood R.C. | 465.65 |
| 4. | G.W.Hinder | Oxford City R.C. | 455.28 |
| 5. | B.R.Hygate | Portsmouth Con.R.N. | 445.22 |
| 6. | A.Brook | Bec. C.C. | 437.72 |
| 7. | I.C.Shaw | Speedwell B.C. | 430.75 |
| 8. | A.H.Harris | Viking R.C. | 430.57 |
| 9. | D.R.Miesner | Brentwood R.C. | 429.95 |
| 10. | A.Mitchell | Edgware R.C. | 426.75 |
| 11. | M.G.Pocknall | Bec.C.C. | 422.91 |
| 12. | L.E.Lowe | Speedwell B.C. | 421.28 |
| 13. | R.I.Burnett | Mersey R.C. | 416.71 |
| 14. | M.J.Wilkins | Surrey R.C.C. | 412.27 |
| 15. | D.Thomas | Long Eaton C.C. | 406.44 |
| 16. | T.Finch | Bon Amis C.C. | 406.22 |
| 17. | J.A.Coulson | Buccaneers C.C. | 403.86 |
| 18. | A.J.Goodall | S.Bucks R.C. | 402.69 |
| 19. | W.E.Squirrell | S.Western R.C. | 401.68 |
| 20. | K.Rising | Comrades C.C. | 399.94 |
| 21. | W.E.Thorncroft | Brentwood R.C. | 397.93 |
| 22. | D.J.E.Stokes | Viking R.C. | 397.52 |
| 23. | P.J.Crowsley | Southboro & District | 396.35 |
| 24. | A.R.Williams | Shaftesbury C.C. | 393.79 |
| 25. | P.Cudmore (T) | Colchester Rov. | 393.10 |
| 26. | G.F.Hayman | Southboro & District | 391.04 |
| 27 | G.F.Attwell | Leyton C.R.C. | 391.04 |
| 28. | D.A.Panting | Cwmcarn Paragon | 389.78 |
| 29. | D.Shaw | Long Eaton C.C. | 389.70 |
| 30. | G.E.Mills | South Bucks.R.C. | 388.00 |
| 30. | W.K.Smith | Speedwell B.C. | 388.00 |
| 32. | R.H.Douglas | Worthing Excel.C.C. | 385.75 |
| 33. | P.Reeve | Buccaneers C.C. | 383.88 |
| 34. | R.Griffith | Crawley Whs. | 382.25 |
| 35. | J.D.Hughes | Dulwich Hamlet C.C. | 370.38 |
| 36. | T.C.Harrison | Ross Wheelers | 346.56 |
| 37. | K.E.Bailey (T) | South Bucks R.C. | 343.82 |
| 38. | W.A.Cliff (T) | Southgate C.C. | 338.30 |
| 39. | J.Cox | Welwyn Whs. | 322.59 |
| 40. | L.A.Howard | Redmon C.C. | 310.59 |
| 41. | G.F.Bailey | South Bucks R.C. | 292.62 |
| 42. | G.W.Miles (T) | South Bucks R.C. | 267.48 |

Teams:

| | | |
|---|---|---|
| 1. | Brentwood R.C. | 1293.53 |
| 2. | Speedwell B.C. | 1240.03 |
| 3. | S.Bucks R.C. | 1134.51 |

## North Road National 1968

| | | | | | | |
|---|---|---|---|---|---|---|
| 1. | E.W.Matthews | * | Altrincham C.C. | ... | ... | 489.470 |
| 2. | N. Carline | * | Morley C.C. | ... | ... | 481.518 |
| 3. | M.Ward | | Leicestershire R.C. | ... | ... | 479.095 |
| 4. | C.Smith | * | East Midland C.C. | ... | ... | 470.172 |
| 5. | J.R.Baines | * | Icknield R.C. | ... | ... | 465.569 |
| 6. | R.C.Goodfellow | * | Beacon Roads C.C. | ... | ... | 462.339 |
| 7. | E.Tremaine | * | Leicestershire R.C. | ... | ... | 458.311 |
| 8. | M.E.Cotterill | | Leicestershire R.C. | ... | ... | 443.347 |
| 9. | D.Bowman | | Leicestershire R.C. | ... | ... | 442.548 |
| 10. | R.E.W.Poole | * | Brentwood R.C. | ... | ... | 442.437 |
| 11. | B.R.King | | Coalville Wheelers | ... | ... | 440.384 |
| 12. | R.W.Usher | | North Road C.C. | ... | ... | 435.417 |
| 13. | D.R.Meisner | * | Brentwood R.C. | ... | ... | 431.116 |
| 14. | P.Jackson | | Shaftesbury C.C. | ... | ... | 430.845 |
| 15. | J.A.Westcott | * | Icknield R.C. | ... | ... | 429.131 |
| 16. | T.K.Morley | | Southgate C.C. | ... | ... | 427.135 |
| 17. | A.J.King | * | North Road C.C. | ... | ... | 427.053 |
| 18. | P.S.Ryan | | Sans Souci C.C. | ... | ... | 425.715 |
| 19. | D.Long | | Sherwood C.C. | ... | ... | 424.265 |
| 20. | R.W.Odell | | Luton Wheelers | ... | ... | 417.627 |
| 21. | J.Cannon | | Herts Wheelers | ... | ... | 414.614 |
| 22. | J.Graves | | Eastern Roads C.C. | ... | ... | 413.119 |
| 23. | B.J.Parslow | | Marlborough A.C. | ... | ... | 412.010 |
| 24. | M.Henighan (T) | * | Comet C.C. | ... | ... | 410.416 |
| 25. | W.D.Goodall | | South Bucks R.C. | ... | ... | 408.064 |
| 26. | W.R.Oakley | | Beacon Roads C.C. | ... | ... | 408.052 |
| 27. | W.E.Thorncroft | * | Brentwood R.C. | ... | ... | 406.821 |
| 28. | P.G.Hollingworth | | East Anglian C.C. | ... | ... | 406.507 |
| 29. | R.I.Burnett | * | Mersey Roads | ... | ... | 403.031 |
| 30. | L.E.Lowe | * | Speedwell B.C. | ... | ... | 401.644 |
| 31. | R.W.Glover | * | Fenland Clarion | ... | ... | 396.373 |
| 32. | D.K.Lusher | * | East Anglian C.C. | ... | ... | 392.406 |
| 33. | H.S.Spelling (T) | * | Wren Wheelers | ... | ... | 391.680 |
| 34. | W.Airey | | Fenland Clarion | ... | ... | 390.864 |
| 35. | J.D.Tribble | | Welwyn Wheelers | ... | ... | 387.402 |
| 36. | W.H.Wootton | * | Hounslow & District Wh. | ... | ... | 385.255 |
| 37. | D.J.E.Stokes (T) | * | Viking R.C. | ... | ... | 384.170 |
| 38. | G.F.Atewell | * | Leyton C.R.C. | ... | ... | 379.967 |
| 39. | W.A.Cliff | * | Southgate C.C. | ... | ... | 379.722 |
| 40. | D.A.Porter | * | North Road C.C. | ... | ... | 374.026 |
| 41. | D.W.Eager | | Eastern Roads | ... | ... | 367.399 |
| 42. | R.A.Holmes | * | Comet C.C. | ... | ... | 366.388 |
| 43. | H.T.Streeton | | London V.T.T.A. | ... | ... | 359.248 |
| 44. | E.L.Newcombe | | Leicester Forest | ... | ... | 351.349 |
| 45. | M.A.Smith | | Welland Valley Wh. | ... | ... | 344.132 |
| 46. | M.R.Purser (T) | | Charlotteville C.C. | ... | ... | 339.895 |
| 47. | J.Beech | | Comrades C.C. | ... | ... | 297.381 |

*DENOTES 24 HR. FELLOWSHIP MEMBER AT TIME OF
RIDE, TO HELP MEMBERS AWARD FELLOWSHIP TROPHIES
AS RESOLVED A.G.M. 1967.

TEAM:

| | | | | |
|---|---|---|---|---|
| 1. | Leicestershire R.C. | ... | ... | 1380.753 |
| 2. | Brentwood R.C. | ... | ... | 1270.374 |
| 3. | North Road C.C. | ... | ... | 1236.496 |

## MERSEY/NATIONAL 1969

| | | | |
|---|---|---|---|
| **1.** | **ROY CROMACK** | **CLIFTON CC** | **507.00*** |
| **2.** | **Eric Matthews** | **Altrincham RC** | **492.88** |
| **3.** | **Stan Turner** | **Brentwood RC** | **480.75** |
| 4. | C. Smith | E. Midlands CC | 473.82 |
| 5. | W. Clayton | Tyne RC | 473.72 |
| 6. | D. Clayton | Tyne RC | 467.68 |
| 7. | A. Robertson | Tyne RC | 455.08 |
| 8. | B. Hygate | Farn. & Camb. CC | 453.36 |
| 9. | S. Richardson | S. Lancs RC | 453.25 |
| 10. | S. Lea | Warrington RC | 451.43 |
| 11. | L.J. Green | Oldham Century RC | 441.02 |
| 12. | D. McNeil | Brentwood RC | 440.08 |
| 13. | C.G. Richardson | S. Lancs RC | 436.02 |
| 14. | C.F.G. Toon | Long Eaton Paragon | 433.88 |
| 15. | L. Hough | Preston Wh. | 431.65 |
| 16. | G. Baxter | Otley CC | 427.90 |
| 17. | R. Yates | Tyne RC | 426.75 |
| 18. | K. Robson | Tyne RC | 426.20 |
| 19. | A. Goulding | Birdwell Wh. | 423.77 |
| 20. | R. Thomas | S. Lancs RC | 422.18 |
| 21. | J. Farrer | Otley CC | 421.68 |
| 22. | M.J. Judge | Seamons CC | 416.86 |
| 23. | D.N. Latham | Lyme RC | 416.44 |
| 24. | E. Bray | Solihull CC | 416.12 |
| 25. | D. Thomas | Long Eaton CC | 414.99 |
| 26. | D. Shaw | Long Eaton CC | 408.60 |
| 27. | B. Blagg | B'ham St. Chris CCC | 408.03 |
| 28. | R.I. Burnett | Mersey RC | 406.25 |
| 29. | M. Jones | Mid Shropshire RC | 403.82 |
| 30. | R. Griffith | Crowley Wh | 402.37 |
| 31. | A. Wright | Southport RCC | 402.18 |
| 32. | D.E. Shuttleworth | Ross & Dist. CC | 396.13 |
| 33. | J.F. Shutler | Altrincham RC | 393.21 |
| 34. | A.D. Young | Notts & Derby Clarion | 393.01 |
| 35. | B. Sanderson | Huddersfield Star Wh | 392.30 |
| 36. | B.H. Waine (T) | Warrington RC | 389.86 |
| 37. | P. Reeve | Buccaneers CC | 389.51 |
| 38. | B. Eyre | Rugby Club Velo | 388.97 |
| 39. | E.A. Fryer | Leicester Forest CC | 388.73 |
| 40. | W.E. Thorncroft | Brentwood RC | 384.76 |
| 41. | J.A. Lovell (T) | Kettering Amateur CC | 380.49 |
| 42. | W.H. Filby (T) | Royal Navy CRC | 378.04 |
| 43. | H.S. Spelling (T) | Wren Wh | 378.02 |
| 44. | N. Maggs (T) | Mersey RC | 375.65 |
| 45. | R.P. Craig (T) | Charlotteville CC | 373.91 |
| 46. | A. Fell | Barrow Central Wh | 364.39 |
| 47. | S. Standard | Bradgate RC | 371.24 |
| 48. | J. Lawley | Barrow Central Wh | 364.39 |
| | J.A. Moore | Barrow Central Wh | 364.39 |
| 50. | J. Smith | Lancaster CC | 364.13 |
| 51. | T. Hall | Long Eaton CC | 363.68 |
| 52. | D.E. Jackson | Preston Wh | |

Team: Tyne RC, 1396.48 mls

Merseyside Ladies C A event (incorporated)

| | | | |
|---|---|---|---|
| 1 | Christine Moody | Birdwell Wheelers | 427.89 * |
| 2 | Wyn Maddock | Notts & Derby Clarion | 386.59 |
| 3 | Joyce Blow (T) | S Lancs RC | 374.15 * |

*Competition record*

## Wessex National 1970

| | | | |
|---|---|---|---|
| 1 | J.R.Baines | Icknield R.C. | 473.52 |
| 2 | D.Clayton | Tyne R.C. | 473.30 |
| 3 | B.R.Hygate | Farnboro' & Camberley R.C. | 454.86 |
| 4 | A.Robertson | Tyne R.C. | 449.07 |
| 5 | I.T.Hickman | San Fairy Ann | 444.57 |
| 6 | D.J.Walker | Portsmouth C.C. | 441.55 |
| 7 | K.Robson | Tyne R.C. | 439.63 |
| 8 | L.E.Lowe | Speedwell B.C. | 425.67 |
| 9 | E.Lobley | Lea Valley R.C. | 424.45 |
| 10 | C.P.Downer | Bournemouth Jub.Wh. | 418.53 |
| 11 | D.M.Culverwell | Hants.R.C. | 411.17 |
| 12 | A.L.Hill | Worthing Excelsior CC | 410.62 |
| 13 | J.Clements | Bath C.C. | 412.64 |
| 14 | C.C.P.Davies | Hants.R.C. | 408.08 |
| 15 | W.Suttie | Bournemouth Jub.Wh. | 402.21 |
| 16 | G.T.Jenkins | Hants.R.C. | 399.45 |
| 17 | J.Mummery | San Fairy Ann CC | 391.43 |
| 18 | K.Smallwood | Farnboro' & Camb.R.C. | 391.27 |
| 19 | D.E.Keen (T) | Lea Valley R.C. | 380.10 |
| 20 | E.R.Holmes | Lea Valley R.C. | 377.74 |
| 21 | E.F.Little | Shirley R.C. | 376.72 |
| 22 | R.Taylor | Bon Amis C.C. | 374.79 |
| 23 | J.H.Taylor | Hants.R.C. | 358.39 |
| 24 | J.A.Shipp | Bath C.C. | 354.79 |
| 25 | P.J.Covey | Viking R.C. | 340.01 |

TEAM:-

| | | |
|---|---|---|
| 1 | Tyne R.C. | 1362.00 |
| 2 | Hants. R.C. | 1218.70 |
| 3 | Lea Valley R.C. | 1182.29 |

The weather in previous weeks leading up to the event had been very hot, and on the day, the sun broke through one hour before the midday start. It was soon extremely hot, very humid, with a strong warm wind, which was to make racing conditions very difficult. Fast starter Brian Morrison battled with Smith for a while after being caught by him. Tony Roberts rode confidently, he was better known for his road racing talents and seemed to be thriving in the hot, windy, hilly conditions.

The hard afternoon circuit around Cowfold, Bolney and Henfield was particularly tough on the riders, with a wind strong enough to blow the riders across the road. To add to their frustrations, a 1200 year old anniversary procession at Henfield made the roads almost impassable for the riders, many of whom weaved through the traffic jams and slowed to walking pace as they passed under the raised arms of traffic policemen.

At the 100 mile point, Smith was slower than usual in 4hrs 42mins. He'd caught Roberts for 5mins, Morrison was next with Sid Hygate at 10mins in 4th place. The wind swung from south east to south west which made conditions even harder for the riders as they rode towards Chichester and the Coast. At 164 miles, Smith was 5 mins inside 'evens' and well ahead of 2nd man Roberts who had stopped for a feed and night clothing. Strangely enough, when the riders were at the far western end of the course and were looking for that wind to blow them back, it suddenly dropped at 10pm. What bad luck!

At 198 miles as the riders left Chichester for the last time to go east and then north, Smith was just on 'evens', Roberts was at 17mins, Dick Usher 26mins, Hygate 38mins, Morrison 48mins and 19 year old Charlie Bruce at 49mins, but riding confidently.

Cliff Smith's 12 hours ran out with 238 miles covered. By this time Dick Usher was the only North Road team member still riding, he was unhappy and wanted to 'pack' but his helpers put him back on his bike. Sid Hygate was now over an hour down on Smith and looking very groggy. The riders retraced via Horsham to Roman Gate, the moon was up but a mist was rolling over the fields. Weird lighting effects occurred high in the sky as cars came over the frequent brows of hills, illuminating the mist and the bands of clouds above.

At Roman Gate, 277 miles, Smith was 20 mins below 'evens' and averaging only 17.5 mph. Roberts was at 28mins, Usher and Hygate had both retired leaving Charlie Bruce in 3rd place. As dawn broke the weary riders went to Guildford as the lonely Windsor section of the road had been omitted this year, due to insufficient marshals to man the many junctions. At 8am the breeze sprang up at the same time as the heat returned.

**Smith** held onto his comfortable lead over those hilly southern roads to the finishing circuit and ran out time with **451 miles. Tony Roberts** despite suffering with cramp in the late stages took a finely judged **2nd** place with **433.29m** and **Charlie Bruce 422.37m. Graham Jenkins** was the fastest trike rider with **372.63 miles.** Only 16 riders finished from 29 starters.

My sincere thanks go once again to Ian Shaw for his fine report, which I have adapted to size. Ian had started in the event but said he was completely beaten by the heat of 80 degrees F and high humidity. He drank more than double his usual amount of liquids but still suffered from dehydration, the hot wind finally finished him off and he retired at approximately 110 miles. Ian felt that he'd taken all of the precautions to stave off the effects of heat over the years in various events, but was finding that as he got older, the heat affected him more.

⪢◇⪡

**The Wessex RC 24hr on July 11th and 12th, hosted the RTTC National Championship,** but still only attracted 45 riders. 1970 proved to be a transition year, with many prominent 24hr 'favourites' having a year out after a hectic three seasons. Matthews had a recurring stomach ulcer, which 'flared up' when he raced or put himself under pressure. Sometimes he could go for weeks without a problem then he would be tempted to race, and it would start again. Carline and Cromack were also absent, but Stan Turner who'd taken a surprise 480 mile 3rd place in the previous years championship was down to start as a favourite in this event, as was Cliff Smith. Dennis Clayton was without his brother Wes this year, due to him still recovering from a spill off his bike. Despite that, the Tyne RC still had a good team with Alan Robertson and Ken Robson. John Baines, Icknield RC, was looked upon as being a possible winner, the first time away from his normal North Road course. Sid Hygate was entered and always rose to the occasion in Championship events.

Prior to the 24hour, Clayton had ridden a 4hr 22min '100' along with Robertson who'd beaten him by a minute in the same event. Stan Turner had just returned from a 1,500mile, 12 day tour to Scotland and back. John Baines had ridden the Hounslow '100' in 4hrs 9mins. John had a similar way of riding a 24hr to Nim Carline, after a very fast start he would then hang on for as long as he could.

The first rider was despatched at 2.01pm on a brilliantly sunny day with the temperature in the low 70's. The humidity wasn't high this time and a north-westerly wind gave the riders plenty of oxygen. The start was just south of Ringwood and the riders had a 'flyer' down to Christchurch. At the 43 mile point on the return journey, Clayton set the pace into a rising wind with Baines at 30 seconds, Turner at 1.5mins and Smith 3.5m. At 70 miles, Baines had slipped to 4th at 5.5mins behind Clayton with Turner 2nd and Smith 3rd.

Back over the 'Forest' to Christchurch, Ringwood and Salisbury, the riders were faced with a strong wind. At 95 miles Clayton led from Turner by 2mins with Smith at 4.5mins. Robertson and Hickman were now riding surprisingly well in 4th and 5th place. Baines was unhappy with burning feet and had slipped to 13mins behind Clayton.

At 135 miles the riders struggled towards a low setting sun with a 'northwesterly' wind still troubling them. Clayton was holding Turner off by 1.5mins, Smith was at 5m, Robertson 13m, Hickman 17m and Baines at 18.5 mins had nearly been caught on the road by Smith. As darkness descended, the field retraced through the outskirts of Salisbury, then via Ringwood almost to Bournemouth. By the turn at 168 miles Turner had taken the lead and Clayton had dropped back to be at 3mins with Smith at 8mins. At this point it was estimated that Turner who was 33mins inside 'evens' would do about 250 miles for the 12 hours.

From 200 miles onwards Turner was well in the lead doing nearly 21mph. Clayton was having trouble eating on the bike and had to keep stopping for food, he was now 11mins behind Turner, Smith was at 15mins, Baines,27m, Robertson, 30m and Hygate, 37 minutes. There was very little cloud cover and the temperature had dropped with a north west breeze still making it tough going.

Dawn had broken at Bear Cross (261m) and Turner who had completed 251m for the 12 hours was still 29 mins inside 'evens', Clayton was still 2nd at 19mins, Smith 3rd at 28mins, Baines was chasing now at 29 minutes. Robertson and Hygate were in 5th and 6th position, riding steadily and pacing themselves evenly. Les Lowe had slowed with the cool temperature in the night and was also having foot trouble.

At 281 miles near Ringwood, Cliff Smith retired, having been affected by the cold, he was lying 4th at the time. At Holdenhurst, on the return from Salisbury at 321 miles, Turner came through at 6.25am still well inside evens, but Baines had moved swiftly through the field and with Smith gone he lay 2nd at 19.5mins, and Clayton was 3rd at 20.5m. There were several retirements at or near here; Lewis, Vetcher and Morris.

Turner was slowing quite noticeably due to an ongoing digestion problem; the sun had broken through as the riders rode a short detour leg to Blandford. Turner looked really rough and 'groggy' and soon reports came back from riders that he was lying on the grass verge with his helpers around him. It was such bad luck for Stan, he'd led the race for over 200 miles and was still on to a 480 mile ride when he packed at 350 miles.

Baines was now in the lead and looking strong, with a 480 mile ride a possibility. Clayton was 2nd at just over 2mins, Sid Hygate was making a huge effort to catch Robertson who was just 2mins in front of him on the road. Sid had a quick stop to take off his night clothing and then hurtled off with that 3rd place medal to ride for. Robertson knew he was 'on' for a team medal and couldn't respond to Sid's onslaught.

John Baines increased his effort, but with 6 hours still to go, he was also riding wisely as he had done throughout the event. Keeping his gears lower than normal he entered the finishing circuit with 407.3 miles covered in 20hrs 34mins, now just 12mins outside a 480 mile ride. Clayton was fighting back at 5.5mins, Hygate was 3rd at nearly 50mins. Baines managed 20mph for the first circuit but Clayton bettered that by 1 minute.

From the 457 miles point, Baines started to lose power, he was completely shattered and also aware how tight his lead was. At 468 miles he still led by just 2 mins, Dennis Clayton never gave up and finally lost by 45 seconds, in the closest ever finish to a 24 hour Championship. Syd Hygate riding at 18 mph on the circuit got his bronze medal. **So John Baines, Icknield RC, won with a personal best of 473.52 miles, his first Championship win. Dennis Clayton's 2nd placed ride of 473.20m was also a p.b. and he led Alan Robertson with 449.07 and Ken Robson with 439.63 to a Tyne RC team win of 1,362.00 miles, their 2nd Championship win.** **Sid Hygate,** Farnborough and Camberley RC, was **3rd** with **454.86m.** At last he had his Championship place and a free ticket to the RTTC awards night.

*This was another excellent report from Ian Shaw.*

John Baines, who had put a terrific 6 months of training in before the event, covering some 8,000 miles, said that the 'going' was very hard at the start and by 100 miles he'd started to lose interest coupled with painful feet which required a change of shoes. He told Les Lowe, who had caught him, that all he wanted to do was carry on to the coast to cool his feet in the sea. Even when Turner and Smith had caught him, it took until 127 miles for him to get going and find some speed. At the 12 hour point he'd covered 241.6 miles and was still feeling okay. Once Smith and Turner had retired he knew that Clayton was the only one to watch out for and he knew on the finishing circuit that he was catching him, but he couldn't raise any more effort.

Three days after his victory, he rode the Oundle Velo '25' and produced a personal best 56m 37secs, on the following Sunday he won a local 100 mile on a hard course with 4hrs 19mins.

Les Lowe who finished 8th with 425.67m also had problems with his feet and lost a lot of time in the 2nd 12 hours, trying to ease the pain. It turned out that a large swelling from a chafed corn had turned septic and a visit to the doctors on the Monday morning was required for penicillin injections.

Stan Turner, after a spell of cramp in the first 100 miles, said that he felt great by the 12 hour point, but was unable to eat any solid food and was relying on just bottles of soup. By dawn he found that John Baines was challenging him and then when they 'crossed' on the Bailey Gate section, Stan realised John was a real threat and getting closer. He arrived at the hill just before the drop to Bailey Gate and his whole body just crumpled, even to the extent of being unable to support his own weight on his arms and saddle. From there everything went blank until he ran out of road. His helpers made frantic efforts to revive him but were in vain and his moment of glory was gone. His recovery took about three hours and the cause of his blackout was due to **very low blood sugar levels.** Stan thinks that this was down to not being able to take solid food; in hindsight, one or two stops for a bowl of rice pudding with honey or sugar, and a piece of cake, may have saved his ride.

*Low blood sugar level is a very tricky problem and can affect people in different ways, and strangely enough, some athletes and sportsmen and women have never experienced it. It's known by various names, 'The bonk, The knock, The wall, The sags' being some. It's a totally different problem to cramp or a build up of lactic acid in the muscles and the correct medical term is Hypoglycaemia (a deficiency of glucose in the bloodstream). I have experienced it many times, right from a very early age, and luckily I've always recognised the symptoms as it starts to drain away your energy and rational thinking. If you know it is coming on and you haven't any food or drink with you, try dropping your pace by half to let your body recuperate, so staving off the worst effects. You will eventually recover just about enough to ride through it until you can eat or drink something very sugary.*

*The symptoms I've experienced when it is at an advanced stage are obviously total lack of power, but the main one is a very similar feeling akin to the first stages of drunkenness. Lack of proper visual focus, nausea, a general moist clammy feeling and breathing becomes shallow. If you don't ease up at these warning signs you will eventually lose the strength from your wrists and hands and start wobbling uncontrollably, ones complete balance can be affected. I have been known to eat a month old rock hard jam sandwich covered in mould whilst on a club run, just to get home. John Withers, in the same state on a winter's club run has resorted to eating sprout stalks still frozen in the ground on a farmer's field.*

*My worst experience was after misjudging the distance of a hard training ride, with no food left in my pockets and my bottle empty. I felt the symptoms overcome me very quickly, dark patches clouding my vision, clammy glistening skin, I was shivery with slight nausea and couldn't hold the handlebars and steer the front wheel. I was now only 200 yards from home with the last steep little hill to climb to my house. I lost my balance and toppled towards the pavement, luckily I stayed upright just long enough to stagger on foot to my front door. After finding the strength to get my keys from my back pocket, I had to support one hand with the other to lift it to the keyhole. Finally I fell through the door hoping that the neighbours hadn't seen me. I devoured cakes, biscuits and chocolate for about an hour and drank sweet tea. I still felt groggy two hours later and realised that I had come close to passing out.*

*Scientific studies have been done and this has led to liquid or 'polymer' feeding for athletes made up mainly of rice derivative carbohydrate powder being mixed with water to supply a riders energy needs. When hypoglycaemia takes over, the body compensates by putting a block on ones power output and calls on ones fat reserves to take over, hence the term 'fat burning'. In recent years professional riders training for the Tour de France are assessed for any excess weight at the beginning of their training programme, then they are sent out on a long ride with just water to exist on. Obviously they are closely monitored, but when they start to feel the effect of hypoglycaemia, they are made to ride, albeit at a slower pace, until they overcome it. Hydration is an important factor in this process.*

---

**The Mersey RC 24hr on July 25th and 26th 1970 was won by Stan Lea, Warrington RC with 441.99 miles. Malcolm Jones,** Mid Shropshire Whls was **2nd** with **432.64m** and **Phil Ashbourn,** Weaver Valley CC was **3rd** with **416.49m. Pete Swinden** came **4th** beaten by just .42 of a mile with **416.07 miles. He led a Birmingham St Christopher's CCC team of John Withers with 410.85, and myself, John Taylor with 377.36m to a winning total of 1,204.28 miles. Terry Kelly rode the fastest trike with 391.51 miles.** Joan Kershaw, Liverpool Eagle RC won the ladies event with the 2nd highest mileage by a woman to date, of **422.34 miles,** and Joyce Blow, South Lancs RC on a bike this time, 2nd lady with 402.12 miles. Looking at these results one will deduce that **Joan Kershaw's mileage would have gained her 3rd place overall in the main event!**

The Saturday dawned dry and windy with plenty of cloud about. By 5pm it was fairly warm as the riders were applauded away from a packed starting lane. The two favourites this year were Stan Lea and Nick Carter. Carter had won the event four times and was staging a 'comeback' after a few years lay off.

Lea started steadily and avoided being drawn into an early battle on the road by his namesake Lionel Lea. He felt that conditions were definitely slower than the previous year where he'd ridden to 10th place in the Championship with 451 miles. The heavy cloud cover made the dark night come earlier than usual. His first 100 miles were covered in 4hrs 50mins and after the Marford leg he found the Welsh Coast road to Nant Hall a very lonely road. On his return south to Whitchurch as dawn broke, he felt surprisingly good but wasn't looking forward to the Nantwich leg and the subsequent run down to Battlefield which Stan reckons is the hardest part of the course. He passed Nick Carter before Whitchurch, sat on a chair eating by the roadside.

Despite his dislike of the Nantwich road he actually enjoyed it this year and his first 12 hours yielded 231 miles. He crossed Carter on his return to Whitchurch and he seemed okay. A spectacular sunny dawn sky was soon forgotten as minutes later the sky turned black and rain started, bringing with it a sharp temperature drop, hence the old saying 'sun before seven, rain before eleven'! Most riders had to don extra clothing, jumpers and woolly hats to preserve their body heat.

*Approaching Battlefield corner the rain got heavier and colder and Stan saw what he though was a small bundle in the road; it was a baby rabbit that had probably been stunned by a car. He got off his bike and put the frightened rabbit under a tree away from the road. With his good deed done for the day, he deserved to win.*

His helpers informed him that he was now 2nd as Pearson was 15 minutes up on him. He still felt good and decided to try and close the gap. He flew past the Edgebolton feed and headed towards Ternhill. He crossed Pearson on the road and was now only 8mins down on him. Lea now felt really strong and kept taking his helpers by surprise as he flashed past. On the return journey through Edgebolton he looked across to the cottage where the breakfast feed was and there was a bike with no 41 on it, Pearson's bike. So Stan was now in the lead, he caught Swinden and Withers on the road and soon started to feel sleepy, even though it was bright daylight. After receiving the cold sponge treatment he perked up again.

Stan maintained his lead and after the hard hilly road from Battlefield to Whitchurch he was looking forward to a half of Shandy when he got to 'The Harp' at Quina Brook. After his liquid reward, the remainder of his ride went smoothly back north to the finishing circuit at Waverton where he covered two laps. Stan had done just enough to win after 20 years of trying.

Malcolm Jones who came 2nd had originally planned to ride the North Road event, having ridden the 'Mersey' twice, he just fancied a change of scenery but his training plans to check out the North Road course never came to fruition. He entered the Mersey anyway and I bet he was glad. His 432 miles was a personal best, it's just a pity he had no team-mates riding. He said that going into the night beyond the Chester area he saw a Minivan go past and then stop up ahead. A chap leapt out and shouted 'hot soup'. Malcolm didn't recognise the van or the helper and was worried that he was taking someone else's food so declined the offer. Later, he saw the van again, helping someone else and he suddenly recognised the helper, it was Don Spraggett. Malcolm said he felt awful for refusing his soup and got his helpers to apologise to Don.

Don Spraggett would help anyone and when he wasn't riding the event or if he'd packed, he would spend hours as a roving one-man support team either in a van or on a bike, laden with pots, pans, kettle, stove, bottles and sponge bucket, all precariously hanging off his saddlebag.

I too rode that Mersey event in 1970 and finished low down in the field, but was just determined to finish for the team. An article by John Withers in the 24hr Fellowship Journal in 1971, explains the poignant reason for us winning the team award. I will relate the first three paragraphs of his article.

*"Very early in the 1970 season, all the active long distance members of the club had decided on what they were going to do about the Mersey event. Barry Blagg had ridden the previous year and had come 27th with 408 miles and definitely wanted to ride again. The rest of us were definitely not going to ride, but tragically, that was not the way it was to be: On the Sunday of the Spring Bank Holiday came the tragic news that Barry had died in an accident walking on his own on Snowdon, while on holiday with his wife and young child.*

*Barry was first and foremost a cyclist for the sheer enjoyment and freedom of it, and his racing came second to that. In the nine years that he was a member of the club he had participated in most of the activities that the club had promoted, in spite of long periods at sea with the Merchant Navy. Not only was he a keen cyclist but he was also a first class companion whose ebullient humour never left him even in the most trying circumstances.*

*It is these characteristics that mark him as one of the best members that our club has had, certainly during my sixteen years of membership He inspired the remaining four 24hour riders to 'have a go' as a tribute to him in this years Mersey, and we had just seven weeks to get ready for this ride."*

John Withers hadn't raced or trained for two years and was very unfit. Pete Swinden, his tandem partner, was probably the fittest of all of us, keeping a solid core of fitness by riding to work and touring miles with the club. He was married like Pat Kenny and myself, and racing was just something we crammed into our busy work and family schedules.

Surprisingly enough, John's enthusiasm for racing always overcame his unfitness and he started well, catching Pete, Pat and myself, in the first two hours. Pat had punctures early in the event and then had lots of wheel problems to a point where he was at the back of the field, and almost out of touch with the rest of us. I rode my usual 'try as hard as I could' race knowing that by the Edgebolton breakfast feed after 12 hours of riding, I would know more about myself after bacon and egg and mugs of tea.

**Pete Swinden,** described by Ian Shaw in previous races as a **'hardman'** knew how to suffer. After all, his knee problems experienced on his tandem proved that. Unfortunately during this Mersey he went off course in the Chester area and lost 20 minutes, but he battled on, determined to finish. We all found the darkness hours to be the best part of the race, with perfect temperatures and plenty of oxygen.

The cold early morning rain had affected Pat Kenny quite badly, he really was riding on his own, off the back of the field. The hilly stretch down to Battlefield was his worst point and even his ever-cheerful helper, Charlie Larkin, couldn't keep him going. He packed around the Edgebolton area.

Pete hadn't re-caught John and for once John must have thought for the first time in 13 years of riding 24hr races, he might possibly beat Pete, but on the way North from Battlefield, around the 300 mile point, Pete was rapidly gaining on John, finally catching him at Prees. After chatting about their various aches and pains, Pete rode steadily away from John, to finish in 4th place with 416.07miles. John grovelled at 15 mph to the finishing circuit and then started to seize up and lose his balance. He landed in the hedge at Huxley Chapel but remounted and stayed upright long enough to finish 6th with 410.85 miles, beating an old friend of ours, ex B.S.A. professional and Tour De France rider, Arthur Ilsley, Birchfield CC by .66 of a mile.

*I finished with 377 miles with tears in my eyes partially due to just being pleased to have survived the ordeal, but mainly out of sadness, thinking about Barry and his wife Carol and baby daughter Julie.*

*I was exactly the same age as Barry, and our daughters were born around the same time. I'd spent many a long hour riding through the night with him to the Welsh coast and back. Nothing ever phased him and he always had a cheeky smile on his face. He'd had one or two scrapes on his bike, as we all had, and one incident always brought a smile to us. His front brake cable had a permanent kink in it at the very top of the curve, which had been caused by a lorry. Barry had been out on a club run and was sat at traffic lights behind a lorry. The lights changed and the next thing he knew, he was being dragged along by the vehicle. His front brake cable had got caught in the tarpaulin rope hooks that hung down from the flat bed of the lorry. He pedalled like fury on his 65" fixed gear until both he and the lorry were going about 25 mph, luckily, the lorry driver changed gear and lost speed doing so (not automatic gearboxes in those days) and Barry was able to yank the cable free!*

*After months at sea, he would just turn up out of the blue with no training, sometimes a little overweight, and thrash us all without getting out of breath, and ride all day. Ironically, when he died, his wife Carol was expecting another child and a boy was born 6 months later and christened Barry in his memory, and he has that same cheeky smile.*

One person I was glad to see riding was Joan Kershaw. She only caught me once during the event as far as I can recall. I'd seen her ride 100's and 12 hour races, producing rides that would put her in the first 5 in the men's event and I always hoped she would ride a 24hr. Her 422 miles was superb and would lead eventually to her forming a team with Ruth Williams and Amy Hooton to establish a Ladies 24hr Team Record.

---

**The North Road 24hr in August 1970 was won for the 8th time by Cliff Smith.** His mileage of **459.226** beat **2nd** man **Terry Bush** by just over 20 miles. Bush's **438.745 miles** was a brave effort by a novice rider. **Charly Bruce** now a 'hardened' distance man, on his second 24hr, faded towards the end, but he still managed **433.716** miles for **3rd** place, an 11mile improvement and personal best. He'd also come 3rd in the Catford in June.

Cliff Smith was challenged early on in the race by S. Cruse, and Smiths 4hr 44m, first '100' put him in line for a steady 'evens' ride. He knew he started as favourite, but with many unknown novices riding he had to keep an eye on the challengers. At the 12hr point, Smith recorded 240 miles, Cruse 232, Bruce 225, Catling 224 and Bush 223 miles.

The night was misty but fairly warm compared with other years. Bush was the first man on the road after the 12hr point, but he had been cut out of a 15mile detour. Smith maintained his 20mile lead, but the battle for 2nd and 3rd places wasn't won until the last hour on the finishing circuit. The men in contention for these places were Cruse, Catling, Ryan, Bruce, Bush and Sutton.

At the end Terry Bush said that as he reached the circuit his helpers informed him that he was only a minute behind the 3rd placed rider and that the chap in 2nd place was looking rough. That was all Bush needed to set the adrenalin pumping, it was a feeling hard to describe, but all of the fatigue left him and his legs went round mechanically. On his last circuit he caught young Charley Bruce and then the magic switched off and he could feel the ache in his legs again. The sight of 'Wilkie' (Eric Wilkinson) the main timekeeper, jumping in the air with enthusiasm for a local Bedfordshire man, kept him going till the end.

When the Southgate CC lost their 3rd man through retirement at 16 hours, it left the **North Road trio of Ryan, Summerlin and Hartley to win the team prize with 1,209.831 minutes.** 23 riders finished from 25 starters. **The fastest trike was R. Griffith, 368.866 miles.** This had been Sid Mottram's 21st promotion of the event, but due to a car accident, he kept control while on crutches, being chauffeured around the course in Pat Phillips' Rolls-Royce.

*Pat Phillips was a well to do Coventry store-owner and businessman. He was a member of the North Road CC and probably joined around the same time as Jack Middleton and his brothers.*

# 1971

**The Catford 24hr** on July 3rd, also incorporated the **National Championship** and as such it boasted 80 riders, one of the highest entry figures for a Catford event since 1955. **Robin Buchan, Norwood Paragon CC won the race with 483.84 miles.** He was an extremely talented rider up to 12 hours, but was a novice at 24 hr riding till now. **John Cahill, North Staffs St Christophers CCC came 2nd with 464.71miles,** he was also an excellent 100 miler and 12hr man, riding his first 24hr. **Wes Clayton, now fully recovered from his 'spill' led a Tyne RC team with 463.03 miles for 3rd place along with brother Dennis, 458.03 in 4th place and Alan Robertson, 5th, with 456.40m to a total of 1.377.46 miles. This was the Tyne RC's 3rd Championship team win in succession.**

The 24hr favourites entered were John Baines as defending Champion, Dennis and Wes Clayton, Cliff Smith, 7 times a winner of this event, Dick Poole, plus many 'novice' newcomers, Robin Buchan, John Cahill, Tom Finney and Mick Coupe.

The weather for the start at 12 noon was hot, sticky, and windy. John Cahill led the race throughout the afternoon, he had a similar way of riding to Nim Carline, one of thrash from the start and hang on. At 64 miles he was 7 minutes clear of the field and riding as if it were a 25mile event and not an all day one. Cahill was pushing massive gears and had already caught Buchan for 10 minutes.

At Steyning, 88 miles, Cahill was still in the lead but he'd lost time to punctures and a bike change. Den Grady was at 3mins and Buchan had 'opened up' and moved into 3rd position at 4mins, Robertson was still well up at 5mins, followed by the Claytons at 8mins and Ivor Hickman. Cliff Smith was unhappy with the heat as were many others. Baines was low down on time but riding with 'dead-legs' due to a heavy cold, he earned everyone's admiration for carrying on riding when very much below par, Hickman pulled out at 130 miles due to sickness.

As the riders continued west towards the coast, the temperature started to fall and darkness came at around the 200 mile point. Cahill still led Buchan by over 4mins, Grady was at 13m, Hygate and Robertson 23m, Wes Clayton 24m, Smith 26m, Dennis Clayton 27m, Coupe 42m, Davey 48m, Poole 53m, Finney, Lowe at 54m, and Baines 55 minutes.

On the return east over the Downs, Buchan was really 'flying'. As midnight approached on the Billingshurst leg at 232 miles, Buchan was the first man on the road by 15 minutes, over 5 minutes up on Cahill. It was calm, mild and very dark and the report on the event said that Buchan looked brand new but Cahill looked rather worn. Grady was at 18mins and the Tyne RC team were looking very solid on the road with less than 5 mins covering all three riders. Cliff Smith was at 30mins and Mick Coupe at 45mins. Pete Smith and Les Lowe were now ahead of Dick Poole at 64 minutes.

At 12 hours Buchan reached 250 miles and looked to be in a class of his own, riding a mainly solo effort at the head of the field. During this period of darkness and with good knowledge of these local roads, Buchan put 43 minutes between himself and Cahill. Dawn rose and between 6am and 8am the sun increased its heat.

At 367 miles only 5 riders had completed the full course. Robin Buchan was 26mins inside 'evens' and looked to be on for a possible 485 mile ride, Cahill looked subdued at 48 mins and Wes Clayton led the Tyne RC team at 65 mins. He was also closing on Cahill.

Buchan was the only rider to complete the new Gatwick Airport detour and yet he was still the first man to reach the finishing circuit. Most riders were visibly affected by the heat as it approached mid-day. Robin Buchan with a lead of 60 minutes had time to stop for a quick freshen up before completing his ride of 483.84 miles, a course and event record for the Catford, and a remarkable performance.

Cahill held onto 2nd place with 464.71miles, just beating Wes Clayton's 463.03m. He led the Tyne RC team to a total of 1,377.46 miles. Cliff Smith held 6th place with 455m, after a slow start. He found the Tyne RC trio's performance an impenetrable barrier. Sid Hygate retained 7th place with 446.70, just 'pipping' Ken Davey by .5 of a mile. Dick Poole took 9th place with 444.58m and with Pete Smith's mileage of 431.23 and Sid Hygate's, they completed the second team, The Farnborough and Camberley CC with a total of 1,333.51m.

Mick Coupe, after a fast start, hung on to take 10th place with 440.58 miles, with John Baines a brave 11th place 438.81m. Les Lowe had foot trouble for the second time but finished with his best Catford ride to date, of 429.54m, he just pipped Den Grady's 429.09m. Grady had a cracking first 12 hours and was prominently placed amongst the leaders early on, but he had also suffered agonies with his feet and resorted to walking up the hills on the finishing circuit.

So ended a very successful Championship event organised and run by Jack Simmons and the Catford CC, with 56 riders finishing from an entry of 80.

---

**The Wessex RC 24hr on the 17th and 18th July 1971, was won by Graham Mann, Hainault Rc with 469.94 miles. Granville Olive,** Oxonian CC was **2nd** with **461.99 miles** and **Eric Lobley,** Lea Valley RC **3rd, 418.86 miles.** One good fortune featured in the event this year, 'the weather' which helped 19 riders to finish from 25 starters.

At Netherhampton (114m) Olive was just a few seconds up on Mann with Bill Vetcher 3rd at 15mins. At the Corfe Castle turn (199m) Mann clocked 9hrs 33mins with Olive at 4mins and they were the only riders to have covered the whole course to this point. Mann's 12 hours expired between Lytchett Minster and the Woodbury Hill turn, giving him approximately 242 miles and Olive 240m.

At the Salisbury turn (297m) Olive had gone into the lead with 15hours 9secs and Mann was at 9mins and this position was eventually reversed in the last 100 miles to the finishing circuit. Thankfully the Organisers had cut over 6 miles of deteriorating road from this return journey, the road in question had undergone extensive drainage work and would have shook the tired riders to bits.

*Graham Mann remembers one or two moments from his winning ride, in which he was challenged throughout by Granville Olive. He said that Olive went past him very early in the morning at such speed, he felt as though he was standing still. Graham suffered another three hours of 'rough patches' by which time Granville Olive was 20mins up, but wasn't gaining any more. This was Grahams chance to pull him back minute by minute until he eventually caught him at 390 miles.*

**The Hampshire RC trio of Bill Vetcher, Mike Walters and J.H. Taylor totalled 1,095.43 miles to win the team race.**

The Mersey RC 24hr at the end of July was won by Mick Potts, Derby Wheelers, with 475.15 miles. Peter Kay, Apollo Whls was 2nd with 457.40 and Eric Tremaine, Leicester RC on a trike was 3rd with 433.93 miles.

Les Lowe along with Terry Poulter helped Mick Potts on his first ride at this distance. Les wrote an article for the 24hr Fellowship Journal and I've used a few paragraphs from his description.

"The field was disappointingly low in number this year and Mick was off No 27 and had only two potential riders behind him, Stan Lea, the winner in 1970, and Christine Moody. Stan didn't start due to the after-effects of a holiday sickness and Christine started with a badly infected throat. She rode pluckily for a long time, but had to eventually 'pack'. Just in front of Mick Potts was Pete Kay, another newcomer to all day racing, Eric Tremaine, on a trike this time, Malcolm Jones, Geoff Toon, Lionel Lea and Brian Eyre.

Within an hour or two of starting, Mick Potts was well inside 'evens' and at 86 miles led Kay by 9mins, Clowes at 15m,and Nicholas at 20mins. With Micks speed on the road, Les and Terry were finding it difficult to feed him, that extra 2 or 3 mph meant them rushing around to get back in the car and on the road to get ahead again. This 20mph plus was held all the way up the Welsh coast road to Prestatyn where Mick lost a few minutes with front light trouble and then was sent on his way South after a quick massage from Bill Gray.

He lost a little time in these next few hours that take in the tough Nantwich detour, but at the 12hour point he recorded 248 miles. Pete Kay at the same time had 238.3m with Clowes, 230m, Nick Carter, 225m, Nicholas 218.7m and EricTremaine 211.4 miles. The Shawbury detours started at 260 miles and after various optional legs, the riders pass back through Shawbury at 327miles to head towards Battlefield and return to Whitchurch. Mick Potts rode virtually all of this distance out in front of the field, on his own. Kay remained his closest rival at 45 minutes.

The return journey to Whitchurch was wind assisted but Potts couldn't take advantage and seemed to have fared better when riding against the wind. As Mick headed towards Wem and the hilly Welshampton section his gain on 'evens' was only 12 mins. His feeding regime had now become even more intense as he headed towards the last quarter of the race and his helpers were hard pushed to satisfy his needs. They nicknamed him 'Oliver Twist' as he always asked for more food.

Back at the finishing circuit, Mick Potts was just on 'evens' but knowing that he was winning he settled down to a steady plod. Les and Terry, his helpers, pleaded with him to raise his speed to 'evens' again but to no avail. It wasn't until Nicholas and Kay caught him that he started to take an interest and fight back. Les Lowe said that as helpers they had to resort to cheering Mick's opposition, just to provoke a reaction. It finally worked and with a lap to go he re-caught them and broke loose to finish at the Bulls Head, Clotton, with 1 minute, 26secs left to run. He absolutely refused to go any further but then he knew he had won by 18 miles from Pete Kay"

At the end Les said that to feed and help a rider doing 20mph for 24hours had put Terry and himself at full stretch with no room for error. I suppose, in hindsight, that realistically they should have had two teams helping.

The Hull Thursday RC consisting of Nicholas, Mason and Barker took the team prize with 1,255.77 miles. Pat Kenny led John Withers and myself to a 2nd team mileage of 1181.26 for Birmingham St Christopher's CCC.

The North Road CC 24hr in August was won by Cliff Smith with 447.624 miles, this was his 9th North Road win. The wind was howling from the west as the 40 riders were despatched from Potton Lane by Eric Wilkinson, timing his 22nd North Road 24hr event. Eric had been presented with a gold medal the night before by the North Road 24hr Society for his 21 years of service.

Cliff Smith was after his 9th win and was the favourite in this event, although Ken Usher was on the card to start. Ken was still capable of a 470mile ride, but heavy business commitments often prevented him from training, and to cap it all he was recovering from a bad accident. Despite these setbacks he'd managed to cram in 4,000 miles training on his trike "to make it harder", but he actually rode a bike in the event.

There were many regulars on the start card; Ken Lovett, Bob O'Dell, Pat Ryan, a one time BBAR rider now enjoying his all day rides, Terry Bush, Derek Porter, 65 year old Harry Streeton, Eric Lobley, Stan Spelling, Ray Burnett, Ivor Hickman, W. (Bill) Coupe and Sid Hygate, who wanted to break his own club record but hadn't much chance in that wind.

Bernard and Ethel Thompson who were Guests of Honour of the North Road CC, were out helping and Bernard was reporting on the event. He mentions travelling up and down the A1 both ways on the new revised course and seeing the riders 'leaning on the wind' at an incredible angle just to stay on the road, not just for a short stretch, but sometimes for miles, where the road was exposed.

At 100 miles, Cliff Smith had taken over the lead; he was defying the wind and settling down to the mammoth task of yet another 19 hours of this special kind of torture. He clocked 5hrs and 20secs for the 100 miles with Eric Lobley, 2nd at 2mins, Ivor Hickman 3rd at 4mins and a new name, Roger Sewell, riding his first 24hr for the North Road CC team, the same as his father Jack and grandfather Charlie had done since the 1920's. Roger was at 5mins, Ken Usher had retired before the 100 miles were out, and Pat Ryan went out before the 12 hour point.

Whenever one saw Cliff Smith he looked just the same, hammering against the wind on the way out and spinning his 50 year old legs round with the wind and leaning expertly as it gusted from the west. He always appeared to be smiling whatever the hardship.

At the 12 hour point Cliff Smith had ridden 234 miles, Hickman 229, Sewell 228.75m and Lobley 227m. At 6am Sid Hygate staggered through the checkpoint, but he was well down in the placings and looked beaten, in fact most riders by the early morning were showing the strain of riding in appalling conditions, all except Cliff Smith "Mr Perpetual Motion"!

What made the event so special this year was the fact that 27 out of the 40 riders finished, but if you had seen them in the first few miles hammering almost in vain along the exposed stretch of the A1, you wouldn't have given any odds on more than half a dozen riders getting to the finishing circuit.

Dawn revealed a 'ravaged' field of riders spread out over two hours on the road and most of them were 2 hours down on their schedules. The final hours were enlivened by the battle for team honours between the North Road and the Lea Valley RC. Ivor Hickman who came 2nd riding for the San Fairy Ann CC recalled matching Cliff Smith for mile after mile up to the 12 hour point, where he had to make a decision whether to overtake Cliff and try to open up a gap, bearing in mind that a battle for supremacy on the road at that point could have been so exhausting. Ivor decided to drop back and take a feed. Just after midnight his helpers greeted him with "Happy birthday to you!" and he celebrated with chicken soup and Jaffa cakes. He wondered what mileage he had done in 12 hours and shortly after leaving the feed, a Rolls Royce glided past and a voice from inside (probably Wilkie's) advised that he had done 229m. Ivor asked who was the unknown rider no 25, as he seemed to be going well? He was told "a gentleman from the North Road CC, Roger Sewell."

Soon after dawn, Ivor caught Roger who was going through a bad patch. After that, apart from the horrendous wind, the ride to the finishing circuit was uneventful, but once there, Ivor's feet started to give him agony followed by saddle-soreness. On his 2nd circuit, Roger Sewell came 'flying past'; he was also competing for that 2nd place. Ivor, not knowing what mileage Roger was on, re-engaged his sore aching feet back into the toe clips and hammered after him, catching him with 20mins to run, and that is how they finished with Ivor beating him by 6.5 miles.

**Cliff Smith took his 9th win with 447.6254 miles, Ivor Hickman was 2nd, 439.766 and Roger Sewell 3rd with 433.218 with Eric Lobley 4th, 428.110m. Roger Sewell led Ken Lovett and A.C. Hartley to a North Road team win of 1,269.895 miles.**

From comments made to the Fellowship Journal, one can only gather that Cliff Smith wasn't happy with the course, having to ride such a lot of miles up and down the A1 on both days, many riders also commented on the rough surface of the finishing circuit.

One of the pluckiest riders that day was Arthur Lancaster of the North Road CC who had been 'dared' into riding by his club mates. He'd had very little preparation and claimed to have a pair of 'wonky' legs, he struggled round the course, refusing to give up and finished with 279.2 miles.


# 1972

**The Catford 24hr** on July 1st and 2nd 1972, was **won by Cliff Smith with 442.42 miles and was his 8th win in this event,** but with one of his lowest winning mileages. **R.T. Powney,** Kingston Phoenix RC was **2nd** with **417.36 miles** and **George Siddle,** Spartan Whls, was **3rd** with **407.13 miles. Dick Poole was 4th, 403.52 miles.** No team finished.

Cliff Smith, in the dying moments of the race, incurred a broken thigh bone when he fell from his bike, and this curtailed his racing for the rest of the season.

16 riders started and 11 finished in this smallest Catford field on record so far.

⮞⬦⮜

**The Wessex RC 24hr** on the 15th and 16th July, 1972, **was won by Granville Olive,** Oxonian CC with **458.99 miles.** He won by a very narrow margin of 1.1 miles from **Stewart McPherson with 457.89m,** and **R.W. McTaggart** was **3rd** with **443.61m.** This years event attracted only 31 riders but included one woman, Jill Dale, of the Long Eaton Paragon CC and one Frenchman, Jean Richard, U.S. Creteil, but he was seconded to the Charlotteville CC for RTTC purposes. Jock Wadley had met up with Jean Richard when riding in France and suggested he tried a British 24hr.

Four teams entered, the favourites being the Farnborough and Camberley RC. On known form, Granville Olive, last years runner up, appeared a likely winner and in the event was to prove so, but only after a terrific struggle with a newcomer to all day riding, Stewart McPherson.

By the time the riders had returned from the New Forest and were back at Ringwood (97 miles) Olive was the second man on the road, but was actual fastest in 4hrs 19m, Bill Vetcher was at 17mins, Richard and McTaggart at 18mins and McPherson at 20mins.

At Lytchett Minster (197 miles) only two riders had covered the full course, Olive and McTaggart, Olive in 9hrs 11mins with McTaggart at 23 minutes. Following the western detours into Dorset, the check at Woodbury Hill (246m) showed Olive maintaining his lead in 12hrs 19mins with McTaggart at 17 mins. McPherson who had omitted a 13.5 mile detour was now coming into the picture, at the Salisbury turn (297m) he clocked 14hrs 49mins. Olive and McTaggart who had ridden the full course so far came through in 15 hours 22 minutes, and 15hrs 43m respectively.

The finishing circuit was reached with 408 miles covered, McPherson was first on in 20 hours 43 minutes, followed by Olive in 21hrs 22mins and McTaggart, 3rd with 21hrs 51mins; but not forgetting McPherson's 13.5 mile deficit at this point, which still puts him very close to Olive. 23 competitors made it to the circuit, all of whom finished.

**Olive** completed 3 circuits putting in a tremendous effort over the last one to run out a worthy winner by just over a mile from **McPherson** who had every reason to be pleased with his first all day ride. **In 2nd place he also led a Farnborough and Camberley CC team of Sid Hygate, with 419.40m and J.F. Davies, 379.57m to a winning total of 1,256.86 miles.**

**Jean Richards** suffered from a lack of knowledge of the local roads and probably a slight language problem but finished with a fine **428.71 miles** and we hoped to see him in future events. **Jill Dale,** after suffering many delays and difficulties in following the course, reached the finishing circuit and put up one of the fastest laps. It was good going for a young lady who had not previously ridden any event longer than 50 miles. Her mileage was **296.**

**Bill Vetcher,** Hampshire RC was 6th with 414.88m and Bill Suttie on a bike rode 410.40 miles for one of his highest mileages over a 25 year period.

—&gt;&bull;&loz;&bull;&lt;—

**The Mersey Rc 24hr** on July 22nd and 23rd 1972 was a **win** for **Robert Stapleton,** Weaver Valley CC with **457.80, 'Lol' Green,** Oldham Century RC was **2nd, 446.99m** and **John Hooper,** Oldbury and District CC, 3rd with **430.58m.**

I will use passages from Frank Fischer's report on the event.

"Of the 42 riders on the start sheet, only 39 started.  It appeared to be very open as to who might win and quite a lot of people were of the opinion that the race may be won by Eric Tremaine on three wheels.  He was known to be chasing John Arnold's trike Competition Record, but Eric's schedule of 465 miles appeared very ambitious. Other well-known riders were Les Lowe, Sid Old, Terry Waring, John Gills and one or two 'unknowns', including Rob Stapleton, son of the Organiser.

At the 23 mile point, several riders turn just on the hour.  It was remarked that Stapleton (No 39) had already caught No 38, Eric Tremaine.  Stan Spelling on a trike arrived very late having lost 17 minutes just after starting when his rear axle seized up.   At the Nant Hall turn, Prestatyn (170 miles) the race was sorting itself out, and of the 39 who started only about a dozen had ridden the full course to here.  Of these, young Stapleton was in the lead with 8hrs 10mins.   R. Thomas, South Lancs RC, was at 4.5 mins, 'Lol'Green at 13mins, followed by three riders all with 8hrs 37mins, J.Taylor (myself), John Hooper and E. Richardson.

*As the slower riders came through we were told that a tricyclist had been in a serious accident about a mile short of the turn and two of the helpers from the feeding team went to see if they could help.  It turned out to be the unfortunate Stan Spelling and he was taken by ambulance to hospital with multiple injuries.  Shortly afterwards another rider, P. Stevenson was also hit by a passing car.  He was also taken to hospital and kept in for observation as it was 3am.*

The last to turn was T. Finch who stopped to have his rear light bulb replaced and mentioned he was riding his third 24 hour in a month.

The return journey to Chester and the south was very misty and as the riders approached Whitchurch, a thunderstorm raged, leaving the roads flooded in many places.

The approximate 12hr mileages were, Stapleton, 240.2m, Green, 233.3m, Hooper, 228.4, Waring, 216.8, Goulding, 216.9 and Taylor, 225.7 miles.

At Wem we were able to find out the latest news on the leaders from Tom Barlow himself.  Stapleton now led from Green by 29 minutes with Hooper in 3rd place at 49mins, then Taylor and Terry Waring on a trike in 5th place. Thomas and Richardson had retired as had Eric Tremaine after suffering mechanical problems with his trike.

The journey from Welshampton via Wem and back to the finishing circuit saw Stapleton still firmly in the lead from Green.   On the circuit, Stapleton was the clear leader from Green, Hooper, Waring, Goulding and Taylor. This was the final finishing order.

**John Gills on a trike rode exactly 400 miles and the Stafford RC trio of T.M. Corbett, Reg Pearce and Rob Prentice won the team prize with a total of 1,150.15 miles.**

**Tom Melia, Mersey RC who was the first man to beat 400 miles in the Anfield 24hr of 1933, finished this Mersey event some 39 years later with 353.12 miles.**   Tom had been riding regularly in 24hr events for over 40 years.  That's endurance for you!

*The final thought from Frank Fischer "what a mixed set of emotions for that excellent organiser, Dave Stapleton. The triumph of his son winning, and the disaster of the accident to Stan Spelling".*

*Frank then added a sad postscript to the article. "Mike Twigg has just phoned me to say that poor Stan died on Sunday morning. I feel I can say no more."*

## Stan Spelling

The cycling world in general, and 24hour riders and Fellowship members in particular, were saddened to hear of the death of Stan Spelling in this years Mersey RC 24 hour. The shock was even greater to those of us who had been present at the event as the news had been circulating that Stan was in hospital with a broken leg, but was otherwise okay.

Stan was a prolific rider of 24 hour events with a personal best of 444 miles in the 1966 Wessex event, but Stan wasn't only a 24hr man he was a complete cyclist, ready to try his hand at any event, equally at home on two or three wheels, and willing on occasions to share the glory (and suffering) with a tandem partner. Social events were also enlivened by Stan's presence. He attended most of the Fellowship A.G.M. weekends and held the office of President of the 24hr Fellowship for three years, and during this time he brought in several new members and upheld Fellowship traditions by competing and helping in several 24's. An ex-navy man, Stan further advertised the Fellowship by having the 'crest' tattooed on his arm.

It is ironic that the point where Stan had some mechanical trouble, and slewed into the path of a car, was one of the quietest parts of the course. It was about 2am near the turn on the Welsh coast road; most of the traffic was from event helpers, and most of this had stopped well short of the turning point. Unfortunately luck ran out for Stan, who had survived several serious accidents in the 'rat race' of London traffic. He will be missed.

*The above passage appeared in the Fellowship Journal and was written by Les Lowe.*

Robert Stapleton gave us a few lines about himself and his ride in an article, from which I've taken some details. He was 23 years of age, 10 stone, and started racing in 1967, some five years before this, his first and only 24hr. His only experience of long distance time trialling was in 1971, riding 246miles for a 12 hour. His racing season started in May with the Dukinfield '50', recording 2hrs 14mins. In early July he rode another '50' in Lincolnshire and finished with 2hrs 4mins. His first 50 miles in the event felt good but then he had a bad patch, which worried him. His helpers told him not to worry and sure enough by the time he'd ridden back past the start he was feeling fine. He caught 'Lol' Green and John Hooper before the oil refinery at Queensferry. He then caught me and became the first man on the road. When he arrived at the Saltney to Marford detour point he called out his number to which Tommy Barlow replied "Good God – already". He'd started number 38 and had now caught everyone.

At Queensferry he was cheered on by the local drunks and chased by a couple of dogs. As for the traffic on the coast road he found that a few cars connected to the riders in the event were the cause of at least two incidents to himself, where he had to brake hard and swerve to avoid them. By the Whitchurch to Nantwich leg he'd dropped his speed to below 'evens' and was surprised at the gap he'd opened up on the next rider, Lol Green. Whilst down in the Shawbirch area he slid on loose gravel and came off, cutting himself and buckling his back wheel. With both items fixed, he then battled on through floods. Hot drinks and soup kept him going to the finishing circuit and once on the circuit he was informed that he was 30mins up on Green, and all that he had to do to win was to stay upright and move in a forward direction.

＞◇＜

**The North Road Championship 24hr** on 26th and 27th August 1972 started an hour earlier than normal at 11.01am. It was a chilly start, cloudy with a northerly breeze, not as windy as last year but still enough wind to flatten the grass on the road verges.

There were 64 riders on the card for this event, but for the first time in years there was no former 24hr Champion, of any year, present. Robin Buchan suffered an early season accident and hadn't found any form at all; John Baines was absent and also Cliff Smith, due to a broken thigh bone from a fall that came at the end of his Catford ride some two months previously.

Due to the missing past Champions it was felt that this event was going to be a very open race and there was much speculation as to who was favourite. A shortlist from the start card showed the Clayton brothers, Dennis and Wes, plus Alan Robertson would possibly give the Tyne RC their fourth successive Championship team win. Rod Goodfellow, Stan Turner, George Bettis, Ivor Hickman, who'd ridden to 2nd place in the windswept 'North Road' of 1971, Jeff Lewis, Ken Lovett, Roger Sewell, Don Spraggett and last but not least, Eric Tremaine, who was having a good season. He was after John Arnold's trike record, which stood at 457.33 miles. Although it was a nineteen year old record, it was still thought by many as virtually unbreakable, after all, John Arnold had put nearly 35 miles onto an Albert Crimes record.

Eric had already had a try at Competition record in the Mersey event a month earlier and had suffered mechanical problems and a broken frame. He felt that fate was against him at the time, although he still believed that the Mersey RC course was good for a record, especially if there was a rising 'south westerly' in the last few hours, to get a push back to the finishing circuit, as so often happens.

Back to the start of this event, and a check at 84 miles showed Goodfellow setting the pace some 2.5 minutes ahead of Wes Clayton, followed by Robertson at 3.5mins, Dennis Clayton at 6.5m, Sewell and Hickman at 9mins, Tremaine at 10.5m, Leat at 11mins, Bettis 12m and Turner who was troubled by a knee injury and was losing time at 22mins.

The riders then headed North up the A1 into a stiff cool north easterly breeze towards Thrapston. At the 100 mile point Goodfellow rode through in 4hrs 31mins, but by the 118 mile point at Brampton Hut, Wes Clayton had ridden very positively and was just ahead of Goodfellow. Bettis was now 6th at 13mins and Sewell a few seconds slower. Turner had 'packed' and Tremaine was at nearly 16mins, he was clearly suffering for his earlier exertions and was now in 10th place.

By 7pm at 148 miles the wind was rising and even cooler still, Wes Clayton despite the exposed roads was romping away ahead of Goodfellow and Robertson, he led them both by nearly 10mins. Dennis Clayton was at 11m, Bettis was now 5th at 12mins followed by Hickman, Leat, Lewis, Tremaine and Sewell. Goodfellow's knee gave out at 160 miles and he retired before the run south in the dark. At 187.73 miles, which is the next turn at St Neots, Bettis had ridden strongly and closed up on Wes Clayton at about 295 miles and then caught him on the Cambridge to Woolpack leg and shot past to take the lead. At 334 miles, back at St Neots, Bettis arrived at 4.27am, Wes Clayton was at 6mins but the efforts of the past 18 hours were showing. Tremaine came through like an express, now realising that trike competition record was still a possibility. He was thrashing as hard as if he was in a 4,000metre pursuit. Ivor Hickman was also looking very strong with only six hours to go, he was looking for a Championship place.

At 8am, the breeze rose as strongly as the previous day and dashed many riders thoughts and hopes for a high mileage. On the finishing circuit at 443 miles, Bettis led the field but Wes Clayton and Ivor Hickman were both gaining slightly on his lead. In 42 miles Tremaine gained 9mins on Bettis, such was his effort over these closing miles.

**George Bettis with 470.526 miles took his first Championship win. Wes Clayton was 2nd with 467.094 and led the Tyne RC to its fourth successive win totalling 1,384.898 miles. Ivor Hickman took 3rd place riding for the San Fairy Ann CC with 464.021m, Alan Robertson was 4th with 460.149m and along with Dennis Clayton's 457.655, completed the Tyne RC team. Eric Tremaine was 5th after an epic final 8 hours, he broke John Arnold's trike record by .56 of a mile with 457.985.** 47 riders finished from 57 starters.

Wes Clayton realised that it was anybodies race this year and he felt positive having had a good build up during his season. He'd previously completed his clubs 200 mile endurance ride with brother Dennis. The ride went from South Shields, Northallerton, Hawes, Kendal, Shap, Penrith, Alston and back to South Shields. During the 24hr he remembers being delayed by the Police on the Godmanchester stretch. They were stopping all of the traffic at the scene of a fatal accident where a hitch hiker had been run down. Wes said the speed of the traffic was frightening.

He rode with even more confidence when he found that Rod Goodfellow and Stan Turner had both 'packed', so effectively removing two threats. One of his worst moments was after taking soup at one of the feeds, he suddenly vomited and momentarily blacked out, falling heavily into a ditch, with his bike lying on top of himself. The problem was made worse by not knowing whether the ditch was on the left hand side of the road or the right, but luckily he got back on and proceeded in the right direction.

Dennis Clayton mentions the night being very long, dark and miserable, but was happy once 6am came, knowing there was less than six hours left to ride. He had a shock at about this time when Tremaine hammered past on his trike followed by Ivor Hickman, who remarked about being dropped by a trike. Dennis said he realised Tremaine was well above the average trike rider so didn't let it worry him too much. He concluded by saying that apart from the night being very long, he also felt there to be a lack of atmosphere in these southern 24's compared with the 'Mersey'.

The common factor amongst all of the riders this year was one of a steady start; nobody went off like a bullet from a gun and most of the top riders only came through very strongly in the last 12 hours.

Eric Tremaine had enjoyed a good seasons build up to the North Road event. He'd had a fast trike 12 hour ride with 248 miles, just missing Comp record by 0.7 of a mile. He'd also broken Comp record for the '100' with 4hrs 27mins 51secs, so came to the North Road 24hr with every hope of Comp record. Eric remembers thinking about being just about on for the record as he headed back towards Cambridge at 318 miles and that John Arnold must have had something that he lacked! He saw his father at Crosshall, he'd ridden out on his old bike, and Eric shouted that the record was 'touch and go'! Ed Green, the President of the Tricycle Association, shouted encouragement as only he could, across two carriageways and could be heard for half a mile.

Tremaine concluded that he was still convinced the record could go higher than this, in fact 460 miles plus; all that is needed is the right man with more luck weather wise and even more ambition to prove people wrong; he hoped we didn't have to wait another 19 years (*that was in 1972 – 36 years ago and we're still waiting*)

George Bettis hadn't really decided to ride the event until late into the season, but after winning the Luton Whls 12hr, he decided to have a go. This was his first 24hr since 1966, he'd not ridden after taking his Doctors advice (I think he suffered from Sciatica). Living in Eaton Socon it put him at the start of the event, much closer than any other rider. George said, semi-jokingly, that he rode past his house quite easily at 75 miles into the event, but when he passed at 400 miles, it was with great difficulty. He knew that when the weather changed from a warm breeze on the Friday to a cool north westerly on the Saturday, that it wouldn't be an easy ride and also knew that the finishing circuit would be very hard at the end. Being a maths teacher, his first few hours were spent calculating what he was likely to do, and more importantly what other people would do.

His feeding regime was very basic; a pound of creamed rice with a little sugar and salt, three times every 100 miles and no other food. Drinks were cold water, tea, coffee or soup if the day was cold. After catching Rod Goodfellow and Alan Robertson on the A1, he started to feel more positive about his ride, and after chasing Wes Clayton for 300 miles he finally caught him before dawn at Cambridge. George finally put a tracksuit top on at 4.30am, knowing that all he had to do was maintain his lead, which at times became difficult, as Wes Clayton was gaining back time on him. He struggled around 2.5 laps of that tough circuit, just managing to stave off the competition.

His parting comment was that he wished there was a National 22hr Championship! George's only concession to aerodynamics was to wear a hairnet, a trend used by one or two riders over the years.


# 1973


*Crash helmets for motorcyclists were made compulsory this year.*

**The Catford 24hr** on 16th and 17th June 1973 was **won by Rod Goodfellow, Beacon RCC with 462.56 miles; Pete Howard,** Kentish Whls was **2nd** with **437.13m** and **Ron Powney 3rd,** with **419.55 miles.** This was the first time Goodfellow had ridden the Catford event, and it was his first long distance venture since 'packing' with a bad knee at 165 miles in the previous North Road Championship event.

The day turned out to be very hot and cooling sponges were the order of the day. Goodfellow rode his usual unflustered race with no big names for him to worry about, as Cliff Smith hadn't started. His closest challenger turned out to be a novice 19 year old Pete Howard, riding for a famous southern club, The Kentish Wheelers. Goodfellow, apart from having his normal lighting problems, the same as most riders up until about 1995, had a relatively trouble free ride, his knees were okay, but he did get a feeling of despondency when the wind changed and blew against him coming back from the coast. He said "around the Washington area, I felt quite fed up and decided to ride no more 24hrs!" but after a sit down feed provided by Ian Shaw and Bill Oakley, he felt a lot better as he rode towards the night and cooler weather. Goodfellow's second 12 hours was spent maintaining his lead with enough speed to beat 460 miles, he found the finishing circuit very rough and bumpy in the lanes, and ridiculously busy on the A22.

Meanwhile Pete Howard who had been cajoled into making up the team with Tony Roberts and Robin Beels, was going well at the 200 mile point, to be inside 'evens' with 9hrs 56mins. Incidentally his team-mate Robin Beels didn't start and Tony Roberts 'packed' before night fall. Just after the ten hour point for some unknown reason, Pete 'slowed' and lost about 30mins in the next 30 miles. When Ron Powney caught him in the night, Pete resigned himself to 3rd place until the finishing circuit when his helpers told him that Powney had gone off course, and missed a detour during the day. At sunrise the temperature dropped and Pete felt very weary, he crashed at about 296 miles; in hindsight he said he should have worn more clothing to retain his energy. He had wanted to break the Kentish Whls club record of 446 miles, but was now just happy to having finished with 437.13 miles and 2nd place.

**The Maldon and District CC won the team race with 1,149.19 miles. The team consisted of The Cruse brothers, R.A. and S.F. and G.H. Wayte.** Out of 18 entries, 16 started and 14 finished; only three riders beat 400 miles.

<hr>

**The Wessex RC 24hr on the 14th and 15th July 1973, was won by Bill 'Batman' Vetcher, Hampshire RC with 438.81 miles. John Fisher, Bath CC was 2nd with 424.79 miles and led Jon Clements and Frank Feakes to a team win of 1,149.62 miles. Fred Newton was 3rd with 420.09 miles.**

**Bill Suttie** riding his 24th Wessex 24 hrs finished with **367 miles on a trike,** and his remarks were that the weather this year was the worst ever, with torrential rain causing flash floods and sheet lightning turning night into day. Bill Vetcher and John Fisher were both riding after being cajoled into doing so by club-mates. Vetcher had seen his first 24hr in 1966 when Carline won the Wessex with 496 miles and decided there and then he would win a 24hr one day!

After many seasons of trying and not producing the results, he'd decided to give 1973 a miss and concentrate on the Wessex Championships in 1974, that is until a young lady offered to help him all through the night in her own car, he said the offer was too good to be true. Bill sent off his entry and that was it. John Fishers year was also a pretty poor one leading up to the 24hr with just a few 25mile events, a training ride to Carmarthen, and a 4hr 36min performance in the Hounslow 100, as his only build up to the 24 hour.

The traffic at the start down to the first turn at Fawley was very heavy. The Frenchman, Jean Richard and Granville Olive came flying past him in the opening hours, as had McTaggart, both of these riders had produced good results on this course and were expected to do well. Stuart McPherson was also riding well in the first few hours. By late evening Olive and McPherson seemed to be in the lead along with Bill Vetcher. The rain started just after 10pm and then the sheet lightning started. Bill said he always associated lightning with thunder and had never experienced one without the other, he even thought he might have been hallucinating. John Fisher said he heard thunder but thought it might have been gunfire from the Army firing ranges on the Purbeck Hills. After an hour or two he realised it wasn't the army. Poor Jill Dale retired in the night, she was absolutely 'freaked out' by the lightning and her helpers were trying to console her, but she couldn't continue in the storm. Lots of riders stopped at Nora Neale's jelly, egg custard and rice pudding sit down feed.

By the Wormwell to Gallows Hill section, Bill Vetcher realised he was the first man on the road with only the possibility of Legge, Wessex RC being anywhere in contention as McPherson, McTaggart and Olive had all packed. Bill thought he may be close to club record held by Simon Searle with 441.25 miles, but without a watch and milometer, it was difficult for him to gauge what his finishing mileage would be. Finally the hilly detour in the Cranbourne area dashed his hopes and by the finishing circuit he realised a ride of over 440 miles wasn't on.

Strangely enough, after training and trying for six years to win a 24hr race, Bill's success came in a year when he just rode for fun. He never did receive the help promised by a 'dolly bird' from his club, it was just a ploy to get him to ride!

<hr>

The Mersey RC 24hr on July 28th and 29th was a National Championship event. It was won by Nim Carline with 490.31 miles. Eric Matthews now riding with the South Lancs RC was 2nd with 480.81 miles. Wes Clayton was 3rd with 465.75 miles and led his brother Dennis who came 4th, with 461.28m and Ken Robson, 427.10m, to another Tyne RC Championship Team win of 1,354.13 miles. The fastest trike rider was Steve Hill, Leicester Forest CC with 422.70 miles.

Although the entry of just 64 riders was rather lower than previous Mersey RC Nationals, it was still a high quality field including defending champion, George Bettis, former champion, Eric Matthews, former multi champion, Nim Carline, former Mersey winner and leading B.A.R.man Mick Potts and former Mersey, Wessex and Catford winner, Rod Goodfellow. Unfortunately Goodfellow failed to start due to the illness of one of his children.

Saturday was very warm with a moderate northerly breeze as 56 riders were despatched by Ron MacQueen from the starting lane. This same northerly breeze would later hinder the riders as they headed towards the finishing circuit the following afternoon. This was Nim Carline's first 24hr after a four year 'lay off'. He was now 46 years of age.

At 53 miles, Carline led the field, Potts was at 1min, Matthews at 4m, Ivor Hickman at 8mins, Wes Clayton and George Bettis were at 9m and Geoff Lee 10m. At 100 miles, Carline passed through in 4hrs 20mins, setting a very fast pace as darkness fell. Mick Potts was at 3m 30secs, Matthews at 7m 46secs, Bettis at 14m 40s and Hickman 17m. Soon after this check point Mick Potts succumbed to an infected throat and Ivor Hickman was knocked off his bike by a car and also 'packed'.

*If I've remembered the year correctly, a few riders were shot at with an air gun while riding on the coast road detour in the Shotton to Conahs Quay area. The exact location is a little hazy but I recall it being outside a large factory entrance on the edge of suburbs, possibly the Courtauld's factory. Both Pat Kenny and Pete Swinden were hit and Pete said he was sure one of the riders had to have treatment for a pellet wound. On a lighter note, Pete also recalled that when his young 4 year old daughter Judy came out to help with her mum Barbara next day, she was intrigued when Pete finished the race and said that he'd been shot on the Prestatyn 'leg' She inspected both of his legs and was mystified as to where the bullet hole was! The incident made the national newspapers the following day.*

**"Are you sure cyclists aren't a protected species?"**

At the 200 miles point, Bettis and Matthews were holding Carline's speed. By the Nantwich detour at Whitchurch the road was enveloped in thick wet mist, making visibility very difficult. By dawn at 237 miles, Bettis had caught Matthews and both riders were nearly 10 minutes down on Carline. Wes Clayton was at 15mins and Dennis Clayton at 29mins.

The riders continued south through the mist to Battlefield Corner and then to Hodnet, at 264 miles Carline continued strongly in the lead, from Bettis and Matthews, but 20 miles later, George Bettis sat up and retired, a victim of the mist and complaining of the cold affecting his feet. This left just Carline and Matthews to battle for the lead. The sun appeared between patches of mist and at the Hodnet turn for the last time at 309 miles, Carline was looking very dour and strained, pushing a huge gear and holding Matthews off by nearly 12 minutes.

A warm morning turned into a hot afternoon and as Carline hammered his way out to Welshampton still pushing huge gears, he was still 35 minutes inside 'evens'. He'd increased his lead over Matthews to 17mins, Wes Clayton was at 40m, and his brother Dennis was at 1 hour. On this difficult and hilly section of rural roads between Wem and Welshampton, Carline averaged 21mph and was estimated to be onto a ride well in excess of 490 miles, but a nagging, stiff, northerly breeze from here to the finishing circuit hadn't been accounted for and Carline eventually ran out his 24 hours with 490.31 miles, a remarkable ride and surely one of the very best performances ever seen.

Eric Matthews who came to the Mersey 24hr in a pretty fit condition after a few good 100 mile results, started steadily and wasn't tempted into scrapping for an early lead with either Bettis, Potts or Carline. He knew that when Carline was on form, nothing would stop him. Eric went through his first 100 miles in 4hrs 27mins and felt good, he intended to open up and raise his game on the coast road to Prestatyn, but when the time came, he started to fade.

He wasn't downhearted though as one of his main aims was to lead a South Lancs RC team to a Championship win. But as the event wore on, every time Eric got within 12 or so minutes of Carline, the gap would open once more. The surprise and relief on hearing that Bettis had retired was overshadowed by Eric having a bad patch from Wem to the finishing circuit, sometimes dropping to 17 mph. Once he was on the circuit he managed to raise his speed to over 19 mph and despite a last lap puncture where he lost valuable minutes, he ran out time with 480.81 miles.

Roy Cromack helped an 'RAF' team mate **Geoff Lee** to **5th** place and **445.77 miles. P.M. Heppleston,** a new name in 24hr racing took **6th** place with a fine **442.52 miles,** riding for the Abbotsford Park RC. **Ken Robson** the 3rd counting rider for the **Tyne RC** rode **427.10** miles for **8th** place. Eric Matthews was backed by Dick Thomas, with 426 miles, and Nick Carter after an illustrious career covering some 25 years or more, was the 3rd South Lancs team member with 423.2 miles. Malcolm Jones, the sole rider for the Mid Shropshire Whls rode 413 miles, just beating Pete Swinden, Birmingham St Christophers CCC with 411.16m. Pat Kenny rode 403 miles but they were without a 3rd man.

**The Tyne RC equalled the Rutland CC's record of five Championship team wins in a row with 1,354.13 miles and the South Lancs RC were 2nd with 1,330.34 miles.**

⎯⎯⇒•◆•⇐⎯⎯

**The North Road CC 24hr in August was won by George Bettis, Bedfordshire RC with the 4th greatest distance so far of 491.171 miles,** beating Dave Keeler's course and event record. After pulling out of the Mersey 24hr when vying for 2nd place and suffering from cold feet brought on by damp misty conditions, George finished his season off with his best ride ever in this North Road event, beating **Les Lowe,** Speedwell BC by over 50 miles. Les said his provisional mileage was 436 miles but his official figures were **439.761m.** Cliff Smith retired in the night and from then on it was almost a foregone conclusion.

George Bettis didn't have a proper schedule to work to, just a list of times for a 20 mph ride. He originally aimed to become the tenth rider to beat 480 miles. He rode on gears ranging from 74" to 93" and drank only water at the start. He stuck to a mainly rice pudding diet eating 3lb to the 100 miles.

At the 100 mile point he was the first man on the road in 4hrs 35mins, he then drew away from his rivals and rode his second 100 in 4hrs 37m, he was now 47mins inside 'evens'.

At Streatham roundabout (256 miles) he was 51 mins inside 'evens' and it was at that point he felt that a 490mile ride was a possibility. During the night the fog and mist was so thick in places that visibility was down to a few feet and even worse when the white line disappeared from the road or a sharp bend had to be negotiated, as is very common in that area. George also had lots of lighting problems even though he had prepared his lights properly and had lots of spares with his helpers. So all in all he lost many valuable minutes on this long, dark, foggy night.

George lived virtually on the course, at Eaton Socon, and so knew the whole area like the back of his hand, having trained over all of the roads and yet he still found it difficult, so imagine what hardships were suffered by riders who were strangers to the area.

At 8am the fog had cleared and daylight took over. George had already completed an extra section of road to Baldock and back, instigated by Cecil Paget, so as not to run out of road on the finishing circuit. He arrived on the circuit at 444 miles, still 38 mins inside 'evens'. It was a tough circuit with the wind in the wrong direction and Eltisley Hill had to be climbed each time. That took four minutes, and George said it felt like climbing Everest. A blast on the horn from the timekeepers following car and it was all over, but what might it have been without lighting trouble, poor visibility for 7 hours and the wind in the wrong direction?

Les Lowe recalls riding shoulder to shoulder with Bettis during the night trying to share the white line that was just visible in places. Les's ride was one of his highest mileages, certainly for seven years. **Den Mills,** Hillingdon CC was **3rd** with **430 miles, Roger Sewell,** even though a touch overweight, was **4th** with **422.75m** and **Graham Jenkins was the fastest trike rider in 5th place with 416.5m and Rob O'Dell 6th, 416m.**

**Den Mills** had probably one of his best rides in this event with 430 miles, as did **Brian Edrupt,** with 387 miles on a trike. Brian had been lured into riding a 24hr by his dad, Arthur. For three or four years prior to this race Brian had accompanied him on his job as Chief Marshal, checking all around the course that there were enough marshals in place at the right time. Brian said he had vivid memories of riding for miles in the pitch dark, only to come across a road traffic island miles from anywhere that was lit up by car headlights and camping lanterns. Here, an army of helpers, marshals and checkers would make sure that every rider was fed, watered and sent off in the right direction, and this would happen all around the course for the full 24 hours. Den Mills and Brian Edrupt are both actively involved with the RRA and along with Keith and Brenda Robbins and the rest of the Committee, they have helped me with advice, details, and permission to use various record data from the handbook.

⇒•◇•⇐

While 1973 will be remembered for its two superb event winning mileages of 490 by Nim Carline and 491 by George Bettis, it will also be remembered as a sad year for quite a few reasons.

*Early on in the season, John Harding, of the Middlesex RC, died in a car accident in Belgium, and then a few months later, Arch Harding, also of the Middlesex RC, but unrelated, was killed by a stolen car outside his home.*

*Arch was a remarkable man who combined great talent for racing with enormous enthusiasm for touring and club riding. Arch Harding's racing career spanned 25 years and he had been a champion at 50 miles, 100 miles and 24 hours. He was also a prolific winner of the Bath Road '100' and will always be remembered as a true all-rounder. On club runs, Arch would regularly take his violin in his saddlebag and accompany the regular singsong at the pub stop at dinner time.*

*Three staunch members of the North Road CC were mown down by a lorry whilst they were participating in the club's annual 'York run'. Terry Johnson and Robert Garard were killed instantly; Club Captain, Peter Bury died a few hours later in Peterborough Hospital.*

Late in the summer there was a most successful event on the K16, Burton 25 mile course, when no less than 120 trike riders paid homage to the late Stan Spelling by competing for the new memorial 25 trophy. Eric Tremaine was the popular winner.

For one reason or another, all of these tragedies have been brought about by cyclists being run down by motor vehicles.

Finally in November, Bill Ellis died at a comparatively young age of 69, after suffering a heart attack. He'd been a member of the North Road CC for 50 years. In 1927 he became the first 'North Roader' to win the 24hr, three years in succession. He also took 1 hour 50mins off the Edinburgh to London record with a time of 21 hours 53mins.

# 1974

**The Catford CC 24hr on June 15th and 16th 1974, was won by Peter Howard with 435.62 miles. He led a Kentish Whls team comprised of Charlie Bruce, who came 3rd overall with 420.68m, and G.J. Axford, 315.89m, to a total of 1,172.19m. D.A.Hadfield,** Norwood Paragon was **2nd with 430.81m.** From thirteen entries, 12 started and 8 riders finished. The very lowest entry in the Catford's history.

Pete's mileage was slightly lower by two miles than the previous years event, when he rode to a very good 2nd place behind Rod Goodfellow. At the 100 miles point, Pete led this 1974 event with 4hrs 20mins, and after starting off last man he had caught the field after 70 miles. He had his problems when he was sick after eating a banana, then a while later cramped up badly in both legs. He was demoralised during the cold night when he was caught by 3 riders, but hadn't realised they had all done less miles than himself. The sun gradually perked Pete up and he felt a lot better after arriving at the finishing circuit, although he went slower and slower, he was amazed to find that not only had they won the team race, he had also won the event!

*I first noticed Pete on the scene when he rode a tandem with Kathy Bellingham, to tackle some road records in the late 1970's and early 80's. He had proved his ability at 24 hours and I feel that on a different course, maybe with better conditions and with possibly a stronger team, he could have ridden to a much higher mileage, possibly 460 or 470 miles.*

*He went on to marry Kathy in the early 1990's and Peter has now taken on his father's original surname, Akoslovski.*

**The Wessex RC 24hr, a National Championship event was won by Rod Goodfellow with 465.45 miles. Granville Olive** was **2nd** with **457.78m** and **Fred Newton,** Wessex RC was **3rd** with **441.11 miles.**

Rod Goodfellow, who had broken the 5th metatarsal bone in his ankle less than two weeks before the event, decided to risk riding with firm strapping supporting the joint. Being a Doctor, he obviously knew the dangers involved, but his medical colleagues were of the pro-active healing persuasion, and felt that exercise could be a good form of healing for any injury like this. Goodfellow knew the course reasonably well, having won the event in 1969 with 450 miles.

Rain fell heavily for 17 hours before the event and stopped just in time to let the riders get away from the start. Heavy traffic in the Ringwood area had made it a 'close run' thing, for many riders and their helpers, trying to get to the start. Apart from a breeze and one or two heavy thundery showers after teatime on Saturday, the night turned out fine with a moon appearing after 11pm, and dawn broke to a clear sky. On the start card, Goodfellow was the last man off, but Fred Newton, a seeded rider from the promoting club, had a delayed start and was set off one minute behind Goodfellow, so apart from Granville Olive, Rod now had Newton to look out for. At the 100 miles, Goodfellow led with 4hrs 24mins with Olive at 2mins, Newton at 6mins, Hickman at 8mins and Spraggett at 10mins. Don Spraggett's name doesn't appear at the 153 mile check due to an accident, when he fell in the rain on the Saturday evening, breaking his collar bone.

At the 269 mile point near Holdenhurst, Goodfellow still led Olive by 9mins and Newton by 33mins. Rod was now just 5 mins inside 'evens'. Heavy traffic on the Sunday plagued the riders as they rode to the finishing circuit at 406 miles, where Goodfellow led in 20hrs 42mins from Olive at 20mins. Both riders continued at just under 18 mph on the finishing circuit for their respective mileages.

Goodfellow had ridden a well judged race, he'd steadily caught up with Olive on the road and passed him to take a lead of 17mins at about 6am, after 16 hours of riding. He knew Olive disliked riding in the rain due to wearing glasses, and on the one or two occasions that it did rain, Goodfellow took advantage and speeded up, whenever it was appropriate. He then gained and held a small lead of 5 to 8 minutes to the end of the race.

Rod recalled getting to the dangerous right turn into Ringwood and onto the wet finishing circuit where his uppermost thoughts were of Cliff Smith breaking his thigh bone on a wet circuit in the closing stages of winning the Catford in 1972. From then on, Rod went round the bends at about 8 mph until the roads dried out.

It had been another tough weekend for all the riders; of the 46 men who started, only 27 finished. **The team race was won by the Farnborough and Camberley** even without their star rider, Sid Hygate, who had packed very early in the event. **R.P. Craig took 5th overall with 427.23m, R. Dowling was 6th with 425.82m and P.A. Smith 12th with 410.60m, to give a Championship Team total of 1,263.65 miles.**

**McTaggart** took **4th** place with **430.64m** for the Oxonian CC but like many others, the Oxonian were without a 3rd man.

*Mrs Janet Tebbutt, Clevedon and District RC was the only lady rider and she finished with 363.92 miles and was no doubt using this event as valuable training for her* **Amateur 1,000 miles record** *attempt on 8th August 1974, a record she broke with a time of* **3 days 9hrs 29mins.** *In very windy conditions, she beat Wynne Wrightsons record by over 6 hours.*

<hr>

**The Mersey RC 24hr** late July 1974 was **won with a fine mileage of 454.97 by George Berwick, Glasgow RC.** He beat the next man, Sid Old by 28 miles. Surprisingly, Old had only been 9 miles behind Berwick at 12 hours with 228m to George's 237m. **Sid Old** who came **2nd** with **426.82** narrowly beat **Nick Carter, 426.09m** by just .83 of a mile. **Carter led a South Lancs team of Cliff Bate (4th) with 418.28 and V.J. McDermott, 368.39 to a winning total of 1,212.76 miles. Dave Jackson was the fastest trike rider with 384.09 miles.**

George Berwick described himself as a 33year old 5ft 4inch Glasgow navvy. He'd been cycling for about 20 years and racing for about 14 years. One of his earliest 24hr races was in 1967, winning the one and only 'Scottish 24hr' with 448.377 miles. George's favourite past time was 'rough stuff', riding and touring with his wife and when the '3 day week' came about, he upped his training to suit his future plans.

A few days before the event, his helper, Peter Duncan, had to pull out with a bad bout of the 'flu'. Luckily Don Spraggett, who had crashed out of the 'Wessex 24' with a broken collar bone, came to the rescue, and sent a telegram to George telling him to just turn up at the start, and that he would provide help and guidance to him and his helpers during the event. George had got helpers with him, Raymond Donnelly and Bill Torrence, but they were complete novices who didn't know the course.

George travelled from Glasgow and arrived at the start with just 15 minutes to go, not the best of preparations, but then George is very adaptable to changing circumstances and to date (2007) has ridden this event over 40 times. He mentioned the language barrier between him and Don Spraggett, having met for the first time at the event, with Don trying to decipher what George was telling him.

George had a very slow patch in the early morning down towards Battlefield Corner, and was riding at about 10 mph. Don got him off his bike for a sit down feed and a short rest, which did the trick.

Les Lowe, who had ridden his bike to the Wessex event a week or two earlier to act as a roving reporter, checker and marshal, had been hoping to use these miles as good training for this Mersey event of 1974. Les mentions the wind being a very strong south westerly, which plagued him and the other riders. After getting a soaking on the road to Battlefield where George had suffered, Les finally rode himself into the ground at Hodnet and retired shattered and demoralised. He remembers seeing George pedalling a low gear, into the wind, in the early morning, in an effort to maintain his lead and so 'cock a snook' at the RTTC National Committee, who had barred him from riding the event the previous year, because he was Scottish, when it was a Championship, or in other words as Les said, to give them the 'Harvey Smith salute'! At the time Les retired he was lying 5th, having been caught by Nick Carter. Sid Old had caught him at the 100 mile point. Pat Kenny who had been up on Les in the early stages, had taken a hammering on the coast road, and Les had drawn well clear of him. Pat finished with 398 miles.

*I rode this event and finished with 373 miles, but I can't for the life of me remember anything about it. I can remember more details from helping Lynne in her races than I can of my own. Thank God for the 24hr Fellowship Journals that have kept me informed as to what I might or might not have done.*

---

The North Road CC 24hr was won by Cliff Smith, with 451.93 miles. This was Cliff's 10th North Road 24hr win, a remarkable record. He beat **Ken Lovett** into **2nd** place with **448.80m**, Rob O'Dell was **3rd** with **421.73m**. **Les Lowe,** at last had some success, and finished **4th** with **416.38m**. **Eric Lobley** was **5th** with **405.29m**.

Colchester Rovers won the team race with 1,090.30 miles. The team consisted of Steve King, 378.26m, Jock Wadley, 375.87, and C.R. Britten, 336.18m. Jock Wadley was a much renowned and revered writer and columnist for various cycling publications and I've used many of 'Jock's' writings in this book.

This was Cliff Smith's first 24hr since breaking his thigh bone in 1972, and he was thought to be not as fit as he wished, his business partner had been ill in the weeks leading up to the event giving him less time for training.

During daylight hours the weather was muggy, with a strong south to south-west wind for the riders to contend with. At the 100 mile point, Tony Hartley led Smith and Lovett but by Eltisley at 184 miles, Lovett had taken the lead from Hartley at 2mins and Smith at 7mins. Derek Porter retired shortly after Eltisley and so put the North Road CC out of the team race. Soon after midnight, Hartley retired, and throughout the night the leading positions remained the same. From 6.30am the wind increased in strength and in the last 7 hours, the race was decided when Smith pulled away from Lovett. The more pressure he applied the more Lovett suffered until Smith finally drew away to an unassailable lead. He seemed to have ridden himself into fitness as the hours ticked by.

---

*Roy Cromack had bad luck on his End to End attempt this summer; he fell heavily in the Exeter area but continued as far as Whitchurch, where he abandoned. This information came to me via Les Lowe who saw him at Telford and Whitchurch.*

1974 had been a quieter year than many others due to most of the favourites having a rest. Entries were well down on other years. Over the four events of 1974, there were 128 entries, 116 starters and 72 finishers.

# 1975

The Catford 24hr on 28th June 1975, was a National Championship won by John Cahill, North Staffs St Christophers CC with 469.44 miles.

It was a sad occasion and was stated to be the last promotion of this famous event, but unlike recent years when entries had become very small, this year's field was excellent in quantity and quality. Many riders had entered as a gesture of respect to an event which had given so many people a lot of pleasure.

Leading entries were, Nim Carline, 6 times champion, Rod Goodfellow, defending champion and a previous Catford winner, and Robin Buchan who won the Catford so brilliantly four years previously when it was the championship. John Cahill who was second to Buchan that year was also a favourite, yet neither of the riders had raced at 24hrs since 1971. Granville Olive who had ridden to second place in last years championship, plus past winners, Cliff Smith, Reg Randall, Ken Smith and John Baines were all in contention.

Conditions at the noon start were cool and overcast with a force four north-easterly breeze. Carline set off at his usual tremendous pace and at 60 miles he led narrowly from Cahill by a few seconds, in fact with a time of 2hrs 33mins, with Robin Buchan at 4mins. Into the early evening and Carline had set a relentless pace, he'd caught Goodfellow and Cahill and obviously many others. At 114 miles he was 43mins inside 'evens', Goodfellow was 2nd at 6mins, with Cahill another 50 seconds adrift. Buchan was at 8mins 50secs, Olive at 9mins 30secs. At 148 miles, Carline and Cahill were locked in mortal combat quite close together on the road, Goodfellow was over 11mins slower than Carline. Buchan was at 13mins and Olive 15mins. Seventeen miles later, Cahill was starting to pick up speed, he'd re-caught Carline on the road and with elapsed time, Carline now only led the field by 4 minutes.

As the riders headed back east after riding the detours around Chichester, it was obvious that Cahill was riding more comfortably and confidently compared with his previous championship ride in 1971. He was riding lower gears, and this had transformed his normal grinding style of riding into a smooth flowing one. Carline was still hammering 'eye-balls out'; Goodfellow and Buchan both looked less fluid and neither looked happy.

Darkness made it difficult to get detailed time checks so it was 4am before the riders progress was logged. Reports came through that Cahill had levelled with Carline and that both had ridden identical 12 hour distances of 255 miles. From midnight to well after dawn the temperature dropped drastically but the leading riders were locked into such a fierce battle, none of them wanted to lose time putting on extra clothing and all of them suffered later as a consequence.

By dawn at 4am, Cahill led overall by 7 minutes from Carline and he led on the road by 15 minutes ahead of the whole field. The only other rider in contention other than Carline was Buchan, who appeared to be recovering. At 328 miles on the Steyning detour, Cahill was 30mins inside evens, but a rising north-easterly was soon to thwart the leaders progress. Goodfellow and Olive were adrift at 34mins and 45mins respectively and seemed to be dropping out of the picture, with Olive showing no signs of the huge effort he was to produce later on the finishing circuit. Cahill's efforts to stay ahead over the last eight hours seemed to have drained him and he was being overhauled not only by Carline but also by a fast moving Buchan, in fact Buchan took over the lead at this point (356m) by 4 minutes. Soon after that Carline climbed off defeated, just before Buchan caught him on the road. Goodfellow who had been struggling with hay fever had also retired by this point leaving Buchan and Cahill in the lead, but who would be third?

By 6am the riders were returning towards the Gatwick leg and the finishing circuit, but the wind was making progress very painful for the tired riders. Buchan developed eye trouble and had to receive treatment from his helpers, so losing valuable time. He was later seen struggling along the windswept Horsham by-pass looking very weary and although he was still in 2nd place at this stage he was suffering badly. He caught a string of slower moving riders, which included Cliff Smith and had a job pulling away from them. Cliff Smith had made an effort to come up through the middle of the field but he was still well below his best form of previous years and eventually finished with 430 miles.

By the time the finishing circuit was reached at 400 miles, Cahill had established a few minutes lead but looked extremely tired, and as witness to the tough conditions, he had only managed 16.6 mph for the last 80 miles to the circuit. Buchan and Cahill both produced very slow times for their first circuit but both riders gradually revived leaving Cahill to forge ahead again. Eventually he ran out time 6 miles ahead of Buchan, a very worthy winner of this very last Catford event.

Granville Olive meanwhile had made a terrific comeback effort in the last few hours of the event. He made an amazing bid for 2nd place by averaging 20mph for his last 4 hours on the finishing circuit, but at the end, he missed the 2nd place by just 70 yards! **The final result: 1st John Cahill,** North Staffs St Christopher's, **469.44miles, 2nd Robin Buchan,** Norwood Paragon, **463.79m** and **3rd, Granville Olive,** Oxonian CC with **463.75 miles. M.J. Titterton,** Gordano Valley was **4th** at his first attempt at 24hrs with **447.97 miles, M.B. Sheppard,** Catford CC, also a newcomer, rode very stylishly for **5th** place with **439.72m.**

**John Cahill led a North Staffs St Christopher's CCC team comprised of Mick Parker, 424.5miles and Tom Finney, 410.07, to a total of 1.304.05 miles,** beating the Oxonian CC team by 9 miles.

*My thanks go once again to Ian Shaw for his excellent report.*

*Jack Holdsworth who won the first Catford 24hr in 1925 shook hands with John Cahill the winner of this very last event.*

*Frank Fischer wrote in that same journal, that, although the winning mileage was not magnificent, the battle for supremacy between five top class riders was. He went on to say that it was quite the most exciting 24hr he'd ever seen. Out of 66 entries, 65 started and 51 riders finished. Jack Simmons, the Organiser, and his club, deserve praise for their efforts over the recent years. Ever decreasing entries and opposition from younger members in the club brought the promotion to an end. This event had been a fitting finale to 50 years of this famous Catford 24 hour race. Keith Hyatt of the Catford CC furnished me with many details, books and documents on the history of this famous old club, formed in 1886. Keith actually rode to one of his highest ever mileages in this final event with 396 miles.*

---

18th June 1975, saw George Berwick set out from Lands End on what can only be described as the longest solo bicycle attempt at the 'End to End' in modern times, before succumbing to defeat. He was attempting to improve Dick Poole's 1965 record of 1 day, 23 hours, 46 minutes 35 seconds.

From the start, George was always 'up' on Dick Poole's record and I will use a couple of relevant observations taken from an article by Don Spraggett who was one of George's main helpers.

"Heavy rain on 'the Pass of Killiecrankie', George put on his nylon jacket and tracksuit bottoms but nobody knew his legs weren't oiled. On the descents there was a considerable chilling effect and waterproof trousers would have been more effective to keep the wet and cold off his legs. George had obviously suffered over the Grampians on this cold wet second night, and by Inverness, he was only 11 minutes up on Poole's record. I got back on the road after Inverness, having had a 1.5hours sleep and rest break and I was very surprised to catch George up so quickly, he had suffered acute knee trouble, which came on after Dingwall. He was now in severe pain and **retired three miles beyond Evanton after covering 748 miles.** *Article courtesy of the 24hr Fellowship Journal.*

*George had another three attempts after that. In 1976 he got to Gretna 478 miles, in 1977 to Carlisle, 469miles and in 1980, Lancaster, 410 miles. The weather being the main reason for the abandonments.*

**The Wessex RC 24hr** on 19th July was **won** by **Fred Newton,** Wessex RC with a massive margin of 41 miles, to record **450.68 miles. J. Mortimer,** Bournemouth Jubilee was **2nd** with **408.82m. R.L. Gee,** Sotonia CC was **3rd** with **403.65m. Mrs Janet Tebbutt** rode **356.18 miles** and **G.V. Adams was the fastest trike rider with 388.07m.** Three riders retired in the night leaving 18 finishers from 21 starters. Three teams finished, the fastest being **Hampshire RC. 1,089.14 miles,** beating the Colchester Rovers by 22 miles, and the Clevedon & District by 57 miles.

---

**The Mersey RC 24hr on 26th and 27th July 1975, was won convincingly by Rod Goodfellow, with 478.69 miles** from **George Berwick,** 2nd with **443.16** and Sid Old, 3rd, with **438.37m. The South Lancs RC won the team race with 1,186.71 miles.** The team members being A.H. Stafford, 420.33, Nick Carter, 414.03 and **Claude Farrar on a trike with 352.35m. Paul Olson,** Liverpool Mercury, riding probably his first 24hr rode **420.87 miles** and **Steve Nicholas,** a popular 24hr fellowship member, rode **415.57 miles.**

Rod Goodfellow wrote a description of his ride and from it I've gleaned a few relevant details. I think Rod's near evens ride from a field of just 26 starters was excellent. It is noticeable that his first 12 hours mileage was 251 miles and this required a very brave effort to produce 226 miles second 12 hours, for his end result against very little competition.

Rod mentions packing at 320 miles in the Catford Championship a few weeks earlier, due to his eyes drying out and leaving him with very poor vision. The day of the race came and Rod who is a doctor had to work until 1.30pm. After a hurried journey to Tarvin he arrived at the start with just 20mins to spare. He knew his main opposition would be Sid Old and George Berwick. Berwick started very fast but a puncture in the opening miles left Rod to take the lead.

After the initial rural lanes section of the course was behind him, Rod found the remaining 400 miles quite boring with just a few highlights to remember it by, such as the coast road to Prestatyn, which had been drastically improved with various lit sections and that the aroma's from the various take away establishments in Queensferry were now of oriental cuisine. The Whitchurch to Nantwich detour, usually a 'graveyard' section, he quite enjoyed due to the dawn breaking, bringing with it the dawn chorus.

"It's fish, chips and mushy peas."

On the Wem to Welshampton section, he recalled being strafed by a twin engine fighter plane from the Potato Marketing board, which sprayed him for 'blight'. Another long and lonely plod took him back to the finishing circuit where he hoped to have been inside 'evens' but was disappointed to find he was just outside the 20 mph mark. He decided to ease his aching feet and lost a few more minutes and then set about trying to catch some riders on the circuit. He was almost past caring but after 2.5 laps he caught his first rider in 390 miles, the more riders he caught the faster he went, to finally finish at Huxley Chapel with 478.6m, and then wished he hadn't stopped to ease his feet!

So another good result, from 27 entries there were 26 starters and 21 finishers, plus 2 ladies, **Ethel Brambleby,** Hounslow and District Whls with **354.85m** and **Miss Amy Hooton,** Prescot Eagle RC with **332.54m. Dave Jackson,** Preston Whls, was the **fastest trike** rider with **371.39m.**

⮜⬦⮞

A month later on the 23rd and 24th August, **Gordon Hart,** Luton Whls, **won** the **North Road CC 24hr** with **452.142 miles. Cliff Smith,** who had been looking for his 11th win was still slightly below par and produced **444.003 miles** for **2nd** place. Roger Sewell had been one of the favourites and in fact led up until the 12 hour point with 236 miles. At 286 miles, Sewell and Hart were level when shortly afterwards, Sewell broke a crank. A spare bike proved unsatisfactory and he subsequently retired. Despite local heavy rain, Gordon Hart went on to win, with Smith 2nd, **D. Cruse, Maldon and District** was 3rd with **424.631m** and led R.A. Cruse and **G.R.F. Yuill** to a team win of **1,121.849 miles. J.A. Lovell,** Kettering Amateur was the **fastest trike** rider with **332.837 miles** and from a start card of 26, 17 riders finished.

## 1976

*Mini road islands are introduced this year.*

*In early* **May 1976,** *the 24hr Fellowship learned of the death of* **Robin Buchan.** *He was a tough rider who had won the Catford National in 1971 and he'd ridden to 2nd place in the Catford CC Championship 24hr in 1975.*

In late June the Wessex RC hosted possibly the hottest 24hr in history. It was won by Dick Usher, North Road CC with 425.42 miles The Wessex RC decided that upon the demise of the Catford event normally held in mid-June, that they themselves would avoid clashing with the Mersey RC event and so use the June date of 26th and 27th, 1976. A heatwave had just started and the weather got hotter and more sultry on the 2nd day, leading to retirements from this already depleted field. It was reckoned that the temperatures at Southampton had reached 95 degrees F, and Les Lowe, who packed at about 7 hours, said he thought that, on the claustrophobic tree lined stretches of the course, it was probably even hotter! Fred Newton, last years winner and this years favourite had several spells off the bike in the mid afternoon sun and was well down in the field placings, nearly 30mins behind the leader. By early evening many riders had retired, and a travelling marshal following the last man on the road told bystanders that he felt that at this rate, it would be doubtful if any more than half a dozen riders finished!

At the 129 miles check, Dick Usher, North Road CC, led the race with 6hrs 39mins. His brother Ken was 2nd at 3mins and Mike Greethead was 3rd at 4.5mins. At this point, Bill Kiddle, the timekeeper, predicted that the winner would cover less than 430 miles. By the morning only 10 riders remained and the temperature was to reach even higher than Saturdays, and with the exception of Dick Usher, the other riders were moving painfully slow and clearly they'd all had enough. It had certainly been 24hrs of pure hell. A few riders gave up on the finishing circuit, including Ron Geere, who collapsed with 1.5 hours to go, and also Pat Kenny, Birmingham St Christopher's CCC. Ten riders gallantly recorded mileages but I would think that only 6 or 7 actually rode the complete 24hrs. The outright **winner** was **Dick Usher** with **425.42 miles**. **Mike Greethead** was **2nd, 395.70m** and **R.L. Gee,** Sotonia CC was **3rd, 391.11m**.

*On July 20th 1976, an American Spacecraft 'Viking' landed on Mars and sent back TV pictures.*

*Just one week prior to the Mersey RC 24hr, Janet Tebbutt, set out from Lands End to attack the amateur End to End record held by Edith Atkins. Despite a hard westerly wind which plagued her to Perth, and heavy rain as she climbed Shap, she pushed her way North to be eventually rewarded with a southerly wind for the last 200 or more miles, so reaching John o' Groats to break the record with 2days 15hrs, 24mins and 20secs.*

⟹◆⟸

**The Mersey RC 24hr, 24th and 25th July 1976, was won by Rod Goodfellow with 476 miles. He again beat George Berwick,, Glasgow RC into 2nd place, but by a much smaller margin this time of just 12 miles with 464.11m. Vin Denson, a retired Tour de France professional took 3rd place with 449.31miles. Denson led a Redbridge CC team comprised of Eric Angell with 444.34m and E.J. Pheby 434.07, to a team win of 1,327.72 miles.**

Rod Goodfellow at the end of 1975 had decided to wind his long distance racing career up with an attack on the End to End in 1976, but a change of plans and a career move in the N.H.S., from Birmingham to Lancashire, altered his plans once again. By mid year, 1976, he'd abandoned his End to End plans and decided to ride the Mersey RC 24hr.

He started last man off with George Berwick 2 mins ahead of him. He took ages to catch George and 80 miles to overhaul the complete field. His first 12 hours was a re-run of his win the previous year and he clocked up 251 miles. There was more interest for him in this years event with riders to catch in the second 12 hours and on the run back to the finishing circuit against the wind, his helpers were urging him to try for 480 miles, but his legs only wanted him to do 460 miles. With a last 5 mile burst at 23 mph, he ran out time with 476 miles. He had proved that one can still produce an excellent ride at 24hours in the middle of a varied and disrupted racing season. He'd moved house in May, the day after the Anfield 100, and had worked all the hours possible due to missing personnel and he'd still triumphed at his favourite race!

George Berwick had ridden to a very good 2nd place mileage of 464.11 after a first twelve hours of 240 miles. The weather for the event had been cool and breezy at the start with cloud cover during the night to keep a comfortable temperature for the rider. At dawn the temperature dropped and heavy white mist lay over the fields and river banks. Vin Denson had secretly always wanted to ride a 24hr but his professional road racing status had prevented him riding until now. After experiencing bottom bracket trouble early on in the event he settled down to enjoy the rest of his ride, and like Ken Usher, he enjoyed a pint at midday.

Les Lowe, after suffering a puncture early on in the Queensferry area, also had trouble with broken toeclips at around 11 hours. He rode well in this years Mersey, after the disappointment from abandoning the Wessex 24hr in the extreme heat. He obviously found the Cheshire and Shropshire temperatures more to his liking. He recorded one of his best mileages with 436.51m. Graham Dayman of the Royal Sutton CC rode his one and only 24hr in this event. He had been so instrumental in helping Pat Kenny and myself on our record breaking at all levels. He was a very positive helper, his energy levels were boundless, and he was always so cheerful. He finished with 395.46 miles. In later years he took up marathon running and his job, distributing health products to gymnasiums connected him to the sport of weight lifting. Graham still keeps very fit and active and can be found helping and officiating at many high profile sporting events in not only the UK but also abroad.

I also rode that event in 1976 and I tried as hard as I could right from the start, ignoring all the advice of my peers to take it steady. My first 12 hours produced 226 miles and I really though that if Carline could ride like that, then so could I. I took a bit of a packet after 12 hours but I'm glad I rode as hard at the start because it helped me to finish with a personal best of 418.55 miles. Athletes such as Andy Wilkinson and Eric Matthews can control their starting efforts, so as to save energy for their 2nd 12hrs, but I found that however fast or slow I started I'd never got much left in the later stages, so for a person of my capabilities, 'going from the gun' was as good a way as any to ride. Pat Kenny my team mate also rode but suffered throughout to finish with 361.60 miles. From 38 starters, 29 finished.

"Yesterday, you were saving yourself for today.
What are you saving yourself for today?"

In this event the **ladies team 'The Prescot Eagles RC' established Competition record with 1,106.41 miles. The team comprised of Mrs Joan Kershaw with 404.82 miles, Mrs Ruth Williams, 360.76 and Miss Amy Hooton, 340.83m.** This record would stand for 29 years, and of course the ladies race is to be found in the ladies separate history in Chapter 5.

---

The North Road CC 24hr, a National Championship event was won by George Bettis, Bedfordshire RC with 482.603m, 2nd John Cahill, North Staffs St Christophers CCC, 467.912 and 3rd, Les Holmes, Luton Whls, 461.229. He led a Luton Wheelers team of Gordon Hart, 446.175 and Rob O'Dell, 415.824 to a Championship Team total of 1,323.22 miles, just beating the North Road CC trio of Ken Lovett, Dick Usher and Ken Usher by 3 miles. W.H. Wootton took the trike prize with 385.699 miles.

After the longest, hottest summer for many years, the weather chose Saturday 28th August to break, and it broke with a vengeance. It was a dismal scene at Little Paxton at the start of the event. Racing capes cracked in the strong wind and the rain poured down mercilessly as competitors and spectators alike huddled in cars, under hedgerows and trees, finding what shelter they could. Riders schedules were abandoned, but despite the weather, all of the big hitting favourites started, including Bettis, Carline, Cahill, Coupe, Olive, Baines, Tremaine, Blower, Hart, Lovett and the Usher brothers, Dick and Ken. What a field – quality and quantity, 86 entries for Sid Mottram's 27th and final 24hr promotion.

By the 100 mile point, the Timekeeper, Eric Wilkinson, returned the following riders times: Bettis led with 4hrs 30m 32s, Cahill at 31secs, Carline 4min 21s, Coupe, 8m, and Bowen 12m. The north easterly wind was troubling the riders on the exposed sections of road and Bettis who lived on the course knew all of its good and bad sections, he took advantage of this knowledge and surged ahead.

The action at dusk is often a turning point in a 24hr race and several 'hopefuls' must have despaired as the race leader swept past them. Lights and night clothing were donned as the skies cleared and the wind abated. The temperature was cool with the damp chill which strikes after heavy rains. Cambridge at 12 hours saw Bettis with a mileage of 253.5, Cahill, 250, Carline, 245.5, Holmes, 244.5 Olive and Blower, 238m, Tremaine and Hart, 236 miles.

As the riders made their first foray into the 'fens' at Wilburton , the tentacles of mist were just visible but by the early hours of Sunday morning as the riders tackled the Earith, Sutton and Soham detours from Streatham, they were surrounded by thick mist with visibility down to 5 yards or less. Nim Carline and Pete Etheridge collided head on outside Wicken Village, Etheridge was on a trike. Both riders suffered concussion, severe bruising and badly strained neck muscles. Etheridge also had a broken cheek bone and they were both taken by ambulance to Addenbrooks Hospital, Cambridge, and kept in for a week.

Bettis was still firmly in command on the road but with the intensity of peering into the dense mist for 7.5 hours he missed his feeding team at 310 miles. His regular feeding regime was 1lb of rice pudding every 35 miles and he was way past his normal feed time. He stopped and asked a crowd of club folk if anyone had any food to spare, and Steve Pontin produced a bar of chocolate which George ate with difficulty, being used to liquid rice pudding. His main worry once he got back on his bike was to the whereabouts of his helpers; (his wife, father and 10 year old son) had they crashed or broken down? He knew he could only continue without his regular rice pudding for another hour at the most and was so relieved to find them at Kisby's Hut. His speed over this 50 mile stretch had dropped dramatically, but after putting on tracksuit bottoms he started to recover as he felt the benefits of food and warmth. Even a puncture just before the finishing circuit couldn't slow him and he was finally stopped by Ron MacQueen at 483 miles, still feeling quite fresh.

Bernard Thompson interviewed George Bettis after his Championship win and asked him what his season had been like up to the event. George said that he started his serious training in November using a heavy winter bike with a motorbike battery for his lights. He averaged over 'evens' during training and by the time the 24hr event arrived, he'd covered nearly 15,000 training and racing miles. His main time trialling distances were 100's and 12 hours. But he was also a useful 50 miler and proved it by winning the 'Harrogate Nova' event just one month after the 24hr with 1hr 51mins.

In an 8 week period he'd won the 'ECCA' 12hr by 10 miles with 267.96 miles on August 8th. On August 15th he won the Northants DCA 12hr with 265.35 miles. On August 22nd, 5th place in the Southend and County 50 mile with 2hrs 1min, August 29th, Championship 24hr win, 482.6 miles, September 5th, Yorkshire Century '100' 3hrs 56-59 for 3rd place, September 12th, he won the Luton Whls 12hr by 10 miles with 265 miles, September 19th, Century '100' 4hrs 10mins 32s, a win again by 9 minutes and then the 50 miles as mentioned earlier. What an amazing 8 weeks! Bernard Thompson finished by saying that George's best bike was an old battered steel handle-barred machine that had seen better days. 'With thanks to the late Bernard Thompson and Cycling for permission to use these details'

The fog and mist was very slow to clear even during daylight and it had caused many riders to fall by the wayside during the night. Cahill plodded wearily on to the circuit for 2nd place, Owen Blower never recovered any speed after an early morning puncture, but Les Holmes riding his first 24hr made a dramatic recovery from dawn onwards to take 3rd place. I've just noticed looking down the result sheet that I also rode that event and finished with 404 miles. Two 24hrs in 1 year, Oh to be young again! All of the North Road CC events I rode were affected by mist in the night so I probably didn't think that this year was anything out of the ordinary.

*I do recall, in this event, that my eyes were very tired from peering into the fog to see the white line in the centre of the road during the night. After bumping the kerb a couple of times, I realised I was drifting off to sleep and decided to stop and curl up on the grass verge. It was just breaking dawn and I can remember sitting on my haunches with my head between my knees, eyes closed, and hearing the dream like sounds of tubular tyres swishing on the damp road surface as the riders passed in front of me. I paid heed to the words of one of my mentors, John Withers, who had told me that to relax the eyelid muscles for just a minute or two by closing them was enough to combat tiredness. He was right, but I was lucky that the cold damp conditions also kept me from going into a deep sleep.*

In hindsight, the collision between Carline and Etheridge is almost a re-run of the North Road event of 1923, when at around the 100 mile mark, Frank Armond, was 'put out of the running' when he collided 'head on' with W.S. Gibson of the Century RC. Both riders were very badly cut about the head and nose.

So, nothing changes.

John Cahill, in an article to the 24hr Fellowship Journal, gave some explanation for his 2nd placing in the North Road event, quite a few miles behind George Bettis. He'd spent a fortnight in Germany shortly before the event, he was riding in the Taunus mountains, overlooking Frankfurt, when he crashed, tearing ligaments in his left shoulder. The ride home up the Rhine, across Holland and Belgium, became even more painful after developing an abscess in his 'saddle area'! The two ailments caused considerable distress during the event and in the second 12hours he was reduced to riding with one arm and easing himself out of the saddle.

To add to the problems, he lost his helpers for quite a while when they stopped to help Nim Carline and Pete Etheridge after their collision. John wasn't trying to make any excuses for his lower mileage and he described George Bettis's winning ride as 'brilliant'! After taking a month or two to heal his wounds, John set about a 10 month training programme to win the Mersey RC 1977 championship event.


# 1977


**The Wessex RC 24hr** June 25th and 26th 1977. The weather at the start was dull and overcast with a westerly wind, it was dubbed as Dick Poole's comeback year, after a nine year break. He was aided by Sid Hygate and Mike Greethead. The traffic on the main roads around Ringwood and the New Forest was becoming a menace and a threat to this event, with riders having to weave in and out around slowly moving cars with caravans. In fact, Phil Downer, Bournemouth Jubilee Whls, was a victim of one such incident, where an impatient driver decided to pull out of a queue and do a turn in the road. Phil sustained bruises and a wrecked bike! The race was a wide open one with a sprinking of good riders, Ken Usher, Dick Poole, Fred Newton, Tom Ellis, D.J. Grundon, R.J. Elliott and a team of Frenchmen from the U.S. Creteil club, J. Richard, J.E. Gagneur and J.S. Duvivier. 27 riders started and after a few hours the riders in the lead were Usher, Newton, Poole and Elliot. By 100 miles, Usher had retired, and Elliott went through in the fastest time with 4hrs 38mins. Newton was at 4mins and Poole at 10mins.

After a few heavy showers interspersed with sunshine, Dick stopped for dry socks but was soon on his way. Dick deliberately didn't want to start too fast and by 155 miles, he'd slowed to 6th place behind Elliott with 7hrs 30mins, Newton was at 13mins, Ellis at 18mins, Richard 22mins, and Poole at 34mins. Sid Hygate was quite concerned that Dick Poole's food supplies wouldn't be enough for 24hrs and so called at Bisterne, the H.Q, to pick up some more supplies including rice pudding. Fred Newton called in for a sit down feed of bacon and egg. He seemed loathe to hurry back onto his bike, and it is thought he probably got cold here which would account for his overall drop to 6th place with a ride of 422 miles.

At the 12 hour check Dick went through with 226 miles covered and now lay 2nd to Elliott. At dawn, 290 miles, Elliott went through in 15hrs 36mins, Poole and Richard at 4mins, Ellis at 6mins, Grundon and Newton at 22m. With 8 hours to go it was feared that Dick would run out of food so contingency plans were made and one of the helpers, Glenda Fisher, went home to raid her larder at 5am, so that Dick could keep going.

Elliott caught Dick on the road and led him by 5mins, and as the riders headed for the finishing circuit it was thought that Elliott would win from Poole with Grundon 3rd, but once Grundon reached the circuit, he put in some very fast lap times which seriously challenged Dick's position, but he was able to respond and beat him by nearly 4 miles.

The final result was R.J. Elliott, CC Breckland, 1st with 443.35 miles, Dick Poole, Farnborough and Camberley Bikit, 2nd with 435.24m and 3rd, D.J. Grundon, Westerley RC, 431.58m. U.S. Creteil won the team race with 1,227.94m from the Hampshire RC 1,216.49 miles. From a field of 27, 20 riders finished.

---

**The Mersey RC 24hr National Championship** on 23rd and 24th July 1977 **was won** by **John Cahill,** North Staffs St Christopher's CCC, with **477.25m. Mick Coupe,** also N. Staffs St Christophers was **2nd** with **467.50 miles** and **Ian Dow,** Oxford City RC was **3rd** with **458.87 miles. With Mick Parker riding 415.33 miles, North Staffs St Christopher's won the Championship Team prize with 1,360.08 miles.**

The favourites for this year's event were George Bettis, Rod Goodfellow, John Cahill, Mick Coupe, George Berwick and Ian Dow. Although George Berwick being a Scotsman, was not eligible for an English National Championship medal.

By 100 miles, John Cahill led the race with 4hrs 32m 52secs. At the 117 mile checkpoint, Cahill was well ahead with 5hrs 23mins, Bettis was 2nd at 5mins, Goodfellow 3rd at 13m, Dow at 14m and Coupe at 16m. The ride up the coast road to Prestatyn was a struggle into a stiff westerly wind, Cahill pulled out all of the stops on this tough stretch turning his 97" gear quite comfortably. By Whitchurch, George Bettis had faded and he retired. The Mersey RC 24hr isn't his favourite event and he has yet to win on this course. By the return leg from Nantwich at 241 miles, Cahill was 40mins up on Goodfellow who was troubled with a stomach ailment, which was to see him retire after 15 hours.

Cahill's 12 hours distance was 253 miles. 2nd to Cahill at 12hrs was Ian Dow, with 243 miles, a 19 year old 'novice' rider but a superb fixed wheel exponent, and 3rd at 12 hrs was Mick Coupe with 238 miles. George Berwick was 4th with 235m and George Fish 5th, with 234m. The return to the finishing circuit via Wem and Welshampton was another tough ride into a westerly. During the event it was noted that Ken Hughes and Ken Price were riding again after years out of action.

Ian Dow, a newcomer to 24hr racing admitted to being seized by nervousness at the start. He took John Gills' advice not to get caught up in 'on the road' battles in the first few hours, and at dusk he started to overhaul riders who had passed him earlier on. Ian recalls passing through Whitchurch after 12 hours which gave him 239 miles and left him disappointed, but the actual Mersey RC result sheet has him down as riding 243 miles at 12 hours. He jokingly talks about struggling against a tough wind in the night and wondered whether he had missed the turn at Prestatyn and was heading towards Snowdonia!

At about 15 hours after a battle with George Berwick he suddenly realised the enormity of the event and felt sick. At Redbrook after 370 miles, he closed the gap on Goodfellow who climbed off just before being caught. The long road to the finishing circuit saw Ian counting the number of hours and minutes to go. The monotony was broken at one point when a van went past, on the back of which was printed '24hr Recovery Service'. Ian said he was ready to climb into the van and then realised it wasn't connected to the event. This brought on fits of laughter from Ian and prevented him from riding in a straight line! He remembers entering the finishing circuit to cheers and clapping; it was a terrific moment for him. From there onwards he achieved almost 20 mph to finish 3rd, for a magnificent first time ride.

From an entry of 55 riders, 51 started and 31 finished.

At this time in the history of the 24hr time trial and indeed any distance of time trial on the road, the 'fixed wheel single geared bicycle' had almost gone out of fashion with the advent of reliable multiple gearing systems, giving up to 12 speeds. Ian Dow was one of the last 24hr champions to use a fixed wheel in preference to gears, with only Karl Austin (as at 2007) the only winner and regularly placed 24hr rider to still use a 92" single fixed gear. The multiple gear mechanisms on the market at this time in 1977, were Huret, Simplex and Campagnolo. although Sturmey Archer hub gears were still available, they were only used on ladies and gents town, commuting and touring bicycles, and of course by Cliff Smith.

The North Road CC 24hr on 27th August, was **won by Dave Cruse, Maldon and District CC with 432.656 miles, 2nd was Les Lowe, Speedwell B.C. 424.174m, 3rd Dick Usher 419.182, he led his brother Ken with 414.945m and Pete Ambrose 359.183, to a Willesden CC team win of 1,193.310 miles.**

A very windy afternoon was followed by a superb moonlit night and a glorious Sunday morning. George Bettis and Cliff Smith were the two favourites to win, but George Bettis pulled out before the start with a bad knee, leaving the race wide open. At 16 hours, Cliff Smith had trouble with his bike and for the first time ever in a 24hr, he hadn't brought a spare machine.

At one time, it was thought that Les Lowe may win, so adding the famous Speedwell BC to the list of winners, but Dave Cruse seized the opportunity in the last few hours, finishing very strongly with 432.656 miles. From 23 starters, 18 finished.

# 1978

The Wessex RC National Championship 24hr saw **John Cahill, North Staffs St Christopher's produce his first 20 mph ride to record 482.25 miles   Keith Wright, Chippenham and District/John's Bikes, 469.48 miles was 2nd, Graham Mann, Hainault RC was 3rd with 466.50m. Mick Coupe took 4th place with 461.69 and with Mick Parker's 421.84, North Staffs St Christopher's CCC took the Championship Team prize for the second successive year, with a total of 1,365.78 miles.**

At the 100 mile check, Cahill with 4hrs 28m 41s led from Coupe by 2mins, Knight at 4mins, Woodman 6mins, Mann was 5th and Wright 6th, Howard 7th and Berwick 8th. The heavy holiday traffic at Totton where the 100 mile check was made, had riders literally 'rubbing bumpers' as the cars impeded their progress.

The night turned bitterly cold and the strong wind that had been nagging the riders since the start, continued to blow throughout the night. Back at Ringwood the riders had covered 195 miles, Cahill was firmly in the lead with 9hrs 9mins 50secs. Mann was 2nd at 20mins, Coupe 3rd at 29mins, Wright at 30mins, Woodman at 35mins and Howard, 37mins. Between here and 259 miles, Pete Howard retired and Cahill passed in 12hrs 46mins, now 40 mins clear of 2nd placed rider Mann, Wright was 3rd, Coupe 4th.

Despite the bitterly cold night, Cahill rode through it in his silk racing vest and shorts. His only concession was to don a woollen jersey after dawn. Dick Poole thought it was the coldest 24hr night he could remember.

Sunday was another cold windy day as the weary riders finished their slog around the finishing circuit. Cahill being over 10 miles in the lead was assured of another Championship victory with Wright and Mann battling it out for the places.

Graham Mann in a 24hr Fellowship article describes being caught by Cahill. "Next came the long grind from Southampton to Christchurch, into the strong wind, and then with it on our sides up to the top turn at Whyle. It was on this leg that John Cahill caught me, and it brought home to me how strong he was, as I couldn't even hold him for a short time. As he passed I gave him some verbal encouragement but didn't get much of an answer as his mouth was full of food, but he looked relieved to catch me, presumably another one he didn't have to worry about.".

Graham's next encounter was with Mick Coupe who he caught shortly after dark and then embarked on a struggle with him all night. Graham said "He would ride for about 2 hours really hard, knocking hell out of my reserves, but with me just able to hold him at about half a minute and then just as I was on the verge of cracking completely, he would stop with his helpers for anything up to about 5 or 6 minutes and I would get a breather for 30 or 40mins until he caught me again, and so it went on. If only he knew how close he was to breaking me!"

Graham for some reason was turned off various detours around dawn, even though he was up with the leaders, this threw him for a while but he soon recovered and led the race on the road back to the finishing circuit, where he completed almost five circuits for 3rd place with 466.5 miles.

George Berwick, unusually so far south from his beloved Scotland, took 5th place with 438.24m.   Knight of the Gordano Valley with 437.48 led a team consisting of M.J. Titterton and M.J. Horwood  to a 2nd team total of 1,290.26m.  R.E. Fox, Becontree Whls CC was 7th with 437.40m, Sid Hygate, making a long awaited comeback, took 8th place with 434.05 miles and Cliff Smith was 9th with 431.32 narrowly beating Woodman by .18 of a mile.

� decorative divider⟩

**The Mersey RC 24hr** on 22nd and 23rd July 1978 was **won** by **Colin Chambers,** Sharrow CC with **454.68 miles. J. McAllister** was **2nd** with **452.10** and **Ian Dow** was **3rd** with **438.53 miles.**

From looking at the start sheet, it would have been anyone's guess as to the favourites, although there were some well known names towards the back of the field.   Les Lowe, Sid Old, Malcolm Judge, George Berwick, Ian Dow, John Arnold, Middleton CC on a trike was the last man off, perhaps making a comeback? after all it had been nearly 30 years since he took the time trial and record breaking sport by storm, mainly on a trike but also on a tandem trike with Albert Crimes.

Ian Dow was more than likely one of the favourites; this bespectacled young student had broken onto the scene in last years Mersey National Championship by coming 3rd with 458.87 miles.   In a 24hr Fellowship article he describes getting to the start of this Mersey (1978) event bursting with 'overconfidence' and 12,000 miles in his legs since Christmas.  At the beginning of his article he asks the question –

*"If you are terrified by something, you can also be drawn towards it by an irresistible force, this being apparent in mountaineers and some cliff-top suicide cases.   Could it have something to do with why we ride the 24's?"  Ian went on to say that "all the ingredients for a bad ride were there and sure enough, I produced one.   I spent the first 10 hours battling hard trying to shake off a lousy sluggishness and then blew-up.   At 12 hours I realised I couldn't go on, speed was down to single figures and the weather, already bad, was deteriorating. Then Joe Pilling re-caught me, oh yes, he was going to finish alright and in a fit of youthful insanity, I decided to follow his example and so I plodded on for another 200 miles.*

*While lapping the 15mile finishing circuit, outside the hour, I swore that pride would be restored and an entry for the North Road 24hr was in the post next day!"*

I too rode that Mersey 24hr in 1978, I'm pleased that I did so, for two reasons.  The first being that I actually got to riding alongside John Arnold, although I can't remember whether I caught him or whether he caught me.   He retired in the night with a bad back, but was still very chatty when I was with him at about 125 miles.   The second reason was that this would be the last Mersey RC event that went up the Welsh coast road to Prestatyn and back, in fact the furthest north that subsequent events would venture to is Christleton Island, so no more Saltney to Marford and back, Queensferry and the bright lights and gas 'burn off' pipes at the oil refinery.   That part of the course is now confined to the history books.

I have no other descriptions of how Colin Chambers won the event or how John McAllister took 2nd place, so I cannot comment.   George Berwick came 4th with 429.38m and Don Spraggett, 5th, 414.17m.

From 34 entries, 34 started and 19 finished.

⟨decorative divider⟩

**The North Road CC 24hr on the 26th and 27th August 1978, was won for the first time by Ian Dow, Oxford City RC with 472.549 miles.   Don Saunders, Breckland CC was 2nd with 464.218 miles and popular North Roader, Ken Lovett, was 3rd with 441.319 miles.  The team race was won by the Hertfordshire Wheelers with 1,141.562 miles.**

The event was run off in very fine weather but the night was bitterly cold. Thirty riders started and twenty finished.

Ian Dow, after grovelling to 3rd place in the Mersey event just a few weeks previously was determined to make amends.  In that short space of time, he put in some very tough training miles, riding between 150 to 250 miles every other day at an average of 18 mph, using a low 69" fixed wheel gear.  He said:

*"I think it counted as tough even by George Bettis standards.  Mad? Possibly, but I was prepared to do it for three and a half weeks and it would be great to look back on.  After a couple of weeks of this, I rode a 4hr 9min, 100 miles and I knew then that 470 plus miles was on.  Being only 20 years of age and at that, often mistaken for a 15 or 16 year old, I knew I had some laughs in store.*

*I started recklessly catching the whole field (30 riders) from the back, in 70 miles, and passing the '100' check in 4hrs 32 mins.  It was all or nothing this time.  Another '100' went by in 4hrs 43mins; 253 miles for the first 12 hours, only a mile short of a personal best.  The night closed in but I was still going strong.  Just how long could I keep this up?*

*I soon discovered, coming down through St Neots shortly after 2am, I ran smack bang into a 'brick wall' very reminiscent of the one I had suffered in the Mersey.  I looked down to see if I had sprung a leak, but there was no trail of rice pudding; was this the end?*

*It has since transpired that a lot of people had been confidently standing back waiting for me to 'blow' and here they thought their predictions had been right, but I wasn't giving up, and after a long, desperate fight, I pulled myself together again.*

*The sun rose, only six hours to go, I was a few minutes up on schedule and not too much the worse for wear. Onto the circuit and the world was filled with music.  My final effort was soon producing 'evens' and it looked like a 474 miles ride, but I had misjudged it and with 15 minutes to go I lost everything.  This time I really was finished and I crawled to the last timekeeper for 472 miles.  And then, aahh, what bliss, to lie on the grass in the warm sunshine and drop off to sleep".*

His helpers, Connie and Bing Wilson had looked after his every need for this classic win with such a high mileage.

*My thanks to Ian for his honest and amusing description.*

---

And so, the end of another year of declining entries and interest in 24hr racing.  Roy Cromack, the current record holder, blamed the softening attitude of riders who hardly ever ride out to events and do most of their racing on 'dragstrip courses'.  For this, he blamed the structure of the British Best All Rounder Competition, a competition biased towards short distance, speed and fast roads.

*Ironically, these are the very words and thoughts that I have re-iterated when describing Lynne and Marina's position in the women's BBAR some 27 years later, a situation made even more noticeable due to women only having to ride distances of 25, 50 and 100 miles for their best all round performances, unlike the men.*

Eric Matthews suggested a long distance competition based on a 100mile, a 12hr and a 24hr to be run by the 24 hr Fellowship.  Ian Dow, one of our youngest ever 24hr winners felt that more publicity would help enormously, after all, how could anyone be interested in something they didn't even know exists?  He blamed the current 'Cycling' magazine and suggested the idea of a purely time-trialling magazine.

# 1979

The month of May 1979 saw the first of 3 attempts on the Lands End to John o' Groats tandem trike record by Pat Kenny and myself, John Taylor. The record we were attempting to beat had been held by Albert Crimes and John Arnold since 1954, and included the 12hr, 24hr End to End and 1,000 mile records.

Pat and I had broken many Midland RRA records and three National RRA records between 1976 and 1979, as a build up to the End to End and seemed to spend every spare moment either training or racing on the tandem trike. Pat knew the history of their attempt and that Crimes and Arnold had lots of time off the tandem trike during their record ride, due to illness, food and toilet stops, plus a bath and a sleep stop, all amounting to possibly four hours or more. If we had a similar wind to them and took little or no time off the machine other than for the absolute essentials, then we stood just the slimmest chance of breaking the End to End record.

It was a very tight record as Crimes and Arnold were two of the toughest champion cyclists Great Britain has ever seen. It was deemed that their End to End performance was years ahead of its time, and was two hours faster than the solo record held by Sid Ferris.

*At that time, I felt that it was almost an irreverence that I should be part of an attack on such prestigious records, but Pat had broken John Arnolds trike 24hr RRA record in 1965, and he was a firm believer in chance. By using various graphs showing their progress against what we could possibly produce in mph by not stopping, it was a feasible proposition and in practice it nearly worked. Although we would have missed the record by approximately two hours if we had continued for the last 80 miles, I now feel vindicated for attempting their record. With the knowledge that we had a poorer wind on the 2nd day and one that turned against us, plus the time we lost with my knee problem, I feel now that we weren't 'disgraced' by our effort.*

The day Pat and I started we had good weather and a good wind. At the 24hr point we had covered 448 miles, leaving just 422 miles to cover in the remaining 28 hours, which equates to approximately 15 mph. When we reached the top of Shap the wind dropped and it remained calm and unhelpful from then on. We had various problems from Carlisle onwards which cost us valuable time. A badly swollen knee from Edinburgh onwards, plus a total lack of wind from Shap to Inverness being our main worries but we battled on towards Inverness. After the Aultnamain climb a tough North Easterly wind blew against us. With just 4 hours left to go and with 80 very tough miles remaining which included the two major climbs of Helmsdale and Berriedale still to do, the consensus of opinion from our helpers and timekeeper Roy Moss, was that the record was now irretrievable, and we climbed off at Bonar Bridge. It was deemed that we would be approximately two hours outside the record.

We were obviously disappointed but at the same time I was pleased to have got so close to a Crimes and Arnold record. The opinions of all our back up team, including Alan Richards, Tony Shardlow, Graham Dayman and timekeeper Roy Moss, was that we should make another attempt as soon as was practically possible.

Two months later, we started again from Lands End, but the weather forecast had misled us and the predicted wind didn't arrive, but a stifling 80 degree breeze did. To cap it all, the top tube of our tandem trike broke whilst riding along the Bridgwater Flats. Alan Richards put us on his spare machine, and he motored back to his bike shop in Birmingham where he brazed a new tube into place. By the time we reached Wolverhampton, we were down on schedule. We transferred back onto our own machine but without a helping wind we couldn't achieve the speed needed, and 'packed' at Trentham Gardens near Stone.

One month later we had one final try, using a new route through Glasgow and the West of Scotland, but after 20 hours of rain we abandoned at the far end of Loch Lomond, beaten once again by the elements and time.

As I write this particular part of the 24hour and connected RRA record breaking history, I am reminded even more so of the toughness and invulnerability of this record. Last night 3/8/07, I went out to Gailey Island with Liz and Lynne. Gailey is where the A449 crosses the A5 in Staffordshire and is part of the current End to End route. We waited for Ralph Dadswell and Dave Johnson, on a tandem trike, to come through on their attempt. At 11.30pm they were 30 minutes down on a schedule that matched Crimes and Arnold's ride. Ralph and Dave had got very close to the Crimes and Arnold's 12 hour record of 257.75m en route at Worcester; close enough in fact to have it re-measured, due to road improvements at Indian Queens, which affected total distances. Later, as I contacted the telephone H.Q. provided by Allison and Martin Purser, I was told that the riders had a rough time climbing 'Shap', but had recovered enough to get very close to the 24hr record of 466.25 miles, also held by Crimes and Arnold; in fact close enough to also have measured.

Later that day, I found that they had abandoned their attempt on the climb to Beattock Summit around the 500 mile distance. No specific reason was given at the time of enquiring, only tiredness. The wind and conditions at that time were still favourable.

Ralph currently holds upwards of thirty five RRA records, including the trike End to End and also nine with Marina Bloom on the Tandem Trike. He is the most prolific record breaker in the history of the RRA and also holds the RTTC tandem trike 24hr competition record with Dave Johnson, a ride of 466.72 miles.

This record of Crimes and Arnold is now 54 years old as at 2008 and looks like being on the shelf for a very long time. John Arnold at 80 years of age was ringing up the telephone H.Q. regularly, urging the riders to 'go faster'.

I always felt that Jackson and Hargraves were perfectly capable of breaking these tough records, the fact that they were both event winners at 24hrs made them even more suitable. Both Stuart and Edwin had produced solo 24hr rides well in excess of Pat's and mine and had proved themselves on various RRA tandem trike records during those years.

Later on the day Dadswell and Johnson packed, I had a call from Mike Johnson (no relation to Dave) who was out helping on the attempt from the Wigan area onwards. He said that they still had a very good wind behind them when they packed so maybe it was a psychological reason. The fact that they had possibly failed at the 12hr and 24hr records after getting so close may have had an adverse effect on them. The fact that Crimes and Arnold also had a very long rest break at Abington just beyond Beattock, had possibly been overlooked. When they 'packed' they had covered approximately 500 miles with 340 miles left to do in 25 hours to break the record. John Arnold phoned me the day after Dadswell and Johnson failed, and he recalled Albert saying to him "we've got to go faster, we can break two days if we try even harder." John said all he could think of was keeping body and soul together to reach John o' Groats.

Currently, I don't know what the answer is, but whoever is thinking of attempting this record needs to be capable of 450 miles on a bike. It obviously needs to be two very evenly matched riders of similar size, and they need to have trained together over a period of 2 years or more, on a tandem trike, with both riders capable of riding either the front or the rear of the machine.

It would be very interesting to see what Marina Bloom and Lynne Taylor could do together, either on a tandem or a tandem trike over this long journey?

*Margaret Thatcher became the first woman Prime Minister on May 4th 1979*

In 1978 plans had been put in place for a 'one-off' **National Championship 24hr** to be run by the **North Midlands Cycling Federation.** Trevor Wilkinson was to be the Organiser and Frank Minto was to be the Detour Controller, along with a team of experienced helpers, who annually ran an association 12hour on this proposed course. Christine Minto would be heading a team of timekeepers.

Those plans were put into action on Saturday 16th June 1979 at 15.01 when Jimmy Hall of the Rutland CC started in the first 24hr event to be promoted by a Yorkshire club or Alliance, since the Yorkshire Vegetarian event in 1939. The late Benny Hudson, a prolific 24hr man, and Ted Potter would have been proud, in fact it was symbolic that the start was opposite the 'Ted Potter' seat on Blyth Green.

Following Jimmy Hall were 51 experienced and inexperienced 24hr riders on an almost triangular course stretching from Austerfield in the north to Lincoln in the east and to Gunthorp (Notts) in the south, plus obviously any deviations and detours. Last years team champions were there including the individual champion, Cahill, Coupe and Parker. Tom Finney was 4th man as an extra rider for the team. Local heroes, Mike McNamara, 'Ticker' Mullins and Graham Barker seemed to be the only really serious challenge to the St Christopher's lads and they all received a rapturous applause as they left the starting line. Nim Carline was also one of the top favourites although things hadn't always gone to plan for Nim in recent rides. John Baines was another 'local' rider looking for a decent ride.

A warm afternoon and evening saw the field on its way with the champions battling for supremacy. Nim, naturally hoping for a win on local roads took the lead and at the Green Tree, Hatfield (98.1 miles) Carline rode it in 4hrs 21mins, Mullins at 4m, Coupe at 5mins, Don Saunders at 6m, Mortimer 7m, Cahill at 9mins, Alan Peachey also at 9mins, Barker 11mins, McNamara 14m and Finney 19m. After a detour to Austerfield the course retraced southwards down the A1 to Newark. A warm clear night was enjoyed by the riders on an almost traffic free A1. At Newark, 183.6 miles Carline still led the field in 8hours 22mins. Coupe was 2nd at 11mins, Cahill 3rd at 15mins and Mullins 4th at 18mins.

A very dark night saw the riders leave the A1 as they turned eastwards through Newton-on-Trent to Lincoln racecourse at 219.3 miles. The course now retraced back to Newark and at 239.4miles Carline and Coupe were equally timed at 11hrs 21mins with Cahill 3rd at 1min. Crossing the A1 at Newark the riders went southwest towards Nottingham; early morning light dispersed the darkness. A slowly rising sun promised a warm second 12 hours and the riders times at 256.9 miles were Coupe and Carline at 12hrs 12mins, Cahill at 1min, Mullins at 5m, Mortimer at 22mins, Barker at 29mins and McNamara at 52mins. Alan Peachey was at 1hr 3mins, Mick Parker at 1hr 18mins and level with Finney. The North Staffs St Christopher's lads were winning the team race by **7secs** from the Rockingham CC and the Morley by **45secs.**

By Blyth Church only Cahill, Coupe, Mullins, Carline and Barker had ridden the full course up to here (341.5 miles). Cahill in 16hrs 21mins, Coupe at 6m, Mullins at 12mins, Carline at 38m and Barker at 54 mins. By 371 miles at Cantley, Mortimer had packed; this excluded the Morley from the team race, and 7 miles later, Carline also retired.

By the start of the finishing circuit at 418.9 miles, Coupe led in 20hrs 21mins, Cahill was 2nd at 5mins, Mullins was 3rd at 10mins and Barker 4th at 1hr 7mins. At 23 hrs the Progress Board showed the same position, Coupe 472 miles, Cahill 469, Mullins 466, Barker 448, McNamara, 435, Peachey 429 and Parker 417 miles. The first 6 riders all produced personal bests at the finish and wisely none of them had been tempted to scrap with Nim Carline in the early stages of the race.

**Mick Coupe was 1st with 492.682 mile, John Cahill 2nd, 489.010 led a North Staffs St Christophers CCC team including Mick Parker, 435.706 miles to a 3rd successive Championship team win and a new Competition Record of 1,417.394 miles. Tom 'Ticker' Mullins came 3rd with 485.436 and led Graham Barker 469.044m and Mike McNamara, 454.827, to a 2nd team total of 1,409.307 miles for the Rockingham CC, which also broke Comp record,** but it came too late to be claimed as, the St Christopher's had already finished with a greater mileage.

From 51 riders, 35 finished, in this well run event.

＞•◇•＜

One week later on 23rd June, **The Wessex RC 24hr was won** by **George Berwick** with **443.39 miles, Cliff Smith** was **2nd** with **439.1 miles** and **Rob Dowling** was **3rd** with **422.47miles.**

16 riders started and 13 finished.

It states on the result sheet that no team finished but on closer inspection, I noticed that **Chris Davies with 399.18 miles, led a Hampshire RC team consisting of R.G. Davies and P.J. Smith to a total of 1,144.78 miles.**

＞•◇•＜

*On 11th July 1979, **Paul Carbutt** set off from Lands End to tackle the first attempt on the End to End since pre-war days, by a Professional Cyclist, riding for Viking Cycles. This talented rider had been a National Champion at 50 and 100 miles, also 12hours and was the BBAR winner in 1977. He had also ridden in the Olympics as a team time trial rider and had ridden to 3rd place in the Milk Race of 1977.*

*During his End to End ride, over the 'Devils Beeftub' climb, he collapsed at the side of the road, exhausted from heat stroke, but after his back up team had cooled him down he continued through Scotland, to take the record from Dick Poole by 23 minutes, with a ride of **1day 23 hours, 23mins, 1sec.** Paul joins a small select band of riders who have broken this record without having previously ridden a 24hr race, others include Pauline Strong and Andy Wilkinson, plus a few earlier lady riders who weren't allowed to ride 24hr time trials.*

<hr />

**The Mersey RC 24hr on 28th and 29th July was won by Al Mansley,** East Liverpool Whls, with **445.756miles. Stan Spraggett was 2nd with 432.640m** and **J.C. Hulme, Mersey Rc 3rd with 431.302m. He led a Mersey RC team consisting of B.G.Rawling with 401.437m and Dave Denman, 355.224, to a team win of 1,187.963 miles.** They narrowly beat a team from the A5 Rangers, by 6.5 miles.

This was the first Mersey RC 24hr using the new course format, with the coast road to Prestatyn getting even busier at night and various detours on the Wirral and north of Chester also getting more difficult to marshal it was decided to concentrate the revised course in Shropshire and roads south of Chester. A new section of course was added this year, from Ternhill to Chetwynd Heath, Newport and return, plus a small detour from Tern Hill to Market Drayton and return.

Al Mansley at 45 years of age was riding his first 24hr race. He'd always had an ambition to ride one from as far back as 1957 and his club's record, held by Les Russell with 407miles in 1948, had always been his target. Between 1957 and 1979 lots of things had cropped up to prevent Al from realising this dream. He had many years off the bike but when his son Barry started cycling, it was then that Al re-kindled that interest.

1979 arrived with snow and he was reduced to running to keep fit during the winter. Easter saw him ride 114 miles in training in one ride and he said that when he fell through the front door, his immediate worry was how was he going to manage another 300 miles, all in 24 hours. He started racing at the end of April on an 88" fixed gear, he stepped up his training with big distances to work and back, turning a normal 6 mile ride into 58 miles. In May he did a 10hr ride covering 174 miles on the Mersey RC course. In June he rode the Windsor-Chester-Windsor audax event and part of it was done in the company of George Berwick. Al calculated that not allowing for the stops on the route, he'd done 380 miles in 23.5 hours which gave him great confidence.

In the remaining weeks to the event, he rode a fair amount of time trials and rode out to all of them and back home. He arrived on the start line at the Mersey RC 24 hr with 5,000 hard miles in his legs and rode on an 86"fixed gear. Dave Threlkeld and his wife Norma, looked after him for the first 100 miles and then his own wife, Vera, brother-in-law Ray, and clubmate Colin, looked after him for the remainder of the event.

John Hulme led for the first 100 miles and Al recorded 5hrs for his first 100. His only problems during the race were having to stop every 70 miles to soak his foot in a bucket of water to ease a tender spot on the ball of his foot. A broken toe clip and loose bottom bracket were his only other worries. He suffered a bad patch struggling into the wind to Shawbirch and on the way back he made himself eat a lot to overcome this. He also struggled on the Wem to Redbrook section and found it to be the hardest part of the course, but the following wind from there to the finishing circuit made it all worth while.

He'd won his first open time trial at 45 years of age with an ambition to ride more 24hr events in the future.

*My thanks to Al for his comments taken from a 24hr Fellowship Journal. Al is currently (as at 2007) the 24hr Fellowship Treasurer, a job he has carried out for quite a lot of years.*

The Gold Medal that Al won for gaining his East Liverpool Wheelers 24hr record was the original one presented to Les Russell in 1948. Les very kindly had it ground smooth and re-engraved with Al's new mileage. *Information courtesy of Dave Threlkeld.*

Mrs Jenny Colman, Scarborough Paragon, also finished in this race, with 370 miles and would have been placed 15th out of 30 male riders.

⟹•◇•⟸

**The North Road CC 24hr 1979 was won for the second year running by Ian Dow, Oxford City RC with 471.091 miles. Ken Lovett, North Road CC was 2nd with 446.256m and Roger Sewell, 3rd, with 443.930. Cliff Smith was 4th with 441.786. Bob Mynott completed the North Road team with a 392.831 mile ride and a team total of 1,283.017 miles.**

Bob Mynott who had been brought out of retirement for this event, hadn't ridden a 24hr for 29 years. He won this event in 1950, with a 459.5 miles Competition Record ride. Ian Dow who had a runaway win in this event wrote a description of his ride and from it I've taken a few poignant passages.

*"After the 1978 season in which I rode two 24hr events, I decided quite firmly, not to attempt another in 1979, and to give racing a miss for a year in fact. You've heard that one before? Well, this resolution was as genuine as any. Through that winter I covered a mileage so low I didn't dare record anything and by springtime my fitness had deteriorated to absolute zero. The first time I'd achieved this state in 7 years of cycling!"*

Then in April, Ian admitted to looking uneasily through the RTTC handbook and with his student career coming to an end, he made skeletal plans for riding a 24hr with a 12hr, four 100's and a couple of 50's thrown in as well. **"It was North Road or bust!"**

In May he started on a training programme similar to the one he'd used the previous year. He experimented with derailleur gears and after losing rhythm and strength, he returned to his favourite fixed wheel.

From an entry of just 22 riders, Ian had worked out who were his main opponents; Cliff Smith, Ken Lovett and Don Saunders. After a brief battle with Don Saunders, CC Breckland, he found himself well in the lead by 100 miles, with 4hrs 28mins. This took not only Eric Wilkinson, the timekeeper, by surprise, but also the detour controllers and marshals.

After an 11am start, the afternoon ran smoothly with good weather, dry with a light breeze. Ian recalled *"towards evening the wind strengthened and blew from the north east and it began to turn cold. Turning into the wind at Tempsford, I was determined to maintain the pace into the night and settled in for a tough fight across into the fens. The route was A45 from St Neots to Cambridge, a road that affords little shelter, and then out onto the concrete wastes of the new Cambridge bypass. This windswept desert witnessed the fall of darkness and I should imagine also the collapse of the hopes of a few riders. It was appalling; what I would have given for the run down Madingley Hill and through the sheltered streets of the town."*

By 12 hours Ian had covered 251 miles and was well on target with six hours of darkness left. His helpers were very well organised and he was using 'the George Bettis method of feeding', one bottle of rice pudding taken every 1.5 hours. This also reduced the amount of times you need to see your helpers.

As the night progressed, Ian found himself losing speed while groping for the road ahead. He became very drowsy and narrowly missed a rider coming in the opposite direction and his worst time was at 4am on the Wimpole Lodge detour. By dawn he found he was 45mins up on Roger Sewell and Ken Lovett, who were scrapping for 2nd place. He now had his heart set on a personal best, which stood at 472.5 miles, but he'd reckoned without a strong northerly wind getting up at his 400 miles point.

Robin Buchan

Rod Goodfellow

Wes Clayton

Dennis Clayton

Graham Mann

Vin Denson

Roger Sewell

Mick Coupe

228

Pat Kenny & John Taylor

Kath & Pete Akoslovski

Al Mansley

Paul Carbutt

Ian Dow

John Woodburn

Joe Summerlin

Stuart Jackson

## Catford National 1971

| 1 | R.W.Buchan | Norwood Para.C.C. | 483.84 |
|---|---|---|---|
| 2 | J.D.Cahill | Nth.Staffs.St.Chris.C.C. | 464.71 |
| 3 | W.Clayton | Tyne R.C. | 463.03 |
| 4 | D.Clayton | Tyne R.C. | 458.03 |
| 5 | A.Robertson | Tyne R.C. | 456.40 |
| 6 | C.Smith | East Mids.C.C. | 455.67 |
| 7 | B.R.Hygate | Farnboro' & Camb.C.C. | 446.70 |
| 8 | K.Davey | Bec C.C. | 446.21 |
| 9 | R.W.E.Poole | Farnboro' & Camb.C.C. | 444.58 |
| 10 | M.Coupe | Nth.Staffs.St.Chris.C.C. | 440.65 |
| 11 | J.R.Baines | Icknield R.C. | 438.81 |
| 12 | P.A.Smith | Farnboro' & Camb. C.C. | 431.23 |
| 13 | L.E.Lowe | Speedwell B.C. | 429.54 |
| 14 | D.J.Grady | Bec C.C. | 429.09 |
| 15 | D.W.Lock | Worthing Excelsior C.C. | 428.54 |
| 16 | T.Finney | Nth.Staffs.St.Chris.C.C. | 428.15 |
| 17 | D.R.Farley | Marlboro' A.C. | 427.71 |
| 18 | K.G.Smallwood | Farnboro' & Camb. C.C. | 424.48 |
| 19 | R.T.Powney | Kingston Phoenix R.C. | 420.06 |
| 20 | B.R.Morrison | London Coureurs | 417.67 |
| 21 | R.Grimes | Sth.Bucks.R.C. | 413.92 |
| 22 | M.J.Waters | Hampshire R.C. | 410.03 |
| 23 | R.C.Johnson | Brighton Mitre C.C. | 407.50 |
| 24 | H.S.Spelling | Wren Wh. | 407.41 |
| 25 | B.J.Parslow | Marlboro' A.C. | 406.28 |
| 26 | T.F.Lee | Balham C.C. | 404.27 |
| 27 | L.Cole | Balham C.C. | 403.48 |
| 28 | R.Addison | Harp R.C. | 402.39 |
| 29 | F.E.Lock | Portobello C.C. | 400.91 |
| 30 | P.D.Friend | Port Talbot W.C.C. | 400.75 |
| 31 | R.W.Beels | Kentish Wh. | 398.68 |
| 32 | A.J.Hamilton | Acme Wh. Rhondda C.C. | 396.73 |
| 33 | C.G.Brown | Oxonian C.C. | 396.31 |
| 34 | B.S.Gifford | Faversham C.&.A.C. | 388.78 |
| 35 | M.L.Badham | Norfolk R.C. | 388.33 |
| 36 | W.H.Filby (T) | East Surrey R.C. | 387.79 |
| 37 | P.F.Bavage | Kentish Wh. | 383.56 |
| 38 | C.B.Woodcock | Worthing Excelsior C.C. | 382.52 |
| 39 | B.R.Smallwood | Kenton R.C. | 380.37 |
| 40 | R.A.Holmes | Lea Valley | 380.05 |
| 41 | R.Storey | Marlboro' A.C. | 378.41 |
| 42 | E.Dore | Crawley Wh. | 377.19 |
| 43 | G.Monk | Crawley Wh. | 376.50 |
| 44 | G.W.Siddle | Spartan W.C.C. | 373.38 |
| 45 | R.H.E.Roach | Peterborough C.C. | 367.72 |
| 46 | G.H.Wayte | Chelmer C.C. | 366.67 |
| 47 | R.A.Lewthwaite | Peterborough C.C. | 363.94 |
| 48 | R.P.Craig | Charlotteville C.C. | 362.62 |
| 49 | K.G.Perkins | Sth Bucks C.C. | 357.12 |
| 50 | W.E.Squirrell | Sth Western R.C. | 355.13 |
| 51 | M.Shaw | Clarence Wh. | 348.77 |
| 52 | K.Reed | Crawley Wh. | 347.47 |
| 53 | M.J.Seago | Wigmore C.C. | 339.91 |
| 54 | J.P.Beutter | Portobello R.C. | 336.71 |
| 55 | F.J.White | Balham C.C. | 322.81 |
| 56 | K.Graham (T) | Wigmore C.C. | 308.90 |

TEAM:
1) Tyne R.C.   W.Clayton D.Clayton A.Robertson   1377.46 miles
2) Nth.Staffs.St.Chris.CCC   Cahill Coupe Finney   1333.51 "
3) Farnboro & Camb.CC   Hygate Poole Smith   1322.51 "

## North Road National 1972

| 1. | G.M. Bettis | Bedfordshire R.C. | 470.526 |
|---|---|---|---|
| 2. | W. Clayton | Tyne R.C. | 467.094 |
| 3. | I.W.E. Hickman | San Fairy Ann C.C. | 464.021 |
| 4. | A. Robertson | Tyne R.C. | 460.149 |
| 5. | E. Tremaine (T) | Leicestershire R.C. | 457.895 * |
| 6. | D. Clayton | Tyne R.C. | 457.655 |
| 7. | K.M. Lovett (C) | North Road C.C. | 455.311 |
| 8. | D.G. Anness (C) | East Anglian C.C. | 452.505 |
| 9. | P. Leat (C) | Maldon & Dist. C.C. | 441.249 |
| 10. | K. Brooker (C) | Luton W.M. | 431.560 |
| 11. | S.F. Cruse (C) | Maldon & Dist. C.C. | 430.500 |
| 12. | J. Summerlin (C) | North Road C.C. | 427.498 |
| 13. | R.W. Odell (C) | Luton Wh. | 424.538 |
| 14. | L.E. Lowe (C) | Speedwell B?C. | 416.808 |
| 15. | J.A. Westcott (C) | Icknield R.C. | 413.753 |
| 16. | B. Davies (C) | Archer R.C. | 413.513 |
| 17. | E.B. Smith (C) | Lincoln Wh. C.C. | 409.423 |
| 18. | R.A. Cruse (C) | Maldon & Dist. C.C. | 409.242 |
| 19. | C.J. Hill (C) | Stevenage C.C. | 407.769 |
| 20. | S.G. Snyder (C) | Newark Castle | 406.739 |
| 21. | G.W. Siddle (C) | Sparton Wh. | 404.561 |
| 22. | R. Griffith (C) | Crawley Wh. | 401.705 |
| 23. | K. Clarke (C) | Fenland Clarion | 401.348 |
| 24. | D.B. Sutton | Wolsey R.C. | 398.493 |
| 25. | J.B. Wadley | Colchester Rovers | 397.163 |
| 26. | G.T. Jenkins (C) (T) | Hants. R.C. | 393.177 |
| 27. | H. Howard | Dulwich Paragon | 389.799 |
| 28. | K.G. Harper | Clifton C.C. | 389.225 |
| 29. | J.L. Lewis | Lea Valley R.C. | 386.898 |
| 30. | S. Hawkes (C) (T) | Oxonian C.C. | 385.249 |
| 31 | B. Lancaster | Fenland Clarion | 380.085 |
| 32. | R.J. Burnett | Cleveland Wh. | 378.023 |
| 33. | D.E. Keen | Lea Valley R.C. | 374.391 |
| 34. | C. Price | Lea Valley R.C. | 373.741 |
| 35. | R.W. Glover | Fenland Clarion | 372.214 |
| 36. | T. Finch | Bon Amis C.C. | 367.847 |
| 37. | M.L. Badham | Norfolk R.C. | 359.136 |
| 38. | R.G. Holmes | Lea Valley R.C. | 358.894 |
| 39. | C.F. Hoare | Southgate C.C. | 355.710 |
| 40. | A.J. Muddiman | Rutland C.C. | 349.844 |
| 41. | H.T. Streeton | Lea Valley R.C. | 347.284 |
| 42. | W. Coupe | N. Staffs. St. Christopher | 342.778 |

TEAM: 1st...TYNE R.C.      1384.898
2nd...LEA VALLEY R.C.   1135.030

* comp record

## Mersey National 1973

| 1. | N. Carline | Morley C.C. | 490.31 |
|---|---|---|---|
| 2. | E.W. Matthews | S. Lancs. R.C. | 480.81 |
| 3. | W. Clayton | Tyne R.C. | 465.75 |
| 4. | D. Clayton | Tyne R.C. | 461.28 |
| 5. | G. Lee | R. .F. C.C. | 445.77 |
| 6. | P.M. Heppleston | Abbotsford Park R.C. | 442.52 |
| 7. | G. Jones | Birkenhead N.E. C.C. | 433.32 |
| 8. | K. Robson | Tyne R.C. | 427.10 |
| 9. | R. Thomas | S. Lancs. R.C. | 426.33 |
| 10. | L. Girvan | Merseyside Whs. | 423.77 |
| 11. | P.E.A. Carter | S. Lancs. R.C. | 423.20 |
| 12. | S. Hill (T) | Leicester Forest C.C. | 422.70 |
| 13. | P.G. Ashbourn | Weaver Valley C.C. | 420.74 |
| 14. | S. Fogden | Bramley Whs. | 418.62 |
| 15. | K. Barry | Altrincham R.C. | 415.25 |
| 16. | S. Old | Mersey R.C. | 413.86 |
| 17. | M. Jones | Mid. Shropshire Whs. | 413.78 |
| 18. | R. Grainger | Cheshire R.C. | 413.55 |
| 19. | P M. Swinden | B'ham. St. Chris. C.C.C | 411.16 |
| 20. | P. Kenny | B'ham. St. Chris. C.C.C | 403.52 |
| 21. | P.L. Broad | Rhos on Sea C.C. | 403.31 |
| 22. | G.E. Morris | Harworth & Dist. C.C. | 401.97 |
| 23. | N. Maggs | Mersey R.C. | 401.43 |
| 24. | E.A. Ware | Shaftesbury C.C. | 398.21 |
| 25. | J. Smith | Chester R.C. | 393.43 |
| 26. | R.P. Craig (T) | Farnbro' & Camberley CC | 382.98 |
| 27. | D.P. Cahill | Hirwaun Y.M.C.A. Whs. | 382.70 |
| 28. | S.M. Taylor | Rutland C.C. | 378.45 |
| 29. | G.E. Jones | Birkenhead N.E.C.C. | 378.04 |
| 30. | A. Grime | Hyde Olympic R.C. | 375.29 |
| 31. | A. Para | Kenton R.C. | 366.91 |
| 32. | B.H. Waine (T) | Weaver Valley C.C. | 359.61 |
| 33. | C. Royle | Weaver Valley C.C. | 351.33 |
| 34. | G.C. Noble | Harworth & Dist. C.C. | 350.68 |
| 35. | B.H. Lancene | Willesden C.C. | 348.89 |
| 36. | A. Noble (T) | Bradford Elite C.C. | 336.12 |

Team: 1. Tyne R.C. 1354.13
     2. S. Lancs. R.C. 1330.34
     3. Weaver Valley C.C. 1131.68.

## Wessex RC National 1974

| | | | |
|---|---|---|---|
| 1 | R.G. Goodfellow | Beacon Roads C.C. | 465.45 |
| 2 | G. Olive | Oxonian C.C. | 457.78 |
| 3 | F.J. Newton | Wessex R.C. | 441.11 |
| 4 | R. McTaggart | Oxonian C.C. | 430.64 |
| 5 | R.P. Craig | Farnboro & Camberley CC | 427.23 |
| 6 | R. Dowling | Farnboro & Camberley CC | 425.82 |
| 7 | D.L. Grundon | Westerley R.C. | 424.22 |
| 8 | R.J. Wells | Oxford City R.C. | 420.53 |
| 9 | F.P. Drinkwater | Sotonia C.C. | 418.45 |
| 10 | P. Rawlinson | Poole Wheelers C.C. | 416.85 |
| 11 | G.W. Hinder | Oxford City R.C. | 416.74 |
| 12 | P.A. Smith | Farnboro' & Cmbly C.C. | 410.60 |
| 13 | C.C.P. Davies | Hampshire R.C. | 409.52 |
| 14 | M. Howard | Leo R.C. | 400.04 |
| 15 | T.F. Ellis | Bexley C.C. | 396.03 |
| 16 | R.L. Gee | Sotonia C.C. | 381.09 |
| 17 | S.J. King | Colchester Rovers C.C | 380.70 |
| 18 | A.C. Whiting | Upton Manor C.C. | 376.88 |
| 19 | G.W. Siddle | Spartan Wheelers C.C. | 374.87 |
| 20 | R.G. Davis | Hampshire R.C. | 370.72 |
| 21 | H.A. Oliver | Upton Manor | 369.60 |
| 22 | B.F. Halsey | Veralum C.C. | 368.18 |
| 23 | B.R. Morrison | South Western R.C. | 365.47 |
| 24 | G.G. Hood | Westerly R.C. | 356.92 |
| 25 | D.T. Legg | Wessex R.C. | 350.14 |
| 26 | D.O. Hollis | Upton Manor C.C. | 336.97 |
| 27 | W.J. Ford | Clevedon & Dist. R.C. | 331.13 |

47 entered, 46 started, 27 finished.

Team covering greatest distance. Farnborough & Camberley C.C.

P.A. Smith, R.P. Craig, R. Dowling. 1263.65 miles.

WOMEN

| | | | |
|---|---|---|---|
| 1 | Mrs. J. Tebbutt | Clevedon & Dist. R.C. | 363.92 |

## Catford National 1975

| | | | |
|---|---|---|---|
| 1. | J.D. Cahill | Nth Staffs St.CH.C.C. | 469.44 |
| 2. | R.W. Buchan | Norwood Paragon | 463.79 |
| 3. | G. Olive | Oxonian C.C. | 463.75 |
| 4. | M.J. Titterton | Gordon V.C.C. | 447.97 |
| 5. | M.B. Sheppard | Catford C.C. | 439.77 |
| 6. | M.W. Hawes | Central Sussex C.C. | 436.90 |
| 7. | P.A.D. McVey | Folkstone & D.C.C. | 436.41 |
| 8. | R.W. McTaggart | Oxonian C.C. | 431.31 |
| 9. | C. Smith | East Mids C.C. | 430.01 |
| 10. | R.F. Randall | Harlequins C.C. | 428.80 |
| 11. | J.R. Baines | Morley C.C. | 428.76 |
| 12. | R.J. Knight | Gordano V.C.C. | 428.35 |
| 13. | L.E. Lowe | Speedwell B.C. | 428.09 |
| 14. | M.J. Parker | Nt. Staffs St. CH.C.C. | 424.54 |
| 15. | I.W.E. Hickman | San Fairy Ann | 421.05 |
| 16. | C. Chambers | Sharrow C.C.X. | 417.02 |
| 17. | D.M. Lucas | Solihull C.C. | 413.46 |
| 18. | R.T. Powney | Kingston PH.R.C. | 412.95 |
| 19. | T.F. Finney | Nth Staffs ST.CH.C.C. | 410.07 |
| 20. | R.J. Griffin | Crawley WH. | 409.14 |
| 21. | W.R. Oakley | Beacon R.C.C. | 404.69 |
| 22. | B. Hedges | Oxonian C.C. | 399.17 |
| 23. | K.H. Hyatt | Catford C.C. | 397.38 |
| 24. | P.F. Burberry | Lewes W.C.C. | 397.19 |
| 25. | J.E. Richardson | V.C.St Raphael | 396.33 |
| 26. | C.C.P. Davies | Hampshire R.C. | 392.45 |
| 27. | B.R. Morrison | Sth Western R.C. | 391.06 |
| 28. | P.G. Stubbs | Catford C.C. | 388.54 |
| 29. | W.H. Wootton (T) | Hounslow Dis.Wh. | 381.91 |
| 30. | J.A. Pratt (T) | Crawley Wh. | 381.80 |
| 31. | J.K. Newlin | Bec C.C. | 379.82 |
| 32. | D.B. Upton | Folkestone D.C.C. | 377.25 |
| 33. | B.F. Halsey | Verulam C.C. | 375.61 |
| 34. | A.R. Sturk | Cardiff Ajax C.C. | 374.57 |
| 35. | G.P. Standen | Surrey R.C.C. | 373.91 |
| 36. | R.G. Davis | Hampshire R.C. | 373.34 |
| 37. | D.H. Wey | Kingston Ph.R.C. | 372.07 |
| 38. | G.W. Siddle | Spartan Wh. | 371.93 |
| 39. | J.P. Calvert | Hiraun YMCA W.C.C. | 366.17 |
| 40. | W.W. Griffiths | Kingston Ph.R.C. | 362.40 |
| 41. | P.A. Elliott | Gemini B.C. | 359.77 |
| 42. | R.G. Jenkins | Lampard R.C. | 359.50 |
| 43. | L.A. Howard | Redmon C.C. | 359.46 |
| 44. | P.A. King | Redhill C.C. | 354.18 |
| 45. | E.L. Brook | Haslemere D.C.C. | 345.40 |
| 46. | T.M. McHale | Ashford Wh. | 344.04 |
| 47. | R.K. Punter | Catford C.C. | 334.07 |
| 48. | J.P. Beutter | Catford C.C. | 333.86 |
| 49. | K. Reed | Crawley Wh. | 330.53 |
| 50. | D.F. Lamb | Gemeni B.C. | 299.92 |
| 51. | B.T. Anniss | Haslemere D.C.C. | 260.62 |

### T E A M

| | |
|---|---|
| Nth Staffs St. Christ C.C. | 1304.05 |
| Oxonian C.C. | 1294.23 |
| Catford C.C. | 1225.69 |
| Kingston Ph.C.C. | 1147.42 |
| Crawley Wh. | 1121.47 |

Entrants 66, Starters 65.

234

### North Road National 1976

| | | | |
|---|---|---|---|
| 1. | G.M. Bettis | Bedfordshire R.C. | 482.603. |
| 2. | J.D. Cahill | N.Staffs. St. Christopher | 467.912. |
| 3. | L. Holmes | Luton Whs. | 461.229. |
| 4. | E. Tremaine | Leicestershire R.C. | 458.639. |
| 5. | G. Olive | Oxonian C.C. | 452.042. |
| 6 | K.M. Lovett | North Road C.C. | 449 439 |
| 7. | G.L. Hart | Luton Whs | 446 175 |
| 8. | O.G. Blower | Leicestershire R.C. | 446 129 |
| 9. | R. Baines | Morley C.C. | 442 262 |
| 10 | J. Fisher | Cambridge Town & County | 439 471. |
| 11. | R.W. Usher | North Road C.C. | 435 620. |
| 12 | P.A. Smith | Coventry C.C. | 434 444. |
| 13. | K.E. Usher | North Road C.C. | 434.174. |
| 14. | D. Saunders | C.C. Breckland | 431.181. |
| 15. | G.R.F. Yuill | Maldon & Dist. C.C. | 429.670. |
| 16. | H.A. Stennett | Newark Castle | 426.289. |
| 17. | D. Woodman | Archer R.C. | 419.153. |
| 18. | R. Owens | Exeter Whs. | 419.116. |
| 19. | D. Cruse | Maldon & Dist. C.C. | 418.449. |
| 20. | A.J. Braithwaite | Notts. Olympic | 418.435. |
| 21. | J.S. Spiers | North Bucks R.C. | 416.402. |
| 22. | R.W. O'Dell | Luton Whs. | 415.824. |
| 23. | R.W. McTaggart | Oxonian C.C. | 412.317. |
| 24. | C.P. Cowlard | Addiscombe C.C. | 407.226. |
| 25. | S. Hawkes | Oxonian C.C. | 406.763. |
| 26. | D.A. Smith | West Suffolk Whs. | 406.719. |
| 27. | S.F. Cruse | Maldon & Dist. C.C. | 405.712. |
| 28. | J.W. Taylor | Birmingham St. Christophers | 404.225. |
| 29. | D.K. Lusher | Norwich A.B.C. | 403.930. |
| 30. | D.B. Upton | Folkestone & Dist. C.C. | 402.037. |
| 31. | D.G. Spraggett | Birkenhead N.E. | 400.933. |
| 32. | B. Billings | Leicestershire R.C. | 400.326. |
| 33. | T.E. Ellis | N. Hampshire R.C. | 395.990. |
| 34. | T.A. Bush | Bedfordshire R.C. | 393.736. |
| 35. | W.H. Wootton (T) | Hounslow & Dist. Whs. | 385.699. |
| 36. | C.C.P. Davies | Hampshire R.C. | 385.031. |
| 37. | D.C. Wall | Reading C.C. | 381.837. |
| 38. | P.M. Horsfield | Cambridge Town & County | 378.661. |
| 39. | D.W. Buswell | Leic. Forest C.C. | 378.558. |
| 40. | F.R. Muir | Norfolk R.C. | 377.209. |
| 41. | M.R. Purser (T) | Charlotteville C.C. | 374.876. |
| 42. | J.B. Wadley | Colchester Rovers | 374 712. |
| 43. | K. Clarke | Fenland Clarion | 374 556 |
| 44 | L.J. Smith | Folkestone & Dist. C.C. | 371 754. |
| 45. | G.W. Siddle | Spartan Wheelers | 365 131. |
| 46 | E.B. Smith | Lincoln Whs | 363 664. |
| 47. | J.B. Raicevic | Hinkley C.C. | 362 459. |
| 48 | J.E. Hartshorne | Leicester Forest | 362 166 |
| 49 | P.W.J. Carey | Chelmer C.C. | 361 931 |
| 50. | P.J. Benstead | Catford C.C. | 358.915. |
| 51. | G. Dring | Coalville Whs. | 353.677. |
| 52. | W. Airy | Fenland Clarion | 352.087. |
| 53. | M. Reynolds | Hinckley C.C. | 349.475. |
| 54. | B.A. Hay | North Road C.C. | 348.136. |
| 55. | J.A. Wilkinson (T) | S. Lancs. R.C. | 343.683. |
| 56. | M.L. Smith | Kettering Friendly | 332.493. |
| 57. | J.A. Lovell (T) | Kettering Amateur | 329.251. |
| 58. | G. Martin | Hinkley C.C. | 321.213. |
| 59. | D.F. Lamb | Gemini B.C. | 317.059. |

Team Luton Wheelers Holmes, Hart, & O'Dell    1323 miles

## Mersey National 1977

| | | |
|---|---|---:|
| 1. | J.D. Cahill, N. Staffs St. Christopher's C.C.C. | 477.25 |
| 2. | M. Coupe, N. Staffs St. Christopher's C.C.C. | 467.50 |
| 3. | I. Dow, Oxford City R.C. | 458.87 |
| 4. | G. Fish, Coventry Olympic Viscount | 446.49 |
| 5. | G. Berwick, Glasgow R.C. | 443.40 |
| 6. | H. Martin, Preston Whs. | 439.75 |
| 7. | D. Woodman, Archer R.C. Cutty Sark | 438.44 |
| 8. | S.R. Spraggett, Birkenhead N.E.C.C. | 430.30 |
| 9. | S. Lea, Warrington R.C. | 426.66 |
| 10. | M.P. Francis, Nova C.C. | 419.76 |
| 11. | R.W. Browning, Nova C.C. | 418.33 |
| 12. | M.E. Jones, Liverpool Century R.C. | 418.23 |
| 13. | S. Cornish, Mid-Shropshire Whs. | 417.50 |
| 14. | (K.D. Hughes, Mid-Shropshire Ehs. | 416.51 |
| | (J.M.W. Murdoch, Edinburgh R.C. | 416.51 |
| 16. | M.J. Parker, N. Staffs St. Christopher's C.C.C. | 415.33 |
| 17. | I. Ross, Nova C.C. | 410.74 |
| 18. | J.B. Raicevic, Hinckley C.C. | 404.77 |
| 19. | J.W Taylor, B'ham St. Christopher's C.C.C. | 402.92 |
| 20. | P.G. Stubbs, Catford C.C. | 401.31 |
| 21. | K. Price, Cardiff 100 Miles R.C. | 398.69 |
| 22. | N.H. Shenton, Gala C.C. | 392.75 |
| 23. | S. Colquhoun, Birkenhead Victoria C.C. | 387.63 |
| 24. | G. Martin, Hinckley C.C. | 375.40 |
| 25. | F. Martin, Dukinfield C.C. | 372.15 |
| 26. | A.J. Worthington, Chester R.C. | 365.67 |
| 27. | P.J. Benstead, Catford C.C. | 365.53 |
| 28. | C.E. Farrar, South Lancashire R.C.    Trike | 364.66 |
| 29. | J.E. Whitfield, Weaver Valley C.C. | 360.28 |
| 30. | R.B. Upton, Folkestone & Dist. C.C. | 360.08 |
| 31. | D.F. Lamb, Gemini B.C. | 318.67 |

Team:-  1.  N. Staffs St. Christopher's C.C.C.     1360.08
            Cahill, Coupe, Parker.
         2.  Nova C.C.     1248.83
            Francis, Browning, Ross.

## Wessex National 1978

| | | | |
|---|---|---|---|
| 1. | J.D. Cahill | North Staffs St.Chris. | 482.25 |
| 2. | K. Wright | Chippenham & Dist/Johns Bikes | 469.48 |
| 3. | G.R. Mann | Hainault R.C. | 466.50 |
| 4. | M. Coupe | North Staffs St.Chris. | 461.69 |
| 5. | G. Berwick | Glasgow R.C. | 438.24 |
| 6. | R.J. Knight | Gordano Valley C.C. | 437.48 |
| 7. | R.E. Fox | Becontree Wheelers C.C. | 437.40 |
| 8. | B.R. Hygate | Farnboro & Camberley/Bikit | 434.05 |
| 9. | C. Smith | East Midlands C.C. | 431.32 |
| 10. | D. Woodman | Archer R.C./Cutty Sark | 431.14 |
| 11. | M.J. Titterton | Gordano Valley C.C. | 428.30 |
| 12. | M J. Horwood | Gordano Valley C.C. | 424.48 |
| 13. | M.J. Parker | North Staffs St.Chris. | 421.84 |
| 14. | R. Dowling | Farnboro & Camberley/Bikit | 415.81 |
| 15. | M.J. Ayliffe | Clarencourt C.C. | 414.36 |
| 16. | D.L. Grundon | Westerley R.C. | 410.85 |
| 17. | C.C.P. Davies | Hampshire R.C. | 409.97 |
| 18. | R.O.D. Luckwell | Gordano Valley C.C. | 408.75 |
| 19. | S.J. Stanton | Bronte Whs./McManus & Poole | 405.10 |
| 20. | B.G. Brown | Gordano Valley C.C. | 404.97 |
| 21. | R.A. Cruse | Maldon & District C.C. | 397.24 |
| 22. | P.T. Smith | Hampshire R.C. | 397.08 |
| 23. | R.L. Gee | Sotonia C.C. | 392.08 |
| 24. | J.A. Hassell | Luton Arrow C.C. | 390.04 |
| 25. | S.W. Moore | Maldon & District C.C. | 389.84 |
| 26. | D.R. Motherwell | Crabwood C.C. | 386.66 |
| 27. | J.R.E. Tole | Rodney C.C. | 384.49 |
| 28. | P.R. Donovan | Chippenham & Dist/Johns Bikes | 382.90 |
| 29. | D.B. Upton | Folkstone & District C.C. | 381.31 |
| 30. | R.G. Davis | Hampshire R.C. | 373.28 |
| 31. | M. Smith (T) | Maldon & District C.C. | 366.77 |
| 32. | D.H. Way | Weybridge Wheelers | 363.33 |
| 33. | P.J. Baker | Sotonia C.C. | 358.90 |
| 34. | P.J. Waters | Farnham R.C. | 356.58 |
| 35. | M.J. Waters (T) | Hampshire R.C. | 352.52 |
| 36. | J-P. Beutter | Westerley R.C. | 344.59 |
| 37. | J.E. Thorpe | Hampshire R.C. | 333.27 |
| 38. | A.C. White | Sotonia C.C. | 333.13 |

Teams:-

| | | |
|---|---|---|
| 1. | North Staffs St.Chris.C.C. | 1365.78 |
| 2. | Gordano Valley C.C. | 1290.26 |
| 3. | Hampshire R.C. | 1180.33 |
| 4. | Maldon & District C.C. | 1153.85 |

55 entered    51 started.

## North Midlands CF National 1979

| 1. | M.Coupe | N.Staffs.St.Chris.CCC. | 252.7 | 492.682 |
|---|---|---|---|---|
| 2. | J.D.Cahill | N.Staffs.St.Chris.CCC. | 252.3 | 489.010 |
| 3. | T.Mullins | Rockingham CC. | 250.9 | 485.436 |
| 4. | G.Barker | Rockingham CC. | 243.8 | 469.044 |
| 5. | M.McNamara | Rockingham CC. | 238.0 | 454.827 |
| 6. | A.F.Peachey | Southborough & District Whs. | 235.6 | 449.818 |
| 7. | M.J.Parker | N.Staffs.St.Chris.CCC. | 231.6 | 435.706 |
| 8. | J.R.Baines | Morley CC. | 226.5 | 434.430 |
| 9. | I.Collins | Lincoln Whs. | 222.8 | 428.998 |
| 10. | W.Fielding | Halifax Imperial Whs. | 226.0 | 425.429 |
| 11. | T.H.Barr | Feltham R.C. | 220.2 | 422.424 |
| 12. | L.E.Lowe | Speedwell BC. | 215.8 | 421.322 |
| 13. | J.Hall | Rutland CC. | 216.3 | 418.909 |
| 14. | B.Billings | Leicestershire RC. | 215.3 | 415.986 |
| 15. | S.J.Bennett | Vegetarian C&AC. | 218.3 | 415.846 |
| 16. | T.C.Siddons | Doncaster Whs. | 214.7 | 413.539 |
| 17. | C.B.Beardsley | S.Elmsall SCC | 217.9 | 411.691 |
| 18. | E.D.Fletcher | Bridlington CC. | 216.9 | 406.432 |
| 19. | D.Hunter | Hull Thursday RC. | 212.6 | 399.752 |
| 20. | P.V.Rawlings | Barnsley R.C. | 204.2 | 397.507 |
| 21. | J.A.Hassall | Luton Arrow | 208.1 | 394.744 |
| 22. | A.E.Rouse | Colchester Rovers CC. | 206.3 | 391.050 |
| 23. | J.Wild | Long Eaton CC. | 212.4 | 387.457 |
| 24. | A.T.Hibbitt | Doncaster Whs. | 209.6 | 386.286 |
| 25. | D.H.Wey | Weybridge Whs. | 198.0 | 378.972 |
| 26. | R.Waddington | Doncaster Whs. | 197.5 | 378.147 |
| 27. | H.L.Browne | Halifax Imperial Whs. | 217.0 | 377.145 |
| 28. | L.Howard | Redmon CC. | 189.9 | 362.755 |
| 29. | S.Charity (T) | Notts.Castle BC. | 198.8 | 361.482 |
| 30. | G.Dring | Coalville Whs. | 183.3 | 349.243 |
| 31. | B.Sanderson | Seacroft Whs. | 187.6 | 347.280 |
| 32. | R.A.Coleby (T) | Colchester Rovers CC. | 181.9 | 339.994 |
| 33. | G.W.Siddle | Spartan Whs. | 179.1 | 335.095 |
| 34. | F.C.S.Payce-Drury | Norwood Paragon CC. | 171.7 | 322.240 |
| 35. | P.Benstead | Catford CC. | 183.3 | 319.004 |

| Teams:- | 1. | N.Staffs.St.Chris.CCC. | 1,417.394 * |
|---|---|---|---|
| | 2. | Rockingham CC. | 1,409.307 |
| | 3. | Doncaster Whs. | 1,177.972 |

* comp record

## North Road National 1980

| | | | |
|---|---|---|---|
| 1. | J.Woodburn | Velo Club Slough | 505.477 |
| 2. | J.Cahill | N.Staffs.St.C.C.C.C. | 497.337 |
| 3. | I.Dow | Oxford City R.C. | 485.005 |
| 4. | M.Coupe | N.Staffs.St.C.C.C.C. | 476.087 |
| 5. | T.Finney | N.Staffs.St.C.C.C.C. | 468.170 |
| 6. | K.Lovett | North Road C.C. | 465.188 |
| 7. | M.Evans | Wigmore C.C. | 454.216 |
| 8. | C.Cowland | London Fire Brigade | 437.749 |
| 9. | H.Stennett | Newark Castle B.C. | 435.352 |
| 10. | G.Berwick | Glasgow R.C. | 434.377 |
| 11. | P.Harridge (N) | Herts.Wheelers | 432.298 |
| 12. | P.Ashbourn | N.Bucks.R.C. | 426.609 |
| 13. | R.Saunders (N) | High Wycombe C.C. | 423.892 |
| 14. | C.Beardsley | S.Elmsall S.C.C. | 422.060 |
| 15. | L.Black (N) | Norwood Paragon | 421.207 |
| 16. | R.Poole | Farboro & Camberley | 420.619 |
| 17. | P.Harsfield | Cmbs.Town & County | 418.256 |
| 18. | M.Smith (T) | Maldon & Dist.C.C. | 415.812 |
| 19. | N.King (N) | North Road C.C. | 415.672 |
| 20. | S.Clarke (N) | Fenland Clarion C.C. | 415.134 |
| 21. | M.Holliday | A.5 Rangers C.C. | 411.972 |
| 22. | D.Mason | A.5 Rangers C.C. | 410.068 |
| 23. | J.Hassall | Luton Arrow C.C. | 403.123 |
| 24. | W.Dunk | North Road C.C. | 394.168 |
| 25. | D.Stevens | Chard Wheelers | 391.797 |
| 26. | K.Clarke | Fenland Clarion C.C. | 391.435 |
| 27. | R.O'Dell | Luton Wheelers | 386.717 |
| 28. | R.Glover | Fenland Clarion C.C. | 385.072 |
| 29. | P.Merson (N) | Ruthin Road Club | 384.478 |
| 30. | Mrs.A.Dunk (N) | North Road C.C. | 379.655 |
| 31. | S.Carpenter (N) | Hastings & St.Leonards | 374.200 |
| 32. | B.Halsey | Verulam C.C. | 370.659 |
| 33. | W.Cliff | Southgate C.C. | 370.033 |
| 34. | P.Coulson | A.5 Rangers C.C. | 369.446 |
| 35. | B.Hay | North Road C.C. | 367.017 |
| 36. | T.May (N) | Nomads (Hitchin) C.C. | 349.410 |
| 37. | M.Badham (T) | Norwich A.B.C. | 344.597 |
| 38. | P.Benstead | Catford C.C. | 339.044 |
| 39. | W.Wood (N) | Spalding C.C. | 338.589 |
| 40. | T.Lynch (N) | North Road C.C. | 335.730 |
| 41.F. | F.Payce-Drury | Norwood Paragon | 334.740 |
| 42. | G.Sadd | Spalding C.C. | 332.691 |

(T) denotes Tricycle.          (N) denotes Novice.

Team:-  1.  N.Staffs.St.C.C.C.C.       1441.634 (Comp.Record).
        2.  North Road C.C.            1275.028
        3.  Fenland Clarion C.C.       1191.641
        4.  A.5 Rangers C.C.           1191.486

61 Entries.    53 Starters.

Ian continued "after 400 miles there comes a 22 mile section to be tackled, straight up the A1 to Norman Cross. With all the other riders turned short, I was left alone to be torn limb from limb by a vicious headwind which scoured this road, and at one point I simply came to a dead halt, staggered across the verge and slumped over a gate, momentarily unable to continue this endless battle. The onslaught was devastating and my predictions sank to about 467 miles".

Ian returned with the wind to the finishing circuit with an all out effort at 'evens' and finished exhausted from his 471 mile ride. He concluded by saying "Sewell had 'died' on the circuit dropping behind Lovett, and with Cliff Smith also in the 440's most of the excitement seemed to focus on candidates for 2nd place. Just as I finished, I was not too far gone to overhear a member of the promoting club remark that had I not ridden, it would have been a good event – they would not only have taken the team award, but also won the event!"

## OBITUARIES 1970 – 1979

In the summer of **1973 Arch Harding** was tragically killed, by a stolen car outside his home. He was a remarkable man and the main driving force behind the Championship winning Middlesex Road Club team with Fred Burrell and Dick Poole. Most of his successful rides were performed after he became a veteran at 40 years of age. Arch was an all round hard riding clubman and tourist at heart, and liked nothing more than a smoke, a drink and a sing song with his clubmates on a Sunday.

On April 10th **1976 Robin Buchan** was found dead at the roadside near Reigate, Surrey, on Sunday morning. His feet were still strapped to his pedals and Police said there was no sign of an accident or collision. His death came as a complete shock to everyone as he had raced the previous day. A postmortem showed that he had suffered a heart attack that could have occurred at any time on or off the bike. He won the 24 hour Championship in 1971 with 483.8 miles and had planned to attack the End to End in 1977. Robin was just 43 years old when he died.

In January **1978 Alec Denton** died after a short illness. He was a keen tourist and a strong 24 hour rider on both bike and trike. Alec was the Vets 24 hour Champion in 1954 and 1958, and had partnered Frank Cowsill to a new tandem End to End and 1,000 miles record in 1952.

In early November **1978 Claud Butler,** one of Britains most famous lightweight cycle builders died after a long illness. His racing bikes became much sought after by racing men and women and he backed many top riders before and after the Second World War. His 'Claud Butler' trade name still lives on to this day, for a range of quality lightweight machines, currently marketed by Falcon Cycles.

In April **1979 Maurice Draisey,** Century Road Club passed away. He was another renowned trike rider, road record breaker and 24 hour man. I last saw Maurice as Pat Kenny and I rode back from London whilst attacking another Midlands RRA record. He waved his walking sticks in the air as a salute to speed us on our way. Maurice was a founder member of the 'T.A', The Tricycle Association.

In August **1979 C.E. 'Ed' Green,** the President of the Tricycle Association, died whilst riding a 50 mile time trial near his home in Cumbria. Ed had a very loud 'booming' voice and as Pat and I climbed through the mist on Shap in May 1979 on our first tandem trike End to End attempt, we could hear him hollering for miles. He won his first North Road 24 hour trike prize in 1948 with 346 miles, and was a regular 24 hour contestant over those thirty years or more. The church was full with some club folk having to stand outside at his funeral. This was a true measure of his popularity. Ed was 71 years of age when he died.

## 1980

The first event of the year was again the **Wessex RC 24hr** on 21st and 22nd June 1980. **It was won by R. May-Miller, Bath CC with 425.00 miles. Rob Dowling,** Farnboro and Camberley CC was **2nd** with **422.43m** and **B. Taylor, 3rd** with **419.62 miles.** From 16 entries, 14 started and 11 riders finished. Again I have no details of this event, what the weather was like etc, and can only wonder how long this event can carry on with such poor numbers and entries.

**The Mersey RC 24hr** late July 1980 was **won by Malcolm Judge, Seamons CC with 454.767 miles, 2nd** place went to **Dave Short, 449.873** with **George Berwick 3rd, 448.696 miles** and **Mick Hallgarth 4th** with **428.427m. The Seamons CC won the team race with Judge, Bates and Hill riding to a total of 1,200.194 miles.**

Conditions at the start were cloudy with plenty of oxygen in the air for the 57 riders. Apart from the new compact course being used, a new starting time of 2pm was also to be used this year. The old 5pm start, stems from the days when riders and helpers alike were subjected to working on Saturday mornings as part of their normal working week.

Ron MacQueen despatched the field, his 32nd consecutive annual duty for the club. There were no 'super fast' starts from any of the riders, but at 50 miles Dave Short led in 2hrs 9mins, Judge was at 3mins, Saunders 4m and Berwick 5minutes.

"Can you cut out the final hymn? I'm racing in a cycle race in half an hour."

At Haughton Moss, the 'Nags Head' supplied numerous pints to the turn marshals and spectators alike. *The broadcast of Steve Ovett's defeat of Seb Coe in the Olympic 800 metres was fuelling the spectator's interest and helping to insulate them against the rain, which had just started.* It was shortly to become torrential and take full toll of the riders en-route to Christleton Island at 86 miles. Battered by the elements, drowned by the spray from passing cars, and in a couple of cases, suffering from mechanical trouble and crashes, no less than ten riders had packed at that point, including 1979 winner, Al Mansley.

By the 100 mile point the rain was easing and the first 7 riders were inside 'evens'. Short was the fastest with 4hrs 39mins, Judge at 4mins, Hallgarth at 6m, Berwick 10mins, Humphries 15m, Richardson 18mins and Bethell 19 minutes.

The 160 mile point at Prees saw riders and helpers alike trying to effect lighting repairs. Four riders had already been stopped for having either poor, or no lights at all. Dave Shorts early efforts had taken their toll and now Berwick was chasing Judge around the Market Drayton to Chetwynd and Tern Hill legs for the first time, then the Shawbirch to Hodnet return slog at 192 miles.

**Frank Mumford** who provided most of the details for this report said *"Berwick's efforts reminded me nostalgically of the 1948 event in which I was chasing Harry Okell down this leg, only to find him asleep in a helpers car at the turn. To escape my abuse, he jumped out and hammered away to such good effect that he won the event and led us to a team victory!"*

After 12 hours of riding, Judge was well in command, just missing 'evens' by a whisker with 239.7 miles, Berwick 236 and Mick Hallgarth 231.9m. It was a long dark warm night, a fair few riders had 'abandoned' leaving 40 still riding. By the morning the detour controllers were having difficulty keeping the field compact.

At Wem (356 miles) only Malcolm Judge, George Berwick, Dave Short and Mick Hallgarth were sent to Welshampton and Redbrook, and on the return Judge was clocked at 25 mph and was gaining on his rivals. Finally the riders reached the finishing circuit and in that last hour, Short was gaining on Berwick but Judge had timed his ride to perfection.

37 riders finished including Bob Jump, G.S. Sunlight with 382.268 miles and Les Lowe with 387.582m, and in the **Merseyside Ladies event, Mrs 'Trottie' Chase became the first Welsh lady rider to finish a 24hr with 356.098 miles.**

After having four unsuccessful attempts at the End to End record, three on a tandem trike with myself, and one on a trike going from the north, **Pat Kenny, Birmingham St Christopher's CCC finally broke the tricycle End to End record with a time of 2 days 10 hours 36mins and 52secs.** He'd taken 22 minutes off Dave Duffields record and had at last realised his lifelong ambition to break the record. Belonging to a club steeped in record breaking and long distance time trialling, Pat felt that it was the normal done thing to keep attacking this record and his perseverance had at last paid off.

I played a supporting role, driving the following car containing the Mersey RC timekeeper Ron MacQueen, and providing hot coffee for the support team and rider, by using a new fangled 'in-car' water heater, which ran off the battery via the cigarette lighter. In hindsight, it was probably a very dangerous gadget (health and safety) but very useful!

Pat had a fair wind as he started away at 8am on the 4th August 1980. Exeter was reached 29mins inside schedule. He averaged 'evens' over the Bridgwater Flats but slowed as he climbed into Bristol. Here, he was greeted by Eric Wilkinson and his wife Jan. Eric was the timekeeper on the North Road 24hr and a very enthusiastic supporter. As we headed north through Gloucester we were joined by Bill Griffiths (father of Phil). Bill was a past 24 hour rider and even faster over shorter distances. He'd always wanted to help on a successful End to End and now he'd got his chance!

Pat's first 12 hours produced 229 miles but at this point he was 15 minutes down on Duffields record at the same point. Night clothes and lights were taken on board at Tewkesbury and a request for a few pennyworth of chips was fulfilled at Worcester. He pressed on, without slowing, to Gailey Island where his family and friends were waiting for him, and at Stafford he was 1.25 hours up on his schedule.

John Arnold marshalled Pat through at Winwick Church and handed Pat his usual gift of peppermint tonic, a 'special' concoction for 24hr riders and End to Enders. I'm told it cures anything from indigestion to baldness! On a more serious note, Pat had been 'slowing' in the 'small' hours but by Preston he'd pulled back to be 29 minutes up on Duffield's figures. His 24hrs ran out with 413 miles covered and he was now climbing well on 'Shap', even though Pat hates hills. It was a clear day and you could see miles of tortuous climbing up ahead. Pat said "I wish it was covered in mist" as I ran alongside him, and he also said he wished Ed Green was still alive to give him a rousing shout on Shap. The wind around the Scottish Border was blowing strongly and troubled Pat as he climbed the 'Devils Beeftub', and rode towards Edinburgh. He had an enforced stop at Penicuik for a complete change into dry clothes and we convinced him that the wind would soon be behind him after crossing the Forth Road Bridge.

Pat battled on knowing that we wouldn't let him climb off until the record became impossible to get. He reached Perth and missed out a scheduled break, which put him only 27 minutes down on schedule, but by Inverness he'd wiped out all of the time he'd hoped to break the record by; some 48 minutes. It was touch and go, and when he stopped for dry socks and shoes at Inverness, Ron MacQueen wagged his finger at Pat and said "no more stops till John o' Groats"! He still had 140 miles to do and just 10.5 hours to do it in. With some major climbs still to come, it wasn't going to be easy.

The tricky bends, climbs and descents on Aultnamain, Helmsdale and Berriedale were all managed with Pat riding like a man 'possessed'. Through Wick and the last 17 miles seemed never ending, but at last the odd shaped towers of the John o' Groats hotel came into view and Pat had made it. 'Mission Accomplished!' No more End to End records for him, unless perhaps as a Timekeeper, Observer or helper. Pat says he can still hear Ron MacQueen's voice now, telling him "No more stops!"

*Pat went on to organise, help, observe, advise and time many records including the End to End.*

*The long distance B.A.R was born in this year. It was the brain-child of Eric Matthews. To qualify, one had to ride a 100 mile event, a 12 hr and a 24 hr. It was won this year by John Woodburn with an average speed of 23.347 mph.*

The North Road CC 24hr Championship event in late August was won by John Woodburn, Velo Club Slough, with the second greatest ever distance of 505.477 miles. John Cahill rode 497.337 miles for 2nd place and led a North Staffs St Christopher's team of Mick Coupe with 476.087 and Tom Finney 468.170 to a new Competition Record total of 1441.634 miles, beating their previous years record by 24 miles. **This record still stands to this present day in 2008.**

Amongst the 61 entries there were some 20 novices or first time 24hr riders. John Woodburn and Pete Wells fell into this category, but of course they were both prolific winners and champions at events ranging from 25 miles to 12 hours. They were taking on experienced 24hr winners and champions such as John Cahill, Mick Coupe and Ian Dow.

Ian who won this North Road event the previous year had been placed one minute behind Mick Coupe, last years Champion, on the start card, but this wasn't allowed to occur by the RTTC, who were thought by the North Road CC, to be interfering in matters that didn't really concern them. Whether Mick and Ian swapped places and numbers on the start line I don't know as the event report doesn't say.

Pete Wells led the race after starting at a blistering pace. He retired during the night but wreaked havoc amongst not only the favourites and the rest of the riders, but also the course detour controllers. It was estimated that he would have beaten 520 miles if he had continued. John Woodburn survived a battle between himself, Pete Wells, Mick Coupe and John Cahill to win with a mileage just 1.6 miles short of Competition Record.

**Ian Dow** came **3rd** after being knocked off his bike by a young girl on a bike. This resulted in him having to ride with bent handlebars for 200 of his **485 miles.** North Roader Ken Lovett had been chasing Bob Mynott's club 24hr record for years and this time he got it with 465.185 miles. **Mrs Anne Dunk became the first woman to finish a North Road 24 hr with 379.655m,** and finished just over 14 miles behind her husband Bill, also a North Roader. They became only the 2nd husband and wife to finish in the same 24hr event as each other. The first being Bob and Ruth Williams, back in the Mersey RC event of 1967.

Ian mentioned at a later date that the battle between Cahill and Woodburn was the fiercest he had ever seen in a 24hr race with Cahill pushing himself beyond all imaginable barriers in his effort to win. At 12 hours the mileages were Woodburn, 270, Cahill 268, a personal best for him by five miles. Soon after this the inevitable happened; they both blew. But out of the wreckage came the second and third greatest mileages to date: 505.47 (Woodburn) and 497.34 (Cahill).

Ian went on to describe how he battled with John Cahill towards the end of the event and will never forget the dying moments when John caught him - hearing a whoosh of air and feeling the thud of a giant arm across his back, which carried them both forward for a few seconds. They were both beyond words but none were required.

## 1981

**The Wessex RC 24hr** on 20th and 21st June was **won by Stuart Jackson on a trike with 456.59 miles.** This 'novice' 24 hour rider missed Eric Tremaine's Competition Record by just 1.3 miles but led a **Farnham RC team of Edwin Hargraves and Barry Annis to a new trike 24hr Competition Team Record of 1,230.38 miles,** beating the old record by over 13 miles. **Erwin Quistorff,** Clarencourt CC was **2nd** with **445.26m** and **Edwin Hargraves 3rd** with **437.51 miles. M. Smith** of the Maldon CC was **4th** with **431.63m** and **Dick Poole,** who seemed to be making a comeback, was **5th** with **415.01m.** Writing this report with hindsight, I'm pretty sure this is the first and only time that a trike rider has won a fully open 24hr time trial since the Second World War.

The following remarks and passages from Stuart Jackson appear to portray a very light hearted attitude to racing, but in all reality his later partnership on tandem trike with Edwin Hargraves, and indeed all of his races and road records, were tackled with the utmost seriousness, to give some very outstanding results. He spent many touring holidays with both Edwin and Ian Dow, 'stacking in the miles'. The camaraderie between these three riders was immense, but they were deadly serious opponents when a Championship Title or a race win was at stake.

*"Clubmate Edwin Hargraves and I had long deliberated upon the delights of 24hr riding. By 1981 we could procrastinate no longer, and we decided that we should ride on trikes. This would have the advantage that if either of us went particularly well, a Competition Record was possible, and if we didn't, we could always pretend that we were not taking it seriously."*

They needed a third team member and so recruited Barry Annis, who had tried riding a trike and didn't really like it, but he was willing to have a go on Stuart's old trike and complete the team. Stuart continued:

*"In fact, Barry had more experience than Edwin or I, having competed in the last Catford 24hr in 1975. During this event the Catford marshals had been very curious as to how he had managed to disappear completely for 6 hours during the night, eventually discovering that Barry had spent the time asleep in a launderette in Chichester!"*

Stuart had lots of trouble during the event and so did Edwin, mainly due to lighting and punctures in Stuart's case. An electrical genius friend of theirs had rigged up a device using a 6 volt system, but it hadn't been tested before the event. This led to both riders having trouble with flickering lights and both eventually changed back to standard lights. When Stuart found out that Edwin had suffered the same problem he said *"I laughed at the thought of Dave having two trikes wrapped around his neck by irate competitors as they gasped their last breath!"*

He mentions being bored in the night, but thinking it must be even worse for Ian Dow on his fixed wheel and not having the monotony broken by deliberating whether to change gear or not. Stuart also thought that Les Lowe probably rode along calculating his average speed and the average cost in pence per tyre per mile, over the last 27 years. (In hindsight, I think Pat Kenny now holds this distinction, but over a period of 50 years and 870,000 miles or more!)

Second placed rider, Erwin Quistorff, was only 19 years old. Between 1978 and 1980, he'd won his Club's senior 'BAR' when only a junior, and almost all of the Club trophies. Late in 1980 he decided he wanted to ride a 24hr, but didn't know how to go about it. A two week tour of the south-west with Rob Douglas, riding with heavy saddlebags, gave him stamina and then a few 175 mile rides mixed with his Sunday racing gave him his overall fitness.

As he sat on the start line, he looked around and wondered what other 19 year olds were doing on that hot June day? His first 100 miles went by in 4hrs 50mins, including a puncture, but during the night he really felt rough, a feeling he'd never experienced before. By the morning nothing had improved and he had to be cajoled into carrying on. He removed his nightclothes and lights, then, on the long gradual descent to Wimborne he started to feel better. He passed riders on the way back to the finishing circuit and once he was on the 15 mile circuit, he lapped at 40mins. He originally planned to beat 400 miles but at the end he had covered 446.

⇒•◇•⇐

Early in July 1981, John Woodburn made his first attempt at the 'End to End' record. He waited at the Hotel in Sennen for a few days, hoping to get a better wind, but picked up a virus which made him feel weak. He had a check up with a local G.P. who advised him to rest, but the pressure on John to start his ride was immense, so on the following Monday he set out from Lands End, still with a high temperature, but pressed on regardless. He 'rolled' the bike along to Preston at just over 'evens', a pace that would have severely damaged any lesser mortal. He rode on through Scotland but eventually abandoned on the 'Pass of Killiecrankie' a mile or so short of Blair Athol, approximately 630 miles. I saw John on that attempt at Wellington (Telford) and he was already freewheeling down the hills, and appeared to lack the 'urgency' required for such a record. We were unaware at the time of his underlying illness.

A short while later on 25th and 26th July, the **Mersey RC 24hr National Championship was won by John Woodburn, Manchester Whls.** Favourites for this event were John Cahill, Mick Coupe and John Woodburn. Waiting in the wings should any of these three falter were many other strong 24hr men, such as Brian Morris, Mid Shropshire Whls, Tom Finney, North Staffs St Christopher's CCC, Malcolm Judge & George Berwick. Half of the field were 'veterans' including most of the favourites!

The weather at the start was cloudy, overcast and without wind. There were 57 solo male riders entered plus 2 ladies, Mrs Janet Tebbutt and Miss Kathy Bellingham, two tandems and a tandem trike were entered this year. Jenny Colman and her husband were the first tandem away, followed by Joe Summerlin and his son, and thirdly the tandem trike with Pat Kenny and myself. The timekeeper, Ron MacQueen, timing his 33rd Mersey, was joined by Eric Matthews who was learning the ropes with the watch, in preparation for taking over when Ron retired. In case you were wondering why Eric was timekeeping and not riding as a challenging favourite was due to him being crippled, having had his leg amputated. He'd cut his knee some time previously while gardening and it had become infected. Septicaemia had set in and it was too late to treat, leading to gangrene and finally amputation. A terrible tragedy for anyone to bear, let alone a champion record breaking long distance cyclist, but he seemed to take it all without fuss and appeared happy to be amongst racing cyclists at a 24hr, but holding the stop watch instead of the handlebars.

Another tragedy was noted at the start, one of the seven non-starters was number16, R. Wilkes, Ogmore Valley Wheelers. He'd been killed in a traffic accident earlier in the week and it had also involved another of his club mates.

On a lighter note, the tandem trike that Pat and I rode in that event had received a major transmission repair and overhaul prior to the race, involving new chains and freewheel etc. As we started away, the linking chain between the front and rear pedals became unshipped, leaving us feeling a little embarrassed in front of all those people. It was even more embarrassing as we rode off with our pedals out of 'cinque' to each other due to hurriedly replacing the chain in the incorrect positions. In hindsight we did see the funny side of it all but we were to lose over an hour with recurring transmission problems during the event. We weren't the only ones making an unusual exit from the start lane as No 53, C. Beardsley was chased by a loose dog as he started. His sprint lasted more than just a few yards to rid himself of the attacking dog.

From the onset it was obvious that Woodburn, No 56, intended to catch triple champion John Cahill, No 50, as a stepping stone to his target of Cromack's record of 507 miles. He caught him after 40 miles and started a dour battle that was to rage all through the night. The only hindrance was when Cahill had lighting problems.

On the early Alpraham Green section at 23 miles, confusion was caused in the narrow lanes when a combine harvester out of control, narrowly missed Dave Stapleton's (the Organiser) car. Riders on that stretch were also baulked by frightened cows charging wildly along the road. This road was subsequently deemed to be unsafe for use in a cycling event and in future years was deleted from the route card. George Berwick's bottom bracket stripped at 50 miles losing him valuable time and miles.

At the 100 miles checkpoint, Woodburn was fastest with 4hrs 21mins, Morris was at 6m, Cahill nearly 11m and Coupe at 13mins. On the return to Prees, Cahill re-caught Woodburn despite front light problems, but Woodburn fought off the challenge and gradually pulled away to an unchallenged lead from there on despite losing his helpers when they ran out of petrol. The night was cloudy, dark and showery, but the riders had to put up with more than that in the form of lunatic drivers giving them very near misses. Both Howarth and Don Spraggett crashed when forced off the road, leading to them both retiring.

At the 12 hour point, only six men were beating 'evens', Woodburn 255, Cahill 252, Morris 248, Finney 243, Wilson 241.78 and Coupe 241.48m. At 300 miles Woodburn was in real trouble, repeatedly being sick and dropping down to 15mph. The organiser, Dave Stapleton, who was in the area keeping his eye on the field asked his driver Pat Sirett, if he had any peppermint anti-sickness remedy on board. Luckily he had and over the course of the next 30 miles, they cured his sickness and got him back onto normal feeding. Apparently overfeeding had been the cause of the sickness. This loss of speed meant that Competition Record was out of the question and John Woodburn did just enough to keep ahead of the field to maintain command.

Dawn brought with it a tough southwest wind, which further dashed the hopes of many of the riders. Jenny Colman's knee gave trouble at 16 hours so causing the tandem to retire. Leaving Wem at 356 miles, Brian Morris was knocked off his bike by a witless newspaper girl also on a bike. He sustained abrasions to his head and shoulder and lost time recovering from shock. The delay almost certainly cost him his 3rd place, as 19 miles later he was re-caught by Coupe.

Morris suffered a bad cut on his face and was from then on hampered by a painful headache for the final 100 miles. Ironically Morris is a Newsagent who rarely got a Sunday morning off to race.

1980's winner Malcolm Judge suffered badly with 'hot foot' and retired on this section. At Redbrook, Woodburn turned 21.5 minutes up on Cahill. Bernard Thompson the famous reporter for the Cycling Magazine managed to get John Woodburn to pose for a good photograph by freewheeling down one of the many hills on that section. It's good to remember that they did send out a reporter/photographer to important races back in the not so distant 1980's.

Coupe was not without incident himself, having two collisions with spectators necessitating two bike changes. The sun on the finishing circuit was uncomfortable for the tired riders, but Woodburn completed 5 laps at an average of 19.6 mph, Cahill had 4 laps at 18.3mph and Coupe despite his two crashes, did 3 laps at 18.4 mph. The tandem trike with Pat and myself on board creaked and groaned around 3 laps at 16 mph to finish with 407 miles.

So, at the end, **John Woodburn won the 1981 Championship 24 hr with 488.428 miles,** beating John Cahill by 12 miles. **Cahill with 475.483 and Mick Coupe, 3rd with 467.591 led 6th placed man, Tom Finney, 448.787, to a 5th consecutive Championship Team win with 1,391.861 miles. Brian Morris** took **4th** place for the Mid Shropshire Whls with **465.569m. Kathy Bellingham** was the **fastest lady** with **372.549 miles** and **Mrs Janet Tebbutt** was **2nd** with **349.037m.**

<hr/>

**The North Road CC 24hr in 1981** held on August Bank Holiday, was **won by Ian Dow with 474.44 miles. Cliff Smith** was **2nd with 450.60 miles** and **Les Lowe** riding one of his best 24hr races was **3rd with 435.96m.** Ian Dow's ride, although not as high a mileage as his previous years 3rd place Championship of 485 miles, nevertheless proved that he was a very worthy winner, riding virtually unchallenged from the very start. A pure time trial. **Cliff Smith** was looking for his 11th win in this event after a few years of fairly low mileages due to making a full recovery from a broken thigh bone. **At 60 years of age he raised the veteran's record from 401 to 450 miles in this event.**

John Woodburn had been down to start and had expressed his intention to break Competition Record in this event after missing it in the previous years Championship on this course, by 1.5 miles, but after the exhaustions of the failed 'End to End', a winning Mersey RC Championship 24hr and winning the National 12hour all in the space of a few weeks, John failed to start.

Perfect conditions were recorded for this event, very little wind, warm but not oppressive, with cloud cover during the night to keep the cold and mist at bay. Traffic conditions for this August weekend were also good. The Officials and Detour Controllers had been geared up prior to the event for a possible 520 miles of road to be found and this led to a bit of over zealous detour cutting for the slower riders. One such victim was Les Lowe who was turned short at Brampton Hut. Les being an experienced North Road event participant knew that his projected capable mileage would exceed the 4 circuit limit and voiced his opinon to Eric Wilkinson, who authorised a leg to Tempsford and back for him, much to the astonishment of riders returning to the circuit. Les's 2nd place in the VTTA (veterans) Championship pleased him but he said his ride was completely overshadowed by Cliff Smiths. **The only team to finish were the Spalding CC.**

**Mrs Anne Dunk** tried so hard to beat 400 miles in this event but a bout of sickness and the resulting weakness, which had her walking the hills on the finishing circuit, put paid to her hopes and she finally ran out time with **395.22m.** **Mrs Jenny Colman** had overcome the knee problem she had experienced in the Mersey event and finished with **361.36 miles.** Her cheerfulness throughout the event so impressed Bill Frankum, one of the North Road 'elders', that he offered her a special medal if she finished, and despite her tiredness she completed the event and duly received the medal.

# 1982

*On April 2nd 1982 Argentinian Forces captured Port Stanley on the Falkland Islands. British Forces were then deployed. On May 2nd the 'General Belgrano' battleship was sunk by a torpedo, killing 360 Argentinians. On May 4th 'HMS Sheffield' was sunk and 22 of our troops were killed. On July 12th Argentina surrendered. Some 254 British Servicemen were killed and 750 Argentinians died in those two months.*

---

**The Wessex RC event** on 19th and 20th June 1982 was a **National Championship and won by Stuart Jackson with a course and event record of 496.487 miles.** 2nd place went to **Brian Morris** with **476.1 miles** and 3rd, **Ian Dow** with **466.305m.** **Brian Morris led a Mid Shropshire Whls team of Cliff Dean with 398.008m and Don Spraggett with 395.055m to a total of 1,269.163 miles.** **Terry Icke** was **4th** with **460.563m** and **Esther Carpenter** was the only lady to finish with **365.710 miles.**

Ian Dow mentions Stuart Jackson beating him overwhelmingly and although Jackson was credited with only 496.487 miles, it should have been over 500, as he was led off course by an official on the finishing circuit. Luckily he'd done enough to beat Nim Carline's 1966 event record by a tenth of a mile. Brian Morris with 476m started very fast and blew up, and Ian Dow said his painful plod to 466 miles came from his own poor preparations. He started in a brand new pair of untested shorts, which were too tight so restricting position and movement.

Ian suffered a strained muscle in his lower back and then said that the usual symptoms of failure became apparent: indigestion, bad patches, cold in the night, freewheeling downhills and then walking early in the morning to stamp some warmth into his cold feet. From an entry of 46, 42 started and 34 finished.

Reporter for the Cycling Magazine, Chris Davies, mentioned that Stuart Jackson's win was his first National Championship 24hr title. It was a brilliant ride of sustained power, which hardly faltered throughout the entire 24hrs. It came after a blustery Saturday afternoon, with an hour of heavy rain which threatened to disrupt the race completely when 4 cars and a coach collided near Ringwood, shortly after the start, leaving the 42 riders little room to squeeze slowly past a mile long queue of cars.

Brian Morris with his rapid start was fastest at the 100 mile point with 4hrs 27 mins. Most of that mileage was ridden against the wind and only 10 others were inside 5 hours for the 100 miles. Dow riding gears instead of his usual fixed wheel was second at 11mins, Jackson at 12mins and Cahill the race favourite at 13mins. He was making 'heavy weather' of the race and was alarmed to be turned short of a detour at Cadnam after 217.5 miles. He retired at Lyndhurst 25 miles later.

By this point Jackson was well in command leading Morris by a mile, with an estimated 255 mile first 12 hours. He never faltered as he made the most of the calm conditions on a moonless night beneath a star studded sky.

By dawn, Morris and Dow were in 2nd and 3rd place with Terry Icke, Poole Whls, a novice at 24 hours riding well in 4th place, and this is what the final result showed. The youngest rider in the race was Andy Wren who silenced his critics by finishing with 411 miles.

*My thanks to Chris Davies and 'Cycling' for these race details.*

Nobody had realised at this time that this was to be the last Wessex RC 24hr, but just looking at the low entry, even though it was a Championship, should have given some indications as to its demise.

This year of 1982 was to be a phenomenal one for End to End rides, three in fact. The first one being Mick Coupe on the 29th June; he was attacking Paul Carbutt's record from 1979. Pat Kenny timed Mick away from Lands End at 12 noon and he was soon speeding north. He produced 3hrs 50mins for the first 100 miles but paid for it by cramping up in both legs shortly after, when riding the 'Bridgwater Flats'. This End to End was, for Mick, the culmination of his successful 24hr racing over the last few years, having been in the winning North Staffs St Christopher's Championship Team for five years in succession. He'd also won the Championship in 1979 with a colossal 492 miles. He was now riding for the Horwich CC sponsored by Derek Partington who had a successful cycle shop in the area. He was a very generous man and together with his wife they were very enthusiastic about helping with long distance racing. **Mick reached Scotland inside 24 hours and became the first RRA record breaker to do so.** He broke Ken Joy's record by over 7 miles with **482.5 miles.** For the next few hours Mick suffered badly as he rode into Scotland with the wind against him and by the time he reached 'the Grampians' the wind had dropped for him to be an hour up on Carbutt's record. Mick was the first man to use the newly opened Kessock Bridge over the Beauly Firth and he attacked the hills between here and John o' Groats as though he had just started a race. He took 44 minutes off Carbutt's record with **1day 22hours 39mins 49secs. At 46, Mick is the oldest man in modern day times to have broken the record.**

⟹·◇·⟸

**One week later, Eric Tremaine,** who was the Competition Record holder at 24hrs on a **trike,** also set out on the **5th July** to attack the most coveted record on the books 'The End to End', held by Pat Kenny since 1980 with 2 days 10hrs 36mins. Eric was uneasy about the record right from the start as a previous trip over the End to End route by car had made him realise what he was up against.

His first few hours during the attempt were hot, which didn't suit Eric, and by the 12 hour point he'd covered 225 miles, slightly less than Pat Kenny had done. He had a very slow 100 mile stretch between Stafford and Lancaster partially due to lighting problems the bane of most cyclists at that time, and had been for many years. Don't forget L.E.D's hadn't been invented at this time. Joe Summerlin got himself ready to time the first 24 hours assisted by Ivy Mitton and John Williams, but Eric failed to beat Pat's 24hr record by nearly 2 miles with 429.6 miles, just beyond Lancaster. By Edinburgh Eric had pulled back time to be over 2 hours up on schedule. The rough roads in Scotland, particularly in the Perth area had Eric suffering with his hands being badly swollen and numb. He had quite a few comfort stops between here and Inverness but wind conditions were much more favourable than on Pat's attempt and Eric still remained well up on schedule. He rode that final hilly 100 miles magnificently to beat Pat Kenny's record with **2 days 6hrs 18mins 35secs.** Ironically, Eric's 'End to End' record only came about due to him missing a planned emigration to Canada due to the recession. He'd always wanted to break the record but feared it would never happen.

⟹·◇·⟸

**One week later on Friday 13th July, John Woodburn** set out on his **2nd 'End to End' attempt.** He'd abandoned the ride in 1981 after reaching Blair Athol due to an underlying virus and the record he was attacking now (Mick Coupe's) was even faster. Like all good End to Enders, John had used 24hr time trials to test his ability in 1980 and 1981, winning the Championship in both of these years with 505 miles and 488 miles respectively. He was now 45 years of age and 'ripe' for doing it.

John had a very strong south westerly wind to help him from the start, but then had 50 miles of torrential rain from Bodmin Moor onwards. At the 12 hour point he was 2 miles up on Mick Coupe's mileage with 263 miles. By Lancaster he was 19mins up on Coupe's figures and he ran out his first **24hrs by reaching Ecclefechan with 494.25 miles, another new 24hr record for the RRA,** by nearly 12 miles. At Perth, Woodburn was almost 1.5 hours up on Coupe but it wasn't over yet. John recalls climbing Drumochter feeling very cold, especially on the downhill runs. Dawn broke as he climbed Berriedale with ease. By John o Groats he'd taken 1hour 36mins off the record for **1day 21hrs 3mins 16secs.** George Hunton was the timekeeper along with Pat Kenny as the Observer. Jack Fletcher of 'Trueman Steels' had sponsored John's ride. Also on John's helping team were Keith and Brenda Robins. Brenda and Keith are both RRA Officials and have helped on many of John's long distance exploits, looking after his feeding, clothing and general well being over the years. They have also supplied all of the items required for the slick running of major prize presentations over the last 40 years, maybe more. Items such as Winners sashes and Championship caps, lunch menus and table place mementoes at the Triennial RRA dinners and annual RTTC BBAR presentations.

---

**The Mersey RC 24hr** on 24th and 25th July was **won** by **Rod Goodfellow with 456.744 miles. Charlie Robson** was **2nd** with **447.891 miles** and **Dave Short, 3rd** with **436.475m.** Eric Matthews had now finally taken over the role of Principal Timekeeper from Ron MacQueen who had held it since 1949. As the first of 36 solo's and 3 tandems rolled away at 2pm the sun shone to give a warm start to the event. Police interest in the proceedings was very evident after last year's altercation with a combine harvester at Alpraham Green.

At the 100 mile point, nine men and the tandems were inside 'evens', Goodfellow with 4hrs 33mins, Short at 6mins and Robson at 15mins At Whitchurch the sunny, sultry afternoon gave way to a cooler evening as the riders either detoured to Nantwich or went straight on to Battlefield. By the time Goodfellow had returned from Nantwich he had taken the lead with only Dave Short to stay within striking distance till Chetwynd Heath at 181.44 miles. Here the times were – Goodfellow, 8hrs 36mins, Short at 17m and Robson at 32 mins.

The chill of the night took its toll of the field and limited those beating 230 miles at 12 hours. Goodfellow 244, Short 237, Robson 232, Slater 230 and the Kenny and Lowe tandem, 233 miles. The checkers and detour controllers were using 'c.b' (citizen band) radios and this method helped Peter Barlow to keep the field together. Battlefield the last time saw Spraggett and Slater retire while Bethell succumbed near Wem with 4 hours to go.

On the return to the finishing circuit the wind turned to blow from the north making it tough for the riders. Goodfellow managed 3 circuits, scything his way through the weary riders, to take his 4th Mersey win, equalling Nick Carters record. The tandem with Pat Kenny and Les Lowe was hammering around the circuit, making up time for that lost whilst treating 'hot-foot'.

I helped Pat and Les in that event and I noticed during the event that Les who was on the back was tending to lean out to the offside to see past Pat and instead of counter acting this by leaning to the nearside, Les ended up with a very stiff neck and a bad back, nevertheless they rode to **430.52 miles** and so set up a **new Competition Record.**

The second tandem to finish of S. Barron and E. Smith, Lincoln Whls, recorded 425.932 miles, while **Jenny Colman and her husband** from the Scarborough Paragon CC produced **401.769** for 3rd placed tandem and the **best on record so far. The Otley CC were the only team to finish. The members of the team** being **P. Yates with 391.264m, J. Churchman with 376.087 and L. Howcroft with 368.953m for a total of 1,136.304 miles.**

On a more amusing note, Frank Mumford who recorded and wrote about all of the Mersey RC 24hr events, even to the point of describing the bikes and the new fashions in equipment etc. After describing this years advancement in technology and equipment, he said "I couldn't help thinking of the rusty relic on which John Arnold won the 1954 event with 466.73 miles, using odd wheels, a Sturmey Archer cable joined with knots, and spanners lashed to the top tube!"

The North Road CC 24hr August 28th 1982, was won by Hedley Stennett, Newark Castle CC with 458.060 miles. Ian Dow, Oxford City Rc was 2nd with 422.798 and B. Taylor, Addiscombe CC 3rd with 420.288m. M. Green, G. Dennis and D. Porter won the team prize for the North Road CC with 1,148.744 miles. The event was run off in very fine weather and the anticipated duel between Dow and Stennett unexpectedly went Stennett's way when Dow cracked in the night. **Mrs Anne Rogers,** North Notts Olympic just missed 400 with **398.855 miles.** Two other ladies finished, **Mrs Lorna Webb,** Bedfordshire RC, **337.137m** and **Miss Judy Dakin** on a *trike* with **322 miles.** **Les Lowe** was the fastest trike with **393.234 miles,** a new project for him, but a lasting one, as Les joined the 'T.A' (Tricycle Association) and later had many fast rides to his credit.

Geoff Dring who was out helping that weekend and also reporting on the race for the Fellowship Journal, gave the leading 100 mile times as: Dow 4hrs 37mins, Portress and Riley at 2mins, Stennett at 7mins and Green at over 11mins. Lee Scampton at 12mins and Taylor, Lockett and Don Spraggett all at 13mins.

At the 12 hour point Dow led with 244 miles, Stennett had moved into 2nd place with 241m, Portress 236, Taylor 232, Spraggett 231, Riley 229 and Green 228 miles. At this point Dow's lack of training showed, he was expected to pull away from Hedley Stennett but suffered badly during the night.

*A poignant few lines from Geoff Dring as he marshalled at the 'Black Cat' roundabout with Richard Hulse, paints the picture. Geoff thought all of the riders were now safely on the finishing circuit but noticed Richard still peering down the road. Geoff shouted "you can come back over here now Richard, there can't be anyone left on the road". Richard replied "Ian Dow is still to come". Geoff believed that Ian was surely already on the circuit, probably one of the first on, and that if he wasn't on, then he must have packed. However, it says much for the sportsmanship of Dow, that despite terrible suffering and possible humiliation, he did eventually arrive onto the circuit to run out time, and still managed 2nd place.*

Ian Dow describes his 'disastrous season' in another Fellowship article. His 3rd place in the Wessex Championship 'plodding to the bronze medal with 466 miles' for which he blames his own poor organisation. Before the event, he also mentions picking up a bug in the Mersey 24hr but I can find no record of him riding that event. I will now use word for word, a passage from Ian's description of probably one of the lowest points of his racing career, titled - 'Defeat and Total Defeat'.

*For the fifth consecutive year I was pushed off from Little Paxton layby to head south for Wimpole Lodge, unsuspecting of the nightmare that lay ahead. It was well into the night, somewhere out on the 'Fens' before my fruitless toils gave way to a real bad patch. My early lead went the same way as the light from my 'Ever Ready' Rear guard lamp, and at twelve hours I was recaught by an unknown rider at Soham. Only 244 miles: the possibility of an extra-long ride had vanished. Now all I could hope for was that I could still win the event. What I did not know was that the unknown rider was Hedley Stennett, but what I did think I knew was that he knew that he could not expect to beat me. As is customary in 24-hour events we exchanged greetings, good luck and gentleman's conversation. I explained that I was not having a good ride and was only hoping for about 460 miles – I didn't consider it wise to admit my true state.*

*The ensuing battle lasted many hours and was fought to the bitter end, which came at the Baldock turn in the half-light of pre-dawn. The struggle against darkness was over but my body was utterly spent, every turn of the pedals an agonising and demanding effort. The tenuous thread that had held me to the fight with Stennett had broken, and the victor disappeared unchallenged. Then began the ordeal of trying to salvage enough to strike back – some five or six hours remained, still time for Stennett to falter. But my condition worsened, the deficit stretched rapidly to half an hour, and then the final blow: hic-ups! The merciless spasms were too much. I practically fell from the saddle at Mother's feet begging pitifully for a fried breakfast. I was close to tears. The continuity of my effort was over. I stopped long enough to demolish an omelette – the dream of a 24-hour career come true – but it was nothing to a later stop.*

*With still about three hours left I climbed off for what I thought would be the last time. A change of clothes, more hot food and drink to coax some life into my dead body, and what I needed most of all: rest. To end the suffering was all that mattered now. The outcome of a long and soul-searching debate with understanding parents was that I should continue, somehow, no matter how slowly, so that I could say 'I finished'. And so I went on hic-upping miserably, alone up the North Road on my final leg, and would still be there now in a roadside grave, had not Bob Williams of the Mersey stumbled upon my haggard form and nursed it back to Brampton Hut and anxious helpers. When I reached the circuit, with a scant fifteen minutes to run I said 'that's it' and made another final dismount, only to be lifted back onto the machine by enthusiastic supporters. On I had to go until the very last second was up, and only then could I finally say, once and for all, 'NO MORE'.*

*I unstrapped with 423 miles and, would you believe it, second place, by about two miles. Had I not been returned to the treadmill at the start of the circuit I'd have lost it – so to any readers who were there: thanks!*

*If the proverbial man in the street bows down to us long-distance men as a 'race-apart', a nonsensical attitude I come across a lot, then maybe this sorry tale can help to dispel the image. We are as fallible and human as anyone!*

My thanks to Ian Dow and the 24 Hr Fellowship for this literature.

―――――>•◇•<―――――

So 1982 has been a very varied year for 24 hour riding, but a fantastic year for 'End to End' record breaking, three in all plus two RRA 24hr records were included in these rides. The last time 3 End to End records were broken was in 1929, when Tom Hughes broke the trike record only to lose it a few weeks later to Les Meyers. That same August also saw Jack Rossiter take the record on a bike with 2 days 13hrs 22mins. All three of these rides in 1929 used an all-land route for the first time, as ferries in Scotland were disallowed. Similarities can be drawn between the three riders in 1929 and our modern day three all using the new Kessock Bridge over the Beauly Firth, but whereas in 1929 the route became longer, in 1982 it became shorter and would become even shorter when the road across the Dornoch Firth was opened later, giving a distance of approximately 840 miles.

―――――>•◇•<―――――

# 1983

*Seat belts are made compulsory for front seat passengers this year.*

Although it had been hoped to run the Wessex 24hr in its usual early July slot, a decision had been taken by the Club not to hold the event fearing that it would suffer an even lower entry than normal due to the ECCA (Eastern Counties Cycling Association) staging the Championship 24hr on June 25th and 26th. The course for the ECCA event started at Leaden Roding, which is near Bishops Stortford, the circuit was also based here and was 17 miles around. The extremities of the course were Cambridge and Newmarket in the north, Harlow in the west, Stanway in the east and Orsett, near the Thames, in the south. The final legs and detours before returning to the finishing circuit, were in the Chelmsford area.

**The ECCA National Championship 24hr** on the 25th and 26th of June, **was won by Stuart Jackson with 488.84 miles, 2nd, Hedley Stennett with 464.40 miles and 3rd Edwin Hargraves, 457.40 miles. Stuart Jackson along with Hargraves and Craig led the Farnham RC to a Championship Team win with a total of 1,360.13 miles.** Maldon and District CC were 2nd team with 1,254.03 miles and Gemini BC 3rd, 1,235.39m. Eric Tremaine came 4th on a trike trying to improve his own record, but had to settle for 447.02 miles. George Berwick was 5th with 446.85 miles.

**Anne Mann, Hainault RC won the ladies 24hr with a New Competition Record of 438.16 miles,** an improvement of 10.3 miles on Christine Minto's record from 1969. 2nd lady was Ann Rogers, North Notts Olympic CC with 412.55 miles, 3rd Mrs Jean Burrow, 407.99 and Mary Horswell 4th with 394.15m. A fuller report of the ladies race is written in the Ladies History, Chapter 5. From 74 entries, 68 started and 59 finished.

The Mersey RC 24hr held on 23rd and 24th July 1983 was **won by Brian Morris, Mid Shropshire Whls, with 474.143 miles.** S. Cook, Cheltenham CCC was 2nd with 463.205 m, G. Wardle, Macclesfield Whls was 3rd with 448.359m,George Berwick, West Pennine RC was 4th with 442.440m. He led D. Painter with 391.548 and G. Smith, 387.274 to a West Pennine RC team win of 1,221.26 miles.

One of the favourites, Rod Goodfellow, failed to start but I think he would have had a hard fight on his hands, especially from Brian Morris. **Ian and Bridget Boon** still managed to **establish a 421.893 miles mixed tandem record,** even after a 20 minute late start and also losing a few minutes at a turn early in the event.

At the 100 mile point, Morris led with 4hrs 30mins, Gerry Smith was at 2 mins, Cook and Holland at 16mins, Wardle at 17mins and Berwick at 22mins. At Ternhill the only lady in the event, Sheila Simpson, crashed while taking food and broke her collarbone, she subsequently retired for hospital treatment.

Between 9pm and midnight, intermittent thunderstorms flooded parts of the course, literally converting Prees Island into just that! Lynton Threadgolds band of young 'Mersey Roaders' dispensed hot drinks to the riders as they progressed around the Prees-Battlefield-Ternhill triangle. On the 'Chetwynd' leg, Gerry Smith collided with a cow-girl while dodging her animals in the dark, this led to his premature retirement and his valiant bid for honours.

Morris had been the first man on the road since 160 miles and was drawing away from Cook, Berwick, Wardle and Holland. The grim misty night saw Norris, Spraggett, Cresswell and Denman retire between 188 and 202 miles. A cool windless dawn gave a promise of a better 2nd day and so it proved to be. At the 12 hour check, Morris led with 251, Cook 237, Berwick 232, Wardle 230 and Holland 227. Geoff Manson's mobile feeding squad kept the weary riders going throughout, with 'goodies' handed up in musettes.

A cruel twist of fate ended Bob Jump's ride at 312 miles. In the quiet lanes while approaching Wem, he was knocked down by a lunatic motorist. Bob sustained head and leg injuries requiring medical treatment. Morris rode these same roads very cautiously, remembering his accident in the 1981 Championship when he collided with a papergirl, his injuries and loss of time certainly cost him 3rd place that day.

Morris was the first rider to reach the finishing circuit after completing the full course to the cheers of the crowd. The result board at Austins Hill manned by Johnny Helms and John Williams, marked the riders progress as the lads went by. Many of the riders were avid Audax and Randoneur competitors who were using their results gained in this event to count towards their 'performance' to enter the Paris-Brest-Paris' (P.B.P). This had been Dave Stapleton's 22nd running of this famous event.

The North Road 24hr 27th and 28th August 1983 was **won by Rod Goodfellow, North Lancs RC with 453.561 miles.** G. Wallis, Kenton RC was **2nd with 435.506m** and **J. Weston,** Notts Clarion CC was **3rd with 415.971m.**

19 riders started and 17 finished. The weather was bright sunny and warm. Geoff Dring reporting for the 24hr Fellowship Journal, checked the 100 mile times with Eric Wilkinson. The leader was Rod Goodfellow with 4hrs 30mins. G. Wallis at 6m, R. Lockett at 18m, J. Weston at 21mins, W. Lantry at 22m, K. Clarke at 24m and Don Spraggett at 27mins.

Geoff was very impressed by Hugh Culverhouse of theWeybridge Whls. This gutsy rider had only the use of one leg. To get maximum effort from his right leg he pulled hard against the handlebars and slid along his saddle to get a circular pedalling action, his left leg was held immobile and straight at the knee, resting on a fixed crank and pedal.

This year there was a night circuit of some 31 miles off the A1 based on Milton, Ely, Witchford, Haddenham, Wilburton, Histon and back to Milton. It proved to be successful, keeping the field contained and eased the pressure on marshals. At 12 hours Goodfellow led with 243 miles, Wallis 232, Weston 226, Beardsley 225, Usher 221, Spraggett and Clarke 219m.

On Sunday morning the weather turned cold and drizzly with a gusty wind. Despite Goodfellow having problems with his knee, he led to the end and won with 453 miles. **But the most heroic ride of the weekend was that of Hugh Culverhouse who finished 11th with 394.705 miles.**

*In later years, **Hugh** had two attacks on the 'End to End' route. His first ride was completed in **78 hours** and in 1987 he had a second successful attempt and took nearly 10 hours off with **69 hours 5mins 4secs**. I saw him ride through the Midlands on this attempt and was amazed at his speed and strength. The steep climbs of 'Shap Fell' and the 'Devil's Beeftub' were painful for him, but he overcame all odds to break his own record.*

<hr />

We are now in a period of time where the Mersey RC 24hr and the North Road CC 24hr are the two main events each year, with just the odd special event, usually hosting a Championship. The Mersey RC and the North Road CC host the RTTC Championship on alternate years.

# 1984

*In March 1984, Arthur Scargill led the Coalminers Union out on strike against Pit closures. The strike lasted a year and the Union was eventually crushed in 1985 by Margaret Thatcher. Her political decisions caused the end of a way of life and work, affecting thousands of men and their families.*

**The Mersey RC 24hr on 21st July, was won by Malcolm Green, North Roads CC, with 460.132 miles.** Rod **Goodfellow was 2nd with 454.792 and Simon Doughty was 3rd with 442.061m. Worcester St John CC took the fastest team prize with 1,222.752 miles. The team consisted of a regular Mersey 24hr rider, Roger Alma, with 411.688, R. Gillfillan with 410.489 and R. Ashman with 400.575m.**

The event Organiser, Dave Stapleton was assisted this year by Jim Turner who was offering a prize of £75.00 for any rider breaking the Competition Record of 507 miles.

At the start the discussion centred on scratchman Rod Goodfellow's chances of pulling off a record breaking 5th win, having scored 475m in 1967, 478m in 1975, 476 in 1976 and 456 in 1982. None of the field had bettered 456 miles in recent years. **No one particularly rated Malcolm Green with a previous personal best of 411 miles, he was to win with an improvement of 49 miles.**

The checkpoint at 47 miles had the tandem of Cruse and Smith with 2hrs 2mins, Goodfellow was at 3mins, Doughty at 4m, Green 6m, and Ithell at 7mins. At the 100 miles check, the tandem still led with 4hrs 32mins, Goodfellow was 2nd at 5mins, Green at 8mins, Doughty 12m, and Robson at 18m. At the 201 mile check, Goodfellow had taken the lead after a very tough battle in 9hrs 53mins, Green was at 14mins, the tandem at 21mins and Doughty at 24m. The riders were now encountering some mist and a really cold night, but despite this, many of them did not bother with 'longs' or tights.

The battle still raged between Goodfellow and Green with the 'Doctor' being re-caught by Green at 276 miles. This really got the adrenalin flowing and Goodfellow put in a massive effort to pass and open up a lead of 6 minutes at 311 miles. Green responded to the early morning warmth from the sun on the drags to Redbrook and again caught Goodfellow at the turn, 368 miles, with nearly 4.75 hours to go. By the time the finishing circuit was reached at 408 miles, Green had a 5mins lead on time over Goodfellow.

Each bend and turn on the finishing circuit of 17 miles was lined with helpers and supporters, cheering the 36 solos's, 5 trikes and both tandems that had made it to here. Green seemed quite fresh and turned in lap times of 52 minutes with a last lap burst of 50.5 minutes, while Goodfellow had 2 laps of 56.5mins and the last one at 55mins.

Green with 460.132 had ridden a very even race with a 235 miles first 12 hours and 225 for his second half, whereas Goodfellow had almost 240 and 214 miles. Doughty with 442.061 had a first 12hours of 228m and 2nd of 214m. George Berwick won his earlier battles with Don Spraggett and drew away to come 4th with 436.983 miles, while Spraggett had lots of mechanical problems and finished well down with 368.801m. Dick Usher, Spalding CC rode 407.669m while brother Ken who stopped 18 minutes before his 24hours was up, finished with 399.194 miles.

The **tandem pair of S. Cruse and R. Smith** after starting very fast, tailed off halfway through but finished very comfortably with **438.334 miles** for a **new Competition Record** by nearly 8 miles. The previous record being held by Pat Kenny and Les Lowe. **John Jackson,** Macclesfield Whls was the **fastest trike** with **396.073 miles** and Les Lowe was 2nd with 384.216m, while Mark Brooking and Jane Ramsdale on the tandem trike rode 364.531m.

**John Williams used a computer in this event for the first time to produce a finishing forecast and result.**

≫━━◆━━≪

*There are now 20 million cars on Britain's roads.*

**The North Road CC National Championship 24hr in 1984 was won by Stuart Jackson, Farnham RC with 494.16 miles. Ian Dow was 2nd with 486.99 miles and Peter Hoffmann, RSCK Ludwigsburg was 3rd with 471.53m.** Hedley Stennett just missed 3rd place by .31 of a mile, but as Hoffmann was not eligible for the RTTC Championship due to his German Nationality, I assume that **Stennett took the Bronze medal with his 471.22 miles. Mick Coupe was 5th with 470.02m and led a Horwich CC team of Tom Finney who was 6th with 461.15m and John Cahill 443.64 to a Championship Team winning total of 1,374.81 miles.**

The mileage of the first two riders, Jackson and Dow, does not reflect the misfortunes that both of these riders had suffered. Jackson's demise was from not being turned at Brampton Hut in the last few hours of the race, and so losing 18 minutes which at the speed he was averaging was worth approximately 7 miles. Likewise, Dow was turned away from the last optional detour at Biggleswade (which most of the field had ridden) and he was turned left to the finishing circuit with 3 hours still to go. His helpers who were waiting for him on the detour to Baldock started to panic and so did Ian. This was the turning point in Ian Dow's ride; he knew he wouldn't see his helpers for a long time, and he was now getting hungry due to not seeing them. As he started on his 2nd circuit he punctured and it then seemed that his ride was over and lost, but one of the crowd of spectators sorted it out for him and he was on his way again after a few minutes time loss.

Later he saw his father with a spare wheel in his hand. Ian said his feeling then was that his entire race had been won and lost on the circuit. In that last three hours he'd dropped a staggering 7 miles to Jackson. The man who had the 3rd highest mileage, Peter Hoffmann, was over in England to ride long distance events with a view to attacking the End to End record. *The problem now of course is that a first 24hours of 490 miles plus is needed to secure this 850 mile record.*

Coupe, Finney and Cahill were definitely proving that they weren't one hit wonders, having won the Championship team honours 6 times as North Staffs St Christopher's and now for the first time in the colours of the Horwich CC Partington Cycles. They went on to win another 4 Championships for the Horwich CC making a total of 11 wins for this team in one form or another.

The main two men, Coupe and Cahill, had 9 team appearances each, Tom Finney had 7, Mick Parker 4, and Ron Stoneman 3. This year, Finney had one of his best rides, mileage wise; Cahill suffered badly with knee trouble but carried on bravely for the team prize. **R. Geere, Farnborough & Camberley, was the fastest trike 369 miles.**

The weather for the event was good, warm and breezy on the Saturday with the night staying warm and clear. Eighty one riders started, one of the largest fields for many years, 59 riders finished including just one lady competitor Mrs Esther Carpenter, Southborough & District CC, who rode 375.24 miles. It's also pleasing to note that 24 of the finishers were first time 24hr riders, including the complete Saracen RC team of Phil Carbutt, Mike Harborne and Mike Hazelwood.

# 1985

**The Mersey RC National Championship 24hr** on 27th and 28th July 1985 was **won by Ian Dow with 480.55 miles, Gerry Smith was 2nd with 473.55 miles and Steve Armstrong was 3rd with 465.65m.** Although the **Edinburgh RC team** comprised of **Berwick, Borland and Murdoch** were the **fastest** with **1,251.54 miles,** their win could only be recognised by the Mersey RC, as **being Scottish they were not eligible for RTTC National Championship awards, and so the title went to the Horwich CC, comprised of Coupe, Stoneman and Parker, with a total of 1,240.77 miles.**

Steve Armstrong who came 3rd gave us a few details of his ride in the event. The weather at the start was bright and warm but with a strong wind coming from the southwest. Steve had previously ridden some decent 12hr races but an accident in 1982 had left him with a troublesome back. 1984 saw him ride to 7th place in the North Road Championship 24hr, with 449.5m, and although he was pleased with his ride he felt that he could do better, so he planned to make this Mersey Championship his main goal.

A lacklustre season up to late June left him a little despondent and then a personal best of 4hrs 7mins set him up ready for the Mersey event. Despite an acute pain in his right knee one week before the 24hr, which luckily disappeared a few days later, he felt ready both physically and mentally. His feeding consisted of fruit and chocolate bars, yoghurt, creamed rice and fruit cocktail in a 50/50 mix, and bananas. Drinks were mainly electrolyte, mineral energy drink, also decarbonated 'coke' and a 'recovery' drink, which looked and tasted like a milkshake.

He had planned an inside 'evens' schedule up to 12 hrs and was hoping to top 210 miles for his 2nd half of the ride. He had studied the start sheet; it included top riders such as defending champion Stuart Jackson, and previous medallists and winners, Ian Dow, Brian Morris, Mick Coupe, Edwin Hargraves and with Gerry Smith, John North and Simon Doughty all entered, he knew it would be a tough battle for a possible medal.

Mick Coupe got off to a poor start when his rear wheel pulled over in the frame only yards away from the start line and then it was Steve's turn to go. Strangely enough a few moments after he had started, he heard a rubbing noise; he'd also pulled his rear wheel over. *This wouldn't happen in 2008 as all lightweight race bikes have vertical drop-outs and have had for quite a few years.* By 31 miles he had caught Mick Coupe, Ian Dow was pulling away from him, Morris and Doughty were still close behind him. Stuart Jackson was not on form and was already struggling. Steve said he thought many people appreciated his sportsmanship by starting as the defending Champion and he asked the question "how many of our shorter distance stars would have made a similar gesture?" On the next headwind section back to Nantwich he caught Edwin Hargraves who was making a steady start. At 52 miles he passed Gerry Smith who had obviously had some mechanical trouble.

A large crowd had gathered at the 'Nags Head' at Haughton Moss to have a few beers and see the riders turn in the very narrow lane. The southerly wind made the ride down to Whitchurch a hard slog for the riders and Steve was surprised to go through the 100 mile point in 4hrs 34mins. The return leg from Nantwich back to Whitchurch was also a very tough one, Ian Dow was now about 10 minutes 'up' on Steve at this point.

While stopped to put on night clothing and lights just south of Whitchurch, Steve was passed by Coupe, Hargraves and Smith. He started away again from his helpers feeling very overdressed but it wasn't long before the rain came and he re-passed Morris, Smith and Coupe as they too donned night clothing and he regained his 2nd place. It was dark now and the rain got heavier, Steve experienced his first bad patch near Hodnet, Gerry Smith caught him just before Tern Hill traffic lights and drew away up to Prees Heath. It was at that point that Steve wondered whether he had started too fast. He lowered his gears and settled into a better rhythm and felt much stronger on the leg towards Newport. Back at Hodnet (211 miles) saw him taking a short break with his helpers as he'd missed them in the dark and wondered whether they were awake enough to help him on the long stretch back to Prees.

Dow was approximately 20 minutes clear of him as he passed through 12 hours with about 244 to Dow's 250 miles. Gerry Smith had ridden 241m as had Simon Doughty with Edwin Hargraves the only other rider beating 'evens' with 240m. Gerry Smith produced the ride of his life in this event and his steady 241 mile first 12 hours was followed by a well judged 232 mile 2nd half.

With Brian Morris about 10 minutes down, Steve felt that he may now have a chance at a medal and knowing that Dow was ahead of him, it would probably be a silver one. The rain was showing no sign of stopping and he had a few slippery moments, which made him ride more cautiously. John Thompson of the Anfield B.C. took a lot of catching, eventually going on to an excellent 439mile ride. Steve caught Don Spraggett near Shawbury and from then on was 2nd on the road. This did not last long as Gerry Smith was gaining on him and as dawn broke, Smith caught him on his second trip down to Chetwynd. He let him get clear knowing there was still a long way to go and plenty of time to make another challenge.

Back at Hodnet (302m) some of the roads were awash in places. Morris had packed already and Mick Coupe was 45mins down on Steve, with Simon Doughty at 10mins he was the only other challenger for a bronze medal at this point. Steve was now feeling very tired but after some encouragement from Ethel and Bernard Thompson around the Wem area, he picked up a bit more speed.

*Bernard was out in his camper van as always, taking photos of the riders and reporting this Championship for the 'Cycling' magazine as he always did, giving excellent coverage, sometimes two whole pages with photographs, as befitting this famous event (unlike the almost non-existent coverage of modern day 24hr events as in 2007)*

Before the turn at Redbrook (368 miles) Steve was amazed to see that Gerry Smith had almost caught Ian Dow and it looked as though a tough battle for the gold medal was looming for Ian. On the tail wind section back to the finishing circuit from Whitchurch, Stuart Jackson had stayed out to cheer the riders through. Between Christleton Island (Chester) and the circuit at Waverton, Steve had to stop for refreshment, he was going through a very bad patch and when he remounted he decided to go on the attack and see if he could ride through it. Luckily this method worked and he managed to cover over 2 laps at 19 mph and so finished with 465.65 miles and a bronze medal.

Steve Armstrong went on to thank his helpers Lynne Marshall, Steve King and Mark Botteley, who had got him through some very bad patches. Poor weather had taken its toll not only on Steve but all of the riders, but despite this, 45 riders finished with 23 beating 400 miles.

**Mrs Jill Richards,** Cardiff Ajax CC was the **sole lady rider** that day and so won the Merseyside Ladies CA 24hr with **382.684 miles. The mixed tandem of Ian and Bridget Boon raised the record to 443.27 miles** so becoming the fastest tandem in the event. **Les Lowe,** Speedwell B.C. and **Jim Hopper,** Tricycle Association (Mids) created a **new tandem trike record** that day and claimed **419.15 miles.** P. Dade and G.V. Adams finished the tandem race in 3rd place with 416.15 miles.

At last, after 5 years of trying, Ian Dow took his first 24hr Championship title. Ian was a very popular rider with everyone. He was a very modest man who was always looking at his own fallibilities and if he found a solution to a problem with his riding, he would let everyone have the benefit of that knowledge through his writings and articles in the 24hr Fellowship Journals. His highly amusing and honest descriptions of his rides, not only his good ones but also his slower ones, and also his 'training tours' with Edwin Hargraves and Stuart Jackson, made good reading to any aspiring 24hr rider.

In an article entitled 'It's Tough at the Top' taken from a 24hr Fellowship Journal, Ian Dow describes his feelings in the winter of 1984. Ian starts his article by saying that the statement 'It's tough at the top' is rubbish, and went on to say that it was 'tough' coming 3rd all the time and then only 2nd in the 1984 Championship, when nothing short of victory had been considered.

He brooded through the winter of 1984/85, he'd made some silly mistakes in 1984's race but felt passionately that victory could be his in 1985 as long as he didn't make any more mistakes. At the same time he couldn't imagine anyone ever beating Stuart Jackson, Champion for the last 3 years, his track record was formidable, 4 rides, 4 wins, twice close to 500 miles! Ian thought of nothing else that winter, except how to beat Stuart. They toured together over the Easter holidays, but Ian found it difficult to judge Stuart's fitness, they both rode the 'Anfield 100' at Whitsun, but with Ian having a puncture and Stuart riding his trike, there was still no indication as to who was on best form. Ian knew that only victory in the Mersey would settle the score and put his mind at rest.

The day came, Ian was without his usual staunch helper, his father, who was recuperating after an operation. His brother Steven was going to drive and help, despite being a total non-cyclist, he knew of Ian's commitment and ambition to win this event and that's all that mattered. On the way to the event from Oxford they had noticed a heavily gusting wind from the west, buffeting the car on this exposed part of the M6 around Birmingham, although the day was generally bright, sunny and very pleasant.

Ian describes getting to the start with plenty of time to spare, unlike Stuart Jackson. For a while he thought Stuart wasn't going to turn up and defend his title, but a few minutes before the start his rusty old Peugeot came hurtling round the corner and rattled to a stop alongside Ian's car. Out fell 'Carruthers' (Stuarts nickname, Ian's being 'Blenkinsopp') and out fell a couple of bikes to which Stuart hurriedly fitted bottle cages. Ian said he couldn't believe how such a great Champion could be so disorganised for his title race, when he'd had all year to prepare.

The race started and Ian felt good, he was very fond of the first 100 miles of the Mersey course, steeped in tradition as it is. After about two hours it became clear to Ian that something was wrong with Stuart, he was losing lots of time to Ian, so much time in fact that Ian knew it wasn't just a tactical ploy on Stuart's part. At around 120 miles, Ian realised that Stuart had 'packed'. He immediately felt relieved, but the news also came as a distressing anti-climax. He'd been fully wound up for an absolute 'leg-breaker' of a battle with Stuart that wasn't going to happen now. He said "the adrenalin stopped flowing as if a tap had been turned off and I relaxed, there was only one snag, at 120 miles a 24hr title has not been won! far from it".

Night fell and so did heavy rain, the roads were awash and Ian who wears glasses said he almost came to a standstill a few times as he struggled to see the road. Ian said "rain or no rain, however, the wondrous Mersey crowds were in place on every corner, their cheers heartier than ever. It was so good to see the outgoing Champion join them and encourage the riders throughout the rest of the event. I spotted him standing in his cape in the middle of the night and it struck me that a lesser mortal would have been back at home in bed."

During this time it never occurred to Ian that any other rider was challenging him. From Shawbirch Island, where a miserable dawn was breaking, to Redbrook, is a 56 miles stretch of road devoid of turns. He'd been told he'd got a 20 minute lead and so he climbed off at Wem for a quick rub down which took 6 minutes, and on reaching Redbrook, 368 miles, he turned, checked his watch and started rolling back towards Welshampton, thinking he'd probably see his first rider in ten minutes or so. What happened next, took him completely by surprise, a cape clad figure approached him and less than 2 minutes separated them on the road, it was No 60, Gerry Smith; Ian was No 59. Ian thought, "what the hell has happened?" he shouted to his helpers "has that rider done the whole course?" and the reply was "Yes, he has!".

The thought of being beaten at this late stage exploded Ian into action, he shot off back towards the finishing circuit and recalls the bike shuddering and shaking over the rough roads from the effort he was putting in. His brother, Steven, shouted that he'd gained back two minutes but Ian knew that wasn't enough and made his legs 'howl' with pain and luckily the rain washed the tears from his eyes as he tried his hardest to get well back into the lead. He said "I had got my battle, but not with Stuart Jackson, it was with the legendary Gerry Smith whose only previous serious attempt at all day racing had ended spectacularly in the unforgiving side of a cow!"

The chase lasted for 40 miles until Ian turned at Christleton at 408 miles. This was the moment of truth, every second counted as Ian watched for his rival, one minute, two minutes, three – there he is! They waved, Ian had gained 4 minutes back, after 1 lap of the finishing circuit the lead had opened to 8 minutes and after the 2nd lap it was evident that the plucky challenge from Gerry Smith was over, but nevertheless, Ian kept the pressure on to make certain of the win and to top 480 miles.

Ians last paragraph gave praise to the other top riders. He said "Gerry Smiths's ride of 473 miles at the age of 53 and in the atrocious conditions of that event, was surely a superb performance. I wonder what he could have done 20 years previously? After the event I learnt of other heroic rides, - of Steve Armstrong's bronze medal ride, dogged with back trouble who slogged his way to 465 miles, Horwich CC's Mick Coupe who continued bravely after two crashes rather than let his team down, and many, many more!"

≫•◊•≪

**The North Road CC 24hr** held on the August Bank Holiday weekend saw an exceptionally large number of entries for a non-championship event, 74 riders were entered including 2 solo lady riders and 2 tandems.

14 riders failed to start on a day that was 'tolerably fine' during daylight but one which deteriorated rapidly with the onset of night, which was windy and bitterly cold. The cold decimated the field and some riders were reduced to walking to restore the circulation in frozen limbs.

**Pieter Hoffmann** from the German Federal Republic and riding for the Komet Ludwigsburg Club, **won the event with 469.98 miles. Stuart Jackson,** Skipton CC rode a **trike** that year, he was looking for a Competition Record but chose the wrong day to try. Despite the weather he finished with a very creditable **444.13 miles** for **2nd** place. **Malcolm Green was 3rd with 436.72m and led a North Road CC team consisting of Gordon Dennis with 429.70m and Mrs Anne Dunk, 365.78m to a total of 1,233.20 miles.**

Alan Reinsch, RC Cannstatt, a friend of Peter Hoffmann, came fourth despite a very nasty fall during the event, with 435.77 miles. Mrs Jean Burrow, Hainault RC was the fastest lady with 382.97m from Mrs Anne Dunk. The fastest of the tandems, A. Fielding and P. Horsfield, rode to 401.34 miles, just beating the mixed crew tandem of G. Yuill and Miss Judy Tait, by 2.46 miles.

Out of 38 solo finishers only 11 riders beat 400 miles.

*The whole of this report on the North Road CC event was taken from a book entitled 'The Second Fifty Years of Road Riding (1935-1985)', a history of the North Road CC by D.H. Gates, K.M. Lovett and the late F.C. Sellens. My sincere thanks go to the Committee of the North Road CC for their permission to use data, results and information in the writing of my book on the 'History of the 24 Hour Race'.*

# 1986

*On April 27th 1986 fire broke out at Chenobyl, Russia's largest Nuclear Reactor and caused a massive radiation leak, which killed many people.*

*The M25 is completed in this year.*

This year saw the inclusion of a special event run by **The North Midlands Cycling Federation for the RTTC National 24hr Championship, 28th and 29th June. It was won by Ian Dow, Oxford City RC, with 488.896 miles. John Woodburn, Manchester Wheelers, was 2nd with 482.873m and Stuart Jackson was 3rd with 468.152m. Tom Finney with 443.637 narrowly beat Clubmate, John Cahill, by .042miles and led Ron Stoneman with 430.916m to a Horwich CC team winning total of 1,318.148 miles, to take the Championship team title for the 3rd year in succession.** Graham Barker, Rockingham CC was 4th with 460.493m and David Williams, Mersey RC was 5th with 456.649m. This was Ian Dow's 2nd successive Championship 24hr win and as President of the 24 Hour Fellowship he was in a very good position to give a blow by blow account of the event, and the lead up to it in the weeks beforehand.

*1986 – The Hot One. The build up to the 1986 Championship was quite unlike anything I had seen before. No less than two years earlier, Ticker Mullins had announced in 'Cycling' that he was intending to attack Competition Record in the event, and had joined one of the big sponsored clubs specially to do so. He was preparing exclusively for the '24' from then until the event. His one previous ride had yielded 485 miles and gained him a bronze medal in 1979.*

Newly qualified veteran, Sandy Gilchrist, Manchester Wheelers team-mate of Mullins, was the dark horse of the race – a first class 12 hour man making his debut at 24 hours.

The Manchester Wheelers team was completed by the much-feared John Woodburn, who had never been beaten in a '24' and had ridden 505.5 miles in the vintage championship of 1980.

Stuart Jackson had entered again, no doubt back to full fighting form after his disappointment of 1985; Gerry Smith was alive and kicking, and past champions Cahill and Coupe of Horwich were also names to watch. Quite a field.

It was quite obvious that nobody expected me to win. The Daily Telegraph previewed the event as follows: "In the national 24hr time trial championship which begins this afternoon, and is based on the A1 trunk road at Blyth, John Woodburn will try and regain the title he has held twice previously". All the talk was of how much the Wheelers could add to the team record and how Roy Cromack's record was going to be broken.

However, it seemed to me that the Manchester Wheelers team was a recipe for disaster. They were not so much a team as three deadly rivals who were more likely to smash each other into the ground than break records. I hoped so anyway!

There were two men in the field that really worried me – Stuart Jackson and John Woodburn, in that order. Carruthers was without doubt still my most feared adversary. Anybody who had seen him in the final quarter of the 1984 Championship would understand. John Woodburn is a tremendous rider and star at all distances, but looking at his previous rides, it appeared that he did not have Stuart's deadly weapon of a fast finish. It seemed to me that if I could be up on him at dawn then I would still be up at the finish in the afternoon, and that, theoretically, made him beatable.

The weather leading up to the day was windy and baking hot, and Saturday June 28th must have been the hottest day of the year. While the Manchester Wheelers team posed for photographs on Blyth village green, I relaxed in a nearby pub with Dai Sankey and the Welsh boys who were trying to get me drunk before the start.

Just before I was pushed off, Bob Williams of the Mersey found his way through the crowd to tell me that they believed I could retain the title. They had faith! It was the perfect send off.

The heat was such that racing was out of the question. I wouldn't last five minutes in that. Instead I pulled on my white cap and poodled off at not much more than a touring pace. From my privileged position as last man off reading the race was a simple matter. Woodburn was No 50, Gilchrist 60, Jackson 65, Mullins 70 and myself 76. As early as 20 miles Gilchrist was noticeably storming ahead with a massive 5.5 minute lead over me. I had expected him to start fast but not that fast! John Woodburn was pulling away steadily while most of my other rivals were holding roughly level. Mick Coupe was engaged in a reckless duel with his minuteman Mullins but by the time I had caught him at about 70 miles, he had been dropped and was in a very poor state. Soon afterwards he packed, most unusual for him.

I was glad I had pulled in my horns during the heat of the afternoon for I could see other riders wilting all over the place. In the cool of the evening, I began to move and was soon pulling back time. The position at 100 miles, as far as I could determine, was: Gilchrist 4.28, Woodburn 4.34, myself 4.36, Mullins and Jackson 4.40. Soon after this point, my brother handed me a note showing that I was drawing level with Woodburn. Excellent news.

The wind died away and a welcome darkness descended onto the flat North Nottinghamshire countryside. I devoured a chicken leg and a pint of soup and was promptly recaught by Ticker. This would not do. After giving my food a chance to go down I began to put my fitness to the test. The night stretched ahead for about five hours and I knew that I had to use it to build up a winning advantage over Woodburn and Jackson. It was time to go. The gear lever went forward and the power that I had been holding back began to flow. I felt perfect. Mullins fell back and soon I had put Stuart behind me. Sportingly, I resisted the temptation to take all his feeds – we looked the same in the dark with our twin front lamps. The next rider I caught was Les Lowe, but Les cut our discussion short, telling me to get on with the job and chase after Woody and Gilchrist!

Shortly before turning at Lincoln I saw the lights of two riders coming towards me close together. I guess it had to be Gilchrist and Woodburn. So they were battling, but I was gaining on them both. I was going very well indeed. So well in fact, that periodically I had to say to myself, "slow down, Ian, this is a 24 not a 12" Otherwise I would have blown.

"SORRY, wrong number"

Down at Winthorpe Island, 252 miles, and just under 12 hours, the sky was beginning to pale and Roy Cromack gave me a hearty shout. In the dawn chill I stopped along the A46 on the way to North Hykeham for extra embrocation, and this time there was no mistaking the Manchester Wheelers duo! Gilchrist looked miserable, Woodburn invincible as they approached, about a hundred yards apart. They were 8 minutes in front on the road, from which it was not difficult to deduce that I was 18 minutes up on Woodburn and 8 on Gilchrist.

Soon the return from North Hykeham would throw light on the fortunes of Jackson and Mullins. As it turned out Ticker was actually not far behind, but he had obviously been trying very hard and I hope he will not be offended when I say that he looked awful. Carruthers was nowhere. He was so far behind that I lost track of him altogether.

One by one the dangermen were going down. Turning north again at Winthorpe I started to feel particularly fit. It was a fabulous early midsummer morning, no cars littered the roads, the air was crisp and invigorating, and I was winning! Suddenly a large blue obstacle appeared, weaving gently in the road ahead. What was it? It was almost stationary and it looked a bit like a cyclist. As I drew up to it I could see that I was right – it was, or had been, a cyclist. It lifted itself up off its saddle and stood up straight on its pedals, its head hanging down in front. Looking up as I sped past I recognised the inverted features of Sandy Gilchrist. His ride was over: a magnificent athlete but the '24' had beaten him.

Ten hours to go. Now it was between myself and John Woodburn, with him lying 8 minutes in front on the road. Back up the Trent Valley to Gainsborough it felt like heading for home and I particularly enjoyed this stretch. It was a nice winding road with a few easy hills to break the monotony. Over to the left, through the early morning mist, a colossal power station grew out of the cornfields. I felt brilliant, and was cruising effortlessly well in excess of 20 mph. At this stage I was aiming for about 496 miles and hoping to catch Woodburn. John Woodburn however, did not want to be caught.

Near Markham Moor at about 330 miles, I caught a glimpse of Ticker Mullins rooting around in the back of a car – he had obviously jacked it in, leaving Woodburn to battle on alone.

As the sun climbed across the sky so the wind rose from the east. It grew in ferocity until the east-west legs across the fenlands to Crowle and Westwoodside had me crawling along at 17's in a 72" gear out to the turn and racing back at over 23's in 100" coming back. My target of 496 became impossible, and eventually I felt so beaten by the heat and the wind that I lost interest in mileage and concentrated all my effort into holding Woodburn.

He was fighting hard now – time was running out. Enthusiasts at the roadside were urging me to catch him, but every time I started to close the gap he would counter my move. It was a good race but a gruelling one. Back at the finishing circuit the massed crowd on Blyth Green was the biggest I have ever seen at a '24' and it was a huge moral boost on every lap. Round and round we went, locked 8 minutes apart and that is how it stayed.

The first to congratulate me on finishing was Roy Cromack himself, and that was a great moment for me. I myself would like to congratulate Trevor Wilkinson and the NMCF on putting on such a superb '24'. Surely one of the best ever.

The two tandems entered both gained **Competition records.  Firstly the 'Boons' Ian and Bridget** raised their own 'mixed' Comp record to **463.334 miles,** and then **G. Adams, Redbridge CC and M. Smith,** Maldon & District CC added 28 miles onto the previous **men's** record with **466.56 miles.**

*The controversial subject of declining entries had constantly crept into conversations whenever 24 hr events were mentioned. The long distance sport had already lost the Catford CC event in 1975 and also the Wessex RC 24hr in 1983, and although it was felt by some fairly newcomers to the sport of 24hr riding that the introduction of these 'special' events run by various cycling associations on behalf of the RTTC and given Championship status, to be a good thing and so bringing 'new blood' into the sport, there were many of the 'elders' and regulars who could also see the damage of declining entries it was causing, to the two remaining established annual events.  I will now enclose a short passage that appeared in the Mersey RC's official description of their event in 1986 by Frank Mumford.*

*"Although our event included the VTTA (Veteran Time Trials Association) National 24hr Championship, we knew that the rival RTTC-inspired National Championship held one month previously would reduce our field, as already spelt out by Peter Barlow who had been involved in the 24hr scene for 50 years.   Even so, we hardly anticipated a fall to 45 solos and 1 tandem, and we also worried about the 'knock on' effect it would have on the North Road CC 24hr promotion, which coincidentally obtained 44 solos and 2 tandems.*

*It is time to seriously consider whether the total of 150* **potential** *riders that there are each season should periodically be split 3 ways by the intrusion of the RTTC special promotion, to the detriment of the two clubs faithfully organising their own classic 24hr event every season.   Our event involves some 250 officials and costs £1,000 to run and is largely funded on a subscription basis; any further erosion of the entry would inevitably diminish interest and commence the downward spiral to which the Catford and Wessex events have already fallen victim."*

━━━━◆━━━━

**The Mersey RC 24hr** 26th & 27th July 1986 was won by **Mike Stoaling,** Wessex RC with **450.58 miles, Eric Millington,** Wolverhampton Whls was **2nd** with **448.58m,** and **Ken Usher,** Peterborough CC, 3rd with **447.69m. Mark Holden,** Milton Keynes CC was **4th** with **440.93m.  R. Ashman,** Worcs St Johns CC was **5th** with **427.81m.   George Berwick** who was 6th with **426.61** led an Edinburgh RC Team comprised of **W. Borland, 408.56m and J. Thomson, 375.97 miles,** to a winning total of **1,211.14 miles.**

Speculation before the start as to who might win centred on previous winners, Goodfellow, Green or last years 2nd placed rider, Gerry Smith.   Other riders in the frame were Usher who won in 1960 and 1962, and always a dark horse, also four up and coming Audax riders; Haswell, Millington, Stoaling and Ashman who respectively had clocked 428, 426, 418 and 411 miles previously.
Mark Holden, a 24hr novice, but with a decent 247 miles 12 hour to his credit, could also prove to be in with a chance.

The course again this year was based on a start at Tarvin with the hub of the action being at Prees and Ternhill, where Tommy Greep and Peter Barlow kept the field together with various 'detours'.

The 39 starters were calmly monitored by Dave Stapleton, the Event Secretary, before Timekeeper, Eric Matthews, sent them on their way. Frank Mumford, the Mersey RC 'scribe' who gave us this information every year, also kept a record of the riders equipment, clothing and bikes and it makes interesting reading.   The riders ages varied between 19yrs and 77yrs, and out of the 39 machines there were 26 different makes, 6 were Raleighs, 4 Longstaffs (including 3 trikes) 3 Harry Quinn, 3 Peugeot and 3 alloy framed bikes.   There were no Sturmey Archer gears and no 'low profile' bikes this year.   Dave O'Neill who usually ran as 'Lanterne-Rouge', or the 'last man' most years, a position he enjoyed, was the only fixed wheel rider, most now preferring multiple gears.

A few riders failed to start, those being Green, Smith, Garner, Flavell and most poignantly, Stan Argill, who had died under the wheels of an overtaking lorry in daylight on a dual carriageway the previous week. Frank Mumford had visited him in hospital after a previous accident in Majorca and had been told by him that it was the 12th time he had been injured by careless drivers. Frank concluded that this last fatal one was his 13th. Having not long ago written of Stan Spelling's tragic death makes me realise that both of these riders had survived so many previous traffic accidents, and I wondered what the common factor was that made them so vulnerable?

With Green and Smith out of the picture, it looked like Rod Goodfellow might get his 5th Mersey win, but it was felt that the £100.00 prize money on offer from Jim Turner for breaking Competition Record (507 miles) was safe. Jim was soon to take over the running of this famous event from David Stapleton.

Roadworks requiring temporary traffic lights over a good length of road, possibly a mile of uphill riding, for the Tarporley by-pass made a very hazardous start for the riders. I rode that event and on my way by car to the start I waited in traffic that had built up at the lights. Whilst there I checked the length of time allotted to get through the lights and more importantly to a cyclist riding uphill, how much extra time-lag and 'overlap' had been allowed by the contractors for the road to clear for slow moving traffic, before opposing traffic got the green light. I considered at that time that it certainly wasn't enough, and that the resultant cyclist climbing the hill from a standing start had no chance of covering the distance before traffic came from the opposite direction. There was also insufficient room for a wide vehicle to pass a cyclist in safety on this section of road. At the beginning of my ride, I had already decided to start away early before the green light, but only if the road was clear. In this way I felt that I might clear the road works safely. Unbeknown to me and three other riders, an off duty policeman sat in the traffic queue behind us, took our race numbers and reported us. I was later summoned to attend Chester Law Courts to explain what I felt was an unfair and dangerous situation, caused by road contractor's ignorance of cyclists speed over an uphill section of road. The judge listened to my explanation but I was still fined £12.00, however, he did say on reflection that he felt the prosecution had been a waste of police and court time. Funnily enough this was the only item I can remember from the event, after all my 380 miles was hardly worth a mention.

At the 100 miles checkpoint only 8 solo riders and the tandem of M.J. Brooking and J. Jennings, Willesden CC, beat 'evens'. The tandem 1st with 4hrs 35mins, Millington 2nd at 3mins, Goodfellow 3rd at 9mins, Stoaling at 14mins, Holden and Ashman at 16m, Usher 17m, Jackson 20m and Haswell at 23m.

Of the 32 remaining riders at Whitchurch, only 13 were sent on the Nantwich detour by Tom Greep while the remainder were thankfully sent straight on to Battlefield. Bill coupe (Mick's father) at 77 years of age, retired here due to suffering with fractured ribs. Don Spraggett 'packed' on the way to Nantwich as did 2nd placed man Goodfellow. Ken Usher was at this stage moving very well having caught Ashman so proving there was still life in the old maestro yet! He eventually caught Millington on the Newport stretch before 182.4 miles.

Stoaling was now gradually drawing away from the field on this moonlit warm night. In the battle for the trike prize, Smith was faster than both Jim Hopper and Jackson at 84 miles, but by 192 miles Hopper had re-caught Smith. A titanic scrap ensued between these two tough riders and Hopper took the lead at 267m and from there on went unchallenged to finish with 391.76 miles. Les Lowe and Dave Denman both retired at around the 12hr point.

The fastest rider, Stoaling had covered 234.3 miles, Usher 233.9, Millington 230.4, Haswell 227.8 and Holden 225.3m. By the end of the Shropshire circuit and detours only 4 men had covered the full course of 384m. Stoaling with 20hrs 21mins, Usher at 11mins, Millington at 20mins and Holden at 34mins.

On the return to the finishing circuit Millington went into overdrive in an effort to try and beat Stoaling but even after producing the two fastest laps of the 17 mile circuit of 55mins and 50mins. He still had to settle for 2nd place while Stoaling won his first 24hr with 450.58 miles, a magnificent improvement of 32 miles on his previous best. Eric Millington did however net the VTTA Championship award and the Winnerah Trophy with 448.81m beating the gallant Ken Usher by just over a mile.

John Nicholas, an Audax UK Supremo at that time was pleased to see that 12 of the 26 finishers were 'Randonneurs', super tourists, and filled all but one of the fastest seven places.

I've just noticed that Tim Dolphin , Paddington CC, finished one place above me and by nearly three miles extra. This man had already ridden in the previous few years and carried on to ride most years up to 2002.   As far as I know he rode without a helping car and travelled up to the event by train.  24 hours later he rode from the finish to Chester Station to take the train home, back to London.   He was a tough character to do this but he was also a very friendly and much liked rider.

The **tandem** of **Brooking and Jennings** finished with **410.45 miles** and **Jim Hopper, 'TA' Midlands won the trike race with 391.76 miles.**

*I'm pretty sure this is Jim's first performance at 24hrs, having been away as a merchant seaman for many years.  Jim hasn't missed a year to this day (as at 2008) and in twenty years, has crammed more racing miles in on a trike than most riders could manage in a lifetime.  To this day, I cannot recall ever seeing Jim on a bike.  In this 20 year period, Jim has also ridden thousands of miles in audax events including many over the P.B.P. (Paris-Brest-Paris) route.*

———⟹•◆•⟸———

**The North Road CC 24hr,** August Bank Holiday 1986, was **won by Pieter Hoffmann,** Komet Ludwigsburg, with **457.30 miles, Rod Goodfellow,** North Lancs RC was 2nd with **452.68m** and **Gordon Dennis,** North Road CC was **3rd** with one of his best performances ever of **444.21 miles.**

**Hugh Culverhouse,** Weybridge Whls, rode **385.53 miles** in preparation for his **'R.A.AM.' (Race across America) a 3,000 mile coast to coast 'epic'.**   This brave rider only had the use of one leg but it didn't stop him travelling vast distances.  **He broke the record in October with 13 days 11hours 1minute.**

On the 'mixed' tandem, **Ian and Bridget Boon** were trying to break their own Competition Record of 463 miles but had to settle for **449.84 miles,** so beating the tandem of Brooking and Jennings who rode to 421.25m.

56 year old Geoff Murray who rode 303.80 miles on a trike remembers the weather being good during Saturday but with a cold night and showers around the Cambridge area.  He had great difficulty seeing the road in the dark lanes and felt that the promised moonlit night which came at 5am was too late!

Geoff remembers Pieter Hoffmann storming past him just before Newmarket after taking the lead in the latter stages of the race from Rod Goodfellow.   Geoff suffered a number of punctures but despite this he finished his first 24hr race.

Only 21 riders from a field of 45 finished, plus 2 tandems.

# 1987

**The RTTC National Championship** was again run as a special event by the **South District Council of the RTTC,** on Saturday 20th June, and was **won by Ian Dow,** Oxford City RC with **500.10 miles,  his 3rd Championship win in succession** and his first time over 500 miles.  **Rod Collins,** Bristol South CC was 2nd with **483.104m** and **Stuart Jackson,** Skipton CC was 3rd with **475.488 miles.   Ralph Dadswell** was 4th riding for the Antelope R.T. with **460.647m,** John Cahill was 5th with **460.590** and led a Horwich CC team to their **4th successive Championship victory with a total of 1,347.01 miles.** Mick Coupe with **447.652** was 6th and Tom Finney with **438.763 completed the team.**

The course for this event was very similar to the one used for the last Wessex RC 24hr in 1982.  Based mainly in the Ringwood area but now using more of the main roads in the area instead of the rural lanes.    The weather leading up to the event was foul, cold, wet and windy with Friday being the worst day of all.  Incredibly Saturday was dry, sunny, and the wind had dropped to a mere stiff breeze.  Ian Dow's main opposition would come from his training companion 'Carruthers', alias Stuart Jackson, and a newcomer to 24hr racing, Rod Collins.  Ian knew that Rod was a top 12 hour rider as he had been beaten by him in the 'Border 12 hour' by 6 miles where Collins had ridden 272 miles.

From the very start Collins forged ahead dramatically and for a while Jackson held him level but then faded. At 100 miles Ian caught Stuart, apparently his front gear changer had fallen off leaving him on the large chain ring. Ian remarked that for a man who was a National Champion and potential 500 mile man, he needed to concentrate more on his bike preparation. After all, in 1981, he'd missed trike competition record because his lights and tyres let him down.

Ian's ride went very well until he reached the night circuit where he started to lose the 18 minutes he'd gained on his schedule for 490 miles. One consolation was that he'd caught Rod Collins at midnight after 9 hours of riding and he wasn't looking at all well. Ian's night circuits were all run off at around 'evens' pace (20 mph). Eddie Mundy and his wife Pat had been out all night cheering him on and Ian said she had grown in size on every lap from putting more and more clothes on to keep out the cold! Ian had re-caught Stuart who had missed a detour and enjoyed a quick chat with him, but then Ian got directed back towards Ringwood and away across the forest to Cadnam.

At the first light of dawn he was climbing the A31 out of Ringwood and was happy to be 12 minutes up on his 490 schedule. Even at this early hour there was a light but steady flow of traffic. He turned at West Wellow and on the way back he estimated that he was 15 miles up on Stuart and 6 or 7 miles up on Rod Collins. Although he knew that all being well, a win was assured, he didn't feel that a 500 mile pace was being held. He had trouble trying to eat at 5am and wanted some fresh soup which would prove difficult for his helpers to find at that time. He caught Mick Coupe on Castle Malwood Hill and Ian thought he heard Mick gasp "this is my last one!" At breakfast time Ian had a bad patch, which dropped him down to 17 mph. This ate into his gain on schedule and by the time he recovered he only had 7 minutes in hand to beat 490 miles. The day was perfect for him in every way and his helpers got fresh soup to him. He then made up his mind and told his helpers he was going for 500 miles!

He reached the finishing circuit at 420 miles with 3hrs 43 minutes to go, he now needed 21.5 mph for 80 miles but knew it would be very tough. The circuit was 17 miles round and his helpers were stationed on opposite sides of the circuit; his mum and brother Steve on one side with drinks and tinned pears, his girlfriend Tracy and his dad were at Winkton with drinks and a sponge. A first lap of 49mins took his speed almost to 21 mph, but he now needed to cover 61 miles in 2hrs 46mins giving 22mph; it seemed an impossible task.

A second lap of 47mins left 44 miles to go, in 1hr 59mins. He was catching riders all around the circuit. A third lap of 46.5mins took him over 22 mph and the roar of the crowd at Moortown Green could be heard for miles. Ian now needed 22.4 mph for the remaining 27 miles. He knew exactly where the 500 mile point was and what he had to do to get there. Down to Christchurch the wind was dead against him, and he now needed to do the last 10 miles in 26 minutes; all this after riding for 24 hours!

On the Christchurch by-pass a queue of traffic had built up at Somerford roundabout, Ian in desperation took the outside lane and passed all the cars pedalling like fury. With 4 miles to go and 10 minutes left he flew up the last hill to the 'Cat and Fiddle' past the timekeeper, at 498 miles, who was waving his arms frantically shouting "five minutes to go"! Ian prayed for there to be no traffic at the last crossroads, he was lucky, with one last burst he arrived at the timekeeper at 500.24 miles with just 20 seconds over 24 hours! He'd done it.

Stuart Jackson and Rod Collins had both run out their time at the same place as Ian and while Ian lay wrapped in a blanket tended by his girlfriend Tracy, Stuart sauntered over to take a look at Ian and said "serves you right!" Ian remarked that for anyone to have ridden 475 miles and look as fresh as Stuart did, proved that he hadn't been trying at all.

If Ian was exhausted, then Rod Collins was comatose. Ian had never seen anyone in such a state as that, in fact the prize presentation back at H.Q. had to be completely re-arranged around Rod Collin's chair – he could not move out of it. His head lolled from side to side and he was unable to speak. Ian said "I couldn't shake his hand because he was too weak to raise it, instead I rubbed his head, it was all I could think of. I will never forget that scene."

Mrs Jean Burrow, Hainault RC who only got a ride in the event at the very last minute due to intervention by Les Lowe, proved herself worthy of entry in a men's championship by riding 419.13 miles, taking 17th place from 40 finishers. Together with her father, Bill Suttie, they became the first father and daughter to ride in the same 24hr event, although Bill failed to finish. *(Lynne and I have the distinction of being the only father and daughter to actually finish in the same 24hr, and also as part of the Walsall Roads CCC team with Dave Edwards, in the Mersey of Year 2000.)*

Jean suffered with sleepiness having rarely ridden at night or through the night. At dawn she had a bad patch that was to last for 6 hours, but when a crowd of her friends from the Hainault RC turned up to cheer her on, she started to pick up again. By mid morning she was catching riders who had passed her in the night, and finally she reached the finishing circuit to record a personal best of 419 miles.

My thanks to Ian Dow and Mrs Jean Burrow for their input and comments on the event.

<hr/>

**The Mersey RC 24hr, 25th and 26th July 1987, was won by Tony Flavell, Wolverhampton Wheelers, with 442.52 miles. Ray Haswell, Wessex RC was 2nd with 432.83 miles and George Berwick, Edinburgh RC 3rd with 425.43m. He led Borland and Thomson to a team win of 1,172.95 miles. Jim Hopper was the fastest trike rider with 381.48 miles now riding for the Mercia CC.**

Flavell who won the event was the first person I'd seen wearing a skin suit in a 24hr time trial. If I remember rightly it was black and yellow and he wore three quarter length leg warmers from start to finish even though the weather was warm during daylight hours on both days. Another different item of clothing he wore throughout was a tight fitting hood, this 48 year old triathlete had complete control of the race from start to finish. That's not to say he wasn't challenged, in fact at the 47.3 mile point, Eric Millington, his team mate was only 2 minutes down on him with Dave Williams, Mersey RC and Steve Jackson at 4mins.

At 100 miles Flavell led with 4hrs 40mins, Millington was at 4minutes, Pete Akoslovski (formerly Howard) was at 9mins. Around the 12 hour point, Williams, Millington, Akoslovski and Jones all retired. The temperature had dropped rapidly but Flavell recorded 232.94 miles for the 12 hours.

Meanwhile, the Chief Timekeeper. Chris Salter, who was on his way back to Prees from Ternhill at about 1.30am, with some leading time checks was mown down from behind by a motorist who claimed he had wobbled. At Shrewsbury hospital he was found to have a fractured skull and heavy abrasions. Salter who had taken over the main duties with the watch in 1987 due to Eric Matthews having intensive radiation treatment, had luckily had the foresight to synchronise watches with Eric and with that aid, Matt Gleave was able to step into the breach to give us accurate timing at the end.

The run back to the finishing circuit from Wem fork, a journey of some 19 miles, was undertaken against a hard wind. Flavell was the fastest with 1hr 4mins, Holliday was 2nd at 2mins, Haswell and Berwick at 4mins, Taylor at 5mins, Jackson 6mins.

Once back to the haven of the 17 mile finishing circuit the riders speeds were boosted by the supporters around the circuit, and Flavell recorded 2 laps of 56 minutes each. I rode that event and apparently had the fastest lap of all, 55mins, but the ride of the day surely went to Roy Cook, North Road CC, who did 3 laps with one of them being 58 mins, not long after recovering from recent heart surgery! After a 17 year lay off, he produced a personal best in this event, with 394.36m.

Tony Wiggin, a friend of mine from Birmingham St Christopher's CCC took 20th place with 348.52 miles. After protestations of "I couldn't ride non stop for 24 hours" he was finally convinced, by ex 24hour man and Tandem 'End to Ender' Pete Swinden, that he could.

This was Dave Stapleton's 26th and last promotion of the event and it was a little sad to see just an entry of 37 riders. Dave would be handing over the reigns of Organiser and Secretary, to Jim Turner, who had for the last few years been shadowing Dave and also working as the Chief Marshal. Tom Greep was to take over the job of 'Course Controller' from Peter Barlow, and Anne Turner was to become Event Treasurer.

Once again, most of these details about the event were provided by Frank Mumford who mentioned at the beginning that with the event being run on a subscription basis, it was able to offer prizes to a total value of £375, plus trophies and a commemorative plaque to each rider finishing. With excellent feeding, medical attention, marshalling and help, all for the lowest entry fee of £4, it was sad to see just 37 entered, and it would be an even smaller entry for the North Road event a month later. (In fact just 31 despite it being the 'vets' championship) Frank said that the misgivings he had voiced about the RTTC drawing entries away from the two regular promoting clubs had come true. With riders being attracted away from these regular promotions, he felt that the situation could only get worse. A feeling I sympathised with 100% as I could see the danger of what was happening in the 1970's. I vowed never to ride a 'special' event for this reason. I had already seen the North Road CC event getting more sparsely marshalled every year and the riders receiving less back up in the way of feeding from the Organisers over the recent years as compared to the Mersey event. I didn't realise until later years, how dissent from many of the younger members of the North Road CC had already started to affect the event, with many of the members not even bothering to attend the event! I had noticed though that quite a few of the hard core of officials from the Mersey RC event were also present at the North Road 24hrs, people such as the Williams family, Jim and Anne Turner, Shelagh and Edwin Hargraves and likewise Roger Sewell who was on the North Road Organising Committee also gave help at the Mersey event.

The August bank holiday weekend was a disappointment to John Woodburn. He climbed off his bike after 434.5 miles, his dream of capping an unparalleled racing career with the 'RRA' 1,000 mile record that has stood for 17 years to Reg Randall ended at Newark after nearly 23 hours. The stiff wind from the south-west was the final straw and John said to timekeeper Joe Summerlin, that he had been pushing his luck to tackle such a tough record at 50 years of age.

**The North Road CC 24hr** 29th and 30th August 1987 was **won by Pieter Hoffmann,** Portas RT Beifigheim, with **466.22 miles. Mark Holden,** Milton Keynes CC was **2nd** with **453.83m** and **Ken Usher,** Peterborough CC was **3rd** with **446.23 miles.** The weather was very hot, but according to Richard Hulse, not as hot as in 1981. This was Hoffmann's 3rd consecutive win in this event. Mark Holden rode to a personal best mileage and Ken Usher at 53 years of age was proving that he hadn't lost too much speed and enthusiasm since his winning rides in the early 1960's. Alan Reinsch, another German rider and a friend of Hoffmanns took 4th place with 436.34m. Gordon Dennis was the only 'North Roader' and finished with 414m.

I took 6th place with 407.92 miles, I was now riding for the Walsall Roads CC, the same club that Lynne, my daughter, had joined. I felt that I might possibly recruit one or two younger riders to form a 24hr team, but in hindsight, this wasn't to happen until the mid 1990's, although I did manage to cajole one or two into riding 12 hour events, namely Stuart Pearce, John Edwards, Dave Edwards, Dave Merriman and eventually Mike and Lynne Taylor. Stuart Pearce went on to ride the Mersey RC event in 1988 and rode 388 miles.

Sixty three year old Ken Hartley, Calder Clarion CC rode 400.79 miles in this North Road event. He'd come to 24hr racing rather late in life. As an 18 year old he had ridden for the Monckton CC with such riders as 'Shake' Earnshaw, Alf Martin, Arthur Hollender and Eddie Larkin. Then came a 30 year lay off until joining the Calder Clarion in 1978. He'd always wanted to ride a 24hr and had his chance when the Championship was run on Yorkshire roads in 1986, he produced 416 miles. **Les Lowe, Speedwell BC was the fastest trike rider with 364.36 miles. Miss Sian Charlton, Anerley BC with 316.27 was the fastest lady,** and Miss Sue Loveder, Kettering Amateur CC 2nd with 307.02.

On October 15th 1987 'The Great Storm' swept the UK with winds over 100 mph; this caused massive structural damage throughout the land and uprooted thousands of mature trees.

# 1988

*This was the centennial year of the RRA*

**The North Road CC 24hr on the 2nd July was a National Championship event and was won by Stuart Jackson, Skipton CC with 481.36 miles. This was Stuart's 4th Championship win. Ian Dow was 2nd with 479.16m and Pieter Hoffmann was 3rd with 446.15 miles. Gordon Dennis's 406.46miles led David Sewell and Mrs M. Chaney to a North Road CC Championship team win of 1,139.28 miles.**

For 1988, a motion had been passed by the RTTC Committee allowing women riders to participate and compete, not only for individual medals, but also for team medals against and with the men. This ruling applied not only for 24hr Championships but also for 12hour events. From here onwards this rule applied and still applies today (2008).

**Mrs Felicity Beard, Doncaster Whls, won the trike prize with 382.22 miles. She also raised the Ladies Trike Competition Record by over 8 miles.**

At last, the Horwich CC team, formerly all North Staffs St Christopher's CCC riders had lost their strangle-hold on the Championship team medals having won 10 times in one form or another since 1975. These 5 men who dominated the team medals were Coupe, Cahill, Finney, Parker and Stoneman, but one gets the feeling that they will return one day!

*Looking at my copy of the Championship result sheet, I'm assuming that as Pieter Hoffmann being German was in 3rd place and R.W. McTaggart being Scottish in 4th place with 427.49 miles, neither of them were eligible for our Championship, so Phil Oxborough in 5th place with 424.98 would take the bronze medal and 3rd place in the Championship. I'm pretty sure that Pieters performance in this event was his last but one in the country, as mentioned in a previous report, his original intention was to gain experience for attacking the End to End record, but when questioned after his 3rd place ride in 1984, he didn't sound quite so confident and blamed his age of 45 as being the trouble.*

*He was a tough rugged rider built in the same 'stayers' mould as Woodburn and Cahill. His 19hour overland journey in his camper van from Hamburg, taking turns to drive was just a small part of his 24hr weekend. His interest in the 'Lands End to John o' Groats record had been kindled after his epic ride from Hammerfest in North Sweden to Syracuse in Sicily, a journey of 3,523 miles in **14 days,** an average of 252 miles per day.*

*My sincere thanks to the late Bernard Thompson and 'Cycling' for these details.*

Joe Summerlin, Leics RC returned this year after a long time away from 24hr riding, he produced 362.37 miles, but then a lot of his time is taken up as a timekeeper.

An article in the 24hr Fellowship Journal by Martin Brass, describes how feeding Stuart Jackson in this event was like trying to fill a 'bottomless pit'! Martin describes Stuart's insatiable appetite being matched only by his determination to wrestle the 24hr title from Ian Dow. He said that Stuart's appetite was never really satisfied, just postponed for a short while, surely he couldn't eat all that rice pudding! His other needs were a continuous supply of bananas, honey sandwiches, dates, drinks and soup.

At the 100 mile point, Stuart went through in 4hrs 31mins a remarkable time considering that a fair wind had risen. Ian Dow went past in 4hrs 30mins. This wind made it a hard job for the helpers as well as the riders. Trying to decide whether Stuart was losing time to Ian on the very long stretches into the wind, and trying to keep the soup, tea and rice pudding hot, in the night.

Stuart stopped for a quick massage to a painful back. Bill Horton provided the massage as Martin informed him that at 251 miles (the 12 hour point) he was a couple of miles up on Ian. Dawn was cold, two punctures in fairly quick succession still couldn't dent Stuarts ambition, with seven hours to go he was 15 mins up on Ian Dow.

On the way back from Chatteris, Stuart had a toilet stop and complained that he was having a 'bad patch'. Martin knew that Ian was now only 9mins down on Stuart, those minutes got less and less and by the finishing circuit there was just 30 seconds in it.

Stuart responded well and on his 3rd circuit he'd pulled away from Ian by 6mins, to win a very hard race on a very hard day.

*Another article in the same Fellowship Journal by Stuart, has him describing his worst moments in the early morning after losing time to punctures and the incessant wind. He remembered struggling against a headwind to get to a Fellowship weekend at Thorpe in March, Ian Dow coming up from Oxford had a very easy ride, and then to cap it all off, the wind dropped and was of no use to him returning home to Yorkshire next day. Les Lowe's remarks suggested that if he (Stuart) was to beat Ian by just a small margin in the Championship then he could ascribe it to that effort against the wind that March weekend!*

On the first return leg of the 24hr into that strong wind, Stuart realised what a battle he was up against, he reflected on the increasing incidence of strong winds and wondered "is this a manifestation of the unstable weather patterns associated with the 'greenhouse effect?' An example of the camaraderie and spirit of long distance cycle racing was made evident to Stuart as he approached the level crossing gates on the return from the Mildenhall leg at 142 miles.

Stuart said "Neither Ian or I were able to make up anytime on the other, every second was vital. I noticed the orange Dormobile belonging to Ian's father Don, who was helping him, having recovered remarkably from recent open heart surgery, followed closely by a kidney transplant. To my utter disbelief, I saw Don run to the pedestrian gates over the railway line, which he opened to let me through. Here was a man who knew how much those few seconds could mean to me, yet he desperately wanted Ian to win; a man who was more patched up and repaired than one of Russ Mantle's tyres, yet he was running as fast as he could to help me. It took a few minutes for the wind to clear the tears from my eyes."

Stuart continued with praise for his helpers Martin and Bill. They hadn't missed a feed for him and saved him valuable minutes with his punctures. He blamed his bad back on the wind, being tall, the only way to fight the wind was to get down low or to pull extra hard on the brake hoods, so cramping his back muscles.

Stuart hardly remembered the last three hours on the finishing circuit, he thinks it was so painful that his bodies own defence mechanism detached his brain from the hardest parts. He did however see the unmistakable figure of Granville Olive waiting on the roadside to feed Dick McTaggart and it reminded Stuart of how he came to be there, suffering in a 24 hour. These two were to blame. It was the inspiration of their example years ago when he lived in Oxford, that prompted him to ride his first 24 hour.

All that lingered of those memories on the circuit was a jumbled vision of Bill and Martin giving him drinks and shouting time checks. Pieter Hoffmann was valiantly trying to remain upright and groaning his newly mastered words of English "it is of no use". Then came that wonderful moment when Stuart could stop. After three years in the wilderness, it had taken his hardest ride ever to come back for a fourth Championship win.

⟹◆⟸

**The Mersey Roads CC 24hr** held on 23rd and 24th July 1988 was a nostalgic one for Dave Stapleton. He was presented with a clock for his 26 years of unbroken service in promoting and organising this event. The Citation was read by Bob Williams, the Mersey RC President, and the honours gracefully done by Ian Dow. In replying, Dave praised the loyal subscribers and supporting friends of the club, who had made it all possible.

It's sad that only 44 solos and 4 trikes were entered, but unfortunately, 'Cycling Weekly' overlooked the comprehensive write up sent three weeks earlier by energetic Jim Turner, the new promoter, thus the event received no publicity beforehand. This omission also reduced the usual huge gathering that normally is present during the event.

**The event was won by John Cahill, Horwich CC with 452 miles. Dick Newport,** East Surrey RC was **2nd** with **437.56m** and **Tony Flavell,** Wolverhampton Wheelers with **433.31m** was **3rd. He led 4th man, Eric Millington and J. Gent, to a team win of 1,255.63 miles.** 'Super Randonneur', **Andy Major,** rode **426.19m** and **Roger Sewell, North Roads CC** was **6th** with **424.29m.**

The heavy showers and perverse crosswinds were to shatter the hopes of most riders as to any 'personal best' aspirations. The £100.00 prize for a new Competition Record offered by Jim Turner also seemed safe. A fairly cold almost freezing night didn't lend itself to any speedy rides. Cahill had been the obvious favourite to win, but Rod Goodfellow was still chasing that elusive 5th Mersey win. Eric Millington, Mark Holden, Ken Usher and Tony Flavell were all in the running for a prize. Dick Newport, a 'novice' at 24hrs but with a 253 mile 12 hour was also a hopeful contender.

Chris Salter was the principal timekeeper, seemingly recovered from his accident when run down by a car in last year's event. He was stepping in for Eric Matthews who was too ill to attend. At the 100 mile point, Cahill led Goodfellow by 3 minutes with 4hrs 33mins. Bevan was 3rd at 6mins, Millington and Sewell were at 7mins. After the Nantwich detour back at Whitchurch, the two leaders were still 2mins apart on the road. Other riders still going strongly here were Colman, Flavell, Millington, Roger Sewell and Jack Parker.

By 152 miles, Goodfellow, after a huge effort, had opened up a 10mins gap on the road, but at 12 hours, Goodfellow and Cahill had both done 240 miles, Newport 231m, Sewell 229m, Millington, 228 miles. In the trike race, Jim Hopper led John Jackson by 3 miles with 203 miles and Jim Ithell, 197 miles.

Goodfellow faded after 12 hours and Cahill caught him at 280 miles and an hour later, Rod, feeling unwell, retired. Newport rode very strongly through the night and at Wem Fork (357 miles) only he and Cahill had covered the whole course, but with Cahill 54 mins in the lead, he was the only one sent on the next detour. On the 19 mile stretch back to the finishing circuit, buffeted by strong cross winds, Tony Flavell, proved to be the fastest in 57 minutes, Millington and Sewell took 1 hour, Stuart Pearce, Walsall Roads CC, 1 hr 2mins, Brian Davies, 1hr 4mins, but both Cahill and Newport were struggling at 1hr 9m and 1hr 11mins respectively.

Once back at the finishing circuit, John Jackson, on a trike produced the fastest 17 mile lap time of 56mins (a trike record) reminiscent of Crimes and Arnold days. Cahill, Millington and Major all rode leg-breaking laps of 59mins. Jackson's record lap time helped him to beat Jim Hopper for the trike prize, by nearly two miles.

Tim Dolphin was the only rider to have ridden both the North Road event and this 'Mersey', recording 376m and 373.96m respectively and John Reaney at 70 years of age, rode 350 miles, to set a new 'VTTA' age record.

After last years efforts by Tony Wiggin, he was joined this year by fellow Birmingham St Christopher's CCC clubmate, Bob Beaman. Tony recorded 339.74 miles and Bob, after many bouts of sickness, rode to 310.73 miles. He was another rider who doubted his own ability to finish a 24hr but with advice and help from Pete Swinden, John Withers and myself, he finally reached his goal. These events improved the capabilities and confidence of both men, who were 46 years of age.

━━━►•◆•◄━━━

*Also in this year of 1988, John Murdoch and George Berwick broke the London to Edinburgh tandem record with 18hrs 42mins, so beating R.C. Smith and A.E. Collins 38 year old record, by 19 minutes.*

*On December 21st at 7.19pm 1988, Pan American Flight 103 en route from London Heathrow to New York, exploded over Lockerbie in the Scottish Borders, killing all 259 passengers and air crew and at least 11 people of the ground. An Arab extremist bomb is believed to have been the cause of the disaster.*

# 1989

The first 24hr event of the year was again the **North Road CC** on June 24th/25th. **It was won by Phil Oxborough with 469.04 miles.** Pieter Hoffmann was **2nd** with 453.17m and **John Crosby** Cardiff Ajax was **3rd** with **452.35m.** R.C Newport, East Surrey RC took **4th** place with **434.25m** and **Jim Ithell** riding a bike for a change was **5th** with **410.04m,** riding for the Derby Mercury RC. Ken Hartley who came to riding 24hr events late in life was 6th with 391 miles. Bob O'Dell and Eric Lobley almost 'tied' with mileages of 388.69 and 388.48 respectively. Brian Davies who was more at home on the Mersey RC course rode 386 miles and **J.M. Jackson, Macclesfield Whls took the trike prize with 384 miles.**

---

**The Mersey RC 24hr National Championship** event on the 29th July, **was won by Ian Butcher, Bedfordshire RCC with 493.53 miles, Stuart Jackson, Craven CC was 2nd with 472.54m and Phil Oxborough, St Ives CC was 3rd with 435.61 miles.**

Jim Turner organising his 2nd event managed to drum up a field of 78 riders, but there were quite a few non-starters, including Ian Dow who was injured and sportingly spurred Stuart Jackson on to a possible win. John Cahill was also a non starter. Pete Wells was a favourite but although he was a past 12hour champion he hadn't previously got past 14 hours in a 24hr. There were past masters such as Coupe, Finney and Berwick and there were new contenders, Oxborough, Holden, Major and local man, Kavanagh. Ian Butcher looked a possible candidate, having a 280 miles 12 hour and some very fast 100's to use as experience.

32 riders were complete novices at 24hr riding and 41 of the entries were of veteran status. Flavell had to remove his tri-bars before starting the event to comply with RTTC regulations. He was a triathlete and triathlon is a sport that allows such aids to speed. The tandem of Tony Cundy and Bob Stokes pulled out a 386 miles ride and deserves a special mention, as Bob, the stoker at the back, is blind, so that the steersman had to take on board all of the feeds and drinks and steer at the same time, making them both heroes.

Ian Butcher led the race from the very start with metronomic pedalling compared with the huge gears of Pete Wells. Phil Oxborough had his doubts about starting, due to a sore throat, but seemed fairly happy in the early stages.

"hurry up, he's only a mile away.
I can hear his cough."

There was a festive air at Haughton Moss, the pub landlord at the 'Nags Head' had seen the crowds of spectators and had opened early to everyone's delight, including some of the riders. At the 100 mile checkpoint Butcher led with 4hrs 25mins, Pete Wells and Stuart Jackson were at 14 mins. At Tern Hill, Tom Greep instantly assessed the riders potential and either opened or closed detours to suit the riders speed. Wells who was 21mins down on Butcher at 172 miles, packed with severe back pain. I have to admit that I've seen him in agony at the end of some very fast 50's and 100's, hardly able to straighten up and with sweat absolutely pouring from him! He left me in no doubt as to how he suffered to achieve his results.

Heavy showers throughout the night dampened the spirits of many of the riders but Butcher pedalled gears of 72" and 76" fluidly to maintain a lone lead. He reached the Newport turn earlier than expected but the Section Marshall was alert to the problem and turned him. He had a puncture but received speedy help from the Horwich CC support car, typifying the spirit of the event.

The leading mileages at 12hours were, Butcher 257m, Jackson 243m, Oxborough 232m, Major, Finney and Kavanagh 224m. Butchers lead of 14 miles was now unassailable, but the margin for him to break Cromack's record was too narrow; maybe if the weather had been kinder it might have been on. As I recall, it was a warmish if somewhat damp night. I too was plagued with punctures on the Newport section and the temptation to return home some 30 miles away was too much, and so I retired.

With the onset of dawn, the monsoon arrived, drenching the riders, with continuous heavy rain until late morning. At the 341mile check there were still 47 intrepid riders determined to finish, their slog north to the finishing circuit was against a bruising wind. Butcher covered this 19 mile stretch in 1 hour with Stuart Jackson just 4 mins slower; amazingly the tandem trike of Mark Brooking and Miss Jane Ramsdale was 3rd fastest with 1hour 6mins.

Once on the finishing circuit Butcher and Jackson regularly equalled the circuit **record** of 50 mins previously produced by Eric Millington. Jim Ithell on his trike did 1hr 3mins and ladies solo rider, Jan Kirkham, rode a superb lap of 57 mins eventually totalling 351.76, to win the ladies event from Sian Charlton. **Tom Finney with 416.79m led Ron Stoneman and Mick Coupe to a Horwich CC 5th Championship Team win totalling 1,226.26 miles.**

*Journalist Ken Matthews who was 'Cyclings' reporter in the north-west back in the good old days before 'e' mails, mentioned that the strong wind was the cause of the slow first 100 mile results. In fact only 13 of the 43 finishers beat 5 hours. Butcher was out in front, on his own, all night after the first 60 miles and was apparently upset at not seeing many people through the night. The only two riders to complete the full course without detours were Ian Butcher and Stuart Jackson. As Butcher stepped off his bike, his first words were "that was a hell of a night!" Despite also saying "never again" he later expressed the view that he could crack the record with similar standards of preparation and fitness and that the weather was an all important factor.*

*He thanked his superb helpers and paid tribute to the Mersey RC organisation. Jim Turner had worked hard to assemble the 2nd best entry on record, of 78 riders and was rewarded by a successful promotion.*

**Pete Wells** efforts hadn't all gone to waste as in that same year of 1989 **he broke Cliff Smith's Edinburgh to London record by 1 hour 1 minute, to record 17hrs 48mins 4secs, and also raised 'Shake' Earnshaw's 50 years old 12 hour record to 283.6 miles.**

*November 9th 1989 saw the fall of the Berlin Wall dividing East and West Berlin giving freedom to East Germany.*

## OBITUARIES 1980 – 1989

On October 13th **1981 Frank Armond** died at the age of 94. He had been a member of the North Road CC since 1914, some 67 years. His first race was a 24hr and he proved to be a 'feared' rider for many years, competing against champions such as Selbach and Rossiter. Frank's ashes are scattered at the Bidlake Memorial Garden at Girtford, Bedfordshire.

In December **1981, Tommy Barlow** died at the age of 90. He'd ridden 318.5 miles in the Anfield 24hr in his earlier days but was much better known for his organisational skills, his timekeeping, his course and route details for many time trials and his expertise in keeping a field of 100 riders fairly compact on the road by the use of 'optional detours'. Tommy was the mathematical brains behind the B.A.R. competition for over 40 years. He was also heavily involved with long distance road records, especially the 'End to End', for such riders as Bert Parkes, David Duffield, Crimes and Arnold, plus many more.

On 8th July **1982, Ed Tweddell** died aged 74. He broke no less than 15 RRA road records, mainly on a tandem trike with various partners, and was a 'trike man' for most of his life. Ed was a regular 24hr rider over a 30 year period and also broke many northern and regional road records.

In June **1984, Les Meyers** died aged 89. He had been a member of the Southgate CC for 62 years and in 1929 he broke the tricycle Lands End to John o' Groats record in 3days 19hrs 56mins, using an all land route. Les was mainly a trike rider and did much to promote long distance riding in his club.

In April **1985, Albert Crimes** died aged 64. He was probably the toughest long distance trike rider this country has ever seen. He died after a long battle with cancer. Albert was the first trike rider to break the 20 mph barrier for 12 hours in 1953. His many long distance records with John Arnold on a tandem trike are legendary and his separate solo trike End to End and 1,000 mile record proved his superiority on three wheels, in fact, his 1,000 mile record of 2days 21hours and 37mins, still stands to this day, some 50 years later, as do his tandem trike records with John Arnold. (See Chapter 8, **'Nostalgic Moments'**)

In July **1985, Wyn Maddock** died at the age of 78. She was one of the sports greatest veteran time triallists, excelling at all distances from 10 miles to 24hrs. Wyn came from a mining family and had a staunch Socialist background. She was a proud member of the Heanor Clarion CC. Wyn was the victim of several bad accidents in her last few years, but she had survived to be an inspiration to many, including myself.

In April **1986 Jack Rossiter** died aged 88. He had been in failing health for some time. Jack was wounded in the First World War but went on to win the North Road CC 24hr four times, in 1920, 1923, 1924 and 1926. He also won the Catford event in 1926 and 1928. Jack broke many long distance road records, his most notable being the End to End and separate 1,000 mile records.

In **1986 Ron MacQueen** passed away aged 82. In his life he timed more than 1,000 events over a 50 year period including 35 successive Mersey RC 24hr events, and numerous End to End attempts for such riders as Janet Tebbutt, Paul Carbutt and Pat Kenny.

In January **1987 Lilian Dredge** passed away aged 83. Lilian was one of the first record holders under WRRA rules and her success set the benchmark for all future women record breakers in this country. This great pioneer was the first to cover the Lands End to John o' Groats and 1,000 miles route in 1934. Lilian's activities helped to dispel the negative predictions that came from the male hierarchy who controlled the sport of cycling.

In **1987 W.A.G. 'Wag' Onslow** died aged 73. He was a member of the Stourbridge CC and had raced on a bike and trike at all distances from track racing to 24hr time trials over a 50 year period.

Also in January **1987 Stan Harvey** died aged 87. He rode his first 24hr at the age of 49 in the Championship event of 1949. He won the event with 439.97 miles and beat many much younger riders. Stan was a member of the record breaking Addiscombe CC in 1950, 1951, & 1952 and was an enthusiastic cyclist all of his life.

In the Spring of **1988 Ray Page** passed away after suffering from angina for some time. Ray was a solid 24hr Fellowship Organiser and rider and he had been in the winning Mid Shropshire Whls Championship team in 1964, with Ken Hughes and Stan France. Ray's mileage that day was 423.1.

In April **1989 Jim Letts** passed away aged 84. He was a Founder Member of the Ealing Paragon and an RRA record breaker. In 1947 he teamed up with Syd Parker and set the tandem trike Lands End to John o' Groats and 1,000 mile records, comfortably breaking the standards set by the RRA. Two years later, Jim broke Bert Parkes tricycle End to End record by 3hrs 40 mins to record 3 days, 9 hours, 27mins. His tandem trike partner, Syd Parker is still alive to this day as at 2008, aged 93.

In the spring of **1989 Eric Matthews** died from septicaemia, an illness he had borne bravely. Peter Barlow who wrote Eric's obituary went on to say that he was an unassuming man who nonetheless showed qualities of great determination in his riding and went on to win the Mersey RC 24hr three times. Eric was a former RTTC 24hr National Champion and the first man to officially beat 490 miles in 1964. He injured his leg in a gardening accident and in 1977 he lost his leg. In later years he took up timekeeping, helping the sport whenever he could. Eric became Principal Timekeeper for the Mersey RC in 1983 and took over from Ron MacQueen.

Amongst Eric's many other qualities were modesty and courtesy, which made him so respected by everyone who knew him. Nim Carline rated him very highly as an opponent and had tipped him to become the next holder of the End to End record.

In early **May 1989 Bill Griffiths** suffered a fatal heart attack at 69 years of age. He was a noted 25mile man in his hey day but later took a lot of interest in the longer distances, coming 2nd in the VTTA 'BAR' in the 1970's, the same year as his son, Phil, won the BBAR. In 1967 Bill rode the Mersey RC 24hr and produced 431 miles. In the early 1980's Bill was a valuable crew member on Pat Kenny's trike End to End, and later, John Woodburns.

In **June 1989 Felicity Beard** was tragically killed whilst competing in a 50 mile time trial on the A38 near Lichfield. She was 36 years old and had only been cycling for about nine years. In 1982 'Fliss' took to riding a trike and from 1987 onwards she collected the lions share of women's tricycle competition records from 30 miles to 24 hours. 'Fliss' was a lovely lady, a delightful presence at any time trial result board and tea stall, but she was missing that day in the Tamworth RCC '50' HQ and all that was left was the blanket of black cloud and the bewildered grief of those left behind. *These details were taken from an obituary by the late Bernard Thompson.*

In **December 1989 Charles Holland** died aged 81. He was a road record breaker, time triallist and Tour de France rider in the 1930's and 1940's.

# 1990

This was to be a very exciting decade for many reasons, not only for the 24hr riding and Competition Records but also for long distance RRA records being broken by both men and women, especially over the 'Blue Riband' route, the End to End.

Women riders would from now on feature very strongly in 24hr events. They no longer took the smaller mileage lower placings anymore. They had something to prove and they knew they were as tough as the men and the longer the duration and distance i.e. 12hr, 24hr, the closer their performances got to the mens.

*On February 11th 1990, Nelson Mandela was released from prison after 27 years of captivity. He had been imprisoned for his actions and beliefs against apartheid.*

*The Poll tax was introduced by Margaret Thatcher's government in March of this year, causing riots in major cities.*

We start the year with the **North Road CC National Championship 24hr** on June 23rd and 24th. It was **won by Phil Oxborough with 455.45m, 2nd** was **Ralph Dadswell** with **443.05m** and **3rd John Baines** with **434.21m. Phil Oxborough led G. Ford and G. Williams to a St Ives CC Championship team victory of 1,281.65 miles.** John 'Bomber' Baines who came 3rd said he now required a silver medal to get the full set as he had won the Championship gold in 1970. Mark Toon, a 16 year old, from the Truro CC rode a very commendable race to finish with 308.86 miles. Historically, I think, Mark becomes the youngest rider to ever finish a 24hr race. The riders experienced heavy downpours throughout Saturday and Graham Thompson, who recorded the race details for the North Road Gazette, describes the overall weather conditions as 'unpleasant'.

*My thanks to Graham Thompson who was the President of the North Road CC at that time, and Mrs Mary Cook, the Secretary of the club, for furnishing me with the details covering the years 1989 – 1991.*

For a more accurate description of the weather and conditions experienced during this tough event, I've taken a few details from Bernard Thompson's report:

"The few, those who rode or marshalled in this North Road event, and those who have long and accurate memories, will recall the high winds and drenching rain that swept across the Cambridgeshire Fens, seriously tapping riders' reserves even before entering a long cold night. There have been wetter Championships than this, stronger winds maybe, but this combination of wind, rain and cold, proved a deadly cocktail that tested Oxborough's exacting preparation to the limit.

A 10am start from Ely rugby club saw a field of 50 riders and one tandem start this tough event. 12 riders were 'novices' and only half of the field made it to the end, with just 8 riders beating 400 miles.

**Malcolm Judge**

**Anne Mann**

**Rod Collins**

**Hugh Culverhouse**

**Pieter Hoffman**

**Gordon Dennis**

**Brian Morris**

**John Cahill**

**Eric Tremaine**

**Stuart Jackson**

274

**Ian Butcher**

**John Baines**

**Alan Roberts**

**Mick Potts**

**Glen Longland**

**Phil Oxborough**

**Don Spraggett**

**D Brabbin, M Cunnington, R Sewell**

**Phil Barlow**

**Steve Abraham**

**George Berwick**

## Mersey National 1981

| | | | 100 miles | 12 hours | 24 hours |
|---|---|---|---|---|---|
| 1. | J. Woodburn (V) | Manchester Whs. | 4.21.05 | 255.00 | 488.428 |
| 2. | J.D. Cahill | N.Staffs.St.Chris. | 4.31.56 | 252.11 | 475.483 |
| 3. | M. Coupe (V) | N.Staffs.St.Chris. | 4.33.49 | 241.48 | 467.591 |
| 4. | B.Morris (V) | Mid.Shrops.Whs. | 4.27.02 | 248.04 | 465.569 |
| 5. | D.J. Wilson (V) | Ferryhill Whs. | 4.35.34 | 241.78 | 451.092 |
| 6. | T. Finney | N.Staffs.St.Chris. | 4.35.58 | 243.46 | 448.787 |
| 7. | C. Robson (V) | Eastbourne Rovers | 4.57.39 | 230.24 | 447.491 |
| 8. | K.J. Prince | B'head Victoria | 4.45.44 | 227.04 | 435.197 |
| 9. | V. Palk (V) | Altrincham Ravens | 4.39.21 | 232.15 | 432.500 |
| 10. | J.A. Sirett | Dursley R.C. | 4.57.01 | 222.89 | 428.431 |
| 11. | T. Weston | Notts. Clarion | 4.47.13 | 227.69 | 420.900 |
| 12. | D.J. Williams | Weaver Valley | 4.43.44 | 229.75 | 416.330 |
| 13. | M.J. Daley (V) | B'head N.E. | 5. 7.43 | 218.96 | 411.546 |
| 14. | E. Conlan (V) | Mersey Roads | 5. 7.47 | 218.35 | 411.385 |
| 15. | B.F.S. Bailey (V) | Cheltenham & County | 5. 2.31 | 214.67 | 404.763 |
| 16. | S.P. Carpenter | Hastings & St.Leon. | 5. 3.52 | 213.86 | 398.798 |
| 17. | S.J. Nicholas | E.Lancs. | 5.22.00 | 202.04 | 396.052 |
| 18. | I.T. Hilditch (V) | Weaver Valley | 5. 9.12 | 206.70 | 392.720 |
| 19. | D. Hunter (V) | Hull Thursday | 5. 8.34 | 213.20 | 389.795 |
| 20. | J.A. Bethell (V) | City of Stoke | 5.15.37 | 208.47 | 388.045 |
| 21. | G. Berwick(V) (Not Eligible for R.T.T.C. awards) | | | | |
| | | Glasgow R.C. | 5.19.39 | 215.49 | 387.594 |
| 22. | M.L. Roberts | Macclesfield Whs. | 5.19.34 | 202.04 | 380.679 |
| 23. | C.B. Beardsley (V) | South Elmsall | 5. 5.24 | 201.22 | 376.712 |
| 24. | R.G. Davies | Wyre Forest | 5.18.26 | 195.72 | 375.306 |
| 25. | G. Williams | Ruthin R.C. | 5.22.13 | 200.18 | 373.079 |
| 26. | N.E. Chapman (V) | Chester R.C. | 5.13.58 | 209.60 | 373.025 |
| 27. | R. Dumbell | Stockport Clarion | 5.20.42 | 204.84 | 368.080 |
| 28. | M.L. Roberts (T) | Wrexham R.C. | - | 189.84 | 360.062 |
| 29. | M.L. Badham (T) | Norwich Amateur | 5.35.27 | 194.21 | 358.651 |
| 30. | R. Hill (V) | Seamons | - | 181.20 | 343.280 |
| 31. | F.C.S.Payce-Drury (V) | Norwood Paragon | - | 186.99 | 335.418 |
| 32. | M. Simpson | Ruthin R.C. | 5.29.14 | 186.54 | 329.277 |
| 33. | J. Smith (V)(T) | Lancaster C.C. | - | 175.63 | 322.754 |
| 34. | D. O'Neill (V) | Nat.St.Chris. | - | 168.68 | 319.668 |

Team Winners   N.Staffs.St.Chris.  -  Cahill, Coupe & Finney  -  1,391.861 miles.

Tandem Event -

| | | | | | |
|---|---|---|---|---|---|
| P.Kenny/J.W.Taylor (TT) | | B'ham St.Chris. | 5. 9.32 | 210.30 | 407.499 |

53 solos entered - 46 started.  (V) Denotes Veteran.  (T) Denotes Tricycle.
(TT) Denotes Tandem Tricycle.

Merseyside Ladies C.A. Result.

| | | | | | |
|---|---|---|---|---|---|
| 1. | Miss K. Bellingham | Veg. C & A C | 5.19.18 | 183.20 | 372.549 |
| 2. | Mrs. J. Tebbutt | Clevedon & Dist. | - | 168.82 | 349.037 |

## Wessex National 1982

| | | | |
|---|---|---|---|
| 1. | S. Jackson | Farnham R.C. | 496.487 |
| 2. | B. Morris | Mid Shropshire Whlrs. | 476.100 |
| 3. | I. Dow | Oxford City R.C. | 466.305 |
| 4. | T. Icke | Poole Whlrs. | 460.563 |
| 5. | I. Barnett | Morden C.R.C. | 446.768 |
| 6. | G. Berwick | West Pennine R.C. | 428.382 |
| 7. | R. Dowling | Fanboro & Camberley | 423.923 |
| 8. | S. Paulton | R.A.F. C.C. | 422.286 |
| 9. | J. Burrows | Wessex R.C. | 419.407 |
| 10. | E. Hargreaves | Farnham R.C. | 413.132 |
| 11. | A. Wren | Wessex R.C. | 411.882 |
| 12. | R. Haswell | Wessex R.C. | 409.327 |
| 13. | R. Owens | Exeter Whlrs. | 408.784 |
| 14. | P. Dade | Bournemouth Jubilee Whlrs. | 401.710 |
| 15. | C. Dean | Mid Shropshire Whlrs. | 398.008 |
| 16. | D. Spraggett | Mid Shropshire Whlrs. | 395.055 |
| 17. | R. Gee | Sotonia C.C. | 394.781 |
| 18. | R. Burden | Ashford Whlrs. | 385.864 |
| 19. | R. Alma | Worcester St.Johns C.C. | 384.715 |
| 20. | R. Geere (Tricycle) | Farnb & Camberley | 379.905 |
| 21. | E. Dunston | New Forest C.C. | 377.968 |
| 22. | C. Beardsley | South Elmsall S.C.C. | 372.881 |
| 23. | D. Stevens | Exeter Whlrs. | 372.643 |
| 24. | Esther Carpenter | Hastings & St.Leonards C.C. | 365.710 |
| 25. | P. Wren | Exeter University | 364.651 |
| 26. | G. Davis | Hampshire R.C. | 362.271 |
| 27. | A. Burr | V.C. Venta | 358.232 |
| 28. | S. Trott | Exeter University | 349.491 |
| 29. | M. Winson | Chippenham & Dist. | 348.275 |
| 30. | W. Pasley | Farnboro & Camberley | 346.797 |
| 31. | B. Anniss | Farnham R.C. | 338.526 |
| 32. | G. Peddie | Redhill C.C. | 304.171 |
| 33. | G. Thompson | Reading C.C. | 300.481 |
| 34. | F. Payce-Drury | Norwood Paragon | 295.346 |
| Teams | 1. | Mid Shropshire Whlrs. | 1269.163 |
| | 2. | Farnham R.C. | 1248.145 |
| | 3. | Wessex R.C. | 1240.616 |

Entrants - 46      8 D.N.F.      4 D.N.S.

## ECCA National 1983

| Pos. Name | Club | 100m | 12hr. | 24hr |
|---|---|---|---|---|
| 1 S. Jackson | Farnham R.C. | 4.28.39 | 263 | 488.84 |
| 2. H. Stennett | Newark Castle C.C. | 4.43.15 | 240 | 464.40 |
| 3. H. Hargraves | Farnham R.C. | 4.47.40 | 237 | 457.40 |
| 4. E. Tremaine (T) | Leicester R.C. | 4.48.07 | 235 | 447.02 |
| 5. G. Berwick | West Penine R.C. | 4.54.56 | 229 | 446.85 |
| 6. C. Robson | Eastbourne Rovers C.C. | 4.56.20 | 229 | 439.36 |
| 7. M. Gibson | Maldon & District C.C. | 4.49.00 | 230 | 435.42 |
| 8. J. Hall | Rutland C.C. | 4.49.31 | 225 | 429.12 |
| 9. P. Mead | Elite C.C. | 4.55.07 | 225 | 428.29 |
| 10 E. Playford | Gemini B.C. | 4.38.26 | 237 | 425.38 |
| 11 R. Mills | Thanet R.C. | 5.07.49 | 220 | 423.42 |
| 12 W. Ithell | Heanor Clarion C.C. | 4.59.17 | 219 | 419.56 |
| 13 R. Smith | Essex Roads C.C. | 4.57.42 | 223 | 417.31 |
| 14 G. Bell | Glossop Velo R.C. | 5.00.09 | 216 | 416.58 |
| 15 P. Tomlinson | Unity C.C. | 4.48.19 | 222 | 416.48 |
| 16 W. Lantry | Diss & District Wh. | 4.57.42 | 219 | 415.02 |
| 17 T. Wakefield | Gemini B.C. | 5.07.22 | 213 | 414.01 |
| 18 R. Craig | Farnham R.C. | 5.03.07 | 222 | 413.89 |
| 19 S. Honeyball | Addiscombe C.C. | 5.09.43 | 221 | 413.20 |
| 20 M. Parker | Horwich C.C. | 5.03.57 | 224 | 413.09 |
| 21 S. Cruse | Maldon & District C.C. | 5.15.41 | 211 | 411.46 |
| 22 N. Manley | Maldon & District C.C. | 5.05.27 | 220 | 407.15 |
| 23 R. Walker | Elite C.C. | 5.22.46 | 206 | 405.26 |
| 24 S. Argill | Beeston R.C. | 5.14.57 | 210 | 405.04 |
| 25 J. Budd | Redmon C.C. | 5.07.35 | 216 | 404.77 |
| 26 R. Alma | Worcester St. Johns | 5.04.14 | 211 | 404.31 |
| 27 G. Dennis | North Road C.C. | 5.21.18 | 207 | 404.02 |
| 28 V. Rodriguez | Morley C.C. | 5.13.05 | 213 | 403.93 |
| 29 T. Dolphin | Lea Valley R.C. | 5.12.55 | 207 | 402.95 |
| 30 D. Barker | Rodney C.C. | 5.08.02 | 212 | 399.81 |
| 31 J. Laker | Ashford Wh. | 4.49.03 | 224 | 394.37 |
| 32 S. Broom | Becontree Wh. | 5.11.58 | 210 | 390.46 |
| 33 R. Ager | Melton Olympic C.C. | 5.26.40 | 203 | 384.57 |
| 34 L. Lowe (T) | Speedwell B.C. | 4.56.14* | 202 | 383.60 |
| 35 J. King | Hertfordshire Wh. | 4.56.21* | 199 | 383.08 |
| 36 W. Hester | Leo R.C. | 5.25.19 | 199 | 381.56 |
| 37 C. Beardsley | South Elmsall C.C. | 5.08.32 | 208 | 381.40 |
| 38 K. Wawman | Addiscombe C.C. | 5.26.04 | 211 | 376.94 |
| 39 D. Chisnell | Gemini B.C. | 5.29.00 | 206 | 375.57 |
| 40 A. Hilliard | Upton Manor C.C. | 5.10.48 | 197 | 374.27 |
| 41 S. Hubbard | Diss & District Wh | 5.24.27 | 201 | 373.13 |
| 42 E. Dunstan | New Forest C.C. | 4.50.09* | 195 | 367.07 |
| 43 R. Coleby (T) | Colchester Rovers C.C. | 4.51.22* | 203 | 358.59 |
| 44 D. Upton | Folkstone C.C. | 5.26.14 | 192 | 354.59 |
| 45 S. Carpenter | Hastings & S.Leonards CC. | 4.52.09* | 193 | 353.36 |
| 46 J. Clifford | Thanet R.C. | 5.07.50* | 183 | 348.38 |
| 47 K. McDonald (T) | Glade C.C. | 5.02.33* | 190 | 345.33 |
| 48 D. Steward | Maldon & Dist. C.C. | 5.17.17* | 183 | 345.30 |
| 49 E. Mackey | Medway Velo C.C. | 5.03.13* | 181 | 345.28 |
| 50 W. Norris | Maldon & Dist. C.C. | 5.10.12 | 196 | 344.65 |
| 51 E. Mascall | Hertfordshire Wh. | 5.22.38* | 182 | 342.92 |
| 52 T. Trickett | Rutland C.C. | 4.50.39* | 196 | 337.78 |
| 53 S. Moore | Maldon & Dist. C.C. | 5.01.45* | 191 | 333.56 |
| 54 G. Peddie | Redhill C.C. | 5.48.15* | 186 | 330.85 |
| 55 P. Benstead | Catford C.C. | 5.06.13* | 179 | 326.06 |

| Team: | | | |
|---|---|---|---|
| 1. | Farnham R.C. | 1360.13 | miles |
| 2. | Maldon & Dist. C.C. | 1254.03 | " |
| 3. | Gemini B.C. | 1235.39 | " |

Entries 74          Starters  68

### E.C.C.A. LADIES 24  1983

| Pos. Name | Club | 100m | 12hr. | 24hr |
|---|---|---|---|---|
| 1. A. Mann | Hainault Road Club | 4.58.32 | 231 | 438.16** |
| 2. A. Rogers | North Notts. Olympic CC. | 5.07.04 | 220 | 412.55 |
| 3. J. Burrow | Hainault Road Club | 5.14.07 | 215 | 407.99 |
| 4. M. Horsnell | Chelmer C.C. | 4.51.05* | 208 | 394.15 |

At 87.3m *

** Competition record.

## North Road National 1984

| | | | |
|---|---|---|---|
| 1 | S Jackson | Farnham R C | 494.16 |
| 2 | I Dow | Oxford City | 486.99 |
| 3 | P Hoffman ( *) | RSCK Ludwigsburg | 471.53 |
| 4 | H Stennett | Newark Castle C C | 471.22 |
| 5 | M Coupe | Horwich C C | 470.02 |
| 6 | T Finney | Horwich C C | 461.15 |
| 7 | S Armstrong | Melton Olympic C C | 449.51 |
| 8 | G Wallis | Kenton R C | 448.65 |
| 9 | P Ashbourn | Milton Keynes C C | 446.18 |
| 10 | J Cahill | Horwich C C | 443.64 |
| 11 | O Goodspeed | Century R C | 430.19 |
| 12 | C Robson | Eastbourne Rovers | 427.18 |
| 13 | R Collicott | Westerley R C | 424.10 |
| 14 | S Avely | Tooting B C | 424.04 |
| 15 | K Usher | Spalding C C | 423.87 |
| 16 | W Lantry | West Suffolk Wh | 423.39 |
| 17 | G Dennis | North Road C C | 420.11 |
| 18 | M West | Milton Keynes C C | 419.99 |
| 19 | W Ithell | Belper B C | 419.71 |
| 20 | J Richardson | Willesden C C | 419.14 |
| 21 | C Beardsley | S Elmsall S C C | 416.69 |
| 22 | P Carbutt | Saracen R C | 413.68 |
| 23 | A Wey | Weybridge Wh | 412.36 |
| 24 | L Scampton | Welland Valley Wh | 412.23 |
| 25 | R May-Miller | Milton Keynes CC | 411.67 |
| 26 | D Spraggett | Mid Shropshire Wh | 409.81 |
| 27 | J Chaney | Lampard R C | 409.54 |
| 28 | R Craig | Farnham R C | 406.67 |
| 29 | B Ward | Norwich A B C | 405.81 |
| 30 | S Pilsworth | Cambridge T & C C C | 404.04 |
| 31 | G Jones | Kent Valley RC | 401.25 |
| 32 | M Harborne | Saracen R C | 401.22 |
| 33 | J Weeks | Alford Wh | 400.64 |
| 34 | W Hester | Leo R C | 398.89 |
| 35 | R O'Dell | Luton Wh | 396.55 |
| 36 | D Whitehead | 29th Wheelers C C | 394.03 |
| 37 | N Bristow | Milton Keynes C C | 393.83 |
| 38 | D Wilson | Ferryhill Wh | 390.33 |
| 39 | D Sankey | Hirwaun Wh | 390.22 |
| 40 | R Waghorn | Congleton C C | 387.60 |
| 41 | K Wawman | Addiscombe C C | 385.45 |
| 42 | C Holmes | Hillingdon C C | 381.08 |
| 43 | M Hazelwood | Saracen R C | 380.79 |
| 44 | S Argill | Beeston R C | 380.61 |
| 45 | A Lee | Reading C C | 378.18 |
| 46 | S Rowe | Cardiff Ajax C C | 375.87 |
| 47 | J King | Hertfordshire Wh | 375.39 |
| 48 | R Geere (T) | Farnborough & Camberley | 369.02 |
| 49 | P Potter | Audax T T | 366.00 |
| 50 | T Quinton | Saracen R C | 365.25 |
| 51 | D Lyness | Hertfordshire Wh | 360.01 |
| 52 | R Pell | Peterborough C C | 358.38 |
| 53 | C Dodge | Taurus C C | 355.99 |
| 54 | C Tremaine (T) | Kettering Amateur C C | 354.32 |
| 55 | K Jones | Barnsley C C | 344.67 |
| 56 | P Benstead | Catford C C | 338.23 |
| 57 | R Schulman | Norfolk R C | 327.34 |
| 58 | T May (T) | Nomads (Hitchin) C C | 263.36 |

Team Result

| | | |
|---|---|---|
| 1 | Horwich C C | 1374.81 |
| 2 | Milton Keynes C C | 1277.84 |
| 3 | Saracen R C | 1195.69 |

## Mersey National 1985

| | | | | | | |
|---|---|---|---|---|---|---|
| 1 | I.S. Dow | | Oxford City R.C. | 4.27.19 | 250.08 | 480.55 |
| 2 | G.C. Smith | | Merseyside Whlrs | 4.42.49 | 241.57 | 473.55 |
| 3 | S.R. Armstrong | | Melton Olympic C.C. | 4.33.41 | 243.74 | 465.65 |
| 4 | S.P. Doughty | | C.C. Woking | 4.33.47 | 241.01 | 453.34 |
| 5 | H.E. Hargraves | | Cardiff 100 mls R.C.C. | 4.45.28 | 240.30 | 448.20 |
| 6 | J.F. Thompson | | Anfield B.C. | 4.59.43 | 229.93 | 439.53 |
| 7 | J.A. Sirett | | Nutwood Bicycle Club | 4.51.19 | 232.47 | 439.41 |
| 8 | M. Coupe | | Horwich C.C. | 4.39.43 | 232.14 | 434.02 |
| 9 | E.J. Millington | | Wolverhampton Whs. | 4.53.28 | 224.77 | 426.95 |
| 10 | W.W. Borland | X | Edinburgh R.C. | 5.04.27 | 219.40 | 419.74 |
| 11 | G. Berwick | X | Edinburgh R.C. | 5.10.29 | 217.26 | 418.43 |
| 12 | T.G. Roberts | | Brighton Excelsior C.C. | 4.57.22 | 223.34 | 417.52 |
| 13 | R.J. Stoneman | | Horwich C.C. | 4.58.35 | 213.53 | 415.41 |
| 14 | R. Smith | | Clifton C.C. | 4.56.15 | 222.55 | 415.12 |
| 15 | N.J. Copplestone | | Ormskirk St. Annes | 5.09.00 | 220.88 | 413.75 |
| 16 | J.W. Murdoch | X | Edinburgh R.C. | 4.53.46 | 230.36 | 413.37 |
| 17 | R. Haswell | | Wessex Road Club | 5.03.39 | 217.86 | 412.36 |
| 18 | R. Ashman | | Worcester St.John's C.C. | 4.54.11 | 218.15 | 412.10 |
| 19 | C. Robson | | Eastbourne Rovers C.C. | 5.05.34 | 215.79 | 412.04 |
| 20 | D. Sankey | | Hirwaun | 5.03.58 | 217.80 | 411.15 |
| 21 | R.C. Hoof | | Newport C.C. | 5.05.51 | 214.75 | 410.04 |
| 22 | V. Rodrigues | | Morley C.C. | 5.06.14 | 213.43 | 402.84 |
| 23 | D.G. Spraggett | | Mid Shropshire Whs. | 5.15.37 | 216.00 | 402.56 |
| 24 | C. Chambers | | Sharrow C.C. | 5.14.21 | 211.94 | 396.03 |
| 25 | J. Snock | | Cardiff 100 mls R.C.C. | 4.57.15 | 228.26 | 393.79 |
| 26 | E. Spencer | | Tridenton C.R.C. | 4.59.16 | 211.93 | 393.56 |
| 27 | M.J. Parker | | Horwich C.C. | 5.14.13 | 208.41 | 391.34 |
| 28 | K. Dodds | X | Gala C.C. | 5.07.13 | 220.81 | 391.09 |
| 29 | S.R. Roberts | | Brighton Excelsior C.C. | 5.05.57 | 219.67 | 390.77 |
| 30 | J.W. Taylor | | Birmingham St.Christopher | 5.33.12 | 206.50 | 389.98 |
| 31 | A.G. Williams | T | Cheltenham & Co. C.C. | 5.33.09 | 200.33 | 380.48 |
| 32 | P. Potter | T | Tridenton C.R.C. | 5.20.29 | 205.76 | 377.80 |
| 33 | R. Alma | | Worcester St. John's C.C. | 5.15.53 | 196.91 | 375.87 |
| 34 | J.M. Jackson | T | Macclesfield Whs. | 5.34.41 | 196.08 | 375.07 |
| 35 | K.R. Blackburn | | C.C. Woking | 5.12.55 | 205.09 | 369.49 |
| 36 | R.I. Burnett | | Cleveland Whs | 5.55.53* | 181.46 | 353.12 |
| 37 | N. Window | | Nova C.C. | 5.44.15* | 193.61 | 351.92 |
| 38 | T.W. Hall | | Tyne R.C. | 5.48.51 | 190.37 | 347.93 |
| 39 | W.H. Swann | | Long Eaton C.C. | 5.50.34* | 185.25 | 347.82 |
| 40 | J.G. Searle | | Settle Whs | 5.54.27 | 182.26 | 343.59 |
| 41 | N.H. Shenton | | Mersey Roads Club | 5.49.42 | 175.74 | 324.97 |
| 42 | P.R. Newton | | Macclesfield Whs. | 6.09.39* | 167.01 | 308.80 |
| 43 | G. Peddie | | Redhill C.C. | 6.42.39* | 158.71 | 308.11 |
| 44 | S.J. Light | | Mersey Roads Club | 6.33.10* | 155.99 | 293.57 |
| 45 | D. O'Neill | | Merseyside Vets. | 6.43.54* | 153.33 | 288.86 |

X Riders from Scottish Clubs not eligible for RTTC National Championship
   Awards, but are eligible for Mersey Roads Club awards.

T = Tricycle

* indicates time at 100m point has been increased pro-rata to allow for
   mileage omitted.

Team Result 1. Edinburgh R.C.. G. Berwick, W.Borland, J.Murdoch = 1251.54
             2. Horwich C.C.   R.Stoneman, M.Coupe, M.Parker = 1240.77

| | | | | | | |
|---|---|---|---|---|---|---|
| 1. | I.Boon & Mrs. B.Boon | Tandem | | | | |
| | Bristol D.A., C.T.C. | Bicycle | 4.25.11 | 238.98 | 443.27 | * |
| 2. | L.E.Lowe & J.W.Hopper | Tandem | | | | |
| | Speedwell BC/TA (Mids) | Tricycle | 4.57.38 | 225.25 | 419.15 | * |
| 3. | P.Dade & G.V.Adams | Tandem | 4.36.25 | 226.96 | 416.73 | |
| | Bournemouth Jubilee Wh/Redbridge C.C. | Bicycle | | | | |

MERSEYSIDE LADIES ASSOCIATION EVENT

Mrs. J. Richards          Cardiff Ajax C.C.                382.684


73 entries    68 started    52 finishers.               * comp record

## NMCF National 1986

| | | | 12HR | 24 Hour |
|---|---|---|---|---|
| 1 | IS Dow | Oxford City RC | 253 | 488.896 |
| 2 | PJ Woodburn | Manchester Whs' Club | 248 | 482.873 |
| 3 | SW Jackson | Skipton CC | 248 | 468.152 |
| 4 | G Barker | Rockingham CC | 240 | 460.493 |
| 5 | DR Williams | Mersey Roads Club | 240 | 456.649 |
| 6 | TF Finney | Horwich CC | 232 | 443.637 |
| 7 | JD Cahill | Horwich CC | 240 | 443.595 |
| 8 | G Berwick+ | Edinburgh RC | 228 | 438.617 |
| 9 | RJ Wallis | Medway Velo | 230 | 436.832 |
| 10 | R Gilfillan | Worcester St John's CC | 230 | 436.512 |
| 11 | RJ Stoneman | Horwich CC | 224 | 430.916 |
| 12 | J Naylor | Huddersfield Star Whs | 226 | 427.559 |
| 13 | IR Jenkins | Acme Whs (Rhonda) | 227 | 426.528 |
| 14 | P Robertshaw | Rutland CC | 223 | 426.069 |
| 15 | C Chambers | Sharrow CC | 218 | 424.238 |
| 16 | RP Ludlow | Melton Olympic CC | 218 | 421.738 |
| 17 | D Twineham | Selby CC | 220 | 418.185 |
| 18 | E Spencer | Lincoln Whs | 222 | 416.323 |
| 19 | K Hartley | Calder Clarion C & AC | 213 | 416.253 |
| 20 | P Potter | Lincoln Whs CC | 221 | 412.261 |
| 21 | MJ Parker | Horwich CC | 218 | 411.772 |
| 22 | R Ashman | Worcester St John's CC | 212 | 411.294 |
| 23 | TC Siddons | Doncaster Whs CC | 211 | 408.746 |
| 24 | K Jones | Rutland CC | 207 | 404.267 |
| 25 | LE Lowe | Speedwell BC | 215 | 403.464 |
| 26 | JL Clarke | Chesterfield Spire RC | 215 | 401.358 |
| 27 | MR Holden | Milton Keynes CC | 202 | 400.311 |
| 28 | R Goodburn | Doncaster Whs CC | 213 | 399.608 |
| 29 | PV Rawlings | Barnsley RC | 198 | 398.752 |
| 30 | JW Hall | Rutland CC | 217 | 397.272 |
| 31 | R Kendell | Doncaster Whs CC | 203 | 389.598 |
| 32 | GA Stevens | St Neots CC | 212 | 382.572 |
| 33 | P Lond | Scunthorpe RC | 208 | 381.850 |
| 34 | A Sides | Rotherham Whs CC | 195 | 380.103 |
| 35 | TJ Dolphin | Paddington CC | 196 | 378.203 |
| 36 | P Donovan | Savernake VC | 203 | 376.968 |
| 37 | JH Reaney | Doncaster Whs CC | 194 | 375.885 |
| 38 | SA Argill (T) | Long Eaton Paragon CC | 192 | 370.486 |
| 39 | DG Spraggett | Mid Shropshire Whs | 210 | 366.399 |
| 40 | MTS Spink | Leeds Westfield CC | 198 | 365.482 |
| 41 | N Atkinson | Scunthorpe RC | 194 | 363.094 |
| 42 | C Broadhurst | Rutland CC | 194 | 354.372 |
| 43 | TW Hall | Tyne RC | 183 | 334.960 |
| 44 | GW Siddle | Darlington Velo Klub | 164 | 319.261 |

Team:
1. Horwich CC — 1318.148
2. Rutland CC — 1227.608
3. Doncaster Wh. — 1197.952

| Ian & Bridget Boon | mixed tandem comp record | 463.334 |
| G Adams & M Smith | men's tandem comp record | 466.66 |

## South DC National 1987

| Pos | | | | 12 | 24 hours |
|---|---|---|---|---|---|
| 1 | I Dow | Oxford City R.C. | | 257 | 500.099 |
| 2 | R Collins | Bristol South C.C. | | 255 | 483.104 |
| 3 | S Jackson | Skipton C.C. | | 247 | 475.488 |
| 4 | R Dadswell | Antelope R.T. | | 238 | 460.647 |
| 5 | J Cahill | Horwich C.C. | | 243 | 460.590 |
| 6 | M Coupe | Horwich C.C. | | 238 | 447.652 |
| 7 | R McGregor | Stevenage C.C. | | 236 | 443.530 |
| 8 | J Richardson | Willesden C.C. | | 237 | 443.135 |
| 9 | W Wilson | Bath C.C. | | 232 | 441.048 |
| 10 | T Finney | Horwich C.C. | | 235 | 438.763 |
| 11 | R Stoneman | Horwich C.C. | | 226 | 431.753 |
| 12 | R Wallis | Medway Velo | | 222 | 422.350 |
| 13 | R Masset | Charlotteville C.C. | | 213 | 421.689 |
| 14 | K Dean | Mid-Devon R.C. | | 226 | 421.285 |
| 15 | R Hasewell | Wessex R.C. | | 224 | 420.996 |
| 16 | M Holden | Milton Kenyes C.C. | | 221 | 420.092 |
| 17 | Mrs J Burrows | Hainault R.C. | | 219 | 419.132 |
| 18 | J Clark | Wessex R.C. | | 230 | 418.588 |
| 19 | M Parker | Horwich C.C. | | 224 | 416.851 |
| 20 | R Dowling | Farnborough & Camberley | | 217 | 416.543 |
| 21 | S Avely | Tooting Bicycle Club | | 221 | 414.106 |
| 22 | R Patten | Wessex R.C. | | 214 | 413.379 |
| 23 | V Lisztwan | Coventry Olympic C.C. | | 209 | 406.019 |
| 24 | M Brass | Skipton C.C. | | 224 | 405.298 |
| 25 | J Comrie | Reading C.C. | | 208 | 402.838 |
| 26 | F Newton | Wessex R.C. | | 203 | 393.585 |
| 27 | R Waghorn | Congleton C.C. | | 209 | 390.106 |
| 28 | A Lee | Reading C.C. | | 209 | 389.789 |
| 29 | E Stagg | Bournemouth Jubilee Wheelers | | 205 | 388.809 |
| 30 | A Brown | Radstock C.C. | | 203 | 382.911 |
| 31 | R Smith | (T) Clifton C.C. | | 205 | 379.449 |
| 32 | C Roberts | Farnborough & Camberley | | 186 | 376.949 |
| 33 | R Norton | Congleton C.C. | | 199 | 373.561 |
| 34 | R Gee | Sotonia C.C. | | 199 | 370.794 |
| 35 | R Woodcock | Hampshire R.C. | | 177 | 350.258 |
| 36 | J Robertson | Bristol South C.C. | | 188 | 347.877 |
| 37 | E Mackey | Medway Vale | | 175 | 337.939 |
| 38 | G Siddle | Darlington Velo Klub | | 180 | 337.852 |
| 39 | F Moorhouse | Wessex R.C. | | 170 | 337.535 |
| 40 | G Peddie | Redhill C.C. | | 151 | 302.198 |

TEAM

1  Horwich C.C.

(J Cahill  M Coupe  T Finney)        1347.005

2  Wessex R.C.

(R Haswell  J Clark  R Patten)        1252.963

## North Road National 1988

| | | | | |
|---|---|---|---|---|
| 1 | | S W Jackson | Skipton C.C. | 481.36 |
| 2 | | I S Dow | Oxford City R.C. | 479.16 |
| 3 | | P Hoffmann | Portas-Beifigheim | 446.15 |
| 4 | | R W McTaggart | Gala C.C. | 427.49 |
| 5 | | P Oxborough | St. Ives C.C. | 424.98 |
| 6 | | T F Finnery | Horwich C.C. | 414.77 |
| 7 | | J R Crosby | Cardiff Ajax C.C. | 406.56 |
| 8 | | G R Dennis | North Road C.C. | 406.46 |
| 9 | | L E Lowe | Speedwell B.C. | 398.67 |
| 10 | | R J Stoneman | Horwich C.C. | 396.97 |
| 11 | | S Stanton | Abertillery and Dist. Whs. C.C. | 396.58 |
| 12 | | D E Sewell | North Road C.C. | 393.86 |
| 13 | | A R Smith | Anerley B.C. | 392.22 |
| 14 | | P B Howells | Penn C.C. | 384.88 |
| 15 | T | Mrs F A Beard | Doncaster Whs | 382.22 * |
| 16 | | M J Parker | North Staffs. St.Christophers C.C.C. | 380.67 |
| 17 | | R W O'Dell | Luton Whs. C.C. | 380.28 |
| 18 | | R Harris | Beacon R.C.C. | 377.28 |
| 19 | | T J Dolphin | Paddington C.C. | 376.09 |
| 20 | | I T Kent | East Anglian C.C. | 365.70 |
| 21 | | F J Summerlin | Leicestershire R.C. | 362.37 |
| 22 | | J A King | Hertfordshire Whs. | 357.40 |
| 23 | | D L Keen | Lea Valley R.C. | 354.11 |
| 24 | | T Greenhill | Ratae R.C. | 350.43 |
| 25 | | Mrs M Chaney | North Road C.C. | 338.96 |
| 26 | | H Tattersdale | Kettering Amateur C.C. | 322.93 |
| 27 | | Miss S J Charlton | Anerley B.C. | 309.60 |
| 28 | | H Ramsey | Colchester Rovers C.C. | 301.44 |
| 29 | | Miss S E Loveder | Kettering Amateur C.C. | 277.26 |

Team  North Road CC  Dennis, Sewell, Mrs M Chaney   1139.28

* Competition record

## Mersey National 1989

| Pos. | Name | | Club | 100 Miles | 24 Hours |
|---|---|---|---|---|---|
| 1. | I. Butcher | | Bedfordshire R.C. | 4.25.39 | 493.53 |
| 2. | S.W.Jackson | | Craven C.C. | 4.39.53 | 472.54 |
| 3. | P. Oxborough | | St. Ives C.C. | 4.50.21 | 435.61 |
| 4. | A. Major | | V.C. Venta | 5.02.47 | 419.06 |
| 5. | G. Berwick | | Edinburgh R.C. | 5.12.51 | 418.12 |
| 6. | I.D. Padley | | Reading C.C. | 4.58.42 | 417.02 |
| 7. | A. Flavell | | Wolverhampton Wheelers | 4.58.36 | 416.85 |
| 8. | T.F. Finney | | Horwich C.C. | 4.59.23 | 416.79 |
| 8. | P.S. Kavanagh | | V.C. Halton | 5.00.36 | 416.79 |
| 10. | S.M. Jackson | | Macclesfield Wheelers | 4.40.15 | 412.11 |
| 11. | P.G.E. Tyler | | Cestria C.C. | 5.02.39 | 411.73 |
| 12. | R. Stoneman | | Horwich C.C. | 4.57.47 | 409.55 |
| 13. | S.A. Jackson | | Macclesfield Wheelers | 4.58.40 | 407.39 |
| 14. | B.F.S. Bailey | | Seamons C.C. | 5.11.43 | 400.80 |
| 15. | M. Coupe | | Horwich C.C. | 5.05.43 | 399.92 |
| 16. | D.W. Williams | | Ogmore Valley Wheelers | 4.49.59 | 394.24 |
| 17. | M.Holden | | Milton Keynes C.C. | 4.55.39 | 393.32 |
| 18. | T.J. Morris | | Skipton C.C. | 4.48.18 | 392.15 |
| 19. | P.M. Swinden | | Birmingham St, Christophers C.C. | 5.20.15 | 386.13 |
| 20. | R. Sant | | Weaver Valley C.C. | 5.15.41* | 385.04 |
| 21. | J.W. Hopper | T | Mercia C.C. | 5.28.02 | 383.74 |
| 22. | A.K. Hoare | | Cardiff Ajax | 4.56.52 | 378.57 |
| 23. | W.J.Ithell | T | Derby Mercury | 5.34.20 | 373.69 |
| 24. | L. Morris | | Wigan Wheelers | 5.18.37 | 366.61 |
| 25. | E.R.M. Jones | | Pembrokeshire Velo | 5.32.51 | 366.60 |
| 26. | P. Coleman | | Pembrokeshire Velo | 5.03.58 | 364.26 |
| 27. | K.J. Richardson | | Mersey Roads Club | 5.37.53 | 363.88 |
| 28. | Miss. J.G. Kirkham | | Redmond C.C. | 5.13.37 | 351.76 |
| 29. | K.D. Gowans | | V.C. Halton | 5.39.59 | 349.73 |
| 30. | T.J. Dolphin | | Paddington C.C. | 5.41.15 | 342.63 |
| 31. | T.W. Hall | | Tyne R.C. | 5.36.10 | 341.27 |
| 32. | I.W. Blackstone | | Middlesex R.C. | 5.38.58 | 337.63 |
| 33. | A.R. Wiggin | | Birmingham St, Christophers C.C. | 5.29.40 | 336.76 |
| 34. | E.J. Mackey | | Medway Velo | 5.17.41* | 334.88 |
| 35. | M. Howard | | Tamdem Club | 5.06.51* | 331.02 |
| 36. | J. Higgins | | V.C. Halton | 5.40.57 | 328.58 |
| 37. | A.M. Glass | | North Road C.C. | 6.12.48 | 318.99 |
| 38. | P. Annells | | Didcot Phoenix | 5.22.22* | 307.15 |
| 39. | T. Alma | T | Worcester C.C. | 6.08.17 | 290.84 |
| 40. | C.R. Holland | | Derby Mercury | 6.14.57 | 289.51 |
| 41. | Miss. S.J. Charlton | T | Anerely B.C. | 6.10.32@ | 279.90 |
| 42. | R.A. Beaman | | Birmingham St, Christophers C.C. | 6.06.34 | 278.46 |
| 43. | S. Light | | Mersey Roads Club | 5.46.32* | 275.46 |

T Indicates Tricycle - *Indicates the rider was directed to omit 9.77 miles before the 100 mile point
@Indicates the rider was directed to omit 14.66 miles before the 100 mile point
Team Result:- Horwich C.C. 1226.26 Miles ( T.F. Finney, R. Stoneman, M. Coupe,)

**MERSEY ROADS CLUB 24hrs** Tricycle Association Trophy Official Result 29th/30th 1989

| | | | | |
|---|---|---|---|---|
| 1. | J.W. Hopper | Mercia C.C. | 5.28.02 | 383.74 |
| 2. | W.J.Ithell | Derby Mercury | 5.34.20 | 373.69 |
| 3. | T. Alma | Worcester C.C. | 6.08.17 | 290.84 |
| 4. | Miss. S.J. Charlton | Anerely B.C. | 6.10.32@ | 279.90 |

**MERSEYSIDE LADIES CYCLING ASSOCIATION 24 HOUR** Official Result JULY 29th/30th 1989

| | | | | |
|---|---|---|---|---|
| 1. | Miss. J.G. Kirkham | Redmond C.C. | 5.13.37 | 351.76 |
| 2. | Miss. S.J. Charlton | Anerely B.C. | 6.10.32@ | 279.90 |

**MERSEY ROADS CLUB TANDEMS 24HOURS** Official Result 29th/30th 1989

| | | | | |
|---|---|---|---|---|
| 1. | A.B. Cundy & R.E. Stokes | Shirley R.C. Tamden Bicycle | 5.01.22 | 386.54 |
| 2. | M. Brooking & Miss.M.J. Ramsdale | Willesden C.C. Tamden Tricycle | 5.19.56 | 372.64 |

285

## North Road National 1990

| Pos. | Name | Club | Miles |
|---|---|---|---|
| 1. | P. OXBOROUGH | St. Ives CC | 455.45 |
| 2. | R. DADSWELL | Antelope RT | 443.05 |
| 3. | J. R. BAINES | Selby CC | 434.21 |
| 4. | J. R. CROSBY | Cardiff Ajax CC | 432.10 |
| 5. | G. V. FORD | St. Ives CC | 419.66 |
| 6. | D. R. WILLIAMS | Mersey Roads Club | 410.99 |
| 7. | G. J. WILLIAMS | St. Ives CC | 406.54 |
| 8. | M. J. HOLDEN | Mersey Roads Club | 404.95 |
| 9. | T. W. REYNOLDS | CC Breckland | 400.30 |
| 10. | T. J. DOLPHIN | Paddington CC | 392.36 |
| 11. | P. W. SMITH | Eagle Road Club | 366.51 |
| 12. | S. G. MILLS | Selby CC | 361.83 |
| 13. | B. M. MONAGHAN | North Road CC | 361.05 |
| 14. | E. G. MACKEY | Medway Velo Club | 359.69 |
| 15. | I. R. PERKINS | Coalville Whs. CC | 355.66 |
| 16. | G. R. MARKS | Addiscombe CC | 354.56 |
| 17. | J. A. KING | Truro CC | 353.45 |
| 18. | G. MALAM | Cardiff Ajax CC | 352.42 |
| 19. | R. D. DENMAN | Mersey Roads CC | 350.33 |
| 20. | W. J. PYE | Mersey Roads CC | 347.10 |
| 21. | R. SHEARS | Selby CC | 341.05 |
| 22. | M. J. SINCLAIR (T) | Weybridge Whs. CC | 317.63 |
| 23. | M. A. TOON | Truro CC | 308.86 |
| 24. | H. W. RAMSEY | Colchester Rovers CC | 299.76 |
| 25. | S. J. LIGHT | Mersey Roads Club | 246.16 |

**TANDEM**

| | | |
|---|---|---|
| R. J. GILBERT | Welland Valley Whs. CC | 337.57 |
| N. J. HOLMAN | | |

**TEAMS**

| St. Ives CC | | Mersey Roads Club | | Selby CC | |
|---|---|---|---|---|---|
| Oxborough | 455.45 | Williams | 410.99 | Baines | 434.21 |
| Ford | 419.66 | Holden | 404.95 | Mills | 361.83 |
| Williams | 406.54 | Denman | 350.33 | Shears | 341.05 |
| | 1281.65 | | 1166.27 | | 1137.09 |

Pete Wells led comfortably at 150 miles with 6hrs 55mins, Oxborough at 7mins, Dadswell at 12m and Baines at 20mins. A short time later Wells retired, with recurring back trouble, and Phil Oxborough took the lead. At 4pm it looked as though the end of the world was nigh, with car headlights cutting through the 'murk'. Thunder and lightning shattered the Fens like the soundtrack of a graveyard scene in a horror movie and the rain lashed the poor riders on these exposed roads".

At Streatham (221 miles) Oxborough had been riding for 10hrs 33mins and Dadswell was at 20 mins, but Oxborough took a lengthy rest and by the 12hour point he'd covered 244 miles to Dadswells 241m. John Baines led John Crosby by 10 miles with 236m and by now the wind and weather had improved despite turning cold. Dadswell was trundling a big gear compared to Oxborough in an effort to gain the lead, but it wasn't to be.

The wind came back to trouble the slowing riders in the last few hours of the race, with Phil Oxborough running out a worthy winner by over 12 miles from Ralph Dadswell and over 21 miles from John Baines.

1990 was also the year that 'Tri-bars' became officially allowed in time trials run under RTTC rules. It was a method of aiding the rider to obtain a low crouched 'tuck position' to make them more streamlined. 'Tri-bars' had previously been used in triathlons in this country but like a lot of new innovations I think the idea first came from America. Ian Dow, the 24hr Fellowship Editor was quick to endorse their use, quoting a 1 mph improvement on his journeys. He went on to say *"since Cromack's 507 miles record 22 years ago we have seen low profile bikes, disc wheels, aero tubing, aero helmets, skin suits, energy drinks, clipless pedals, computers and 'L' shaped cranks, and all have failed to add one single inch to the 24 hour record. But here is something which really seems to make a difference"*.

**"Not only does it improve the airflow, but it keeps me dry as well."**

This was also a controversial year, with the RTTC National Committee trying their hardest to find a way of denouncing the 24hr, saying that such a minority sport wasn't worthy of Championship status anymore. They had also voiced concerns about night-time safety issues with tired riders attracting Police attention.

The Secretary of the 24hr Fellowship, Malcolm Green, along with Jim Turner and Roger Sewell drafted a letter counteracting every item that the RTTC were proposing. This strong retaliation was successful and I'm glad to say that there has been very little interference from the RTTC ever since.

———⟩◆⟨———

**The Mersey RC 24hr** on the 28th and 29th July, was **won by John Clarke, Rutland CC with 436.65 miles. Paul Colman**, Pembrokeshire Velo was 2nd with **421.57 miles** and led Roy Jones and V. Howells to a team win of **1,137.03 miles. George Berwick**, Edinburgh RC was 3rd with **420.52 miles. Mrs Sheila Simpson won the Merseyside Ladies CA award** and came **5th** with **408.07** miles, and **Jim Hopper** was the **fastest trike rider** with **401.08m** beating newcomer **Ron Sant** by 13 miles. John Clarke, the winner, produced a personal best ride by 35 miles.

*The course this year was a new one designed to eliminate 'u' turns, a new ruling from the RTTC, yet strangely enough in the year 2007, a 'u' turn was used in the National Championship 100 run in Lancashire. The turn involved pulling into a lay-by on the busy A6 at Garstang and then turning in the road. I was absolutely amazed, apparently the rule doesn't apply in Lancashire!*

A new start venue and HQ at Farndon Sports Club proved very successful but of course the age old 'u' turns at Wades Green, Clive Green, Haughton Moss 'Nags Head' and Nantwich were all gone, relegated to a bygone age. With the support from the mobile feeding stations dotted around the course, the 200 marshalls and a comprehensive medical first aid station with qualified nurses, it was felt that any rider without a support car could ride this event and not have to worry about such things. The event earned praise and congratulations from everyone, including the Police.

At 100 miles, near Ternhill, Hoare led with 4hrs 53 mins. Clarke was at 2mins, Jackson at 4mins and Colman 9mins. Many riders had suffered punctures by this point due to newly laid chippings. The weather during the day was hot, but the night turned very cold and dark. A car accident meant that the Newport to Weston-under-Lizard stretch couldn't be used during the night. At Hodnet, the genial drunks that tried to marshal the riders in the 1989 event had been replaced this year by drunks in an uglier mood, some climbing over the marshal's car.

At 12hours Clarke was the fastest with 229 miles, Colman 225m, Berwick 218m, Viney 215m. Clarke reached 300 miles still in the lead and was the only rider to complete the full course. Sunday dawned to another hot oppressive day.

Whereas we had lost some of the 'old' roads that occurred in the first 100 miles, we had retained Prees, Battlefield, Shawbury, Shawbirch and Hodnet, with the proviso that Battlefield could only be negotiated as a left turn. The Police had also banned the use of Christleton Island at Chester for cycle events, so it meant using a new finishing circuit based on Farndon, Coddington, Waverton, Saighton, Bruera and back to Farndon.

Despite 19 riders not finishing, 80 year old Billy Swann, Long Eaton CC, produced a new age record of 297.88 miles. Pembroke Velo became the first Welsh team to win the team prize in this event, beating Weaver Valley CC by nearly 55 miles. Nobody beat 'evens' on the new 16 mile finishing circuit and Colman had the fastest lap of 53 minutes.

Two of the better-known retiree's were Nick Carter at 193 miles from circulation problems. This 70 year old had a winning mileage in this event of 464 miles in 1955, and Pete Duncan retired with sickness at 70 miles. This famous 62 year old had a 440 mile trike best in 1954. *My thanks to Frank Mumford for some of these details.*

One young rider I took an interest to in this event was Pete Winwood, Walsall RCC. He joined the staff at my shop, Bridgtown Cycles, in 1988, and after hearing of his trans-world trips, I suggested he tried a 24 hour. "I've never raced before" was his reply, but that was no excuse, and jokingly I said that a '24 hour result becomes part of your job description!' In all seriousness, he produced 380.48 miles which I felt for someone who hadn't time-trialled before was a superb ride, a ride which gave him an even greater confidence in his abilities.

*The same Saturday morning of that Mersey RC 24hr weekend saw the start at 8am of another epic ride.* **Pauline Strong** *started on her long quest from* **Lands End to John o' Groats** *in order to attack Eileen Sheridan's 1954 record of 2days 11hours 7mins. By the time Pauline reached Knutsford at 342 miles, she was almost 2 hours behind schedule and was already suffering with bad knees, a bad back and extreme tiredness. She was allowed a 15mins sleep at Wigan before pressing on Northwards. Pauline climbed Shap, arriving at the summit by 10.15am Sunday, she was still two hours down on schedule but felt better when she reached the Scottish Border just after midday. Two hours later the heavy rain started, this rain continued for the next 200 miles or more, requiring her to make many stops for dry clothing and hot soup. By 4am Monday, she was on the last part of her journey from Inverness.*

**Pauline arrived at John o' Groats** *at 2.50pm, Monday, to a rapturous welcome. She'd broken Eileen's record by over 4 hours with* **2days 6hrs 49mins and 45 secs.**

*A broken collar-bone only weeks before the record had prevented her from riding a 24hr in preparation and so made her record even more amazing. Pauline became one of the very few riders who hadn't used a 24hr race as preparation. Paul Carbutt was another and surprisingly Andy Wilkinson also. A common factor to all three riders is their background careers of top class road racing interspersed with regular BBAR placings and Championship rides.*

*Two months later in September 1990,* **Andy Wilkinson** *'Wilko' to his friends was to start on his epic journey from* **Lands End.** *After many postponements due to bad weather, he finally got away on 26th September. Heavy rain soon after Penzance made for a miserable and dangerous start to his journey, with heavy holiday traffic stuck in jams along the route in the West Country. He had a complete change out of wet clothing at Bristol and also put his lights on for the drab conditions.*

*Although he had rain, he also had a reasonable wind, which enabled John Williams to report that Andy was about 2.5 hours up on a schedule to beat John Woodburn's record by 16 minutes. Later in the ride a road closure and a closed level crossing gate required Andy to carry his bike on his shoulders, cyclo-cross style. By Wigan he was soaked through again and had to stop for dry clothing for the fourth time. He was now running out of dry clothing especially shorts, but he still battled on. Shap was climbed into a headwind and pouring rain and Edwin Hargraves reported that he had covered 423 miles in 20 hours and they were hoping for a possible new 24hr record, but Andy was now having a very rough patch and was falling asleep. A stop was made at Penrith, but despite this he still managed 489.9 miles for the 24 hours, but missed Woodburn's record by 5 miles.*

*Plans were put into place to have his wet clothing taken to timekeeper Dave Harris's house in Edinburgh to be dried by a contingency of his neighbour's tumble driers. Dave's wife Margaret then would take the dried clothing up to Inverness for the rest of the journey.*

*By the time Perth was reached Andy was suffering from sleep deprivation and strong coffee had failed to work. After a stop at Dunkeld he got to the Kessock Bridge before tiredness set in again. Andy was still at this time over 3 hours up on schedule and he attacked the climb of Aultnamain in pouring rain. He descended at such speed on the winding narrow downhill that Les Lowe and John Williams were worried that the following car would aquaplane, but once onto flatter roads after Bonar Bridge the adrenalin and power started to drain from him. He had many stops for sleep and warm clothing as he climbed through the 'Ord of Caithness'. Jim Turner was worried that Andy was becoming hypothermic as he rode slowly along, shivering and unable to control the handlebars. Between here and the John o' Groat's hotel, Andy lost every last bit of time he'd gained on schedule, consequently at Wick he had just 60 minutes to cover the last 17 soul destroying miles. He suddenly realised the urgency required and when he sprinted over the line at the hotel, he'd beaten John Woodburn's record by just 58 seconds. This is the narrowest margin ever on this record, with a new time of* **1day 21 hours 2mins and 18secs.**

*Andy was the first rider to use tri-bars, polymer feeding and a heart rate monitor, but on reflection, Andy felt that tri-bars in the latter half of the journey was a mistake as the fixed torso position that it gave, lulled him into sleep, with the tired rider leaning on the bars and nodding off. At 27 years of age, Andy became one of the youngest riders in modern times to break the record.*

## 1991

In January 1991, the Mersey Road Club's eldest Founder Member E.G. 'Guy' Pullan died, he was aged 88.

He had been present at many Anfield 24hr races and was responsible for the smooth handover when the Mersey RC took over the realms of continuing the 24hour in 1937. He held many responsible posts with the Mersey RC the CTC and the Liverpool District RTTC Council. He was a keen tourist and a striking figure and stylish rider on his black and chrome plated Raleigh RRA bike.

*This obituary was courtesy of Ken Matthews.*

*The Gulf War 'Desert Storm' also started in January this year.*

**The North Road CC 24hr** on June 24th and 25th 1991 was **won by Phil Oxborough, St Ives CC with 452.58 miles.** John Baines, Selby CC was 2nd with 430.01 miles. **Mick Holliday, A5 Rangers CC was 3rd with 420.24 miles.** S.F. Cruse, Maldon and District CC was 4th with 414.92 and led Miss E. McCarthy with 403.02 and D. Wood, 370.07m to a team win of 1,188.01miles. George Berwick was 5th with 413.57 miles.

On July 13th & 14th 1991 Jim Hopper and Ron Sant broke four Regional tandem trike records in one ride. Harold Nelson had suggested to Ron that the NRRA (Northern) 24hr record belonging to Tweddle and Cookson of 385.25 miles needed updating. It was a 1933 record and was the oldest one left on the Northern Roads Record books, and also that a much newer standard at 100km needed setting. Pat Kenny and Les Lowe were contacted for advice and they suggested putting in for the MRRA (Midland) 12hr & 24hr at the same time, and also include the RRA 24hr held by Crimes and Arnold since 1954.

Plans were put in motion. Jim's wife, Margaret set to, contacting all the relevant associations, and with George Longstaff lending them his own tandem trike, they were then all set for the assault. Tony Shardlow was the timekeeper and other officials were Pat Kenny, Les Lowe, Pete Swinden, John Williams and myself. Margaret was in charge of the feeding as usual and Ian Hill, Ben Steven and Barry Donaldson were the drivers. The start was at Tern Hill and the course took in Prees, Ludlow, back to Ternhill, A5 Weston under Lizard, Lichfield, A51 Stoke, A50 Uttoxeter, Derby, Bakewell, Nottingham and Newark. The weather was mixed and very wet and windy at the start.

It was a fairly trouble free ride, they set the 100 km standard, then broke the MRRA 12 hour, held by Pat Kenny and myself, by just over a mile, with 236.37 miles, and set the MRRA 24hr with 436.750m. They realised towards the last four hours that they probably wouldn't break the Crimes and Arnold record, but they did add just over 50 miles onto the NRRA record of Tweddle and Cookson.

This was both Ron and Jim's first foray into long distance record breaking and they went on Jim's philosophy that 'trikies never pack', and that 90% of the effort comes from between your ears!

*Sadly, three of the members of this party are no longer with us. Margaret Hopper, Ron Sant and George Longstaff. George passed away in 2003, Ron in 2004 and Margaret in 2005.*

<hr>

**The Mersey RC National Championship 24hr was won by Mick Potts, Derby Mercury with 486.65 miles. Phil Barlow, Kiveton Park CC was 2nd with 472.14m and Phil Oxborough was 3rd with 465.56 miles. Simon Pedley with 430.28 miles and Graham Moult with 394.32m completed a Derby Mercury Championship Team win of 1,311.25 miles. Mrs Sheila Simpson, Doncaster Whls, was the fastest lady in the Merseyside Ladies CA event with 426.18 miles.**

**Rod and Peter Goodfellow broke the tandem competition record with 501.35 miles and became the first father and son to complete a 24hr race on a tandem at record speed.**

Jim Turner's persuasive charms had managed to raise a record entry of 92 riders, including 8 trikes, 2 tandems, and 1 tandem trike. Jim would turn up at high profile functions and time trials and offer you the 'greatest day out riding your bike that you've ever had with all the food you could eat'. When you ask what is involved he would pull out a Mersey RC 24hr entry form from a secret pocket in his large overcoat, then as Gethin Butler once said " he's gotcha"!

With most of the past high mileage favourites and champions not entered, it was wondered as to who might win. Would it be Phil Guy, a good 12hr man and BBAR rider, but a novice at 24hrs; or Phil Oxborough who'd just won the North Road event in very tough conditions; or Mick Potts who'd been cramming in thousands of miles of training this year? He'd also won this event 20 years previously with a 475 mile ride; or Phil Barlow, he was a very fast 100 miler and always a possibility in such a wide open race, even though he was also a novice.

There were many past winners seen at the start, such as John Arnold, Cliff Bate, Nick Carter, Roy Cromack, Ian Dow, Malcolm Green, Stuart Jackson, Stan Lea, Alec Smith, Robert Stapleton, Kath Akoslovski, Joan Kershaw and Christine Minto; all were either on helping, marshalling or supporting duties during the event. Frank Mumford was there, looking around and making notes on bikes, clothing and equipment being used by the riders. He was also 'The Scribe' who produced most of the detailed history of this famous event. His humorous remarks always make me smile when I'm looking through his event details, remarks such as Les Lowe's dilapidated Mercian bike earning him the 'John Arnold accolade'! 69 riders sported computers, 41 various tri-bars, 32 with clipless pedals, 19 helmets. Very few riders started with lights in position, most of them would pick them up at Prees, and even fewer carried more than marginal food 'rations'.

Six machines had rear disc wheels, including the Goodfellow's tandem where the 'sonic booming' (the drumming sound made by these hollow wheels) must have spurred on their victims, as from last position, no.100, they were to mop up and catch the whole field. Phil Guy, back pedalling on the start line with consequent reverberations from his rear disc wheel, prompted the query 'winding up the clockwork?'

With all this hi tech equipment evident in the last two or three years, Frank asks "imagine what competing triathletes might introduce – movable saddles, Kevlar spokes, shades, and given the chance, male bikinis!"

Chris Salter, the Principal Timekeeper, was also the main architect of this new course, which was now devoid of any 'u' turns and right hand turns unless performed around a traffic island. The only problem that this course posed was one of heavy traffic flow at times, but luckily very few incidents occurred. Ian and Bridget Boon who were hoping for a record ride on the mixed tandem had a very rushed start when their car got to the HQ with only minutes to spare. Rod and Peter Goodfellow were the first to help unload their tandem and get them away with just a one minute late start.

At 50 miles, the Goodfellow tandem was the fastest in 2hrs 5mins, Barlow 2nd at 5mins, Potts 8mins, Boons 10m, Ayres 11mins, Guy and Pedley at 12 mins, Oxborough at 13m and Leach at 14m. By the 100 mile check point the Goodfellows had a clear lead of 13mins in their quest for a 500 mile comp record, with 4hrs 13mins, Phil Barlow was at 13mins, the Boons tandem at 21mins, Potts at 22mins, Pedley 27m, Ayres & Guy at 28m and Oxborough at 29m. The ladies were Sheila Simpson with 5hrs 5mins and Jean Burrow at 21mins. In the trike race Jim Hopper with 5hrs 15m led Pat Kenny by 23mins and Ron Sant by 25mins.

At Prees Island the faster riders were sent left to Tern Hill while the slower riders went straight on to Battlefield. With heavy traffic plaguing the riders, the job of separating the fast from the slow, to go either left or right, proved to be a tricky one for Tom Greep, Roy Cromack and RTTC Observer, Dave Stapleton, who was worried about the possibility of accidents, but all went well by using C.B. radio's to give the No's of riders approaching and so direct them onto the correct road.

At 172 miles the Goodfellows had a 25 minute lead with 7hrs 33mins. Barlow was 2nd with 7hrs 58mins with Potts at 29mins, the Boon's tandem at 37m, Guy at 41m, Ayres at 44m and Oxborough at 50m. At 10.5 hours Steve Ayres retired out of the running. At 12 hours only the two tandems and 3 solos had beaten evens. The Goodfellows were fastest with 261 miles, Potts 2nd 250m, Barlow 249m, Guy 245m, the Boon's tandem 243m and Phil Oxborough with 238 miles.

The weather conditions for this weekend were perfect for speed with just a little mist in the Newport area around dawn. Many riders had troublesome lights, and the RTTC Observers were worried about the safety issues it posed. Even having two lights front and two rear could not guarantee a safe passage in the darkness, even if it was a proprietary brand name such as 'Ever Ready', 'home made' lighting systems quite often proved more reliable.

At 300 miles the Goodfellow tandem still led with 14hrs 1min, Mick Potts was 2nd at 39 mins, Phil Barlow at 45mins, Phil Guy at 56m. It was thought that the Goodfellows would break the 1986 record of 466.56 miles held by Adams and Smith, but the 'Elders' and those in the know, felt that 500 miles was an impossible task. They now had 10 hours to cover 200 miles, a very narrow margin when you consider that Rod had only just recovered from mumps and Peter was relatively inexperienced, but the weather conditions were favourable and with Mick Potts still to catch and only a minute ahead on the road, they had a good incentive.

Amazingly Potts stretched his lead to 4 minutes at 348 miles and he wasn't caught until 373 miles. The effort told on him and he reached the circuit at 412 miles, some 7 minutes down on schedule. The fastest solo lap of this 15 mile circuit was ridden by Turner with 44mins, Potts, Murphy and Oxborough rode a 45 min lap. The tandem knew they had to ride above 20 mph and rode laps of 57mins, 50mins, 45m, 43m and finally a lap of 42m ridden in 'red mist' mode.

At the end it was Potts who had 4 circuits, Barlow and Oxborough with three, to take the first three places. John Leach was 4th with 453.08 and Alan Bate 5th with 448.18m. Surprisingly Phil Guy who had ridden consistently suddenly stopped with over an hour to go, and finished with 422.4m. Mrs Sheila Simpson took 10th place overall with 426.18 and 2nd fastest ride in this event by a woman since Christine Minto's ride in 1969.

The best performance by a novice was that of Hugh Canning, 421 miles, for Birmingham St Christophers CCC, he was the fastest of five St Christopher's riders that day, the others being, Pete Swinden with 381.34m, and struggling with a bad back, Pat Kenny (trike) with 361.69m. Tony Wiggin, 330.20m and Bob Beaman, 261.42m after hours of sickness.

**Jim Hopper, Mercian CC had the fastest trike ride with 404.63 miles.** The Horwich CC team of M. Roscoe, Ron Stoneman and Tom Finney were 2nd with 1,244.13 miles.

The tandem record of 501 miles by father and son team of Rod and Peter Goodfellow was not all plain sailing. Son Peter was much taller than his dad who was steering the tandem. This gave Peter a cramped position on the rear, causing him to suffer numbness in the saddle area, which led to trouble in passing water. Peter also experienced severe tiredness towards the end of the race, falling asleep and then hallucinating, but after a quick stop for food and Coca-Cola, he perked up again. They both found the hills very hard through not being able to get out of the saddle as easily as on solo bikes. Rod said he felt that the companionship of riding a tandem especially with his son, had enabled him to get round one more 24hr race, as at 52 years of age, he'd lost the enthusiasm to ride on his own nowadays.

Although they had a 'special' long wheelbase tandem made for them by M & B Cycles of Dronfield, they still couldn't attain a perfect position, but it was obviously good enough. Their lighting was a 'one off' design, a 10volt 4 a.h.battery, consisting of 5 industrial nicad rechargeable 'd' cells, in a feeding bottle carried on the frame, powering a quartz-iodide headlamp and standard dynamo type rear. They also had a secondary rear L.E.D. lamp, a design which hadn't been on the market long, their secondary front light was a standard bulb using type, by a Japanese firm called 'Cat-Eye'.

Mick Pott's preparation for this event had been very thorough. He was a very tough rider and even at 50 years of age, could strike fear into many of the younger men he raced and trained with. Apart from the 24hr Championship being one of his goals, he also wanted to do well in the 'PBP' (Paris-Brest-Paris), which came later, in September.

His earlier months of mileage were done on a low-geared fixed wheel bike. By March the Audax events had started giving him a variation to his training. By the end of April he'd totalled over 6,000 miles and by the end of June he'd covered 9,729 hard miles, but things hadn't been easy having sustained damage to his right hip in a fall, requiring hospital treatment.

The month of July came around and Mick tapered his training down, even he knew that at 50 years of age, recovery was slower, and that rest was as important as 'miles'. He had managed to recruit a team of 3 more riders; Jim Ithell, Simon Pedley and Graham Moult. Jim had provided all the members of the team with extensive details of the course and the event so that they were all very well prepared.

Right from the word 'Go' Mick felt good, using gears of 90" and 95", riding mainly on the tri-bars for the whole of the 24hrs. He had his first stop at 130 miles to put lights and thermal vest on, he shouted at his helpers for not having his chair ready, but they knew he would be short tempered during the event and they were prepared for his outbursts. He said although his Vista rear LED light was brilliant, his standard front lights gave him lots of problems. His wife, Joy, being very safety conscious, tried three times to swop lights for him until on the third occasion he said to her "stop trying to give me a bl—dy light, just feed me!" Luckily she didn't drive off and leave him, but Mick later said that he'd been washing up ever since!

His third stop came at Tern Hill (300 miles) to take off lights and tights and have a bowl of grapefruit. He was hoping to get caught by the tandem on the Newport section, merely so that he could have a chat. On the return to Tern Hill he found that Phil Barlow was only 8 minutes down on him, but Mick recalls feeling good and thinking that Barlow would have to be feeling even better than him to beat him.

On the High Ercall leg the tandem eventually caught him and then Mick knew it wouldn't be long before reaching the finishing circuit. He'd seen Simon and Graham and so knew that his team were still in with a chance of a win.

During the morning he made use of his smaller chain ring and gears to give his legs a rest. By the time he reached the circuit he was 20 minutes clear of Barlow, he knew then that he would win and really enjoyed his last few hours. Although Mick's ride was fairly uneventful, Simon went off course for 8 miles and Graham spent some considerable time off the bike being sick. Mick's last remarks were "I'm sure both of them will be back with bigger mileages in the future, and I will be there to feed them!"

---

In 1991, **Ralph Dadswell** broke Pat Kenny's 26 year old **London to Edinburgh Trike Record,** by 1hr 20mins with **19hourts 27mins and 54 secs.** Also on that same ride, **he continued for the 24hr record** also held by Pat and raised the record by 15 miles to record **449 miles.**

Ralph's two appearances in previous 24hr time trials plus these two tough records were all to stand him in good stead for his assault on the epic 'Lands End to John o' Groats' record in 1992.

# 1992

*Speed Cameras are used for the first time this year on Britain's roads.*

**The North Road National Championship 24hr event on June 20th & 21st was won by Andy Wilkinson, Port Sunlight Whls, with 501.96 miles, Mick Gray, Crest CC was 2nd with 481.08 miles and Ian Gray, Derby Mercury 3rd with 473.17 miles. Ian Gray led Graham Moult and Simon Pedley to their 2nd National Championship Team win of 1,288.13 miles.**

The event this year had managed to attract an entry of 64 riders of whom more than half were novices. The favourites, apart from Mick Potts and Mark Holden were all novices, newcomers to the art of 24hr riding, but they all had pedigrees. Andy Wilkinson had taken John Woodburn's End to End in 1991, so you were left in no doubt that he was a 'stayer' having ridden 489 miles for his first 24hrs to Gretna Green, in almost continuous torrential rain. Glen Longland was also everyone's favourite, the first man to reach 300 miles for 12 hours and becoming BBAR with that same ride. Steve Marchant was included as was Pete Pickers and all had sub 4 hr hundreds to their credit.

By the morning of the event the wind blew steady and very strongly. 57 riders started plus 1 tandem trike and 3 tandems. The field also included 3 women, Sheila Simpson, Jean Burrow, and Celia Prescott. Andy Wilkinson was No 50 and Glen Longland was 60, and many were surprised that by the 50 mile point Wilkinson had developed a small lead, with 2hrs 7mins. Longland was at 3mins, Marchant at 4m, Ian Gray at 8m, Pedley at 9m, Mick Potts and Mick Gray were both at 11mins with Pickers, King and White at 12mins. Stuart Jackson who gave many of the details of this event for the Fellowship Journal said that the traffic on the A142 West of Ely was particularly heavy and very fast, and with aggressive drivers it became frightening. Having already been forced off the A1, he felt that we would all end up being pushed into the sea by the motor maniacs!

At the 100 mile point everyone was scratching their heads and asking what was the matter with Longland; there was no doubt that Wilkinson was drawing away with 4hrs 25mins, Longland at 8mins, Ian Gray at 18mins and Mick Gray, Dadswell and Potts all at 20 mins. Phil Oxborough had retired soon after 50 miles with a bad back and Steve Marchant retired soon after 100 miles.

The leg from Littleport to Mildenhall put paid to the hopes of many riders. Stuart Jackson who was 'feeding' the riders on this section at 132 miles said "I watched Wilkinson glide by apparently without effort, then waited for Longland, and waited. 20 minutes later a very unhappy Pete Pickers grimaced past. He'd been caught for 20 mins and then dropped for another 20. Dadswell came through having gained 8 minutes on him and still the wind roared and still we waited for Longland. Eventually the 'Antelope' star 'jerked' uncomfortably past, 21 minutes adrift of Wilkinson, he was not looking the smooth stylish athlete that I had seen so many times before. It was not suprising that he did not complete this leg and Mick Potts also decided he had gone far enough at about the same point, when 28 minutes down on Wilkinson".

Mick Gray and Ian Gray were a minute apart on the start sheet with numbers 25 & 26, apparently Roger Sewell had done this to add a little interest to the proceedings, both being novices and both being tough 'road men'. Ian Gray was an Australian now living in England and had been recruited by the Derby Mercury to boost the strength of the team. Mick and Ian's rivalry in the 24hr was intense, with a tough battle on the road ensuing. This obviously helped them to overcome the thought of racing for 24 hrs. The elastic broke at 14 hours and by 350 miles, Mick Gray was 28 minutes up on Ian.

At the 200 mile point Wilkinson was virtually riding on his own with 8hrs 50mins. Dadswell retired which inspired John Baines, he'd been Champion in 1970. Graham Moult and Neil Roberts also moved up in the field, with Baines winning the tussle at this stage. Andy Major was now lying 4th whilst Mark Holden who'd had a very slow start had moved into 6th place.

At 400 miles Wilkinson with 18hrs 53mins was 1 hour up on the 2nd man, Mick Gray, and still had the possibility to take the 507 mile record but he was going through a very rough patch. Being so far ahead of the field he'd been sent on an 18 mile optional detour twice, from Stetchworth to Four Went Ways and this had really slowed him badly taking 5hrs 18mins, for his 4th 100 miles. He did pull through his rough patch and managed to accelerate to 'evens' for his last 100 miles, lapping the fnishing circuit of 18 miles in 54 minutes, but the wind of the previous day had taken its toll of him. Nevertheless he'd won the Championship with 501.96 miles, which is what he'd set out to do.

Mick Gray was 2nd with a distance of 481.08m and Ian Gray 3rd on 473.17m. Stuart Jackson asked "when last did novices take all three medals in the National Championship?"

During the event it was noticed that Andy Wilkinson's second 100 miles had taken the same time as the first - 4hrs 25mins. When thinking that his second '100' was very fast, one forgets that the first '100' was extraordinary in that it contained possibly 40 miles of tough headwind riding and it was felt that this probably did more to demoralize Longland than anything else, plus the fact that Andy looked so smooth doing it.

When Longland climbed off, he said he had every intention of riding another 24hr but his team-mate Pete Pickers said he had absolutely no intention of riding another 24hr under any circumstances!

Mark Holden who came 6th with 419 miles in this Championship was chosen for a random drug test for caffeine to which he proved positive. The guidelines are 12mg per litre of urine. The test is there only to detect 'megadosing' on caffeine tablets – it being scientifically accepted that ordinary tea and coffee drinking provides no athletic benefit. It is also known that the urine test is actually a very poor indicator of blood caffeine level, the level that counts. However, under extreme conditions such as a 24hr race it is possible to fail it without 'megadosing' as Mark did. He did admit to drinking 14 litres of tea in the last 14 hours of the race. It is claimed that if a rider is badly dehydrated at the end of a race, such as a '100' then just three cups of tea could be enough to fail the test!

Ian Dow in his editorial recap of the season said "That out of all the tough riders entered and expected to either win or break records, only Wilkinson survived, the others falling victim either to the fearsome wind, sickness, tactical errors or demoralisation". Ian goes on to mention *"how many people in the South, including the Editor of Cycling Weekly, hadn't realised how good Andy Wilkinson was, and when Ian made the comment that Longland was not the only rider capable of a 300 mile twelve hour, he'd received some very strange looks.*

*Andy Major who improved over 20 miles to finish 4th with 444 miles reported riding with the wind at 30 mph and against it at 13 mph. He likened that experience to 'sensory deprivation', hearing nothing above the deafening roar of the wind and seeing nothing but dead straight roads across a dead flat landscape.*

*Wilkinson's speed alone does not destroy his opponents, it is his style. To see Wilkinson in action is frightening, he is almost completely motionless, or appears so, there is no betrayal of any effort whatsoever and not a sound. In fact he creates so little a disturbance that you can easily miss him when he goes past, and if you do see him, you see a man who is not trying at all.*

*Then you look at your watch! You check and recheck and then stand and stare after him. I have never felt anything as chilling as the sight of Wilkinson gliding slowly into that impenetrable wall of wind, faster than the fastest 12 hour rider could go."*

These words and passages above describing Andy's riding style are by Ian Dow who has also ridden over 500 miles in 24 hours, which adds even more power to his words. I have followed Andy Wilkinson's long distance career very closely having been present when many of his 24hr rides were done. The only concession I can add to these words to prove that he really is human and does have the odd frailty, is that while helping Lynne since 1993, I've seen him suffer with a bad back on occasions. In later years he resorted to riding the Mersey 24hr on a slick tyred mountain bike, to alleviate this problem and I found it even more amazing to see him glide past at 23 mph on his mtb giving a nod and a smile and looking even less like a dedicated time triallist. But as Ian said, looks can be deceptive!

*Edwin Hargraves recently remarked how well 'Wilko' stood up to the two very long body, mind, and soul destroying detours he was sent on by the North Road CC Organisers and Controllers. It was felt by many bystanders and observers to be a heartless and futile way of riding a time trial, on your own, with no one to catch or even see, on route, almost like an extra punishment for being talented, but then after all, Andy is a Northerner!*

⇒•◇•⇐

**The Mersey RC 24hr one month later was won by Ian Gray, Derby Mercury, with 463.02 miles. Richard Johnson, North Shropshire Whls was 2nd with 450.30m, Graham Smith, Severn RC was 3rd with 447.15 miles. Bridget Boon, Severn RC with 437.62 miles was 4th. She just missed Anne Mann's Competition Record by .5 of a mile and with Ian Finch's 361.21 miles, the Severn RC took the team win with 1,245.98 miles.**

With the absence of mega-milers such as Dow, Jackson and Wilkinson, it was felt that Ian Gray, Phil Oxborough or Peter Goodfellow would be contenders for top honours in the mens race, and either Bridget Boon or Sheila Simpson for the ladies title.

86 solos plus 3 tandem trikes were entered, in all 42 of the entrants were new to the 24hr event, including 15 who had not raced beyond 50 miles. The temperature was kind, with a gentle south-westerly wind which gave the odd shower in the night. Peter Goodfellow who was No 85 behind Gray No 80, went off from the start like a rocket, but only caught Gray after 61 miles. A scrap ensued with both riders in sight of each other on the road for 159 miles. At 176 miles Gray recaught Goodfellow and gradually drew away to lead by 8 minutes at 222 miles, 21 mins at 261 miles and finally 38 mins by 294 miles, where Goodfellow abandoned – sick.

Richard Johnson, No 87, riding his first 24hr with the judgement of a veteran, wisely didn't try to match Gray and Goodfellow or try to ward off the pursuing Oxborough, No 90, who caught him at 42 miles. This effort by Oxborough had proved too much so early on in the race and Johnson re-caught him fairly soon and by 53 miles had a 3 minute lead on the road.

Oxborough plugged on but eventually retired near 200 miles. Tony Fouldes at 66 years of age was still riding for his old club, the Rutland CC, and inspired by Jim Halls efforts in the last few years, was also riding a steady race. He finished with an amazing 412.38 miles, to take the 'VTTA' award. His best mileage ever had been in 1955 with 460 miles, a time lag of 37 years.

Once again Prees Island posed problems for the section detour controller Tom Greep, although his job was made easier with a 'CB' Citizen Band radio (like the lorry drivers use). This method had been in operation for quite a few years now and had proved very useful. An additional hazard this year was motorised 'yobs' practising hand-brake turns on the Islands approach roads in the night, until sorted out by the Police.

Frank Mumford who provided most of these details said that seeing the tandem trikes taking tight island turns and bends reminded him of the days when watching Crimes and Arnold break records in the 1950's. Frank said that the only difference, was that these modern day 'stokers' weren't thumping their steersmen on the back with cries of "Push you idle 'B------' as John was want to do with poor Albert.

Pat Kenny and Pete Gifford were the fastest tandem trike with 382.09 miles, Mike Johnson and Richard Hills were 2nd with 376.88 and Mrs M.V. Staines and Mr. J. Staines were 3rd with 332.25 miles.

One or two extra points of interest here, Ian Hill, Mercia CC had a 44 miles improvement this year, with 405.06m, compared to Hugh Canning whose 421.02 this year, was just .01 of a mile better than last year. Karl Austin, Congleton CC made his debut in this year's event also with 421 miles.

*Bridget Boon, when told at the finish that she had just missed Competition Record by a whisker said "Oh well, I'll just have to ride another one!" This was Bridget's first solo performance after having a lot of success on the tandem with husband Ian. We shall see more 'tough' rides from Bridget over the next few years.* **(A fuller account of the Ladies History is in chapter 5)**

*16 year old Simon Baddeley, Kidderminster CTC, became the youngest ever rider to finish a Mersey 24hr with 322.09 miles and finished one place ahead of the oldest rider in the race, John Reaney, at 74years of age. He finished with 313.17m and Karl Austin rode the fastest finishing circuit lap, in 48 minutes.*

---

Stan Turner, a very experienced 24 hr rider having ridden to over 480 miles himself, helped Mick Gray, in this years North Road event, to a silver medal with 481.08 miles. Stan gave some tips to anyone who wanted their man or woman to aspire to a top mileage Stan had done his homework in finding out what the local weather would do over that weekend. He knew that Force 4 to 6 winds would blow until sunset on the Saturday and then the night would be calm and fairly mild, but with mist patches at dawn, then sunrise would bring a warm day. This information helped Stan to be able to instruct Mick not to push too high a gear into the wind and to ride at a pace that was comfortable, pedalling and not pushing. Grovelling on too high a gear is a tactical error that many long distance 'stars' have made in the past and indeed this year's North Road event proved that.

Also knowing when is the right time to stop your rider to put on night clothing and lights, and when to take them back off in the morning. Stan waited until Mick had got a fair enough lead over Ian Gray and then got him off and ready with his night attire and back on again before being caught. This then put Mick's opponent at the disadvantage of having to stop for the same treatment. Also knowing who your opponent's helpers are and recognising them during the event gives you some idea as to where their rider is on the road. An intimate knowledge of the course and where the Marshalls should be is another very useful aid, especially when your man is out virtually on his own at the front of the field.

Work to a rota so that one helper can have something to eat and drink and perhaps a short sleep while the other takes over and then swop roles, this saves the situation where so often in the past, the whole crew have had to stop for hours to sleep and so lose track of their rider.

Being strict with your rider is an art that can take years to learn, but Stan was an RTTC Coach and National Coaching Secretary and a 'BCCS' Senior Coach, his decisions were made wisely. Mick wanted to stop and take off his night clothing when the temperature was still fairly low and Stan said "No, we'll wait till its' warmer". As the sun rose he pulled Mick in for his stop. He dismounted and sat on the road, he was in a distressed state and didn't want to carry on, he was so tired and he'd had enough. Stan at this time had to be ruthless with him, pointing out how far they had all come and that he wasn't prepared to let him to just 'throw the towel in'! Stan lifted him off the road, got him back onto his bike, and told him to get on with it and that he would soon pick up, which of course he did, without anymore problems. It was probably a good job that Mick's wife Sue, who was also on the helping team, was fast asleep at the time and missed the incident. The reason why I say this is because if you are either married to or related to the rider in some close way, it is very difficult to stand by and hear or see somebody else telling them what to do, even if it's the right thing to do.

*I have first hand knowledge of this type of situation from helping Lynne Taylor, my daughter, on most of her 24hr and record breaking 'End to End' rides. Moments such as the middle of the 2nd night in the Grampians on her first solo attempt where her eyes were so tired from trying to peer into a black wet road surface, she wanted to stop for 30 minutes but the team only let her have 5 mins because the record was so tight.*

---

**On Monday August 10th at 8am Ralph Dadswell rode away from Lands End to attack Eric Tremaine's trike End to End record.** Ralph had a fast start with a good wind and reached the 200 mile point beyond Bristol in less than 10 hours, putting him 30 minutes ahead of schedule. By 8pm he'd reached Tewkesbury at 240 miles for his first 12 hours. At Stafford with 300 miles covered in 15hrs 35mins he was 20 minutes up on record. By Knutsford the wind had dropped and at Warrington he was 10 minutes behind schedule. Although he had many people out helping him to get through Wigan and Preston, he arrived at Lancaster 35mins down. 400 miles took him 22 hours and as daylight returned, Ralph started to feel a bit depressed, there was no wind and he felt sluggish. He realised that with over 400 miles left to do it was going to be a tough job.

He wasn't going to beat his own 24hr record of 447 miles and so he decided to stop at Kendal at 7.15am for a quick feed and revitalisation. Ralph swapped to his brother Tim's trike with much lower gears for the climb of 'Shap Fell', but just over the summit he sheared the inner ring off the chainset so had to swop back to his own machine. A new chainset was purchased and fitted at Carlisle so he swapped machines once again just in time for him to climb the 'Devil's Beeftub' and ride towards Edinburgh. A heavy shower, which flooded the roads, dampened his enthusiasm and he decided to have another 10 minutes sleep. His mind was already playing tricks on him, he envisaged tackling the Grampians after a good nights sleep and then realised he was on a record attempt and couldn't take any sleep!

While crossing the Forth Road Bridge he picked up a puncture and the team had difficulty changing the wheel but in 5 minutes he was back on the road to Perth which was in a poor state of repair. At 600 miles he was 1hr 40mins behind schedule with 34hrs 50mins elapsed. Another demoralising ride over the Grampians to Inverness left Ralph hallucinating, he recalled seeing people ahead with drinks, only to reach them and find they were trees!

His memories of the route from his previous reconnoitre of the journey left him with doubts in his mind. He kept stopping and asking the team if he was on the correct route, he was having the same sleep deprivation problems as Andy Wilkinson had experienced. After being convinced that he was on the correct road by showing him the map, he then asked them the question "what am I doing here, where am I going and why am I out on my trike in the wind and rain when they were all sitting in the van?" After being given a stern answer by Audrey Hughes, the timekeeper, he continued to John o' Groats to record **2days 5hrs 29mins,** so beating Tremaine's record by 49mins 35secs.

*It's amazing what problems sleep deprivation can cause and the same can be said about hypothermia, but when both problems occur at the same time, it can put a normally very astute, bright, calculating person, into a 'zombie' like state. Both of these physical states can be used as a method of torture, did I hear 'Human Rights' mentioned?*

Ralph recalled "things flooded back to my brain as people shook my hand and congratulated me. Suddenly it all made sense, oh dear, why oh why had I wasted all that time?"

*These details were taken from an article written by Ralph Dadswell with odd comments and observations from myself.*

# 1993

The 50th Mersey RC 24hr on 24th and 25th July was a National Championship and incorporated the Merseyside Ladies CA event. It was won by Phil Barlow, Kiveton Park CC with 490.88 miles. Glen Longland, Antelope RT was 2nd with 477.46 miles and Paul Bland, Kiveton Park CC was 3rd with 468.51 miles. Peter Goodfellow with 448.81 completed the Kiveton Park CC team who won the Championship with a total of 1,408.20 miles. (an event record) Keith Silvester, Mid Shropshire Wheelers was 4th with 467.92 miles. Mrs Christine Roberts took 5th place overall and broke the Ladies Competition Record with 461.45 miles, beating Anne Mann's 10 year old record by over 23 miles. Mrs Bridget Boon, Severn RC was the 2nd lady and 9th overall with 446.88 miles. She too beat the existing record by 8 miles. Another 5 solo lady riders rode that day, Lynne Taylor, Sue Gray, Celia Prescott, Mrs J.M. Wilson and Helen Sandelands. **Jane Ramsdale stoked a tandem trike for Mark Brooking, producing 401.22 miles, a new mixed Competition Record. (For complete details of the ladies rides in this event and indeed all other 24hrs see Chapter 5)**

This years entry of 101 was a record for this event and Jim Turner was overjoyed. The field included 4 tandems and over 60% of the riders had previously ridden a 24hr, seven of them having done rides of 450 miles plus. Several teams were entered, Derby Mercury, Mersey RC, Kiveton Park CC, Antelope RT, Mid Shropshire Whls, Severn Rc and Walsall RCC.

Standard wired-on tyres were now the 'norm' with 78% of riders using them and only 22% using tubulars. 83% used computers, 63% tribars, 60% clipless pedals and safety helmet use was 27%. Carbon tri and quad spoked wheels were used by 8 riders. It's interesting to note that this year most riders had fitted a rear 'Led' light, although technically illegal, they at least were more reliable. Front 'Led's had been developed and were used by a few riders mainly as a 'back up' light, as it gave a neon yellow light.

*It's interesting to note that Christine mentions riding with 2 'Cateye' halogen bulb- using front lamps and the amount of light they provided. We'd had 60 years of absolutely rubbish battery lights and suddenly we have good ones. Okay, they cost possibly double the price of the British ones but they were good, very good. The downside was they weren't British, they were Japanese and I'm afraid that by now all of our industry had disappeared. What amazed me about the new forms of lighting was that models were being improved on, year by year, better seals, longer battery life, lighter in weight, better beams, the list is endless.*

The weather was hot on the Saturday with a tough wind for the riders until night- time. Showers in the night gave way to a windy Sunday with intermittent sun and showers, but generally warm.

The first time check at 51 miles which was mostly a wind assisted run, gave Barlow at 2 hours, Ian Silvester at 5mins, Longland 6mins, Bland and Pedley at 9mins, Peter Goodfellow and Keith Silvester at 12mins. At 96 miles, Christine Roberts (No 65) had caught Bridget Boon (55) but the two were closely matched on the road until 250 miles. The starting sequence of the latter half of the field was to generate some ferocious scraps between the faster riders, with eventual winner Barlow (No 90) catching rival Longland (85) in 39 miles, he went on to scythe through the field by 185 miles, ridden in 8.25 hours.

Nightfall saw no cessation of effort from the top riders, with Barlow, Longland, Goodfellow and Ian Silvester so far ahead that they were sent on an extra leg around midnight to keep them within the field. At this time Barlow had 13 mins on Longland, but a gastric upset sometime later slowed him and he was recaught at around 248 miles. Fortunately first aid was on hand, dispensed by feeding supremo 'H' (Harold Nelson). From his magical medical chest at Hodnet, where an 80ft long tent had been erected, serving as a café, medical HQ, rest room and sleeping quarters. From this club emblem decorated palace, 'H' could supply corpse reviving potions, 'T.L.C.' massage, a few strokes from the butt end of a ragman's trumpet, or anything else, to keep the infirms going – except stimulants! Following 'tea-addict' Holden's bother with the 'RTTC' after his 'North Road' in 1992, 'H' ensured that only decaffeinated drinks were given today, to avoid drugs charges.

Suitably dosed, Barlow was soon flying again, re-catching Longland for ten minutes at 330 miles. Longland was now suffering with the 'knock' (low blood sugar levels). He took a couple of stops to recuperate but lost a lot of time and momentum here. At 12 hours, only 6 riders were beating 'evens'. Barlow 253miles, Longland 249m, Bland 247, Goodfellow 246m, Keith Silvester 243m and Christine 241m.

Earlier detouring of the faster riders gave Bridget the honour of reaching the finishing circuit first, to sustained applause from the waiting fans. With all body sensors in the 'red zone' she accomplished 3 laps of the 15 mile circuit in 52, 52 and 53 minutes, so beating Anne Mann's record by 8.75 miles. But it's a tough sport, Christine recorded 3 laps of 51, 51 and 50mins, eventually bettering the record by 23.25 miles.

*Christine is of course a very fast rider and a multi champion at 100 miles. She had recently ridden 253 miles for a 12hr race, but even so, her 461.45 mile ride was way beyond expectations, showing what can be achieved with dedication, thorough preparation and attitude of mind.*

*Christine had overcome serious injuries after being hit by a car at the end of a time trial in 1987. After a long spell off the bike to recover mentally and physically, she came back to winning form in 1990 and then built herself up for this record breaking occasion. I was out helping Lynne that weekend and my recollection of Saturdays weather was of stifling heat, coupled with a brick wall of a wind. I watched the battle evolve between Christine and Bridget and my memories were of Christine 'turning over' a huge gear from very early on, as if to stamp her authority on the race.*

*Phil Barlow told 'Cycling Weekly' that the wind was horrendous and not conducive to record breaking, so this makes Christine's ride even more remarkable.*

Barlow took the Gold medal with 4 circuits of 49, 46, 45, and 45 minutes to the acclaim of about 1,000 spectators manning the circuit. His 237 mile second 12 hours of riding giving a total of 490.88 miles proved that he was a stayer. Keith Silvester who came 4th with 467.92 miles, narrowly missed the bronze medal by .59 of a mile. The irony of it all is that he stopped a minute early before his time was up, possibly losing him 3rd place.

**Jim Hopper with 398.54 miles was again the fastest trike rider.**

Peter Goodfellow had a problem trying to fit proper training in for this event, with his medical 'finals' only 5 weeks before the event, he knew he wouldn't be at his very best. A crash in a road race left him with a sprained shoulder but this didn't put him off. During the 24hr he fed on 'Maxim' and rice pudding with alternative hand ups of fruit with sugar. His first 12 hours gave him 246.2 miles, but he was now suffering hip pain which he'd never experienced before, he desperately wanted to 'pack' but his helpers coaxed him along, assuring him that it would all be worth it, especially for the team, and he was glad they kept him going.

After the event he took up his hospital post and started work a few days later. He was walking with a limp, but smiled when his new colleagues told him he would be tired after working all night!

Ian Dow, in his comments as the Editor of the 24hr Fellowship Journal, said that the overall standard of rides in the Championship was high this year, the highest for a long time. Eleven riders beating 440 miles (including 2 women) and this has only happened 6 times ever before (but not with women), the most recent being in 1969. The total entry of just over 100 was probably a record, although there were fields of 100 riders in the 1950's before the limit was raised to 120, so let nobody say that 24hr popularity is declining, after all, the mens 100 mile Championship had only 75 entries this year (1993).

*Once again I thank Frank Mumford and Ian Dow for their comments and amusing descriptions.*

—————⇒•◇•⇐—————

I will again use paragraphs from Ian Dow's editorial to introduce this years North Road 24hr event, which had resorted back to its usual slot on the calendar of August bank holiday, 28th & 29th.

"Within days of the 'Mersey', Bridget Boon was out on her bike again, packing in the miles as if the 24hr had been nothing but a dream. Having missed the record by half a mile last year, and being thwarted by Christine reaching the record point before her this time, she then made one of the greatest acts of defiance in 24hr history and entered the North Road 24hr. It was obvious she had set her heart passionately on owning that Competition Record, and would let nothing get in her way.

Bridget had evidently made a perfect recovery in the five weeks between the events, and the elements, for once, sided with her and gave the North Road event a good day. For the first time in her life she beat 'evens' for 12 hours, covering 243 miles in the first half, but with most of the 8 hour night falling in the second 12 hours, and with a nasty bout of sickness towards the end, the record slipped away and she finished 4 miles short.

*Nonetheless however* **Bridget had won the North Road 24hr** *by nearly 40 miles. (Just imagine the reaction from the 'old timers', after all it had only been a few years since women had been allowed to join the club).* **Her two rides this year must rank alongside Eric Matthew's double of 486 in the Mersey and 489 in the North Road National Championship of 1968.** *(that is a comparison and an accolade worth having!)*

—————⇒•◇•⇐—————

**The North Road CC 24hr, August 28th & 29th 1993, was won by Bridget Boon, Severn RC with 457.14 miles. Peter Bishop was 2nd with 417.72 miles and John Baines was 3rd with 416.84m. Jim Hopper with 392.87 was the fastest trike rider and together with Dave McGeachie Clarke who came 4th with 414.06 and John Walker with 349.47 miles, the Derby Mercury took the team honours with 1,156.40 miles.**

This win by Bridget is the only time in the history of timetrialling that a woman has won a 24hr event. Bridget's main rival during this race had been Robert Fry, Willesden CC. He led at the 12 hour point with 246 miles, to Bridgets' 243, Peter Bishop, Heron CC rode 228, McGeachie Clarke 225, & John Baines 221. But at 14 hours, Robert Fry dropped away, finally to finish with 386.28 miles. A nasty bout of sickness in the last third of the race saw Bridget's speed drop, so putting paid to her breaking the record, but nevertheless she won by nearly 40 miles.

Jim Hopper recalled that towards the end of the race Bridget came past him and said "at last, I've been trying to catch you for 22 hours!" For his 392.8 mile ride he gained a North Road silver medal for being the fastest trike rider, as have all winning trike riders in this event down through the ages, in fact 95 years. The North Road CC have been the only club to also list the fastest trike rider every year, right the way back in time on their start cards, as well as the solo bicycle winner. I think this custom goes back in time to the days when trike riders were plentiful and made up a fair percentage of the field. Looking back at old line drawings and photos back to the 1890's, one sees almost as many famous riders astride trikes as bikes, with such rough roads they were probably more stable.

On a lighter note, Jim said there was a large gathering at the result board waiting to see who had won. Margaret, Jim's wife, was standing with Jim's other helpers, Johnny Bevan and Ian Hill, when Bridget's name went up as the winner. One old chap in the crowd was heard to mutter that it was a disgrace and that women should be at home looking after the house etc. The 'old chap' was none other than one of the North Road CC officials. Jim said that the lads had a job to stop Margaret thumping him!

Ian Dow in his Editorial summing up of the event said that the sickness may have been caused by an over concentrated solution of 'Maxim liquid polymer drink. It is something that all riders need to avoid, the trauma that sickness can bring on, especially when exherting oneself, can be debilitating and with Bridget missing the record by 4 miles, one wonders whether the benefits from polymer feeding in real endurance long distance racing, are not in some way outweighed by the problems that it can cause.

Stuart Jackson, in an article titled **'The Hi-tech Revolution: Science or mere Fashion?'** asks if any of these new innovations that have appeared over the last few years, have actually made any difference. Most of the riders who start off in the event on just polymer feeding soon end up adding to their diet with either ham or tuna butties. As a helper Stuart recalls being at a feeding station during the night with helpers trying to find something solid to give their riders, who were demanding food other than tasteless watery liquid. He also added that a rider taking nothing but polymer liquids has to spend extra time with toilet stops to get rid of excess fluid, especially at night when the temperature has dropped, and the rider isn't sweating much.

Stuart had some excellent rides to his credit, some over 490 miles, and all performed on nothing more than basic rice pudding and maybe a little fruit cocktail. For drinks he used just normal fluids such as squash or tea. He also asks where is the evidence that tri bars are beneficial in a 24hr as at 1993. Roy Cromack's 507 miles record still stood, and even amongst the lower placed riders, the performances hadn't altered. Pulse meters, disc wheels and tri spoke wheels also failed to add any mileage and Stuart remains to be convinced, but also added that there had been so much change technologically it could possibly create an improvement in the near future.


# 1994


*On May 6th 1994 The Channel Tunnel opened linking mainland Britain to France and the rest of Europe.*

**The Brighton Mitre CC 24hr, 25 & 26th June.** The Brighton Mitre Cycling Club Centenary fell due in this year, and Miker Hayler had always felt it would be a fitting way to celebrate his club's historical centenary by running a 24hr race, on roughly the same roads and in the same area as the Catford CC had used from 1925 to 1975. It was not a championship event but it did draw a field of 35 riders, some of them newcomers from mainly southern areas, with only George Berwick and Les Lowe classed as 'northerners'.

Bridget Boon was the favourite to win this event and everyone knew she would be going all out for the Competition Record. At the 100 mile point Ian Dow, who was helping in the event, waited to give the riders a sponge. He fully expected to see Bridget come through first on the road, but Marc Cunnington, Swindon RC came first in 4hrs 37 minutes. He'd caught her for 6 minutes and by the time she came past she was 8 minutes down on him. Marc's previous years performance in the 'Mersey' of 422 miles gave no indication of what he was really capable of.

The next time Ian could check Bridget's progress was on the night circuit. At the 12 hour point Marc had ridden 240 miles and Bridget 239.4, with James Reynolds 3rd, 233.5 miles. Ian felt that 239.4 wasn't quite enough for Bridget as it still left 222 miles to do in the 2nd half. The race was becoming a ding-dong between the two of them. Ian worked it out that allowing for tiredness, Bridget should be through 'Earwig Corner' on the outskirts of Lewes at 2.45am, but knowing that Marc was up on her, he expected him through first. Imagine his excitement when Bridget came through first - smack on time!

James Reynolds was next through, he was far too cheerful, Ian reckoned. With the circuit being 39.8 miles Ian hoped to see Bridget back at 5.00 am, that would leave her with 149 miles to do in 7hrs 50mins: 19 mph – just possible? But the first rider back was Marc followed some 30 minutes later by James Reynolds, sadly Bridget had packed at 16.5 hours, having ridden 305 miles. Attention now focussed on Marc and James, Marc could do 450 if he kept the pressure on and James possibly 430 miles.

Once Ian had got back to the finishing circuit he was surprised to find out who was still in the race. George Berwick had come to grief at Steyning after bending a wheel, but he still finished with 371 miles. Peter Dean was still riding, earlier he'd had a nasty spill when taking a sponge from Ian, he'd cut and grazed himself very badly, but after having his hand and wrist bandaged he carried on to finish with 355.7 miles. Paul Whitehead who'd ridden a fast first 100 of 4hrs 49mins and 215 for his 12 hour, finished with 368 miles.

A cracking battle was going on for 3rd place between Tim Dolphin and Richard Griffin, with Tim winning it on the very last lap with 405.45 to Griffin's 404.08 and James Reynolds was almost on his knees losing 10 minutes each circuit to the winner, Marc Cunnington.

Ian Dow concluded with "Looking around the H.Q. I could tell who had really tried. Marc Cunnington sat in silent blankness waiting for his award, while behind me there was a muffled thud as James Reynolds collapsed on the floor, out cold, he had given everything".

No matter that only 5 riders had beaten 400 miles, what mattered most was that a '24hr' had been run in the south for the first time in 7 years, and had been successful, riders, helpers, marshals, organisers, good course, they were all there. It had been a perfect summer's day of 20 degrees C, comfortable humidity and nothing more than a light cool breeze from the west.

Marc Cunnington remembers being back on the A22 and overtaking Bridget. He offered her some words of encouragement as he could see she was going through a bad patch. He was later to learn that illness had forced her retirement, this must have been a difficult decision having come so far. Keith Valters had worked out a schedule for Marc of 452 miles, which proved accurate to the mile. Once on the finishing circuit his pace slowed to a crawl, so slow in fact that he asked Duncan, one of his helpers, how close was the Competition between him and James Reynolds, and within a few minutes came the reply "neck and neck"! This was enough to spur Marc into action on his last circuits. Duncan afterwards confessed to having tricked him. Marc said "It was rather mean but at least it revived my competitive spirit, and added a mile or two on".

James Reynolds lost his helpers during the event and after suffering lighting problems he was confronted with the problem of having no food left, he remembers a helper's car passing him and stopping just ahead of him on the road. James thought "Good, I can now cadge some food". As he got to within 50 yards the car pulled away again. This happenend three times until James hadn't got the strength to chase him anymore. "Finally, I caught him and begged some cake. He told me that he had been guiding me through the lanes near Wivelsfield thinking I was lost and not realising I was desperate for food." James puts his fainting fit, causing him to collapse at the HQ, down to getting very hungry during the night and never fully recovering.

**The final results were Marc Cunnington 1st with 452.704 miles, 2nd James Reynolds with 427.131 and 3rd Tim Dolphin, 405.454miles. Peter Holland was the fastest trike rider with 399.082 miles and Medway Velo were the only team to finish. The team members being Ken Stokes, Ernie Mackey and S. Franklin, with 1,068.118m.**

⟫•◇•⟪

*Phillip Barlow, Kiveton Park CC started from Lands End in ideal conditions and by 100 miles he was 33mins inside schedule, but a diversion at Bristol and the onset of pleurisy whittled his time advantage down to just 12 mins at Worcester. Barlow rode on through the night but finally climbed off, exhausted and shivering, just north of Lancaster at 5am next morning. The pleurisy was apparently a complicaton of a chest infection after a heavy cold in weeks prior to the attempt.*

⟫•◇•⟪

**The Mersey RC 24hr including the Merseyside Ladies CA event on 23rd and 24th July 1994 was won by Andy Wilkinson, Port Sunlight Wheelers, with 496.16 miles. Christine Roberts, Crewe Clarion Wheelers was 2nd with 442.67m and won the MLCA event. Lynne Taylor, Walsall Roads CC was 3rd with 418.20 miles. No team entered.**

*A couple of paragraphs at the start of Frank Mumfords report on the race, sums up the situation that weekend. "When the start card revealed that 502 miler and End to End record holder Andy Wilkinson was the last solo off, most other riders opted for 'Plan B' but cheered up when they saw that he'd handicapped himself by riding a mountain bike. When a mountain biker did 355 miles in the 1993 event, the pundits dismissed this as an heretical aberration; they were now to be confounded when Wilkinson did the second greatest mileage in the events history, surpassed only by Cromacks record of 507 in 1969.*

*Even worse for the 'Machos', ladies took 2nd, 3rd and 7th places!* These were superb rides done in rough weather; Saturday afternoon was oppressively hot, scary thunder and lightning enlivened a warm night and monsoon rain fell pre-dawn, with heavy showers thereafter. A strong south to south-west wind blew throughout, making the first 100 miles very hard."

Wilkinson 'Wilko' started in scratch position at the back of the field, he quickly rode into the lead catching other 'short-markers' Christine Roberts at 34 miles, Roger Sewell at 40 miles, Bob Newell at 50 miles and Lynne Taylor at 85 miles. As the event wore on, Wilko had to be sent on extra detours to keep him within the field.

Christine, although feeling the effects of a hard season, was heading for runner up spot by catching most of the field in the first 150 miles. Although her original intention had been to raise her own Competition Record to possibly 480 miles, I think she'd realised that the weather so far had put paid to that plan. She was obviously going for a 2nd place or even a win, if anything went amiss with Wilko. Apart from Christine there were four more ladies entered, Lynne Taylor, Anne Learmonth, Helen Sandelands and Sian Charlton, although these last two retired later in the event.

Anne Learmonth, a hardened Audax rider rode strongly throughout, and had a running battle on the road with Jim Hopper on his trike. It was a battle that was to last some 300 miles or more, with Jim Hopper recording 398.37 miles and taking second place in the VTTA awards behind 68 year old Tony Fouldes, Rutland CC, who rode 392.65 miles. Anne at her first attempt at a 24hr time trial rode 402.13 miles, a very creditable ride.

Karl Austin had the 3rd best mileage of 220 at 12 hours, but took a terrible 'packet' on the Sunday morning. His mum, Joyce, who helped in most of his races, said he was 'on his last legs'. He made it to the circuit and completed one lap to finish with 391.74 miles. Lynne Taylor had a good ride that day to take 3rd place just beating newcomer Dave Brabbin by 3 miles.

I helped Lynne that weekend and apart from gaining a personal best she also overcame most of her fears of thunder and lightning, as indeed most of the other riders must have done. In the early evening as dusk was falling, the sky was lit periodically by sheet lightning. I think this was the first time she had ever ridden in these conditions and as I handed up her drinks, I could hear the intrepidation and shrieks of amazement in her voice as the road was lit up by the flashes and the thunder crashed around us. On the road from Battlefield to Hodnet you could see for miles as the flashes turned night into day. As the storm started to move away, you got that funny feeling that it would roll around Shropshire all night and come back vividly when you least expected it: and it did, many times.

I got used to seeing Wilko in that event and although my immediate thoughts of him riding it on a mountain bike were ones of it being almost an irreverence, I was soon being amazed by his speed, in fact I found it almost unbelievable. Working in the bike shop, I knew that a mountain bike, however you modified it, would always be about 6lbs heavier than a decent road bike. The tyres, although of a slick smooth rounded nature, would still be equivalent to a 28mm section or the old English "inch and an eighth". Occasionally during the event I would see him doing his shoulder and back excercises and realised then that a mountain bike actually gave him a slightly easier more comfortable position than a road bike. His ride that day blew all of the theories about lightweight and aerodynamics right out of the water. In a 24hr race it's mind over matter, and all the best equipment in the world won't make you win, only training, fitness, ability to suffer and the will to win, can do that.

I mean no disrespect to any of the other riders that day, but 'Wilkos' ride was awesome, 496.16 miles with no-one to push him, beating the next rider by 53 miles. It's also interesting to note that Wilko's 2nd 12 hours mileage of 239 miles was a perfect example of his 'controlled' and steady riding. It's an art or a skill that not many riders possess. Many of the past high mileage winners have aspired to those mileages by the 'Nim Carline' method of 'going like hell' from the start and hanging on to the finish. Sometimes with competition from other high mileage men in that same race, they either blew each other apart, or pushed one rider to a massive mileage.

Lynne that day equalled my own personal best of 418 miles on only her 2nd ride, and I felt now that I would be better off helping with her future career.

42 solo riders and 1 tandem started and 25 solos and 1 tandem finished.

The tandem was manned by Ron Van Hesswijk and Dai Harris, for 385.83miles. George Berwick with 376 miles was well on his way to equalling Jack Spackmans record of 55 x 24hr rides.

━━━━▶•◆•◀━━━━

**The North Road CC 24hr National Championship on the August bank holiday weekend was won by Glen Longland, Antelope RT with 475.40 miles. Steve Wharton, Paddington CC was 2nd with 439.81 miles and Graham Moult, Derby Mercury was 3rd with 438.11 miles. He led Simon Pedley with 397.40 and Dave McGeachie Clarke, 382.89, to a Championship Team win of 1,216.90 miles.**

Glen Longland had what must have been his best ride so far: He was only 2 miles slower than on his Mersey last year. His 475 miles was performed on a much harder day this year. With a poor entry of only 34 solos and a very strong westerly wind that blew for the full 24 hours, it made his ride a very good one.

The expected tussle between Longland and Phil Barlow came to little, as Phil packed quite early, obviously not feeling well, but it did lead to a fast first 100 miles of 4hrs 22mins for Glen who was quoted in 'Cycling Weekly' as thinking now, that only Andy Wilkinson could break the 24hr record. In other words, after three attempts, the record had finally beaten him – or was he just trying to take the pressure off for another try?

There were three other contenders for the other two medals. 'Steve Wharton, a novice, Graham Moult and Andy Major, it was just unfortunate that they were riding different optional detours to each other, because their positions in the medals were not clear until after the finish. As it turned out, Wharton (silver) with 439m and Moult (bronze) were less than a mile apart, while Andy Major stoically accepted his 3rd Championship 4th place with 434.58 miles.

Jim Hopper and Ron Sant rode a tandem trike to 410.47 miles.

<h1 style="text-align:center">1995</h1>

**The Mersey RC National Championship 24hr on 29th and 30th July 1995 was won by Andy Wilkinson, Port Sunlight Whls with 501.39 miles, Paul Bland, Kiveton Park CC was 2nd with 475.08 miles and Philip Leigh, Kent Valley RC was 3rd with 461.58 miles. Simon Pedley with 429.30 miles led Dave McGeachie Clarke with 417.14m and Jim Hopper (trike) 408.92m to a Championship Team win for the Derby Mercury of 1,255.36 miles.**

**Lynne Taylor came 7th overall with 441.40 miles to win the Merseyside Ladies CA event.**

The promotional efforts of Organiser Jim Turner had once again attracted a large field of 86 riders of whom 4 were ladies. Six trikes started plus a mixed tandem crewed by Norman and Sylvia Powell, Wyre Forest CRC; they finished with 347.76 miles.

It was felt that 'Wilko' Andy Wilkinson could be seriously challenged by Phil Barlow or Paul Bland or maybe even get pushed beyond 507 miles, and who knows, there were some newcomers riding who were all either good 12 hour men or 100 milers. Riders such as Rob Eperjesi who had a Welsh 12 hour of 262m, Adrian Pudsey (258) Aitken (250) Costain (262) and Elliot 4hrs 10mins (Trike 100). Phil Leigh was a tough road man but unknown at time trials.

Likewise Christine Robert's Competition Record could be under threat, by either Bridget Boon or Lynne Taylor. Although Christine herself was entered, she admitted to feeling under the weather and hadn't felt right since her 4hrs 28mins Anfield 100 earlier in the season, but with Bridget Boon failing to start, it was thought that her record was probably safe. Seven teams were entered including the current champions The Derby Mercury, and past Champions, Kiveton Park CC.

The weather on the Saturday was of sultry heat relieved only by a coolish night with a light south to south-west breeze. By the 100 mile point, Wilko had caught virtually the whole of an 80 strong field, to record 4hrs 16mins. Bland was at 18mins, Leigh at 22m and Costain at 23 mins. There were a few retirements, Barlow, Eperjesi and Ben Elliott. He had been hit by an approaching car, overtaking another car, the wing mirror had smashed into his hand bruising it very badly, and he was persuaded to stop for hospitalisation. Christine who had been 6 mins down on Lynne at the 100 mile point and not feeling right decided to pack at Prees. The game Reverend Tyler who was suffering from a poisoned leg battled on probably not realising the danger he was in.

Wilko, riding a mountain bike for the 2nd year running, was out in front at the 12 hour point with 269 miles (an improvement by 12 miles over the previous year). He was 21 miles ahead of second placed Paul Bland, with 248 miles, and Phil Leigh, a tough southern roadman who'd never time trialled above 50 miles, was 3rd at 12 hours with 246 miles, Doughty 242 miles and Costain 241m, but he was fading badly and would eventually retire at 14.5 hours after a hard learning experience. Riders below 'evens' at 12 hours were Lally, Austin and Lynne Taylor, all with 229 miles, Wicks 219 and Jim Hopper (trike) 214 miles.

The Sunday dawned hot but the gentle breeze helped to push the riders back to the finishing circuit where Wilko covered 4 laps of the 14.9 mile circuit with 2 laps at 43 mins (the fastest of the day) and his last two at 47 and 45mins. He finished at Rod Goodfellow's timing station and was completely 'sold out' but still cheerful with a 501.39 mile ride to his credit, becoming the **lst person to beat 500 miles twice.** Runner up Bland also did 4 laps clocking 46m, 50, 49 & 49 mins, while bronze medallist Leigh, struggled with 3 laps. Lynne rode 4 laps of 51, 52, 50 and a grand finale of 48 minutes.

The Rev. Paul Tyler with a poisoned leg collapsed on the finishing circuit after one lap and he ended up being taken to hospital where he was released 4 days later.

Andy Wilkinson had been on target for Competition Record up until the closing hours of the race, when backache finally ruled out the finishing speed he needed. Lynne had improved 22 miles to another personal best of 441.40 miles and still finished fresh. Maybe Lynne will be the next serious challenger for Christine's record: we shall see.

Karl Austin rode an 81" fixed gear to a personal best of 434.95 miles. Hugh Canning, Walsall Roads CC had a slow start this year, and recorded 413 miles, narrowly beating Brian Davies by .26 of a mile. The Reverend Tyler was given a mileage of 405.39 with 71 minutes still to run. The current Editor of the Fellowship Journal, Ned Millington, rode 403.9 miles, Tom Lodge, the retired Wessex 24hr Organiser, at 62 years of age, rode 379 miles. Tom also supplied much of the information I required for the early Wessex events, and he also has a very fast short-distance son, named Harry. Tim Dolphin who was almost as prolific at 24 hours as wee Georgie Berwick, rode 372 miles to George's 387m.

49 solos and 1 tandem finished this tough event.

⇒•◇•⇐

**The North Road CC 24hr on August 26th and 27th 1995, was won by Marc Cunnington, Swindon RC with 449.79 miles. Dave Brabbin, Douglas Valley RC was 2nd with 438.58 and Ben Elliott who'd crashed out of the Mersey with a damaged hand, was 3rd with 415.98. Charlie Bruce was 4th with 411.21 miles and led Ernie Mackey and Ken Stokes to a Medway Velo Team win of 1,131.2 miles.**

The favourites before the start were Marc Cunnington, winner of last years Brighton Mitre with 452 miles, young Ben Elliott (Trike 100 mile record holder) had ridden 248 miles for a 12 hour only two weeks previously on a trike, but he was on a bike in this 24 hour. Steven Wharton, last years silver medallist in the Championship and Dave Brabbin, an 'up and coming' 24 hr man, destined to win one day.

Andy Major who gave a few details on this 24hr and was helping at one of the feeding stations with Ian Dow said he was amazed at the amount of time some of the riders spent at the feeding station, eating soup and drinking 'decaf' tea. After rarely stopping in an event himself except for the absolute essentials, he said that some of them were wasting possibly 3 to 4 miles while sat there, but then Andy was probably forgetting that not everyone had a car full of helpers seeing to their every need, twice an hour. On the odd occasion where I've been glad of a sit down feed in a 24hr, I've always ridden away afterwards feeling much more positive and in a happier frame of mind. With the influx of Audax riders over the years and the increasing amount of riders who don't belong to a club full of dedicated time trialists, I'm not surprised at this trend. There will always be the top 5 or 10 riders in an event who do not use a feeding station, but then not everyone can be that focussed and if it helps the other 70% of the riders to last out the 24 hours then it is justified. The 'Harp' at Quina Brook and the breakfast feed at Edgebolton were my favourites, the aroma of bacon frying as I rode towards Edgebolton was sometimes too much to resist!

Back to the North Road event and the 12 hour point showed Marc Cunnington in a clear lead with 240 miles, Dave Soloman and Charlie Bruce were both at 227 miles, Dave Brabbin 225, Tim Dolphin and Ben Elliott were on 221 miles. The race was now on for 2nd place and it was thought that Elliott who was riding within himself, was going to come to life in the second half. He showed this promise by riding the 43 mile night circuit in 2hrs 20mins, some 10mins faster than the other leading riders, but in the early hours he began to fade.

At this point, Dave Brabbin, with his wife Eileen helping him, was picking up very strongly and riding into 2nd place. As dawn broke after a warm night, the wind reappeared across the 'Fens' with the riders hard to keep a check on due to being on different detours, and it wasn't until they were on the finishing circuit that their progress could be checked. Cunnington was still winning but fighting to lap at 18 mph. Elliot had come to life again and was lapping at almost 'evens', and Brabbin was almost matching him.

Cunnington finally finished with 449.79m but Andy Major asked the question "After winning his 2nd 24hr out of 4 races, what is he capable of in a Championship event with a dedicated back up team?"

Dave Brabbins 2nd place was a personal best by 10 miles, after riding so consistently, but Ben Elliotts ride was one of confusion for the onlooker. He claimed afterwards that he didn't enjoy it and it clearly showed, apart from a fast burst in the night and a turn of speed on the finishing circuit, he had a job to get motivated for the other 20 hours.

Charlie Bruce who took 4th place with 411.21 was making a comeback after a 25 year lay off. Previously in 1970 he'd ridden to a place in the winning team with 422 miles and enjoyed it so much he rode the North Road event that same year, and came 3rd with 433.716 miles. So what could he have aspired to in those 25 years?

# 1996

**2nd April 1996 'Wilko' attacks End to End.** *(See text after the Mersey Report)*

*On the Spring Bank Holiday the 26 and 27th May 1996,* **Jim Hopper** *broke the RRA standard set for a trike of 19.5 hours for the 346 mile journey between* **Pembroke and Great Yarmouth.** *Here are a few details of that ride taken from an article by Jim that appeared in the 24hr Fellowship Journal. Pat Kenny was the Timekeeper and Observer for the record. Ian Hill was again the driver and Margaret, Jim's wife, looked after his food and clothing etc and all of the details for the ride. The route started from outside Pembroke Castle gates and went via Carmarthen, Llandovery, Brecon, Willersley, Ledbury, Tewkesbury, Broadway, Shipston-on-Stour, Buckingham, St Neots, Thetford, Norwich and finished on the Britannia Pier, Great Yarmouth.*

*Jim started into a south-easterly wind, very low cloud and rain. By Brecon he was 29 mins down on schedule, but by the 100 miles point, he'd almost averaged 'evens' with 5hours 2mins. He battled on through Lugwardine, where an Observer who lives on the route gave them all hot drinks. He climbed the south end of the Malverns on Hollybush Hill and dropped towards Tewkesbury. Observers in East Anglia were phoning Pat's mobile phone and reporting a strong to gale force westerly wind; it was just what Jim wanted.*

He climbed through the Cotswolds to Buckingham and the A5. The 12 hours went by with 225.4 miles covered, the promised wind blew him along the Cambridge bypass and at Newmarket he was 9 mins up on schedule. At the Norwich bypass he was 28 mins up and he reached the Britannia Pier at 2.15pm with a **new record set at 18 hours 15mins 47 secs.**

In the past, Jim had broken a few regional tandem trike records wih Ron Sant, but this was Jim's first RRA record. After years of regular appearances in the Mersey RC 24 hr and riding a few Paris-Brest-Paris audaxes, he'd put that mileage, experience and stamina to good use. He'd gone through some very poor weather and conditions on this record, across some very tough terrain, but as Jim says 'Trikies never pack'.

Jim told me a story recently about when he first started cycling back in the late 1950's. His first long club run was a 100 mile reliability trial and involved riding to the start and then riding home afterwards from the'tea stop', a total journey of some 120 miles. He was only 14 at the time and although his father was a cyclist, nobody had told Jim what a reliability trial was, or what to expect. He was wearing only shorts and a football shirt and being mid-winter he was freezing for most of the day. The route took him over some tough climbs in the Peak District and he was inadequately dressed or equipped for such a journey.

Jim arrived home late on the Sunday night after being out since daybreak, he was absolutely shattered, hungry and cold, and thought he might get a little sympathy from his dad but to no avail. It was 'off to bed' and school next day.

Jim said he learnt very quickly from that day's experience, and that, I think, is probably what has made him such a tough character, and a cheerful one as well. I was a little luckier than that. Birmingham St Christophers had at least 6 regular young lady riders who looked after me when I started. Maybe that's why Jim always beat me in races. I also had two loving sisters who were both older and both were keen touring cyclists and Mom always cooked me a Sunday dinner – so maybe I was a little spoilt?

---

You may have noticed that the North Road event had reverted back to the original August Bank Holiday date on the calendar for these previous few years, but under pressure from the RTTC, if the North Road wanted to promote their event as a championship, they were told it had to be run in June, for maximum daylight hours, and although this wasn't really a beneficial time for riders, coming so early in the season, and without the chance to have ridden many 100's, the club decided to give way and promote Championship events in this early month. Concern over lighting was said to be one issue but the irony of it is, that lights have never been so good. With the advent of L.E.D.'s and very reliable bulb-using battery lamps, albeit ones produced in 'Pacific Rim' countries, lighting isn't the safety problem it once was.

---

**The North Road CC National championship 24hr, 29th & 30th June 1996, was won by Malcolm Whitehead, Velo Club Deal, with 465.75 miles. Marc Cunnington , Swindon RC was 2nd with 452.82 miles, and David Brabbin, Wigan Whls C & AC 3rd, 449.08 miles. David Howes, Derby Mercury RC was 4th with 442.21 and he led Jim Hopper on a trike with 384.39 miles and David McGeachie Clarke, 362.26, to a Championship Team win 1,188.86 miles.** This was their 5th Championship team win with the last three in succession.

Even though this was a Championship event it still only mustered an entry of 47 riders of whom only 30 finished. *For my narrative of this event I've used passages, observations and remarks by Eileen Brabbin who was out helping husband David, throughout the event.*

David had abandoned in the previous years Mersey National at about 15 hours due to the effects of dehydration. He was fairly new to 24hr riding at that time and for him it was a lesson well learned. You can tell someone about the dangers of dehydration on a regular basis, but there is nothing like feeling the after effects at first hand to make the advice sink home. Nausea, headache, cramp and collapse, it can cause all of these problems. Luckily for Dave he didn't suffer with it this year, but he did have a very bad time during the night from sleepiness.

The favourites for this race were Malcolm Whitehead, Mike Perrin, Marc Cunnington and Dave Brabbin. Eileen said that by the 12 hour point it was clear that there was a leadership battle going on between Whitehead and Perrin. This battle continued through into the early hours, when Mike Perrin started to fade as he was leaving the night circuit. Despite having a couple of spills, Malcolm Whitehead kept his lead as he headed towards the finishing circuit. The competition was now hotting up for second place. Marc Cunnington was managing to keep up the 15 minute lead he had over David, who was now suffering with tired eyes.

Dawn breaking helped to ease Dave's tiredness problems and with about 6 hours to go it looked as though he might get 2nd place as he piled on the pressure to try and crack Marc, but he responded by digging even deeper to retain his 2nd place.

Eileen said that funnily enough, the fact that the 'North Road' had been a National Championship hadn't really registered with David. His achievement was only really brought home at the prize presentation; he had been that intent on keeping a wary eye on his rivals, he hadn't registered the enormity of the race.

Kathryn Smith was the only lady rider. She finished with 320.94 miles

≕⟫·◇·⟪≕

A month later **The Mersey RC 24hr on 28th and 29th July was won by David Brabbin with 462.41 miles, Karl Austin was 2nd with 449.77 and Adrian Pudsey was 3rd with 445.94m. Lynne Taylor was 4th with 438.97 miles and won the Merseyside Ladies CA event. The fastest team was the Mersey RC with David Lloyd, 395.17m, Brian Davies, 393.22m and Paul Cull, 355.53m, giving a total of 1,143.92 miles.**

Our top riders and past Champions were all involved with events elsewhere this year. Andy Wilkinson, and Ian Butcher were concentrating on the BBAR, Phil Barlow was road racing, Mick Potts, Sheila Simpson and Bridget Boon were audaxing, while Christine Roberts was preparing for her 'End to End'. Frank Mumford's quick round up at the start, to check the riders fads, fashions and new fangled items of equipment noticed that the triathlon tandem of Geoffrey Simmons and Trevor Greenwood was constructed with a Double Alsop Beam; that is to say that each riders seat post and saddle is mounted at the end of a horizontal flexible beam, that has no seat tube to support it.

Karl Austin found that an 81" fixed gear was too low last year, and opted for a 92" this year. Six carbon fibre and metal matrix framed bikes were being used this year, as aluminium is thought to give too harsh a ride over a 24hr period.

Another 'first' this year was Paul Ward, one of the competitors, who was carrying a mobile phone. Frank said "its good to talk".

The weather started warm with a pleasant moonlit night and mid morning rain to refresh the riders as they reached the finishing circuit. The wind was light and variable throughout. The course this year had been redesigned in order to omit the traffic-infested detour via Tarvin, Nantwich and Crewe, in the earlier stages of the event, instead the riders were shuttled up and down the A41 and A49 to Battlefield.

At the 95.7 mile check at Prees Island the course controllers and marshals performed their usual gyratory miracles of fastest riders left, slowest right. Karl Austin was the first through in 4hrs 16mins with Adrian Pudsey 2nd at 2mins, Brabbin at 10m, Chris Lowe at 14m and Lynne Taylor at 16m. The field was more compact now, as a result of accurate detour controlling. The riders headed off towards Newport and finally to turn at Pickmere Island on the A41/A5 junction near Weston Under Lizard.

There were a good many scraps taking place during the night, as some riders tired or even retired, and some found their speed. Karl Austin and Adrian Pudsey were battling for the lead on the road, but a long stop before midnight by Austin, enabled Pudsey to catch him at 197 miles. This fired Austin into action again; he recaught Pudsey and broke clear.

The 12hr point saw Karl in the lead with 242 miles, while David Brabbin had crept up into joint 2nd place with Pudsey, both with 239 miles. Lynne was next with 228 miles, Chris Mullin 225m, and Jim Hopper (trike) having a storming ride with 220m. Both Adrian Pudsey and Lynne Taylor were fighting sickness. Dave Brabbin who had started off steadier than most riders was now starting to work his way towards the front of the field. At 301 miles, Karl Austin, Adrian Pudsey and Dave Brabbin were the only riders to have covered the full course and were sent on an extra leg to Pickmere and back, to allow the rest of the field to stay in contact. This was the stretch that David Brabbin attacked on, he caught Adrian at 314 miles and Karl at 325 miles. Karl managed to stay within a few minutes of Brabbin for a further 40 miles before fading away, never to recover any of his losses.

In the early hours just after dawn the race was decided. Brabbin only dropped 13 miles on his 2nd 12 hour period, whereas Pudsey dropped 33 miles, Austin 35 miles and Lynne Taylor 18 miles. The 15.3 mile section from Prees back to the finishing circuit at Handley was for some a very fast stretch, but for others it was a struggle, according to how much life they had left in them. Chris Mullins was the fastest in 42 mins, but then suffered once on the circuit. Brabbin took 43 mins and Lynne Taylor 46 mins, Lynne also took the fastest circuit of the day with 46 mins and the next amount of circuits (4) but then she had omitted a leg to Pickmere in the night while feeling sick.

The twisty hilly circuit proved a real struggle for Austin on his 92" fixed gear. Jim Hopper gave it his all, truly earning the VTTA Championship with his 417.3 mile age group record, and a personal best by 9 miles at 54 years of age. The triathlete tandem just missed 400 miles with 399.57m and with no less than 14 riders bettering their 1995 distances on the old course, it was deemed that this course was faster.

A special award was presented to David Stapleton for his long service to the sport and it was noted that Harold Nelson had earned himself a 'B.E.M.' for his dedication and service to the sport, as a masseur, coach and mentor.

From 41 starters only 30 finished plus 1 tandem.

※ ⬦ ※

Before I move onto 1997, I must mention just a few more **achievements that Andy Wilkinson accomplished in 1996.** I said earlier in the year, that along with Ian Butcher he was hoping to get a top placing in the BBAR. This he did handsomely, but first of all, let us go to the **2nd April 1996,** a time when most BBAR aspirants would be riding a few local 25's and 50's to measure their progress, but where was Andy Wilkinson? He was just about to start away from **Lands End Hotel** in a **'Faired Windcheetah Recumbent' tricycle.** I say 'in' because he was basically lying semi-prone inside a Perspex and glass fibre bubble built onto a recumbent tricycle. He was going to try and establish an **'End to End'** record for an unorthodox form of cycle/ tricycle. It wasn't going to be recognised by the RRA as there wasn't a category for this type of machine but they (the RRA) were quite happy for the attempt to go ahead with RRA officials in place to record and observe every aspect of the ride.

He'd suffered delays and problems early in the ride, the first one being at Bristol with a broken axle and then again when Shap was reached the temperature outside had dropped rapidly causing condensation and misting on his windscreen. He'd also had traffic jams to contend with earlier in the West Country, but despite all this he reached Gailey Island, **295.5 miles in this first 12 hours.** He reached just beyond 'Crook Inn' for an **estimated 24hr distance of 530 miles** and so far he had a speed in excess of **22mph!** Fog around the Edinburgh area made visibility even more difficult for Andy but despite all this **he reached Perth in 28 hours, and was now 3hrs faster, at this point, than anyone had ever recorded.**

He conquered the Grampians and although there was snow all around and at the roadside, he only had rain, mist and a misted screen to contend with. At the Drumochter Summit he was 2hrs 25mins up on his schedule. This was followed by a hair-raising drop into Inverness, but Andy was having real problems with his left leg requiring 'time out' for massages.

Andy decided to forego any more planned stops so that he could put the record inside 40 hours, but thick mist and fog on the 'Ord of Caithness' again caused visibility problems. The last tortuous climbs of Helmsdale and Berriedale played havoc with Andy's legs and **he finally reached John o' Groats at 11.14pm with an unofficial record of 1 day, 17hrs, 4mins, 22secs.** He'd taken just under 4 hours off his own bike record set in 1990.

At the end he thanked all his helpers, RRA Officials and in particular Bob Dixon, who had provided the recumbent, and concluded by saying *"I continue to dream that one day the efforts of all involved will be rewarded by official recogniton of the ride".* The RRA to this day (2007) haven't provided a category for this type of machine but they have put a special inclusion of Andy's ride in their 'Official History' contained in the handbook.

The reason for this epic long distance ride to be so early in the year was two-fold. The first was so that Andy didn't get 'cooked' in the enclosed machine and secondly it gave him time to recover physically and mentally to be ready for his assault on the 'BBAR'. Andy had two months to do this and in that time he underwent training and therapy from Peter Keen who recognised that Andy had a terrific heart that was capable of enormous effort over a long period of time, but he needed to alter his training regime to acclimatize his muscles, heart and brain, to shorter and much faster efforts. Along with Alan Roberts, who also helped with training and sorting out which 'BBAR' events to ride, Andy used his two months well.

Apart from these phenomenal 'strives' he was making, he was also working long hours at the family Nursery business. Andy's job was to plant and manage the trees and shrubs on a daily basis, with Christmas time being the peak period. Apart from riding and racing with the Port Sunlight Whls, he was being sponsored by Adidas-Scicon.

Two months later he produced **Competition Record for 50 miles in 1hr, 37mins, 26secs, also Comp Record for 100 miles in 3hrs, 27mins, 39secs, and finally Comp Record for 12 hours with 300.27 miles making a winning 'BBAR' speed of 28.236mph, obviously another record.**

Paul Histon, apart from being the course section marshal for Jim Turner in the Mersey 24hr had also formed a great friendship with 'Wilko'. He had also seen just what Andy was capable of after watching him tackle the long stretches in the 24hr, out on his own at the front of the field, from the comfort of the marshalling car. Both Paul and Jim were on Andy's recumbent 'End to End' record and were instrumental in helping Andy on his 'BBAR' rides.

I would say that Wilko came from the same sort of mould as Nim Carline and Beryl Burton, tough outdoor workers, out in all weathers with hard training rides after work. The only difference I think is that Andy was open to suggestions of using new methods of feeding and training, experimenting with equipment such as tri-bars, pulse meters and speed training. Whether on the day all the new technology had contributed to these fantastic rides I don't know, if he can produce over 500 miles on a mountain bike without any real challengers, then it makes you wonder?

Andy was a more controlled and disciplined rider than most of his predecessors and this I think may have been his secret weapon. He very rarely got drawn into a battle on the road with any of his rivals and often his 2nd 12 hours of a 24hr race would produce over 47% of his total mileage.

After easing off over the winter and experimenting with track racing and in particular 'pursuiting' Andy came into 1997 wondering how he was going to repeat his successful 1996 season. After a few lack-lustre rides at various shorter distances, he no doubt felt that this wasn't to be a good year for him, a bit of an anti-climax. The only rides he'd been enjoying were his training and clubrun rides and consequently he'd put a little bit of weight on. It was on the way to a sporting course time trial with Paul and Jim that the plot was hatched to have a go at the 24hr record. So after some very useful advice from Roy Cromack, the previous holder of the 507 mile record, Andy decided to enter the Mersey event.

*In June of this year 1997, Christine Roberts attacked Pauline Strong's* **'Lands End to John o' Groats record.** *I saw Christine as she came through Fordhouses near Wolverhampton with 290 miles covered and she was already 45 mins up on a schedule to beat the straight out 24hr record. She had a steady wind behind her and was pedalling smoothly. Pete Swinden who was an Observer in the feed car said that on the climb of Shap the wind was well behind her at almost gale force. Christine got almost to Carlisle and* **broke the 24hr Record with 467.30 miles,** *but her helpers had noticed during the night on the downhill sections of road, she was freewheeling, sometimes even braking, and not taking full advantage of the conditions. Christine continued almost to Edinburgh where she abandoned the attempt*

*After sustaining serious injuries in a collision with a car in 1987 Christine had recovered physically, but the crash had left her with a severe phobia of riding on main roads, with flashbacks to the accident leaving her feeling very insecure when racing.*

⋙━◆━⋘

**The Mersey RC 24hr National Championship was won by Andy Wilkinson, Adidas Scicon, with a new Competition Record of 525.07 miles. Brian Walker, G.S. Metro was 2nd with 483.33 and Gethin Butler, Norwood Paragon CC was 3rd with 472.55 miles. Gethin led a Norwood Paragon CC team consisting of Steven Roach, with 403.49 miles and Ross Bartlett, 390.44m to a winning total of 1,266.48 miles. Lynne Taylor, Walsall Roads CC came 12th overall and won the Merseyside Ladies CA event with 418.08 miles.**

I will start the report of this historic race by quoting a John Williams remark, made while waiting for the riders to start, in the blustery wet conditions then being experienced. He said **"If anybody was to beat 500 miles in these conditions, they would definitely be 'Supermen' and would qualify, as such, to wear their underpants on the outside of their tights!"**

53 riders including 3 women set off to a wet and windy start and by 53.5 miles most of them arrived at the checkpoint drenched. Butler was the fastest in 2hrs 15mins, Steve Marchant was at 1min, 'Wilko' at 4mins, Walker at 10m and Lynne Taylor was at 22m. Gethin Butler who was undoubtedly one of the best time triallists and roadmen that this country has ever seen was hoping to follow in his Grandfather, Stan Butler's footsteps (or wheeltracks). Stan had won the Championship 24hr in 1950 with 458 miles and had broken Competition Record but of course, Gethin was an unknown quantity at 24 hours, as was Brian Walker.

There had only been 3 riders start with a fixed wheel, 'Auk' rider Steve Abraham on an 87", Karl Austin 92" and Brian Walker on 104", but Walker changed to a multi- geared bike after 50 miles and two punctures. Paul Bland, Edwin Hargraves, Marc Cunnington, Paul Costain, Chris Mullin and Steve Marchant were also in the running for a medal as well as those riders already mentioned, with Dave Brabbin off last man as he had won last year's event.

By 86 miles, Butler had caught Cunnington, Mullin, Bland and Walker and at the 95.7 mile check he led with 4hrs 9mins. Walker, 16 minutes slower than Butler, Bland 20m, & Austin 22m. Lynne at this point with 4hrs 45 mins was just one minute up on a 'jaded' Christine, who eventually retired before midnight at 173 miles.

At the 12 hour point as the riders fought their way around the Shropshire circuit, 'Wilko' began to assert his mastery and experience with 268 miles. Butler rode 264, Walker 255, Costain and Marchant 248, Brabbin 240. A dark, starless night made it difficult to check the riders, with 'bunching' making it even more difficult as 5 riders would all pass in 1 minute. Some of the early 'fliers' were now finding sleepiness a problem as they rode into their 2nd 12 hours. Wilko who'd already caught Walker at 142 miles, finally caught Butler, at 275 miles, he'd been turned 3 miles short by mistake at Market Drayton and was also suffering back-ache and a sore saddle area, together with lighting problems. Walker finally caught Butler at 328 miles after a 268 mile chase.

Bland climbed off at 210 miles while Cunnington persevered until 275 miles. Edwin Hargraves' handlebar stem cracked at the halfway point and he lost time waiting to get on a spare bike, but he still finished with 440 miles.

During the night, 'Wilko', Butler and Walker had been sent on an extra Ternhill to Newport detour to try and keep the field compact. Butler and 'Wilko' returned back to Ternhill quite close together on the road but Walker was a long way back. The wind had eased and the showers had cleared. A half moon appeared making checking easier. It was now a much cooler temperature for any riders who were still in shorts. At 6am 'Wilko' was first on the road and still looking fresh, strong and fast. Butler was 2nd but looked distinctly tired and clearly resigned to being beaten. Walker had taken a new lease of life and was looking a lot better than Butler, but of course he was a long way back on the road.

The time check showed 'Wilko' had 7hrs 37mins left to ride. If he could maintain 'evens' he would do just over 515 miles, which his helper Ian Burns, confirmed was his scheduled target. Emerging from the Shawbirch detour, Wilko had gained a further 4 mins over 'evens'. On the way back to the finishing circuit, a check was made at Prees to watch the riders progress. Wilko was well ahead and estimated to be on a 522 mile ride, while Walker and Butler were close enough to be about level with each other.

*Jim Turner mentioned to me that while he was turning and checking the last few riders at the Pickmere Island turn, well south of Newport, he had a phone call from Paul Histon who was driving the 'lead' car, to say that 'Wilko' had just entered the finishing circuit. Jim said that a direct route from Pickmere to the finishing circuit was probably 40 miles, but the course that Andy had ridden to get there was over 70 miles. That puts Andy's ride into perspective.*

After dashing to the finishing circuit John Williams was able to check Wilko's times and it makes exciting reading. At 11.36 & 56 secs am **he'd completed 451.97 miles,** with 3hrs 28min & 4secs left to run. On **lap 2** which he completed in 40m 34secs, **he'd completed 466.89m** with 2hrs 47mins 30 secs left. By **lap 3** which took him 44 mins he'd completed **481.81 miles** with 2hrs 3mins 30secs left. By **lap 4** ridden in 43mins 10secs he'd completed **496.73 miles** and by **lap 5** which he did in 43mins 46secs, he'd already broken the record handsomely with **519.66 miles** and still with 36mins 34 secs left to ride.

After another quick dash around the circuit John Williams checked Wilko at **Coddington Church with 524.4 miles** done and still going at an incredible speed with just about a minute to go, finishing with an amazing **525.07 miles.** It's also amazing to note that **his first 12 hours had produced 268 miles and his 2nd 257 miles.**

Brian Walker came 2nd after drawing away from Gethin Butler in the closing quarter of the race, he finished with 483.33 miles, a brilliant ride for a first time at 24 hours and in such good company. His first 12 hours had given him 255 miles and his 2nd had yielded 228 miles. Gethin who came 3rd with 472.55 miles after leading for so long during the event, was completely spent. He'd ridden 264 miles in his first 12 hours and 208 in his second. Steve Marchant, another novice, took 4th place with 467.18 miles. Paul Costain finishing his first 24hr took 5th place with 458.47 miles and Karl Austin was 6th with 443.77 miles.

*Frank Mumford who provided a lot of the background text about this event asks tongue in cheek "Seriously, what more did any avid 24hr follower expect to see? Knowing that 'Wilko' with 7 successive 'Anfield 100' wins, plus being the 1996 'BBAR' winner with all events at Competition Record speed, a triple winner at 24 hours with two 501 mile rides, and one at 496 miles, plus an 'End to End' record holder twice over, was taking on Gethin Butler and other young hopefuls in the 1997 Mersey. It was thought that maybe the lure of a special prize of £1 per mile if Competition Record was broken, donated jointly by Roger Sewell, the North Road Promoter, and Jim Turner, the Mersey Promoter, plus the £150 1st prize from the Mersey RC, with £25 on offer for the fastest lap of the finishing circuit, which totalled £700 in all, was his goal. Maybe it was the RTTC Gold medal and the M.R.C. Cup, that inspired Andy's effort, but I doubt it, as he donated £175 back to the 24hr subscription fund a short time later. No, I'm pretty sure it was just that 24hr record he wanted."*

Surprisingly enough 'Adidas Scicon' who had sponsored Andy's rides over that 2 year period, received more press coverage after Andy's 24 hour record, than for his and other Adidas team member's rides of the previous year. Andy rode a Giant Cycles 'monocoque' frame fitted with Shimano transmission and gears, with special Kevlar spoked wheels; the cycle had been designed by Mike Burrows.

**Roy Cromack** also wrote a lengthy and interesting article on Andy's preparation and ride. I have chosen just a few poignant passages from that writing.

"I offered to prepare schedules for him and did my best to convince him that special physical preparation was unnecessary for a good '24' and that the mind was far more important. I prepared schedules for 507.1 miles, 515 miles and 525 miles.

Riding out to the start of the event through a downpour and helped by an ever increasing tailwind, I pondered on his prospects. My biggest fear for Andy was that he would fight the wind too hard, particularly on the first leg down to Battlefield Corner in an attempt to hold his 515 miles schedule. I suspected that Gethin would start too fast as well and wondered whether Andy would have the will power to allow Gethin to open up a substantial lead.

At the start I was staggered by some of the bikes to be used. The first one was Brian Walker's with a pursuiters position, disc rear wheel and a pursuiters 102" fixed gear; it took him just 50 miles to realise how unsuitable it was and change to a slightly less fierce machine equipped with gears. Gethin was on his usual time trialling bike, also equipped with a rear disc wheel, despite his knowledge of the course, having ridden some of the bumpiest parts in the recent '100' where the unsuitability of a low profile bike should have been manifest. The wind as I rode via Malpas to Prees Heath was 'stiff' and as the cloud cleared the wind strengthened. It did not look like a record-breaking day, but this was a geriatric record, which I felt was vulnerable in almost any conditions. Although Andy was a few minutes adrift of Gethin at 50 miles, he was still up on the 515 mile schedule and well enough in charge to give me the 'thumbs up' when I yelled at him to keep it steady.

At about 5am I found that Andy was over 20 mins up on Gethin, later, as the riders emerged from what I am sure was a difficult leg from Pickmere via Newport to Tern Hill, I learned that they had both covered an extra 34.2 miles. At this point Andy was well in charge and heading for 520 miles plus. He was far from cheerful when he stopped to take off his long sleeved top on the Shawbirch leg, but I took that as a good sign; at least he was taking things seriously.

We drove up the course from Whitchurch and caught a very smooth looking Andy just before the 'Black Dog' at Waverton. Despite a hard 30 mile run from Battlefield, directly into a north-westerly breeze, he'd still managed to gain on schedule. He looked to be suffering quite badly, locked in a cage of concentration, but then he should have been suffering at this stage.

We drove to the first timekeeper after 507 miles, he was an old adversary of mine, Derek Johnson, and I joined a small group, **cheering the first man ever to hold 4 Competition Records simultaneously.** Even the timekeeper was on his feet, Barbara, my wife, was jumping up and down, beside herself with excitement, perhaps grounds for divorce under the circumstances. I had to fight back the tears, and they weren't tears of disappointment at losing my record.

With one lap to go, we moved onto the next timing station and as 5 minutes past 3 arrived the tension rose even higher, but right on time the familiar figure appeared. For a moment he seemed not to have heeded our shouts for him to stop, but he came to a halt about 50 yards down the road. After being lifted from his bike and helped onto the grass he lay flat out for several minutes before struggling into a sitting position to receive the congratulations of a group of awe-struck admirers.

On my way back to the HQ I was in a trance. I had expected to relinquish the record much sooner than I actually did and not wait 28 years, and then I began to wonder years after, whether the late Tommy Barlow had been right, when he told me it would never be beaten. To be able to hand over to a rider of the calibre of Andy Wilkinson was a privilege which exceeded my expectations, and to have played even a very small part in his ride was jam on both sides of the bread. In the conditions and under the circumstances, Andy's performance was nigh on perfect. The weather and the poor state of Shropshire's roads have, however, left a glimmer of hope for those who follow; a ride of similar quality on a good day, in the North Road event would bring a distance in excess of 540 miles. Food for thought perhaps for Gethin Butler, that a 24 hour race is not simply two 12 hours one after the other."

*My thanks to Roy Cromack for these words.*

After 'Wilko's' incredible 1996 record-breaking 'BBAR' season, it was feared that 1997 would probably be an anti-climax for Andy, and it very nearly was. After gaining recognition and publicity for his sponsors, Andy was meant to follow through into 1997 by attempting to win the World Championship Track Pursuit as his next target. At the close of 1996 Andy went about his job of providing hundreds of Christmas trees for his families nursery business on the Wirral. This had involved many long hours, 6 or 7 days a week, digging and cutting the trees. Some nights he didn't ride home until midnight after working in the fields under floodlighting. This was a normal annual procedure for Andy and is probably what gave him his underlying stamina and strengths, working outdoors in all weathers and conditions along similar lines to another famous market gardener, Nim Carline, who along with Beryl Burton farmed rhubarb on his smallholding in Yorkshire. Their staminas and speeds were evident over a 30 year period.

I spoke to Andy in 2006 and told him I was about to write a book on the History of the 24 hour, and had he got any background and details about his ride that I didn't already know about. He started by saying that he headed towards January 1997 feeling very strong although he hadn't done much on the bike due to work commitments. He rode the track a couple of times and soon took to it quite well and felt at home 'riding the boards'. In training sessions he was soon having to ease back so as not to lap some of the 'future Olympic favourites'. He then told me he was scheduled to ride various events during early spring leading up to a trial on the track for the pursuit. That's when things started to go 'haywire' for him and it became a disastrous start to his year. Andy couldn't find any form for racing, let alone pursuiting, although he felt generally strong and fit, when it came to the trials to make the pusuit squad, he'd had a cold and various niggling health problems. This resulted in him failing to beat the time limit required to make the grade.

Andy said he was at an all time low, his sponsors were relying on him to perform well in the pursuit, but it wasn't to be. After another month or two of 'lack lustre' riding it was now May and Andy was trying to find other outlets to perform well at, one or two road races, sporting course time trials etc. Meanwhile the sponsor's backing was fading for Andy and they were concentrating on the other riders in the 'Adidas Sci-con' squad who were riding stage races. This left Andy out on his own.

One day he contacted Jim Turner and Paul Histon, his mentors from his previous record breaking year of 1996 and told them what was happening and the low spot he was experiencing, how he felt and could they give him any help or inspiration? Andy was rapidly losing his speed and what fitness he'd got and was even putting on weight, he was also getting depressed which takes a lot to admit to, but if anybody could help and understand his needs at that time, it was Paul and Jim. Andy had entered a sporting course time trial on the north-eastern side of the country and asked them for a lift and some help during the event. On the way there he downloaded all his thoughts and doubts to them, about whether, or how, he could resurrect his season and please his sponsors.

As it happened Andy won that event which brought a bit of a sparkle back. On the journey home he suggested riding the 24hour and 'going for broke'. Paul and Jim were doubtful about his overall fitness, stamina and lack of training miles that he would normally have gained by this time in the year and tried to dissuade him, but they also said that if that would give him a goal to aim for, then they would support him all they could.

So with just two months to go to the event, Andy set about a plan to recover his fitness and to better the 24hr record. He mentioned asking Roy Cromack's advice, which I've already described. Also lots of race reports have appeared about Andy's tremendous record that day, but Andy only remembers his trials and sufferings during the event. He said that although it was a fair day and night weather-wise, it was not brilliant, with crosswinds, and a very cold night. His main recollections were of the final hours of the race and although he had been lapping the finishing circuit in just over 40 mins, after 5 circuits with 3 to go, he was so desperately tired and couldn't wait to finish. In fact when the final seconds of the 24 hours were up and Jim Turner dropped the wet cloth (*the reason why a wet cloth is used is that being wet it will be too heavy to blow away*) on the road to mark the exact spot, Andy wanted to stop, but the car containing the main timekeeper came alongside and told him to continue to the next timing station, probably well over a mile further on. He was now very upset and frustrated at having to prolong the agony, he was desperate to get off his bike and lie down. Andy remembers being near to tears and banging his handlebars in anger at not being allowed to stop, but two minutes later, his wishes were granted at Timekeeper 8.

I passed that spot around the same time, not realising just how fantastic Wilko's ride was. I saw Andy's dad, Stan, out on the circuit and thought then how proud he must have felt. I was busy helping Lynne after her hard 418 miles ride.

I was surprised when Andy said that knowing how he felt at various stages during the race, he could have squeezed a bit more effort from himself and that another 10 or 15 miles was a possibility, on the flat North Road course perhaps, and knowing Andy, he wasn't just being modest! Its hard for us lesser mortals to get to grips with, but top riders like Andy have a problem containing their speed in the early quarters of the race and keep below 25 mph, otherwise they wouldn't reach 8 hours, let alone 24. In hindsight I doubt if any future record breaker will ever get to ride the North Road course.

In undertaking this ride, Wilko had showed **true grit, blood, sweat** and **tears.** The **true grit** being the determination to retrieve what he could from a patchy lack lustre early racing season in 1997, riding even though he knew he wasn't at a physical peak of total fitness. The **blood** was pumping through a large heart at anything from 100 to 200 beats per minute for the whole 24 hours, as the course takes in a fair amount of hills. 'Hinstock' on the way back from Newport is a good one, and 'School Girl Hill', so called because it peaks at the entrance to a private girls school on the road to Battlefield (Shrewsbury) and Prees by-pass hill on the A49, is another. The **sweat** which soaked Andy and left a white salty powder encrusted on his clothes and skin wasn't the normal perspiration or moisture that one gets from the usual body hot spots, such as arm pits etc, it's a permanent oozing from all over the body in an effort to cool the main trunk and brain. I've seen many top riders in this state and my most vivid recollection was of seeing Pete Wells winning a '50 mile' in record time on the K17 Burton Road near Lichfield. He was absolutely drenched in sweat at the finish and stood with his bike and both were 'dripping' equal amounts. His leather saddle was soaked and he stood on wet patches on the road edge. At that point I thought "if that's what I've got to do to become famous, then I'm never going to make it!" The **tears** were of despair from Andy when his speed dropped during a very cold night, it took all the energy he could muster to reach the warmth of daylight with his necessary speed intact. Also there were tears of frustration at the very end of his ride when he was told to continue past his 24hr point and ride on to the next timekeeper.

All of these emotions and qualities are to be found not only in most top riders, but also in seasoned 24hr competitors of varying abilities, even novices experience these conditions. The **true grit** starts at the training stage with long hard miles some 9 months prior to the event, and then having the courage to enter the event. The **blood** needs to be in good condition and a balanced diet will generally ensure this. Everyone who plans to ride a 24hr must make sure that their heart, lungs and circulatory system are in tip top condition and perhaps a well-man or well-woman clinic at the Doctors wouldn't go amiss to re-assure that all is well. The **sweat;** most racing cyclists are used to sweating for an hour or two when training or racing, they may even get away without drinking much more than a cup of tea or a small 500 ml bottle of cordial, but for prolonged training sessions and long rides on a regular basis, then a different re-hydration regime is required. Regular drinking before, during and after the ride is of paramount importance, whether you use a carbohydrate polymer drink such as 'PSP' from 'Science in Sport' or the carbo and electrolyte combined drink called 'Go' which helps replace minerals lost through sweating, is of personal choice. You may wish to drink just water or cordial, which is ok but neglects your carbohydrate intake, thus requiring a snack of either a nutrition or muesli bar or jam butty etc. Whatever method you choose to use for re-fuelling must be practised with and used on a regular basis during all of your rides.

In that 9 months training and preparation period it is worth experimenting with different ways of taking carbohydrates. Try different makes of nutrition bars as some of them are very dry and hard to swallow. Get used to riding and eating regularly, that's what the pockets are for in a racing vest. Wherever and whenever possible, eat and drink little and often', choose a downhill or wind assisted and 'safe' section of road to practice the art of eating and drinking on the bike. Don't rely on hoping it will all come right on the day of the 24hr race, have a feeding plan for your helpers to work with and also have some alternative items of food such as tinned peaches, fruit cocktail, rice pudding, custard, porridge, hot tea or coffee, soup, malt loaf. Be careful; steer clear of too much fresh fruit or proteins such as meat or cheese, and if all else fails, it may help to get off the bike, sit in a chair, and eat a bowl of cornflakes while having a wash or a change of clothes at the same time.

Failure to replace the liquids lost through sweating can cause headaches, nausea, stomach and muscular cramp and a general malaise and lethargy. If neglected for a long period of time it can affect kidney and liver function. Failure to replace the carbohydrates can lead to hypoglycaemia (lack of blood sugars) which if ignored will cause total breakdown of cohesion, speed will drop drastically and a drunken like state will overcome the rider. The first signs of the symptom known as the 'bonk' or the 'knock is one of lightheadedness and a general weakness in the upper body, arms and hands. If it is tackled straight away with a rapid carbo intake then the drop in performance can be minimised. If it is allowed to go unchecked, almost to the state of collapse, it may cause the rider to abandon the race completely.

And finally, the **tears** are usually tears of relief at the finish or when one still has an hour to ride and is finding it impossible to push ones body any further or any faster than walking pace. These were the same tears that Wilko experienced, **tears of frustration and exhaustion.**

I think now is an appropriate moment to explain how riders are timed and checked for final mileage on a 'finishing circuit', which is nowadays usually about 15 miles in length. There are usually 8 timekeepers in that distance, spaced fairly evenly, only their exact distance from each other is relevant. The most important thing is that the timekeepers are positioned in a spot where they are not in anybodys way or impeding traffic flow, or too near to a busy junction, space is also required for the rider to lie down and possibly be picked up by a helper's car. Once the rider reaches the circuit, he or she, is checked and timed at each timekeeper they pass, and their time is logged onto a finishing sheet. The timekeepers would have all previously synchronised their timepieces with the Head Timekeeper and each timekeeper would be assisted by a Recorder whose job is to write the riders number and time down, and also to assist in recognising riders as they pass; especially when two or three pass all in the same 20 seconds.

When a rider is about to run the 24 hours out, the normal procedure, if between two timekeepers, is to carry on another mile or so to the next timekeeper and over-run your time. A calculation is then made as to what your average last circuit speed was, and to deduct the time over-run by. Each timing station has a set of exact mileages reached at that particular station. Each timekeeper will also 'log' the amount of times you have gone past him, so it is very important that the rider shouts his or her number and also has that race number prominently displayed on ones clothing at all times.

Most riders who have finished a 12 hour or 24 hour race will know how this works, but I just wanted to clarify to the reader as to how final accurate mileages are calculated, recorded and verified by the Organiser of the event, usually within an hour of the last rider finishing.

Incidentally there have been numerous riders over the years who have stopped exhausted at a timekeeper with a minute or two to go, subsequently to find out that they have either missed out on a top placing in the event, or a personal best, by stopping too soon. Many overall placings and even team prizes have been lost this way. If for some reason a rider doesn't make it to the finishing circuit, either through illness, accident or exhaustion etc, they are given the distance at the last marshalling or checking point they were recorded at, on route to the finish.

'Detours' or 'optional legs' are a method of making sure the faster riders are kept usually within 20 miles or approximately an hour of the main field of riders. These sections of road are accurately measured and usually have a traffic island at each end, so that the 'Detour Controller' can direct and see the rider's number in safety. The marshal or 'controller' will be situated just before the optional leg and will assess and signal as to which riders are sent on this extra mileage. When the full course is talked about, it's the complete printed route and mileages, including all of these 'optional legs'. This is the 'full course' distance printed in detail on the start card, all the way to the finishing circuit, usually a distance of about 460 miles (as at 2008). The latest Mersey RC 24hr course is made up with two or three circuits or loops of road, linked together with sections of main road. As mentioned earlier, if slower riders drop well behind the pace it doesn't matter, they will just do one or two circuits less than the faster riders.

Incidentally, the method of 'following out' a rider as they are breaking Competition Record whether male or female, on bike, trike, tandem or tandem trike, has now been discontinued in the Mersey RC 24hr event, so Rod Goodfellow, the Chief Timekeeper, informs me. Whether it is still a method used in the 12hour events I don't know, Rod said it is now left up to the discretion of the Organiser and Timekeeper on the day, and that there is no official CTT ruling on this subject.

Wilko's 'following out' in 1997 was probably the last time this method was used. As the 24hr point was reached, a wet cloth* was dropped onto the road verge as the last second was timed and called out. That exact spot was then indelibly marked and surrounding road details would be noted, details such as a lamp post, field gateway, drive entrance, drain cover, telegraph pole etc. At the earliest opportunity the distance from the timekeeper to this exact mark and location on the road would be measured by an official course measurer riding a bike with a revolution counter on his wheel. Usually this procedure is repeated once or twice to make sure that it is correct. The wheel would have been previously calibrated and checked against a 'known measured mile'. Whereas this method has now been discontinued for the **CTT/RTTC** purposes it is obviously still in use for 12hr and 24hr performances under **RRA** road record rules.

⟹◆⟸

**The 99th North Road CC 24hr 23rd and 24th August 1997 was won by Marc Cunnington, Swindon RC with 468.91 miles, Dave Brabbin, Wigan Whls C & AC was 2nd with 466.61 miles and Roger Sewell was 3rd with 429.35 miles,** riding for the Hounslow and District Whls (despite being the Organiser for this event). 4th was Ken Baker, Colchester Rovers CC with 416.90, Tim Dolphin was 5th with 411 miles. **Charlie Bruce who was 6th overall with 384.90 miles led the Medway Velo Club to a team win of 1,112.54 miles, Ken Stokes with 377.28 and Ernie Mackey, 340.36 m were the other two members of the team.** Steve Abraham, Lampard RC rode 393.66 for 7th place, Kevin Langham, Leics Forest CC with 392.52 finished just ahead of **trike rider Jim Hopper, Derby Mercury, who rode 389.05 miles.**

In retaliation to the incredible record breaking two seasons that Andy Wilkinson had produced, Glen Longland took the opportunity in 1997 to add over 16 miles to Pete Wells' RRA 12 hour record with an astounding 309.5 miles. (If you recall, Wilko, added just .29 of a mile onto Glen's RTTC 12 hour Competition Record with a mileage of 300.27 in 1996).

## 1998

**The 100th North Road 24 hour and National Championship in June 1998, was won by Ian Butcher with 501.31 miles. Paul Holdsworth was 2nd with 476.5m and Rob Richardson, 3rd with 459.5m. With Marc Cunnington taking 4th place, this gave the Hounslow and District, the Championship team win with 1,374.94 miles.**

Timekeeper, Joe Summerlin, despatched 54 solo riders including 3 ladies who put the men to shame by all finishing. Three tandems also started, all facing a fresh breeze and cool conditions at this 10am start.

Heavy rain drenched the riders around the 50 mile point but all the seeded riders were setting a good pace. By the 100 mile check at Chatteris, the rain had blown through and Ian Butcher led with 4hrs 23 mins. Paul Holdsworth was at 1 minute, Winterbottom at 3 mins and Brian Walker at 4 mins. At South March with about 222 miles covered Butcher went through still in the lead with just over 10 hours elapsed, Walker was at 1 minute on the road, with other fast riders in close contention.

On the Soham to Stow circuit, the 12 hour distances showed Butcher still in the lead with 263 miles, Walker 261 m, Holdsworth 260m, Richardson 256 and Cunnington 247m. Jim Hopper was the fastest trike at this point with 209 miles. As the night drew on the battle for 1st place was between Butcher and Walker. At the end of the 1st lap at Stow, the gap was 9 mins, Walker had closed up within 3 minutes by the 2nd lap, but by the 3rd lap he'd cracked and the gap was 18 mins. Butcher's constant pace had told, and Walker retired on the way back from Soham, so losing a silver Championship medal. By the finishing circuit the silver and bronze medal placings were being contested by Holdsworth and Richardson, 10 miles apart, but the main interest centred on whether Butcher would reach his 500 mile target. Finally, at the Wilburton timekeeper, his quest was over, he'd reached 501.31 miles.

Hounslow riders, Holdsworth and Richardson, were both first time riders at 24 hours.
The three ladies were Jeanette de Giorgio, Gail Summerlin and Janet Lowe.   39 solos, 2 tandem trikes, and 1 trike finished.

*This report was by Jim Ithell, the 24hr Fellowship Chairman, who was meant to ride, but a long haul flight had left him lethargic and instead he did a useful job of reporting, marshalling and checking the riders.   Jim mentions that the Secretary of the Fellowship, John Hassall, had started but packed in the night with a bad knee.*

*On a lighter note he mentions Andy Wilkinson being at the start on his super new motorbike, he was now enjoying his retirement from racing and was here to see others suffer! (Little did he know that a tandem and a young lady awaited him just 2 years later)*

*Another funny moment Jim recalled was when marshalling a busy spot at Haddenham, a young lady attending a wedding at Haddenham Church walked past, Jim mentioned to the other marshals that the young lady seemed to have been very short of material for her wedding outfit.   One of the lady marshals overheard Jim's remark and suggested that if the men had that much life in them perhaps they should be riding.*

**Jim Hopper** for his efforts on producing the **fastest trike ride of 389.99 miles** in this the 100th Anniversary of running the North Road CC 24 hour, received not only his usual Silver medal but also a commemorative glass goblet with an etched image of 'G.H.S.' George Herbert Stancer, astride his trike.

The tandem trike crewed by Peter Holland and Brian Richards with 390.84 miles beat the tandem trike with Jim and Vera Staines who rode 298.15 miles.

⟫⬥⟪

**The 55th Mersey RC 24 hour on 25th and 26th July 1998 was won by Edwin Hargraves with 462.20 miles riding for the Abercynon RC, Karl Austin, Congleton CC was 2nd with 435.96m.   Mark Wilcox, Holme Valley Whls was 3rd with 430.37 miles. Lynne Taylor, Walsall RCC was 4th with 427.61 miles and won the Merseyside Ladies CA event and the Turner Cup for the 4th year running.**   No teams were entered and **Jim Hopper was the fastest trike rider with 406.72 miles.**

This year saw the 'swansong' of Chris Salter who had been the Principal Timekeeper for 11 years.  His retirement at the end of this event made way for quadruple Mersey RC winner, Rod Goodfellow, to take over.   The weather at the start on Saturday was warm and sunny with light cross-winds, the night was cool with brief showers and a very cold dawn.

Edwin Hargraves, who had recently relinquished his job as Secretary of the Road Records Association, 'RRA', so that he could concentrate on his cycling, was a 'regular' at this event and indeed many other 24's over the years. He had been placed many times in the top 6 riders at this discipline.  He was caught early at the 25 mile point by Karl Austin, who had set off like a released coil spring, but Edwin was undeterred by this rider pushing a huge fixed gear, and in turn Edwin re-caught him at 82 miles.

The 100 mile check saw the two leaders well away, Austin was now back in the lead with 4hour 36m and Hargraves at 4mins. Horne, Condor RC, riding above expectations was at 13 mins with Lynne Taylor and J. Streets at 15mins. After 100 miles, the pace tended to settle down as the survivors rode the night circuit.  Karl Austin and Edwin Hargraves rode neck and neck on time until Edwin broke away at 190 miles leaving Karl struggling to turn the big-geared fixed wheel.  Frank Mumford describes it as 'struggling' but in hindsight I see Karl probably twice or three times a year in long distance events, either 100's, 12's or the 24hr riding the same fixed wheel bike and I am convinced it wouldn't make a scrap of difference what bike or gear he rode, I think he would end up with the same mileage.

Apart from Lynne, there were two other women riding that day, Yvonne Unsworth and Francis Challenor. Yvonne packed at 197 miles with nearly 12 hours ridden. She had been ill with sickness, her efforts at trying to improve on her previous years mileage of 341 had taken its toll. Francis Challenor, another friend of Lynnes was determined to finish and even though she was the last rider to reach the finishing circuit at 12.30 she gallantly rode 330.21 miles.

The first rider onto the finishing circuit was Mark Wilcox at 11.12am and with 24 finishers reaching the circuit over a 1hr 18min period, it shows the skill involved at the section detours by Course Controller, Tom Greep. Lynne Taylor rode the two fastest laps of 49 mins each, while Edwin Hargraves, the only rider to complete the full course, took the 3rd fastest of 50 mins, as did Langham and Wilcox.

Ninety year old Ethel Scothern of the Newark Castle, a long time supporter of the 24 hour, was celebrating her birthday by riding the opposite way around the circuit to cheer the riders on. At the opposite end of the age scene, brothers John and Trevor Green, Holyhead CC, respectively 14 and 16 years became the youngest ever 24 hour participants. John finished with 245.75 miles after a carefully planned ride interspersed with regular breaks. George Berwick rode his 40th Mersey RC 24 hour with 357.23 miles. Mike Bloom, Marina's husband, rode 410.74 miles that day.

Lynne donated her 4th place £50.00 award to John Green in recognition of his courageous ride. It was rumoured that he may lead a schoolboy team in next years event.

So, at last, a win for Edwin Hargraves who first came to fame in 1981 when riding a trike and helping his Farnham RC team mates, Stuart Jackson and Brian Annis, to break the Trike Team Competition Record for 24hours with a total of 1,230.38 miles. Edwin who came 3rd with 439.51 miles on a trike in that 1981 Wessex event went on to break six RRA records with Stuart Jackson on a tandem trike, and also a solo London to Pembroke trike record. This Mersey RC win of Edwins' was to be his last serious competitive event, as an outbreak of the stomach bug, Ecoli, leading to a pulmonary embolism, curtailed his actions for over 2 years and left him too weak to race.

"I still think he's too young for a 24-hour event"

*Sadly it was noted that 1937-38 and 39 winner and regular helper at the Mersey 24hr event, Alec Smith was absent, ill. He passed away on Sunday 13th September 1998.*

**On 5th August 1998 Miss Jodi Groesbeck and Adrian Harris** set off from **Lands End** to try and beat a 72 hrs 'standard' set by the RRA for a 'mixed' tandem ride over the 'End to End' journey. The main feature that made their ride unique was that they both lived full time in America, although Adrian was an Englishman. They flew in from the U.S. on a fortnight's holiday, having already mustered their helpers and officials prior to their trip. They arrived in the U.K. on the Saturday and started out on Wednesday. Jodi, who does most of the steering on the tandem, was amazed at the holiday traffic on crowded roads that she had never seen or ridden on before. Despite experiencing breathing problems caused by the heavy traffic in the south they arrived at Bristol in approximately 10 hours. They rode through the Midlands during the hours of darkness, relying on their helpers, Observers and Marshals. They made it to Lancaster in 22 hours. After their ascent over Shap they finally got to Scotland after experiencing horrendous traffic conditions on the A74, risking life and limb in the spray and heavy crosswinds. The remaining 350 miles were relatively trouble free, they even climbed Helmsdale and Berriedale without undue strain, and arrived at **John o' Groats in 2 days 8 hours 28 mins, so breaking the standard by 15 hours 32 mins.**

In 1999 despite drastically falling entries in both the North Road and Mersey Rc events, it was still felt necessary by the RTTC Council to invite the Brighton Mitre to run their event as the National Championships.

The literature that introduced the event for the Brighton Mitre stated 'this "24" hour event is the very last of its kind on southern roads this century, in fact, if future traffic forecasts are anywhere near accurate, it could possibly be the final '24' ever to be held in this part of the Country!  Having organised a special one-off event to mark the Brighton Mitre's centenary in 1994, and with the approach of the Millenium, it was felt an "End of Century" 24hr would be an appropriate finale.'

In closing, the literature stated that the club recognised and appreciated the 'Catford CC' and the 'Wessex RC' 24 hour events run on southern roads, and that without either of them, many clubmen in the south, especially the older generation, would never have witnessed the many epic battles by the 'stars' of the past.   Riders such as Gus Andrews, Stan Butler, George Laws, Reg Randall, Ken Price, Nim Carline and Cliff Smith.

The event drew 66 entries, of whom 56 started and 37 finished.  One or two new 'stars' emerged from this event and all of them were first time 24hr riders or 'novices'.

**The Brighton Mitre CC, National Championship 24hr, on 26th and 27th June, 1999 was won by Dave Shepherd, Rother Valley CC with 483.917 miles.  Andy Payne, GS Stella was 2nd with 474.157m and Andy Cook, Chippenham and District Whls was 3rd with 455.639 miles.**  Nik Gardiner, Mid Oxon CRT was 4th with 444.895 miles.  Chris Martin, Lewes Wanderers CC was 5th with 438.173m, Chris Shepherd was 6th with 433.354m and John Pugh, Godric CC, was 7th with 429.97 miles.  **Paul Cribb who was 8th with 429.1 miles led Trevor Rush and David Palmer to a Bognor Regis CC Championship Team win with 1,125.801 miles.**  Anne Marie Manley, Bournemouth Jubilee Whls with 359.6 miles and Janet Lowe, San Fairy Ann CC with 353.4m were the only ladies to finish.

The weather for the event was hot at the start and fairly breezy.  The evening cooled off, but the breeze remained to trouble the riders for the full 24hrs.  It rained on and off from dawn to the finish.  The course started north of Worthing at the Dial Post near Horsham, it was centred mainly in East and West Sussex, and came as far west as Tangmere.  There were 4 different circuits, afternoon, evening, night and finishing.

Looking at the result sheet one can see that Dave Shepherd, the winner, who had already proved himself to be an excellent half day rider, rode a good 1st 12 hours of 251.7 miles in this event and 232 for his 2nd half as did Andy Payne, 245 and 229, and Andy Cook, but Nik Gardiner who had the 2nd fastest first 12 hours of 248.9 miles lost time during the 2nd half of the event, resulting in him dropping approximately 25 miles before reaching the finishing circuit.   His 2nd 12 hours yielded just 196 miles despite him riding the fastest lap of the 11.26 mile finishing circuit with 32mins 4secs.

Although Andy Payne rode the fastest 1st 100 miles in 4hrs 29mins with Gardiner 2nd at 2mins, it was Shepherd with 4hrs 36mins who rode steadily throughout to win this Championship event, his first 24 hour.  Marina Bloom, CrawleyWhls, who was in 10th position at the 12 hour point, faded out and retired with back pains in the early hours of the morning, as did Brian Walker.

Dave Shepherd, Nik Gardiner and Marina Bloom, would go on and prove to be 'stars' in future years.

*John Pugh, Godric CC, who was probably 60 years old at the time of this event, came 7th with a very good mileage of 429.9 miles.  He started riding 24 hour races in the very early 1960's at the same time as myself and always seemed a tough hard rider which reflected in this very good result.*

The Mersey RC 24hr on 24th and 25th July 1999, was won by Karl Austin, Congleton CC with 448.16 miles, Simon Doughty, Weaver Valley CC was 2nd with 426.79m and Lynne Taylor, Walsall Roads CC, was 3rd with 424.89m. There were no eligible teams.

Intense heat from the 2pm Saturday start until dusk took its toll of the riders, slowed most 100 times and caused the premature retirement of many seasoned performers. The first to retire inside 5 hours were Sewell, Hassall, Hall, Loader, and Bailey, Vessey and Ackerley went within 7 hours. Marina Bloom and Peter Goodfellow who both started very fast were gone by 10 hours. Simon Corbett and Ian Hill both retired from crash injuries before 14 hours, Dave Brabbin was the last to retire at 18.75 hours with food poisoning when lying in 2nd place.

Karl Austin and Gerry Jones were the only riders to complete the full course. Austin had caught Jones by 72 miles and the pair where within sight of each other until 93 miles. Similarly, Simon Doughty caught Lynne Taylor at 15 miles and was 4mins up on her at 43 miles, undeterred, Lynne closed up at 140 miles despite being off colour. She held Doughty until 195 miles and even the expert help from Wilko couldn't keep her riding at that speed.

Many scraps were the order of the day. The 100 mile check showed Austin with 4hrs 46mins, he was drawing away from Brabbin and Doughty who were at 8mins and Lynne and Gerry Jones at 10mins. The onset of dusk showed just how good the riders lights were. Technology had come on in leaps and bounds to make the lighting bright, safe and good to see by.

At 12 hours Austin had clocked up 235 miles to Brabbins 231, Jones 230, Doughty 229, and Lynne's 224 despite still being off colour. The dawn sun breathed new fire into tired aching legs as the riders completed their circuits in Shropshire.

The 15.25 mile stretch to the finishing circuit at Handley was a tough one into an unhelpful breeze. Frogatt was the fastest with 48 mins, followed by Karl Austin and Lynne, who had now recovered with 53 and 54 mins respectively. Once on the circuit, B. Evans, Manchester Whls, had the fastest lap of the day with 47 mins, followed by Austin with 48m and Steve Abraham 49 mins.

**Jim Hopper on a trike took the Winnerah Trophy as the best veteran on standard with 389 miles at 57 years of age.** John Green improved on his previous years total with 305.4 miles at 15 years of age, and **Lynne took the Turner Cup again for the 5th successive time with 424.89 miles.**

*A few weeks later, eight of these Mersey RC 24hr survivors rode the **Paris-Brest-Paris Randonee of 752 miles. Simon Doughty won the Combination Prize by having the 2nd best Mersey RC 24hr mileage of 426 miles and the fastest British PBP performance of 60 hours 14mins.** Berwick was 2nd in 65 hours 37m, Abraham 68hrs 22m, Hopper on trike, 71hrs 40m, Froggatt, 70hrs 37m, Bond, 75hrs 27m, Peacock, 85hrs 54m, and Knight 86hrs 54m.*

*Archivist, Frank Pulman, pointed out to the 'Fellowship' that George Berwick had now surpassed the post-war completed events of Jack Spackman and Cliff Smith and questioned what his final total would be.*

⟹•◇•⟸

The 101st North Road CC 24hr on 28th and 29th August 1999 was won by David Brabbin, Wigan Whls CC with 463.05 miles. David Solomon, Whitewebbs CC was 2nd with 426.95 miles and David Steer, South Eastern RC was 3rd with 424.13m. Colin Knapp, Middridge CRT and Paul Tyler, Cestria CC, on a tandem trike, raised the Competition Record to 428.94 miles, and **Marina Bloom** overcame previous back problems to finish with **353.97 miles.** She was the only lady competitor.

From 19 solo starters, only 12 riders finished, including **Ken Usher, who was the fastest on a trike with 381.77 miles.**

**The only team entered, the Medway Velo Club, consisting of Ernie Mackey, Charlie Bruce and Ken Stokes, failed to complete the 24hrs due to Ken's tragic death.**

*Ken was returning from Newmarket and approaching Fordham when a vehicle struck him from behind, causing him severe head injuries. The vehicle did not stop. After being treated at the scene, Ken was taken to Addenbrooke's hospital. He passed away on the following Tuesday morning without gaining consciousness.*

---

Frank Mumford, who supplied much of the narrative for the Mersey RC event, sums up the year of 1999, and I will pick a few points from his summary, which puts the year into perspective. He stated that the Brighton Mitre Championship in June had attracted 66 entries with 37 finishers. A month later in July the Mersey RC event saw a drastic reduction in entries of just 37 with 22 finishers, and at the end of August the North Road event, even though it was a Veterans (VTTA) Championship, it still only drew 19 entries and 1 tandem trike, with just 12 solos and the 'long barrow' finishing.

For the Mersey RC it had been a depressing fall in numbers compared with the glory days of 1991-1995 when 85 to 97 riders had entered. Despite a massive prize list and a very modest entry fee of £8.00, Frank felt that without the event being a National Championship things wouldn't improve.

Sadly the North Road CC's 101st 24hr race was to be its last, as Roger Sewell, the Organiser, had been deterred by low prizes and worse, waning support from the North Road club membership in recent years. With Ken Stokes tragic death from a hit and run accident, it was the last crushing blow for an event that had run since 1886, had survived two world wars and was finally defeated by apathy.

The Mersey RC Organiser, Jim Turner, made it his intention to run the Millenium year 2000 event as his last promotion. He'd had 13 glorious years since taking over from Dave Stapleton and the club hoped to find a willing organiser to work alongside Jim and finally take over the ropes under Jim's guidance.

---

On 17th September, Phillip Leigh, of the Kent Valley RC attacked Andy Wilkinsons End to End record, although Phil was primarily a road man, he'd also time trialled from 10 miles to 24 hours He'd taken 3rd place in the Mersey RC National Championships behind Andy Wilkinson and Paul Bland, with a mileage of 461.

His attempt started well, he averaged 23mph to Exeter but a cloudburst at Bristol seemed to turn his luck. It was thought that a chemical spillage on the road from a tanker was the cause of a skin irritation in the saddle area, as spray from the rain had soaked him. Despite regular medical attention, from thereon it became agony for him to sit on the saddle.

The wind dropped as he passed through the Midlands but he continued through to Carlisle well down on schedule. He reached the Scottish Border but by the Forth Road Bridge he realised he had to average 'evens' (20 mph) for another 270 miles. At 31 hours into the ride, he abandoned. His was the first End to End to use the internet for people to gain access to information on his attempt.

## OBITUARIES – 1990 – 1999

**1990 - John Withers** died at 52 years of age. He suffered a sudden heart attack whilst touring in France with other members of Birmingham St Christopher's CCC. John was the main inspiration for the long distance time trialling and road record breaking in the club over a 20 year period. He rode the tandem with Pete Swinden and broke numerous road records. John was a regular 24hr contestant and was equally happy riding either the North Road 24hr or the Mersey event, his best performance being 430 miles in 1961. The pinnacles of John's racing career were the RRA tandem '1000 mile' record in 1964, and later the tandem 'End to End' in 1966, both records with Pete Swinden still stand to this day, over forty years later.

1991 – **Ken Hartley** died on May 28th after riding a tandem 10 mile time trial with Alan Wray. Ken was a much loved character who came into the world of 24 hour racing late in life. We will never know why Ken waited until he was 62 before his first attempt, producing 416 miles in the sweltering heat of the 1986 championships. His fluid, slightly rocking style gave an aura of perpetual motion and his placid temperament left him resolutely smiling through difficulties that would have brought others to their knees. Apart from his age record at 24 hours Ken also held various tandem age records from 100 miles to 12 hours and planned to ride many more, but died suddenly at 67 years of age. *These details were taken from an article by Ian Dow for the Fellowship Journal.*

1991 – **Phil Downer** was killed by an oncoming motor cyclist as he was riding home from work in nearby Wimborne, in late 1991. 49 year old Phil was a much loved family man and tackled all aspects of cycling, touring, club life, time trialling at all distances including a 418 mile 24hr in 1970. He was a much respected committee member of the South DC and the Dorset CA and a course measurer for those areas. A packed congregation at his funeral was a measure of his popularity.

1992 - this was a bad year for losing our 24 hour stalwarts. In August **Cliff Smith** was taken to Leicester Hospital after a collision with a car, he subsequently suffered two strokes, leading to a blood disorder which caused his death at 71 years of age. Cliff carved out an amazing racing career despite a disability received from World War Two when, as a gunner, his spine was shattered by the constant vibrations of the huge anti-aircraft guns. Despite this, he rode 38 twenty four hour races and won 18. He also gained many top five placings and two Championship Team honours. Cliff won the North Road 24hr ten times and the Catford event eight times. His first event was in 1955 and his last was at 60 years of age in 1981 with 450.6 miles, breaking his 'age record' by a massive 49 miles! These performances were truly amazing for a man who faced the almost impossible task of riding a bike after lying in an army hospital bed for seven years. *These details were taken from an obituary by the late Bernard Thompson.*

On 24th August **1992 – Trevor Wilkinson** died from cancer, aged 62. Although he time trialled at all distances up to 12 hours, he was better known as an Organiser and an Administrator of the sport and played a large role in the Mersey RC 24hr feeding and marshalling teams, for a period of some 25 years. He later took to timekeeping and could be found on the finishing circuit of this famous event. During those 25 years, Trevor also ran two 'special' 24hr races for the 'NMCF' as RTTC Championships and both were very successful.

In the autumn of **1992 – Richard Hulse** passed away just before his 79th birthday, after a short illness. He was a keen supporter of the good things in cycling, the camaraderie, the hard touring, long distance time trials and road records. Richard was a stickler for detail and dress code and usually wore specially tailored cycling suits, white shirt, collar and tie. He rode a Raleigh Record Ace, that he had earned as a lad by passing his matriculation exams, and needless to say, that was also immaculately kept. Although Richard rode a few 24hr time trials around the late 1940's he preferred to play a supporting role as either a roving marshal or observer. *Les Lowe gave these details of his obituary.* I too remember Richard very well and to see him stood with his cycle was akin to looking at a Patterson sketch of the 1930's. His friends in the North Road CC nicknamed him 'Carbide' due to him always using this type of lamp on his bike.

In December **1992 – S.P.V. 'Stan' Bray,** Solihull CC died of a stroke at the age of 73. He was a dedicated cyclist in all aspects of club life and a prolific writer. He rode seventeen 24's, his first being the 1949 Mersey RC National Championship, with 422 miles covered, coming 4th and leading the Solihull CC team to victory. Stan's best distance was 455.7 miles in 1958. In later years he rode a couple of 24's on a trike and broke the vets age record with 401.7 miles. Stan was virtually a founder member of the 24hr Fellowship in 1960 and also broke many Midland RRA road records. *His son, Eddie, at a later date rode 416 miles in the Mersey RC 24hr but admitted to preferring shorter distances.*

**Jack Spackman** died in **1992,** he retired from 24hr racing at 55 years of age having ridden 55 all day events. Jack then took up long distance walking and competed regularly. He was a founder member of the 24hr Fellowship and when he wasn't competing he would help in the events, and also observe on road record attempts. His favourite machine was a trike and he was a much respected elder statesman for our sport; his knowledge of long distance cycling was a valuable source of information.

In **1993** – **Frank Shubert** died suddenly at his home in Cheltenham aged 87. He was the winner of both the Irish RC 24hr and the Yorkshire Veg C & AC 24hr in 1933 and 1935. Frank was a lifelong cyclist and a prolific winner of distance races in his day and also wrote many detailed reports for the Fellowship Journal, so providing valuable material for this history.

**Sid Genders,** Walsall Roads CC died in Miami aged 73 in **1993.** He was a founder member of the 24hr Fellowship and was an authority on diet and preparation for endurance events as well as being a tough 24hr rider. He put his knowledge into practice in 1969 by setting out from Penzance to become the fastest solo East to West Atlantic rower, and also the oldest at 51 years of age. His 160 day crossing via Antigua was 20 days faster than John Fairfax's. Sid practised for his Atlantic crossing by rowing in his spare time on Edgbaston Reservoir.

**Steve Nicholas** was murdered by bandits while passing through Ghana in **1993.** Steve paved the way for British riders in the P.B.P. (Paris-Brest-Paris) and would be pleased to know that the tradition is continued by our riders every 4 years. He led the Hull Thursday RC to a team win in his first Mersey RC 24hr in 1971 and also played a very active role in the 24hr Fellowship.

**Stan Butler** died in May **1993** at the age of 83. He was a lifelong member of the Norwood Paragon CC and partnered Frank Southall to many tandem records before the Second World War. Stan rode in the Olympics of 1932 and also had many top 'BAR' placings. In 1950 he crowned an impressive career with victory in the National 24hr Championship, breaking Competition record with 458 miles. Stan was the father of 60's and 70's roadman, Keith Butler, and daughter Valerie, and was Grandfather to Allison, Megan and End to End and 1,000 miler, Gethin Butler.

**Malcolm Challinger** died in **1993.** He was a regular helper at many 24hr events along with his wife Rose. Malcolm chronicled many early 24hr track races as well as many more up-to-date reports of events for the Fellowship Journals. His writings have provided excellent information for this 24hr history book for which I'm indebted to him. Malcolm's ashes were scattered at Hodnet Corner on Sunday morning during the Mersey RC event of 1993.

**Sid Ferris** passed away in **1993** just one month after his wife Eileen. He was 85. Sid was a tough time triallist and record breaker. He won the North Road 24hr 3 times and later took the RRA 24hr record as a professional for Raleigh-Sturmey Archer. Sid was a legend in his own lifetime and went on to break not only the Edinburgh to London but also the Lands End to John o' Groats and 1,000 mile records.

**Frank Fischer** died in November **1993** aged 85. He was a member of the Kentish Whls and in 1945 he rode the first North Road event after the war and did 362 miles. Frank was a 24hr Fellowship member and supplied various articles and information about the early years. He lived in Stafford for a good many years and finished his days there.

Long distance Expert – **Jim Hanning,** Veg C & AC, Redmon CC and St Austell Wheelers, died in **1994,** at 64 years of age. He won the Catford 24hr in 1958 with 462.9 miles and had 2nd placed rides in both the Wessex RC and North Road 24 hr events around that time, in such company as Dave Keeler, Peter Duncan, Ron Coukham and Ken Price. Later in life Jim moved to Cornwall for his work and finished his days there.

**John Cahill's** death in September **1994** at 52 years of age came as a shock to everyone and another link with long distance time trialling has come to a close. John came from a family of cyclists and racing men and he was the cousin of team-mate Mick Coupe. His career spanned many tough years and he was a rider in the Nim Carline mould, with great strength, heart and determination. John's tactic was to muscle his way to as big and early a lead as possible, and then defend it. Three Championship golds, four silvers and nine team medals tell the tale. John was found with a head injury by the side of the A34 road, not far from his home and died 24 hours later in hospital. He played a central role in a deep family and club tradition which was the envy of all his rivals, and to my generation of 24hr riders, John was an inspiration. *Obituary details were by Mick Coupe and Ian Dow.*

**Ken Davis,** a popular North Road CC long distance rider died on 14th November **1994** aged 67. Amongst his many performances, a 422 mile ride in 1954 and a personal best of 445.24 miles in 1956 were highlights of his racing career. Ken had been a stalwart member of the club for over 46 years and in that time he'd been Club Captain, Secretary and Timekeeper.

**Eric Wilkinson** died on 16th January **1995** aged 81. He'd won the first North Road 24hr after the Second World War in 1945 and was a revered National RRA and RTTC Timekeeper, timing the North Road 24hr event for 42 years. Eric 'Wilkie' was a former trike Competition Record breaker in the 1930's and went on to time many RRA road records including the Swinden-Withers tandem 'End to End' in 1966. Eric was often supported by his wife Jan and he was one of the most enthusiastic timekeepers I have ever met.

**John Cull,** President of the Mersey RC, died on 7th February **1995** from cancer. He was 58 years of age. John was a backbone member of the club and held many important positions, and for this he was awarded an Honorary Life Membership. I remember him for always playing a supporting role at the Mersey RC 24hr, every year without fail. The year following his death, Paul, his son, rode the 24hr race in his father's memory and recorded 355.53 miles.

In **1996 – John Walker** of the Derby Mercury died suddenly at 56 years of age. John was a regular rider in both the Mersey and North Road CC 24hr events and Jim Turner recalled his high spirits and the friendly banter that would be exchanged at the feeding stations. John's final years 24hr mileage was 376.55 in the Mersey RC event.

**Phil Johnson,** Manchester Whls passed away in **1996.** He was the father of TA stalwart, Mike Johnson, who himself in recent years has provided immense help for many long distance road record breakers, including 'End to Enders'. Mike recently told me that his father's house was on the main End to End route at Newton Le Willows and during his time had played host to many record breakers who stopped for a meal and a sleep on their journey north. Mike remembers his father Phil getting him out of bed when he was young so that a record breaker could have a sleep.

**Beryl Burton** died in the spring of **1996,** she was 59 years of age. Her absorption in the sport won her 25 'BBAR' titles and her total domination of womens time trialling will be impossible to repeat. She won World Championship titles during her career but ironically the one discipline that beat her was the 24hr time trial. Beryl's attempt to win the Gold medal on offer to the first person to beat 500 miles in 24 hours ended at around 350 miles with very painful knees, and at the time she climbed off she led the field, and was on course for a ride well in excess of 500 miles. Beryl still holds the ladies 12 hour Competition Record with 277.25 miles ridden in 1967, and her mileage at that time also beat the current men's record held by Mike McNamara with 276.52 and then Martyn Roach with 277.17 miles. Beryl had suffered various health problems since the 1980's and had been the victim of more than her share of road accidents. By 1995 she was a shadow of her former self and her riding had become a real effort. Beryl was found dead with her bike at the side of the road.

I wrote to Wes Clayton, Tyne RC, requesting photos for this book and he informed me that his brother **Dennis Clayton,** who had shared many a battle with him in 24 hour races, had died while riding his bike in **1997.** Tyne RC won the Championship team medals five years in succession from 1969 to 1973 and Dennis was in the team on all of these occasions.

Two obituaries were reported in the 24hr Fellowship Journal of February **1999.** The first one was **Ken Price,** a great all round rider of the 1950's era, possibly his best long distance achievement was breaking Competition record for 24 hours with 478.55 miles, thus winning the Catford event of 1955. Ken also became President of the Fellowship in the 1960's.

The second obituary was **Alec Smith,** the winner of the first three Mersey RC 24 hours in succession, before the Second World War, 1937/8/9 with distances of 420.5, 437.5 and 438.75 miles. Alec always intended to make a comeback to the sport in later years but played a supporting role instead.

On 23rd March **1999 - Charlie Taylor** died at 79 years of age. He rode his best 24hr with 352 miles at 66 years of age and he was a member of the Mersey RC for 20 years. Frank Mumford recalled that whenever hard riders gathered, memories of his wry humour, happy disposition and contempt of 'wimps' would ensure he was not forgotten.

**Alf Arnold,** brother of trike man John passed away early in this year of **1999.** He had throughout his life been a great support not only for John but also for many other time triallists and record breakers.

**Edgar Seeley** died in **1999** at 87 years of age. He was a top time triallist and RRA record breaker in the 1930's and rode to 2nd place in the Catford 24hr of 1934 with 428.625 miles. In 1935 he raised the Competition Record to 444.75 miles and this record stood until 1954. Frank Robertson was convinced that Seeley was capable of 460 miles, but business commitments caused him to retire in 1936. Frank went on to comment that he came 3rd to Edgar Seeley in the Catford of 1935 but with a more modest 404.8 miles. Seeley's rides had earned him the title of the new 'Demon Rider'.

In August **1999 – Ken Stokes** died tragically after being struck by a hit and run driver whilst taking part in the North Road CC 24hr on the 28th and 29th August. The vehicle did not stop. Ken was treated at the scene and then was transferred to hospital where he passed away without gaining consciousness on the following Tuesday morning. Ken rode his first '24' in the Brighton Mitre event of 1994 with 383 miles, he'd led the Medway Velo team to two VTTA awards and was looking for a third win when tragedy struck him down at 60 years of age.

# Y 2000

The famous Mersey RC 24hr has attracted many 'star' riders over the years and I would go as far as saying that 70% of End to End attemptee's have used a 24hr as a yardstick to measure their capabilities and progress in preparation for the ultimate time trials 'The End to End' and '1,000 miles'.

Lynne was no exception, she followed on riding 24hr events where I left off. She started by riding the Mersey in 1993 with a mileage of 394 and by 1995 had progressed to 441 miles. It was the same year that Wilko had won with 501 miles. I helped Lynne on many of her long distance trials from 100's to 12hrs and 24hrs, and I felt that with her smooth, steady, unflustered style of riding, she had the makings of a good End to Ender. She persevered year in year out and was obviously there riding when Andy Wilkinson broke Competition Record with 525 miles in 1997.

The years and months went by, Andy and Lynne were quite often guest speakers at various functions and club dinners, whenever possible. They either went on bikes or a tandem. 'Wilko' at this time was in virtual retirement from time trialling and probably thought that he had done it all, but Jim Turner and Paul Histon had other plans, they realised that the 'mixed tandem' record could be taken down by a few hours, especially if Lynne and Wilko were riding it. With the men's tandem record standing at 2 days, 2 hours, 14mins to Pete Swinden and the late John Withers, it was thought that even their record was vulnerable.

Andy and Lynne trained from mid 1999 on the tandem, despite living 120 miles apart. Lynne had her usual racing season on the bike and by the spring of year 2000 they were ready. The 'back up team' comprised mainly of people and officials involved in the Mersey RC 24hrs; Anne and Jim Turner, John, Bob, Ruth and Jonathan Williams, Christine and Frank Minto, Mike Johnson, Paul Histon, Ron Sant, Lynne Mckie, Pat Kenny, who timed the start, and Dai Davies who took over timing from the 12hours point right through to the finish. Colin Baldwin and the late Bert Owen were travelling masseurs and helpers; Andy's parents Judith and Stan, provided a 'comfort' wagon throughout the journey. Shelagh and Edwin Hargraves provided a telephone and 'internet' H.Q.

**8am 13th May 2000** saw the **tandem pair** start away from Lands End. By Okehampton at 100 miles they had slowed a little due to the hills and the heat to be just 10mins inside evens. They had both started with suntan cream on their skins, but when they removed their extra clothing, wet due to heavy mist, they should have replenished their skin protection, as later in the day they were both suffering from sunburn on their exposed limbs.

At Bristol they were still inside 'evens' but happier due to cooler conditions. At the 12hr point they had covered 247.5miles to reach Severn Stoke. At 10.57pm they passed through Gailey Island with 294 miles covered. Out through the Potteries to Holmes Chapel, Warrington, Winwick Church, Preston and Garstang at 4.10am where a comfort stop was taken. They had covered 390 miles in just over 20 hours.

Jim Ithell

Paul Bland

Ron Sant , Jim Hopper & George Longstaff

Mick Gray

Marc Cunnington

Andy Wilkinson

Ian Gray

Phil Leigh

Ralph Dadswell

326

Christine Roberts

Wilko "525"

Brian Walker

Lynne Taylor

David Brabbin

Edwin Hargraves

Les Lowe

Wilko Windcheetah

Bridget Boon

327

# PHOTO PAGES CONTINUED

**Page : 228**  **Robin Buchan,** 24hr Champion in 1971.  **Rod Goodfellow** receiving the North Road cup in 1983. **Wes Clayton** leading his brother **Dennis** to a Tyne RC Championship team win in the Catford event of 1971. **Graham Mann,** winner of the Wessex RC 24hr in 1971 with 469.9 miles.  **Vin Denson** 'Mersey' 3rd place with 449 miles in 1976. **Roger Sewell** riding the North Road 24hr in the early 1970's. **Mick Coupe,** 24hr and End to End record breaker, 1982.

**Page : 229**  **Pat Kenny and myself** breaking the Birmingham to London and back record. **Kathy & Pete Akoslovski** breaking another MRRA record. **Al Mansley** just starting his winning Mersey RC 24hr in 1979. **Paul Carbutt** BBAR and professional End to End record breaker in 1979. **Ian Dow,** triple 24hr Championship winner, 1985/86/87.  **John Woodburn,** 24hr Champion 1980/1981 and End to End record breaker, 1982. **Joe Summerlin** being pushed off in the North Road 24hr in 1972, by Peter Bury; **Eric Wilkinson** is the timekeeper with Geoff Edwards and Frank Armond looking on.  **Stuart Jackson,** quadruple 24hr Championship winner 1982/83/84/88.

**Page : 274**  **Malcolm Judge,** Seamons CC, Mersey RC 24hr winner 1980. **Anne Mann,** Competition record 24hr in 1983.  **Rod Collins,** silver medallist with 483miles in 1987. **Hugh Culverhouse,** End to End & Race across America with only one useable leg in 1987.  **Pieter Hoffman,** North Road 24hr winner in 1985. **Gordon Dennis,** 3rd in the North Road 24hr with 442.2 miles.  **Brian Morris,** silver medallist 24hr Championships 1982 with 476 miles.  **John Cahill,** triple Championship 24hr winner 1975-1978.  **Eric Tremaine,** trike 24hr Competition record breaker in 1972 and End to End in 1982.  **Stuart Jackson,** trike 24hr team Competition record in 1981.

**Page : 275**  **Ian Butcher,** Champion 24hr rider in 1989 with 493.5m, and 1998 501 miles.  **John Baines,** Championship winner in 1970 with 473.5 miles.  **Alan Roberts,** top time triallist and advisor to the Champions. **Mick Potts,** 24hr Champion at 50 years of age in 1991. **Glen Longland,** 24hr Champion in 1994. **Phil Oxborough,** 24hr gold medallist in 1990.  **Don Spraggett,** regular Mersey RC contender with a PB of 471.8 in 1968. **Marc Cunnington,** 1997 North Road winner, 468.91 miles, **Dave Brabbin,** 2nd 466.61 and **Roger Sewell,** 3rd, 429.35 miles.  **Phil Barlow,** champion in 1993 with 490.88m.  **Steve Abraham,** Audax and 24hr hardman. **George Berwick,** prolific 24hr rider for forty years.

**Page : 326**  **Paul Bland,** silver medallist in 1995 with 475 miles. **Jim Ithell,** North Road National in 1992, taking the trike prize with 360 miles. **Jim Hopper** and **Ron Sant** with **George Longstaff,** record breakers in July 1991. **Marc Cunnington,** winner of the Brighton Mitre event in 1994 with 452.7 miles. **Andy Wilkinson,** winning the Mersey RC Championship 1995, with 501.39 miles on his mountain bike. **Mick Gray,** 2nd in the North Road Championship 1992, with 481 miles. **Ian Gray,** (no relation to Mick) 3rd in that same event with 473 miles. **Phil Leigh** on his End to End attempt in 1991.  **Ralph Dadswell** waiting at the start of his End to End record in August 1992.

**Page : 327**  **Christine Roberts,** the current ladies Competition record holder in 1993 with 461.45 miles. **Andy Wilkinson 'Wilko',** top BBAR in 1996 and 24hr record holder in 1997. **Brian Walker,** silver medallist in 1997 with 483.33 miles, seen here in short distance mode.  **Lynne Taylor,** cornering on the Mersey RC finishing circuit in 1997 with 418 miles.  **Les Lowe** in the ECCA National 1983, with 383.60 miles. **Dave Brabbin,** Mersey RC 24hr winner in 1996 with 462.4 miles. **Edwin Hargraves** multi RRA record breaker and Mersey RC 24hr winner in 1998, with 462.2 miles.  **Andy Wilkinson's** 'Windcheetah' in the Highlands in April 1996. **Bridget Boon,** North Road winner in 1993 with 457.14 miles.

**Page : 378** **Karl Austin,** Mersey RC 24hr winner in 1999 with 448.16 miles. **David Shepherd,** Brighton Mitre Championship winner in 1999, with 483.9 miles, and Mersey RC Championship winner 2002, with 482.128 miles. **Gethin Butler,** Mersey RC Championship winner 2000 with 509.25 miles, current RRA 24hr, End to End and 1,000 miles record holder. **Jose Pinon Shaw,** regular top three championship 24hr rider, personal best 472.78m in 2007. **Keith Coffey,** silver medallist in 2005 with 475.897m **Nick Cave,** bronze medallist in 2006 with 472.492. **Neil Skellern,** very stylish rider and silver medallist in 2006 with 477.653m. **Simon Doughty,** 4th, Mersey 24hr Championship in 1995 with 459 miles. **Lynne Taylor,** riding the second fastest women's 24hr in 2007, with 459.29m. **Nik Gardiner,** 4 times Championship winner and the 2nd highest mileage ever, 513.65. **Eamonn Deane,** 24hr Champion in 2007 with 501.04 miles. **John Warnock,** silver medallist in 2007 with 489.32 and 2008 with 491.39 miles.

**Page Ladies : 379** **Kate Green,** the first lady rider over 300 miles, with 308 in 1908. **Lilian Dredge,** pioneer record breaker, the first to ride from Lands End to John o' Groats and 1,000 miles in 1938. **Marguerite Wilson,** the youngest End to End record breaker at 21 years of age in 1939. **Edith Atkins,** the first lady to beat 400 miles in a straight out 24hr record of 422 miles, and took many other place to place road records, including the End to End and 1,000 miles in 1953. **Eileen Sheridan,** the Hercules professional and most prolific ladies road record breaker in history. **Wyn Maddock,** veteran 24hr rider in the late 1960's. **Joyce Blow,** the first lady 24hr trike Competition record breaker in 1968.

**Page Ladies : 408** **Joan Kershaw** led the Prescot Eagles ladies team to a Competition record in 1976. **Ethel Brambleby,** Merseyside Ladies CA winner 3 years in succession from 1973. **Christine Minto,** the first RTTC Competition record breaker at 24hrs with 409.16 miles. **Ruth Williams** on the starting line at the Mersey 24hr in 1967 with officials, Peter Barlow, Eric Wilkinson, and Organiser David Stapleton looking on as Ron Macqueen checks his watch. **Janet Tebbutt** climbing the Devil's Beeftub on her amateur End to End in 1976. **Ann Dunk & Fiona Steel** attacking a tandem 12 hour record.

**Page Ladies : 409** **Christine Roberts,** current RTTC and RRA 24hr record holder. **Felicity Beard** 24hr trike Competition record holder 1988. **Anne Mann,** Comp record holder in 1983 with 438.16 miles. **Jean Burrow,** personal best 1987 with 419.18 miles. **Mrs Sue Gray** on the finishing circuit of the Mersey RC 24hr in 1993, with 383.72 miles. **Bridget Boon,** the only woman to ever win a 24hr race. **Pauline Strong,** End to End record breaker in 1990 with 2 days 6 hrs 49mins 45secs.

**Page Ladies – Colour : 470** **Sheila Simpson** battling against the wind in 1992 with 401.76 miles in the North Road 24hr. **Christine Roberts,** 100 mile Champion in 1987, 1990 and 1994. **Bridget Boon** on her way to a 446.88 mileage in the Mersey 24hr 1993. **Carol Westmorland** winning the Mersey RC ladies event with 445.412m in 2006. **Tracey Maund,** Walsall RCC team Competition record breaker at 100 miles, 12hrs & 24hrs, seen here in the Welsh 12 hour in 2003. **Ann Wooldridge,** 3rd lady in 2005 with 395.5 miles. **Marina Bloom,** RRA 12 hour record holder 274 miles and Mersey RC ladies Champion with 447.334 in 2005. **Lynne & Liz,** mother helping daughter to a 459.29 miles ride in 2007.

**Page : 471** **Jim Hopper** on his way to finishing another Mersey RC 24hr. **Lynne & Andy** climbing Berriedale in 2000 with just 2 hours to go to reach John o' Groats, being hydrated and urged onwards by **Paul Histon. Eileen & David Brabbin** breaking the 24hr tandem Competition record in 2002 with 464.92m. **Lynne** receiving the 'Turner' cup from **Jim Turner** with **John Williams,** the President of the Mersey RC. **Ralph Dadswell & Marina Bloom** taking another RRA record. **Ian & Bridget Boon** tandem Competition record breakers in 1983/85 & 86, with 463.33 miles.

**Page : 472** **Men over 500 miles.** **Rod & Peter Goodfellow** on their way to tandem Competition record in 1991 with 501.35 miles. **Ian Butcher,** North Road Championship winner in 1998 with 501.31 miles. **Ian Dow,** National Champion in 1987 with 500.1 miles. **Roy Cromack,** the first man to beat 500 miles in 1969 with 507. **Andy Wilkinson,** the current 24hr record holder with 525.07 miles in 1997. **Eamonn Deane,** winning the Mersey RC 24hr in 2007, with 501.04. **Gethin Butler,** RRA 24hr End to End and 1,000 mile record breaker in 2001 with a p.b, 509.25 to his credit. **Nik Gardiner,** Mersey RC winner in 2008 with the 2nd highest mileage recorded 513.65. **John Woodburn,** North Road Championship winner in 1980, with 505.47 miles.

## Mersey National 1991

| Pos. | Name | | Club | 100 miles | 12 hours (approx) | Final Mileage |
|---|---|---|---|---|---|---|
| 1. | **MICK** | **POTTS** | **DERBY MERCURY** | 4.35.00 | 250.2 | **486.65** |
| 2. | **Phil** | **Barlow** | **Kiveton Park CC** | 4.26.12 | 249.0 | **472.14** |
| 3. | **Phil** | **Oxborough** | **St. Ives CC** | 4.43.25 | 238.4 | **464.56** |
| 4. | John | Leach | Rossendale RC | 4.44.40 | 235.5 | 453.08 |
| 5. | Alan | Bate | New Brighton CC | 4.49.24 | 237.8 | 448.18 |
| 6. | Graham | Williams | St. Ives CC | 4.49.48 | 237.3 | 447.51 |
| 7. | George | Berwick | Edinburgh RC | 4.56.40 | 227.6 | 436.00 |
| 8. | Martin | Staines | Worcester St. Johns CC | 4.55.12 | 228.9 | 433.00 |
| 9. | Simon | Pedley | Derby Mercury | 4.40.34 | 230.5 | 430.28 |
| 10. | Sheila | Simpson (Mrs) | Doncaster Wheelers | 5.15.02 | 220.7 | 426.18 |

| Pos. | Name | Club | Mileage | | Pos. | Name | Club | Mileage |
|---|---|---|---|---|---|---|---|---|
| 11. | P. Guy | Mid-Shrops. Whs. | 422.40 | | 37. | D. Willoughby | Pembrokes. Velo | 379.87 |
| 12. | H. Canning | B'ham St. Chris. | 421.02 | | 38. | J. Burrow (Mrs) | Shaftesbury CC | 375.60 |
| 13. | M. Roscoe | Horwich CC | 420.08 | | 39. | R. Breedon | Chelt. & Co. CC | 374.98 |
| 14. | J. Clarke | Rutland CC | 416.70 | | 40. | W. Pykett | Beauvale CC | 371.60 |
| 15. | J. Hall | Rutland CC | 416.10 | | 41. | M. Webb | Waltham Forest | 371.38 |
| 16. | R. Stoneman | Horwich CC | 415.75 | | 42. | P. Windwood | Walsall RC | 362.80 |
| 17. | M. Tongue | ABC Centreville | 415.21 | | 43. | P. Kenny (T) | B'ham St. Chris. | 361.69 |
| 18. | J. Clark | Wessex RC | 415.15 | | 44. | I. Hill | Mercia CC | 359.79 |
| 19. | M. Wilmer | Kent Valley RC | 408.99 | | 45. | M. Turner | ABC Centreville | 359.12 |
| 20. | T. Finney | Horwich CC | 408.30 | | 46. | S. Chalkley | K'minster CTC | 354.85 |
| 21. | J. Hopper (T) | Mercia CC | 404.63 | | 47. | R. Rix | Thurcroft CC | 350.76 |
| 22. | D. McGuiness | Southport RCC | 404.08 | | 48. | T. Murphy | Mersey RC | 348.73 |
| 23. | D. Hanson | Prescot Eagle RC | 403.23 | | 49. | N. Holgate | Southport RCC | 347.50 |
| 24. | B. Davies | Wrexham RC | 401.49 | | 50. | M. Howard | Waltham Forest | 340.71 |
| 25. | T. Dolphin | Paddington CC | 395.27 | | 51. | K. Gowans | VC Halton | 331.83 |
| 26. | G. Moult | Derby Mercury | 394.32 | | 52. | A. Wiggins | B'ham St. Chris. | 330.20 |
| 27. | R. Abram | Southport RCC | 394.20 | | 53. | E. Mackey | Medway Velo | 328.27 |
| 28. | J. Viney | Prescot Eagle RC | 392.33 | | 54. | D. Carter | South Lancs RC | 327.13 |
| 29. | A. Hoare | Cardiff Ajax CC | 392.12 | | 55. | S. Tebbitts (T) | K'minster CTC | 321.55 |
| 30. | R. Simpson | Edinburgh RC | 389.01 | | 56. | G. Siddle | Darlington Velo | 317.01 |
| 31. | T. Morris | Skipton CC | 387.89 | | 57. | M. Greenblatt | Mersey RC | 314.61 |
| 32. | G. Bell | Glossop Velo RC | 387.17 | | 58. | A. Parker | Mersey RC | 311.01 |
| 33. | R. Sant (T) | Weaver Valley | 385.66 | | 59. | J. Reaney | Brodsworth RCC | 301.54 |
| 34. | J. Featherstone | Weaver Valley | 382.76 | | 60. | S. Light | Mersey RC | 296.30 |
| 35. | P. Swinden | B'ham St. Chris. | 381.34 | | 61. | R. Beaman | B'ham St. Chris. | 261.42 |
| 36. | A. Magee | Westmead Team | 379.93 | | | | | |

**Team:** Derby Mercury (Potts, Pedley, Moult), 1311.25 miles.

**Tandem:** R. Goodfellow (N. Lancs RC) and P. Goodfellow (Sheffield University CC), 501.35 miles. *

**Lady:** Mrs. Sheila Simpson (Doncaster Wheelers), 426.18 miles.

* comp record

## North Road National 1992

| | | | |
|---|---|---|---|
| **1.** | **Andy Wilkinson** | **Port Sunlight Wh** | **501.96** |
| **2.** | **Mick Gray** | **Crest CC** | **481.08** |
| **3.** | **Ian Gray** | **Derby Mercury** | **473.17** |
| 4. | Andy Major | Alton CC | 443.95 |
| 5. | John Baines | Goole Vermuyden | 427.69 |
| 6. | Mark Holden | Beds. Road CC | 419.81 |
| 7. | Graham Moult | Derby Mercury RC | 417.15 |
| 8. | Neil Roberts | Mapperley CC | 416.49 |
| 9. | Pete Bishop | Heron Racing Club | 410.45 |
| 10. | Fred Lyn | Seacroft Wh | 404.66 |
| **11.** | **Sheila Simpson** | **Weaver Valley** | **401.76** |
| 12. | Simon Pedley | Derby Mercury RC | 397.81 |
| 13. | Richard Griffin | Crawley Wh | 391.45 |
| 14. | Clive Chappe | Reading CC | 386.22 |
| 15. | Ron Gager | Redmon CC | 382.59 |
| 16. | Tony Deadman | Maidenhead & Dist | 378.91 |
| 17. | Stephen Barratt | Merthyr CC | 378.32 |
| 18. | Vernon Dancey | Cheltenham & Co. | 373.14 |
| 19. | Jean Burrow | Shaftesbury CC | 372.50 |
| 20. | Ernie Mackey | Medway Velo | 364.07 |
| 21. | Peter Baumber | Cambridge CC | 360.69 |
| 22. | Jim Ithell (T) | Derby Mercury RC | 360.11 |
| 23. | Brian Powney | Kingston Phoenix | 355.44 |
| 24. | James King | Truro CC | 354.01 |
| 25. | Tim Dolphin | Paddington CC | 352.87 |
| 26. | Roger Harris | Beacon Roads CC | 344.72 |
| 27. | Mark Toon | Choughs RC | 310.76 |
| 28. | Peter Martin (T) | Ratae RC | 286.73 |

**Tandem:**

Peter & Mary Horsfield   Redmon CC   336.40

**Team:**

Derby Mercury RC   1288.13
(Gray, Moult, Pedley)

## Mersey National 1993

| | | | 98.62 miles | Est. 12 hrs | 24 hrs |
|---|---|---|---|---|---|
| 1. | **PHIL BARLOW** | **KIVETON PARK CC** | 4-08-20 | **253.8** | **490.88 miles** |
| 2. | **Glenn Longland** | **Antelope RT** | 4-19-04 | **249.5** | 477.46 |
| 3. | **Paul Bland** | **Kiveton Park CC** | 4-20-50 | **247.2** | 468.51 |
| 4. | Keith Silvester | Mid Shropshire Whs | 4-26-40 | 243.3 | 467.92 |
| 5 | Mrs. Christine Roberts (Competition record) | Crewe Clarion | 4-31-55 | 241.0 | 461.46 |
| 6. | Bob Newell | Lincoln Whs | 4-35-15 | 237.0 | 457.77 |
| 7. | Simon Pedley | Derby Mercury RC | 4-30-10 | 239.7 | 450.91 |
| 8. | Peter Goodfellow | Kiveton Park CC | 4-25-40 | 246.2 | 448.81 |
| 9. | Mrs. Bridget Boon | Severn RC | 4-48-50 | 236.8 | 446.88 |
| 10. | Andy Major | Alton CC | 4-46-20 | 233.9 | 444.98 |

| | | | | |
|---|---|---|---|---|
| 11. G.S. Barker | Rockingham CC | 235.0 443.71 | 54. D. Barry | Hinckley CRC | 188.4 332.20 |
| 12. G.R. Moult | Derby Mercury RC | 219.4 430.55 | 55. Miss H.Sandelands | Mersey Roads Club | 181.5 331.58 |
| 13. D.R. Williams | Mersey Roads Club | 231.8 429.53 | 56. M. Howard | Waltham Forest CTC | 182.9 331.27 |
| 14. M.T. Wilmer | Kent Valley RC | 224.5 425.43 | 57. G. Davies | Bath CC | 173.6 327.76 |
| 15. M.F. Cunnington | Swindon RC | 224.7 422.04 | 58. F. Taylor (T) | Harboro Concord CC | 165.9 314.50 |
| 16. J. Baile | Unity CC | 225.4 421.65 | 59. T. Frenzel | Cwmcarn Paragon | 167.3 313.99 |
| 17. S.A. Underwood | Hampshire RC | 219.3 421.40 | | | |
| 18. I. Hill | Mercia CC | 217.8 417.21 | | | |
| 19. J. Hatfield | Ravensthorpe CC | 222.8 415.77 | | | |
| 20. D. McGreachie-Clarke | Derby Mercury RC | 218.6 415.02 | | | |

**_Tandems_**

1. Mark Brooking / Jane Ramsdale (TT) — Willesden CC / Seacroft Whs Comp record — **401.22**
2. P. Kenny/P. Gifford — Birm St Chris/Midland TA — 338.17
3. M. Pickover/D. White — Loughborough Students — 336.93

_Team:_ Kiveton Park CC   1408.20 miles (Event Record)

| | | |
|---|---|---|
| 21. B. Davies | Mersey Roads Club | 215.4 407.44 |
| 22. S. Cornish | Mid Shrops Whs | 223.0 406.35 |
| 23. I.A. Finch | Severn RC | 216.7 401.68 |
| 24. J. Ellis | Kiveton Park CC | 207.8 400.78 |
| 25. K. Austin | Congleton CC | 223.8 399.11 |
| 26. J.W. Hopper (T) | Derby Mercury RC | 211.2 398.54 |
| 27. P.B. Winwood | Walsall Roads CC | 208.7 397.68 |
| 28. G. Berwick | Edinburgh RC | 207.5 396.71 |
| 29. K.S. Morte | Mersey Roads Club | 207.9 396.69 |
| 30. Miss L.E.A. Taylor | Walsall Roads Club | 214.4 394.06 |
| 31. A. Magee | Stockport Clarion | 213.1 392.97 |
| 32. D.W. Harris | Bynea CC | 199.6 390.39 |
| 33. M.S. Webb | Waltham Forest CTC | 206.0 386.52 |
| 34. W.J. Ithell | Derby Mercury RC | 206.7 385.56 |
| 35. N. Millington | Mid Shrops Whs | 200.0 385.39 |
| 36 Mrs S Gray | Derby Mercury RC | 217.3 383.72 |
| 37. K. Langham | Leicester Forest CC | 205.1 379.58 |
| 38. P. Packwood | Cannock CRC | 199.3 379.20 |
| 39 Miss C Prescott | Beauvale CC | 210.3 377.87 |
| 40. T.J. Morris | Skipton CC | 205.3 376.11 |
| 41. T. Deadman | Maidenhead & Dist. | 205.1 373.30 |
| 42. P. Gee | Hainault RC | 207.6 371.49 |
| 43. J. Pratt | Brighton Excelsior | 201.4 371.44 |
| 44. Mrs. J.M. Wilson | Bath CC | 194.8 366.04 |
| 45. B.S. Donnan | Chelt. & Co. CC | 188.2 363.23 |
| 46. R. Goodbier | Evesham & Dist.Wh. | 190.0 356.98 |
| 47. I. McAll | Hinckley CRC | 190.3 355.93 |
| 48. R. Johnson | Brighton Mitre CC | 197.3 353.44 |
| 49. D.M.C. Buck | Somer Valley CC | 194.1 343.67 |
| 50. T.J. Dolphin | Paddington CC | 188.1 342.02 |
| 51. A. Griffiths | CC Woking | 193.4 338.27 |
| 52. M. Greenblatt | Mersey Roads Club | 181.2 338.13 |
| 53. E.G. Mackey | Medway Velo | 181.9 334.62 |

North Road National 1994

| | | |
|---|---|---|
| **1. GLENN LONGLAND** | **ANTELOPE RT** | **475.40** |
| **2. Steve Wharton** | **Paddington CC** | **439.81** |
| **3. Graham Moult** | **Derby Mercury** | **438.11** |
| 4. A. Major | Alton CC | 434.58 |
| 5. R. Newell | Lincoln Whs. | 423.64 |
| 6. G. Williams | St. Ives CC | 400.63 |
| 7. S. Pedley | Derby Mercury RC | 397.40 |
| 8. C. Yates | Otley CC | 395.42 |
| 9. R. Griffin | Crawley Whs. | 384.90 |
| 10. D. McGeachie-Carke | Derby Mercury RC | 382.89 |
| 11. A. Smith | Long Eaton Par. | 381.97 |
| 12. K. Langham | Leic. Forest CC | 381.73 |
| 13. T. Dolphin | Paddington CC | 381.25 |
| 14. D. Solomon | Whitewebbs CC | 376.58 |
| 15. W. Clough | Cambridge CC | 374.13 |
| 16. P. Dean | Hillingdon CC | 364.17 |
| 17. G. Berwick | Edinburgh RC | 359.29 |
| 18. P. Packwood | Cannock CC | 344.21 |
| 19. G. Nye | Shaftesbury CC | 333.37 |
| 20. D. White | Loughborough Students Union CC | 309.53 |
| 21. H. Tattersdale | Kettering Am. CC | 293.69 |

Team: Derby Mercury RC, 1216.90 miles.

Tandem trike: Jim Hopper (Derby Mercury RC) & Ron Sant (Weaver Valley CC), 410.47 miles

## Mersey Roads National 1995

| Name | Club | AUK mem. | Previous best 24 | Age | VTTA Pos. | VTTA plus | 100.5m | 12hrs (est) | Best f-ct lap (mins) | Final mileage |
|---|---|---|---|---|---|---|---|---|---|---|
| 1. **Andy Wilkinson** | **Port Sunlight Whs** | | **502-91** | 31 | | | **4-16-01** | **269.1** | **43** | **501.39** |
| 2. **Paul Bland** | **Kiveton Park CC** | | **468-93** | 42 | 1 | **87.22** | **4-34-52** | **248.4** | **46** | **475.08** |
| 3. **Philip Leigh** | **Kent Valley RC** | | | 35 | | | **4-38-47** | **246.3** | **54** | **461.58** |
| 4. Simon Doughty | Willesden CC | | 452-85 | 34 | | | 4-39-48 | 242.0 | 51 | 459.07 |
| 5. Kevin Lally | Rutland CC | A | 409-94 | 26 | | | 5-01-40 | 229.0 | 45 | 443.80 |
| 6. John Leach | Rossendale RC | | 453-91 | 50 | 3 | 76.94 | 4-48-56 | 233.4 | 51 | 442.17 |
| 7. **Lynne Taylor** | **Walsall Roads CC** | | **418-94** | 26 | | | **4-52-58** | **229.0** | **48** | **441.40** |
| 8. Adrian Pudsey | Hereford & Dis. Wh | | | 46 | 4 | 58.57 | 4-39-55 | 228.7 | 48 | 435.04 |
| 9. Karl Austin | Congleton CC | | 421-92 | 31 | | | 4-54-24 | 229.0 | 48 | 434.95 |
| 10. Simon Pedley | Derby Mercury RC | A | 450-91 | 37 | | | 4-55-50 | 229.1 | 46 | 429.30 |
| 11. Pete Wicks | Richmond & Darl'n | | 403-94 | 48 | 5 | 56.34 | 4-56-41 | 219.4 | 51 | 427.10 |
| 12. Dave McG-Clarke | Derby Mercury RC | A | 415-94 | 30 | | | 5-05-29 | 214.5 | 52 | 417.14 |
| 13. Nigel Hood | ABC Centreville | A | 382-92 | 32 | | | 4-50-31 | 222.4 | 49 | 417.10 |
| 14. Hugh Canning | Walsall Roads CC | A | | 51 | N | | 5-33-04 | 207.4 | 52 | 413.89 |
| 15. Brian Davies | Mersey RC | | 413-72 | 52 | 6 | 53.91 | 5-17-20 | 219.3 | 52 | 413.63 |
| 16. Melville Kirkland | London St. Chris. | A | | 46 | N | | 5-11-44 | 213.0 | 48 | 411.55 |
| 17. Jim Hopper (T) | Derby Mercury RC | A | 404-91 | 53 | 2 | 81.50 | 5-22-00 | 214.8 | 56 | 408.92† |
| 18. Chris Mullin | Weaver Valley CC | A | | 41 | N | | 5-08-58 | 217.2 | 58 | 406.62 |
| 19. Paul Tyler | Cestria CC | | 411-89 | 37 | | | 4-50-41 | 229.3 | 59 | 405.39 |
| 20. William Dean | Southport CC | A | | 40 | N | | 5-16-08 | 212.2 | 56 | 404.78 |
| 21. Ned Millington | Oswestry Paragon | | 385-93 | 48 | 10 | 32.64 | 5-15-58 | 208.6 | 53 | 403.90 |
| 22. Robert Owens | Hereford & Dis. Wh | | | 41 | 16 | 9.43 | 5-35-47 | 202.9 | 53 | 400.50 |
| 23. Phil Packwood | Cannock CRC | | 379-93 | 32 | | | 5-03-36 | 211.4 | 59 | 397.55 |
| 24. Mick Wilmer | Kent Valley RC | A | 425-93 | 47 | 13 | 22.84 | 5-16-41 | 215.2 | 64 | 396.37 |
| 25. John Featherstone | Wigan Whs C&AC | A | 382-91 | 48 | N | | 5-12-05 | 206.0 | 55 | 395.10 |
| 26. Steven Massey | Mercia CC | | | 18 | | | 5-12-08 | 208.5 | 47 | 392.22 |
| 27. Grahame Hargreaves | Ratae RC | | | 50 | N | | 5-09-29 | 211.4 | 59 | 392.10 |
| 28. Andrew Ashcroft | Lancashire RC | | 377-94 | 31 | | | 5-17-49 | 207.3 | 60 | 389.84 |
| 29. George Berwick | Edinburgh RC | A | 464-76 | 54 | 11 | 32.25 | 5-29-41 | 203.4 | 59 | 387.61 |
| 30. Kevin Langham | Leicester Forest CC | | 381-94 | 34 | | | 5-22-32 | 205.3 | 58 | 386.51 |
| 31. Stewart Bond | Preston Whs | A | | 51 | N | | 5-26-17 | 206.5 | 58 | 385.69 |
| 32. Steve Sayers | Cleveleys RC | | 355-94 | 34 | | | 5-45-35 | 190.0 | 54 | 385.53 |
| 33. Peter Holland (T) | Southboro' & Dis. | | 399-94 | 48 | N | | 5-38-29 | 205.1 | 59 | 384.31 |
| 34. Tom Lodge | Salisbury RC | A | | 62 | 8 | 45.65 | 5-34-10 | 197.3 | 52 | 379.34 |
| 35. Martin Staines | Worcester St. Johns | A | 433-91 | 36 | | | 4-13-14* | 202.0 | 54 | 375.40 |
| 36. Tim Dolphin | Paddington CC | A | 405-94 | 44 | 17 | -9.56 | 5-13-19 | 204.5 | 63 | 372.65 |
| 37. Ron Lee (T) | San Fairy Ann CC | A | | 59 | 7 | 53.03 | 5-37-31 | 196.0 | 66 | 365.87 |
| 38. David Unsworth | Hereford & Dis. Wh | A | | 57 | 14 | 16.70 | 4-38-00* | 186.6 | 54 | 363.26 |
| 39. Frank Newton-Adair | Ellesmere Port CC | | 337-94 | 45 | 19 | -17.68 | 5-37-58 | 189.1 | 53 | 361.16 |
| 40. Michael Froggatt | Swindon RC | | | 31 | | | 5-59-49 | 186.4 | 64 | 353.46 |
| 41. John Walker | Derby Mercury RC | | 349-93 | 54 | 18 | -16.49 | 5-40-05 | 190.6 | 58 | 352.88 |
| 42. Joe Summerlin (T) | Leicestershire RC | A | | 62 | 9 | 43.99 | 6-18-22 | 183.0 | 65 | 349.90 |
| 43. Graham Axford | Addiscombe CC | | 317-73 | 41 | 20 | -42.12 | 6-04-50 | 186.3 | 121 | 349.01 |
| 44. Brian Richards | Thanet RC | | 376-93 | 56 | 12 | 25.45 | 6-06-03 | 185.6 | 61 | 344.53 |
| 45. Chris Lowe | Swindon RC | | | 36 | | | 4-47-04* | 166.6 | 54 | 330.28 |
| 46. James Roberson | Bristol South CC | A | 347-87 | 44 | N | | 6-03-35 | 170.9 | 69 | 318.52 |
| 47. Les Lowe (T) | Speedwell BC | A | 393-82 | 64 | 15 | 13.63 | 4-50-00* | 171.3 | 71 | 314.91 |
| 48. Richard Hull (T) | Willesden CC | A | | 34 | | | 4-51-00* | 168.9 | 97 | 303.69 |
| 49. Paul Ward | Kinder Racing Team | A | 322-94 | 30 | | | 5-14-20* | 154.2 | 63 | 298.81 |
| **Tandem:** Mr & Mrs S. Powell | Wyre Forest CRC | | | 57/55 | | | 4-11-17* | 196.9 | 80 | 347.76† |

* - 77.68 miles, N - Non-VTTA member; T- tricycle, † - VTTA age record

**Merseyside Ladies CA winner:** Lynne Taylor

**Team Race:**  1. Derby Mercury RC  (Pedley, McG-Clarke, Hopper)  1255.36 miles
2. Hereford & Dist. Whs (Pudsey, Owens, Unsworth)  1198.80

## North Road National 1996

| Posn | No. | Name | Club | Miles |
|------|-----|------|------|-------|
| 1 | 40 | Malcolm Whitehead | Velo Club Deal | 465.75 |
| 2 | 47 | Marc Cunnington | Swindon Road Club | 452.82 |
| 3 | 25 | David Brabbin | Wigan Whs C & AC | 449.08 |
| 4 | 32 | David Howes | Derby Mercury RC | 442.21 |
| 5 | 10 | Adrian Pudsey | Hereford & Dist.. Whs | 430.01 |
| 6 | 30 | Michael Perrin | Sherwood CC | 419.89 |
| 7 | 42 | Ray Charles | Elmet CRC | 418.06 |
| 8 | 46 | William Lantry | Velo Club Elan | 417.02 |
| 9 | 13 | Richard Griffin | Crawley Wheelers | 409.64 |
| 10 | 12 | Kevin Younge | Kings Lynn CC | 406.82 |
| 11 | 33 | Kevin Langham | Leicester Forest CC | 395.55 |
| 12 | 45 | David Solomon | Whitewebbs CC | 394.99 |
| 13 | 27 | Michael Merry | Willesden CC | 390.77 |
| 14 | 21 | Robert Owen | Hereford & Dist.. Whs | 384.80 |
| 15 | 26 | Tim Dolphin | North Road CC | 384.48 |
| 16 | 18 | Jim Hopper (T) | Derby Mercury RC | 384.39 |
| 17 | 06 | George Berwick | Edinburgh RC | 380.22 |
| 18 | 37 | Grahame Hargreaves | Ratae RC | 379.36 |
| 19 | 23 | Andy Bentley | Velo Club Elan | 376.12 |
| 20 | 43 | David Gray | Glasgow United CC | 374.48 |
| 21 | 05 | David McGeachie-Clarke | Derby Mercury RC | 362.26 |
| 22 | 31 | Anthony Richardson | Hereford & Dist.. Whs | 360.90 |
| 23 | 29 | Peter Holland (T) | Southborough & Dist. Whs | 351.75 |
| 24 | 39 | John Walker | Derby Mercury RC | 347.79 |
| 25 | 22 | Kathryn Smith (L) | Sherwood CC | 320.94 |
| 26 | 09 | Henry Tattersdale | Kettering Amateur CC | 318.37 |
| 27 | 24 | Mark Brooking (T) | Willesden CC | 318.26 |
| 28 | 44 | James King | Truro CC | 313.87 |
| 29 | 38 | Paul Ward | Mersey Roads Club | 293.08 |
| 30 | 19 | Andrew Davidson | Gatwick Cycling Team | 275.99 |

T = Tricycle rider. L = Lady rider.

## Team Event - Result

**Derby Mercury Road Club 1188.86 miles.**

**(David Howes, Jim Hopper, David McGeachie-Clarke)**

## Mersey National 1997

| Place. | No. | Name | Club | 95.7 mil | 12hrs | 24hrs | |
|---|---|---|---|---|---|---|---|
| 1. | 65 | Andrew Wilkinson | Adidas-SciCon | 4.09.30 | 268.05 | 525.07 | ✳ |
| 2. | 50 | Brian Walker | G. S. Metro | 4.17.48 | 255.02 | 483.33 | |
| 3. | 60 | Gethin Butler | Norwood Paragon C. C. | 4.03.58 | 264.19 | 472.55 | |
| 4. | 68 | Stephen Marchant | South Eastern R.C. | 4.09.01 | 248.51 | 467.18 | |
| 5. | 69 | Paul Costain | Port Sunlight Whs. | 4.41.19 | 248.75 | 458.47 | |
| 6. | 45 | Karl Austin | Congleton C. C. | 4.25.35 | 235.09 | 443.77 | |
| 7. | 56 | Chris Mullin | Weaver Valley C. C. | 4.27.11 | 235.70 | 443.35 | |
| 8. | 47 | Edwin Hargraves | Cardiff 100 Miles R. C. | 4.41.13 | 234.04 | 440.89 | |
| 9. | 37 | Simon Pedley | Derby Mercury R. C | 4.31.05 | 228.26 | 432.18 | |
| 10. | 67 | Adrian Pudsey | Hereford & Dist. Whs | 4.32.31 | 228.48 | 428.12 | |
| 11. | 33 | Stephen Lau | Surrey Cycle Racing Lg | 4.50.08 | 224.36 | 426.20 | |
| 12. | 52 | Lynne Taylor | Walsall Roads C. C. | 4.45.01 | 223.01 | 418.08 | |
| 13. | 61 | Steven Abraham | Lampard Road Club | 5.03.31 | 218.18 | 417.76 | |
| 14. | 53 | Tony Glover | G. S. Metro | 4.51.46 | 216.70 | 416.46 | |
| 15. | 63 | Kevin Aitken | South Pennine R. C. | 4.38.58 | 231.01 | 415.67 | |
| 16. | 35 | Hugh Canning | Walsall Roads C. C. | 4.56.30 | 218.76 | 413.11 | |
| 17. | 44 | John Streets | Scarborough Paragon | 4.48.16 | 213.34 | 406.87 | |
| 18. | 64 | Steven Roach | Norwood Paragon C. C. | 4.26.21 | 218.61 | 403.49 | |
| 19. | 48 | Tim Dolphin | North Road C.C. | 5.05.52 | 204.29 | 400.31 | |
| 20. | 30 | Jim Hopper (Tri) | Derby Mercury R. C. | 5.07.58 | 208.70 | 397.15 | |
| 21. | 27 | John Pugh | Godric Cycling Club | 5.07.24 | 209.19 | 395.33 | |
| 22. | 38 | Kevin Langham | Leicester Forest C. C. | 5.06.13 | 205.48 | 392.91 | |
| 23. | 51 | Ross Bartlett | Norwood Paragon C. C. | 5.02.46 | 194.69 | 390.44 | |
| 24. | 49 | Alan Sutton | Elgin Cycling Club | 4.47.07 | 214.76 | 383.27 | |
| 25. | 42 | David Gray | Glasgow United C. C. | 4.56.41 | 203.65 | 378.96 | |
| 26. | 20 | Harold Heyworth | Derby Mercury R. C. | 5.04.55 | 206.01 | 376.58 | |
| 27. | 23 | Michael Froggatt | Swindon Road Club | 5.17.31 | 196.27 | 371.57 | |
| 28. | 41 | Graham Young | Mercia Cycling Club | 5.23.21 | 196.70 | 370.18 | |
| 29. | 40 | Jon Jennings | Norwood Paragon C. C. | 4.48.48 | 197.74 | 368.32 | |
| 30. | 34 | Alf Short | Wigan Whls C. & A. C. | 5.32.21 | 187.59 | 362.19 | |
| 31. | 25 | George Berwick | Edinburgh Road Club | 5.46.23 | 187.24 | 355.85 | |
| 32. | 22 | Brian Richards (T) | Thanet Road Club | 5.44.05 | 183.41 | 348.81 | |
| 33. | 15 | Yvonne Unsworth | Southport C. C. | 5.28.33 | 190.33 | 341.75 | |
| 34. | 26 | Richard Corcoran | Rutland Cycling Club | 5.45.48 | 175.84 | 334.87 | |
| 35. | 31 | Ernest Mackey | Medway Velo | 5.37.45 | 173.54 | 333.51 | |
| 36. | 10 | Mike Gowers (Tri) | Ford Cycling Club | 5.23.10 | 162.29 | 285.95 | |

### TANDEM

| | | | | | | | |
|---|---|---|---|---|---|---|---|
| 1. | 1 | Stephen Light | Mersey Roads Club | - | 112.16 | 231.88 | |
| | | Paul Ward | Mersey Roads Club | | | | |

| 1ST TEAM | | 2ND TEAM | |
|---|---|---|---|
| Norwood Paragon C. C. | | Derby Mercury R. C | |
| Gethin Butler | 472.55 miles | Simon Pedley | 432.18 miles |
| Steven Roach | 403.49 miles | Jim Hopper | 397.15 miles |
| Ross Bartlett | 390.44 miles | Harold Heyworth | 376.58 miles |
| TOTAL | 1266.48 miles | TOTAL | 1205.91 miles |

* comp record

North Road National 1998 (100th anniversary)

| POS | No. | NAME | | CLUB | DISTANCE |
|---|---|---|---|---|---|
| 1 | 55 | Ian Butcher | | Team Sanjan Design | 501.31 |
| 2 | 40 | Paul Holdsworth | (N) | Hounslow & Dist Whls | 476.51 |
| 3 | 45 | Rob Richardson | (N) | Hounslow & Dist Whls | 459.50 |
| 4 | 60 | Marc Cunnington | | Hounslow & Dist Whls | 438.93 |
| 5 | 56 | Ken Baker | | Colchester Rovers C. C. | 420.01 |
| 6 | 41 | John Pugh | | Godric C. C. | 414.21 |
| 7 | 54 | Gordon Hart | | Icknield R. C. | 410.31 |
| 8 | 15 | David Mackey | (N) | San Fairy Ann C. C. | 407.94 |
| 9 | 6 | Kevin Langham | | Leicester Forest C. C. | 404.22 |
| 10 | 52 | Charlie Bruce | | Medway Velo Club | 401.61 |
| 11 | 36 | Richard Griffin | | Crawley Whls | 400.40 |
| 12 | 42 | Michael Bloom | | Crawley Whls | 393.71 |
| 13 | 21 | John Baines | | Elmet C. R. C. | 393.04 |
| 14 | 58 | Steve Abraham | | North Bucks R. C. | 390.07 |
| 15 | 5 | Jim Hopper | (I) | Derby Mercury R. C. | 389.99 |
| 16 | 24 | Tim Dolphin | | North Road C. C. | 388.79 |
| 17 | 12 | David Solomon | | Whitewebbs C. C. | 386.18 |
| 18 | 46 | Simon Pedley | | Derby Mercury R. C | 385.62 |
| 19 | 11 | John Heseltine | (N) | Stourbridge C. C. | 384.34 |
| 20 | 16 | Steve Sayers | | Cleveleys R. C. | 383.70 |
| 21 | 57 | Alan Pedliham | (N) | Willesden C. C. | 377.11 |
| 22 | 53 | Ian Kellaway | (N) | Coventry C. C. | 375.67 |
| 23 | 49 | Jeanette DeGiorgio | (LN) | Shaftesbury C. C. | 373.31 |
| 24 | 26 | Peter Lowe | (N) | San Fairy Ann C. C. | 371.35 |
| 25 | 48 | Damon Peacock | (N) | Central Lancashire R. C | 370.35 |
| 26 | 17 | Robert Franks | (N) | Stourbridge C. C. | 369.68 |
| 27 | 38 | George Berwick | | Edinburgh R. C. | 366.05 |
| 28 | 3 | Ron Gager | | Crawley Whls | 345.85 |
| 29 | 2 | David Steer | (N) | South Eastern R. C. | 341.91 |
| 30 | 7 | Chris Vessey | (N) | Hounslow & Dist Whls | 341.27 |
| 31 | 14 | Ian Simmonds | (N) | East Anglian C. C. | 340.08 |
| 32 | 32 | Harold Heyworth | (T) | Derby Mercury R. C. | 338.18 |
| 33 | 31 | John Lee | (N) | Icknield R. C. | 332.30 |
| 34 | 29 | Ernie Mackey | | Medway Velo Club | 328.44 |
| 35 | 39 | Gail Summerlin | (LN) | Leicestershire R. C. | 327.68 |
| 36 | 1 | George Arnot | (T) | North Road C. C. | 320.13 |
| 37 | 22 | Janet Lowe | (LN) | San Fairy Ann C. C. | 313.40 |
| 38 | 4 | Mike Gowers | (T) | Ford C. C. | 274.44 |
| 39 | 34 | Paul Ward | | Mersey Roads Club | 270.08 |

| | | | | | |
|---|---|---|---|---|---|
| 1 | 65 | Peter Holland | (TT) | Southborough & Dist Whls | |
| | 66 | Brian Richards | (TT) | C. C. Bexley | 390.84 |
| 2 | 61 | Jim Staines | (TT) | Mildenhall C. C. | |
| | 62 | Vera Staines | (TT) | Mildenhall C. C. | 298.15 |

## TEAM

| | | |
|---|---|---|
| 1st Team | Hounslow & District WHS | 1,374.94 miles |

Engraved Glassware & N. R. Silver Plated Medal 1,139.96

| | | |
|---|---|---|
| 2nd Team | Crawley Wheelers | 1,139.96 miles |

N. R. Bronze Medals

## Brighton Mitre National 1999

| Pos. | No. | Name | Club | 100 Mls H.M. | 12hrs (Est) Mls | FINAL 24 hr |
|------|-----|------|------|------|------|------|
| 1 | 45 | Dave SHEPHERD | Rother Valley CC | 4.36 | 251.7 | 483.917 |
| 2 | 40 | Andy PAYNE | G.S.Stella | 4.29 | 245.5 | 474.157 |
| 3 | 50 | Andy COOK | Chippenham & District Whs | 4.44 | 232.8 | 455.639 |
| 4 | 60 | Nick Gardiner | Mid Oxon. CRT | 4.31 | 248.9 | 444.895 |
| 5 | 52 | Chris Martin | Lewes Wanderers CC | 4.46 | 231.7 | 438.173 |
| 6 | 56 | Chris Shepherd | Rother Valley CC | 4.49 | 235.1 | 433.354 |
| 7 | 41 | John Pugh | Godric CC | 5.05 | 229.9 | 429.973 |
| 8 | 46 | Paul Cribb | Bognor Regis CC | 4.46 | 228.0 | 429.115 |
| 9 | 63 | Bob Buchanan | Bec CC | 5.00 | 221.3 | 428.396 |
| 10 | 10 | James Reynolds | Maldon & District CC | 5.01 | 223.2 | 427.473 |
| 11 | 15 | David Nash | Crawley Wheelers | 5.13 | 213.9 | 416.950 |
| 12 | 38 | Richard Griffin | Crawley Wheelers | 5.16 | 212.8 | 411.055 |
| 13 | 54 | Steve Abraham | North Bucks RC | 5.06 | 219.9 | 410.186 |
| 14 | 27 | David Steer | South Eastern RC | 4.54 | 220.8 | 403.943 |
| 15 | 17 | Tony Gale | Lewes Wanderers CC | 5.24 | 207.3 | 399.740 |
| 16 | 35 | Marc Cunnington | Hounslow & District Whs. | 5.05 | 209.9 | 386.048 |
| 17 | 62 | Kevin Langham | Leicester Forest CC | 5.06 | 213.5 | 380.402 |
| 18 | 30 | Roger Sewell | Hounslow & District Whs. | 4.55 | 206.0 | 379.299 |
| 19 | 53 | Julian Rickard | Epsom CC | 5.27 | 200.2 | 376.248 |
| 20 | 20 | Tim Dolphin | North Road CC | 5.37 | 193.4 | 369.709 |
| 21 | 14 | Peter Lowe | San Fairy Ann CC | 5.28 | 197.0 | 369.530 |
| 22 | 23 | Jim Thomas | Prescot Eagle RC | 5.31 | 199.0 | 367.927 |
| 23 | 51 | Adam Wankowski | Stowmarket & District CC | 5.22 | 198.7 | 367.924 |
| 24 | 49 | Stewart Bond | Preston Wheelers | 5.34 | 201.3 | 366.591 |
| 25 | 43 | Julian Gee | Sotonia CC | 5.23 | 196.5 | 362.364 |
| 26 | 29 | Michael Friday | Catford CC | 5.43 | 194.0 | 359.731 |
| 27 | 26(W) | Annemarie Manley | Bournemouth Jubilee Whs. | 5.52 | 191.5 | 359.652 |
| 28 | 37 | George Berwick | Edinburgh RC | 5.40 | 188.4 | 358.907 |
| 29 | 33 | Jay Chisnall | Brighton Mitre CC | 5.33 | 191.5 | 353.878 |
| 30 | 3(W) | Janet Lowe | San Fairy Ann CC | 5.58 | 190.5 | 353.403 |
| 31 | 24 | Trevor Rush | Bognor Regis CC | 5.56 | 196.8 | 348.531 |
| 32 | 13 | David Palmer | Bognor Regis CC | 5.49 | 190.5 | 348.155 |
| 33 | 34 | Keith Balcombe | Brighton Excelsior CC | 6.01 | 179.0 | 343.415 |
| 34 | 16(T) | Peter Holland | Southborough & District Whs | 5.58 | 185.0 | 342.526 |
| 35 | 21 | Chris Vessey | Hounslow & District Whs | 5.56 | 175.8 | 321.968 |
| 36 | 8 | John Manville | Brighton Mitre CC | 5.40* | 146.0 | 302.337 |
| 37 | 4(T) | Mike Gowers | Ford CC | 6.08* | 160.7 | 294.412 |

```
         T E A M    R E S U L T
(1st)  Bognor Regis C.C  ( 46, 24, 13 )  =  1125.801 miles
(2nd)  Hounslow & Dist Wh.( 35, 30, 21 )  =  1087.315 miles
```

## Mersey National 2000

| Name | Club | | 100mls | 12hrs | 24hrs | Age |
|------|------|--|--------|-------|-------|-----|
| 1 .G.Butler | Preston Whs. | | 4:15:52 | 270.31 | 509.25 | 31 |
| 2. S.Edwards | Rhondda V.CC. | | 4.31.48 | 252.91 | 487.70 | 37 |
| 3. D.Shepherd | Rother V.CC. | | 4.34.57 | 249.95 | 481.52 | 39 |
| 4. R.Townsend | Halifax RC | | 4.13.26 | 261.70 | 476.97 | 30 |
| 5 M.Botteley | Letchworth V.C. | | 4.37.29 | 241.23 | 461.46 | 33 |
| 6. N.Farr | Mid Shrops.Whs. | | 4.48.33 | 236.87 | 455.59 | 45 |
| 7. K.Austin | Congleton CC | | 4.33.04 | 242.55 | 453.50 | 36 |
| 8. G.Jones | Wrexham R.C. | | 4.43.28 | 236.70 | 444.33 | 54 |
| 9. M.Smith | Maldon & Dis.CC | | 4.47.48 | 234.19 | 434.45 | 41 |
| 10. Lynne Taylor | Walsall R.C.C. | | 4.39.13 | 230.50 | 433.68 | 31 |
| 11. C.Williams | Hereford & D.Whs. | | 4.59.57 | 226.43 | 429.08 | 34 |
| 12. N.Stewart | Wigan Whs.C&AC | | 4.48.05 | 221.42 | 428.02 | 35 |
| 13. A.Rhodes-Paterson | Congleton C.C | | 4.44.25 | 231.62 | 422.60 | 31 |
| 14. A.Tout | Cardiff Byways RCC | | 4.58.12 | 216.80 | 420.27 | 35 |
| 15. G.Knight | Macclesfield Whs | | 4.47.28 | 224.25 | 413.38 | 42 |
| 16. J.Froggatt | Dukinfield C.C. | | 4,52.25 | 225.01 | 412.38 | 31 |
| 17. D.Lewis | Cardiff BywaysRCC | | 4.57.01 | 217.28 | 411.64 | 44 |
| 18. C.Hughes | Hereford & D.Whs. | | 5.09.10 | 219.77 | 409.27 | 40 |
| 19. S.Abraham | North Bucks RC | | 5.18.42 | 204.25 | 406.90 | 25 |
| 20. C.Knapp | Middridge CRT | | 4.45.54 | 218.58 | 404.10 | 40 |
| 21. K.Langham | Leicester Forest CC | | 4.56.58 | 215.05 | 403.63 | 39 |
| 22. P.CooK | Derwentside CC | | 4.49.18 | 223.11 | 398.90 | 38 |
| 23. J.Hopper | Derby Mercury RC | | 5,09.52 | 215.06 | 398.71 | 58 |
| 24. M.Philipson | Derwentside CC | | 5.10.30 | 215.35 | 397.28 | 36 |
| 25. R.Beverly-Smith | Hereford D.Whs | | 5.22.05 | 204.62 | 393.07 | 30 |
| 26. D.Peacock | Central Lancs RC | | 5.15.55 | 208.14 | 390.58 | 41 |
| 27. D.Edwards | Walsall R.C.C. | | 4.59.12 | 215.35 | 380.60 | 50 |
| 28. I.Kellaway | Coventry C.C. | | 5.28.22 | 194.22 | 375.83 | 40 |
| 29. J.W.Taylor | Walsall R.C.C. | | 5.29.52 | 199.08 | 371.62 | 56 |
| 30. B.Bailey | Seamons C.C | | 5.35.25 | 199.97 | 370.19 | 63 |
| 31. G.Shepherd | Fife Century RC | | 5.26.43 | 2.02.62 | 369.71 | 47 |
| 32. M.Daly | B,head NECC | | 5.39.24 | 199.82 | 368.14 | 61 |
| 33. G.Berwick | Edinburgh RC | | 5.43.30 | 193.15 | 367.55 | 59 |
| 34. A.Wankowski | Stowmarket DCC | | 5.23.13 | 192.99 | 363.60 | 48 |
| 35. R.Waghorn | Congleton CC | | 5.17.57 | 199.48 | 360.12 | 54 |
| 36. J.Trott | Camel Valley T.C.C | | 5.10.31 | 200.65 | 359.15 | 33 |
| 37. N.Wood | Coventry C.C. | | 5.42.43 | 196.22 | 350.76 | 68 |
| 38. T.Bailey | Chester R.C. | | 5.54.34 | 187.39 | 350.49 | 47 |
| 39. B.Bottomley | West Bromwich RC | | 5.48.57 | 191.26 | 349.45 | 30 |
| 40. B.Loader | Sydenham Whs | | 5.47.51 | 179.71 | 348.42 | 67 |
| 41. R.Brown | Stockport Clarion | | 5.26.59 | 204.62 | 347.64 | 24 |
| 42. D.Stokes | Johnstone Whs | | 6.11.12 | 179.70 | 347.33 | 56 |
| 43. F.Laussman | Coventry CC | | 4.41.56 | 218.24 | 339.14 | 41 |
| 44. T.Walne | ST Budeaux CC | | detoured | 182.90 | 339.01 | 45 |
| 45. Sharon Clifford | Coventry RC | | 6.00.09 | 181.04 | 337.70 | 40 |
| 46. J.Taylor | Derwentside CC | | 5.41.08 | 186.54 | 337.27 | 35 |
| 47. G.Catherall | Anfield BC | | 6.06.37 | 179.88 | 336.29 | 26 |
| 48. I.Miesen | Willesden CC | | 5.45.25 | 176.69 | 328.77 | 32 |
| 49. C.Vessey | Hounslow Dis; Wh. | | 6.25.32 | 185.87 | 321.00 | 56 |
| 50. Heather Swift | Central Lancs | | 6.32.31 | 161.57 | 312.29 | 43 |
| 51. J.Briggs | De Laune CC | | detoured | 172.59 | 311.35 | 35 |
| 52. M.Gowers | Ford CC | | 6.21.02 | 165.23 | 301.32 | 60 |
| 53. D.Barry | VTTA Birmingham | | 6.21.02 | 170.92 | 300.95 | 51 |
| 54. P.Ward | Mersey RC | | detoured | 139.99 | 253.40 | 35 |

| Tandem | | | | | | |
|------|------|--|--------|-------|-------|-----|
| D & E.Brabbin | Wigan Whs | | 4.37.47 | 239.42 | 406.51 | 43 |

Winning Team: Congleton C.C. K.Austin = 453.50, A.Rhodes-Paterson = 422.60, R.Waghorn = 360.12,
Total = 1236.22.

Winning V.T.T.A. Team: Coventry C.C. N.Wood = +31.85, I.Kellaway = -17.92, F.Laussman = -54.61,
Total = - 40.68.

As they started away again Andy was shivering almost uncontrollably and it's thought that a touch of sunstroke could have been the reason. By 7am they were climbing Shap. They reached 2 miles north of Shap Village at 8am, so giving them 444 miles for their first 24 hours, and they were over 3 hours down on a schedule to beat the mens tandem record held by Swinden & Withers with 2days 2hrs 14mins.

By 12.51pm they had reached Moffat 510 miles; they climbed the 'Devils Beeftub' magnificently and once over the top, Andy and Lynne picked up a helpful wind. John Williams who had been the 'back-room' Organiser of this attempt had advised the 'on-road' team Organiser Jim Turner, to implement a slower schedule just based on beating the mixed tandem Groesbeck/Harris record. This put them back up on a more realistic schedule and target.

The Forth Road Bridge saw Andy looking very tired and a sleep was called for. He was also worrying about the hills that lay ahead such as the Grampians. Once refreshed, the riders continued to Perth where another break was taken. By 8.14pm they were back on the road to BlairAthol at 640 miles. They now had 200 miles left to ride and 19 hours to do it in. It was a cold night in the Grampians but without much wind. Andy was very tired but they eventually reached Inverness at 4.42am with 720 miles covered. The tandem had reached 60 mph on the last descent.

Another stop for sleep was taken, Andy was as usual under a huge pile of blankets trying to keep warm, and it was here that Jim and Paul told me that Andy is often affected in this way when he is on the brink of exhaustion! They now had 120 miles to cover as they climbed away from Inverness via the Kessock Bridge. Lynne commented to Andy that it would only be like riding the Shenstone 200K Audax, a journey they had covered just prior to this attempt.

Hugh Canning who was driving the support van commented "Lynne still amazingly fresh – Wilko 'man of steel' feeling dreadful but hopefully pushing on." The phrase 'running on empty' was used on this occasion to describe Andy's resilience. By 8.11am, Helmsdale had been climbed after just 48 hours of riding. At 9.07am Berriedale was topped with 796 miles ridden and 44 to do. Wick was reached at 10.28 with 17 miles to go, Lynne was feeling very sore underneath but otherwise OK. Andy freewheeled on the downhill sections to ease the pain on her backside.

At last, 11.19am and John o' Groats was reached in **2 days 3hrs 19mins 23 seconds.** A five hour beating of the old record!

For Andy it was one 'End to End' too many, or too far, but at least it had given Lynne her first viewing of the route she would use on her solo attempts, and I think it gave her great confidence for her future rides. Apart from being sore in the saddle area she was otherwise in good shape and didn't appear phased by her 51 hour journey.

This record, apart from being the first of the new Century, was also the forerunner to a rash of End to End and 1,000 mile records akin to the heady days of 1982 when three End to Ends were broken in less than 3 weeks.

⟫═⟩◆⟨═⟪

Later, on 29th and 30th July 2000, **The Mersey RC National Championship 24hr was won by Gethin Butler with 509.25 miles, Stephen Edwards, Rhondda Valley CC was 2nd with 487.70 miles and David Shepherd, Rother Valley CC with 481.52 was 3rd. Lynne Taylor, Walsall Roads CC was the fastest lady with 433.68 miles. Karl Austin who was 7th overall, with 453.5 miles, led Adrian Rhodes-Patterson and Rob Waghorn, to a Congleton CC Championship team win of 1,236.22 miles.**

The weather for the event as I recall was generally very good, except for a cloudburst at the start, which flooded the road between Farndon and Broxton. I can recall pedalling through ankle deep water and then climbing from Broxton Island on roads that were steaming in the mid afternoon heat. I had decided, unwisely, to make a comeback at 56 years of age, to try and help the Walsall RCC to win the team race, along with Lynne and Dave Edwards. I say unwisely because despite all of the advice I usually give to other people as to training and being fit enough for a 24hr race, I thought I could manage with just 6 months training, which included a 100 mile time trial and a couple of training rides over 100 miles, the result being 371.6 miles. I then felt rough and very lethargic for 6 months or more, but then I suppose I was lucky in as much as I recognised the symptoms of overdoing it, and didn't try to do any more events that year. The team aspired to 3rd place behind the Congleton CC and the Hereford and District Whls CC, but at least we broke the Walsall RCC club record that had been established in this very same event some 50 years previously, by Sid Genders, Bill Perrett and Bill Bradley. Lynne and I became the first father and daughter to finish in the same 24hr race.

But enough said about me, and again I use Frank Mumfords words to describe this first event of the new century. Frank said that the weather was reasonable after the cloudburst, with a light and variable wind, a cold night with some mist, and then a sunny Sunday with another cooling shower on the finishing circuit. There were only 3 non-starters from an entry of 67. No '500 milers' had entered, Edwards and Townsend were known only for their 12hour performances. Eileen and David Brabbin were on a tandem, they rode 406.5 miles and Dave confessed to being the weak link by lack of training.

At the 100 mile point, eleven riders were inside 4hrs 46mins as follows, Townsend, 4hrs 13mins, Butler at 2mins, Edwards at 18m, Austin at 20m, Shepherd at 21m, Botteley, 24m, Lynne 26m, Laussman 28m, Jones at 30mins, Patterson 31m and Knapp 32mins.

Butler had scythed through the field in warding off Rob Townsend who'd set off like a released spring, catching Nigel Farr, Steve Edwards and Dave Shepherd, but by 133 miles, Townsend was tiring, compounded by wheel and lamp trouble, this probably robbed him of 3rd place as his helpers weren't at hand. Lynne caught Knapp at 12 miles and he didn't lose sight of her till 75 miles. She caught Gerry Jones at 100 miles and then he raised his tempo at 133 miles and repassed her to escape to an 11 miles advantage at the finish. 1999 event winner Austin, off last man, struggled to try and catch anybody in the early stages of the race, but his 4hr 33mins first 100 and his 242.5 miles 12 hours put him 5th overall at the halfway stage, but having only a 91" fixed gear to push he struggled to raise his pace in the 2nd 12 hours and covered only 211 miles.

At 12 hours Butler had covered 270 miles, which I think is one of the greatest mileages ever for the first half of a 24hr race. Townsend was still challenging him with 261 miles while Edwards had 252 miles and Shepherd 249m, but they were about to lift their pace. Lynne Taylor, the fastest lady, was suffering with 230 miles ridden, but helper Wilko was at hand to administer T.L.C.

As the dawn broke and the run rose to fire the riders up for the last 6 hours or more, the riders were finishing the Shropshire circuits and looking forward to heading north to the finishing circuit. The first rider to get to the finishing circuit was Steve Edwards, who incidentally had the fastest time for the 16.8 mile stretch from Prees to Handley, of 46 minutes. He got there at 10.48am with time to complete 5 laps of this 14.9 miles circuit, as did Butler, Shepherd, Jones, Lynne, Abrahams, Williams and Tout. Once on the circuit, Gethin Butler rode the fastest lap in 41 mins, equalling Wilko's 1997 record.

**Jim Hopper was again the fastest trike and the fastest Vet with 398.71 miles.** Lynne took the Turner cup, for winning the Merseyside Ladies CA event, for the 6th year running. Sharon Clifford rode 337.70 miles and Heather Swift, 312.29 miles.

Roy Cromack had been out to check on the riders progress during the event and noted that Gethin had covered an extra 26 miles, over the full course of 405 miles, to everyone else.

Gethin looked disinterested on the circuit and only raised his pace when he realised that the old 507 mile record was slipping away from him. Roy thought that Rob Townsend had disappeared during the night, but he duly appeared and ploughed round the circuit looking quite strong. It turned out that his main helper had cleared off during the night, taking much of his food and warm clothing with him. This, compounded by wheel and lighting problems, left Rob with 4th place. Roy chatted to Wilko on the circuit, full of 'bounce' as ever but admitting that the tandem End to End had not been the best two days of his life!

Ned Millington, the current Editor of the 24hr Fellowship Journal, wrote an introductory article in October's edition and I've taken one or two poignant observations from it. "Many people expressed surprise that Gethin Butler would ever ride another 24hr, but he proved us wrong. Possibly the key was simply that, at whatever cost, he did actually finish in 1997, and so could rationalise the result until he felt he owed himself a ride that would do justice to his ability. The first ride could now be looked back on as a marker – a positive achievement in fact, as he was no longer in uncharted territory and could put his bad experience to good use. Had he not finished in 1997, I'm certain the psychological barrier of coming back would have been insurmountable.

The absence of Wilko must have entered into his mind-set, but there were other very good contenders to reckon with, if he got it wrong again, defending Champion, David Shepherd, last years winner Karl Austin, Stephen Edwards, and Rob Townsend. Although Butler finished well ahead, he was pushed hard in the first 12 hours by Rob Townsend."

At the award ceremony, Gethin revealed that his granddad, Stan Butler, had won the National Championship just 50 years ago with 458 miles on what now would be considered very low-tech equipment. This mileage would today have gained him 6th place.

Jim Turner was duly thanked for his 13 years of outstanding service as Promoter, Secretary and Organiser of the event, along with Anne, his wife, who promised to carry on as treasurer for the event.

Jim's reply and comments were *"I would like to thank all the people who have been involved in any way in this remarkable feat of endurance for the past 13 years. I have made so many friends during this time who have either ridden the event or helped out in so many ways and given up so much of their time, and contributions to the subscription fund. I feel very lucky to have been associated with such quality people. The job has been difficult, but without your support it would have been impossible.*

*My congratulations to Gethin on a wonderful ride, which goes into the record books as the 2nd best distance of all time, a truly great rider, and a worthy winner of the Brazendale cup. He said he would be back and he did it in style, well done!*

*Congratulations also to Stephen Edwards of the Rhondda Valley in his first 24hr, a truly great and classic rider and past champion, David Shepherd, who also had a good ride in 3rd place, we would like you both to come back and ride next year.*

*Our tandem pair winners, David and Eileen Brabbin, are very capable of getting that record of Bridget and Ian Boons'. They will be back, you can count on it! My congratulations to all the other finishers, you are a credit to the cycling game. Also my sincere thanks to all the Officials, I hope you will all give the same support to Doug Clark who will be in charge for next year's event.*

*My final thanks go to the sub-committee and feeding team, you have all been a credit to the event and a lot of riders pass on their thanks."*

With the sad demise of the North Road 24hr this left the Mersey RC as the sole promoters of a 24hr National Championship time trial. It has been and always was an excellent event and to this day remains as **'THE'** 24 hour.

Although Jim Turner had officially retired, he still remained in the background to help Doug Clark with his onerous task of running a 24 hour. Jim had already been instrumental in many riders successes either in time trials or road records and this new found leisure time gave him chance to help plan a few riders almost immediate futures.

## 2001

*On February 11th 2001, Ellen MacArthur finished in 2nd place in the Vendees Globe Yacht race, taking 94 days.*

*On February 20th 2001, 'Foot and Mouth' broke out for the first time in 20 years, causing transport movement restrictions around the country. Millions of animals had to be destroyed.*

The Mersey RC National Championship 24 hour held on 28th and 29th July 2001 was won by Gethin Butler with 485.88 miles. Tim Bayley, Arctic Racing Team was 2nd with 469.82 and Chris Shepherd, Rother Valley CC was 3rd with 462.99 miles. Tim Bayley led Andy Proffitt and Damian Coleman to an Arctic RT Championship team win of 1,268.52 miles. Lynne Taylor was again the fastest lady with 423.13 miles and Jim Hopper was the fastest trike rider with 408.56 miles, but looking at the results I see that M. Smith, Maldon CC also on a trike pushed him to within 1.4 miles with 407.17 m. Jim Hopper took the Vets award.

Chris Shepherd, who came 3rd, is David's brother, so at least he was helping to keep the family name held high. Tim Bayley who came 2nd was an unknown quantity as a 'novice' rider, but proved himself well, and Gethin Butler was possibly, like Lynne, saving a little bit of energy back for his forthcoming End to End, but in all seriousness, I think the unremitting heat during the event, put paid to many riders hopes of beating their recent personal bests. Saturday pm was very hot, the night was mild but dark, and Sunday was again very hot, relieved only by a rising north west breeze late in the event, which hindered the riders return to the finishing circuit.

The tandem ride of Eileen and David Brabbin was probably one of the only success stories of the day, with a 33mile personal best of 439.54 miles, taking them ever closer to the Boon's record.

At the 83.8 mile turn, Gethin was the fastest with 3hrs 31 mins and 2nd fastest was Chris Hopkinson, Matlock CC at 16 mins, Tim Bayley was 3rd at 18 mins. With the course now utilising circuits, it was difficult to get a clear picture of rider's intermediate performances during the event. At 237 miles, Butler was first on the road in 11hrs 7mins with Chris Shepherd at 1 minute.

By the early morning Butler had a clear lead and reached the finishing circuit first at 11.01am, having taken 49 mins for the 16.8 mile stretch into the wind to get there. Although Hopkinson had ridden it in 46 minutes, he still finished in 6th position with 440.93miles. Many of the first 11 riders had very respectable finishing circuit laptimes, i.e. Ginty 49mins, Proffitt 48min, Shepherd 50m, Botteley and Hopkinson 52m, but they had all lost too much time during the event, probably from the heat, for it to make much difference. Karl Austin's lap of 89 minutes reflects the off-colour ride he had, to finish with 411 miles, some 42 miles slower than his previous years ride.

Surprisingly the entry of 44 was the lowest recorded for a Mersey RC hosted RTTC National Championship since the mid 1960's. Possibly the juxtaposition of the Isle of Man week and Audax UK's London-Edinburgh-London 884 mile ride in the week leading up to the Mersey had siphoned-off some riders. Incidentally 'AUK' distance legends, Abraham and Berwick had just finished the 'L.E.L.' while Butler and Shepherd had ridden the subsidiary 520 mile event, what heroes! George Berwick also completed his 27th Mersey event and his 40th in total. Sadly, one of the Mersey 24hr regulars Kevin Langham was no longer with us. He'd passed away while just riding his bike and was found at the roadside earlier in the year.

Andy Wilkinson had helped Lynne to her 7th consecutive win, and he spent a nostalgic few minutes before the event in such company as John Arnold, Nim Carline, Nick Carter, Al Mansley, Mick Potts, Les Lowe, Edwin Hargraves and Johnny Helms. New Organiser, Doug Clark and his wife Doris were very much in control while Jim Turner was seeing to last minute duties as Chief Marshall.

⇒◇⇐

Three weeks later on 21st August, Ralph Dadswell and Marina Bloom were opposite the Rowland Hill statue in King Edward Street at 6.32 am. Albert Ayton, the timekeeper sent them on their way to attack the 'mixed' tandem trike RRA record 'standards' for the London to York – York to Edinburgh – 12 hours – London to Edinburgh and finally the 24hr. They achieved all five records in one ride. The London to York in 8hrs 56mins 4secs, the 12 hour with 265 miles, the York to Edinburgh in 10hrs 44mins and 20 secs and the London to Edinburgh in 19hrs 40mins 40secs. They turned and retraced south at Edinburgh to run out time and break the 24hr record with 451 miles. What an achievement.

Although Ralph had broken many RRA records himself, some 33 in fact, including these five, Marina, despite riding one or two regional RRA records, mainly with Ralph, was virtually unknown at long distance riding. She had a couple of 24hr performances around the 350 mile mark, but from what I recall she had lots of back problems during these events. I feel that this 5 in 1 RRA record with Ralph gave her terrific confidence and from that day in 2001 onwards, she became a force to be reckoned with in all aspects of long distance racing, from 100 miles to 12 hours to 24 hours.

*For a fuller report of this amazing ride, see the* **Ladies History in Chapter 5.**

*On 11th September 2001 a tragedy occurred in America, when Terrorist suicide bombers flew aircraft full of passengers into the top storeys of the Twin Towers Trade Center in New York, causing the towers to collapse. The number of dead has been estimated at 3,000. No one has claimed responsibility, but many believe it is the work of Al Qaeda. With the American way of putting their month before their day, it is now known as* **'9/11' day.**

Just over two weeks later on **26th September 2001, Lynne Taylor,** Walsall RCC, set out from **Lands End** at 8am to attack Pauline Strong's 'End to End' record of 2days 6hrs 49mins 45secs. Lynne, after over 40 hours of rain and very unhelpful conditions throughout her journey, finally reached **John o' Groats in 2days 5hrs 48mins 21secs** and broke Pauline's record by 1hr 10mins. *(for more details see Chapter 5 – Ladies History).*

One day after Lynne started, **Gethin Butler,** rode away from **Lands End** at 10am in much better conditions to attack Andy Wilkinson's 'End to End' record of 1day 21hrs 2mins 18secs. On the way, he added just over 11 miles onto John Woodburn's 24hr record set in 1982 and set a new RRA record of **505.8 miles** by reaching the Beattock bypass. Gethin had the advantage of being able to start 1 day later than Lynne, due to him putting in his notice of intention to attack the record prior to Lynne's notice. This gave him the first choice of date and time to go.

*After reading in Chapter 2 about the closely fought battles between Heppleston and Ferris over the Edinburgh-London and 24hr in 1938 and 1939, where both men were on the road almost within an hour of each other on both occasions, and with the distinct possibility of one catching the other, I wonder just how these attempts had been allowed to take place? In 1938 Charlie Holland actually started on the same route, sandwiched timewise between Heppleston and Ferris. In hindsight I feel that if Lynne had been allowed to start on the same day as Gethin, she would almost certainly have been very close to 2 days for the End to End and 2 days 12 hours for the 1,000 mile record. With as good a wind as Gethin had on that day she may also have snatched the 24hr record on route. As Pat Kenny always says, apart from obviously being fit, record breaking is all about taking chances and having a bit of luck with the wind and conditions, and he should know.*

*But rules are rules, and after all it made 2002 another nail biting year.*

Gethin had warmer, dry conditions with an excellent wind gusting west-south-west at 18mph for the start of his journey through the south west. He reached Filton just north of Bristol with 199 miles covered in 8hrs 24mins. At this point he was 54 mins up on schedule. By the 12 hours point he was just south of Wolverhampton with 279.5 miles covered. He reached his hometown of Preston with approximately 404 miles covered at 4.25am, he'd been on the road just 18hrs 25mins. By Lancaster he was an hour up on schedule, thick mist on Shap made the climb and descent a tricky and dangerous affair, but Gethin was heartened by the numerous clubfolk at the summit to see him through. By Gretna Green, tiredness was taking its toll. He had hoped to get to the top of the Devil's Beeftub for his 24hrs but fell just slightly short.

He climbed the 'Beeftub' in low cloud and got to the top soaked through and cold. Gethin was now racing into the unknown having only ever ridden beyond 24hrs in an audax event. After realising that he'd broken the 24hr record he was daunted at the thought of having another 330 miles to do, plus the remaining mileage if he went on to attack Reg Randall's 1,000 mile record. Gethin admitted at this point to feeling quite depressed and disinterested in racing, he climbed off at the top of the Beeftub and had a rest and some hot Bovril.

Jim Turner, who had organised the record attempt, hovered around Gethin as he lay there, and tried anxiously to coax him back onto his bike. Jim knew that he couldn't afford to lose sight of the record and the urgency required to get going again. Don't forget, Jim had been present at 'Wilko's' record and knew what was required.

Gethin, after a stop that wiped out his 50 minute gain on schedule, got back on the road but felt equally as bad some 40 miles later. He took another 10mins sleep in a bus shelter at Penicuik and that refreshed him, he got beyond the Forth Road Bridge and had a pep talk from Gillian, his wife, and eventually reached Perth. As he left the suburbs to join the lonely A9 he remembered the words Jim Turner had spoken to him at Lands End. **"No one who has got past Perth on one of my attempts has packed or failed!"**

He put his lights on at Pitlochry for his second night and amazingly started to pick up speed and reached Inverness in a happier mood. As Gethin crossed the Black Isle just 2 mins up on schedule, he knew that with the wind coming off the sea, his next 80 miles were going to be his hardest ever, with 3 more climbs to ride.

I was there at John o' Groats at the end of his ride to see him cross the line in **1day 20hrs 4mins & 20secs. He'd beaten 'Wilko's record by nearly 58 minutes.** We had been there since Lynne's arrival the previous day and were quite concerned when Jim had phoned us and said that Gethin had gone through a very bad patch before Edinburgh, that he'd lost all of his gain on schedule and his interest to carry on, but we knew that Jim wouldn't let him give up that easily.

When Gethin arrived at John o' Groats the weather was awful with gusting winds coming off the sea. The air was damp with mist and cold and squally showers at 6am. But after a short break he announced that he was going for the 1,000 mile record with just another 160 miles to cover. Colin Baldwin gave him a massage and with dry clothing on he went on his way at 7.30am. After more breaks for dry clothing and sustenance, **Gethin finally completed his 1,000 mile** journey just before 6pm with a time of **2days 7hrs 59mins.** He had taken 2hours 41 mins off Reg Randall's record from 1960, and had become the first solo male to take the 1,000 mile record and the End to End in one ride since Sid Ferris some 64 years ago.

*For a full report of Lynne's 'End to End' please go to the Ladies History in Chapter 5 or my first book on the history of the End to End – 'The End to End Story'.*

*When reading these reports you realise the importance of riding 24hr events. Both Gethin and Lynne must have gained their confidence for tackling a journey of 840 miles by riding the Mersey events, and you will have noticed that many of their helpers, organisers and officials for these long distance records are to be found doing much the same job at the only annual 24hr epic on Shropshire and Cheshire roads.*

## 2002

The Mersey RC National Championship 24hr 27th and 28th July 2002 was won by David Shepherd, Rother Valley CC with 482.128 miles. Jose Pinon Shaw, Central Lancs RC took 2nd place with 470.044 miles, and 3rd placed Mark Botteley, Fenland Clarion missed a silver medal by less than .5 of a mile with 469.698 miles. Brian Walker who came 6th overall with 453.791 miles led Chris Hopkinson with 396.791m and Steve Gelder 387.271, to a Pete Read Racing Championship team win with 1,237.853 miles.

Lynne Taylor took 9th place overall with **438.042 miles,** but was challenged throughout by Marina Bloom, Crawley Whls, who produced a 427.5 mile ride. Five other ladies finished, Ursula Betterton, Ann Wooldridge, Claire Ashton, Gail Summerlin and Philippa Crocker.

**Eileen and David Brabbin, Wigan Whls, raised Bridget and Ian Boon's mixed tandem competition Record to 464.924 miles.**

With the new RTTC ruling stating that any stretch of road could be used up to 6 times on any calendar day, this meant that the Organisers of the event could now change the course so as to avoid using the busiest roads, and to make the course more compact, so as to require less marshals and checkers. It meant that provided there was a traffic roundabout at both ends of a stretch of road, then the riders could be sent up and down this section of road for up to 6 times in one day, making it a useful method to keep the faster riders never too far away, or ahead of other slower riders. The Quina Brook circuit at teatime Saturday and at dawn Sunday could take the riders off the main road for a while as traffic built up. Work was continuing on the new Hodnet bypass and as such hadn't caused many problems. Finally the stretches of road from Ternhill to Market Drayton and back and also Tern Hill to Pickmere via Newport and return, were both dispensed with.

Frank Mumford mentions in his report that, for legal reasons, the Mersey Roads CC had now abandoned the practice of having running helpers handing up drinks and food, in case riders are brought off accidentally – it's the compensation culture raising its ugly head once again! From now on, riders wanting food and drink at an official feed will have to stop and collect their supplies.

The weather at the start was hot but thankfully not as hot as 2001. After a warm cloudy night with a westerly wind, a rising south-westerly wind next day helped the riders on their way to the finishing circuit. The RTTC Observer was suitably impressed this year by the quality of the riders lights and virtually no exceptions; how things have changed in ten years thanks to Japanese and Chinese technology, and the rapid development of the L.E.D. (light emitting diode). Some of the much brighter headlights i.e. between 10watt and 20watts would have cost a fair amount of money, in fact probably in the region of £200/300 in 2002, with probably the need for a spare back up battery if the 20 watt was used

'Would you care to place your order for your drink at 200 miles?'

for more than a few minutes. But if a rider did a fair amount of night riding then it was well worth the money spent. Isn't it just a pity that Great Britain couldn't produce decent cycle lighting.

With Andy Wilkinson helping Lynne in this event and Gethin having a quietish year after his End to End the previous year, it was felt that a winner could come from any number of riders who had previously and in recent events covered 450 plus. Men such as Steve Edwards, Dave Shepherd, Brian Walker, Mark Botteley, Jose Pinon Shaw, Karl Austin and Chris Hopkinson.

Jim Hopper, although off colour, was looking for his 5th trike win. Lynne Taylor was hoping for her 8th consecutive ladies win, but found stiff opposition from Marina Bloom, who had previously been disappointed with abandonments. Chris Hopkinson was confident that he was fit enough to offer some stiff competition after a spill the previous year had left him requiring a plate and pins to hold a broken leg together. He started off this event most promisingly with the fastest first 100 miles of 4hrs 23mins, only to crash at 170 miles damaging both his plated leg and elbow. After being patched up he insisted on continuing for the sake of the team.

At the calculated 100 mile point, Hopkinson was in the lead with 4hrs 23mins and had left his immediate challengers well behind. Pinon Shaw was at 3mins, Walker at 8mins, Shepherd at 11mins, Edwards and Briggs at 14m, Botteley at 16m, the Brabbins tandem looked to be on for the record with a 4hr 38min 100 mile. Lynne Taylor led Marina at this point by just 4mins with a 4hrs 48mins ride, and Karl Austin settling down in between them (timewise) with 4hrs 50mins.

By the 12hour point the riders were strung out on the 52 mile Prees, Tern Hill, Battlefield, Ternhill and back to Prees, circuit, and two riders were calculated to be level with 251 miles, Shepherd and Pinon Shaw. Others beating 'evens' at this time were, Briggs 244 miles, Tandem 243m, Botteley 242m. Stewart had ridden 236m, O'Donoghue on his way to a new Irish 24hr record, 235m, Walker 233m, Jones 230m, Austin 229m with Lynne and Marina both with 225 miles.

The riders made their way onto the Quina Brook circuit just after dawn and settled down to piling in the miles on rural lanes before the final dash to the finishing circuit later in the morning. Brian Walker was the fastest rider on the stretch between Quina Brook and the finishing circuit, with a time of 36mins for the 13.5 miles. Shepherd and Botteley both rode 39mins, Pinon Shaw, O'Donoghue and the tandem clocked 40 mins. Hopkinson, Stewart and Abraham did 41mins.

Once the finishing circuit was reached it was Walker again who had the fastest time of 38mins, obviously in an effort to make up for his slow first 12hours. Austin had a fast lap of 39mins, not an easy task with the tight bends and steep gradients on a 95" fixed wheel. The Brabbin tandem produced a 40minute lap in a last desperate effort to make up time lost through a puncture and a couple of bad patches. Dave Shepherd, Mark Botteley and Andy Briggs managed a 41minute lap in an effort to consolidate their leading positions.

Lynnes best lap was of 43 minutes compared to Marina's 47mins, and Marina had put up such a brave effort in this event to produce her best ever ride. And that was it, all over for another year, Dave Shepherd rode himself into the ground to hang on and win this event and also take the fastest 'VTTA' Vets award. Jose Pinon Shaw improved 29 miles to take 2nd place by .3 of a mile from Mark Botteley who rode a steadier ride with a first 12hour of 242 miles and a 2nd 12hrs of 227 miles. The tandem pair of Eileen and David Brabbin did succeed in breaking Ian and Bridget Boon's record by over a mile with 464.924 miles. They had been riding a tandem since their marriage some 20 years ago, but it was mainly for leisure and touring purposes. Their first 24hr event in 2000 produced 406 miles, which is incredible considering Eileen's admission that she isn't a real cyclist, as she had never mastered a solo bike. Their next 24hr was a year later in 2001 and despite the very hot conditions which Eileen described as like riding through treacle, they rode 439 miles, even after having over 2 hours off the tandem. Eileen had always helped Dave over the years when he rode solo, and I was always very impressed by the way she managed to find her way round the course and feed him on her own, night and day, but then she is a woman and they can multi-task.

"YOU know I have to relax before a race."

As I mentioned earlier, David Shepherd rode himself into exhaustion and looked completely drained at the finish. He had to be helped from the car at the H.Q. and sat on the step outside trying to recover. He was applauded, congratulated and presented with his cap, jersey, cup and medals while still sprawled on the step. He managed to raise his arm and gave a smile in recognition of his achievements. He later went to hospital where he was kept in overnight for checks until he recovered the next day. Dave's condition at this time sounds to be very similar to Rod Collins' when he came 2nd to Ian Dow in 1987 in the South DC National Championship with 483 miles. The prize presentation had to be completely re-arranged around his chair and Ian Dow said on that occasion that Rod appeared to be in an almost comatosed condition. So when anyone casually says they feel exhausted, I smile to myself and think of these riders at the end of their 24hr ordeal!

On October 1st, 2nd & 3rd 2002, Lynne Taylor broke her own solo bicycle End to End record by 1hour 3mins, giving a new record of 2days, 4hrs, 45m, 11secs,. She then went on to break Eileen Sheridans 48 year old 1,000 mile record by 8hrs 22mins, with 2days 16hours 38mins. On this record Lynne only had favourable conditions from Inverness onwards.

*For a fuller report on these two records go to Chapter 5, year 2002, Ladies History, or find a full End to End and 1,000 mile History in my first book titled "The End to End Story" 100 years of Cycling Records by John Taylor.*

## 2003

*March-April – British Armed Forces join U.S. troops to invade Iraq and topple Saddam Hussein.*

The Mersey RC 60th 24hr also hosted the CTT (Cycling Time Trials) National Championship on 26-27th July and was won by Gethin Butler, Preston Whls, with 471.21miles. Neil stewart, Wigan Whls was 2nd with 456.643 miles and Richard Thoday, Matlock CC was 3rd with 451.356 miles.

**Marina Bloom, Walsall Roads RCC with 413.255 miles, led Lynne Taylor with 411.141 miles and Tracey Maund, 405.305 miles to a new Ladies Competition Team Record and a National Championship Team win with 1,229.70 miles,** beating Gethin Butler's Preston Whls team of Chris Hopkinson and Stewart Bond, into 2nd place, by 3 miles. **They are the first all-woman team to gain such an award in an Open National Championship,** and they added 124.3 miles onto a 27 year old record previously held by Joan Kershaw, Ruth Williams and Amy Hooton of the Prescot Eagle RC.

Jim Hopper was the fastest trike rider with 357 miles.

The closure of the A442 Shawbirch leg and temporary traffic lights at Hodnet on the A53 caused the Organisers to implement a series of changes at the start of the event whereby riders were sent onto the finishing circuit that ran past the HQ and start area. Up to five laps of this circuit was covered which meant climbing quite a steep hill called the 'Cock o' Barton' bank up to five times. After this series of circuits the riders continued to Broxton Island and turned right through to Grindley Brook and Prees in the normal way. The first man on the road at Grindley Brook was the last man to start, No 70, Gethin Butler, at 4.20pm, Chris Hopkinson was at 2 mins. Gethin stayed in the lead after going to Tern Hill and back via Prees, and to the start of the Quina Brook evening circuit at 5.41pm, and Hopkinson was at 9mins.

The first of the women riders on the road at Quina Brook was Marina Bloom at 6.06pm, Lynne was 3mins faster than Marina at this point. Heavy rain just before dusk chilled the riders and it was clear that warm and waterproof clothing would be needed this year. Some of the riders struggled on the section from Prees to Battlefield and back as night fell, with the hills feeling long, hard and never ending.

Lighting was excellent this year with the advances in technology, and the improvement and developement of the front L.E.D. from a lime green or yellow light to a bright bluish white.

Lynne who had been going well earlier had a bad night and was well down on previous performances at the Battlefield check. She had developed a chill even though she had lots of warm clothing on. Lynne's brother Mike and Neil Peart were looking after her this year and as Liz and I drove out to pick up the race at dawn, we found her off the bike and trying to eat and get warm, not far from Prees Green on the A49. Conditions were quite weird along that stretch of road at 5am; we travelled through thick cold wet mist into bright sunshine and then back into mist. Lynne said she had got soaked a few times by heavy rain and couldn't stop being sick.

With just the stretches of road between Tern Hill – Prees and Battlefield in use during the night, it was a lonely plod for a lot of riders. Gethin, however, was eating up the road, he was riding so fast he kept passing through the whole field, and was the only rider sent from Prees to Battlefield for a 5th time at 6.29am. He was back in 1hr 43mins for the 28 miles.

In previous years the riders would have gone from Tern Hill down to Newport and sometimes as far as Pickmere Island at the junction with the A5 near Weston-under-Lizard. Frank Mumford who for the last 40 or more years, had written the race report for the Mersey RC 'Record' and the 24hr Fellowship Journal, always tried to include a little bit of history and 'hear-say' into his reports and one of his favourite stories was of Lady Pigott's ghost being present in the Chetwynd area on the Newport road. She was looking for her murderous husband and wherever she went she left an icy atmosphere. The stretch of road around Chetwynd was prone to pockets of cold mist during the night, and of course anybody susceptible to ghost stories could get a little spooked when passing through the area. There is also another spooky area on that section where it is heavily wooded either side of the road and the high trees almost touch in the middle to form a dark archway or tunnel that runs for about a mile. I've also beaten 'evens' through there a few times! But sadly, Frank has laid down his pen and I now use Bob William's report to form my race history.

Just after 7am the first riders started to enter the 12.5 mile Quina Brook circuit, where the hedges can provide shelter and more warmth than the wide main road. Gethin caught many more tired riders once he got onto the circuit. After 3 laps he was sent north towards the finishing circuit, back through Grindley Brook at 10.15am having passed nine more riders on that stretch. All of the Walsall RCC ladies team were either on the finishing circuit or on their way by 10.37am. The sun was now trying to shine as the riders either 'grovelled' or 'flew' around the last circuits. The road surfaces on these rural lanes are very rough, and being on a circuit, one never seems to get the reward of a bit of downhill after climbing uphill. Although Gethin had an unassailable lead, Neil Stewart, Richard Thoday and Chris Shepherd (David's brother) still had some speed in their legs.

From an entry of 67 solos, 62 started and 47 finished. One Tandem with Mary Corbett and Norman Harvey, Sotonia CC finished with 366.9 miles and one tandem trike with Ursula Beterton and Colin Knapp finished with 268.9 miles.

*Congestion charges for London's motorists were introduced in 2003.*

# 2004

**The Mersey RC National Championship 24hr on the 24th-25th July 2004 was won by Niklaus Gardiner, Time Trial.Co.Uk RT with 479.131 miles, Jose Pinon Shaw was 2nd riding for Preston Whls with 470.799m, and Andy Briggs, Doncaster Whls was 3rd with 460.603 miles.**

**Lynne Taylor was 6th with 443.145 miles and led another successful ladies team of Marina Bloom, 434.062 and Tracey Maund with 415.629m to a Walsall RCC Championship Team win of 1,292.836 miles. They also broke their own Ladies Competition Record. This total also beat the Matlock CC team** consisting of Chris Hopkinson, Richard Thoday and Eric Ruthenberg, by 56 miles.

So for the second year running an all ladies team has beaten a mens team for the National Championship title in this, the toughest endurance race in time trialling.

The weather forecast had shown a low pressure and windy wet weather from the north-west, so the most we could hope for was 'mixed' conditions. The event started off dry, but grey and overcast, and a bit cool if you were marshalling on a drafty corner or island. In fact, most of the marshals I saw were dressed in virtual winter clothing and even gloves, especially in the night.

The tandem with George Shepherd, Mersey RC, and George Berwick, Edinburgh RC, led the field for the first hour or two. They had started at the head of the field along with Norman and Sylvia Powell, Oldbury & District CC, also on a tandem, although the Powells would retire before nightfall. The two 'Georges' eventually finished with a 392mile ride. After a smooth first 100 of 4hrs 59mins they looked very workmanlike during the night but by daylight George Berwick, the 'stoker' looked a little ragged and the tandem wasn't going quite so smoothly.

At Prees Island with 95.5 miles covered the tandem still led the field on the road at 5.33pm but the faster riders were now hammering along. The first of the ladies through was Kathryn Smith at 6.06pm, followed by Ann Wooldridge, Gail Summerlin, Claire Ashton, Marina Bloom, Lynne Taylor and Tracey Maund. The last lady at this point being Heather Swift at 6.59pm. Lynne was going well and at this point was making time on the other ladies, as well as several men.

The riders were now passing onto the Quina Brook circuit and the tandem was still first on the road, and completed 5 circuits, along with the faster riders. Dan Howard on a trike was the last rider to go onto the finishing circuit, but was run down by an elderly driver who said she was dazzled by the sun. Luckily he wasn't too badly injured but his trike was badly damaged. This was Dan's first 24hr and it was hoped that this experience wouldn't put him off riding it in future years.

Lighting again this year was excellent and I recall standing at Prees at about 9pm and thinking theres a lot of motorbikes or mopeds coming, but I couldn't hear any noise, their lights were dazzling and most riders had two rear L.E.D. lights and some even resembled a cars rear foglight.

Chris Hopkinson was going well in the earlier stages but by late evening he was fading and having to stop for many short breaks; incidentally, he had the fastest 100 mile time with 4hrs 18mins, beating Andy Briggs by 1min 20secs. Pinon Shaw had the 3rd fastest 100 with 4hr.27m and Nik Gardiner 4th with 4.31, but of course it's the overall end result that matters. Having noted Hopkinsons fast first 100 mile times over the last 4 or 5 events, makes you wonder if a steadier starting speed would be more beneficial for a better overall finishing mileage. Lynne who finished in 6th place and beat him by 6 miles had a first 100 time of 4hrs 41mins.

Rain fell as the riders finished their night sections going from Prees to Tern Hill, Battlefield and then returning to Prees to start it all over again. By dawn the heavy squalls of rain were petering out and we hoped to get a bit of warmth later on, but it wasn't to be, and by 8.30am the rain was bouncing off the bonnet of the car and the roads were strewn with small branches and twigs from the trees being buffeted by a tough wind.

The Quina Brook circuit, although it gave slightly more shelter to the riders at this point, was very slippery and grit strewn, causing the riders to ease up on the many sharp bends and turns. This circuit was closed off earlier this year to make sure the riders got safely through the buffeting crosswinds coming through the Cheshire Gap and landing on the Broxton Hills, as they headed north to the finishing circuit.

The finishing circuit was equally as slippery and gritty with spatterings of mud at many farm entrances. The positions on the road had already been fought for and won by late morning, although it was difficult to keep track of what the leading riders had or hadn't done. On the finishing circuit Lynne was lapping in roughly the same time as Nik Gardiner but then she has had 12 years experience of these roads.

At the end, Gardiner had a fine win but must have wondered just what he had to do to achieve 500 miles. Nik had his first 24hr experience in the Brighton Mitre event in 1999, with 444 miles, but since then had concentrated more on his BBAR career, getting many high placings. Jose Pinon Shaw had, as usual, given his absolute all and looked to be in a poor state at the finish but he'd had some underlying health problems, so it wasn't surprising. Andy Briggs was, as far as I can recall, riding his first 24hr and so his 3rd place with 460.6 miles was a very creditable ride, as was Tony Grassby who was 4th with 448.2m. Ferdinand Laussman riding for his age award had his best ride ever with 446.29 but ironically the event was on his birthday and he didn't in the end qualify for the award. Marina Bloom had her best 24hr so far with 434 miles, even though she had fallen in the night on a slippery manhole cover and hurt her back. She pushed Lynne to a new personal best of 443 miles, where at one stage after bouts of sickness, we thought that Lynne wouldn't beat 430 miles.

In the veterans placings, Graham Barker, Rockingham CC at 57 years of age, won the award, with 426.7 miles, and Gerry Jones, Wrexham RC was 2nd at 58 years of age with 413.6m. Both of these men had ridden to high mileages and good positions in various 24hr races in the past.

*For a full report on the ladies race go to Chapter 5.*

From an entry of 72 solo riders, 68 started and 61 finished, plus 1 tandem.

## 2005

*On 8th February 2005, Ellen McArthur completed her lone single-handed circum-navigation of the world in the record time of 71 days, 14 hours, 18 minutes.*

**The Mersey RC National Championship 24hr on 23-24th July 2005, was won by Nik Gardiner, Time Trial.Co.Uk.RT with 493.081 miles. Keith Coffey, BEC CC was 2nd with 475.897m and Neil Skellern, Congleton CC was 3rd with 453.828 miles. Marina Bloom with 447.334 miles led Lynne Taylor with 412.807 miles and Rob Meredith, 396.3m, to a Walsall Roads CC National Championship team win of 1,256.520 miles. This was a massive personal best for Marina by nearly 12 miles, and gave them their 3rd consecutive team win.**

**Ralph Dadswell and David Johnson rode 466.723miles on a tandem trike and so improved Competition Record by 37 miles.**

Road works at the very start of the event led to some quick alterations to the course, but Doug Clark and Rod Goodfellow were unflappable and the old road in Barton Village was used. The course had undergone other changes this year with the Hodnet bypass being put to good use to link up with the Shawbirch road, and this would form a near 40 mile night circuit, that could be broken into smaller sections quite easily if required. Pleasant sunshine greeted the riders at the start, and out of an entry of 71 riders, 11 failed to start and 47 finished plus the tandem trike.

The first 100 miles was a hotly contested one by the two leaders, Nik Gardiner, No 70 and Keith Coffey, No 69. They both did identical rides one minute apart on the road with 4hrs 18mins 18secs. Mark Abela, Kent Cycles RC, was the 3rd fastest with 4-24-49 and eventually came 5th overall with 452.252 miles. Paul Robinson was 4th fastest with 4hrs 27mins 49s, and Neil Skellern also dead heated with Paul Alderson for the 100 miles in 4-29-49; Alderson finished 8th with 431.8 miles.

Marina was fastest of the ladies with 4hrs 44m 21s and Lynne 2nd, just 3 mins slower. The riders went onto the Quina Brook circuit from late afternoon onwards. Some did 5 laps, but Mark Abela, Paul Robinson, Neil Skellern, Keith Coffey and Nik Gardiner all did 7 laps. By the time the riders reached Shawbirch in the dark for the first time, Nik Gardiner had moved up through the field, he turned at the island at 11.12pm. and led Keith Coffey by 9mins. Marina had turned at 11.02 and led Lynne by 35 mins. Lynne was suffering from a heavy cold but wanted to carry on for the team and the fact that she looks forward to this event from the day after she finishes the previous years Mersey RC 24hr.

The wind had dropped but riders were reporting heavy rain at Tern Hill and Mike Johnson's comfort stop at Espley Island did a roaring trade all night even though everything was free. Sunday morning at Prees saw dawn rise at 4.30 as riders passed on their final journey to Shawbirch. At 6am when most of the field had returned, it was decided to send Nik Gardiner back to Shawbirch as he was way out in front of the field. He was the only rider to do this extra section of road. He returned from this 39mile leg at 8.01am and entered the Quina Brook circuit to loud cheers from the crowd of club folk gathered.

A wide load was on route from Whitchurch to Chester and so it was decided wisely by the Organisers to keep the riders on the Quina Brook circuit until it passed. Janet Tebbutt at 69 years of age had slowed down and only managed one lap. A few showers kept the riders alert as they now made their way to the finish at Handley where the final circuits would see the riders finish off their mileages. The tandem trike pair of Dadswell and Johnson seemed very smooth on these narrow twisting lanes and I did wonder at the time as to whether there was an ulterior motive for their ride, after all, their 466.723 mile Competition Record was just half a mile further than Crimes and Arnold's 1954 RRA record gained on route to John o' Groats. Could they be planning an attack, after all, neither of them were young men any more?

I think Nik Gardiner would have known at around 18 hours into the ride that 500 miles would be 'touch and go' but to see him as late as the 22 hour point still piling the pressure on, showed his dedication. To maintain 'evens' on that finishing circuit required not just speed but also skill, with many tight bends and villages to go through and with showers making the surfaces slippery, he gave his all, finishing with an amazing 493.081 miles. Maybe 500 next year!

An outstanding ride from Marina Bloom, with Lynne and Rob Meredith, secured the Championship Team honours for the Walsall Road CC, their 3rd consecutive win. Three other ladies bravely finished that day, Ann Woodridge, Ann Bath and Janet Tebbutt. Ann Wooldridge's 394.5 miles was a personal best for her on her third ride in a 24 hour.

Jim Hopper had the fastest trike performance again, and his 391 mile ride in this years event gave no indication as to the sad bereavement he had suffered in March, when his wife Margaret had passed away after a short illness. Margaret had been Jim's main supporter in all of his races over the last 20 years and although she didn't drive, she always managed to muster a good faithful team of Jim's mates for his support crew on his long distance events; men such as John Bevan, Ian Hill and Jim Ithell.

Margaret was always cheerful and gave a shout to every rider that passed. Her speciality was handing up slices of melon on the finishing circuit, very refreshing when the weather was hot. She gave Lynne lots of support over the years and was there on the roadside with Jim when she rode through the Midlands on all of her 'End to End' records. On the 24hr Margaret would jokingly ask Lynne if she wanted to borrow her lipstick to look at her best on the finishing circuit.

Jim's ride this year was expected though for he knew he would be in trouble from 'above' if he didn't turn up and do a good ride. Margaret is sadly missed by all who knew her.

Another person missing from this years line up for the 24hr was Tim Dolphin, Hounslow and District Whls. He last finished this event in 2002, I think with 378 miles, but failed to start in 2003. He was always a very cheerful and independent rider, who relied only upon the help from the official feed stations. He would catch the train from London where he lived, early on the Saturday morning, ride from Chester Station to the start, ride the event, and then ride back to Chester station, for the train back to London. He used this same routine for at least 20 years to my knowledge.

Tim moved to Marlow in 2000 and the change in surroundings and circumstances seemed to suit him. His failure to start in 2003 was down to him damaging his knee a few weeks prior to the race. In 2005 he was diagnosed with a heart problem, which would prevent him riding his bike competitively again, and it seems that at that time he suffered a bout of severe depression. Roger Sewell, who gave me this information about Tim's last few months, said that he was a great guy with a voracious appetite, had a laid back attitude and did most of his training in the local gym. Tim was an inspiration to us all with his gritty determination and will be missed by all who had the pleasure to know him.

This had been Doug Clark's 5th promotion of the event, along with his wife Doris, he'd made a smooth transition of leadership and was now to hand over to Jonathan (Jon) Williams, Bob and Ruth's son, who had been waiting in the wings, always there every year, performing many duties and giving solid support. He would now be the new Promoter and Organiser for 2006. At the prize presentation, Sam Moffatt, the Mersey RC President thanked all of the people involved with the smooth running of the event, especially those from other clubs who faithfully turned out every year to take up various duties around the course. Paul Olson gave a good introduction to the prizewinners as Compere for the event, and Rod, David, and Maggy Goodfellow slaved away in the backroom to produce a quick result sheet. And that was it for another year, now everyone could return to their 'normal' lives.

# 2006

A sad start to 2006 came very early when Frank Mumford passed away on 4th January. He had been a staunch member of the Mersey RC since 1939, and had been largely involved in writing the club history in later years. He raced at all distances but his main passion was the longer rides, especially the 24 hour. Frank was in the winning club team regularly from 1951.

He compiled the annual 24hr race report for the Club Journal 'The Record', and this report was adopted by the 24hr Fellowship Journal. To get the material for his writings Frank would wander around at the start of the 24hr every year and ask the riders for bits of information on their equipment, or how they felt etc. It all made very interesting reading and I've used his accurate, if sometimes amusing narratives, including his ghost stories etc, for a lot of my Mersey RC 24hr history.

He has seen and reported on riders from the Alpaca jacket and fixed wheel era to the modern day skinsuit, aero helmet, tri-bar, disc wheel, carbon-fibre brigade. He was born in 1915 and had seen many changes in his lifetime.

I am indebted to Frank, the Mersey RC and the 24hr Fellowship for permission to use material for this History of the 24 Hour.

**The Mersey RC National Championship 24hr, 22-23rd July 2006, was won by Nikolaus Gardiner, John's Bikes, with 504.023 miles. Neil Skellern, Congleton CC was 2nd with 477.653m and Nick Cave, Leicester Forest was 3rd with 472.492 miles. The fastest lady was Carol Westmorland, Border City Wheelers, with 445.412 miles. Jim Hopper was again the fastest trike rider with 393 miles. Paul Robinson was 6th overall with 461.423 and led a Cardiff Byways RCC team consisting of Mike Pain with 440.440m and David Lewis 409.163m to a National Championship Team win of 1,311.023 miles.**

**Richard Thoday and Chris Hopkinson rode a tandem to 473.795 miles. The second highest mileage ever, after the Goodfellow's.**

2006 proved to be a very good year for a lot of riders as far as the 24hr race was concerned. Nik Gardiner's consistency paid off and he reached his goal of 504 miles; since his first event in 1999 he'd now improved 60 miles. It was realised at 12 hours that he stood a chance of beating 500. His first 12 hours of 267.5 miles left him with just 233 miles to do in his second half. His speed put him well in the lead at 12 hours by nearly 16 miles over Howard Waller, Oxford City RC. Howard faded with a 210 mile second half to finish in 5th place with 461.757m. The 3rd fastest at 12 hours, Nick Cave, with 248.9m, finished very strongly and maintained that 3rd place for a bronze CTT Championship medal, and Neil Skellern, who lay in 4th position at 12 hours with 246 miles, had a very strong 2nd half with 231 miles and took the silver medal.

The top three riders, all had very smooth styles as befitting their mileages and positions. Graham Barker, Rockingham CC who took 4th place overall with 465.253m was proving that over 27years of riding 24 hour races hadn't blunted his speed and enthusiasm; this year he had improved 5 miles on his 4th placed North Midlands Championship ride in 1986, which was a very hot event. I think his best ride ever was 469m in the 1979 N.M.C.F. Championship.

Paul Robinson had changed clubs this year from the Ystwyth CC to the Cardiff Byways RCC, and improved nearly 40 miles on his previous years mileage to lead the team win. Super Audax UK rider, Steve Abraham, South Bucks RC, produced an amazing 436.889 miles, without any help other than what he carried with him, or stopped for at the feeding stations around the course.

David Lewis, the 3rd man in the Cardiff Byways winning team is another avid Audax rider as are many of the present day 24hr competitors. Dave has been a regular rider in the 24hr over a number of years, he is easily recognised by his long flowing dark hair and tanned good looks.

It was felt this year, that possibly the more compact course helped midfield riders to improve their performances with competitors being closer together and gaining a uniformity of speed in relationship to each other. It also helped with official feeding, and the riders own helpers had less chance of missing them or getting lost themselves.

This was Jon Williams first organisation of this famous event and he must have been pleased to have an entry of 70 riders with just 4 non-starters and 9 non-finishers, plus the 3 tandems all started and finished. It was thought that having 7 teams finish this year was a record, and with the Cardiff Byways fielding 2 finishing teams and the Deeside Thistle CC also with 2 teams, it made the team race even more remarkable.

The tandem of Thoday and Hopkinson went well for the first 12 hours and they recorded 263 miles, but from what I saw of them after that, they really didn't ride all that well together and they must have had a fair amount of time off the machine to record only 210 miles for their 2nd half. With Richard Thoday on the front and being a very tall rider, it looked as though the tandem was at least 12 inches too short in length. With just aero tri-bars it left them with very limited positions, more suited to riding a 25mile than a 24hr. By early morning on the Quina Brook circuit they were just ambling along at about 15 mph with Hopkinson leaning out on the back either to his right or his left and looking very uncomfortable.

Carol Westmorland's 9th placed ride of 445.412 miles was an excellent first time performance although we shouldn't have been surprised at this result after seeing her 12hour results over the years. Carol had ridden the same events as Lynne and Marina, and she'd matched them for mile after mile. Lynne levelled with Carol for the first 12 hours, in fact Lynne was just 0.1 of a mile ahead of her at that point with 232.209m while Marina trailed slightly with 229.2 in 3rd place for the ladies race.

Carol said to Lynne that she was soon to be married and that she'd always wanted to ride a 24hr and felt that there was no time like the present! Lynne had up to this point had a fairly normal season, but with excessive working hours due to her brother Mike opening a brand new cycle store, coupled with the ongoing heatwave, she came to the 24 hour without her usual pre-event training, and feeling a little jaded. She didn't start to lose her position on the road to Carol until mid morning, on the Quina Brook circuit, and although she fought back well, she couldn't match Carol's speed over the last few hours on the finishing circuit.

Marina meanwhile had been suffering from a niggly back pain long before the first 12 hours were up and she did well to finish with 416.4 miles, but knew that with only 3 riders, she had to finish for the team, however in the end they took 3rd place to the Cardiff Byways CC and the Congleton CC.   Rob Meredith, with lots of help from his wife Suzie, this year produced another personal best of 425.75 miles, and so became the 2nd counter in the Walsall RCC team.

The weather, as I recall for the event, was hot throughout with some heavy stormy rain showers late on Saturday giving way to a very hot Sunday.

# 2007

**The Mersey RC National Championship 24hr on July 21st and 22nd, was won by Eamonn Deane, a 49 year old postman, with 501.04 miles riding for the Bournemouth Jubilee CC.   John Warnock, Twickenham CC was 2nd with 489.32 and Jose Pinon Shaw was 3rd with 472.78 miles.   Lynne Taylor took a very hard won 4th place, just missing the Womens Competition Record by 2 miles with 459.29 miles.   A.P.I. METROW won the Team Championship medals with 1,307.118 miles.   The team comprised of Paul Robinson, Chris Hopkinson and Chris Asher.**

This report of the 24hr race isn't an hour by hour account, it is more of a general outlook on the whole event as seen from the passenger seat of Lynne's support van.   The format for the course had to be altered this year, due to heavy floods ruling out the use of the Quina Brook circuits.   At the start many riders left the timekeeper wearing a race-cape and many had narrow mudguards fitted, a sensible idea, as some roads had patches of surface floodwater.   Conditions were cool and drizzly but with little wind.

There was a large clan of Scottish riders, mainly from the Deeside Thistle CC and the Edinburgh RC.   They had brought along a 'piper' who gave each Scottish competitor a patriotic send off with a short rendition of 'Scotland the Brave'.   George Berwick rode his 47th Mersey event and finished with 314 miles, riding for the Edinburgh RC.

The strongest team on paper looked to be the Congleton CC with Neil Skellern, Karl Austin and Graham Barker, and the 2nd strongest, the Walsall Roads CC with Lynne Taylor, Marina Bloom and Rob Meredith.   Individual male riders I thought would do well were, Neil Skellern, Eamonn Deane, Jose Pinon Shaw, Karl Austin, Graham Barker, Ian Silvester and Steve Abraham, in that order.   I hadn't accounted for John Warnock who came 2nd due to him having no history at 24hrs and the fact that he was positioned very early in the starting order.   I felt that this could be Neil Skellern's or Jose Pinon Shaw's year, without the presence of Nik Gardiner, and I also knew that Eamonn Deane, as well as being a past 12 hour National Champion in 1998 with 273 miles, had been contacting Jonathan Williams as to what was required for a successful 24hr winning ride.

Of the women, I obviously chose Lynne, knowing her form and determination to get the record and the Turner Cup for the 10th time.   I placed Marina 2nd and probably a Scottish lady 3rd.

At the 100 mile point, John Warnock led with 4hrs 17mins 03secs. Paul Robinson was at 29 seconds, Ian Silvester at 2mins 29secs and Pinon Shaw was at 3mins 17secs.   Deane took 4hrs 21mins 32secs and Lynne 4hrs 37mins.   By night we could see Deane, No 75, Silvester No 60, Robinson No 40, Skellern, 85, and Pinon Shaw No 65, were all pulling away from the rest of the field.   We didn't notice John Warnock go through, probably because he hadn't got a late O or 5 number at the fast end of the field.

Karl Austin was riding his own race and wasn't getting embroiled in any early battles.   He had one or two stops for clothing etc and we noticed that Lynne had pulled well ahead of him.   Neil Skellern, although riding very smoothly as usual, seemed to take ages to catch Lynne who was No 69.   He had a first 100 of 4hrs 30mins but then he slowed drastically to record 238 for 12 hours.   The last we saw of him was sitting with his helpers at Shawbirch, he'd changed out of his skinsuit and aero helmet and was fully clothed in woolly hat and warm night clothing including a waterproof jacket.   He was quietly protesting to his helpers about not feeling too good.   Whether the cold and damp had got to him I don't know, but he must have packed shortly after 12 hours as his last checkpoint was at 247 miles.

At the 12 hour point John Warnock led by nearly 10 miles with 265.91m compared to Deane's 256.71 miles and Pinon Shaw's 255.57m. Paul Robinson was 4th with 244.78m, closely followed by Ian Silvester with 244.06m and Lynne was in 7th place with 239.15miles. To break the womens record she now had to ride a 2nd 12hours of 222.4 miles. Paul Histon who was helping her to try and get the record was bubbling with enthusiasm and telling her to hold 'evens' pace for as long as she could. We both knew that as soon as she got to the finishing circuit, it would be almost impossible to ride at 'evens' with the rough surface, tight bends and hills to negotiate.

At 3.30am there was a bluish streak in the sky and by 4.30am dawn had broken. The night had flown by but a lot of riders were visibly slowing and appeared to be on 'auto-pilot'. The feeding station at Espley Island near Hodnet, manned by Mike Johnson and Yvonne Crane, was a hive of activity throughout the night. It provided a welcome respite for tired riders to have a sit down on a proper seat and close their tired eyes for a minute or two, only to be rudely awoken and sent on their way after a cup of hot coffee, tea or soup. Mike and Yvonne also provide hot drinks for the helpers and plenty of hot water for the thermos flasks. Along with Geoff Manson and Lynton Threadgold, they are a very valued part of the Mersey 24 hour race.

Luckily, the main roads were fairly dry during the night, which made the road surfaces easier for the riders to see. Lynne suffered two punctures and both were due to a broken lorry brake disc that had shattered to bits, like shrapnel, and was strewn across the carriageways between Prees and Tern Hill in the night. With Lynne riding very close to record pace, these were two stops that she could have well done without! Paul was monitoring and restricting her drinks and cutting her 'comfort stops' or 'calls of nature' to an absolute bare minimum, in fact, I think she only had approximately 12 mins in total off the bike, in 24 hours. Marina had ridden 227.7 miles in the first 12 hours and appeared cheerful, but by breakfast time she'd had enough and eventually packed at 306 miles. Rob Meredith, Lynne's surviving Walsall RCC team-mate, was also looking very rough and complaining of a bad stomach. We managed to avoid telling him that Marina had 'packed' and that there wasn't a Walsall RCC team left. We suggested that he pottered on for a few miles and that he might feel better when the sun came up. Knowing how important the 24hr is to Rob, we felt that if we could keep him going with a bit of 'kidology' it was worth it. An hour or so later he was seen hammering along in his usual way, and I'm glad to say he finally finished with 408.25 miles, his 2nd fastest 24 hr ride of all.

By mid morning the last few riders had been turned back at Espley Island to take the long haul north to the finishing circuit. At this point Lynne was still on record pace, but only just. Her feeding was mainly hot rice pudding and hot tea, to combat the chilly damp morning. My job was to provide the rice and the tea and I left it to Paul to sprint alongside Lynne and hand it up, as well as give her terrific vocal support. No 16, John Warnock, came past Lynne on a couple of occasions; he was wearing minimal racing kit and seemed to ride very fast for an hour or two and then stop at his helper's car for a break, only to hammer away again, rather reminiscent of Mick Coupe's style of riding. We still weren't aware that he was onto a 490 mile ride at that time due to us being focussed on helping Lynne, it was obvious that Eamonn Deane and Jose Pinon Shaw were both riding to medal positions, but with the layout of the course, there was no quick way of checking other riders progress.

By midday Sunday most of the marshals and helpers had regrouped onto the finishing circuit. Once there, Lynne's speed dipped slightly below evens and she was now dropping behind her schedule for the Competition Record. There were only a few short lengths of road on the circuit where Lynne could average 'evens', and every bend, rough surface and hill saw her speed drop, but still she tried with such determination. However Paul tried to calculate her final mileage due to the course re-adjustment; he kept coming up with a figure of 459 miles to finish at Timekeeper 1, on the main road. Finally his predictions came true and Lynne came to a halt for a well-deserved rest, but sadly, she had missed Christine's record by just over 2 miles.

Although Lynne was obviously disappointed, she was also elated to have got so close to the record and to have ridden the 2nd greatest distance ever by a woman in 24hrs under time trial conditions. Mark Holt and Jose Pinon Shaw also finished at this timekeeper but in different states of tiredness. Mark who had been helped throughout by a team of Port Sunlight lads and lasses, including 'Wilko' looked just glad to be finished and was quite happy to chat and relax now that it was all over, his 419 miles was a personal best for him.   I met up with Mark a week or two later at a 24hr mountain bike endurance race that both he and Lynne rode, and Mark admitted that he enjoyed the mountain bike race slightly more, due to being able to have a little rest and take a 'lap-out' every now and then. He also mentioned bacon sandwiches, and a good selection of rousing 'pop' music during daylight hours, as being a 'plus' for the mountain bike race!

At the other end of the scale, Pinon Shaw had literally collapsed into an almost comatose state, his breathing was very shallow and he wasn't reacting to any outside noise or efforts at communication.   'Wilko' was asked for his advice and help as he himself often went into a near death like state of exhaustion after all of his great 'epic' rides. After what seemed like ages, Jose, gradually flickered back into the real world, he was an awful colour, his face was haggard and a shade of parchment.   He'd given his all to finish with 472.78 miles.   Later, at the awards ceremony, Jose was just able to hobble the short distance across the room to pick up his bronze Championship medal and he now had a smile on his face.   John Warnock wasn't at the awards ceremony due to him having a long journey home that same day, but nevertheless, his 489 miles ride was much appreciated by all of the 24hr fraternity.   I hope he returns again in 2008 as I'm sure that he is capable of at least 500 miles.   Another rider who made his efforts look easy was, of course, the winner Eamonn Deane.   He always seemed to be in control and stayed on his low profile time trial bike for the whole 24hrs.   I've got to admit, he looked very comfortable throughout with smooth pedalling to the end.   Being a tall rider, I would have expected him to have a few back problems, but none were mentioned. At 49 years of age this superbly fit rider from Bournemouth who is also a triathlete and a postman, has still got a few years left to see if he can add to his winning mileage of 501, and challenge 'Wilko's' 10 year old record.

Lynne came 4th overall, she was so close to the record, and now knows what she has to do in the future.   Although she looked a little more weary afterwards than in previous years, she still hasn't taken herself to the state of collapse as other 'stars' have done.   Christine and Alan Roberts were out at this event and at the H.Q; they both knew how hard Lynne had tried, and Christine commiserated with her, which was a very sporting gesture.   In the past they have both given Lynne lots of support and advice on her riding at all levels, and this has instilled great confidence in her.

Considering the size of the field mustered by Jon Williams, for this only his second organisation, there were very few reported incidents.   From 85 solo entrants and 1 tandem, there were only three; the first being Mark Holt who had a telephone directory thrown at him from a passing vehicle during the hours of darkness at Prees Village.   The second was a short while later at Shawbirch where Lynne had something thrown at her, again at close range, from a car window, as she encircled the island.   The only other incident was when 80 year old super-vet Ron Longstaff touched the kerb when taking a drink on the finishing circuit.   He fell from his bike and smacked his head on the ground, sustaining bruises and lacerations to his face.   He was deemed to be physically okay but his son took him to hospital for a check up, just to be on the safe side.   I don't have the details as to how much time he had left to run, but the result sheet shows his last recorded checkpoint to be 326.795 miles during this event.   Ron had ridden a first 100 miles in 5hrs 13mins and a 12 hour of 193.5 miles, at 80 years of age!   I'm just a youngster of 64 and I'm beginning to feel very inadequate, but Ned Millington, the 24hr Fellowship Journal Editor, assures me I shouldn't feel too bad about it, as Ron is a 'living legend' and mentions that he's been winning races since the 1940's, in fact he won the Mannin Veg road race on the Isle of Man in 1948.   His training for this 24hr race had

been a regular 300 miles a week, and this does leave me with one question "Why has he left it so late in life to experience the obvious joys of a 24 hour race?"

A few more rides worthy of a mention before concluding are firstly the winning team, A.P.I. Metrow.   With the retirements of Neil Skellern from the Congleton CC and Marina Bloom from the Walsall RCC, it left Paul Robinson, Chris Hopkinson and

Chris Asher, to win the Championship Team medals for the A.P.I. Metrow, with 1,307.11 miles. This beat the Congleton CC into 2nd place by nearly 27 miles, and the Deeside Thistle CC 'A' team who came 3rd with 1,235.54 miles. This Scottish club fielded 13 riders and all of them finished, making this another 'first' for the Mersey event by having nine teams finish. Stephen Massey was a surprise 5th with 452.89 miles riding for the Derby Mercury RC and Ian Silvester, San Fairy Ann CC was 6th with 446.92 miles.

Jim Hopper looked cheerful throughout and I think he enjoyed the 24 hour much more than the previous weekends Championship '100'. At 63 years of age, Jim was the fastest trike rider with 376.46 miles, but sadly we are seeing less and less trikes being ridden in events now, especially the 24 hour. The average age of trike competitors seems to be 60 years old at least. Jim would have been the 2nd fastest 'veteran' in the 'VTTA awards', but the goalposts had apparently been mysteriously moved this year, and the awards were restricted to bike riders only. In a roundabout way, this ruling from the VTTA seems to hark back to over 50 years ago, when John Arnold rode the 2nd fastest mileage in the Championship event, but wasn't allowed an RTTC medal or place, due to him riding a trike.

**Do they not realise that a trike is rated, across the board, approximately 10% slower than a bike, due to it having 3 points of contact with the road?**

*I draw my approximately 10% comparison from riders who excel on both machines, Stuart Jacksons performances for example, where in 1981 he produced 456.59 miles on his trike and in 1982 he rode 496.49 on his bike. They were both event winning performances and at the end of my 1965 Mersey RC 24hrs report, there are more relevant details on trike matters. At the beginning of 2008 I was told that a trike 25 mile event, due to take place during the season on the 'K16' course near Lichfield, had been cancelled for safety reasons, but bike events on the same course are to be allowed.* **I wonder if there is a vendetta?**

Graham Barker a rider with probably 40 years experience at 24hr racing took the fastest veteran award on standard with 428.69 miles riding for the Congleton CC this year. He was helped as usual by a very able Margaret Allen, who was Womens RTTC Champion at 10, 25, 50 and 100 miles time trials, both as an individual and also as a team member between 1967 and 1994. What Margaret doesn't know about how to suffer to get results isn't worth knowing, and I'm sure she put Graham through his paces during this event!

*In hindsight, I would have been interested to have seen what mileage Margaret could have ridden in a 24 hour, as she had some pretty impressive 100 mile times during her career.*

Steve Abraham wasn't quite up to last years high mileage but nevertheless he was very pleased with his 436 miles, riding completely reliant on the official feeds as if complying with Audax rules. He rode to and from the event on his bike, through a fair amount of rain on the Friday, breaking his journey both ways to stop off at Bridgtown cycles, just off the A5 near Cannock, for a cup of tea and a rest. Mike Taylor (my son) now owns and runs the business with Lynne, Andy Bond and a dedicated staff of cyclists. Steve must have had a round trip of over 700 miles in 4 days.

Bob Williams' description of the 24hr reminded me just how wet it had been and of all the problems caused by over 2 months of heavy rain. Many riders had to detour just to reach the H.Q. before the start due to flooded roads, but luckily only Stuart Archard had to have a late start for this reason. Bob said that despite the conditions, only 8 riders failed to finish; Graham Barker won the Winnerah Memorial Trophy and apparently it was the legendary timekeeper from Aberdeen, 'Nobby'Clarke, who organised the bagpipes for the Scottish invaders. *Sadly he passed away in December that same year of 2007.*

Mike Rainton, just two weeks previous to the 24hr, had finished a successful 5 day End to End charity event for the Bishop Simeon Trust, raising £2.700 and wrote an article for the journal. In it he mentions that when he nervously told his family of his intention to ride the 24hr, he was told "Grandad, you are mad!" His training partner Mike Wood, who also went on to help Mike throughout the whole episode, also questioned his sanity, but when promised free cups of tea forever, he kindly agreed to help.

Mike remembers arriving at the H.Q. feeling nervous, anxious and scared. Whilst he was on the starting line he also felt very emotional. He had planned to break the ride into 8 three-hour segments, so as not to be too daunted by the prospect of riding solidly for 24 hours. Mike suffered badly during the night but once daylight appeared he felt better, despite the cold dawn giving him a headache. Once he was on his way back to the finishing circuit he picked up speed, confident in the knowledge that he would now complete his mission, and prove to them all that he wasn't really mad!

I spoke to Mike at the H.Q. and he was over the moon, one could see that this was probably one of the most euphoric moments of his life, with having completed the 'End to End' journey and this 332.4 mile 24 hour, all in the space of three weeks, it would be a hard act for him to repeat, or even improve on, but there's always next year.

Joel Sothern, a plucky American from California, riding for the Ultra Marathon C.A. finished with 419.98 miles, and later wrote an appreciative article describing the unique experience he'd had as a 'Yank in King Arthurs Court'. Joel described the dismal wet weather and 90% humidity as 'raining cats and dogs' as opposed to the British 'bucketing down'. *(I thought they were both our sayings?)* *However, he praised the 'volunteers' (marshals and checkers) for being on duty for hours on end, in wet bone chilling cold, to make sure no-one went off course. Joel Sothern described the event as without doubt the best organised and supported that he'd ridden, even though riding on the wrong side of the road and negotiating 'circles' (islands) was a new and daunting challenge to him. He thanked Chris Hopkinson for encouraging him during the ride and was amazed to find that the 'Good Samaritan' who gave him a lift from the finishing circuit to the H.Q. was none other than Andy Wilkinson. Joel summarised by saying that for him it was the 'cycling experience of a lifetime' and heartily recommended that other Americans give it a try.*

I'd always wondered exactly what illness Jose Pinon Shaw had suffered around 2003. I knew that it had been a very life-threatening time for him but I hadn't realised just how serious, as I'd seen him win the 24hr silver medal in 2004 with 470.7 miles.

*In an interview published in the Preston Wheelers Club magazine, Jose stated that he was diagnosed with Non-Hodgkins Lymphoma in 2003. After two operations, six months of chemotherapy and three months of radiotherapy, he was back on his bike again. He went on to say that just 9 months after completing his treatment, he took the 24hr silver medal in 2004, much to the shock and amazement of his Consultant, who had told him that it was unlikely he would ever ride competitively again. Jose said it felt great to prove him wrong.*

After taking up cycling much later in life than most of us and then starting to ride competitively at 33 years of age in 2001, he's certainly made up for lost time. I've seen him racing in Championship 100's and obviously all of the 24hrs he's ridden in and he's a tough focussed rider, who gives every ounce of his power, strength and endurance. In a 24hr race, he 'runs on empty' towards the end and always seems close to collapsing once he has got off his bike. One instinctively knows that here is a rider who has set his body clock for 24hrs and has given his all.

*When asked if he had any specific ways of training or reasons for his success, Jose said* **"I try to ride every race as if it is to be my last one ......... you never know, by the end of the race, I may have decided that it was!"** *Jose concluded with even more poignant words* **"I'm sure you know of people who have had cancer and think it's the end .......... please tell them my story just to prove it isn't."**

*My thanks to Jose Pinon Shaw, the Preston Wheelers and the Mersey RC 'Record' for allowing me to print this amazing story.*

So that was it, another classic 24hr Championship run to its conclusion, this being the 64th edition. More details of this 2007 event can be found in Chapter 5, The Womens History.

**The Mersey RC National Championship 24 hour 26/27th July**

The event started in hot sunshine and without a hitch, opposite the HQ at Farndon at 13.01. Geraint Catherall was the first man away from an entry of 66 solo riders including 2 trikes and 2 ladies. Three tandems also started at the end of the main field, an all male one with Hedley and Southworth, VC167, a mixed crew tandem of Sharp and Cox, Ystwyth CC, and an all female one of Barnes and Norman, Twickenham CC.

*The course this year was back to its regular format after the floods of 2007, and took in the Quina Brook circuit once again and the Organisers had complete freedom to use any section of the course as often as they needed to on both days. From the start, the route travels 16.6 miles south through Broxton, Grindley Brook to Prees Island and the start of a 39.475 mile large circuit. This circuit is comprised of main roads linking Tern Hill, Hodnet Bypass, Espley Island, Shawbirch Island (Telford) and retrace via Tern Hill to Prees. After two of these larger circuits are completed, the riders then travel a short distance north past Prees to take the Wem road through Tilstock and Quina Brook to rejoin the A49 back to Prees, to complete a 12.6 miles circuit of rural lanes. Most turns and junctions are to the left or are made at islands, making them as safe as possible. With direction arrows 'caution cyclists' signs, plus experienced marshals and checkers at each turn, nothing is left to chance. The Quina Brook circuit is repeated until almost nightfall and then the riders are directed onto the larger circuits once again.*

*Nik Gardiner number 55 produced a superb 4hr 10min first 100 miles and had caught the complete field by the time he'd reached the first Quina Brook circuit. He then proceeded to lap the 12.6 miles in exactly 34 minutes including the climb on the Prees bypass and lots of roughly surfaced lanes. This year's event was a totally new experience for me, for once I was just a spectator for the first time in 50 years, due to Lynne not riding. I've been involved with this historic and popular event since 1958 either as a helper or a rider, and it was quite a novelty to stand and chat at various locations around the course, instead of dashing off to get ahead of Lynne to give her a drink or rummage in the back of the van to find her night clothes etc. To top it all off, Liz and I stopped at Prees just as dusk was falling for an 'all day breakfast' at Lynn's Raven Café; how decadent!*

*Inside we found members of the 'Williams CC', the Minto's – Christine, Frank and Phillip, and members of the Mersey RC, having a quick break for a bite to eat while the riders tackled the larger circuit south to Tern Hill. These faithful stalwarts had been on duty for nearly 8 hours checking and marshalling and would be ready for the riders on their return. Rod Goodfellow had a quiet spot in the corner of the café to feed the progressive results into his laptop and from this information he would be able to double check 100 mile and 12 hour results for later on. Rod was the Principal timekeeper and later he would leave Prees and set up his computer at the HQ where, along with his son David and his wife Maggie, he would produce a provisional result sheet once all of the information had been collected from the timekeepers around the finishing circuit. Rod of course knows the 24 hour race scene inside out having performed at top level, winning many races including this event 4 times over a period of 25 years. In 1991 he broke the tandem competition record with his other son Peter, with 501.35 miles also on this Mersey course.*

*I spoke to Sheila Hardy, the RTTC Observer, as she checked proceedings at Prees Island, and she said whereas a few years ago competitors lighting, or lack of it, would have been one of her concerns, it was riders using 'Walkmans' or personal stereos that had become the modern problem. Riders were also seen using mobile phones and one even texting as he rode along, and these are all issues she has to address. As time triallists we have to be seen doing the right things when riding on the roads, and making sure we don't bring the sport into disrepute. I use a 'Walkman' or personal stereo at home occasionally and then I'm in a world of my own. I know I would be a very inattentive rider if I used one on the road. Apart from that, I don't think there were any other rider issues and from what I saw on and around the course, the standard of riding was good, even on the finishing circuit where riders are at their limits of exhaustion.*

Prees was a very busy place with riders pulling in either to sample the cuisine at Lynn's Raven Café or to use the toilets. It is the nerve centre of the race almost from the start, right through the night and well into late Sunday morning as the riders push north towards the finishing circuit. Wherever the rider is on the course, he or she is never more than 20 miles away from food or help, with Mike Johnson and Yvonne Crane providing a mobile feed and rest unit at Espley Island and later at Handley on the finishing circuit. One could even put on weight if they stopped long enough at these places, but I'm sure Mike Johnson would soon have you on your way, after all he's ridden this event on a tandem trike and he knows that 'time is miles'. A three minute stop loses you one mile.

In 1992 Mike rode 376.88 miles with Richard Hills and produced a performance just 5 miles less than Pat Kenny and Pete Gifford, also on a tandem trike. Since then Mike has played a mainly supporting role not only in this event but also on many long distance RRA records either as a driver cum helper, or as an Official Observer. Being an ex-rugby player and lorry driver, he is built like a brick wall and has terrific stamina. His knowledge of the roads in the UK and many towns and cities makes him an ideal support team member and driver on any record attempt. He also has a very calming influence during attempts and I have good knowledge of this from his help on Lynne's epic records.

Neil Skellern rode a more planned race this year after his disappointment from pulling out after 12 hours in 2007. He started steadier this year, particularly with 26 degrees of heat to contend with in the first few hours. When I saw him at Prees around 8pm, Edwin Hargraves informed me that he was now upping the pace and picking his way through the field to establish himself amongst the leaders who were Nik Gardiner and John Warnock. With Jose Pinon Shaw being a non-starter, this made things a little easier for the top men this year.

Most of the riders had already been turned on to the larger circuit towards Tern Hill but I noticed Nik Gardiner being directed to do another circuit of Quina Brook. Edwin said that Nik would complete 8 circuits (approximately 100 miles) before being sent to the luxury of smoother roads towards Tern Hill and beyond. Nik's lap times had been so consistent over this 12.6 mile collection of rural lanes that Edwin was able to predict his arrival to within 30 seconds each time! It was here that I realised Nik was 25 miles ahead of the rest of the field except for perhaps John Warnock.

As mentioned earlier Lynne hadn't entered this year due to BBAR commitments and a totally different method of training under the guidance of her coach and mentor, Paul Histon. Liz and I met Lynne and Paul at Prees as dusk fell, she'd travelled up from the Shaftesbury 50 where she had recorded a personal best of 1hr 56mins 31secs, and was obviously over the moon but said she felt very strange standing there and cheering other riders on their way. This was the first time in 15 years that she hadn't ridden and normally her whole season is based around the 24hr, even when End to End records and BBAR positions are involved. Lynne was particularly eager to give Marina a shout and had her chance when she turned towards Tern Hill at dusk.

Here I chatted with 24hr fellowship members, Brian Griffiths, Ned Millington and an old opponent of mine from wayback, Malcolm Jones of the Mid Shropshire Wheelers. You can imagine their recollections of the good old days and mention was made of looking forward to the ride up the 'Prestatyn leg' and the Whitchurch to Nantwich 'graveyard' leg. I also had chance to chat with Alan Roberts who tries to get out to as many races as possible, despite being in a wheelchair. Christine usually accompanies him whenever she can, although she still tries to find time to race and train. They're both pretty clued up when it comes to who's done the best rides and Alan still manages to enthuse about bikes, equipment, and methods of training which he has done all of his life. When I asked Christine if she would ever contemplate riding another 24hr her eyes glazed over a little and she chuckled at the thought. She still looks incredibly fit and I saw her next day riding around the finishing circuit the opposite way, cheering riders on. I suppose that if you still hold Competition Record at 24 hrs with 461 miles you don't have to prove anything or worry about riding another one.

Jim Hopper appreciated a 'cheer' as he flashed past on his trike to a 365 mile ride. He knew that he would be the fastest trike rider as long as he finished, due to 72 year old past champion, Ken Usher, not starting. It had been stiflingly hot until about 9pm and by then the sun was setting and the temperature dropped to a welcome 20 degrees C, by which time most riders had put extra clothing on. There were a hardy few who continued in just their daytime racing kit or maybe just a thin top and arm warmers, but kept their legs bare. I spoke to a couple of riders after the event, who had ridden all night with bare legs and they both said they'd suffered with painful knees and in hindsight should have put leg warmers or tights on, to cover the clammy cool skin which can lead to over cooling of joints and muscles.

*I know many older riders like myself will look back with nostalgia to the days when probably 50% of the field would ride through the night without any extra clothing on , especially if it was a hot weekend. In times past, the race leaders were always loathe to stop and put on tights or thin trousers because of the time lost factor, but some would submit to putting on a woolly jumper or race cape. I think in this modern day and age there is enough evidence and data to show that heat loss to a point of being too cool can soak up a lot of available energy and power output from a rider, energy that could be put to better use.*

The night went well for most riders with fairly mild conditions and very little wind. We were sad to find that Marina had packed in the night from drowsiness, which left Rose Leith to take the honours. By mid morning most of the slower riders had left the quiet hedge lined lanes of the Quina Brook circuit and were on their way to the finishing circuit. Gardiner was well in the lead from Warnock by over 20 miles but it was difficult to pick out other riders progress on a circuit. It was thought at this point that Gardiner could possibly achieve 515 miles and that Warnock would probably repeat his previous years mileage. Neil Skellern had gone through the night unscathed but was roughly 40 miles down on Gardiner and 20 miles behind Warnock.

After chatting to the lads from St. Christopher's CCC, Pete, Derek, Alan and the two Bobs, I realised that there were very few race officials left at Prees and that the main action was taking place on the finishing circuit. Originally I had planned to visit various parts of the circuit to see how the riders were progressing, but then I realised after experiencing five very exciting minutes at Timekeeper Six, Coddington Church, it would be futile to go elsewhere. All the action was there; the marshal who blew his whistle at the approach to a blind bend, a short blast indicated a solo rider and a long one was for a tandem; the timekeeper, the recorder and the number checkers were all busily working under a blazing hot sun. Luckily most riders came along separately although there were the occasional two or three together, due to the intricate nature of the finishing circuit, but I'm sure the officials would have coped easily, whatever their task.

The odd tractor and trailer going to and fro laden with hay and a couple of loose farm dogs, all made for the occasional stressful moments due to the narrowness of the lane, and the speed of the tired riders. I suddenly had a thought, or moreover a flash back, that this rural scene at TK6, Coddington Church, is about as close as one can get to how things were for riders at the start of the 20th century. It was reminiscent of the scene portrayed in the early photos of Shorland and Bidlake on the Great North Road, and also of John Arnold cornering his trike around the 1950's earlier in this book.

Parishioners leaving the church after morning service asked us what was going on and how long did the race last? When we informed them that it was nearly the end of a 24hr race, and that the fastest rider was just about to complete a 510 mile ride, and that most competitors would cover upwards of 350 miles including a 70 year old, they were amazed. The looks on their faces when they realised that the riders had been pedalling virtually non stop since the previous dinner time left many speechless, but then timekeeper No 6 has been stationed here outside the church steps and the old red phone box, annually, for at least 20 years, so I did wonder why the sudden interest?

One elderly churchgoer stepped onto the road and commented that she thought cyclists were a nuisance as they prevented her from getting past in her car and slowed her down. Jim Turner tactfully remarked that this was only a time trial and that the riders rode in single file, which appeased her somewhat, but she then remarked that it was the large bunches of riders she got annoyed with. So nothing has changed in over 100 years, were still upsetting the motorists whatever roads we choose to ride on! **It's a good job she wasn't driving a horse and carriage (see year 1894 Chapter 1).**

Jim Hopper was only too happy to finish here and then he freewheeled downhill to his helpers car manned by John Bevan and Ian Hill, his regular 'crew'. Colin Bezant No 35 also finished here and promptly leapt off his bike and jumped over the churchyard wall to lie flat out on the cool grass next to the gravestones in the shade of a huge oak tree. Luckily it was after the congregation had gone home otherwise he might have suffered the rough end of an irate elderly ladies walking stick!

At the end Nik Gardiner was lapping at 44 minutes per circuit, he now looked extremely tired but still managed a smile in acknowledgment of our cheers every time he passed. Lynne thoroughly enjoyed herself and many riders were surprised to see her standing on the circuit cheering them on. Karl Austin with 450.16 produced one of his best rides ever and was prominent throughout, he turned his big fixed wheel gear and stormed forcefully around the hilly twisting finishing circuit, he was also lapping in 44 mins similar to Gardiner.

Graham Barker in his tussles with Jim Gresty was lapping at around 46 mins, but the rider with the fastest lap of the day 40mins 50secs, was another fixed wheel hardman, Steve Abraham on a 94" gear, although at the end he said he was only trying to make up for time he'd lost during the event. It's not easy riding a 24hr under any circumstances let alone riding without any mobile help, although he has topped 440 miles using this method, but I hope that for once in his life Steve tackles a 24hr with dedicated mobile help just to see what he could do. I knew that this year he'd lost half a tooth just before the race and was having difficulty eating. He finished with 382.17 and rode his usual journey home next day to Milton Keynes, stopping off for his customary cups of tea at Bridgtown Cycles and had a chat to Lynne and Mike.

Graham Barker had a much better ride this year even though he was beaten in the age awards by Jim Gresty. Graham had a spirited battle with Jim throughout the event, which intensified on the finishing circuit to a nail-biting conclusion. I took up a cool spot on the church steps and listened to Edwin Hargraves reeling off the rider's numbers and actual passing times and then their respective lap times. He would regularly check his figures with Recorder, Ian Price (the son of Ken Price, the 24 hour Competition Record breaker in 1955). Jim and Anne Turner were making double checks on the riders along with Shelagh Hargraves, all were making sure that no one slipped through the net without being timed and recorded to the exact second.

HELMS.

"Tell daddy where you've hidden his watch - he's got to time a bike race."

I had forgotten just how much intricate work, with two electronic watches and writing sheets of numbers and times, went on at each timing station, and this was just one of seven such timekeepers. Edwin was able to tell us with the information he had, that at 1pm all barring accidents, Jim Gresty, lapping at 18mph would beat Graham Barker for the Vets award. He also knew that Nik Gardiner would win from John Warnock and Neil Skellern.

Back at the HQ Margaret Allen who had helped **Graham Barker,** said that his lower mileage last year in 2007 was due to a lot of knee pain, caused by his tights being put on skew-whiff creating pressure on his kneecaps. Graham rode originally with the Rockingham CC when they were a force to be reckoned with in the past, and he's been performing at high levels in 24hrs ever since, probably for a period of forty years or so. This year he again helped the **Congleton CC** along with **Neil Skellern** and **Karl Austin,** to another **Championship Team win of 1,359.84 miles.**

**Joel Sothern,** Ultra Marathon CA, who rode in 2007 with 419.98 miles said then that he would return and bring more of his American long distance comrades with him to do battle in 2008. He kept to his word with Marc Veorinelle, Cao St Cyr and Padraig Marrey, Western Lakes CC, all eager to participate in this 120 year old history of ours. **Joel** improved on his previous years ride by a good margin of 23 miles with **442.37** and received the Mick Pott's award for his efforts. Joy Potts, Mick's wife presents this award annually to the rider with the highest mileage at 50 years of age or over, in memory of Mick who won the Championship in 1991, when he was 50 years of age, with an amazing 486.65 miles.

**Nik Gardiner** looked very weary at the end but then he had just completed the second highest mileage in history. This performance of **513.65 miles** put him 4 miles above Gethin Butler (who is now winning marathons) but 11 miles below Wilko's record of 525.07 miles. Nik said that this was definitely his last 24 hour, but I've heard him exclaim that before, along with many other 24 hour riders! He has a very young family including a new born baby. He mentioned having had many sleepless nights recently and I did wonder whether this makes him an ideal candidate to become the next 'End to End' attemptee?

Whereas last year we had an invasion of Scottish riders from the Deeside Thistle, this year it was the regular Edinburgh RC crew of George Berwick, Graham Jones, Graeme Wylie and John Connaghan, with 1,055.21 miles. Apart from the Americans and the Scots, the only other invasion was the Irish trio from the Sorrento CC, Rose Leith, Paul O'Donoghue and John O'Sullivan. They were the 3rd fastest team with 1,141.58 miles. **Daniel Mathers** upheld a Seamon's CC tradition of having a tough 24hr man in the club with a fine **455.95 miles 4th place** and Steven Massey with 442.42m led Jim Hopper and Peter Turner to 2nd team place with 1,169.45 miles, for the Derby Mercury RC.

**Rose Leith,** Sorrento CC **won the ladies event** and the **Turner Cup** this year with **352.95 miles,** and also created a new Irish ladies 24hr record. She said she thoroughly enjoyed the event although admitting to not having done enough hard training. Rose also holds the ladies Irish End to End record but says there is a definite lack of competition at the longer distances in Ireland and if the team want to ride a decent 100 miles, 12hr or 24hr event they have to take the ferry to mainland Britain to do so. Her time for this punishing 592 kilometre End to End route is 21 hours.

Three tandems started and three finished. The all male tandem of Aiden Hedley and Andrew Southworth, 'VC167' finished with 395.85 miles, and won the 'Johnson Trophy'. The mixed crew of Jasmine Sharp and Andrew Cox, Ystwyth CC rode 359.99 miles and the all female tandem of Charlotte Barnes and Elizabeth Norman, Twickenham CC, rode 329.49 miles. All three were solid rides as I know how hard it is to keep a tandem going for 24 hours. The compatibility required of the riders and the hope that they will still be friends afterwards, these qualities are strenuously tested for 24 hours.

So finally, **Nik Gardiner,** Johns Bikes, with **513.65 miles,** won this years Mersey RC Championship event. This was his 4th Championship win and he now joins the ranks of elite riders who've won more than 3 gold medals, Stuart Jackson has 4 and Nim Carline has 6.

**John Warnock,** Twickenham CC, who I predicted could be the next man over 500 miles, didn't quite make it, but nevertheless produced a superb silver medal ride with **491.39 miles.** He looked so steady and unruffled throughout and at the end he went up to collect his medal from Sheila Hardy and showed no signs of fatigue.

**Neil Skellern,** Congleton CC, took a well-earned bronze medal with **467.74 miles.** He just needs a gold medal now to get the full set. Maybe next year?

Ned Millington, in this years 24hr Fellowship Journal, reminds us that this event was once more recognised as the Premier event in Europe, by virtue of its inclusion in the Ultra-Marathon Cycling Association of America's calendar of long distance events as the European Championship, as well as being a counter for their European and World Cup series of events.

This event was Jon Williams' 3rd successful Championship promotion and Mersey RC President Sam Moffat and Paul Olson, the MC at the HQ, both thanked Jon and all of those involved with the event, and made the riders and their crews most welcome at the awards ceremony.

Both Wilko's 525 miles and Christine's 461miles Competition Records are safe for another year, but there is always 2009. As I mentioned in the introduction of this book, someone will always wonder what mileage they could achieve in 24 hours, and this event is the only official and accurate way of finding out.

**Ralph Dadswell and Dave Johnson's 2007** tandem trike **12 hour record** attempt has been ratified by the RRA Committee as **259.4 miles.** Then on the 1st October 2008, **Ralph and Paul Mace** claimed a new time of **13 hours 37mins 35 secs,** for the **Lands End to London** tandem trike record. They also improved the **12 hour** figures to **262.5 miles** and both records are subject to ratification.

# OBITUARIES : 2000 – 2008

## 2000

**Vernon Lilley** passed away on the **8th April 2000,** after suffering a short illness combined with the chronic lymphatic leukaemia he had been fighting for several years. Vernon reached the age of 87 despite his illness. Amongst his many other cycling exploits he also rode 379.6 miles in the Mersey RC 24hr of 1976 at 64 years of age.

**Steve Hawkes** died tragically on **7th May 2000,** whilst competing in the Mid Oxon CRT 25 on the Botley course. He was 62 years old. His first 24hr race, the 'Catford' of 1969 gave him 414.6 miles and 3rd place. John Gills informed us that Steve joined the 24hr Fellowship while lying on the grass verge after the event. His last 24hr was in 1976 with 406.7 miles, but he continued to race at distances up to 12 hours until 1992, many races were on a trike. Steve held many official posts in cycling club life and was the Chairman of the 24hr Fellowship from 1983 to 1994. *Obituary details were written by Dave Free.*

**Andy Burnett** died early in **2000,** he was a staunch 24hr rider and an enthusiast all of his life. Andy started his long distance career in the late 1940's with some very respectable mileages over 400 and various top five placings. In 1999, just before he died, Andy donated a full set of Journals for the Fellowship archives.

**Ken Hughes** died on **31st July 2000** aged 68. He was a hard riding clubman and led the Mid Shropshire Whls team to victory in the National Championship race of 1964, along with Stan France and Ray Page. 'Taff' Brissenden gave me details from Ken's obituary and mentioned that Ken had turned his talents to performing with a folk band alongside Taff who played the accordian. The band were called the 'Castle B' and they still perform to this day in the Shrewsbury area. Ken rode a fixed wheel for most of his races and I remember him 'battling' on the Mersey Rc 24 hour with members of my own club, Pete Swinden, John Withers and Pat Kenny. Ken also provided a few race descriptions and from them I've used passages and details from the early 1960's for this book.

**Ron Smith** died on **24th December 2000** aged 85. He road a ten shilling bike his father bought him at the age of eight. Ron joined the Atonia CC and time trialled for many years, preferring the longer distances. He rode three 24hr races, his best being 352 miles in 1953 to get the club record. Ron gave us his tale of the 'Wessex ghost' shortly before he died, and it appears in the Wessex race report of 1955, Chapter Three.

## 2001

**Les Heald** passed away on **April 27th** aged 88. He was a staunch Fellowship member from the very early days. Some of his best performances were ridden on the Mersey RC course in the 1950's. Les gained many South Lancs RC team places with rides over 430 miles.

**Geoff Guy** passed away early in **2001,** he was one of the best 24hr specialists of pre-war and immediate post Second World War years. On his first Catford 24hr ride in 1937 he covered 419.625 miles, and with Frank Robertson and A. Oxbrow set a Team Competition Record, which stood for some 10 years. Geoff won the Catford event for the next two years running with 433m and 427miles. After the war he resumed racing and again won the Catford in 1948 with 430 miles and led Purves and Shillibeer to another Competition Team Record of 1,284 miles. When Geoff wasn't racing he could be found helping his Vegetarian C & AC clubmates to their numerous victories in the following years. Frank Robertson said that Geoff was a very good friend in those happy carefree days and that he has fond memories of club riding with him.

**Kevin Langham** collapsed and died whilst riding his bike in the early summer of **2001,** he was only 40 years of age. Kevin regularly rode both the Mersey and the North Road 24 hours and just loved riding his bike, never complaining. He rode for the Leicester Forest CC and had many 24 hr performances over 400 miles. I only learned of Kevin's passing at the start of the Mersey event in 2001.

**Roy Moss** passed away in **2001,** he was heavily involved in the sport as a timekeeper in Wales. Roy was also an RRA timekeeper and timed Pauline Strong's End to End in 1990. When Pat Kenny and I failed on our End to End record attempt in 1979, there was no reproach from Roy, only words of encouragement to try again. Alzheimer's disease cut Roy's life short, as it has done for many other cyclists.

**Bert Owens** passed away this year, he had been a regular helper at the Mersey RC 24hr as a member of Harold Nelson's team of Masseurs who could be found throughout the 24 hour giving 'new legs' to many weary riders. Bert was a friendly character and always willing if there was a job to do. His last big mission was helping on the mixed tandem End to End for Andy Wilkinson and Lynne Taylor in May 2000. He was on the support team and worked alongside masseur Colin Baldwin.

## 2002

**Eric Lobley** died on **July 2nd 2002** from leukaemia at 71 years of age. Eric was a founder member of the Lea Valley RC and inspired others to ride 24hr races. His best performance in a Championship event was coming 9th with 424 miles in the Wessex RC National in 1970.

**Arthur Lancaster** who died on **October 12th 2002** aged 87 was a tireless worker for the North Road CC and a member for 67 years. He raced at most distances from 10 miles to 24hrs. His son, Andrew, told me that his father was a keen helper and supporter on the North Road event and he can still remember vividly, the feeling of excitement as a boy, at the prospect of staying up all night. Andrew said he couldn't remember making it much past midnight, only waking up at dawn on the back seat of his dad's car with a crick in his neck, as he bumped up another grass verge somewhere east of Cambridge. Arthur was a life member of the Road Records Association and served on its Committee for many years. (*See the last paragraph of the North Road 24hr in 1971*)

## 2003

**Roy Lomas** of the Kentish Whls died in **2003.** His daughter Pauline informed the Fellowship that he had ridden twenty three pre and post war 24 hour races, despite only having one leg. Roy had lost the use of his other leg due to a childhood illness, and in one particular month he rode two 24's and a 12 hour. Two of Roy's championship performances I've located are the Catford in 1947 with 323 miles and the North Road of 1948 with 329 miles.

**Ira Thomas** died in **October 2003** aged 90. He was well known on Shropshire and Cheshire roads as he'd seen and been involved in every 24hr in the north west since 1926, both as a rider and official with two clubs, the Mid Shropshire Whls and the Anfield B.C. His ashes were scattered at the old Battlefield Corner near Shrewsbury.

**George Longstaff** passed away in **2003,** he was a well known and respected cycle engineer who produced hand built bikes, trikes, tandems and tandem trikes, for riders worldwide. George suffered a stroke whilst riding and never recovered.

## 2004

**Paul Carbutt** died in **May 2004** aged 53, from motor neurone disease, a debilitating illness for which there is no known cure. Paul broke the 'End to End' record in 1979 after a glorious cycle racing career, rising from amateur clubman, time triallist and road man, to winning the 'BAR'. He rode as a professional for Viking cycles and Paul's last public appearance was in 2003 when he received a standing ovation as he lined up with many other famous End to Enders to watch a film taken on John Woodburn's record in 1980; a film that had lain undiscovered in a shed for 20 years. I spoke to Paul on the telephone a few weeks before he passed away and he asked me how my book on the End to End history was proceeding as he knew I had written about him. I replied that it was due to be published very shortly. Paul sounded very positive even though he'd completely lost the use of his limbs, and I didn't realise at that time that he wouldn't live long enough to read his story.

Ron Sant died suddenly on **13th September 2004,** he'd suffered a heart attack whilst leading a cavalcade of veteran cyclists through Telford, at 70 years of age. Ron came into long distance racing later in life than most, riding his first 24 hour at 56 years of age. He was a tough character on both bike and trike, and his knowledge encompassing the history of cycles knew no bounds. He was a great help when I needed details for both of my books, as he'd left a legacy of relevant literature for me to plunder. Ron gained the Audax gold medal for riding from Lands End to John o' Groats inside 80 hours and had helped on many road record attempts over that same journey as an Official Observer in the last few years of his life. No one knew that Ron was ill but apparently he had an underlying heart problem and had stopped racing. He was an Observer on the last three End to Ends and he said he was now looking forward to a rest from 'record duties'. He broke Midland and Northern road records with Jim Hopper on the tandem trike in 1991 of which there is a photo in this book, taken on the day, with George Longstaff, who'd kindly lent them the machine.

Don Spraggett died in late **Autumn** of **2004.** He was a prolific mile-eater, one of the 'old school' of riders. Don had a long and lasting 24hr career and was a force to be reckoned with in the 1960's. He rode to many high placings, especially on his home course the 'Mersey' event. Don's highest mileage was 471.88 in 1968 riding into 2nd place behind Eric Matthews. He would help anyone in an event and even when he'd 'packed' on the odd occasion he would stay out on course and help others. Don was one of the instigators of secreting food parcels and drinks around the course the day before an event, hiding any items that would help him in ditches or behind hedges, for consumption during the event. Ned Millington mentioned that Don would lend the benefit of his expertise to one and all from the roadside, at all the hours of the day and night, as many found out who were on the receiving end of his uniquely tasty and never to be forgotten rice pudding.

Harry Wilkinson passed away in this year. He was a well known time triallist both before and well after the second world war and one of the old time hard riding clubmen who would ride miles to an event, whether it be a 100 miles or a 12 hour, ride the event, and then ride home again. He took many Vet's age awards and later he helped look after riders during events. Harry provided 'comfort stops' with his van on Lynne's solo End to End in 2001, he travelled the full journey with John Arnold and gave much needed support on route.

# 2005

Margaret Hopper passed away in **March 2005** after a short illness. She had been a 24 hour Fellowship member for many years and looked after her husband Jim on his numerous races and road records along with a crew of Jim's friends. Margaret had a cheery word for everyone and Lynne always looked forward to seeing her during the Mersey RC 24hr for the support she gave. Needless to say, Margaret is missed by all of us. (*also see Mersey race report 2005*)

Bob Mynott a lifelong member of the North Road CC passed away in **2005** at 85 years of age. He won the North Road 24hr in 1949 and the following year broke Competition Record with 459.5 miles. In 1979, Bob came back to his old love of 24hr riding and recorded 394 miles at 59 years of age, to help his club win the team race.

Tim Dolphin also passed away in this year. He was a lone rider and competed without motorised helpers in both the North Road CC and the Mersey RC 24 hour events in the same year. (*for more details see the 2005 race report.*)

# 2006

Frank Robertson passed away early in this year. He was a rider from the 1930's and a good friend of Edgar Seeley and Sid Ferris. Frank rode his first 24hr in 1935 and came 3rd to Seeley with 404.8 miles, and went on to ride many more. In later life Frank emigrated to Australia but remained a member of the 24hr Fellowship. He continued throughout his life to send information about riders from those early years, and I've used many of his details for this book.

Frank Mumford died on **4th January 2006** at 91 years of age. He had been a lifelong member of the Mersey RC since 1939. Frank was in the winning team in 1947, 1948, 1950 and 1951, his highest mileage being 407.7 miles. In later years as well as club riding over long distances at weekends, he also became an avid audax rider. Frank served the club well and was a keen organiser. Before the start of the Mersey RC 24 hr, Frank could be found chatting to riders and gleaning snippets of information about their fitness, or details about their bikes, equipment and clothing, and all of this information would form part of his report on the rest of the race for 'The Record'. My writing of the History of the 24hr race relies upon Frank's very detailed yet sometimes comical descriptions and phrases, that stop us from taking ourselves too seriously.

**Mick Potts** lost his struggle for life in **January 2006** aged 64. A stroke caused his death after a four year battle with cancer. Jim Hopper said that Mick, who he had known for most of his life, was one of the hardest riders he'd ever known. In 1991 Mick won the Mersey RC National Championship 24 hour with 486.6 miles at the age of 50. His only other performance had been in winning it 20 years previously with 475 miles. During his long and glorious racing career, Mick had turned his hand to all forms of competition from track racing to road. He competed internationally and time trialled at all levels up to 24 hours. Later he turned to audax riding and rode the 'PBP' Paris-Brest-Paris twice, breaking the record for an Englishman.

**Mick de Moulpied** died in March 2006 after struggling since the late 1990's with Alzheimer's Disease. He was born in Guernsey but lived most of his life at Selly Oak in Birmingham. During his life, Mick organised many road record attempts for various riders. Dave Duffield's trike records were all planned and organised by Mick as well as record rides by Swinden and Withers and also for Pat Kenny and myself. He took up time keeping in later years and worked tirelessly for the Midlands RTTC area and also as an RRA Timekeeper and Official. In his earlier years as a racing clubman, Mick organised the Beacon Road Club's annual Birmingham to Weston and back reliability trial, and usually rode it himself as part of his 24 hour training. His best result was in the Mersey event of 1961 with 404 miles.

**Malcolm Judge** died in **2006,** he was one of the backbone members of the Seamons CC, and he won the Mersey RC 24hr in 1980 with 454 miles but his personal best is 455 miles, a club record that still stands to this day. Johnny Pardoe wrote a cycling tribute to Malcolm, sometimes known as 'Seamus' or 'Judgy'. He recalled their long history in the club together and their quest to race on the 'fast' courses, which meant riding long distances on bikes to get there, long before cars became affordable. One amusing incident Johnny recalled was "riding over to Blyth, Notts, to ride a 50 mile event. On arriving at the 'White House Café' we went through the weekly ritual of removing the mudguards, changing the sprockets and generally getting very oily. Malc asked him if he'd got a rag and Johnny replied 'Sorry Malc, but there's one on the fence over there'. It turned out to be Nim Carline's shirt! 'Sorry Nim' Johnny said, and they made up for it by inviting Nim to be the Guest of Honour at their annual club dinner." Malcolm went on to win the club 'BAR' competition 8 times and was also the club 12 hour Champion no less than 9 times.

**Ron Coukham** passed away around this time after suffering from Alzheimer's disease for quite a long while. Ron had been a tough member of the Rutland CC, alongside Stuart Thompson, Graham Fouldes, George Steers, Joe Leversidge and Jim Halls, between 1955 and 1959, winning Championships and pushing the Team Competition Record higher on two occasions. Ron could later be found playing a supporting role in many 24 hr races, always putting something back into the sport he loved.

# 2007

On **January 10th, Wyn Wrightson** passed away. She held the ladies amateur 1,000 miles record from 1953 to 1974 and broke many Western Counties road records.

On the **1st April 2007, Ron Diplock** died aged 86. Ron worked tirelessly for his club, the Ealing Paragon CC, and also the CTT and RRA both as a Timekeeper, Observer and Course Measurer. His best 24 hr performance was 421 miles. After the turn of the Millenium, Ron was due to measure parts of the 'End to End' route so that the 1,000 miles record could be accurately finalised for Gethin and Lynne, but illness prevented him from his mission and his health deteriorated rapidly.

On **May 29th, Norman 'Nim' Carline** passed away aged 79 from Pagetts Disease. As mentioned so far in the race reports, Nim was revolutionary in his method of riding long distance events, throwing caution to the wind, ignoring all of the previous methods of winning a 24 hour. He would 'ride like fury' from the very start (his own words) in an effort to demoralize the opposition. In most cases he succeeded with some breathtaking winning performances and record mileages. Nim made races exciting by giving his all, 100%, and whenever and wherever he rode there was always a nailbiting atmosphere. He always said that young Eric Matthews would be the one to succeed him, with his slightly steadier, more scientific approach to tackling the 24 hour. Nim trained very hard and worked long hours at a very physically demanding job and this showed through in his stamina and ruthlessness with himself in races. In 24hr circles he is spoken of in awe and stands head and shoulders amongst the 'legends' of long distance racing. Even in 2008 younger champions and record breakers such as Andy Wilkinson, Gethin Butler and Nik Gardiner, respect his winning ways and mileages. I last saw Nim at the Mersey 24hr in 2005, wearing his traditional flat cap and normal sports jacket. He marshalled the Whitchurch bypass island for 13 years and Jim Turner acknowledged his stalwart help on the 24hr scene, never losing interest in the sport. The cycling world has sadly lost another great champion.

In **June 2007 Will Townsend 'OBE'** died aged 102. He'd been an untiring worker and Official for both the RRA and the RTTC for most of his life, and claimed to have been at every BBAR concert since the 1930's.

**David Stapleton** died this year aged 93. He had been the Secretary and Organiser of the Mersey RC 24 hour for 30 years, prior to Jim Turner taking over the role in the 1980's. Dave had to contend with many crises during that time and he'd handled them very well. He was a very thorough man and always made sure that the riders were well looked after during the event, whether they were doing 300 miles or 500. Dave's son Robert won the Mersey event in 1972 with 457 miles at his first attempt but in that same event, trike rider Stan Spelling suffered an accident which proved fatal, prompting Frank Fischer to remark "what a mixed set of emotions for that excellent Organiser, David Stapleton." I last saw Dave in 2006 after the 24hr at the Farndon HQ. He was still helping with race details, and apart from being a little deaf, he seemed fine.

**Gerry Jones** died after a short illness about this time, aged 61. I first noticed his results when he rode for St Christopher's CCC in 1959 with 402 miles, and then riding for the Wrexham RC 41 years later in 2000, when he produced 444 miles.

In **November, Bernard Thompson** passed away. Apart from being a well known Writer, Reporter and Photographer, Bernard had travelled in his motor home with his wife Ethel, to many high profile cycle races, including End to End records. He covered many Championship time trials as a Reporter for 'Cycling' and his black and white photos and action shots of the 'Star' riders are all part of our history. Fortunately before Bernard passed away, Peter Whitfield managed to convince him to have his photos put onto a compact disc for all to see. Bernard had got to know many riders over 40 years of reporting and consequently he was called upon to pen many Obituaries during that time.

**Paul Cull,** Mersey RC died in **December 2007** from a brain tumour. He'd been ill for quite some time. In 1995 he bravely rode the Mersey 24hr in memory of his father John. Paul rode 355 miles that day with very little training.

**Jim 'Nobby' Clarke** the noted Scottish Timekeeper died on the **23rd December 2007** after a long fight against illness. I found a 24hr result that he produced in the Wessex National Championship in 1958 of 413 miles riding for the Royal Navy CA. He was a great help in 2001 when he came to our aid to time Lynne over the line at John o' Groats, having travelled up from Aberdeen.

# 2008

**Eddie Mundy** died suddenly on **9th January,** he collapsed after riding to the Addiscombe CC clubroom. Up until the time of his death he still handled much of the paperwork for both the Addiscombe and the RRA. To me he had been the main contact for record breakers and most RRA correspondence came from him. He broke and held Competition Record for the 24hrs, firstly in 1950 with 455.91 and then 467.5 in 1952, being part of the Addiscombe record-breaking team during these years. Eddie was a tough, sturdily built man, a tower of strength, true to his club all of his life, and a tireless worker for the RRA. He'd been a submariner during the Second World War and had many friends, resulting in the church being packed at his funeral. He will be greatly missed.

**Tom Finney** died in **February** of **2008.** He was a tough 24hr rider and was a regular member of the North Staffs St Christopher's team and then the Horwich CC Championship 24hr team for a period spanning 14 years from 1975 to 1989. In 1980, along with John Cahill and Mick Coupe, he rode to a Team Competition Record of 1,441.59 miles; Tom's 468 miles that day was one of his best performances ever and this team record is still unbroken as at 2008. Mick Coupe is now the only member of that famous trio still alive. In the 1970's Tom was a member of the Army CU and attempted the End to End, backed up by a team of military personnel. I saw Tom ride through the Midlands and it seemed strange to see khaki clad helpers leap out of a Land Rover to help him. Tom packed before he reached Scotland due to unfavourable conditions.

**Bill Perrett** died in **February,** he was 92 years of age and had been in poor health for quite some time. Bill owned a popular bike shop in Bloxwich near Walsall, and he was also a life long member of the Walsall Roads CC. In 1949, along with Bill Bradley and Sid Genders, he rode the Mersey RC 24hr and produced 388.74 miles, to set a Walsall RCC team record that day which stood for 50 years. Bill worked tirelessly to promote the South Staffs CA time trials for a period of 40 years back in the good old days when we still had some excellent fast courses quite close to home. Bill will probably be remembered by Midlands riders more for this work than anything else.

**Fred Cowling,** Tyne RC, passed away also in the **Spring** of **2008.** His earlier exploits at riding for 24 hours had obviously sewn the seed for the lads from the Tyne RC to give it a try and this led to the successes in the 1970's. Fred was a regular contributor to the Fellowship Journal.

**Bernard Blow** passed away in the **summer** of **2008** from Alzheimer's Disease, he was 82. Bernard along with his wife Joyce, was one of the founder members of the 300,000 miles club. One 24hr result I managed to find for Bernard, and I daresay there were more, was 385 miles in the Mersey RC Championship in 1953, riding for the South Lancs RC. Bernard's wife Joyce, a Champion trike rider at all distances up to and including the 24hr, nursed him round the clock, to the very end of his life.

**Ken Matthews** passed away in **July 2008,** after suffering poor health for quite some time. Ken was a life long member of the Kirkby CC and a talented road man. Later he became better known as a Reporter for the Liverpool Echo and covered all the cycling events and riders in the North West of England. Ken was also 'Cycling's' man in the North West and gave credibility and exposure to talented racing men and women from Staffordshire in the south, going as far north as Cumbria.

**Bill Coupe** died in **August 2008,** aged 99. He was one of our last surviving links to the Anfield 24hr having ridden the penultimate event in 1935, and coming 2nd with 377.75 miles. Bill was a lifelong cyclist and still active on the 24hr scene whilst well into his seventies. I have used some of Bill's observations and writings around the 1930's in this book, and they help to colour the picture and give us an insight as to those times pre and post Second World War.

**Ivy Mitton** passed away on **11th October 2008.** She had been a life member of the RRA and a valuable Timekeeper and Observer for many years. Ivy was always willing to be of assistance to record breakers over any distance, whether it be a National or Regional RRA record. Ivy suffered many physical setbacks in her life, but overcame them all to continue with her work and pastime, assisted by her husband, Peter. Both of them were 24 hr Fellowship members.

**Gordon Brennan** died on **October 9th 2008.** He held the 100 miles and Liverpool to Edinburgh records, both on a trike, and was always supportive of other record breakers over the years.

## Mersey National 2001

| Place | No | Name | Club | 100 mile | 24 Hrs |
|-------|-----|------|------|----------|--------|
| 1 | 50 | Gethin Butler | Preston Wheelers | 4.13.17 | 485.88 |
| 2 | 35 | Timothy Bayley | Arctic Racing Team | 4.33.06 | 469.82 |
| 3 | 48 | Chris Shepherd | Rother Valley CC | | 462.99 |
| 4 | 49 | Mark Botteley | Fenland Clarion CC | | 443.61 |
| 5 | 17 | Jose Pinon | Central Lancs RC | 4.51.11 | 441.66 |
| 6 | 40 | Chris Hopkinson | Matlock CC | 4.32.13 | 440.93 |
| 7 | 23 | Steve Ginty | Southport CC | 4.52.49 | 431.35 |
| 8 | 39 | Lynne Taylor | Walsall RCC | | 423.13 |
| 9 | 43 | Bryan Ackerley | Wrexham Roads/Fibrax | | 411.32 |
| 10 | 45 | Andy Proffitt | Arctic Racing Team | | 409.85 |
| 11 | 26 | Jim Hopper (Tri) | Derby Mercury RC | | 408.56 |
| 12 | 44 | Michael Wiseman | Hertfordshire Wheelers | | 407.37 |
| 13 | 34 | Mike Smith (Tri) | Maldon & District CC | | 407.17 |
| 14 | 25 | Karl Austin | Congleton CC | 4.47.54 | 397.87 |
| 15 | 22 | Michael Phillips | Drighlington BC | | 392.95 |
| 16 | 30 | Damian Coleman | Arctic Racing Team | | 388.85 |
| 17 | 10 | Timothy Dolphin | North Road CC | | 386.97 |
| 18 | 38 | Ritchie Tout | Cardiff Byways RCC | | 385.74 |
| 19 | 21 | Steve Sayers | Fleetwood RC | | 379.31 |
| 20 | 27 | Steve Abraham | North Bucks RC | | 360.41 |
| 21 | 19 | Neville Holgate | Southport CC | | 354.05 |
| 22 | 24 | Ian Kellaway | Coventry CC | | 352.97 |
| 23 | 29 | George Berwick | Edinburgh RC | | 350.84 |
| 24 | 18 | Campbell Crombie | Johnstone Wheelers | | 350.75 |
| 25 | 8 | Dave Stokes (Tri) | Johnstone Wheelers | | 343.01 |
| 26 | 13 | Jeremy Briggs | De Laune CC | | 342.18 |
| 27 | 28 | Rob Waghorn | Congleton CC | | 330.10 |
| 28 | 33 | George Shepherd | Fife Century RC | | 324.74 |
| 29 | 20 | Chris Vessey | Hounslow & District Whs | | 324.25 |
| 30 | 9 | Heather Swift | Central Lancs RC | | 314.78 |
| 31 | 16 | Calum McIntosh | Edinburgh RC | | 309.85 |
| 32 | 47 | Simon Corbett | Wrekinsport CC | | 305.27 |
| 33 | 15 | Gareth Gregory | Port Talbot Wheelers | | 241.53 |

### TANDEM RESULT

| | | | | | |
|---|---|---|---|---|---|
| 1 | 2 | Eileen Brabbin<br>David Brabbin | Wigan Wheelers | 4.48.25 | 439.54 |

### Team Result

**Arctic Racing Team - 1268.52 miles: Tim Bayley, Andy Proffitt, Damian Coleman**

### Ladies Winner
**Lynne Taylor  (Walsall RCC) 423.13**

## Mersey National 2002

| Pos | No | Name | Club | 100 mile | 24 hrs |
|-----|-----|------|------|----------|--------|
| 1 | 55 | David Shepherd | Rother Valley CC | 4.34.49 | 482.128 |
| 2 | 54 | Jose Pinon | Central Lancs RC | 4.26.56 | 470.044 |
| 3 | 59 | Mark Botteley | Fenland Clarion CC | 4.39.49 | 469.698 |
| 4 | 56 | Andy Briggs | Kiveton Park CC | 4.37.42 | 461.001 |
| 5 | 61 | Neil Stewart | Wigan Wh. | 4.46.49 | 453.992 |
| 6 | 57 | Brian Walker | Pete Read Racing | 4.31.03 | 453.791 |
| 7 | 25 | Paul O'Donoghue | Sorrento CC | 4.46.49 | 449.620 |
| 8 | 58 | Karl Austin | Congleton CC | 4.50.42 | 443.625 |
| 9 | 50 | Lynne Taylor | Walsall RCC | 4.48.42 | 438.042 |
| 10 | 46 | John Falconer | Caithness CC | 5.03.29 | 435.503 |
| 11 | 52 | Gerald Jones | Wrexham RC Fibrax | 4.45.29 | 432.473 |
| 12 | 4 | Clifford Jackson | Pembrokeshire Velo | 5.04.42 | 428.437 |
| 13 | 45 | Marina Bloom | Crawley Wh. | 4.52.36 | 427.502 |
| 14 | 62 | Robert Osman | Clifton CC | 4.51.22 | 426.973 |
| 15 | 22 | Richard Thoday | Matlock CC | 4.48.42 | 423.868 |
| 16 | 37 | Steve Abraham | North Bucks RC | 5.41.26 | 410.664 |
| 17 | 47 | Ritchie Tout | Cardiff Byways RCC | 5.24.58 | 401.426 |
| 18 | 43 | Paul Cook | Derwentside CC | 4.55.42 | 400.468 |
| 19 | 60 | Chris Hopkinson | Pete Read Racing | 4.23.49 | 396.791 |
| 20 | 53 | Graham Smith | Severn RC | 4.56.29 | 389.713 |
| 21 | 10 | Alex Doig | Deeside Thistle CC | 5.20.15 | 389.469 |
| 22 | 17 | Roger Squire | Wrexham RC Fibrax | 5.14.22 | 389.440 |
| 23 | 51 | Steve Gelder | Pete Read Racing | 5.08.26 | 387.271 |
| 24 | 31 | Jim Hopper T | Derby Mercury RC | 5.30.01 | 382.317 |
| 25 | 33 | Tim Dolphin | Hounslow & Dist. Wh. | 5.39.05 | 378.469 |
| 26 | 40 | Tony Bailey | Chester RC | 5.35.15 | 378.339 |
| 27 | 14 | Dave Minter | Tamworth RCC | 5.46.26 | 373.074 |
| 28 | 6 | Bill Carnaby | Hounslow & Dist. Wh. | 5.51.54 | 372.865 |
| 29 | 34 | Campbell Crombie | Johnstone Wh. | 5.57.40 | 366.642 |
| 30 | 30 | David Lewis | Cardiff Byways RCC | 5.05.15 | 364.338 |
| 31 | 32 | Ian Kellaway | Coventry CC | 5.53.46 | 363.251 |
| 32 | 18 | Andrew Harrington | Deeside Thistle CC | 6.04.30 | 358.696 |
| 33 | 21 | Neil Williams | Cadiff Byways RCC | 5.40.08 | 354.606 |
| 34 | 41 | George Berwick | Edinburgh RC | 6.10.19 | 353.882 |
| 35 | 19 | Paul Whitehead | Hampshire RC | 5.52.53 | 347.708 |
| 36 | 29 | Tom Ellis | North Hampshire RC | 5.49.23 | 344.062 |
| 37 | 20 | Ursula Betterton | Cleveland Coureurs | 6.12.47 | 341.427 |
| 38 | 39 | Ann Wooldridge | Gloucester City CC | 5.30.15 | 332.582 |
| 39 | 7 | Claire Ashton | Wrekinsport CC | 6.36.05 | 328.863 |
| 40 | 42 | Geraint Catherall | Anfield BC | 5.57.58 | 328.231 |
| 41 | 1 | Dave Stokes T | Johnstone Wh. | 6.37.00 | 328.178 |
| 42 | 35 | Julian Gee | Sotonia CC | 5.50.05 | 327.234 |
| 43 | 16 | Mark Shannon | Edinburgh RC | 6.17.19 | 324.304 |
| 44 | 5 | Thomas Hall | Tyne RC | 6.51.53 | 311.226 |
| 45 | 12 | Douglas Haig | Deeside Thistle CC | 5.38.30 | 305.596 |
| 46 | 2 | Gail Summerlin | Leicestershire CC | | 294.145 |
| 47 | 15 | Philippa Crocker | Dursley RC | | 264.791 |
| 48 | 8 | Graham Halden | Leek Cyclists' Club | | 262.118 |

### TANDEM RESULT

| 65 | Eileen & David Brabbin | Wigan Wh. | 4.38.56 | 464.924 * |

### TEAM RESULT

| 1 | Pete Read Racing: | Brian Walker | 453.791 |
|---|---|---|---|
| | | Chris Hopkinson | 396.791 |
| | | Steve Gelder | 387.271 |
| | | | 1237.853 |

| 2 | Cardiff Byways RCC | 1120.370 |
|---|---|---|
| 3 | Deeside Thistle CC | 1053.761 |

* comp record

## Mersey  National 2003

| Place | No | Name | Club | 100 mile | 24 Hrs |
|---|---|---|---|---|---|
| 1 | 70 | Gethin Butler | Preston Wheelers | 4.16.50 | 471.210 |
| 2 | 50 | Neil Stewart | Wigan Wheelers | 4.33.08 | 456.643 |
| 3 | 46 | Richard Thoday | Matlock CC | 4.40.03 | 451.352 |
| 4 | 40 | Chris Shepherd | Rother Valley CC | 4.41.46 | 445.473 |
| 5 | 55 | Paul O Donoghue | Sorrento CC | 4.35.31 | 436.069 |
| 6 | 30 | Nick Cave | Leicester Forest CC | 4.47.53 | 431.940 |
| 7 | 64 | Graham Smith | Severn Road Club | 4.48.12 | 422.441 |
| 8 | 36 | Gerald Jones | Wrexham Road Club | 4.43.27 | 418.890 |
| 9 | 58 | John Hatfield | Ravensthorpe CC | 4.50.29 | 418.281 |
| 10 | 32 | Marina Bloom | Walsall Roads CC | 4.46.07 | 413.255 |
| 11 | 51 | Lynne Taylor | Walsall Road CC | 4.41.16 | 411.141 |
| 12 | 61 | Chris Hopkinson | Preston Wheelers | 4.43.13 | 405.636 |
| 13 | 62 | Tracey Maund | Walsall Roads CC | 5.21.20 | 405.305 |
| 14 | 52 | David Lewis | Cardiff Byways RCC | 5.03.16 | 403.620 |
| 15 | 49 | Patrick Schalbetter | CATS MBC | 5.00.03 | 401.034 |
| 16 | 38 | Michael Phillips | Drighlington BC | 5.11.34 | 398.920 |
| 17 | 20 | Steven Abraham | North Bucks Road Club | 5.34.01 | 392.134 |
| 18 | 69 | Miles Jenkins | Chester Road Club | 4.47.24 | 391.637 |
| 19 | 34 | Roger Squire | Wrexham Road Club | 5.44.28 | 391.122 |
| 20 | 66 | Roland Elsdon | Rugby RCC | 5.06.56 | 385.717 |
| 21 | 57 | Eric Ruthenberg | Matlock CC | 5.12.03 | 380.603 |
| 22 | 35 | Ian Kellaway | Coventry CC | 5.13.29 | 378.798 |
| 23 | 4 | Campbell Crombie | Johnstone Wheelers CC | 5.29.05 | 378.385 |
| 24 | 68 | Jonathan Morgan | North Shropshire Wheelers | 5.14.17 | 377.013 |
| 25 | 16 | James Roberson | Cardiff Byways RCC | 5.18.58 | 373.895 |
| 26 | 13 | Michael Friday | Catford CC | 5.40.40 | 372.482 |
| 27 | 67 | Rob Waghorn | Congleton CC | 5.28.11 | 368.998 |
| 28 | 27 | Simon Simpson | Johnstone Wheelers CC | 5.31.31 | 368.017 |
| 29 | 43 | Ann Wooldridge | Walsall Roads CC | 5.19.55 | 365.420 |
| 30 | 23 | Roger Cliffe | Solihull Cycling Club | 5.20.49 | 364.064 |
| 31 | 48 | Jim Hopper (Tri) | Derby Mercury Road Club | 5.31.16 | 357.868 |
| 32 | 6 | Dick Law | Solihull Cycling Club | 5.35.54 | 356.344 |
| 33 | 28 | Giudo Reynolds | Solihull Cycling Club | 5.48.24 | 355.576 |
| 34 | 9 | Claire Ashton | Walsall Roads CC | 5.34.38 | 355.396 |
| 35 | 63 | John Hassall | South Pennine RC | 5.36.03 | 352.367 |
| 36 | 18 | Stewart Bond | Preston Wheelers | 5.44.53 | 349.829 |
| 37 | 44 | Paul Whitehead | Hampshire RC | 5.29.35 | 347.586 |
| 38 | 26 | Robert Watson | North Hampshire Road Club | 5.50.30 | 344.432 |
| 39 | 25 | George Berwick | Edinburgh Road Club | 6.03.39 | 335.979 |
| 40 | 22 | Mark Shannon | Edinburgh Road Club | 6.00.43 | 335.839 |
| 41 | 10 | William Leaper | Mersey Roads Club | 6.10.52 | 312.132 |
| 42 | 21 | Arthur Vince | VC Camelot | 6.36.30 | 308.790 |
| 43 | 39 | Geraint Catherall | Anfield BC | 6.41.24 | 308.536 |
| 44 | 15 | Graham Trickey | Border City Wheelers | 6.33.44 | 302.745 |
| 45 | 59 | Chris Vessey | Middlesex Road Club | 6.07.28 | 301.483 |
| 46 | 11 | Dave Stokes (Tri) | Johnstone Wheelers CC | 6.27.06 | 300.217 |

**TANDEM RESULT**

| | | | | | |
|---|---|---|---|---|---|
| 1 | 3 | Mary Corbett Norman Harvey | Sotonia CC | 5.00.15 | 366.922 |

**TEAM RESULT**

**Winning Team**
**Walsall Roads CC**

| | | |
|---|---|---|
| Marina Bloom | 413.255 | |
| Lynne Taylor | 411.141 | |
| Tracey Maund | 405.305 | |
| **Total 1229.701** | ✷Comp record | |

**Second Team**
Preston Wheelers                 **Total 1226.675**

**Third Team**
Solihull Cycling Club            **Total 1075.984**

## Mersey National 2004

| Place | No | Name | Club | 100 mile | 24 Hrs |
|---|---|---|---|---|---|
| 1 | 80 | Niklaus Gardiner | timetrial.co.uk RT | 4.31.31 | 479.131 |
| 2 | 55 | Jose Pinon Shaw | Preston Wheelers | 4.27.31 | 470.799 |
| 3 | 70 | Andy Briggs | Doncaster Wheelers | 4.19.51 | 460.603 |
| 4 | 62 | Tony Grassby | Dinnington RC | 4.35.32 | 448.265 |
| 5 | 72 | Ferdinand Laussmann | Coventry Cycling Club | 4.39.12 | 446.299 |
| 6 | 65 | Lynne Taylor | Walsall Roads CC | 4.41.52 | 443.145 |
| 7 | 60 | Chris Hopkinson | Matlock CC | 4.18.31 | 436.638 |
| 8 | 52 | Marina Bloom | Walsall Roads CC | 4.55.32 | 434.062 |
| 9 | 50 | Karl Austin | Congleton CC | 4.47.32 | 432.995 |
| 10 | 57 | Graham Barker | Rockingham CC | 4.48.13 | 426.719 |
| 11 | 75 | Richard Thoday | Matlock CC | 4.42.13 | 423.692 |
| 12 | 48 | Roger Squire | Wrexham Roads Club | 4.51.14 | 422.293 |
| 13 | 47 | Tracey Maund | Walsall Roads CC | 5.02.53 | 415.629 |
| 14 | 73 | Gerald Jones | Wrexham Roads Club | 4.52.36 | 413.641 |
| 15 | 46 | Robert Watson | North Hamshire road Club | 5.08.15 | 410.627 |
| 16 | 18 | Dale Sturman | West Suffolk Wheelers | 5.10.13 | 410.483 |
| 17 | 23 | Anthony Wheatley | West Bromwich CTC | 5.13.33 | 404.397 |
| 18 | 78 | David Lewis | Cardiff Byways RCC | 4.56.09 | 403.731 |
| 19 | 29 | Robet Gray | Loughborough Phoenix CC | 5.07.54 | 396.525 |
| 20 | 19 | Ka-Wai Li | West Bromwich CTC | 5.16.14 | 396.193 |
| 21 | 79 | Paul O Donoghue | Sorrento CC | 4.46.52 | 396.148 |
| 22 | 51 | Steven Abraham | North Bucks Road Club | 5.39.34 | 396.081 |
| 23 | 35 | Kathryn Smith | Nottingham Clarion CC | 5.01.55 | 395.555 |
| 24 | 67 | Michael Heesom | Merseyside Wheelers | 4.49.13 | 388.429 |
| 25 | 40 | Ann Wooldridge | Walsall Roads CC | 5.04.14 | 388.029 |
| 26 | 33 | Robert Meredith | Walsall Roads CC | 5.20.54 | 385.417 |
| 27 | 77 | John Lindsay | Wills Wheels CC | 5.19.38 | 376.197 |
| 28 | 69 | Eric Ruthenberg | Matlock CC | 5.08.15 | 375.808 |
| 29 | 58 | Jim Hopper (Tri) | Derby Mercury RC | 5.25.15 | 373.143 |
| 30 | 66 | Giudo Reynolds | Solihull CC | 5.48.48 | 371.844 |
| 31 | 56 | Phil Holden | Seamons CC | 5.06.19 | 369.998 |
| 32 | 43 | Ritchie Tout | Cardiff Byways RCC | 5.18.54 | 365.072 |
| 33 | 68 | Paul Whitehead | Hampshire RC | 5.06.33 | 364.980 |
| 34 | 20 | Daniel Fisher | Willesden CC | 5.27.57 | 359.612 |
| 35 | 11 | Simon Simpson | Johnstone Wheelers CC | 5.35.56 | 359.042 |
| 36 | 49 | Campbell Crombie | Johnstone Wheelers CC | 5.53.01 | 358.044 |
| 37 | 38 | Dave Stokes | Johnstone Wheelers CC | 6.19.48 | 355.376 |
| 38 | 45 | Jimmy Froggatt | Wills Wheels CC | 4.45.02 | 354.245 |
| 39 | 59 | Ian Kellaway | Coventry Cycling Club | 6.04.07 | 353.383 |
| 40 | 76 | Christopher Riley | Wills Wheels CC | 5.19.58 | 353.275 |
| 41 | 14 | Paul Hodgkinson | Matlock CC | 5.29.36 | 349.074 |
| 42 | 71 | William Wright | Wills Wheels CC | 5.09.22 | 347.203 |
| 43 | 32 | Bob Harber | Brighton Excelsior CC | 5.31.34 | 346.666 |
| 44 | 44 | Alf Williams | Port Talbot Wheelers CC | 5.31.36 | 345.272 |
| 45 | 16 | Tony Pember | Cardiff 100 Miles RCC | 5.53.57 | 343.197 |
| 46 | 30 | Geraint Catherall | Anfield BC | 5.39.16 | 342.691 |
| 47 | 28 | Eric Cittanova | Wills Wheels CC | 5.51.33 | 340.280 |
| 48 | 24 | David Burton | Wills Wheels CC | 5.32.35 | 327.740 |
| 49 | 64 | James Roberson | Cardiff Byways RCC | 5.49.40 | 326.014 |
| 50 | 9 | William Leaper | Mersey Roads Club | 5.55.15 | 320.444 |
| 51 | 10 | David Barry | sport.fagley | 5.58.16 | 319.371 |
| 52 | 34 | Robert Morton | Seamons CC | 5.45.43 | 317.982 |
| 53 | 61 | Stephen Poulton (Tri) | Cheltenham & County CC | 6.26.43 | 310.289 |
| 54 | 42 | Chris Vessey | Middlesex Road Club | 6.06.42 | 307.454 |
| 55 | 12 | David Tickle | Seamons CC | 6.23.56 | 303.048 |
| 56 | 37 | Mark Shannon | Edinburgh Road Club | 6.20.48 | 293.718 |
| 57 | 17 | Heather Swift | Central Lancs RC | 6.30.23 | 287.713 |
| 58 | 22 | Arthur Vince | VC Camelot | 6.39.19 | 286.253 |
| 59 | 41 | Gail Summerlin | Leics RC | 7.08.20 | 279.673 |
| 60 | 21 | Michael Buckley | Tunstall Wheelers | 5.23.14 | 276.357 |
| 61 | 31 | Graham Halden | Leek Cyclists' Club | | 243.557 |

**TANDEM RESULT**

| Place | No | Name | Club | 100 mile | 24 Hrs |
|---|---|---|---|---|---|
| 1 | 2 | George Shepherd | Mersey Roads Club | | |
| | | George Berwick | Edinburgh Road Club | 4.59.54 | 392.291 |

**TEAM RESULT**

**Winning Team**
To receive the RTTC Championship Shield, 3 RTTC Championship
Medallions, plus £30 each and the Booth Memorial Shield.

**Walsall Roads CC**
| | |
|---|---|
| Lynne Taylor | 443.145 |
| Marina Bloom | 434.062 |
| Tracey Maund | 415.629 |

Total 1292.836 Comp Record

**Second Team**
Matlock CC  Total 1236.138

**Third Team**
Cardiff Byways RCC  Total 1094.817

## Mersey National 2005

| Place | No | Name | Club | 100 mile | 24 Hrs |
|---|---|---|---|---|---|
| 1 | 70 | Niklaus Gardiner | timetrial.co.uk RT | 4.18.18 | 493.081 |
| 2 | 69 | Keith Coffey | Bec CC | 4.18.18 | 475.897 |
| 3 | 53 | Neil Skellern | Congleton CC | 4.29.49 | 453.828 |
| 4 | 67 | Graham Barker | Rockingham CC | 4.41.21 | 452.749 |
| 5 | 38 | Mark Abela | Kent Cycles RC | 4.24.49 | 452.252 |
| 6 | 45 | Marina Bloom | Walsall Roads CC | 4.44.21 | 447.334 |
| 7 | 30 | Steve Abraham | North Bucks RC | 4.51.23 | 443.416 |
| 8 | 68 | Paul Alderson | South Western RC | 4.29.49 | 431.832 |
| 9 | 64 | Roger Squire | Fibrax-Wrexham RC | 4.46.26 | 430.537 |
| 10 | 66 | Karl Austin | Congleton CC | 4.32.21 | 428.052 |
| 11 | 52 | Paul Robinson | Ystwyth CC | 4.27.49 | 422.638 |
| 12 | 46 | Roland Elsdon | Rugby RCC | 4.49.23 | 421.104 |
| 13 | 43 | Mark Leadbetter | Unattached, SCU | 4.52.23 | 420.600 |
| 14 | 40 | Robert Watson | North Hampshire RC | 4.43.21 | 418.114 |
| 15 | 27 | Daniel Fisher | Willesden CC | 4.55.55 | 415.505 |
| 16 | 36 | Edgar Reynolds | Solihull CC | 5.10.37 | 413.792 |
| 17 | 49 | John Pugh | Godric CC | 4.52.55 | 413.785 |
| 18 | 55 | Lynne Taylor | Walsall Roads CC | 4.47.55 | 412.807 |
| 19 | 33 | Philip Kelman | Deeside Thistle CC | 4.54.21 | 412.400 |
| 20 | 22 | Dale Sturman | West Suffolk Wheelers | 5.10.23 | 408.189 |
| 21 | 63 | Eric Ruthenberg | Matlock CC | 5.02.32 | 401.258 |
| 22 | 20 | Andrew Sherwood | Mid Oxon | 5.06.55 | 400.792 |
| 23 | 63 | Robert Meredith | Walsall Roads CC | 5.17.58 | 396.379 |
| 24 | 35 | Ann Wooldridge | Walsall Roads CC | 5.12.58 | 394.549 |
| 25 | 57 | Ray Retter | North Devon Wheelers | 4.54.37 | 393.143 |
| 26 | 51 | Jim Hopper (Tri) | Derby Mercury RC | 5.07.58 | 391.495 |
| 27 | 48 | Anthony Wheatley | CTC West Bromwich | 5.11.45 | 389.243 |
| 28 | 39 | Paul Stephens | Ross on Wye & District CC | 5.01.23 | 388.171 |
| 29 | 14 | Phillipe Van Doornick | Solihull CC | 5.25.32 | 382.345 |
| 30 | 54 | Colin Knapp (Tri) | Middridge CRT | 5.28.29 | 373.582 |
| 31 | 32 | Hefin Jones | Ross on Wye & District CC | 4.58.18 | 372.925 |
| 32 | 47 | Phil Holden | Seamons CC | 4.58.03 | 369.965 |
| 33 | 65 | Chris Hopkinson | Matlock CC | 5.04.20 | 369.280 |
| 34 | 28 | Roger Clarke | Tyneside Vagabonds CC | 5.08.26 | 354.390 |
| 35 | 23 | George Berwick | Edinburgh Road Club | 6.01.09 | 346.419 |
| 36 | 10 | Ann Bath | Kingston Phoenix RC | 6.01.03 | 342.767 |
| 37 | 42 | David Rapley | Charlotteville CC | 4.47.21 | 342.463 |
| 38 | 13 | Geraint Catherall | Anfield BC | 5.54.38 | 341.540 |
| 39 | 34 | Michael Friday | Catford CC | 5.52.40 | 338.311 |
| 40 | 9 | Andrew Barratt | Lyme Racing Club | 5.28.26 | 332.343 |
| 41 | 24 | Dean Peach | Walsall Roads CC | 5.48.29 | 327.083 |
| 42 | 19 | John Rowlinson | Seamons CC | 5.56.43 | 313.113 |
| 43 | 15 | Janet Tebbutt | Cavalier CC | 6.27.02 | 311.336 |
| 44 | 12 | Gareth Gregory | Port Talbot Wheelers | 6.34.24 | 307.297 |
| 45 | 29 | Doug Haig | Deeside Thistle CC | 5.41.22 | 304.600 |
| 46 | 7 | Arthur Vince | VC Camelot | 6.51.37 | 302.009 |
| 47 | 25 | Dave Tickle | Seamons CC | 6.47.59 | 291.285 |

### TANDEM TRIKE      * Comp record

| Place | No | Name | Club | 100 mile | 24 Hrs | |
|---|---|---|---|---|---|---|
| 1 | 72 | Ralph Dadswell David Johnson | Antelope RT High Wycombe CC | 4.25.58 | 466.723 ✱ | competition record |

### TEAM RESULT

**Winning Team**
To receive the RTTC Championship Shield, 3 RTTC Championship Medallions,
plus £30 each and the Booth Memorial Shield.

| Walsall Roads CC | Marina Bloom | 447.334 |
|---|---|---|
| | Lynne Taylor | 412.807 |
| | Robert Meredith | 396.379 |
| | Total | 1256.520 |

**Second Team**

| Seamons CC | Total | 974.363 |
|---|---|---|

## Mersey National 2006

| Place | No. | Name | Club | calculated 12 hour Distance | 24 hour Distance |
|---|---|---|---|---|---|
| 1 | 70 | Nikolaus Gardiner | John's Bikes | 267.500 | 504.023 |
| 2 | 60 | Neil Skellern | Congleton CC | 246.041 | 477.653 |
| 3 | 54 | Nick Cave | Leicester Forest CC | 248.931 | 472.492 |
| 4 | 58 | Graham Barker | Rockingham CC | 245.349 | 465.253 |
| 5 | 65 | Howard Waller | Oxford City RC | 251.598 | 461.757 |
| 6 | 43 | Paul Robinson | Cardiff Byways RCC | 241.389 | 461.423 |
| 7 | 51 | David McLoughlin | Dundrum Town Centre Orwell | 241.794 | 456.400 |
| 8 | 62 | Robert McCready | Inverclyde Velo | 235.513 | 449.827 |
| 9 | 52 | Carol Westmorland | Border City Wheelers CC | 232.078 | 445.412 |
| 10 | 24 | Mike Pain | Cardiff Byways RCC | 242.214 | 440.440 |
| 11 | 67 | Karl Austin | Congleton CC | 235.280 | 438.750 |
| 12 | 57 | Steven Abraham | North Bucks RC | 232.347 | 436.889 |
| 13 | 61 | Lynne Taylor | Walsall RC | 232.209 | 434.412 |
| 14 | 68 | Roger Squire | Fibrax Wrexham RC | 225.933 | 429.642 |
| 15 | 15 | Philip Kelman | Deeside Thistle CC | 229.771 | 429.070 |
| 16 | 63 | Tim Melville | Team AW Cycles | 226.052 | 426.862 |
| 17 | 7 | Robert Meredith | Walsall RC | 226.052 | 425.757 |
| 18 | 13 | Dale Sturman | West Suffolk Wheelers | 220.242 | 422.458 |
| 19 | 19 | Ray Retter | North Devon Wheelers | 228.570 | 419.263 |
| 20 | 44 | Chris Asher | VC167 | 232.078 | 416.929 |
| 21 | 69 | Marina Bloom | Walsall RC | 229.231 | 416.449 |
| 22 | 56 | Melville Kirkland | Willesden CC | 219.597 | 415.512 |
| 23 | 6 | Andrew Sherwood | Farnborough and Camberly CC | 231.093 | 414.957 |
| 24 | 25 | Robert Watson | North Hampshire RC | 221.261 | 412.178 |
| 25 | 29 | David Lewis | Cardiff Byways RCC | 218.188 | 409.163 |
| 26 | 59 | Martin Lucas | Willesden CC | 206.659 | 407.076 |
| 27 | 38 | Ian Kellaway | Coventry CC | 210.523 | 403.828 |
| 28 | 48 | Geoff Smith | Sussex Nomads CC | 213.663 | 394.024 |
| 29 | 27 | Jim Hopper | Derby Mercury RC    T | 206.360 | 393.240 |
| 30 | 11 | Ritchie Tout | Cardiff Byways RCC | 218.876 | 390.576 |
| 31 | 26 | Bruce Bricknell | Deeside Thistle CC | 194.562 | 389.276 |
| 32 | 17 | Giudo Reynolds | Congleton CC | 200.851 | 387.555 |
| 33 | 34 | Peter Lee | Cardiff Byways RCC | 203.551 | 385.490 |
| 34 | 20 | Phil Holden | Seamons CC | 206.196 | 382.560 |
| 35 | 66 | Eric Ruthenberg | Matlock CC | 213.268 | 382.180 |
| 36 | 46 | Ian Horne | Derby Mercury RC | 204.008 | 370.663 |
| 37 | 14 | Jeremy Meades | Lewes Wanderers CC | 206.726 | 369.083 |
| 38 | 42 | Scott Taylor | Deeside Thistle CC | 201.676 | 360.454 |
| 39 | 8 | Peter Wilson | Royal Air Force | 191.099 | 360.219 |
| 40 | 49 | Robert Morton | Seamons CC | 195.310 | 359.765 |
| 41 | 5 | Geraint Catherall | Anfield BC | 189.725 | 355.463 |
| 42 | 32 | Jason Smith | Deeside Thistle CC | 196.507 | 353.050 |
| 43 | 31 | Bob Harber | Brighton Excelsior CC | 192.695 | 343.161 |
| 44 | 40 | Chrystal Sheldon | Kingston Phoenix RC | 180.472 | 339.111 |
| 45 | 16 | George Berwick | Edinburgh RC | 177.954 | 336.547 |
| 46 | 37 | Mike Beattie | Deeside Thistle CC | 187.443 | 336.364 |
| 47 | 12 | Ann Bath | Kingston Phoenix RC | 190.171 | 335.468 |
| 48 | 39 | Andrew Johnson | Cardiff Byways RCC | 189.196 | 334.914 |
| 49 | 36 | Robert Morris | CC Topp | 182.176 | 333.016 |
| 50 | 30 | James Mepham | Verulam CC | 188.465 | 330.488 |
| 51 | 10 | Andrew Barratt | Lyme Racing Club | 186.663 | 315.472 |
| 52 | 2 | Janet Tebbutt | Cavalier CC | 162.687 | 313.459 |
| 53 | 23 | Dave Stokes | Johnstone Wheelers CC | 157.805 | 305.625 |
| 54 | 33 | Michael Wigley | Seamons CC | 172.257 | 300.966 |
| 55 | 9 | Mark Shannon | Edinburgh RC | 163.446 | 288.775 |
| 56 | 21 | Douglas Haig | Deeside Thistle CC | 172.960 | 275.070 |
| 57 | 47 | Roy Deakin | Lyme RC | 118.483 | 222.704 |

### TANDEM RESULT

| | No. | Name | Club | 12 hour | 24 hour |
|---|---|---|---|---|---|
| 1 | 76 | Chris Hopkinson Richard Thoday | API Metrow Matlock CC | 263.267 | 473.795 |
| 2 | 72 | Aidan Hedley Steve Bateman | VC167 VC167 | 205.312 | 401.392 |
| 3 | 74 | Colin Knapp John Carr | Middridge CRT Cleveland Wheelers | 203.352 | 380.619 |

### TEAM RESULT

| | | |
|---|---|---|
| 1 | Cardiff ByWays RCC | 1311.023 |
| 2 | Congleton CC | 1303.958 |
| 3 | Walsall RC | 1276.619 |
| 4 | Deeside Thistle CC | 1178.799 |
| 5 | Cardiff ByWays RCC | 1110.980 |
| 6 | Seamons CC | 1043.291 |
| 7 | Deeside Thistle CC | 964.484 |

Merseyside Ladies CA  winner
Carol Westmorland

## Mersey National 2007

| Place | No. | Name | Club | calculated 12 hour Distance | 24 hour Distance |
|---|---|---|---|---|---|
| 1 | 75 | Eamonn Deane | Bournemouth Jubilee | 256.71 | 501.04 |
| 2 | 16 | John Warnock | Twickenham CC | 265.91 | 489.32 |
| 3 | 65 | Jose Pinon Shaw | Preston Wheelers | 255.57 | 472.78 |
| 4 | 69 | Lynne Taylor | Walsall RC | 239.15 | 459.29 |
| 5 | 41 | Steven Massey | Derby Mercury RC | 235.49 | 452.89 |
| 6 | 60 | Ian Silvester | San Fairy Ann CC | 244.06 | 446.92 |
| 7 | 40 | Paul Robinson | API Metrow | 244.78 | 442.95 |
| 8 | 53 | Dale Sturman | West Suffolk Wheelers | 227.51 | 441.42 |
| 9 | 55 | Karl Austin | Congleton CC | 232.15 | 439.33 |
| 10 | 50 | Chris Hopkinson | API Metrow | 227.12 | 436.84 |
| 11 | 35 | Steven Abraham | North Bucks RC | 226.81 | 436.55 |
| 12 | 57 | Philip Kelman | Deeside Thistle CC | 230.30 | 435.85 |
| 13 | 45 | Graham Barker | Congleton CC | 233.23 | 428.69 |
| 14 | 58 | Chris Asher | API Metrow | 224.58 | 427.31 |
| 15 | 6 | Paul Alderson | South Western RC | 239.89 | 427.05 |
| 16 | 84 | Joel Sothern | Ultra Marathon CA | 220.13 | 419.98 |
| 17 | 24 | Mark Holt | Port Sunlight Wheelers | 225.21 | 419.33 |
| 18 | 82 | Roger Squire | Wrexham Fibrax RC | 218.20 | 417.98 |
| 19 | 64 | Mike Pain | Cardiff Byways RCC | 234.65 | 414.61 |
| 20 | 36 | John Hatfield | Ravensthorpe CC | 218.82 | 413.18 |
| 21 | 21 | Giudo Reynolds | Congleton CC | 213.29 | 412.34 |
| 22 | 23 | Martin Lucas | Willesden CC | 208.23 | 409.87 |
| 23 | 72 | Robert Meredith | Walsall RC | 221.85 | 408.25 |
| 24 | 73 | David Gostelow | Wrekinsport | 209.36 | 402.70 |
| 25 | 9 | Bruce Bricknell | Deeside Thistle CC | 211.29 | 401.21 |
| 26 | 19 | Kenneth Bryson | Deeside Thistle CC | 209.21 | 398.48 |
| 27 | 78 | Aidan Hedley | VC 167 | 210.98 | 396.53 |
| 28 | 51 | John Connaghan | Edinburgh RC | 207.39 | 389.20 |
| 29 | 7 | Ginny Pollard | Deeside Thistle CC | 205.49 | 384.75 |
| 30 | 61 | Bob Richards | RNRMCA | 206.27 | 383.27 |
| 31 | 70 | Paul O'Donoghue | Sorrento CC | 201.21 | 378.54 |
| 32 | 28 | Jim Hopper | Derby Mercury RC   T | 200.30 | 376.46 |
| 33 | 46 | David Lewis | Cardiff Byways RCC | 207.38 | 374.23 |
| 34 | 8 | Andrew Dade | Cardiff Byways RCC | 199.82 | 368.03 |
| 35 | 14 | Linda Reid | Deeside Thistle CC | 197.56 | 363.82 |
| 36 | 13 | Peter Lee | Cardiff Byways RCC | 189.18 | 362.98 |
| 37 | 52 | Scott Taylor | Deeside Thistle CC | 205.64 | 362.61 |
| 38 | 63 | Paul Fallon | Ross on Wye CC | 197.78 | 361.99 |
| 39 | 4 | Damon Peacock | Southport CC | 203.47 | 361.39 |
| 40 | 68 | Jason Smith | Deeside Thistle CC | 192.30 | 357.63 |
| 41 | 59 | Kenny Watson | Deeside Thistle CC | 198.44 | 355.71 |
| 42 | 26 | Phil Holden | Seamons CC | 205.84 | 353.29 |
| 43 | 29 | Robert Morton | Seamons CC | 182.55 | 349.02 |
| 44 | 22 | Mark Gray | Derby Mercury RC | 193.22 | 348.02 |
| 45 | 1 | Lindsay Goldbeck | Deeside Thistle CC | 183.66 | 346.03 |
| 46 | 71 | Geoff Smith | VC Etoile | 192.76 | 345.12 |
| 47 | 47 | Allan McCourt | Deeside Thistle CC | 178.87 | 344.16 |
| 48 | 18 | Geraint Catherall | Anfield BC | 176.08 | 340.29 |
| 49 | 20 | Peter Trodden | Harrogate Nova | 175.84 | 337.10 |
| 50 | 17 | Stephen Airey | Catford CC | 178.36 | 334.01 |
| 51 | 44 | Michael Rainton | VC Baracchi | 178.69 | 332.42 |
| 52 | 48 | Bob Loader | Sydenham Wheelers CC | 171.40 | 330.06 |
| 53 | 30 | Andrew Barratt | Kidsgrove Wheelers | 181.04 | 327.29 |
| 54 | 27 | Ron Longstaff | Zeus CRT | 193.55 | 326.79 |
| 55 | 37 | Stephen Poulton | Cheltenham & County CC | 168.17 | 324.82 |
| 56 | 76 | Alexander Whyman | Deeside Thistle CC | 190.77 | 321.37 |
| 57 | 31 | Mike McConville | Seamons CC | 177.79 | 319.39 |
| 58 | 81 | Stuart Archard | Chippenham & District Wheelers | 178.82 | 318.40 |
| 59 | 33 | Joe Applegarth | Houghton CC | 183.26 | 317.12 |
| 60 | 11 | George Berwick | Edinburgh RC | 163.01 | 314.76 |
| 61 | 62 | Ben Green | Manchester Wheelers | 163.00 | 313.33 |
| 62 | 5 | Mebs Bobat | Deeside Thistle CC | 173.54 | 304.95 |
| 63 | 12 | Michael Friday | Catford CC | 170.14 | 304.33 |
| 64 | 54 | Douglas Haig | Deeside Thistle CC | 172.62 | 300.57 |
| =65 | 49 | Alan Purchase | Kidsgrove Wheelers | 149.02 | 252.69 |
| =65 | 56 | Mark Shannon | Edinburgh RC | 158.09 | 252.69 |

### TANDEM RESULT

| | | | | | |
|---|---|---|---|---|---|
| 1 | 86 | John Carr | Cleveland Wheelers | | |
| | 87 | Colin Knapp | Middridge CRT | 213.87 | 299.47 |

### TEAM RESULT

| | | | | |
|---|---|---|---|---|
| 1 | API Metrow | P. Robinson, C. Hopkinson, C. Asher | | 1307.11 |
| 2 | Congleton CC | K. Austin, G. Barker, G. Reynolds | | 1280.38 |
| 3 | Deeside Thistle CC | P. Kelman, B. Bricknell, K. Bryson | | 1235.54 |
| 4 | Derby Mercury RC | S. Massey, J. Hopper, M. Gray | | 1177.39 |
| 5 | Cardiff Byways RCC | M. Pain, D. Lewis, A. Dade | | 1156.87 |
| 6 | Deeside Thistle CC | G. Pollard, L. Reid, S. Taylor | | 1111.18 |
| 7 | Deeside Thistle CC | J. Smith, K. Watson, L. Goldbeck | | 1059.37 |
| 8 | Seamons CC | P. Holden, R. Morton, M. McConville | | 1021.72 |
| 9 | Deeside Thistle CC | A. McCourt, A. Whyman, M. Bobat | | 970.48 |

## MERSEY ROADS RESULT 2008

| Pos. | No. | Name | Club | Cat | 24 hour Distance |
|---|---|---|---|---|---|
| 1 | 55 | Nikolaus Gardiner | Johns Bikes | | 513.65 |
| 2 | 60 | John Warnock | Twickenham CC | | 491.39 |
| 3 | 58 | Neil Skellern | Congleton CC | | 467.74 |
| 4 | 56 | Daniel Mathers | Seamons CC | | 455.95 |
| 5 | 40 | Karl Austin | Congleton CC | V | 450.48 |
| 6 | 45 | Steven Massey | Derby Mercury RC | | 442.42 |
| 7 | 47 | Joel Sothern | Ultra Marathon CA | | 442.37 |
| 8 | 54 | Graham Barker | Congleton CC | V | 441.61 |
| 9 | 42 | Jim Gresty | North Shropshire Wheelers | V | 437.87 |
| =10 | 16 | Michael Thompson | VC 167 | | 428.45 |
| =10 | 27 | Paul O'Donoghue | Sorento CC | | 428.45 |
| 12 | 34 | Clayton Knight | Shaftsbury CC | V | 415.63 |
| 13 | 12 | Roger Squire | Wrexham Fibrax RC | | 413.71 |
| 14 | 30 | Graham Jones | Edinburgh RC | V | 408.83 |
| 15 | 9 | Bob Richards | RNRMCA | | 399.37 |
| 16 | 35 | Colin Bezant | CC Basingstoke | | 392.55 |
| 17 | 23 | Richard Newey | Agiskoviner | | 389.39 |
| 18 | 43 | Stewart Wilson | Nene Valley | | 384.86 |
| 19 | 53 | Henry Martin | Oxford University CC | | 384.22 |
| 20 | 20 | Steven Abraham | North Bucks RC | | 382.17 |
| 21 | 38 | GSA Smith | Settle. WWW. Wheelers | | 367.54 |
| 22 | 3 | Jim Hopper | Derby Mercury RC | T | 365.19 |
| =23 | 37 | Thomas Deakins | Flitch Crono | | 363.56 |
| =23 | 26 | Ashley Holmes | Deal Tri | | 363.56 |
| 25 | 33 | Peter Turner | Derby Mercury RC | V | 361.84 |
| 26 | 15 | John O'Sullivan | Sorento CC | | 360.63 |
| 27 | 10 | Stephen Dart | Mid Devon CC | | 360.06 |
| 28 | 24 | Rose Leith | Sorento CC | W | 352.50 |
| 30 | 1 | Geraint Catherall | Anfield BC | | 340.67 |
| 31 | 4 | Malcolm Matcham | VC Venta | V | 337.61 |
| 29 | 28 | David Unsworth | Hereford Wheelers CC | | 326.10 |
| 32 | 7 | Michael Wigley | VC 167 | V | 325.00 |
| 33 | 32 | George Berwick | Edinburgh RC | V | 323.78 |
| 34 | 36 | Graeme Wyllie | Edinburgh RC | | 322.60 |
| 35 | 29 | Matthew Chambers | Didcot Phoenix | | 321.69 |
| 36 | 11 | Joe Applegarth | Houghton CC | | 286.73 |
| 37 | 5 | Arthur Vince | Yeovil CC | | 260.44 |

## TANDEM RESULT

| | | | | | |
|---|---|---|---|---|---|
| 1 | 61 | Hedley / Southworth | VC 167 | | 395.85 |
| 2 | 62 | Sharp/Cox | Ystwyth CC | M/W | 359.99 |
| 3 | 63 | Barnes / Norman | Twickenham CC | W/W | 329.49 |

## TEAM RESULT

| | | | |
|---|---|---|---|
| 1 | Congleton CC | N. Skellern, K. Austin, G. Barker | 1359.84 |
| 2 | Derby Mercury RC | S. Massey, J. Hopper, P. Turner | 1169.45 |
| 3 | Sorento CC | P. O'Donoghue, J. O'Sullivan, R.Leith | 1141.58 |
| 4 | Edinburgh RC | G. Jones, G. Berwick, G. Wyllie | 1055.21 |

Gethin Butler

Karl Austin

David Shepherd

Jose Pinon Shaw

Keith Coffey

Nick Cave

Neil Skellern

Lynne Taylor

Simon Doughty

Nik Gardiner

Eamonn Deane

John Warnock

378

Kate Green

Lilian Dredge

Edith Atkins

Marguerite Wilson

Eileen Sheridan

Wyn Maddock

Joyce Blow

# CHAPTER FIVE

## THE LADIES 24 HOUR HISTORY
## PART ONE – EARLY DAYS

Before the turn of the century in the 1880's, the 'Press' deemed it undesirable for 'Fragile Female Forms' to perform athletic feats of strength or cycle on rides of abnormal endurance. A **Mrs Allen** of Birmingham rode 200 miles on a tricycle in 24 hours. The ride took place around the week ending 7th July 1885. She rode a 'Humber' machine weighing 65lbs. It was not documented as to what event or context the ride took place in, whether it was a private trial or record attempt, and it isn't known whether other riders took part.

**Kate Green** 'GHS' (George Herbert Stancer) writing for the 'Cycling' journal in 1955, reported Kate Green's death in Buxton Hospital. She was 78 years of age. 'GHS' described her record breaking performances as being of 'man calibre'. Her career of speed and endurance cycling had taken place mainly on Yorkshire roads which at that time were in a diabolical state, the surfaces being of very poor quality. The roads were feeling the destructive effect of motor traffic, which at that period often meant steel studded wheels similar to the ones seen on steam powered lorries and tractor units, at 'classic' steam rallies and transport festivals. Pneumatic tyres were still being developed.

Cycling performances and mileages recorded at that time must be regarded in their proper relationship to the conditions under which they were achieved. This is why Kate Green was outstanding. In **1906 she rode a 'paced' 100 miles** event in **5 hrs 38 mins 53 secs.** She also covered **193.75 miles in 12 hours.**

'Un-paced riding' didn't develop so rapidly in the Northern Counties as elsewhere, but by **1908** this keen Yorkshire 31 year old had decided to concentrate on un-paced time trials. She attempted a **24 hr** race, something new in women's cycling, achieving **308 miles.** In this connection, it must be mentioned that a T.W. Monkhouse of the Yorkshire Road Club was the first man in the Northeast to record over 300 miles with 304.75 just some ten years previously.

Not satisfied with her 1908 performance of 308 miles, Kate made another attempt at a 24 hr race a year later but was unfortunate with the weather. Heavy rains had turned the road surface into thick clinging filthy mud. 'GHS', himself a very good rider and Official Observer was in the Yorkshire area that weekend, and he agreed to take on a spell of following Miss Green, with the result that he rode for well over 100 miles on his tricycle. He concluded "in spite of the poor conditions which included some fog, **Kate Green** covered **313 miles,** and my chief recollection of the performance centres on the composure of the rider. When she finished in the morning she might well have been just back from an all night club-run".

Kate Green was one of the very few ladies who ever rode in competition against the men. The 'Yorkshire Road Club' of which she was a member did not accept female entrants for their races and handicap events, but the 'Leeds Road Club' did, and it's in their events that she succeeded in beating 50% of her male opponents.

Most of her leisure cycling was with male companions, for the distances that she rode with ease would, in those days, have been beyond the capacity of the average club girl even in the county that had been more progressive than any other in encouraging women to enter cycling competitions.

Miss Green toured the British Isles extensively and helped record breakers whenever their routes were within riding distance of her home. Kate worked tirelessly as an RRA Observer as well as being an ardent organiser for the 'CTC' Cyclists Touring Club. It would be some 27 years before a woman with her strength, speed and stamina came along. Shortly after her record breaking career, Britain endured its First World War - 'The Great War' 1914-1918. Many young men gave and lost their lives for their country. This in turn put the growth of cycle sport and club life on hold for five years.

In the early 1900's it was a male dominated society in Great Britain, although there had been a successful suffragette movement campaigning for better women's conditions and voting rights since the 1860's, it was 1928 before women finally got the vote at 21 years of age, due to the efforts of Emmaline Pankhurst. Women were still held back from prominent positions in all walks of life – politically, professionally, academically and athletically.

Cycle racing, believe it or not, was actually a rich man's sport, hence in the 1880's to 1920's a lot of long distance record breakers were either Doctors, Academics, Entrepreneurs, Landed Gentry or Company Directors, who could afford to have days away from their homes and workplaces, or pay for 'Pacers' and their lodgings, cycles and train fares. They also had the finances to employ Masseurs, Trainers etc, not forgetting Timekeepers and Observers Fees and 'RRA' charges.

The men who owned and ran the cycling and sporting journals at that time were also against female participation in what had been, up until then, a male dominated sport. Most pastimes and sports were equally as guilty of not allowing women to take part i.e. football, cricket, horse racing, hunting, shooting, fishing, athletics, boxing and finally golf, which has probably the worst record of all for not allowing women to participate or even enter a club-room, denying integration at any level up until very recently.

Eventually one or two influential female cyclists, such as Lilian Dredge, whose husband Freddie was a successful racing man, and Evelyn Stancer 'GHS's wife, who also went under the name of Petronella, voiced their opinions to their male colleagues. They drew on enough support from other women cyclists to form a nucleus in 1934   that was to become the 'WRRA' (Womens Road Records Association). Mrs Lyn Stancer, formerly Mrs Evelyn Parkes, was appointed President and Miss Jessie M. Springall became Hon. Secretary and Treasurer.

During the period 1935 to 1940, seventy one claims to records were passed using thirteen different record routes, all records were open to bicycle, tricycle, tandem and tandem tricycle. I think we can say that apart from the previous lone efforts of one or two outstanding ladies, the 'WRRA' in 1934 was the start of organised women's cycle racing in Great Britain, albeit mainly of a record breaking and time trialling nature.

**1936 Lilian Dredge** was the first lady to produce a record mileage for **24 hours with 339.5 miles** under WRRA rules, some 26 miles further than Kate Green's ride in 1909 although I suspect Mrs Dredge had better road surface conditions, but who knows?

Lilian was a professional rider for Claud Butler who was, at that time, probably one of England's most popular and well known hand built lightweight cycle manufacturers, who went on to have 5 or 6 sales and service outlets in the London area. In his advert dated September 30th 1936 in the 'Cycling', he claims that her performance took place, riding into a headwind for most of her journey, which at that time was the furthest ever ridden by a woman. "A remarkable tribute to the endurance of this plucky lady rider and her Claud Butler machine"! **Lilian,** later in 1938, went on to become **the first woman to ride from Lands End to John o' Groats ( 870 miles )** and then carry on to complete **1000 miles** all in the same journey. **The End to End** took **3 days 20 hours 54 mins** and the **1000 miles** took **4 days 19 hours 14 mins,** a truly remarkable pioneering performance for women's cycle sport.

Ethel Brambleby time trialled at all distances from 10 miles to 24 hours, her racing career covered some 50 years from the 1930's to the 1980's. She reminded me as to how much opposition there was from the male cycling fraternity to women racing. The 'WRRA' at that time stipulating that 'female' record aspirants must not let the side down and appear unladylike with their efforts, as this would fuel the ego's of the hierarchy who ran the sport !

Women racing in most time trials until 1988 had to start before the men, in most cases at 5.00 am in the dark and cold. In fact in the mid 1960's Beryl Burton commented that if she had been allowed to start, placed in the middle or towards the end of the men's field, she could have improved women's competition record at most distances much earlier in history, due to being much warmer and less tired from not having to get up so early.

Although there had obviously been races and time trials taking place since about 1886 (North Road CC 24 hr) 1889 (Anfield BC 100 mile and 24 hr) and in most years when the country wasn't at war, men's competition record performances at all distances date from around 1934. There are very few ladies mentioned until **Marguerite Wilson,** in **1938** is listed in the 'RTTC' Handbook as having ridden 215.5 miles in 12 hours to produce the **first 'RTTC' competition record** riding against other ladies starting at one minute intervals. This result is also listed as best on record in the 'WRRA' record book in 1938, although Miss Wilson's performance is preceeded by R. Wright with 205.25 miles in 1937 and Pearl Wellington with 211 miles in 1938 for 12 hours time trialling.

A short passage from an article by Frank Robertson in the 24hr Fellowship Journal, November 75, entitled 'Down Memory Lane for 24 hours' "I rode quite a lot with the 'vegetarians' during the winter of 1931, these 'club runs' were usually of some 150 miles including a proportion of rough stuff, and were led by such famous riders as Len Cave, Sid Ferris, Ted Brumell and George Phillips.

Digressing for one moment, there was just one lady member who attended these runs regularly, she often came straight off night duty as a nurse to do so. She was shown absolutely no mercy by the male riders but she was always there at the finish of the run. Her name was Pearl. Later she went on to break many WRRA records as **Pearl Wellington.** I noticed in the record books that her **12 hr of 211 miles, Lands End to London** and **24 hrs 377 miles** were all done in **1938.** It is possible it was a 'three in one' ride.

**Marguerite Wilson** became the next rider to push the distance ridden in **24 hours to 396 miles in 1939.** She was by then a professional riding for 'Hercules', a Birmingham cycle manufacturer, more known for producing general cycles for all the family. She tackled the 24 hour as a good preparation for the forthcoming 'End to End' and 1000 mile ride which incidentally took place on the 1st to 4th September 1939. She finished at John o' Groats as strict wartime blackout restrictions were being implemented in this coastal village overlooking 'Scapa Flow' in the Orkney's, a sensitive naval operations area.

This was to be one of the last of her rides covering a total of 22 records over a 4 year period. **Marguerite Wilson** was only 21 years of age when she took the **End to End** record with **2 days 22 hrs 52 mins** and **1000 miles** in **3 days 11 hours 44 mins.** Definitely the youngest rider to do so, since G.P. Mills in the 19th Century.

Up until the next ladies 24 hr record breaker in 1953 most of our previous aspirants of the 20th century have had to dress in black from head to toe so as not to give the impression they were racing or taking part in a competition. The material for the jacket was a tough hard wearing 'alpaca' weave with large blazer type pockets at the lower front. The black tights were also of a tough weave and very unflattering, although Marguerite Wilson would have looked good in any circumstances, as would all of our lady record breakers. She was photographed in the Grampians with her sleeves rolled up – Wow – bare arms!

The Second World War destroyed not only the lives of millions of brave men and women, it also disrupted home life in Great Britain. People were uprooted, cities bombed into rubble, roads and bridges wrecked by German air raids. Whereas the First World War took five years out of our cycle racing and club's history, the Second World War saw some nearly eight years lost before people returned to rebuilding their lives. Although the 'North Road CC' held a 24 hr race in 1945 some troops still hadn't returned home by then. Food rationing and the poor state of the roads and towns prevented most races from being re-instated, and the first Mersey 24 hr event after the war was in 1947.

**1953 Edith Atkins** an amateur rider from the 'Coventry Road Club' produced an amazing improvement of some 26 miles taking the **24 hr record to 422 miles.** On the way to this record Edie had broken the **London to York, 12 hr, London to Edinburgh,** a '4 in 1' ride. Edie was also the first woman to beat 400 miles in 24 hrs. This petite Coventry housewife who was managed by her husband Ron, again followed suit later that year and took Marguerite Wilson's **'End to End'** record with **2 days 18 hours 4 mins** - a 4 hr 48 minute improvement.

**1953 Eileen Sheridan** was without a doubt the most prolific of all our women cycle record breakers. This petite 7 stone 4ft 11ins athlete nicknamed 'The Pocket Hercules' who had started cycling in the early 1940's had an illustrious amateur career, and became a very powerful and formidable opponent in road time trialling circles. She had proved herself as early on as 1944, winning club races from 10 miles to 100 miles, putting not only many female but also male competitors behind her. **In 1949 she won her first 12 hour race with 236.6 miles and broke women's RTTC Competition Record by almost 17 miles.**

In 1950 Eileen won the ladies championship 100 mile time trial with 4 hrs 37 mins 53 secs. Taking 5.5 mins off comp record. In 1951, Eileen was awarded the Bidlake Memorial Trophy for her outstanding achievements, possibly the highest accolade a racing cyclist could ever attain.

A Coventry housewife and secretary, Eileen Sheridan was supported by her husband Ken, throughout her amateur and professional career, spanning some 10 years. In 1952 Eileen turned professional, riding for Hercules Cycles, who wanted her to break all of the solo women's records on the books. In 1953, a short while after Edie Atkins had raised the 24 hr record, Eileen's manager, Frank Southall, suggested that she should build up for her attempt on the 'End to End' and 1000 mile record by attacking three records in one ride. **Eileen took the 12 hr with 250.5 miles, the Lands End to London with 14 hrs 36 mins 18 secs** carrying on to take the **24 hr with 442.75 miles.** In early July, Eileen went on to fulfil her lifetimes ambition of breaking the **End to End with 2 days 11 hours 7 mins** and going on for the **1000 mile record of 3 days 1 hour.** Eileen's **1954 24 hr record of 446.25 miles** which was a straight out WRRA ride was to be the last women's professional category 24 hr ride against the clock. In 1980 the WRRA abolished the distinction between amateur and professional and from then on recognised only the 'best on record' whatever the status of the rider.

In WRRA (RRA) terms it would be some 43 years until **Christine Roberts** improved on Eileen's mileage to record **467.30 miles in 1997.** This record was broken while Christine was attempting the End to End that failed just before Edinburgh. Christine's 24 hr ride of 467.30 miles was a magnificent one. Although she had a very good directional wind helping her, the course does take in many towns, some quite large: Penzance, Exeter, Bristol, Gloucester, Worcester, Wolverhampton, Warrington, Preston, Lancaster and Carlisle. There are also some leg numbing hills on the route especially in Cornwall, Devon and around the Bristol area. The record would also have included Shap, a nine mile tortuous winding climb to over 1000 ft that would have come in the last third of the ride. So, another 'epic' ride in the history of Womens's RRA long distance record breaking. **This concludes the list of women's 24 hr results from the RRA Handbook.**

Eileen Sheridan became the figurehead for women's cycling issues from the 1950's onwards. She was vivacious, looked very good on and off the bike, eloquent and an ambassador for our sport. She appeared in lots of magazines and on news films and radio. Her professional career with 'Hercules Cycles' meant lots of attendances at cycle trade exhibitions and appearances at high profile shows such as 'The Ideal Home Exhibition' in London.

Eileen encouraged many club girls to take up racing when she starred in a cine movie in the late 1950's about her cycle racing performances. Although her racing career finished in 1954, she continued her links with cycling, even though she now had a young family to look after. These links to the sport are still evident today as she regularly attends the annual 'RTTC' 'BBAR' presentation and most 'RRA' functions. She has also been a regular after dinner speaker covering a period of some 50 years.

At just over 80 years of age she is still in touch with a lot of riders and record breakers and has a very knowledgeable view of the sport and is 'up to speed' on what is currently going on.

Over the last 50 years Eileen has encouraged men and women riders to aspire to greatness. She has attended many championship events and presented the prizes. My daughter, Lynne Taylor, has benefited greatly from Eileen's support for her record breaking. The encouragement and friendship shown to Lynne over the last 10 years or more has helped her to achieve three End to End records and the 1000 mile record. Eileen being one of the first to congratulate Lynne over the phone upon breaking the records, even though the 1000 mile record had belonged to Eileen since 1954.

I spoke to Eileen at the 2007 CTT BBAR 'do' in January and she said she wished somebody would go for her London to Portsmouth and back record of 6 hrs 56 mins 40 secs set in 1954. I said it would be a tough one even 53 years on. Long may she have the heart and strength to attend many more functions.

*For more details on Eileen's End to End and 1000 mile records, go to Chapter 3, 1954.*

# PART TWO - THE RTTC ERA

Most of the action for women's 24 hr time trialling performances starts in the late 1960's in the Mersey R.C. event incorporating the Merseyside Ladies CA 24 hr. I apologise if the ladies history sounds complicated so far, the reason being that it has been handled by two different organisations, the WRRA and the RTTC. From here on it becomes simpler with mainly RTTC performances.

## 1967

**Christine Minto (Nee Moody)** Her ride becomes **The First RTTC Competition Record with 409.16 miles. Christine's ride was to set the benchmark for all women's 24 hr rides from this day on.** Two other ladies rode that day, **Mrs Ruth Williams and Mrs Wyn Maddock.** They started numbers 6, 7, and 8 amongst the men at the beginning of the field. Ruth covered **403.7 miles** and that must have made everybody in the promoting club very proud. Her father-in-law and the whole Williams family were heavily involved with the club and the running of this famous 24 hour race, and have been for 70 years. Ruth has helped or officiated at this and many other Mersey R.C. events since the 1960's. She can be found on the last weekend in July, checking riders through at Prees, along with Christine who is nowadays, Mrs Christine Minto, a celebrated and revered time keeper working tirelessly for the sport with her husband, Frank, who ran the 'BBAR' result tables, taking over from Tommy Barlow many years ago. Frank and Christine have both been involved with long distance time trialling and record breaking as well as organising and timing many open events in their Yorkshire district.

*Here is a passage taken from a Mersey R.C. resume by John Reid, printed in the 24 hr fellowship journal of 1967.*

"The special highlight this year was the little bit of history made by incorporating the first ever open 24 hr event specifically for women. Three brave girls entered, three brave girls started, and by jove, three brave girls finished – all getting their silver standard medals. They were, Chris Moody (Birdwell Wheelers) 'our' Ruth Williams who made husband Bob 'go all the way' and evergreen Wyn Maddock (Notts and Derby Clarion) at 60 years of age, who rode with a slight fracture of the shoulder bone, sustained in a brush with a car whilst training a week before the event, and who earned herself a write up in 'The Guardian'.

Weather conditions for the event were just about perfect as all the riders were despatched by Ron Macqueen from 5 pm on the Saturday evening at Austins Hill. Good progress was made by Christine, off No 6, who at the 100 mile point was still the first rider on the road with 5 hrs 5 mins elapsed. Ruth was at 10 mins and Wyn at 41 mins but Rod Goodfellow, Beacon Roads, was closing fast and was only 2 mins behind at this point.

After a dark run up the coast road to Prestatyn and back to Vicars Cross Island at Chester (185 miles) Christine goes through with 10 hrs 9 mins elapsed, Ruth 10.21 and Wyn 11.18. It's a clear dawn as the 'girls' pass the 205 mile point at Whitchurch. They are all riding very strongly. Ruth is now 30 minutes up on husband Bob.

At the 12 hr point Rod Goodfellow had a very convincing lead over Ken Usher with 252 miles – could this be a record ride in the making ? A fine sunny morning greets the riders as they wind their way to Battlefield Corner (Shrewsbury) past the feed at Edgebolton to Tern Hill.

Christine goes to Tern Hill and is sent back by Tommy Barlow, the Course Detour Controller, who shouts words of encouragement to her, she calls back "don't worry, I'll finish!" Shawbury corner just after Hodnet comes next and then to the Shawbirch turn, Wellington (Telford). Back at Hodnet the riders had now covered approximately 300 miles and Goodfellow still had a very clear lead over Howard Bayley, Solihull CC. He'd now overcome the 'collywobbles' to slip into 2nd place on the road.

Back at Shrewsbury, Battlefield Corner, and right along the A49 to Whitchurch where left through the lanes to Tilstock and Wem. Christine misses a 'detour' that takes the riders out to the border with Wales. This puts her first on the road again. Meanwhile Goodfellow had completed all of the extra loops of road and was thundering along behind Christine, just a few minutes ahead. They headed north back towards the finishing circuit at Chester.

Ruth followed a few minutes behind Goodfellow, past the 'Harp' at Quina Brook, the last feeding station of the day; meanwhile, Christine is still leading Goodfellow over the 'Broxtons' now only 8 miles to the finishing circuit but at Handley Church, Rod finally caught her and hammered on to enter the circuit to tumultuous applause from the many club folk there waiting to see history evolve. He was followed just over a minute later by Christine. Their respective positions at that time on the road meant that if Rod could keep the pressure on with 3.5 hours to go, he could beat 'evens' with a 480 mile ride and Christine's estimated mileage could be a possible 410. It was a gloriously hot afternoon, just what you don't need at the end of a 24 hr race. The effect of many hours of riding under a blazing hot sun take their toll and the hoped for targets of a lot of riders fail to materialize. Both Rod and Christine gradually slow as they lap the circuit. Christine ran out of time just less than a mile short of 410, and Rod with 475.38. Howard Bayley slogs a huge gear round the circuit to finish second with 458.69 miles and Ken Usher came back strongly for 3rd place with 455.17 miles. Local man, Stan Lea, gained a fine 4th with 450.37 miles

In all 30 riders got onto the circuit to complete the 24 hrs ride. Bob Williams, Ruth's husband, finally finishes his first 24 hr with 415.28 miles, so beating Ruth by just 12 miles".

**Mrs Wyn Maddock,** who I think was already a grandmother and 60 years old by then, provided a fine **366.67 miles.** She was what one can only describe as a genteel, graceful lady, who had a kind word for everyone.

She always had a thin lace handkerchief tucked into a wrist bracelet or watch strap and one would imagine it had a dab or two of either lavender water or eau de cologne.

I can't ever recall seeing her with a club racing vest on; she usually wore a white blouse or top and dainty shorts. She was very lithe and slim and could keep up a steady 17 to 20 mph for hour after hour and never showed any signs of fatigue or distress.

Wyn rode until she was in her late seventies. She was injured when knocked off her bike by a car, and this eventually cut short her life. She died in 1985 aged 78 years. I remember riding many time trials from the age of 14 and at all distances against her and she very rarely altered her pace. The Oldbury 12 hour was one of her favourite rides I would see her on. A very gracious lady.

The sit down feed at Edgebolton took place in an arch doored entrance at the side of a terraced cottage on the main road. It had a cobbled floor and was furnished with kitchen table and chairs for the weary riders to ease themselves into. All manner of breakfasts were to be had from porridge and cornflakes to bacon, sausage and egg. Nothing was too much trouble. Ablutions if needed were performed up the garden path in a 'privy' with a wooden bench seat with a hole cut into it. The feeding station was manned by a team of club folk who would help ease you on or off your bike, or if you didn't want to stop they would offer you a bottle of tea and a sponge.

'Here comes a Wobbley Wheelers rider. Give him the cheap blackcurrant without the glucose.'

The 'Harp' at Quina Brook is another famous landmark in this event, being the last feed of the day, it was operated from about 11 am to 2 pm on the Sunday. I've stopped there a few times in the past in 24 hr events. It's an old village pub where a front parlour is set aside for the riders. Tables were laden with dishes full of trifles, custard, blancmange, jelly, rice pudding, and plates of sandwiches and salad with gallons of tea or juice. It was a godsend on many occasions.

Sadly, none of these feeds are used in the modern day 24 hr although the present day course still goes past the Harp at Quina Brook, which is now a private dwelling.

# 1968

**The Merseyside Ladies CA 24 hour: Christine** again rode to another **Competition Record in 1968** by improving her own record by 11 miles to produce **420.05 miles** on the way to this new record she had beaten **Joyce Blow** on a trike who recorded **371.68 miles.** This was to become a new **Womens Trike Competition Record for 24 hrs.** Joyce and her husband Bernard, went on to be founder members of the 300,000 mile club, along with Les Lowe, Pat Kenny, Chris Davies and many others, all being 24 hr riders. The leader on mileage (to date in 2007) is Chris Davies with approximately 890,000 miles & Pat Kenny with 840,000.

# 1969

**Christine Minto's** next ride was in 1969, although it was somewhat overshadowed by Roy Cromack's 507 mile competition record winning ride in the same event. **Christine's mileage** was also a new **Womens Competition Record of 427.86 miles.**

In that same **Merseyside Ladies CA Event,** Joyce Blow pushed her own **Trike Competition Record** up to **374.15 miles.** It was to be a record that stood until 1988.
Wyn Maddock, Notts & Derby Clarion, put up a marvellous personal best ride of **386.59 miles.**

**Beryl Burton** also rode this race but retired at 350 miles with painful knees. For more information on her ride look at the history of the Mersey Road Club **Men's** event of 1969.

It will be 14 years before Christine's record is broken. In the 'in-between years' there were still some very good rides performed by the ladies.

# 1970

**Merseyside Ladies CA.**       **Joan Kershaw** - Prescot Eagles R.C. beat Joyce Blow to win with **422.34 miles** to Joyce's fine **402.12.** Joyce was on a **bike** this time. Fred Cowling in the 24 hr Fellowship Journal of 1971, mentioned riding sandwiched between the two girls on the way south to Whitchurch just as dawn was breaking. He remembered both of them having regular stops along this stretch, and being overtaken regularly by them. Joan was suffering from backache and was trying to relieve the pain. With more than 13 hours still to ride, it wouldn't be easy. Fred later recalls plodding along in the Wem to Quina Brook area at 337 miles. Joyce sprinted past on her '70' fixed gear. They scrapped all the way to the Welsh border at Welshampton to turn at Redbrook pump, a terrible stretch of road coming so late in the ride. He said it made the journey much more interesting and bearable.

"I MUSTN'T stay gossiping – I'm five minutes down on schedule."

**Joan Kershaw's** ride of **422.34** was less than 20 miles behind the men's winning mileage of Stan Lea with 441.99 miles and only 10 miles less than Malcolm 'Mal' Jones, Mid Shropshire Wheelers. He had a cracking ride with 432 miles in only his third 24 hr race. *(Joan's 422.34 miles would have put her 3rd overall in the men's results)*

# 1972

Jill Dale, Long Eaton Paragon, achieved 296 miles in the Wessex 24 hr.

# 1973

**Ethel Brambleby** bridged the gap from 1973 to 1976 with three consecutive rides of **326.17, 340.62** and **354.85** miles - an even 14 miles improvement each year. Ethel rode for the Hounslow and District Wheelers, a club she has been with most of her life. (all three rides were done in the Merseyside Ladies)

# 1974

In 1974 **Janet Tebbutt** was the sole lady rider in the Wessex RC 24hr with **363.92 miles.**

Later that year on August 8th Janet set out on the longest journey of her life, The **WRRA Ladies Amateur 1000 miles record.** She had modestly chosen one of the slowest records on the books but obviously the longest, requiring terrific stamina and determination. Janet used a star shaped course based on Bristol and using some of the same roads as used in the Wessex RC 24 hr. She had two hours sleep the first night, somewhat less on the second and a mere 20 minutes on the third night. Thick mist, strong winds and heavy rain plagued her ride but she still took over 6 hours off Wyn Wrightsons 21 year old record, with **3 days 9 hrs 29 mins..**

# 1975

**Janet Tebbutt** gained 15th place with **356.18 miles** in the **Wessex RC 24 hr.**

# 1976

**Joan Kershaw** had by this time galvanized a team of long distance ladies, who were all interested in riding for 24 hrs. **Ruth Williams** who had shone in the **1967 24 hr** with **403.70 miles,** and 3rd team member, **Amy Hooton** who had ridden to **2nd** lady behind Ethel in 1975 with **332.54 miles.**

**The Mersey RC Event** of 1976 was a very successful one for lots of people. Rod Goodfellow won the event with a remarkable 476 miles, just 4 miles off evens pace, knocking George Berwick into 2nd place with a cracking 464.11 miles; his best ever I think. Third was the ex tour de France rider, Vin Denson, who had always fancied the all day event; he recorded 449.31 miles.

For me, the highlight of the weekend was a historical one for **Joan, Ruth and Amy 'The Prescot Eagles'.** They provided the **first ladies team ever in a 24 hr race,** setting a **new RTTC ladies team competition record of 1,106.41 miles.**

**Joan** rode to **404.82 miles, Ruth** battled long and hard to achieve a Mersey RC silver medal position with **360.76 miles,** and **Amy Hooton** gained a bronze with **340.83.**

## THIS TEAM RECORD WAS TO STAND FOR 29 YEARS.

The other significant reason for me to remember the event was that I produced my best ever mileage of 418.55 miles. It was my eighth 24 hr race and I had improved every year from a 360 mile ride, taking it for granted that I would improve a bit each year, but little did I realise at the time that it would remain my personal best 'PB'. One always has ambitions of higher mileages and better performances, and although I did ride another 10 events spread out over the next 24 years till year 2000, I never could push myself hard enough to match my ambition.

One other little success for me in that event was beating Joan Kershaw at last. To me she was such a good rider to look up to in events going right back to 1959. Joan never showed signs of distress, always looked cool and elegant on a bike. In the events that I rode in from schoolboy age, she always nodded when going in the opposite direction, and when she passed you from behind there were always words of encouragement.

In the 1980's Joan re-emerged with her own Prescot Eagles 'team' of two daughters, Louise and Mandy who were equally as elegant. Joan's family team won the medals for being 1st team in the **1985 'Ladies Championship 100'** **with 14 hrs 9 mins 19 secs.** Amazingly enough it was just one second slower than her first ever 100 mile championship team win in 1962 with J. Kennedy and G. Graham, some 23 years previously. **Ruth Williams** is another rider who has shared team honours with Joan over various distances in the 1960's.

Joan's solo championship wins are the 50 mile in 1962 and the 25 mile in 1965. She also led the Liverpool Eagle RC Ladies 'Best All Round Team' to wins in 1960, 1963, 1966 and 1975.

Probably my first recollection of her was when riding in my first Oldbury and District 12 hour race, one I'm sure I rode annually for about 35 years. Joan caught me going out along the A38 Burton on Trent road before it became a dual carriageway. The road was shrouded in 'will-o-the-wisp' patches of mist in those days with no traffic to disperse it. She glided past effortlessly, and created an everlasting impression.

There was now a three year gap with no action at all for the ladies. It would be 7 years before an improvement on the ladies bike record and 12 years for the ladies trike record at 24 hours, but I will try to fill in as many performances as I can find for those 'in-between' years, starting in 1979.

# 1979

**Jenny Colman** was the sole lady rider in the **Merseyside Ladies CA 24 hr** this year with **370.05 miles,** riding for the Scarborough Paragon CC.

# 1980

**Mrs Dorothy Chase** of the Cardiff Ajax CC became the first Welsh girl to run out time in a 24 hr time trial with **356.098 miles.** The event was the **Merseyside Ladies CA.** She beat one of her own clubmen, A.R.Sturk by 2 miles and overall beat 7 men. The riders experienced very heavy showers going into the Saturday night, but the weather cleared to give a good day with a 'balmy' afternoon on the finishing circuit. The event took place in late July as usual

Just one month later, **History was made in the North Road CC National Championship 24 hr, when Mrs Anne Dunk became the first woman rider to finish,** in this their 82nd Annual promotion since 1886. Anne who is a member of the host club produced a strong ride, finishing with **379.655 miles** beating 12 men in the process. This event took place over the August Bank Holiday.

# 1981

**The Mersey RC 24 hr** in late July saw my old training partner, **Miss Kathy Bellingham (later to become Kath Akoslovski)** riding her first 24 hr race. A member of the Vegetarian C & AC and the Warwick RC, she produced a fine ride of **372.549 miles** on a not too easy day and night, overcast with intermittent showers and then a very hot sun on the finishing circuit.

Later that year Kathy went on to take Eileen Sheridan's **London to Birmingham record** by 7 mins with **5 hrs 12 mins 18 secs.** That was just one of 4 national RRA ladies records she broke around that time. Another excellent one being a **58-52** for the **trike 25 mile record** in **1981,** nearly a 9 minute beating of Jenny Noad's record. Apart from National RRA, Kathy has broken and still holds many Midlands and Regional Road Records on all forms of machine and with various tandem partners including Lynne.

A recurring knee problem from an injury sustained earlier in her cycling career has prevented her from racing at full strength since 1986. She married Pete Howard, a previous Catford Winner of 1974 with 435.62 miles. Pete, later took his fathers original Russian name of Akoslovski to continue the line. Pete and Kath have a son Thomas, who is a BMX Champion and very active in the sport.

Another famous lady record breaker who rode the **Merseyside Ladies Event** that same day as Kathy is **Mrs Janet Tebbutt.** She finished with **349.037 miles,** another fine mileage in a career spanning some 50 years. This 24 hr came just 5 years after her successful assault on the **Ladies Amateur End to End** with **2 days 15 hrs 24 mins.** Janet at nearly 70 years of age is still racing long distance and in 2006, I've just noticed she produced **313.459 miles. How does she do it ?**

I rode that event in 1981 on the back of Pat Kenny's tandem trike and boy did we suffer. We shipped the 'linking' chain at the start and lost about an hour during the event trying to keep the cranks in some sort of synchronization. We eventually finished, grubby with oil and grime, for a 407.499 mileage.

Looking back on this ride brings a smile to my face although it didn't at the time. I would be on the down stroke with my right leg and Pat would be on the way back up with his right. It was a very lumpy performance. Every hour or so Pat would leap off and bash the eccentric bottom bracket round to try and improve matters. Cornering became a wheel and hair raising experience – 'The Last of the Summer Wine' springs to mind, or should that be 'Laurel and Hardy'?

One month later in the **North Road CC 24 hr, Anne Dunk** once again rose to the occasion to produce a **395.22 miles** ride taking 6th place in the main field. Here are some passages relating to the event taken from The North Road Gazette and The 24 hr Fellowship Journal. *"for most club members around the course, the highlight of the event was Anne's ride, for she really raced, every inch the true competitor, holding fourth place for much of the time, catching Bob O'Dell seven minutes before the 100 mile point. Her challenge raised Bob's effort and for the next 12 hours we had one of those 'epics', which are the fascination of the time trial game. Anne rode herself into the ground, finally succumbing to the 'old bogey' (not you Bob) feeding trouble, leading to sickness. This reduced her to walking up the hills on the finishing circuit. That she was so near to 400 miles was a shame, but surely we have a rider who can approach the ladies record of 427 miles – given better luck with her diet.*

*Finally the other lady entrant, Jenny Colman from Scarborough who rode cheerfully throughout and at times was to be seen liberally dousing herself with water. Bill Frankum was so impressed that in a moment of admiration he offered her a medal if she finished, which she duly did, and subsequently the committee agreed to this specially donated award with pleasure. Next year Jenny hopes to be back with her partner on a tandem Viva La 24."* **Jenny Colman's** mileage of **361.36** was just 9 miles less than her Mersey ride of 1979.

# 1982

The **North Road 24 hr** saw **Mrs Ann Rogers,** North Notts Olympic climb to 10th position in the main field beating 13 men in the process with another ride so tantalisingly close to the 400 mile mark with **398.855 miles.** Two other ladies finished this historic event, **Mrs L. Webb** of the Bedfordshire RC with **337.137 miles** and **Miss Judy Dakin,** CC Breckland, on a **trike** with **322.561 miles.** Judy became the **First Lady Trike Rider** to finish in the **North Road event.** I wonder what old past 19th century winners, G.P.Mills, F.T.Bidlake, Holbein, & Marriott would have said? "Hmmm, not even trike riding is sacred any more!"

# 1983

On June 25th & 26th, The Eastern Counties Cycling Association 'ECCA' promoted a 'Special RTTC National Championship 24 hr', using roads east of London, Cambridge, Harlow, Southend, Chelmsford and finishing on a circuit at High Roding just north of Chelmsford. I've chosen some memorable lines and passages from an article by Anne Mann, published in the 24 hr Fellowship Journal shortly after the event. *"I don't suppose I would have ever ridden a 24 hr if our local 'ECCA' had not accepted the 'RTTC' offer to promote the championship in 1983, with the 'ECCA' deciding to incorporate a woman's event.*

*It was late October 1982 that the first firm thoughts were made, and I decided then to just ride steadily through the winter and see how things went. Jean Burrow also expressed an interest in riding and we were anxious to get one of our other girls to prepare for an attempt on the team record. Unfortunately however, no one else was at all keen to ride and we both agreed that you can't twist peoples arms to ride a 24hr and we had to put thoughts of the team out of our minds.*

*It was by now late December and my husband Graham, who had ridden three 24 hr races, winning a bronze medal for 3rd place in the Wessex RC 24 in 1978 with 465 miles, began to sow the seed of an idea that I could beat Christine Minto's record of 427.86 miles.*

*This thought I at first rejected, as I did not want to set myself too high a target and then fail; Preferring to aim for 400 miles and anything over that being a bonus. That mention of the solo record however, was enough to make me keep the idea at the back of my mind from then on.*

*It was obvious that Graham would not be able to do the helping 100% so Ann Illingworth (a regular team competition record breaker riding with various clubs in the 1960's including the Hainault RC, at distances of 25,30,50 and 100 mile) volunteered to assist him which pleased me, being a great friend over many years, and I knew she would give me maximum effort and support."*

Anne's normal time trial training was usually only a few hours fitted into a busy family home schedule, but for the 24 hr she realised she had to increase her hours and mileage on the bike. Her performances and form in 1983 'fluctuated' from week to week. A trip to the doctors didn't show anything up at the time, but she was later diagnosed as having had mild glandular fever. Anne rode two 100 mile events and five 50's with a fast 1 hr 1 min for 25 miles and a 2 hrs 3 mins for 50. She felt that a BBAR place was possible, but the important event was the 24 hour.

*'The start sheet arrived and it transpired that there were four girls entered, Mary Horsnell, Jean Burrow, Ann Rogers and myself, in that order. Graham knew that Ann Rogers had ridden a good 24 hr last year and as such was considered the most serious threat in the event, as both Mary and Jean were 'novices' and their abilities as local riders were known better.*

*Graham suggested that I should start very positively and hopefully catch and drop all three riders in the first 100 miles and then ride my own event, and although I had no intention of 'racing' I did think that this was a sound idea".*

After a trouble free start, Anne continues *" I was in a very contented frame of mind as I headed off towards the 100 mile mark, which took 4 hrs 58 mins. I was now 10 minutes up on the next lady and headed off up the E1 course towards Cambridge. Prior to the event I had not ridden in the dark for 14 years and in case it put me off I didn't include this aspect in my preparation. In the event however, the night was my best period physically. It was cool and calm and I had no trouble with lights or identification of helpers etc. Ann would come towards me with a flashing light and tell me what was being handed up, and Graham would run in the headlights from the car. In the 12 hours on the return from Harlow, I had covered 232 miles and was still riding quite steadily although obviously slowing gradually.*

*Dawn broke and I went into my worst period, on the South End Road leg. Afterwards, Graham said it was the only part of the event where he was concerned about my finishing. From the turn on the A12 to the finishing circuit I was really grovelling (or so it seemed at the time), but in retrospect there must have been many riders in far worse condition than me. The 'cut out' (detour) marshals made me go down the last leg to Birch, which I was dreading. Apparently I missed the closing time by 4 minutes and I had no option but to continue down the detour. The indifferent surfaces and the loneliness of this leg was the straw that broke the camels back.*

*My legs went completely and, all in all, I think that having to complete this stretch cost me about 3 miles overall, but regulations are regulations and that is it. I found it heart breaking at the time, but what it did mean however, was that I had time to get to the circuit and, having done the full course, I knew I would break competition record before I reached the circuit. This was a good feeling and this incentive tended to buck me up a little again. Graham asked Harry Burnett, one of our club members, to go ahead and stop when his car speedo indicated where the existing record distance was. The feeling of joy as I rode past him was immense. By this time my legs had 'gone completely' and even a slight gradient forced me out of the saddle and into considerable pain.*

*Once on the circuit I had 30 minutes left to ride and as I passed the zero timekeeper I got a lot of cheers from my family and friends in the club and ECCA, many of whom had given me up as they thought I was long overdue by their calculations, not realising that I had ridden the whole course.*

*From the first timekeeper there is a slight rise up to 'High Roding' and I was forced to walk up this as I just could not put enough pressure on the pedals to go forward. Having got to the top however, I had trouble at first getting back on my bike again and so it continued with me only able to achieve 6 miles in the first 30 minutes I had on the circuit, finally finishing at George Martindale having achieved 438.12 miles and immediately being surrounded and pampered by family and friends, all jumping up and down with excitement and shaking hands. It was a wonderful feeling and one I will treasure forever."*

Anne's mileage would have put her in 7th place in the men's championship event, which was won by Stuart Jackson with 488.84 miles.

So, **Anne Mann, 1st lady** with a **new competition record of 438.12 miles; 2nd lady, Ann Rogers,** North Notts Olympic CC with **412.55 miles;** 3rd was **Jean Burrow, 407.99** and **4th Mary Horsnell** with **394.15 miles.**

Jean Burrow, in a later journal, said that she'd ridden to various 24 hr 'get-togethers' with her dad, Bill Suttie, when she was a teenager. One of the venues was in Dorset and she rode home afterwards, overnight to Bournemouth. Jean was impressed and influenced by stories from Sid Hygate and John Fisher and this is what helped kindle her interest.

I know another young lady who was also spurred on by stories from her father and by listening to his friends when they got together to talk about 24 hr riding and record breaking, but that comes later!

<hr>

**At the end of July, in the Mersey RC 24 hr,** there appeared to have been little action in the ladies event, due to Sheila Simpson falling heavily at about the 160 mile point. After completing the 100 miles in 5 hrs 26 mins, heavy thunder, torrential rain and lightning swept across the course, flooding the roads. Between 9 pm and midnight, conditions were very tricky. Apparently, Sheila fell very heavily when taking a feed in the dark and broke her collarbone, having to retire for treatment.

One other woman was riding the event that day, on a tandem, with her husband Ian. Her name was **Bridget Boon,** and they were making their debut at 24 hr riding. They were both hard riding club tourists from the Bristol and Clevedon area. Timekeepers put them just outside 'evens' (20 mph) for the first 100 miles with 5 hrs 4 mins. The 12 hr point yielded 216 miles and they finished in great style according to Frank Mumford, the Mersey RC 'scribe' in his usual brilliant report on the event. They lapped the finishing circuit three times with 50, 49 and 53 minutes to set up a **mixed tandem competition record of 421.893 miles.** *Up to that time a performance by Jenny Colman and her husband in the Mersey RC event of 1982 of 401.77 miles had stood as 'best on record'.*

## 1984

This was a lean year for women riders, in the **Merseyside Ladies 24 hr,** Jane Ramsdale 'stoked' the tandem trike with T. Brooking and although she had a suspect knee at the time, they finished with **364.531 miles.** Tandem trikes are very hard work at the best of times, let alone ridden with a bad knee. The 'stoker' (rider at the back) gets the worst position, having to sit way behind the bottom bracket and also having a top tube that is never in a constant position due to the rear wheels causing it to oscillate from side to side, so catching ones knees very hard when one is least expecting it.

<hr>

A month later in the **North Road 24 hr, Esther Carpenter** of the Southborough and District CC was the only lady in a Championship field of 86 men. The daylight hours were warm and sunny and the night was dark but mild and clear. Esther put up a fine **375.24 miles** to become the only Ladies solo bike 24 hr performance of 1984.

## 1985

In the **Merseyside Ladies CA 24 hr** incorporated with the Mersey RC National Championship Event, just one sole lady rider, **Mrs Jill Richards,** Cardiff Ajax CC finished with **382.68 miles.**

A ride of that distance deserves merit due, as does the **mixed tandem** ride of the **Boons, Ian and Bridget.** A distance of **443.27** with a fast first 100 miles of 4 hrs 25 mins, & a 12 hr of nearly evens, 239 miles. They rode a very well judged race with this being only their second attempt at the distance. This mileage was a **new competition record.**

They beat a male tandem of P. Dade and G.V. Adams by 26 miles and a tandem trike crewed by Les Lowe and Jim Hopper by 24 miles, so good results there for everyone, but I do think it helps when you have an opponent in the race, i.e. two or three tandems, half a dozen trikes, and five or six ladies at least, competing with each other.

Ian Dow, Oxford City RC won the event in his usual smooth manner with a 480.55 mile ride beating Gerry Smith, Merseyside Wheelers by 7 miles exactly. Steve Armstrong came third with 465.65 miles. A good weekend for 52 riders.

———◆———

A month later in the **North Road CC 24 hr, Mrs Jean Burrow beat Anne Dunk** by 17 miles. Mrs Burrow's mileage was **382.95.** Anne's mileage of **365.78** helped Malcolm Green with 437.72 and Gordon Dennis, 429.70 to **secure the team win for the North Road CC,** with a mileage of **1233.20.**

The weather had been tolerable and dry on the day but with the onset of night, became bitterly cold, made worse with a strong wind. The cold decimated the field and reduced some of the riders to walking, so as to restore the circulation to frozen limbs.

**Miss Judy Tait** and Mr G. Yuill both from the Maldon and District CC rode a **tandem** with a mileage of **398.88.** They were just beaten by A.Fielding and P.Horsfield on a tandem with 401.34. Peter Hoffmann with 469.98 miles won the event with Stuart Jackson 2nd on a trike with 444.13. Two superb mileages on the day. From 60 starters only 36 solos and the tandems finished.

## 1986

**Saturday June 28th** saw another 'one off' **24 hrs Championship** event promoted for the **RTTC by the NMCF (North Midlands Cycling Federation).** The weather was very hot on both days. The event started on the hottest part of the day with the two ladies going off 1st and 2nd at 2.00 pm. Anybody who tried to 'race' in those conditions ran the risk of overheating, sunstroke and exhaustion, so a cautious start was required. The two ladies did very well to finish and it doesn't look as though their performances were affected too much. After a warm night came the relentless sun and heat. A strong wind rose later in the morning to trouble the riders even more, but despite all of this, **Mrs Jean Burrow beat Celia Prescott** by just over 10 miles with **403.364** to Celia's **393.013,** coming 26th and 31st respectively.

The 'Boons' had improved year on year with their **tandem 24 hr results** and had followed suit in this event with a fine **463.334 miles** ride. **Another new competition record.**

The overall championship was won by Ian Dow with 488.896 miles, an amazing ride considering the heat. Ian had decided not to get embroiled in a battle with the other five or so favourites, but played a waiting game, picking them all off slowly, one by one, with John Woodburn and Stuart Jackson finishing 2nd and 3rd with 482.873 and 468.152 respectively.

———◆———

Two months later, the **Boon's** rode **tandem** again in the **North Roads CC 24 hr** hoping to beat evens, but by looking at the overall results of the solo riders, I would think it was a hard day. The Boons dropped a little on their mileage with **449.84,** which would have given them third place amongst the solo's. It will be interesting later on to see what their individual results are for 24 hrs on bikes.

Peter Hoffmann, Komet Ludwigsburgh won the event with 457.30, Rod Goodfellow was 2nd with 452.68 miles and Gordon Dennis 3rd with 444.21 miles. One other tandem finished, M. Brooking and J. Jennings, Willesden CC with 421.25.

# 1987

**The South DC Special Promotion 24 hr Championship** was the first 24 hr of the season on the 20th June. **Mrs Jean Burrow** was the sole lady rider in the event and came in 17th position in a field of 40 men finishers. Jean nearly didn't get a ride as it was a championship for men only, but after many letters of protest to the RTTC both by Jean and Les Lowe, she was finally allowed to ride, with the proviso that she couldn't win any awards. Her **419.132 miles** was a personal best in this her fourth 24hr. Jeans ride was all the more remarkable, only finding out two months before the event that she was to be allowed to ride. Two months is fine preparation time wise for a 50 or 100 mile event, but a stamina race like a 24 hr needs 6 months preparation. Being a busy mum with two children also meant that training time was restricted. After sorting out all the feeding arrangements, not only for herself but also for her children, Louise and Jamie, who were staying the night with friends. Jean felt she was ready to race.

Graham Mann who had helped his wife Anne to a competition record 24 hr result in 1983 was helping Jean in this race along with husband Mick, and they proved to be an excellent team. Jean, in a 24 hr fellowship journal, mentions how she caught her father Bill at about 90 miles. He wasn't feeling too good and retired shortly afterwards. The severity of the hills on this course was one of Jeans drawbacks and the drowsiness on the night circuit was another. Her eyelids were so heavy she said she was afraid to even blink for fear of ending up in the ditch.

The period immediately after the dawn saw Jean grovelling, hardly moving at any more than walking pace. Lots of riders came past her in this period leaving her demoralised & she was also now experiencing problems with eating, but she knew she couldn't 'pack' and let everybody down. On the hill near Bere Regis she got her lowest gear turning and started to catch a few riders back and so started to regain her position on the road. With her morale now lifted she started to pull back time knowing the finish was only a short while away. Jean fancied rice pudding but husband Mick was picking up the children and his car had got all of the food in it. After a panic stricken few moments, her friends, Pete, Doreen and Graham frantically scoured the local shops and struck lucky. The rice pudding saw her through to the finishing circuit where she ran out time at 2.25 pm.

---

There was no action by the ladies in the 1987 Mersey and the 24 hr season concluded with 2 rides in the **North Road event**. **Miss S. Loveder** produced **307.02** riding for the Kettering Amateur CC. She was pushed into 2nd place by **Sian Charlton** with **316.27 miles**. This North Road CC event had been another of European flavour with Pieter Hoffmann winning again with 466.22 miles from Mark Holden 453.83. This invasion by Pieter was one of many successful rides he made around this time.

# 1988

This was the Road Records Association Centenary Year

From 1988 onwards women were allowed to integrate in the main field of male riders and were allowed to compete for medals and team places in championship events.

1988 saw action from the ladies in only one event - **The North Road CC 24 hr** Championship promotion. **Mrs Felicity Beard, 'Fliss'** riding a **trike** was the fastest lady with **382.22 miles** beating **Mrs M. Chaney, 338.96, Miss Sian Charlton** was 3rd with **309.60** and **Miss S.E. Loveder** with **277.26 miles** was **4th**. Fliss Beards Competition **trike record** put her 15th in the men's championship field. A championship won by Stuart Jackson with 481.36 miles, narrowly beating Ian Dow by two miles. **Her record still stands to this day.**

# 1989

**In January the Women's Road Records Association merged with the RRA**

In 1989 the Mersey RC 24 hr saw the only action for the ladies with **Miss Jan Kirkham** from the Redmon CC producing the best ride with **351.76 miles** beating **Sian Charlton's trike** mileage of **279.90**. **Miss Ramsdale** rode a **tandem trike** with Mr Brooking and rode a fine **372.64 miles**. The Championship was won by Ian Butcher with a massive 493.53 miles from Stuart Jackson with 472.54 miles. The 'mixed' tandem trike mileage became the **'best on record'** at this time.

## 1990

After crashing out of the 1983 **Mersey 24 hr** at 150 miles, **Mrs Sheila Simpson** made her comeback in this event of **1990**, taking a very well deserved **5th place** with **408.07** miles. Sheila was only 28 miles behind the winner, John Clarke of the Rutland CC. Thirty two finished out of 51 starters.

The early stages of the event were under an oppressive sun, with an unhelpful south easterly breeze. It was on a new course designed to cut out U turns. At 12 hours, Sheila had covered 211 miles and was riding strongly even though the night had turned cold.

Her experience at riding Audax events helped her to establish a new ladies age record and put up the best Merseyside Ladies CA figures for 20 years.

———◆———

Between 28th and 30th July, **Pauline Strong** broke Eileen Sheridan's **End to End** record with **2 days, 6 hrs, 49 mins and 45 secs.**

Heavy traffic caused delays in the West Country and a 13 mile traffic jam in Cornwall made for dangerous riding and time lost on her schedule, but Pauline rode on.

At Knutsford Pauline was nearly two hours down on schedule, she was suffering with bad knees at Wigan, 365 miles. By 7.30 am next day, the wind was rising in her favour as she pushed on through Lancaster. Pauline climbed Shap extremely well and reached the summit at 10.15 am, still only two hours down on schedule.

Carlisle was passed and she reached the 'Welcome to Scotland' sign at 12.30pm with a one arm punch in the air. Roy Moss, the timekeeper, said that the schedule from there on became more generous. Her knees were now heavily bandaged over her wrinkled tights (She called them her Nora Batty's).

By 500 miles at 2 pm, heavy rain was falling as she made her way towards Moffat. After climbing the Beeftub in thick wet mist she stopped at the summit for hot soup and more clothing, but the long descent towards Edinburgh left her freezing cold and Pauline lost most of the time she had gained back. Throughout Sunday night she had numerous changes of clothing due to the heavy rain. By the time the Slochd summit had been reached it was estimated that Pauline had averaged 15.8 mph and to break the record she needed to do 10.7 mph to the finish. A one hour rest was taken as Pauline was hallucinating and she had to be persuaded to continue. Despite a very painful left buttock she showed tremendous courage and amazed everyone by pulling back time towards the closing stages from Inverness to the end.

Pauline said that her knees were so swollen she was unable to bend them and had to ride out of the saddle to try and make them bend. She remembered thinking that she wouldn't wish this amount of pain and suffering on her worst enemy!

I rang Roy Moss in the following car in the Highlands on Sunday night about 10 pm and he said it was touch and go, but if she could keep going and not lose any more time she could still get the record. I went to bed and relived my own journeys over those desolate roads and tortuous climbs – I didn't envy her at all.

When I rang on Monday morning I heard the good news that she had broken the record by over 4 hours. I was amazed by the sheer enormity of her ride against all odds.

Pauline tried three more times to reduce the record down to 2 days, once in August 1991, getting as far as 500 miles where very strong winds forced her to abandon, and then in May 1992, she tried again but fell heavily at about 150 miles, bruising her ribs. She finally abandoned around midnight unable to breathe without pain.

Late August that same year was her third and final attempt getting as far as Carnforth where painful, strained, tendons in her leg brought her to a halt, with heavy rain falling, it was a wise decision.

Pauline's successful End to End in 1990 was the first to use a mobile telephone. It was about the size of a house brick, but never the less proved very useful in the remote regions of England and Scotland.

# 1991

**The North Road CC** event was held in late June. **Miss E. McCarthy** took **6th** place overall in this her first attempt at 24hr racing.

What a commendable ride, helping her clubmates from the Maldon and District CC to the team win. Phil Oxborough, St Ives CC won the event with 452.58 perhaps in preparation for the Mersey Championship event just one month later. Only 15 riders finished. The entries for this once very popular event obviously have been affected by being so early and so close to the Mersey promotion.

---

One month later, the **'Mersey' 24 hr** turned out to be one of the best ever. The results of the event rewarded Jim Turner and everyone involved with the running of it for all of their hard work.

**Sheila Simpson,** Doncaster Wheelers, **won the Merseyside Ladies CA 24 hr** with **426.18 miles.** This time, she came 10th overall and took revenge on the previous years winner, John Clarke, by nearly 10 miles. **Mrs Jean Burrow,** Shaftesbury CC beat 23 men to finish with **375.60 miles.** Mick Potts won the event in convincing style with 486.65 miles at 50 years of age, a very popular winner. 61 solo riders finished plus the Goodfellows; Rod and son Pete, who broke tandem competition record with 501.35 miles.

# 1992

**The first 24 hr** in 1992 was again the **North Road CC** in late June. It took place in a fearsome wind, many of the favourites packed when their expected mileages were not forthcoming, but that was in the men's field. Of the ladies, **Sheila Simpson,** riding now for the Weaver Valley CC came through it all well to take 11th position with **401.76 miles.** Again her Audax experiences had seen her through some rough patches into the wind in this probably her toughest 24 hr. **Jean Burrow** put on a good ride with **372.50 miles,** and the only other lady to finish was **Mrs Mary Horsfield** of the Redmon CC stoking the tandem for husband Peter and producing **336.40 miles.**

Celia Prescott had started the event and was lying in a very good position at 12 hours, with 223 miles, but then promptly stopped and refused to go any further. Her helpers couldn't believe it, so lost for words were they that they asked Stuart Jackson if he could talk her into continuing, but to no avail. Celia said she wasn't enjoying it, and that she only continued beyond 60 miles because she had eaten so much the day before! (*enjoying it – who said it would be enjoyable?*)

---

One month later we saw much better conditions for the **Mersey Roads 24 hr** with just a spattering of light showers, mainly in the night and a light south west wind playing gently throughout and helping the riders back to the finishing circuit on the Sunday morning. With over 60 riders entered it promised to be a good event.

There were many scraps on the road very early on. Frank Mumford who reported for the Mersey RC 'Record' and the 24 hr Fellowship Journal, mentions Robert Fry, a super randonneur, when sandwiched on the road between George Berwick, Bridget Boon and Sheila Simpson at around the 60 mile point, he suddenly 'took off' and caught up with Rod Goodfellow and Ian Gray (two of the favourites), and then finally 'disappeared from our screens' around the 120 mile point.

Sheila Simpson who had ridden a hard North Road CC event only a month previously with 401 miles, gradually lost time on Bridget Boon who then became the first rider on the road. Bridget's was one of the most heroic rides of the day; she rode 'eyeballs out' on the finishing circuit, recording successive laps of 50, 52 and 50 minutes, **but just missed Anne Mann's 1983 Competition Record of 438.16 by .5 of a mile.** One consolation was that **Bridget** had set a new **'MLCA' Merseyside Ladies Cycling Association course and event record with 437.62 miles.**

Meanwhile **Sheila Simpson** had fought to keep her position in the field and came **2nd** to Bridget with **407.52 miles.** The **3rd** lady to finish was **Corri Farquharson** with **345.07 miles. Mrs M.V.Staines** of the Mildenhall CC crewing the **tandem trike** with her husband was the only other lady entrant. They finished with **332.25 miles.**

Ian Dow, when mentioning highlights of the season, picks out Bridget Boons 'exceptional' solo debut and blamed a last minute course modification for robbing her of the competition record, to which Bridget simply shrugged her shoulders and said 'Then I'll have to do another one!' Incidentally her mileage put her in 4th place overall, from a field of 52. Ian Gray won the event with 463.02 miles.

Bridget shares some secrets of her first solo 24 hr:

*"After a hard season in 1991 and carrying the fitness gained into the spring of 1992 we decided to ride the North Road event on the tandem. After 14 hours we abandoned the ride but it did give us some much needed racing miles. With just 4 weeks to the Mersey 24 hr we rode as many 100 mile time trials as possible. The Severn RC had a team entered (a first); myself, Ian (DNS) Graham Smith and Ian Finch. We each had a car supporting us, each car with at least two drivers and maybe a third person as well. These people were friends from the Bristol DA and mostly 12 hour and Audax men and women.*

*Ian and Bruce Pilsworth were feeding me, and the aim being a bottle and sponge every half hour with eats on demand. The food and drink was fairly simple. All drinks contained Maxi-Jul. During Saturday this was mixed with plain water with occasional fruit juice; overnight with tea, coffee and complan. On Sunday I complained about all these thick drinks and was given lucozade and fizzy orange, still with Maxi-Jul. Back to tea on the finishing circuit but fortified with glucose.*

*The food eaten was one piece of malt loaf, half an egg sandwich, half an apple, a small bag of rice pudding and three Nesfit energy bars. This would all fit in one hand. The bike was an Argos 753 conventional machine with tri-bars, and Michelin Hi Lite tyres Lighting was two 6V Halogen headlights and one rear light, all powered by a sealed lead-acid battery.*

*Of the ride itself, I can only remember parts. The intention was to keep evens for the first hundred (4.56.35 actual) and 230 miles for the first 12 hours (225.6 actual) to avoid tiring myself too early. Ian and Bruce were giving me time checks through the night.*

*I had seen Ian F. and Graham only once each as I went into the dark. The night passed with no major hitches, stopping to change batteries at 1.30 am and once or twice to relieve a mild stomach upset. I was glad when daylight came and I could see people again. I saw Graham still going strong at around 5 am and Ian F. on the way back from Newport for the last time. Ian had not had a comfortable night but it was great to feel we still had a team going.*

*I left Shawbirch with a tailwind back to Hodnet and had a slow spell that I could do nothing about when I was cut from the B-road leg from Shawbury corner. I saw Ian F.'s feeding team at Battlefield who shouted at me and I began to move again. On the way to the circuit, I re-caught everyone who had passed me in my slow spell. Jim Turner had told me I was lying fourth overall, and I wondered where everyone else had gone. Ian and Bruce told me "evens to the circuit and eighteens around it and the records your's". I managed evens to the circuit, and the first time round it I was careful to 'sus out' the bends, junctions etc. I felt elated to reach the circuit and know that whatever happened I had finished. All around the circuit friends were shouting me on.*

*I headed for Timekeeper One for the fourth time thinking 'Good, I can stop here' … but no such luck, on to Timekeeper Two, hoping to cover enough distance in 90 seconds to take me to the record. Finishing at the front door of the Black Dog at Waverton, glad that it was all over, I climbed into the back of the car and ached.*

*Back at the Headquarters I spoke to numerous people out of the car window – thanks to you all for your misplaced congratulations – and managed to walk to the result board after Jim Turner had announced the prize winners.*

*At the time it was thought that I had beaten Anne Mann's record of 438.16 miles by 0.4 of a mile, but on checking, my mileage came down to 437.62, so nearly, but not quite.*

*Graham and Ian finished with 447 and 361 miles respectively, enough for the team prize, and the best result from a club in our area for a long time. So if we didn't make all our targets, it was nice to go home with that."*

From an article in The Fellowship Journal – by Bridget Boon

# 1993

### What An Exciting Time for Ladies Time Trialling

This passage by Ian Dow, Editor of the Fellowship Journal in 1993, sets the scene.

**"This year will almost certainly be remembered for the rides done by ladies – Christine Roberts 461 miles and Bridget Boon's two rides of 446 and 457 taking the women into a totally different league from anything we have seen before."**

Male pride was beaten to pulp as Christine's ride earned her fifth place in the Championship and Bridget's 446 ninth – both riders handsomely beating Anne Mann's old competition record of 438 miles.

The Mersey did not actually get a particularly good day; overall it was about average, a breezy Saturday afternoon, good warm night, but then quite a strong head-cross wind back up to the circuit and finally heavy showers.

Christine is of course a very fast rider; she was 100 mile Champion in 1987 (4-13) and '90 (4-25) and had recently done 253 miles for a 12 hour. But even so her mileage of 461.45 was way beyond expectations, showing what can be achieved through thorough preparation, efficient teamwork, and above all, attitude of mind.

Christine's split mileage was 240/221, a very even ride – exceptional for the first attempt, while Bridget's was 236/211 showing that her improvement over last year 225/212 was gained entirely in the first half. She had a bad time in the third quarter but recovered and was travelling faster than Christine on the circuit.

<hr>

Within days of the Mersey, Bridget was out on her bike again packing in the miles as if the '24' had been nothing but a dream. Having missed the record by half a mile last year and being thwarted by Christine reaching the record point before her this time, she then made one of the greatest acts of defiance in 24 hour history and entered the North Road. It was obvious that she had set her heart passionately on owning that Competition record, and would let nothing get in her way.

Critics were quick to write off her chances of beating Christine's mileage but they underestimated the determination of this remarkable woman. Bridget had evidently made a perfect recovery in the five intervening weeks, and the elements for once sided with her, and gave the North Road a good day. For the first time in her life she beat evens for 12 hours, covering 243 miles in the first half, but with most of the eight hour night, falling in the second half and a nasty bout of sickness towards the end, the record slipped away and she finished four miles short. The sickness incidentally was probably caused by over-concentrated liquid feed (Maxim) which is something we all need to be careful to avoid.

Nonetheless, **Bridget had won the North Road 24 by 40 miles** (just imagine the reaction from the old guard) and completed her third top quality 24 in two seasons. **"Her two rides this year must rank alongside Eric Matthews' double of 486 in the Mersey and 489 in the NR/National of 1968."**

This next passage is Christine Roberts' own story of her record breaking ride also taken from the Fellowship Journal 1993.

*"I first started thinking about riding a '24' after watching Phil Guy in the 1991 Mersey/National. It was a beautiful weekend, but what struck me most was that in between going out to watch Phil start, going home for some tea, back out to give a final cheer before the night, going home to bed, having a lie in, and eventually going out to the finishing circuit, people were continually riding! It seemed the ultimate test, and once the seed was sown, it was nurtured by a couple of half decent 12's, the most satisfying thing being that my left knee, badly damaged in an accident in '87, stood up to the pressure really well.*

*The 24 being the goal for '93, our season took on a slightly different pattern from other years, concentrating on local events, instead of B.A.R. chasing up and down the country. I'm afraid I'm not at all technical when it comes to training! I just like riding my bike; in fact, as I work full time, my usual routine is about a 20 minute ride into work on my 'work' bike, often with panniers, and then if I can manage it a three hour plus ride home, again usually with panniers. It doesn't bother me if the bike is heavy because I think it's more the time and effort spent on the bike rather than speed that counts, and anyway it feels really good, on a weekend, riding my racing bike.*

*That said, I think its important to listen to your body and a long ride was often followed by a day just going back to work. I did about 8,200 miles up to the event, not a great deal, but I was happy and relaxed with the way things were going. The only really long ride I had was five weeks before the event when I rode up to Carlisle on the Friday, rested the Saturday, and rode home again on the Sunday, 300 miles in total, averaging over 18's because luckily the wind was favourable in both directions.*

*I only rode two 100's before the '24', the first being the Anfield on May bank holiday, a must for checking that things are progressing well, and the second, the Manchester Wheelers 100 on 17th July, perhaps a bit close to 'the' day, but a useful experiment with the bottles!*

*Alan and I were very fortunate in having the assistance and advice of Andy Wilkinson, especially on feeding, so for the Manchester '100' I was trying a purely liquid feed, alternating between Maxim and Maxim and Isostar mixed. Andy had arranged a handlebar bottle cage to try, the idea being to minimise shoulder and arm movement, further enhanced by the use of a straw. However, if you seal around the straw to prevent splashing it causes a vacuum when you suck, and totally defeats the object, in fact so much so that I was quite relieved when I dropped a bottle, so I could concentrate on racing, rather than gasping for breath trying to suck a miniscule amount of liquid! Eventually I reverted to a normal bottle, still on the handlebars, but I hadn't taken on board the required amount of feed. I think the fact that it poured down for the last hour and a half saved my performance. Soon afterwards we were told that you need a tiny hole in the top of the bottle to break the vacuum and sure enough it worked a treat, so the straws were back in favour!*

*As 24th July approached, we became even more avid weather watchers than normal, and personally my goals were reducing to just getting round. However, after reading Alan Ray's "End to End" book, it became apparent that favourable weather conditions were the exception rather than the norm for record breakers, so although the Saturday was windy, I considered it a bonus being bright and dry.*

*However, I soon changed my mind after the first few pedal revs, struggling so much up the hill to Borras, that I was sick! I wondered who would make the first witty comment in the car and later was told it was Alan's 'it's early days yet' which I understood became quite an annoying catch phrase!*

*Paul Bland caught me for three minutes about a mile before Broxton, but once over that shock, the race settled into a steady routine. I really enjoyed the first 100 miles, probably because it was around Crewe, and there were lots of friends out giving me a shout. However, I wasn't so keen on the hourly ham butties handed up to provide protein and whenever I was allowed I preferred a banana. Even I realised though that too many bananas might result in a stomach upset, so towards the end, when given the privilege of choice, I agreed to a "butty, bloody butty!"*

One of the things that surprised me most was how quickly it went dark, and I was quite disappointed to have to have lights on not much after 9 pm. I also made the mistake of putting on too much extra clothing and had to make an unnecessary stop to take something off. My contact lenses had also been misplaced, and then to top it all, the handlebar bottle cage snapped off just after Battlefield. This I considered a major blow, because I'm an over cautious bike handler at the best of times, and the thought of fumbling around all night searching for the normal bottle position did nothing for me at all! However, I was really impressed with the amount of light the two handlebar mounted Cat-eye halogen lamps threw out sideways and soon realised it wouldn't be such a problem. That said, my right arm and shoulder ached quite a bit towards the end of the race, which vindicated Andy favouring a handlebar bottle cage.

One other upset occurred just after it started raining about 10pm. I was pulled into the lay by about four miles from Prees, and being dazzled by magnified raindrops on my glasses, I hit a drain and felt my back wheel slide. I managed to stay upright, but I was badly shaken and quite upset as I fumbled to put my found lenses in. If I'd had to stick with my specs I might have called it a day then, but the lenses were a god-send and I soon became more relaxed. Ironically, not long afterwards it stopped raining and the night ride almost became a pleasure, especially dropping back down to Newport for Pickmere with the stars twinkling through broken cloud.

Coming back down to earth with a bump though, Bridget passed me on a downhill stretch heading for Ternhill. I'd caught her for ten minutes at about 90 miles and here we were back together again at 200! I marvelled at her confidence – how did she know she wouldn't hit anything and lose control? I realised I'd been lost in my own little world, but here was a reminder that this was a race! I retook her on the climb to Tern Hill, concentrated hard on the drag to Hodnet and managed to pull away. Alan and I had been aware of the dangers of being involved in a tussle, it being of prime importance to ride your own race, but fortunately that was the only occasion in the whole 24 hours.

From then onwards there were no other real problems other than the gradual aches and pains the odd dropped bottle or banana, and the far too frequent heavy showers. I had dreaded the leg to High Ercall and it was just as bad as I expected, the chipped road surface being the worst I'd ever experienced. I made a mental note never to ride a '25' round there, and was so relieved to return to the main road at Shawbury. I suppose that was the worst leg and in fact the '50' split in that area proved it but what surprised me most was that even though I felt so rough I was still catching people.

The run to the finishing circuit was supposed to have a tail wind and for once the weathermen were right and it was S.W. However, the closer I got to Prees, the more I began to realise the record was on and an average speed of 13 mph was going to do it. I toyed with the idea of taking off my leggings and long sleeved jersey, but the showers soon cooled that.

Onto the circuit and I checked with Alan at which timekeeper I should finish to reach the record. "Yes, but you're not stopping there!" came the answer. Even I'd realised I'd far too much time left to run, but even so, I actually managed to raise a smile when I passed Donna and Nigel Stoddard's sign 'Old Competition Record' and everyone gave a cheer at the "Black Dog".

I wish I'd been able to raise my game on the circuit, especially as so many people were out giving their support, but I must admit to just wanting to get on with it and finish. I'd managed to time it so I had the climb from Aldford to Churton in the last few minutes, but this time I still had 1.5 minutes in hand. There was quite a crowd gathered at the White Horse and I felt a little ungrateful continuing round the corner to a huge cheer, but I was going to make the most of the descent into the lanes, which was just as well really, because with Andy leaning bodily out of the car window beckoning me to follow, there was no way that they were going to stop.

And then the relief. The end. The success. The pride. The pain. The tears, and everyone wanting to help. Alan, Andy, David, Donna and Nigel rallied round as they had for the whole 24 hours, and pampered me. It was wonderful but I also felt a little sad when Alan pointed out that my actual finishing spot was exactly where Phil Guy had had to call it a day after 22.5 hours in 1991.

*For Phil and me, I hope there will be other '24's' but for different reasons we'll remember the first. One things for sure though, for a solo performance, it takes a hell of a lot of teamwork to complete the event. Just one person's name goes into the record books, but without the support of the previously mentioned five, it wouldn't have been possible.*

**Thanks for sharing a day in the life."**

Christine had at last triumphed over the odds that can beset a champion. Although she doesn't dwell on the past, I feel that knowing the facts can help one make fairer and more rational judgements of performance with this information at hand.

Towards the end of 1987's season Christine, after winning the 100 mile championship earlier with 4 hrs 13 mins 11 secs, was struck by a car when riding a time trial. This incident saw Christine hospitalised for a long time and unable to ride. After operations and much treatment and a couple of years without racing, she regained enough confidence to start training and racing. She came back in 1990 to win the 100 mile championship again with 4 hrs 25 mins 26 secs, but Christine admitted she was never very comfortable on fast main road courses with heavy traffic, especially in wet conditions, or poor visibility. Memories of her accident kept flashing before her eyes and coming back to haunt her, so this massive win and Competition Record ride in 1993 was her reward for missed opportunities due to injury. Incidentally, she came back in 1994 to take the 100 mile championship again with 4 hrs 19 mins 4 secs.

I was out helping Lynne that weekend in 1993 on the first of her many 24 hr rides. Ian Dow reported breezy conditions in his article, but my recollection of Saturday afternoon and evening's weather was of stifling heat coupled with a brick wall of a wind. I watched the battle evolve between Christine and Bridget and my memories were of Christine 'turning over' a huge gear from very early on as if trying to stamp her authority on the ride.

Phil Barlow who that day won the men's championship, from Glenn Longland and Paul Bland, with 491.136 miles said when questioned by 'Cycling Weekly' that as far as he was concerned the wind was 'horrendous' and not conducive to breaking the men's 507 mile record.

In Frank Mumford's 1993 Mersey report he noted that Christine had caught Bridget (off 10 mins earlier) by 96 miles and was 17 mins faster at the 98.6 mile point, 4 hrs 31 mins 55 secs to Bridget's 4 hrs 48 mins 50 secs. The two were only minutes apart on the road at the 250 mile point. Christine's 12hrs gained her 241 miles to Bridget's 236.8 miles. Christine was one of only 6 riders to beat 'evens' at 12 hours. Frank concluded his ladies report with: *"Dawn broke and brought a blustery west wind, gnawing at the 'survivors reserves', but the beckoning haven of the finishing circuit provided the incentive for them to flog-away at the pedals. Earlier detouring of the faster riders gave Bridget the honour of reaching the finishing circuit first, to sustained applause from the waiting crowd. With all body sensors in the 'red zone' she accomplished 3 laps of the 15 mile circuit in 52, 52 and 53 minutes in the effort to beat Anne Mann's record, succeeding by 8.25 miles. But it's a tough sport; Christine was to record 3 laps of the 15 mile circuit of 51, 51 and 50 minutes, bettering the record by 23.35 miles!"*

Christine's final comment "that was a week and a half's training in one day! I'm not a big mile-eater as I work full-time. I'm still stiff all over right now, and I hope I recover soon because I'm entered for the National 100 mile at Bristol next Sunday. My whole year has been based on this 24 hr race."

To conclude this historical weekend's ride by the ladies, I will start with **Lynne Taylor who came 3rd in the Merseyside Ladies CA promotion with 394.06 miles.** This solid ride was to become the first of many and I felt that, probably for the next few years, I would be helping Lynne in this event, rather than riding it myself. The urge for me to compete in this enduring annual time trial was getting less and less each year, but I still love the atmosphere just as much as ever. Lynne came 30th out of 59 solo riders, with another 25 failing to finish.

**Mrs Sue Gray,** Derby Mercury RC was **4th lady** with **383.72 miles,** in this her debut at 24 hr riding. **Celia Prescott** also completed this event with **377.87 miles. Mrs J.M.Wilson,** Bath CC was **6th lady** with **366.04 miles.** So far, this is the most ladies ever to finish in a 24 hr race. With **Miss Helen Sandelands,** Mersey RC getting good local support to produce **331.58 miles. Miss Jane Ramsdale,** Seacroft Wheelers, partnered Mark Brooking to a new **mixed tandem trike record with 401.22 miles,** which still stands to this day.

One footnote that reiterates what I have said about the importance of carrying on round the finishing circuit until told to stop by the timekeeper was proved in this Mersey event.

Keith Silvester, Mid Shropshire Wheelers, rode very strongly throughout, as did Paul Bland, Kiveton Park CC. Paul just pipped Keith by 0.6 of a mile. Keith had fought back from about a six mile deficit on the circuit, lapping well above 'evens', attempting so he thought to take the bronze medal from Christine. Unaware of Paul Blands position, Keith stopped at a timekeeper with 1.5 minutes left to run, and lost the bronze medal. I doubt if he will do that again!

=⊳·◇·⊲=

**One month later,** on the August bank holiday, **Bridget Boon won the North Road CC 24 hr outright,** beating the next rider, Peter Bishop, by nearly 40 miles with **457.14 miles.** Bridget was trying to avenge her defeat of just one month earlier and was hoping to claim a new record. Her 12 hr mileage of 243 miles in the event was bettered only by Robert Fry of the Willesden CC, by 3 miles. He was the rider in 1992's Mersey who battled it out in the early stages with leading riders, catching and dropping some of them, including Bridget and then he 'packed' at about 118 miles.

In this, the North Road event however, he still led Bridget until about the 14hr point, where she reeled him in. Bridget continued to pile the pressure on and spent many hours on her own at the head of the field. The weather was near perfect and it was thought she could just break the record but with no competition it was going to be a tall order. She had to cover 78 miles in the last four and a quarter hours to get the record and while she went tantalisingly close, she just failed by 4 miles.

For some unknown reason, Robert Fry climbed off on the finishing circuit covering just 140 miles in his last 12 hours. Peter Bishop, Heron CC, was 2nd with 417.72 miles and John Baines was 3rd with 416.84 miles. **Jean Burrow** rode strongly to finish with **375.81 miles. Bridget** hadn't broken the record but she will go down in history as the **first and only woman to win an open 24 hr time trial (as at 2008).**

Roger Sewell, the event secretary, quipped "talk about a blow for women's lib, a lot of men thought it was bad enough allowing women members in the North Road – and now we have a woman winning the open '24'". (It took until 1978 before the elders of the North Road CC were outvoted to allow women to join the club and become full members)

It's ironic that after a 10 year wait for an outstanding ride to materialise, three occur within the space of a month. Firstly, Christine's 461.45 miles, then Bridget's 2nd place ride of 446.88 miles, followed by Bridget's own history making 457.14 miles ride in the North Road cc 24 hrs, beating all of the men, not by just a few miles, but by nearly 40 miles.

# 1994

The year started off very sparsely for the women, the **'Brighton Mitre'** special centenary event in June organised by Mike Hayler, had Bridget Boon and Marc Cunnington as the two top favourites entered. Everybody felt that this may be Bridget's best chance at the record if the conditions were right.

Ian Dow who was out at the event checking, marshalling and generally helping, reported that it was a perfect summers day. Bridget at that time was the most talked about rider in 24 hr circles. There was a lot of pressure on her to break the record. Bridget came through the checkpoint at 100 miles in 4 hrs 45 mins 49 secs. She had already lost 8 mins to Marc Cunnington, but she was still fairly cheerful. She had been training very hard for this event, conditions were still good, 20 degrees C, no more than a cool breeze from the west, could she do it? Ideally she needed to be inside 4 hrs 30 for the first 100 but there was plenty of time to pick up speed. Bridget knew that Christine Roberts was riding the Mersey 24 in a months time and that Christine had made plans to attack her own competition record and try and top 480. So, no pressure there then !

At the 12 hr check, Marc and Bridget were virtually dead level both doing approximately 240 miles. The next 6 hours would be crucial for Bridget, she needed to keep close to evens in that time and would be looking for no less that 350 miles at 18 hours. At 2.45 am Bridget came through ahead of Marc, onto a 39 mile circuit. After a long wait Marc came through at 5.06 pm but sadly Bridget had packed. The last recorded distance and time for her was 305 miles in 16 hrs 29 mins. Ideally she needed 325 at that point and she knew she was beaten. Marc Cunnington went on to win with 452.704 miles. *(My thanks to Ian Dow for this report)*

The only other lady in the event was a regular evergreen, **Ms Sian Charlton** finishing with a mileage of **282.993 on a trike.**

⋙·◇·⋘

One month later in the **Mersey Road CC 24 hr,** the much awaited tussle in the Mersey where Christine was hoping to better her own 461 miles record, never quite materialised, but here is a quick resume of the ride using some material from Frank Mumford's description.

*"Saturday afternoon was oppressively hot, scary thunder and lightning enlivened a warm but oxygen filled night, with monsoon rain falling pre-dawn. Heavy showers fell throughout the next day and a strong south/south west wind blew the riders towards the finishing circuit.*

*Although **Christine** didn't break any records, she did come **2nd overall** with a fine mileage of **442.67,** beaten only by Andy Wilkinson with 496 miles and nobody minds being beaten by 'Wilko' do they? It's possible that Christine's efforts the previous weekend in winning the National 100 mile championship again had affected her.*

***Lynne Taylor,*** *Walsall Roads CC proved to be another 'rising star' with **418.20 miles** coming overall 3rd.*

**This was a first for ladies in the history of the Mersey RC 24 hr. Women had taken 2nd and 3rd place ahead of the men.**

After a very lean spell for 24 hr events and ladies in particular, we are now seeing an upsurge, especially in the Mersey RC events which are very 'user-friendly' with their approach to feeding and care. After all it was in this event some nearly 30 years ago that women were first treated to this 24 hr ritual that their male counterparts had been enjoying and enduring since 1885. **Anne Learmonth** took **7th** place with a very good first time ride of **402.13 miles.**

Some dour tussles arose as the riders penetrated deepest Shropshire. Christine caught Lynne at 130 miles but had only drawn away a minute by 153 miles. Anne Learmonth had a battle-royal with fellow audax rider, Jim Hopper, on his trike. She caught Jim just after 40 miles but there was only a minute or two in it when the two riders entered the finishing circuit after another 320 miles."

As mentioned, the night enlivened the riders, with loud thunder raising their tempo. Vivid lightning illuminating the roads and refreshing rain pelting them around dawn. I remember following Lynne on a couple of occasions at a distance, just to make sure she was okay as I knew she wasn't too good with thunder and lightning. She didn't mind looking out of her bedroom window at it and we've had some pretty spectacular storms at home, living at the top of the hill. In the spring of 1969 a bolt of lightning took out a telegraph pole and electrical installations opposite our house. I too like looking out at thunderstorms, but I also enjoy riding through them. I know it can obviously be dangerous but there is such an increase in oxygen at the time, coupled with a feeling of being very close to nature, one has to live a little dangerously every now and then! Torrential summer rain I also find very invigorating to ride in.

Lynne said at a later date "to overcome racing through these conditions, either in 100's, 12 hrs or 24 hrs or End to Ends, one needs to experience them in training. Lynne reminded me that she asked if she could stop at the van while the storm was so close and I said "yes, I'll stop just up the road". She carried on to say that every time she got within sight of the van I moved off and eventually she rode out of the storm.

This was to be the last action for the ladies this year, as the North Road event was an all male entry.

**Jim Turner, The Mersey RC 24 hr Organiser and Secretary** for the event was renowned for recruiting riders, with offers of 'the best day out in your life' or 'eat all you can in 24 hrs for £5.00'. By early spring he had cajoled many new riders into giving 'all day' riding a try.

It was an **RTTC Championship** event and as such had attracted 86 riders, the 4th largest field ever. Top names had entered including Andy Wilkinson, Phil Barlow, Phil Leigh, Marc Cunnington, Karl Austin and Dave Brabbin. For the ladies, Christine Roberts was out to push her own Competition Record up higher still, given better conditions. Bridget Boon was hoping to push her p.b. (personal best) even further. Lynne Taylor who had improved from 394 to 418 miles, felt that the confidence she had gained from the last two years and the friendship, help and advice from Christine and Alan Roberts, could lift her over the 440 mile mark.

There were 35 entrants from the Audax UK ranks, some of them in training for the forthcoming Paris-Brest-Paris, some three weeks away.

The Saturday turned out to be very sultry and conditions were only relieved by the cool evening. Bridget Boon failed to start, so making it a two-way battle for the ladies.

At the 25 mile point Lynne had a 2 minute lead on Christine, but by the 100 mile check Christine had drawn ahead of Lynne by 5 minutes. This looked to be turning into an interesting tussle, but we were disappointed as Christine climbed off at Prees, leaving Lynne to prove herself against the men. In fairness, Christine, said she'd been feeling off-colour since her 4 hr 28 minute Anfield 100.

At the 108 mile point, Paul Bland caught Lynne but she held him to within minutes until the 200 mile check. On the night 'detours' to Shawbirch, an idiot motorist was reported to be allowing his passenger to slap the riders as the van went past and overtook. Its registration number was taken and reported to the local police but they showed no interest. Lynne was one of the riders affected by this, as was another Walsall RCC rider, Hugh Canning.

Lynne lost some more time on this dark stretch when her front lamp disintegrated, luckily, a gallant male competitor helped her to find the bits and re-build it. Some of the riders at the 12 hr check had beaten evens, Wilko 269 miles, Bland 248 miles, Leigh 246, Austin and Lynne both doing 229 miles. Conditions now were much more placid and bearable than the thunderstorms of the previous year.

Daylight brought the heat back with only the trees in the lanes giving any shade or comfort to the riders, but they did have a breeze blow them helpfully to the finishing circuit at dinnertime.

Wilko was predictably the fastest on the 14.9 mile circuit, covering 4 laps successfully in 43mins, 43mins, 47 mins and 45 mins, to finish with a superb 501.39 miles on his lightweight slick-tyred mountain bike fitted with tri-bars. Andy had suffered back pains in previous events and felt that comfort was ultimately more important than pure speed over a long distance, such as his 500 plus miles. Actually when you look at him tucked into his tribars, his position is very similar to that of a road bike.

While helping Lynne, I would see Andy sit up every hour and lean back and stretch himself, on other occasions he would stand on his pedals and freewheel but lean right forward over his bars and arc his back inwardly. Another trick to ward off stiffness and pain, was to do arm and shoulder exercises while on the move. Lynne rode very strongly throughout, she knew the course very well and now knew that she was capable of pushing herself for 24 hrs without 'blowing up'. On the finishing circuit Lynne completed 4 laps of 51, 52, 50 and a grandstand finish of 48 minutes.

Paul Bland, Kiveton Park CC came 2nd with 475.08 miles and Phillip Leigh, Kent Valley RC 3rd with 461.58 miles. **Lynne was 7th with 441.4 miles, and became only the third woman ever to beat 440 miles.** One other lady finished that day, **Sylvia Powell,** stoking the **mixed tandem** to a fine **347.76** miles with husband, Norman. He was a top BBAR man of the 1960's and 70's, when riding for the Oldbury and District CC. They broke various VTTA age records that day.

There had been in all 28 retirements, one being Lynne's friend and workmate, Rob Eperjesi, who pulled out at about 80 miles, just going into the evening. I think his main problem was trying to pace himself to an easier 'push' than normal.

Rob was more used to sub one hour, two hour and 4 hour rides, for 25, 50 and 100 miles. I think the night would have been a good test for him.

In the **North Road CC 24 hr** a month later, **Mrs Mary Horsfield** was the only lady to finish with **301.52 miles** again crewing the tandem with her husband, Peter. No other ladies finished.

Later that year Lynne wrote an article for the 24hr Fellowship Journal entitled: **'I COULD NEVER RIDE ONE'.** In it she reveals the story behind her 441 mile ride in the Mersey RC event. I have taken a few passages and lines from that article.

*" 'I could never ride one', were my thoughts and words whenever I heard my dad John, talking to his friends about RRA records, End to Ends and the Mersey 24 hr. His friends being Pat Kenny, Pete Swinden, Les Lowe and the late John Withers.*

*In my younger days I used to help in the Oldbury 12 hour and later the 24 hour. At the feeding stations on the Oldbury 12 hr I have good memories of boxes of Mars bars, Marathon bars, bread pudding, tins of rice pudding, raisins and sugar cubes. My brother Mike and I used to love it at the end because we would share the left over Mars bars. These days you wouldn't have much to look forward to at the end 'food wise' because I, like many others, now use the energy drinks, Maxim and Isostar.*

*This big question happened a few years ago when I was waiting to start the Anfield 100. Jim Turner saw me and asked me if I was thinking of riding the Mersey 24 hr. I replied 'you've got to be joking, I don't think I could do it!' My dad said that I ought to give it some thought and have a go; at this point I'd only ridden a couple of 12 hr races".*

Lynne then mentions booking a holiday that coincided with that particular Mersey 24hr weekend and thinking 'yes, I've got out of that one', but in 1993 curiosity got the better of her plus the fact that I'd mentioned (only jokingly of course) that I'd written into her contract of employment at the bike shop, that she must ride a 24 hr every year! Another deciding factor was at the RTTC Championship night in January, Alan Roberts mentioned to Lynne that Christine was riding the 24 hr and Lynne said she was thinking about it but wasn't sure. At that point Alan shouts to Christine for all to hear "Lynne is riding the 24 hr too". That was it, she had no choice but to ride.

After riding her first 24 hr in 1993 covering 394 miles, Lynne found everyone so friendly and supportive, she then had the 'bug' to ride another one. After training hard for 1994's event doing winter rides with Christine, Lynne came to her 2nd 24 hr with lots more confidence, and finished with 418 miles. Lynne said "I was thrilled to bits coming 3rd, standing next to Christine who was 2nd and Andy who had won. This was a great day"

In 1995 Lynne said that although she felt confident at the start of the 24 hr she still felt very nervous. I helped her in that event with Pete Swinden who has a lot of experience at distance riding. Apart from getting 'hot foot' and then the disappointment of Christine 'packing' and also her friend Rob, at roughly the same point, she had a trouble free afternoon and early evening. She had a chat with Hugh Canning, another Walsall Roads CC rider, who was going well as darkness fell. Shortly after this Lynne was punched by someone leaning out of a van, and the same thing happened to Hugh on the same stretch of road. This upset Lynne, but after vocal support from Pete and Roger Winwood and Pete's wife Lisa, Lynne got on with her ride. The rest of the night went smoothly and after a 10 minute sleep stop at 6 am, Lynne was pleased to see her mum Liz, who had taken over from Pete Swinden.

Lynne recalled *"I carried on fine, not tired at all. I was pleased to see Rob and his dad Louis had come back out to see the event. I thought I was on for about 420 miles or at the most 425. I saw Christine on the finishing circuit cheering me on so I tried my hardest. I needed 425 miles for my club gold standard and at the end I could not believe I had done 441 – it still hasn't sunk in properly. I got my gold standard, and broke the club record".*

Lynne went on to thank everyone involved with the event and then paid tribute to Albert Southall, her masseur and coach, who passed away the day after the 24 hr race.

## 1996

**The North Road CC 24** Hr was a Championship Year but it still only attracted one woman rider, **Kathryn Smith,** in her first 24 hr race. She clocked up **320.94 miles** and beat 5 men in the process. The race, run in late June attracted just 45 entries. The event was won by Malcolm Whitehead with 465.75 miles with Marc Cunnington and Dave Brabbin 2nd and 3rd. Thirty riders finished.

<hr>

A month later in late July, **the Mersey RC event** was won by Dave Brabbin -Wigan Wheelers with 462.41. Frank Mumford takes up the story "The weather was fairly kind, a warm start was followed by a moonlit night, a showery dawn and a mild day with variable breeze.

At the 25 mile point, Lynne came through with l hr 8 mins on a par with Brabbin, Millington and Cunnington. With the absence of Sheila Simpson and Bridget Boon, who were 'audaxing' and Christine Roberts who was preparing for the End to End, Lynne was the only female contestant left after Sylvia Powell retired early in the evening.

At the 95.7 mile time check, Lynne was lying 5th with 4 hrs 32 mins and riding strongly. Evening time saw a few early retirements which left Lynne lying in 4th place at the 12 hr check, with 228 miles. Adrian Pudsey was 3rd with 239, Brabbin 239 and Karl Austin in the lead with 242 miles.

By dawn, the battle between Dave Brabbin and Karl Austin for the lead was over, with Brabbin pulling away after 301 miles. Lynne suffered sickness during the night but rallied round after dawn with a strong ride to the finishing circuit. Once there **Lynne** rocketed around the 14.9 mile circuit with the fastest lap of the day 46 minutes. She finished with **438.97 miles** just 2 miles under her best performance the previous year."

**Christine Roberts** who already held the RTTC ladies competition record for 24 hrs with 461.45 miles, set off on her quest from Lands End to try and break the coveted End to End record held by Pauline Strong and to try and increase the RRA 24 hrs record on the way. The 24 hr record she was trying to beat belonged to Eileen Sheridan and was 446.25 miles.

The ride started well and with a good wind it looked as though there was a possibility of breaking the records. By the time she had climbed Shap the wind had become almost gale force and **Christine broke the 24 hr record with 467.30 miles** but things weren't running smoothly and Christine was unhappy when descending. After having many stops for 'pep' talks with her helpers, Christine finally climbed off just before Edinburgh, obviously very disappointed, but at least she had broken another 24hr record. **An RRA record.**

## 1997

**The Mersey RC 24 hr** was a championship event this year and was also the only event to have women riding. **Lynne's 418.08 miles** ride was just a fraction of a mile shorter than her second ride in 1994. Frank Mumford went on to describe Lynne as being 'dainty' and having been the fastest lady for the last three years. But the ride of the day was undoubtably Wilko's 525 miles which I have chronicled elsewhere in this book.

The weather during the event was unkind with rain early and late, strong contrary winds, south westerly then veering north, with a chilly night. Lynne reached the 95.7 mile check in 4 hrs 45 mins and was a minute up on a jaded Christine Roberts who retired at 173 miles. **Yvonne Unsworth** at 54 years of age (looking 35) took the **3rd** best on standard in the VTTA (Veteran Time Trial Association) awards. Despite being ill during the night with a digestion problem, **341.75 was her final mileage.** Yvonne went on at a later date to help Lynne on her 2002 End to End and 1000 mile record, where 15 mins sleep is a bonus for helpers or riders alike. So a 24 hr race was good experience for Yvonne.

Lynne was 12th overall and unchallenged for the ladies prize. She was below her best of 441 miles in 1995 due to work commitments and demands of 6 days a week in the bike shop, but at the awards ceremony she had shed all signs of fatigue and brought a sense of glamour to the occasion.

To have been on the finishing circuit at the same time as 'Wilko' who was breaking competition record was a wonderful feeling, with clusters of club folk all waiting in anticipation to see him through. The 'buzz' and the cheers as he went through, lapping the twisting and difficult rural circuit at 22 mph. All this effort at the end of 24 hours of non stop racing which saw him beat all of the field bar Brian Walker, by a minimum of 50 miles and two thirds of them by over 100 miles.

**What a man, What a weekend!**

Finishing the season on a sad note, **Sunday 31st August 1997** saw me up at 3.30 am to load the bikes and kit into the van for Lynne to ride the Merseyside Association open 12 hour starting at Prees.

I had the radio on quietly in the kitchen hoping to catch a weather forecast although I was pretty sure it was going to be wet anyway. I couldn't understand why the radio was playing such melancholy music and then heard the newsreader say that Diana, Princess of Wales, had died in a car crash in Paris. I had a job to believe it but I switched the radio off so that Lynne didn't hear it. We got to the start and with it being wet, the riders were only getting to the timekeeper a minute or two before their start time, and so didn't get much time to chat. I thought if I could keep the sad news away from Lynne she might do a decent ride. She started at 6.16am and throughout the day the radio played really sad music, broken only by regular reports about Diana's death. The weather fitted the occasion, it rained for most of the day and it was very grey. Lynne said she thought that the little clusters of people out helping were very quiet and subdued but then some people are like that.

Paul Costain won the event with 261.8 miles, Christine Roberts was 7th with 244.14, Lynne was 9th with 241.7 miles, Derek Everton , Cannock CRC 212 miles and Frances Chaloner rode 193 miles..

Luckily Lynne didn't realise what had happened until she finished and was having a cup of tea in the 'Raven' and saw the news on the television. I am not a Royalist, I'm neither for or against, but felt that Diana was 'normal', and I found the events of the following days and weeks were quite touching and impossible to ignore. This was definitely one of those occasions when I knew exactly what I was doing on that particular day.

# 1998

The first event in this year was **The North Road CC 24 hr,** held in late June and incorporating the **RTTC Championship.** It was also an historical event in as much as it marked the 100th anniversary of the first unpaced scratch road ride.

It attracted 60 solo riders including 3 ladies (all veterans) and 4 tandems. The ladies being **Jeanette de Giorgio** of the Shaftesbury CC with the highest mileage of **373.34** miles, **Gail Summerlin** Leicester RC **327.68** and third **Janet Lowe** with **313.40** miles, riding for the San Fairy Ann CC. The women had the distinction of all finishing, unlike twenty of the male solo riders. The weather in the first part of the event was distinctly cool with a fresh breeze. Late afternoon saw gale force winds and cold torrential rain, with many riders grovelling out to an easterly turning point.

The main interest was the battle of the giants, Ian Butcher at 12 hrs had amassed 263 miles to Brian Walkers 261 with Paul Holdsworth 260 miles. It was a very cold night, still with an easterly wind. For most of the riders it was just a matter of survival, especially for the ladies, who I'm pretty sure were all first time riders on a bike in a 24 hour event.

━━━⟫•◈•⟪━━━

**The Mersey RC 24 Hour** a month later in July fared no better, with 40 solos entered including 3 ladies, but only a total of 24 finished on a much better day. The difference being only two out of the three ladies finished. At the 57 mile check Lynne had covered it in 2 hrs 42 mins. Yvonne Unsworth, Southport RC, 3 hrs 06 mins and Frances Chaloner, Stafford RC 3 hrs 26 mins.

At the 100 mile point Lynne went through in 4 hrs 51 mins, but Yvonne and Frances were cut from the main course and detoured so missing a time check. At the 12 hour point, Yvonne was feeling ill and packed. Frances did 175.73 and Lynne 219.89 miles.

Frances, also a friend of Lynne's, reached the finishing circuit at 12.30 am, a gallant effort, she was determined to finish. She had chatted to Lynne regularly about riding long distances and Lynne had said to her "You must ride the Mersey 24 hr, I'm sure you can do it, you will get very well looked after by the organisers, helpers and marshals".

**Frances did finish with 330.23 miles.** She was elated and pleased to have done it. (She still talks about it some 8 or 9 years later and always tries to get out to see Lynne in the last few hours of the event).

Out of the 25 finishers, **Lynne** had the fastest lap time of 49 minutes (twice) riding as if supercharged, eventually to finish **4th** with **427.1 miles.** Edwin Hargraves, an old adversary of mine from tandem triking days, won the event. Everyone was so pleased for him, such a nice guy who usually plays a supporting role with his wife Shelagh, either marshalling, timing or organising. Edwin had pulled out 462.20 miles at 48 years of age, knocking Karl Austin of the Congleton CC into 2nd place with 435.9 and Marc Wilcox, Holme Valley Wheelers, riding his first 24 hr event, in 3rd position with 430.37, another very good ride for a 'novice'.

On the 5th August 1998 Jodi Groesbeck and Adrian Harris set a new mixed tandem record of 2 days 8 hrs 28 mins for the End to End. For more details, go to the Men's History, Chapter 4.

# 1999

In 1999, another famous old club **The Brighton Mitre CC** celebrating its 105th year, promoted the first 24 hr to take place on June 26th & 27th. It was billed as **The Last Championship 24 hr race of the Century.** It was held on southern roads with a HQ at Washington on the A24 south of Horsham. Of 56 starters only 37 completed the 24 hrs. Two of those finishers were ladies. **Anne Marie Manley** riding for the Bournemouth Jubilee Wheelers with **359.65 miles,** and **2nd lady** was **Janet Lowe** riding her 2nd solo 24 hr and improving 40 miles on her previous years ride with **353.40,** only 16 miles less than her husband Peter this time.

The event was won by a very stylish Dave Shepherd of the Rother Valley CC, riding his very first 24 hr with 483.917 miles, a very well judged race. The main driving force behind the promotion of this race was Mike Hayler.

A month later the **Mersey RC** attracted just 36 starters of whom only 22 were to finish. Intense heat was the main cause of so many retirements. Four women were entered: Heather Swift, Gail Summerlin, Marina Bloom and Lynne Taylor.

By the 10 hour point Marina had retired due to a recurring back pain. She had also packed in the 'Brighton Mitre' event just a month previously with the same problem. In the Brighton event Marina had ridden into 9th place with 225 miles at 12 hours and then climbed off. The problem with back pain isn't like sickness or digestive problems, which can sometimes be overcome later in the event. Back pain generally only gets worse and can sometimes turn into a more serious situation if ignored.

Gail Summerlin bravely battled on aided by Timekeeper husband, Joe. She was trying to improve on her North Roads performance of the previous year but it wasn't to be, and she retired before 17 hours.

Another 'retiree' from food poisoning was one of the favourites, Dave Brabbin at 18.75 hours. This left Karl Austin whose 12 hr mileage was 235 compared to Brabbins 231, Gerry Jones 230, Simon Doughty 229 and Lynne who was off colour with 224 miles. The dawn sun breathed new fire into the riders aching legs as they were finishing their Shropshire circuits and looking forward to turning north towards the finish.

Joan Kershaw

Ethel Brambleby

Christine Minto

Ruth Williams

Janet Tebbutt

Ann Dunk & Fiona Steel

**Christine Roberts**

**Fliss Beard**

**Anne Mann**

**Jean Burrow**

**Sue Gray**

**Bridget Boon**

**Pauline Strong**

Lynne pulled back quite a lot of places to finish 3rd just 2 miles behind Simon Doughty and worthy winner, Karl Austin, who had ridden his own race since daybreak with nobody challenging him for position. Karl's mileage was 448.16 miles, Simon's 426.79 and **Lynne's 424.89.**

**Heather Swift,** Central Lancs RC finished with **287.94 miles.** She was using the event as good training miles for her forthcoming Paris-Brest-Paris PBP Audax, which sadly she failed to finish. **Lynne won the Turner Cup for the 5th consecutive year.**

<hr>

Sadly the **North Road CC** event which had been running for 114 years was to be their last one. Run in August with a field of just 19 solos and 1 tandem. Seven riders failed to finish but one success story was **Marina Bloom,** Crawley Wheelers, who overcame her back problems to finish with **353.97 miles.** We shall see and hear a lot more of Marina over the next few years. Dave Brabbin, Wigan Wheelers, overcame the digestion problems that terminated his Mersey ride, to win this event with 463.05 miles. He rode very strongly throughout and was never really challenged.

One of the seven riders who failed to finish was Ken Stokes, Medway Velo. Ken was returning from Newmarket to Fordham when a vehicle struck him from behind causing severe head injuries from which he never recovered. He was just 60 years of age. This tragic death plus steadily falling entries and lack of support from members of the promoting club was the final straw for Roger Sewell, the event organiser who decided to call it a day. So ended the longest running annual chapter in our history.

# 2000

**13th – 15th May saw Andy Wilkinson and Lynne Taylor break the mixed tandem End to End in 2 days 3 hrs 19 mins 23 secs.** For a full report of this record please refer to the Men's history.

With the demise of the North Road fixture, a lot of pressure was now put upon the sole surviving event, **The Mersey RC.** Luckily, lots of people wanted to ride a 24 hr to mark this histories millennium year. 54 solo riders finished plus 1 tandem from a field of 63 starters. I even got dragged in to form a Walsall Roads CC team with David Edwards, an ardent mile-eating Audax man. He'd also been press-ganged into riding by Lynne Taylor, my daughter. It was a good event, it had to be, as it is now the only 24 hr event in the calendar unless there is a special CTT promotion. There were three lady solo bike riders this year, Heather Swift, Sharon Clifford and Lynne.

Eileen Brabbin, after years of dashing round in the car helping husband David to his many victories, decided to see what a 24 hr was really like from a riders perspective. Eileen couldn't ride a bike; believe it or not its quite a common thing, we get a lot of ladies in the bike shop from all walks of life who have never mastered balancing on a bike, or have never been in a position to even try riding a bike. It's hard to imagine, I know, but it wasn't all that many years ago where if an overpowering parent said 'you're not having a bike, they're dangerous!' that was it, no bike. Eileen was racing for the first time ever in a 24 hr on a tandem, what bravery!

From the 54 finishers, 21 riders plus the tandem beat 400 miles and Gethin Butler produced a superb 509.25 miles. The event had got off to a very warm but wet start for the early riders in the field. I was No 17 riding in ankle and bottom bracket deep flood water around the Broxton area. I was soaked through from the torrential rain that had blown through the 'Cheshire Gap'. It was exhilarating, the roads were steaming. I knew that just up the road towards Whitchurch it would be hot, dry and sunny; I guessed right. When I finished the next day my socks and shoes were still damp and the soles of my feet were all wrinkled and peeling.

**Heather Swift** beat 4 men to finish with a 24 mile improvement on last years figures with **312.29 miles.** It was a very evenly paced ride, having covered 161.57 in the first 12 hours. **Sharon Clifford** of the Coventry RC finished **2nd lady with 337.50 miles** in this her debut at a 24 hr ride. **Lynne** won the **Turner cup** for the **6th year with 433.68 miles** coming 10th overall. After a fast first 100 miles of 4hrs 39 mins and a 12 hr of 230 miles, Lynne suffered sickness during the third quarter of the ride.

The wind was light and variable, Saturday night was cold with some mist patches and Sunday was warm with heavy showers refreshing the riders on the finishing circuit. Lynne, like many others, completed 5 laps of this tough rural circuit finishing 'on empty' even with Wilko's help.

She was possibly feeling a bit jaded and fragile from having completed her first End to End on the tandem with Andy only two months previously in May. She was also recovering from a very bruised backside which most rear tandem riders or 'stokers' suffer.

**Year 2000** was also a sad occasion in as much as The Mersey RC 24 hr was losing its very popular promoter **Jim Turner and his wife Anne** who had organised the event for 13 years.

In that time they had the good support of the Mersey RC Committee and membership, plus the regular helpers, marshals, timekeepers and good friends, possibly some 200 people in all, who form a massive team to oversee the running of this annual event. It had been a hard year for all of us up to this point. Jim Turner apart from carrying out his final Mersey job, had already organised Lynne and Andy's Liverpool-Edinburgh RRA tandem success and consequently their successful tandem End-to-End. The End-to-End in particular being very stressful for Jim when various aspects of the ride started to make it a nail biting time.

Various other members of the faithful 'crew' who run the Mersey, in particular the Williams family, Ruth, Bob, John and Jonathan, plus the Minto's, Christine and Frank, the Goodfellows, Mike Johnson, George and Brenda Jackson all helped on the record. Paul Histon, Lynne Mckie, Yvonne, Colin Baldwin, Pat Kenny, Dai Davies, Ron Sant, and Hugh Canning were also on the End-to-End team along with myself. John Williams Snr was the 'backroom' organiser and Jim was the 'on road' organiser for these attempts.

Apart from these last three epic occasions i.e The Mersey, The Liverpool to Edinburgh and The End to End, the Williams family would also have put on a road race, various time trials, helped in the Anfield 100, and would finish off the season with helping in the West Cheshire 12 hour in mid August. These are all jobs they have been doing for near on 40 years to my knowledge, in one way or another.

History-wise I think **Lynne and myself are the first father and daughter to finish in the same 24 hr** and I'm glad I finished, for the sake of the team, although we only came third, behind winners, Congleton CC and 2nd Hereford and District Wheelers.

One final distance I forgot to mention was that of the Brabbin's tandem 406.51 miles. They got the 7th fastest 12 hr of 239 miles. Dave Brabbin admitted that he'd been the 'weakest link'. Roy Cromack said in his description of the event that to hear Eileen say she wasn't really a cyclist left him 'totally staggered'!

# 2001

**The Mersey RC 24 hr** in 2001 was under the direction of a **New Organiser – Doug Clarke.** Jim Turner was there in the background to help with the transition as he had promised. Again the event was to be the only one for 2001. Numbers were down on the entries of year 2000 but not too bad with 33 riders finishing plus the Brabbins tandem again.

**Heather Swift** increased her previous years mileage to **314.78 miles. Lynne was the fastest lady again, with 423.13** for her 7th consecutive 'Turner Cup' win. **Eileen Brabbin** had obviously enjoyed last years 24 hr enough to try again on the tandem. Either that or perhaps she found riding with husband David less of an effort than helping him. They improved by a massive 33 miles to finish with **439.54.** I wonder at this point as to what sort of force would Eileen be on a bike, as she looked very comfortable with the effort?

Gethin Butler won the event with 485.88 miles, some 24 miles down on the previous year, but he didn't get 'stretched' quite so hard in the first quarter of the event as last year. It's still a very good result and one that put him in good stead for what he was about to embark upon just 2 months later – The End to End. Lynne was in the same frame of mind, and under the same set of circumstances. She knew that given reasonable conditions and with her experience gained from the 'Wilko' tandem records last year, she stood a good chance of getting Pauline Strong's

End to End record. Lynne knew that she was physically better prepared than Pauline had been, in as much as Pauline hadn't had the luxury of riding a 24 hr prior to her attempt. Although she had entered one, she had an accident and broke her collarbone, so putting her preparation on hold. This makes the fact of Pauline breaking Eileen Sheridan's record even more amazing.

Lynne's attempt was to take place a day before Gethins, due to RRA rules. (Gethin who had booked his attempt before Lynne, got priority as to the date he chose), and we all know 'what a difference a day makes' weather wise that is!

I couldn't help feeling at this point in July, that this years 24 hr event had been a slightly lack-lustre copy of the year 2000 one, but then I'm now only a helper and armchair critic and what do I know? Frank Mumford, writing one of his last reports on the 2001 event blames *the heat, unremitting, enervating heat which scourged away most riders hopes of beating their recent 'personal best'*.

Saturday night into Sunday was very mild, very dark and Sunday dawned very hot, relieved only by a north west breeze which arose late in the event and hindered the riders return to the finishing circuit.

---

A few weeks later, in September, Lynne rode the West Cheshire 12 hr and finished with 249 miles. She went up to John Williams who was working out all of the finishing positions and mileages on his computer. He asked Lynne to sign the RRA notice for the forthcoming attempt. Like Jim Turner, as soon as one job is finished for him, another turns up. Riding this annual 12 hr event normally would be the icing on the cake for Lynne, bringing a long season to a close, but not this year, she knew there was one final mission to complete.

This year, Jim was the organiser and 'on road' Director of Gethin's high profile End to End attempt and John Williams was Lynne's. One can now see how closely the record breaking and End to End scene is inextricably linked to the 24 hr events, not just by the riders, but by the same organisers, officials, helpers and marshals etc.

---

While all of this activity has been going on in the Lynne Taylor and Gethin Butler camps in 2001, **Marina Bloom,** Crawley Wheelers had been having a normal season so far with 25's, 50's, 100's, culminating about August with the Sussex 12 hr. She then declared to **Ralph Dadswell,** master of the trike and tandem trike scene and prolific breaker of records, that she was ready for what can only be described as a '5 in 1' RRA record. They had to beat a pretty fast, stringent time limit for a mixed **tandem trike** crew for no less that five records – **'London to York', 'York to Edinburgh', 12 hour, 'London to Edinburgh'** and finally returning south from Edinburgh for the **24 hour record.**

**On 21st August 2001** after a pretty 'hairy' start just south of the Smithfield Market area of London, (the actual start point is opposite the Rowland Hill Statue in King Edward Street) they managed to pick up a favourable breeze after being delayed by heavy traffic. They were to reach York via the A1 with various detours as the A1 becomes the A1.M motorway. Hatfield, Welwyn, Biggleswade, Buckden, Peterborough and Stamford were reached on schedule. 100 miles had gone by in 4 hrs 30 minutes. By Markham Moor they were 20 mins up on schedule. Blyth, Bawtry and they were on the run into York via Thorne.

So York was the first record in 8 hrs 56 mins 4 secs, well inside the standard set by the RRA, by over 2 hrs. Through Easingwold, Thirsk, Northallerton and Darlington, where they were over 30 mins up with favourable conditions. The flat roads were now left behind as they progressed towards Durham where the 12 hour point was reached with just over 265 miles covered so far – what a ride! On now through Chester-Le-Street and past the 'Angel of the North' at Birtley. Newcastle came and went and the hills were now taking their toll on the two riders as 300 miles was passed. A change to warmer clothing at Morpeth, ready for the cold night in the hilly borders. Seventy miles on the A697 took them to the A68 just south of Soutra. Despite the very hilly terrain, Wooler was reached still well inside schedule to Coldstream.

The road became a series of short steep 'drags' followed by a drop and then climb again, not the best of terrain for a tandem trike. At Greenlaw they had only 15 mins in hand with 22 miles left to Edinburgh and 1 hr 22 mins to do it in. With 372 miles already covered in the middle of the night and a large climb still to overcome, things were looking grim. But with words of encouragement from their helping team, Marina and Ralph managed to find a fair amount of downhill through Dalkeith and sprint into **Edinburgh.**

They snatched the record by 40 seconds as they reached the North Bridge Post Office. You might think that it was all over now, gaining 4 records by getting to **Edinburgh** in **19 hours 40 mins 40 secs,** but there was still the 24 hour record to beat, with just under 400 miles covered and over 4 hours left, anything was possible.

The riders retraced out of Edinburgh towards Berwick on Tweed. After various detours due to road signage being wrong, the riders went via Musselborough and Dunbar. With 435 miles covered, a mechanical problem occurred when the chain jammed between the chain rings losing them 10 minutes. With just over an hour to go and 435 miles completed they 'went for broke' towards Berwick, reaching just beyond the English Border before collapsing in a heap about a mile short of Berwick on Tweed. **This established a new 24 hour record of 451 miles for a mixed crew tandem trike.** It also included the **York to Edinburgh** record in **10 hrs 44 mins 20 secs.**

This magnificent 5 in 1 record of Marina's and Ralphs took place in **August 2001,** just one month before Lynne and Gethin's solo End to Ends and although Marina already had a few high profile ladies records, I think these latest ones helped trigger Marina's career as a long distance racing specialist. *(My thanks to Ralph Dadswell for the use of information from his article that appeared in The Fellowship Journal.)*

⇒•◇•⇐

**Between 26th and 30th September 2001, Lynne and Gethin both achieved their goals.** I now include a short passage from the 24 hr Fellowship Journal written by Charles G. Robson, The Fellowships Competition Secretary.

*"I am sure you will all have read in 'Cycling Weekly' about the epic rides of Gethin Butler and Lynne Taylor, from Lands End to John o' Groats. Gethin beat Andy Wilkinson's record by almost an hour with a time of 1 day, 20 hrs, 4 mins 20 secs, and on the way took the 24 hr place to place record from John Woodburn with a distance of 505.8 miles. As if this was not enough, he managed to get back on his bike and set a new 1000 mile record of 2 days 7 hours 59 minutes, taking 2 hrs 41 mins off Reg Randall's 1960 record. Let's also remember the quality of Randall's ride setting a record which lasted over 40 years on a more primitive machine. Lynne who set off the day before Gethin, not only endured the most horrific weather, but also had to mentally put up with being down on schedule for most of her ride. Her time of 2 days 5 hrs 48 mins 21 secs took just over an hour off Pauline Strong's record and was a triumph of positive thinking over adversity. I am sure we shall see her making another attempt, as she herself reckons she could improve her time by around 5 hrs with better conditions and a more favourable wind."*

The circumstances and proximity of these two epic rides are very similar to Eileen Sheridans and Crimes and Arnolds rides. Using lines and passages from my first book **'The End to End Story'** I will try and show the likeness.

"Lynne had just broken Pauline Strongs' 11 year old record by 1 hr 10 mins. We all felt very emotional at this point. Out of 53 hours of riding, Lynne had endured at least 45 hours of rain. Based on her physical state at this point, 'the team' took the decision not to continue for the 1000 mile record. John Arnold and Harry Wilkinson who had provided a mobile comfort stop at various points on the journey were now going to motor back down the A9 to see Gethin Butler coming through the Highlands. After a good nights sleep, Lynne and the helping team were up at 5am to cheer Gethin in at 6am.

We had been informed of his progress up through Scotland by mobile phones. He put up a new 24 hr record of 505.8 miles, and despite taking a packet and 'blowing' after Edinburgh, he was still up on schedule by 1 hour.

As he came down the road from Wick the wind was gusting so strongly, he went through the finish line at John o' Groats so fast, we thought he would plough into the hotel wall. After all of the greetings and congratulations for breaking the End to End record, he announced that he would continue after a short break for the 1000 miles.

We had witnessed history being made by two of the country's top long distance riders within 24 hours. The last time anything like this happened was in 1954, over 50 years ago, when Eileen Sheridan broke the End to End and 1000 mile record, and the following day, Albert Crimes and John Arnold broke the 12 hour, 24 hour, End to End and 1000 mile records on a tandem trike.

Eileen was there to greet them outside the hotel, the three riders chatted for a few minutes before Crimes and Arnold carried on to complete their 1000 miles record journey. Eileen's team had given the lads a whole cooked chicken to finish their journey with."

The John o' Groats hotel is now boarded up and sadly not in use, but one could imagine the riders and support crews staying there and celebrating.

Lynne's first solo End to End had been meticulously planned by John Williams and ideally Lynne should have started on the Thursday, the day that Gethin had booked, but RRA rules and protocol meant that this couldn't be allowed.* So Lynne started the day before Gethin in drizzly murky damp conditions. The little wind she did have was behind her as she bypassed Penzance. At 60 miles she was just 5 mins inside evens and the rain was getting heavier. Lynne questioned us with 'where's the wind?'

We saw Jim Turner and Gethin's team of helpers including Ron Sant, Dai Davies, Observer and Timekeeper respectively and Colin Baldwin, Masseur and driver, on their way south to Lands End for a Thursday start. Jim had already phoned Paul Histon and told him that the weather was fine in Exeter.

At Okehampton with 100 miles ridden in 4 hrs 56 mins Lynne went into a three quarter headwind as she skirted Dartmoor. The spray from the lorries on the busy A30 made for a scary ride at times especially at incoming slip roads. Lynne passed through Exeter still inside evens but experiencing heavy rain and heavy traffic. At Taunton she dropped below evens after stopping for dry shorts and more wet weather clothing. Andy now reduced her drinks to 500 ml (one small bottle) per hour. By 5.15 pm she had covered 181 miles in 9.25 hours.

With the closure of the usual route through Bristol due to a landslide, Lynne had to take the very narrow hilly route over the Clifton Suspension Bridge where a great team of marshals, including Bridget Boon, under the guidance of Geoff Lonsdale, saw her safely through Bristol. It was now bucketing down as Lynne pushed on through heavy peak hour traffic. Her 12 hrs yielded 225.4 miles before Gloucester was reached. A wrong turn in the city lost her about 5 mins. We saw Neville Channin and Anne Wooldridge here and Neville wrote to Lynne afterwards saying how sorry he felt seeing her emerge out of the gloom, without any helping wind and already being well down on schedule. But he also knew she wouldn't give up.

Another wrong turn on the approach to Worcester and a stop to change on to her night bike with better lights meant more lost time. Another stop at the Mitre Oak on the Kidderminster Road was taken to take on board Lynne Mckie as a female support for Lynne. John Arnold was also here with Harry Wilkinson. They were providing three or four comfort stops using Harry's van in the next 600 miles.

Wolverhampton was reached by midnight and Gailey Island with 297 miles covered at 12.30 am. A huge crowd of friends and family members had gathered to see her through and we took on board Pete Swinden and Pat Kenny, our next two observers to Gretna Green, and said goodbye to Christine and Frank Minto who had been with us since Lands End. On route between here and Winwick Church we saw many of Lynne's 24 hr compatriots. Margaret & Jim Hopper, Les Lowe, Karl Austin, Neil Peart, Dave Brabbin and Tom Greep. The rain had eased over the last three hours but by Warrington it was raining heavily again. At 5.37 am she'd covered 384 miles and was now putting on double layers of clothing as the cold and wet conditions were getting to her. So far she has had about 20 hours of rain.

At Kendal she took a 30 mins comfort break before climbing Shap. She had managed 420 miles in 24 hours. It was still very wet with no wind as she started back on the road. John Arnold commented as to how pale and drawn Lynne looked, not her usual self and who knew what lay ahead for her. Andy Wilkinson looked at me questioningly as I was secretly thinking "How long can she go on without any help from the weather?"

John Williams internet report following a phone conversation with Wilko said "on the 2nd day, after another stop for a short sleep, time down on schedule was 4.5 hours and the attempt was at a crucial point. Having failed to get the first two records, the 12 hr and 24 hr, it was apparent that Lynne would also fail to reach John o' Groats if she slipped any further behind.

Crossing Shap Fell in blinding torrential rain and mist, with no help from the wind, the attempt director began to contemplate the possibility of abandoning". John then went on to say that "fortunately Lynne had other ideas and knuckled down to holding her speed and defying the elements". Paul Histon was I'm afraid, the only one besides Lynne who was really enthusiastic about continuing.

By Carlisle, Pat Kenny reckoned Lynne was about 4.5 hours down, but if she could forego a scheduled 1 hour break at Gretna, she could recoup quite a lot. At Gretna we swapped observers. Pat Kenny and Pete Swinden went back home and Bob Williams and Mike Johnson joined us.

Lockerbie was reached with 504 miles covered by 1.55 pm. Lynne stopped for more dry shorts and peppermint tea on the Beattock Summit. She reached Edinburgh in the tea time rush hour but with directions from Carol Dietman and her friends, Lynne got safely through and crossed the Forth Road Bridge.

At 7.15 pm with 586 miles ridden, Lynne was enjoying dry roads and she said she could feel a little push from the wind and yes, she would like to get beyond Perth for her next stop. That's positive thinking for you, and Wilko said it was the best news he'd heard since the start. At 9.30 pm with 607 miles done she was away again, on the soul destroying A9 main dual carriageway, but at least she couldn't get lost could she? Lynne now had 230 miles to do in 16.5 hours – an average of 14.5 mph – not easy after all of this effort. Harry and John who'd provided the break at Perth were now motoring on to Inverness and would set up another comfort stop there.

At 2 am with 685 miles completed, Lynne had just 12 hours 49 mins to do 155 miles. She was now very sleepy and wanted to stop but Andy said she must hurry now to Inverness. It's very cold, high in the Grampians and by the time she dropped towards Inverness the wind was against her, Lynne was cold and could only manage 30 mph down the steep drop.

A 22 mins break at Inverness did the trick. Twelve minutes sleep, a quick massage and hot rice pudding and she was away again with just 9 hours left to cover 120 miles, with 3 or 4 tortuous climbs left to do on the 'Ord of Caithness' and a block headwind every time she rode by the coast. It was not going to be easy but by 10.50 am Lynne started the climb of Berriedale with the team running alongside her; Paul, Lynne Mckie, Mike Johnson and Andy.

By 12.55 pm she was 2 miles north of Wick with just 15 miles to go, heavy rain, poor visibility and very strong side winds were still plaguing her, but she wasn't giving up now and at 1.48 pm she finally dropped down to the John o' Groat's finish line for Nobby Clarke to time her in with a new record of **2 days 5 hours 48 mins 21 seconds.**

After all the congratulations we had to make a decision as to Lynne carrying on for the 1000 mile record. Another 160 miles plus, in 19 hours with atrocious conditions and another 10 hours of darkness. Lynne's face was ashen and she had to be helped off her bike. I think we made the right decision for her not to continue for the 1000 miles. After a long hot shower, Lynne had to have a fan heater blowing hot air on her for about three hours to bring her out of hypothermia. But what an achievement.

On arrival home late next day, it was noted how strong the wind was, it blew from the south at a gusting 20 mph for 3 or 4 days!

*Having recently researched the long distance 'RRA' record breaking exploits of Sid Ferris, Cyril Heppleston and Charles Holland in 1938 particularly over the Edinburgh-York-London and 24 hour route, I find it an amazing fact that all three professionals were despatched individually from Edinburgh Head Post Office within the space of 75 minute. Admittedly, Ferris, Heppleston and Holland were initially on slightly differing routes from Edinburgh, but all three would have been heading down the A1 towards York probably within 30 mins of each other on that day. This leads me to wonder what contingency plans were in place should one rider appear to be catching another?*

# 2002

The main story for the ladies is that this is the year where Marina Bloom came through very strongly with newfound confidence in the **24 hr** which was a **National Championship,** promoted by our one and only **Mersey RC** in July. I was out again helping Lynne with Neil Peart, a very talented time triallist at all distances up to 12 hours, who regularly helps Lynne in her longer events.

Lynne had a real challenge throughout the event from Marina, with Lynne winning by 10 miles, which sounds a lot but up until the last few hours it had been a pretty close ride between the two girls. Lynne had to really fight hard to 'raise her game' at the end.

Five other ladies rode that weekend, **Ursula Betterton,** Cleveland Couriers, **was 3rd lady** with **341.427 miles, Ann Wooldridge** was **4th** riding for Gloucester City CC with **332.582 miles** after losing so much time during the night with sickness which she thinks is from drinking too much Maxim in the hours after midnight. **Claire Ashton** of the Wrekinsport CC was a bit slower with **328.863** but was very happy just to finish. Claire has come from Audax riding so knows that finishing the course is the main goal. **Gail Summerlin** finished with **294.145** miles after quite a few D.N.F's over the last few seasons so this ride was pleasing to her and husband Joe. **Philippa Crocker** was 7th fastest lady with **264.791 miles.** For Ursula, Ann, Claire and Philippa, this was their first foray into 24 hour racing. I hope they enjoyed it. **The Brabbins** on a tandem again improved another massive 25 miles to record **464.924 miles,** beating the Boon's 16 year old record by over a mile. The expression on Eileen's face as much as said 'I wish I'd taken this up years ago'!

**Lynne came 9th** in the overall field with **438.042** to take **The Turner Cup** once again. **Marina Bloom** was **13th** overall with **427.502,** a massive personal best for her by 63 miles. David Shepherd, Rother Valley CC rode himself into the ground to win the event with 482.128 miles, a 12 mile beating of 2nd man Jose Pinon Shaw of the Central Lancs CC with 470.044 miles and in a close run 3rd place, Mark Botteley, Fenland Clarion CC just 0.346 of a mile slower than Pinon Shaw with 469.698 miles.

Ann Wooldridge on her debut in 2002 wrote an article for the Fellowship Journal entitled **"A Foray into long distance cycling".**

*"Years ago I decided that one day I would ride a 24 hr event. This year I finally was ready for the challenge. I had actually decided to enter after the 2001 National 24 hr Champs had taken place, and Lynne Taylor had successfully achieved her Lands End to John o' Groats record. I felt that I was mentally ready. So during the dark winter months I assembled my team of helpers. This consisted of Toby, Mike Davis, Neil Calder, Pete and Sheila Humble, Ed and George Unsworth, and for the later stages my brother and his wife. Then I booked a B&B to accommodate us all for 3 nights with people getting up at various un-hospitable hours, eating, and enough drivers to carry out personnel changes.*

*I started my specific training during the winter, part of which consisted of long steady mind-bending turbo sessions. Then we went on an early season training camp. Every week I did a long ride on a Monday to build up my base, and to ride non-stop, feeding myself en route. At the start of May I did what is my favourite ride of this year, I cycled from Gloucester, round the top of London and down to Canvey Island – 192 miles in 11 hours and 34 mins. I find one-way rides to be very good for motivation. SPOT ON TARGET – average speed 16.6 mph. Lynne Taylor sent me down some lights from her shop to use for the night and to get used to, and gave me lots of valuable information.*

*Then the specific planning for the 27th and 28th July took place with maps, route details, bottle training.*

*On Friday, we drove up to Whitchurch and met in the B&B. Then a meal and a good nights sleep. The race started at 2pm. The weather was very hot. Sheila rubbed plenty of sun cream into my bare skin as I was getting quite nervous. The boys were busy and the HQ was a hive of activity. My van had my night bike ready, change of clothes, food supplies, toiletries, water etc, and a board with white lights on in the shape of an A to be switched on at night so I would recognise my helpers in the dark – absolutely essential.*

*2.39pm and I was off into the unknown. I rode steadily and started drinking quite soon as it was so hot. There was also a headwind. The course had been easy to memorise and is based around Prees Island at Whitchurch, very compact, with a huge café, toilets, carpark etc. And lots and lots of spectators. I rode on and on, fuelling myself and taking bottles on board. I suddenly had to take my helmet off because I was getting a headache, and then it magically disappeared. This daytime riding up to 9.40 pm was done on my Argos lo-pro. Then I stopped to put on a jacket, swap bikes and put on reflective arm bands etc ready for the night. My Tommasini was the bike I would now stay on for the remainder of the event.*

*The next five hours were on lovely quiet roads with the odd spectacle of cyclists silently riding on and on. Around midnight it was very black and all along the roadsides were supporters with various lighting systems to attract their riders. It was nice to see Ian and Bridget Boon at Shawbirch Island and Graham Smith's supporters (Severn RC) but suddenly at 3 am just after a good first 12 hours I pulled over and was violently sick. Not just once, which would have been ok but 4 times. This was totally unexpected and something I hadn't even considered. I was so empty after retching for a while and felt very very weak. How on earth would I manage to carry on for another 11 hours?? A feeling of desolation began to creep into my head ... I couldn't let my team down!!*

*After a rest and some encouragement I managed to drink a bit of water and eat a tiny square of bread. Not much – my tummy was completely empty. I didn't want to smell another banana, or anything sweet. A bit of a problem! I was made to get back on my bike and carry on. I did so, spinning a tiny gear. I passed Graham who was asleep on the grass, also having a bad patch. By now the sky was not so black and little animals were getting up. I found that I had to stop every single 10 miles for a wee (water was going straight through me) and some rice pudding – the best food ever invented for long distance racing! A cup of tea and a nice fresh roll that Toby bought me (in desperation) turned my stomach. At 6.50 I had to stop at Prees Island for a sleep and toilet stop. Looking at my mileage I knew I had a long way to go. Then I gradually began to get stronger.*

*Halfway round the Quina Brook circuit I changed my clothes again, had a quick wash and brushed my teeth. Much better! Toby was darting around on his Brompton and things began to look up. It was essential to keep seeing my van now...a welcome sight. The day began to get very hot again. All I could drink was water, but I could eat a little better. I felt much fresher and my mind was very sharp. I didn't have any problems with tiredness at any time in the ride. I knew I would finish now with well over 300 miles, so was happy. At 11.50 I got onto the finishing circuit. It was extremely hot. My helpers positioned themselves at various spots in case I needed them. Christine Roberts was riding round, and my favourite Gethin Butler came over for a chat when I was eating yet more rice pudding. Then as the time got towards 2.39 I couldn't wait to stop. 'Stop at the next timekeeper' was like music to my ears! There was my van waiting for me! I sat down on a cushion and Neil undid my shoes and put my feet in a bowl of water...and Mike gave me the most delicious packet of plain Walkers crisps to eat!! Just right.*

*After a while we drove back to the HQ for showers and a rest. I was so happy to have succeeded and very pleased with my team (certainly the best looking one there!) On seeing my mileage I was quite stunned to see 333.277 miles after all the stops and problems I had encountered, and my average cycling speed was 16.71 mph – 0.01 mph higher than I had aimed for. Had I not stopped for what added up to several hours I would have been very near to 400 miles. The feeling of achievement was tremendous, and the realising of a 10 year goal was just fantastic. And I now had insight into what not to drink – MAXIM ... even though I had used it successfully for years and years. The first of my 24 hour races had been completed. The funny thing was that my legs didn't feel too bad, obviously tired, but riding a small gear stopped any stiffness occurring. But because of my food problem I used up all my natural fat stores as energy and it took 3 weeks to recover from the event. I looked like a skeleton the next morning!! But all this is experience for next year!"*

Apart from a couple of 50 mile events, **Lynne** finished her long distance time trialling season off with **244.48** miles in the **West Cheshire 12 hour,** just 15 miles behind winner Rob Nelson with 259.61.

With this performance Lynne now felt confident that she was ready for her 2nd forthcoming End to End and with the main aim of completing the 1000 miles. This ride was due to take place before the weather deteriorated in October.

In this year of **2002, Marina,** riding for Crawley Wheelers CC came **4th** in the **Womens BBAR** and **Lynne** came **5th.**

Lynne was so pleased to at last have someone in competition with her and both Lynne's and Marina's results especially in the 24 hr proved this. I know that Lynne, Marina, Claire Ashton and Ann Wooldridge were on friendly chatting terms at the end of events etc. It must get very lonely when you are the only woman in a predominantly male club, and I think this was the case for all of them. The men in a club can easily make a team of 3 decent time triallists, but to get 3 girls performing regularly at all distances for more than one season is very difficult unless there is a sponsorship deal or monetary involvement. None of the girls I've mentioned have ever been in a sponsored club or would ever wish to be as far as I know. They like being free spirits, to come and go as they wish, but I think they were all looking for an extra goal to aim for in their sporting careers.

Marina & Lynne had both been racing seriously for about 14 years or more at this time, Ann Wooldridge even longer. Claire Ashton had come into club life after riding lots of very long Audaxes but was now enjoying mixing her riding with time trials They all knew about Lynne's End to End exploits and had kept in touch or went out to see her through en route in year 2000's mixed tandem and 2001 attempt. Lynne had also kept an interested eye on Marina's record breaking, mainly with Ralph Dadswell and Lynne also knew that Marina, apart from riding a good 24 hr, was a very tough 12 hour rider, so they had a lot in common. I know that apart from them all making contact with each other, they were also in touch with Jim Turner who was about to put the final plans into place for Lynne's 2nd solo End to End.

Lynne's training and racing throughout the year of 2002 had gone well, her 5th place ladies BBAR position was made up of a 59.42 for 25 miles, 2hr 00m 26 secs – 50 miles and 4 hr 12mins 47secs – 100 miles. I always felt that if the emphasis for short distance speed ie: 25 mile events was removed and a 12 hour performance was used as in the men's BBAR, then **Marina and Lynne** would be scrapping it out for **1st and 2nd places** in the competition, not 4th and 5th.

More importantly, for Lynne's mental and physical state, she had ridden a good 12 hr of 244 miles and a 438 mile 24hr. For a record like the End to End and 1000 miles there are no better or 'softer' alternative methods of training, you have to go out at all hours and 'put the miles in'. Ride the 50's, 100's 12 hrs and 24 hrs that are available, ride in all conditions, winds, rain, freezing cold, boiling hot, thunder & lightning, heavy traffic, because on a ride the length of great Britain, plus 160 extra for the 1000 miles, one can encounter any or all of these conditions, not to mention riding in the dark for 2 nights without sleep, and then another day!

On **October 1st, 2nd & 3rd 2002, Lynne broke her own solo Bicycle End to End** by 1 hour 3 mins giving a record of **2 days, 4hrs 45mins 11secs.** She then went on to break Eileen Sheridan's 48year old **1000 mile record** by 8hrs 22 mins with **2 days, 16 hrs, 38 mins,** with conditions only turning favourable for Lynne in the last 17 hours of the ride.

It had all started the previous year in 2001 as Lynne was helped off her bike at John o' Groats her first words were "I've got to do this again haven't I Dad?" This was such a positive thing for her to say after such a gruelling ride, the hardest two days of her life. I replied "Yes, you could put the record inside two days with the right wind and weather!"

So the following month we asked Jim Turner if he could organise another attempt and he said he would be glad to, but that he would have to direct it from home, as the last two End to Ends and 1000 had taken quite a lot out of him. Being there on the road handling all the problems as they arose had put quite a strain on him, taking weeks to recover from. A new team of helpers this year including Mike, Lynne's brother, Neil Peart, Yvonne Unsworth, Colin Baldwin and a new timekeeper, Tony Shardlow who was not only a regular RTTC timekeeper in the Midlands but was also steeped in RRA tradition and experience. Mike Johnson, Pete Swinden and Ron Sant were again observers, but both Pete and Ron said that they had been on so many record attempts as Observers that they really could do with a rest, once this was over. I was there on the team as a mechanic and spare driver, but really my favourite roll was to be there to record and describe events that happened along the way as the 1000 mile journey unfolded. Christine Minto was again to be our start timekeeper swapping with Tony at Gretna.

My first job was to make Lynne a new bike as the Giant Cadex she had used on her 2001 record was quite heavy compared with some of the latest machines and equipment available, also her Campag Shamal wheels had both gained about a teacupful of rain water in each rim by the end of her ride. I used an Orbea frame made from Columbus Alloy Tubing with a carbon fork and wishbone rear stays for comfort, finished with Shimano Dura ace components and wheels. The weight was now down to approximately 18 lbs. Lynne had an excellent season, which gave her great confidence as she was about to undertake this epic journey.

After waiting a month for a good wind, a decision was made to start on the 1st October. A 12 to 15 mph south westerly wind had been forecasted and it was felt that if we didn't take this opportunity to start then it would be too late in the year as we were already down to 11 hours of daylight and even less in Scotland, with possibly minus temperatures in the 'Grampians'.

She started in the dark at 6 am and passed along the Penzance by-pass some 30 mins later, observed by Elaine Hancock. By Launceston with 77 miles ridden in 3hrs 48 mins, the sun was just breaking through patchy pockets of mist. By Exeter the light winds had disappeared and drizzle had settled in.

Lynne reached Bridgwater, 160 miles, in 8 hrs 17 mins and was now riding in torrential rain. She had already had two or three changes of clothing to stay comfortable for the latter part of her journey. We had been told numerous times that the weather was fine just 40 miles ahead of us, but we were beginning to despair. At Bristol, Lynne was 1 hr down on schedule and as wet as the previous year.

"There's no need to water the garden, Lynne Taylor's going on another record attempt"

Heavy peak time traffic hindered her and by the 12 hr point she had only covered 213 miles. As she rode into her first night things weren't looking too good, but as we stopped her for a dry set of clothes and massage near Worcester, Lynne was still cheerful and positive saying that her main aim was the 1000 miles of which there were 750 left to do!

Large crowds of club folk saw her through Gailey Island at around 11pm and many of them popped up en-route as far as Congleton. By 6am she had reached Carnforth with 410 miles covered in her first 24 hrs but she was still 10 miles behind last years performance at this time. The climb of Shap was completed in the dry this year and she reached the summit by 8.34am. She should have been here at 5.11am, and so is drastically down on the record but a 1 hour scheduled break is foregone and so technically by Carlisle she was only 2 hrs 20mins adrift. Lynne reached Johnstone Bridge 503 miles at 12.35pm and was now over halfway towards her 1000 miles. By the Forth Road Bridge at 4.46pm Lynne had narrowed her losses down to 1 hr 39 mins and took a short break at nightfall to put extra clothing and lights on. She was looking forward to reaching Perth and finally got there at 7.21pm. Out on the A9 the drizzle started, and combined with the darkness, she was experiencing very tired eyes.

As Lynne climbed higher on the A9 the drizzle turned to sleet and by Blair Athol she was struggling to keep going. It looked doubtful at this point as to whether the End to End record was obtainable, but Lynne knew that if she could stay awake and just keep going at about 12 mph she could possibly break Eileen's 1000 mile record. At 2 am Lynne reached the Slochd Summit with 702 miles covered. She was now 1 hr 40 mins behind schedule but now less than 20 miles from Inverness. We had noticed her occasionally freewheeling and braking, I thought that perhaps there was a problem with her bike, but when I mentioned the subject to her at the end, Lynne said she was slowing for the traffic lights. She had actually been hallucinating and reliving the heavy traffic conditions and traffic lights in Bristol!

Lynne crossed the Kessock Bridge and over the Beauly Firth at 3.25am with just 120 miles to cover. Earlier, as we crossed the Grampians we had heard a very promising weather forecast. It was actually a shipping forecast for that north-easterly region we were in, but we didn't detect any improvement until she reached the Black Isle.

By the Tain bypass Lynne had gained back another 23 minutes and was now only 1hr 17mins behind schedule. It was dry, not too cold and she had a tailwind and a beautiful dawn to look at on her right and out at sea. Lynne now realised that with the gains she was making she could get both the End to End and 1000 mile records. She'd climbed Helmsdale and Berriedale by 8.22am and with 796 miles covered was only 44 mins behind a schedule that was made to run at 12 mph.

The clubmen from the Caithness CC and the Wick Wheelers had been alerted as Lynne had got closer to John o' Groats and they were putting the final details into motion for her 1000 mile record route. After nearly being taken off the road by a huge Tesco lorry, Lynne reached Wick at 9.50am and to equal her existing record she'd got 17 miles to do in 1hr 58 mins. It was a glorious day as Lynne finally dropped down to John o' Groats with **a new record of 2 days 4 hrs 45 mins 11 secs.**

After quick congratulations she retraced up to the Guest House where she had a quick shower, a bowl of soup, fresh clothes and a massage from Colin Baldwin. **No-one in the history of the RRA has taken their own End to End record, paced or un-paced on consecutive years on the same category of machine. Lynne is also the first person since G.P.Mills in 1895 to break an End to End record on three consecutive years.**

After a 5 mins sleep and receiving congratulations and support from Eileen Sheridan by phone, Lynne restarted her last 160 miles, plus an extra distance of approximately 10 miles for safety's sake at 12.02 pm. The road runs along the coast to Thurso with magnificent views of the Orkneys. By mid afternoon it had turned breezy and cool with intermittent showers, a bit like April with double rainbows out at sea. It was hoped that she would be finished by midnight but she had until 7am the next morning to break Eileen's record of 3 days 1 hr. As she retraced to Wick for the second time at 5.15 pm she had covered 929 miles.

Lynne now had 80 miles left to do and was averaging a steady 18 mph. At Castletown she'd covered 954 miles by 7.33 pm and was 1hr 35 mins inside schedule. On the return to Thurso we saw a wonderful display of 'Aurora Borealis' or Northern Lights out at sea and lighting up the sky over the Orkneys. By 10.37 pm she'd covered the exact **1000 miles,** just beyond Thurso traffic lights, with a total time of **2 days, 16 hrs, 38 mins** but still had to complete her extra 12 miles just to be on the safe side, after what happened to Dick Poole in 1965. Alasdair Washington and Malcolm Gray of the Caithness CC and members of the Wick Wheelers had made this possible so that Tony Shardlow could accurately pinpoint Lynne's mileage. Lynne had completed her remaining 160 miles as fast as Gethin had the previous year. What a marvellous end to a nail biting 64 hours where both records looked doubtful, especially on the first day.

That brought 2002 thankfully to a close, but a month later sees the training for next season start, interspersed with after-dinner speeches and prize presentations at various cycling clubs around the country with as many functions ridden to, as possible, by bike.

Marina had been the catalyst for the girls coming together to join Lynne with a view to forming not only a long distance team, but possibly also a BBAR team. At the Walsall Roads CC dinner in late November 2002, there were 4 new female faces, Marina, Ann, Claire and Tracey Maund from the Cheltenham CC, with guests Anne and Jim Turner. Jim gave a speech and said what outstanding female talent the club had amongst them. He re-capped on Lynne's exploits since year 2000 and I think it was from that night onwards that Marina, Tracey, Ann and Claire approached the club to apply for membership. Jim offered his services to manage and advise them on what events to ride and a strategy as to how he could support them now that his End to End duties were over.

# 2003

By early June, the ladies team of the Walsall Roads CC had already come together in one or two early season events, notably the **'Anfield 100'**. **Marina** was the **fastest lady** with **4 hrs 33mins 59 secs.**

**Lynne** for some inexplicable reason couldn't get her head together and finished outside evens. **Claire Ashton** finished with **5 hrs 33 mins 33 secs** and they were the **3rd team winners.**

What a difference, two weeks later, on the 15th June a gloriously hot day (too hot for racing) the ladies rode the Burton and District CA 100 on the A50 Uttoxeter-Stone-Rocester-Derby course. What a good start to the season it was, Lynne, Marina, Tracey all pulled out personal bests. **Lynne** with **4 hrs 2 mins 12 secs** for **fastest lady.** **Marina, 4 hrs 09 mins 54 secs. Tracey, 4 hrs 14 mins 27 secs,** , Ann, **4 hrs 35 mins 08 secs** and Claire just 12 secs outside evens with **5 hrs 00 m 12 secs.**

**They broke the National Ladies 100 mile Team Competition Record by over 19 mins, with a time of 12 hours 26 mins 33 secs.**

There was such excitement watching them all rise to the occasion, with 15 miles to go it looked as if Lynne could possible go inside 4 hrs, but cramp locked her leg muscles in the last 5 miles due to dehydration although she had consumed about 6 litres of liquid. Things were now looking very good for the 24hr in two weeks time as 100 mile time trials are about the best training and performance guides prior to a 24 hr race.

I will now include my own report and description of the event written at the time from the sidelines, helping and driving on such occasions.

⸺⸺◆⸺⸺

**Walsall RCC Ladies Assault of the 24 hr Team Record – Mersey RC 24hr 2003**

The team are now getting 'edgy', we are well into July and the 24 hr is looming. They are ringing and 'texting' each other, unheard of in my day 'texting'? I wonder what G.P Mills or G.H.S. would have made of it! Even John Arnold has now got a mobile phone.

Had they done enough miles? The 24 hour course was altered from it original format. The work on the Hodnet by-pass had put paid to the run down to Shawbirch island near Telford, and then literally a week before the event, temporary traffic lights at Hodnet forced the organisers to abandon the Ternhill-Hodnet-Battlefield section altogether. The course now consisted of up to 5 circuits of lanes, 13.5 miles in the headquarters and starting area, then a run up the A41 to Prees and then 4 circuits of 12.5 miles round the Quina Brook and Tilstock area which took the riders into early evening. Section 3 consisted of Prees to Ternhill, retrace to Prees, left through Preston Brockhurst, climbing 'Schoolgirl Hill' then run downhill through Hadnall to turn at Battlefield island, one mile from Shrewsbury, then retrace to Prees island and do it all again up to 3 times. Each lap was 42 miles and this took the riders well past daybreak and beyond where more repeats of the Quina Brook circuit took them till mid morning and then a long stretch towards Chester where the last series of circuits started off left at Handley on the A41.

This took the riders back into the lanes past the Headquarters at Farndon where left and within a mile or so a vicious climb to Barton to complete the circuit at Handley. The road surface on the circuits left a lot to be desired, basically chippings that had gone smooth in places, but broken up regularly by winter exposure and water and tractor damage.

This plus up to 20 hard climbs of 'Schoolgirl Hill both ways, that's six, plus Prees bypass hill 10 times plus the start and finishing circuit hill at Barton at least 8 times making possibly 24 climbs in all.

Lynne was her usual self 'shall I ride the Club 10, will it do me any good'? Have I done enough miles? This is a girl who hasn't stopped or eased off for 5 years, having amassed 3 End to Ends and 1000 Mile records in the last 3 seasons totalling 50,000 miles. Obviously I replied "of course you've done enough miles!" Her weight was now well below 9 stone. In fact when you look at Marina, Lynne, Tracey and Ann they are all so slight in build you wonder just where does the power come from? When you look at a lot of the male riders they have big shoulders, big thighs and calf muscles and weigh anything up to 12 stone, and the girls still fly past them after 100 miles. I almost feel sorry for the poor chaps, what have they got to do to beat the women?

Ann had been texting Jim Turner for advice and asking Lynne odds and ends on feeding etc. Last minute nerves I think. Claire was quite confident from all the audaxing she had done. Being comfortable with one's own company and decisions and relying on no one else but yourself, a good outlook, but sometimes if you want to improve you have to let someone else into your world to bring out the best in you. As long as Claire could improve on last year's mileage by at least 30miles she would be happy.

Marina had husband Mike to advise her. He doesn't use polymer feeding (i.e. Maxim, PSP etc) relying on basic carbohydrates such as rice pudding, bread pudding, butties and mainly water, which proved very good on the day. I don't know what Ann and Tracey existed on but it certainly suited them. I don't think they suffered any sickness bouts. Lynne's brother Mike, and Neil Peart who had teamed up on the End to End and 1000 miles, were helping Lynne this year. Watching the forecast prior to the event it looked as though it might be a bit mixed. The Cheshire Gap is a bit like the Bermuda Triangle and seems to have its own weather system coming in over the Welsh hills from the coast, through the Gap, towards Chester and Whitchurch.

Lynne wanted to get up to the Headquarters with just enough time for comfort, she doesn't like chatting too much before an event, there's always a chance that negative thoughts can get hold of you. She often gets people coming up while she's waiting to start on the line and they say "I'm surprised you didn't beat the hour last week Lynne" or "there's some tough roads out there" of which she is perfectly aware. She even had one chap come up to her just before a '25' and say "did you know old so and so has died Lynne?" which for Lynne ruined her ride. Colin Baldwin, her masseur on the End to End and 1000, says people often look at the hole and not the doughnut! Claire had left her taxi at Prees with lots of food and drink and spares in it. She had to pass it about 20 times so it was ideal for location. Ann's husband Toby, and Mike Davies, a clubmate, were helping her, and Tracey's husband Colin was doing the hard work for her.

The way the course was split into circuits meant you hardly ever came into contact with the other girls or their helpers, which means that no-one has a clue as to the performances by anyone else.

When I rode years ago with just a wrist watch on (and clothes of course) I could always tell how the rest of the lads were doing or where the leaders were; even at night one gets an inkling as to the speed or riding style of opponents coming towards you and of course you could judge how far they were beating you by, or vice-versa, not very often in my case.

The start came – Lynne was sent on her way at 1.51pm. The day turned out to be very warm up until mid-afternoon on the Saturday, which was very helpful. Then a few heavy squally showers blew across the riders late afternoon, giving them a good soaking. I've said before that none of the girls have any excess weight or fat to protect them so they tend to be quickly affected by the cold and wet when in racing kit. I know Ann was in tights and protective top before the evening rain set in. Lynne started to be sick going into the darkness. Mike and Neil were at a loss as to what to give her although she produced a fast 100, 4hrs 40mins, beating most of the men. She was now starting to lose a lot of time off the bike trying to get food inside her and keep dry and warm. Her 12hr wasn't too bad 225 miles but when in the early hours of the morning Liz and I went out to Prees, we found her off the bike in a lay-by having a massage and change of clothes. She had got very cold in the night and although the sun was breaking through in places, other areas of the road were cold and misty. Mike and Neil still don't know whether the sickness is from a chill or the feeding regime, so they revert back to Maxim every other drink and try rice pudding etc. When she gets back on the bike she rides very well, and there is no sign of any problem from her riding style, but Mike says she has already lost 2 hrs off the bike – at worst that's 30 miles. She seems to be quite cheerful now and moving well.

We saw Anne and Jim Turner checking numbers up towards Prees, and Jim says from his reckoning they would get Competition Team Record, and possibly win overall team from the Preston lads. The problem as I've said with circuits, is that there are always riders you miss and don't see for hours. It wasn't until we got onto the final circuit after watching Lynne claw back some distance, that we saw Marina riding very strongly. She had suffered with her back but had pulled through ok. We didn't see Tracey until almost the very end. She looked very determined. Somebody said she was winning the Ladies event, which didn't surprise me. We saw Ann quite often, well covered all during the event, in fact I don't recall seeing her in shorts at all. Claire rode a very strong ride, she always seemed cheerful and thankful for the encouragement.

The 24hrs were nearly up and everyone in the team would finish barring accidents of course. The final finishing circuits were awful as I say, the surface was rough and there were lots of hills that being a circuit you never got the equal benefit of going back down them; everyone said they hoped that next years event would be better routed to give more 'out and home' sections.

This was it; the final mile, Lynne finished in the lay-by on the A41, so relieved it was all over, there were tears in her eyes, she had suffered so much and she also knew she'd probably lost the 'First Lady' and no ninth consecutive win, but she was happy the team had broken comp record. Everyone went back to HQ.

The word was buzzing around that Tracey and Marina had beaten Lynne, but to be honest nobody knew who had done what, and it remained like that for over 2 hours.

Most people went home so that by the time of the prize presentation there were only a few officials and prize winners left to receive the awards. Remember a lot of people had been up all night and have up to 300 miles to drive home. One thing was certain – Gethin had won with 471 miles. Lynne had a bit of a 'ding dong' with him on the last circuit; Gethin saying it was a call of nature that slowed him down, allowing Lynne to get ahead, said with a twinkle in his eye! The girls, all five of them, had their photos taken in front of the result board, all were relieved and elated to have finished. **They had won overall team prize from Gethin's team, Preston Wheelers, by about 2 miles and broken the Ladies Team Competition Record with 1229.7 miles,** adding approximately 120 miles to a record previously held by Joan Kershaw, Ruth Williams and Amy Hooton since 1977 riding for the Prescot Eagles CC.

Lynne said she now felt ok, if a little sore in the throat and lungs area. I think this was as a result of being sick. Liz & I had come across her in a field gateway about an hour before the end heaving and retching, her whole body trembling from the effort. She said she had nothing left inside her and her throat was sore from the bile. An old friend of Lynne's from York, Frances and her partner and two dogs had driven over to see Lynne at the finish. She was so pleased they had done it. Frances had painted Lynne a lovely water colour of her on the finishing circuit last year and it captured the mood and surroundings beautifully.

**This years (2003) Mersey RC 24 hr Championship** event report, usually written by Frank Mumford, is now written by Bob Williams as Frank has now 'laid down his pen', after years at the task. I have picked some details from Bob's report that are relevant mainly to the ladies position in the event.

"At 17.41 hours (Sat pm) at the start of the Quina brook circuit, Gethin arrived first with Chris Hopkinson at 17.50. The first of the women riders was Marina Bloom No 32 at 18.06, Lynne No 51 at 18.21, Tracey No 62 at 18.24, Ann Wooldridge No 43 at 18.45, Claire Ashton No 9 at 18.28 and Gail Summerlin No 5 at 18.55. (Both Tracey and Gail having done only 3 laps of the starting circuit).

After very heavy rain at night fall, Lynne, who had a bad cold, was well down on previous performances at this point. At the Battlefield check the second time round, Lynne went through at 35 mins past midnight with Marina at 01.32 but Marina had done an extra lap of the Quina Brook circuit, 12.5 miles, five laps to Lynne's four. Gethin Butler was the only rider to cover 6 laps of the circuit. With all of the Walsall Road CC women still riding well, it looked like the Women's competition team record could be broken.

Gethin was going so fast he kept passing the main field. He was the only rider to be sent from Prees to Battlefield for a 5th time. The cold rain that had plagued the riders in the night had stopped sometime in the early hours and the dawn sun was weakly trying to shine.

The riders were meanwhile retracing back to the Quina Brook circuit at 7.00 am. The circuit is kept open long enough to allow the riders time to get from there to the finishing circuit at Handley. The five Walsall RCC Ladies were all still riding strongly as they passed Grindley Brook with the following times: Claire at 9.42 am, Lynne 9.52, Marina 10.17, Tracey 10.22 and Ann at 10.37. Gethin was still well in the lead but Neil Stewart, Richard Thoday and Chris Shepherd still had some speed in their legs.

At last the 24 hr Championship drew to a close, all the Walsall Road ladies did sterling rides. Marina, Lynne, and Tracey won the overall team prize from the men, **the first time in history that an all women team has beaten a male team in any National Championship. They improved the ladies Competition Team Record to 1,229.70 miles."**

Gethin won the event with 471.21 miles, Neil Stewart was 2nd with 456.64 and Richard Thoday, 3rd with 451.35, Chris Shepherd was 4th with 445.47. The ladies gained high overall positions in the field of 47 finishers. **Marina 10th with 413.255, Lynne 11th with 411.141 and Tracey 13th 405.305 miles. Ann 29th with 365.42** a personal best for her and **355.57 for Claire** another p.b. in **34th place.** Two more ladies completed the course that day, **Mary Corbett** on the back of a tandem behind Norman Harvey with **366.922 miles** and **Ursula Betterton** on the back of a tandem trike with Colin Knapp, **268.932 miles.**

A fortnight later **Marina won the ladies 12 hr Championship with 240.32 miles** on a very hard day.

On **7th September 2003** the Walsall Ladies Team 'invaded' South Wales to ride **The Welsh National 12 hour Championship.** Here are some of the remarks and comments from Edwin Hargraves who with his wife Shelagh, had organised this time trial championship. The text is taken from the result sheet of the event. He thanked the helpers, supporters and officials, also Jim and Anne Turner, for their help and recruitment of riders to make it a top class field.

"In July, after the Mersey 24 hr, Lynne Taylor announced to the world that the Walsall Road Ladies next major event was the Welsh 12 hour. Shortly after that the entries started to roll in and I knew we were in for a classic event, with many of the best long distance riders in the country coming to Wales to ride our event. As far as we know we have never had a ladies team riding our 12 hr. The Met Office predicted gales, rain, floods etc and we know that the course isn't the fastest in the country. Lynne was reported to have said that it wasn't worth getting out of bed unless she could do 250 miles. (no pressure there then !)

**Congratulations to Lynne on improving Welsh Ladies Competition record,** (previously held by Louise Jones with 245.240) and to **Marina and Tracey** in establishing a **Welsh Ladies Team Record.** The team's aim was to take the National Competition Record and it is said that they missed it by such a narrow margin." (1.87 miles)

Gethin won the men's event with 274.578 on a fairly hard day, with a very cold frosty start for the first 5 hours. **The Ladies Welsh Team Record** established was **725.746 miles.** The team comprised of **Lynne 248.967, Marina 242.035 and Tracey 234.762. Ann Wooldridge** put up a fine **221.603 miles** for **4th Lady** and 25th overall from a field of 57 finishers.

**Two weeks later on 21st September 2003, The National 100** took place, it had been postponed 4 months due to road works on the A50. The event was run for the CTT by **The Long Eaton Paragon.** Lynne likes this course because she can ride out to the start. **Ruth Dorrington won** the Women's Championship with a nail-biting finish from Lynne. Ruth's winning margin was just 5 seconds so **Gold for Ruth with 4hrs 11 mins 53 secs, Silver for Lynne with 4hrs 11 mins 58 secs, and Bronze for Marina** with an outstanding **4 hrs 12 mins 06 secs.** Marina was just 8 seconds away from silver and 13 seconds from Gold! What a close finish, I'm pretty sure that's the closest finish in history for a Ladies Championship 100.

**Ann Wooldridge** rode a fine race with **4 hrs 34 m 39 secs** giving the **Walsall Roads CC Ladies the team win of 12hrs 58 mins 43 secs.** What a cracking end to the year. Needless to say Kevin Dawson broke the course and championship record with 3 hrs 22 mins 45secs. I reckon at that sort of speed he could top 700 miles for a 24 hour!

After a very hard season, **The Walsall RCC Ladies** attained good **BBAR** results and positions. **Marina** came **3rd** with **24.94 mph average** and **Lynne 4th with 24.87 mph.** They also took **lst ladies BBAR team with Tracey** being the third counter.

On **4th October, Marina** partnered **Ralph Dadswell** on a **tandem trike** to establish a new **RRA mixed record** between **Birmingham and London (112 miles).** In spite of heavy traffic at both terminal cities they beat the RRA standard by over an hour to record **4hrs 57 mins 20 secs** for their journey. Only 11 minutes slower than the men's record held by Dave Pitt and Pete Stonebanks.

So ends a superb racing season for the long distance ladies of the Walsall Roads CC.

# 2004

I think it was felt that the season of 2003 would be a hard act to follow, but even knowing what tough rides all the girls had endured in the Mersey RC 24 hr, they still felt that there were a lot more miles that they could add to the record.

The season started as normal for Lynne in February, with the club events. Her first **100** was as usual the **Anfield** in May. This uses much the same roads as the 24 hr race. **Marina** was the **fastest lady** with **4 hrs 29 m 34 secs** with **Lynne** just 29 secs slower with **4 hrs 30 mins 03 secs.** Nik Gardiner won the event with 3-51-39 from Wayne Levet 3 hrs 55-13 secs.

The next **100** was the **Burton & District CA** held on a very cold and windy afernoon in June. Everyone suffered and so did their times, all except the winner, Kevin Dawson, with 3hrs 37 mins 25 secs. But he's not really human is he? He can't possibly feel pain I'm sure. The ladies times were **Tracey, fastest,** with **4 hrs 27 min, Lynne 4 hr 31 m 02 secs and Marina 4 hrs 31 mins 04 secs.** Astounding, just 2 seconds between Lynne and Marina but so good to see Tracey take the fastest time. I am sure that the '100' is one of her best disciplines. **Ann Wooldridge** also had a very good ride with **4hrs 37 mins** proving she is also a tough nut in hard conditions. **Claire** rode to a fine **5 hrs 20 mins 04 secs,** a good performance on that day. With just one more '100' to perform before the 24 hr race Lynne and Marina travelled to the Yorkshire C.F. event hoping to get a decent time for their BBAR results. Lynne just pipped Marina on the day with 4hrs 22mins 09secs to Marina's 4hrs 23mins 30 secs. So, over three totally separate 100 mile events in three different areas, its amazing, they are so evenly matched with Marina's total time being just 54 secs less than Lynne's.

I've used from here on, an extract from my own description of the Mersey 24 hr written the day after the event, entitled:

## A DAY OUT FOR THE LADIES:

The weather forecast had shown a high pressure with good weather in the south being pushed away by low pressure and windy wet weather from the north west and into Wales, so the most we could hope for was 'mixed' conditions. The event started off dry but greyish and overcast, a little bit cool if you were marshalling on a drafty island. In fact most of the marshals we saw were dressed in virtual winter clothing and even gloves, especially in the night.

The Walsall Roads CC had two teams in this year, comprising of Lynne, Marina, Tracey, Ann, Claire and Rob Meredith. All our riders got away okay, glad to be on the road at last. After early evening Rob was riding without helpers, relying on going past Prees where the café was open all night, and also where his car was parked, so he could help himself. We found Mike Johnson and Yvonne providing a wonderful service to the riders and helpers with food and hot drinks, filling flasks from a caravan just before the Hodnet by-pass and later, on the finishing circuit at Handley. His ribald quips to the riders keeping them amused, he's provided this service for quite a few years now, enabling more audax riders to ride without back up teams.

Lynne prior to the start had said she wanted to enjoy this one and give it her 'best shot'. She started No 65 and said she was worried she wouldn't catch anyone, being this far back, but her fears were allayed when she started riding through the field one by one. The course was a well-known, much used, Prees-Ternhill-Hodnet-Battlefield variation of roads, using the new Hodnet by-pass, and proved very popular with the riders and helpers alike, from what I gathered. The switch onto the Quina Brook circuit in the early evening relieved the boredom for a few hours. At the 100 mile point, after one lap of Quina Brook Lynne had just caught Marina for 13 mins and was 7th fastest overall on the road with 4-41-52.

Chris Hopkinson led the field with 4-18-31 from Andy Briggs 4-19-51, Jose Pinon 4-27-31, Nik Gardiner the favourite 4-31-31, 'Hoppy' had started very fast but like we always say 'see who's left at the finish'! Lynne was obviously feeling good, Neil Peart was looking after her. I joined him at 80 miles after being picked up at the shop in Cannock by Phil and Pauline St John, who follow all of Lynne's races and exploits as if she were one of their own family. They were both pleased to see her going so well, and stayed out until nearly nightfall.

Lynne had also caught Tracey off No 47 by the 100 mile point. Marina's 100 was 4-55, Tracey's 5-02, both girls still riding smoothly. Ann Wooldridge was next with 5-04 looking smooth and comfortable dressed in tights, ready to combat the cooling breeze.

Our next rider was Rob Meredith at 56 years of age with 5 hrs 20 mins, and then Claire Ashton another 18 minutes adrift and although she seemed cheerful, she knew she was not riding at her best. Rob was going totally into the unknown at this point having never time trialled above 50 miles before.

Another of the lady favourites riding, Kathryn Smith, who had ridden into bronze medal position in the championship 100 a week previously went through in 5 hrs 1 min 55 secs, so didn't appear to be a threat to Lynne at this point. I always think that while not wanting to burn yourself out in the first 100 of a 24 hr, you still need to be trying at 90-95% of your normal effort as this gives you a psychological boost if you produce a reasonable time. Lynne normally does 4hr 30m for the Anfield 100, so was not 'hanging about' with this performance.

Phil St John headed for home after wishing her well and hoping she could get a p.b. At this point in time I felt that the weather wasn't really good enough for a p.b. with a stiff breeze hassling the riders on the open stretches, and the threat of rain in the air. Lynne had experienced problems with feeding and had got very cold with the early rain on last years 24 hr. Her usual diet of carbo drink every hour with a small 'butty' in between hadn't worked very well resulting in sickness and lots of time off the bike, so this year she wasn't sure what to do.

She had reduced the strength of the carbo drinks and was taking quite a lot of water in between. We were also trying her out with rice pudding every other hour, but by midnight she was getting bouts of 'stitch' which was affecting her breathing and making her stomach uncomfortable again. We could tell something wasn't right as her average speed had dropped off quite drastically, from being nearly 20 mins inside evens at 100 to just on evens at 200 miles. We estimated her 12 hour mileage to be 235. Up to now she had been off the bike for about 10 mins and a p.b. looked unlikely, leaving well over 207 miles to get in the second 12 hours.

Marina was battling back at this point and we were now back on the original Prees-Ternhill-Hodnet-Battlefield section until the very early morning. It was difficult to tell who was still going in the mens field although I had seen Nik Gardiner, Jose Pinon Shaw and Chris Hopkinson, who Lynne had caught back on the road before the 12hr point.

He seemed to ride erratically, one minute 'storming' along in a massive gear, catching everyone, and then an hour later bodging along struggling to turn the big gears. Marina had caught Lynne, she was riding very strongly, her husband, Mike, was keeping her on a very strict feeding regime of rice pudding and water with the occasional drop of coffee. All we could do now was to stop Lynne losing too much of the advantage she had gained over Marina by the 120 mile point.

We were relieved to see Tracey and Ann still going very strongly, with looks of total determination on their faces. Claire, although having encouragement and help from Mari Guy, had packed around the 12 hour point but stayed out after having a sleep in the car, to see the rest of the event. I spotted Rob Meredith a couple of times battling on. I didn't know what sort of mileage he was up to but he seemed to be going at a steady 15-16 mph. Lynne was so pleased when we told her the team was still going and Rob was doing well.

Apparently he rode the whole event on 'Endura' liquid drink, but at the end he complained he still hadn't got completely rid of the 'spare tyre' round his waist, so I suggested maybe finish off the season with the local 12 hour on that course, and that should do it!

By dawn heavy squalls of rain were falling patchily on the course, the riders had now covered 270 miles plus, and were looking forward to perhaps a bit of warmth later?

Lynne had to have a change of clothes at Battlefield at about 6.00 am as her clothing was damp and her shorts rubbing her. She wanted to wake herself up after feeling dozy so she started back on the road with just shorts, top and arm warmers, with a chest protector to keep her stomach warm. She lost about 12 mins here but at least she was now a bit more comfortable.

Neil and myself were trying to work out what she could end up with, on a projected estimated mileage, if nothing else went wrong, like heavy rain or strong winds or more sickness. The most we could come up with was 435 miles. Lynne seemed pleased with that, saying as long as it wasn't as low as last year. They all progressed, at about 18 hrs into the ride to the Quina Brook circuit, where it made a change to be in the lanes again. The full course up to here was 366.4 miles and Lynne had done just over 350 miles with approx 5 hrs to go. It was now raining quite heavily. On high ground you could look up the 'Cheshire Gap' towards the Welsh hills shrouded in rain, and with westerly winds it was coming our way.

Liz had come out in the car, bringing the traditional bacon, sausage and lettuce sandwiches with a drop of sauce. They went down well, although I had to finish them off at work on the Monday. Liz took over the driving of the van from me so I could have a snooze in the car before the 'grand finale'. I dozed off just after Lynne went through with one lap to go. I programmed myself to have about 40 minutes. The rain was bouncing off the bonnet and I pitied the poor riders on the main road going up to the Prees bypass hill, getting a double soaking from the spray off the passing vehicles. I awoke with a start and looked at the car clock. It was still raining heavily and the clock said 9.45. I looked back up the road to the Prees bypass hill and not a rider in sight. I stood in the rain for a while, which was quite cold, the trees were shedding bits of twigs and leaves, and I thought its going to be a hard ride up to the finishing circuit. I waited 5 minutes, no riders, not much traffic – had I slept 12 hours and was it 9.45 at night? I told myself 'no' somebody would have missed me by now wouldn't they? and anyway it would be nearly dark.

I got back in the car and drove fairly fast up to Prees Island knowing that the Quina Brook circuit closed at 10.30 am. There were no helpers on the roadside: At Prees there were a few marshals and regulars packing up to move on. I got to the Wem road junction and saw riders going straight on towards the finishing circuit, the numbers varied from 7 to 70. Where could Lynne possibly be. I motored on past lots of riders, some going well, some obviously in distress with bad backs or sore backsides, or both, most riding with that 'fixed' stare. I eventually passed Marina in a bright orange race cape around Broxton, which meant either Lynne had packed or was a long way ahead. I joined the circuit at Handley and went round backwards, the opposite direction to the riders.

I found a nice spot to stop in, well off the road and waited. First came Ann, then Tracey, what a relief, they were still going. After what seemed an age, Lynne came flying through. It appears that she was within a minute of Marina, going into the Quina Brook circuit. Marina went round one more time, the circuit closed early and Lynne got sent straight on to the finishing circuit. At the end of Lynne's first circuit of 13.252 miles Marina had just entered at timekeeper No 1 within sight of Lynne. This put Lynne ahead by about 6 miles. By this stage Marina was suffering with a bad back, having to lift herself off the saddle periodically and arch her back to relieve it. I hadn't realised that she had come off her bike after hitting a slippery drain cover by Prees. This is what had probably affected her back. I motored the opposite way round again to almost the same spot as before, and had a quick chat with Liz and Neil. Neil looking very positive at this point, reckoning Lynne should be on to a p.b. To me it didn't seem possible with the wind and rain they were having, on the slow winding narrow wet gritty muddy circuit. Most of the riders were having to freewheel and brake gently on all the bends and junctions.

427

With nearly two hours to go, Lynne had got 34 miles to do to equal her previous best of 441 miles. Again Ann and Tracey came through still with that determined look on their faces, hardly acknowledging my shouts of encouragement. Rob Meredith came past looking tired but still pedalling steadily on. Lynne was now only taking water and sponges to wipe the mud and grit off. I worked it out that at her present speed she would probably run out of time just before Handley at Timekeeper No 1. Neil had obviously convinced her she could get a p.b. by keeping this current speed up, which she duly did, to run out with 443.99 miles.

I saw Marina as her time was running out on the main A41 looking very tired. It was impossible to know who had won the men's and what teams were still in the race, **but one thing I was sure of, the girls had broken comp record again, and that alone is fantastic.** I didn't know at the time whether Tracey had beaten Ann, but I knew they had both done good rides, as had Marina, Lynne and Rob.

It was such a reward for me to see them all victorious in their own ways, knowing the euphoria that follows a successful 24 hr. Lynne apparently was lapping in virtually the same time as Nik Gardiner, mind you, she should do, she knows that circuit like the back of her hand now.

Now comes the clearing up and the presentations back at the Headquarters at Churton. The event was absolutely faultlessly run, the Organisers and Officials once again doing a marvellous job, from the marshals who patiently waited for hours on windy corners in the middle of the night, Mike Johnson and Yvonne with the support caravan and all the timekeepers and recorders, they all put in 110% effort.

It was a wonderful weekend for the Walsall Roads CC. I thought the arrangement of the course made it very safe and other than the odd rider, the standard of riding was very good, very safe and sensible. The lighting front and rear for virtually everybody was the best I've ever seen. To get 61 finishers out of a field of 80 is a real credit to Doug Clark and the team. On reflection afterwards, **Tracey** had pushed herself so hard to get a p.b. **416.5 and 13th place,** also a comp team record place, she lay huddled in a sleeping bag on the floor so as not to miss the awards.

**Marina,** likewise, had suffered so much in the last six hours to get **8th** place with a new p.b. and Comp record team place with **435.65,** pushing and battling with Lynne to force **Lynne** into **6th** overall (beating Chris Hopkinson) plus comp record team again with a new pb of **443.99** which is I think the fourth biggest mileage after Christine Roberts Comp Record of 461.65 in 1993. **All three Walsall RCC girls also beat the men's teams once again to take Championship 24 hr team medals and a new ladies competition team record of 1,295.87 miles.** This added 66.17 miles onto their 2003 record.

**Ann Wooldridge** took **25th** place out of 61 finishing with **388.43 miles.** This mileage alone would have got a new comp team record if either Lynne, Marina or Tracey had failed to finish. For Rob, I have every praise doing his own thing. I should think he's thoroughly pleased with himself, producing a ride of 387 miles and realising an ambition that most cyclists couldn't aspire to.

Despite the ladies breaking the Team Competition Record and beating the men's 24hr teams for the last two years running, very little was ever printed, just the bare results as I recall by 'Cycling' magazine, but then perhaps someone had been cheating in the Tour de France again! My main 'beef' with this pathetic lack of publicity is that in any other endurance sport or open championship, the fact that the women's team had beaten the men's team and won, would have made headlines in most newspapers sports pages, as well as national press dailies and TV media, let alone the magazine that covers that particular sport. To do it two years running and get nothing more that a line or two of results in 'Cycling' beggars belief.

⟹•◆•⟸

Two weeks later **The Ladies Team** consisting of **Marina, Tracey and Lynne** rode the 'ECCA' (Eastern Counties Cycling Association) 12 hour. The aim was to attack and try to improve the National Ladies 12 hr Team Competition Record of **727.33 miles** held by the Coalville Wheelers since 1997. That team consisted of Liz Milne, Kathy Platts and Celia Foskett.

The ECCA course was based on 4 circuits linked by the A11, taking in the outskirts of Newmarket, 'Fourwent Ways', 'Six Mile Bottom', Stetchworth, Sawston, Royston, Duxford, Fowlmere to finish on a circuit in the Little Chesterton - Sawston area.

The course had good potential as Kevin Dawson had produced course and event record in 2003 with 296.957 miles. I do wish he would try a 24 hr! Come on Jim, work your persuasions on him. The girls gave the chaps a good run for their money and many of them must have thought 'how on earth do we beat them'? **Lynne** took **7th** place overall with a p.b. of **251.51 miles.** **Marina** was **9th** with **247.224** and **Tracey 12th** with **244.742** which gave them the **Ladies Team Competition Record by 16 miles with 743.476 miles.**

Nick Bowdler, Farnborough and Camberley Wheelers won the event with 274.087 miles.

The season was nearly at a close but Lynne and Tracey were still in need of a slightly better 100 mile time for the BBAR but it was a very windy day on the exposed Cleveland course in late August. Lynne finished with 4 hrs 23 mins 25 secs, and Tracey 4 hrs 23 mins 35 secs. Another close result – just 10 seconds between them. Dawson won the event with another incredible 3 hrs 35 mins 58 secs.

In between these 100 mile BBAR qualifying events, the ladies were still trying to improve their 25 and 50 mile times in an effort to increase their speed in a competition which is biased towards shorter distances, so relying on purely float mornings, aerodynamics i.e. head down with aero helmet on or downhill and dragstrip courses. I'm sure there are better ways of proving that you're the best, not just at the shorter distances but also events that require endurance. As mentioned before if a 12hr could be included then riders could do more qualifying rides on their local roads and still be in with a chance of a BBAR position without all the car travel chasing fast courses (carbon footprint). This is only my own opinion of course and as a historian of long distance cycle racing, maybe I'm a tad biased.

**Carol Westmorland,** Border City Wheelers, **won the 12hr Championship in 2004 with 243.19 miles.** She is another tough rider who Lynne and Marina have to consider when she's riding the same events as they are, as 1st place is usually fought out between these three.

# 2005

*On 8th February 2005 Ellen MacArthur completed her single-handed circumnavigation of the world in the record time of 71 days 14 hours 18 mins. This hadn't been a race against other competitors as in the Vendees globe race of 2001, it was a lone attempt against the clock and the worst elements that the worlds oceans could throw at her.*

*I watched her video camera transmissions over the Christmas Holiday on TV in the comfort of a warm house while she was battling huge seas in a hostile ocean. There were very touching times during those transmissions especially when the weather had taken a turn for the worse and was battering her flimsy boat, or when she was becalmed in the 'doldrums' and losing whole days at a time. There were also problems when her nautical equipment failed her and left her in despair. She spoke truthfully and openly about her innermost fears and loneliness and I could relate to some of those feelings, not so much for myself, but for Lynne on her two solo End to Ends and 1000 mile records.*

I know it's a totally different sport and on a massively different timescale, and yes Lynne had got a following car and people to see on route, but on the start line outside the Lands End Hotel, before dawn, with nothing but darkness, the lapping of the waves below the cliffs, the mournful cry of the seagull and the thought of keeping body and soul together whilst giving a maximum output on your own for up to two and a half days, it must seem just as daunting a task.

I compare Lynne getting beyond Penzance and onto the wide dual carriageway with 990 miles to go, with Ellen MacArthur just losing sight of England over the horizon, with the world's oceans to conquer. The rebuffs from the weather, the times when behind schedule (for Lynne it was hours, for Ellen it was days). The doubts and despondency that Ellen had, luckily Lynne didn't have, and it was us, her helpers and followers including myself who couldn't see how she could possibly carry on in such poor conditions on both occasions. We despaired for her.

The lump in my throat and tears of jubilation I experienced when Lynne broke her records against all odds, were also evident when I stood on the headland at Falmouth Harbour with Liz and our friends Pauline and Martin in 2005 and watched that fragile catamaran drift into harbour with Ellen MacArthur jumping up and down on the deck and waving to the crowds as she completed her mission.

The main difference being that Lynne had just a Timekeeper and Observer to see her over the finishing line at John O'Groats as opposed to heavy cannons firing a salute as the yachtswoman passed the end of the harbour amidst tug boats spraying their jets of water high into the air. Of course there was also the thousands of people lining the docksides to welcome her home, not to mention the millions watching on TV around the world. In comparison Lynne's records seem to have been broken amidst an air of secrecy and subterfuge.

---

The first decent test to see how the form is progressing for the 24hr is the classic **Anfield 100** on the May bank holiday weekend. **Lynne** was the fastest lady from **Marina** by 9 minutes. **Lynne 4hrs 31 mins 52 secs** and **Marina 4 hrs 41 mins 14 secs.** Louise Schuller, Finsbury Park CC making a long trip north was the 3rd fastest lady with 4 hrs 46 mins 43 secs. A good ride on a hard course. Malcolm Cox won the event with 3 hrs 54 mins 13 secs and Neil Peart, Walsall Roads CC was the fastest on a fixed wheel with 3 hrs 59 mins 22 secs. All very good rides on a very undulating, multi-directional course.

On a sad note, the rider 4 minutes slower than Marina, 60 year old Maurice Broadbent of the Rhyll CC with 4 hrs 45 mins 23 secs, was riding in what was to be his last 'Anfield 100'. (Four members of the Rhyll CC were tragically run down and killed, by a car, in early January 2006. Maurice was one of them.)

Three weeks later on a very hard day, **The Burton and District CA 100 mile event** saw **Carol Gandy** take the **lst lady** prize with **4 hrs 21 mins 28 secs, Tracey Maund** was 2nd with **4hrs 24mins 06secs. Lynne was 3rd, 4hrs 25 mins 16 secs and Marina** close **4th, 4 hrs 26 mins 05 secs.** Just two minutes separated the results of the Walsall Roads ladies. I say it was a hard day because 67 riders failed to finish on this tough open, exposed, dual carriageway course. Out of 48 hardy heroines and heroes who finished only 7 riders beat 4 hours. Marc Wolstenholm won the event with 3 hrs 53 mins 58 secs.

The next testing ride before the 24 hr was the **National Championship 100** run by the Westerley RC. Marina was the fastest Walsall Ladies rider coming **4th** with **4 hrs 33 mins 58 secs. Lynne 5th** with **4 hrs 37 mins 23 secs** and **Tracey Maund 7th** with **4 hrs 38 mins 55 secs. Ruth Eyles,** Beacon RC won the Championship with **4 hrs 20 mins 13 secs,** from **Carol Gandy 4hrs 26 mins 10 secs. 3rd** was **Michelle Ayres 4 hrs 30 mins 48 secs.**

Lynne thought it was a hard course and day, harder than the Anfield. I think it bears out what she says when you consider only seven male riders beat 4 hrs, with Michael Hutchinson the winner 3hrs 36 mins 38 secs, 2nd Zak Carr at 10 mins with 3 hrs 46 mins 40 secs and 3rd Kevin Dawson 3 hrs 47mins 57 mins.

Zak Carr became another rider who tragically lost his life, killed by a speeding motorist. Zak was a top competitor at all distances up to 12 hours and was a talented tandem rider, breaking competition records on a tandem for 10, 25, 30, 50 & 100 miles & 12 hours. All records are still standing to this day. I know he had plans to ride a 24 hr but sadly I shall not be able to write of his exploits.

**The Walsall RCC Ladies won the Championship Team Race for the 2nd time with 13 hrs 50 mins 16 secs.**

---

Six days later on **23rd July 2005, the Mersey RC Championship 24 hr** took place. This year there was a new night circuit due to the opening of the Hodnet bypass. Its distance was almost 40 miles, taking in Espley Island on the Hodnet bypass to Prees, via Tern Hill and retrace back through Espley Island to turn at Shawbirch Island. The night 'comfort' stop is on this circuit at Espley where riders can get hot drinks and food, helpers can top their flasks up and chat with the crowd that gathers there to see how the race is unfolding around the 12 hour point.

Mike Johnson and Yvonne Crane have been running this mobile unit for quite a few years now, having taken over the job from Harold Nelson 'B.E.M.'. Nik Gardiner was the only rider beating 'evens' well into the night.

It had been a bright sunny day for the start, but the evening turned cool, with a beautiful sunset. Marina was taking 2 hrs 15 mins for the circuit but Lynne was definitely off colour with a bad cold. There is no chance of her packing, having based her whole season around this event, she normally enjoys it so much.

The tandem trike crewed by Ralph Dadswell and Dave Johnson put up the 6th fastest 100 with 4 hrs 25 mins 58 secs. Dead-heating at the 100 mile mark were Nik Gardiner and Keith Coffey, riding his first 24 hr with 4hrs 18 mins 18 secs.

Marina, 4hrs 44m 21s, Lynne 4hrs 47 m 55s, Ann Wooldridge, 5hr 12m 58s, Ann Bath, 6hr 01m 03 secs and Janet Tebbutt, 6hr 22m 02 secs.

The dark chilly night drew on, there were some reports of showers, quite heavy ones in the Ternhill area and by midnight, Lynne's cold was holding her back to be just over 30 mins slower than Marina. Eventually the night passed, without incident, and the riders moved on to the Quina Brook circuit around 6am, some doing 5 laps or more. The circuit starts by turning left off the Whitchurch bypass and onto the Wem road. It's a winding, rural, hedge-lined road with a few rough patches, going through Tilstock Village, and continuing to Quina Brook which is just a collection of houses and cottages. The old pub 'The Harp' is still there but is now a private dwelling. It used to be a main feeding station in years gone by. I can still see those bowls of trifle and rice pudding even now. (only dreaming) After turning left at Quina Brook the road drops quite sharply and is interrupted by a few tight bends just to make you concentrate. It eventually links back up with the main road just before Prees village bypass where the course goes left along the A49 on a new road over the village. Needless to say, it's a hill and eventually it brings you back to the Prees café stop and 'The Raven' to join the Whitchurch bypass. The full circuit is 12.261 miles and provides a safe haven where the riders can gather their senses before returning to the busier main roads.

Steve Abraham, a prolific Audax rider who generally rides a fixed wheel bike and is now producing some very good results in the 24hr as others do in the spirit of Audaxing, without mobile help, carrying all of his own provisions, lights, drinks, clothing etc. In his usual 'write up' or article he produces most years for the Fellowship Journal, he says *"Marina, who started 15 mins behind me was looking very strong, but I seemed to be holding her off. The next one I wanted to check upon was women's End to End Record Holder, Lynne Taylor. She is very easy to spot because of her riding style. There are lots of very good riders in the Mersey RC 24 hr, they look as if they are gliding along, but Lynne looks as if she's floating on air, as if by magic. I was just starting to wonder if I'd missed her when there she was, but something was different this year. She was floating along, but not quite as fast as usual. Something I couldn't put my finger on, something not quite right there!"*

The riders were kept longer than usual on the Quina Brook circuit due to a heavy 'wide load' using the main Chester road to the finishing circuit. At least the riders had a helpful push from a south-westerly breeze to the finish area. Dougie Clarke had really excelled himself on this his last promotion of the event. He'd had to overcome road works and alter the starting point. The first part of the event had to be detoured through the lanes, then there was the wide load, and to cap it all, the finishing circuit also had to be changed due to last minute road works - so well done Doug!

**Marina had a well deserved win for the ladies with 447.334 miles** and 6th position overall. **Lynne** struggled but finished with **412.807** so securing a team win for the 3rd year running, but this time with Rob Meredith improving to **396.379** miles in this, only his second 24 hr. It was another **Championship Team win** for the Walsall Roads.

**Ann Wooldridge** was the **3rd lady** with **394.549** just missing a team place, but producing a fine personal best for her in her 3rd try at the distance. **Ann Bath** Kingston Phoenix RC riding her 1st 24 hour at 56 years of age, finished very pleased with herself and so she should be, with **342.767 miles. Janet Tebbutt** at 69 years of age rode steadily throughout to record **311.336 miles.** 'Dogged determination' is the trade mark for this former amateur End to End and 1000 mile record breaker from the mid 1970's.

Forty seven solo's finished, plus a record breaking tandem trike ride of 466.723 miles from Ralph Dadswell and Dave Johnson. Dean Peach, a friend of Lynne's from the Walsall RCC finished with 327.083 miles. Lynne had inspired him to ride the End to End for charity earlier in the year and she then talked him into using his fitness to ride the 24 hr !

Nik Gardiner won again in fine style, getting closer each year to the magic 500 miles with 493.081 miles. Keith Coffey, 2nd with 475.897 miles. Its good to see new riders getting into long distance racing. 3rd was Neil Skellern, Congleton CC, a regular and a team mate of Karl Austin's with 453.828. Graham Barker, Rockingham CC was a fine 4th, just 1 mile slower with 452.749, helped by Margaret Allen, the 25, 50 & 100 mile champion in the late 80's.

Here is an article written by Ann Bath, who only started riding a bike at 42 years of age. She rode in her first 12 hr race at 54 and now her first 24 hr at 56, demonstrating that its never too late for women to enjoy the thrill of cycle racing! She hopes with this article to persuade more people to participate.

*My first 24 hour: many asked why? The idea started when I found out that no woman in my club's 68 year history had ever done one. I'd only been doing time trialling for 6 years – but I'm up for a challenge. I joined the 24 hour fellowship and enjoyed reading their back journals they sent. But I started getting nervous when I read another woman's first attempt – she had nine helpers, I was only planning on having one! I really only started serious long distance mileages from May and averaged about 250-300 miles weekly including one ride of well over 100. I started riding out and back to time trials, although 34 miles before a '50' didn't do much for my time! My longest ride was home to Lyme Regis on my road bike which is set up identically to my racing bike. I had panniers holding all my food and drink and spare clothes. It was 163 miles and I left at 4 am, practising using my new Enduro lights. I'd forgotten there was a 15%, mile long hill at 160 miles which was certainly character building.*

*Then the day dawned nearer; my partner and I booked into a Good Beer Guide Pub at the HQ at Farndon 2 nights before. We checked out Lynn's café at Prees Island. I had already decided that my one treat during the 24 hours was to have one shortish midnight café stop. We also planned where the car would be left for the majority of the race, parked at Prees Island. It is an estate and Steve would sleep in it while I did the night 39 mile circuits, otherwise he was going to be too sleepy to drive us home to Surrey on the Sunday evening. I would carry a phone for emergencies and a spare car key, so I could get into the car when he was having a curry or enjoying some local real ale.*

*On the Friday I prepared the food and drink and filled up several chill-boxes – in retrospect I made far too much! Friday evening we had a short walk across a river into Wales and I had a huge pasta meal and 2 puddings. I slept very well both nights. I was off at 1.10pm on Saturday, so it was a relief to get on the bike again, and I was very excited. I was just determined to finish, but how many miles should I try to expect to do? My secret aim was to try and do 368 miles and get a National Age Record, but I was pretty sure this would be out of my reach on my first attempt, as it would be a steep learning curve. I used my lightweight steel Roberts bike, but no tri-bars, and we had put a mud-guard on the back as rain was forecast. The weather was quite cool, but it was very pleasant after the heatwave 6 days before in the National 100, where I got awful cramps at mile 97. I carried a Camel-Back\* and had a goodie bag that sits on the top tube, filled with various snacks including small savoury sandwiches. The time seemed to go quickly and the marshals and spectators were very encouraging. I stopped at the car to pick up more supplies, then it was off onto the shorter 12 mile Quina Brook circuit. I really liked this circuit as you couldn't get bored, and then after a few circuits it was back to the car to put on my night jacket, change Camel-Backs and off on the 39 mile circuit again.*

*There were feed stations at Prees and then 10 miles down the road at Hodnet so you were never more than 20 miles from food and drink. It got darker and I enjoyed seeing the sunset, I have always enjoyed cycling at night for some strange reason, so was actually looking forward to the night cycling. The marshals continued being so encouraging and cheerful, it seemed amazing to have so many out there all night. Then it was pitch dark – some of the roads didn't even have a white line on the left hand side, but my lights were amazing, and I also wore a light-weight head lamp, which was very useful as I could see my speedo, distance covered and heart rate monitor.It was great seeing other riders on the road and their helpers parked in lay-bys. My jacket was not quite warm enough and there was some rain, but I didn't end up changing it. As you approached Prees Island at the end of each circuit the lights got brighter and brighter and then you were there, with all the people cheering you on – it was amazing. They were even shouting 'come on Ann' or 'come on Phoenix' even when my club jersey was covered up by my night jacket.*

Back to the car and this time Steve wasn't there – he was in the pub as planned and then having a curry.  So I stocked up on more food and drink and off again.  Then after 11 and a half hours it was decision time – stop now for my midnight café stop, or go on another 39 mile circuit.  Decided to stop – wonderful crumble and custard and a coffee, but in retrospect I lost 35 minutes and also if I'd stopped later my 12 hour time would have been more than 186 miles.  Steve then slept in the car again.  Then suddenly I realised dawn was approaching and that was great  - but for the first time I felt very slightly sleepy, and made good use of the Hodnet feed to have a coffee and banana which did the trick.  I had not long just passed someone having a sleep at the roadside.  At Hodnet they were encouraging a sleepy tricyclist to get out of a chair and back on his bike! I just couldn't give the race less than 100% as the marshals were just so encouraging; I felt like a superstar all day and night! Lots of the top riders were giving encouragement and Lynne Taylor said 'come on Ann' and I was really chuffed!  Keith Coffey kept giving encouragement when he passed – he was our club guest speaker at our Awards evening in February and when he heard I was doing a 24 he said he may too – he did incredibly well to be second in his first attempt.

I'd decided to have my usual cereal at around 7 am, and changed my shorts but kept long thin leggings on.  Steve said I did seem to have a bit of a low patch during the night and seemed to spend too long choosing what to take with me, but strangely I didn't really notice it, as I had started getting rather a sore behind, as expected, and it was foremost in my mind.  Then it was off back to the 12 mile Quina Brook circuit, and Steve said I seemed to pick up after breakfast – it was as if I'd started a new day of cycling, most strange!  I felt really good on these circuits and was managing nearly 16 mph.  I realised I'd had far too much time off the bike to get anywhere near 368, but the main thing was that I was so enjoying the experience and the whole atmosphere of the event.

Amazingly, maybe due to spinning light gears as much as possible, my legs didn't feel too bad, and I didn't have any back-ache.  Getting cramp in the 100 taught me a huge lesson about not pushing heavy gears.  But at about 21 hours I started to get a very painful left hand, and found it difficult to keep it on the tops.  Still considering I didn't have any other major problems I felt I'd been pretty lucky in my first attempt.  I seemed to keep going round the Quina Brook circuit; what I didn't realise until later was that we had to wait for a huge slow load to go before going to the finishing circuit.  Then off we were sent – and I knew the finish was in sight!  We seemed to have a lovely tail wind to the finishing circuit, just what was needed as a final morale-booster.  The organisers were amazing, as first the start had to be moved due to road works, then they had the slow load to contend with, and then the finishing circuit had to be changed to a shorter one at the very last minute.

It was a bit hilly with quite narrow roads in places, but just the thing to keep you on your guard, and I found concentrating on the twists and turns made the time go quickly.  I couldn't believe that I felt better and stronger than on the finishing circuit of a '12'.  The support and cheers were fantastic - but at one hour to go I'd run out of food and drink and didn't have an emergency gel, but in the end couldn't be bothered to stop.  Then my time was up, and there was Steve who had miraculously worked out which time-keeper I'd stop at!  I was over the moon, and it confirmed what many had said – that it is the best event on the time trial calendar.  I just felt privileged to be part of it, and indebted to all the marshals and others whose encouragement helped me achieve what I did.  Back to the headquarters and confirmed so quickly that I'd done 342 miles. Later I studied my heart rate graph and splits and realised I'd had over two hours off the bike – much more than I'd planned: I was very surprised how the minutes here and there added up.  So next year will be very different, probably much harder !

It was my turn to sleep in the back of the car going home, out like a light for about 5 hours.  Home at 9 pm and then slept well again and off to work Monday with a big smile on my face.  The buzz and feeling of achievement stayed with me for at least 2 weeks.  After a few days off the bike and eating loads, the following weekend we went on a 180 mile 3 day tour, carrying tent and sleeping gear, so I was delighted at my fast recovery.  Putting in the extra miles in preparation just made me realise how much I love all aspects of cycling – whether its leisure cycling, touring, racing, even just cycling to work or the shops.
I really would recommend anyone having a go at the 24 hour as it really is such an amazing event.  For the modest entry cost, you are so well supported with food and drink, if you want it, free food at Lynn's all night café, the priceless cheers and smiles all night long, and to cap it all, a medal and 24 hour Mersey embossed individual photo.

So roll on next year, when I really will try and do over 368 miles !
Ann Bath – Kingston Phoenix Club

*\* Camel-Back is a 2 or 3 litre bag containing a drink. It is held on ones back with shoulder straps. The liquid is delivered to the mouth by a thin pipe from the bag, with a non return valve in the mouthpiece. This method of hydration has evolved from the Mountain Bike scene.*

⟫·◇·⟪

Three weeks later, on a cold wet and windy day, on an exposed, tough, meandering North Midlands course, the ladies, **Marina, Lynne and Ann Wooldridge** rode the **Championship 12 hour** run by the NMCF (North Midlands Cycling Federation). Michael Hutchinson won the event with 285.7 miles, Nik Gardiner 2nd 276.91. **Marina** was the **fastest lady 244.94** from **Lynne** with **242.13** and **Carol Westmorland** was **3rd** with **241.99.** As mentioned earlier in the book these three ladies are so evenly matched with just 3 miles difference covering their performances. They took 14th, 15th and 16th places out of a field of 47 finishers. **Ann Wooldridge** was the **4th** placed lady with **220.88 miles.** A very good ride on a hard day, although it actually brightened up towards late afternoon. **Sue Elsdon** and **Debora Hailes finished** with **211.95** and **210.44** respectively.

At the end of the season **Lynne** travelled over 250 miles by car to Port Talbot to record **59.03 mins** for a personal best **25 mile** performance which took her to **4th place** in the **Womens BBAR. Tracey Maund** took **5th place,** just 0.32 mph slower and with **Marina's** high placing they took the **BBAR Team Win** for the **2nd year running** - so ending another jam packed season with the 24 hr as one of their main goals.

# 2006

This year was to be a tough one for the ladies of the Walsall RCC with Tracey Maund and Ann Wooldridge not too keen on the long distances any more. Lynne was finding racing and training very difficult compared with other years due to helping her brother Mike (my son) to move the family cycle business from an old Victorian shop to a brand new purpose built 6,000ft retail store. Lynne like all of us was working up to 14 hours a day for 6 days a week from March until the opening of the new store in June. The work took its toll with excessive heat being another factor and she rode only 25 races in the whole of 2006, compared with 42 in 2005.

The upside of 85 degrees heat is that Lynne generally fares better than most people in it. Again she tries to spend as much time as possible in hot conditions outdoors, especially on a bike, so that if the weather on the day of an event is very hot, she has got an advantage over others.

**The Anfield 100** at the end of May was actually quite cold. Nik Gardiner won the event from Hywel Davis with 3hrs 54m 31secs to 4hr 00m 26s. Nik's ride was the only sub-four hour one which shows the tougher conditions. **Lynne** was the **1st lady** with **4hr 37m 49 secs. Marina was 2nd lady** at 7 mins with **4h 44m 25 secs** and **Kathryn Smith,** Nottingham Clarion was **3rd,** just inside evens with **4h 58m 50 secs.**

A month later the **Burton and District CA 100** turned out to be a very good day. **Lynne** recorded **4hr 7m 06 secs,** and at the end said she felt very good and very strong. She came 33rd overall out of 75 finishers. Ruth Dorrington turned in a time of **4hr 11m 06secs** and **Marina** was **3rd** Lady with **4hr 21 m 20 secs.** It was a good start to the year for all of them.

The event was won with another very fast time of 3h 33m 12secs by Michael Broadwith from Ian Cammish and 27 riders beat 4 hrs. Neil Peart came 4th to be Walsall RCC's fastest rider with 3h 41m 24 secs, which helped him towards his eventual 5th place in the 'BBAR'.

⟫·◇·⟪

Another month later on the 22nd July, **The Mersey RC 24 Hr** got on its way under the guidance of Jon Williams, his first time as Organiser, having performed all the various other duties in the event for over 25 years. Lynne wasn't too sure how she would perform, having had very little rest from work. Her only training was riding to and from the shop usually at unearthly hours, but she was still keen to do battle.

When the day came, the Walsall Ladies were a depleted team, Ann and Tracey found they'd had enough of focusing on the long distance scene. It is a hard, dedicated life to keep returning year after year, as Marina and Lynne have done. Rob Meredith was again to be a key member of the team and proved himself worthy, beyond his wildest dreams, with 425.757 miles. This year he had a lot of help from his wife Suzie, which I think makes a heck of a difference even though the feeding stations are superb in their location etc, there's nothing like having somebody looking after you every hour, saying 'come on, I haven't come all this way for you to pack in now'!

This years event attracted a field of 70 solo riders, 2 tandems and 1 tandem trike, of whom 57 solo's finished including **7 teams** which I am pretty sure is a **record for this event,** and possibly equals the record for **any** 24 hr event. The weather if my memory serves me correctly was hot throughout with some heavy stormy showers on the Saturday, petering out to give a very hot Sunday.

Carol Westmorland, Border City Wheelers CC was entered this year. It was her debut at 24 hr riding and she wanted to experience just one before she got married in late August. Lynne and Marina had fought many battles with her in time trials especially 100's and 12hrs in the past few years and knew she was very capable of winning.

At the 12 hour check, there was absolutely nothing between Lynne and Carol. Lynne was actually 0.1 of a mile up with 232.209 miles but with the compaction of the course which helps with the grouping of the riders, it's very difficult to tell on a circuit as to the positions of certain riders as there is always the chance that they may have missed a circuit. At the 12 hr point Marina was over 2 miles down on Lynne but was still riding very strongly despite a niggling back pain.

Just after dawn, the riders went on to the Quina Brook circuit and stayed on there until mid morning before heading north to the finishing circuit. I was again helping with Liz, Lynne's mother, so that Neil Peart could have some 'shut-eye' as he'd helped Lynne non-stop since leaving home before the start of the event.

We had a little 'cut through' lane on the circuit where we could detour through to the main road at the end of Prees Village, and could then see the riders again as they came along the main road. At one point I noted Carol's passing time was slower than Lynne's and I though perhaps Lynne had decided to push on to take the lead but this was just a blip, probably caused by Carol stopping for natural causes. I had also thought that maybe Carol was tiring, after all , this was her first 24 hr race, but no, by late morning Lynne had slowed slightly and Carol had started to pull away.

Marina had struggled through the 'early hours' and into the morning, she just wanted to finish, knowing she had only a few hours left to suffer with maybe another championship winning team place. Lynne tried her hardest to respond to our shouts of encouragement, but I could tell she hadn't got enough speed left to hold Carol who was steadily gaining on her. Meanwhile Rob Meredith was having the ride of his life, ploughing along, gnawing at the miles left to do. I thought that he was probably a circuit down on the girls and didn't realise until the results came through that he'd been ahead of Marina from about 18 hours.

The finishing circuit was reached after a long slog up the main road. Once there, a fine battle ensued, with **Carol Westmorland** catching Lynne while she was stopped for a call of nature. Carol then pulled away to a convincing lead and went on to be a worthy winner of the ladies event with **445.412 miles** with **Lynne** so pleased just to finish with **434.412 miles.** **Marina** gamely battled on to take **3rd** placed lady with **416.449.** **Rob Meredith** was over the moon to be 2nd counter in the Walsall Road CC team with **425.757 miles.** The team came 3rd behind the Congleton CC and winners Cardiff Byways CC with 1311.023 miles.

Three more ladies finished this 24 hr long battle against tiredness and heat. **Chrystal Sheldon** of the Kingston Phoenix on her 1st 24hr with **339.111** miles and **Ann Bath** with **335.468** miles on her 2nd ride to try and improve her club record. **Janet Tebbutt** riding for the Cavalier CC at 70 years of age finished with **313.459 miles.** Another superb 24hr ride for her.

Nik Gardiner, Johns Bikes, won the event and joined the elite '500' mile club at last with 504.023 miles. At the 'CTT' BBAR presentation in January 2007, Nik said 'beating 500 miles had been his lifelong ambition' and that 'he really enjoyed those extra 4 miles'! Neil Skellern, Congleton CC rode strongly for 2nd place with 477.653 miles and Nick Cave, Leicester Forest CC was 3rd with 472.429 making his debut.

———⇒◇◁⇐———

Three weeks later, **Lynne** battled her way around a very windy **West Cheshire 12** hour, again becoming **1st lady** once more with **232.80 miles.** She was hoping to wind her season up with a ride over 240 miles, but again tiredness took its toll. Only one other lady finished, Sarah Corbett with 180.17 miles. Neil Skellern rounded off a fine season with 269.12 miles beating Rod Brooks by .5 of a mile.

Lynne was still determined to stay in the 'BBAR' and when a few of the lads from the Walsall Roads CC said that they were riding the Port Talbot Wheelers 25, **Lynne** said 'count me in'. The 250 mile round trip was worth it as she produced a personal best of **57.58 miles,** to retain **5th** place in the **2006 Womens BBAR. Marina** was placed **10th** and **Carol Westmorland 12th.**

One or two points of RTTC (CTT) history are worth mentioning here. From 1988 the ladies were permitted to be integrated in the main field of male riders, receiving start positions according to their previous performances. In certain circumstances, as with the layout of the men's starting order, a woman could request either an early, middle or late field placing and probably get one, at the discretion of the organiser.

From that date onwards, women were also allowed to contest the 12hr and 24hr National Championship races for individual and team medals, whether it be an all female team or a mixed one. Whereas it is rare for a woman to win a 12hr or 24hr race (except in Bridget Boon's case in 1993) it's been quite common since that date to see a woman take 2nd or 3rd spot in a non-championship event, whether it be a 12hr or 24 hr race. The 24hr is unique in as much as there is now only one event left on the calendar and men have always taken the Championship individual medals, but I think that the possibility of a female winning a National Championship 24hr or at least getting silver or bronze is getting closer and closer.

From 2003 a Championship category and status at 12 hrs and 24 hrs was introduced for women, but unlike the men there were no 2nd, 3rd, silver or bronze medals, just a gold for the fastest lady. My feeling is **'do they not deserve a CTT medal - have they not tried as hard?'**

It is pleasing to note that the Walsall RCC Ladies took the 24hr Championship Team Award in 2003 and 2004, and in 2005 a mixed team, comprised of Marina Bloom, Lynne Taylor and Rob Meredith took the honours.

Rob came into the sport late in life, after losing his son George in a mountaineering accident. Rob set up a charity in his son's name to give adventure breaks and holidays to disabled and under-privileged children. The charity is named 'The George Meredith Trust'. Rob started riding his bike over longer and longer journeys and distances to raise money for the charity, but never considered himself to be anything special. He suffered one or two horrendous accidents at this time, breaking lots of bones and had to have many pins in his body to hold him together This set him back each time but he was so determined to continue to ride and work for the charity, he ignored the pain.

Lynne first met him when he came into the shop for some bits and pieces for his bike. When she found out what had happened in his life she was amazed at the distances he'd covered and suggested he join the Walsall RCC to gain more experience if he wanted to race and ride with company. Lynne also remembered Rob's son George, as she had taught him trampolining at the local Sports and Leisure Centre. The friendship grew and she gradually managed to convince Rob he was capable of riding a 24hr and that he would 'enjoy' riding the Mersey RC event.

His regular comment or saying when broaching the subject would be "I couldn't do that, I'd never be any good or fast enough for 24 hours". But he was good and he's now completed three events, improving massive amounts each time to 425.757 in 2006.

This event in 2006 had been Jon William's first venture into organising a 24hr time trial. With his years of experience of helping at all levels he did the job very thoroughly. He drew on the help of probably 200 people plus members of his own family including Samantha and Barry.

Whereas many people are quite happy to do a job for a few hours and maybe even move onto another, such as marshalling or feeding, there has to be someone in sole charge to make decisions, before, during and after the event. Someone to co-ordinate those willing helpers. This event hopefully is the first of many for Jon to whom we owe our thanks.

## 2007

## "A MISS IS AS GOOD AS A MILE (OR TWO)" - No pun intended

### The Mersey RC National Championship 24 hr on July 21st and 22nd 2007

This is an account of Miss Lynne Taylor's brave attack on the RTTC Ladies 24 hr Competition Record of 461.45 miles, held by Mrs Christine Roberts since 1993. This report is not so much a blow by blow hourly account of the race, it is a recall of my memories and thoughts throughout the event and so tends to wander a little. It is also a general outlook on the whole event as seen from the passenger seat of Lynne's support van - by her proud father John.

Lynne dedicated her ride to the memory of Iris Dunster who passed away on June 1st 2007.

That weekend in 1993, when Christine pushed the Competition Record to 461.45 miles, was also Lynne's first attempt at 24 hrs. It was a hot windy Saturday followed by a showery windy Sunday. As we stood in the hall for the prize presentation and Christine painfully made her way to the front to collect her awards, to a well-deserved ovation, I wondered then if Lynne would ever rise to Championship or record status. Her 394 miles seemed a long way off Christine's 461 miles, some 67 miles in fact. An almost impossible bridge to cross?

Although we had the kind offer of help from Phil St John and obviously myself on the Saturday and Sunday, plus Liz, Lynne's mum early on the Sunday morning, we felt that this year could possibly be just a repeat of last year. Although we had helped Lynne year in and year out in fourteen events, we were only capable of normal parental enthusiasm and felt that if Lynne was to improve a vast amount she needed somebody who could lift her spirits. In the past, Neil Peart has been a stalwart helper throughout Lynne's career, but wasn't available this year.

Lynne had experienced a more relaxed year working at the Bike Shop, she had even been able to have her regular day off during the week to train. She still felt though that her season so far had just been ordinary, although I wouldn't class a 2hr 2min for 50 miles and 4hrs 14mins Burton 100, plus Championship Team in the National 100, with Marina and Carol, as 'just ordinary'.

There had been cancellations and course changes again this year, which had left gaps in her season, one exception to this had been her 3rd place – Elite Category ride in the six hour mountain bike cross country endurance race; her first exploit on a MTB. Lynne said it had been one of her best training workouts ever and she was looking forward to a 24 hr MTB Enduro race in August.

Jim Turner had heard about Lynne's plight of only having just Phil, myself and Liz helping, and set about recruiting Paul Histon, who now runs his own Company installing garage doors. He was obviously a very busy man but said he would be delighted to help Lynne. He had been her main motivator in the past on her mixed tandem End to End with Andy Wilkinson, where Paul's persuasive powers had seen Andy through some very bad patches from Exeter to Inverness.

437

Paul was also on Lynne's first solo End to End the following year when over 40 hours of rain affected the ride. Lynne and Paul were the only ones confident that the record could be broken. Paul had also been in the back up team on many of Andy's Competition and RRA record breaking rides in the mid 90's along with Jim Turner; they formed a formidable team, and I am sure that the two of them together could have convinced the Pope he was a protestant!

When Paul hands up a bottle or food for Lynne he runs with her for 200 yards or more giving advice and encouragement. Although Lynne is self motivated for most of the races she rides and training she has to put in for something as big as attacking records, I felt that to get Comp Record she needed more than the help and encouragement I could give her. Lynne had won the 'Turner' Cup nine times and had a personal best of 443.14 miles, and Christine's record seemed to be getting more unbeatable as the years progressed. Paul knew that Lynne was capable of getting the record and set out a schedule of 4 hrs 40 mins for her first 100 miles, 243 miles at 12 hours, tailing off to 19 mph and then 18's in the later stages, leaving a remaining 12 hrs of 219 miles.

After a very hot promising month of April 2007, the weather had got gradually worse week on week, with flooding being the main threat to everyday life. By early July many parts of the Midlands and Southern England had already experienced problems. A large dam had over-spilt in Yorkshire and by the week of the Mersey RC 24 hr many towns and villages on the River Severn, Avon, Wye, Thames and Trent were under water and I did wonder whether this years event would be the first cancellation in its history, but strangely enough, this small part of Shropshire and Cheshire was virtually untouched.

The day of the event arrived, the 21st July, as we drove up to the start at Farndon we passed the entrance of the road to the Quina Brook night and morning circuit of some 13 miles, just as Council workmen were putting signs and barriers in place to close the road off. (Panic Stations)
Lynne rang Jonathan Williams straightaway but all was calm. He already knew, apparently a van was stuck in floodwater on the circuit. The Organisers were now going to 'play it by ear' as to whether the circuit would be used. As luck would have it for the riders, they were kept on the main roads between Prees, Ternhill, Espley Island and Shawbirch for about 18 hours with the finishing circuit starting at Handley being the only other deviation.

The Quina Brook circuit and finishing circuit are comprised of lovely idyllic rural lanes with a few sharp bends to negotiate and one or two hills to climb, and they are meant to offer the riders a quiet safe haven to clock up the miles before going back onto the busy main road again. They are ideal for touring on and admiring the views in daylight and dry conditions, but a real 'trial' in dark, damp or wet conditions with many potholes hidden under large puddles and large patches of wet stinking slurry and mud at farm and field entrances. I know that Lynne soaks the back of her mitts with Olbus oil so that she can combat the smell of animals by sniffing her hand. If one is already suffering with sickness or a dodgy tummy, these bad smells can only make one worse, so this circuit closure was probably a blessing in disguise for her.

At the start of the event many riders left the timekeeper wearing race capes and waterproofs, many had narrow mudguards fitted. A sensible idea as the main road to Broxton had drifts of floodwater lying across its surface. Conditions were cool, drizzly and damp but without any wind. This year there was a massive contingent of Scottish riders mainly from the Deeside Thistle CC and the Edinburgh RC. They'd bought along their own master of the Bagpipes who piped each Scottish rider away from the start line with a short rendition of 'Scotland the Brave', and they were brave, their fastest man being 43 years of age Phillip Kelman, with 435 miles and amazingly all 13 Deeside Thistle riders finished including a complete team of ladies. Ginny Pollard took the fastest ladies veteran award with 384 miles, 2nd was Linda Reid with 363 miles and 3rd Linsay Goldbeck 346 miles.

The strongest team on paper looked to be Congleton CC with Neil Skellern, Karl Austin, Graham Barker and Guido Reynolds. The 2nd strongest on paper were the Walsall Roads CC comprising of Lynne Taylor, Marina Bloom and Rob Meredith, and 3rd the API-Metro team of Chris Hopkinson, Paul Robinson and Chris Asher.

Of the women I obviously chose Lynne, knowing her form and determination to get the record and the Turner Cup for the 10th time running. Marina 2nd and possibly a Scottish lady 3rd. I had thought Lynne could possibly be in the first five overall and possibly 3rd if the weather was really bad. (Men can be real cissies if it rains hard!) Lynne's start time came, Paul made sure she'd had a fast 10 minute warm up with a jacket on before she answered to the timekeeper. She started wearing a gilet and leg warmers in addition to normal racing kit, and kept these extra items on throughout the ride with just the addition of overshoes and a fluo-yellow thermal top in the night.

Paul said he intended to see Lynne every 10 miles and that he would probably do the full course in the van in case of a puncture or mechanical problems. It's lucky we did as Lynne had two front wheel punctures and we were on hand to help. Her first one was in the night just as she approached Prees Island.

We were parked waiting to time her when we heard this ear-piercing shriek 'PUNCTURE' from about 200 yards away. She rode to us wobbling on a completely flat tyre, having ridden over something hard and sharp. Lynne thought it was possibly a brick and that she'd wrecked her wheel. Within a minute we had her back on the bike with a new wheel in place. The offending item that had caused the puncture was part of a lorry brake disc that had disintegrated, scattering dangerous debris on the A41, all the way from the end of the dual carriageway to Prees Island. So somewhere between there and the Holyhead Ferry there was a lorry with no brakes. The complete disc had broken into more than ten segments just like shrapnel, razor sharp, and red-hot.

Paul kept his eyes open as he drove back along the road and removed four or five pieces from the carriageway. He said he could feel the heat from the metal through his trainers as he tried to dislodge the chunks of metal from the tarmac. When Lynne finished she discovered a large bruise on her shin when she removed her leg warmers. She had felt something hit her leg but the adrenalin rush caused by the panic of the puncture overrode the pain.

A few hours later on the same stretch of road in daylight she had another front wheel puncture, but luckily on both these occasions we had been parked within earshot or sight and effected quick wheel changes. It is hard to calculate the minutes that punctures cost you, it isn't just the actual time you are stopped for, it's the loss of momentum and confidence to get back to a positive state of mind.

Paul had arranged that her toilet stops would be kept to an absolute minimum and that we would incorporate whatever else needed doing to her or her bike at the same time. In total I think she was physically stopped for about 12 minutes - a record for Lynne. An example of how valuable time can be lost apart from her punctures, was around midnight when Lynne rode towards where we had just a drink to give her. She screeched to a halt and said 'I want a toilet stop'. I dashed to the back of the van to find the bucket when Paul said 'You've only just been an hour ago, get back on and do another two hours or more then you can have a quick stop'. Lynne protested and then carried on for another five hours without stopping. I felt terrible for making her go on and would gladly have let her stop, which in hindsight would have been another mile off her total.

Paul was right of course, and funnily enough at the end of the event he said to her 'You didn't really want to stop did you?' to which Lynne replied 'No, I just wanted to have a quick chat to cheer me up'. So you see, it isn't always a good thing to have a family member related to the rider, on the helping team. Lynne is very self-motivated and my requests for 'more speed' rarely have the same impact as when Paul tells her, so I tend to stick to tea making.

Earlier in the event, at the 100 mile point, we had been too busy helping Lynne to note what the men were doing, but Paul was pleased, Lynne was on schedule with 4hrs 40 mins but the actual result sheet has her down at 4hrs 37 mins. The fastest man was John Warnock with 4hrs 17mins 03secs.

Karl Austin was riding his own race and wasn't getting drawn into any early battles. He had one or two stops for clothing etc and that was when I noticed that Lynne had pulled well away from him. At the 12hr point Lynne was in 7th place with 239.89 miles and Marina was 2nd lady with 227.7 miles.

Although Marina appeared cheerful she was suffering with a bad back. She bravely continued on until well after daybreak, eventually retiring at 306 miles.

In the meantime, Paul was meticulously logging Lynne's exact mileages and times at each island, as the normal course details couldn't be used as a running total due to the closure of the circuit. He wanted to make sure that at the end his total tallied up with the timekeepers. Whenever Neil Peart has helped Lynne he has also done the same thing, leaving nothing to chance as organiser's computers and provisional result sheets aren't always right. Lynne was still up on schedule but obviously at 12 hours she had dipped a fraction under 20 mph. She still appeared to be 'on evens' for hours after that, gradually dropping down to 19 mph and then 18's on the finishing circuit.

Back to the race and a 'bluish' streak was just visible in the black sky at about 3.30am and by 4.30 it was light. The night seemed to have flown by and a lot of riders were now on auto-pilot. Lynne had to sponge her face and eyes a couple of times to stave off tiredness. She wears wrap around sunglasses during the day and yellow light enhancing glasses at night in an effort to protect her eyes and stop her eyelids drying out in the breeze.

Paul had said at the start that he didn't want me to get too tired and that I should stop at Mike Johnson's mobile feeding station at Espley Island on the Shawbirch detour and have a rest, but Lynne was going so well and I was so 'keyed up' there was no way I could relax, but we did call in at the caravan to get flasks full of hot water to make tea and hot rice pudding for Lynne. Mike was his usual self, witty, scathing, insulting (only to me of course) but I can take it. His ribald quips and risqué remarks leave one chuckling to oneself as they are recalled later on. Mike was aided by Yvonne Crane and both were doing a marvellous job once again, keeping riders going through the night and then again later on the finishing circuit at Handley.

Geoff Manson and Lynton Threadgold were also on the feeding team, dotted around the course. Mike Johnson happened to look in the back of our van and commented that it looked to be in a worse muddle than when he drove it on the 'End to End' in 2001, and he wondered whether I'd tidied it up since then!
Lynne's feeding had consisted mainly of liquids up to the 100 mile point, a litre of water followed by a litre of SIS PSP Carbo and a litre of SIS Go, Electrolyte and Carbo. From the 100 mile point we introduced the odd butty and energy bars and as night fell we started to give her hot sweet tea and hot rice pudding.

She still carried either water or a carbo drink in case she couldn't eat, so as to stave off 'the knock'. We were trying to minimise her liquid intake in an effort to cut down her toilet stops. Over the last few years Lynne has experienced bouts of sickness in many of her 24hr races and record breaking, and by giving her warm drinks etc we were hoping to avoid a repeat of this problem. Although she had a night bike already set up with powerful lighting etc we decided to keep her on her daytime bike equipped with Cateye front and rear led. "We felt that as the main roads used during the night were relatively dry, the available light would reflect back from the surface of the road and she would be okay with just a constant beam front led. Her day bike is obviously lighter.

Rob Meredith, Lynne's team-mate was still going but by early Sunday morning he'd suffered two hours of stomach trouble losing a lot of time. We caught up with his wife Susie, who was stationed not far from Tern Hill and Rob was leaning on the car and looking most upset with the thought that he couldn't carry on and that he would let the team down. I suggested that he just pottered around for an hour or two and see how he felt. He painfully rode away and I told Susie that Marina had already packed so there wasn't a Walsall Roads CC team left, but didn't want to say it in front of Rob in case it demoralised him. You have to be a bit crafty sometimes!

Rob takes his long distance riding very seriously and I knew that to finish an event was very important to him. He'd had surgery only a few months previously and it was wondered whether he would be fit enough to race. I'm more than happy to say that Rob finished with 408.25 miles. His 100 mile time was 4hrs 50mins and his first 12 hours had been 221.8 miles. At 59 years of age he'd come 23rd from 85 entries.

By mid-morning the last few riders were turned at Espley Island to take the long haul North to the finishing circuit via Tern Hill, Prees, Malpas, Broxton and Handley. At this stage Lynne was still on for the record and Liz rang Lynne's brother Mike with the good news. We knew it would be tight and Paul was pushing her very hard and restricting her drinks. He was running flat out alongside her telling her how she was going and what she had to do to get the record. I bet his Achilles tendons were a bit sore on Monday. My main role was making tea and hot rice pudding, a less strenuous job I'm glad to say.

Liz had come out early on the Sunday morning with Phil St John, mainly as support for Lynne but also as reserve drivers and transport had there been a problem. Liz took over my role in the van with Paul while I had a break. Phil took over the driving and we stationed ourselves on the main road. Phil had been out on the course the night before with his wife Pauline. They are a much valued support for Lynne. It was good to see Pete Swinden, Bob Beaman and Derek Everton giving Lynne a cheer at Prees. They'd ridden up from Cannock to see her.

After a few hours break I suddenly had a thought. What if Lynne punctures again or needs to get on the spare bike, it would put the van into panic mode. At times Phil and I were quite a long way from Lynne and without any spares we weren't really of much use, except for vocal support. I put this to Paul next time we caught up with him and he saw the point I was making. Lynne was now on the finishing circuit so once again I climbed back into the van knowing that the circuit was wet, dirty, gritty and with pot holes, and if needed I would be there to help with a wheel change. (My 25 years of working in the bike shop had taught me a few useful skills). We had noticed No 16 go dashing past looking as if he was riding a 25 mile race, wearing just the bare minimum race kit, no arm or leg warmers. We felt that the temperature was still very cool and that he must be just a novice, but how wrong can you be?

He flew past Lynne a couple of times, we were right, he was a novice rider in as much as it was his first 24 hr race. But he certainly wasn't a novice in any other way as he came 2nd with a superb 489.32 mile ride. I predict a 500 mile ride from him one day, maybe next year?

By 12 o'clock midday all of the marshals and helpers had regrouped on to the finishing circuit. Lynne's speed had dropped slightly below schedule as she negotiated the bends and poor surfaces on the circuit. Paul felt that it was touch and go now. The speed Lynne had averaged on the main roads had now dropped below the required 19 mph; every stretch of downhill was followed by a left or a right turn which could only be negotiated at about 10 mph, but she still tried with such determination. She hadn't eaten anything for quite a while and had kept her liquid consumption low so as to prevent an unwanted toilet stop.

Lynne's brother Mike and his wife Kate turned up with little Noah, Lynne's nephew, who at 10 months of age was enjoying all of the shouting, cheering and clapping and was adding a few shrieking noises of his own. Paul had worked out roughly where she would finish, probably back out on the main road at Timekeeper No 1. At last there were not enough minutes left in the hour and she over-ran her time slightly. Paul was almost too afraid to ask the timekeeper what mileage he made it.

All Paul's reckonings amounted to 459 miles, exactly the same amount as the timekeeper. What a pity, just 2 miles short of Christine's record, a record Lynne respected greatly. Although obviously disappointed she was also elated to have got so close to the record and to have achieved the 2nd greatest distance in 24 hours ever ridden by a woman under time trial conditions.

I thought she might have been in the first five overall, but was amazed when I saw the results board at the H.Q. Fourth place amongst all of those classy riders. Jose Pinon Shaw and Mark Holt also finished at the same timekeeper. Mark from the Port Sunlight Wheelers had a 419.33 mile ride. Andy Wilkinson and a team of lads and lassies from the club had been helping him throughout.

Andy was now trying to revive Jose who was in a seriously bad state and looked near to death. He'd pushed himself so hard to get 3rd place and a ride of 472.78miles. After what seemed ages, he stirred back into life and was able to talk and eventually move his limbs. Andy was probably the only one equipped to deal rationally with Jose's physical state, after all, Andy had been in that same state so many times himself during his epic long distance time trialling and record breaking career.

Later at the awards ceremony Jose was just able to hobble the short distance across the room to pick up his medal. Paul's estimated mileage for **Lynne** was very similar to the official result **459.291 miles.** I was quite surprised to learn that the method of using the chief timekeeper in a car to 'follow out' the rider if it was thought that Competition Record was possibly being broken has now been discontinued, and that calculations are now made on average speed and elapsed time between the timekeepers.

I spoke to Jim Turner who organised the Mersey RC Event for 13 years up until the year 2000. He said that 'following out' was the method used to verify the accuracy of Andy Wilkinson's ride in 1997 and also Christine's in 1993. Jim said he also used the same method on Rod and Peter Goodfellow's tandem record on that same course in 1991. The reason why he particularly recalled 'Wilko's finishing point was the look of devastation and disappointment in Wilko's eyes at being told he had to ride to the next timekeeper. Jim said 'I will never forget that look'. Apparently there is now no ruling for or against this method and it is left to the discretion of the chief timekeeper and organiser on the day. The exact spot where Wilko finished is marked every year with a large board displaying 'Wilko 525'.

So that was it, another classic 24hr run to its final conclusion, an event that has been held since 1937, this being the 64th edition.

| | | | |
|---|---|---|---|
| 1st | Eamonn Deane – Bournemouth Jubilee Wheelers | | 501.04 |
| 2nd | John Warnock – Twickenham CC | | 489.32 |
| 3rd | Jose Pinon Shaw – Preston Wheelers | | 472.78 |
| 4th | Lynne Taylor – Walsall Roads CC | | 459.29 |

Championship Team: A.P.I.Metrow                                              1,307.11 Miles
(Paul Robinson, Chris Hopkinson, Chris Asher)

It was good to catch up with old friends once gain during the event and at the Headquarters, including the Williams family of Ruth, Bob, John, Jonathan, David, Samantha, Janet and Barry. Edwin and Shelagh Hargraves who were checking along with Anne and Jim Turner. Every time we saw Jim he was more and more hopeful that Lynne was 'onto a ride'. Although he stood to lose a £200.00 donation if she broke Competition Record, knowing Jim he would be most happy to do so. Along with the Merseyside Ladies CA he already donates a cash prize and the 'Turner Cup Trophy' to the winning lady.

Rod Goodfellow, a past champion 24hr man, is principal timekeeper and along with his wife Maggie and son David, provides the crucial results sheet. The event obviously relies on a team of timekeepers and recorders, Christine and Frank Minto and son Phillip, Keith and Pippa Orum, Brenda and George Jackson, Margaret and Eric Fogg, Chris Salter and Jimmy Carroll, Les Johnson and Celia Elliot. But jobs that are equally as important as any others, the marshals and course officials who check the riders through. I'm afraid they are too numerous to mention but most of them are on duty for the full 24hrs.

Our thanks also go to Sheila Hardy who had the unenviable task of presiding over this National Championship as the RTTC (CTT) representative along with Liverpool District Observers, Derek Johnson and Bob Williams. Sheila's job is to make sure that time trialling rules are adhered to and that rider's safety isn't compromised in any way during the event. A job she does with tact and charm.

'Lynn's Raven Café' at Prees Island had stayed open all night and indeed more than 24 hours. They provided a welcome respite for riders, helpers, marshals and officials. Our thanks go to Lynn and her team for providing this service. Doug and Doris Clark, Mersey RC stalwarts, along with Dave and Beryl Denman, cheerfully carried out many 'behind the scenes' duties back at the HQ.

The camaraderie that this 24hr race brings has to be seen to be believed. The purely amateur status of this sport makes one feel proud to be part of it, and the slick organisation puts many professional events in the shade.

The 'Tour de France' is always on at the same time as this famous 24 hour race and when anybody asks me if I've been watching the Tour, I usually reply that I'm too busy helping Lynne in her races where the only substances required by the riders are either hot tea, coffee or rice pudding.

### 'They are time-trials – Races of Truth'

Back home once more, the bottles are washed, the rubbish is thrown away, and the van is emptied. Two days later Eileen Sheridan rang to congratulate Lynne and also commiserate with her for missing the record. At over 80 years of age, she can still recall many of her exciting record-breaking exploits of the 1950's. When I mentioned about

Paul Histon being such a positive support for Lynne and that he had been her 'mentor' on many occasions, especially during her End to End, Eileen recalled Frank Southall, her manager, being such a massive support for her in the days when she had to break what seemed like almost impossible records. Eileen attributed many of her successful records to his guidance and enthusiasm.

Dave Threlkeld 'Photographer Extraordinaire' from the north west, also rang to see how Lynne was, and to offer his congratulations on such a high mileage. Dave has also been there to support Lynne over the years, as she passed through his patch in various races, capturing the moods of the riders in various races, also their every expression, and goose pimples on occasions. Dave was out at Prees for most of the night taking some wonderful action shots and then back at the Headquarters for the prize presentation. He said he felt like a dog with two tails!

Finally it was good to see Roy Dunster from Cornwall. He'd travelled up through the floods on Friday to see the race and especially to see Lynne. His wife Iris, had very recently passed away and my memories of Iris and Roy were being there at Lands End usually as dawn was breaking, together with their Golden Retriever dogs. Roy and Iris had been such a good omen and positive support for Lynne over the years. They were there at the start of all three of her End to End records in 2000, 2001 and 2002. Lynne regularly kept in touch with Iris and Roy; she said it was so good of him to make the journey and support her so soon after his bereavement, but I'm sure it's what Iris would have wanted.

# 2008

**This years Merseyside Ladies CA and the Turner Cup was won by Rose Leith, Sorrento CC with 352.50 miles,** and helped Paul O'Donaghue and John O'Sullivan to a 3rd place team mileage of 1,141.58 miles. Rose also won the Charlie Taylor Memorial Trophy.

As you may have realised, Lynne Taylor wasn't riding this year, due to her chasing fast 'BBAR' times, but Liz and I motored to the event around 7pm and met Lynne at Prees. She'd come directly from the Shaftesbury '50' after producing a 1hr 56mins 31secs ride, some 300 or more miles away. Paul Histon, her coach, had driven her up to the Mersey event, and they were both over the moon with the days outing and result. Lynne's first words on arrival were "how are Marina and Rose Leith doing?" and I said that Rose had just stopped for night clothing and that Marina had just gone through, past Prees to start her 5th Quina Brook circuit and would be back round in 45 mins or so. This was Rose's first 24 hour time trial and she was taking it steady due to the heat.

This was Marina's first attempt at a 24hr without team backing since 2003. In 2007 she had 'packed' around the 14hr point and since then she had struggled to reach top form again. Marina left the Walsall RCC ladies team at the end of 2007 and joined her local club the Rugby RCC. Dusk was falling when Marina came back to Prees and she was directed onto the larger circuit towards Ternhill. Lynne shrieked words of encouragement and Marina recognised her voice straight away and glanced back in response. After a very filling meal at 'Lynn's Raven Café' taken in the company of the Minto's, Christine, Frank and Phillip, and also members of the Williams cc plus Dave and Beryl Denman, we made our weary way back home around 1am for a few hours sleep only to return next morning to see how the race was progressing. Lynne said she'd had a very restless sleep and was awake every hour to check on the time, she was re-living some of her past 24hr races, instead of dropping off to sleep.

We arrived back at Prees next morning only to be told that Marina had packed around 13 hours and 237 miles, after feeling very drowsy and bumping the grass verge a couple of times, which unnerved her. Lynne was very upset at this news because she knows the efforts and sacrifices one had to make in the build up to a 24hr or any long distance event.

Maybe it was the monotony of riding a fixed wheel gear coupled with the heat of the previous day that caused the drowsiness, or maybe it was the loneliness of that long dark stretch down to Shawbirch and back that caused it, I don't know, but I do know what the disappointment of retiring in a 24hr feels like, having had three such occasions myself.

**Rose Leith** now knew that all she had to do to win was to finish, which she did with **352.50 miles.** She took the Mersey Ladies CA award and won the Turner Cup, and she also created a new Irish ladies 24hr record that day. I spoke to Rose at the H.Q. after the race and apart from slightly bloodshot eyes she looked pretty good after such an effort. Rose admitted to not being able to train as hard as usual this year, and also mentioned that to ride any time trial longer than a 25 or 50 miles event, she has to travel to mainland Britain to do so. So I suppose we should consider ourselves very lucky to have such a large calendar of events at all distances to choose from, even if it is a shrinking one.

When Rose realised that I was Lynne's dad, she mentioned that there is an Irish End to End record from Mizen Head to Fanad Head and she holds the record for this 592 kilometre journey with a time of 21 hours. Rose enquired as to whether Lynne would ever consider attacking this record? I then asked her if she knew of the 'IRC' (the Irish Road Club) and Rose said yes and this it was now known as IRC-Ushers. She also knew that the club had been involved in long distance racing many years ago. I informed her that Bill Finn had organised a number of 24hr races in Ireland for the IRC before the Second World War, and that an Englishman, Frank Shubert, had won the event on a few occasions with rides of 400 miles plus. So Rose's win today brought us full circle!

In early November I accompanied Lynne to the Barrow Central Wheelers 75th Anniversary Dinner and Dance. Lynne was the Guest Speaker and also presented the prizes and annual awards. Whilst there I chatted to Gethin Butler and naturally the subject turned to 24 hour and End to End records. He spoke about breaking the 24 hour record at Moffat and then realising that he was only halfway there for the 1,000 miles, and still had over 330 miles to do to get to John o' Groats. With the time spent off the bike and battling against his own negativity in Scotland, Gethin reckons that there is possibly another two hours to come off the End to End and 1,000 mile records. Although I was there at John o' Groats when Gethin arrived, I hadn't realised that his 'short break' before continuing for the 1,000 was approximately one and a half hours.

Later that evening, Johnny Pardoe introduced me to 86 year old Harry Knipe who formed part of the Barrow Central Wheelers winning team in the Mersey RC 24 hour of 1959. Harry rode 375.1 miles on a trike that day and said he remembers it well. I asked him if, with his unusual surname, he was related to R.L. Knipe, who rode the first paced mileage over 400 in the Anfield of 1902 with 406.5 miles? Harry said no, he wasn't, but the name Knipe was a local one found mainly in the Barrow in Furness area.

Here is a selection of long distance Road Records appertaining to this book. There are of course many other shorter records on the association's books.

## LAND'S END TO JOHN O'GROATS
### BICYCLE
*Shield presented by the Anfield Bicycle Club in 1894*

| | | Days | Hrs | Min | Sec |
|---|---|---|---|---|---|
| 1891 | G P Mills | 4 | 11 | 17 | |
| 1892 | T A Edge | 4 | 00 | 40 | |
| 1892 | L Fletcher | 3 | 23 | 55 | |
| 1894 | R H Carlisle | 3 | 14 | 15 | |
| 1894 | G P Mills | 3 | 05 | 49 | |

*Unpaced*

| | | Days | Hrs | Min | Sec |
|---|---|---|---|---|---|
| 1903 | C J Mather | 5 | 05 | 12 | |
| 1904 | F W Wesley | 4 | 07 | 25 | |
| 1905 | G A Olley | 3 | 20 | 15 | |
| 1907 | T Peck | 3 | 12 | 53 | |
| 1907 | W Welsh | 3 | 08 | 04 | |
| 1908 | G A Olley | 3 | 05 | 20 | |
| 1908 | T Peck | 2 | 22 | 42 | |
| 1908 | H Green | 2 | 19 | 50 | |
| 1929 | J W Rossiter | 2 | 13 | 22 | |
| 1934 | H Opperman | 2 | 09 | 01 | |
| 1937 | S H Ferris | 2 | 06 | 33 | |
| 1958 | D J Keeler | 2 | 03 | 09 | |
| 1958 | R F Randall | 2 | 01 | 58 | |
| 1965 | R W E Poole | 1 | 23 | 46 | 35 |
| 1979 | P A Carbutt | 1 | 23 | 23 | 01 |
| 1982 | M Coupe | 1 | 22 | 39 | 49 |
| 1982 | P J Woodburn | 1 | 21 | 03 | 16 |
| 1990 | A Wilkinson | 1 | 21 | 02 | 18 |
| 2001 | G Butler | 1 | 20 | 4 | 20 |

### TANDEM BICYCLE

| | | Days | Hrs | Min | Sec |
|---|---|---|---|---|---|
| 1895 | G P Mills & T A Edge | 3 | 04 | 46 | |

*Unpaced*

| | | Days | Hrs | Min | Sec |
|---|---|---|---|---|---|
| 1938 | L Innes & W A Thompson | 2 | 14 | 48 | |
| 1952 | S F Cowsill & A E Denton | 2 | 08 | 47 | |
| 1960 | J A Bailey & J Forrest | 2 | 04 | 48 | 03 |
| 1966 | P M Swinden & W J Withers | 2 | 02 | 14 | 25 |

### TRICYCLE
*Shield presented by the Palatine C C in 1929*

| | | Days | Hrs | Min | Sec |
|---|---|---|---|---|---|
| 1885 | T R Marriott | 6 | 15 | 22 | |
| 1886 | G P Mills | 5 | 10 | 00 | |
| 1893 | G P Mills | 3 | 16 | 47 | |

*Unpaced*

| | | Days | Hrs | Min | Sec |
|---|---|---|---|---|---|
| 1929 | T Hughes | 3 | 21 | 55 | |
| 1929 | L J Meyers | 3 | 19 | 56 | |
| 1949 | H Parkes | 3 | 13 | 03 | |
| 1949 | J K Letts | 3 | 09 | 27 | |
| 1950 | H Parkes | 3 | 00 | 38 | |
| 1957 | D P Duffield | 2 | 20 | 09 | |
| 1957 | A Crimes | 2 | 12 | 37 | |
| 1960 | D P Duffield | 2 | 10 | 58 | 29 |
| 1980 | P Kenny | 2 | 10 | 36 | 52 |
| 1982 | E Tremaine | 2 | 06 | 18 | 35 |
| 1992 | R Dadswell | 2 | 05 | 29 | 01 |

### TANDEM TRICYCLE
*Shield presented by T Hughes in 1954*

*Unpaced*

| | | Days | Hrs | Min |
|---|---|---|---|---|
| 1947 | J K Letts & S W Parker | 2 | 22 | 41 |
| 1954 | A Crimes & J F Arnold | 2 | 04 | 26 |

## LADIES LAND'S END TO JOHN O'GROATS
### BICYCLE
*Crystal vase presented by Mrs C M Watts*

| | | | Days | Hrs | Min | Sec |
|---|---|---|---|---|---|---|
| 1938 | L Dredge | Pro | 3 | 20 | 54 | 00 |
| 1939 | M Wilson | Pro | 2 | 22 | 52 | 00 |
| 1953 | E Atkins | Am | 2 | 18 | 04 | 00 |
| 1954 | E Sheridan | Pro | 2 | 11 | 07 | 00 |
| 1976 | J Tebbutt | Am | 2 | 15 | 24 | 00 |
| 1990 | P J Strong | | 2 | 6 | 49 | 45 |
| 2001 | L E A Taylor | | 2 | 5 | 48 | 21 |
| 2002 | L E A Taylor | | 2 | 4 | 45 | 11 |

## ONE THOUSAND MILES
*Unpaced*
### BICYCLE
*Shield presented by G A Olley in 1925*

| | | Days | Hrs | Min |
|---|---|---|---|---|
| 1907 | G A Olley | 4 | 09 | 03 |
| 1907 | W Welsh | 4 | 07 | 41 |
| 1908 | T A Fisher | 3 | 19 | 01 |
| 1909 | W Welsh | 3 | 15 | 57 |
| 1930 | J W Rossiter | 3 | 11 | 58 |
| 1934 | H Opperman | 3 | 01 | 52 |
| 1937 | S H Ferris | 2 | 22 | 40 |
| 1956 | A Render | 2 | 16 | 50 |
| 1960 | R F Randall | 2 | 10 | 40 |
| 2001 | G Butler | 2 | 07 | 59 |

### TANDEM BICYCLE

| | | Days | Hrs | Min |
|---|---|---|---|---|
| 1952 | S F Cowsill & A E Denton | 3 | 07 | 41 |
| 1964 | P M Swinden & W J Withers | 2 | 18 | 09 |

### TRICYCLE
*Shield presented by Bartleet Memorial Committee in 1945*

| | | Days | Hrs | Min |
|---|---|---|---|---|
| 1938 | G E Lawrie | 4 | 06 | 32 |
| 1956 | D P Duffield | 3 | 12 | 15 |
| 1958 | A Crimes | 2 | 21 | 37 |

### TANDEM TRICYCLE

| | | Days | Hrs | Min |
|---|---|---|---|---|
| 1947 | J K Letts & S W Parker | 3 | 12 | 25 |
| 1954 | A Crimes & J F Arnold | 2 | 13 | 59 |

## LADIES ONE THOUSAND MILES
### BICYCLE
*Wooden plaque presented by BR & A Edrupt in 2005*

| | | | Day | Hrs | Min |
|---|---|---|---|---|---|
| 1938 | L Dredge | Pro | 4 | 19 | 14 |
| 1939 | M Wilson | Pro | 3 | 11 | 44 |
| 1953 | W Wrightson | Am | 3 | 15 | 53 |
| 1954 | E Sheridan | Pro | 3 | 01 | 00 |
| 1974 | J Tebbutt | Am | 3 | 09 | 29 |
| 2002 | L E A Taylor | | 2 | 16 | 38 |

## MENS
### PEMBROKE TO GREAT YARMOUTH
*Unpaced*
### BICYCLE

| | | Hrs | Min | Sec |
|---|---|---|---|---|
| 2003 | C Hopkinson | 16 | 58 | 02 |

### TRICYCLE
*Shield purchased with the bequest from C H & W E Perry in 2000.*

| | | Hrs | Min | Sec |
|---|---|---|---|---|
| 1996 | J W Hopper | 18 | 15 | 47 |
| 1997 | R Dadswell | 17 | 54 | 06 |

## Ladies Pembroke to Great Yarmouth

2004 Marina Bloom 16.51.56

## TWENTY FOUR HOURS
### BICYCLE
*Shield presented by the North Road Cycling Club in 1893*

| | | | Miles |
|---|---|---|---|
| 1886 | G P Mills | | 295 |
| 1888 | P A Nix | | 297 |
| 1889 | M A Holbein | | 324 |
| 1890 | M A Holbein | | 336 ½ |
| 1892 | M A Holbein | | 359 |
| 1892 | F W Shorland | | 366 ½ |
| 1893 | F W Shorland | | 370 |
| 1894 | C C Fontaine | | 376 |
| 1895 | M A Holbein | | 397 |
| 1897 | M A Holbein | (MP) | 403 ½ |
| 1897 | G Hunt | | 411 ½ |
| 1898 | F R Goodwin | (MP) | 428 |
| *Unpaced* | | | |
| 1900 | T G King | | 346 ½ |
| 1901 | T G King | | 357 |
| 1901 | H Green | | 394 |
| 1922 | M G Selbach | | 397 ¼ |
| 1923 | C F Davey | | 402 ½ |
| 1931 | E B Brown | | 416 ½ |
| 1934 | H Opperman | | 431 ½ |
| 1934 | F W Southall | | 454 |
| 1935 | H Opperman | | 461 ¾ |
| 1938 | C Heppleston | | 464 ¾ |
| 1938 | S H Ferris | | 465 ¾ |
| 1939 | C Heppleston | | 467 ½ |
| 1954 | K H Joy | | 475 ¾ |
| 1982 | M Coupe | | 482 ½ |
| 1982 | P J Woodburn | | 494 ¼ |
| 2001 | G Butler | | 505.8 |

### TANDEM BICYCLE

| | | |
|---|---|---|
| 1894 | J van Hooydonk & P Highall | 317 |
| 1894 | E Oxborrow & H H Sansom | 340 |
| 1895 | G P Mills & T A Edge | 377 |
| 1895 | J A Bennett & M A Holbein | 397 ½ |
| *Unpaced* | | |
| 1913 | C H Turnor & E Webb | 381 ½ |
| 1921 | F E Armond & F G Thomas | 399 |
| 1921 | C W Shadford & R E Wilson | 412 ½ |
| 1924 | G W Bridges & G E Sibthorpe | 417 |
| 1932 | A E Morris & S Brown | 429 ½ |
| 1932 | W G Phillips & A G Oxbrow | 430 ¾ |
| 1933 | V J Viel & J W Dougal | 461 ½ |
| 1950 | R C Smith & A E Collins | 467 |
| 1959 | J A Bailey & J Forrest | 492 |

### TRICYCLE
*Shield presented by the North Road Cycling Club in 1893*

| | | |
|---|---|---|
| 1885 | C H R Gossett | 231 ¾ |
| 1886 | A H Fletcher | 250 ½ |
| 1887 | G P Mills | 264 |
| 1889 | W C Goulding | 280 |
| 1890 | F T Bidlake | 289 |
| 1891 | M A Holbein | 311 ½ |
| 1892 | M A Holbein | 337 |
| 1894 | F T Bidlake | 356 ½ |
| 1913 | H G Cook | 360 ½ |
| *Unpaced* | | |
| 1908 | F W Wesley | 326 |
| 1914 | H G Cook | 339 ½ |
| 1925 | H T G Page | 349 ¾ |
| 1928 | F Hancock | 366 |
| 1933 | J W Rossiter | 385 ½ |
| 1952 | J F Arnold | 428 ½ |
| 1965 | P Kenny | 431 ½ |
| 1991 | R Dadswell | 447 |

### TANDEM TRICYCLE

| | | |
|---|---|---|
| 1887 | C W Brown & W C Goulding | 259 |
| 1887 | G P Mills & R Tingey | 298 ½ |
| 1893 | F T Bidlake & M A Holbein | 333 |
| *Unpaced* | | |
| 1919 | C H Turnor & A Newsholme | 333 |
| 1926 | F G Thomas & M Dunn | 347 ¾ |
| 1927 | A E Houghton & T E White | 375 |
| 1933 | E Tweddell & H T Cookson | 385 ¼ |
| 1938 | B F C Gough & G E Lawrie | 392 ¾ |
| 1951 | E G E Widdows & J M P Robinson | 404 |
| 1952 | E Tweddell & J W Stott | 412 ½ |
| 1954 | A Crimes & J F Arnold | 466 ¼ |

## LONDON TO EDINBURGH
### BICYCLE
*Shield presented by T G King in 1901*

| | | | Hrs | Min | Sec |
|---|---|---|---|---|---|
| 1889 | F W Shorland | | 44 | 49 | |
| 1891 | P A Ransom | | 43 | 25 | |
| 1892 | R H Carlisle | | 32 | 55 | |
| 1894 | G P Mills | | 29 | 28 | |
| 1894 | C C Fontaine | | 28 | 27 | |
| 1895 | W J Neason | | 27 | 38 | |
| 1897 | J Hunt | | 26 | 46 | |
| 1899 | F R Goodwin | (MP) | 25 | 26 | |
| *Unpaced* | | | | | |
| 1903 | F Wright | | 31 | 48 | |
| 1904 | E H Grimsdell | | 28 | 03 | |
| 1904 | G A Olley | | 27 | 10 | |
| 1905 | E H Grimsdell | | 26 | 10 | |
| 1905 | R Shirley | | 23 | 43 | |
| 1928 | W A Ellis | | 21 | 53 | |
| 1931 | E B Brown | | 21 | 49 | |
| 1937 | S H Ferris | | 20 | 19 | |
| 1938 | C Heppleston | | 19 | 13 | |
| 1939 | C Heppleston | | 18 | 57 | |
| 1965 | C Smith | | 18 | 49 | 42 |
| 1989 | P G Wells | | 17 | 48 | 04 |

### TANDEM BICYCLE

| | | | | |
|---|---|---|---|---|
| 1894 | E Oxborrow & H H Sansom | 27 | 33 | |
| *Unpaced* | | | | |
| 1905 | E Bright & P H Miles | 27 | 54 | |
| 1923 | H M Green & L M Lamouroux | 27 | 14 | |
| 1925 | F G Thomas & L C Cockerill | 23 | 18 | |
| 1930 | E B Brown & C Neale | 21 | 35 | |
| 1936 | A B Smith & F E Marston | 20 | 18 | |
| 1950 | R C Smith & A E Collins | 19 | 04 | |
| 1988 | J W M Murdoch & G Berwick | 18 | 42 | 23 |

### TRICYCLE
*Shield presented by J van Hooydonk in 1929*

| | | | | |
|---|---|---|---|---|
| *Unpaced* | | | | |
| 1905 | F W Wesley | 32 | 42 | |
| 1926 | H T G Page | 26 | 33 | |
| 1939 | B F C Gough | 26 | 16 | |
| 1939 | T F Maddex | 25 | 17 | |
| 1949 | E Tweddell | 24 | 11 | |
| 1965 | P Kenny | 20 | 48 | 52 |
| 1991 | R Dadswell | 19 | 27 | 54 |

### TANDEM TRICYCLE

| | | | |
|---|---|---|---|
| *Unpaced* | | | |
| 1938 | B F C Gough & G E Lawrie | 23 | 37 |
| 1950 | E Tweddell & J W Stott | 23 | 32 |
| 1951 | E G E Widdows & J M P Robinson | 22 | 57 |
| 1956 | E Tweddell & C Sandham | 21 | 16 |

## LADIES LONDON TO EDINBURGH
### BICYCLE

| | | | Hrs | Min | Sec |
|---|---|---|---|---|---|
| 1953 | E Atkins | Am | 21 | 37 | 54 |
| 1954 | E Sheridan | Pro | 20 | 11 | 35 |

## LONDON to EDINBURGH MIXED TANDEM TRIKE

2000 R Dadswell & Mrs M Bloom 19 hrs 40 mins 40secs

## LADIES TWENTY-FOUR HOURS
### BICYCLE
*Silver Cup presented by 'Cycling'*

| | | | Miles |
|---|---|---|---|
| 1936 | L Dredge | Pro | 339 ¾ |
| 1938 | F Wren | Am | 355 ½ |
| 1938 | P Wellington | Am | 377 ¼ |
| 1939 | M Wilson | Pro | 396 |
| 1953 | E Atkins | Am | 422 |
| 1953 | E Sheridan | Pro | 442 ¾ |
| 1954 | E Sheridan | Pro | 446 ¼ |
| 1997 | C Roberts | | 467.30 |

## 24 HOUR MIXED TANDEM TRIKE

2000 R Dadswell & Mrs M Bloom 451 miles

## TWELVE HOURS
### BICYCLE
*Shield presented by A J Wilson in 1893*

| | | | Miles |
|---|---|---|---|
| 1889 | M A Holbein | | 175 ½ |
| 1890 | M A Holbein | | 177 ½ |
| 1891 | P C Twentyman | | 181 |
| 1891 | G Smith | | 190 ½ |
| 1891 | F W Shorland | | 192 ½ |
| 1892 | F W Shorland | | 194 ½ |
| 1893 | F W Shorland | | 195 |
| 1894 | W Brookbanks | | 202 ½ |
| 1894 | F W Shorland | | 211 |
| 1894 | A A Chase | | 213 |
| 1895 | M A Holbein | | 217 ½ |
| 1897 | M A Holbein | (MP) | 219 |
| 1897 | G Hunt | | 224 |
| 1897 | E Gould | | 226 ½ |
| 1899 | F R Goodwin | (MP) | 245 |
| *Unpaced* | | | |
| 1898 | A F Ilsley | | 187 |
| 1898 | E Gould | | 191 |
| 1898 | E Gould | | 201 ½ |
| 1900 | H Green | | 226 ½ |
| 1926 | J W Rossiter | | 242 |
| 1934 | H Opperman | | 243 |
| 1934 | F W Southall | | 253 |
| 1938 | H James | | 259 ¼ |
| 1939 | H Earnshaw | | 276 ½ |
| 1989 | P G Wells | | 283 5/8 |
| 1991 | P G Wells | | 292 7/8 |
| 1997 | G Longland | | 309.5 |

### TANDEM BICYCLE

| | | |
|---|---|---|
| 1889 | P C Wilson & M A Holbein | 163 |
| 1892 | H Arnold & J P K Clark | 179 |
| 1893 | A Brown & M A Holbein | 200 |
| 1894 | F Busvine & A Smythe | 204 ½ |
| 1895 | J W Stocks & M A Holbein | 221 |
| 1897 | A E Walters & M A Holbein | 230 |
| *Unpaced* | | |
| 1900 | E P Clarke & E C Coles-Webb | 205 |
| 1900 | H Charles & D K Hall | 210 ½ |
| 1901 | E A Cully & E H Grimsdell | 219 ½ |
| 1909 | E H Grimsdell & M R Mott | 221 |
| 1920 | E W Hill & J Quantrill | 232 |
| 1924 | E W Franklin & W R Donovan | 236 |
| 1927 | V S Bowman & A West | 249 |
| 1930 | C Marshall & L Cave | 253 |
| 1935 | E Milliken & W F Stuart | 274 ¾ |
| 1960 | B Wray & A Brook | 279 3/8 |

### TRICYCLE
*Shield presented by S F Edge in 1925*

| | | |
|---|---|---|
| 1888 | G P Mills | 147 |
| 1889 | W Ward | 151 |
| 1889 | W C Goulding | 151 |
| 1890 | A F Ilsley | 159 ½ |
| 1890 | G R White | 164 |
| 1891 | M A Holbein | 174 ½ |
| 1892 | M A Holbein | 183 ½ |
| 1894 | W W Robertson | 184 ½ |
| 1894 | E J Steel | 190 ½ |
| 1894 | F T Bidlake | 194 ½ |
| *Unpaced* | | |
| 1901 | R S Cobley | 177 ½ |
| 1901 | W T Hall | 197 |
| 1927 | A H Glass | 205 ¼ |
| 1928 | M Draisey | 210 ½ |
| 1934 | A L Abram | 222 ¾ |
| 1938 | S W Parker | 230 |
| 1955 | D P Duffield | 230 ¾ |
| 1961 | D P Duffield | 239 5/8 |
| 1981 | S W Jackson | 248 3/8 |
| 1991 | R Dadswell | 248 ¾ |
| 1995 | R Dadswell | 251.6 |
| 1995 | R Dadswell | 257.5 |
| 1996 | R Dadswell | 266.3 |

### TANDEM TRICYCLE

| | | |
|---|---|---|
| 1890 | J Rowley & H Arnold | 164 |
| 1891 | A J Wilson & J J McCarthy | 164 ½ |
| 1892 | A Brown & M A Holbein | 177 ½ |
| 1893 | F T Bidlake & M A Holbein | 181 ½ |
| *Unpaced* | | |
| 1912 | E A Bentley & L Cohen-Price | 182 ½ |
| 1925 | J E Patmore & C W Patmore | 185 |
| 1925 | D F Nash & H J Scutchings | 220 ½ |
| 1932 | J S Jonas & S del Banco | 229 ½ |
| 1942 | R Morford & G E Lawrie | 232 ¾ |
| 1951 | E Tweddell & J W Stott | 242 ½ |
| 1954 | A Crimes & J F Arnold | 257 ¾ |

## LAND'S END TO LONDON
*Unpaced*
### BICYCLE
*Shield presented by A J Wilson in 1909*

| | | Hrs | Min | Sec |
|---|---|---|---|---|
| 1902 | J E Naylor | 25 | 25 | 32 |
| 1902 | L W B Martin | 22 | 16 | 16 |
| 1903 | J E Naylor | 22 | 07 | 18 |
| 1905 | F T Bone | 21 | 34 | |
| 1907 | C W D C Ball | 20 | 59 | |
| 1910 | F C Higgins | 20 | 40 | |
| 1920 | F E Armond | 19 | 46 | |
| 1923 | C F Davey | 17 | 51 | |
| 1923 | M G Selbach | 17 | 47 | |
| 1923 | C F Davey | 17 | 29 | |
| 1931 | E B Brown | 16 | 35 | |
| 1934 | F W Southall | 15 | 08 | |
| 1935 | H Opperman | 14 | 09 | |
| 1938 | C Holland | 13 | 44 | |
| 1952 | R J Maitland | 13 | 07 | |
| 1953 | K H Joy | 12 | 54 | |
| 1954 | R J Maitland | 12 | 34 | |
| 1994 | G N Longland | 12 | 01 | 37 |

### TANDEM BICYCLE

| | | | | |
|---|---|---|---|---|
| 1905 | L Drake & A Payne | 21 | 06 | |
| 1923 | G W Bridges & F E Sandford | 20 | 46 | |
| 1923 | E Merlin & H Fowler | 19 | 37 | |
| 1928 | V J Viel & W S Gibson | 17 | 26 | |
| 1930 | C Marshall & L Cave | 15 | 52 | |
| 1936 | L Innes & W A Thompson | 15 | 25 | |
| 1947 | L E Copping & J M Sloper | 15 | 04 | |
| 1948 | R C Smith & A E Collins | 14 | 01 | |
| 1955 | R T Powney & F L Powney | 13 | 27 | |
| 1961 | B Wray & A Brook | 13 | 18 | 05 |

### TRICYCLE
*Shield presented by F C Higgins in 1928*

| | | | | |
|---|---|---|---|---|
| 1912 | H Prichard | 24 | 54 | |
| 1923 | F G Thomas | 22 | 02 | |
| 1932 | J W Rossiter | 19 | 01 | |
| 1948 | A L Wilkins | 17 | 44 | |
| 1952 | E G E Widdows | 17 | 22 | |
| 1959 | G A J Lewis | 16 | 32 | |
| 1959 | R N West | 15 | 26 | |
| 1974 | F W Cubis | 14 | 48 | 22 |
| 1981 | S W Jackson | 14 | 05 | 10 |
| 1996 | R Dadswell | 13 | 16 | 13 |

### TANDEM TRICYCLE

| | | | | |
|---|---|---|---|---|
| 1939 | B F C Gough & W J Turner | 19 | 53 | |
| 1950 | E G E Widdows & J M P Robinson | 17 | 52 | |
| 1951 | E Tweddell & J W Stott | 16 | 21 | |
| 1952 | E G E Widdows & J M P Robinson | 16 | 12 | |
| 1977 | P Kenny & J D Gills | 14 | 19 | 46 |
| 1979 | S W Jackson & H E Hargraves | 14 | 18 | 16 |

## LADIES LAND'S END TO LONDON
### BICYCLE
*Silver cup presented by the Dunlop Tyre & Rubber Co Ltd*

| | | | Hrs | Min | Sec |
|---|---|---|---|---|---|
| 1935 | L Dredge | Pro | 22 | 13 | 50 |
| 1938 | F Wren | Am | 19 | 56 | 00 |
| 1938 | P Wellington | Am | 18 | 42 | 00 |
| 1939 | M Wilson | Pro | 17 | 09 | 00 |
| 1952 | E Atkins | Am | 17 | 13 | 31 |
| 1953 | E Sheridan | Pro | 14 | 36 | 18 |
| 1970 | A Horswell | Am | 13 | 43 | 33 |

### TRICYCLE
*Silver replica bequeathed by Mrs L Dredge*

## LADIES TWELVE HOURS
### BICYCLE
*EPNS Cup presented by Arthur Rayner 1970*

| | | | Miles |
|---|---|---|---|
| 1937 | R Wright | Am | 205 ¼ |
| 1938 | P Wellington | Am | 211 |
| 1938 | M Wilson | Am | 215 |
| 1939 | M Wilson | Pro | 230 |
| 1952 | E Sheridan | Pro | 231 |
| 1953 | E Atkins | Am | 234 ¾ |
| 1953 | E Sheridan | Pro | 238 |
| 1953 | E Sheridan | Pro | 250 ½ |
| 1970 | A Horswell | Am | 259 |
| 1992 | P J Strong | | 259 ½ |
| 2005 | M Bloom | | 274.0 |

### TANDEM BICYCLE

| | | | |
|---|---|---|---|
| 1937 | A Caley & M Gallagher | Am | 217 ¼ |
| 1939 | E Broughton & R Wallace | Am | 220 |
| 1939 | F Wren & E Nicholas | Am | 227 ½ |
| 1959 | J Terry & A Bendall | Am | 241 ½ |

# CHAPTER SIX

## THE GRADUAL DECLINE AND POSSIBLE REMEDIES

I would like to continue with my comments on the decline in our long distance sport, a subject I touched upon at the end of the 1963 Mersey 24hr race description. I tried to describe our values then and the way things were at that time and I will now move forward 45 years to compare the changes in lifestyle from 1963 to present day 2008. They are vast changes that I think have led to the gradual decline, not only in our particular branch of the sport, but also many other sports that require more than two hours devoted to them.

I was aged 19 in 1963, the year of that event, so you could say I was 'footloose and fancy free'. I wasn't thinking about marriage or owning a house or mortgage and I had an old A35 van I used as support transport for long distance racing. I played in a rock group in the winter months and socialised at a local Catholic youth club. I earned just enough money to pay for my keep at home with my widowed mother and my pocket money was spent on bikes and entering races etc.

The thought of having lots of money or even wanting lots of money wasn't my wish at that time, only to be as fit as possible and to ride in time trials every year. I endeavoured to support the club runs whenever I could, but if my spare time was rationed then I just 'trained' or rode as far and as fast as I could in those few hours available.

I married Liz in 1968 and acquired a mortgage and a house, like many other similar aged people I knew, it was the normal 'done thing' at that time. Looking back in hindsight I realise times were financially hard. I lived 15 miles from my work in Birmingham and tried to ride there every day rather than use a car. Liz & I had a daughter, Lynne, and a son, Michael, in those first three years of marriage but I still strived to race every year and round up my season with a 24hr and 12hr event, usually the 'Mersey 24' and the 'Oldbury 12'. Liz, in later years, always reminds me that I paid for new tubulars and to enter events, even though Lynne hadn't got new shoes to wear.

At that time in the early 1970's I didn't feel aware of any peer pressure to keep bettering myself financially, adverts were just adverts, they weren't denouncing and deriding as current adverts are, where anyone who is lacking the latest 'must have' items is seen to be leading a dull life or is of a sub-culture. I didn't feel that I was missing out on anything because I chose to ride a bike and didn't have a promising career; I actually felt sorry for anyone who didn't cycle or have time to take part in a physical sport or past-time, or live a healthy outdoor life. My 24hr performances scattered over nearly 40 years and 17 solo all-day events range from 366 miles to a mediocre 'could do much better' 418 miles. I knew my weaknesses and limits.

There were very few large Corporate Companies or Conglomerates vying mainly for your money, but more inconspicuously for your time, or Companies that ran leisure complexes, theme parks etc. It wouldn't have been an option for many people I knew in the 1960's, they hadn't really got much spare income to spend on leisure and entertainment pursuits at that time. Pubs in those days were generally only open from about 11am to 2pm at dinnertime and then 6pm to 10.30pm at night. Only the fairly "posh" ones had a menu that involved more than a packet of crisps or salted peanuts. Taking the family out for Sunday lunch, which in 2008 usually lasts all afternoon, certainly wasn't in vogue then. A Sunday dinner for most cyclists was one that your Wife or Mother had cooked and put on a plate to keep for you. If you were lucky you ate it about 10pm, hotted up on a pan of boiling water with the gravy solidified around the edges of the plate, but you never complained because you knew what the answer would be! *This makes me realise that after the bicycle as the Number 1 invention of our times, the microwave oven must take 2nd place.*

In the 1960's one or two lads in the cycling club were interested in football and followed the interests of teams such as Birmingham City or Aston Villa. They would see the occasional game and listen for the football results on Saturday teatime. That was their limit of involvement and apart from a little friendly rivalry and 'ribbing', that was about the extent of their interest. In this modern day it's an all time and money consuming business that is blasted at you night and day, 7 days a week, whereas it used to be just Saturday afternoons. Sport today seems to be designed to fit in with television coverage.

Advertisers are keen to have their 'prime slot' before during or after a football match or an event, or in the case of the Olympics, the whole event is scheduled to coincide with television companies and advertisers world-wide rather than for the benefit of the sport or the sports person. People's concentration levels whether participating or just watching seems to be very low. One hour maximum for youngsters and two hours for adults.

My local evening newspaper in 2008 has a minimum of six full pages, six nights a week devoted purely to football, and if there is a local 'Derby' or 'clash', it can be upwards of 12 pages. We've become a nation of 'sports watchers' and armchair critics rather than participating in a regular exercise or outdoor pursuit ourselves. I would go as far as to say that 50% of the population watching sport on TV at every opportunity, class themselves as being 'sporty', even if they are shouting at the screen whilst eating, drinking and smoking themselves to an early death.

When we lost to Croatia at football in 2007 we had Politicians, Heads of Industry and Commerce, talking about the vast monetary cost and loss of esteem that the English nation would suffer because we were out of the competition. I cringed when I heard those remarks and hoped that they weren't speaking on my behalf.

Computers, or home P.C's; how many lives, or hours of life, have they consumed? It has led us to be a nation of bargain hunting 'buy it on line' penny pinchers who then wonder where their local shops, services and jobs have gone to. I'm sure the Government-led media have made many, once normal people, fearful of paying the recommended retail price in case they look foolish in front of their friends. It's actually given the meekest of people a 'tool' to shop with, and bargain prices to make them become demanding, forceful, and sometimes abusive, to shop staff. The internet has brought us a lot of bad things even worse than 'shopping on line' – pornography; how to make bombs; identity cloning; vast uncontrollable bank fraud; bad eyesight and posture; loss of conversation (or did the television finish that off?). It's producing generations of children and adults who cannot write properly, or think for themselves, or use a library to extract information from a book to stimulate their brains. People assume that if it can't be found on the internet, then it doesn't exist.

In 2008 we have children and youths bullying each other and teachers, either on line or on their telephones. People are putting unregulated derogatory remarks 'on line' so affecting others. We are becoming so controlled by telecommunications I do wonder what the future holds? I've even heard different age groups admit that losing their mobile phones would make them almost as devastated as losing a member of their own family! What is happening to us as a Nation, I fear to think?

Supermarkets and out of town store shopping, that's another wonderful and rewarding 'family experience'? As a cyclist and road user I would put it in the same category as a giant car boot sale. It blocks the local suburbs and main roads up at certain times especially at weekends. Even motorway exit lanes get 'backed up' for miles with people going shopping at large retail complexes. Proper cyclists in my local area have had to re-route many of their leisure and sporting rides due to these commercial enterprises, in fact many of our time trial courses have been spoilt or made dangerous in this way. The Battlefield to Tern Hill section of the Mersey Road 24hr course had to be deleted due to a large retail outlet being built with an entrance close to the island, shortly after the Millenium. This gradual erosion of our courses and pastime is happening nationwide and it is for all these reasons that I hope you can see why I have touched on all these subjects and that I haven't completely flipped and lost the plot. Whether you agree with my rantings or not, I've had to mention these contributory factors, which I feel are causing our sports decline.

If you are of the generation that was lucky enough to have ridden a cycle for sport or pleasure in the 1950's, 60's and even 70's, then you may recognise and understand my fears for future generations of not just amateur cyclists, but for any younger person wanting to take up a sport or traditional hobby and pastime of any kind.

The gradual decline of performances and entries in 24hr races or even a passing interest in anything classed 'endurance' has been discussed at length by like minded members of the 24hr Fellowship in their Journals over a number of years now. Obviously I am not talking about the top echelon of competitors and winners that we've had over those years, or any particular events, or whether an event was of Championship status, no, I'm talking generally, across the board. These declines have affected most of the events for the last 40 years to a point where we now have only one event that receives on average about 65 riders of all capabilities every year.

Even with the vast improvements in bikes, their weight, aero-dynamics, gearing efficiency etc, or the wealth of knowledge on the subject of diet in sport specifically for endurance racing, hasn't altered the situation. We've seen the advent of polymer liquid feeding and electronic aids such as magnetic or electronically controlled resistance rollers that can be linked to a virtual reality screen so that you can ride your favourite race in the garage while monitoring your heart rate etc. With the vast improvement in clothing and thermal wear that copes with all conditions, it makes the list almost endless. **I won't include road surfaces,** because apart from any improvements that have been provided for just car, lorry and motor bike traffic including such items as anti-skid patches at danger spots so that they can brake more efficiently from 90 mph in the wet, and cambered sections that sometimes stop lorries and cars from rolling over due to incompetent driving, **I don't think the surfaces have improved at all, certainly not for cyclists.** Whether main or trunk roads, fast 'B' roads or rural lanes, the plethora of potholes, rough ribbed surfaces, badly sunken service and utilities channels cut either across or parallel to the carriageway, and rural roads that are 'patched' on a weekly basis to stop them from reverting to cart tracks, all prove my point.

The traffic calming measures introduced to most areas have not really had the desired effect, with many drivers speeding up between obstructions, the bollards, chicanes and kerb build-outs have all made conditions much worse for cyclists, with traffic impatiently trying to get past the obstructions and restrictions.

No, the cyclists in the 1960's and 70's, certainly from a speed perspective, had better faster quieter road surfaces than today's riders, but when I analyse the one 24hr course I have either ridden on or helped on for 50 years, the Mersey RC course, to the point where I've known all of the surfaces of these roads and all of the different route variations over the years, I would say that the modern day road conditions are roughly about the same here as in the 1960's. I think the fact that 500 miles has been beaten on this course seven times including 'Wilko's Competition Record, speaks for itself.

I can think of more reasons for declines in riders participating in events and their performances, which tie in with my previous gripes about the erosion of our cycling leisure time. **The main one is the lack of time spent on the bike, on the road in all conditions and at various hours of the day.** I'm not just thinking about someone specifically preparing for a one off 24hr, that they are not likely to repeat, I'm targeting the 'would be' regular 12hr and 24hr and possible future long distance record breaking aspirants in general.

There have been many articles over the years on how to train for specific races over varying distances and durations, but little has been written, broadly speaking, for ultra-long distances such as a 12hr or 24hr. It's as if it doesn't exist, and most of the literature that I've read has been aimed mainly at disciplines of two or three hours duration.

Many sports coaches and therapists advocate the use of fairly short bursts of exercise such as interval training, which may get results at 50 or 100 mile races, but isn't really suitable for endurance events. In fact a lot of the current cycling magazines carry 'soundbite' articles that suggest you don't have to waste hours training on the road and that anything is achievable using their methods.

I know that 'mind over matter' is an attitude that can carry a rider through many things, but I don't know of many good long distance riders who would expect to do a good ride on very little training. They may 'pull off' the odd ride after a weeks holiday or a short enforced lay off the bike, but most of them will have previously put in a good period of 'core training and mileage' which means probably a minimum of 350 miles a week of hard riding on the road over many months. For 24hr racing, the old saying 'you only get out what you put in' is a very relevant one.

To do well and keep performances high, year after year, for 12hr and 24hr racing you must train in a dedicated manner, and I don't mean sitting on a bike mounted on a turbo home trainer in the garage, unless conditions outside are too dangerous to ride in. Use a bike on the road that's fairly heavy preferably with mudguards for all conditions so that even the rain doesn't put you off. Fit a luggage rack with a pack or bag of some sort strapped to it to carry food, spare clothing, tools, tubes and waterproofs.

Use decent lights at all times when required and reflectives wherever possible, I personally advocate using a very good lightweight helmet but that is one's own choice. If your bike then totals up to being 50% heavier than your race bike, that's even better still. After riding your heavier bike for training, I suggest finding a safe 20 mile circuit comprised of mainly left hand turns and time yourself riding at race pace on your heavier bike. Take a note of the time taken to complete one circuit and then a couple of days later, at the same time of day and with similar conditions, ride just as hard on your race bike and you should see a possible ten or fifteen per cent improvement in your time. This is not to say that one must or should always ride a heavy bike when not racing. Getting one's ultimate 'speed with comfort' position is also of vast importance not just for a 4 hour ride but also for an all day and night effort.

If in doubt about the suitability or position of any of your bikes, then I suggest that you use a decent lightweight cycle shop, with staff that actually participate in time trials, and take their advice. They will also be able to point you in the right direction as to suitable clothing, lighting, transmission, tyres, energy food and drinks, and they may even have time to give tips on training and how to prepare for long distance riding, especially if you visit 'Bridgtown Cycles' near Cannock, where Lynne Taylor and her brother Mike work, and have been associated with the sport for over 25 years.

Modern day riders who have used and still use this tough, 'hands on' approach to their time trialling and training are: Glen Longland, Gethin Butler, Ian Dow, Andy Wilkinson, Ian Cammish, Lynne Taylor, Christine Roberts, Marina Bloom, Neil Peart, Steve Abraham, the list is endless.

Use the bike for commuting and leisure time transport, it's surprising just how many miles one can accrue in this way. When visiting relatives who are sympathetic with your effort, or if going on holiday, get your wife, partner, or husband etc. to take the car while you ride the bike and either meet them there or halfway on the journey. Try at least one or two overnight rides to build up that confidence in the dark and if you can find like-minded company to ride with, that's even better still, although night riding isn't absolutely essential, it does help. In the 1980's Cannock to Holyhead and back was one of my favourite overnight rides, after work on a Saturday. Although this sort of character-building activity and pressure can play havoc with a marital or family relationship, you are only on this earth once and only a relatively small percentage of your adult life is needed to realise these ambitions. Obviously if you want to return year after year to race, then yes, that percentage grows.

Attitudes and negative vibes and jibes targeted towards anyone or any sport that lasts any longer than a couple of hours have also added to the decline of our sport. These attitudes have generally been expressed by 'non sporty' people, and there are and always have been, many who fall into this category. The expression 'you must be mad' comes to mind. I've even heard it uttered by short distance time triallists and roadmen. When I was younger I found that the more adverse the comments were about my cycling and long distance riding and racing, the more determined and obstinate I became. Sadly this isn't the case with many of the younger people today, they worry too much about their image and what their friends will think of them, and finally they bow to peer pressure.

Sweating or perspiring from effort, how many people, other than sportsmen or women, do that anymore in this day and age. It's definitely not in vogue for 60% of the population, for them it's a bodily function that only happens during a fever or after having a really hot curry, from being obese, or at a rave whilst on 'ecstasy'. Sadly the main weekly 'Cycling' magazines attitude hasn't helped the situation much for the last 20 years or more. They've gradually squeezed out any proper informative articles or coverage of 24hr racing or long distance record breaking, quoting such reasons as: lack of space due to the coverage of the 'Tour de France' which seems to last for at least 9 months, also the 'Vuelta', 'Giro', Schoolboys 10 mile championships etc, etc, the list being endless. However, there are numerous pages of articles devoted to testing the latest 'blinged' (I do hate that word) carbon fibre race bikes in the Alps, or to testing the 'must have' pair of wheels at only £1,500 a pair. Numerous photos of readers mates riding a local club '10' dressed like Lance Armstrong in a prologue time trial, have also taken up columns of valuable space.

Where have all the regional reporters and contacts gone to? Apart from the Advertising Department, the European and Domestic road race coverage Dept, the rest of the magazine (the part that used to be interesting) seems to be run by probably only one person and is now down to one page.

Even more sadly disturbing, is the fact that our own governing time trial organisation, the RTTC has, over the last 30 years, tried to undermine any growth that the longer races such as the 12 hour and 24 hour should have had. The future of the 12 hour race as part of the 'BBAR' has been in question for a very long time now, but thank goodness, we still have a real time trial worthy of being in that competition. After all, how can you be classed as the 'best all round time triallist', if you only race up to 4hrs or even less?

The 10 mile time trial which was deemed a 'novelty' or ladies and junior's event when I started racing in the late 1950's is now looked upon as a major sporting distance. Early in 2008 I spoke to Colin Baldwin, a qualified cycling and sports masseur who also organises and officiates in events in the Southport area, and he mentioned that a 10 mile event on the 'Levens' course at Brock had attracted over 170 entries from riders whereas 50 mile events in the same area were lucky to get a field of 50 riders.

The 24 hour has been a lost cause to the RTTC for many years now, they even tried to deny it from having a Championship status, and how much more of a Champion cyclist can you be, than the winner of a 24 hour race, or to come 2nd or 3rd, or by being part of a team, better than anyone else's team? They have also quoted safety issues, especially at night as being a weak point, but again, statistics and race reports have proved that there isn't an issue at all. We've even been warned about drinking too much tea and coffee, and that just about sums it up!

But I will stop there, on this subject of decline since 1963, and the causes and possible solutions. I bet you're glad I've not mentioned white vans, road humps, huge triple axle 40 ton lorries with possibly even larger 60 ton models with trailers to come. Cheap imports; 'political-correctnesses' such as children being degraded and humiliated by being encouraged to compete in a sport or team game against each other; Government disinterest and the 'selling off' of school playing fields for housing; 'carbon footprint'; 'climate change'; immigration; 4x4 vehicles; cycle lanes that are a joke; obesity; drug and drink abuse; irresponsible TV companies, hedge cutting;etc,etc.

If you want to read the 'inside story' of how top rider Ian Dow tackled his training and racing over a period of 15 years, 1975-1990, then go back to the reports covering those years, in particular the North Road event of 1978 and the 'NMCF' Championship of 1986. There was nothing scientific about Ian's training, just sheer hard miles over the winter and then devoting a specific period of 4 weeks intense training just prior to his first North Road win with 472 miles.

Interestingly, Ian's 500 mile win in the South DC event of 1987 was ridden prior to tri-bars being allowed in RTTC events, and of course so were those of Roy Cromack and John Woodburn in 1969 and 1980 respectively.

By 1957 Raleigh had become the largest cycle manufacturer in the world. It had acquired many other brand names by this time including Rudge-Whitworth, Triumph, Three Spires Cycles of Coventry and BSA (New Hudson & Sunbeam).

A new factory producing Sturmey Archer gears, costing just over a million pounds, now took the total ground area, covered by the complete works, up to 60 acres, but Raleigh didn't have an easy time, and a slump in cycle sales was recorded. A boom in moped sales and the ease of paying for goods by Hire Purchase meant that many people could now afford cars, mopeds and household luxury goods such as fridges and televisions etc. General cycle use was now in decline at this period in time.

In the 1960's it was felt that Raleigh were not making enough good quality racing machines and they set about rectifying the problem by taking Carlton Cycles under their wing. Gerald O'Donovan of Carlton was given his own workforce and specialist workshops at Ilkeston devoted purely to lightweight hand-built racing bike production.

By the 1970's Raleigh were supplying and sponsoring racing teams in various countries and had a large involvement as 'TI-Raleigh' with the professional scene under the direction of David Duffield and Peter Post. To keep Raleigh producing popular cycle models for all ages and user groups they used the services of designer Alex Moulton who introduced the 'RSW' range of small wheel and compact folding cycles. In 1970 Alan Oakley, Raleigh's Chief Designer came up with a new design, 'The Chopper', which proved a huge success in the U.K. followed by the 'Grifter' and then a bmx range called 'Burner'.

In the 1980's an all terrain bike soon followed called a Bomber. This full size 26" wheel bike was one of the forerunners of the mountain bike, a craze that started in America and swiftly caught on in the UK, and eventually world wide.

Since 1880 Raleigh had built up an export market supplying 140 countries, including many of the Commonwealth countries worldwide; they also had a huge operation in America. By 1980, shortly before I joined the trade and opened my first small cycle shop, trade was already dwindling. The mountain bike boom hadn't yet started, Raleigh was obviously still the major UK cycle manufacturer with Falcon-Coventry Eagle Cycles and Dawes still in the running as British cycle makers. At that time they were all trying to stave off competition from European manufacturers such as Peugeot and Kalkhoff.

We had survived the '3 day week' in 1973 leading to the 'winter of discontent' and in March 1984 a miner's strike, which lasted a year, again saw the country plunged into uncertainty. Like the slump and depression of the 1930's, various parts of the country that relied solely on coal mining were decimated leading to huge job losses. Many of these communities to this day have never recovered and Margaret Thatcher's personal vendetta against the coal miners led by Arthur Scargill, and her determination to close many pits which she claimed as a 'great victory', went a long way to create a vast gulf in people's fortunes, 'the have's' and the 'have not's'. Her 'free-market' deregulation policies plus the privatisation of many of our major industries, services and institutions, exacerbated since then by the present Labour government has, I think, led to the greed in the financial market and the poor state we are in today 2007-2009.

By the mid 1980's China, Japan and many Pacific rim countries were expanding their cycle industries and markets to go worldwide. The quality of components from Japan right from early days has always been good, innovative and user friendly, and made serious 'in roads' affecting the sales from major European component manufacturers. Cycles and accessories from Taiwan, an island just off the coast of mainland China, have in my estimation, also been of good quality, and the 'Giant' brand name has been a major player for well over 20 years.

By the mid 1990's Raleigh had lost its grip on the UK market even though they had a massive dealer structure nationwide, making them a household name for bikes. With a good marketing scheme and a large and varied component and accessories range, they should have been able to compete, but by the year 2000 most of the factory workforce had gone. The 60 acres of land had been sold off to keep the shareholders happy and Raleigh went the same way as the other existing British brand names, Falcon, Claud Butler and Dawes, just selling boxed bikes from Pacific rim countries to the trade, through a handful of representatives and a small computerised office.

I had visited these British factories in the 1980's still thriving and bustling and to me it seems such an awful waste of our skilled workforce now they are all closed. I do wonder what will happen to the supply of general purpose cycles into this country once the Chinese workers start asking for better wages, so making their products more expensive, but I'm afraid there will always be a developing third world country willing to supply us with cheap bikes.

We still have a few skilled frame makers producing small amounts of hand built, individually made specialist cycles and components, but there are no 'volume' manufacturers left at all. As mentioned elsewhere in this book, our roads are clogged by huge lorries transporting thousands of boxes full of foreign goods, including cycles, from one huge warehouse or store to another.

On reflection, the history and the fortunes of Raleigh seems to have mirrored our own long distance cycle racing very closely, since the 1880's.

# CHAPTER SEVEN

## VISIONS OF THE FUTURE

## DREAMS OR REALITY

My ultimate **'Dream Visions'** for the future of long distance cycling, and indeed most forms of cycling, are many. My first vision would be that time trialling, especially at 100 miles, 12 hours and 24 hours, becomes a National and Olympic sport.   Likewise, the current Olympic distance triathlon would be increased to an 'Ironman' and any sporting events (excluding the original Olympic track centre disciplines) would be looked upon as 'novelty' events, if they only took a few minutes to complete.   The marathon at 26 miles would still be staged, but there would also be a 50 mile and 100 mile run.

In my dream future, athletes, cyclists, swimmers, runners and any other participants in long duration events would be given much more encouragement, appreciation and recognition for their efforts and achievements, not looked upon as 'freaks' and 'nutcases', (just two of the modern day descriptions from people who cannot aspire to high achievements themselves).

I would also hope that my dream vision could include a more intense participation by the 'media' and that they publish more than just 'tongue in cheek' rhetoric and eye catching headlines as is presently experienced.  We need a more meaningful and informative coverage of long distance events such as 12hr and 24hr time trials, plus maybe even a road record or two, like the Edinburgh–London or the 'End to End'.   I'm sure these articles would be well received, as would 'retro' articles on past riders and champions.

Maybe there will be a TV sports channel or media in the future interested in broadcasting tough endurance events, one that doesn't just show 'wall to wall' golf, football, cricket, tennis, motor racing etc.   After all, we've already had over 40 years of television where many of the programmes have just been popularist 'junk for the masses'.  Maybe then, we will see some proper sporting heroes and heroines and profiles of pioneering outdoor 'stars' whose life styles are worth emulating, rather than the ones who are only driven by obscene amounts of money.

Hopefully a new cycling publication of the future would pay attention to its reader's wishes and devote 80% of its pages to cycling and cyclists in this country with the emphasis on time trials and amateur club sport.  It would publish details of forthcoming future events, preferably the longer ones.  Event coverage, promotion and support would have to be impartial, with equal space and time given to both sponsored and non-sponsored events.   The same impartial reporting coverage would also apply to individual riders and teams alike.

Only racing from the British Isles or UK would be featured in the main, with scant coverage of the Vuelta, Giro, and Tour de France, and only on the weeks that they take place, not for 40 weeks of the year, as is commonplace at the moment.  After all, most people if they are really interested in European professional events, will have seen them live on Sky TV or other channels, so making magazine coverage at least 3 days old.   'Sportive rides', 'Tap de Tours', and events of a similar nature, which are basically over priced reliability trials, would also receive the same scant recognition.

In the winter months when space is plentiful, cyclo cross events would get good coverage, especially the longer ones like the 'Three Peaks'.  'Hill climbs'; are also another specialist sport for the 'off' season, but quite often are of very short duration, some only taking a few minutes.  A round up of news from genuine cycling clubs around the country would always be a welcome item to read, perhaps discussing future strategies and the hopes of their members.   Clubs could also disclose their location, where their popular rides are, and what days and times they meet, this could go some way to attract new members.  A club's annual dinner and prize presentation could also be of interest to read about, especially if it was a 50th or centenary celebration.

Articles on time trial 'stars' past and present and in-depth, meaningful interviews with each of the top six men and women 'BBAR' riders would make useful information for young aspiring time triallists, followed by a good coverage of the BBAR prize awards.  Maybe this magazine of the future could be used as an interactive forum for riders to exchange race information or give advice on how to prepare for longer races.   Safety issues could also be discussed, maybe grievances could also be 'aired' and a 'think tank' for the future of our sport would also be useful.

Advertising would probably have to take up the other 20% of space, but not to the point where it is so prevalent and interspersed that the publication looks like a weekly mail order catalogue. Hopefully this new publication would act as a useful tool in the drive to resurrect our flagging sport of time trialling, after all, the media in the past as well as being a mouthpiece of the cycle trade, has always provided a platform for the captains and guardians of our sport for over a 100 years. I can't think of a leader or 'Captain' that we can boast of at this present time, or even a prominent spokesperson, but hopefully my dream future will include one or two modern day equivalents of F.T. Bidlake and 'G.H.S.' George Herbert Stancer who can guide us through these 'nanny state' car orientated, money and image obsessed times we are in.

I firmly believe that publicising what we do and the way future riders can participate is the only way forward. Ian Dow in the early 90's, when he was the Editor of the 24hr Fellowship Journal, asked the question "are people actually aware that there is a 24 hour time trial?"

Long distance racing gets very little publicity, either before during or after the event, and even in the past it was only the professional riders whose deeds were publicised nationally, in newspapers, on radio, or newsreel films. Eileen Sheridan was probably the most well known women's sports personality in the 1950's and Reg Harris, the track sprinter was one of the mens. Events at that time, whether time trials or RRA records were 'Private and Confidential' and prior publicity was not allowed, consequently the world outside of the sport was not aware of what was happening until after the event. Amazingly nearly 60 years later, nothing has changed. Both Lynne and Gethin's End to End and 1,000 miles record rides were carried out amidst an air of almost secrecy and subterfuge, both riders received nearly a full page between them in our own press, even though there is no rule or law banning publicity in this modern age.

I also feel that there are still strained relationships and bad vibes coming from the Transport authorities, the Police, the Motoring lobby and the general motoring public, believing that the roads are for them only, and that cyclists and everyone else moving at a slower pace are a real nuisance and shouldn't be on the road at all. The poor pedestrians rank even lower than cyclists! Horses and their riders seem to be the only slow moving road users to receive consideration and that is only because horses can be unpredictable and leave a motorist with a few big dents should there be an altercation. We haven't got an outspoken guardian of our sport willing to 'fight for our rights' even though we have had one or two high profile court cases fought and often won by the CTC solicitors. These actions have been taken where the rights of cyclists have been totally ignored or overruled by the Police and they are all actions that have been taken in the 'rear guard' defence of cyclists. What we really need is a pro-active, progressive 'front guard' defence committee or promoting body made up from representatives of all the governing bodies and branches of our sport

"Do you want all the road?"

i.e. The CTT, BC, CTC, BTA, RRA and Audax UK. This 'committees' sole purpose would be to protect and promote cycling's future position and rightful place on the road, not only as a sport, but also to extol all of the benefits that cycling can bring to a nation.

With obesity and overcrowded roads being a major issue, and now in 2008 the economic downturn as well as the protection of our environment, I feel that cycling is an obvious solution to many of these problems. A financial 'fighting fund' could be made available by either Lottery money, donations from cycling clubs and organisations, also a levy of a few pence could be added onto each entry fee for events run by all of the various sections of the sport as previously listed.

Government ministers could be lobbied and maybe we will be lucky enough to win support from a controversial outspoken figure like Ken Livingstone or Boris Johnson. They are not politically afraid of ruffling a few feathers and making a nuisance of themselves every time the question of obesity and the health of the nation is talked about from a remedial perspective and not a preventative one, or the acute transport problems surrounding us daily. Global warming and most active people's carbon footprint could also be reduced by cycling if only they had a safer environment to ride in. After all, when have we ever heard a politician propose cycling as a possible sensible sustainable, cheap solution to any of these problems? I can see them all in Parliament now, waving their papers and bleating like sheep.

It is questionable as to whether any of the present day cycling publications would be worth using to promote cycling as a sensible option, to address the problems I've mentioned previously, they all seem to be unconcerned about such serious issues as it would be deemed as using up non profitable column inches. Even the CTC's own regular publication seems to be guiding cyclist's interests away from the road and onto tracks and trails. The publicity, protection and promotion of our sport and cycling generally for future generations seems to be very low on anyone's list of priorities or even non-existent. There seems to be no 'joined up' action or proposals to get the Government to promote and make cycling an important issue.

I did think that our terrific success at the Olympics and the huge haul of gold medals could possibly raise the profile of cycling and it probably did for about a fortnight, but within hours of the games finishing I was almost bundled off the road by an impatient motorist and then a day later was hit a glancing blow by a passing tractor and trailer. I suppose two Olympic champions hurtling around a track on aero dynamic bikes, dressed in figure hugging lycra and wearing aero helmets bears little resemblance to the average cyclist on the road. A non-cycling person could be enthusing about Bradley Wiggins winning another pursuit gold medal and then 10 minutes later, driving his car and blasting his horn at a cyclist who happened to be in his way. This is how probably 60% of the motoring public view cyclists, good to watch on the television in the Olympics, but a real nuisance on the road!

The cycle trades investment in our future is now wholly influenced and controlled by foreign companies. To the large cycle and accessory manufacturers and 'Pacific Rim' suppliers, the UK market is too insignificant to bother with, as it represents too small a percentage of their world-wide sales. They have no planned and co-ordinated strategy to promote cycling other than in their own individual brand brochures and cycling press. Our future growth as a sport and means of transport isn't in their hands, like the cycling press they are just preaching to those who are already converted.

We need a high profile charismatic spokesperson who could become the 'voice of cycling' not just for the sporting issues but also for cycling in general. He or she would appear on various TV chat shows, breakfast time, television programmes such as the 'One Show' and general news programmes, sporting quizzes etc. They would have a regular column in one or two high profile daily newspapers and generally make themselves available to comment on any cycling issue or to give an opinion on any subject or concern affecting cycling and cyclists at any time.

The spokesperson would also need to be present either as part of a committee or as a voice for cycling whenever any transport policy making is in progress. He or she needs to be able to 'bend the ear' of any high profile media figures such as Jon Snow, who is a cyclist himself, Jeremy Paxman and indeed any programme maker involved with either health, transport or global warming.

Other sports such as football, cricket, athletics and rowing have traditionally had their figureheads, mentors and role models, who have helped to shape their sports future and after watching our own successful stars on the track and road at the Olympics, I did wonder if there was a budding cycling leader and spokesperson amongst them who could take that role, but I doubt it.

The only positions in cycling that some of our past sporting stars have taken are either as cycle shop and cycle business owners or as manufacturer's representatives. Ex World Champion pursuiter Hugh Porter is probably the only one who has a regularly heard voice in cycling circles with his excellent race commentaries on all branches of the sport, but I'm afraid he is the only one. I can only think what powerful figureheads other Olympic champions have become for their sport, Dame Tanni Grey Thompson, Sir Steven Redgrave, Lord Sebastian Coe, and cyclists have no one!

I can only think of the impact that 'Greenpeace' has had on Politicians and Government Ministers worldwide. They originally carried out some very controversial campaigns, I say controversial only because of the way they obtained worldwide publicity through their risky manoeuvres, but the end result is that they are now watched and supported by millions of people and their spokespersons are listened to by governments worldwide. 'Friends of the Earth' are another organisation who have stood up and given their opinions on many controversial issues including climate change and the natural world around us.

Our cycling ambassador and committee of dedicated people hopefully wouldn't have to use any controversial actions or risky manoeuvres to gain their free publicity at every opportunity, but I'm afraid that without any recognition we will not be able to go forward and stake our positions and push for our rights in a nation full of 'petrol-heads'.

To re-iterate the reasoning and the importance of my last few paragraphs, I open my local evening newspaper in October 2008 and I see a colour coded map of England with the areas of high mortality portrayed. Northern cities such as Glasgow, Newcastle upon Tyne, Liverpool and Manchester are all high risk areas.. Parts of the West Midlands and Staffordshire where I live are also rated moderately at risk. Just below this mortality map is a totally separate article on the decreasing amount of cycle lanes and how the 'CTC' campaigners found that the Government in 2001/2 created 405km of cycle lanes but in the years 2006/7 that figure had slumped to 140km.

Why the figures are quoted in Kilometres I don't know, maybe it looks a larger amount, after all 140km is only 94 miles for the whole of England. The 'CTC' campaigners also quoted that their members thought the lanes were 'too narrow', not in the right place and randomly came to a stop. In my area near Lichfield we recently had cycle lanes installed on one main road into the city for about 2 miles. It involves a 4ft width of red tarmac on either side of the road, plus various traffic 'furniture' such as bollards and road narrowing chicanes have also been installed. But the irony of it all, is that the cycle lanes have actually reduced the carriageway width for the motorist. This obviously makes the motorist unhappy and so alienates us once more. The road passes through suburbs, and house drives lead directly onto the road where cars and delivery vans park outside the houses, rendering the cycle lanes absolutely useless. The cyclist is then forced back out onto the main carriageway.

A better safer future could be attained for cyclists, whether at club level, racing, sporting, touring or even commuting, if there was a total ban on the glorification of speeding cars and powerful cars, whether depicted in adverts or on consumer programmes such as 'Top Gear'. I'm sure most people are aware of what the presenter of that programme thinks of cyclists and pedestrians or indeed any poor soul who gets in his way while he is having fun in his car. What a waste of viewing time and fuel and what an irresponsible TV company, one I have no choice but to pay my licence fee for.

Getting up to speed as quickly as possible and being pressurised to maintain that speed as a novice driver, either before, during or after passing the driving test, as is the current teaching trend should be discouraged. Many drivers, especially the young, continue to drive much too fast for our crowded narrow roads and conditions, to a point in 2008 where not one of the major car insurance companies will insure an individual driver under 21 years of age. Death and accident rates at 17 years of age are 10 times higher than for a person of 35 (these figures apply mainly to 17 and 18 year old males). This is why many youngsters are caught driving illegally without insurance.

To tie in speeding cars with the thinking on 'global warming' a subject I've felt very strongly about since around 1970 when I tuned family cars for fuel efficiency with diagnostic equipment for a living, I would ban the manufacture and sale of any car or vehicle that couldn't produce economy figures way above what are generally accepted at present day. A car or vehicle that carries up to eight people would have to produce 70 mpg and a car that takes up to five people at least 90 mpg.

For years now, manufacturers have spent millions on the looks of a car and what speed and performance figures it can produce. Companies have competed with each other to see who can supply the most gadgets in their cars, but not one of them has bothered much about fuel consumption figures. Adverts for new cars and vehicles usually have technical jargon including fuel consumption and economy figures written in very small print under the advert, I also found that the varying consumption figures were quite difficult to understand.

For years I couldn't understand why fuel economy was almost bottom of the list of priorities when it came to producing a car but at last in 2007 and 2008 I've noticed innovative manufacturers such as Citroen actually laying claim that under stringent varied road testing they have vehicles that now produce over 80 mpg, so that is a step in the right direction and I hope others will follow suit.

We have the technology and knowledge and the manufacturing base to produce 'hybrid' engines and power units that incorporate all of the latest fuel saving innovations, so it shouldn't be too difficult. The only problem will be found in trying to change the 'mindset' of the general motoring public who will be loathe to give up their fast, gas guzzling monsters, their luxurious 'personal spaces' and 'comfort protection zones' on wheels.

Speed limits would be cut to 60 mph on motorways (adding just over 10 mins onto a 100 mile journey, 50mph on all major trunk and 'A' category roads that are shared with cyclists, pedestrians and other non-motorway traffic, and 40 mph on all rural roads, lanes and 'B' roads, where safe to do so. The suburban and pedestrian area limits we have at present, of 30 and 20mph respectively are about right. These new limits will automatically save fuel drastically not only for cars but also for vans, lorries and buses. I think it will create a safer environment not only for pedestrians and cyclists, but also for all other road users and wildlife.

All trainee learner motorists and motor cyclists would undergo at least a years tuition, not only regularly behind the wheel of a car with a proper instructor but also with time spent on a bicycle, learning the art of courtesy to others, roadcraft, coping with all conditions, all weathers and also night riding. Learning to survive on a cycle in these environments whilst coping with high-speed traffic would be a real eye-opener for most people new to cycling. All this, coupled to a more stringent road driving test would make things much safer all round and reduce the actual amount of drivers and cars on the road. At present day we have in the region of 37 million drivers and probably more than 30 million cars.

The age for learning to drive would be increased to 20 years old with a driving test no sooner than 12 months after the first official lesson. Anyone losing their licence through the totting up of points system or for dangerous or drunken/drugged motoring offences would automatically be banned 'for life'. Injury or death caused by dangerous driving would also incur an automatic ban for life and a proper custodial sentence with a minimum of five years actually served by the offender, whatever the circumstances. All children above the age of five would be taught to ride a cycle properly at school and made to integrate safely with pedestrians on shared use pavements and paths. They would at a later age, possibly twelve, be taught roadcraft, the highway code and then how to ride on suburban roads, or shared use paths to get to school safely on their own. After all, at the moment we have probably two recent generations of drivers on our road, who have never cycled or even walked to school, on or along a road. They may have had a BMX cycle or mountain bike and they may have even done a paper round on a bike or on foot, but a lot of them have never been taught roadcraft on a proper road. They get taken to school by their parents and they then either progress to a motor scooter or moped for a year or two or get behind the wheel of a car, using their parents insurance.

Any future new road building, other than motorways, would have to include proper cycle tracks or shared use paths on both sides of the road wherever physically possible, to run parallel to the carriageway but separated safely away from the road edges by a safety margin or barrier. The parking of motor vehicles for any purpose would be strictly prohibited on or across these cycle lanes. The proviso would also be in place for any competent cyclist who normally rides on the main carriageway, and has a lawful age-old right to do so, would be regarded by law as a vehicle and allowed to ride on the carriageway. All existing roads would also have to include properly planned and thought out cycle routes, lanes or shared use paths different to the 'Mickey Mouse' ones we have at present.

I also feel very strongly about 'crime and the causes' and I'm absolutely convinced that certainly amongst young males, a lack of sporting facilities and opportunities are to blame. Being denied the chance to belong to a sporting team or club group of any sort as opposed to drifting around in a 'gang', is a definite factor fuelling today's crime rate. A recent survey in 2007 revealed that 70% of British teenagers take no part in organised sport after the age of 16. When the Government 'sold off' the school sports fields and cut the time spent on the sports field or in the Gym from the weekly school curriculum I felt it was a criminal act in itself. As a 'stroppy' teenager myself I benefitted greatly from sport, either running myself into the ground playing various ball games on the local recreation ground, or playing table tennis and socialising at a Catholic youth club. I cycled for hours on end, in all weathers, coming home too exhausted to be troublesome, just hungry, tired and in need of a wash.

I joined Birmingham St Christopher's Catholic Cycling Club at 13 and never looked back. I had become a proper cyclist and had a duty not to let my club or family name down.

I also firmly believe that until the crime rate, both on the streets, in the Cities and our suburbs or on the main highways is dealt with, we will limp along as a Nation, struggling day to day from one crisis to another. I would increase the 'useful' manpower of our police force by an extra 50% until the problems are significantly reduced. If the Government refuse, due to lack of funding, I can only think how biased and unfair their handling of the 'Northern Rock' bank and their commitment to shore up any dodgy ailing financial institution to the tune of over 200 billion pounds of our money was. Unfortunately, with all of the old fashioned values gone and with 'u' turns by the Government and local authorities almost on a weekly basis, it's a wonder that anarchy hasn't broken out!

"FANCY that - it's been lovely here all day."

But in all truth, my **'Realistic vision'** for the future of long distance time trials at 12hours and 24hours and epic place to place RRA road records, is one of continuing decline in entries and general performances. Strangely enough, Audax events at all distances from 100 kms to 1200 kms seem not to have been affected by this malais. Maybe it's the fact that they are ridden at a fast touring pace with small groups of riders spread out along fairly quiet 'B' roads and lanes, that makes the events more attractive to riders of all abilities, than riding a time trial.

Endurance or 'Enduro' off road mountain bike races from six hours to 24hours also seem to be very popular still. I have first hand knowledge of both these sports, the difference being that Audax events generally are run on a voluntary, cost covering basis, as opposed to mountain bike races which are costly to enter and are usually heavily supported and sponsored by the cycle trade, and run for a profit.

The efforts of the faithful, hardworking non profit making club organisers and secretaries of not just long distance time trials but events at most distances seem to be thwarted by red tape in the form of course safety, police regulations, last minute road closures and course alterations all on a regular basis. Even on a wet day, events have to be cancelled due to spray from vehicles affecting visibility.

Maybe the fact that the Mersey RC 24hr is run on a subscription basis and relies upon donations from interested individuals and groups, as well as the entry fees from riders, has kept it going all these years, I don't know, but I do know that the North Road CC event that ran for over 100 years, ceased to exist after 1999 due to rapidly reducing entries, plus a lack of interest and enthusiasm from a majority of its own club members. The last event organiser and secretary, Roger Sewell, who was as passionate about 24hr racing as members of his own family had been for 90 years, worked so hard along with 24hr Fellowship members and stalwarts from the Mersey RC to keep the event running. He even provided prize money from his own pocket (although he wouldn't want me to mention that) but in the end he was forced to abandon this once proud annual promotion.

*As a protest to some of the North Road member's apathy, Roger Sewell joined the Hounslow and District Wheelers and rode the North Road 24hr in 1997, coming 3rd with 429 miles whilst still promoting and running that same event on behalf of the North Road Club.*

Ken Stokes tragic death during the last North Road event which I think was probably the only fatality in its 114 years history, made the decision final. While the tragic circumstances were not the fault of either the rider or the events promoter, but instead due to a callous hit and run driver, it is still the innocent parties who've suffered.

Bob Williams who generally lays out and prepares the Mersey RC 24hr course every year by placing direction arrows and the 'caution – Cycle race in progress' signs around various junctions and locations, has found that this job has required more skill and safety consciousness year upon year, as do the jobs of marshals and number checkers at various locations on the course, due to speeding and inconsiderate drivers.

The marshals are all very vulnerable but as cyclists they know what vulnerability really means in today's traffic conditions. They've been doing this job for years and many of them are 'bordering on elderly', but they know that without their help the event would eventually cease. Whether there is a field of 30 riders or 100, it doesn't make any difference to the total amount of helpers required, it's always at least 200. This event is the only survivor, whereas all others have eventually failed and I wonder how long can these good people keep coming back year after year to provide us with this wonderful unique event?

I certainly hope I'm wrong with my **Realistic Visions** and predictions, and I sincerely hope and wish Jon Williams and the Mersey RC all the success they deserve for the future running of this event, one I've been associated with for 50 years.

I mentioned earlier in Chapter 6 about owing it to yourself to try at least one 24hr race in your life, as sadly I've heard many riders say "I wish I'd had the courage to ride one, but I'm too old now and my back wouldn't last out that long". I'm sure that many good riders have reached the end of their careers or at least gone 'past their best' days and thought "I wonder what mileage I would have done if I had trained properly and ridden a 24hr?" and the same goes for their doubts about road record breaking. Their thoughts must have been even more fuelled when riders they knew they could beat at 100 miles or 12hour events, then went on to gain a high place or win in a Championship 24hr or break a long distance road record.

In my lifetime I'm glad to say that I've probably influenced at least 20 riders, maybe more, to ride a 24 hour. Lynne can certainly double that figure and have the satisfaction of knowing she's advised many individuals and teams riding for charity on their End to End attempts and subsequent successes on a 'non-record' basis. They've all initially had the mindset that they couldn't possibly last the distance or the hours and we've suggested methods of training in an effort to instil an air of confidence in themselves, and virtually all of them have finished either the 24hr or the End to End or even both in some cases, all with good results.

The overwhelming opinion from them was that they'd all gained terrific self-esteem and confidence. All of them to a man (or woman) has said that it was definitely one of the best periods of their lives, especially when they finished and realised what they had achieved. In the case of 24hr time trialling, many of them went on ride more events.

If my history of these races has made you interested in any way, please go and have a look at the one last remaining annual 24 hour event on the calendar. It's held generally around the last weekend in July on roads in Shropshire and Cheshire. The event starts from Farndon near Wrexham at 1pm on Saturday and finishes on a circuit near Farndon from 1pm on Sunday. If you wish to enter then that's even better still. If in doubt as to your abilities and requirement for this event, then contact the Mersey RC website. After all, what other highly organised and relatively inexpensive, highly aerobic, amateur, outdoor sport is there that lasts for 24 hours?

Our long distance cycle racing that has a 125 year history is absolutely unique, but if it did sink into complete decline due to reasons mentioned, then that would be a very sad day, as it is a race that would be very difficult to revive in later years.

# CHAPTER EIGHT

## REFLECTIONS, REASONS FOR WRITING AND NOSTALGIC MOMENTS

This rich, unique history has absorbed my interest for the last 50 years, as long distance riding has played a large part in my life, primarily as a youngster drinking in the atmosphere that surrounded me during those early years of 24 hour riding and helping on record attempts, so much so, that I wanted to compete every year. Even though I was only a very average rider, I did have dreams that one day I would beat 450 miles and attain a top three placing or perhaps even break a road record and get my name in the RRA handbook, I would then own a much coveted certificate to frame and hang on the wall at home.

Well, I did break a few road records with Pat Kenny on a tandem trike and I did go on to complete seventeen 24 hour races, but I think I earned as much pleasure and feelings of achievement by helping others to reach their goals, such as being on Pat's trike End to End in 1980 as chief cook and bottle washer and driving the following car with Ron Macqueen to time his ride. After observing on Mick Coupe's End to End in 1982, my next call to duty was helping Lynne to achieve her long distance goals from 1990 onwards.

My absorption of knowledge and the work involved in archiving the material for this book has been made more exciting and interesting knowing that I was part of the history. Along the way I had the chance to see all of the greatest long distance riders since the late 1950's and was lucky enough to rub shoulders with many of them. I suppose that subconsciously I was storing information, which may not have been of interest to others at the time. I probably eavesdropped many conversations, either before, during or after races, or at gatherings such as club dinners and road record meetings. The added wealth of knowledge imparted to me by my team-mates, John Withers, Pete Swinden and Pat Kenny has certainly been a great help. Later on I became an avid reader of the 24 hour Fellowship Journal and over the years I have collected articles and photos of my long distance heroes from the cycling press.

Around 1980 I opened a small cycle retail business and apart from it curtailing the hours I could devote to my bike riding, it also diminished some of the excitement and interest I had in cycling, both as a sport and pastime. I was present at the launch of nearly all of the new innovations and products in the cycle trade from most of the major companies since 1985, which included second and third generation aluminium and alloy frames, carbon and aluminium composites, disc wheels, carbon tri and four spoke wheels. Japanese indexed gearing, cassette hubs for multi speed gearing from six to ten sprockets (cogs) giving up to 30 gear combinations and ratios, all operated from the brake levers. Aerodynamic products such as tri-bars, aero helmets, modern training and racing aids such as turbo trainers, carbohydrate drinks (polymer feeding) and probably the most important of all to us 'night riders', decent lighting at long last.

Strangely enough it was probably the late 1980's when I was first made aware of 'l.e.d.'s' (light emitting diodes) by George Legg, a cycle trade representative for Kirk and Merrifield, a Birmingham wholesaler. He showed me this very small 'piercing' point of red light no bigger than the plastic plug in the end of a 'biro' and said to me that this new little light would revolutionise the cycle lighting industry, and asked if I wanted to place an order? I said that I wasn't convinced, and that I couldn't see how something so small and insignificant could possibly catch on or conform to British Standards, and were there any plans to make one for a front lamp? George said that they were working on it. I declined his offer and then put an order in for some more British made but very unreliable Ever Ready lamps!

"I've got one of those oval head tubes to reduce the resistance."

In the late 1980's the French 'Wonderlite' lamps came onto the British market and although they didn't provide much of a beam to see by, and also had poor brackets, they at least didn't suffer from bad internal connections and 'dodgy' switches. I learned of their reliability when my untested 6volt home made system failed in a Mersey RC 24hr and Ian and Bridget Boon kindly lent me their spare Wonderlamps, which lasted all night.

Time moved on and we pioneered forward from one tiny red 'l.e.d.' to multi-l.e.d.'s and multi-mode lights. Eventually the lights got brighter with better reflectors and all round visibility. Almost at the same time we had a neon yellow front 'l.e.d.' which gradually progressed and was then developed into a bright bluish white 'l.e.d.'. The race was now on to produce a white 'l.e.d.' that not only threw a beam but could also provide peripheral visibility to other road users, so that we could see and be seen. Obviously all of this research, development and manufacture was done in Japan and China, from the early 'l.e.d.' rear light through to the modern day lithium battery powered 20 and 30 watt front lights.

Road bikes in 2008 could now cost from as little as £300 to as much as £7,000 but weigh less than 6kg or 12lbs. Strangely enough, most of the research and development we have witnessed on the road bike scene covering the last 25 years, we have the 'mountain' or 'all terrain bike' to thank for. The explosion in popularity, marketing, development and sales of this 'off road' bike has captured the imagination of almost every age group, and its success has given the cycle industry worldwide, enough funding to take us forward, from the standard steel tubed 14 speed racing cycle of the 1980's to the 30 speed aerodynamic carbon fibre composite lightweight machines we now have in 2008.

In the 1980's and 1990's the British cycle industry went through many recessions and economic set-backs and one only has to look at the fortunes or misfortunes of Raleigh as one of the supposed leaders of the cycle industry, to see this. The mountain bike burst onto the scene in the mid 1980's, and I recall wistfully thinking around the mid 1990's, how lucky the industry had been to have a product, whether one likes mountain bikes or not, that has resurrected the fortunes of the trade and I shudder to think where the cycle trade would be today without it.

All of these products and innovations as they evolved, I had to view in a cold calculated business like manner, as a retailer rather than as a keen cyclist, with the consuming passion that I'd had since 13 years of age. In those early teenage years, I'd gazed longingly at the frames and components on display at Priory Cycles on the Stratford Road in Birmingham, and drooled over the latest imported equipment and bikes at Wilson's Cycles in Aston. If I was lucky enough I sometimes caught a glimpse of a famous local time triallist or an 'independent' roadman of the day as he called into the shop for parts. Another place and time where I lost myself to cycling dreams was watching the frame builder at work in the front window of a small bike shop in Carters Green, West Bromwich.

Eventually in the 1990's my only interest left in the sport was the 24 hour and long distance road records scene, where I tried to make myself available to help whenever I could. I did manage to race a few times during this period of 20 years between 1980 and 2000, but my spare time away from the shop has been mainly devoted to helping Lynne in her racing career. However, this was made even more difficult by the fact that she also worked in the bike shop so that when we were both away, her mum Liz and Dave Merriman, our mechanic, had to cope with everything.

Customers, friends and cycling club associates often commented about how interesting it must have been working in a bike shop, and asked if I had any plans to write a book about my experiences. I thought long and hard about the idea but couldn't view the prospect with much enthusiasm. I had however written a few reports and descriptions of Lynne's 24 hour rides by this time, mainly for a possible future historical documentary for her. I realised while doing this, that I actually got immense pleasure from writing, not only about Lynne's rides, but also about the 24hr races in general.

During the 1990's Lynne met Eileen Sheridan and they became good friends. Lynne wrote to Eileen regularly and when Lynne told her she was attempting the End to End on a tandem with Andy in 2000, their correspondence became even more intense. Eileen sent Lynne her own autobiography, which included the build up to her own solo professional 'End to End' and '1,000 miles' records in 1954. It was a book I had read in my earlier days, but when I read it the second time it had a whole new meaning. Over the years, if I wanted to find a documented and accurate description of a famous 24 hour or End to End record etc, I would spend hours trawling through at least 30 years worth of 24 hr Fellowship Journals and by the time I had found it I had usually been distracted many times by other interesting articles and material found there.

The day after returning home from Lynne and Andy's successful End to End in May 2000, I sat down and wrote an almost hour by hour description and account of their ride and had a few copies printed off to send to people who had helped out. A year later, Lynne announced that she was attempting the solo ladies record and I then happened to read Alan Ray's history of the End to End; it was a book that had been presented to Lynne at the Mersey RC dinner, by Paul Olson.

After reading Alan's book, I realised that it was the only existing history of the End to End records, and covered mainly high profile solo bike rides by men and women, but ended with Dick Poole's record in 1965. None of the trike, tandem or tandem trike records were mentioned in any detail, if at all, and I felt then that one day I would redress the situation and write a book covering the complete history of record rides over this famous journey, and also include the 1,000 mile record descriptions.

The recurring gastric problems that I experienced from the year 2000 onwards now gave me the chance to start writing seriously, and you will see from here on how it all affected me.

I think here, at this point in the book, it is worth mentioning a few peculiarities, phenomenons and physical distresses that can be experienced both by riders and helpers alike on long distance races. During and after my last three End to Ends and 1,000 miles, where I've either been a driver, helper, mechanic, or Observer and gone the complete distance from Lands End to John o' Groats, I have experienced some weird sensations. My first was partial loss of bowel and bladder control, which I found out later, is not an uncommon thing after being active and awake for 60 hours or more. Dai Davies, the timekeeper on three out of the last five successful End to Ends from 1998 was noted as not eating for the whole of these journeys and drinking just enough to stave off dehydration. When questioned about this, he told me he'd flown Hercules transport aircraft in the 1970's and 80's with the R.A.F. This meant being in the cockpit for very long hours, and it was his way of dealing without needing the toilet at a crucial time on a flight or later on a record attempt.

I personally find that sleepiness doesn't affect me at all while I am on the move, whether it be a 12hr, 24hr or an End to End. The adrenalin from following the rider, or getting out to cheer them on, or pass up food and drink every half hour, stops you from even thinking about sleep. This adrenalin fuelled concern is even more intense when it's a member of your own family you are helping. However much food and drink I took along for the journey for myself, I found that I was existing for seven or eight hours or more without even thinking about either. I've tried to sleep when told to, but found it impossible to do so on the move. When helping on 24hr races I can be active day and night and it isn't until I leave the HQ after the race that I find my eyes will not stay open. In those situations Liz drives me home.

On Lynne's first solo End to End, I drove the following vehicle a fair percentage of the journey and found no problem at all until I reached the traffic lights at Wick after 820 miles, and when I stopped I found that I was pulling the handbrake on really hard and still felt that the van was trying to surge forward. When I looked around at stationary objects at the roadside I realised it was me who had a small problem with 'constant forward movement', not the van. This phenomenon had been caused by travelling in a forward direction for over 50 hours.

I'm pretty sure that hallucinations, when they occur to riders on these epic journeys from 24 hours to End to Ends and 1,000 miles, are caused obviously by sleep deprivation combined with tricks caused by either cars lights or daylight, creating a perceived shape or image that isn't really there. One example was on the A9 in the Grampians at about 3am on the second night, Lynne went past a long lay-by that had several waist high black and white posts with reflectors on the top, lining the edge of the road, and she honestly thought that they were a row of penguins patiently watching her go by.

Many riders have hallucinated in daylight, mistaking post boxes and rubbish bins for people, and even wishing them good morning. I liken it to dreaming with your eyes open, and I'm sure many people have experienced getting home having either ridden or driven for miles over a familiar route that contains traffic lights, junctions, roundabouts, and suddenly panicking from having no memory of that particular part of their journey. "Did I stop at the lights, or at that junction; have I left a trail of destruction behind me?" The answer is no, because you've been on auto-pilot and probably driving quite normally whilst day dreaming about something else. This is very similar to our rider who appears to be riding fairly normally even whilst having mild hallucinations.

A different phenomena, one that I have witnessed on at least three occasions, is when 'stokers' on either a tandem or tandem trike, have pedalled quite hard and reacted to position and balance adjustments and instructions from the steersman, whilst fast asleep. Pete Swinden remembers having a long conversation with his stoker John Withers, who was pedalling hard but apparently fast asleep on the tandem as they headed towards John o' Groats. John said that he had no recollection of that particular part of the journey or of the conversation. Strangely enough, although most tandemists can ride either the back or the front, it is very rare throughout the history of long distance time trailing and road record breaking, that a 'stoker' has swapped places with a 'steersperson'. I use the word steersperson because Miss Jodi Groesbeck and Adrian Harris did swap places on their End to End record, but I think it was mainly because Jodi was an American and Adrian was British and he went on the back of the tandem after Bristol so that he could map read through some of the more difficult towns and cities.

It almost makes commonsense for both riders to do a 'turn about' every now and then, without too much difficulty 'position wise' as the steersman regularly suffers from mild exposure and the worst conditions, when rain, wind, or cold, are experienced. Likewise the stoker quite often overheats on the back and would probably benefit from a 'refresher' on the front. In hindsight, both Pat Kenny and Andy Wilkinson both suffered from exposure on the front of their respective tandem trike and tandem rides. I did however swap with Pat after he had got freezing cold dropping down into Inverness on our first End to End attempt. I took the next section over Aultnamain while he got warm and had a sleep on the back as we hurtled down the other side towards Bonar Bridge. It was a white-knuckle experience for me, and a nice snooze for Pat who rested his head on my back. Although it gave him a much needed break, we were too far behind schedule for it to be of much use, and the attempt was abandoned at around the 48 hour mark with nearly 800 miles covered.

On Andy & Lynne's mixed tandem End to End in 2000 after crossing the Grampians, Andy would have benefited from having a short break and going on to the back of the tandem, and if the truth was known, a swap in the first 24hrs wouldn't have gone amiss either.

I've included these details on sleep and sleep deprivation in this history because I feel that it could be of interest or importance, safety wise, to anyone planning on riding or helping for the first time, and that it may give them an insight as to what can happen. I cannot express strongly enough the safety aspect of all this, especially after a 12 hour or 24 hour time trial, when either the rider or their helper feels that they will be safe to drive home, even if it is only an hour away.

By standing or sitting in the HQ for an hour or more waiting for the results, and winding down in a less oxygenated space, after ones adrenalin has stopped flowing, can be a crucial time to make the right decision. If there isn't a fairly fresh 'reserve' driver, I strongly recommend that an hour or two of sleep be taken. It could be just enough to relax and re-strengthen the eyelid muscles for the journey home. There isn't a successful formula for staving off the need for sleep as everyone is different. Some people need a full eight hours and are physically lacking without it, some people manage quite well with very little sleep and show no signs of tiredness. As far as I know there is no way of storing extra sleep before an event. Lynne has started her last three 'End to Ends' having had little or no sleep on all three occasions. The first time was the mixed tandem record, and by the time she and Andy had finished their 'pasta loading' it was time for bed, but a combination of nerves and indigestion kept Lynne awake for most of the night. With the experience she has gained over the last fourteen years or more, Lynne doesn't panic if she can't sleep. She knows that resting with her eyes closed for a few hours is usually enough.

I strongly advise the wearing of protective wrap-around glasses; yellow tinted light enhancing ones for dusk to dawn and UV protective tinted or clear for the daylight hours. Glasses not only protect your eyes from dust, stones and insects, but also stop your eyes drying out and the eyelids taking a battering from the persistent airflow. If five minutes sleep isn't enough, then try 10 minutes, but anymore than that usually puts the rider into a deeper sleep, where the whole body starts to shut down into a state that is difficult to recover from, or to quickly recoup the higher heart rate or lungs and muscles work load required. Obviously road safety is very important, but most riders are highly charged with adrenalin and fully concentrated enough to continue. It would also be wise for the helpers to keep a constant look out for their tired rider and if they didn't respond properly to vocal instructions or were very slow to react, I would suggest they make their rider have another sleep.

After the frenzy of record breaking around the start of the new Millenium I wrote and published my first book on the complete 'History of the End to End and 1,000 mile records', and I'm glad to say that it was well received in such a specialist niche market.  Strangely enough, as if by a twist of fate, the time taken for writing the book and the many hours needed to research it, came about as a result of illness, where my health had been affected, probably by irregular eating whilst helping on these long haul 50 hour epics.   Three End to Ends, three years in succession and the stress levels induced during these rides, probably played a part in creating 'IBS' – (irritable bowel syndrome).  I.B.S. eventually progressed to gallstones and led to me being off work from the cycle shop for over a year.   During that time I sat for hours on end each day writing, sometimes until 2am; this led in turn to my developing a 'DVT' (deep vein thrombosis) in one leg.  Needless to say I spent the next six months on Warfarin tablets and standing up to finish writing my first book.    To use a modern day phrase or saying "how lucky or unlucky was that?"   I returned to work for a couple of years and trade was steady but didn't seem to be increasing much.   I then decided that I'd really had enough and it was time that the younger members of my family took over the business to take it forward.   Mike, my son, who already had a sound business experience behind him and had honed his skills in the cycle trade in my absences, decided to move the business a short distance away and open a large retail store.   He was backed by Liz, his mum, and Lynne, his sister, with their years of experience and expertise in the trade and with lots of new staff to cope, I was finally 'put out to graze'!

I felt contented with my first book, well almost contented, and many people had written to me saying how they had been transported back in time whilst reading it.   Some readers who had actually been involved in the End to End from the 1940's onwards said they were reduced to tears by the nostalgic reports I had included.    For these acclamations I was more than pleased, but was still niggled by the lack of publicity and interest shown by the media and the hierarchy of our sport, for anything more than a hundred mile race.

Where were the large headlines, the pages of photos and narrative, the revealing stories about how a 24 hour race was won, or an End to End and 1,000 mile record was conquered.  Who were the riders, how did they win, or break records; what were their training methods; what were their fears before or during the ride; what made them do it; but more importantly, where were the people who should have been championing these magnificent endurance record rides as they happened, or even after they happened? Maybe the riders themselves have got to do their own promotions and pester the media until their stories are told?   I don't have the answer, but I do know that most of the record breakers are very modest people and wouldn't dream of praising their own achievements.

It is for these reasons that I have tried to redress the situation with these two books.   For many years I felt a little uneasy that our past written history had been tucked away in over 40 years worth of 24 hour Fellowship Journals, as if belonging to a bygone age or a secret society.   I honestly thought that someone else would eventually write a book covering these histories, but to no avail, all of the other possible historians, archivists and authors had either passed away, or were too busy riding their bikes.   Maybe they also were too modest to praise their own past achievements, I don't know, but the consensus of opinion from people involved in the sport was that they were happy for me to write the history, so with the blessing of the 24 hour Fellowship, the RRA and the major clubs that were involved, I set about my lengthy task.

Whereas my first book covered 48 record End to End and 1,000 mile rides from 1929 to present day in reasonable detail, this new book would be on a comparatively massive scale.   With a possible 300 or more races to write about and thousands of riders in that 125 year period, it was going to be a tough job.   There were times when I had my doubts, and I felt that the subject was too vast for me to cover or to cram into one volume.   Apart from the somewhat repetitious annual 24 hour races to write about, I also wanted to keep the readers interest alive with reports on some of the longer 'place to place' records that took place in those same years.

As well as just documenting facts and figures, I also wanted to whisk the reader back in time by writing a little on the social history of those times, firstly to the Victorian era, then the Edwardian age and the beginnings of motoring and then the two World wars.   Through various recessions, depressions and numerous decades of change including the 'space-age' to present day, our long distance road records and 24 hour cycle racing has survived.   From its very inception in the 19th Century through the 20th Century to the new Millennium, this unique history is still intact even though it may not appear quite as buoyant, exciting and expanding as in its much earlier days.

I hope my various comments on certain controversial subjects and topics throughout the book haven't offended too many readers. They are mainly general 'gripes' aimed at large organisations, committees and governing bodies, as opposed to individuals. Where I've criticised a situation or a social dysfunction or lifestyle, I've also tried to suggest a solution to improve matters. My opinions are purely my own, but I know that they are possibly ones that are also shared by a fair proportion of cyclists, particularly the older ones.

One encouraging feature I experienced early in January 2008 was the applause and terrific reaction to Peter Whitfield's speech as Guest of Honour at the CTT 2007 'BBAR' awards in Nottingham. Whereas, in previous years, I have come away from the prize ceremony feeling increasingly more negative about our future, this year I came away feeling very good. I know they are only words, but the way the audience clapped and cheered when he spoke about the almost total lack of media publicity, participation and appraise our time trialling stars have received in the recent past and are still receiving, it was as though he had been reading everyone's thoughts. When he also mentioned the obsessive coverage of the 'Tour de France' and anything foreign, to the detriment of our own home-grown British sport, I felt he was very close to getting a standing ovation, except perhaps from any media reporters present, if there were any. It's as though he had wakened a shared feeling in all of us.

Peter has recently written and published two books dealing not only with time trial stars past and present, but also riders from all aspects of the sport, all with excellent photos. Both books are brilliant and much needed documents of our time, as I hope my own books will become.

Later there was a conveyor belt style of awards presentation, where I still wasn't too sure who our 6 female and 12 male 'BBAR' recipients were, or exactly who our CTT time trial Champions were, as there are now various and numerous different series, categories and age group awards, very similar to football with its various different sponsors, cups and leagues. I was however, pleased to see and hear Lynne Taylor and Eamonn Deane, both 2007 champions of the 24 hour race. They took to the microphone and praised the Mersey RC 24 hour event, and the people who help every year under the guidance of the William's family, Jonathan, the Organiser in particular. Both Champions proclaimed "long live the 24 hour".

# NOSTALGIC MOMENTS

My first item of nostalgic interest is also tinged with sadness. It concerns John George MacDonald, otherwise known as 'Mac', a Scotsman based in Birmingham for his work. He belonged to the Speedwell B.C. along with Richard Hulse and Sid Capener. Like Richard, 'Mac' had ridden a few 24hr events around the late 1940's and into the early 1950's. I think he rode 4 events in all and his best mileage was in the North Road event of 1947 with 340.43 miles. 'Mac' as a 24 hour man would have been very interested in the Crimes versus Arnold trike battles in the Mersey events from that time and up to 1954.

1953 was actually a very exciting time when these two men who had kept raising the 24hr competition record through their battles finally found a victor. John broke Albert's trike record by nearly 37 miles for a new record of 457.33 miles! That winter, Albert and John announced their intention to attack the 12hr, 24hr, End to End and 1,000 miles record on a tandem trike. Naturally 'Mac' was interested and decided to take a holiday to his beloved Scotland and on the way North he would see if he could help or be of any assistance to the record breakers. He took the train part way to get ahead of the riders on route, and as far as I know he did this on quite a few occasions, he would marshal or help to feed them and then get ahead again via the train.

Whenever a report appeared in the journals or 'Cycling' press at that time, it just said 'J.G. MacDonald of the Speedwell B.C. had died on route, while helping the record breakers in the north of Scotland'. I was always intrigued by this statement and wondered what really happened, was he alone when he died, what about his family etc? Where was he buried, how old was he, how did he die?

Late in 2006, John Arnold wrote to me and sent photos of a very descriptive black marble gravestone, the inscription being **"This stone was erected by the riders to the memory of John George Macdonald of the Speedwell Bicycle Club, Birmingham, who collapsed and died on the road at Everly Freswick on the 12th of July 1954 aged 52 years, after helping on the Lands End to John o' Groats and the 1,000 mile tandem tricycle record attempts from the 10th to the 12th of July 1954. 'Mac' now rests peacefully in his beloved Scotland".**

John went on to say in his letter that after the records were broken in 1954 he tried on several occasions to find 'Mac's' grave in Wick Cemetery. The correct version of the story that John managed to find on record in the local press at Wick, was that 'Mac' had arranged his cycling tour so that he could be present when Crimes and Arnold arrived at John o' Groats. He left Walsall and travelled north by train to meet the tricyclists and handed them a drink as they passed over Bonar Bridge early on the Monday morning. He then travelled to Wick by train and together with members of the Wick Wheelers CC he assisted in the marshalling of the route for the completion of the 1,000 miles over the roads of Caithness. The pair were due to finish their record ride at about midnight back at John o' Groats. 'Mac' was riding with a group of Wick Wheelers when he complained of feeling cold and unwell. The group stopped to help him. He put on his cycle cape and sat down to rest at the roadside. Mr Pat Macleod went to a nearby house for help but 'Mac's condition had deteriorated rapidly and he became unconscious. He was taken to a local house belonging to a Mrs R. Horton at Freswick and was then taken by car to John o' Groats, where a Dr Gill from Canisbay declared that Mr Macdonald was dead.

Some years later, Peter Barlow and Joe Davis who had been in the motorised support team for the record attempt, returned to Wick but were unable to find 'Mac's grave. John Arnold went on to say that before Albert Crimes died in 1985, he'd travelled to Helmsdale with his wife Marjorie, but Albert was too ill to continue with the task of finding the grave, and returned home. Finally in 2006, John took two journeys by train up to the 'Ord of Caithness' to find the grave and have a headstone made and inscribed. John's first trip north was cut short by a landslide across the railway line before Wick. Undeterred he returned later and was eventually successful in his efforts. This had been a duty that John felt he must complete, as his own health hadn't been too good in recent months.

So after 52 years, this sad mission has been accomplished, as John had promised to Albert.

Whilst researching John MacDonald's results in various 24 hour events, I came across a name I had been searching for, for ages, that of Barry Blagg, a close friend of mine from the 1960's and you will see later as to why I had been looking for a result sheet with his name on. We had raced together, toured together, ridden through the night to his parent's caravan on the Welsh coast beyond Barmouth, and spent many hours and days in each others company. Whereas I would train for a specific event and prepare properly, he would just turn up, take off his saddlebag and race, at any distance, and usually beat me. We both rode for Birmingham St Christopher's CCC and considered ourselves to be the 'back-bone members' along with John Withers, Pete Swinden, Pat Kenny, Reg Plant and Ant. Burke to name but a few. 'Baz' got married shortly after me in 1968 and we both had daughter's born around the same time. He was a merchant seaman and the life suited his easy going, laid back character. Baz would be back at sea for up to 3 months at a times, and then turn up on the doorstep unannounced at any ungodly hour, and invite himself in for a cup of tea and a natter. He would then catch up with club life as if he hadn't been away. Baz was very softly spoken with a cheeky grin and bright blue eyes, looking like a cross between Steve McQueen, George Peppard and Ewan McGregor.

In 1969 he rode his second 24 hr event, The Mersey RC National Championship, which Roy Cromack won with 507 miles, Baz was the only rider from St Christopher's CCC that year, which was unusual as we normally fielded a full team or more. He finished with 408.03 miles with no specific training at all. Nearly a year later whilst on a Spring bank holiday, in a caravan near Snowdon with his wife Carol and daughter Julie, he went off one dinnertime to walk in the mountains alone. Barry was never seen alive again, he'd fallen and his body was found at the bottom of a steep 'scree' slope.

At his funeral there was a church full of friends, relatives and young couples with children. It was a very sad day and his wife was also six months pregnant with their second child, to be a boy also named Barry in his father's memory. We vowed there and then to form a team to ride the Mersey 24hr also in Barry's memory.
(The details are to be found in the event of 1970)

In June 2006, some 36 years later, I had a phone call at work. "Hi, is that John? – it's Barry Blagg." I caught my breath in astonishment, my brain told me it couldn't possibly be him, he was dead. It took a minute or two to sink in, it was Barry Junior, that same soft voice. He said he wanted to know what his dad was really like, as all he knew was what his mother had told him. Barry who was now 35 years old had searched through his fathers few belongings and found a tarnished old silver medal with a 'Liver Bird' motif on one side and 408.03 miles engraved on the back, and wanted to know what it was all about.

There was then a large gathering of old St Christopher's members and we managed to assure Barry that his dad was one of the nicest guys you could ever have had, as a friend, a clubmate and a father.

On a more general scale I have vivid memories from my early efforts at the Mersey 24hr. Riding past cottages and houses at about 10pm with bedroom lights on and secretly wishing it was me going to bed, as the bravado of riding a 24 hr race had diminished a little after six hours of effort; hurrying past the burning gas flares and miles of pipework and gantries lit up like Blackpool pier at Queensferry oil refinery near Chester: - being scared witless as trains hurtled out of the darkness from cuttings that ran alongside the unlit stretches of coast road between Chester and Prestatyn around 1am.

Woodsmoke drifting across the road and lights going on when passing isolated cottages around dawn, as farmers got ready to tend their cattle in the Broxton area; - racing from Prees, hoping to get past the farm at Sandford before the cows crossed the road after milking, especially if the roads were wet; - the wonderful smell of bacon and eggs drifting in the morning air at the Edgebolton breakfast feed.

Climbing away from Grindley Brook towards the finishing circuit, with old timers shouting "come on lad, all the way now!" – made even better with a gusting southerly wind 'howling' in the telephone wires; - the sound of clapping as you entered the lane to the finishing circuit at Waverton, and better still the timekeeper shouting "you can stop now, you've finished here".

Seeing all the star riders in the North Road Championship of 1960, trying to destroy each other in the early stages, Dave Keeler, Ron Coukham, Cliff Smith, Fred Burrell, Dick Poole, John Arnold and Stuart Thompson. I couldn't believe my eyes and later in the evening, I saw Arch Harding riding along smoking a cigarette after downing a quick pint; - John Arnold cornering at speed on his trike in a later Mersey event.

Being at Bridgnorth and seeing Dick Poole's fixed stare as he glided back into the darkness on the first night of his End to End; - hearing and almost feeling the effort and speed as Nim Carline came past me, turning a huge gear to try and pull away from Eric Matthews who was going just as fast, but making it look so effortless, as he just 'tapped' the pedals around.

Seeing Pat Kenny's wind battered face as he climbed off his trike at John o' Groats and his look of relief at having at last broken the record in 1980; - seeing the tears of jubilation from Mick Coupe's helpers and family as he became the first man to reach Scotland from Lands End in 24 hours, accompanied by a thunderstorm and a rainbow across the A74 at Gretna in 1982.

The lump I had in my throat when I rang Pauline Strong's HQ and found that she had broken the End to End record in 1990, as her prospects had looked very doubtful the previous evening when battling through heavy rain when crossing the Grampians.

Seeing 'Wilko' on the finishing circuit as he flew round those last tight bends in the back lanes at the end of his record 525 miles in 1997; - Lynne taking 3rd place overall behind Karl Austin and Simon Doughty in 1999 and me thinking 'at last we have a decent 24hr rider in the family, now I can retire'; - following Andy and Lynne's tandem record as they plummeted downhill towards Inverness at nearly 60 mph. This came after some very soul searching and tough times during their previous 24 hours of the ride; - ringing Lynne's mum Liz and her two Grans during that same record attempt at Wick and telling them that Lynne and Andy would be finished within the hour. Liz said she was so relieved, as none of the family had slept properly for two nights thinking about the riders; - Lynne climbing to the Slochd summit on the second night of her first solo End to End record; she looked very small and lonely in that vast mountain range; - hearing next day whilst on that same record via mobile phones, that Gethin who was 24 hours behind Lynne had broken John Woodburn's 24hr record by 11 miles with 505.8 and had reached the Moffat area. The downside was that he'd stopped, exhausted and had lost the 50 minutes he'd gained on schedule and that Jim Turner was frantically trying to get him back on his bike. I felt deeply for Jim at that moment in time; - some 15 hours later, seeing Gethin hurtling downhill towards the John o' Groats hotel in the dark, just after 6am, and then amidst the gusting, wet, gloomy dawn, calmly announcing that he would go on for the 1,000 miles after a short break; - one year later on Lynne's 2nd solo record, after a 45 hour struggle against poor conditions and whilst crossing the Grampians, hearing a shipping forecast while I was in the following van.

The forecast said 'southerly winds, backing west for northern coastal waters'. Tony Shardlow, the timekeeper, Colin Baldwin, the masseur, and myself were ecstatic with such good news; - 20 hours later while returning along the coast towards Castletown we experienced one of the best examples of the 'Northern Lights' or 'Aurora Borealis' out at sea. The shivering columns of light were just hovering over the Orkney's like a gigantic halo.

It certainly took Lynne's mind off the fact that she still had over 50 miles left to complete her 1,000 miles record, on her 3rd dark night; - looking in the wing mirrors and seeing the teams of helpers and the cavalcade of Scottish supporters and cyclists following us, as Lynne hammered out those final miles of her 1,000, beyond Thurso and the Castle of Mey.

In September 2008, Liz, Lynne and myself travelled to the National Cycle Collection and Museum at Llandrindod Wells, at the request of Eileen Sheridan. She was unveiling an exhibition of memorabilia illustrating and relating to her amazing long distance cycle record breaking career in the 1950's, and wanted Lynne to be present as the current End to End and 1,000 mile record holder. We were all so proud to be there, especially Lynne, as she regularly keeps in touch with Eileen who has been such an inspiration to her over the years.

Whilst there I had a good look around the Museum, which contains exhibits from the 'Hobby Horse', 'Boneshaker' and 'High Ordinary' age, right through to the present day carbon fibre racing machines. I noticed photos, books, artefacts and cycles belonging and relating to some of our past long distance riders and record breakers, Frank Southall, Sir Hubert Opperman, Sid Ferris, to name but a few. There was even a memorial headstone from the grave of Maurice Selbach, a 24hr rider and record breaker from the 1920's.

We had a wonderful day and were made most welcome by the curator David Higman 'MBE', Trevor Jarvis, the Treasurer, and all the 'Friends of the Museum Trust'. Set in this historic Welsh market town surrounded by scenic countryside, I can highly recommend this venue for a day out.

The last nostalgic and touching moment for me came when I was putting these final chapters together. Noah, my Grandson who was born in 2006 on the day I started writing this book, points to a photo on the wall and says to Poppy, his baby sister 'Look, Lynney on her bike'!

If you wish to ride a 24 hour time trial or feel that you would like in some way to get involved with this historic event, then please contact the Mersey R.C. organiser Jon Williams at oggy-merseyroads@hotmail.com

Likewise, details on Road Record breaking can be found at www.rra.org.uk

Details of the 24 hour Fellowship can be obtained from the secretary John Hassall, 23 Hadrian Avenue, Dunstable, Bedfordshire LU5 4SW.

Sheila Simpson

Christine Roberts

Bridget Boon

Carol Westmorland

Tracey Maund

Ann Wooldridge

Marina Bloom

Lynne & Liz Taylor

Jim Hopper

Lynne Taylor, Andy Wilkinson & Paul Histon

Eileen & David
Brabbin

John Williams, Lynne Taylor, Jim Turner

Ralph Dadswell, Marina Bloom

Ian & Bridget Boon

# Men over 500 miles

**Rod & Peter Goodfellow**

**Ian Butcher**

**Ian Dow**

**Roy Cromack**

**Andy Wilkinson**

**Eamonn Deane**

**Gethin Butler**

**Nik Gardiner**

**John Woodburn**

# CHAPTER NINE

## MY 'IMMORTAL LEGENDS', HEROINES AND HEROES OLD & NEW

Cycling has played a very large part of my life since the age of 13, and many of my formative years of club life were influenced by three good friends, Pete Swinden, John Withers and Pat Kenny. Pete was a stockily built powerhouse of a man, although he was a touch shorter than me he had a terrific lung capacity and never seemed to get tired. Pete usually rode a single speed fixed wheel, but occasionally resorted to a Sturmey Archer fixed drive multi-geared hub using mostly high ratios whether for touring or racing. He went nearly everywhere on his bike, as we all did, despite owning a car. Pete dressed in fairly normal casual clothing of the day when riding and only wore a club racing vest during time trials or record attempts.

Racing wasn't Pete's priority and he preferred to ride with the club or tour, but when he did race, it was usually anything from a 100 mile event upwards in distance, and if he took his mudguards and saddlebag off, you knew he meant serious business. He had lots of friends, hobbies and pastimes outside of cycling and was always ready to give up his time and help others with their projects.

I learned a lot from Pete and I gained confidence as a youngster just by analysing his lifestyle and trying to emulate his 'mind over matter' attitude to his riding. He didn't have to rely on the latest cycling equipment, or any specific training routine to produce the solid results he achieved whether in time trials or later, his many Midland and National road records on a tandem.

John Withers, on the other hand, was of a much slighter build in his earlier racing days and also at the time of his record breaking. He was originally a Dental Technician but in later life he worked in Accountancy. I spent many Sundays riding in his company and learned a lot about the countryside, how to study and read a map, and plan journeys. One of John's other passions at that time was youth hostelling, and I enjoyed some long trips including a tour of the West Country with John and another youngster much faster than myself, Dave Guy, who went on in life to become a Barrister.

Trike riding was another art that John taught me on the car park at the 'Cat in the Window' café just south of Knowle in Warwickshire. I had many near misses that day while learning to control the 'Barrow' but after an hour or two I eventually mastered the art. Dave Guy, meanwhile, who had been stood quietly watching and probably learning from my mistakes, asked if he could give it a try. He clambered aboard the trike and rode away in a straight line - first time.

John Withers was the first rider in our section of St Christopher's to ride a 24hr race and he was soon hooked on the long distance time trialling scene. He became a 'mine of knowledge' on the subject and was soon reeling off the names of his heroes. John was always full of enthusiasm for racing and it's from him that I acquired my zest for the sport and my thirst for knowledge of these heroes we had seen flashing past, riders such as Dave Keeler, Reg Randall, John Arnold and Arch Harding.

I was now 14 years old and although John and Pete were only four or five years older than myself, to me they were real men, they rode 12 hr and 24 hr races and I helped them whenever I could. Pat Kenny spurred on by John and Pete's exploits took up long distance racing and joined the team after a few years. I eventually became the reserve rider and 4th team member. I helped on Swinden and Wither's RRA tandem 1,000 miles in 1964 and Pat Kenny's Edinburgh to London and 24hr trike record in 1965 and also his trike End to End in 1980.

I realised early on that I was amongst record breakers and heroes who were my friends and whilst helping them I also realised that they really suffered at various times on their rides, John in particular on the '1,000' when his rain sodden leather saddle started to collapse causing him to have terrible open sores on his backside which he endured for another 400 miles. Pete also suffered with a very painful knee on their tandem End to End in 1966, and had to have hospital treatment first at Perth and then again later at Inverness. Pat's sufferings on his trike record were mainly from psychological pressure to succeed against increasing winds and other adverse conditions once he reached the Scottish borders. His expert and intimate knowledge of the End to End route and the mathematical and chronological deductions he made as he reached various points on the route, usually down on schedule, all combined to work against him.

473

When you are young you think that you'll probably live forever, as will all of your close friends and family. I thought athletes and sporting role models were virtually indestructible at that time in life, around my early teenage years. I don't remember how old I was when I made a conscious decision that there was no such thing as immortality and that the promise of 'everlasting life' that my strict Roman Catholic faith had instilled in me, was probably just an ideological myth, and a ploy to get me to lead a perfect life. But I still couldn't perceive that a rider who had broken the longest road records in the UK could possibly have a physical defect such as an undetected, underlying heart and circulation problem.

So when later in life I was contacted with the tragic news of John Withers death in 1990, while he was touring in France, it came like a bolt out of the blue. He was with a small group of St Christopher's 'lads', Pete and Phil Swinden, Tony Wiggin, Bob Beaman, Steve Cronshaw and Phil Bratton. They'd just had a midday meal and were about to ride away, when John just keeled over onto the edge of the road and died. His heart had given out, there were no warning signs, no last words, he'd gone.

One can't begin to imagine the shock for the lads who were with him and for Pete who had to break the news to his family by phone. Strangely enough I had accepted my own father's early death at 48 when I was only 11 years old, because he had been ill for a long time with heart disease. It was in 1955 and long before by-pass surgery and heart drugs had been developed. I find it amazing now to think how far we have progressed in all medical matters since then.

When looking back at our past heroes and heroines and analysing their physical attributes and athletic lifestyles, it's surprising to find out just how many of them have had ongoing health problems, either before, during or after their racing careers. Starting with Sid Ferris who was blind in one eye, as is Pete Swinden, and both from their childhood days. Sid had to have his eye treated and dressed when on a long distance race, and always wore an eye patch. John Arnold suffered badly with his feet almost for the duration of his long distance career and resorted to wearing industrial 'clogs' bolted to his pedals to alleviate the pain. Cliff Smith spent a long time in hospital after the war and had to wear a spinal support casing due to injuries he'd suffered as a gunner on the heavy artillery. Cliff was a most unlikely looking competitor due to his gaunt, haunched appearance, but looks can deceive and he became a feared adversary and one of the most prolific winners at 24 hour racing.

Dave Keeler also suffered with a recurrent back problem due to his height, as did June Pitchford who eventually finished her racing career riding in a very upright position. Albert Crimes suffered terribly with his stomach on both his tandem trike and solo trike 'End to Ends' and Eric Matthews had a stomach ulcer that would 'flare up' intermittently causing him to miss races and sometimes a whole season. Mick Coupe overcame rheumatic fever twice in his life, leading up to his successful long distance career, but despite all of these setbacks, didn't they all do some amazing rides? Even Roy Cromack had a 'pacemaker' fitted in later life.

John Withers was another of these tough characters and his illness had probably been progressing for many years, until it manifested itself on that fateful day, but John wasn't alone when he died, or in the way that he died, as other famous riders have also sadly expired at the side of the road: Beryl Burton, Jon Cahill, Roger Page, the cyclo-cross star, and Joe Gilkes, the roadman. The only difference being is that they were alone in their final moments.

Sadly my book came too late for many riders, their mortality beat me to it. Even while I was writing I experienced 'De-Ja-Vu' moments where I would be describing an event, and within hours I was being informed of the death of one of the main characters in my race report. First of all, we heard of Dave Stapleton's death and a short while later Gerry Jones, then Nim Carline followed by Eddie Mundy. I know its all down to fate, but I started to wonder whether the 'grim reaper' was looking over my shoulder to see who I was writing about next, as the only person I knew to be ill at the time of writing, was Nim Carline.

Although they and many other riders and 24hr personnel have all gone before us, at least their deeds and achievements are preserved in this book for all to see.

If I was asked to list my all time top riders starting with the women, I would narrow it down to five. Starting with Eileen Sheridan, our first lady ambassador and female figure head of our sport of time trialling and road record breaking in the 1950's. The media coverage of her exploits gave us a romantic and nostalgic view of how things were done over half a century ago.

Coming forward a few years we saw the rise in prominence of undoubtedly the greatest woman cyclist and time triallist in the world, Beryl Burton. Her 30 year career saw her totally dominate the sport of time trialling and leave a legacy of Championship and 'BBAR' wins that will be impossible to surpass. Ironically her only failure was at 24 hour riding, due to painful knees, but her 12 hour ride of 277 miles in 1967, which at the time beat the men's Competition Record, performed in that same event, speaks for itself. Her total of prolific solo time trial competition records, some 50 in all, will never be bettered by either sex, and neither will her 72 Championship wins.

Christine Roberts is our next 'big hitter' at 24 hour racing in the 1980's and 90's, her tussles with Bridget Boon around those same years were legendary, and still are. Christine's strength and the ability to turn a big gear to gain results gave her the big mileages that still stand to this day, both as a Competition Record in the time trial scene with 461.45 miles, and also 467.30m for the lone Road Records Association 24 hr mileage.

During her climb to supremacy at 24hr riding, Christine was closely shadowed by Bridget Boon, and between them they raised the stakes and the mileages that made women's performances very respectable against the mens' in those same events and both riders helped the cause that saw women start to take regular top five overall places in 24 hour events. In fact Bridget became the first and only woman ever to win a 24hr race and that was in 1993. Previously to that Bridget had raised the mixed tandem Competition Record with her husband Ian in three successive years with rides of 421.89, 443.3 and 463.3 miles.

Our present day female icon of the long distance road scene is Lynne Taylor, for her persistent and successful assaults on the End to End and 1,000 mile records, and her ten 24hr wins from 15 successive rides, not to mention her ladies Team Competition Records at 100 miles, 12 hours and 24 hours, with Marina Bloom and Tracey Maund. All for a non sponsored Walsall Roads Club team.

Like Eileen, Lynne is an ambassador for our sport, but rarely gets the platform to portray her feelings and views on the sport via the media as Eileen did. She does however attend club dinners throughout the winter as Guest of Honour, where she manages to encourage and enlighten others with her talks on the sport of long distance racing and record breaking. I hope I'm forgiven for praising and continually writing about Lynne's achievements since 1993, but then she has ridden and won more 24hr races since 1993, than any other woman in history. As Michael Hutchinson exclaimed "fifteen!" when sat next to Lynne at the 2007 'BBAR' awards. With a personal best of 459.2 miles, 3 End to End's and a 1,000 miles record, this certainly makes Lynne the UK's greatest woman endurance cyclist ever, and after all, I am her Dad.

For my true grit male legends of the past, it has to be Albert Crimes and John Arnold, even though their tandem trike partnership only spanned about two years, and their individual 24hr and record breaking careers about 14 years.

The prophetic statement Jock Wadley made in 1954 after their epic 12hr, 24hr, End to End and 1,000 mile journey "they had cornered so fast in their last few miles, it was feared they would crash and fall, but Albert and John did not fall, and neither I think will the 4 records they achieved!" To this day, 54 years later, that statement still rings true, their records still stand, as a testament to their strength and endurance, as does Albert's solo trike 1,000 miles at 2days 21hours and 37mins ridden in 1958.

The most exciting and courageous rider I saw in my days of 24hr riding was Nim Carline, over a 20 year period. In that time he won a record six 24 hr Championships in an eleven year period between 1962 – 1973. He also pushed the Competition Record up to 496 miles in 1966 by his aggressive style of riding. His method of dominating a race from the very start, and then winning the battles that ensued from this, was admired not only by his supporters and bystanders, but also by other riders, and even some of the 'stars' he was beating.

My modern day 24 hr and long distance road record man obviously has to be 'Wilko', Andy Wilkinson, who currently holds the 24hr Record with 525 miles, and at that same time in 1997, he also held Competition Record at all of the BBAR disciplines, and he is still the current holder of the 12 hr record with 300.27 miles. Andy's End to End forays speak volumes for his courageous recoveries, and throughout his 25 year career, that has also encompassed many distinguished road race titles, he has never relinquished his role as a clubman. He regularly meets up with his fellow riders in the Port Sunlight Wheelers, and always looks forward to 'rough stuff' riding in North Wales with the lads.

When it comes to the modesty stakes 'Wilko' certainly takes 1st place after stating at the end of his 24hr record that he could foresee someone producing a 540 mile ride, on the right day and on possibly a flatter course.

But then I can't possibly leave out that other Mr Nice Guy and current End to End and 1,000 mile record holder, Gethin Butler, who like Andy has had a full career both as a roadman and a top time triallist at all distances over a number of years. Another notable similarity to Andy, which is a little unusual in this day and age, is that Gethin is also a 'dyed in the wool' clubman who loves just riding his bike and is happier touring or Audax riding than he is flogging himself around a time trial course. Gethin can also be found helping others on a regular basis, in long distance events, just like 'Wilko'. In more recent times Gethin has turned to marathon running, and in 2008 won the Blackpool marathon in 2 hrs 33 mins.

I know that throughout this history people have said that certain mileages and records will be impossible to beat, but in the case of Gethin's End to End and 1,000 mile record, and not forgetting the 24hr record he put up on route, I think all three RRA records will stand for many, many years to come, along with Wilko's 525 miles.

I could be accused of living in the past, but that is what Historians do. Our past history of long distance cycle racing has certainly been a good one, and I sincerely hope our future proves to be even better.

Finally, if the unthinkable does happen and we are driven off most of the useful roads in Britain, then perhaps someone in the future, out riding in a club group around an enclosed traffic free circuit, on a 2 hour 'endurance' ride will say "I wonder how far I can ride in 24 hours?"

| RTTC LADIES over 400 MILES in 24 HOURS | | | |
| --- | --- | --- | --- |
| YEAR | RIDER | MILES | *comp record* |
| 1993 | Christine Roberts | 461.45 | √ |
| 2007 | Lynne Taylor | 459.29 | |
| 1993 | Bridget Boon | 457.14 | |
| 2005 | Marina Bloom | 447.334 | |
| 1993 | Bridget Boon | 446.88 | |
| 2006 | Carol Westmorland | 445.412 | |
| 2004 | Lynne Taylor | 443.145 | |
| 1994 | Christine Roberts | 442.67 | |
| 1995 | Lynne Taylor | 441.4 | |
| 1996 | Lynne Taylor | 438.97 | |
| 1983 | Anne Mann | 438.16 | √ |
| 2002 | Lynne Taylor | 438.042 | |
| 1992 | Bridget Boon | 437.62 | |
| 2006 | Lynne Taylor | 434.412 | |
| 2004 | Marina Bloom | 434.062 | |
| 2000 | Lynne Taylor | 433.68 | |
| 1969 | Christine Moody | 427.86 | √ |
| 1998 | Lynne Taylor | 427.61 | |
| 2002 | Marina Bloom | 427.502 | |
| 1991 | Sheila Simpson | 426.18 | |
| 1999 | Lynne Taylor | 424.89 | |
| 2001 | Lynne Taylor | 423.13 | |
| 1970 | Joan Kershaw | 422.34 | |
| 1968 | Christine Moody | 420.05 | √ |
| 1987 | Jean Burrow | 419.18 | |
| 1994 | Lynne Taylor | 418.2 | |
| 1997 | Lynne Taylor | 418.08 | |
| 2006 | Marina Bloom | 416.449 | |
| 2004 | Tracey Maund | 415.629 | |
| 2003 | Marina Bloom | 413.255 | |
| 2005 | Lynne Taylor | 412.807 | |
| 1983 | Anne Rogers | 412.55 | |
| 2003 | Lynne Taylor | 411.141 | |
| 1967 | Christine Moody | 409.16 | √ |
| 1990 | Sheila Simpson | 408.07 | |
| 1983 | Jean Burrow | 407.99 | |
| 1992 | Sheila Simpson | 407.52 | |
| 2003 | Tracey Maund | 405.305 | |
| 1976 | Joan Kershaw | 404.82 | |
| 1967 | Ruth Williams | 403.7 | |
| 1986 | Jean Burrow | 403.36 | |
| 1991 | Eilean McCarthy | 403.02 | |
| 1994 | Anne Learmonth | 402.13 | |
| 1970 | Joyce Blow | 402.12 | |
| 1992 | Sheila Simpson | 401.76 | |

## MEN over 490 MILES in 24 HOURS

| YEAR | RIDER | MILES | comp record |
|------|-------|-------|-------------|
| 1997 | Andy Wilkinson | 525.07 | √ |
| 2008 | Nik Gardiner | 513.65 | |
| 2000 | Gethin Butler | 509.25 | |
| 1969 | Roy Cromack | 507 | √ |
| 1980 | John Woodburn | 505.47 | |
| 2006 | Nik Gardiner | 504.023 | |
| 1992 | Andy Wilkinson | 501.96 | |
| 1995 | Andy Wilkinson | 501.39 | |
| 1998 | Ian Butcher | 501.31 | |
| 2007 | Eamonn Deane | 501.04 | |
| 1987 | Ian Dow | 500.1 | |
| 1980 | John Cahill | 497.34 | |
| 1982 | Stuart Jackson | 496.49 | |
| 1966 | Nim Carline | 496.37 | √ |
| 1994 | Andy Wilkinson | 496.16 | |
| 1984 | Stuart Jackson | 494.16 | |
| 1989 | Ian Butcher | 493.53 | |
| 2005 | Nik Gardiner | 493.081 | |
| 1969 | Eric Matthews | 492.88 | |
| 1979 | Mick Coupe | 492.682 | |
| 2008 | John Warnock | 491.39 | |
| 1973 | George Bettis | 491.171 | |
| 1993 | Phil Barlow | 490.88 | |
| 1958 | Dave Keeler | 490.311 | |
| 1973 | Nim Carline | 490.31 | |
| 1964 | Eric Matthews | 490.03 | √ |

## POST SECOND WORLD WAR Records

| YEAR | RIDER | MILES | comp record |
|------|-------|-------|-------------|
| 1958 | D H White | 484.75 | √ |
| 1956 | D H White | 484.64 | √ |
| 1955 | K Price | 478.55 | √ |
| 1955 | S Thompson | 474.12 | √ |
| 1954 | S Thompson | 469.66 | √ |
| 1952 | E Mundy | 467.52 | √ |
| 1952 | G A T Laws | 463.29 | √ |
| 1951 | G Andrews | 461.31 | √ |
| 1950 | R F Mynott | 459.5 | √ |
| 1950 | S M Butler | 458.18 | √ |
| 1950 | E Mundy | 455.91 | √ |
| 1948 | G Basham | 454.2 | √ |

## PRE SECOND WORLD WAR Records

| YEAR | RIDER | MILES | comp record |
|------|-------|-------|-------------|
| 1935 | E B Seeley | 444.75 | √ |
| 1933 | S H Ferris | 431.25 | √ |
| 1931 | J W Dougal | 430.75 | √ |
| 1930 | E J Doubleday | 416.25 | √ |
| 1928 | W A Ellis | 413.5 | √ |
| 1927 | W A Ellis | 410.5 | √ |
| 1925 | J E Holdsworth | 408.5 | √ |
| 1919 | M G Selbach | 405 | √ |

## RTTC  TRICYCLE COMP RECORDS,MEN, over 410 MILES

| YEAR | RIDER | MILES | comp record |
|------|-------|-------|-------------|
| 1972 | Eric Tremaine | 457.89 | √ |
| 1953 | John Arnold | 457.33 | √ |
| 1981 | Stuart Jackson | 456.59 | |
| 1983 | Eric Tremaine | 447.02 | |
| 1985 | Stuart Jackson | 444.13 | |
| 1954 | Pete Duncan | 440.90 | |
| 1981 | Edwin Hargraves | 437.51 | |
| 1956 | Albert Crimes | 436.50 | |
| 1956 | Pete Duncan | 435.12 | |
| 1971 | Eric Tremaine | 433.93 | |
| 1965 | Pete Duncan | 433.56 | |
| 1964 | Jim Shuttleworth | 424.81 | |
| 1953 | Albert Crimes | 424.33 | |
| 1959 | Ken Usher | 423.23 | |
| 1973 | S Hill | 422.70 | |
| 1952 | Albert Crimes | 422.40 | √ |
| 1965 | Johnny Pardoe | 419.94 | |
| 1951 | John Arnold | 419.26 | √ |
| 1962 | Howard Bayley | 417.37 | |
| 1996 | Jim Hopper | 417.30 | |
| 1967 | Jim Shuttleworth | 416.90 | |
| 1973 | G T Jenkins | 416.54 | |
| 1962 | T Kelly | 415.:89 | |
| 1980 | M Smith | 415.81 | |
| 1965 | T Kelly | 415.27 | |
| 1951 | Stan King | 415.05 | |
| 1958 | T Kelly | 414.04 | |
| 1963 | F C Brown | 414.02 | |
| 1955 | D Duffield | 414.00 | |
| 1949 | Albert Crimes | 411.79 | √ |
| 1950 | Jack Kings | 411.50 | |
| 1961 | T Kelly | 410.78 | |
| 1968 | M Henigan | 410.42 | |
| 1965 | B Kirkham | 410.08 | |
| 1949 | L Holt | 409.00 | √ |
| 1949 | Cliff Prior | 402.11 | √ |
| 1948 | Len Holt | 392.65 | √ |
| 1948 | Syd Parker | 391.04 | √ |
| 1939 | George Lawrie | 387.34 | √ |
| 1936 | A G Oxbrow | 382.50 | √ |
| 1928 | Frank Fisher | 365.25 | √ |
| 1920 | T H Pryor | 354.50 | √ |

## LADIES TRICYCLE COMPETITION RECORDS

| YEAR | RIDER | MILES | comp record |
|------|-------|-------|-------------|
| 1988 | Felicity Beard | 382.72 | √ |
| 1969 | Joyce Blow | 374.15 | √ |
| 1968 | Joyce Blow | 371.68 | √ |

## MENS 24 HR TRIKE TEAM COMPETITION RECORDS

| YEAR | TEAM | MILES | |
|------|------|-------|---|
| 1981 | Farnham R.C. | 1230.38 | S W Jackson, H E Hargraves, B T Annis |
| 1959 | Crouch Hill C.C. | 1216.53 | K Usher, D Hutchinson, H James |
| 1954 | South Eastern R.C. | 1054.30 | D Ivey, A Waller, L Smalldon |

## LADIES 24 HR TEAM COMPETITION RECORDS

| YEAR | TEAM | RIDERS | MILES |
|------|------|--------|-------|
| 2004 | Walsall R. C. C. | L Taylor, M Bloom, T Maund | 1292.84 |
| 2003 | Walsall R. C. C. | M Bloom, L Taylor, T Maund | 1229.7 |
| 1976 | Prescot Eagle R. C. C. | J Kershaw, R Williams, A Hooton | 1105.41 |

## MENS 24 HR TEAM COMPETITION RECORDS

| YEAR | TEAM | RIDERS | MILES |
|------|------|--------|-------|
| 1980 | North Staffs St. Christophers CCC. | J Cahill, M Coupe, T Finney | 1441.59 |
| 1979 | North Staffs St. Christophers CCC. | M Coupe, J Cahill, M Parker | 1417.39 |
| 1960 | Middlesex R. C. | F Burrell, A Harding, R W Poole | 1407.23 |
| 1958 | Rutland CC. | R Coukham, S Thompson, G Steers | 1402.69 |
| 1955 | Rutland CC. | S Thompson, R Coukham, G Fouldes | 1397.13 |
| 1952 | Addiscombe CC. | E Mundy, G Andrews, S Harvey | 1361.94 |
| 1951 | Addiscombe CC. | G Andrews, S Harvey, J F Watts | 1351.92 |
| 1950 | Addiscombe CC. | E Mundy, S Harvey, S Armstrong | 1341.95 |
| 1949 | Vegetarian C & AC | J Purves, W Shillibeer, E G Guy | 1284.19 |
| 1947 | Luton Whls C.C. | R Goodman, E S Ellingham, H Walker | 1283.5 |
| 1937 | Vegetarian C & AC | F N Robertson, E G Guy, A G Oxbrow | 1254.62 |

## MALE TANDEM

| YEAR | | MILES |
|------|------|-------|
| 1991 | R C Goodfellow & P B Goodfellow | 501.35 |
| 1986 | G Adams & M Smith | 466.56 |
| 1984 | R W Smith & S Cruise | 438.33 |
| 1982 | L E Lowe & P Kenny | 430.51 |

## MIXED CREW TANDEM

| YEAR | | MILES |
|------|------|-------|
| 2002 | Mr & Mrs D Brabbin | 464.92 |
| 1986 | Mr & Mrs I Boon | 463.33 |
| 1985 | Mr & Mrs I Boon | 443.3 |
| 1983 | Mr & Mrs I Boon | 421.89 |
| 1982 | Mr & Mrs J Coleman | 401.77 |

## MALE TANDEM TRICYCLE

| YEAR | | MILES |
|------|------|-------|
| 2005 | R Dadswell & D Johnson | 466.72 |
| 1999 | C Knapp & P Tyler | 428.94 |
| 1985 | L E Lowe & J Hopper | 419.15 |

## MIXED CREW TANDEM TRICYCLE

| YEAR | | MILES |
|------|------|-------|
| 1993 | M Brooking & Miss J Ramsdale | 401.22 |
| 1989 | M Brooking & Miss J Ramsdale | 372.64 |

## SENIOR LONG DISTANCE B.A.R.

| YEAR | No. | WINNER | MPH |
|------|-----|--------|-----|
| 1980 | 40 | John Woodburn | 23.347 |
| 1981 | 26 | John Woodburn | 22.717 |
| 1982 | 38 | Stuart Jackson | 21.73 |
| 1983 | 35 | Stuart Jackson | 21.915 |
| 1984 | 43 | Ian Dow | 22.374 |
| 1985 | 41 | Ian Dow | 22.178 |
| 1986 | 52 | Ian Dow | 22.178 |
| 1987 | 37 | Ralph Dadswell | 21.473 |
| 1988 | 35 | Ian Dow | 21.69 |
| 1989 | 26 | Ian Butcher | 22.314 |
| 1990 | 34 | Phil Oxborough | 20.875 |
| 1991 | 33 | Phil Barlow | 21.937 |
| 1992 | 40 | Richard Johnson | 21.112 |
| 1993 | 43 | Phil Barlow | 22.539 |
| 1994 | 37 | Marc Cunnington | 21.778 |
| 1995 | 37 | Marc Cunnington | 21.592 |
| 1996 | 27 | Malcolm Whitehead | 22.478 |
| 1997 | 24 | Gethin Butler | 23.813 |
| 1998 | 28 | Paul Holdsworth | 22.472 |
| 1999 | 23 | Nikolaus Gardiner | 22.873 |
| 2000 | 21 | Gethin Butler | 23.879 |
| 2001 | 13 | Chris Hopkinson | 22.561 |
| 2002 | 17 | Andy Briggs | 22.05 |
| 2003 | 23 | Gethin Butler | 23.314 |
| 2004 | 29 | Nikolaus Gardiner | 22.963 |
| 2005 | 22 | Nikolaus Gardiner | 23.314 |
| 2006 | 25 | Neil Skellern | 22.992 |
| 2007 | 14 | Jose Pinon Shaw | 22.004 |
| 2008 | 9 | Neil Skellern | 22.383 |

No. indicates the number of eligible riders in the competition that year.
The long distance 'B.A.R.' chart and results are courtesy of the 24hr. Fellowship competition secretary, Charles Robson who has a 447 mile ride to his credit in 1982.
Note the decline in number of riders completing all three disciplines
100 mile, 12hours and 24 hours, from its peak in 1986 (52) to present day (9).